A Companion to the New Testament

Since this *Companion to the New Testament* was first published in 1970, new methods of interpretation and sustained research into the environment of Jesus and of the early church have combined to correct former misunderstandings and to set old problems in a new light. This fully revised second edition now follows the New Revised Standard Version (NRSV) to provide a running commentary on the text of the New Testament while taking account of the findings of recent scholarship. Using no technical language, it aims to set the text in the context of the time and place in which it was written and to clarify its meaning in the light of modern methods of research and interpretation. Accessible and up to date, this work will be invaluable to clergy, students and all who have a serious interest in the New Testament.

DR A. E. HARVEY was formerly a Lecturer in Theology at Oxford University and Sub-Dean of Westminster. He is now retired and is a Fellow of the George Bell Institute.

THE NEW REVISED STANDARD VERSION

A Companion
to the New Testament

SECOND EDITION

A. E. HARVEY

CAMBRIDGE
UNIVERSITY PRESS

PUBLISHED BY THE PRESS SYNDICATE OF THE UNIVERSITY OF CAMBRIDGE
The Pitt Building, Trumpington Street, Cambridge, United Kingdom

CAMBRIDGE UNIVERSITY PRESS
The Edinburgh Building, Cambridge, CB2 2RU, UK
40 West 20th Street, New York, NY 10011–4211, USA
477 Williamstown Road, Port Melbourne, VIC 3207, Australia
Ruiz de Alarcón 13, 28014 Madrid, Spain
Dock House, The Waterfront, Cape Town 8001, South Africa

http://www.cambridge.org

First published 1970
Reprinted 1971   1973
First paperback edition 1979
Second edition 2004

Printed in the United Kingdom at the University Press, Cambridge

Typeface Minion 10/12 pt   *System* LATEX 2$_\varepsilon$ [TB]

A catalogue record for this book is available from the British Library

Library of Congress cataloguing in publication data
Harvey, A. E. (Anthony Ernest)
A companion to the New Testament: the New Revised Standard Version / by
A. E. Harvey – 2nd edn
p.   cm.
Includes bibliographical references and index.
ISBN 0 521 78297 X – ISBN 0 521 78834 X (pbk.)
1. Bible. N.T. – Commentaries.   I. Title.
BS2341.2H37 2004   225.7 – dc22   2004040782

ISBN 0 521 78297 X hardback
ISBN 0 521 78834 X paperback

Contents

CONTENTS

Preface

The first edition of this *Companion* was commissioned forty years ago by the Oxford and Cambridge University Presses as an aid to the general reader of the recently published New English Bible (New Testament, 1961). This was the first ecumenically authorized translation into modern English; but it remained in currency for barely thirty years. In 1989 it was replaced by the Revised English Bible, which effectively made its predecessor obsolete.

As a result, the *Companion*, though still in circulation, ceased to be an appropriate tool for the study of the New Testament. If reprinting were to be considered, it would clearly have to be adjusted to the text of a version in more general use. Since the New English Bible's natural successor, the Revised English Bible, failed to capture the market in the way that had been hoped, the publishers were obliged to recommend that any revision of the *Companion* should adopt the text of a more widely established version. For a number of reasons the New Revised Standard Version was the obvious candidate.

But it soon became clear that a revision would involve more than simply adapting the commentary to the phraseology of a new text. Substantial changes – some would say advances – have taken place in New Testament studies during the last thirty years. New methods of interpretation, and sustained research into the environment of Jesus and of the early church, have combined to correct former misunderstandings and to set old problems in a new light. Added to which, my own career of study and exposition, research and teaching, has enabled me to bring what I hope is a more mature and better-informed judgment to bear on many issues raised by the text. As a result, though some sections have received only light revision, others have been substantially rewritten.

The principles which have guided me throughout were set out in the Preface to the First Edition (1970), which is reprinted here. In this revised edition, the style and format have remained the same. Since it was these in particular that appear to have found favour with the readers of the first edition, it would have been presumptuous of me to think I could improve on them by substantial changes. All that is new in this edition will be found, not in the arrangement of the commentary, but in the details of its interpretation. Some changes are little more than stylistic improvements; others go to the heart of the interpretative enterprise. In any case, my purpose, now as before, has been, not to impose my own reading of the text, but so far as possible to lessen the obscurities, and to enlarge the possibilities of understanding, which lie before any reader today who is open to the fascination and the challenge of the writings which make up the New Testament.

I must record a debt of sincere gratitude to many people: to those learned reviewers of the first edition whose careful reviews have helped me to avoid many errors; to my colleagues and students, whose probing questions have honed my approach to biblical and theological questions over many years; to Professor Bruce Metzger, for courteously responding to my queries about textual and translation decisions taken by the NRSV translators; to Professor Stephen Mitchell of the University of Exeter and Robert Morgan of the University of Oxford, who have read sections in draft and given me invaluable advice; and not least to Dr Non Vaughan-Thomas, who has generously shared her secretarial expertise and enabled me to create a serviceable typescript on a sometimes recalcitrant computer.

A. E. H.

All Saints, 2003

NOTE: The English text referred to throughout is that of the New Revised Standard Version (1989).

Almost all the footnotes refer to questions of text and translation that are raised in the NRSV footnotes.

Wherever there is a break in the text of the NRSV, the opportunity has been taken to insert a sub-heading along the lines of the rubrics at the foot of the page in most editions.

The Index makes no pretence of being a concordance to the New Testament: it is intended merely to guide the reader to those pages on which each item or topic is mentioned or discussed.

In this edition I have added a list of Old Testament passages which are referred to in the text.

Preface to the First Edition (1970)

In this *Companion* I have been concerned with questions which anyone may be expected to ask who approaches the New Testament in general, and the New English Bible translation of it in particular, without any previous introduction. These questions are not always the same as those which occupy professional scholars; yet it is mainly their research which has made it possible to attempt to answer them. All that I have learnt from them I gratefully acknowledge; and I am aware that there are countless things I have still failed to learn.

This book could not have been written at all had it not been for the generosity of the Governing Body of Christ Church, Oxford, which readily accepted that I should devote to this work the main part of my time as a Research Student of the House. It would also hardly have been completed had it not been for the stimulus of eight months spent in Jerusalem in 1966–7, which again I owe to the liberality of Christ Church, as well as to the hospitality of the Right Revd Campbell MacInnes, then Archbishop in Jerusalem, and of others in St George's Close, Jerusalem. I am also deeply indebted to the Ecole Biblique and its Director for permission to make use of its magnificent library during my stay in Jerusalem.

I should not have presumed to offer so ambitious a book for publication had it not first received the scrutiny of men wiser and more learned than myself. Chief among these is the Revd Dr C. H. Dodd, who was one of the first to conceive the project of a book such as this, who constantly encouraged me while I was writing it, and who patiently read and weighed every word of the typescript. After him, I owe the greatest debt of gratitude to the Revd Professor C. F. D. Moule, who read more than half the book in typescript and helped me with a large number of suggestions.

Others who have read parts of the typescript and made valuable comments are Père P. Benoit OP, the Very Revd Dr Henry Chadwick, Professors J. Duncan M. Derrett and E. R. Dodds, Mr E. W. Gray, the Revd J. L. Houlden, Mr Kenneth Pearce, Mr C. H. Roberts and Dr G. Vermes. Besides these, there are many others without whose help the work could hardly have been done: my colleagues at Christ Church, who patiently responded to my insistent questions on matters lying within their special competence; my pupils, who helped me to keep my mind fresh on the basic questions which confront any student of the New Testament; and finally some of the students at St Augustine's College, Canterbury, who helped me with the proofs.

Two men, who in their different ways helped me most, died before the book was published. One was Dr C. A. Simpson, Dean of Christ Church, who read much of the typescript, made characteristically candid and thoughtful comments on it, and sustained me through this long task with his warm-hearted encouragement. The other was my father: the small share which I may have inherited of his integrity, his powers of analysis, and his unusual ability to ask searching questions about what others take for granted, is largely responsible for any originality which this book may have. I have tried throughout to ask the questions which he would have asked and to seek the answers which he would have regarded as honest. The book, indeed, was written for him, and owes more to him than he ever knew.

To the memory of these two men I gratefully dedicate this *Companion to the New Testament*.

A. E. H.

St Augustine's College, Canterbury
March 1970

THE NEW TESTAMENT

The word TESTAMENT is a technical term with a long history. Strictly speaking, the English word, like the Latin word from which it is derived, means a legal arrangement, a 'will'; and the same was true of the Greek word, *diathēkē*, of which 'testament' is a translation. But it is obvious that what has been known since the early centuries of the church as the New Testament is not a legal document and has little in common with a will. That it bears this name is the result of a particular turn in the fortunes of the Greek word.

When, in the third century BCE, a group of Jewish scholars translated the Hebrew scriptures into Greek for the use of Greek-speaking Jews in Alexandria and elsewhere, they found themselves confronted by a number of words in the original which had no equivalent in the Greek language. One of these was the Hebrew word *berith*, of which the usual English translation is 'covenant'. This word was an important one in the history and religion of the Jewish people: it expressed one of their fundamental convictions about the relationship between God and human beings. God, they believed, had shown in the distant past his readiness to protect and care for his own people. He had miraculously rescued them from slavery in Egypt and settled them in a land of their own. He had undertaken to continue this relationship of commitment towards them, and demanded that they, for their part, should observe in their lives and their worship those principles that he had revealed to them on Sinai and which were known to them as 'the law'. All this was described in the Jewish scriptures as the 'covenant' into which God had entered with his people. Indeed, the Jews' conception of this covenant embraced their deepest convictions about the faithfulness, the justice and the mercy of God. It was not like a legal contract: the fact that Israel failed to fulfil its obligations did not mean that God was released from his undertaking. Rather, it was an expression of the absolute commitment of God to his people despite all the faithlessness they showed in return. In rendering this important word by the Greek word *diathēkē*, the translators virtually gave a new meaning to a familiar legal term. Thereafter, any Greek-speaking person who was familiar with the scriptures knew that *diathēkē*, though it normally meant 'will' or 'testament', was also a technical term for that 'covenant' which the Jews believed God had made with his own people.

The documentary evidence, so to speak, for this covenant consisted in a collection of sacred books which had been formed gradually over the centuries and which, by the time of Christ, had already been complete for about two hundred years. The collection was not homogeneous. It consisted of books written at different times for different purposes, and it was some time before an agreed text was established for all of them. The Jews distinguished

1

three broad divisions: first, the law (the five books attributed to Moses); then the prophets (which included most of the historical books); and finally the remaining books, which they called simply 'the writings'. The first of these divisions, since it included the code of religious and civil laws under which they lived, they regarded as the most important. Consequently, when they wished to refer to the whole collection, they sometimes called it simply 'the law'. Otherwise they called it 'the writing' or 'the writings', that is, 'scripture' or 'the scriptures'. These scriptures were regarded with the greatest reverence. Elaborate precautions were taken to prevent the smallest alteration to the text, and the leather scrolls on which they were written were reverently preserved in the temple and the synagogues. It was not just that they were more important, or more authoritative, than other books. They were in a class by themselves. They were believed to have been inspired by God, and they formed the basis of all worship, all education and all justice in every Jewish community.

The first Christians, being Jews, inherited the same reverence towards the scriptures. When they referred to them, it was sufficient to call them simply 'scripture' or 'the scriptures'. No other writings had any importance for them, even if they occasionally made use of some that were believed to be inspired but that were not generally accepted into the canon of the Hebrew Bible. It would not have occurred to them to think that these scriptures had in any way lost their unique authority merely because a new way of understanding them had been made possible by Christ. On the contrary, they continued to take it for granted that these scriptures contained the authentic record of God's dealings with his people, and (following the example of Jesus himself) they soon began to find in them numerous prophecies and oracles which seemed to have come alive for the first time in the light of their faith in Christ. In Christ, God had done something absolutely new for humankind, yet it was something that fulfilled and complemented, rather than superseded, the historic faith of Israel. Only in matters of worship and detailed observances did they come to believe that certain parts of the law no longer applied to them. The matter was neatly expressed by Paul in one of his letters. God's previous covenant with his people should be called no longer 'the covenant', but 'the old covenant'. For now God (as was promised even in the Hebrew scriptures) had made a new covenant through Christ (2 Corinthians 3). The documents of the old covenant were the scriptures – indeed on one occasion Paul actually called them 'the old covenant' (2 Corinthians 3.14), in order to help Christians, who now had a 'new covenant', to place them in the right perspective. And the terminology seems to have stuck. By the end of the second century CE the church seems to have got used to calling the original Jewish scriptures 'the old covenant' (the Old Testament), in contrast to which the formative writings of the Christian faith inevitably began to be known as 'the new covenant' (the New Testament).

For Paul, of course, no authoritative Christian writings existed. Indeed, he made much of the contrast between the old covenant, which was expressed in written documents, and the new covenant, which was "not of letter but of spirit" (2 Corinthians 3.6). The first generation of Christians drew their faith, not from a book, but from a living experience. Nevertheless circumstances made them into writers. Paul himself kept in touch with the widely scattered churches he had founded by writing them letters in which he strengthened their faith and discussed important points of doctrine and conduct. These letters are the earliest Christian writings we possess, and they were followed by others from other Christian leaders, who may or may not always have been in Paul's position of needing to communicate with a distant church, but who adopted the form of an apostolic letter in order to consolidate the faith of their fellow Christians. Meanwhile it seems that the need began to be felt to preserve in written form the sayings of Jesus and the events of his life. To meet this need several Christians, probably in different parts of the church, composed the books which have been known, since they were written, as 'gospels'. These relate the story of Christianity from its very beginning in the life and work of Jesus and are the source of virtually all our knowledge about him; but they appear to have been composed later than Paul's letters, during the second half of the first century CE. One of them was followed by a second volume (the Acts of the Apostles), which carried the story on into the history of the early church.

Thus the first Christian writings were the result of particular circumstances and particular needs encountered during the early decades of the church's existence. At first, Christians did not need a new set of scriptures; their faith was sustained by the spirit active among them, and their teaching was based partly on the Old Testament as interpreted in the light of their new experience, and partly on facts and traditions which were remembered by their elders and which could be traced back to Jesus or his immediate followers. But, as living contact with this first age of Christianity began to die out, it became necessary to assemble whatever writings still survived from that period in order to provide a solid and authentic basis for Christian teaching and also to have a standard of Christian truth to appeal to against the attacks and innovations of heretical thinkers. The task was complicated by the fact that there were already books in circulation which purported to have been written by one or another of the original apostles but which were in fact the work of later imitators. The church had to decide which of these writings were authentic. In theory it had a simple criterion: only those which had been written by an apostle could be accepted. In practice the matter was not so easy, since some of the generally accepted books were originally anonymous, and some which bore the name of an apostle were suspected of being the work of the next generation. It was not enough that a writing claimed to be 'apostolic'; it must be known to have been written in the first seventy years or so of the church's existence and to have held a firm place in the esteem of the majority of Christians. In essentials, the selection was settled by the end of the second century, though the inclusion or exclusion of a few books continued to be debated for much longer. On the evidence available, it can be said that the church did its work well. Almost all the writings now included in the New Testament belong unmistakably to the first generations of Christians – roughly the first century CE – and have a note of authenticity which is lacking from other surviving documents which the church might have been tempted to include.

As soon as the selection was established, it inevitably changed its character. By the end of the second century the New Testament came to be regarded, like the Old, as 'scripture'. Its various writings, regardless of the original differences between them, were all treated as inspired documents of the Christian faith. Christianity became, like Judaism, a religion of a book. The methods which had long been used to discern the Word of God in any verse of the Old Testament began to be used on the New. The New Testament, along with the Old, began to be called 'the Bible', which means simply 'the Books'. This Bible, like the Old Testament before it (which it still included), became in turn a book different from all other books, to be interpreted in a special way and possessing in every part a unique degree of authority and truth.

It was only in comparatively recent times that it began to be realized that this approach does violence to the original diversity and vitality of the individual writings which make up the Old and New Testaments. However strongly it is believed that they owe their place in scripture to the fact that their writers wrote under the inspiration of the Holy Spirit, to regard them all as equally authoritative in every detail is to do an injustice to their original diversity. This *Companion* is written in the conviction that the New Testament gains in cogency and intelligibility when it is taken for what it originally was, that is, a collection of writings each of which was produced under particular circumstances. Sometimes these circumstances are lost beyond recall; but often it is possible to reconstruct them with reasonable certainty and so to recapture something of the urgency and authority which these writings possessed for their first Christian readers.

All the books of the New Testament have come down to us in Greek. It is possible that some of them, or some small parts of them, originally existed in Aramaic, which was Jesus' first, if not only, language, and were translated within a few years into Greek; but as we have it the New Testament is written in the language which was understood (if only as a second language) by the majority of people in the eastern half of the Roman empire in the first centuries of our era. Our best evidence for this language is the mass of letters and documents – many of them written in colloquial Greek – which began to be discovered in the nineteenth century, written on papyrus and preserved in the sands of Egypt. Many passages in the New Testament that were formerly thought to have been written in a form of Greek without parallel elsewhere have been found to conform with the style and idioms of those who were using Greek to conduct their daily business. But the New Testament writers were also capable of writing in a more literary style, as well as owing a debt to the Greek translation of the Hebrew scriptures. To understand their work, we need to know something of the culture of what is loosely called the Hellenistic world, that is, the civilization which, since the imperial ventures of Alexander the Great, had come progressively under the influence of Greek ideas and Greek institutions, even though the political centre had passed to Rome. But Christianity was born in the one part of the Roman empire where there had been determined resistance to the influence of Greek civilization. Though the great majority of Jews in the world lived outside Palestine and spoke Greek, their culture remained essentially Jewish. In Palestine itself they spoke mainly Aramaic, a language which had spread over much of the Middle East since the days of the Persian empire, and their lives were still regulated by observances laid down in their scriptures. Even in the Dispersion they kept themselves at a certain distance from the ideals and institutions of Greek culture, and were the one race allowed to dissociate themselves completely from the official religion of Rome. The society of which we read in the New Testament is therefore not that of the Greco-Roman world in general but of that particular part of it which jealously retained its national religion and culture and way of life.

It happens that not many documents have survived which are evidence for this particular region of the Roman empire. Very few non-Jewish writers had any interest in it; and the Jews in Palestine were far from being prolific writers. The discovery of the Dead Sea Scrolls after the Second World War did something to dispel the darkness. They reveal in considerable detail the life and beliefs of a particular religious movement that was flourishing in Palestine in the time of Jesus. Our only other contemporary record is that of Flavius Josephus, a Jewish aristocrat who was involved in the Jewish War of 66–70 and who subsequently wrote both a history of that war and a complete history of the Jewish people in the hope of gaining sympathy at Rome for the Jewish cause. Another Greek-speaking Jewish writer, Philo of Alexandria, was meanwhile devoting his life to interpreting the Jewish scriptures in terms that would make sense to people educated in Greek philosophy. By temperament and circumstances Philo was remote from the concerns of the Jews in Palestine. Yet his writings were intended for readers of similar background to those addressed by early Christian writers, and they can occasionally be usefully compared with passages in the New Testament.

Apart from this there is very little indeed. A few Jewish writings of a visionary and symbolic character (known in modern times as 'apocalyptic') were preserved in translation by the Christian church (which also had its own 'apocalypse' among the writings of the New Testament). Otherwise the characteristic Jewish distrust of any authoritative writings apart from the scriptures continued right into the second century, and it was only in about the middle of that century that the Jewish rabbis began to write down and codify the traditions which had been handed down to them. These rabbinic writings became voluminous in the centuries that followed, and often contain genuine recollections of customs, events and doctrines of first-century Palestinian Judaism. But their evidence is always fragmentary and often misleading. The picture they present of life in Jerusalem before its destruction in 70 CE is frequently idealized beyond recognition.

In this respect the New Testament stands very much by itself. Much of it is first-hand evidence for conditions and events of which we would otherwise know nothing. Where we can check it against independent sources of information it is usually reasonably faithful to the facts. Where we cannot, we have to judge its historical reliability on its merits. On the whole, the historical evidence it provides is consistent and plausible, and for reconstructing the circumstances in which any part of it was written the most important information is usually to be found within the New Testament itself. Yet it is still necessary (and this is one of the purposes of this *Companion*) to supplement this information so far as possible from the little we know about the history, religion and culture of the Jewish people in Palestine and in the Dispersion during the first century CE.

Not that the Christians were ever merely Jews, or Christianity simply a form of Judaism. The Christian religion and the Christian church represented something new and unique in the ancient world. Yet Jesus was a Jew, and so were all his first followers and all the founders of the first churches. Christianity stood closer to Judaism than to any other religion or philosophy of life, and its history and beliefs were written in predominantly Jewish terms for the first century of its existence. The clearest instance of this is the constant use of the Old Testament which is made by nearly every New Testament writer. Sometimes whole passages are quoted, sometimes just a word or a sentence; sometimes there are subtle allusions and sometimes a writer seems deliberately to imitate the style of the Old Testament without actually quoting it. There is nothing surprising in this. The only form of literature with which most of these writers were familiar was either scripture itself or else some kind of commentary on it; and it was natural that they should see their own work in the same light, however new the message was that they had to convey. To us their use of scripture, and the interpretation they placed on particular passages, often seems recondite and artificial. It presupposes a long tradition of Jewish scholarly interpretation which was based on principles very different from those which would be acceptable today. But this does not alter the fact that the Old Testament was the most important single element in the background shared by all the New Testament writers.

Like most editions of the New Testament, the NRSV does not make it possible for the reader to recognize every quotation of or allusion to a passage of the Hebrew scriptures. But even if it did, it would not always be easy to turn up the relevant passage of the Old Testament and identify it with the reference in the New. Most modern English translations of the Old Testament are based on a Hebrew text which did not become fully standardized until the early centuries of our era. In the time of Christ it is unlikely that every synagogue and religious group in Palestine used an identical text of the scriptures. Moreover, although in Palestine they were read in Hebrew, the reading was usually followed by a translation into Aramaic; and throughout the Dispersion the Jews read and listened to the scriptures in a Greek translation. The most famous of these Greek translations, the Septuagint (so called because of the tradition that it was compiled by a team of seventy translators), was made in Egypt in the third century BCE and had a wide circulation. It still exists, and by comparing it with the quotations that occur in the New Testament we can tell that this was the translation most frequently used by most Christian writers. But they did not always use exactly the version which we now possess. Sometimes their Greek translation seems to have been slightly different from that of the Septuagint, sometimes they seem to have quoted a version based on an Aramaic translation, and occasionally they may have made their own translation from the Hebrew. If all these translations had been strictly accurate by modern standards this would not greatly matter. But in fact they show striking variations from each other – sometimes the translators seem to have misunderstood the original, sometimes they rephrased it to make it (as they thought) more comprehensible to their readers. In addition to this, the Septuagint contained more books than were subsequently admitted into the Hebrew text that has survived. These books, having been 'hidden away' by the Jewish scholars of Palestine on the grounds that they were not sufficiently important or authoritative to be included in scripture, have, since the Reformation, been printed separately in Protestant Bibles under the title 'Apocrypha' (literally, 'hidden books'). In the NRSV they are placed under the heading APOCRYPHAL/DEUTERO-CANONICAL BOOKS.

For all these reasons, the use of the Old Testament in the New is not always easy to recognize and its function in the argument is often difficult to follow. In this matter as in others, this *Companion* attempts to elucidate the writers' usage and so to bring out the tremendous importance which the Old Testament had for them as a prime source of inspiration and truth. Even the title, THE NEW TESTAMENT, can hardly be understood apart from that other term, 'the Old Testament', from which it was ultimately derived.

THE GOSPELS

To the modern reader, the word GOSPEL denotes the kind of book that has come down to us under the names of Matthew, Mark, Luke and John. But in the early church it was some time before the word took on this meaning. It is clear from the letters of Paul that 'the gospel' existed before any of the 'gospels' came to be written. *Euangelion*, 'gospel', was the name given by the first generation of Christians to the message they had to impart. Literally, it meant 'good news'.

If we are to judge by the accounts in the Acts of the Apostles, when this message was first preached it consisted of a fairly brief summary of those facts about Jesus of Nazareth which had caused his followers to believe that he was the promised Messiah, or Christ. For the purpose of convincing their Jewish hearers, it was doubtless on these facts that the first preachers needed to concentrate, along with the consequences of those facts for faith and conduct. But Jesus, though he wrote nothing himself, had also been a teacher, a prophet, a healer and exorcist, a miracle-worker and a controversial expositor of law and scripture. Many of his acts and sayings must have been reverently preserved in the memories of his followers and were available to give flesh to the bare bones of the original proclamation. Moreover, new questions soon began to be asked. For example, the Christians found themselves in controversy with the Jews over such matters as sabbath observance and food laws: what had been Jesus' attitude? They were liable to be under threat from the Roman authorities if their religion seemed in any way to invite sedition: had Jesus said and done things to provoke the hostility of the occupying power in Palestine? Problems were arising about moral conduct and discipline within the Christian communities: had Jesus left any instructions that were relevant? These and many other questions inevitably arose in the course of the early decades of the church's existence and may have provided an additional incentive to recall and preserve the details of the life and teaching of Jesus.

We do not know how soon these details began to be written down in collections of sayings or connected narratives. But between about 65 and 100 CE four books were written in Greek which gathered together much of what was already recorded or was still remembered about the life and work of Jesus. The form of these books was unlike anything that had been written before. To a certain extent they could be called 'biographies' (for ancient biographies omitted much that would be obligatory today); but they also had a clear religious and missionary purpose. What they contained was the original 'gospel' proclaimed by the church, though cast in extended narrative form. They were known by the title of the message they embodied

(THE GOSPEL) and were distinguished from one another by being ascribed to Matthew, Mark, Luke and John.

These four names do not tell us much. They were almost certainly intended to stand for the four men who appear in the New Testament under the names of 'Matthew', 'John Mark', 'Luke the beloved physician' and 'John'. But it is no more than a tradition of the church, going back to the second century CE, that attributes the gospels to these men; the books themselves are anonymous, only two of them make any claims for their authors, and the environment they reflect is not, for the most part, that which one would have expected if they had been written by men who were among the earliest followers of Jesus. Nevertheless, there must have been some reason for preserving these names: two of them (Mark and Luke) are not even the names of apostles. It may well be that at some stage the tradition contained in the gospels passed through the hands of the men whose names they bear, even if not all of them were the actual authors.

More significant is the relationship between the four written gospels, and particularly between the first three. The gospels according to Matthew, Mark and Luke all tell what is essentially the same story. Sometimes they tell it in almost identical language; at other times they diverge substantially from each other. Usually they agree, sometimes they disagree; and each of the three preserves material that is absent from both the others. Mark is the shortest, and contains very little which does not appear in Matthew or Luke or both. On the other hand, Matthew and Luke have a number of passages in common which do not appear in Mark. In short, the relationship between the three is close, but very complicated. They appear to have originated in different places for use in different Christian congregations: no church would have needed a second or third so similar to the first, and it can have been only when they began to be circulated more widely (and when the methods of book production made longer books possible) that they were bound up in the same volume. On the other hand, they cannot have been written quite independently of each other. The occurrence of almost identical passages in two or even three gospels is explicable only if one writer had access to the work of another.

There is no completely convincing explanation of all these facts. In modern times the most popular hypothesis has been that Mark was composed first and was used by both Matthew and Luke; that Matthew and Luke also used another source, now lost, consisting mainly of sayings of Jesus (hence the appearance of passages common to both of them but absent from Mark); and that each of them had access to traditions not available to either of the others, which they worked as best they could into the narrative framework provided by Mark. To account for all the facts this explanation needs considerable refinement and cannot be said to have been proved correct: some scholars continue to use a different model. But as a working hypothesis it has probably aided the study of the first three gospels more than any of the other possible combinations, and it is adopted in this *Companion*, not because it can be proved to be true, but because it is impossible to make sense of the evidence without some explanation of this kind. Moreover, it would have been a waste of space and of the reader's time to provide as full a commentary on the same passage each time it appears in different gospels. It was therefore a matter of practical convenience, as well as a deliberate exploitation of the most widely held hypothesis, to make the commentary on Mark more detailed than either of the other two. Any passage which occurs in Mark and in one or more of the other gospels is fully discussed only in its context in Mark. The commentary on the parallel passage in another gospel is confined to pointing out significant differences. Further, where a passage occurs in both Matthew and Luke (but not Mark), the discussion will normally be found under Matthew – though this again is merely for the reader's convenience: it is not intended to suggest that Luke had read Matthew (although theoretically this is also possible).

More important consequences follow from adopting this hypothesis, however, than the arrangement of this *Companion*. If Matthew and Luke used Mark, then Mark must have been written first. It seems unlikely, for various reasons, that any of the gospels was written earlier than the death of Paul or later than the end of the first century of our era. To allow time for Mark to have been circulated and then rewritten by Matthew and Luke, it seems sensible to place Mark near the beginning of that period – say between 65 and 70 – and the other two a decade or two later. John's gospel is usually thought to reflect external conditions and a stage in the development of Christianity which are somewhat later than those reflected in the other three, and is therefore dated between 90 and 100. But all these assumptions are open to challenge, and there is virtually nothing against which to check the proposed dates. Even the catastrophic event of the fall and destruction of Jerusalem in 70 CE is not certainly alluded to in any New Testament writing.

There is another consequence of accepting this hypothesis which bears more directly on the interpretation of each gospel. When a passage occurs in Mark and in one or both of the other 'synoptic' gospels, there are often notable changes, sometimes slight, sometimes quite substantial, which have been made in Matthew and Luke. If one studies these changes one can often see a pattern beginning to emerge: it is as if each gospel writer had a particular approach of his own to the material he was recording, an approach which he expressed by subtle editorial changes or rearrangements. Whereas the selection of sayings and episodes he was working on may have been the result of the particular concerns of the churches which originally preserved them, he appears to have had a literary and theological strategy for enabling the reader to see the significance of the story he was telling. The case is still clearer when we come to John, whose gospel tells a story notably different from the others and in a new and distinctive style. It has usually been assumed that

John, like Matthew and Luke, used Mark, though if he did so he used it with much greater freedom than they did. But he clearly also had other sources of information, and some of these may even be older and more authentic than those available to Mark. However this may be, it has been realized since very early times that he was recasting his material in a more consciously literary and 'spiritual' style so as to express in his own way the genius of Jesus' teaching and the significance of his life and work. Sometimes his narrative and chronology are incompatible with those in the other gospels, and we have to make a choice. It is usual to regard Mark's gospel (assuming it is the earliest) as providing the most reliable historical information. But we do not possess the material which Mark himself may have been editing and possibly rearranging for his own purpose. It is possible that he, as much as John, imposed a certain pattern on his sources (such as a much simpler account of Jesus' movements between Galilee and Jerusalem) in order to bring out the significance of the events he was recording. It is clear that none of the gospels was ever intended merely to present a bare chronicle of Jesus' doings. Each of them is also 'gospel', good news.

Detailed analysis of the gospels has shown that much of the material out of which they were composed originally consisted of small independent units, sometimes amounting only to a single saying, sometimes running to the length of a complete episode. It was the writers of the gospels who put these units together to make a coherent narrative, and sometimes placed them in a different order or in different contexts. It follows that it has never been possible to write a 'life of Jesus' in the modern sense of a narrative charting his development and progress through a period of years: apart from the beginning and the end, we simply cannot be sure in what order the various episodes took place, and we cannot always disentangle their original significance from the interpretation which each of the gospel writers has placed upon them. (This is particularly the case with some of the parables.) But it does not follow from this that it is impossible to get behind the written gospels at all. On the contrary, the individual contribution of each of the writers is slight and subtle; to present the message in their own way they each had to be content with relatively small touches – hence the difficulty of establishing exactly what the agenda was of each. It is as if the material they had to work on, having been reverently preserved by their fellow Christians and being already broadly familiar to their hearers or readers, set a strict limit to their editorial freedom. At any point we must be prepared to see their hand at work; but it seems never to have been a free hand. What has come down to us under the names of Matthew, Mark, Luke and John is a story which, in its essentials, the writers could never have created themselves.

Even this does not necessarily take us back to Jesus himself. By the time the gospel writers set to work the traditions they possessed about Jesus had already been collected and preserved by the church and had been put to use (and possibly adapted) for the purposes of preaching, teaching and defending the faith. They had also at some stage been translated from Aramaic (Jesus' language) into Greek, with all that that implies of subtle accommodation to a different culture. The gospels as we have them often betray the marks of these developments. The circumstances and needs of the early church, and the characteristic editorial strategies of each evangelist, are discernible in the form in which Jesus' sayings and the events of his life have been preserved. Yet, as literary critics may remind us, the story has a power and consistency such that it must either be based on fact or be the work of a literary genius. But that it was originally the work of any single writer is excluded by the existence and intricate relationship of the four gospels; and the story, however composite its present form, contains elements such as could hardly have been created by the church. It is for these reasons that we may still say with some confidence that the gospels, despite the mysterious and complicated history of their compilation, preserve an authentic recollection of the life and teaching of Jesus of Nazareth.

THE GOSPEL ACCORDING TO

MATTHEW

Jesus' ancestry

1.1 **An account of the genealogy.** To the modern reader this may seem a daunting beginning. Even the most laboriously painstaking modern biography would hardly begin with a complete line of descent from a remote ancestor. But in the Jewish culture there were good reasons for doing so, and the reader would know what to look out for. Was Jesus of impeccably Jewish descent (a true **son of Abraham**) – and, if not (as the unexpected listing of four women, arguably all Gentiles, might suggest), what were the implications? Had he a mission for the world as well as for his own people? Was he of the tribe and family from which people (or at any rate most people, but there were rival views) expected a **Messiah** to come? Might there be some significance in the exact moment in history at which he had been born? (Counting by generations it was three times **fourteen** – a multiple of the symbolic number seven – from Abraham.)

16

17

1   These questions all arise from the title by which Jesus is introduced: **the Messiah.** This Hebrew term, meaning 'the Anointed One', was translated into Greek as *Christos*, and gave Jesus the name by which he was to become universally known. It was an old title, originally used of the first kings of Israel. But in the time of Jesus it was reserved for a divinely appointed but fully human figure whom (it was widely believed) God would soon send into the world to inaugurate a new and blessed age for the benefit of his chosen people (or of the elect among them). Was Jesus this Messiah, this Christ? His work and teaching were such that the question was bound to be constantly raised. In public, he never gave an altogether unambiguous answer to it, though some may have begun already to call him 'Jesus the Christ' to distinguish him from other men called 'Jesus' (*yeshua*, a common name). There was a moment when the crucifixion seemed to rule out the claim that he was Messiah; but after the resurrection his disciples became convinced that the claim was true, and began to refer to him regularly as Jesus 'the Christ', and soon simply as 'Jesus Christ'. By calling him **Jesus the Messiah** in its opening words the gospel declares itself to be addressed to people who are prepared to take this claim seriously while they read or hear the story.

The list itself is clearly less concerned with exact historical accuracy (which was unattainable anyway) than with the theological message that might be read off from it: other comparable lists in the Hebrew scriptures and later literature are similarly adjusted or supplemented to convey the desired message

13

of, say, legitimacy or purity. From Abraham to Zerubbabel Matthew's genealogy runs through the well-known leaders of the Jewish people. Where it can be checked against similar lists in the Old Testament (such as in the first chapters of 1 Chronicles) it shows some discrepancies; but no single and authoritative genealogy of the leading families of Jewish history existed in Matthew's time, and it need cause no surprise that Matthew's list differs slightly from others, particularly since it had to be adjusted a little to fit into a fourteenfold pattern.[1] After Zerubbabel the line branches off from the main stem in order to reach the immediate ancestors of Jesus, and we have no means of checking it. It is quite different from the table in Luke (3.23–38); but this does not necessarily prove either of the tables to be a fiction. The evangelists may have had access to family papers or family memories, preserving one or more family trees (perhaps through different parents or grandparents). Both of them believed they could show that Joseph was among the descendants of

6 **David**; and this was a key link in the chain of evidence to support the claim
16 that Jesus was indeed **the Messiah.**

But Joseph was not Jesus' father. Matthew had two apparently incompatible things to say about Jesus: first that he was a descendant of David (as the Messiah was generally expected to be), and secondly that he was born in a unique way without a human father, and so could be acknowledged (as he is later in the gospel) as, in a special sense, 'Son of God'. But Jewish law and custom would have offered an obvious solution. If a Jew formally adopted and named a child, that child became his son. This, along with Jesus' divine sonship, is the theme of the rest of the chapter.

The miraculous birth

18 **Now the birth of Jesus the Messiah took place in this way.** The birth was miraculous: it was God, and no human father, who caused Mary to conceive. In the Old Testament the creative power of God was called his 'spirit'; and it would have come naturally to a Jewish writer such as Matthew to use the same language: **she was found to be with child from the Holy Spirit.** But Matthew (unlike Luke) does not linger over this miraculous circumstance; he goes straight on to the human consequences. Mary was **engaged to Joseph**, which meant under Jewish law that she was fully committed to marry him; the contract would have already been signed and it remained only for the marriage ceremony to take place and for the bride to take up residence in her husband's house. Her pregnancy, if suddenly discovered at this stage by the bridegroom, would normally cancel the engagement, justify a divorce
19 and bring shame and financial loss to the bride's family. **Being a righteous man**, Joseph could not condone this apparent scandal. He must either bring

---

[1] Actually the list has only forty-one names instead of forty-two, but this may be the result of an accident in the transmission of the text.

his fiancée publicly before a court to prove her guilty or else repudiate the marriage contract and **dismiss her quietly**. But a further divine intervention, related in the form of a dream and an angel, made him take responsibility himself. If the world were to believe that he had had intercourse with his betrothed before their marriage, it would not greatly matter: this was not regarded as a serious impropriety in Jewish society; and by adopting and naming the child he took him formally into his own family and ensured that, like him, Jesus could rightfully be called a 'son of David'.

Matthew, however, is not concerned only to settle these practical details. He compresses into this short paragraph some important clues to the wider significance of Jesus' birth. The name 'Jesus' itself meant 'saviour', and described 21 something of Jesus' destiny (**"he will save his people from their sins"**); and the manner of Jesus' birth had a striking parallel in Old Testament prophecy. One of Matthew's particular contributions to the gospel story was to demonstrate that not merely the suffering, death and resurrection of Jesus but also many other episodes had been prefigured or foretold in scripture. In doing this his methods were not always such as modern scholarship would countenance, though they would have aroused fewer scruples among Jewish scholars 23 of his time. Here, for example, the original Hebrew of Isaiah 7.14 has, not **"the virgin"**, but 'a young woman', and it is unlikely that Isaiah, in this prophecy of future abundance and divine favour, meant anything so improbable as a virgin birth. But in the Greek translation of the Old Testament, which Matthew appears generally to have used, the word could (though did not necessarily) mean 'virgin', and so to Matthew's mind the text could be regarded as a startlingly exact prophecy of the event he had just recorded.

The wise men and Herod

2.1 **In the time of King Herod**. Herod the Great died, after a long reign, in about 4 BCE. Matthew's narrative implies that Jesus was born not less than two years before this (verse 16), but also not much more (verse 19) – say 7–6 BCE. This is somewhat earlier than the traditional date (between 1 BCE and 1 CE), but the idea of dating world history by the birth of Christ was not invented until five hundred years later, and the date then chosen was the result of a mistaken calculation. Matthew's date is not improbable in itself; the only difficulty is to reconcile it with the chronology in Luke's gospel (see below on Luke 2.1).

In any country where astrology was taken seriously – as it was in most countries in the ancient world, and particularly in those which lay immediately to the east of Palestine – a new star such as a comet, or a notable conjunction of the planets, would quickly attract attention, presaging an important new turn in human affairs. Conversely, it was believed that it was the very regularity of the stars which guaranteed the orderly course of history, and it followed that any really significant event must necessarily be accompanied by some striking phenomenon in the heavens. The birth of Jesus was such an event; and if the following story now reads more like legend than history, it is easy to see how such a legend could have originated, particularly since similar legends were told in Jewish folklore about the birth of Moses (as they were in other cultures about the births of great rulers); and there are indications throughout the gospel that Matthew may have regarded Jesus as, in some sense, a second Moses.

On the other hand, the story, at least in broad outline, is by no means incredible. The visitors from the east are called, in the Greek, *magi*. The word originally came from Persia, where it denoted influential and respected religious leaders; but in ordinary Greek usage it had come to mean something less respectable: sorcerers or magicians. What does it mean here? These men were certainly not 'Three Kings of Orient' – that is a later legend based on the prophecy in Isaiah 60.3. And they may not have been altogether harmless 'wise men'. But one kind of knowledge they did possess – astrology; and it is certainly correct to call them (with the NRSV footnote) *astrologers*. Their observation of the star had satisfied them that some change was pending in the west, that is to say, in Palestine; and they felt sure enough of their

2 interpretation to put to Herod a specific question, **"Where is the child who has been born king of the Jews?"** Herod, who doubtless intended to make his own arrangements about the succession to his throne, preferred to regard the star as a presage of that other 'king' whom the Jews were awaiting, the Messiah. Many passages of their scriptures were read as pointing forward to this figure, and it was to be expected that the religious leaders of the Jews, and particularly

4 **the chief priests and scribes** (who were the professional expositors of these scriptures), would be able to answer the astrologers' question. Their answer could by no means be taken for granted: many opinions were abroad about the circumstances in which the Messiah would appear. But there was a prophecy in Micah (5.2)[2] which was certainly understood by some as an oracle about the birthplace of the Messiah. In Matthew's story the immediate function of the prophecy is to direct the astrologers to the village not more than six miles from Jerusalem where they would find what the star had led them to expect; but in the wider context of the gospel its apparent fulfilment serves to strengthen the claim that Jesus was the expected Messiah, a 'son of David' (for Bethlehem had been David's home).

Even in antiquity it was felt to be impossible that the star should actually

9 have gone **ahead of them** or **stopped over the place** in such a way as to guide them on their short journey. Clearly the language is poetic rather than

2 literal;[3] nevertheless, the statement that they had seen the star **at its rising** continues the astrological theme. (The Greek word, which normally meant

---

[2] Matthew quotes this in a version a little different from that either in the Hebrew or in the Greek of the Septuagint, and combines with it a few words from 2 Samuel 5.2.

[3] The translation **the star had stopped** in verse 10 is a pedantic attempt to make it more plausible – see the literal meaning in the NRSV footnote.

in the East, was also used in this technical sense of *rising*.) The purpose of the astrologers in seeking the child was to pay him homage. When they found

11 him they offered him **gifts of gold, frankincense and myrrh** – traditional products of the wealth and luxury of the east. (Compare Isaiah 60.6 for gold and frankincense – that passage may have been in Matthew's mind – and Song of Solomon 3.6 for frankincense and myrrh.) Their gifts showed that they recognized him as the 'king' of whom the star was a sign; and they – Gentiles, perhaps representing the entire world – were the first to give their allegiance to one who would be crucified as 'king of the Jews'. Herod's interest, however, was more practical: to eliminate one who might grow up to be, if not a pretender to his throne, at least a cause of unrest in Judea. It would be in keeping with what we know of the character of Herod that he was

16 **infuriated**, and **sent and killed** all suspect children. His reign, especially in its closing years, was marked by many atrocities. But although this act has come to be known as the 'massacre of the innocents', Matthew may not mean that he killed *all* the children of two years or under. The phrase, **according to the time that he had learned**, makes good sense in astrology ('learned' is a significant word in the Greek, meaning that he *enquired very precisely*): only those children born at the exact season of the conjunction of the stars would have been a threat to him – possibly quite a small number. Matthew's concern, at any rate, was not so much to portray the savagery of Herod as to discern the larger significance of the episode. He saw it, first, as a direct fulfilment of a prophecy of Jeremiah (31.15). Rachel, the wife of Jacob and

18 mother of two of the 'tribes' of Israel, is there imagined as **weeping** for her descendants who are being deported by the Assyrian conquerors past the northern frontier town of Rama. Matthew evidently thinks of her lamenting near Bethlehem, perhaps because there was an old tradition (Genesis 35.19), which is still preserved by a monument today, that Rachel's tomb was close to Bethlehem. Secondly, Herod's brutality was the motive for the flight of Jesus' parents into Egypt, and this too placed Jesus in the line of a great national tradition: God had "called [his] son" – the people of Israel – "out of Egypt" (Hosea 11.1). Jesus, who was 'God's son' *par excellence*, lived through a similar exile and a similar return.

23 **He made his home in a town called Nazareth**. Galilee was ruled by Herod Antipas, one of Herod's sons, and theoretically the danger might have been as great there as in Bethlehem. In practice, however, Nazareth was probably safer. It was a small and rather isolated town in the hills of Galilee, with none of the Davidic or Messianic associations of Bethlehem. We even read in John's gospel that no one would have expected a native of Nazareth to make any mark on history (1.46, "Can anything good come out of Nazareth?"). But the fact was that Jesus certainly had his home there and was known as a 'Nazorean' (or 'Nazarene'[4]), and indeed Christians were for many years

---

[4] The form used by Mark and sometimes by Luke.

also called 'Nazarenes' in Palestine. One of Matthew's purposes in the whole of this chapter has been to insist that this 'Nazorean' was nevertheless born in Bethlehem, as a true descendant of David should have been (though it is Luke who gives a practical explanation of how this might have come to be so). Even in the name **Nazorean**, however, Matthew finds some significance. But here we are at a loss. The Old Testament does not contain the words, **"He will be called a Nazorean."** Perhaps the nearest phrase occurs in the narrative of the birth of Samson: Samson was to be a "nazirite" (Judges 13.5), which meant an ascetic under vows to God. But Matthew may have had in mind a more subtle allusion to the Hebrew word *netser*, 'branch', which occurs in various biblical texts (especially Isaiah 11.1) that were held to be prophecies of the Messiah.

John the Baptist and Jesus' preparation

3.1 **In those days.** The phrase is perhaps deliberately imprecise. Many years have passed in the little gap between chapter 2 and chapter 3. Jesus has grown up. Judea is now under direct Roman rule, the reign of Archelaus, Herod's successor, having quickly come to an ignominious end (6 CE); while the northern and eastern parts of the country, Galilee and Perea, are still under the more or less independent rule of Herod's son, Herod Antipas. It is in connection with this Herod Antipas that **John the Baptist** makes a brief appearance in the pages of another writer nearly contemporary with the author of this gospel, the Jewish historian Josephus. Josephus' interest in him is more political than religious (though he does acknowledge his moral stature), but his account agrees in the basic facts. The popular interest in John appeared to Herod Antipas as a threat to peace, and in due course Herod imprisoned him.

When Mark introduces John the Baptist he concentrates entirely (apart from a few words devoted to the nature of his baptism) on his rôle as the herald and forerunner of Jesus. Matthew, though he quotes the same prophecy from Isaiah (40.3), presents him at the outset as a moral challenge in his own right, making his proclamation in the manner of an Old Testament prophet. John certainly resembled a prophet, both by his clothes (compare the description of Elijah in 2 Kings 1.8), and also by his appearance in the **wilderness of Judea**. Large tracts of Palestine, one of them reaching right up to the neighbourhood of Jerusalem, were (and in many cases still are) bare and uncultivable, as against the densely populated farmlands of Galilee or the vineyards of other parts of Judea. Traditionally, a prophet was a man who pondered his message in an austere environment, away from the amenities of sophisticated life. John conformed with this tradition; and his message was correspondingly

2 simple and direct. **"Repent"**: the word meant not so much personal remorse for a particular fault or offence as a complete and general re-orientation, away from the compromises and casuistries of contemporary political and

religious life towards a single-minded attention to the just demands of God. The **"kingdom of heaven"** is the same concept as the 'kingdom of God' (the form usually found in the other gospels), only in a somewhat more reverential Jewish dress – the Jews sought to avoid using God's name, and preferred to speak of 'heaven', 'angels' and the like. A preliminary definition of it might be: God's rule, that longed-for state of affairs when human beings will willingly and spontaneously do the will of God. **"Has come near."** The question is, how near? From the Greek word alone, it is impossible to tell. But it is clear from what follows that John is giving urgent warning of coming judgment. Most Jews expected this some time in the future. John proclaims that it is very near indeed: his word (like that of Jesus, whose preaching, in this gospel, begins in exactly the same way) is meant to drive the point home: it is no longer in the uncertain future, it is **near.**

7 Among the crowd were **many Pharisees and Sadducees** (on whom see below on Acts 23.6). It does not strictly follow from the Greek that these people came **for baptism.** They may have simply come to watch. They represented a higher level of society than (presumably) the rest of the throng, and in Matthew's account (unlike Luke's) they are singled out for attack by the Baptist just as, later in the gospel, they (or usually just the Pharisees) are consistently criticized by Jesus. The ground for John's attack is that they

9 claimed a certain immunity from the coming judgment: **"We have Abraham for our ancestor"** – a classic Jewish defence that is criticized also by Paul in Romans 2. John – in words used also by Jesus (7.19) – sweeps aside this assumption of divine favouritism, and returns to the arresting element in

11 his proclamation. The one who **is coming** is certainly (as in Mark) a person infinitely greater than himself, and his baptism will be, not just a ritual washing with water, but a personal encounter with the **Holy Spirit.** He is also to be an Elijah figure (the language recalls Malachi 4; Sirach 48), a man of **fire,** bringing immediate judgment.

We know, and Matthew's readers knew, who it was for whom John was preparing a way. It was Jesus. But we should not necessarily read this back into the narrative. For in many respects Jesus does not fit the portrait given here. Jesus himself still expected a coming judgment, even if, later on, his own coming came to be understood as a kind of anticipation of it; and as for an Elijah figure, Jesus regarded John, not himself, as Elijah (11.14). Matthew, in any case, does not state explicitly that John recognized Jesus as the one who was to come. What he recognized was simply something exceptional about Jesus which seemed to make it inappropriate to baptize him (like others) 'confessing his sins'. It looks, indeed, as if this may have been a difficulty felt by the early Christians. They knew that Jesus had been baptized by John, and that John's baptism was for 'the forgiveness of sins'; they knew also that Jesus was without sin. So why was he baptized? This passage may have

15 been moulded to provide an answer: **"to fulfil all righteousness".** What this means has prompted much debate. It may be that Jesus was "fulfilling" all the

scriptural prophecies about him which focused on "righteousness"; it may be that he was seen to be validating the rite of baptism for all future generations of Christians; it may be that even the Messiah could undergo a re-orientation towards perfect righteousness, and so could repent and be baptized. However this may be, the rest of the account of Jesus' baptism follows Mark closely

17 (Mark 1.9–11). The same combination of scriptural texts was heard **from heaven** (though possibly only by Jesus); but this did not conclusively identify him as the one whom John was expecting. Indeed, John was still in doubt some time later (11.2–3).

4.1   **Then Jesus was led up**. Mark, at this point, simply records a period of contest with the devil in the wilderness. Matthew and Luke evidently knew a fuller version of the story, and one which puts it in a somewhat different light. In Mark, one has to imagine a sustained struggle between Jesus and the devil, Jesus being meanwhile aided and fed by angels. Here, Jesus *first* undergoes a prolonged fast (he is only afterwards waited on by the angels, verse 11) and is

3 *then* approached by the devil in the character of the **tempter** and exposed to three 'temptations' or tests. The first of these tests was a natural consequence of his hunger and could have taken place on the spot. The other two are

5 also vividly set in Palestinian scenery – **the pinnacle of the temple** is usually thought to be the south-east corner of the immense terrace constructed by Herod the Great around the temple area in Jerusalem, from which there was a sheer drop of some 45 metres (150 feet) into the Kidron valley below; and many hill-tops in the Judean desert offer impressive views over the Jordan valley to the mountains beyond, which could well be described as a

8 microcosm of **all the kingdoms of the world and their splendor**. Thus the actual tests could not have been carried out in one region of the Judean desert; they must have taken place in Jesus' mind. In which case it must be asked, in what sense is it likely that the story represents a historical episode in the life of Jesus? One feature of the story bears on this question. All Jesus' replies are quotations from the book of Deuteronomy: Deuteronomy 8.3, 6.16 (in answer to the devil's quotation of Psalm 19.11–12) and 6.13 – and a learned swapping of texts was (at least in later centuries) a common form of rabbinic disputation. Furthermore, these verses in Deuteronomy occur in the context of the period of 'testing' which the people of Israel themselves underwent in the wilderness. It is clear that the biblical narrative has influenced the form and perhaps even inspired the content of the story recounted by Matthew and Luke: Jesus was re-enacting in his own person the formative experience of the desert generation. But this is not to say that Jesus did not experience something of the kind himself. The disciples could well have been aware that Jesus treasured these verses of Deuteronomy, and had come to perceive their significance for himself during his period of retreat in the wilderness. The remaining details would not have been hard to fill in.

12   **When Jesus heard that John had been arrested**. Like Mark, Matthew regards the moment of John's arrest – which he can assume that his readers

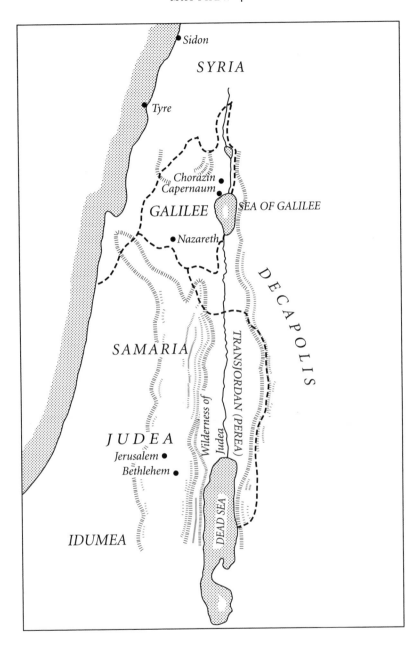

know about, and which he describes only later on – as the point in time at which Jesus appeared publicly in Galilee. But he is a little more specific than Mark about the details. **He withdrew** – not, probably, to avoid the same fate as John's; for Galilee, just as much as Perea (where it is likely that John was arrested), belonged to the territory of Herod Antipas. Rather (though it is not said that this followed immediately), he may well have wished for a period of 'withdrawal' after the rigorous testing in the desert. Matthew also knew (or at least inferred) that since so many of the events he was about to record were enacted on the shores of the Sea of Galilee, Jesus must have

13 moved from Nazareth (which is some 30 miles from it) and **made his home in Capernaum**, the most important Jewish town on the lake; and this enabled him to invoke another prophecy. The passage he quotes from Isaiah (9.1–2), with its old tribal names for the region, was written when Galilee was under

15 foreign control (and was therefore **of the Gentiles**), and prophesied its restoration to the people of Israel. Matthew sees in Jesus' appearance **by the sea** (and perhaps also in the eventual Christian mission to the Gentiles) a different and more significant fulfilment of the prophecy.

17 On Jesus' proclamation (which in Matthew is identical with that of John the Baptist), see below on Mark 1.15.

18 **As he walked by the Sea of Galilee.** Matthew follows Mark (1.16ff.) in placing this episode at the beginning of Jesus' work. It was necessarily located by **the Sea of Galilee** – which is what the Jews called it, though in reality it was a lake, the Lake of Tiberias. The main fishing waters are still at the north end of the lake, where warm springs enter it near the site of Capernaum.

The Sermon on the Mount

But Matthew then widens the scene. Jesus' preaching and healing – of which

23 he is about to give examples – extended **throughout Galilee**. It was concentrated, for the purpose of teaching, on towns such as Capernaum and Chorazin, where there would be a large synagogue and where the sabbath congregations would offer him a good opening for his work (see on Mark 1.21); but we are also to picture him as a healer and preacher, moving about over a wide area and attracting great crowds, not only from Galilee and the

25 rest of Jewish Palestine (**Jerusalem, Judea and from beyond the Jordan**), but also from the more cosmopolitan world of the **Decapolis** (the 'Ten Towns', a league of wealthy Greco-Roman cities to the south-east of Galilee).

Since at least the time of Saint Augustine the next three chapters of Matthew's gospel have been known as *The Sermon on the Mount*, follow-

5.1 ing the cue given in the first words of chapter 5, **he went up the mountain**. We may be tempted to ask, which mountain? But the original Greek is less precise, and means 'up into the hill country', that is, away from the populous coast of the lake into the more lonely foothills to the west and north. Jesus' purpose in thus going 'up the mountain' was usually to get away from the crowds, either in order to pray (Matthew 14.23) or to talk privately with his disciples (Mark 3.13). Accordingly, the opening of his discourse here is specifically addressed to his **disciples** (who are mentioned here for the first time, and may be assumed to be a group which has grown out of individual decisions, such as those of Simon and Andrew, to 'follow' Jesus, 4.18–20); and the traditional picture of Jesus standing on a high place addressing the multitude is unwarranted by these opening verses. However by the end of the discourse (7.28), we find that *the crowds* "were astounded at his teaching". If we wish to accept these chapters at their face value as the record of a single occasion we shall have to assume that the crowds caught up with Jesus while he was talking, and that what began as the giving of teaching to a group of disciples ended, by force of circumstances, as a sermon addressed to a large congregation.

This is possible; but the apparent change in the audience between the beginning and the end is not the only indication that these chapters are something other than the record of a particular occasion. Some of the sayings throughout the 'sermon' must have been originally intended for the disciples, some for the crowds; some of them are found in other gospels in quite different contexts; and some, by the time Matthew included them, may have been somewhat altered by the early church (or even by radical and ascetic groups of followers) into a form more appropriate to their own situation. Moreover the discourse as a whole hardly constitutes a 'sermon' in the modern sense. There is a logical development of thought in certain sections, but there is no overall theme, and it is hard to imagine the discourse being delivered on a single occasion and listened to by a single audience. In short, it fits the facts better if we regard these chapters as a collection made by Matthew (or the source he was using) of Jesus' spiritual and ethical teaching, arranged under certain headings, and provided with an introduction and conclusion which (since these occur also in the 'sermon' in Luke's gospel, 6.20–49) may well reproduce a pattern which Jesus was accustomed to use in his teaching. Such a collection would certainly have been useful for teaching purposes in the early church, and this may be one of the reasons Matthew incorporated it in his gospel. Another reason may be that Matthew saw Jesus as, in some respects, a new Moses: Jesus' teaching on the 'mountain' corresponded to, and was indeed, an authoritative commentary on, Moses' proclamation of the law on Sinai.

These possibilities must be borne in mind throughout the next three chapters. But they do not necessarily affect our estimate of the 'sermon'. For, however it came into existence, it remains the most comprehensive and ethically radical account of Jesus' teaching to have come down to us. It was regarded by the author of the gospel as a fair summary of what Jesus taught – if he was following Mark he may well have thought that this was something essential that needed to be added to the story near the beginning. At times we may detect evidence of subsequent editing and retouching by Matthew or by the tradition which he preserves. We may suspect that on some points Jesus may originally have expressed himself differently or have had specific situations in mind which are no longer remembered. Yet we shall never in fact be able to replace this discourse by something different, nor are we likely to recover a more faithful picture of Jesus' ethical teaching than that which Matthew gives us. These are the words through which we must still hear (or at least overhear) the voice of Jesus; this is the *Sermon on the Mount* which, down the centuries, has left an indelible mark on the church and on the world.

3   **"Blessed are . . ."** This is a typical formula in moral teaching from the time of Homer onwards, and comparable lists of those who are 'blessed' were not unknown in Jesus' culture. These 'beatitudes' are a way of expressing the generally accepted values that underlie particular moral commands. We all wish to be 'blessed'– usually in a material sense, with fulfilling work, adequate income and happy domestic life, but often also in the deeper sense of an assurance that we qualify for the long-term rewards of religion; and moral teaching is designed to help us recognize and adopt for ourselves the kind of conduct which will contribute to these ends – and if the ends are not achieved in this life it has often seemed reasonable to believe that there will be just compensation after death.

But the form of a 'beatitude' can also be used to propose a value that is *not* generally accepted but perhaps should be. Those with which the 'sermon' begins are by no means conventional; indeed, in the form which they have in Luke's gospel (6.20ff.) they are very radical indeed. In Matthew their radicality is mitigated by the fact that most of them may be read as invitations to behave in a certain way, rather than as bald statements that those who are poor, bereaved and so forth are thereby 'blessed'. Yet they still represent a striking reversal of the priorities which most people have always accepted as leading to 'blessedness'.

"Blessed are the poor in spirit." The phrase, in the original Greek, sounds unnatural, though it actually occurs in Hebrew in the Dead Sea Scrolls and may have been current in Jesus' time. It is best understood in the light of a characteristic Old Testament conception of poverty. In the corresponding phrase in Luke (6.20), Jesus says simply, "Blessed are you who are poor". In many ancient cultures, including the Jewish, this would have sounded paradoxical, if not actually nonsense. It was riches, or at least a comfortable income, which showed that one was blessed – though it was often added that for true blessedness one needed to be virtuous as well. But there was one strain of Jewish piety (represented particularly by some of the psalms) which gave a deeper dimension to poverty. In this tradition, 'the poor' had become a religious as well as a social category. As opposed to those among the truly rich who were also (as so often) influential, extortionate and oppressive, 'the poor' were those who, being in modest circumstances, kept intact their own righteousness and piety. However much they appeared to be the losers in the social scale, they could be sure that they would ultimately be rewarded and vindicated by God. This tenacious faith of 'the poor' was decisively endorsed by Jesus; but, as we shall see, he included those who were physically, even desperately, poor, and took them seriously enough to do what no moral teacher (at least in his own culture, if not in any culture) had ever done before; that is, he addressed his teaching directly to them: in his eyes they were as capable of moral responsibility and as worthy of reward as anyone else.

4 **"Blessed are those who mourn, for they shall be comforted."** Out of context, this could sound like the kind of pious sentiment which is the stock in trade of any minister of religion: 'Believe in God, and your mourning will find consolation.' But such an anodyne sentiment hardly belongs here. Jesus' beatitudes (at least in Matthew) are based on the promise of a state of affairs in the future different from the present: it is then that mourning will be replaced by comfort. And in any case the Greek word has a wider meaning than 'mourn'. It can mean simply 'grieve' – over one's own or others' shortcomings, over the state of the world, over the lack of faith or integrity around one. The promise that these things will be reversed is 'comfort' way beyond the scope of conventional piety.

5 **"Blessed are the meek."** Almost identical words occur in Psalm 37.11. This meekness (which in the Old Testament is the mark of those who accept their humble status without bitterness) is one of the characteristic traits of 'the poor'; and the confidence that it would be rewarded, and that people of this character would be vindicated over against those who customarily trampled on them, had already found expression in at least one tradition of Jewish spirituality.

6 **"Blessed are those who hunger and thirst for righteousness."** Luke, again, preserves a more radical version (6.21), "Blessed are you who are hungry now". Hunger goes with poverty, and we know that Jesus was serious about the genuinely poor being blessed. But in Matthew's version the beatitude is a challenge also to those who are not physically hungry: an active yearning for righteousness – in the sense, not just of personal rectitude, but of the establishment of a just state of affairs – is a moral priority underlying much of Jesus' most challenging teaching.

After the first four beatitudes, three of which are more radical than any-thing which is to be found in the Old Testament or contemporary Jewish 7–9 piety, the series continues with three more which seem rather to commend certain virtues than to propound a new scale of values. These, which can be paralleled in Jewish writings, are lacking in Luke's more radical list, and they give the opening of the 'sermon' a conventional tone of ethical instruc-tion rather different from the abrupt pronouncements in the first beatitudes.

10 Only the last – **"Blessed are those who are persecuted for righteousness' sake"** – returns to the proclamatory style of the opening. There had been many in Jewish history who had been **persecuted for righteousness' sake.** Religious people trusted and prayed that, despite their apparent humiliation,

these martyrs had been accepted by God and would one day be vindicated. Jesus gave his authoritative endorsement to this faith.

1, 10   The first and last in this series of beatitudes state that **"theirs is the kingdom of heaven"**. Is this a promise for the future, or is there a sense in which the kingdom is already present? This is a question which runs right through the gospel. It is raised by Jesus' very first words, "The kingdom of heaven is upon you" (see above on 3.2). There is a sense in which the kingdom must always be future: if God is truly 'king', the present state of the world cannot be the final and intended form of his 'kingdom'. But equally it would be blasphemous to deny that God is already 'king'. His kingdom must therefore always be understood as *both* present *and* future. This ambivalence is reflected in Jesus' teaching; but he also saw himself (or was seen by the earliest Christians) as bridging the present and future dimensions, in that he fulfilled the prophecy, "The spirit of the Lord G o d is upon me, because the L o r d . . . has sent me to bring good news to the oppressed . . . to comfort all who mourn" (Isaiah 61.1–2). The beatitudes proclaim a message: the coming of Jesus inaugurated a time that had been foretold in scripture and in which many of the world's accepted values would be challenged.

11   **"Blessed are you."** The language suddenly becomes personal: no longer the broad sweep of a teacher propounding general moral truths, but the direct address of a master to his followers. It seems too early in the gospel scheme to think that those who had so recently begun to follow Jesus would already be suffering revilement and persecution. It was the church, after Jesus' resurrection, which first began to experience these things, and it is they who will have gratefully remembered Jesus' warning and Jesus' promise (if indeed, they did not actually adapt them to their own situation). Similarly, the metaphors which follow – of salt and lamp – clearly apply, not to any casual listeners, but to those who have already committed themselves to discipleship.

13   **"You are the salt of the earth."** We now use salt mainly for flavouring, and so the metaphor suggests to us a small but necessary element in that total mixture which is human civilization (and this, in fact, is precisely what many would say the Christian contribution to history has been). But in antiquity salt was equally important for *preserving* food; and the metaphor may be similar to that used by a Christian writer of the second century, 'Christians are the soul of the world' – for they are responsible for its continuance in life. But how does salt **lose its taste**? Chemically, it can never lose its saltiness. But in the various stages of use to which it was put it could become progressively less and less pure until finally it was useless, and then there was no way its saltiness could be **restored**.

14   **"The light of the world. A city built on a hill."** The two metaphors probably belong together. Isaiah had declared it to be the destiny of Israel to be a "light to the nations" (49.6); and the symbol of this destiny was the city of Jerusalem set on a hill, to which the peoples of the world would come to worship the one

true God. Jesus' disciples were to inherit this destiny, and could be described
15 with the same imagery. The only surprise is the appearance of a **bushel
basket** (an unlikely translation, introduced in the NRSV, of a word for a
measuring vessel: see below on Mark 4.21): the occurrence of this saying in a
quite different context in Mark is one of the pieces of evidence which make it
likely that the 'Sermon on the Mount' is a subsequent collection of teachings
rather than the record of an actual sermon.

17   **"Do not think I have come to abolish the law or the prophets."** Jesus'
ethical teaching was not all innovation. Like the teaching of his contemporaries, it took as its point of departure the comprehensive code of behaviour
contained in the books of the Old Testament attributed to Moses, which was
not only 'the law' as administered in the courts but also a guide to the moral
conduct required by their religion. It also reflected the great moral insights
contained in the writings of the prophets, and took account of the traditional
wisdom expressed in proverbs and maxims. Sometimes Jesus' teaching was
so radical that it seemed to be in direct contradiction to 'the law', and some of
the first Christians were quick to draw the conclusion that Christianity made
the whole law obsolete. But Matthew's arrangement of the teaching seems
designed to show that even where it appeared to be most at variance with
normal Jewish practice it was still a legitimate development of the original
'law': **"I have not come to abolish but to fulfill"** – and 'fulfilling' the law could
mean not merely observing it punctiliously but divining its true meaning and
fashioning one's whole way of life accordingly. Consequently Jesus' followers,
whatever their enemies might say (and we can probably overhear this debate
at several places in Matthew's gospel), were as committed to 'fulfilling the
law' as any of their Jewish antagonists.

    To demonstrate this, Matthew appears to have arranged the first section of
his collection of Jesus' teaching in the form of a new interpretation of the law
of Moses – as indeed, Jesus may have done himself: it was a natural way for
20 a Jewish teacher to proceed. The **scribes and Pharisees** (that is to say, those
who were expert in the law and held to the Pharisaic way of life) devoutly
believed that the law of Moses, though formulated many centuries before, was
still valid in their own day as a comprehensive guide to conduct; and in order
to bring it up to date they evolved certain rules of interpretation by which its
ancient provisions could be shown to apply to present-day circumstances.
Jesus' quarrel with these men (and again this is a debate which continued into
the next generation and which we can often overhear as the gospel progresses)
was that their interpretation had become so subtle and casuistical (though
we now know that it was also often remarkably humane) that it was in
danger of frustrating the original intention of God's law. But in offering his
own interpretation Jesus was not taking the law less seriously than they did.
He too regarded it as divinely inspired, and therefore unalterable down to
18 the smallest **letter** (the *yod* or 'jot' of the Hebrew alphabet) or **stroke of a
letter**, and as of eternal validity; and as regards the keeping of its provisions

20 (as interpreted by Jesus), his followers must have a **righteousness** that **exceeds that of the scribes and Pharisees**. This, at least, seems to have been the view expressed here of the relation between Jesus' teaching and the law. But the question was not an easy one, and was greatly to exercise the mind of Paul; nor was it always answered in the same way by every New Testament writer.

21 **"You have heard that it was said to those of ancient times."** The phrase is repeated, with slight variations, six times in this chapter. In each case it refers to a familiar provision of the law, and prepares for a new interpretation. '**You shall not murder**' is the sixth of the Ten Commandments. But the rest of the sentence, '**whoever murders shall be liable to judgment**', is not in the Old Testament (though it is of course implied), but is the kind of addition which lawyers made to the original text in order to show its practical application. But the addition enables Jesus to sharpen the point he wants to make by paradoxically adopting technical legal language to press home what turns out to be a moral injunction. One who commits murder must be brought before a court for judgment, whereas a mere expression of anger or insult cannot normally lead to a trial. So why does he say that this too will be

22 **liable to judgment** (or the judicial **council**)? One's first reaction is that this is impossible: no legal system could cope with every fit of anger being a legal offence. But then he goes on: **"if you say, 'You fool', you will be liable to the hell of fire"** (literally, *Gehenna*, the burning refuse pit below Jerusalem that was a current image for hell fire) – that is to say, he was not talking about a human court at all, but about something more serious: the judgment of God; and in the eyes of God, the ultimate arbiter of morality (this is his point), anger and insult may be just as serious as murder.

23–4 Before the series is continued, two practical examples are given which illustrate the same point. Both are vividly drawn from daily life. In the temple at Jerusalem one of the commonest sights will have been that of individual Jews bringing beasts or birds to be sacrificed at the great altar in the central court. Some of these sacrifices were laid on them by law on certain occasions (Luke 2.24), some were offered voluntarily as thank-offerings or as offerings to atone for some transgression. From the point of view of the temple cult, a personal grievance would have seemed a small matter compared with the due completion of the sacrifice; but from Jesus' statement that any offence against one's brother or sister is as serious as murder it followed that personal reconciliation must be of more importance than any ritual act – and he drives the point home by the slightly grotesque picture of the worshipper depositing an offering (possibly a live animal!) in the temple while going off to seek the offended party through the tortuous streets of the city.

25 **"Come to terms quickly."** This again seems drawn from life – and, signif-icantly, from the life of the poor, not of the comfortably off (to whom moral

26 teaching is usually directed). It follows from the end of the saying (**"you will never get out until you have paid the last penny"**) that Jesus was thinking of someone who was critically in debt and was being sued by a creditor. It

28

was natural (though of course sometimes risky, and certainly disapproved of by some moralists) to play for time by, say, pretending that the debt did not exist, or by finding a pretext for needing more time. The risk was that it would come to court, and imprisonment was normal for defaulting debtors. But this was not only imprudent: any attempt to evade repayment of debt was an offence against the more radical morality taught by Jesus.

27 **"You have heard that it was said, 'You shall not commit adultery.' "** Jesus' interpretation of the law is resumed, this time with the Seventh Commandment (Exodus 20.17), interpreted in the light of the Tenth ("you shall not covet your neighbor's wife"). Other moral teachers stressed the danger of the wanton or lustful glance: Jesus characteristically sharpens the point by

29, 30 saying that it may *amount to adultery.* The metaphor of the **right eye** and the **right hand**, being embedded in the same context, seems to refer to sexual behaviour – and so it has often been taken in Christian history; but a similar saying occurs both later in the gospel (18.8–9) and in Mark (9.43–7) in a different context, and it may originally have had nothing to do with adultery.

31 **"It was also said, 'Whoever divorces his wife . . .' "** Jesus' teaching on divorce is extremely rigorous, and will be discussed at length when it occurs later (19.3–9) and in Mark (10.1–12). But this passage is notable as one in

32 which an exception is allowed: **"except on the ground of unchastity".**

33 **"You shall not swear falsely."** Perjury was an offence against the law (Leviticus 19.12), and vows made to God had to be fulfilled (Deuteronomy 23.21). Moreover reverence was required for the divine name, so much so that a Jew would not normally utter it at all and oaths were made on lesser entities such as the temple. But the law said nothing (how could it?) about casual swearing: only moral pressure could discourage it. Jesus seems character-istically, to be suggesting that the absoluteness of the law with regard to perjury should be extended to everyday conversation. So, **"Do not swear at**

34 **all."** To imagine that Jesus meant to prohibit the taking of an oath even for official purposes, such as an appearance in court, is probably to be too literal: the injunction has the characteristic note of Jesus' uncompromising ethical demands, aimed at the commonest form of swearing and alerting his hearers to its danger.

38 **"'An eye for an eye and a tooth for a tooth.' "** This, the *lex talionis,* is a basic principle of elementary justice and was written into the Old Testament (e.g. Leviticus 24.19). Originally a measure for bringing the instinct of revenge under control by limiting the compensation which could be demanded for an injury, it had become a theoretical criterion for assessing damages in court, and its application inevitably gave rise to differences of opinion. Jesus may have had debates of this kind in mind; but instead of contributing to them he allowed the principle to stand without any attempt at mitigation and simply told his followers not to invoke it. Instead of claiming damages or standing on rights, they should willingly accept insult (even the particular indignity

39 of being struck on the **right cheek** with the back of the insulter's right hand),

41 and when asked to perform a service should offer to do even more – the circumstance envisaged may be the requisitioning of transport by a Roman soldier: once again Jesus is concerned for the poor, who would have nothing

40 to offer as surety for a loan except their **coat** or their **cloak** and would have no servant or beast of burden to offer but only their own backs.

43 **"You shall love your neighbor and hate your enemy."** Only the first half of this sentence stands in the Old Testament (Leviticus 19.18). But, as we know from Luke's gospel (10.29) as well as from Jewish writings, people asked: Who is my neighbour? And the answer given was usually: Any fellow Jew, with the addition (in some more liberal quarters) of particularly deserving Gentiles. The rest of the world (since it consisted, by definition, of Gentiles and idolaters, God's 'enemies') could be treated with something considerably less than love; and as for one's personal enemies, even if one might occasionally be in a position to be generous towards them, they must normally be treated with caution, if not with actual vindictiveness. All this is expressed, in a language which had a tendency to call things either black or white, by the phrase **"hate your enemy"**, which many of Jesus' contemporaries would have felt to be implied in the command to 'love one's neighbour'.

44 Jesus' interpretation rejects all such casuistry: you must **"love your enemies"** – and this becomes, whether in Jesus' own intention or in the tradition of the early church, no longer a matter of Jewish attitudes to Gentiles, but of the attitude of individuals towards their personal enemies, of Christians towards their persecutors, or even (occasionally) of citizens towards foreign colonists. The injunction in Leviticus, "you shall love your neighbor as yourself", was already demanding enough. Jewish moralists made it more manageable by restricting the category of 'neighbour'. But Jesus, with unprecedented radicalism, proposed it as a universal rule of personal ethics and character-

46 istically drove the point home with an *a fortiori* argument. **Tax collectors**

47 were regarded as practising an immoral profession, **Gentiles** had (in Jewish eyes) an inferior moral code. Yet even they 'loved their neighbour' in the limited sense that had become attached to the injunction in Leviticus. But this partiality towards friends, colleagues and fellow Jews was in contrast to

45 the impartiality of God, who (as a proverb expressed it) **"makes his sun rise on the evil and the good"**. God's goodness knows no bounds, he makes no distinctions – and therefore he has no patience with the distinctions we tend to make ourselves between one kind of 'neighbour' and another.

48 **"Be perfect, therefore."** In Greek thought, perfection consisted in an advance towards higher levels of knowledge and self-discipline. To the Jews, it meant a whole-hearted and uncompromising conformity with the ethical standards and practical provisions of the law. The Greek meaning occurs in Paul; but here the meaning is likely to be one more familiar in the Jewish culture: perfect conformity with the divinely given law. And as God was the ultimate model for all human behaviour (as in Leviticus 19.2, "You shall be holy, for I the LORD your God am holy"), so God's generous and impartial

love must be the standard for all human loving, raising (like much else in the 'sermon') the level of moral demand to a height which, however impracticable at times, has continued to inspire the conduct of Christians and non-Christians alike right up to the present day.

6.1 **"Beware of practicing your piety before others."** The word 'piety' does not convey the full meaning of the Greek word, which is, literally, *righteousness*. It means the full practice of the law, understood as a complete guide to moral conduct. This involved not only religious observances but also 'acts of charity' (particularly almsgiving) that were not laid down in the law at all but had come to be regarded as essential to the virtuous life. Jesus had no quarrel with these, but only with the attitude with which they were often performed, particularly by those who most insisted upon them, the Pharisees (to whom Jesus – or subsequently the church – seems to have given the opprobrious

2 name **"hypocrites"**, which originally meant 'actors', 'showmen'). It seems to have been the custom to announce any substantial gift at the meeting of the congregation either **in the synagogues** or at an open-air gathering **in the streets** (though nothing whatever is known about the use of a trumpet for the purpose – was the phrase already proverbial?). By contrast, Jesus'

4 followers must give **in secret**. Again, the Jews regularly prayed (standing) at certain times of day, either in a synagogue or wherever they happened to be. This too gave opportunities for ostentatious piety, particularly if one chose

5 out **street corners** for the purpose. Finally, there was a tendency to admire anyone who knew and could recite especially long prayers (and here there is a sideways glance at heathen worship as well as at the synagogue: it is Gentiles

7 who typically **heap up empty phrases** – a rare word in the Greek, sounding rather like 'babble'); by contrast, Jesus prescribed a very short and condensed prayer for his followers.

9 **"Pray then in this way."** Into this series of contrasts between Jewish and Christian religious practices is slipped the Lord's Prayer. It is possible that it may be another example of the same thing: Jesus may have originally taught it in opposition to traditional Jewish forms of prayer (though Luke offers a quite different reason, 11.1). But in detail there is little in Jesus' prayer which would have been difficult for Jews to pray, and many of its clauses belonged equally to Jewish spirituality; its originality lies rather in its extreme economy and directness, which does indeed contrast with the more elaborate prayers which every Jew was expected to recite daily.

The prayer occurs twice in the New Testament, once here in Matthew and once in Luke (11.2–4). In each case the basic elements of the prayer are the same, but Luke's version is considerably shorter. Jesus may, of course, have taught the prayer in both forms; but it is not difficult to think of reasons why, in the different churches for which Matthew and Luke wrote, two different versions of the prayer should have existed. If, for instance, Luke's version is original (which is the prevailing scholarly view), Matthew's version could be an early expansion of it under the influence of other Jewish prayers; while if Matthew's is original, Luke's could be an abbreviation of it for the benefit of a church less accustomed to Jewish forms of prayer. In any case, it is the longer form which since very early times has become standard in the church, though in one significant detail Christian usage has usually preferred the language of Luke ('sins' rather than 'debts').

"Our Father in heaven." Prayers written exclusively for private use are a comparatively modern invention. Jesus' prayer, like all formal Jewish prayers, was primarily intended to be used in corporate worship by a group or congregation. This gives content to the word **our**. In most religions of the world God is at one time or another addressed as Father, but not always in the same sense. For the Greeks, God was 'father' in the sense of creator: he was therefore everyone's father. From this we inherit such ideas as the universal fatherhood of God and the equality of all human beings before him. The Jews, on the other hand, tended to think of God as Father in a much more particular way: God was 'father' to Israel in that he had a special relationship with his people and guided and protected them 'like a father'. Consequently when Jews prayed, 'Our Father', they were not usually thinking of the whole of humanity: there was a sense in which God's 'fatherhood' was exclusive to themselves. What then would Jesus have meant by **"Our Father"**? There is no evidence in the gospels that he was un-Jewish enough to endorse the Greek idea of God's universal fatherhood; but neither is he likely to have accepted the exclusive attitude of the Jews that only they were the true 'children of God'. Jesus' own attitude lay somewhere between. He himself was in a special sense 'son of God', and God was in a unique way his Father. Moreover, those who followed him became, along with him, God's 'children', and were entitled to address God with that singularly intimate Aramaic word which passed at once into the praying of the earliest Christians: *abba*, Father (see on Romans 8.15). Luke's version of the prayer, which begins with the single word 'Father', probably reflects an original which began with this distinctive word, *abba*. Such apparently easy familiarity with God might have seemed shocking to the Jewish mind, and it may have been as a concession to Jewish feelings that Matthew's version replaced it with the more formal address (which can be paralleled in contemporary writings), **Our Father in heaven**.

"Hallowed be your name." The NRSV has retained the archaic word, which is probably now known to most people only through its occurrence in the Lord's Prayer. To 'hallow' is to separate from all that profanes. There is a part of creation where God's name is already perfectly hallowed – **in heaven**; the prayer is that this hallowing should be extended to earth, that the whole of creation should become consonant, instead of discordant, with the divine purpose. Two implications of this are drawn out in the next two clauses. First, **"Your kingdom come."** Much of Jesus' teaching in the gospel concerns this 'kingdom'. God is king – that is axiomatic. But his reign is not yet universally acknowledged. Jesus often draws attention to those moments in the present – often quite unexpected ones – when an individual's response to an ordinary human situation makes this reign actual; but he also constantly looks ahead to the time when God, by his own act, will make his kingdom universal. The prayer presumably embraces both kinds of 'coming'. Secondly, **"Your will be done."** The meaning of this, again, follows from the 'hallowing' of God's name. It does not express (as it might in some religions) a resigned acquiescence in an inscrutable providence, but a longing for God's purpose to be fully realized **on earth as it is in heaven.**

11   **"Give us this day our daily bread."** This is unlikely to be merely metaphorical: most Jewish prayers included a petition for bread, and no formal Jewish meal would ever be eaten without thanksgiving to God, who provides food for our use. But the clause says, not just bread, but **daily bread**. The adjective is puzzling. This particular Greek word occurs nowhere else in literature, and we can only guess at its meaning here. Still less can we recover the Aramaic word which Jesus originally used. It is true that a 'religious' interpretation is possible. Bread had a special significance for Jesus: the bread which he broke became a means of communion; and it is possible that, apart from the satisfaction of hunger, this petition with its mysterious adjective contains a reference to the supernatural nourishment given by Jesus to those who worship him – a suggestion made by Jerome at the end of the fourth century, who introduced the word *supersubstantialis* into his widely used Latin translation. But even if this meaning is present it can hardly be the whole meaning. The natural thing would be to pray simply for 'bread'. But Christians apparently were to pray only for enough for today (or, at most, *tomorrow* – see the footnote in the NRSV). We need bread today, because the present weighs upon us, life is to be lived and we have work to do. But tomorrow – next week, next year – is in the hands of God.

12   **"And forgive us our debts."** 'Debts', in Jesus' culture, was a perfectly intelligible way of speaking of offences against another or against God, and Luke's version ('sins') may be just as faithful a translation of Jesus' original word. But we cannot assume (any more than we could in the case of 'bread') that the meaning is entirely metaphorical. Debts, we believe, have to be repaid: there is a moral, and often a legal, obligation to do so. The Hebrew scriptures made it obligatory to remit debts every seventh year (Deuteronomy 15.1–2). By the time of Christ commercial conditions had made this virtually impossible (loans became very scarce in the sixth year!) and a way had been found to circumvent it. Here, then, was a way in which Christians could observe the spirit as opposed to the letter of the law – they could continue to remit debts in the seventh year! But this would hardly account for the presence of the petition in such a tightly knit prayer, and the metaphorical sense of debts, meaning *sins* (as in Luke), must be present, and is indeed made explicit in the brief commentary which follows the prayer, where the
15 word is 'sins' or **"trespasses"**. Yet one aspect of 'debts', as opposed to 'sins', remains crucial. To forgive a debtor involves telling the debtor that the debt is remitted, not just telling God that one 'forgives'. So with 'sins': it is not

enough to confess to God; we must also make it up with the person sinned against (which is the harder part!).

13 **"And do not bring us to the time of trial."** 'Trial', instead of the traditional word *temptation* (see the NRSV footnote), is a more faithful rendering of the Greek word. 'Temptation' is a psychological concept, suggesting a struggle within the individual between good and bad impulses. But this kind of psychological analysis was not characteristic of Hebrew thinking. The nearest corresponding Hebrew concept was that of 'testing'. In the Old Testament, many of the afflictions suffered by the people of Israel, and many personal catastrophes which befell pious individuals, were understood as a 'test' imposed by God. How one would ultimately be judged would depend on how one survived this 'test'; and the more urgently that judgment was expected (and some scholars believe that the whole prayer is coloured by this sense of urgency) the more reason there was to dread any decisive moment which might bring out the true worth of a person and so irrevocably determine God's final verdict.

"Rescue us from the evil one" – or *from evil* (as in the NRSV footnote). The Greek word can mean either, and translators have to make their choice. Perhaps in the long run it makes little difference whether a personal devil is seen behind the phenomenon of evil. In Jesus' time it was natural to think in that way; today it may seem less so. But the reality of evil, with which the follower of Jesus is in perpetual conflict, is acknowledged either way.

In many Christian traditions the prayer ends with an ascription of glory to God. But these words (*For the kingdom and the power*, etc., as in the NRSV footnote) are absent in most early manuscripts and were almost certainly added under the influence of Jewish prayers when the prayer began to be used regularly in public worship. The original prayer taught by Jesus seems to have contained no liturgical elaborations; indeed, the most striking thing about it is the directness and simplicity of its petitions.

16 The last of the warnings against hypocrisy concerns fasting. Fasting was a recognized practice, and was becoming more widely observed in Jewish circles at the time this gospel was written. There was always a temptation to draw attention to one's abstinence. Christians were also to fast, but their 18 fasting must be **in secret**.

So far, the teaching of the 'sermon' seems to have been in deliberate opposition to other religious authorities, particularly the Pharisees. It now becomes more general, and continues a tradition that goes back to Old Testament writings such as Proverbs or Sirach: the tradition of Hebrew (but also international) 'Wisdom', which was based on the intensely practical experience of 'the wise' combined with firm religious values, and was typically expressed in proverbs.

19 **"Do not store up for yourselves treasures on earth."** This advice was already centuries old, and was usually taken as an encouragement to generous almsgiving. Here it has a strongly Palestinian flavour: the 'treasure' is not the

gold of a rich town-dweller locked away in a strong-room (for gold does not 'rust'!) but the cherished possessions of country people, such as clothes and carpets[5] stored in a corner of a mud-brick house where thieves could easily **break in** (literally, dig their way in) through the walls.

22   **"The eye is the lamp of the body."** Before the modern era, vision was assumed to be caused by the eye sending out light rays. Thus far, the saying sounds like a proverb. But it develops into a more complex and puzzling metaphor, exploiting the moral connotations of an 'eye'. The NRSV says **healthy**. The Greek is more suggestive: *'sound'* or even *'generous'*; while **unhealthy** could equally well be *'evil'*. Physically the eye was held to give out light; but morally any evil intentions could be said to spread the darkness that is within.

24   **"No one can serve two masters."** Not, of course, literally true – slaves were occasionally shared between two owners; but true enough to have been already part of proverbial wisdom. Most people would think it possible to combine a reasonable concern for the things of this world with the service of God. Jesus is characteristically radical: **"you cannot serve God and wealth"** – literally *mammon*, a word that seems to have covered all kinds of property and money matters.

25   **"Do not worry."** The word 'worry' occurs four times, and is the key word
26   of this paragraph. The imagery belongs again to the countryside. **"Look at the birds of the air"** – Jesus makes his point with a certain humour, conjuring up the absurd picture of birds carrying bags of seed and reaping-hooks.

28   **"Consider the lilies of the field."** For a few brief weeks in the spring the fields in the Holy Land are a mass of colour with wild flowers, to be compared with the proverbial splendour of Solomon. 'Lilies' is the traditional translation, but we do not know exactly which wild flower Jesus was thinking of – it
30   could have been the Anthemis or Easter daisy. As for the **grass of the field**, the image is clear enough: a few days of hot sun and all the scrub growth turns brown and dry and can be used in the peasant's baking-oven. God has no less concern for us than for birds and flowers. Moreover, God has given
33   us a more serious concern – to work for his **kingdom** and his **righteousness**.
34   **"Today's trouble is enough for today"** – which is not the sigh of someone who has become resigned to misfortune but a programme of action. There is plenty of work to be done today, combating and overcoming the evil around us. We are not to take on in addition a useless burden of anxiety about the evil which will have to be faced tomorrow.

7.1   **"Do not judge, so that you may not be judged . . . the measure you give will be the measure you get."** One of the most powerful generators of proverbs is the almost instinctive belief that there is a law of retribution in

---

[5] If **rust** is a correct translation one must add things such as metal tools. But the meaning of the Greek is uncertain: it may mean other destructive agents like insects – see the NRSV footnote.

human affairs, and that the harm you do to others will be returned on your own head, if not in this life, then in the next. But Jesus' sayings, even if they have the same proverbial sound, go a good deal deeper. Here, it is not stated by whom you may be judged; but everyone would have known what was meant. The unexpressed subject is God, the 'judgment' is the verdict God will one day pass on every one of us, and we are not to anticipate it (for instance, by keeping a certain kind of person out of our religious society).

2 The same goes for the **measure you get** – not from your fellow human beings but from God: you cannot expect him to be generous in his verdict on you if you are rigorous in your verdict on others. As for the hypocrisy of criticizing others before you look carefully at yourself, the world's literature is full of proverbs about it. Jesus' example is characteristic of him, in that it is almost
3 grotesquely exaggerated – a **speck** and a **log**.

6 **"Do not give what is holy to dogs."** Proverbial again. Dogs were more likely to be fierce scavengers or hunters than pets, and the word 'dog' was often one of abuse. It is of the essence of serious religion that it contains truths and practices which must be guarded from desecration by unbelievers.

7 **"Ask, and it will be given you."** No one in Jesus' culture doubted the efficacy of prayer, but (since prayers often seem to go unanswered) it was assumed that a prayer must fulfil certain conditions (sincerity, humility, etc.) in order to qualify for an answer. Jesus' teaching, by contrast, appears to be quite unconditional, and proceeds from the premise (which also underlies the Lord's Prayer) that God, being Jesus' Father in a unique way, is therefore also Father of all who follow Jesus. And if God is the Christian's Father, then he will treat his children as a father should – with some discipline, certainly, but with at least the patience and generosity which even ordinary human parents are sometimes capable of showing; and Jesus' examples here (the
9, 10 **stone** and the **snake**) display his characteristic irony.

12 **"In everything do to others as you would have them do to you"** – the Golden Rule. A similar rule of thumb for moral conduct was current in Jesus' day, and was indeed, thought to sum up **the law and the prophets**. But generally (both in Jewish and pagan culture) it took the negative form, 'Do not do to others what you would not wish them to do to you.' This is significantly different from Jesus' rule, not just because avoiding evil is a colourless concept compared with doing good, but because there is a different presupposition. Beneath the negative form there is an implied threat: Do not do to others what you would not wish them to do to you, *otherwise* they will begin to do just that. But in Jesus' rule there is no threat. Treat others as you would like them to treat you, *otherwise* – what? Otherwise they may not do for you all you wish they would? But no one ever expected they would! There is no 'otherwise'! Jesus' maxim is not prudential at all, but sums up the radical altruism of his ethic: this is how you are to treat others – regardless!

13 **"Enter through the narrow gate."** Moralists in antiquity often represented the choice between good and bad as a decision between 'two ways', the narrow,

difficult path of virtue and the easy road of licentiousness. Jesus stands in the same tradition, but gives the metaphor new life by combining the image of a road with that of a gate – one should perhaps imagine oneself in a walled city, with its principal gate leading on to a main road while a small gate leads to a mountain path. Moreover, he does not seem to be content with the usual moral (not many are virtuous, but make sure you are yourself). By the gate

14 **that leads to life** we must understand the path of Christian discipleship; and it has been true ever since the beginning of Christianity that, relatively speaking, **there are few who find it.**

15 "**Beware of false prophets.**" It is difficult to identify the people Jesus had in mind; but it is certainly true that during the first century or so of the church's existence 'false prophets' constituted a practical problem. Genuine 'prophecy' was a gift that was highly esteemed in the church, and itinerant prophets were warmly received. But this hospitality could easily be abused. It was not difficult to play the part of a prophet, and the churches soon had to devise some means of 'testing' the inspiration of their visitors. The tests they used are described in some early Christian writings (there is an example in 1 John 4.1), and here it looks as if a general principle of moral

16 judgment – **you will know them by their fruits** – which was spoken by Jesus in various contexts (Matthew 12.33; Luke 6.43) came to be applied to this specific problem; though the way it is expressed here (**grapes from thorns, figs from thistles**) has the hallmark of Jesus' ironical style.

Much the same goes for the following paragraph. We do not hear of Jesus

21 being addressed as "**Lord, Lord**" in his lifetime; but in the church it immediately became an article of faith that Jesus *was* 'Lord', and Christians were by definition those who acknowledged 'the Lord Jesus'. But was it enough simply to make this confession of faith? Was it enough even to speak inspired words and perform miraculous cures and exorcisms 'in his name'? Were such people necessarily Christians, and would they be accepted by Christ at the

22 final judgment? By no means. "**On that day**" it will be by our adherence to the kind of teaching given in this 'sermon', more than by our professions of faith or our psychic powers, that we shall be judged worthy of entering the kingdom of heaven.

24–7 The 'sermon' ends, like other discourses of Jesus, with a parable. Two houses may look outwardly the same; but one, foolishly built on the sandy bed of a wadi, is suddenly inundated by a raging torrent which, after a few days of Palestinian rain, will rush down the valley and destroy all but the firmest building. Outwardly, two people's lives may look much the same. But when the moment of testing comes, all the pretensions of one will collapse into ruin.

The 'sermon', as we have seen, is both rooted in the moral and legal tradi

29 tion of the Old Testament and at the same time full of novelty. The **scribes** to whom people would have been accustomed to listen gained 'authority' for their teaching by quoting the opinions of previous revered masters. Jesus

quotes no one, yet he offers interpretations of the law that are radical and
28 challenging. It is no wonder that the crowds were **astounded**: this teaching
has continued to have an astonishing impact ever since. But where did Jesus
29 get his **authority**? Perhaps simply from his personal charisma; but the reader
of the gospel already has an inkling of something more profound: he claimed
to have received absolute authority from God (see 28.18).

Healings and exorcisms

By placing the 'sermon' so early in his account, Matthew (unlike Mark)
gives prominence to Jesus' activity as a teacher, even perhaps (as some
believe) representing him as a new Moses. He now returns to the order
of events in Mark and devotes a few paragraphs to examples of Jesus' heal-
8.2–4 ing, beginning with the cure of a leper. In Mark (1.40–5), this episode is told
in greater detail and with an eye to its social and religious implications;
but Matthew (as often) shortens it by omitting everything except the
bare narrative. The only emphasis he appears to lay on the story is not
(as in Mark) the behaviour of the leper who has been cured but (characteristically for Matthew) on Jesus' anxiety to conform with the law:
4 **"offer the gift that Moses commanded"** (the details are in Leviticus,
chapter 14).
5 **When he entered Capernaum.** The next episode (which is also in Luke
(7.1–10) but not in Mark) is evidently recorded for the sake of the conversation between Jesus and a military officer. Much of the point of the conversation lies in the fact that the man who appealed to Jesus was a **centurion** (the
Roman title for an officer in charge of about a hundred men). This does not
reveal his nationality: whether he was in the service of Rome or of one of the
vassal kings (Herod Antipas or Philip), he could have been recruited from
any part of the eastern empire. But we do know one thing about him: he is
unlikely to have been a Jew (for Jews did not normally serve in any army in
Palestine). The episode is therefore one of the very few in the gospel which
illustrate Jesus' attitude towards Gentiles. The conversation is almost identical in Matthew and Luke, though the two evangelists seem quite independent
of each other when it comes to narrating the episode itself.
6 **"My servant."** The Greek is ambiguous: it could mean 'servant' or 'son'. In
Luke (7.2) it is certainly a servant, a slave; and the motive is that the centurion
'valued him highly'. In Matthew the centurion appears to be involved emo-
tionally, and 'son' is a translation that explains things better. At any rate, Jesus'
7 immediate response to this request by a foreigner was favourable: **"I will come
and cure him."** But the soldier, sensing the impropriety of a Jew of Jesus'
renown entering the house of a junior officer – or else out of pure diffidence –
8 requested Jesus merely to **speak the word**, and made a comparison (which
is the other main point of the story) between the authority of himself as an
9 officer and the authority of Jesus. Just as he, being **a man under authority**

himself, had soldiers under him and could get his will done by his subordinates (though himself under orders from his superior), so, he believed, Jesus had supreme authority over those powers of evil which caused such things as paralysis. Jesus surely did not need to go and encounter the particular evil force concerned; he had only to **speak the word** and the whole regiment of the devil would obey him. To credit Jesus with such authority was a sign of remarkable faith; and Jesus was led to comment on the contrast between such faith and the much more reserved and sceptical attitude which he had found

10 **in Israel** – or which he was about to find: the episode may have been placed by Matthew at an earlier stage in the story than that to which it originally belonged.

11 **"I tell you, many will come from east and west."** This saying occurs in a different context in Luke (13.28–9) and was doubtless remembered for its own sake, apart from any particular occasion. It is added here as a comment on the episode which has just taken place. The general expectation was for a future age of glory, often pictured as a heavenly feast, presided over by the great patriarchs of the past. In the language of those prophets who wrote when the Jewish nation was exiled far away from Jerusalem (e.g. Isaiah 49.12), there would at the same time be a great coming together of people **from east and**

12 **west** – but these, of course, would be Jews, **heirs of the kingdom.** Jesus here turns this conventional imagery on its head: it is a great variety of people who will flock in to enjoy the promised kingdom, while those who so confidently looked forward to it will be **thrown into outer darkness**, which in this gospel tends to be painted in lurid colours: **there will be wailing and gnashing of teeth.**

14–17 The next two brief paragraphs follow Mark's gospel (1.32–4) with only slight abbreviation. In Mark, the events are included in his account of a sabbath day's activity, so that the words 'at evening' (Mark 1.32) are significant: only after the sabbath ended at sunset was it permissible to travel any distance or carry the sick. Matthew, by his rearrangement and by dropping all

16 mention of the sabbath, has robbed these same words (**That evening**) of their significance. Characteristically, he sets Jesus' activity in relation to a

17 prophecy of Isaiah (53.4). This comes from a chapter which the church soon came to see as one of the key Old Testament passages bearing on Jesus; but Matthew quotes the text in an unusual version which appropriately makes it apply, not to salvation from sin (its usual sense), but to healing from disease.

Two sayings on discipleship follow, which may not originally have belonged so early in the story: not enough teaching has yet been given about the Son of Man to make verse 20 comprehensible. The sayings themselves have a proverbial ring; but on their own they would be merely mystifying. They get their meaning and their radical thrust from the narrative setting: it is when they are addressed to a potential follower that they become characteristic of Jesus' challenging style – which makes it seem likely that it was on some such

19 occasion (even if later on) that they were originally spoken. **"Teacher, I will**

follow you." Following a revered teacher was not a particularly daunting project in itself: many teachers had disciples who spent all their time with them. But the radical nature of 'following' Jesus is such that it does not even have the security enjoyed by birds and beasts. Similarly, the request to 'bury one's father' before enlisting with Jesus' followers was entirely reasonable: attending to the burial rites of one's closest relations was an absolute duty, normally taking priority over anything else. It is unlikely that anyone would have invented Jesus' extraordinary command to neglect even this for the sake of following. Few doubt that this saying is authentic. Indeed, it is characteristic of Jesus to keep the edge of his teaching sharp by admitting of no exceptions. *Never* refuse to forgive, *never* divorce, give away *everything* – this is Jesus' style, and we have to come to terms with it as best we may. (We can allow, perhaps, for a characteristic note of exaggeration.) But there is also of course

22 a more general application. Taken metaphorically, **"Let the dead bury their own dead"** is a haunting maxim, inviting us to leave the ranks of those whose minds are closed to new possibilities and to become, through discipleship, really 'alive'.

23   **And when he got into the boat, his disciples followed him.** The word **followed** is a little odd: 'his disciples went with him' would be more natural. But 'following' is what this section is about, 'following' was the vocation of the church which came after; and this may be the first of the subtle alterations and adjustments to the story as we know it from Mark (4.35–41), by which Matthew appears to have adapted it to the needs of a Christian community that was struggling against discouragement like a small boat caught in a storm, apt to imagine that its Protector was asleep. This record of Jesus' magisterial words to the raging elements (whether or not there was an actual miracle – the storm could have subsided anyway) may have been intended to reasssure the church that its destiny was, after all, in safe hands.

28   **When he came to the other side, to the country of the Gadarenes.** It is likely that a small strip of the south-eastern shore of the lake belonged to the important Greco-Roman city of Gadara (which lay about 7 miles away), and to this extent Matthew's correction of Mark's 'Gerasenes' somewhat eases the geographical difficulty of the story (for Gerasa lay much further away; *Gergesa* (see the NRSV footnote) is unknown); at the same time the name of the city, as well as the presence of a herd of pigs, still gives the impression of a predominantly non-Jewish environment. The story reproduces that given by Mark (5.1–20), but is told more briefly, and in a less sensational form. The man possessed (according to Mark) by a whole legion of unclean spirits becomes (unexpectedly, but there are other instances of this in Matthew) **two** violent demoniacs; and the enormous herd of two thousand swine becomes

30 simply **a large herd**. Moreover, the emphasis here is quite different. In Mark's version the interest is focused on the state of the man before and after the exorcism and upon the crowd's reaction to the cure. But here the two sufferers claim our attention only once. The scene is played out entirely between Jesus

and the demons, who recognize him (it is only supernatural beings who
29 do so) as **Son of God**, and expect from him an unwelcome anticipation of
that punishment which (according to popular Jewish mythology) the devil
and all his company were to receive at the end of time. They beg to be
allowed to make a spectacular demonstration of their power (a recurrent
feature of exorcism stories), and this duly takes place in the destruction
of the pigs. The consequence is very different from that in Mark's version:
instead of a vociferous witness being left behind in gentile territory, there
was a unanimous reaction of hostility. Matthew's scheme does not seem to
allow for any form of mission to the Gentiles at this stage.

9.2   **And just then some people were carrying a paralyzed man.** (the NRSV
omits the important words, *to him*: they were not just passing by chance.)
The story is told more fully by Mark (2.1–12) and Luke (5.17–26), and the
people's exploit in lowering the stretcher through the roof – which is not
mentioned by Matthew – seems a necessary presupposition of the story if
the words **When Jesus saw their faith** are to make good sense. **"Take heart,
son; your sins are forgiven."** Since it was believed that one was unlikely to
recover from an illness unless God had forgiven one's sins, this was sufficient
reason for Jesus to say, **"Take heart"**: if the paralytic's sins were really forgiven
he could now expect to recover. But the unspoken accusation of blasphemy
incited Jesus (as in the other accounts) to make a demonstration of his
authority to pronounce forgiveness of sins by miraculously performing a
8 cure. **The crowds**, in Matthew, not merely were stunned by the miracle but
appreciated, perhaps, that it was a decisive answer to the charge of blasphemy.
Jesus' act proved that God had indeed, granted him such authority.

9   **He saw a man called Matthew.** In Mark (2.15–17) and Luke (5.27–8) the
name of the customs official (the only kind of tax collector who would work
in an office or **booth**) is Levi. There can be no doubt that this is the same
incident as in the other two gospels; all the main features of this and the
following paragraphs (down to verse 17) are the same. The only important
difference is the name of the disciple. One reason for the change is probably
that Levi does not occur in any of the gospel lists of the twelve, and the writer
of this gospel (or a later hand, if it was desired to bring the reputed author
of the gospel into the narrative) wished to attach the story to one of the
known apostles (it is only in this gospel (10.3) that Matthew is called a 'tax
collector').

The narrative continues exactly as in Mark (2.15–17), save that Jesus'
13 reply to his critics includes a quotation from Hosea (6.6), **"I desire mercy,
not sacrifice."** Possibly Matthew was dissatisfied with Jesus' brusque and
proverbial reply to the Pharisees and deliberately introduced the quotation
from Hosea, which was a classic formulation of the superiority of spontaneous acts of compassion and generosity over the fulfilment of the temple
ritual, and which Jesus (again according to Matthew) also used on another
occasion (12.7 below). In this way Jesus could be portrayed as meeting the

Pharisees on their own ground of the interpretation of scripture. **"Go and learn what this means"** was, incidentally, a standard phrase in learned Jewish arguments.

14–17 In verses 14–17 Matthew runs very close to Mark (2.18–22) and Luke (5.33–8), but adds a characteristic touch at the end. The drift of the sayings in Mark, and still more in Luke, is that Jesus' new message is incompatible with the old observances. But for Matthew this must have seemed too radical a programme. Christianity may have been a new interpretation, but it by no 17 means superseded the law of Moses. So he adds, **"both are preserved"**.

A short section follows devoted to miraculous healings, which are told very briefly, but in such a way as to bring out the fact that the miracles were performed in response to a gesture of faith. In Mark's version (5.21–43), as 18 in Luke's (8.40–56), the **leader of the synagogue** (who is actually just a 'ruler' in Matthew's text, but the translators have filled in the title from the parallel accounts in the other gospels) came to Jesus when his daughter, though critically ill, was still alive: he asked only for healing, and it was Jesus who took the initiative when it was known that the child had died. But here the child is already dead, and the man's faith in Jesus is demonstrated in that he believed from the outset that Jesus could perform the miracle, exceptional even in Jesus' activity, of restoring the dead to life. Similarly, the story of 20–2 the woman with haemorrhages is much shortened, but is told in such a way as to bring out the woman's faith and Jesus' approval of that faith. Nevertheless, even within this brief scope, Matthew adds two touches of what we 20 would now call local colour. Jesus' garment had a **fringe**, which in the Greek is a technical word for the fringe or tassel which Jews were bidden to wear on each corner of their cloak (Numbers 15.38); and the house of bereave- 23 ment had already attracted **flute players**, whose profession it was to attend mourners.

The gospel contains a number of stories of Jesus curing the blind. There is one in both Matthew (20.29–34) and Luke (18.35–43) which follows the story as told in Mark 10.46–52. But here Matthew has an additional version, told more briefly than the others but preserving two typical features: first, 27 that the blind recognize Jesus as **Son of David** (which all the evangelists agree was correct in a sense, but was not normally discerned by those with whom Jesus came into contact: there may be something symbolic in the fact that it is only the blind who 'see' this); and secondly, Matthew on each occasion 27 unexpectedly introduces, not one, but **two blind men**, just as in 8.28 he equally unexpectedly introduces two demoniacs. In this very brief account 29 Matthew is careful, once again, to emphasize the men's faith: **"According to your faith let it be done to you."** The injunction is added, which occurs 30 less frequently in Matthew than in Mark, **"See that no one knows of this."** Perhaps it was the particular intuition which the blind men had about Jesus' identity ('Son of David') which Jesus (at least according to Matthew's scheme) did not wish to be widely known at this stage.

32–4   The last in the series, the exorcism of a demon from a dumb man, is told only in the briefest outline. Since Jesus is dealing here, not with the patient, but with a demon which has assumed control over the patient, there is no question of the individual's faith. Instead, the interest of the story is shifted to the reaction of the onlookers – and the comment of the Pharisees becomes the trigger for an extended discussion in a similar episode later on (12.24–8).

The mission of the twelve

The kernel of the following section is to be found in Mark (6.7–13). Jesus, at some stage in his work in Galilee, commissioned his disciples to go out independently of him as missionaries and healers, and the instructions and advice which he gave them are recorded in each of the first three gospels. But it was perhaps inevitable that the early church, when it meditated on these sayings, was more interested in their application to its own circumstances and problems than in the actual historical situation in which Jesus originally pronounced them. There was consequently a tendency, both to collect together the scattered sayings of Jesus which seemed to have a bearing on church life, and to hand them down in a form that was appropriate to the time. This tendency, which is present even in Mark's much briefer collection, has clearly influenced this section of Matthew. In the first place, the setting of the discourse has become artificial. In Mark (6.7,30) and Luke (9.2,10) the disciples are sent out on a mission, and when they return they give some account of their exploits. In Matthew too they are "sent out" (10.5); but it is never said that they actually go, and there is no reference to their coming back: Matthew has characteristically allowed the importance he attaches to this substantial discourse of Jesus – one of several in this gospel – to crowd out the details of the circumstances that inspired it. In the second place, the conditions prevailing in the church when Matthew wrote are clearly discernible in the form in which some of the sayings are recorded (especially 10.17–20, 40–2). And in the third place, Matthew has added to the original collection a number of sayings about the future which lies ahead of the Christian community, sayings which occur in a quite different context in other gospels and which have little relevance to the situation of the twelve disciples supposedly about to depart on their first missionary expedition. In short, Matthew has edited his material in such a way that it has become, not so much the report of words which Jesus may have used to commission his disciples, as a manual of Jesus' sayings relevant to the work and witness of the church.

Before proceeding to this commissioning of the disciples, Matthew introduces two similes to characterize, first, the people among whom they would work, and secondly, the urgency of the mission on which they would be sent.

36   The people were **like sheep without a shepherd** – a comparison familiar from the Hebrew scriptures (e.g. Ezekiel 34.5), occurring in another context in Mark (6.34), but serving here to fix in the mind one of the commonest

designations of Christian ministers: they were to be 'shepherds'. The disciples,
37 moreover, were to be like **laborers** when **the harvest is plentiful**, and the
church must urgently pray that God would liberally increase the number of
those called to this urgent task – or so Matthew understood the saying. But
just as the 'fishers of people' saying probably had a different meaning before
it became a commonplace in the church (see below on Mark 1.17), so with
the harvesting metaphor. The harvest was one of the commonest biblical
38 images for the last judgment; and the Greek phrase, **Lord of the harvest**,
would naturally lead the mind to the divine judge himself. The labourers
at this ultimate harvest were traditionally to be the angels (as they are, for
instance, in the Revelation); but the followers of Jesus were to have their
place on the tribunal at this judgment, and might also have a share in the
harvesting. **"Ask the Lord of the harvest to send out laborers"**, on Jesus'
lips, may well have been a command to pray for the immediate beginning of
the judgment, hastened no doubt by the efforts of his followers.

10.1   **Then Jesus summoned his twelve disciples.** We have not been told before
that he had twelve; but the existence of the twelve was so taken for granted in
the church that it was hardly necessary to introduce them: they were simply
his twelve disciples. Just as there were twelve legendary tribes of Israel, so
there were to be twelve leaders of the new people of God. Matthew's list is
much the same as Mark's (3.16–19). But only a few of the names are known
personalities. The important thing was that the group existed and consisted of
2   **apostles** (which means 'sent out' on a particular mission) whom the church
subsequently recognized as its founders. It followed that the instructions
given to them were given, through them, to the church.

5   **"Go nowhere among the Gentiles."** By the time this gospel was written,
Gentiles outnumbered Jews in the church and the Christian message had
penetrated deep into non-Jewish lands. This command of Jesus, recorded
only by Matthew, is therefore extremely puzzling. It is true that Jesus himself
seldom ventured into genuinely gentile territory; but Matthew reports his
specific command, after the resurrection, to "make disciples of all nations"
(28.19), and there are at least hints in Jesus' teaching that he thought of his
message and his mission as something far wider than a religious movement
within Judaism. Why then is Jesus here reported to have limited the scope
6   of the mission to the **house of Israel** (by which Matthew, like other Jewish
writers, means the Jewish population of Palestine)? Two solutions suggest
themselves, but neither is entirely satisfactory. Either the command was (or
was subsequently understood to have been) a temporary limitation which
was removed after the resurrection; or else perhaps the church for which
Matthew was writing was one still engaged in a difficult mission to the Jewish
people, tempted to abandon the task and join the more successful mission to
the Gentiles, but needing to be recalled to its first duty by the recollection of
some stern words that Jesus had once uttered: **"go rather to the lost sheep
of the house of Israel"**.

7   **"As you go, proclaim the good news."** The task of the missionaries was to extend the preaching and healing work of Jesus. Sufficient descriptions of this work are given in the course of the gospel, and little space is devoted to it here. Instead, the discourse is concerned with the way these missionaries

8   are to conduct themselves. **"You received without payment; give without payment."** Some of the powers which the disciples were to exercise, such as healing and exorcizing, were possessed by others, who accepted payment and hoped to make a living by their exceptional gifts. But Christian missionaries were to bestow the benefits of these powers as freely as they had received them. Their manner of life, at least on this occasion, must be one of absolute

10 poverty – **no bag for your journey**, either for provisions or for receiving alms (see on Mark 6.8); not even **sandals, or a staff** (which are allowed in Mark's version), either as a sign of a more extreme asceticism, or else because coat, stick and begging pouch was the uniform of wandering philosophers who accepted a beggar's reward in return for their wisdom. How then were they to live? **"Laborers deserve their food."** This was a proverb which occurs with more than one application in the New Testament. However Jesus originally meant it, the early church soon adopted it as a principle. As in other religious societies, the travelling preacher was to be given hospitality in believers' houses, rewarding them only with the customary greeting of peace (though this was not a mere formality: it could be revoked if necessary!). A readiness to hear and receive was a test of qualifying for salvation: if a town or a house failed to pass it, the traveller, by 'shaking off the dust', would demonstrate that it would have no part in the kingdom – just as a Jew, entering Palestine, would shake off the dust of gentile countries which could not share the sacred destiny of the Holy Land. Its punishment, said Jesus, would be worse even

15 than that of the proverbially sinful cities, **Sodom and Gomorrah**. Doubtless Jesus would have been thinking of the judgment brought upon themselves by those who gave no hearing to the first preaching of the gospel; but possibly the church, when it recalled these words, applied them to the experience of its own members in inhospitable Jewish towns.

However this may be, the sayings which follow plainly reveal a perspective different from that of twelve men sent out on a brief preaching tour. Matthew, in fact, has drawn into this discourse a number of sayings which Mark and Luke place considerably later in the narrative. In those gospels, the sayings are prophecies of the sufferings which Christians will have to endure, and describe some of the traditional tribulations (such as strife within families) which will presage the approaching crisis. In Matthew, they refer equally clearly to the period, not of Jesus' lifetime (when there is no evidence and little probability that the disciples suffered persecution) but of the church; and they are grouped here for convenience, even though they hardly fit the

16 context. Apart from the opening warning (**"be wise as serpents and innocent**

17–22 **as doves"**), which sounds like an old proverb, the next few verses all occur in Mark's chapter of prophecies (Mark 13). But Matthew adds a startling

23 new saying: **"you will not have gone through all the towns of Israel before the Son of Man comes"**. The 'coming' of the Son of Man is a phrase which usually seems to stand for the moment when this phase of history will come to an end, the judgment begin and the righteous be finally vindicated; and the saying looks at first sight like a prophecy of Jesus which was soon proved false. Yet Matthew, half a century later, felt able to include this saying in his 'manual for the church'. Was he writing for a community of Christians engaged in the difficult task of preaching in Jewish cities and encouraging them to persevere despite discouragement and persecution, on the grounds that there were still plenty of towns for them to work through before the end? Or did he understand the figure of the Son of Man in a more sophisticated way, as he in whom the righteous were represented and, in a sense, already vindicated? If so, in so far as Christianity had already begun to receive a ready hearing, it could be said that the Son of Man had already 'come'. As in other passages (and see especially below on Mark 9.1), we must beware of imagining that Jesus, when he used the language in which his contemporaries speculated about the future, was indulging in predictions as naïve as some of theirs.

24 **"A disciple is not above the teacher."** The same proverb occurs in Luke (6.40) in the context of the 'sermon'. Here it is applied to persecution of the disciples, who can have nothing worse to endure than their master did

25 (though, by the end of the story, what could have been worse?). On **Beelzebul**,

26 see below on Mark 3.22. **"Nothing is covered up that will not be uncovered"** – another proverb, usually somewhat pessimistic: acts of which one is ashamed tend to come out, if not in one's lifetime, certainly at the judgment. But perhaps there is a more positive thought here (as probably also at Mark 4.22): the gospel, in its beginnings, was essentially a mystery, something covered up and hidden, known only to a few. But Christians need not be discouraged: one day there would be 'revelation', a full manifestation to the whole world,

27 and in the strength of this promise they should meanwhile **proclaim from the housetops**. The worst that could happen to them would be physical death; while to falter in their mission would expose them to the judgment of God,

28 who alone is able to **destroy both soul and body in hell**. God's concern for them was as certain as for the sparrows that are sold as poor people's food in

33 the market – so long as they were faithful. But **whoever denies** Jesus **before others** loses the right to call God 'Father', and will not be acknowledged by Jesus himself.

34 **"Do not think I have come to bring peace to the earth, but a sword"** – and yet, "Blessed are the peacemakers" (5.9)! To approach this paradox, we need to remember the scriptural maxim, "There is no peace . . . for the wicked" (e.g. Isaiah 57.21). The establishment of peace involves the suppression or exclusion of the wicked, which will hardly happen without the use of the sword. But this saying may also have originally belonged in the context of Jesus' predictions about the time immediately before the judgment. One of

the terrors of that time (it was widely believed) would be internecine fighting and the break-up of family loyalties (see below on Mark 13.12). In this sense Jesus, by precipitating this climactic period of history, would be bringing, not peace, **but a sword** – and the early church, seeing families divided by the new faith (for Jewish communities were evidently as intolerant of conversions to Christianity in the first century as they were until quite recent times), saw here a sign of the approaching crisis.

In view of this, loyalty to Jesus must take precedence over all other loyalties – in Luke's gospel this is expressed even more strongly (14.26) – and the sayings which follow take on their full meaning in the light of the subsequent experience of the church (see below on Mark 8.34–6). In verses 40–42 one can even overhear something of the church's structure and nomenclature. Travelling 'prophets' were frequent visitors to local churches and (so long as they were genuine) it was a duty to give them hospitality. **A righteous person** seems, for a time at least, to have been a name used by Christians for one another; and **one of these little ones** was a familiar way of referring to the poor and the gentle, the 'little flock' out of which the church was characteristically composed (see below on Mark 9.42). In short, the theme of this short paragraph is the same as that which is worked out on a grand scale in the parable at the end of chapter 25: "just as you did it to one of the least of these who are members of my family you did it to me" (25.40).

11.2   **When John heard in prison**. The explanation of John's imprisonment is given below, 14.3–5. We learn here for the first time that he had a following of disciples: according to Luke (3.10–14) – and we also know this from the Jewish historian Josephus – he had significant teaching to give on moral questions. But his main importance for Christians lay in his rôle as precursor. His message was centred on one who was to come after him, whom he thought of as a Man of Fire, bringing universal judgment; or as Elijah, who (many believed) was to make a supernatural return shortly before the last judgment; or perhaps even as the Messiah, who was to inaugurate a new age. Matthew's account of the first meeting between John and Jesus makes it appear that John recognized in Jesus at least some marks of the person whom he had been predicting. But since then Jesus' activity, though clearly out of the ordinary, had scarcely measured up to the sensational programme expected of such a figure. To this extent his question is understandable: **"Are you the one who is to come?"**

Jesus' answer, as so often when he was questioned about himself, was somewhat ambiguous. There were prophecies in the Old Testament (see especially Isaiah 35.5–6; 61.1) which foretold a time when physical infirmities would be cured and social evils righted; and the usual interpretation of these passages was that this golden age would begin with the coming of the Messiah. Jesus' miracles had already fulfilled the spirit, and in some cases the letter, of these prophecies. This meant, surely, that a new age was dawning. But how far Jesus himself corresponded with the popular image of the inaugurator of that new age was another matter. In particular, he was certainly not the victorious warrior whom the populace had often been led to expect. His activity raised questions rather than compelled allegiance. People had to make up their

6 minds for or against him. Hence – **"blessed is anyone who takes no offence at me"**.

7   **Jesus began to speak to the crowds about John**. There were many different versions current of the programme which popular Jewish speculation envisaged for the end of the era and the dawning of the promised new age. They tended to revolve around some exceptional person, be it an Elijah *redivivus* or a Messiah. But they did not normally make room for *two* such figures (though the Dead Sea Scrolls do allow for two Messiahs). Therefore, given the fact that Jesus appeared to be such a person, it was something of a problem (doubtless for subsequent generations of Christians as much as for the contemporaries of these events) to fit John the Baptist into the scheme. Jesus sharpened this

7 question for his hearers. When they went out **into the wilderness**, what had they expected to find? Not, obviously, something as ordinary as **a reed shaken by the wind** (which may or may not be metaphorical: either an actual reed, or a man as feeble as a reed); nor yet something so crudely sensational as a splendidly dressed figure in the depths of the desert. A desert preacher

9 was likely to be one thing only: a **prophet**. But this prophet was different in

10 that he was a **messenger** – the prophecy which fitted him (Malachi 3.1) is given here exactly as at the opening of Mark's gospel. The new state of affairs which he heralded was quite different from the social changes others sought

12 to effect through **violence** (this is one possible meaning of the enigmatic and somewhat ambiguous Greek phrase – see the NRSV footnote: there were certainly some violent revolutionaries around at the time). It was even now being brought about by Jesus; and if you could accept that, then you could accept that John was, after all, the great messenger of popular expectation,

14 the **Elijah** who was to come, the last figure in the old era of the law and the prophets. But to recognize this, you had to be able to recognize what was unprecedented in Jesus, and this insight was not given to everyone, just as not everyone could grasp the message of the parables. And so here (as several

15 times in connection with parables): **"Let anyone with ears listen!"**

All this endowed John the Baptist with great significance. Yet Jesus said

11 that **"the least in the kingdom of heaven is greater than he"**. Why? Perhaps because all normal ideas of greatness are turned upside down in the kingdom, so that the first become last, the last first. Or else because John the Baptist only announced the kingdom and came too soon actually to belong to it. It is true that Jesus nowhere else suggests that you have to belong to a particular era in order to enter it. But there is a number of sayings which do imply that the appearance of Jesus had opened an entirely new chapter in history, and that the least of his disciples enjoyed a privilege which had been denied to the greatest figures of the past (see below on 13.17).

16   "To what will I compare this generation?" The little parable that follows is
about two groups of children playing a game of marriages and funerals. One
group makes the appropriate music, the other responds with the appropriate
actions. Both John and Jesus had, in their different ways, presented a challenge and demanded a response; but their hearers, like sulky children, had
19 answered, 'You are not playing it right.' "Yet wisdom is vindicated by her
deeds." In the Hebrew tradition, 'wisdom' was less a matter of philosophical
profundity than of careful observation of experience; and the test of such
'wisdom' was whether it was borne out in real life. The response invited by
both John and Jesus might seem at first sight to run counter to the 'wisdom'
of ordinary common sense; yet it would turn out to be true 'wisdom' and
be **vindicated** by the rewards which it would bring. (This, at least, is one
possible meaning of the saying; but it occurs in a slightly different form in
Luke 7.35, and its meaning remains uncertain.)

21   **Chorazin** lies a few miles inland from Capernaum. It was a smaller and
less pretentious town (to judge from the surviving remains), and this is the
only indication in the gospels that Jesus worked there. A miracle at **Bethsaida**
is recorded in Mark 8.22–6. Jesus' saying here suggests that the purpose of
his **deeds of power** was to move people to repentance. In the gospel accounts
they certainly made a strong impression: people came back for more and
praised God for what they had seen. But we also hear of frank opposition
and scepticism on the part of certain individuals, and it may be (in view of
this saying) that whole communities showed a less positive reaction. Jesus
adopts the tone of an Old Testament prophet: Amos (1.9–10), Isaiah (23),
Ezekiel (26–8) and Zechariah (9.2–4) had all made of **Tyre and Sidon** a
classic example of cities that deserved the wrath of God; Isaiah (14.13–15)
23 had said of Babylon that, even if it thought of itself as **exalted to heaven,**
it would soon be **brought down to Hades**; and **Sodom,** from the book of
Genesis onwards, was the sinful city *par excellence*. But even these cities
were excusable compared with the impenitent witnesses of Jesus' 'deeds of
power'.

25   **At that time Jesus said**. Verses 25–30 have a solemn ring. Whether or not
the sayings they contain originally belonged together (or were even all spoken by Jesus), they are cast in a form which was quite frequently attributed
to teachers in antiquity. The last chapter of Sirach, a book that was written
about two centuries earlier, is composed on much the same pattern (thanksgiving for benefits received, verses 1–12; claim to special knowledge, 13–22;
invitation to others, 23–30); it also contains many phrases which are strikingly similar to the words of Jesus. Similarly the Stoic philosopher Epictetus,
not many years after Jesus' death, appealed to others to follow his way of life
28 in a sentence of exactly the same structure as **"Come to me . . . and I will
give you rest."** Therefore if Jesus, at some stage, made a general appeal for
people to come to him for instruction, this was a well-established way for

him to do so (or for an editor of his sayings to picture him doing so). In addition, as we shall see, there are clear allusions to things said of Moses in the Old Testament, and the passage serves to strengthen the impression given elsewhere in this gospel that Jesus is to be understood as, in a certain sense, a 'new Moses'.

25 **"I thank you, Father."** Since the nineteenth century this saying has been called 'a meteor from the Johannine sky'. Certainly Jesus' intimacy with God, as of a son with his father, is a leading theme of the Fourth Gospel, and these words of Jesus, which seem unexpected here, would cause little surprise there. Nevertheless the ideas they express are not out of place. The contrast between the misguided learning of the Pharisees and the privileged insight of the least of Jesus' followers underlies many episodes in this gospel, and the claim that Jesus was to God as a son is to his father, and that his followers, through their solidarity with him, come to share his sonship and thereby have the right to address God as Father, runs through much of the Sermon on the Mount and is presupposed in the Lord's Prayer. Terms such as 'knowing', 'hiding' and 'revealing' might suggest the kind of religion in which mystical or esoteric 'knowledge' of God is the main object, to be obtained by initiation into successive degrees of illumination. Almost from the beginning, there was a tendency to assimilate Christianity to this kind of religion (see below on Colossians 2.16ff.); and these verses have often been regarded as evidence for similar influences. But the terminology also has its home in Jewish religious thought and experience. To the Jew, God was not 'known' to the one who searched unaided for religious truth: God 'chose' to reveal himself to his people, whom he 'knew' in the sense that he had chosen and identified them. In return, the people 'knew' God, in the sense that they gave him their allegiance and were the recipients of his self-revelation. All these ideas were present in the biblical accounts of the cardinal experience of Moses (see especially Exodus 33.11–23; Numbers 12.1–8; Deuteronomy

29 34.9–12) – who was also incidentally remembered as 'gentle' (Numbers 12.3). But now the vehicle of this revelation was Jesus, and its recipients were no longer, as of right, the ethnic people of Israel but those who were chosen by Jesus to share in the privilege of his sonship and to enter into the Son's intimate 'knowledge' of the Father.

"Take my yoke upon you." All religious leaders lay a 'yoke' on their followers, just as any king lays a yoke on his subjects. People's allegiance can be expressed only in acts of submission and obedience. Moreover, to encourage that allegiance, any teacher or ruler will certainly promise 'rest' to those who are under the yoke, and the extent to which that 'rest' will seem worth having will depend, in part, on the severity of the previous régime. Now it was a common figure of speech that the law of Moses which governed the lives of the Jews, despite the many blessings and privileges which it conferred, was nevertheless, a 'yoke' which had to be borne with discipline and patience; and one of Jesus' complaints against the Pharisees was that in their

efforts to make the ancient law applicable to present-day conditions they had succeeded only in making the law more oppressive. At least a part of what Jesus would have meant by 'his yoke' must be understood in this context: even though he expected from his followers (at least according to Matthew) explicit obedience to the law, yet by directing them back to the spirit that lay behind the letter of the law, by assuring them that their prayers, uttered in the way that he taught them, would be heard and answered, and by promising blessings both now and in the future to those whom society had tended to
30 exclude and victimize, he was able to say, **"my yoke is easy, and my burden is light"**. But at the same time the saying has a generality and a nobility which transcend this particular context.

29   **"I am gentle and humble in heart."** These words are not primarily a description of Jesus' moral character; they define the kind of 'king' that Jesus was – one who was "humble" (21.5) and who "humbled himself" (Philippians 2.8). His 'kingship' was so different, his rule implied such a reversal of the usual structures of authority, that his 'yoke' had nothing to do with oppression or blind obedience. Christians, indeed, were soon to call it "freedom" (James 1.25).

In chapter 12 the narrative turns from discipleship to controversy. Jesus' principal opponents (at least according to this gospel) were the Pharisees, and the first issue raised is that of sabbath observance. Basic sabbath rules were laid down in scripture and were taken for granted by the entire population; but the Pharisees had developed a more rigorous system of observances, and it was the casuistry often involved in these that Jesus criticized. Matthew, in the next two episodes, follows much the same tradition as Mark (2.23–3.6) and Luke (6.1–11), but in each case introduces a somewhat more technical argument which shows Jesus meeting the Pharisees on their own ground.
12.1–6 In the first, after referring his opponents to the somewhat indecisive case of David, Jesus adds (using a technical scholarly formula **"Have you not read . . . ?"**), a logically more powerful argument. It was agreed that the necessities of the temple service made it necessary for the priests to break a sabbath regulation – for instance, by offering sacrifices daily (Numbers 28.9–
6 10). *A fortiori*, if **"something greater than the temple is here"** it will provide exemption for other kinds of 'reaping'. An appeal to the general principle
7 expressed in Hosea 6.6, that **mercy** (which includes many kinds of charitable acts) is of more value than ritual observances, rounds off the argument. The validity of this reasoning depends of course ultimately on the authority
8 which Jesus claims for himself. So here (as in Mark and Luke): **"For the Son of Man is lord of the sabbath"** – not by any means with a view to abolishing it, but as an authoritative judge of the priorities to be observed.
9–14   In the second episode the challenge to Jesus is answered in Mark and Luke by a simple counter-challenge: "Is it lawful to do good or to do harm on the sabbath?" Here, Jesus' reply takes the form of another argument *a fortiori*. It would have been admitted by his critics (though possibly with

51

some reservations) that it was permissible to rescue a sheep on the sabbath. How much more then to do good to a human being!

15–21   The following paragraph appears to offer an explanation of a rather puzzling feature of Mark's narrative. Mark records that, while Jesus was performing cures, the unclean spirits by which some of the sufferers were possessed shouted out that he was the Son of God, and Jesus "sternly ordered them not to make him known" (3.12). Matthew uses exactly the same language but omits all reference to the spirits. What in Mark takes the form of a dialogue with supernatural powers appears in Matthew as a simple command given to the crowds. This does not make the command less puzzling: why did Jesus insist on this secrecy? Matthew seems to suggest by his introductory words

15   (Jesus **departed**: the Greek word suggests 'retiring' or 'withdrawing') that the motive was simply prudence: he wished for the time being to avoid further controversy with the Pharisees. But he also has a more subtle explanation to offer. One of the Old Testament passages which seemed to Matthew (and doubtless to the early church) both to foretell Jesus' coming and to explain his destiny was the opening of Isaiah 42 – the prophecy of a 'servant' who would establish justice in the world. An allusion to this prophecy seems to underlie

18–21 the words heard at Jesus' baptism (3.17); here Matthew quotes it in full, in a version that does not follow either the Hebrew text or the Septuagint Greek version precisely – possibly the verses had been already much pondered in the church (or by Matthew himself) and slightly modified in the process. At any rate, this version brings out the point that was important for Matthew,

19   namely the silence and modesty of the servant: **"He will not . . . cry aloud, nor will anyone hear his voice in the streets."** It was in conformity with this prototype, Matthew suggests, that Jesus maintained his mysterious secrecy.

    The following episode is told by Matthew and Luke in a form somewhat different from that which it has in Mark (3.22–30). It begins with a brief account of an exorcism, which aroused in the bystanders a reaction of con-

23   siderable expectancy: **"Can this be the Son of David?"** It was widely believed at the time that God would soon bring into being a new age by means of a divinely appointed agent (a Messiah), who would be the true successor of King David and could therefore be called (not because of his genealogy but because of his destiny) 'the Son of David'. Some believed that this person existed already, but that his identity would remain unknown until the time for his appearing should come. When that moment came he would manifest himself with exceptional powers. Jesus' miracles naturally gave rise to the question, **"Can this be the Son of David?"**

24   The Pharisees were ready with an alternative explanation: **"It is only by Beelzebul, the ruler of the demons, that this fellow casts out the demons."** Jesus' reply is here very close to that in Mark's account (3.22–6) but has an additional point of some interest. It shows that there were exorcists about of whom the Pharisees approved; therefore the argument used against Jesus would apply equally to them. No, the Pharisees were wrong and the people

(in a sense) were right. Jesus' exorcisms were indeed, a sign of something

28 new: **"the kingdom of God has come to you"**.

29 The comparison with the **strong man's house** is almost exactly as in Mark
30 (3.27) but in verse 30 Matthew adds a proverb expressing the challenge of
Jesus' teaching. Jesus appears to say the opposite in Mark 9.40 ("whoever is
not against us is for us"), but the contradiction is probably only apparent:
the meaning of proverbs depends on the purpose for which they are used
32 (see below on that passage in Mark). The saying about the slander against
the Spirit is as difficult here as it is in Mark (3.28–30), even though Matthew,
like Luke, has the additional words, **"Whoever speaks a word against the
Son of Man will be forgiven."** It is possible that the experience of the early
church has influenced the form of words. It was one thing, out of ignorance
or perversity, to misunderstand the church's teaching about the nature of
Jesus Christ (i.e., in Jesus' language, 'to speak against the Son of Man').
But if, confronted by the manifest power of the Spirit in the church, people
continued to revile and persecute its members, then there seemed no further
hope for them, **either in this age or in the age to come** (as Matthew puts it,
using a standard Jewish idiom).

33 **"Either make the tree good and its fruit good."** This is essentially the
same saying as in the Sermon on the Mount (7.16–20). There it was applied
to the problem of discriminating between true and false prophets; here it is
part of an attack on the hypocrisy of the Pharisees, whom Jesus (in Matthew)
34 treats with great asperity (**"brood of vipers"**). Any form of casuistry tends
to focus on words and actions rather than on the intentions of the heart;
Jesus, by contrast, regards motivation as all-important: the reason God will
36 judge severely even **every careless word** is that such words are a sure sign of
underlying intentions.

38 **"Teacher, we wish to see a sign from you."** This request occurs in Mark
(8.11) and is there refused without any reason being given. Here the refusal
is expanded by a reference to Jonah. The book of Jonah was much revered. It
contained a message both of hope and of warning. All the other Old Testament
prophets had met with resistance, unbelief, even outright rejection; but Jonah
had preached, and (much to his discomfiture!) the whole city of Nineveh
had attended to him and repented. This was the hopeful side of the message:
repentance was always possible, and God would reward the penitent as he
had rewarded Nineveh. But Nineveh was not a Jewish city! This was the note
of warning: was there anything in Jewish history to compare with Nineveh's
41 repentance? And the warning is taken up by Jesus here: **"The people of
Nineveh will rise up at the judgment with this generation and condemn
it"** – a moral that could also be drawn from that other Old Testament story
42 of the visit of the Queen of Sheba to Solomon (1 Kings 10). But Matthew,
unlike Luke, has worked in another motif from the legend of Jonah. The
decisive 'sign' which Jesus ultimately did give to that 'generation' was the
resurrection, and the church (whether or not there was any warrant for this

40 in Jesus' original saying) very soon came to see Jonah's legendary sojourn **in the belly of the sea monster** as a prefiguration of Jesus' brief sojourn in the grave.

43 **"When the unclean spirit has gone out of a person."** Given the naïvely realistic language of an age which believed implicitly in spirit-possession, this was, and remains, a valid description of what we would now call a psychological danger, that of curing an obsession without putting anything positive in its place. So Luke understands it (11.24–6); but Matthew applies

45 it to a whole **generation**. It is hard to be sure of the meaning. Perhaps the idea was that, after an imperfect repentance provoked by Jesus' teaching, that generation would soon be exposed to the dangers of still worse religious and political leaders than they had before – a danger which (at least from a Christian point of view) had been abundantly fulfilled by the time Matthew wrote.

46–50 The scene which closes the section is given almost exactly as in Mark (3.31–5).

Parables

Matthew now devotes a further chapter to the teaching of Jesus; but this time it is teaching of a new kind. So far, it has taken the form of rules, precepts and

13.3 advice for the conduct of life. But it was well known that Jesus also **told them many things in parables**, and Matthew, who follows very closely the account given in the corresponding chapter of Mark, now presents a collection of these parables, and at the same time casts Jesus in a new rôle: that of an inspired teacher of divine mysteries.

The collection begins with a parable of sowing, told almost exactly as in Mark. Just as, however good the harvest, there will always be some wastage, so, despite the apparent success of Jesus' work, there would always be some who opposed it and so excluded themselves from the kingdom. But if this was how the parable was intended by Jesus to be understood (see on Mark 4.1–10), it was not for this reason that Matthew set it down here. Matthew, in common with Mark, possessed another and more recondite interpretation; and he evidently saw Jesus' parables, not as illustrations intended to make his meaning clearer (which was the most common sense of the Greek word), but as cryptic sayings intelligible only to the initiated (which was one of the meanings of the corresponding Hebrew word). There was good precedent for an inspired teacher clothing his teaching in mysterious imagery. Visionaries who believed that they had been vouchsafed glimpses of the destiny which God had for the world would naturally express the content of their visions in cryptic form; for they were, in effect, divulging 'mysteries' or secrets the full manifestation of which was reserved for the future. Meanwhile it was only to themselves and to the privileged few who had the knowledge and understanding to grasp the meaning of their cryptic discourses that these things were revealed. An example of this kind of writing is the Revelation of John, which springs from the tradition of Jewish 'apocalypses' that began with the book of Daniel and ran on to at least the end of the first century CE. Jesus himself was remembered to have conformed with this tradition when he gave some teaching on his vision of the future (see below on Matthew 24 and Mark 13). In Matthew the parables seem to be regarded as part of the same kind of teaching. In the centre of the picture stand the disciples,

11 a privileged group to whom it has been given **to know the secrets of the**
17 **kingdom of heaven.** Even the prophets and kings of the Old Testament, for all their remarkable insight and vision, did not reach that point of initiation into the purposes of God which the disciples have already reached – and they will go further still: Matthew applies to them a saying of Jesus which
12 stands isolated in Mark (4.25), **"to those who have, more will be given".** The disciples, unlike the people of Israel of old, have been given "eyes to
9 see and ears to hear" (Deuteronomy 29.4), and this makes them a uniquely privileged group, in contrast to the bemused crowds who are straining to catch the import of Jesus' teaching from the shores of the lake. But what then of these crowds? Why is their fate so different from that of the privileged
10 few? This is the sense of the disciples' question, **"Why do you speak to them in parables?"** (which in Mark appears as a question, not about the hearers, but about the parables themselves). And the answer is that here,
14–15 once again, is a fulfilment of prophecy. Matthew quotes (at far greater length than Matthew or Luke) from Isaiah 6.9–10. His quotation follows word for word the Septuagint version of the Greek Bible, which gives a somewhat different sense from the Hebrew. Jesus is not likely to have used this version, but it does not follow that he did not on occasion make use of the same passage in Hebrew (see below on Mark 4.11–13) – only that Matthew has been at work editing the material. The word in the passage that has caught
15 Matthew's imagination is **understand.** It is not opposition or indifference or perversity that has kept the crowds from accepting the message, but a lack of understanding; and Matthew has subtly altered the interpretation of the parable (an interpretation which may not go back to Jesus himself: see below on Mark 4.14–20) in order to make the point that the reward belongs to one
23 who hears the word and **understands.**

The second parable is also drawn from ordinary agricultural practice; indeed the farmer's problem was not at all unusual. It was to be expected in
25 any cornfield that there would be **weeds,** and one of the most troublesome was that species of *darnel* (the likely meaning of the Greek word) which in its early stages is almost indistinguishable from the young blade of corn.
26 Nothing could be done about it, therefore, until **the plants came up and bore grain:** by then (in fact somewhat before then) it would be easy enough to distinguish the weeds. There were then two possible courses of action, both of which were quite common practice, but each of which had disadvantages. Either the weeds could be pulled out when the corn was still green – but

darnel had strong roots and there was a danger of pulling up the corn at the
30 same time; or else they could be left to **grow together until the harvest** –
but then it had either to be carefully separated out in the reaping (which
would have been done not by the farmer's own people alone but by a force of
hired labourers), or else sieved out in the threshing; for the seeds of darnel
are poisonous. In the parable, the farmer chooses the second course, and this
alone would have given Jesus a point: Do not try to weed out your ranks and
form a sect of holy and virtuous people. There will be time enough for this
at the judgment (for which 'harvest' was a familiar symbol).

But in the present form of the parable this familiar scene is turned into
an anecdote by the addition of a curious feature. The presence of weeds in
a field would not normally be a great surprise: it was the commonest of the
28 farmer's difficulties. But here there is a different explanation: **"An enemy has
done this."** This is not improbable. Stories are told of village feuds being
carried on in this way. On the other hand, it does not add anything to the
point of the parable, which appears to lie in the wheat and the weeds 'growing
together' until harvest. The detail of the **enemy** becomes significant only if the
parable is in reality a different kind of story, an allegory or cryptic discourse
in which each term stands for something else. 'Harvest' is a conventional
image of judgment. The description of the harvesting in verse 30 is difficult
to visualize in terms of wheat and weeds, but is apt enough if the real material
being harvested is a cross-section of good and bad human beings; and in this
case the 'enemy' is a necessary character, since it is the devil who prompts
our evil deeds.

In this form, at any rate (which may or may not be the form in which Jesus
originally spoke it – some believe that he made little use of allegory), the
parable fits appropriately into its context in Matthew's gospel. The story, like
the previous one, is deliberately mysterious, and only the privileged few are
given the key to its meaning. Moreover, since its theme is the judgment, it falls
naturally into place in the teaching of one who (in Matthew's presentation)
had a special vision of the future to impart to his chosen disciples. As in the
37–43 case of the previous parable, Matthew has an esoteric interpretation to offer.
This again has a number of features characteristic of Matthew's editing, and
there are serious reasons for doubting whether it can go back to Jesus himself.

The next two parables, at any rate, seem more characteristic of Jesus in
that they are given without any clue to their correct meaning. If they had
been intended to receive the same kind of esoteric interpretation, then each
element in them would presumably have to have been a cryptogram for
31 something else; and, given one correspondence (**the kingdom of heaven is
like a mustard seed**, or like **yeast**), one would have to ask what, for instance,
the person who sowed or the woman who baked stand for. But it is unlikely
that Jesus meant them in this sense. The phrase **the kingdom of heaven
is like . . .** does not necessarily (or at least did not in the language which
Jesus spoke) mean that the kingdom corresponded with just one person or

thing in the parable, but that it was illustrated by the parable as a whole. The point of comparison in each case seems to be simply the contrast: the tiny

32 seed and the full-grown **tree** (there is more than a touch of Jesus' liking for exaggeration when he calls the spindly mustard plant a 'tree'), or the small

33 amount of **yeast** that leavens a whole day's baking.

34 **Without a parable he told them nothing**. Matthew, of course, does not mean that Jesus never spoke to the crowds at all without a parable – after the Sermon on the Mount that would be nonsense. But in his rôle as a revealer of the secrets of the future, his speech to the crowds (Matthew wishes us to understand) was always cryptic, and only his disciples were given the key to his meaning. Matthew again finds a scriptural model for this. The passage he

35 quotes is Psalm 78.2, with a slight modification of the second line: **what has been hidden from the foundation of the world** is a phrase which describes the kind of revelation being given by Jesus better than the literal text in either the Greek version or the Hebrew. Although it is from a psalm, it could

34 legitimately be regarded as **spoken through the prophet**, since David (the reputed author of the psalms) was also believed to have 'prophesied'.[6]

The next two parables belong together and make the same point: the total

44 commitment demanded by the kingdom of heaven. To buy a field, the man in the first parable had to sell everything he had: he was therefore a poor man, doubtless working in the field as a hired labourer. Having found the treasure, he was not necessarily obliged to report it to the field's owner, but he could not expect to be able to acquire it unmolested until he became the

45 owner himself. The **merchant** of the second parable would have been a far more prosperous person. He is to be imagined passing through Galilee on his way from the pearl-fishing seas of the east. On his last journey he was able to acquire an exceptional pearl for which he willingly surrendered his entire stock, knowing that it would make his fortune when he brought it to the dealers in the big cities.

The last parable is drawn from one of the commonest scenes on the lake

47 (here called **the sea**, which was the way the local inhabitants referred to the Lake of Tiberias). The point about the net is that it catches **fish of every kind**, which are sorted out only afterwards – and this presumably (as in the case of the wheat and the weeds) was the original point of the parable. Do not try to sort out the good from the bad in this life by forming a little sect of specially pious people and despising all who will not join you on those terms: all the sorting necessary will be done by God at the judgment.

49–50 The interpretation added by Matthew does not conflict with this, but it shifts the emphasis from the present to the future, and treats the parable as another cryptic description. This is consonant with Matthew's picture of Jesus in his rôle of an expounder of the secrets of the future to a privileged

---

[6] Why some manuscripts attribute the words to Isaiah is a mystery – see the NRSV footnote.

few; but it may, once again, represent a later understanding of the parables themselves.

Mark's parable chapter ends with a summary of the way in which Jesus addressed the crowds (4.33–4). Matthew slightly alters this by focusing attention on the disciples who (unlike the uncomprehending group in Mark)
52 alone have the privilege of 'understanding'. The ordinary Jewish **scribe**, in the course of his training, built up an immense store of the **old** – that is, of knowledge of the scriptures and of the traditional interpretations of them that were handed down and elaborated by generations of scholars. But the training of Jesus' disciples, as sketched in this chapter, gave them something **new** to offer as well.

Matthew's account of Jesus' visit to Nazareth follows Mark closely (6.1–6), and only two slight changes have significance. Jesus is called, not 'the carpen-
54 ter', but **the carpenter's son** – perhaps Christians were uncertain whether Jesus had actually practised the craft or were unwilling to acknowledge it;
58 and Mark's "he could do no deed of power there" is altered to **he did not do many deeds of power there**. Matthew was not prepared to concede that Jesus' power had such limitations.

14.1   **Herod the ruler.** Mark calls him 'king', which is doubtless what he was popularly known as; but Matthew, more precisely, gives him his official title of *tetrarch*, or **ruler**. The tetrarchy of Herod Antipas included the whole of Galilee, and this was the ruler whom Jesus had to reckon with until he travelled up to Jerusalem. Herod's attitude to religious movements of the kind started by John the Baptist was clearly an important factor in the story; and
1–12 Matthew, who has already alluded to John's arrest in 4.12, now introduces the full story, which is told exactly as in Mark (6.14–29),[7] with the omission of a few details.

13–36   The news of this execution sets in motion the sequence of events which ensues. The narrative closely follows that in Mark (6.32–56), leaving out a few
21, 24 details, and showing only a slight tendency to enhance the miracles (**besides women and children . . . far from the land**) and to present the disciples in a better light. Peter's venture on the water, however, is told only by Matthew and may even have been elaborated by him to illustrate two favourite themes: the importance of faith for a disciple and the impulsiveness and unreliability of Peter's character at moments of crisis – traits which were to have serious consequences later on.

15.1   A critical question from some **Pharisees and scribes** from Jerusalem provokes Jesus into a vigorous counter-attack. When Mark comes to this incident (7.1), he elucidates it for non-Jewish readers by adding an explanation of the Jewish customs alluded to. Matthew omits these notes – which is another reason for believing that his readers were primarily Jews, and would have known

---

[7] Except that the dancer (according to most manuscripts) is called **the daughter of Herodias**, whom we know from Josephus to have been called Salome.

2   at once that the Pharisees' comment, **"they do not wash their hands before they eat"**, touched a question, not of hygiene, but of ritual purity. Precisely

3   what the **tradition** was that Jesus was attacking and what the target was of his counter-attack on the Corban oath (the term is omitted by Matthew, but the argument is the same as in Mark), are difficult questions – see below on Mark 7.1–13; but the underlying tendency of Pharisaic tradition to overlay God's

8–9 law with **human precepts** is neatly summed up in the quotation from Isaiah 29.13 (which Matthew, like Mark, quotes according to the Greek version) and is here, as elsewhere, made the target of Jesus' criticism. No wonder

12 the Pharisees took **offence**! But Jesus, in the presence of his disciples, went further still. These religious leaders prided themselves on being "guides to the blind" (Romans 2.19). Jesus casts this back in their teeth by calling them

14 **blind guides** themselves.

Woven into this controversy is a saying which appears in a very simi-

11 lar form in Mark (7.15), **"it is not what goes into the mouth that defiles a person, but it is what comes out of the mouth that defiles"**. This say-ing certainly sounded a little mysterious (one of the meanings of the word

15 **parable**), and needed interpretation; and the interpretation added by Mark ("Thus he declared all foods clean") made it apply specifically to the question (much discussed in the early church) whether Jewish food laws still applied among gentile Christians. Matthew omits this: if his congregation consisted of Christian Jews the question would have seemed less important. Never-

17–19 theless, he gives an explanation of the 'parable' in order to make sure of the

16 disciples' **understanding**. Then, with a slight twist at the end, he brings it

20 round to the point where the section started: the ritual washing of hands.

21–8 The section which follows is of some interest in view of the subsequent history of the church. The question to which the passage offers an answer is: What was Jesus' attitude to Gentiles? Matthew follows Mark's version of the story (7.24–30) but may have felt that it left the question somewhat in the air. According to Mark, Jesus seemed both to endorse the usual Jewish attitude of exclusiveness towards all non-Jews, and at the same time to make an unex-plained exception for the benefit of a woman who was "of Syrophoenician origin". Matthew endeavours to bring more logic into the story by adding a few details which may be in part his own invention or else drawn from

22 another version of the same story. The woman came **from that region** – that is, in all probability, from some village at the north end of the Jordan valley, where the administration was carried out from the coastal city of Tyre (or even Sidon), but the population was still mainly Jewish. She is here called a **Canaanite**, which is a piece of antiquarianism on the part of Matthew: Canaanite is the Old Testament term for those inhabitants of Palestine, such as the Phoenicians, whom the people of Israel found already in occupation. But it serves to underline the biblical foundation for the apparent exclusive-

24 ness of Jesus' reply, **"I was sent only to the lost sheep of the house of Israel."** More clearly than the lively, and perhaps slightly humorous, dialogue that

follows, this first reply leaves no doubt of Jesus' attitude towards Gentiles: his mission was not to them. But Matthew also makes clear (as Mark does

28 not) why an exception was made for the Canaanite woman: she had **faith**. As in the case of the Roman centurion (8.5–10), so here: non-Jews, if they have faith enough, can qualify for the kingdom. Whether or not this was originally Jesus' attitude, it soon became that of the early church. It governs the thought, for instance, of the first few chapters of Paul's letter to the Romans.

Matthew continues to follow closely the order of events in Mark's gospel, but gives them a more logical sequence. What in Mark is a single miracle (the healing of a deaf and dumb man, 7.31–7) becomes in Matthew a whole series of miracles. The effect is the same: the prophecy of Isaiah (35.5) is

30 seen to be fulfilled – the three words, **lame, blind** and **mute** all occur in that passage – and the people, doubtless recognizing the significance of these

31 events, **praised the God of Israel**. But the setting in Matthew's gospel, with the

29 crowds flocking to Jesus where he was seated somewhere **up the mountain**,

32–9 also sets the scene neatly for the feeding miracle that follows. The same considerations apply to this narrative as to the version in Mark (8.1–10); Matthew has made only slight alterations, perhaps partly to increase the

32 impression of Jesus' mastery of the situation ("**I do not want to send them away hungry**" for Mark's "If I send them away hungry", the enlargement of

38–39 the crowd by **women and children**). **The region of Magadan** is Matthew's alteration of Mark's 'Dalmanutha'. But from our point of view this is no improvement: Magadan, like Dalmanutha, is completely unknown.

Matthew has already given a full report of the question of a 'sign' (12.38–9), doubtless drawn from a source other than Mark; but here, for all that,

16.1–4 he continues to follow Mark's order and relates it again, closely following Mark (8.11–12), but omitting Mark's reference to Jesus' 'deep sighing' and adding an allusion to **the sign of Jonah** which was mentioned in the earlier conversation.

Matthew's treatment of the next episode is highly significant. He normally presents the disciples as a privileged group of men, constantly in the company of their teacher and in a unique position (unlike the crowds) to grasp the meaning of Jesus' teaching. But as he followed Mark's gospel he was now confronted by an episode which was the occasion for the severest criticism ever made by Jesus of the disciples' ability to understand him (8.14–21). He succeeds, however, in giving it a somewhat different turn. The elements are

6 the same: the saying on **the yeast of the Pharisees and Sadducees**, and the crossing of the lake without provisions. But Matthew's combination of them is subtly different. Instead of concentrating on the disciples' total incomprehension of the significance of the feeding miracles, Matthew shifts the emphasis on to Jesus' somewhat enigmatic saying about yeast. It was this that the disciples had failed to decode correctly. Matthew follows Mark in suggesting that they had naïvely thought he was talking about actual bread;

12 but he then explains that the real, deeper, meaning was **the teaching of the**

Pharisees and Sadducees. Once more, the disciples are shown as the recipients of an esoteric interpretation of a saying of Jesus. Whether this was what Jesus would have intended is perhaps doubtful. In Mark the corresponding phrase is "the yeast of the Pharisees and the yeast of Herod", which can hardly mean anything but the common desire of the two authorities to do away with Jesus. In Matthew, Herod is somewhat unexpectedly replaced by **the Sadducees.** This party certainly had some teaching of its own (of which we know very little beyond what can be inferred from Matthew 22.23); but it was an aristocratic party, more political than religious, and would hardly have been interested in trying to influence people at the social level of Jesus' disciples. By the time Matthew wrote, in any case, they had disappeared as an effective force in society, and they make only one further appearance in this gospel (22.23). But the Pharisees remained the one influential party after the fall of Jerusalem in 70 CE, and this warning against their teaching may be Matthew's response to the opposition with which they began to threaten the church.

13   **The district of Caesarea Philippi,** some miles north of the Sea of Galilee, is the scene (as in Mark) of an important moment in the unfolding of the true nature of Jesus. But this moment, in Matthew's treatment, becomes also a means of drawing attention to one of the the disciples who has so far been generally mentioned only as one of the group, but who now begins to become prominent in the story (not always to his credit) and who was subsequently a leading figure (if not *the* leading figure) in the early church: Simon Peter.

    "Who do people say that the Son of Man is?" This is (to us) a strangely oblique way of speaking, but there can be no doubt that Jesus' question is really about himself – the sequel makes this plain – and in any case, the question is clearly not a theoretical one about that mythological figure who occasionally appeared in Jewish speculation as the 'Son of Man', but about the flesh-and-blood person who is speaking. The stage reached so far in the popular estimate of Jesus was that of moderately tense expectancy: he claimed to be bringing the promised kingdom appreciably nearer, and therefore he might well be one of those Old Testament figures who, it was popularly believed, would return to earth to prepare for the coming new age. Indeed, John the Baptist himself had appeared to fulfil so faithfully the rôle of an Old Testament prophet (particularly Elijah), and had at the same time proclaimed such an urgent message, that Jesus might even be a reincarnation of him – a belief in the possibility of reincarnation was certainly held by some. But Simon Peter had advanced to a further stage in understanding who Jesus

15 was: **"You are the Messiah, the Son of the living God."** That Jesus was in fact these things was taken for granted by the church when Matthew was writing; and by relating that Peter offered and Jesus accepted these titles, Matthew incidentally allowed his readers to feel that the language they were accustomed to use of their Lord had been endorsed by Jesus himself.

But the significance of the narrative, apart from marking a crucial stage in the development of the disciples' understanding (and possibly also of Jesus' self-understanding), is mainly the light it throws on Peter. Matthew has inserted a saying that occurs in no other gospel. So far, he has represented the disciples as a group of men who are given the unique privilege of private and esoteric teaching, while the crowds who listen to Jesus are left in doubt and even bewilderment about his real meaning. One of them, however, has now shown that he has advanced further still, to the point where he can receive a direct revelation from God. Recognizing Jesus as 'Son of God' is something exceptional in the gospel story (normally it is only supernatural beings who do so). It could not have been revealed by ordinary **flesh and**
17 **blood**. Those who achieve this recognition are **blessed** – and it is doubtless implied here that all those Christians who come to acknowledge the same truth for themselves are similarly 'blessed'.

But if Peter, up to this point, is the prototype of all Christians who confess Jesus to be Christ and Son of God, the next part of the saying sets
18 him apart. **"You are Peter, and on this rock . . . "** Matthew has already said more than once that Simon was "called Peter", and Mark states that it was Jesus who gave him this name. Unlike, for instance, the name given to two other disciples ("Boanerges", Mark 3.17), Simon's new name stuck to him, and he is known indifferently throughout the New Testament as Simon or Peter (or its Aramaic equivalent, Kephas). Jesus' intention in so naming Simon is here explained for the one and only time in the New Testament: Peter (in Greek *Petros*, in Aramaic *Kephas*) means 'stone' or 'rock'; and the significance of the name is now worked out, giving its bearer an apparently unique rôle to play in the subsequent history of the church.

Since it is clear from the New Testament that Peter was in fact not, or at any rate not for long, the universally acknowledged leader of the church (the church in Jerusalem was under the leadership of James the Lord's brother); and since, on the other hand, it has been of primary concern to one whole section of the church for many centuries to assert the absolute supremacy of Peter and of his successors over the church at large, the authenticity and meaning of this passage have been a subject of long-standing controversy.
18 Further, the word **church** is very rare in the gospels (it occurs only here and at 18.17), and even though the concept of a community of followers may be implied in Jesus' teaching as a whole, it remains surprising to find him using the precise word 'church' (which in Greek was used mainly for a political assembly or, in the Bible and later Jewish literature, for an assembly of the people), and it is tempting to think that it was only after the Christian church had come into existence that such a saying could have assumed its present form. On the other hand, the building metaphor, as applied to the church, seems to have been used from very early times by Christians, particularly by Paul. The metaphor is not unparalleled in Jewish writings, but it remains a

striking one, and there is no reason why it should not go back to Jesus himself. Moreover, if Jesus gave Simon a name which means 'stone' or 'rock', it need not surprise us if at some moment he put the two ideas together and ascribed to this disciple an important rôle in the 'building' which was to come. To this extent the saying may well go back to Jesus, even if the subsequent evolution of a Christian 'church' has modified the form in which we now possess it.

"**The gates of Hades.**" It may seem surprising to find 'Hades', a word drawn from popular Greek mythology, instead of the Hebrew *sheol*. But both words meant the same: the shadowy dwelling place of all the dead, apart from the blessed few (in Greek myths) who attained the Elysian fields, or the occasional individuals in scripture (such as Enoch and Elijah) who were taken directly to heaven. So either term might be used by a Jewish author writing in Greek. Hades had 'gates', preventing any possible return to the land of the living; but the church, through the resurrection, now has the power to bring the dead through those gates to a new life. Again, it is easier to understand the birth of this saying after the resurrection of Jesus than before it; for it was the resurrection that assured Christians that the power of death had been overcome. Yet if Jesus did in fact make predictions of a general kind about the community which was soon to arise in his name, these predictions could well have included some form of this saying. The
19 expression **the keys of the kingdom of heaven** appears to be explained in the sentence which follows; but unfortunately 'binding' and 'loosing' have a number of possible meanings which range from determining the possible options allowed by law (as a lawyer might in disputed matters), to making the decision to excommunicate a sinful member of the church. It is not altogether easy to reconcile this responsibility of Peter's (or of any single church leader) with the more democratic procedure described in chapter 18 below, or indeed with the Christian message of forgiveness to all who sincerely repent. The interpretation of these words depends, again, on whether it is thought credible that Jesus should have given detailed directions for the organization of the church and on whether it is admitted that the subsequent practice of the church may have influenced the form in which the sayings have been handed down.
21–8 The remainder of the chapter reproduces the corresponding passage in Mark (8.31–8) with only a few alterations. The final saying, on the coming of the kingdom, has been modified significantly. One of the rôles of the Son of Man (suggested by the Son of Man passage in Daniel 7) was to assist
27 at the judgment, when everyone would receive their reward for **what has been done.** So far the saying merely endorses what was probably quite a
28 widespread belief. But the sequel, **"there are some standing here who will not taste death before they see the Son of Man coming in his kingdom"**, is more startling. It appears to predict, erroneously, some radical change in the lifetime of Jesus' own disciples. To alleviate the difficulty, Matthew, unlike Mark, makes the saying turn, not on the kingdom itself, but on the

figure of the Son of Man, and in so doing may be trying to reconcile it with the experience of the church; for there was a sense in which Christians had already seen **the Son of Man coming in his kingdom** – compare Stephen's vision in Acts 7.55–6. But the saying still retains much of the strangeness that it has in Mark (see below on Mark 9.1).

17.2   **He was transfigured.** Matthew's account of the 'transfiguration' follows closely that in Mark (9.2–8), and the details, as in Mark, frequently suggest a symbolical interpretation, even if (again as in Mark) they do not necessarily demand it. The small changes made by Matthew nevertheless all point in one direction. Moses comes before Elijah, so that the two figures are clearer symbols of the law and the prophets, Moses the law-giver being given first place; and certain small touches, such as the radiance of Jesus' face (not just his clothes) and the awe felt by the disciples after (instead of before) the heavenly voice, bring the experience of Moses on Mount Sinai more vividly to mind (Exodus 34.29–35). These details perhaps show Matthew at work, presenting Jesus as a new Moses. The scene is followed, as in Mark, by the

10   disciples' question about Elijah, **"Why, then, do the scribes say that Elijah must come first?"** The scribes would have taught the traditional interpretation of Malachi 4.5 (Elijah would come "before the day of the L O R D" and

11   even **restore all things**). But nothing would have prepared them to imagine this Elijah appearing unrecognized and enduring punishment. Jesus helps the disciples to envisage this and so to recognize John the Baptist as the divinely ordained precursor. This would also help them (and the reader of

12   the gospel) to understand how such a fate could also befall the **Son of Man**.

14–21   The exorcism which follows is related more briefly in Matthew than in Mark (9.14–29), and nothing is said about faith being required in the sufferer or his parents. Nevertheless, Matthew still makes *faith* the point of the story. To the question, why Jesus' disciples (and perhaps also the early Christians) do not always succeed in their exorcisms, the answer in Mark is: they do not pray enough! The saying of Jesus given here suggests a different answer: they have not sufficient faith!

    A further prediction of the fate in store for the Son of Man is recorded here as it is in Mark and Luke, but with a characteristic difference. In the other gospels the disciples failed to 'understand'. But Matthew will not have the disciples come short of understanding; for they are to be the teachers of those who come after. So here, on the contrary, they understand so well that

23   they are **greatly distressed**.

24   **The collectors of the temple tax.** The Greek has simply the *didrachma*, which could conceivably mean a Roman tax. But the 'double drachma' was equivalent to the 'half-shekel' which Jews, not only in Palestine but all over the Roman empire, were obliged (morally if not legally) to pay as an annual tax for the upkeep of the temple. The translators have therefore assumed that it was the **temple tax** that was being demanded. The amount of this tax was relatively small; it was just twice the labourer's wage for a day's work (20.2),

and the obligation to pay it was generally accepted by rich and poor alike. Nevertheless, certain classes of people were exempt, some because they were not full citizens (such as slaves or Samaritans), some because they were particularly privileged as priests. The question of the collectors, therefore, did not necessarily amount to asking whether Jesus was a rebel against the law; he might have had a status qualifying him for exemption. And this is precisely

25 what Jesus explained to his disciples later on, **when he came home**. The **kings** of whom the Jews had experience were those vassal kings whom the Romans allowed to administer parts of Palestine under the general jurisdiction of the empire. The **tribute** which these rulers exacted was a capitation tax levied on all subject peoples; the 'tolls' were customs dues. Roman citizens were exempt from both these – Jesus calls them **their children**, literally, 'their sons', which was a way of saying those who enjoyed the privileges of Roman

26 citizenship; but all **others** (literally, *foreigners*) were subject to them. Jesus' answer implied that, just as Roman citizens were exempt from provincial taxes, so certain people might have a similar immunity with regard to taxes for the temple – as was the case with priests; and Jesus claimed a status at least comparable with theirs.

27 Nevertheless, Jesus complied with the collectors' demand. The story of how he did so is reminiscent of many folk tales, and is often thought to be the kind of legend which might very soon have attached itself to the person of Jesus: similar stories came to be told of famous Jewish rabbis by way of emphasizing their exceptional holiness. Alternatively, some saying of Jesus – a parable or simile – might in the course of telling have been changed into a story about Jesus himself. Nevertheless, the story has a significant bearing on the issue. The fortuitous (or miraculous) bonanza in the fish's mouth made it possible for the tax to be paid without admitting any liability or raising doubts about Jesus' exceptional status. The **coin** in the fish's mouth was (according to the Greek) a *statēr*, which corresponded to four drachmas or two people's temple tax, and sufficed for Jesus and for Peter (perhaps representing the small group of disciples). Matthew alone records this story. It may have been preserved (or possibly modified) in a Jewish-Christian church because of its bearing on what could have been a delicate question for Jews converted to Christianity: should they or should they not continue to pay the temple tax? They may have found their answer in the words, **"so that we do not give offense to them"**, and have been inspired by the story to look for their own ways of paying without admitting that they still had a legal liability to do so.

Conduct within the church

18.1 **At that time the disciples came to Jesus and asked**. The chapter constitutes one of the five substantial discourses with which this gospel is punctuated. It is addressed specifically to the disciples, but the topics it deals with are unmistakably those which were later to arise in the life of the church. **"Who is the**

greatest in the kingdom of heaven?" The question looks innocent enough; but the context in Mark (9.33–4) reveals why it was originally asked – the disciples had been discussing "who was the greatest" among themselves. We can probably detect in Matthew's handling of this his desire to present the disciples in a more favourable light: he simply omits the disreputable argument which was the original cue for the question. Whether or not the church was interested in the order of precedence which may have obtained among Jesus' first followers, it was certainly interested in the order of precedence which should be observed among its own members and in the problems of organizing its community life; and it doubtless found the sayings of Jesus collected here relevant to these questions.

2 **He called a child, whom he put among them.** In the narrative in Mark (9.36), Jesus answers the disciples' question with the same gesture: he makes them concentrate their attention on a child, and declares himself present even

5 in such an insignificant person. Matthew repeats this: **"Whoever welcomes one such child in my name welcomes me"**, but he adds to it other children-

3 sayings. **"Unless you change and become like children."** 'Change' (literally *turn*) is a scriptural synonym for the more common 'repent' (see Mark 4.12, where it occurs in a quotation from Isaiah). But in what respect must they become like children? What Jesus' original meaning may have been is a deep question, and is discussed below in connection with Mark 10.13; but in the immediate context given to the saying by Matthew – that of order and priority in the church – the point is probably quite simple. As the text goes on to say,

4 **"Whoever becomes humble like this child"**, not so as to become literally child-like (for children are not necessarily humble in character), but so as willingly to occupy a child's humble place in the community.

In the corresponding passage in Mark, sayings about children lead on to sayings about 'little ones' (9.42), but there are signs that this is an artificial connection: 'little ones' seems to have been a name given to the weaker and more insignificant members of the Christian fellowship. The case is even clearer here. The notion of a small child 'having faith in Jesus' is a modern one; in antiquity, children were assumed simply to go along with their parents in their religious allegiance. One became a Christian 'with one's household', and nobody asked questions about the strength of the children's 'faith'.

6 Therefore when Matthew presents us with the phrase **"one of these little ones who believe in me"**, we must beware of assuming that the discourse is still about children and not about members of the church. In the church,

7 **stumbling blocks** are bound to appear, in the form of persecutions, heresies and betrayals; but deliberately to add to these by making life still more difficult for the 'little ones' would be a serious sin – and one which would naturally be included in this discourse when applied to the life of the church.

8 **"If your hand or your foot causes you to stumble."** Almost the same saying occurs in the Sermon on the Mount (5.29–30) in the context of personal renunciation. Why does Matthew repeat it here? Possibly because he found

it in the corresponding passage of Mark (9.42–7); or perhaps because he saw a new meaning for it in this context. Paul wrote of the church as the 'body' of Christ (1 Corinthians 12 and elsewhere). Offensive members must be thrust out rather than the whole community be corrupted. By contrast, the

10 **little ones** must never be despised, for they have their **angels** in heaven. The function of angels in Jewish literature was twofold. First, they constituted the court of heaven, offering unceasing praise and worship; secondly, they acted as the messengers and agents through which God intervened in human affairs. (There is a number of examples in the early chapters of Matthew and Luke.) Popular belief also ascribed a third function to them, that of guardian angels for individuals and nations. (This is clear from Acts 12.15 and became officially recognized in Jewish writings in the following centuries.) But these guardian angels were not excused their duties in heaven: they still had their place in the heavenly court. As to the order of precedence of these angels, it was usually thought that only a very few actually had the privilege of standing in God's presence and (to use a courtly metaphor) of '**continually** seeing his face'. If the guardian angels of these 'little ones' had this dignity, what must be the worth in God's sight of those whom they guarded!

12 **"If a shepherd has a hundred sheep"** – an easy supposition: this was a reasonable-sized flock for a single-handed shepherd; and if one went astray, he would not necessarily abandon it just to keep close to the flock. But the parable is given a quite different application from the more famous one it has in Luke's gospel. There, all the emphasis is on the joy of the shepherd when the lost sheep is found; here, it is on the duty of the shepherd not to let a straying sheep get lost – an obvious lesson for church leaders with regard

14 to their **little ones.**

15 **"If another member of the church sins against you."**[8] These sentences are not (like what has gone before) mere exhortation: they lay down a strict procedure to be followed. From the language, it is almost possible to date the words to a particular phase in the growth of Christianity. There was already a

17 **church**[9] – that is to say, the saying can hardly have existed in this form in Jesus' lifetime, before any formal 'church' was established. But this church was still profoundly Jewish: it treated its recalcitrants as a Jewish community would

17 treat **a Gentile and a tax collector** – which appears to mean that no such people could be members! Yet the actual procedure it followed was by no means typically Jewish. It is true that the Dead Sea sect had a very similar procedure (and the similarity between these verses and a passage in the Scrolls shows, at the very least, that at this stage this Jewish church was in touch with ideas that had shaped other religious movements); but the patience which

---

[8] The words **against you** are omitted in the oldest and most authoritative manuscripts, in which case the saying applies more obviously to church discipline than to personal quarrels.

[9] In the Greek text the word for **church** occurs in verse 17, but not in verse 15, where **member of the church** has been introduced into this translation to avoid the word *brother.*

Christians were to show towards a sinner (expressed in its most radical form
21 in Jesus' reply to Peter about forgiving **seventy-seven times**) is very different
from the normal procedure of the synagogue, where exclusion normally followed conviction automatically. Nevertheless, moments would come when
the church would have to apply this ultimate sanction. When this happened,
there was a saying of Jesus which could be held to authorize their disciplinary
18 action (see above on 16.19): **"whatever you bind on earth will be bound in
heaven"**.

19 **"If two of you agree on earth."** This 'agreement' was the united prayer
of the church, for the church was the place where two or three individuals
were gathered together 'in Christ's name'; and just as a later rabbi could say,
'When two sit together occupied with the words of the law, the divine glory
is in the midst of them', so the fact of being united in the worship of Christ
guaranteed his presence among them.

The king and his debtors

23 **"The kingdom of heaven may be compared to a king."** The parable is clearly
intended to illustrate the teaching which has just been given about forgiveness, and makes its point, as so often in Matthew, by a touch of exaggeration.
The scene is the court of a **king:** Jesus may have been thinking of one of the
sons of Herod the Great who ruled as vassals of Rome, or else of a more distant and perhaps legendary oriental monarch. Among the men who served
this king were officials (some of whose status may still have been that of
slaves) entrusted with the taxation of his realm, or even local governors set
24 over certain areas of the kingdom. **One who owed him ten thousand talents
was brought to him.** Here is the first touch of exaggeration. This sum would
have been more than the total tribute paid by Galilee to Rome in fifteen
years – an immense amount, but it would be just conceivable for a local
governor to fall into arrears to this extent; if he did, he would presumably
have enriched himself enormously by so doing, and the king could hope to
27 recoup much of the debt by confiscating the man's property. **Out of pity for
him**, however, the king **forgave him the debt** – which could mean either
outright cancellation or an indefinite postponement of repayment. By contrast, another, much more junior, official owed the first the modest sum of
28 **a hundred denarii** (less than half a year's wage for a labourer). The first
had every right to bring him to court and, if convicted, have him jailed; but
31 the affair, as being between court officials, was noticed by **his fellow slaves**
(who might also be officials or courtiers), with the consequences described.
At the end of the story there is a touch, if not of exaggeration, at least of the
exotic: the Jews did not practise torture, and did not normally suffer it at the
hands of the Romans other than in times of war or insurrection; but they
had all heard of the methods practised by oriental despots, and torturing was
not an unheard-of way of forcing a debtor to reveal what assets and credits

he possessed. Jesus' parable describes a situation which, by being somewhat larger than life, makes the point all the more cogently.

Marriage and possessions

19.1 **He left Galilee.** The geography, both here and in Mark (10.1), is somewhat obscure. One of the pilgrims' routes from Galilee to Jerusalem crossed the Jordan south of the lake, followed the east side of the valley through

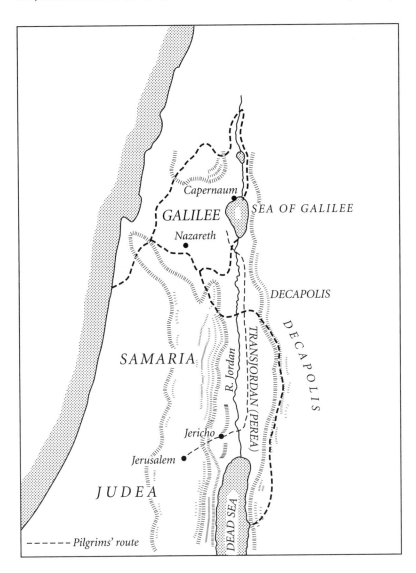

'Transjordan' (technically Perea, which like Galilee was part of the territory of Herod Antipas) and then re-crossed the Jordan to Jericho in Judea. If Jesus took this route it would have effectively taken him **beyond the Jordan**; and

3 since Perea was predominantly Jewish the presence of some **Pharisees** need cause no surprise. The difficulty is that Matthew calls this part of the country

1 **the region of Judea**. Either he was careless in his geography or else he was using the name (as was sometimes done) for Jewish Palestine generally.

The Pharisees' question reflects a controversy which certainly existed in the time of Jesus. The relevant passage in the law runs, "Suppose a man enters into marriage with a woman, but she does not please him because he finds something objectionable" (or *shameful*) "about her, and so he writes her a certificate of divorce" (Deuteronomy 24.1). The possibility of divorce, in this passage, is taken for granted, and the grounds on which it is permitted are defined as "something objectionable". But what does this phrase mean? The most rigorous school of thought considered that it referred only to adultery; but those more favourable to divorce interpreted it in the most general way possible, to cover quite trivial misdemeanours by the wife. We know that at the time of Jesus this wider interpretation was the usually accepted one: the historian Josephus, for example, tells us that he divorced his wife because he was 'displeased with her conduct'; but at the same time there were some who disapproved on moral grounds of such permissiveness and wished to encourage marital fidelity by tightening up the application of the law. Jesus was evidently being challenged to enter this debate when he was asked (according to Matthew, who was evidently familiar with this controversy),

3 **"Is it lawful for a man to divorce his wife for any cause?"** (literally, *for any and every cause*).

Jesus' answer was characteristic. Instead of confining the discussion to the text in question, he drew attention to another part of scripture which could be invoked to provide positive teaching about marriage. From these texts (Genesis 1.27; 2.24, on which see below on Mark 10:1–12) no legal

6 consequences followed; but the moralist could infer that the spouses are **no longer two, but one flesh** – that is to say, their union is so profound that it must be intended to preclude divorce.

The Pharisees' objection to this was perfectly fair. If the law of Moses explicitly allowed for divorce, how could anyone say that divorce was contrary to the will of God? But Jesus was concerned, not with a legal, but with a moral question. The fact that the law permitted and regulated a certain practice (in this case in the context of regulations about second marriages) did not mean that the practice was necessarily right or good, particularly if the relevant

8 clauses were arguably in the nature of concessions to human frailty: **"It was because you were so hard-hearted that Moses allowed you to divorce your wives."** The concession was a secondary development. The real will of God could be read off from the account of creation; and this should be the guiding

9 principle for family life. **"Whoever divorces his wife . . . commits adultery."**

Adultery was a very serious offence; in theory it incurred the death penalty. Jesus was in no position to influence the way the law was interpreted in the courts, nor was he presumably suggesting that divorce should be punished by death; but by calling divorce as serious as adultery he showed his radical disapproval of it.

Yet according to Matthew (unlike Mark and Luke) Jesus' reply is not only a moral judgment. By allowing for a practical exception, **except for unchastity**, he engaged with the technical discussion of the interpretation of the law, and showed that he sided with those who interpreted the law on divorce as strictly as possible. It is characteristic of this gospel that Jesus should be represented as taking part in a legal argument of this kind; moreover the exception subsequently provided an escape route for the church from the extreme rigour of Jesus' position when it came to formulate its own standard for Christian marriage (and many believe therefore that this exception derives from the church rather than from Jesus). Mark's gospel, by contrast, which omits any legal exception, records only Jesus' unqualified condemnation of divorce as such – which is indeed, the more striking and characteristic part of his teaching on the subject.

10–11 The meaning of the following short paragraph depends on how much of it goes back to a historical conversation between Jesus and his disciples and how much is an addition by the church in the interests of making Jesus' radical ethical teaching more practicable. That the sequence of thought is due to Matthew is suggested by a comparison with the corresponding passage of Mark (10.10–12). There, Jesus' pronouncement on divorce is followed by a private conversation with the disciples about the practical implications of it. Matthew follows the same pattern, but gives it a quite different content: the disciples' question is a more pointed one, and Jesus' answer leads to a fresh saying altogether. It appears that Matthew has taken advantage of the change of scene recorded by Mark in order to add an important piece of ethical teaching, ostensibly for the benefit of the disciples but in reality of greater relevance to the life of the church.

Seen in this light, the disciples' question, if a little banal, is quite natural. Jesus' teaching on marriage seemed to set an impossibly high standard: might it be better not to marry at all? The answer given was a saying of Jesus about the renunciation of marriage which seemed, by implication, to accept the point of view of the disciples and to concede that his teaching could not be carried out literally by more than a few. Marriage without the possibility of divorce, he seemed to be saying, is an impossible ideal. The only safe way is to renounce marriage – but of course that is something that

11 **"not everyone can accept"**. Thereby, the church might well feel authorized to countenance divorce (at least on grounds of adultery) among its own members; Jesus' absolute teaching about indissoluble marriage was never intended to be observed to the letter except by those few who could be sure of not transgressing it – by renouncing marriage altogether.

This is a possible reading of the passage. Some of Jesus' teachings in Matthew's gospel certainly seem to have been adjusted to conditions subsequently prevailing in the church. If we assume, however, that the dialogue is historical, and transpose it back into the context of Jesus' lifetime in Palestine, we get a very different result. One matter that was taken for granted in his culture was that a man was normally under obligation to marry and beget children. "Be fruitful and multiply" (Genesis 1.28) was regarded as a command binding on all; and only certain rigorous sects, which regarded ritual pollution caused by intercourse as a still more serious matter than the command to bring up children, ever thought of recommending a celibate life. Against this background, the disciples' objection takes on a
10 different sense. **"If such is the case with a man and his wife, it is better not to marry."** But (in view of the divine command) it cannot ever be 'better' not to marry; therefore that cannot be 'the case': marriage without the possibility of divorce is absurd. Read in this way, the disciples' objection is a real one: it seeks, by a *reductio ad absurdum*, to show that Jesus' teaching cannot hold; the means of divorce permitted by the law must be in the nature of things. Jesus' reply goes some way to meet the point: to most people it will seem like this, but there will be some (and here the disciples must be in mind, and those followers of Christ who will be their successors) who, by God's appointment, will be able to fulfil the nature of marriage as God originally intended it to be.

12 **"There are eunuchs."** The word 'eunuch' is surprising in a Jewish context. Eunuchs were a foreign phenomenon, and usually the subject of derision and contempt. The word, however, was used as the Greek equivalent for the Hebrew word meaning *sexually impotent*, of whom lawyers recognized two categories, those born impotent and those subsequently made so by illness or accident. Those in both categories were excluded from public worship in the temple and were denied certain legal and social rights. The first two clauses of Jesus' saying accurately describe these two classes of men, and in themselves say nothing of interest. The only significant thing about them is the fact that Jesus referred to such people at all; but we shall find that it was characteristic of him to give unexpected prominence to socially unacceptable or disadvantaged people – tax collectors, prostitutes, Samaritans, the very poor – and 'eunuchs' were certainly among them. But apart from this, the function of these first two clauses is entirely to build up expectation of what will come next. And what *could* come next? In Jewish law, these two categories exhausted the possibilities: there was no other kind of 'eunuch'. Jesus must have startled his hearers when he revealed that the point of his epigram was to do with a foreign custom which caused revulsion among his own people: self-castration.

Throughout the history of the church, **eunuchs . . . for the sake of the kingdom of heaven** has been taken as a metaphor for the voluntary renunciation of marriage. It is the text appealed to again and again as the authority for a form of discipleship that was rare in that culture but became well established in Christianity: celibate monasticism. It is possible that this was Jesus' meaning; but it seems unlikely that he would have envisaged this in his lifetime (and most of the disciples were in fact married); moreover the metaphor, if it is one, would more naturally be to do with self-control in sexual matters than with celibacy. (Both Jewish and Greek literature have examples of this usage.) Indeed, preoccupation with this assumed metaphorical sense may have prevented critics from noticing the truly startling character of the saying. Literally, the only self-castrated 'eunuchs' anyone in Jesus' world was likely to have seen were the priests of the pagan goddess Cybele, who voluntarily mutilated themselves in order to follow their religious vocation. There is some evidence that these existed in Palestine and could have been seen by Jesus and his hearers. But how could their unnatural action be **for the sake of the kingdom of heaven**? It was certainly for the sake of a religious vocation. Could Jesus have been bold enough to suggest that even these unlikely persons could set an example of the commitment required if one were to be serious about following him? If even pagan devotees will do *that*, what should you be prepared to do yourself? Perhaps, among other things (so Matthew may have taken it), renounce the possibility of divorce!

From this point to the end of the chapter Matthew follows Mark closely (10.13–31), and it is necessary here only to draw attention to certain small changes he has introduced.

13   **Then little children were being brought to him in order that he might lay his hands on them and pray**. Mark writes simply "for him to touch": Matthew adds that what they wanted was 'prayer', that is, a blessing such as a parent or respected teacher might be asked for. He omits one of the sayings recorded by Mark, but retains the essential one for the sake of which the

14 incident was doubtless remembered: **"it is to such as these that the kingdom of heaven belongs"**.

16   **Then someone came to him**. Matthew appears to have inferred from the
20 enthusiasm of his approach (as described by Mark) that he was a **young man** – which may give a certain edge to the end of the story: his parents are likely to have been living, and one of his most sacred duties was to provide for them. How could he give everything away? Apart from this, Matthew has eliminated some of Mark's more striking details. In particular, instead of the pointed exchange, "Good Teacher . . .", "Why do you call me good?", he makes the conversation open with a standard religious question,

16 **"What good deed must I do to have eternal life?"** (which makes Jesus'
17 answer, **"There is only one who is good"**, appear a little irrelevant). Good works, particularly almsgiving, were generally regarded as a qualification for a reward in heaven, and the young man may have desired some direction on what kind of munificence he should aspire to. Jesus directed him instead to **"keep the commandments"**, mentioning some of the Ten Commandments,
19 and adding the very general commandment from Leviticus (19.18), to **love**

your neighbor as yourself. But he attached no value, apparently, to any extra works of piety which his questioner may have had in mind. The only

21 alternative he gave was **to be perfect,** which takes us back (in this gospel) to the demanding ethic of the Sermon on the Mount (5.48) and involves total commitment – the drastic response required is highlighted by the extreme

24 comparison of the **camel** and the **eye of a needle** (on which see below on Mark 10.25).

The reply to Peter on the question of rewards gives a specially privileged place to the disciples in a way characteristic of Matthew's treatment of them.

28 The imagery of the saying about **thrones** stems from the book of Daniel (7.9–14): "As I watched, thrones were set in place . . . the court sat in judgment . . . I saw one like a human being [literally, *a son of man*] coming with the clouds of heaven." The significance of Jesus' title, 'Son of Man', in Matthew's gospel is concentrated in the rôle which this figure was to play in the judgment, and those of Jesus' followers who had been admitted to know the 'secrets of the kingdom' (13.11) would also play their part in the same scenario. **The twelve tribes of Israel** was an archaic title that could be used for the contemporary Jewish nation. A possible meaning of the saying (which has a totally different context in Luke 22.48 and therefore must have existed independently of any particular occasion) is that the nation as a whole would be 'judged' by those few individuals who had accepted Jesus as Lord. But 'twelve tribes' was a phrase that could also be used to describe the New Israel constituted by the church (see below on Revelation 7.4–8); and the saying could equally well mean that the disciples were to 'judge' the church, in the sense (which followed the Old Testament concept of 'judging') of assuring its members of their vindication and rightful reward. This second sense leads more naturally

29–30 into the following saying, which is again concerned with rewards in heaven. Matthew is still apparently following Mark (10.29–31); but he smoothes out the apparent concern for material rewards in Mark's version by omitting the words, "in this age".

20.1 **"The kingdom of heaven is like a landowner."** The setting of the parable is vintage time in Palestine, the only time of year when unskilled labourers would be needed in a vineyard. Normally the landowner would hire as many as he needed first thing in the morning; but the story required that he should have miscalculated and taken the rather unusual step of relying on what was evidently a high level of unemployment and engaging further labourers right

6 up to **about five o'clock** (literally, *the eleventh hour*). At the end of the day he was bound by law (Leviticus 19.13) to pay the stipulated wage to those who had done a day's work; but with regard to the rest he could either wait till they came again the next day and made up the full time (this was the usual procedure) or else, if the work were finished, pay 'whatever was right' (or *just*) for the number of hours worked. On this occasion he instructed his

8 manager to settle the labourers' wages, **beginning with the last** – that is to say, the eleventh-hour labourers who were not to be allowed to go home and

return in the morning but were to be paid off at once. The surprise came in
9 the fact that they were paid **the usual daily wage** (one *denarius*).

Matthew has shown how he understood the parable by rounding it off
16 with a form of the maxim he has just quoted (19.30), **"the last will be first,
and the first will be last"**, which was highly relevant to the subject in hand
(the correct ordering of the Christian community). But this can hardly have
been the original point of the parable: the fact that the last to be employed
were paid first is an unimportant one in the story; all the emphasis is on their
being given, not first place in the queue, but equal treatment with the others.
This is not the only occasion in Matthew's gospel when a parable is given an
inappropriate conclusion (see below on 25.1–13), and we have to ask what the
original point is likely to have been. We may guess (but, as in the case of most
of Jesus' parables, it can be no more than a guess) that the question which
caused Jesus to tell it was not that of the priorities to be observed in the future
church but of his own converse with 'tax collectors and sinners'. According
to strict justice, those who had devoted their whole lives to observing the
law in all its detailed provisions (as the Pharisees recommended) deserved
a greater reward than men and women who, after lives of irresponsibility
or even immorality, had responded at the eleventh hour to the preaching
of Jesus. The parable could have challenged any of Jesus' hearers to see the
question of ultimate rewards from the point of view of a God who is not only
just but generous.

Not to be served but to serve

17–33 For the rest of the chapter Matthew follows Mark closely (10.32–52) apart
from a few changes of detail. As so often, he appears to have been unwilling
to allow the disciples to appear in an unfavourable light, and the blame for
their ambitious pretensions is laid, not on James and John themselves, but
on their mother. (The difficult saying about 'a baptism' in Mark is also
omitted.) The healing story is a doublet of the one told already (9.27–31),
30 but the blind man of Mark (10.46–52) has become **two blind men** (not the
only time this happens in Matthew), and the theme of 'faith', which was
prominent in the previous version (9.29), is passed over without mention.

Going up to Jerusalem

21.1 **When they had come near Jerusalem and had reached Bethphage.** Matthew
has the same topography here as Mark. The road from Jericho, just before
it reached the crest of the Mount of Olives, had a turning off to the left
leading to the small village of Bethphage and after that to Bethany. It was the
natural place for Jesus to pause while obtaining a mount for his entry into
Jerusalem. All the gospel accounts, though they differ in a number of details,
see this episode as symbolic and interpret it with reference to Old Testament

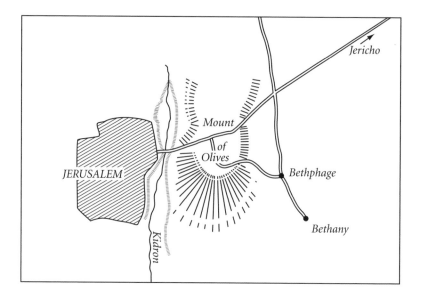

prophecies of a coming Messiah, in particular Zechariah 9.9 (see below on Mark 11.1–10). Matthew characteristically makes this correspondence quite

4 explicit – **This took place to fulfil what had been spoken through the prophet** – and quotes the verse from Zechariah in full, prefacing it with

5 a phrase from Isaiah (62.11), **"Tell the daughter of Zion"**. He also adds a curious detail, however: there were two beasts, a **donkey** and a **colt**. It is true that the prophecy of Zechariah has a double description of the animal – **mounted on a donkey, and on a colt, the foal of a donkey** – but this was a common idiom of Hebrew poetry which often, in two halves of a single line, likes to say the same thing in slightly different words. So far as we know, no Jewish interpreter ever thought of reading Zechariah's words as if they meant two animals; but Matthew (who, as we have seen, liked things in pairs) seems to have done so – unless of course he knew of a tradition that Jesus entered Jerusalem with two mounts and then offered a literal interpretation of Zechariah to explain it. But he gives no explanation of how Jesus actually

7 used the two animals: they **put their cloaks on them, and he sat on them** gives no help to the reader who tries to visualize the scene.

9 **The crowds . . . were shouting**. If they were all shouting the same thing, it must have been either a brief phrase (such as *Hosanna*) or something they knew by heart. Matthew, like the other gospels, assumes they were singing part of Psalm 118, of which the relevant verses (25–6) are as follows:

> Save us (*Hosanna*), we beseech you, O LORD! . . .
> Blessed is the one who comes in the name of the LORD.

The psalm was used at a number of annual festivals, and in the course of its liturgical use the Hebrew word *Hosanna* seems to have lost its literal meaning ('save us now'), and to have become a general cry of acclamation or shout of praise. Both Matthew and Mark are content to leave it as it stands without translating it into Greek and without offering any explanation of its meaning. The reason must be that this was one of the Hebrew words (*amen* was another) which the Greek-speaking church had taken over into its worship, so that it would have been already familiar to Matthew's readers.

Matthew makes one significant change to the text of the psalm. He adds, **to the Son of David**. It is an important theme of the gospel that Jesus' Messiahship was confirmed by his ancestry, which could be traced back to David. The crowds, therefore, if they had shouted out this title (which is unlikely if they were singing a psalm), would have shown that they recognized Jesus as Messiah, or at least that an age was dawning which would have some resemblance to the time of King David, and this would explain

10 Matthew's comment that **the whole city was in turmoil**. There is a further small detail to be drawn from Matthew's topography: Jesus did not enter the temple area directly (as he could have done), but by way of a détour through the city. But the recognition that here at last was the promised Messiah was apparently not sustained. Once he was in the city, the crowd seems to have dropped the portentous title, 'son of David', and given to enquirers the

11 much less sensational reply, **"This is the prophet Jesus from Nazareth in Galilee."**

It seems, then, that Matthew may have allowed the subsequent faith of the church, which thought of Jesus riding triumphantly into Jerusalem as the promised Christ, to colour his description of the scene. At any rate, Jesus' status as Messiah is hinted at much less obviously in what follows. (On

12 the details of Jesus' action in the **temple** precincts, see on Mark 11.15–17.)

14 The healing of **the blind and the lame** could be regarded, by those alert to ancient prophecies being fulfilled, as the breaking in of the promised age to be brought by the Messiah; but equally it could be regarded as of no decisive

15 significance, which was the view of **the chief priests and the scribes**. Matthew contrasts them, not with the formerly enthusiastic crowds (whose attitude had now become uncertain), but with the **children . . . in the temple**, who continued the acclamation that started on the Mount of Olives, **"Hosanna to the Son of David!"** Matthew has recorded elsewhere (19.14) Jesus' saying that it is children who are closest to the kingdom; and the fact that these ones intuitively recognized Jesus as the Messiah is foreshadowed in the words

16 of a psalm (8.2), **'Out of the mouths of infants and nursing babies you have prepared praise for yourself.'** In the Hebrew the last phrase of this text has, not 'praise', but 'strength'. Matthew's quotation is according to the Greek version and fits the situation perfectly. But the Hebrew or Aramaic text that would have been used by Jesus would have been less appropriate; and our impression is thereby strengthened that Matthew has written up this

section fairly freely in order to bring out the ambivalence of Jesus' reception in Jerusalem.

19 Matthew somewhat abbreviates the story of the **fig tree**, but follows Mark
23–7 closely in the dialogue about John the Baptist (see below on Mark 11.20–
28 33). He then inserts a parable not found elsewhere. **"A man had two sons."**
The parable itself is perfectly clear and of wide application, and its pointed
23, 32 direction at the **chief priests and the elders** is plausible enough: **"the tax collectors and the prostitutes are going into the kingdom of God ahead of you"**. These were two classes of people whose way of life most flagrantly (in
29 the view of observant Jews) expressed a clear **'I will not'** to the commands of God but for whom Jesus consistently and (it seemed to his enemies) shockingly kept open the possibility of 'changing their mind'. Thus far, the point is clear enough; but Matthew has added a second saying about John the Baptist which is a little difficult to relate to the preceding parable, and is perhaps better understood separately (a similar saying in Luke 7.29–30 has
32 a quite different context): **"John came to you in the way of righteousness."**
This was John's reputation even outside the Christian community. Jesus' opponents could hardly claim that it was his own allegedly 'unrighteous' way of life that was preventing them from responding to him when they had been equally unresponsive to the preaching of 'righteous' John.

33 **"Listen to another parable."** The interpretation of this parable is discussed at length below on Mark 12.1–12. Except for a slight increase in the number of slaves sent to collect the rent (making it easier, perhaps, to see them as an allegory of the Old Testament prophets), the details of the story are the same as in Mark. But if, in Mark, the story already shows signs of having had an interpretation imposed upon it by the early church, in Matthew this is very much clearer. The passage of Isaiah (5.1) on which the opening words are based continues (verse 3): "And now, inhabitants of Jerusalem and people of Judah, judge between me and my vineyard." Hence, perhaps, the extra dramatization in Matthew when Jesus puts the question to his hearers,
40 **"What will he do to those tenants?"** The reply, at any rate, shows a clear tendency to fasten an interpretation on the parable. The main crime of the tenants was their maltreatment of the landowner's slaves and their murder of the son; but Matthew makes it sound as if their real guilt was that they did
34 not let the owner **collect his produce**. This, applied to the Jewish people, was a constant theme of Jesus' preaching (at least according to Matthew): they
43 had failed to produce the **fruits** (or the 'produce' – the word is the same in the Greek) of the blessings which God had bestowed on them. Consequently (and Matthew draws out a consequence that was in fact only slowly realized by the church even if it was implied by much that Jesus said), **"the kingdom of God will be taken away from you and given to a people that produces the fruits of the kingdom"** – that is, the Gentiles! The parable thus becomes, in Matthew, an attack on the Jewish people as a whole and a prophecy of the success of the gentile mission; and it is perhaps by a slight oversight that he

reproduces from Mark the statement that the chief priests and the Pharisees
45 **realized that he was speaking about them.**

22.2 **"The kingdom of heaven may be compared to a king."** A parable occurs
in Luke's gospel (14.16–24) so similar to this one that both must go back
to the same original. But in Matthew the story is considerably less lifelike,
sometimes even far-fetched, whereas in Luke it seems to spring straight from
daily life. It is tempting to see here what was originally a straightforward
story with a simple point having been transformed, in the course of telling,
into an elaborate allegory. The setting has become a royal wedding feast.
Invitations had been sent out to the notables among the city-dwellers, and
when the day came the king, following the courteous custom of the time,
3 **sent his slaves** to inform the guests that all was ready and to conduct them
to the palace. But – **they would not come!** No reason is given for their rude
and disloyal behaviour (in contrast to Luke's version, where their excuses are
given in great detail); and at this point the story becomes frankly implausible.
Why should the king, after receiving the first affront, have demeaned himself
still further by sending a second set of slaves with a renewed invitation? And
6 why should the invited guests have then **mistreated them, and killed them?**
It is possible that the story is a coded description of a political rebellion
against some known ruler, which would explain some of the unlikely details.
Alternatively it may be an allegory, and an allegory has a logic of its own.
A wedding feast was a familiar image for the heavenly kingdom promised
to the elect people of God. 'Slaves' (or *servants*) – the prophets – had been
repeatedly sent to invite the guests to prepare themselves (by repentance),
but had been ignored, maltreated or even killed. As a result, Jerusalem (as the
prophets had foretold) had been taken and destroyed, once by the Assyrians
centuries before, and now (by the time Matthew's gospel was written) by
the Romans. The story so far reads like an allegory of these events. But what
of the wedding feast? Was God's purpose now frustrated and his promise
void? Regardless of verisimilitude the story continues as if only an hour had
8 passed. **"Those invited were not worthy"**, but there were others to whom
9 it could be offered instead. **"Go therefore into the main streets**, that is, the
public places where people congregated. It was a fact, both of Jesus' practice
and of the missionary experience of the church, that the gospel, having been
rejected by the Jews and their leaders, was offered to Gentiles, who included
10 (of course) **both good and bad.**

11 **"But when the king came in to see the guests."** The story goes on, but
the sequel is again quite implausible. How could those who had just been
'gathered' from the streets have been expected to provide themselves with
wedding robes? There is no evidence for the solution sometimes proposed
that a festal garment was issued to each guest on arrival; and even if this had
been the case, the failure of one guest to put it on would be incomprehensible.
To make sense of it we have to assume that another, and originally separate,
allegorical parable has been added by Matthew and somewhat inexpertly

welded into a single story. The kingdom of heaven is like a royal wedding feast: and woe to anyone who comes not properly prepared (with repentance? with righteous deeds?). The penalty will be exclusion; and on the last day

13 the consequence will be **weeping and gnashing of teeth** – the characteristic phrase in Matthew to denote the torments of hell. And (as elsewhere) a maxim is added that doubtless goes back to Jesus but does not altogether fit

14 the context here: **"many are called, but few are chosen"**.

15–45 The four questions and answers that follow are very much the same as in Mark (12.13–37), but Matthew builds up a slightly more dramatic scenario by presenting them as a series of attacks by different sections of Jesus' opponents – Pharisees, Sadducees, a lawyer – while the people stand by in amaze-

41–5 ment. The scene culminates in a powerful counter-attack by Jesus which silences his questioners. Within the conversations themselves the hand of

34–40 Matthew can be seen in the third (on 'the greatest commandment'). In Mark, the question is asked by a lawyer who turns out to be an admirer of Jesus and who earns Jesus' approval by his approach to the law. But here the question

35 has a different tone, and is asked deliberately **to test him**. In what sense was it a 'test'? Did his enemies want to see whether he was familiar with the scholarly debate they engaged in themselves over the correct logical ordering of the laws? Or did they suspect him of placing so much emphasis on some laws that he was improperly and dangerously indifferent to others (as the story in Mark suggests that he did)? If so, Jesus' reply (in Matthew) gave them no grounds for criticism: that the rest of the law could be deduced from these two commandments was a perfectly orthodox position that was actually held by some. In saying this, Jesus was making the kind of technical judgment his opponents made themselves; and the scene contributes to Matthew's careful portrait of Jesus as a perfectly correct (even though sometimes highly original) interpreter of the law.

23.2 The discourse which follows consists of a sustained attack on **the scribes and the Pharisees**. In the time of Jesus these two groups were by no means identical. The scribes were a professional class who underwent a formal and exacting training in the law and were then qualified to undertake the education of others, to sit as justices in the law courts and to give their rulings when appealed to on questions of law and conduct. For these services they received no payment, and most of them followed another profession at the same time; but since the law of Moses governed both the correct performance of the temple ritual and decisions in all Jewish law courts, their learning gave them considerable authority, and they were beginning to displace the old priestly aristocracy as the most influential class in society. The Pharisees, on the other hand, had no official status as such. The origin of their name is obscure, but their emergence as a distinctive party is usually thought to date from the time of the Maccabean revolution (second century BCE), when, under the name of 'Hasideans', they "offered themselves willingly for the law" (1 Maccabees 2.42) and became the most devoted and intransigent defenders of the Jewish way of life against Hellenistic influences. Their successors, the Pharisees of Jesus' day, were thus not so much a professional class as a school of thought. They found in scripture, not only a code of law sufficient for the religious and civil ordering of the community, but a detailed and comprehensive system which (given their own traditional method of interpretation) could be shown to govern every aspect of daily life. To demonstrate this, they formed themselves into fellowships whose members were committed to carrying out every detail of the law according to its Pharisaic interpretation, and to keeping themselves ritually pure by shunning the society of all those less observant than themselves (hence perhaps their name, which probably means 'separated'). These fellowships did not consist only of scholars; indeed, the majority of Pharisees were laymen. But they formed an increasingly important element in Jewish society, and both in their teaching and in their personal lives the Pharisees treated scripture with a seriousness and a determined obedience which far exceeded that of society as a whole.

The natural way for Pharisaism to extend its influence was through the administration of justice and through education; and in the time of Jesus many of the scribes had become Pharisees. Nevertheless, the two groups remained distinct. The scribes were qualified professionals, the Pharisees were exponents of a style of observant life; and not all scribes were Pharisees or all Pharisees scribes. Consequently, though both may have had failings which came under sharp criticism from Jesus, these failings were not necessarily the same in each case. The scribes, though required to be professionally competent in the law, were not thereby committed to make their lives morally superior to other people's, and as a class they may often have deserved the charge of oppressing others while knowing how to keep on the right side of the law themselves. The Pharisees, on the other hand, aimed at a very high standard of observance and strove to bring their personal lives into conformity with a detailed and comprehensive interpretation of the law. In so doing they may well at times have allowed an elaborate system of outward observances to obscure the moral thrust of the law (though there is independent evidence that their legal judgments were often singularly humane), and to lead them into an exclusiveness which ignored the real needs of their fellow men and women. To this extent, there may have been some justice in Jesus' accusation of 'hypocrisy'.

Why then in this chapter of Matthew (as often in Luke, though not in Mark or John) are the two classes grouped together as the objects of Jesus' attacks? Some of the charges brought against them fit the scribes, some the Pharisees, but not all fit both. Moreover, Luke's gospel (especially 11.37–52) makes a distinction between those of Jesus' criticisms which were aimed at the scribes and those which were aimed at the Pharisees. The reason may be simply some confusion in the tradition. But it must also be remembered that in any case, by the time Matthew's gospel came to be written towards the end of the first century CE, the social make-up of the population was no longer what it had been in the time of Jesus. Jerusalem had fallen; and in the dispersed and disorganized Jewish population authority and influence had passed to a 'school' of learned men which had recently been founded at Jamnia, on the coastal plain west of Jerusalem. These men were Pharisees; and from then on there ceased to be any real distinction between them and the scribes; for, in their efforts to consolidate and codify the traditions and observances of the Jewish nation (despite the destruction of the temple), the Pharisees gained complete control over the administration of justice and education. The Judaism with which Christianity was confronted when Matthew wrote his gospel was therefore becoming increasingly Pharisaic; and we can probably overhear, in these reports of Jesus' attacks on the scribes and the Pharisees, something of the polemic which was being carried on by Christians in response to attacks by the leaders of neighbouring synagogues.

"The scribes and the Pharisees sit on Moses' seat." This is not just metaphor. An imposing stone seat has been found in the ruins of more than one ancient synagogue, placed in the centre of the rear wall facing the congregation (which is where the synagogue elders sat). This may have been called **Moses' seat**. But in any case, the name indicates the function of the person who sat there. Moses both promulgated the law and acted as judge. His successors continued in the same tradition, interpreting the law and giving judgment on transgressions of it. Christians, as much in Jewish as

3 in gentile communities, were to be law-abiding: **"do whatever they teach you and follow it"**. But these professional judges and interpreters were not to be regarded as models of behaviour. Their knowledge of the law enabled them to discover exemptions and saving clauses which lightened the burden

4 for themselves, but they did not **lift a finger** to make the same relief available

3 to all, and so it could be said of them that **they do not practice what they teach.**

5 **"They make their phylacteries broad."** Observant Jews followed the biblical injunction (Deuteronomy 6.8–9) to 'bind the words of the Lord to their foreheads' by wearing a small cubic box, secured by straps to the back of the neck – perhaps it was these that they made **broad**. The boxes looked similar to the amulets or charms carried by those who believed in magic and for which the usual word was **phylacteries**, and there may be something derogatory in the use of this word for the Jewish custom. Similarly, Deuteronomy 22.12 imposed the wearing of "tassels" at the edge of the cloak, and these **fringes** could doubtless be made ostentatiously long. Such affectations, along with

6 the desire for a **place of honor** and for marks of public respect (which is singled out in Mark's gospel, 12.38–9), were characteristic of a profession that was perhaps becoming increasingly conscious of its influence and offering subtle temptations to the vain and ambitious.

8 **"You are not to be called rabbi."** 'Rabbi' became the formal title for an ordained lawyer or teacher in the period after the fall of Jerusalem in 70 CE when authority in religious matters became concentrated in the school of

Jamnia. In the time of Jesus it was simply a term of respect, given spontaneously to established teachers. While the disciples had Jesus, their 'master', with them, it is unlikely that anyone would have thought of calling them 'rabbi'; but later, when the leaders of the Christian community began to exercise authority in a way somewhat similar to the leaders of local synagogues, there may have been a tendency to follow Jewish practice and use the by now formal title 'rabbi'. But the Christian church, if it was to remain faithful to Jesus' teaching, must be in important respects distinct from the Jewish

9 community and must eschew such titles. This must apply also to **"father"**, which (outside the family) was normally reserved for the patriarchs ('our father Abraham' and the like) but was also beginning to be applied to espe-

10 cially distinguished teachers. As for **instructors**, this translation catches the unusual flavour of the Greek word. Perhaps the title was being tried out in the church when Matthew wrote, or perhaps it was simply a Greek equivalent of 'rabbi'. But it came under the same condemnation. Christians (for this saying can hardly have been spoken in its present form by Jesus, who never explicitly described himself as 'Messiah') **have one instructor, the Messiah.** Only one principle could properly govern authority and seniority in the church,

11 one which Jesus propounded on several occasions (20.26; Mark 9.35): **"The greatest among you will be your servant."** And this in turn depended on a principle exhibited in God's dealings with human beings which had already

12 found expression in the Old Testament (Proverbs 29.23; Job 22.29; etc.): **"All who exalt themselves will be humbled".**

13 **"But woe to you."** Seven of these 'woes' follow, aimed indiscriminately at the scribes and Pharisees and perhaps again influenced by the strained relations existing in Matthew's time between the church and the Pharisaic leaders of Palestinian Judaism. **"You lock people out of the kingdom of heaven."** It is true that the exclusive fellowship of the Pharisees, which imposed strict observances on its members, could be held to imply that all others were outside the kingdom and that it could not be entered except by adopting the same rule of life; but the attack springs to life if transposed to a later period, when the Christian community was thought of as an (at least partial) realization of the kingdom, while Jews not only refused to join but stopped others from joining. Moreover, some sections of Judaism (though so far as we know not the majority) undertook vigorous proselytizing, and this may have happened in direct competition with the Christian mission. We can probably detect the language of very strained relations when one side calls

15 the other **a child of hell.**

16 **"Blind guides."** Jesus called his opponents this more than once (15.14; Luke 6.39), and the phrase became part of the language of Christian polemic against the Jews (Romans 2.19). The attack here amplifies a similar passage in the Sermon on the Mount (6.33–7): no casuistry can mitigate the seriousness of oaths and vows, which are all, even if they do not seem so, in reality in the name of God.

23 **"You tithe the mint, dill, and cummin."** This was typical Pharisaic elaboration of the law (Deuteronomy 14.22–3) that all Israelites must pay tithes of their grain, wine and oil: the Pharisees extended this even to herbs. Doubtless none of them would have admitted to overlooking **the weightier matters of the law**; but the burden of Jesus' attack on them was that this excessive attention to detail caused them to lose sight of the great principles on which the law was based – which prompted a notable instance of Jesus' taste for

24 almost grotesque exaggeration: to **strain out a gnat** from a bowl of wine was common sense; to **swallow a camel** showed more than a little blindness! This and the following accusation must both have originally been directed specifically against the Pharisees (as they are in Luke 11.39–42).

25 **"You clean the outside of the cup and of the plate."** The ritual cleansing of vessels used in the worship of the temple was being extended by the Pharisees to the cups and dishes of daily household use (to make the home 'holy'), and in the following centuries they were to develop a complicated system of rules applying to almost any household utensil. Jesus saw in this tendency (for this surely is an authentic saying) material for a trenchant simile: all this attention to the outside of crockery vessels was like their attention to the externals of religion. But what were they like **inside**? If they would begin there, the externals would look after themselves. The same thought evidently continues in the next simile, though since Jewish tombs were normally carved

27 out of rock it is hard to see why any would have been **whitewashed.** (Luke indeed seems to imply the opposite when he makes Jesus talk of the danger of not seeing them at all, 20.44.) Possibly the reference is to the white sheen of the limestone ossuaries in which the bones were eventually laid. But the point is the same: all efforts to make such things **look beautiful** would not affect the fact that the contents were repugnant and ritually 'unclean'.

29 **"You build the tombs of the prophets."** We know nothing of any prophets' tombs in the neighbourhood of Jerusalem. The so-called 'Tomb of Zechariah', which still stands in the Kidron valley, is a Hellenistic monument and was not associated with the prophet until later. But we do know that legends were growing up in this period about the lives, deaths and burial places of Old Testament prophets; and at Hebron there were certainly famous monuments which were (and still are) reputed to be the tombs of Abraham, Isaac and Jacob, the **righteous** of the remote past. But this did not alter the fact that the ancestors of Jesus' contemporaries (and this last 'woe' seems to apply to the Jewish nation as a whole rather than to scribes and Pharisees in particular)

30 had taken part in **shedding the blood of the prophets.** Only one such murder is mentioned in the Old Testament, that of a certain Zechariah (2 Chronicles 24.20–2); but Jewish legend had added five more of the great prophets to the list of national martyrs. Jesus, who was widely acknowledged to be a 'prophet', may well have seen his own impending death as an episode in the same tradition, and these words challenge his opponents to play their appointed part in the grim drama.

34   **"I send you prophets, sages, and scribes."** Here an old theme of scripture is adapted to the coming destiny of the church. Just as God "sent prophets among them" (2 Chronicles 24.19), so Jesus is made to say (he could hardly have done so in his lifetime), that he would **send** those who were to become the leaders of the Christian communities, among whom there would be 'prophets' (see above on 10.41), 'sages' and 'teachers', whose fate might follow a pattern which filled the Old Testament from cover to cover: the death of

35   **Abel** was the first murder in the book of Genesis (4.8), that of Zechariah the last in 2 Chronicles, which was at that time the last of the books in the canon of Hebrew scriptures. (This Zechariah may or may not be, or have been believed to be, the same as the author of the book of Zechariah, whose father was indeed, – unlike the 2 Chronicles prophet – called **Barachiah**.)

37   **"Jerusalem, Jerusalem."** Jerusalem was not in fact, or even in legend, the place where many of the prophets had met their death; yet it was the symbolic centre of the national and religious life of a people which had again and again rejected the prophetic voice. Jesus, to end this discourse of condemnation, once again assumes the rôle of a prophet destined to suffer a similar fate, upbraiding the city which should have accepted his message, using the classic metaphor of the protective wings of a bird (Deuteronomy 32.11; Isaiah 31.5; etc.) and prophesying, as if he saw it before his eyes, the days when the

38   great **house** of the temple in the midst of it would be made meaningless by the departure of God from its sanctuary along with the destruction of its magnificent buildings. It was not to be Jesus' destiny to reverse this terrible sequence of events by compelling the inhabitants to repent. On the contrary, their very recognition of him would come only, if at all, when (perhaps at his ultimate vindication in glory) there rose spontaneously to their lips the

39   traditional acclamation (Psalm 118.26), **'Blessed is the one who comes in the name of the Lord.'**

A discourse on the future

24.1   **As Jesus came out of the temple.** The setting for this discourse is as vivid and realistic as in Mark (13.1–3). The immense scale of Herod the Great's architectural achievement on the temple mount evoked both the disciples'

2   admiration and Jesus' prophecy that **"not one stone will be left here upon another"**; and Jesus' extended answer to the disciples' astonished question about this prophecy was appropriately delivered on the Mount of Olives, which commands a magnificent view of the whole temple area. The elements of the answer are the same as in Mark's version, and Matthew has made only a few rearrangements and additions. The catastrophes and tribulations which were normal in history were to be intensified; the faithful would be put to a severe test. But these things would not be merely fortuitous; they would be signs of a new age about to come. The disciples' question (in Matthew) certainly invited such an answer. They did not wish to know merely when the

temple would be destroyed; they realized that such a staggering reversal of Jerusalem's present splendour must presage still more significant events; and the only two events which they could envisage as being on the required scale

3 were the **coming** of Jesus (presumably in glory: this is post-resurrection language) and the **end of the age.** They realized (with that deeper insight which Matthew, unlike the other evangelists, ascribes to the disciples) that all these things must be related; and they asked Jesus for further precision.

4 His reply includes conventional elements: the danger of being led **astray,**

7 the intensification of **famines and earthquakes.** The persecution of the faithful also belonged to the conventional picture of the bitter period before the

8 end (which Matthew, like Mark, calls by the technical name, **the beginning of the birth pangs**); but Matthew has already recorded sayings about this in an earlier discourse (chapter 10) and includes only brief allusions to it here; whereas more space is given to the implications of a period which would

12 inevitably see an **increase of lawlessness.**

14 **"And then the end will come."** The modern reader is disconcerted to find that it does not, but that other calamities are still to be recorded which clearly belong to the time before the end. But it is a feature of the kind of literature to which this chapter belongs (of which we possess a number of Jewish examples, such as 2 Esdras in the Apocrypha, and one Christian example, the Revelation) that the drama is not made to unfold in an orderly progression, but the description keeps turning back on itself to fill in details belonging to an earlier phase. So here: the events now predicted (whatever

15 the precise meaning of the cryptogram from the **prophet Daniel** – see below on Mark 13.14) are not those of the end at all, but of an incursion of military strength into Palestine on a scale that would make immediate flight the only sensible course; and, since mainly Jews would be affected, it is added that it

20 would be as well if it did not happen on **a sabbath,** when all journeying is forbidden and when fugitives would have a crisis of conscience to contend with as well as their other troubles.

24 The danger from **false messiahs and false prophets** is made more precise than in Mark. The fanatics who appeared in the years following Jesus' death proclaiming themselves to be divinely inspired leaders and attempting to lead

26 a nationalist rising did in fact often begin by gathering a following **in the wilderness;** alternatively they might form a conspiracy **in the inner rooms.** But the coming of the Son of Man (as the next verses make clear) would be totally different: it would be as quickly and easily recognized by all as a corpse

28 is spotted by **vultures** (this seems to be the sense of the proverb inserted here). The language used of it is like that of the Old Testament prophets when they looked forward to 'the day of the Lord': disorder among the heavenly bodies (which would certainly be reflected in unnatural catastrophes on earth, Isaiah

31 13.10; 34.4), a **sign** (which is probably an ensign, Isaiah 11.12), a **trumpet call** (Isaiah 27.13; Joel 2.1) and the gathering of the **elect from the four winds** (Zechariah 2.6; Deuteronomy 30.4). All these conventional features

are gathered round Daniel's description of the coming of the Son of Man (Daniel 7.13–14).

32 With the simile of the **fig tree** the discourse moves (as in Mark) from description to exhortation: this must be your posture in the face of all these developments, neither scepticism because of the apparent delay of the end, 36 nor agitated preoccupation with the exact day and hour (which **only the** 42 **Father** knows). The watchword (as in Mark) is **"Keep awake."**

This lesson of wakefulness is illustrated in Matthew with a series of parables and similes which emphasize (at least in this presentation of them, if not in their original form) the suddenness with which the end must be expected and the error of not taking seriously the teaching which has just been given.

37 **"As the days of Noah were."** The narrative in Genesis concentrates entirely on Noah and his family. Apart from the brief statement (6.11–13) that "the earth was corrupt" and that God had "determined to make an end of all flesh", nothing is said about the behaviour of those doomed to destruction. But as the Jews meditated on this story they began to be impressed by the attitude of Noah. Even though there were no signs in advance of the coming deluge, he put such trust in the word of God that he unhesitatingly set about the immense and apparently absurd task of building a great ship on dry land. He became, in fact, one of the classic examples, along with Abraham, of those who unhesitatingly put their whole faith in God in the face of every contrary indication of prudence and common sense (Hebrews 11.7). If Jesus mentioned him in his teaching one would have expected him to draw the same moral: when I preach to you, be like Noah who believed the message of God and not like those others who, since they would neither listen nor 39 believe – **they knew nothing** – were consigned to destruction. But here, all the emphasis is not on Noah but on the men and women who showed by their manner of living that they made nothing of the calamity which threatened them. How different must be the lives of Christians (this seems to be the moral here) who are aware of what is impending! There will be no time for 40 last-minute repentance. Suddenly, in the midst of daily occupations, **one will be taken** (to join the company of the elect) **and one will be left** (to face the judgment).

45 The parable of **the faithful and wise slave** may have had a somewhat different point when Jesus first told it from the simple lesson of vigilance which it illustrates here. The background to it is one of the many estates in Palestine which were owned by foreign magnates and managed in their absence by stewards or agents who were often slaves. Being slaves, the house-hold staff would be rewarded, not by higher wages, but by a position of greater 48 responsibility. Similarly, one who turned out to be a **wicked slave** could be punished, not just by dismissal, but by death – but at this point the details become blurred. 'Cutting in pieces' was not unknown as a punishment for slaves, but seems gratuitously brutal here – there may be some mistransla-tion of the original Aramaic word; and by the end of the parable the landlord

seems to have become the divine Judge and the punishment (Matthew's
51 characteristic **weeping and gnashing of teeth**) that which will be meted out
to all **hypocrites** at the judgment. Clearly the parable, at some stage in its
progress from the lips of Jesus to the written page of the gospel, has been
adapted to yield teaching about the proper behaviour of Christians as they
await the return of their Lord: all the emphasis is now on the suddenness
of the master's homecoming. But the natural structure of the story, with its
balanced contrast between a trust deserved and a trust betrayed, points in
a different direction. Who, among Jesus' contemporaries, had been set over
God's household? And who was ready for the reckoning which might come
at any time?

25.1 **"Then the kingdom of heaven will be like this."** Another parable follows
which Matthew evidently saw as a further illustration of the same theme of
watchfulness and preparedness for judgment. It ends with the same message –
13, 5 **"Keep awake therefore"** – and the detail that **the bridegroom was delayed**
suggests the context in which the parable may have been used in the church.
The glorious return of Jesus was being delayed longer than expected: those
who relaxed their vigilance would be like the bridesmaids who failed to reckon
with the possibility of delay and were not ready when the moment came. But
it can be seen at once that this interpretation of the parable is somewhat
forced. If five of the girls had fallen asleep and five remained awake and
ready, the moral – 'Keep awake therefore' – would have been exactly right.
5 But in the story they *all* **became drowsy and slept**, and there is no suggestion
that there was anything wrong about doing so. The error of the five foolish
bridesmaids was not that they fell asleep, but that they did not allow for the
possibility of delay. Was the original point of the parable, therefore, to warn
Jesus' followers that they must be prepared for a longer period of waiting
than they thought?

We are unfortunately not in a position to fill in the background with any
certainty. Marriage customs vary from place to place and from one period
to another, and we possess no independent evidence of marriage festivities
in Palestine in the first half of the first century CE. In particular, we hear
nowhere else about a procession at night or about attendants with lamps.
On the other hand, one of the high points of marriage festivities all over the
ancient world was the moment when the bridegroom was escorted, either
to the house of the bride, or (with his bride) to his own house. This was the
moment for singing and dancing; and when the procession got indoors the
guests would sit down to the wedding feast. In broad outline the story of
1 the ten bridesmaids fits well enough into this pattern. **"Ten bridesmaids took
their lamps and went to meet the bridegroom."** The 'lamps' one usually
thinks of are the small domestic oil lamps used all over the ancient world,
which consisted simply of a shallow container of oil and a wick fitted into
a hole in one end. But it is difficult to see how such lamps could have been

used on this occasion: they would instantly have blown out when taken out of doors, they were quite inappropriate for carrying about, and in any case, they would have lasted all night without being refilled. Some kind of hurricane lamps are another possibility; but the Greek word used here never (so far as we know) meant this, and anyway, being made of horn, they would have given out a very subdued and unfestive light. Far the most likely kind of lights for them to have used for any dancing or running in procession were torches – and this is what the Greek word normally means. But torches usually consisted of long cones of wood coated with pitch; if this was what the girls were carrying they cannot possibly have needed oil as well. The only convincing solution which has yet been proposed is a custom which has been observed in relatively modern times in Palestine. This consists of wrapping the head of a torch with some material impregnated with olive oil. The torch will then burn for a short time, say a quarter of an hour, after which it will need soaking in oil again if it is to be made to blaze up suddenly or to last for a longer time. If this is what the girls were to carry the fault of the foolish ones was not that they did not allow for the delay but that they came at the beginning without an essential part of their equipment; and, having slept during the time they might have put this right, they had no chance to make good their negligence when the critical moment came. The bridegroom went

10 **into the wedding banquet** with the girls who had lighted his way; but he was not going to admit some more girls, whom he had never seen until that moment.

If this is the true explanation – and it cannot claim to be more than a conjecture – then it gives a very different point to the parable. The moral

13 which Matthew places at the end – **Keep awake therefore** – has already been shown not to fit the parable; and the suggestion that the original emphasis was on the unexpected delay of the bridegroom now fares no better: the fault of the foolish girls was not that they had brought too little oil but that they had forgotten to bring any oil at all. In which case the parable seems to fall into place beside that of the man without a wedding garment (22.11–13). The new life promised to believers (often described in the image of a feast) is freely offered to all – but on condition that they prepare themselves (presumably with repentance and a will to change their manner of life). Those who take this condition lightly must expect to be turned away.

14 **"It is as if a man, going on a journey"**. Precisely what is 'as if' is not said: as with many parables of Jesus the original application was not preserved, though Matthew (as we shall see) found reason to include this one in the general context of teaching about the future. The parable has to be understood in the light of commercial realities in Palestine. Jews were not permitted to practise usury among themselves; therefore the man going abroad could not simply lend his money for investment in someone else's business. He had to find agents whom he could trust to initiate and carry on a commercial

enterprise on his behalf. It was natural that he should choose his servants for this, even (perhaps) if they were **slaves**.[10] Among these, some might have already proved themselves more capable than others, and there was
15 nothing unusual about dividing up the capital, not into equal parts, but **to each according to his ability**. The man would not risk losing a large sum by giving it as working capital to an inexperienced or incompetent agent. The sums involved were substantial. A **talent** was equivalent to 6,000 standard silver coins (*denarii*) – five, or even two, talents was a large sum, and if the agents made a loss they would probably have had to compensate their master out of their own pockets (though it is difficult to see how slaves could do this). If they made a profit (and high rates of profit and interest were normal in antiquity), most of it, as well as the original capital, would be due to be repaid to their master, for though they were to be active in business they were still his agents. It followed that, although they might have to take the risk of losses themselves, they could not expect to enrich themselves by their profits. Their principal reward would be the prospect of promotion in their master's employment.

So much for the setting; now for the characters. Two of them are vividly drawn, the master and the third slave. This slave, compared with the two others, is given only a modest capital sum to work with; clearly he was not regarded as very competent. But a small capital is more difficult to trade with than a large one; he could not expect much of a profit, and there was always the risk of a loss. So he buried the money, which was regarded as the safest way to mind a deposit. And when he had to settle accounts with his master
24 he stood up to him firmly. **"I knew that you were a harsh man"**, that is, one who expected the maximum return on his money and who made as small an outlay as possible (by way of 'sowing' or 'scattering' his money for the benefit of his agents or debtors) and pressed for the highest possible rate of return. The slave feared the risk of losing the capital more than that of forfeiting any credit he might gain from making a profit. We see him, not only as a timid and incompetent businessman, but as a servant with a sense of grievance towards his master.

The description of the master is equally vivid. Far from denying his
27 slave's description of him, he proceeds to substantiate it. **"You ought to have invested my money with the bankers."** In modern terms this might make good sense: a deposit account at a bank is a safe and painless way of securing a small increase on capital. But in antiquity one did not normally deposit money for interest; on the contrary, one paid a bank in return for the safety of the deposit. It is possible that a more literal translation gives a better

---

[10] This is the translation of the word chosen almost everywhere it occurs by the NRSV, even though conventionally (and possibly correctly) it has been rendered *servants*. But it causes difficulty in this passage because it is unlikely that slaves had sufficient rights at law to be able to carry on a business on their own account.

sense: 'You should have given my silver coins to the money-changers.' Gold and silver coins were minted outside Palestine and money-changers charged a small commission for exchanging them for the local bronze coinage. The servant with a substantial capital of such coins could at least have gone into nominal partnership with a money-changer and secured some interest that way. At any rate, the master, true to character, could not accept the slave's point that, with a small capital, it is better to be safe than sorry.

28   **"Take the talent from him, and give it to the one with the ten talents."** This was no punishment: he was due to pay back the capital in any case; and it was only logical for the master to add it to the capital of the slave who had shown himself the best businessman. But, as we read the parable in Matthew, this comparatively trivial detail becomes the most important point in the story. For it appears to be a perfect illustration of a saying of Jesus that is quoted once in another context in Matthew (13.12) and in yet

29   another in Mark (4.25): **"For to all those who have, more will be given … but from those who have nothing, even what they have will be taken away."** Precisely what Jesus would have meant by this saying we do not know (it was probably already proverbial – see below on Mark 4.25). But Matthew seems to have seen in it a commentary on the rewarding of people's spiritual

30   resources at the judgment; for he goes on to consign the **worthless slave** to hell (for which **weeping and gnashing of teeth** is a standard expression in this gospel) and we are left in little doubt that, as he tells this story, the return of the master stands for Christ's return: the reward of the 'good' slaves has been deliberately spiritualized, so that they are not merely given a position

21, 23   of greater responsibility on earth but are invited to **enter into the joy** of their master, that is (as the striking Greek phrase suggests), in the heavenly kingdom. In Matthew's hands, if not before, the parable has become an allegory of the divine judgment.

Was this the original meaning? It is important to remember that today's metaphorical meaning of the word 'talent' is a result of this parable: it certainly did not exist at the time. So we cannot assume that Jesus was speaking about people's 'talents'. On the other hand, it would be characteristic of Jesus (like most story-tellers) to put the emphasis on the last of a series of three. One slave had failed to make anything of the capital entrusted to him. What had Jesus' opponents done with the immense capital of their ancestral religion which had been entrusted to them?

The discourse ends with what is not so much a parable as a grand tableau

31   of the judgment, built up out of a number of separate images. **"When the Son of Man comes in his glory"** is the language of Daniel's prophecy (7.13–

32   15), describing the solemn moment of divine judgment when **all the nations** would become subject to the righteous Son of Man and to the elect, whom he gathered and represented. **"As a shepherd separates the sheep from the goats"** is a simile for judgment as old as Ezekiel (34.17): the Palestinian shepherd might pasture his flocks of sheep and goats together, but at some stage

he would separate them. The white sheep were a natural symbol for the pure apparel of the righteous, the black goats for the dark deeds of the wicked. And finally, a king on his throne was one of the commonest images for the God of justice, who would one day bring all to account for the 'acts of kindness' which they had done or failed to do (the only act described here which seldom occurs in similar Jewish lists is visiting prisoners). All these elements, including even a dialogue between the king and those who appear before him, are conventional enough. But the way these elements are combined and exploited is unique and arresting. That Jesus himself was the Son of Man who would 'come in glory' has already been intimated several times in the gospel, and it followed from the title itself that he would play some part in the judgment. Here the thought is taken a step further: he becomes the Judge, the king who

34 gives sentence – though still in some way subordinate to God (**"you that are blessed by my Father"**). But the real originality of the passage, as well as its beauty and symmetry, lies in the dialogue. That people would be rewarded for their acts of kindness was taken for granted by Jesus' contemporaries; and many would even have been prepared to accept that these acts, rather than the fact of belonging to the Jewish race or having faithfully observed the law, would serve as the principal basis for distinguishing between the blessed and the damned. But the reason given here must have seemed unprecedented: it was not just that acts of this kind were meritorious, but that in doing them to certain people one is doing them to Jesus himself. Who are these people in whom lurks the Son of Man? It is tempting to answer: All who are

40 in need. But it is by no means certain that this is what is being said here. **"Just as you did it to one of the least of these who are members of my family** (literally, *these my brothers*) **you did it to me."** 'Brothers' in this gospel (and indeed, throughout the New Testament) is almost a technical word for fellow Christians. Moreover, Jesus called his 'brothers', not men and women in general, but those who, with him, acknowledge God as their Father. In short, we must hesitate before we assume that the reward of eternal life is promised to all who show kindness to *any* sufferer. Those who will be rewarded appear (at least according to Matthew) to be those who show kindness to *Christians*, for it is in the Christian community that Jesus lives on, bringing men and women face to face with the ultimate issues of life and death, reward and condemnation, just as he did when he preached and worked on earth.

The final days

From this point Matthew follows the account in Mark (chapter 14 onwards) very closely, and it will be sufficient to notice a few details which he has

26.2 changed or added. **"You know that after two days the Passover is coming."** This is exactly the same chronology as in Mark, but here it takes on a deeper meaning: Jesus knows in advance that this particular Passover will be crucial as being the moment when **"the Son of Man will be handed over to be** crucified" – and the stage is set for this 'handing over' at a meeting which only

3 Matthew records **in the palace of the high priest, who was called Caiaphas** (who held office from 18 to 36 CE). Already there is conflict: Jesus is prophesying his crucifixion during the Passover, while his enemies are endeavouring

5 to avoid exactly this. **"Not during the festival"**, they said.

6 **While Jesus was at Bethany.** Compared with Mark's account (14.3–9), Matthew's is less startling. Instead of breaking the neck of the bottle and

7 emptying the entire contents over Jesus' head, the woman merely **poured it** (indeed, the Greek verb is in the imperfect, which means literally *began to pour*), and the value of the ointment is not the prodigious sum of three

9 hundred *denarii* (which Mark gives) but only **a large sum**. Any reader who still found in Mark's version of the story, despite its symbolic meaning, an unnecessarily wasteful gesture would have been considerably less shocked when reading Matthew.

14 **Then one of the twelve.** Matthew alone gives the details of the bargain made between Judas and the chief priests. If it is asked how Matthew knew the exact figure, the answer could possibly be that some Christian was able to find it out afterwards and pass on the information; but it is perhaps more likely that Matthew inferred it from a passage of the Old Testament which he regarded as a prophecy of the events he was recording. Zechariah 11.12 runs, "They weighed out as my wages thirty shekels of silver." In the time of Jesus the equivalent of a shekel was a *tetradrachm*, which was the largest silver coin in currency and which had been minted all over the Greek-speaking world since the time of Alexander the Great. The sum of money would therefore have amounted to 120 *denarii* (about four months' wage for a labourer).

15 The Greek verb here translated **paid** is the same as that for "weighed out" in the Greek version of Zechariah, and Matthew may well have intended the allusion to be picked up. Here the word can mean either 'paid' or (more likely) 'agreed on'.

17 **On the first day of Unleavened Bread.** Strictly speaking this (as in Mark) is inaccurate: these preparations had to be made before sunset, which is when (by Jewish reckoning) the 'first day' of the festival began. With regard to these preparations, the apparently miraculous circumstances in Mark's account of the finding of the room are omitted: here, it seems that the matter was simply

18 prearranged. Jesus had already known that his **time** was **near**.

20–9 Matthew's additions to Mark's account of the supper (14.17–25) are very small. The traitor is explicitly identified as Judas – though perhaps not so clearly and unambiguously that anyone but Jesus and Judas would have realized what was going to happen. It is not said when Judas left the company to carry out his plot; but this point (i.e. after verse 25) is the most likely one; and if the traitor was then out of the room, the slightly greater emphasis in this

27 account (compared with Mark's) on the privileged circle of disciples (**"Drink**

29 **from it, all of you . . . when I drink it new with you"**) is understandable. There is one further addition of significance: that the new 'covenant', like

the old, was to be sealed by blood, and that this was represented by the cup, is an understanding common to all the accounts. Only Matthew adds

28 that (perhaps like the 'new covenant' in Jeremiah 31.31–4) it was **"for the forgiveness of sins"**.

31 **"You will all become deserters."** This is a new translation of a word (*skandalizesthai*) which usually means 'take offence' (as in 5.29; 11.6), but also (as here) can mean something stronger. 'You will all fall away into faithlessness'

31–5 (or even 'into sin') would be a reasonable paraphrase. Jesus' prediction of

36 Peter's denial and the episode in **Gethsemane** are told almost exactly as in Mark (14.26–42): Matthew has merely removed Mark's imputation (14.40) that the disciples' fatigue was such that they were incapable of answering Jesus at all. But in the story of the arrest Jesus' reply to Judas is new and a

50 little mysterious. **"Friend, do what you are here to do"** is a plausible translation of the Greek words, but cannot claim to be certain: it is possible that it is a question (*'What have you come for?'*). In the narrative that follows Matthew makes one significant addition. The scuffle which led to the high priest's slave losing an ear is mentioned only in passing in Mark, but here it leads to

52 two sayings of Jesus. The first, **"all who take the sword will perish by the sword"**, sounds like a proverb – possibly, like another proverb used by Jesus, expressing a reaction against the violent tactics of fanatical rebels against the Roman régime (see on Mark 9.40): Jesus made a point of dissociating himself

53 from any movement of this kind. The second raises the conflict to a different level. As Luke puts it, this moment was "your hour, and the power of darkness" (22.53), which is not just a metaphor but a clear indication of the way the crisis presented itself to the gospel-writers (and doubtless to Jesus). The contest was not merely between Jesus and the secular powers. Behind this was raging a battle against Satan and all the evil powers. We know (especially now from the Dead Sea Scrolls) how this battle might have been imagined in the time of Jesus: huge detachments of angels arrayed in military order lined up against each other in readiness for the final conflict. The discipline and order of the Roman army were projected by these visionaries into the scene of heavenly warfare; hence Jesus' otherwise surprising borrowing of a Roman military term: **"twelve legions of angels"**.

57 **Those who had arrested Jesus took him to Caiaphas the high priest**. Matthew, unlike Luke and John, follows exactly the same order of events as Mark: immediately after Jesus' arrest there was a meeting in Caiaphas' house of **the scribes** (among whom there will have been some Pharisees) **and the elders** (who were probably influential and aristocratic laymen). Matthew,

59 like Mark, calls this a meeting of the **council** (*Sanhedrin*), and it is natural to assume that it was a formal trial. However, apart from the many technical anomalies according to later rules of procedure (see on Mark 14.53), this may well have been no more than a preliminary hearing. It led, after all, not to a judicial verdict but to an agreement among those present that Jesus was

66 one who **deserves death**; and the consequence was not a judicial execution but a decision to hand Jesus over to Pilate. Even if those present were technically judges, and the proceedings were to that extent judicial, there would have been nothing unusual in members of the court themselves presenting evidence against the accused – the system in that respect was totally unlike that of a modern law court. But for any charge to be substantiated, it was necessary for two witnesses independently to give consistent evidence, and

60 this seems to have been the court's difficulty. **At last two came forward.** It seems that valid evidence was obtained on only one count, a saying of Jesus, which in fact John's gospel records in another context (2.14). Matthew's version of the saying is a little milder than Mark's (14.58): not, "I will destroy

61 this temple", but **'I am able to destroy the temple'** – a form which will have given less trouble to Christians afterwards, since it did not raise the question (as Mark's version does) of when and how this promise was fulfilled. Nevertheless, the allegation was serious. 'Prophesying against the temple' had once nearly cost Jeremiah his life (Jeremiah 26) and was the kind of thing which, if uttered in the precincts of the temple, could doubtless be regarded as blasphemous. Here, *prima facie*, was damning evidence; and when Jesus refused to speak a word in his own defence, a case seemed to have been made out. The critical point which proceedings had reached is marked by the fact

62 that the **high priest stood up**; but before declaring the meeting's judgment he had one further question to put which would confirm and explain the evidence so far given. There was a tradition that when the Messiah came he would inaugurate a period of new holiness and significance for the temple in Jerusalem. Could it be that Jesus' saying was not just blasphemous arrogance but was a sign that he believed himself to be the Messiah? If so, this would by no means lessen his guilt – unless of course he really were the Messiah (which, under the circumstances, would have seemed extraordinarily unlikely to his judges); nevertheless, it would make Jesus' saying about the temple intelligible and give the judges a more substantial case to pronounce on. He therefore

63 put Jesus **under oath**[11] to answer the question, **"tell us if you are the Messiah, the Son of God"** (where **Son of God** may be an intrusion from the vocabulary of the early church, though there was a long line of Old Testament figures who, by virtue of their special destiny under God, were called 'sons of God').

Down the centuries, there has been a succession of supposed Jewish 'Messiahs'. Surprisingly, it has not been in their character ever to *claim* messiahship. Their words and actions raise the question; it is for others to acknowledge

64 or reject. Jesus' answer to Caiaphas is in this tradition: **"You have said so."**

---

[11] This may not be a correct translation. To put someone **under oath** is to draw attention to the risk of perjury if the testimony is untrue. But here the problem is to get Jesus to speak at all. *I adjure you* makes better sense. Cf. Leviticus 5.1.

But then, by means of allusions to two Old Testament passages (Daniel 7.13; Psalm 110.1) which described a personage vindicated and honoured by God, Jesus affirmed that at least one of the implications of the title, Messiah, was true of himself. **"From now on"** – not in some theoretical future, but by an immediate reversal of fortune – Jesus would be seen to be vindicated and to have been given a unique status **at the right hand of Power**. Matthew doubtless saw this claim as having been fulfilled by the resurrection and ascension of Jesus: the church did in fact come to acknowledge Jesus as vindicated and glorified. But to the judges this claim seemed merely to aggravate the

66 original blasphemy. **They answered, "He deserves death"** – not necessarily a verdict, but a decision which was to lead to another court (Pilate's) imposing the death penalty. Meanwhile they indulged in some extremely unjudicial personal insult and violence. Here was a test: the Messiah would surely have the gift of prophecy – for instance, he would know who people were without being told. But Jesus offered no such confirmation that he was indeed the Messiah.

69   **Now Peter was sitting outside**. Here Matthew has rearranged Mark's narrative very little, omitting only the curious feature of *two* cock-crows. This story occurs in all the gospels: see on Mark 14.66–72.

27.1   **When morning came**. The key to this episode is the fact, only mentioned in John's gospel (18.31), that the Jewish authorities were unable to carry out a death sentence: the Romans reserved this power to themselves. The further meeting of the Jewish authorities had simply the task of deciding how best to 'hand over' Jesus, which need not have taken them very long. In any case, it was necessary for them to do so as early as possible so as to catch the governor: it was in the early morning that he customarily received such deputations. At this point Matthew inserts an episode which is recorded in none of the other gospels (though it is referred to in Acts 1.18–19): the death of Judas. It comes in a little awkwardly, for the **chief priests and the elders** are at this moment at the high priest's house, whereas Judas' gesture of returning the

5 money presupposes that he and they are **in the temple** – that is to say, in one of those courtyards in the temple precincts where there were arrangements for receiving money (see on Mark 12.41–4). Matthew, in fact, is adding an excursus on the working-out of Judas' destiny without too much concern for its connection with the main narrative (a modern writer would probably use a footnote for the purpose). It is clear that the interest of the early Christians was not merely biographical. There were more significant reasons for the tradition being preserved. One was that the Christian community in Jerusalem came to associate a particular spot with Judas' sinister death.

8 They named it, in Aramaic, *Akeldama* (Acts 1.19), which meant **the Field of**

7 **Blood**; but to everyone else it was known as **the potter's field**. The site of it is fairly certain. The 'Potter's Gate' of Jerusalem lay at the extreme south-east corner of the city, at the mouth of the ill-famed valley of Gehinnom. Nearby

were tombs cut into the rock; the whole area, with its smoking industries, its sinister historical associations and the ritual uncleanness which belonged to a cemetery, was a fit place to bear the memory of the death of a traitor. Precisely what the connection was between Judas and this place was perhaps (by the time this gospel was written) no longer remembered, and it was necessary to work back from the name the Christians themselves had given it. A quite different explanation is given in Acts (1.18–19); here, an inference is drawn which at least shows Matthew's expert knowledge. The
7 area belonged to the temple authorities and was used as a **place to bury foreigners** (for whom, of course, the associations of the place were less sinister – in later centuries it became an honourable burial place for Christian pilgrims). How did they acquire it? What better explanation than that they
6 used Judas' money which, being **blood money**, could not be put into the temple **treasury**? These details are quite correct. Deuteronomy 23.18 runs, "You shall not bring the fee of a prostitute or the wages of a male prostitute into the house of the Lord." *A fortiori*, blood money could not be put into the **treasury** (in the Greek, literally *corban*, another technical Jewish term).

But there was also a more fundamental reason for this interest in the circumstances of Judas' death. It did not present itself to the first Christians as something demanding a psychological interpretation: it was part of a divinely ordered scenario. Such things had long been prepared in the purposes of God and might be expected to be alluded to in prophecy. Sure enough, Zechariah 11.12–13 runs as follows:

> So they weighed out as my wages thirty shekels of silver. Then the Lord said to me, "Throw it into the treasury" – this lordly price at which I was valued by them. So I took the thirty shekels of silver and threw them into the treasury.

This text was always somewhat obscure and different versions of it exist. Moreover, it had a curious variant. Only certain versions give "throw it into the treasury"; the original Hebrew appears to mean 'throw it to the potter'. It looks as if Matthew knew both these versions, and he was also able to exploit the fact that, when translated into Greek, the word meaning 'I took' was identical with that meaning 'they took'. Consequently it required only a little skilful manipulation of the original (which interpreters of his time took very much for granted) to yield an impressive prophecy of Judas' change
9 of heart. One problem remains: why does Matthew say **Jeremiah** (which has already been corrected in some ancient copies – see NRSV footnote)? It is true that there were two well-known passages of Jeremiah in which the prophet "went down to the potter's house" (18.3) and "bought a field" (32.9); but even if these lay at the back of Matthew's mind, it was Zechariah, not Jeremiah, that he was quoting (though there may possibly be an allusion

in his quotation to Jeremiah 18.1ff. and 32.6–9). The most likely answer is that this was simply a mistake; but it is also possible that Christian authors, when quoting from the Hebrew scriptures, used, not a complete copy, but a collection of short prophecies which the church had found particularly relevant to the proclamation and defence of the faith. It is quite likely that these prophecies were not always correctly arranged under their respective authors (for another example, see on Mark 1.2–3).

11 **Now Jesus stood before the governor.** After this digression Matthew returns to the main narrative and records the hearing before Pilate. His account closely follows that of Mark, though it presupposes on the part of his readers less familiarity with the circumstances than Mark's does. Mark's readers were evidently expected to have heard of Barabbas; but here

16 he is introduced with the more precise name, **Jesus Barabbas** (Barabbas, which means simply 'Father's son', was a common name: the addition of 'Jesus' helps to identify the bearer of it); and the scene is given a new element of dramatic irony by the confrontation of two alleged criminals both

17 called Jesus, **Jesus Barabbas or Jesus who is called the Messiah.** Matthew has

19–20 two new details to add to the narrative. One is the intervention of Pilate's wife. (Roman provincial governors had only recently begun to take their wives with them when on foreign service.) Her dream is very much like the kind of portent which ancient historians often recorded before a battle or a crisis. The other detail is Pilate's gesture of washing his hands

24 **before the crowd.** The gesture would be intelligible in any culture, but it was also a classic biblical way of expressing innocence (Deuteronomy 21.6; Psalm 73.13). By recording it, Matthew emphatically attaches the blame for what followed to the Jewish people as a whole, in words that were to have tragic consequences for relations between Christians and Jews for many centuries.

27 **Then the soldiers of the governor took Jesus into the governor's head-quarters.** Matthew is still following Mark very closely – and the fact that he uses the same rather uncommon word (said to be of Persian origin) for 'compelling' (or *commandeering*) Simon of Cyrene is one of the detailed pieces of evidence that support the assumption that he had Mark's gospel in front of him when he wrote. (See the introductory note to the gospels, p. 9). He leaves out the names of Simon's sons (which Mark gives as Alexander and Rufus), presumably because these men, who may have been known to Mark's first readers, were by now of no interest to Matthew's. At the same time he

28 adds or alters certain details. When the soldiers mocked Jesus, they **put a scarlet robe on him**, not a 'purple' one, as in Mark: scarlet was less symbolic of royalty than purple, but in reality much easier to come by – it was the colour of Roman soldiers' cloaks. It is less clear why Matthew substitutes

34 wine **mixed with gall** for Mark's "wine mixed with myrrh" (15.23): possibly a recollection of Psalm 69.21 ("for my thirst they gave me vinegar to drink") influenced him. In any case, the point is the same. The drink was poisonous,

and offered as an insult. And to the description of the mockery to which Jesus was subjected Matthew adds a further touch, drawn again from the repertory of Old Testament poetry describing innocent suffering. The closest parallel is in Psalm 22 (the psalm which provides the most impressive precedent for and commentary on Jesus' suffering):

> "Commit your cause to the LORD; let him deliver –
> let him rescue the one in whom he delights!"
> (22. 8)

But there is another passage which might also have been in Matthew's mind. The first chapters of the Wisdom of Solomon are concerned precisely with the problem of the righteous sufferer, and in chapter 2 the mockery of the unrighteous is described. The following phrases (from verses 13 to 18) will show how closely Matthew's account conforms with what had already become a classical model in Jewish writing:

> He . . . calls himself a child of the Lord. . . . .
> and boasts that God is his father.
> Let us see if his words are true . . .
> for if the righteous man is God's child, he will help him,
> and will deliver him from the hand of his adversaries.

Matthew diverges significantly from Mark's account only when it comes to the moment of Jesus' death. At this point (15.38) Mark mentions an event which seems at least as symbolic as factual: the tearing of the curtain of the temple. In doing so, Mark seems to be writing according to an ancient, even oriental, convention: the reference to extraordinary events accompanying a person's death is an element of commentary on the significance of the moment rather than meticulous historical reporting. Matthew takes this further, and thereby starts a trend which produces a mass of increasingly improbable phenomena in the accounts of the later apocryphal gospels. The
51 symbolism may have in fact begun with **the curtain of the temple** itself. This huge piece of tapestry was a famous sight. It was hung in front of the doors of the main temple building, and could be seen even by non-Jews when they looked through the gateway of the Court of the Israelites towards the temple entrance. The most obvious symbolism in the tearing of this curtain **from top to bottom** was the end of that separation between God and people, priests and laity, Jews and Gentiles, which was inherent in the worship and structure of the temple. But a further meaning may have been suggested by the picture embroidered upon it, which was of the entire firmament of heaven. Not the curtain only, but the heavens themselves, were rent asunder (one of the traditional ways of describing the Day of the Lord); and this was answered on earth by an earthquake. To this extent Matthew's commentary
52 on the moment of Jesus' death has a certain symbolic logic. That the **tombs also were opened** seems less logical; but resurrection was also an element of

the Day of the Lord, even though (as Matthew appears to admit) the time
53 for it was really *after* **his resurrection.**

54 **"Truly this man was God's Son!"** This is a total reversal of the mockery
of a few hours earlier. At the very moment of Jesus' death things had been
seen which could be read as God's vindication of his righteous servant, and
even the foreigners standing by – the centurion and those with him – were
moved to recognize something exceptional in Jesus. In Mark it is Jesus' bearing at his death which impresses the centurion; here it is the accompanying
portents which overwhelm the whole group of soldiers. Their confession
was significant: it was as 'Son of God' (the usual translation of the Greek
phrase – see the NRSV footnote) that the church soon began to worship
Jesus. But if we are to ask what the phrase could have meant in the mouths
of these gentile soldiers, the answer could be that they had heard of persons who, because of their apparently miraculous powers, were called 'sons
of God': the phenomena surrounding Jesus' death, such as an earthquake,
showed that Jesus was one of these. But Matthew's readers are unlikely to
have lingered over historical plausibility. The message of these words is that
at Jesus' death there were even Gentiles who recognized Jesus for what he
truly was.

55 **Many women were also there.** Matthew lists the same names as Mark,
56 except that he seems to identify Mark's Salome with **the mother of the sons
of Zebedee.** But only two of them remain to witness the burial, and only
two return on Sunday morning to the tomb, Mary Magdalene and the other
Mary (28.1). Joseph of Arimathea, too, has undergone a significant change
at Matthew's hands. In Mark he is presented as a devout and influential
Jew, whose main motive in undertaking the burial of Jesus was probably
that of saving the city and its surrounding country from the defilement of
an unburied corpse. But in Matthew his motive is quite different. He is a
57 man who **was also a disciple of Jesus** (which might have been difficult if,
as Mark says, he was also a member of the Sanhedrin: Matthew omits this
detail) and his action is that much more devoted in that he lays Jesus in his
60 own **new tomb.** What in Mark was a hasty burial perfunctorily performed
by a stranger has become in Matthew a work of charity undertaken by an
influential disciple.

62 **The next day.** Matthew alone reports this episode, which accounts for
the presence (in his narrative) of soldiers at the tomb, who then become
important witnesses of the resurrection. It is a little surprising to find Jewish
authorities taking action of this kind on the sabbath, and in any case one
would have thought they should have taken this precaution as soon as Jesus
was buried. Pilate duly provided the guard, however (the Greek has *kustōdia*,
a Latin word appropriate for a contingent of Roman soldiers, not Jewish
temple police), and the Jews, as an additional precaution, placed some kind
of seal on the stone so that any unauthorized opening could be detected.

28.1   **After the sabbath.** The scene is recognizably the same as that in Mark, but is told with less detail and greater emphasis on the supernatural. The
  2 **great earthquake,** the **angel of the Lord** and the paralyzed fear of the guards are all features that belong less to an objective narrative of the discovery that the tomb was empty than to an imaginative description of a supernatural experience. Such importance as the empty tomb itself may have had is still further played down when the vision of the angel is immediately followed by an encounter with the risen Jesus. This brings the women's experience into line with that of the rest of the disciples: it was not the empty tomb but the appearances of Jesus himself that gave them confidence to proclaim the resurrection. The women were simply the first to acknowl-
  9 edge him in his risen state when they **took hold of his feet, and worshiped him.**

Matthew has his own explanation to offer (different from Mark's) of why the discovery that Jesus' tomb was empty was not immediately seized upon and proclaimed by his followers: a counter-story was deliberately put about by the Jews; and since the Christian version of the matter rested only on the testimony of two women, whose evidence was reputed to be proverbially unreliable and would not have been admitted in a court, this could never have had much force in disputes (such as we can frequently overhear in Matthew's gospel) between the early church and its Jewish opponents. Matthew simply reports the two versions of the facts and leaves the reader to decide between them.

  16   **Now the eleven disciples went to Galilee.** Matthew, like Mark, has faithfully recorded (26.32) the somewhat puzzling statement of Jesus that after the resurrection he would 'go ahead' of his disciples to Galilee. The promise has
  7, 10 just been repeated by the angel at the tomb and by Jesus himself; and Matthew ends his gospel by recounting its fulfilment. The mention of the **eleven** seems deliberately precise. The 'twelve' were last mentioned at the Passover supper (26.20). Since then, Judas had defected and killed himself; but although Peter had denied Jesus and the rest had deserted him, these eleven were still (to Matthew's way of thinking, if not in historical fact) the appropriate group to receive the final revelation of Jesus' authority and commission. In any case, they **went to Galilee.** This contradicts Luke's account, according to which all Jesus' appearances took place in or near Jerusalem. But it is possible that Matthew was more interested in the symbolism of the setting than in the geography. He has said nothing previously of a **mountain to which Jesus had directed them:** this phrase does not help us to locate the scene. On the other hand, the greatest moments of Jesus' self-revelation, whether of his true nature (the transfiguration) or of his moral demands (the Sermon on the Mount), were conceived as taking place on a mountain, and just as the definitive revelation of God in the Old Testament took place on Mount Sinai, so Matthew (giving perhaps yet another hint that Jesus was a new Moses)

may well have taken it for granted that the scene he was about to relate took place on a mountain, and that Jesus must therefore have previously arranged this meeting place.

17 **They worshiped him.** The appearance of the risen Jesus is not described and has to be inferred from the disciples' reaction. On meeting the earthly Jesus their greeting would have been respectful, certainly – that of disciples to their master. The only reason for 'worship' (which implied prostration, a subservient action otherwise only appropriate before kings and emperors) must have been some sense of the supernatural – and this is what is conveyed here, though not a word is used to describe what the disciples saw. **But some doubted.** Possibly the vision was ambiguous: was the figure certainly Jesus? Was the strangeness of the appearance sufficient to warrant worship? Nevertheless, their doubt at this stage seems surprising – particularly since Matthew is usually careful to present the disciples so far as possible as models of Christian obedience and understanding. This may perhaps be Matthew's grudging admission of the fact, which is clearly stated in John (20.25), that at least one of the disciples took time to be convinced of the reality of the resurrection.

18 **"All authority in heaven and on earth has been given to me."** This is the fulfilment of the destiny of the Son of Man – "To him was given dominion and glory and kingship, that all peoples, nations, and languages should serve him" (Daniel 7.14). The words provide the answer to the question, What was Jesus' status after the resurrection? He was the one to whom supreme power had been given under God. The church soon had various ways of expressing this, one drawn from Psalm 110:1 – "Sit at my right hand until I make your enemies your footstool" – and others besides. But most appropriate to the triumphant end of the story of the suffering Son of Man were these words from Daniel; and the following sentences offer a commentary on the **authority** which was now exercised by the risen Jesus. It was effective, not when people were blindly

19 subservient, but when they became Jesus' **disciples** by accepting baptism and observing his teaching. However much Jesus may have limited the range of his disciples' mission during his life on earth (as seems clearly the case, for instance, in the 'mission charge' in chapter 10) their task was now worldwide. Indeed by the time this gospel was written, Christianity had spread so far round the civilized regions of the Mediterranean that it was no more than poetic exaggeration to say that it had reached **all nations**. For the language of these sentences is the language of the early church: baptizing and instructing were the main activities of Christian ministers and missionaries, and it is of a piece with the emphasis which throughout his gospel Matthew places

20 on Jesus' ethical teaching that Jesus should say, **"teaching them to obey everything that I have commanded you"**. Doubtless the conviction of the first generation of Christians that this was their task and mission, and that the risen Christ was perceptibly 'with them', went back to an assurance given

in the course of an experience such as Matthew describes. But plain reporting cannot do justice to such experiences; something has to be added to draw out the meaning. And we can hardly be wrong in detecting, in the last words of the gospel, an allusion to one of the very first prophecies which Matthew sees to be fulfilled in Jesus (1.23): "They shall name him Emmanuel, which means, 'God is with us.' "

MARK

Jesus and John

1.1 **The beginning of the good news.** When a messenger brought news of a victory in war or of some stroke of personal good fortune, the correct Greek word for the tidings was *euangelion*, 'good news'. In the Roman empire, happy events of this kind were ascribed to the apparently superhuman power of the reigning emperor. It was the emperor's genius which assured victory, peace and prosperity. He was the saviour of humankind, and the news of a new emperor's birth or accession was always a significant *euangelion*. The essence of the Christian message was that a new saviour had now appeared on earth and had ascended his throne in heaven. It was no stretch of language to call this message a *euangelion*, and the word soon became a technical term in the Christian vocabulary. The equivalent in English has always been the Anglo-Saxon word *gospel* (as in the NRSV footnote), of which **good news** is a reasonable modern equivalent.

The content of this 'good news' concerned (or was proclaimed by) **Jesus Christ, the Son of God**. For some years before Mark wrote (as is evident from Paul's letters), the title 'Son of God' had become attached to Jesus. Nevertheless, in the written gospels it is used only sparingly, and its occurrence here in the very first verses of Mark's gospel is significant: evidently one of the main purposes of Mark's work was to demonstrate that Jesus was in fact the 'Son of God'. To feel the force of this claim, we have to ask what the title would have suggested to Mark's first readers. Among Greek-speaking people, the phrase denoted nothing very much out of the ordinary. The alleged miracle-workers and men of undoubted psychic or ascetic powers who moved about the ancient world were often so described; and the subjects of the Roman empire had become accustomed to the emperor taking the title, 'Son of a god'. But (as is clear from the temptation stories in Matthew and Luke) Jesus vigorously rejected any suggestion of earthly domination. If he was 'Son of God', this did not mean that he was one among the many other 'sons of God' of the ancient world; for he was unique. The meaning of the title for the earliest Christians (and for Jesus himself if he accepted it) must therefore be looked for, not in the secular idioms of Greece and Rome, but in Jewish religion; and here the title was more specific. It meant one who was singled out for an important rôle in the unfolding of the destiny of his people – and for this God would choose by no means only kings and rulers, but also prophets and even particularly wise and pious men.

In recent times the hopes attached to such a one had become concentrated in a single divinely appointed figure, the Messiah (in Greek, the *Christ*) who was to appear at the end of the present age and inaugurate a new era. Tentatively before the resurrection (if we accept the evidence of the gospels) and confidently after it, the disciples recognized that Jesus was indeed this Christ (albeit a very different 'Messiah' from that of Jewish expectation). If so, then the title 'Son of God' was not only appropriate, it took on new meaning by virtue of the exceptional intimacy which Jesus clearly enjoyed with his heavenly Father and of his claim to speak and act with his Father's authority. This was a claim fraught with consequences: its apparently blasphemous implications (if it were not true) were a source of scandal and were one of the reasons which led to Jesus' execution; but if it were true, anyone who acknowledged it would be obliged to acknowledge Jesus' divine authority – and the gospels have the ring of truth when they report only very rare instances of human beings (unlike heavenly voices or demons) making this acknowledgment. But whatever intimations the disciples may have had during Jesus' lifetime that this filial intimacy with God was a fact, the resurrection seemed to prove it. Thereafter they could talk confidently of **Jesus Christ the Son of God**. To convince others of this 'good news' was the object of Mark's gospel.

Exactly what point in this 'good news' could be called **the beginning** is not clear; each of the gospel writers chose a different point for the beginning of the story of Jesus – Matthew chose his birth, Luke the birth of John the Baptist, John the beginning of creation itself. Mark (like the early Christian sermons, as in Acts 10.37) starts later than any of them with the appearance of **John the baptizer**, who is introduced with an Old Testament prophecy.

4
2 Only the second part of the quotation can be found in **the prophet Isaiah** (40.3); the first part appears to be a combination of Malachi 3.1 and Exodus 23.20. Christians may have come to see references to John in all these texts, and after they had been quoted together for some time they may have been thought of as a single passage and attributed as a whole to Isaiah. In any case, the prophecy serves to emphasize that aspect of the mission of John which was of greatest importance to Christians: he was the forerunner of Jesus.

4   **John the baptizer appeared**. The prophecy simply announced "a messenger". Mark now fills out the historical figure, John, who fulfilled the prophecy. He appeared **in the wilderness**. This, for anyone who knew the country, was a sufficient indication: although a large part of the region was desert, it was the arid and wild mountainous area, which begins dramatically just below the Mount of Olives and stretches down to the Jordan valley over 900 metres (3,000 feet) below, which was the 'wilderness' any local inhabitant would think of at once. John's appearance there doubtless helped to emphasize the austere and challenging message which he had come to proclaim. It was also close to the Jordan, where John carried out his work of **baptism**. This baptism was something new. The Jews practised several forms of washing as part of the ritual needed to remove the impurities of sin, and we now know from the Dead Sea Scrolls that in one Jewish sect at least (with which John

may have had some connection) such ritual washing had great importance. But nothing in such practices approaches the radically simple character of John's baptism. Admittedly it was also **a baptism of repentance for the forgiveness of sins**. But it was clearly not performed simply as a supplement to existing rituals. It was proclaimed as something decisive, an act which everyone should submit to, regardless of their previous religious practices. It symbolized a more sincere and radical repentance and was a necessary preparation for a new state of affairs which would shortly come into being. Some of the implications of this are worked out in the narratives of the other gospels. Here it seems to have been sufficient to indicate the barest elements of the scene: a new rite of symbolic cleansing, readily undergone by a great multitude of people, performed by an austere preacher in the wilderness of the Jordan valley, far from the usual centres and institutions of the Jewish religion. The essence of it was that the people, however scrupulously they may have been abiding by the moral and ceremonial laws of their religion,

5 were moved to come **confessing their sins**. John's baptism, like the teaching of Jesus, inaugurated a new challenge to make a symbolic rite the sign of uncompromising moral sincerity.

2 The quotation from Malachi (3.1), "**I am sending my messenger ahead of you**", would have already prepared the reader to think of John as Elijah; for the same Malachi had prophesied (4.5) that Elijah would one day return. The description of John's clothes reinforces the impression: in 2 Kings 1.8 Elijah is described as "a hairy man, with a leather belt around his waist". Moreover, the returning Elijah was to herald the "day of the Lord"; John

7 heralded not only one who was **more powerful** than himself, but one whose baptism would be the immediate prelude to judgment and a new age.

The readers of the gospel knew who this was, and Mark spends no time on the questions which worry the other evangelists, such as whether John recognized Jesus or whether it was appropriate for Jesus himself to be baptized. He relates the important facts in a single sentence and proceeds at once to interpret the significance of Jesus' baptism by John. The dove appears to be a visible symbol of what was essentially an invisible event: Jesus' endowment with the Holy Spirit. The voice from heaven, speaking words drawn from Psalm 2.7 or Isaiah 42.1 (or both), serves to give authoritative confirmation of the title given to Jesus in the first sentence of the gospel: a 'Son of God'

11 who was also **the Beloved** and accepted by God, in a different class from any others who might have been given this title before.

Matthew and Luke each give a detailed account of the 'temptation' of Jesus. According to them, it consisted of certain choices suggested to him by Satan. Mark's account is much briefer, and we must not assume that he intended

13 the same interpretation. Some of the details have biblical precedents: **forty days** was a traditional round number, the time Moses spent on Mount Sinai (Exodus 24.18), the time Elijah spent on his pilgrimage to Horeb; and **the angels waited on him** (providing him with food) exactly as they did on Elijah

(1 Kings 19). But the fact that he was – unharmed – **with the wild beasts** (like Daniel in the lions' den or perhaps like Jonah in the whale's belly) marks the episode out as a trial of strength and endurance which could be described as being **tempted by Satan,** a contest between the Son of God and the powers of evil which remains present in the background of other episodes as the story progresses.

14 **Now after John was arrested** (literally, *was handed over,* the expression typically used for Jesus' fate later on). Mark's readers were evidently expected to be familiar with the story of John's arrest (which Mark in fact relates later on, 6.17–29): it is mentioned here simply in order to mark the moment at which Jesus' work in Galilee could properly be said to have begun – that is, not immediately after the baptism and temptation but after a certain interval. What Jesus was doing in that interval (whether for instance he remained in company with John the baptizer) is not said by Mark, who is less concerned to fill in the gaps in his biography than to divide the narrative into clearly marked sections. For him, the activity of Jesus has two main phases: first in Galilee, where Jesus has much success and also some opposition; and secondly in Jerusalem, where the opposition builds up to his condemnation and death. This simple arrangement is logical and plausible, and is followed with only slight modification by both Matthew and Luke. But the fact that John's gospel follows a different pattern, weaving together Jesus' activity in Galilee and Jerusalem, suggests that Mark's arrangement may be schematic rather than historical; and there are hints even in Mark's narrative that Jesus may have made more pilgrimages to Jerusalem (as a pious Jew living in Galilee would normally have done) than the single one that he records. However this may be, Mark clearly intends Jesus' appearance in his home country to signal the beginning of the first period, that of preaching, healing and controversy. He devotes the next few chapters to giving some typical examples of these activities.

14 **Proclaiming the good news of God.** The modern reader is curious to know what this 'good news', this *euangelion,* consisted of, and will probably find Mark's bare summary of it merely tantalizing. In this respect Matthew, who places the Sermon on the Mount at the beginning of his account of Jesus' work, may seem much more satisfactory (and indeed, Matthew's was a much more popular and frequently read gospel until quite recent times). The reason Mark was content with such a brief summary is probably that when he used this word *euangelion* he could be sure that his readers would be thoroughly familiar with what he meant by it. It was the preaching which they themselves had heard and responded to when they became Christians; and Mark gives here, not the content which Jesus must have given to it when he first preached it, so much as the tone in which he preached and in which indeed, his followers continued to preach for some time themselves.

15 **"The time is fulfilled."** Every Jew would have picked up the meaning. History, as recorded in the Old Testament, was all preparation for a

consummation that still lay in the future. Jesus was proclaiming that the time of preparation was at last over. **"The kingdom of God has come near."** The meaning of this phrase 'kingdom of God' would have been partly understood by anyone: it meant God's rule, which no one could deny in theory but which was still by no means universally acknowledged and so was still 'to come'. But Jesus would give it a new dimension, which would be gradually revealed in his teaching and destiny and in the experience of the church after his resurrection. The point here is that it had **come near.** Unlike his predecessors, Jesus did not merely teach about the kingdom, he proclaimed its imminent arrival. **"Repent, and believe."** It will have made no difference that Jesus' hearers already professed a religion in which repentance played an important part. It will have been no good answering, 'But I repented yesterday.' Jesus' appearance marked the irruption of something new, and the urgency of his teaching demanded (as the next two paragraphs will show) a single-minded and immediate response, a turning away from old habits and attitudes and a total commitment to a new standard and a new master. Christian preaching doubtless still had this urgent and demanding tone in Mark's time and continued to have it long afterwards. Mark is showing here that it had the same tone of urgency when first delivered by Jesus.

Healing activity

16 **As Jesus passed along the Sea of Galilee.** Mark has now set the scene: Jesus is in Galilee, proclaiming the gospel by his deeds, as we shall see, as much as by his words. The next events hardly fall into a biographical sequence: they are presented as typical examples of Jesus' activity, somewhat loosely strung together. The first such event is Jesus' summons to two pairs of brothers to accompany him. How much they knew beforehand, and how much they were prepared for this sudden call, are details which Mark does not trouble to record. The important points for him (as they doubtless were for the young church when it reflected upon the experience of conversion) were the powerful attraction by which Jesus drew them away in the midst of their occupations and the immediacy of the disciples' response. They were

20 fishermen: not peasants (for Zebedee employed **hired men**), but partners in

17 a family fishing business. Jesus said he would make them **"fish for people"**. The metaphor is obvious enough in the context of the life of the later church, where 'fishing for people' meant drawing them in from the pagan world outside into the security of the 'net' of the church. But when Jesus used the phrase he probably meant something different. The fishing net in the Old Testament (e.g. in Jeremiah 16.16) is a symbol of the last judgment: when that judgment comes, men and women will be caught up into it inescapably. Simon and Andrew, James and John are to share in Jesus' work of confronting their contemporaries with a judgment which is already beginning and which (like fish in a net) they cannot escape.

21   **They went to Capernaum.** Jesus, Mark has informed us, came from
Nazareth. But the centre of his activity was to be Capernaum, some 30 miles
away from Nazareth and some 450 metres (1,500 feet) lower in altitude – a
different world altogether from his native highland township. Capernaum
was the largest town on the lake, had a brisk commercial life (it was situated
on the important trade route from Damascus to the Mediterranean) and was
an important centre of the fishing industry. Its synagogue would probably
have been one of the largest in the country (as the existing ruins show it to
have been in the next century), and here Jesus went **when the sabbath came**
for the normal service of prayer, readings from the scriptures and exposition.
The scene is told in detail in Luke (4.31ff.): it was normal for the president of
the synagogue to invite a qualified person to give the teaching, and it was natural that Jesus, who had doubtless already showed himself to be competent
in scripture, should receive such an invitation. Mark (unlike Luke) does not
say what teaching he gave; but we may assume that it took the usual form of
an exposition of a reading from the scriptures. But it was nevertheless, some-
22   thing very different from the normal run of sabbath sermons. **He taught
them as one having authority, and not as the scribes.** It is possible that
Galilean congregations would have been equally impressed by the authority,
or at least the greater learning, of, say, a scholar from Jerusalem, compared
with the less highly qualified local scribes to whom they were accustomed;
but Mark, who has already stated that Jesus was the Son of God, and doubtless
knew that, unlike the scribes, he never appealed to the authority of previous
interpreters but gave his own authoritative interpretation, doubtless had a
more significant kind of authority in mind. He proceeds to illustrate this, not
by an actual example of Jesus' teaching, but by what we could call 'a miraculous cure'. By calling it this, we mis-describe it. Mark sees it rather as another
encounter between Jesus and the forces of evil, and the onlookers have the
same interest. They are impressed by the fact, not so much that the sufferer
27   is cured, as that **"even the unclean spirits . . . obey him".** Popular belief in
Palestine – as indeed, in other parts of the ancient world – was inclined to
find evil spirits (as agents of the devil) at work in many spheres of life. A fairly
obvious case of their activity was any kind of mental or physical illness, such
as epilepsy or some forms of schizophrenia, in which the sufferer behaved
as if 'possessed' or controlled by some outside force. Furthermore, if (as was
usually the case) this condition led the victim to commit acts which were
23   ritually 'unclean', then the outside force was called an **unclean spirit.** The
proper technique for dealing with this condition was exorcism, and the power
to perform exorcisms was not uncommon (Matthew 12.27; Acts 19.13). The
normal procedure was to make the spirit confess who or what it was and then
to invoke the name of a more powerful force in order to drive it out. Clearly
(at least in Mark's understanding) Jesus had no need to invoke any authority
24   apart from his own: the spirit instantly recognized him as **the Holy One of
God** – a phrase roughly equivalent to 'Son of God' – and, after the usual

26 final attempt to manifest its power (in this case by **convulsing** its victim), submitted to Jesus' command and left the people amazed by a new authority, expressed not just in teaching but in mastery of the forces of evil.

30 **Simon's mother-in-law.** We can piece together the family structure: Simon was evidently married, his brother shared the house, and the mother-in-law,

31 when cured, **began to serve them.** Nothing is said to explain the absence of Simon's wife, who would normally have been the person to perform this service. But none of this is of any interest to the narrator. This is the first instance of Jesus' power of healing, told without any of the elaboration (such as the use of charms, spittle or even prayer) customary in such accounts. Yet a fever, in that culture, could be serious. Jesus' ability to cure her by the simple act of taking her **by the hand** would have been enough to create a strong impression on the reader.

32 **That evening, at sundown.** The timing is precise. The sabbath ended at sunset (as even gentile readers of Mark would have known) and only then would it have been lawful to bring (if that meant carrying) **all who were sick** out of their own houses to the house where Jesus was. The two previous episodes have shown how Jesus set about healing and exorcising, and we must

34 infer that he now continued in the same way. That **he would not permit the demons to speak** may anticipate the restraint and secrecy which will be a particular feature of this gospel's account of his activity (see below, p. 145), or it may simply be that he prevented the demons taking the initiative by recognizing and naming him before he could cast them out.

35 **In the morning, while it was still very dark.** The phrase in the original is rough and vivid (*early, still night, very much so*). It is not clear whether Mark is emphasizing Jesus' need for solitude in prayer or his desire to get away from the crowds. Either way, the episode marks the transition from Jesus' initial appearance in Capernaum to his wider mission throughout Galilee.

40 **A leper came to him.** The biblical disease of leprosy cannot have been the same as the terrible paralysis, anaesthesia and rotting of limbs which bears that name today. Descriptions of it in the Bible (see especially Leviticus 13–14) suggest a variety of skin diseases which were certainly difficult to cure but which cannot have been regarded as totally incurable (as modern leprosy would have been), for there are elaborate directions both in the Old Testament (Leviticus 14) and in later Jewish literature about the formalities of ritual cleansing which must be performed by patients when they recovered. The real terror of the disease was experienced, not so much in the physical suffering it involved, as in the ritual 'uncleanness' which was imposed on the sufferer. Strictly speaking (though it is possible that the severity of these rules was partially relaxed in the time of Jesus), a leper was allowed no physical contact with the persons or the houses and possessions of other Jews; and this social ostracism was inspired not so much by the fear of contagion as by the ritual contamination which was believed to be caused

41 by any such contact. If Jesus was **moved with pity** it will have been this

aspect of the affliction which will have moved him most; but a number of early manuscripts offer a significant variant at this point, *moved with anger* – a more difficult reading (for clearly Jesus was not angry either with the sufferer or with the crowds), but quite explicable as a reaction aroused by the inhumanity of the social regulations which added so much suffering to the physical condition of lepers. At any rate, Jesus seems to have been careless of the implications for himself of having touched him – indeed, it is just possi-

45 ble that this is the reason he **could no longer go into a town openly**: as a result of physical contact with a leper he was ritually unclean. Nevertheless, he instructed the leper to conform with the regulations governing recov-

44 ery. Those whose leprosy disappeared had to go and show themselves **to the priest**, who would examine them; if the priest confirmed that the recovery was complete he would allow them to be readmitted to the community after making the prescribed offering (all these regulations can be found in Leviticus 14 and were still in force). Only the completion of this ritual would provide the necessary **testimony** to the community that there would be no further ritual contamination. The stern warning with which Jesus dismissed the leper, telling him to **say nothing to anyone**, may show Jesus' continuing deference to the priestly authorities: he wished to avoid the risk of either the man or the community acting on the physical cure before the ritual ban had been officially lifted; or again this may anticipate that apparent desire for secrecy which will soon begin to accompany Jesus' ministry. But the leper, even if he subsequently travelled to Jerusalem to fulfil his ritual obligations, clearly did not wait before mingling freely with others and spreading the news of his cure.

2.1 **It was reported that he was at home** – back in Capernaum, presumably with the family of Simon (1.29). Much depends on how we imagine the scene. It is unlikely that such a house would have been large enough for Jesus to preach to more than a small gathering of people, though Luke (5.18–19), who was more familiar with the larger houses of Greco-Roman cities, evidently pictured the whole scene as taking place indoors. It is perhaps more likely that Jesus stood outside the house; and this seems to be implied by the statement

2 that there was not enough room **even in front of the door**. Because of the press of people, the four men carrying the paralysed man could not force their way through; so they seem to have found a way up to the roof of the house, perhaps at the side or at the back. Small houses in Palestine normally had flat roofs: one would have thought that they could have let down the

4 pallet (or **mat**, as the NRSV prefers to translate it) from the edge of it, directly in front of Jesus. But if the closely packed throng of people made even this impossible, they must have broken through the dried mud-and-wattle roof and lowered the pallet on to the only spot where there would have been any space, inside the house and *behind* Jesus. Their faith was that Jesus must ultimately turn back into the house and would then be forced to attend to the sufferer.

5   **When Jesus saw their faith, he said to the paralytic, "Son, your sins are forgiven."** It was widely believed that illness came as a direct punishment for sin – a theory that was obviously inadequate to explain the whole problem of suffering (and Jesus certainly did not accept it unreservedly). Nevertheless, no one denied that there was some connection between sin and illness, and to be forgiven by God was regarded as an essential condition for recovery. Now, since people certainly did recover, it followed that God must have forgiven them their sins, either of his free mercy or in response to their repentance or their meritorious acts. But God could not be forced to forgive: he retained his sovereign freedom to give or to withold forgiveness, and no one could presume to know whether God would forgive or had forgiven until unmistakable signs of physical recovery could be seen. Jesus' unequivocal statement, **"Your sins are forgiven"**, therefore embodied a striking claim. He was not just speaking with the voice of a prophet, who by virtue of privileged insight might have known that the man was about to recover and could have inferred that God had forgiven him. Jesus declared outright that the man *was* forgiven, and so implicitly claimed the authority (which of course Mark's readers knew that he possessed) to dispense God's forgiveness

6   himself. The **scribes** were quick to recognize the apparently blasphemous
7   implications: **"Who can forgive sins but God alone?"**

Jesus' claim was certainly blasphemous – unless it was true. Could it be proved true? How (since one's forgiveness is entirely a matter between oneself and God) could it ever be known whether someone had been forgiven? The risk involved in simply stating that someone's sins were forgiven was perhaps not too great: the statement was 'easy' to utter since there could be no evidence to show whether it was true or false. If, on the other hand, the statement implied that the person making it could actually *effect* forgiveness, it was a

9   stupendous and potentially blasphemous claim. It was no **easier** to make such a claim than to effect an immediate physical improvement which, if the forgiveness was authentic, could be expected to follow anyway in due course. Jesus therefore authenticated his claim by what we now call a miracle: by giving the man an immediate recovery from his paralysis he demonstrated that his declaration, **'your sins are forgiven'**, had been effective. Mark does not say whether the scribes were convinced. This is only the beginning of a long series of events which build up the tension between Jesus and the religious authorities. Instead, he brings the episode to a close by describing the impression made on the crowd, who were less interested in the theological point at issue than in the unprecedented evidence of a powerful spiritual authority at work among them.

10   This is the first use of the phrase **the Son of Man** in this gospel. It occurs again, possibly with a somewhat different meaning, later in the chapter, but otherwise its occurrences are all clustered in the second half of the gospel. It never established itself in the early church as a formal title of Jesus, but the evidence of the gospels is unanimous that Jesus frequently used it when

speaking about himself. Why did Jesus refer to himself in this cryptic way, and how did he intend the title to be understood? A century of intensive modern research has failed to offer any certain answer. In his own language (Aramaic) the equivalent must have been *bar nasha*, 'son of a man'; and just as the frequent biblical phrase 'sons of men' (or 'children of humans' in sensitive modern translations) often means nothing more than 'people', so this idiom may have been used in certain circumstances to mean simply 'a man' or 'a certain man'. It is therefore possible that there are some instances in the gospels (for example 2.28 below) where Jesus' use of the expression meant, not anyone in particular, but people in general. But such instances are the exception. Normally it is quite clear that when Jesus talked about the Son of Man he was referring to a particular individual. There are reasons for thinking that in Aramaic the idiom was sometimes understood as an enigmatic and oblique way of referring to oneself – 'someone, you may guess who'. If so, Jesus' use of it may have been of a piece with his characteristic manner of speaking: instead of making explicit claims for himself, he challenged his hearers to make up their own minds whether or not he was a person about whom such claims could be made. Nevertheless, his use of the expression is likely to have had deeper resonances. It may have suggested, for instance, not just 'a man' but 'the Man', that is to say, a particular man who had been singled out by God to perform a significant and perhaps representative rôle in the destiny of his people or even of all human beings. There was much speculation in antiquity about the return of the perfect Man, who would restore human beings to their pristine glory and inaugurate a new era. But the form in which such speculation is most likely to have been familiar to the society in which Jesus moved was that which stemmed from some verses in the book of Daniel:

> As I watched in the night visions,
> I saw one like a human being [*like a son of man*]
>   coming with the clouds of heaven.
> And he came to the Ancient One
>   and was presented before him.
> To him was given dominion
>   and glory and kingship . . .   (7.13–14)

This 'one like a son of man' in Daniel is again a little mysterious – the book was deliberately written in cryptic imagery – but certain things can be said with reasonable certainty. The context in Daniel shows that he appeared before God (the 'Ancient One') at the moment when the judgment of the world was about to begin. He was in some sense a representative figure: he stood for the righteous who (at the time the book of Daniel was written) were being brutally oppressed by a foreign power; and Daniel's vision was that in God's judgment their destiny would be reversed; they would be vindicated for their faithfulness, and there would be given to them that ascendancy among the peoples of the world that was being denied them at the present time. This Son of Man figure certainly inspired the imagination of later thinkers and visionaries. We cannot say for certain how far the idea had progressed in Jesus' day or what associations the phrase would have aroused in ordinary people's minds. But certain elements must have been fairly constant. In particular, the Son of Man was always a personage who was (or would be) vindicated by God's final judgment, and he always had some connection, whether as representative or leader, with those who suffered on account of their faith. When therefore Jesus used the expression – which he did most frequently (at least according to Mark) in connection with his own impending sufferings – he must have been understood by at least some of his hearers to be tacitly claiming that, whatever his present humiliations, he (perhaps with other faithful ones) was destined to be vindicated by God. But none of this enables us to say exactly what he would have meant by saying that **the Son of Man has authority on earth to forgive sins.** He would hardly have intended it to be taken in the completely general sense of 'any human being', since it was the question whether *any* human being could do such a thing which was the point at issue. But whether in this case he was using the phrase as an enigmatic reference to himself or whether he intended to make a larger claim we are in no position to say.

Disciples and critics

13 **Jesus went out again beside the sea.** The exact locality of the call of Levi is left vague by Mark, except that it was near the lake; but we can fill in the details from the geography of Galilee. Capernaum, on the northern shore of the lake, was a station on the important 'road to the sea', which carried trade between the cities on the east side of the lake to the Mediterranean ports. It was also close to the frontier between the territories of Herod Antipas and Philip, and was the centre of the fishing industry on the lake. 14 It was the obvious place for a customs office or **tax booth;** and since Jesus had already become well known in Capernaum, Levi may have had time to ponder Jesus' message before deciding to respond. Curiously, Levi does not appear in the list of the twelve in 3.14–19 below (although his brother James does): this is perhaps why in Matthew's gospel the same story is told, not of Levi, but of one who was known to have been one of the twelve: Matthew.

The social status of Levi can be inferred from the next paragraph. His house[1] was large enough to accommodate a fair number round the table; the

---

[1] In the Greek, verse 15 has simply *his house* and is ambiguous: it could mean Levi's house or Jesus' house. But Jesus does not seem to have had his own house in Capernaum: he apparently stayed in that of Simon's family. Luke, at any rate, understood the house to be that of Levi (5.29), and this is the option preferred here in the NRSV.

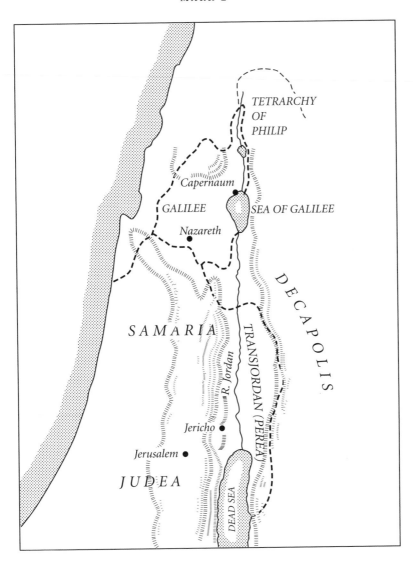

15 fact that the guests were *reclining* (rather than **sitting** – see the NRSV footnote) suggests a formal meal. He was therefore probably a well-off customs
officer in the service of Herod Antipas. But the profession of **tax collectors**
(including customs officials) was one which was frowned on by Jewish society. They were agents – even if indirectly – of the foreign occupying power
(for Herod had to pay tribute to Rome) and their profession encouraged
extortion, since they made their living by taking a proportion of the tax for
themselves. As a result they suffered exclusion from many areas of society and

were even denied certain civic and religious rights. They tended consequently to make their friends mainly among themselves and members of similarly disreputable professions; and a group of such people would be looked upon as, by definition, **sinners.**

16 At the other extreme of society were **the Pharisees**, who not merely avoided contact with such people but constituted a closed society of their own, maintaining a code of ritual observance more rigorous than that accepted by the majority of the people. They would naturally have expected a religious teacher such as Jesus to observe a similarly punctilious rule of life, and this seems to have been a recurring cause of tension between them. In this present instance Jesus' conduct seemed to them particularly shocking. Some of them (who were also **scribes**) observed him not merely conversing with these disreputable members of society but actually sharing a meal with them, which showed both his willingness to be identified with them and also a reprehensible disregard of the ritual uncleanness that might be contracted from the utensils of an non-observant household. And not only this: Jesus had now

15 gathered a number of disciples around him (indeed, **there were many who followed him**: Mark has recounted the call of only five, but now indicates that he had a larger following), and he was allowing these also to associate with disreputable company.

In reply to their scandalized comments, Jesus quoted a familiar proverb – only the sick need a physician – and then boldly applied it to his own rôle in

17 contemporary society: **"I have come to call not the righteous but sinners."** This saying will doubtless have been understood by the church in Mark's time in a general and spiritual sense: it will have been their experience that Christ's invitation had come to them, not as specially virtuous people, but as 'sinners'; and it is possible that their understanding of this saying has influenced the form in which it has come down to us. Nevertheless, these words of Jesus, as well as the proverb, would have been an apt reply to those who criticized the company he kept: he found himself constantly in opposition to those who were widely regarded as the most **righteous** in society, and sought out those who were shunned as **sinners.**

18 **Now John's disciples and the Pharisees were fasting.** Fasting was an obligation laid on all Jewish people on one day of the year; but the members of stricter religious movements tended to lay on themselves additional fast days. This was certainly true of the Pharisees (Luke 18.12) and Mark says that it was true of their **disciples** (though strictly speaking they were a closed society and did not have 'disciples' except in so far as some of them were scribes and had students). We are not surprised to hear that it was also true of the movement initiated by John the baptizer. Seeing Jesus surrounded by disciples, people[2] naturally expected it to be true also of his movement, and when they found that he apparently laid down no such rules for his

---

[2] Or John's disciples and the Pharisees: see the NRSV footnote.

followers they asked the reason. Jesus replied with a comparison. It was the
19 responsibility of the **wedding guests** to contribute gaiety to the proceedings.
Fasting – which meant doing without wine as well as food – would be quite
out of place and was in fact waived even by the Pharisees on such occasions.
"As long as they have the bridegroom with them they cannot fast." By this it
is clearly meant that Jesus' presence with his disciples was a time of rejoicing:
fasting was appropriate to a time of repentance and preparation, but now
the awaited moment had come and the old observances were out of place.
Jesus was not merely initiating a variant of the Jewish religion, his presence
implied a new era. This impact of the new on the old is illustrated by two
21 similes. Old material will not take the strain of a new patch that pulls on it
22 when it begins to shrink; and new wine (which was poured off from the vats
before it had finished fermenting) needed new and supple wineskins, not old
and brittle ones, which would burst under the pressure.

Thus understood, these verses form a connected and intelligible whole. But
the sequence is interrupted by a verse which appears to say something quite
20 different. **"The days will come when the bridegroom is taken away from
them, and then they will fast on that day."** Jesus, we have said, appears to have
been answering a question about fasting by showing in three short similes
that the new dispensation which he had come to proclaim was incompatible
with observances symbolizing repentance and preparation. Why then did he
prophesy a time when they would be resumed? Furthermore it was the firm
belief of the church, expressed in words attributed to the risen Jesus (Matthew
28.20, "I am with you always, to the end of the age"), that the Lord always
was and always would be present among those who acknowledged him. What
moment can then have been in mind when Jesus is reported as saying, **"The
days will come when the bridegroom is taken away from them"**? Was Jesus
already foreseeing (or was Mark presenting Jesus with foresight of) the days
between the crucifixion and the resurrection? If so, this comes a long time
before Jesus (at least in Mark's gospel) makes any explicit allusion to his
destiny in Jerusalem. Or is this a saying which was invented or adapted by
the early church to justify its own later observance of days of fasting? The
verse remains an enigma.

23   **One sabbath he was going through the grainfields**. A short sequence of
sayings and episodes follows which illustrates Jesus' attitude to the most fundamental and widely observed of all Jewish observances. The sabbath was
regarded as one of God's greatest gifts. It was the privilege of the Jew (sometimes even envied by pagans) to observe it and to hand down the tradition of
its observance from generation to generation. Much of this tradition was of
a very positive character: the sabbath was a day for rest and enjoyment, for
family gatherings and of course for attendance at the synagogue. The simple
direction in scripture, "you shall not do any work" (Exodus 20.10) – which
had the force of law in any Jewish community – had been elaborated into a
series of detailed and often oppressive prohibitions, and it is with these petty

restrictions – which were insisted on most rigorously by the Pharisees – that Jesus is shown frequently taking issue in the gospels. One of these is illustrated by the first episode. **His disciples began to pluck heads of grain.** It was expressly allowed in Jewish law for people to satisfy their hunger by taking a handful of fruit or corn from someone else's field (Deuteronomy 23.24–5). Though this had been somewhat modified by the time of Jesus, the action of the disciples would not normally have caused trouble. But on the sabbath, at least according to the Pharisaic interpretation of the law, such an action must be regarded differently: it fell in the same category as reaping (even though no sickle was used), which was 'work' and therefore

24 **not lawful.** Jesus, in reply, appealed to a passage of scripture which the rigorists themselves had some difficulty in explaining. The story about David is told in 1 Samuel 21. David was being pursued by Saul, and, coming to

26 the sanctuary (**the house of God**) which then existed at Nob, demanded food for his men. (The priest concerned – who was not a **high priest** – was actually Ahimelek and not his son **Abiathar**; but Abiathar was one of the two most famous priests in the time of David, and the error, whether it be Mark's or Jesus', is trivial.) It happened that the only bread available was **the bread of the Presence**, the sacred bread which was placed each week before the sanctuary and which could afterwards be eaten only by the priests (Leviticus 24.5–9). Jewish scholars were in some embarrassment to explain how it could have been right for David and his men to eat this bread. Jesus (who necessarily took responsibility for the actions of his followers) may simply have been trying to silence his critics by pointing to an instance where their own tradition of interpretation left them in difficulties; but there may also be an unspoken implication (made explicit in Matthew's account, 12.1–8) that 'a greater than David' was there who, even more than David, had authority to claim exemption from particular regulations of the law.

27 **Then he said to them.** The phrase in the Greek is one of Mark's characteristic ways of binding into the context of his narrative a saying of Jesus which may originally have been remembered in isolation. The saying adds a further touch to Mark's account of Jesus' attitude to the sabbath. Even the Pharisees were prepared to concede that if a human life (or indeed, an animal's life) was in danger it was allowable to ignore a sabbath regulation in order to save it; and they would have agreed that **"the sabbath was made for humankind, and not humankind for the sabbath"**, in the sense that the sabbath conferred a great blessing on those who observed it. It is possible that the following verse – **the Son of Man is lord even over the sabbath** – should be understood in the same way: the Aramaic phrase underlying the Greek for 'Son of Man' could mean simply 'a human being', and the later rabbis might have agreed that 'a human being is lord over the sabbath'. This may be all that the phrase means in this context; but given the implications of 'Son of Man' on other occasions when Jesus uses the title of himself, it may also be understood (as

it may have been understood by Mark and his readers) as a tacit claim to a unique status. Jesus' authority was such that he could legislate even on such matters as the observance of the sabbath.

3.1 **Again he entered the synagogue.** Mark adds one more dispute between Jesus and the Pharisees over the sabbath, this time leading up to a clear breach between them. The presence of a man **who had a withered hand** constituted a test case; for although it was permissible on the sabbath to save a life that was in danger, an act of healing when there was no urgency could constitute a breach of the sabbath regulations. It seems to have been, once again, the sheer

5 inhumanity of such an interpretation which moved Jesus **with anger,** and caused him to challenge the Pharisees with a kind of *reductio ad absurdum*:

4 suppose putting off treatment were actually to do **harm** or even precipitate death, would they still give priority to sabbath restrictions? At any rate, the story is told without any emphasis on the miraculous cure or the reaction of the people; the point is that Jesus' defiance was sufficient to set in motion a

6 plot against his life, the Pharisees seeking political help from **the Herodians.** These men, who reappear later (12.13), were presumably partisans of Herod Antipas and could be enlisted by representing Jesus' movement as a threat to the peace of the district.

The twelve and Jesus' family

7 **Jesus departed with his disciples to the sea** – that is, to the lakeside. The scene changes dramatically from an ordinary sabbath congregation in the synagogue to a huge gathering on the shore of the lake, threatening even to

9 **crush** Jesus by its size and by its insistence to get near him. Mark's list of the districts from which they had come seems to include all the main areas of Jewish population in Palestine (see the map on p. 120). So far, the movement

8 had been confined to Galilee; but now they were coming from **Judea** and **Jerusalem** in the south (omitting of course Samaria, which was regarded as an alien and hostile district), and, still further south, from **Idumea** (the Edom of the Old Testament), from **beyond the Jordan** (that is, the narrow strip of valley and highlands to the east of the river, officially called Perea), and from **the region around Tyre and Sidon,** to the north-west of Galilee, where there were substantial communities of Jews. The list gives a powerful impression of the rapid spread of Jesus' reputation as a healer. Healing involved exorcism,

11 and therefore contact with the **unclean spirits,** who knew (as Mark and his readers knew, but the crowds did not know) that Jesus' power over them came from his being **the Son of God.** Jesus may have had his own reasons for silencing them; but Mark uses the occasion to introduce what seems to be a recurring and enigmatic motif of his gospel, which scholars have come to call 'the messianic secret' and which raises a host of tantalizing questions which become acute later in the gospel (see below, p. 145). Whatever the reason, Mark states that Jesus did not wish his true nature to be widely known.

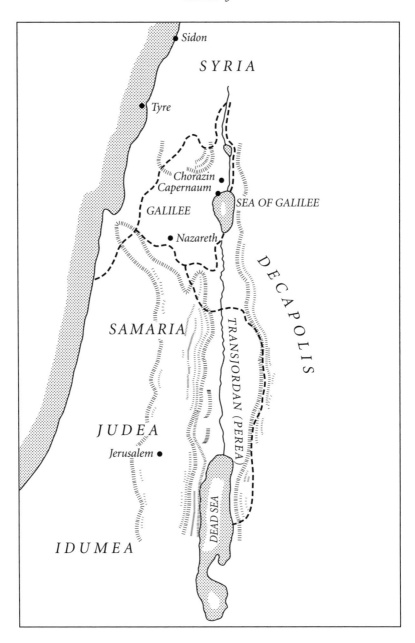

13 **He went up the mountain.** Steep and relatively inaccessible country lay not far from the lake and offered escape from the crowds and a chance to gather

14 his closest followers. **He appointed twelve,** a statement which becomes more significant in verse 16, where they become *the* twelve; and he named them **apostles,** that is to say, *agents* fully authorized to extend and continue his work in his name. These apostles were to become an essential link between Jesus' work on earth and the continuing existence of the church. Some members of this group were well known to Mark and his readers, either because of the part they played in the gospel narrative or because of their subsequent rôle in the church. This goes for the first four in the list, and of course for Judas Iscariot. But the rest seem to have been little more than names, and the lists given in different parts of the New Testament do not always agree. The important thing was evidently not the name and character of each but the fact that they were **twelve,** symbolizing that the new people of God was in important respects the successor of the old Israel with its legendary twelve tribes.

16 **Simon (to whom he gave the name Peter).** The name Peter means 'a stone', as is explained in John's gospel (1.42) and would in any case have been obvious to a Greek-speaking reader; and a reason for the name is suggested

17 in Matthew (16.18). The name **Boanerges** is difficult to translate back into Aramaic. Mark tells us it meant **Sons of Thunder,** which may be right, but it does not take us much further. There is no record of these two disciples ever having been called by this name subsequently, though their suggestion (according to Luke 9.54) that the Samaritans deserved to be consumed by fire

18 fits it quite well. **Thaddaeus** occurs only in Mark's list, replaced in Matthew (10.3) by Lebbaeus, in Luke (6.16) by 'Judas son of James'. The second Simon's added name, **the Cananaean,** is probably equivalent to 'the Zealot' (as in Luke 6.15). Not much is known of the Zealot party before the beginning of the Jewish War in 66 CE, when its members became champions of revolt against the Roman occupying forces; but it is quite likely that this fanatical anti-Roman movement was already active during the previous decades. If so, Simon seems to have been (but perhaps no longer was) a member of it.

Up to this point in Mark's narrative such opposition as Jesus had encountered (which first comes to the surface in 3.6) had been created by his attitude to sabbath regulations. The next two episodes illustrate the beginning of a deeper antagonism. That the activity of Jesus should have collected a large crowd inevitably suggested to some (or perhaps just to his family or close associates – the Greek can bear any of these meanings) that he had **"gone**

21 **out of his mind",** and that the crowds had been attracted by mere curiosity. They therefore thought it necessary **to restrain him.** Meanwhile Jesus was being confronted by a more menacing accusation. It is plausible that some

22 **scribes** should have come **down from Jerusalem** specially to investigate the reports about Jesus. They admitted the reality of Jesus' exorcisms but gave them a sinister explanation. The power by which Jesus drove out the demons

and spirits that caused (it was believed) so much of people's illness was not a good power but a worse power still. The man who professed to cure those who were possessed by devils was in a worse case himself – he 'had' (in the sense that someone 'has' a devil) **Beelzebul**,[3] who was, if not the devil in person (as Matthew states, 12.24), at least a prince among devils. Jesus attacked this as mere sophistry. It was one thing to believe (as Jesus and his contemporaries certainly believed) that there was an objective force of evil abroad which could enter people and make them act in a way untrue to their nature; and it made sense, on this view of the matter, to talk of devils, spirits, demons and so forth in the plural: these were all different manifestations of the same supernatural power. But it was quite another thing to infer from this terminology that different devils or spirits could be played off against each other for the benefit of human beings. Evil was ultimately one single power, and to talk of it being 'divided against itself' was a contradiction in terms. It was as silly as saying that 'Satan could drive out Satan'.

23 Jesus puts his answer in the form of two **parables**. Though many of his contemporaries told parables, it is Jesus who has made the form immortal. But the word itself did not necessarily mean anything so extended and elaborate as most of Jesus' stories. In Greek it meant any comparison or simile; and the Hebrew word to which it corresponds in the gospels had an even wider range of meanings – proverbs, riddles, illustrations and stories. Thus
25 Jesus' answer here consists of two short illustrations, the first from a **house divided against itself**, which could well be a political allusion, the 'house' being a dynastic line such as the Herods: if they quarrelled (as they were liable to do) they could bring their kingdoms to an end. The second uses the
27 figure of **a strong man**. This may be simply an analogy with the contest with Satan: Jesus is 'strong' enough to rob him of his victims. But there may be another meaning. According to the mythology of his time, the monstrous power of evil was due to be 'bound' for a period before the end of the world (Revelation 20.2), so that underneath the comparison may lie an implicit claim of Jesus to be the person destined to bring all the forces of evil into subjection.

On any interpretation, the saying which follows is hard to understand and has caused much agonizing among Christian readers. The first part of it fits easily enough into the general pattern of Jesus' teaching. Some Jewish thinkers had drawn up a whole list of sins which in their view put the sinner outside the range of divine forgiveness – and it must be remembered that the legal code authorized by scripture specified a number of offences punishable by the death penalty or by permanent exclusion from the community. Jesus'

---

[3] The name occurs nowhere outside the New Testament and its origin and meaning are unknown. An old theory is that it is a form of *Baalzebub*, 'the God of Ekron' (2 Kings 1.2), and in view of this theory many Latin versions and the older English translations reproduce the name in the form *Beelzebub*. But all Greek manuscripts have *Beelzebul* (or in some cases *Beezebul*).

teaching stands at the opposite extreme of such thinking, indeed, is a radical
28 departure from it: *anyone* may repent and be forgiven. **"I tell you, people will be forgiven for their sins and whatever blasphemies they utter."** Why then does he make the severe exception which follows? And what does it mean, to 'blaspheme against the Holy Spirit'? Mark indicates the way he
30 understands this himself: **for they had said, "He has an unclean spirit."** Confronted, that is to say, by a clear instance of the defeat of evil powers (which in Mark's theology indicated that the Holy Spirit was at work), they had rejected this clear evidence of God's activity. Mark may have wished his readers to infer that, since no clearer instance could have been given them of the presence of the Spirit, nothing further could happen which would lead them to repentance, and therefore there was no chance that they would adopt the attitude necessary to obtain forgiveness. In the wider context of a doctrine of God's mercy this is a hard saying. But Mark's intention may be more limited. He has to explain how it happened that human beings crucified the Son of God. If they were capable of 'blaspheming' the clearest manifestation of his divine power, then it was understandable that they would not stop short of destroying Jesus. Nothing would move them to repentance; therefore nothing could qualify them for forgiveness.

31   **Then his mother and his brothers came.** It is perhaps surprising that there is no mention of his father. Was Joseph dead by this time? And the presence of brothers (mentioned again in 6.3) is a problem with regard to the later tradition of Mary's perpetual virginity: those who accept it have to adopt the slightly artificial (but possible) explanation that they were half-brothers or even cousins. Mark does not say what happened when his family arrived to 'restrain' him (verse 21); their presence simply gives him the cue for recording a saying of Jesus which may have been remembered apart from any particular
35 context (it may possibly be alluded to in Romans 8.29): **"Whoever does the will of God is my brother and sister and mother."**

The parables

4.1 **Again he began to teach.** Just as Jesus' fame as a healer had drawn such crowds that he had to have a boat ready so as not to be crushed by the crowds (3.9), so his fame as a teacher drew a crowd so large that he **got into a boat.** Mark evidently intended to set the two scenes in parallel, and just as in the first he gave some notable examples of Jesus' work of healing, so now, for the first time in his gospel, he gives a sample of Jesus' teaching.

In fact, however, this sample can hardly have been typical. Admittedly it consists mainly of 'parables', which were one of Jesus' most characteristic figures of speech; but the point of these particular parables is not so much to convey an ethical or religious challenge as to illustrate how the teaching as a whole was to be understood. They answer the question, not *what* Jesus taught, but *how* he taught. In this they continue an important theme from the previous chapter. Just as Jesus' works of healing had provoked opposition as well as admiration, with the result that his opponents, having 'blasphemed against the Holy Spirit', had now lost all chance of repenting and being forgiven, so his teaching was such as to arouse different reactions among his hearers, some of whom would inevitably be deaf to his message – God

9 would not give them **ears to hear**, a phrase which evokes Deuteronomy 29.4 and recalls the obstinacy of the people of Israel in the face of the spectacular benefits they received at the time of the exodus. What was the explanation of this? Why was the teaching of the Son of God ignored or rejected by some of those who heard it? In the case of the acts of healing, Mark was able to give two reasons for this opposition: some thought Jesus was mad, others that he was inspired by the devil. Neither of these reasons would account for the rejection of his teaching. And so Mark opens his presentation of Jesus' teaching with a discourse that bears upon this very question.

3 **"A sower went out to sow."** The first of the parables describes usual farming practice in Mediterranean lands in antiquity. After the harvest (around June) the farmer would probably plough his fields at least once, perhaps several times, during the summer months, both to prevent the dry earth from becoming too hard and to keep it free of weeds. In November or December (the time of the first heavy rains, when there was enough moisture in the ground to allow the seeds to germinate) the field would be sown, the sower casting the seed by hand and probably varying the quantity of the seed to the quality of the soil. Very soon after the sowing the seed would be ploughed in to protect it from the birds. The field would be bounded on at least one side by a path that could not be ploughed over; there would be places where the limestone rock underlying the soil came close to the surface, making for

5 **rocky ground** and soil too shallow to hold enough moisture; there would be
7 areas where the **thorns** or thistles could not be eradicated. A small amount of
4 seed (which is what **some seed** suggests in the Greek) would inevitably fall in these places: a little wastage was inevitable and would not normally be worth commenting on. The important thing was the seed that fell in the productive part of the field. Most of this would grow to fruition, often producing

8 several side-shoots. A return of **thirty** to **sixty** grains from each plant was not unimaginable; only **a hundredfold** sounds like deliberate exaggeration (which, after all, Jesus was fond of).

But if the parable merely describes ordinary farming practice with which his hearers were perfectly familiar, what made it interesting? The answer must be that Jesus, with a touch of vivid and poetic observation, dwells on precisely those details which would not normally be thought to be worth mentioning – the few grains of corn that fell outside the cultivable area. From the farmer's point of view the wastage would be negligible. It would hardly occur to him to notice it and still less to censure the sower for allowing a few seeds to fall on the path. But Jesus, by describing no fewer than three ways in which a small amount of grain might be lost, put all the emphasis on the fact that even when the harvest was good some wastage was inevitable, some seeds would come to nothing. In the same way, perhaps, however successful his own work might appear to be, it was not surprising if there was some wastage, some indifference, even some opposition.

If this is the natural interpretation of the parable, it is also one that is consistent with what we can imagine to have been Jesus' understanding of himself and his mission. He presented an unavoidable challenge, and it was inevitable that some would react against him. But Mark evidently had reason to think that there was a further meaning in the parable, for which a more subtle interpretation was required. Consequently, before going on with the scene of Jesus' public teaching he records some conversation which Jesus had
10 in private with **those who were around him along with the twelve**. This change of scene puts the matter in a different perspective. The emphasis in the parable appeared to be on the small but inevitable amount of wastage: a few will always remain unfruitful even though the main harvest develops abundantly. But now it is the other way round. The phenomenon being explained is no longer the small (though potent) opposition to Jesus' teaching compared with the crowds who press in to hear. It is those who understand it who are now the small minority, and what has to be explained is the fact
11 that the great majority remain **outside** this charmed circle.

This change of perspective perhaps belongs to a shift from the time of Jesus to the time of the early church. Jesus, at this stage in the narrative, had more success than opposition. He was more aware of the crowds who strained to see and hear him than of the enemies who were already plotting against him. But for the early church things were very different. The Christians were a small movement in the midst of a large and (particularly on the Jewish side) hostile world; and to account for this hostility they were glad to find an explanation in a prophecy of Isaiah (6.9–10). That great prophet had been entrusted with the authentic word of God. Yet the people would not listen. Why? It must have been because God had intended it that way and dulled
12 their understanding – that they might '**look, but not perceive . . . listen, but not understand**' – and it was this that prevented them from turning to God and obtaining his forgiveness. Paul is reported to have used the same text when confronted by the opposition of his fellow Jews in Rome (Acts 28.26–7); and doubtless the prophecy helped many Christians in the early days of the church to understand their own position and the unyielding attitude of their neighbours.

Did Jesus quote this text himself? Mark says that he did, and this is quite plausible: there will have been many occasions later on when it may have helped him to understand and interpret the massive opposition which he encountered. But is it appropriate to the context here, where Jesus has more admirers than opponents? Or has Mark (or the source from which he derived his narrative) introduced it in order to explain a somewhat different sense of the word 'parable' from that which is exemplified in the story of the sower?

The word 'parable' (or its equivalent in Jesus' language) could mean a variety of figures of speech, including riddles and enigmatic sayings. The parables of Jesus, though they may have been clear enough to those who first heard them, were doubtless relevant to the circumstances and context in which they were delivered; but when the original setting came to be forgotten they may have seemed less easy to understand and have become 'parables' in the sense of mysterious and teasing utterances. In which case the fact that Jesus taught 'in parables' could be held to explain why some (indeed, a great many, as it seemed to the first Christians) did not accept his teaching: they did not understand it! It was only to his intimate disciples (so this explanation ran),
11 and through them to the church, that Jesus had given the clue, **the secret** (literally, *the mystery*[4]) **of the kingdom of God.**

As one example of the kind of privileged explanation which was necessary (on this view) to understand Jesus' teaching, Mark appends a detailed interpretation of the parable of the sowing. He attributes the interpretation to Jesus, and it may well have come down to Mark along with the parable itself. But scholars have found serious reasons for doubting whether Jesus was the author of it. It contains a number of expressions more characteristic of the later preaching of the Greek-speaking church than of Jesus; its attempt (which involves slight confusion: the seed appears to be both the 'word' and its hearers) to give a one-to-one equivalence between each moment in the story and its meaning contrasts with the single thrust of most of Jesus' parables; the circumstances which prevent the proper reception of the word
17, 19 (**trouble or persecution** or **the lure of wealth**) belong more to the experience of the church than to that of the crowd listening to Jesus' teaching for the first time; and the analysis of different kinds of unbelief, psychologically accurate though it may be, hardly springs from the parable itself but has to be read into it. Mark could plausibly say that if this was how the parables were to be understood they would indeed, be 'mysterious' to anyone who did not possess the clue. If Jesus taught like this, no wonder that (at least in the end) so few followed him. Mark indeed, goes so far as to suggest that Jesus' parables were all like this (though he contradicts this himself with the parable of the tenants of a vineyard (12.1–12), of which the meaning was
13 only too clear to his opponents): **"Do you not understand this parable? Then how will you understand all the parables?"** And at the end of the
34 chapter he explicitly makes the same point: the disciples were privately given the key to all the teaching which to those outside their circle remained simply 'parables' – mysterious and perplexing. This is one of Mark's answers to a question which runs through his gospel: why was Jesus not immediately recognized as the Son of God, teaching with such authority that he could not be gainsaid? Because he deliberately gave his teaching in a form which could

---

[4] This word appears first in Jewish literature in the book of Daniel and has a special meaning: the secret purpose of God which will one day be revealed. See below, pp. 641–2.

be understood only by those whom he let into the 'secret'. If so, then it is possible that he missed the real 'mystery' of this parable, in which there are distinct resonances of the style of apocalyptic writers describing the exceptionally rich harvest (of either good or bad) which God would reap at the final judgment. In this way, perhaps, Mark develops his own understanding of Jesus' parables here, even at the expense of breaking into his first account of Jesus' public teaching – which is resumed without apology at verse 21.

21 **He said to them** – and 'them' is once again the crowds, straining to hear Jesus' teaching by the lakeside, just as on a previous occasion they had pressed upon him to witness his powers of healing. Mark has just reported that Jesus' parables were such as to mystify all except those who belonged to the privileged circle of the disciples and were given the clue to their interpretation. He now gives some examples of precisely this kind of enigmatic parable. All but one of them (the seed scattered on the land, verses 26–9) reappear in Matthew and Luke, who by placing them in a certain context (as in Matthew 13.12) or by making minor alterations (as in Luke 8.16–18) give some hint as to how they understood them. But Mark neither offers an esoteric explanation of them (as he does for the parable of the sowing) nor offers by his editing any suggestion about their meaning. The sayings remain mysterious, apparently illustrating what he has just said about their effect on their hearers. It may be that the point of them was already obscure to him, as it has remained to their readers ever since.

The sayings themselves are characteristically vivid, drawn from life, and sometimes with the ring of proverbs. The **lamp** is the ordinary olive-oil lamp that has been found in thousands among the ruins of the ancient world, shaped like a small flattened tea-pot with the wick in the spout. To light a room it would be put **on the lampstand**. Scholars have laboured to find reasons why someone might think of putting it **under the bushel basket,**[5] **or under the bed**; but we may be content to see here an instance of Jesus' characteristic liking for slightly grotesque exaggeration. Proverbially (the following verses 22 read like proverbs) anything **hidden** (such as the meaning of the parables? 24 or the true nature of Jesus?) will be brought into view one day. Or take the bazaar: the fair and generous merchant does better in the end, but (as in all economies) the poor get poorer, the rich richer (in understanding the parables? in understanding the gospel? in faith?). The seed is sown, apparently by a rather casual farmer who does nothing to it until the moment for harvest has come; the actual growth (meaning the spread of the gospel? or the approach of God's judgment?) continues mysteriously and quietly – the harvest, at all events, was a biblical symbol often used by Jesus for the last 29 judgment, and the words **he goes in with his sickle, because the harvest has come** are a reference to Joel 3.13, where this judgment is described.

---

[5] A new and surprising translation of a word which means a *measuring vessel*. Putting a lamp under any kind of basket would be to invite disaster!

31 The **mustard seed** was proverbially the smallest seed in the ground and, by comparison, the plant which grew from it was prodigious – over 2 metres (6 feet) tall in Galilee. But when Jesus uses language about it which in Daniel (4.12) and Ezekiel (17.13; 31.6) is applied to a massive tree, he seems again to be indulging his taste for exaggeration. We are told that these two parables

30 illustrate **the kingdom of God**, but there is no clue where we should look to see it – in the small beginning and astonishing growth of the gospel? of the church? of faith in the human heart? Mark seems to have kept faithfully to his programme of showing that Jesus' teaching was likely to sound mysterious to the mass of his hearers.

Activity further afield

36 **They took him with them in the boat, just as he was.** Apart from a brief interlude of private instruction (4.10–20), the whole of Jesus' teaching has been given from a boat by the lakeside (4.1), and indeed, all his activity has been located on the west side (or rather in or near the north-west corner) of the Lake of Tiberias. Now, without even getting out of the boat, he is reported to have crossed over to the east side with his disciples. It is a little curious that

35 the crossing should have been undertaken **when evening had come.** They would then have reached the other side two or three hours later, long after nightfall; but the events which followed clearly took place in daylight. Mark may not have been much concerned with such details; but if he was, then he must have envisaged the crossing as having been combined with an all-night fishing expedition, during which it would have been natural for Jesus to take the opportunity to get some sleep; for if the boat was big enough to hold a whole group of disciples (and it seems some were) it could well have had a raised stern and space to sleep underneath.

The episode, at any rate, is recounted quite factually: details such as the

36, 38 **other boats** and the **cushion** may even suggest the memory of eyewitnesses;

37 and the **great windstorm** was of the kind for which the lake is notorious, and which can take even the most experienced fisherman by surprise. But Mark is likely to have been more concerned with its appropriateness as the first of a series of episodes in which Jesus resumed his activity as what we would now call a miracle-worker (though we need not necessarily call this one a 'miracle': it is always possible that the wind would have dropped just then anyway!): Jesus 'rebuking' the wind recalls his 'rebuke' of unclean spirits (1.25; 3.12, where the Greek has the same word). Moreover, there are distinct resonances of the story of Jonah sleeping through a storm and having to be roused (Jonah 1.5–6) – and 'something greater than Jonah' was present (Matthew 12.41) – and of the many Old Testament passages where God himself shows his power over the elements. And Mark may well have been aware also of the message of the story for the early church, struggling with the storms of persecution and hardship – as Matthew and Luke clearly were.

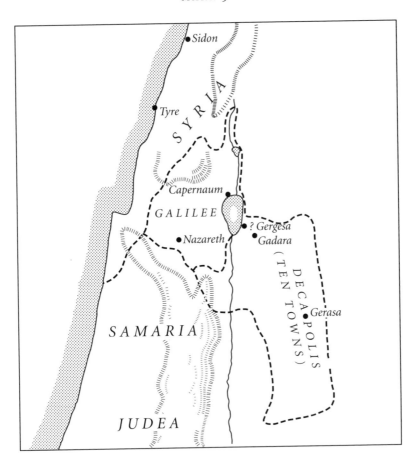

At the same time the emphasis he gives to the disciples' reaction at the end is of a piece with his portrayal of them as painfully slow to come to faith and understanding, despite a manifestation of his power that was sufficient to inspire **great awe.**

41

5.1 **They came to the other side of the sea, to the country of the Gerasenes.** Gerasa was one of the most important of the group of Greco-Roman cities which lay for the most part on the eastern side of the Jordan and which, though subject to Rome, constituted a league known as the Decapolis (the Ten Towns). Later in the century Gerasa began an ambitious building programme and became one of the most splendid cities of the east – its ruins (now known as Jerash) are still spectacular. But even before that, those of Mark's readers who knew little about Palestine were likely to have heard of it. This may be why Mark calls the scene of this episode **the country of the Gerasenes:** with the name, and with the detail of the herd of pigs (inconceivable in Jewish territory), he will have succeeded in conveying the impression of the very

129

different pagan world in which Jesus set foot when he crossed over the lake. But as a matter of geographical detail the name creates difficulties. The scene is laid by the shore, not far from a town (verse 14). Gerasa lay some 30 miles away from the lake, more than a day's walk, and no part of the shore could properly be called 'Gerasene'. A few Greek manuscripts, following the version in Matthew, give *Gadarene* (see the NRSV footnote). Gadara was another city of the Decapolis, somewhat closer than Gerasa: it lay in the hills within sight of the lake. But this city also was too far away to fit the details of the story. A third possibility, *Gergesa*, can possibly be identified with a site on the edge of the lake which has some of the required features, and this name too occurs in some manuscripts. But in any case, Mark may have been more anxious to give the area the feel of a sophisticated pagan environment than to offer geographical precision; and 'Gerasa' would have served this purpose admirably.

Just as the area was exceptional for Jesus' activity, so too the case of pos-
2 session is described as an exceptional one. The **unclean spirit** gave its victim
9 superhuman strength, and its name, **Legion** (a Roman military unit of nor-
mally at least six thousand men), put it in a class apart from the more common cases of possession by even, say, seven demons. Yet on seeing Jesus it reacted
7 just as other unclean spirits had: it recognized him by his name (**Jesus**) and his real nature (**Son of the Most High God**) and acknowledged his superior power. It was doubtless to illustrate Jesus' authority over even such a demon, and even in gentile surroundings, that Mark recorded the story. But there are some further details which make the story exceptional. The first is Jesus' conversation with the spirit. Usually he simply commands it to come out. Here he also asks its name (which was standard exorcist's technique, though it was normally done before, not after, the command to come out, as a way of getting control of the spirit). The second is the title, **Most High God**, which was not a Jewish phrase but belonged to the vocabulary of Hellenistic cults – another detail which gives an exotic flavour to the scene. The third is the destruction of the pigs. It was to be expected in an exorcism that the devil would make a final demonstration of its power before leaving its victim. This usually took the form of a paroxysm in the victim, though stories were told of other violent manifestations (such as a statue being overturned nearby). In this way the onlookers would be assured that the spirit had been decisively
13 overcome. A herd of **two thousand** pigs would hardly have been a common sight even in a pagan land, and their loss would have been a major catastro-phe for their owner – if indeed, they were all lost: pigs are normally capable of swimming! But neither the narrator nor, it seems, the crowd which soon collected was interested in this aspect of the matter. The miracle, in the eyes of all, was the recovery of one who had been possessed by so formidable a spirit.
15, 17 It was because of this that **they were afraid** and begged Jesus to **leave their neighborhood**. Nevertheless, since Jesus would not allow the subject of the cure to go with him, the evidence of the miracle, in the person of a notorious

demoniac suddenly restored to health, was soon widely acknowledged in an area far outside the normal range of his activity.

The two healing miracles which follow are woven into each other in a way that suggests the hand of an expert narrator. (Mark was particularly adept at
22 this.) **Leaders of the synagogue** were officials elected by the community to be responsible (though usually one at a time) for the maintenance and worship of the synagogue, and they were necessarily among the most respected members of the local community. That one of them should have appealed to Jesus was therefore a sign that he had by now achieved considerable fame as a healer. But although the present section of the gospel contains a group of episodes which gives substance to this reputation, Mark does not emphasize this aspect. Instead, attention is focused on the 'faith' of the victim or of the close relatives. It was said of a number of people in antiquity that contact even with their clothes could heal diseases (compare Acts 5.16; 19.12); and this was explained in terms of a magical 'power' going out of them. Mark does not exclude this explanation, but he makes it clear that the cure was never-
34 theless much more than magic: **"Daughter, your faith has made you well"** – she may have come to Jesus as a last resort, having impoverished herself with more 'conventional' healers; but Jesus (or Mark) judges her importunacy to have been a sign, not of desperation, but of **faith**. Similarly with the restoring to life of a little girl who had just died. This was of course the supreme miracle for anyone to perform, and very few had ever been credited with it. The story is told in vivid detail, down to the actual words spoken by Jesus in his own
42 language, Aramaic. Those who witnessed it were duly **overcome with amazement**. But Mark's emphasis is again on 'faith': to the girl's father Jesus says,
36 **"Do not fear, only believe."** And (though this can hardly be conveyed in a modern English translation) the words used of the girl's recovery were highly suggestive to Christian readers. For those (Jews and Christians alike) who believed in a future resurrection, the righteous who had died were in reality
39 **not dead but sleeping**, waiting for the great moment of awakening; and the
41, 42 words translated **get up**, **got up** are those which the first Christians instinctively used to describe the raising of Jesus from the dead. On this occasion Jesus did not merely bring the girl back to life; he gave a symbolic demonstration of the wonderful reality, known to faith, of resurrection from the dead. It is hard to imagine that such a sensational event could have remained
43 unknown. Jesus, when he **strictly ordered them that no one should know**, could have been trying to protect the girl until she had **something to eat** or planning his own escape from the crowds; or else we have here an editorial note by Mark, reinforcing the message that Jesus' true nature was not yet to be fully revealed.

There follows what (at least according to Mark) was Jesus' one visit to
6.1 his **hometown**, Nazareth. He followed his regular practice of attending the synagogue on the sabbath and making use of an invitation to preach in order
2 to spread his message. Inevitably, he made an impression: **many who heard**

him were astounded. Yet the dominant reaction of his audience was sceptical. How could one who had grown up among them and practised a trade,[6] and whose family was still well known to them, pretend to speak as if he had all the training and authority of a professional expositor of scripture? Their
3 scepticism was an obstacle; indeed, they **took offense at him** – in the Greek, a technical expression drawn from the Greek Old Testament for the shattering of faith: the incredulity of Jesus' hearers was a *stumbling block* (*skandalon* – see the footnote in the NRSV) which prevented them from accepting his
6 authority and believing in him. By contrast, their **unbelief** points up the 'faith' that has been a key factor in the two previous episodes. Jesus replied
4 to them with a familiar proverb, which is placed here by Mark (followed by Matthew, 13.57) and is entirely apposite – indeed, the episode might almost have been invented to illustrate it. John, on the other hand (4.44), places it in a quite different context: the occasion on which Jesus actually said it may no longer have been known.

The disciples' mission and the death of John the Baptist

Then he went about among the villages teaching. The Greek is even less precise: 'he *was going*' about'. At some stage during this activity (but Mark evidently did not know at what stage) Jesus enlarged the scope of his work by sending out his disciples as missionaries. They had the double task of carrying
7 on Jesus' onslaught against the powers of evil in the form of **unclean spirits**
12 and of proclaiming **that all should repent**. It was a mission very similar to that which was subsequently entrusted to the church and there can be little doubt that, at least in some of the gospel accounts, the practice and experience of the early Christian missionaries have influenced the record of Jesus' charge to his disciples (see above on Matthew 10). It is hard to be
13 sure, for instance, whether the detail of anointing **with oil** is an authentic element of the disciples' mission (for it is not mentioned anywhere else in connection with Jesus' activity) or is a reflection of the subsequent practice of the church (James 5.15). In either case it is clearly not thought of as a medicinal treatment (for which indeed oil was often used, Luke 10.34), but as an instrument or sign of supernatural power over disease. But even if such details are uncertain, there is no reason to doubt that Jesus, on at least one occasion (Luke records two: see below on Luke 10.1), sent his disciples out on a mission and that his charge to them was faithfully remembered.

The manner in which they were to proceed is vividly drawn. Apart from
8 what was basically necessary for anyone walking across the country – a **staff**
9 and **sandals** – they were not to take any of the provisions of food, clothes

---

[6] The alternative reading, *son of the carpenter and Mary*, is probably an assimilation to Matthew's version, which seeks to dispel the notion (that some may have found repugnant) that Jesus had plied a trade.

or money with which prudent travellers would normally equip themselves before a long journey. There may also be the implication that they were not to go as beggars – the word translated **bag** can mean the pouch in which a beggar, or even perhaps an itinerant Cynic philosopher who despised all possessions, put what was given to him. Two reasons suggest themselves for this command to travel light. First, the mission seems to have taken place in Galilee, which was densely populated: they would never have been far from a village. Secondly (and this is more important) they were to expect hospitality (as any traveller could who had good reason for the visit) and to accept it. They were, however, not to exploit this by moving from house to house in turn: their work was presumably too urgent and their time too precious. On the other hand, the kind of reception they had would be a sign of people's readiness to hear them. If it were unfavourable, they were to perform a gesture which was a characteristic Jewish way of emphasizing the 'holiness' of the land: after being abroad, or in any place regarded as 'unclean', Jews would shake the dust from their feet before they stepped in the holy land so as not to contaminate it. The disciples' gesture would be interpreted in the same way: the place which did not receive them could have no part in the coming kingdom.

Mark separates the departure of the disciples from their return by a narrative which bears only indirectly on the theme of the gospel. It is certainly true that **John the baptizer** was put to death by Herod Antipas: the fact is recorded also by Josephus. It is also true that, just as John's preaching was the forerunner of Jesus' preaching, so his death prefigured Jesus' death and perhaps for that reason won a place in the gospel story. But the vivid details of Mark's account may also be there for their own sake. The story as told in Mark is somewhat different from Josephus' account: according to Josephus, Herod's motive was mainly political, while in Mark it is personal. But Mark's version is perfectly consistent with what is known of Herod's character; and although it is told more in the manner of a *raconteur* than of what would pass for history today (though Herodotus, the 'father of history', has many such stories), it may well have a basis in fact.

14–15 **Some were saying . . . others said**. The rumours to which Jesus' activity gave rise all tended in one direction. There was no special reason to think that one who had been **raised from the dead** would be capable of performing miracles; on the other hand it was a widespread popular belief that the new age, which was confidently expected by many in the near future and would be marked by a decisive triumph of good over evil, would be ushered in by the return of one of the great Old Testament figures, Moses, Elijah or **one of the prophets of old**. In so far, then, as the activity of Jesus seemed to betoken the arrival of this new age, it was natural to identify him with one of these; and following the same line of thought it might even have seemed possible that John the baptizer himself had been someone in the same tradition who would 'come again' at the appointed time in the person of Jesus. (A belief in metempsychosis was not unknown.) Mark, at any rate, by way of introducing the following story, makes Herod think along these lines.

17   **For Herod himself.** Herod Antipas had been tetrarch (and doubtless known locally as 'king') of Galilee and Perea since the death of his father, Herod the Great, in 4 BCE. While returning from a visit to Rome he had fallen in love with Herodias, the wife of his brother. This brother did not possess a kingdom of his own at the time, which may be one of the reasons why Herodias left him and was prepared to marry Herod Antipas. So far as we know, the brother's name, like his father's, was simply Herod: that Mark calls him Philip may simply be because he confused him with Philip the tetrarch, another of Herod's sons, who in fact was not Herodias' husband but her son-in-law. Herod Antipas then prepared to divorce his first wife (who anticipated him by returning to her father's court at Petra) and duly married Herodias, who brought with her the child of her first marriage, Salome. (Josephus gives us her name.[7]) The girl would have been about twenty years old. All sorts of unfortunate results followed from this marriage, including, predictably enough, a war with the Nabatean king of Petra, the father of Herod Antipas' first wife. But in the eyes of strict Jews there was a further reason for disapproval, in that by biblical law it was unlawful to marry a brother's wife while the brother was still alive. This is the background to John the baptizer's remonstrances and Herodias' grudge against him. According to Josephus the scene of John's imprisonment and execution was Machaerus, Herod's frontier stronghold on the east side of the Dead Sea. The gospel narrative is not incompatible with this, though Herod's luxurious palace in Tiberias on the Sea of Galilee would certainly have been a more appropriate setting for the story of the fatal banquet.

Feeding the crowds, disputing with Pharisees

30   **The apostles gathered around Jesus.** For the first and only time in Mark's gospel the disciples on their return from their mission are called **the apostles**. The word, which means literally 'one who is sent out', was a technical term for an agent or a messenger entrusted with an official mission; but in the early church it had just one meaning: it meant the select group of disciples who, having witnessed the resurrection, were entrusted with the task of founding the church. It is a striking fact that this title is so seldom read back into the gospel narrative; but there is perhaps good reason for it here in that the disciples had just acquitted themselves of the kind of task which was performed by agents or emissaries and which was subsequently to be the particular mission of the 'apostles'.

---

[7] Some manuscripts of Mark appear to contradict this, calling the dancer another **Herodias**, a daughter of Herod. See the NRSV footnote.

Jesus' reaction to the crowds who had just frustrated his intention of
31, 34 sailing to **a deserted place** was that they were **like sheep without a shepherd**.
This biblical expression (Numbers 27.17; Ezekiel 34.5) was more than just a
picturesque metaphor for an aimless multitude. It evoked the whole history
and destiny of Israel. God himself had 'shepherded' his people, keeping them
together as one flock in the face of all disintegrating pressures, leading them
into their own land and towards the fulfilment of that moral and religious
ideal which their scriptures held before them. But God had also deputed this
'shepherding' to the people's own religious and political leaders, who had
again and again failed to live up to their responsibility – the classic description
of this failure is in Ezekiel 34. And it was the same (Jesus implies) in his own
time. The religious leaders, particularly the scribes and the Pharisees, had
failed to give the guidance expected of them; this is a recurring theme in the
gospel. And it was because of this failure that Jesus' heart went out to the
crowd – **they were like sheep without a shepherd**. But there was still more
in this phrase. It was promised in scripture (and the hope was still alive in
later Jewish writings) that God would finally send a leader who would be a
true shepherd. Jesus, possibly seeing himself in this rôle, began to fulfil it by
showing, first, that he could **teach them many things**, and secondly, that he
was aware of their physical needs.

The four gospels between them give no fewer than six accounts of a feeding
miracle of this kind, and clearly the church cherished the memory of it. Just
as, in Mark at least, the healing miracles are not presented merely as the feats
of a wonder-worker, so the miracle of the feeding had a deeper significance.
40   The scene is not a picnic but a formal meal. The men are made to sit down **in
groups of hundreds and of fifties** (perhaps recalling Moses' organization of
the people in the desert, Exodus 18.25), and one of the Greek words translated
in groups gives a distinct flavour of a banquet. Jesus proceeds like a devout
Jewish host to say the blessing and break the bread himself. The crowd is thus
brought into table fellowship with him – an expressive symbol of human
solidarity in that culture. The whole scene could hardly fail to be remembered
in later years when the church began to meet together for that eucharistic
meal by which they received spiritual sustenance and experienced their Lord
as still somehow present among them as their host.

The traditional site of this miracle is a small and luxuriant plain in the
north-west corner of the lake, which appears not to have been populated in the
time of Christ and which lay only about an hour's walk west of Capernaum.
If this was in fact the place, and if Mark or the tradition he was using was
sufficiently familiar with the country for us to be able to rely on the details –
and both these assumptions are open to question – then the course of the
following events may be imagined as follows. It had been quite possible for the
crowds to gather on the shore from the neighbouring towns before the boat
reached the spot: the boat had therefore clearly not crossed the lake from one
side to the other (which would have been much quicker than walking all the

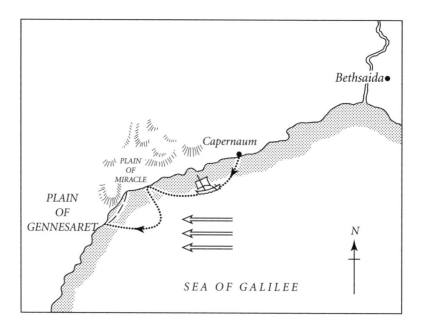

way round) but had simply moved some distance westward along the shore
31 in order to reach **a deserted place**. If it started from Capernaum (which was
the centre of Jesus' activities) then the traditional site of the feeding miracle
would be about the right distance away. After that episode Jesus apparently
intended to do what the crowds had done, that is to say, to walk east towards
Bethsaida after he had climbed away from the shore for some solitude in
which to pray; he would then walk round on foot while the boat returned
the way it had come.

45 Thus, **he made his disciples get into the boat and go on ahead to the
other side, to Bethsaida**. Bethsaida was only a few miles further east than
Capernaum on the other side of the mouth of the Jordan, hardly 'the other
side' of the lake,[8] but a certain distance eastward from the traditional site of
48 the feeding miracle. The disciples, however, found themselves rowing **against
an adverse wind** possibly so powerful that by the early hours of the morning
(literally *the fourth watch* – Mark uses the Roman reckoning) they had not
merely made no headway but were actually drifting (we must suppose) in the
opposite direction. Seeing this, Jesus set out south-westward to meet them
and apparently struck out (in the shallows?) across the water – there is a rocky
hill west of the plain of the miracle which runs right down to the shore of
the lake; Jesus would have lost sight of the boat if he had walked round it or
over it. **He intended to pass them by**, presumably because he wished to get

---

[8] The writers or editors of some early manuscripts saw the difficulty and omitted the
words *to the other side*.

to the land in time to meet them. But once they had seen him he joined them
53 in the boat. So **they came to land at Gennesaret**. The plain of Gennesaret
lay still further to the west, and they were now further from their destination
than when they had set out. Indeed, the adverse wind had prevented them
from making the crossing at all; but they were now at least in a different place
(which is all the Greek need mean by **crossed over**), though not, as it turned
out, away from the crowds.

In some such way as this it is just possible to fit the events recorded by
Mark into the geography of the lakeside. But such topographical precision
is unlikely to have been his main concern. What he had to record was an
apparently miraculous feat which Jesus was remembered to have performed.
As usual he was anxious not to present it as a freak or as an ostentatious
performance by a wonder-man, and so he concentrated on the reaction of
52 the disciples. **Their hearts were hardened** – which is exactly what Jesus had
accused the scribes and Pharisees of previously. The phrase denotes an almost
wilful lack of response to a revelation of God's presence in the world. Just as
the disciples **did not understand about the loaves**, failing to see the event as
a demonstration of Jesus' true 'shepherding', so now, we are to suppose, they
failed to see the implications of his mastery of the elements: their minds still
worked at the level of popular ghost stories, and their dominant reaction was
simply fear.

Yet for all this deeper purpose, the fact remained that Jesus performed
53–6 many miracles, particularly miracles of healing; and the chapter ends with a
brief summary of this constant activity, without any attempt at interpretation.

7.1   **Now when the Pharisees and some of the scribes who had come from
Jerusalem gathered around him**. Almost from the beginning of the gospel
these men have been constantly in the background, representing a sinister
and powerful opposition to Jesus. Not only were they allied to an influential
political party in Galilee (the Herodians, 3.6), they were in touch with the
religious authorities in Jerusalem (whence some of these **scribes** had come,
perhaps for the express purpose of reporting on Jesus' activities). So far,
conflict with them had been focused mainly on specific questions of sabbath
observance. But now their antagonism finds a target in a question of ritual
purity, which provokes Jesus into a fierce counter-attack against the whole
principle on which religious practices were based.

The dispute began because some of Jesus' disciples were observed to be
2 **eating**[9] **with defiled hands**. Mark explains that this meant **without washing
them**. It is certainly true that in the next century (if not earlier) it was a
strict rule among orthodox Pharisaic Jews to wash their hands before eating,
not for hygienic reasons, but in order to avoid the risk of contaminating
their food with any ritually 'unclean' substance which might be on their

[9] The translators have omitted two words which stand in the Greek, *the loaves* – conceivably the fragments left over from the last episode.

hands; and since this rule was not to be found in scripture they appealed
3 to **the tradition of the elders,** namely an oral tradition of interpretation of
the law which was believed (at least by the Pharisees) to go back to Moses.
Whether this rule was observed in the time of Jesus is less certain, though it
may already have been customary among the Pharisees, who could well have
expected Jesus' disciples to be equally observant. Mark's comment, which
is clearly intended for readers unfamiliar with these customs, goes on to
ascribe to **all the Jews** practices[10] which again cannot be documented for
this period but which may nevertheless already have been customary, at least
among some stricter groups. The point was that none of them could be
6–7 directly inferred from scripture; and Jesus' quotation of Isaiah 29.13 is apt
enough, even though the passage was originally directed against the people as
a whole. Here it follows the Greek version of the Old Testament more closely
than the Hebrew, and may therefore owe its form more to church usage than
to Jesus – the same text is used in the same context in 2.22. But in any case its
contrast between 'lips' and 'heart' justifies Jesus' description of his critics as
6 **hypocrites,** with no more commitment to the deeper implications of their
creed than an 'actor' (which is what the word 'hypocrite' originally meant)
who merely spoke his part but did not have to carry it through in his personal
life.

3   Whether or not **all the Jews** observed this rule about the ritual washing of
hands, the offence given by Jesus' disciples must have been similar to their
failure to fast (2.18): they were not adopting those pious practices which
were expected of the followers of any serious religious movement within
Judaism. If Jesus' reply was originally a quotation from the Hebrew text of
Isaiah (and if this was the same as what we now read in our Bibles), it would
7 have ended, "their worship of me is a human commandment learned by rote".
He was endorsing the prophet's criticism of any religious practice which was
unthinkingly followed at the expense of a more profound religious and moral
motivation. In this sense he applied the text to his opponents with the words,
8 **"You abandon the commandment of God and hold to human tradition."**
The many detailed observances which the Pharisees regarded as binding on
themselves and sought to extend to others were based, not on the written law
itself, but on a traditional interpretation of that law which sought to make all
its injunctions relevant to contemporary life. The sheer complexity of these
observances made the mastery of them a matter which tended to crowd out
a balanced understanding of the true spirit of that law; and it is on this point
that Jesus' most characteristic attacks against the Pharisees were made. Their
attempt to secure perfect obedience to the law by fencing it round with a

---

[10] The matter is complicated by uncertainties both of correct translation and of the
manuscript readings: **thoroughly wash their hands** represents the strange phrase *wash
with their fist* (perhaps with cupped hands?) and the list of articles to be purified in some
manuscripts includes *beds.*

mass of detailed observances had resulted (Jesus argued) in a neglect of the fundamental commandments.

But Jesus, in Mark's narrative, carries the attack a stage further. The Pharisees not merely distracted attention from **the commandment of God**; by

9 their detailed applications of it, they were actually **rejecting** commandments by developing traditions that were incompatible with them. This was a serious charge indeed. The actual example chosen by Jesus is surprising. From all we know of Pharisaic tradition it is clear that the Pharisees, like every-

10 one else, placed very high value on the Fifth Commandment, **"Honor your father and your mother"** (Exodus 20.12, and the negative form of it, Exodus 21.17) and were prepared to waive all sorts of other obligations to ensure that it would be observed. The case envisaged by Jesus is that of a son who

11 in a moment of anger says **"Corban"**, which (Mark explains for non-Jewish readers) meant an **offering**, presumably (the translators add) an offering **to God**. But the word could be used as an oath: 'I swear that you shall have no benefit from anything of mine because it is Corban, that is, set apart as an offering to God.' Now the Jews, like many people in antiquity, took oaths very seriously: it was laid down in the law (Deuteronomy 23.21) that oaths must be kept, and fearful consequences could be expected if they were not. Therefore it made no difference if, when the moment of anger had passed, the son repented of his precipitate words. He was now bound by an oath which prevented him from fulfilling his normal duties to his parents. Clearly such a use of oaths had the makings of a serious abuse. It is true that the Pharisees attempted to remedy it by arguing that a large number of popular ways of swearing were not valid oaths at all and therefore constituted no excuse for failing to observe a clear commandment of the law. Nevertheless, there is some evidence that abuses of this kind may have flourished in the time of Jesus and it would have been fair to attack the Pharisees if their tradition appeared to countenance them.

14 **Then he called the crowd again.** This introductory sentence gives no hint of Jesus' motive in making the pronouncement that follows. On the face of it,

15 the saying **"there is nothing outside a person that by going in can defile"** is of a piece with Jesus' prophetic criticisms of some of the religious practices of his day: outward observances are valueless compared with the pure intentions of the heart. But there is no clue to the precise application he had in mind; and we can understand why it was subsequently thought of as an enigmatic

17 saying (which is one of the meanings of the word **parable**). As with the parable of the sowing in chapter 4, Mark appends an interpretation that was given privately to the disciples. This interpretation makes the saying apply specifically to regulations about food; and these regulations were (and still are) an important element of Jewish identity. But is this the point Jesus originally had in mind? The topic was not particularly appropriate to his work among the population of Galilee, where these regulations were taken for granted and where any attempted abrogation of them would have been greeted with

surprise and disbelief. It was only in a mixed Christian community of Jews and non-Jews that the question could have become important. Moreover, the list of evil deeds and vices in Jesus' answer is more typical of the conventional language of Hellenistic ethics than of Jesus' own teaching, and may betray the influence of a more cosmopolitan environment. The principle that 'all foods were clean' was certainly coming to be accepted among Christians by the time this gospel was written; but there is abundant evidence, both in Acts (10.15; 15.29) and in Paul's letters (Galatians 2.11–14; 1 Corinthians 8 and elsewhere) that Jewish scruples over kosher food continued for some time to cause friction among Christians in mixed churches. Jesus' 'parable' doubtless implied a liberal attitude towards such things; but the implication was not fully seen by the church until the whole question of the application of Jewish

19 observances to Christians had been settled. **Thus he declared all foods clean** looks therefore like a comment by Mark, reflecting the conclusion that his church had finally reached in this matter and finding it authorized by Jesus' 'parable'.

24 **From there he set out and went away to the region of Tyre.** The predominantly Jewish region of Galilee was bounded on most sides by territories that were mainly gentile. To the west, the plain lying between the mountains of Galilee and the Mediterranean belonged to the Roman province of Syria, and its inhabitants were called 'Phoenicians of Syria' to distinguish them from the Phoenician settlers who had founded Carthage in Libya. The principal Phoenician cities in Syria were Tyre and Sidon, which were both cosmopolitan Mediterranean ports; but there is some evidence that politically the **region of Tyre** extended eastward over the mountains as far as the upper reaches of the Jordan and therefore included an area where the population was still mainly Jewish. Mark's meaning therefore may be that Jesus travelled to the extreme north of the Jordan valley, where he would still have been among his fellow Jews, not that he took the more drastic step of crossing the mountains into the non-Jewish environment of the coastal plain.

Nevertheless, the point of the following story was that it put to the test Jesus' attitude to Gentiles. What would he do when accosted by a gentile woman – particularly at a time when he apparently wanted no one **to know he was there**? Was he prepared to extend his miraculous and compassionate powers to pagans? Jesus' first response, though a little cryptic and perhaps spoken with sufficient humour not to give offence, was discouraging: everyone knew

27 that the Jews, who believed themselves to be in a special sense the **'children'** of God, were not above referring to non-Jews as **'dogs'**; and Jesus seemed to be going along with this. But the woman, instead of protesting at this exclusiveness, replied to Jesus with respect[11], accepting that Jesus' mission was primarily to his own people, but continuing the metaphor to suggest

---

[11] The word translated **"Sir"** could be merely an expression of politeness; but it could also mean *Lord* and convey considerable respect.

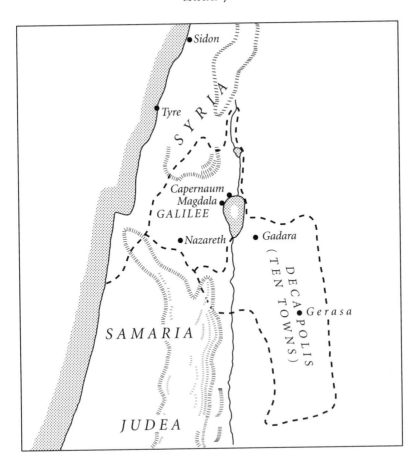

(again perhaps with humour) that there might be something left over for the dogs. She surmised (with a prophetic insight that may well have seemed significant to Mark and to the many gentile Christians in the church for which he was writing) that the ultimate benefits of Jesus' activity could not be limited to the Jewish race. Challenged by this insight, Jesus rewarded her with a rare manifestation of his power: exorcism at a distance.

31   Jesus' return journey **from the region of Tyre** is not easy to trace on the map. If we assume that Mark intended to continue the series of episodes which took place at the outposts of Jewish territory, he could perhaps describe Jesus' south-eastward journey as **towards the Sea of Galilee, in the region of the Decapolis**, even though the Decapolis (on the other side of the lake) was his destination. But **Sidon**, and even its territory which, like that of Tyre, extended far inland, lay considerably to the north. If Jesus went literally **by way of Sidon** he must have made an immense détour, and his journey would have taken many days. If he went even into the territory of Sidon at its nearest

point he must have gone substantially out of his way. We must assume either that Mark was confused about the geography or else that he mentioned Sidon only because, since early times, it was customary to refer to it in the same breath as Tyre.

32 The cure of the **deaf man who had an impediment in his speech** is described in unusual detail. Jesus' procedure recalls that of miracle healers in many parts of the world: typical details are the withdrawal for privacy, the touch, the spittle and the solemn word of command in Hebrew or Aramaic (which would have sounded arresting to Greek-speaking readers, whether or not Jesus was in reality speaking his own language at that point); and the raising of the eyes to heaven and the powerful sigh can also be paralleled from magical techniques (though they may of course indicate something of Jesus' emotions on this occasion). But Mark characteristically avoids giving the impression that it was a magical feat or a typical piece of 'faith healing': he

36 adds once again Jesus' strange injunction **to tell no one** (see below, p. 145);

37 and he records the very strong impression made on the crowds (**beyond measure** – the Greek is emphatic) which suggests that they saw the miracle as a sign of greater things to come. For had not Isaiah prophesied (35.5–6) that in the promised new age "the ears of the deaf [shall be] unstopped . . . and the tongue of the speechless sing for joy"?

8.1 **In those days.** That Jesus performed at least one miracle of feeding a multitude is one of the best attested facts in the gospels, which contain no fewer than six accounts of such an episode. Mark and Matthew each record a second occasion, with only slight differences from the first. Mark seems to have had no information about the time and place of this one; and it is of no help to us when he records that the place to which Jesus crossed over

10 was **Dalmanutha**, since nothing whatever is known of this place.[12] We can assume that the setting was still on the far side of the lake, where the crowd may have included some Gentiles; and the motivation this time is more practical: Jesus' concern was not that they needed 'shepherding' (6.34) but that they

2 had been listening to him **for three days** without food. Yet there are hints that there is more to it than merely a miraculous provision of food when needed.

6 The words **after giving thanks** (which are not in the previous account) may point forward to the later institution of the eucharist (which means literally 'thanksgiving'), and the failure of the disciples to believe and understand

4 (**"How can one feed these people?"**) becomes the cue for a pointed dialogue with them a few verses later (14–21).

11 **Asking him for a sign from heaven.** Coming straight after the report of some remarkable miracles, this request seems surprising. What more

---

[12] This may be why some manuscripts offer the variants *Mageda/Magada* (which is the place, equally unknown, given in Matthew) or *Magdala*, which can be identified with a town on the west side of the lake.

142

impressive 'sign' could have been given than the feats which Jesus had been performing? But from the point of view of sceptical and sophisticated observers like the Pharisees the crucial question about Jesus – whether or not he had the authority of a true prophet – could not be so easily settled. Jesus' miracles, however much deeper meaning may later have been found in them (which is often drawn out by the evangelist), were never entirely cogent or unambiguous. Jesus' exorcisms, it was suggested, could have been carried out in collusion with the devil himself; his healings used recognized techniques of magic; his apparent disregard of sabbath observances called into question his religious credentials. It was not prudent to give one's allegiance to someone simply on the basis of a reputation for miraculous feats. Moreover, Jesus' teaching constituted a direct challenge to existing institutions and traditional piety. If the Pharisees were to own his authority they would be forced to call into question much of their own cherished tradition of interpretation and practice. Naturally the Pharisees (and doubtless many other serious religious people) were unwilling to draw such disturbing conclusions from their encounters with Jesus unless they had a clear and unambiguous 'sign' that he had full authority to say what he said and do what he did. What would they have regarded as such a sign? Here we can only speculate. It may be that there is literally nothing which can be guaranteed to persuade those who cannot be open to new possibilities. But parallels from the Old Testament and from later Jewish sources suggest that a dramatic fulfilment by Jesus of a specific prophecy, or a miraculous confirmation of one of his own predictions, might have confronted them with a challenge that at least some of them could no longer evade.

12 **He sighed deeply in his spirit.** The signs of emotion which, to a notable extent in this gospel, are attributed to Jesus seem to be provoked mainly by impatience with the religious observances and attitudes by which he was surrounded. So here: the religious mentality which will not question its own assumptions without first being given what it will recognize as unassailable evidence makes Jesus impatient. He sees his questioners as representatives of a whole generation which, like the 'generation' of Israelites in the wilderness, is too obstinate to recognize the source and the implications of the wonders done in its midst.

15 **"Beware of the yeast of the Pharisees and the yeast of Herod."** This saying is not elucidated by the story in which it occurs. It is found in a quite different context in Luke (12.1), and it is likely that it was remembered as an isolated and somewhat enigmatic saying of Jesus which Mark thought appropriate to work in at this point. Yeast, because of its impressive power to transform a mass of dough many times the size of itself, was often used metaphorically. Sometimes good influences were compared with it (Matthew 13.33), sometimes bad (1 Corinthians 5.6). The only clue to its meaning here is that it must have been something that the Pharisees and Herod had in

common; and this (since an alliance of Pharisees and Herodians on this very point is recorded in 3.6 above) can hardly have been anything but a common intention to suppress Jesus and his movement.

But the story to which the saying is attached (and in which it plays virtually no part) has a very different point. It gives Jesus an opportunity to castigate his disciples for their still unenlightened response to the great things he is doing in their presence. He repeats the condemnation of them placed by
17 Mark after the first of the two feeding miracles (6.52), **"Are your hearts hardened?"** – a biblical phrase suggesting that they were still in that state of obstinate resistance which had characterized the people of Israel throughout their history in the face of God's self-revelation; indeed, Jesus goes so far as to
18 apply to his disciples those apparently fatalistic words of Isaiah (6.9) which (at least according to Mark) he used of the crowds at large when they failed to understand his parables (4.11–12). In this respect the distinction between the disciples and the crowds seems here to have vanished; indeed in general Mark, unlike Matthew, seldom portrays them in a favourable light. Their rehabilitation was to come later, after Easter, and belonged, not to the gospel story, but to the history of the church. Meanwhile, even after witnessing the feeding miracles, they remained blind. The sections which follow show Jesus taking steps to penetrate their blindness.

Sight for the blind

For Jesus could heal the physically blind. It may be in order to point to a deliberate contrast between his power over blindness and the continuing obtuseness of the disciples that Mark inserts here a second healing story remarkably similar to that given at the end of the previous chapter (the two stories have in common the privacy of the cure and the use of touch and spittle, and what was said above about the conventional aspect of this
22 procedure applies with equal force here). This one takes place at **Bethsaida**, which was on the far side of the Jordan, in the tetrarchy of Herod Antipas' brother Philip. Philip had begun to found a new city on the site named 'Julias' after Augustus' daughter Julia; but since very little is heard of this 'city', and since no buildings of any pretension have been found on the site, it may be that his plans never got very far and Mark may be not altogether inaccurate in
23 calling it a **village**. In any case, there is no reason to think that its population must have been much less Jewish than that of, say, Capernaum, or that Mark intends us to imagine that the blind man was a Gentile. The unique feature of the cure is that it was gradual. If a parallel was intended between the man's blindness and the disciples' failure to understand, it is possible that it was this detail which led Mark to place the story here. The next three chapters relate the gradual (though still only partial) enlightenment of the disciples.

Jesus the Messiah – the transfiguration

From Bethsaida, a day's walk northward through the territory of Philip would
27 have been more than sufficient to reach **the villages of Caesarea Philippi,**
a town that had been re-founded by Philip as a Hellenistic city, without
presumably much affecting the character of the surrounding villages. The
beginning of the conversation may seem a little contrived: Jesus is unlikely
to have needed to ask the disciples for information about what people were
saying, and their answer to Jesus' question has already been given once by
Mark in connection with Herod (6.14). But it serves to point up the significance of the disciples' reply. The people at large had certainly come to see in
Jesus more than a freakish miracle-worker: he also had a pressing message
about God and his purposes for his people, and it was natural to identify him
with one of those prophetic figures of the past (even the immediate past, like
John the Baptist) who, it was believed, would return to earth to herald a new
age. But since this new age had not yet begun in any tangible or visible way,
people hesitated to take the further step of identifying Jesus with that unique
person, the Messiah, who was actually to inaugurate it, even if there might
be signs of its dawning in the liberating activity of Jesus. Moreover, Jesus
himself had not openly admitted to the title of Messiah. But the Christians
for whom Mark's gospel was written believed that Jesus *was* the Messiah:
indeed, they had come to call him, as a matter of course, Jesus 'Christ'. Here,
Mark is insisting that, even before the resurrection, his disciples (for whom
Peter appears as the spokesman, since Jesus' response to what he says seems
on each occasion to embrace them all) had come to recognize the same truth:
29 **"You are the Messiah."**
   This truth, however, was not yet to be openly revealed. The injunction
to silence continues the series of injunctions which Jesus (particularly in
Mark's gospel) gives several times after the performance of a miracle. It is
debatable whether these injunctions go back to Jesus (in which case they
could have been motivated by a desire for privacy, a fear of too much public
excitement, an anxiety to avoid conflict with the government or a sense that
a popular following was a form of temptation to be resisted) or whether
they were, at least in part, inserted by Mark to explain the embarrassing fact
that the majority of Jesus' contemporaries did *not* recognize that he was **the
Messiah**. Here, in any case, the injunction makes a clear distinction between
the disciples and the people in general: the disciples have advanced, despite
their previous failures, to the point of recognizing Jesus as Messiah, whereas
this is something which must still be concealed from the crowd.
   Their progress, however, does not go very far. Jesus goes on to give them
31 some further teaching, which finds no response in them whatever. The **Son
of Man** was a title that suggested a glorious and vindicated figure; but he
was to come into this state of glory only after he, or the righteous people
whom he represented, had suffered and even been martyred for their faith.

It was perhaps natural that popular thought should fasten more on the glory to come than on the necessary condition that the righteous people of God (of whom everyone hoped to be a member) should first undergo severe tribulation; and the effect of Jesus' words here (which are spoken 32 **quite openly,** no longer in parables) is to correct this bias – which he calls 33 a temptation of **Satan** – and to emphasize the things which have got to happen first before glory and vindication can be contemplated. He does this, for himself, in some detail; and the details are an unmistakable description of his own rejection, death and resurrection. According to Mark, therefore, Jesus both identifies himself unambiguously with the Son of Man and gives a detailed forecast of his destiny. How near we stand to historical truth at this point is a tantalizing question. On the one hand it was to be expected that the words in which the church soon became accustomed to recite the bare facts of Jesus' life, death and resurrection should have influenced at least the form in which Jesus' prophecy was remembered, if not its actual content. On the other hand it is difficult to make sense of Jesus' words and actions unless it is granted that he had at least a premonition of the fate in store for him and some consciousness of his ultimate destiny.

34 For some more general teaching on the same theme Jesus **called the crowd** to listen along with the disciples – or so at least Mark or his source arranged this group of sayings. The whole difficulty of this passage is to determine how far the later experience of the church has influenced it. That there has been some influence is difficult to deny. That Jesus' followers should **"take up their cross"**, for example, would have been a startling (though perhaps not impossible) expression in the mouth of Jesus before his own crucifixion had taken place: it could only have suggested the image of a slave or a rebel condemned to death for resistance or rebellion against the Roman occupying power – and what sort of model was that for the Christian disciple? Only when Jesus himself had set an example by 'taking up his cross' and suffering for his faith could the image establish itself as a model for discipleship. Again, whatever teaching Jesus may himself have given about 'denying oneself' and 35 'losing one's life in order to save it' (and this last certainly has something of his characteristic love of paradox), these sayings take on far more relevance and significance if they are read in the context of a struggling and persecuted 38 Christian community. The same goes for the final saying, **"Those who are ashamed of me..."** There may have been moments in Jesus' life (such as that of Peter's denial of him) when this saying would have been to the point; but it reads more easily as a subsequent warning to the church that anyone who is 'ashamed' of Jesus and his **words**[13] – that is, who has not the courage to

---

[13] Some manuscripts (see the NRSV footnote) read *and of mine*, i.e. 'of my followers' instead of **of my words**. In this form the saying would certainly have originated in the church rather than in the mouth of Jesus: for Jesus had no 'followers', in the sense of a steady community of which a wavering member might be 'ashamed', until after the resurrection.

confess allegiance in the face of persecution – cannot expect to be numbered among those who will share the Son of Man's glorious vindication hereafter.

9.1   **And he said to them.** This is one of Mark's characteristic ways of adding a saying of Jesus which did not originally belong in the same context. The saying itself presents great difficulty. Mark's gospel is quite likely to have been written when at least some of those 'standing there' with Jesus were still alive, and the prediction could still have been taken literally. But, understood in its plainest sense, it was soon proved false. Was Jesus simply mistaken (an unwelcome explanation if he was really the Son of God)? Or is this a false report of what he said? Since no one would have thought of attributing to Jesus an apparently unfulfilled prediction if he did not actually make it, it is highly likely to be authentic. But how then are we to understand it? In the context both of Jesus' own teaching and of contemporary popular expectation, **the kingdom of God . . . come with power** could not mean anything less than a decisive intervention by God to inaugurate a new order which would be unmistakably his 'kingdom'. If this is what Jesus in fact predicted in the lifetime of his hearers, then we have to say that he was mistaken; and many interpreters have felt bound to accept this limitation of Jesus' understanding of the future, particularly since it is clear from the New Testament letters that for a time the early Christians certainly expected a decisive event of this kind. On the other hand a number of events, of less finality but of considerable significance in the working out of the divine purpose, did in fact take place before the passing of Jesus' generation. One was the destruction of Jerusalem and the temple in 70 CE, which seemed, at least to Christians if not to Jews, to constitute God's final judgment passed on the Jewish religion; another was Jesus' vindication as Son of Man by the resurrection; a third was the manifest power released in the church which caused the gospel to be spread and accepted on a scale beyond all human expectation and seemed a clear foretaste of the **kingdom of God . . . come with power**. It is possible that Jesus' prediction originally referred to one or more of these events (the first of which would have been readily discernible to a 'prophet' in view of the political situation at the time); in addition to which, the 'kingdom of God' in Jesus' teaching was never a concept confined to the future. His message was that, though the consummation was still to come, vital things were happening even now and vital challenges were being issued in the course of his activity which revealed the 'kingship' of God. Since all his teaching about the coming of the kingdom was thus a great deal richer in meaning than the simple prophecies of doom or glory made by some of his predecessors, it is reasonable to think that the saying here, whatever its original form, was neither so naïve nor so misguided as might appear at first sight.

The episode which follows is traditionally known as 'the transfiguration', 2 **transfigured** being derived from the Latin word which corresponds most nearly to the Greek *metemorphōthē*, 'changed his form'. The narrative is

brief and succinct: it has the flavour of an eyewitness account. But it also
4 lends itself to symbolic interpretation. **Elijah with Moses**, for example, are
clearly not just extras on stage but are intended by their presence to point
to the nature of him with whom they are conversing. But on this occasion
what do they stand for? Elijah was commonly thought of as the first of the
prophets, and Moses was the law-giver (though it is surprising to find him
in second place after Elijah: perhaps he was added to the story later – at any
rate Matthew's account (17.3) reverses the order). Are they symbols of the
law and the prophets which Jesus was destined to fulfil and supersede? Or
does Elijah appear in his usual rôle of precursor of the Messiah? In which
case Moses may be there for the same reason: a key passage in Deuteronomy
(18.18) has God promising to "raise up for them a prophet" *like Moses*, and
there may even have been a belief in the time of Jesus (as there certainly was
at a later date) that Moses as well as Elijah would return at the inauguration
5 of the new age. Again, **"Let us make three dwellings"** is plausible as a factual
6 account: in total confusion (**He did not know what to say**) Peter tried to
offer hospitality on the mountain to the disciples' distinguished guests. But
the word 'dwellings' means literally *tents*, and could be an allusion to the
fact that in the earliest history of Israel it was in a 'tent' that God came to
meet his people (Exodus 33.7–11); and the image of a tent continued to
serve as a description both of the actual temple in Jerusalem and of the true
7 sanctuary of God in the heavens (Hebrews 9.1–14). Again, the sudden **cloud**
was a perfectly natural phenomenon on the mountain top, but was also a
traditional sign of the presence of God (Exodus 16.10; 19.9 and many other
passages); and, since the alleged extinction of the prophetic spirit after the
death of the last of the Old Testament prophets, the **voice** from heaven was
the most frequent of the ways in which God was believed to communicate
directly with human beings. The words spoken by this heavenly voice are
almost identical with those spoken at Jesus' baptism (1.11); the significant
difference here is that they are addressed to the three disciples, who have
2 been very deliberately taken **apart, by themselves** as witnesses (two or three
were sufficient in a court of law), and who are henceforward – though their
subsequent behaviour might seem to belie such privileged knowledge – in
possession of the key to Jesus' true nature. One more symbolic clue to the
7 mystery may lie in the final phrase, **"listen to him!"**: the phrase occurs also in
the passage from Deuteronomy already referred to (18.18) about a prophet
who was to come. Jesus (the vision seems to imply) is this prophet.

The vision, then, is replete with Jewish symbolism: some if not all the
details take on their significance from traditions that originate in the Old
Testament. All the more striking, therefore, is the one verse which describes
the appearance of Jesus' clothes in language of an almost peasant simplicity –
3 **dazzling white, such as no one** (literally, *no fuller*) **on earth could bleach
them**. These recall the white robes assumed to be worn by divine beings

and by righteous humans raised to heaven; but the transformation of Jesus' appearance *while still on earth* is unparalleled in Jewish literature: to find anything comparable one has to go to Greek myths, where gods often enough assume human form and then suddenly, by their dazzling appearance, betray their true nature. But there the parallel stops. Jewish religion, unlike Greek philosophy, did not conceive of another and more glorious reality lying in some sense 'behind' the physical world and occasionally breaking through to human senses. The Jews thought of this other reality, not metaphysically, but temporally. It lay, not in the present 'behind' the outward appearance of things, but in the future: it was the content of God's promises to his people and would one day, by God's gracious intervention, be fully revealed to them. Certainly there is evidence for some of what we would now call 'mystical experience' – Paul is a witness to that. But most Jewish visions were of "what must take place after this" (Revelation 4.1), and it may be that Jesus' transfiguration should at least in part be understood in this sense: Jesus' 'glorification' lay in the future, it was the state he would enter after the resurrection (and some believe that this whole scene is an early Christian reading back of that state into Jesus' earthly life). What the three privileged disciples were being vouchsafed was a glimpse of that which was to come. But in the context of Jesus' teaching and activity the vision was also more than this. Jesus was *already* Son of God and Messiah; therefore he was already (for those who could see it) a figure of glory. In his transfiguration, as in his preaching of the kingdom and in his power over the forces of evil, Jesus brought decisively into the present things which until then Jewish religious thinkers had assumed were reserved for the future.

In Mark a spectacular action of Jesus is often followed by an injunction to secrecy. The transfiguration evidently falls into the same category of things not, or not yet, to be revealed – though in this case it is more in the nature of a vision vouchsafed to a privileged few than a miracle that happened to be witnessed by a number of people. Jesus refers to himself again (as in 8.31) as **the Son of Man**, and for the first time places a limit to the period of secrecy – until he had **risen from the dead**. Whether or not this phrase was later put into Jesus' mouth by the early church (by which time it would have been a natural way of referring to the resurrection), it is highly significant that Mark records that the disciples were puzzled by it, **questioning what this rising from the dead could mean**. As a phrase to describe what was expected to happen at the end of time, when all human beings would be 'raised from the dead' in order to receive judgment and reward or punishment, it could hardly have caused puzzlement: a general 'resurrection of the dead' in this sense was widely believed in. What presumably mystified them about Jesus' saying was that it implied that the Son of Man would rise from the dead not *at* but *before* the general resurrection. If so, his rising could be fitted into the generally accepted scheme only if it was the signal for the speedy coming of the end; and if this is the logic of this somewhat jerky paragraph (but in anything to do with life after death it is impossible to be sure what people may have believed at the time), we can account for the disciples' second question: if the end was to come so soon, why had not all things yet come to pass which were due to happen first?

11 **"Why do the scribes say that Elijah must come first?"** It was the profession of the scribes to determine, by reference to their own tradition of interpretation, the precise bearing of a given passage of scripture upon any matter of conduct or belief. The passage in question here was Malachi 4.5–6:

> "Lo, I will send you the prophet Elijah before the great and terrible day of the LORD comes. He will turn the hearts of parents to their children, and the hearts of children to their parents. . ."

The original prophecy was not too mysterious: before the day of the Lord a new prophet would appear who would be none other than the first of the prophets (who had in fact never died but had been taken up to heaven) and who would return to establish peace in the families of Israel before the end came. But from early times there had been a tendency to elaborate the rôle of this future Elijah. The Septuagint Greek version of the Old Testament, by adding the words 'and a man to his neighbour', had already extended the range of his peace-making from family life to the life of the nation as a whole. By the time of Christ he had become an important figure in the scheme of what was to come, and his rôle had grown from that of domestic

12 peace-making to that of one who would **restore all things** to their pristine perfection. Whether he was to be the precursor of the Messiah, or himself to fulfil part of the expected task of the Messiah, was a matter on which opinions were doubtless divided. But in any case, it seemed difficult to conceive that the end could come without the previous appearance of this Elijah figure; and the words of Jesus, which seemed to bring the end sensationally close at hand, naturally raised the question in the disciples' minds how, in Jesus' scheme of things, Elijah could be fitted in.

Jesus' reply is somewhat obscure. The correctness of a traditional interpretation of a passage of scripture could be established or refuted by reference to another passage, and this seems to be Jesus' procedure here. Prophecies that the Son of Man himself was to **go through many sufferings and be treated with contempt** are not easy to find: the suffering servant in Isaiah 53 is usually thought to come nearest to what must have been meant, and doubtless the Son of Man passage in Daniel 7 was seen to imply that the now vindicated and glorious figure had recently, in the persons of the righteous, suffered persecution. If this were true of the Son of Man, might it not be true also of Elijah? If so, then the disciples could look among their own contemporaries for a man who fulfilled this rôle. If we turn to Matthew (11.14), his account makes explicit what is implicit in Mark. They need not look far: the person in question was John the Baptist.

15 **When the whole crowd saw him, they were immediately overcome with awe**. This is a very strong expression, denoting much more than surprise that Jesus should have appeared at just that moment. Was there still something 'transfigured' in his appearance? When Moses came down from Mount Sinai "the skin of his face was shining" (Exodus 34.30). Since the account of the transfiguration is full of Old Testament allusions, this may well be one more: Mark (the only one of the evangelists to record this detail) may have been thinking of a reflection of glory still visible on Jesus' face some hours after the event and producing awe in all those who saw him.

16–18 It seems an argument had started over the disciples' failure to perform an exorcism. That they were empowered to exorcize is stated in 6.7; but that they should occasionally have failed is not surprising in itself (for some spirits were stronger than others) and must also have given the story a particular interest for the early church, in which exorcism was still practised but doubtless not always with success. What was the reason for these failures? A possible answer lay in words attributed to Jesus and added here by Mark as a piece of private

29 instruction to the disciples: **"This kind can come out only through prayer."** If they failed, it must be because they did not pray enough![14]

The exorcism, the last recorded by Mark, concerns a severe case of what we would now call epilepsy or hysteria but was then ascribed to the activity of a spirit. Jesus' reaction to the all too human scene which met him on his descent from the mountain recalls the impatience and resignation of an Old Testament prophet: in the face of the signal acts of God that had been performed before their very eyes the people remained (as often in

19 their history) a **faithless generation** – the words evoke a passage such as Deuteronomy 32.5. The immediate provocation for such severe language seems to be the attitude of the crowd; for it is they who bring the case to

22 Jesus. But it is then justified by the tentative approach of the boy's father, **"if you are able"**, which showed a clear lack of faith in Jesus' power over the

24 spirits, only partly made good by the father's impassioned appeal, **"I believe; help my unbelief!"** It was apparently the approach of the crowd, however, rather than the candid confession of the father, that spurred Jesus to perform the exorcism and cure the boy, not just of his present fit, but of his illness

25 altogether: **"come out of him, and never enter him again"**. Nevertheless it may have been because of these words about faith, and because of Jesus' statement (which must have been a source of great encouragement to Mark's

23 readers) that **"all things can be done for the one who believes"** (which can also mean, *by* the one who believes), that Mark included this exorcism story.

27 It is possible also (given that the Greek word for **lifted him up** is the same as that for 'raising up' from the dead) that, in the vivid details of the boy being

26 **like a corpse** and of most of the bystanders thinking he was dead, Mark saw

---

[14] Many manuscripts add the words *and fasting*. This looks like an early Christian addition, giving a further reason for failure: they did not fast enough!

a prefigurement of that victory over death which was to be accomplished in Jesus' resurrection and shared by all who have faith in him.

The challenge of discipleship

Mark now devotes a section explicitly to Jesus' instruction of his disciples away from the crowd. The main burden of this teaching was his prediction of the fate in store for the Son of Man, which is here repeated in very much the same terms as before (8.31); and just as on that occasion the disciples

32 refused to accept it, so now **they did not understand** and **were afraid to ask.** For us, who have come to regard 'the Son of Man' as simply a title for Jesus, the teaching seems to be a straightforward statement of what was going to happen, and we find it hard to see how his disciples could have failed to 'understand' it. But 'son of man' to Jesus' contemporaries either meant some unspecified person who might or might not be the speaker (apparently this was an idiomatic use) or else was a reference to the figure in Daniel 7 who was first and foremost vindicated and glorified; he embodied the splendid destiny to which God's righteous and elect people could look forward after their sufferings. The disciples may not have found too much difficulty in Jesus' use of the title as such, for they already saw in him a person of unique power and authority; but the teaching which Jesus was giving them about the rôle that suffering was to play in the destiny of this figure (and doubtless of the community of the righteous whom he represented) was hard for them to square with their preconceptions and was apparently too much for their understanding.

Nevertheless, the teaching was remembered – or at least that part of the teaching which concerned what would be demanded of the community and which gave guidance to that community at times of stress; and there is a

35 certain formality in its presentation, in that Jesus **sat down**, as a teacher would when giving instruction, and **called the twelve** who were to be the chosen recipients of it. It is possible that we can detect in the apparently illogical sequence of these paragraphs one of the ways in which it was held in the memory. For these sayings were clearly not originally spoken in the order, or even necessarily in the context, in which we now have them. There is little apparent connection between them, and several of them occur in Matthew or Luke in quite different, and sometimes more appropriate, surroundings. On the other hand, one saying often contains a word or an idea that occurs again in the next, so that the memory would find it easy to move from one

37 to the other. Thus, **in my name** in the saying about children is picked up by

38, 39 **in your name ... in my name** in the saying about non-Christian exorcists;

42 **a stumbling block** put before 'little ones' is picked up by being 'caused to

43, 44 **stumble**' by one's right hand; **fire** in connection with hell leads on to being

49, 50 **salted with fire**; and this again leads on to two further sayings about **salt**. In short, the apparently inconsequential series of sayings may reproduce a kind of mnemonic system by which the sayings were remembered and perhaps used for teaching in the early church.

To understand these sayings it is therefore sensible to take them separately.

35 (i) The saying **"Whoever wants to be first must be last of all and servant of all"** occurs again at 10.43–4 and in various other places in Matthew and Luke. The context is always that of Jesus' instruction to the circle of close disciples, and it is a norm so radical that only an intimate and highly motivated group would be capable of adopting it into its organization. (Indeed throughout its history even the church has consistently failed to do so.)

37 (ii) **"Whoever welcomes one such child."** This saying rests on a presupposition which was taken for granted in antiquity, as indeed in some respects it still is. Agents or envoys represent the one 'in whose name' they come; to maltreat them is to maltreat the sender. But why should Jesus take a child as an example? It is certainly true that Jesus had (for his time) a remarkable, indeed almost unprecedented, regard for children, valuing them in their own right and not just (like his contemporaries) as potential adults. This saying could thus be a warning to his disciples that they must do the same. But it would also have been characteristic of him to take a child as an extreme example of the proposition that the very least person might in some sense represent Jesus (like the 'little ones' of verse 42) and must be received as such.

(iii) Part of the technique of exorcism was to find out the name, and so undermine the power, of the demon concerned, and then to invoke by name a stronger power that could drive it out. There is nothing surprising

38–9 in the report that a contemporary exorcist, hearing of Jesus' power over a large number of 'unclean spirits', should have been invoking his name without any sense of obligation to join his following. The reaction of Jesus' disciples is human and understandable; that of Jesus suggests that he was anxious to avoid forming any kind of militant and exclusive sect. To make

40 the point, he used what was almost certainly a proverb: **"Whoever is not against us is for us."** The proverb was presumably at home in a political context and expressed a liberal and conciliatory policy as opposed to that of the more fanatical nationalist sects which were continually springing up under the Roman administration in Palestine. The fact that Jesus uses another proverb which appears to say the exact opposite, "Whoever is not with me is against me" (Matthew 12.30; Luke 11.23), does not mean that he contradicted himself. All depends on the context. This second proverb would have been the watchword of the more fanatical parties; and there were certainly aspects of Jesus' teaching which had a certain exclusiveness, and he may well have found it appropriate to express them on occasion by the more exclusive version of the proverb.

41   (iv) **"Truly I tell you"** – one of Mark's characteristic ways of adding an isolated saying of Jesus. The saying occurs in Matthew (10.24) in the context of instructions about the reception to be given to Christian missionaries: the very minimum of hospitality afforded to them assures the giver of some reward.

42   (v) **"If any of you put a stumbling block before one of these little ones."** The reader may still have in mind the child whom Jesus took in his arms in verse 36; but the 'little ones' may in fact just as well be the weaker members of the community, and a commentary on this saying can be found in Romans 14; indeed, it may have been the kind of situation described there which caused the saying to assume its present form.

     (vi) The necessity for radical self-discipline and renunciation of every cause of temptation is described with all Jesus' characteristic vividness and eschewal of compromise. 'Cutting off a hand' or 'a foot' was certainly intended as a metaphor; and since the language is metaphorical it should not be pressed for teaching about hell and eternal punishment. Jesus accepted and used the language of his contemporaries about these things. In the Greek, the word for

44 **hell** is *Gehenna*, the precipitous valley on the south side of Jerusalem which was of baneful memory in Old Testament history (*Hinnom* in 2 Kings 23.10, Jeremiah 7.31 and elsewhere) and was, in the time of Jesus, smoking with the refuse of the city. It was in common use as a word for 'hell', and other

44 conventional touches are added to the saying, like the **unquenchable fire** and

48 the phrase (a quotation from Isaiah 66.24) **"where their worm never dies, and the fire is never quenched"**.

49   (vii) **"For everyone will be salted with fire."** Salt preserves; and that which will make Jesus' disciples worthy of eternal life and preserve them in a state of preparedness for it will be the fire of persecution – at least, that is one possible meaning of this mysterious saying.

50   (viii) **"Salt is good."** The form given to this saying in the Sermon on the Mount shows that it is the followers of Jesus who are to be like salt. For the rest, see above on Matthew 5.13.

     (ix) **"Have salt in yourselves."** This appears to come close to the Greek idiom in which salt means sharpness of mind and speech, like 'seasoned with salt' in Colossians 4.6.

10.1   **He left that place and went to the region of Judea and beyond the Jordan.** The journey was destined to be of the greatest significance. Jesus was leaving the comparative freedom of the somewhat provincial territory of Galilee and would soon be facing a direct confrontation with the religious leaders in Jerusalem. On the way, however, there was no reason for things to be any different for him, since the populations and political conditions through which he passed would have been much the same as they were in Galilee. The shortest route from Galilee to Jerusalem was due south along the mountain range on the west side of the Jordan. But this meant going through Samaria,

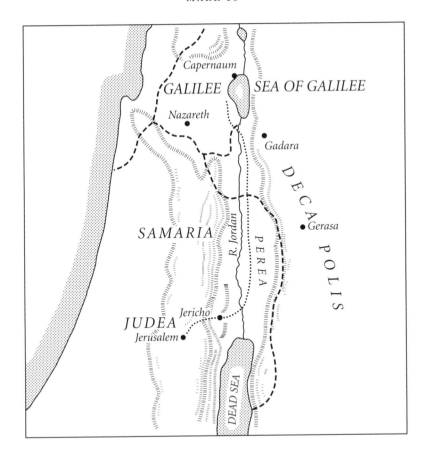

and since relations between the Jews and the Samaritans were exceedingly strained at this period (only John's gospel suggests that Jesus did anything significant there), Jewish travellers often preferred to cross the Jordan south of the lake and proceed down the east side of the valley through territory which was also, like Galilee, under the administration of Herod Antipas and in which the population was predominantly Jewish. This was the territory 'beyond the Jordan', and was called Perea. Travellers would then re-cross the Jordan in order to reach Jericho and enter Judea, having skirted both Samaria and most of the Decapolis and having remained for almost the entire journey on what could reasonably be described as Jewish soil. Mark's description of the route seems confused (placing **Judea** *before* **beyond the Jordan**). It may be that he had no first-hand knowledge of the geography; but whether or not we are to take his words as an exact description, they suggest one of the routes which were normally taken by travellers and pilgrims from Galilee to Jerusalem.

2 **To test him they asked, "Is it lawful for a man to divorce his wife?"** It is not easy to be sure what prompted this question or in what sense it was a 'test'. Divorce in the time of Jesus was easily available and certainly regarded as 'lawful'; but there was discussion on the question of what constituted adequate grounds for it. The only relevant text of scripture (Deuteronomy 24.1–4) was far from precise, and the opinions of the professional interpreters were divided, some taking a strict view and some a more permissive one. Matthew, who seems to have had greater familiarity than Mark with matters of this kind, set Jesus' sayings on divorce in the context of such a discussion (19.3–9). But here the question is completely general: not, Under what circumstances is divorce permissible? but, Is it lawful at all?

On the face of it, this was a question which could hardly have arisen in normal Jewish life. Divorce was a well-established institution, and the only relevant passage in the law of Moses (again Deuteronomy 24) presupposed its legality. On the other hand there were certainly some who disapproved of divorce on moral grounds, and at least one Jewish sect forbade divorce among its members and would have regarded the apparent permission to divorce granted in the law as a 'concession' of which they should not make use. If Mark is reporting correctly and the question was put to Jesus in this general form (and not in the more technical form given in Matthew), it must have been because he was expected, as a moral teacher who perhaps wished to form a sect or movement of his own, to take a rigorous view on the matter and could be challenged to reconcile this with scripture. In this sense the question could have been asked **to test him**.

All ancient Jewish discussions of the matter of which we have any record concentrate on Deuteronomy 24: it was the only relevant legal text. But from a moral point of view it was arguable that other texts were more important – Malachi 2.14–16, for example, expressed strong disapproval of divorce. The ones from Genesis chosen by Jesus in his answer to the Pharisees could be shown to have the same implication and to be more pertinent to the question of the good life than any legal permission which was simply a concession to

5 human **hardness of heart.**

The relevance of the first of the texts quoted by Jesus is not immediately obvious. Genesis 1.27 runs: "God created humankind (*adam*) in his image ... male and female he created them." Why does the text, which begins in the singular (*adam*, 'man') suddenly break into the plural? Whatever the real reason, there is some evidence that there were scholars in the time of Jesus who had an ingenious interpretation based on the legend (made famous by Plato) that human beings were originally androgynous, made up of a male half and a female half, which then got separated and for ever after yearned for each other. Was it this double being – or perhaps just the fact that (in the second creation narrative) Eve was created from Adam – that explained the unexpected appearance of the plural 'them'? In which case the text might be held to support a view of marriage as the reunion of two beings that originally belonged together, a union too sacred to be broken. In any case, the argument becomes clearer with the second quotation, which is from Genesis 2.24 and immediately follows the account of the creation of

7 the woman from the rib of the man. The words **for this reason** are part of the quotation and indicate that the biblical writer is giving an explanation of marriage. As Jesus comments, marriage is the means by which God has

9, 8 **joined together** what originally belonged together. That they become **one flesh** is, of course, a metaphor: in reality they remain two individuals. Jewish interpreters took it to mean an indissoluble kinship, and a venerable (but not necessarily correct) Christian interpretation has inferred that the physical consummation of marriage makes the union indissoluble. But nothing in the text shows how Jesus understood the metaphor. The force of the two

6 quotations from Genesis is simply that **from the beginning** marriage was the divine will for human beings. Whatever provision the law subsequently made to accommodate human 'hardness of heart', there could be no doubt of the original intention.

10 **The disciples asked him again about this matter.** They may simply not have understood this somewhat sophisticated piece of reasoning, or else they were puzzled (as Christians have been ever since) about its practical implications in a society where the possibility of divorce was taken for granted. Jesus' reply to them was quite uncompromising. He was not, it seems, offering a legal judgment: to do this he would have had to address the text in Deuteronomy, and in any case, Jewish law permitted polygamy (at least in theory), and therefore a legal prohibition of divorce would not necessarily have affected the position of the husband who wished to marry another woman. Rather, Jesus was making a moral judgment on divorce in general.

11 **Adultery** was regarded as one of the most serious offences; its social consequences were extremely damaging and it was punished very severely. By calling the remarriage of divorced persons 'adultery', Jesus condemned it in very strong terms indeed. This was surprising enough; it is perhaps still more surprising that in the second half of his reply Jesus suggests that the culprit who takes the initiative might be the wife. This was barely possible under Jewish law; if Mark's gospel was written or read in a place such as Rome it is possible that the saying may have been reformulated to correspond with the more even-handed provisions of Roman law.

13 **People were bringing little children to him.** We cannot imagine that there
16 was ever a lack of small children around Jesus, and doubtless he often **took them up in his arms**; but on this occasion the adults actually brought them to him, evidently with the purpose of obtaining his blessing: it was something commonly asked of a religious teacher. Why the disciples objected is left to our imagination; but Jesus' reaction, as described by Mark (who hesitated less than any of the evangelists to ascribe expressions of emotion

14 to him) was a strong one: **he was indignant.** What was the quality in children which Jesus prized so highly? We have to clear our minds of all those

concepts of children's innocence, freshness of vision and spontaneity of motive which became established in the west only after the Romantic movement and have probably never had much currency in the east. Children, in antiquity, were valued not for their childishness but only for the promise in them of adulthood; and the 'blessing' of a parent or a teacher was sought to strengthen the hope that the promise would be fulfilled: it was a blessing entirely for the future. It is a startlingly new and modern tone which we hear in Jesus' voice when he appears to value children *as children*, in the present and not the future. It is possible, of course, that he was not doing anything of the sort. 'Children' in this passage may be symbols for the poor and meek and humble of heart, even a nickname for Christians (as perhaps in 9.37); or the episode may even (as some maintain) owe its form, if not its origin, to disputes in the early church about whether infants should be baptized. But neither of these explanations does full justice to the saying, **"it is to such as these that the kingdom of God belongs"**, which implies that there is something in children of real religious importance. The nearest the Bible (or any ancient literature) comes to this is a passage such as Psalm 131.2 – "I have calmed and quieted my soul, like a weaned child with its mother" – where the total dependence of a small child on its mother is an image of the dependence, trust and humility we should feel before God. We can only guess how much more than this was intended by Jesus, or indeed, how much more would have been understood by his followers.

17   **A man ran up and knelt before him**. This scene, which contains some notably vivid details, also has a striking beginning. It was not customary for people of dignity to 'run' up to a stranger, or for any Jew to kneel to another – the gesture was associated more with the cringing behaviour expected in the presence of an oriental monarch; and **"Good Teacher"** was a form of address so unusual that Jesus was moved to comment on it. This is hard to convey in English, for in a phrase such as 'Good Sir' the word 'good' is nothing more than an expression of courtesy. The same was true to some extent in Greek society, and a Greek-speaking reader would probably have found the phrase 'Good Teacher' as unremarkable as a modern English reader does. But in Jewish conversation this polite idiom was unknown. To say of someone that he or she was 'good' would not even have been understood as a professional compliment: a Jew would not have said that Jesus was 'good' in the sense of being a good teacher, better than others. To call someone 'good' was to use the word in all seriousness of moral character and personal conduct. And used absolutely, with no qualification, it suggested a moral perfection that belonged to God alone. Hence Jesus' objection. It has often been felt (as it appears to have been felt by Matthew, who alters the sense of the remark, 19.17) that the objection came oddly from Jesus: surely he, if anyone, merited the title 'good'? But it may be that Jesus was objecting less to the word itself, which might in fact have been appropriate to him, than to the attitude of

May 30, 2022 5:19:47 PM
79491

Item: 39085401305715
Title: The Paulist Biblical commentary
Material: Book
Due: 27/06/2022

Item: 39085052521321
Title: A companion to the New
Testament : the New Revised
Standard Version
Material: Book
Due: 27/06/2022

Item: 39085022465427
Title: The complete idiot's guide to the
Bible
Material: Book
Due: 27/06/2022

Item: 39085031232081
Title: Recovering Jesus : the witness
of the New Testament
Material: Book
Due: 27/06/2022

Total items: 4

his questioner, who was prepared to use so serious a concept as a term of courtesy or even flattery.

"What must I do to inherit eternal life?" The question was a standard one. After death, at the general resurrection, we shall all be judged on our record, and those whose good deeds and way of life have merited it will **inherit eternal life** while the rest will be consigned to hell. This, at any rate, was the usual way of looking at it in the time of Jesus and in the circles in which he moved (as it still is for many people), and the ultimate purpose and goal of religious piety and moral conduct was to 'gain a share in the world to come', that is, to **inherit eternal life.** The basic condition for achieving this was the faithful observance of the law of Moses; but it was not difficult to keep the basic laws and observances, and any serious religious quest seemed to demand something more rigorous. It was natural to expect that a teacher such as Jesus would offer a more strenuous ethic than mere law-abidingness. Jesus' reply

19 was almost brusque: **"You know the commandments"**: he simply referred him back, without any refinements of interpretation, to that section of the Ten

20 Commandments which governs conduct towards one's neighbour. **"Teacher, I have kept all these since my youth."** This reply was not pretentious. Many of us could say the same – we have not (at least consciously) broken the law or been had up in court. Jesus, at any rate, did not criticize his reply; on the

21 contrary he **loved him.** Perhaps he valued especially the evident earnestness of the man's question, coming from someone who (as we learn at the end)

22 **had many possessions.** The obvious advice to give him would have been to recommend a drastic increase in charitable giving, for this was certainly

21 valued as a highly meritorious act and a sure way of amassing **treasure in heaven;** and the rich were regarded as fortunate in having the resources to do this on a large scale. But Jesus pushed this far beyond the limit that would have been thought appropriate by most of his contemporaries (some of whom actually discouraged excessive almsgiving, on the grounds that one had a duty not to impoverish oneself). The questioner must give away everything. Only total 'giving to the poor' would answer his situation. And to the question, What should he do then, as a pauper? Jesus had the answer ready: **"Come, follow me."**

The story is one of a personal encounter between Jesus and a particular wealthy man. The question must have immediately been raised (as it has been raised ever since): Would the same apply to everyone who is rich? The normal Jewish view (which was shared by all but the most radical thinkers in antiquity) was that riches were a sign of God's blessing, and that one could turn one's wealth to a source of greater blessing by generous acts of charity. The obverse of this, of course, was that the poor were not blest; and since the rich are always few and the poor many, a more refined view had developed, according to which the poor had other virtues and opportunities for service which they could cultivate, and other evidence in their lives of

God's blessing upon them, which compensated for their lack of privilege. Jesus very strongly endorsed this attitude. He went so far as to say, without qualification, "Blessed are you who are poor" (Luke 6.20). There was some precedent for this; but none for the conclusion which Jesus drew from it, "Woe to you who are rich" (Luke 6.24). When, therefore, Jesus generalized

23 from the case of this particular rich man by saying, **"How hard it will be for those who have wealth to enter the kingdom of God!"**, the reaction of his disciples was one of bewildered astonishment.

25   **"It is easier for a camel to go through the eye of a needle."** Various escape routes have been tried for evading the harsh challenge of this saying. It has been suggested, for instance, (without any supporting evidence) that there may have been a gate in the wall of Jerusalem known as the Needle Gate. But Jesus was fond of almost grotesque exaggeration, and the disciples certainly

26 assumed that he meant what he said: they **said to one another, "Then who can be saved?"** Jesus' reply, again, has generally been regarded as an escape

27 route. **"For God all things are possible."** That is to say, God is of infinite power and infinite graciousness: he will let us into the kingdom out of sheer mercy, despite our reasonably comfortable circumstances. Or so, if we are not actually poor, we may persuade ourselves. But a reader in real poverty will take these words in their most natural sense: Jesus has stated a rule and then adds what is at most an exceptional possibility. The rich are excluded from the kingdom; but God *may*, just occasionally, make an exception!

28   **Peter began to say.** The disciples had responded to the challenge which the rich man had failed to meet. Could they at least be sure of their reward? What could Jesus promise? A leader with both religious convictions and political aspirations (and there were several in first-century Palestine) would

30 naturally promise material rewards **in this age** as well as **in the age to come eternal life.** On the other hand, a teacher whose concern was entirely with religious truth might demand an ascetic life-style and tell his followers to be content with spiritual benefits after death. Jesus' rôle was clearly more of the second type, and the second part of the saying – the promise of **eternal life** – is what we would expect him to have given. But it was also a feature of his teaching that the kingdom is not just future but can be encountered in the present: the rewards normally reserved for life after death might be experienced here and now. It is therefore perhaps less surprising that part of Jesus' answer to Peter's question should have dealt with the question of rewards **in this age.** Nevertheless, the apparent materialism of these promises comes as a shock, even if they are mitigated by the prospect of **persecutions.** But possibly Jesus was merely extending to his disciples his own experience of having gained a new family in place of his own, consisting of all those who 'do the will of God' (3.35), and of finding **houses** to welcome him wherever he went.

31   **"But many who are first will be last, and the last will be first."** In this life? In the life to come? In the Christian community? In society at large? A similarly

disconcerting saying has already occurred in the course of Jesus' instruction to his disciples (9.35), and this one appears in a different context in each gospel (Matthew 19.30; 20.16; Luke 13.30). It was evidently remembered as an isolated dictum, to be inserted by the evangelist wherever it fitted best into the narrative. Its setting in Luke's gospel (an extended description of the unexpected guests who will 'eat in the kingdom') seems particularly apt; but there is no way of knowing Jesus' target when he first said it.

Status and service

32 **They were on the road, going up to Jerusalem.** They were about to come to Jericho, whence the road begins the long, steep climb up to Jerusalem. The summit of the Mount of Olives could already be seen, some 1,200 metres (4,000 feet) above. But 'going up' meant more than this. It described going to Jerusalem as a pilgrim on one of the great festivals – the road may already have been crowded with pilgrims on their way to attend the Passover; and the deliberate and public confrontation which Jesus seemed to be seeking with the centre of religious authority in the land may be a sufficient explanation for the 'amazement' of his disciples and the 'fear' of **those who followed**. Nevertheless, the awed reaction of his followers, though understandable under the circumstances, remains a little strange. Mark may have been deliberately suggesting a presentiment of the dark drama that was soon to begin. Such

33–4 a presentiment, in any case, was immediately confirmed by Jesus' private announcement to the twelve of the fate that awaited him. The two previous predictions of the destiny of the Son of Man (8.31; 9.31) were in general terms, and could well have been spoken out of Jesus' awareness of the nature of the rôle he had soon to play. But this third prediction includes details which are fulfilled precisely in the history of Jesus' trial and execution. Mark may well have wished to credit Jesus with the most literal kind of foresight; but in doing so he may have allowed himself to fill in this saying of Jesus in the light of its fulfilment a few days later.

On the two previous occasions the disciples had failed to understand how one who bore the title Son of Man, which suggested vindication and glory, could be required to face so menacing a future. Here this failure is not mentioned; but the request of James and John perhaps indicates that

37 understanding had still not dawned. **"Grant us to sit . . . in your glory."** They may have imagined that Jesus was about to become a real 'king' in Jerusalem and that they might be his chief courtiers; or they may have been looking forward to the transformation of all things in a new age when they would share Jesus' 'glory' – a saying is recorded in Matthew (19.28) and Luke (22.30) which might have encouraged the question: the disciples were to "sit on twelve thrones, judging the twelve tribes of Israel". In either case they were making the disciples' usual mistake of looking ahead to the future rewards without reckoning on the tribulations which must come first, both for the

Son of Man and for those whom he represented. Jesus' reply contained no
38 rebuke but insisted on this necessary preliminary. **"Are you able to drink
the cup that I drink, or be baptized with the baptism that I am baptized
with?"** Cup and baptism were soon to have a technical meaning in Christian
worship, and this may have influenced the form in which the saying has
come down to us; but the words would have been easily intelligible in Jesus'
mouth. The 'cup' was a common metaphor for any kind of destiny that had
to be fulfilled, whether of suffering or of joy (compare 14.36); and there are
other instances in ancient literature of being 'baptized' as a metaphor for
being overwhelmed by a wave of afflictions. Jesus was in effect challenging
the two disciples to share in that destiny of suffering which must precede his
own glorification. They accepted the challenge, and so qualified for a share
in the Son of Man's glory. But the further privilege of absolute precedence
in the court of heaven was not so readily granted, even (apparently) by Jesus
himself.

43   **"Whoever wishes to become great among you must be your servant"**.
This radical teaching on personal relationships is repeated here (its first
appearance was at 9.35) as Jesus' response to signs of personal ambition
among his disciples; but this time it is based on his own example. The Son of
Man, if indeed, he is the figure described in Daniel 7.13–14, will be exalted
to a position where he will be 'served' by 'all peoples'. But that lies in the
future. Before that (and this is the side of the Son of Man's destiny on which
Jesus lays special stress in these sayings) his rôle is the exact opposite: he
has come to be the 'servant' himself; and since he is a representative figure
it follows that each of those who throw in their lot with his must also be
44 **slave of all**. The full extent of the service which is to be demanded of Jesus is
45 defined in the words which follow: **"to give his life as ransom for many"**. At
first sight this somewhat technical phrase looks more like the later language
of the church than that of Jesus himself. But although there are passages in
Paul and elsewhere which use similar language (e.g. Romans 3.25; Colossians
1.14), there is no other instance in the New Testament of this precise phrase,
and there is nothing in the phrase itself which would necessarily have been
strange to Jesus' own way of thinking. The idea of a 'ransom' was a common
metaphor in the Old Testament: God's interventions on behalf of his people
were often described as acts by which he 'ransomed' them from their enemies;
and since, in the time of Jesus, people thought of themselves as under the
power not only of the occupying Roman forces but of the forces of evil
and indeed of the only too obvious consequences of their national sins and
failures, the metaphor of being rescued from all this by the payment of a
'ransom' was easily intelligible. But how could the death of one man have
such a result? The explanation is often sought in Isaiah 53, where the exiled
prophet seems to have had some intimation that the death of a righteous man
could atone for "the sin of many" (53.12). But, apart from the word **many**,
the saying of Jesus makes no obvious allusion to this passage and it may not

be necessary to look so far for the origin of the idea. Not long after the time of the Maccabees, some two centuries previously, the deaths of those who were martyred for their loyalty to the Jewish religion began to be regarded as some form of expiation for the sins of their nation (2 Maccabees 7.37–8); and it appears that many Jewish thinkers soon came to believe in the vicarious effect of the martyrdom of a righteous man (compare Romans 5.7). If Jesus expressed the significance of his approaching death in terms such as these there is no reason to think that the idea would have been altogether strange to his hearers.

Sight for the blind

46 **They came to Jericho.** The last healing miracle recorded in this gospel is told with much circumstantial detail. The place of it was remembered as the road which led out of Jericho to Jerusalem; there was a **large crowd** around Jesus, possibly of those attracted by his activity, but perhaps more probably of pilgrims who, like him, were 'going up' to Jerusalem for the festival; the subject of the cure is named (which is unusual in Mark) – **Bartimaeus**, which

47 means literally **son of Timaeus**; Jesus is called **of Nazareth** – he is now a long way from Galilee and the bearer of the quite common name 'Jesus' needs to be identified; the blind man addresses him in Aramaic[15] as *Rabbouni*, a particularly respectful form of the title 'Rabbi', which in John's gospel (20.16)

51 is addressed to the risen Jesus; and his answer to Jesus' question **"What do you want me to do for you?"** distinguishes him from the ordinary run of beggars who would simply have asked for alms. All these details could be thought to suggest an eyewitness account. At the same time there are other elements which betray Mark's usual concern to show that the cure was not

47–8 to be understood merely as a remarkable feat of healing. **"Son of David"** is a title which has not been used before in this gospel. Bartimaeus could not have known anything about Jesus' ancestry. But 'son of David' was a possible way of referring to the person who (it was widely believed) was destined to restore the fortunes of Israel: the Messiah, or Christ. The following which Jesus had gathered, and the air of expectancy which surrounded his approach to Jerusalem, could have been sufficient to suggest to the blind man that this Jesus of Nazareth was such a person. But from the point of view of the narrator this recognition had a further significance. A prophecy of Isaiah (61.1, if read in the Greek text, which was used by Luke in 4.18 and would have been known to Mark) promised that such a coming one would 'proclaim recovery of sight to the blind', and Ezekiel also spoke of a Davidic shepherd-figure 'healing the sick' (34.4,23). So far, even the disciples had been slow to recognize Jesus'

---

[15] See the NRSV footnote. Mark, unlike John, does not translate it. His readers, even if they knew little about Palestine, were evidently expected to understand it. The NRSV aids the reader, but eliminates the local flavour, by translating it as **My teacher**.

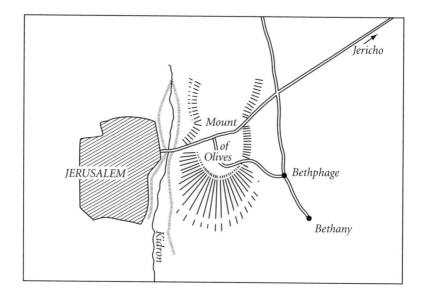

significance. Now a blind man had come to this recognition; and it was in
52 response to this that Jesus had opened his eyes: **"your faith has made you
well"**. If there is any symbolism intended in the previous cure of a blind
man (8.22–6), the same implication is doubtless present here. After a series
of attempts to open his disciples' eyes to his true nature and destiny, Jesus
demonstrates that even the physically blind can be made to see.

Entering Jerusalem

11.1 **When they were approaching Jerusalem, at Bethphage and Bethany, near
the Mount of Olives**. These two villages did not lie on the direct route from
Jericho to Jerusalem, but would have been reached by turning off southward
just before the road began to climb over the crest of the Mount of Olives.
As a way of locating the point reached by Jesus on his journey to Jerusalem
the mention of the two villages is not helpful: they were off the route and at
least a mile apart. But if Jesus was now at the crossroads from which the road
straight on led to Jerusalem while the turning to the left went through the
small village of Bethphage to the larger village of Bethany, the scene was set
2 for him to send two disciples **"into the village ahead of you"** to fetch a colt.

The story that follows, though it had immense significance for the evangelists, is capable of a thoroughly prosaic explanation. Jesus could have made
prior arrangements about a mount, in which case there is nothing surprising
in its having been ready for him; and the gestures and acclamations of the
crowd may have had an equally simple motive. It is often thought likely, for
other reasons, that Mark may have been wrong in implying that Jesus entered

Jerusalem only once, at Passover time. At two other annual festivals it was
8 customary for people to gather green **branches** from the countryside, and
on one of them a prescribed liturgical song was Psalm 118, from which the
9 words **"Hosanna! Blessed is the one who comes in the name of the Lord!"**
are a quotation (verses 25–6). May not the story in the gospels have grown
out of an almost accidental involvement with a crowd of pilgrims on the
road? This would, incidentally, explain why the procession appears to have
had no immediate consequences and provoked no official counter-measures.

But this attempt to deprive the story of the significance so clearly seen by
the evangelists (though in each case in a slightly different way) overlooks one
crucial detail. Jerusalem, then as now, was a holy city. It is a deep religious
instinct, shared by many peoples besides the Jews, that one approaches a place
of pilgrimage on foot. That this was so in Jesus' time is confirmed by later Jewish sources which report an exemption for the elderly or the infirm from the
duty of pilgrimage on the grounds that they would be unable to accomplish
it on foot. Astonishingly, Jesus did the opposite. After making the long climb
up from Jericho on foot he apparently made special arrangements to secure a
mount for the last stretch down from the Mount of Olives to Jerusalem. Such
an ostentatious, unprecedented and (in the eyes of some) surely scandalous
gesture is unlikely to have been invented. It is one of those pieces of historical
information about Jesus which it would be unreasonable to call into question.

Two other details in Mark's account suggest the reporting of a historical
event rather than the elaboration of a legend. One of them is concealed
8 by the NRSV rendering, **leafy branches**, of a word which meant 'straw' or
'brushwood': the purpose is likely to have been the practical one of making
the steep stony path less awkward for Jesus' progress; it is the other evangelists
who interpret this as the ritual greenery carried at festivals. That they **spread
their cloaks**, on the other hand, is a sign that they recognized that the occasion
demanded a gesture fit for a king. The second detail will be obvious to anyone
who has watched or taken part in a street demonstration. The crowd will
certainly shout; but their shouting will take the form, either of a phrase
repeated many times, or of a song they all know. Mark's account conforms
9 with this precisely. The crowd chanted **"Hosanna!"**, which originally meant
'save now' but which had become a word of general religious acclamation;
and they sang a verse from a psalm (118) which was particularly associated
with temple festivals.

Here, then, was Jesus making a striking and public departure from precedent. It was a prophetic gesture, and cried out for interpretation. But, unlike
the Old Testament prophets, Jesus seems not to have offered one. It was left
to the evangelists to draw out the meaning. Mark's interpretation begins
2 with the details of the securing of the **colt**, which is recounted at surprising length, doubtless because of the significance that could be seen in it.
Was Jesus showing miraculous foresight? There is no hint of the amazement and awe normally evoked by his manifestations of supernatural power;

the interest seems rather to lie in subtle aspects of the story. The colt, for instance (which could be the foal either of a horse or of a donkey so far as the word itself goes), had **never been ridden** – an unlikely choice from a practical point of view, but appropriate as a ceremonial mount: it was one on which a mere commoner had never ridden and which had never been
4 made ritually unclean through everyday use. The colt was **tied near a door**, doubtless for practical reasons, but again this evoked a famous, if obscure, oracle in Genesis (49.11) about a future ruler who would bind "his foal to the vine". The requisitioning was apparently acquiesced in by the witnesses on the grounds that the requisitioner had the necessary authority (possibly as a
3 teacher – the word translated **the Lord** could mean simply 'the master', but it also had overtones of special dignity); moreover, Jesus showed his probity by undertaking to **send it back**. All these details build up the picture of Jesus as an authoritative and righteous man following a destiny laid down in scripture.

The significance of the actual procession is explained by Matthew and John in terms of the prophecy of Zechariah (9.9) that the future king would come "humble and riding on a donkey, on a colt, the foal of a donkey". Mark's interpretation is contained in the words he adds to the crowd's singing of
10 Psalm 118: **"Blessed is the coming kingdom of our ancestor David!"** These words come from no known text in scripture or liturgy, and the sentence is too long for the crowd to have chanted it spontaneously. But it recalls a prayer which was said daily by Jewish people for 'the kingdom of the house of David, your righteous Messiah': Mark's addition suggests a heightened expectation of the messianic age to come: by such an acclamation the crowds would have shown that they recognized signs of it in Jesus' carefully staged arrival.

11   **Then he entered Jerusalem and went into the temple.** 'Going up to Jerusalem' reached its goal when the pilgrim descended the west side of the Mount of Olives, crossed the Kidron valley and climbed up the other side to the tremendous terrace on which Herod the Great had built the temple. The terrace formed part of the city wall, and one gate on this side led straight into the immense area of colonnaded porches, open courtyards and subsidiary buildings which surrounded the temple itself. To look **around at everything** Jesus could well have spent some time there; but he soon retired for the night to Bethany, where (if we may supply details from the other gospels) he had friends and the assurance of hospitality.

The story of the cursing of the fig tree is odd in so many respects that it is often thought to have been misreported by the evangelists. Why should
12 Jesus have been **hungry** on the short walk (barely 2 miles) from Bethany to Jerusalem? How can he have expected to find fruit on the tree given that
13 **it was not the season for figs**? And is not his curse on the fig tree both unreasonable in the circumstances and also out of character? Of all these oddities, the greatest is the detail that **it was not the season for figs**. If this

sentence were removed the story, though still puzzling, would at least be plausible; and it is possible to think of reasons why it may not have belonged to the original version. John's gospel, as well as certain details in Mark and the general unlikelihood of a religious teacher staying away from all the festivals, suggest that Jesus may have gone to Jerusalem at other times besides this Passover. If so, the story may have belonged originally to one of these earlier visits at a different time of year – say for the autumn feast of Tabernacles, when figs would have been ripe. But Mark, or the source he was using, allowed for only one visit to Jerusalem, at Passover time, that is to say March-April, too early by some months for any ripe figs to be found on the trees. There was nowhere else to insert a story that was set in the neighbourhood of Bethany; and either Mark or some editor working over the manuscript not long after it was written may have added the explanatory words, **it was not the season for figs**. In the framework of Mark's narrative this was correct. Unfortunately it makes the story barely plausible.

Even if these words are disregarded the story is still puzzling. Why did Jesus curse the tree? Two possibilities can be suggested. One is that the story was originally a parable told by Jesus to express the point that God's patience, like a husbandman's patience, could not be expected to last for ever, and that the parable subsequently became confused with an actual event in Jesus' life. The other is that the action was symbolic, in the tradition of an Old Testament prophet: for all its early promise, the 'tree' of Israel had failed to produce fruit and the time had come for its destruction.

15 **And he entered the temple**, which comprised not only the sanctuary itself and the central buildings connected with the cult but also a series of large colonnaded courts. The whole precinct was sacred, and subject to ritual regulations which were enforced by the Jewish temple police; nevertheless, there is no reason to doubt that people came to the outer courts for many purposes. It was here, under Herod's colonnades, that Jesus taught "day after day" (14.49), and here that crowds gathered to hear him. But the object of Jesus' attention on this first day after his arrival in Jerusalem was apparently quite specific: **those who were selling and those who were buying in the temple**. It is not explicitly said that these people were doing anything wrong; indeed, to some extent their activities seem to have been necessary for the functioning of the temple ritual. All contributions to the temple treasury, for example, had to be made in the purest and most exact coinage known in Palestine, the silver coins minted in Tyre. These could be obtained from money-changers, who charged a small commission; and, at least in the Passover period, these money-changers were officially permitted to have their **tables** (or banks) inside the temple precincts. Similarly, birds and animals for sacrifices, which had to conform to stringent ritual standards, might naturally have been sold close to the place where they were needed. These activities may well have grown and spread beyond the limits that were strictly allowed; there may even have been some debate going on about their propriety in the sacred

area. A religious reformer might well have made them the first target for his attack.

But is this what Jesus was doing? It seems unlikely for a number of reasons. To make any serious impact on what must have been quite an extensive trading area Jesus would have needed the help of supporters; this in turn would certainly have caused the intervention of the temple police, or even the nearby Roman garrison. But there is no hint of anything of this kind in the narrative, and in any case the attack would have been misdirected: it was the temple authorities, not the small traders, who were responsible for the abuses at which they connived.

But if it was impracticable for Jesus to change things single-handed, there was another style of action which would have been more realistic and more appropriate. Old Testament prophets frequently performed a symbolic action to drive home their message: should we not understand Jesus' assault on the trading activities in the temple precincts in the same way? To make his point, he needed only to attack one or two tables or stalls – the commotion need not have been great enough to cause serious disorder. His purpose would have been simply to give vivid expression to his criticism of the temple arrangements: a prophet did not attempt to change things himself but to convince people of the urgency of God's judgment upon their conduct. As a prophetic gesture, Jesus' action would have been both effective and intelligible.

What then did it mean? A prophet usually went on to explain the significance of his symbolic action; and sure enough Jesus is recorded as having done the same. Unfortunately the scriptural quotations with which he is credited are not very helpful, and may in fact be attempts by the evangelists to explain the scene rather than recollections of what Jesus actually said.

17 The first, **"My house shall be called a house of prayer for all nations"**, is drawn from a well-known prophecy (Isaiah 56.7). If Jesus was standing in the so-called 'Court of the Gentiles' in sight of one of the prominent notices forbidding Gentiles to enter the inner courts on pain of death, the quotation would have been entirely appropriate on the lips of a prophet who wished to see the temple a centre of universal worship; but it has little relevance to his action against traders and bankers, who had no responsibility whatever for the exclusion of Gentiles. The second quotation ("a den of robbers") is from Jeremiah 7.11: the prophet was attacking the people of Jerusalem for assuming that, because they maintained the worship of the temple, the violence and idolatry of the city's life would be condoned by God. On the contrary, argued Jeremiah, the presence of such people in the temple showed that they thought of it simply as some sort of protection against the consequences of their unlawful behaviour, rather like a **den of robbers**. If the object of Jesus' attack was the presence of extortionate traders in the holy place, then the description of their trading places as a 'den of robbers' sounds as apt as one could wish. But in fact there has been no suggestion that the tradesmen were

dishonest; it was merely that they were carrying out their trade in the wrong place. Moreover, the word 'robbers' does not catch the meaning either of the Hebrew or of the Greek. The essence of a robber is that he carries out his work surreptitiously. But the word used here means, not a surreptitious thief, but a man of violence, an armed robber or brigand. In the time of Jesus the word was becoming almost a technical term for fanatical rebels against the Roman occupation, who conducted guerrilla warfare, terrorized peaceable citizens and very often had their hideouts in the caves which are to be found in the mountains all over Palestine. We know from Josephus that acts of violence took place in the temple precincts around this period. If so, the saying would have had a point – but again, not as a commentary on the symbolic gesture which Jesus had just performed. In short, both quotations seem unlikely to have been uttered by Jesus on this occasion. The fact that John's gospel (2.17) adds yet another quotation (Psalm 69.9) makes it the more likely that these ones are the work of a narrator searching in scripture for texts that would throw light on Jesus' actions.

So what was the meaning of Jesus' protest? It is possible that it was more easily intelligible at the time than it was to later generations: there may have been some dispute going on about the temple arrangements on which Jesus' gesture seemed a clear comment. But perhaps we can gather a clue from the issue which is raised a few paragraphs later. They asked him, **"By what authority are you doing these things?"** Jesus replied by comparing himself with John the Baptist, whose authority was that of a prophet. When Judas Maccabaeus cleansed the temple of pagan objects in 141 BCE and when his son Simon became high priest, certain matters were left to be resolved "until a prophet should come" (1 Maccabees 4.46; compare 14.41–2). Jesus' action was that of a prophet. Was he then the prophet who was to come?

In the morning as they passed by. The sensational sequel of the cursing of the fig tree gives Mark the cue to introduce three sayings about prayer which, since two of them occur in other gospels in a quite different connection (Matthew 6.14–15; Luke 17.6), were presumably remembered separately. The form of the first was proverbial: 'moving mountains' was already a familiar expression for doing the nearly impossible. Nevertheless, Jesus says **"this mountain"**: the Mount of Olives would have been a singularly striking setting for the saying. From it the Dead Sea can be seen 1,200 metres (4,000 feet) below, and the idea that some cataclysm might 'take it up' would naturally suggest that it would be **'thrown into the sea'.** There may also be in the background (at least of Mark's consciousness) an echo of Zechariah 14.4: "On that day . . . the Mount of Olives shall be split in two from east to west."

"Believe that you have received it." This sounds a little like permission to use the power of prayer for any purpose whatever, along with a hint of how to do it. But Jesus was fond of exaggerations and striking simplifications. The point is surely, as so often in Mark's gospel, the critical importance of 'believing' – that is, of faith. The same point is made explicit in Matthew (21.22), and seems to have been in Paul's mind when he wrote 1 Corinthians 13.2, "if I have all faith, so as to remove mountains".

The third saying (on the necessity to forgive), besides being a characteristic element of Jesus' teaching, reads like a commentary on the Lord's Prayer such as we find in Matthew (6.14–15). Mark does not include the Lord's Prayer in

25 his gospel; but this saying, and the phrase **"your Father in heaven"**, strongly suggest that he knew it and had it in mind.

Controversy in Jerusalem

27 **Again they came to Jerusalem.** According to Mark's scheme (which may be his own invention, and is not followed precisely by Matthew and Luke), this was the second full day of Jesus' activity in Jerusalem. It was taken up with controversy between Jesus and the Jewish authorities, whose supreme council, the Sanhedrin, had its meeting place and offices in or near the temple precincts. The members of this body are often referred to in the gospels as **the chief priests, the scribes, and the elders**: these were the three classes of

28 people who formed the council. Their question, **"By what authority are you doing these things?"**, was more than just curiosity. If 'these things' meant the relatively violent acts of Jesus in the temple area, then the question of 'authority' would clearly arise. The only possible justification for such high-handed action (which clearly was not done on orders from themselves) would have been that the man was a genuine prophet and had received 'authority' from God. And this was serious. If Jesus had such authority, to ignore his warnings could amount to a blasphemous disregard for a divinely authorized messenger. If he had not, it would be their duty to silence him. Either way, the stakes were high, and their question urgently needed an answer.

The problem, of course, was that the question could not be easily answered. No proof was available to justify Jesus' claim to have divine authority. The witnesses of these things had to make up their own minds in the light of what they had seen and heard. It was ultimately the same question as had been

30 posed by John the Baptist, and Jesus was perfectly justified in challenging his questioners to deny that his predecessor was a genuine prophet. The presence

32 of a crowd of people more ready to see the hand of God in the preaching of a John or a Jesus than in the teaching of the official religious leaders put Jesus' questioners at a temporary disadvantage.

12.1 **Then he began to speak to them in parables.** The word 'parable' had a wide range of meanings (see above on 3.23). Sometimes it was an illustration intended to make the speaker's meaning clearer; sometimes it was riddling and enigmatic, leaving its hearers guessing. What is the meaning here? In the chapter devoted to parables earlier in the gospel (chapter 4), Mark seems to have deliberately represented them as obscure and enigmatic to all but those who (like the disciples) were specially privileged to understand them. But

12 here the meaning sprang out more easily. Jesus' enemies saw that **he had told this parable against them.**

1   **"A man planted a vineyard."** At first sight the opening of the story is in the characteristic style of Jesus' parables: the stage is set with a careful description of a familiar scene. The essential features of a Palestinian vineyard are all there: a **fence** constructed all round to protect the precious vines from the depredations of beasts as well as of human beings; a **pit for the wine press**, probably hewn out of rock; and a **watchtower** which was essential for guarding the vineyard, particularly at vintage time. But this straightforward beginning leads into a story which (unlike most of Jesus' parables) has some strikingly implausible details and turns out to be modelled on a famous passage of Isaiah:

> My beloved had a vineyard
> on a very fertile hill.
> He dug it and cleared it of stones,
> and planted it with choice vines;
> he built a watchtower in the midst of it,
> and hewed out a wine vat in it.
>
> (5.1–2)

The details of the watchtower and the wine press are identical; and in the Septuagint Greek version (which Mark, but not Jesus, may have used) there is also a fence. But in Isaiah this is not mere description: the vineyard is an allegory for Israel (it yields wild instead of cultivated grapes). Jesus could not have begun his parable in words so closely reminiscent of this well-known passage without his listeners expecting to find the same kind of allegory in it.

But if the vineyard stood for Israel, then other features of the story would be expected to be equally symbolic. The owner of the vineyard (as in Isaiah) is plainly God. The slaves are the prophets (often called 'God's servants' in the Old Testament) who were consistently maltreated by the people to whom

6 they were sent, some even having been killed; and the **beloved son** can be no other than Jesus himself. The question, Whom do the **tenants** stand for?, is answered by Mark himself: Jesus' interlocutors were the religious leaders

12 of Jerusalem, and **they realized that he had told this parable against them.**

9 The only remaining doubtful point is to determine who were the **others** to whom the vineyard would be given. Reading the story after the event, we have to answer: the church.

If we read the parable in this way as an allegory, it is unnecessary to ask for a plausible explanation of some puzzling details in it. How could the tenants have expected that they would acquire the property by murdering the heir? Why was the owner so imprudent as to send his son into such a dangerous situation? These questions are irrelevant if the course of events was dictated, not by real-life conditions, but by the progress of the allegory in illustrating the relationship of God with his chosen people. But is this correct? If the story is an allegory, it is not the kind of parable that Jesus usually told. If it is not, then why does it sound so implausible?

One solution is to suggest that the parable was invented altogether after Jesus' death, or at least (if Jesus told some such story) that it was so modified and adapted by the church that we can no longer recover the original. Certainly it was the church that recognized Jesus to be God's 'beloved son'; it was the church which saw in Jesus' death the decisive judgment of God on his people; it was the church which clearly represented those 'others' to whom the inheritance would pass – even if these truths were implicit in Jesus' own teaching. May it not therefore have been the church which devised this allegory? On the other hand, is the story really so implausible? Is it not possible to reconstruct the circumstances in such a way that it makes sense alongside the precise and vivid scenes with which Jesus usually illustrated his teaching? The following reconstruction can be no more than tentative, but it may help the reader to choose between these alternatives.

Absentee landlords were a well-known feature of Galilee at the time. They were also inevitably unpopular – and this is the first surprise of Jesus' story: his hearers were invited to be on the landlord's side, not on that of the doubtless impoverished tenants. Planting a vineyard was a long-term investment. In the long run it could be highly lucrative, but for the first few years expenses were liable to exceed profits. No fruit could be gathered for the first three years; but during that time the new vines would need constant tending – the Greek word translated 'tenants' is one used for skilled agricultural workers. No return could be expected from the vines themselves; but it was normal to plant the rows sufficiently far apart for vegetables to be grown between, and these might be sufficient to pay the wages of the workforce and perhaps a nominal profit to the owner. During these first three years it was nevertheless, necessary for the owner to send a representative (who could perhaps be a slave) to collect a nominal rent and maintain the owner's title to the property. But if the workers had been unable to make a profit on the vegetables, the slave's arrival could well have led to a dispute and ended in blows. In the parable this scene is repeated, with a rising level of violence, at the end of each of the first three years (and at this point we may suspect some later allegorization, with the addition of **many others** representing the long line of Old Testament prophets).

In the fourth year matters would be different. For the first time there would be a vintage. This, being 'first fruits', was subject to ritual regulations and temple taxation, and the profits could be appropriated freely only in the fifth year. Nevertheless, it was important for the owner or his accredited representative to make an appearance – Jews were even excused military service for the purpose (Deuteronomy 20.6). Moreover, the owner of the vineyard may have had a special reason to take personal action. His tenants, three years in succession, had refused to pay any rent; and since the only witnesses had been slaves, whose testimony had no legal validity, the tenants might have been contemplating claiming ownership on the basis of three years' undisputed occupation. It would therefore have been essential that in the fourth year he should come himself, or at least send a fully accredited

6 representative. In fact he sent his son, who was **beloved**, that is to say, on good terms with his father and a reliable agent for his father's interests.

But the tenants did not recognize him as an agent representing the owner:

7 they took him for **the heir**, perhaps assuming that the owner had died. It is not inconceivable that they could have made a claim to ownership if the father was dead and the son was intestate, and by throwing the body outside they may have hoped to escape suspicion of foul play. But their plans were fatally flawed, in that the owner was still alive. He unexpectedly arrived, presumably with a strong following, and punished the tenants with death.

Such a reconstruction would make the parable plausible as a story. It may seem unduly complicated; but if there had recently been a notorious case of such a thing in Palestine Jesus' hearers would have had no difficulty in following it. Yet even if it was a real-life story it still had overtones of Isaiah's vineyard, which was a symbol of the people of Israel's faithlessness. To this was now added their systematic ill-treatment of the agents sent by God to help and warn them. Jesus certainly knew himself to be such an agent, and to this extent may have been building his own likely fate into the story. And

12 his adversaries would have had no difficulty in realizing that **he had told this parable against them.**

10 **"Have you not read this scripture?"** (Psalm 118.22). Of course they had; but they did not necessarily know how to interpret it. Some said it referred to Abraham, some to David; but in the early church (which had become used to the strange idea of the Messiah being **rejected**) it was unhesitatingly used of Christ who, through the resurrection, had become 'the head of the corner', or capstone (the literal meaning of the word translated **cornerstone**), of God's new edifice, the church. It has no obvious relevance to the parable, where the murdered son is simply avenged; but Jesus, aware of the opposition gathering against him, may well have used it on this or some other occasion to express his faith in his own ultimate vindication.

13 **Then they sent to him some Pharisees and some Herodians.** We have met these two groups before (3.6) in league together against Jesus, doubtless seeing in him a threat alike to the religious and to the political *status quo*. It is a little surprising to find representatives of Herod's party in Jerusalem (unless they came specially for the festival), since Jerusalem lay outside the territory of any of the Herods and was ruled directly by a Roman procurator; but the **trap** they hoped to catch him in was a political ruse in which they might well have had an interest, in that they were inviting him to show

14 disobedience to the authority of the Roman occupying power. The **taxes** in question consisted of the annual poll tax levied on every citizen of Palestine and paid direct into the treasury of the **emperor**. The question was a subtle

one. The tax was imposed by the Romans, and no Jew who was liable to pay it could refuse to do so without being prosecuted. At first sight, therefore, the question **"Is it lawful to pay taxes?"** sounds academic: in practice there was no option. But, after addressing Jesus somewhat fulsomely as one who taught **the way of God in accordance with truth**, the questioners hoped, perhaps, that he would show himself bound by some rule in scripture which forbade the payment of tax to a foreign power. If he did so he would align himself publicly with those extreme nationalists who regarded the taxes as an intolerable symbol of subordination, and it would then be easy to have him arraigned before the Roman authorities. But the trap was cleverly laid; for, if Jesus produced no learned argument against payment, his reply would amount to an expression of acquiescence in the tax. And, since the tax was by all accounts exceedingly unpopular, such a reply might discredit him in front of the crowd.

15   **"Bring me a denarius."** Coins minted in Palestine – for instance by the Herods – took account of Jewish sensitivity to portraits and pagan images, and the small change in anyone's purse would probably have little on it that would remind one that the country was ruled by a foreign and heathen power. But only copper coins were minted in Palestine; the silver coins in circulation were all – apart from the special Phoenician coins used for the temple treasury – the standard coinage of the empire, bearing the head of the reigning emperor. One of these silver coins, a **denarius**, was equivalent to a day's wage for a labourer, or to half the annual tax paid by every Jew to the temple. The Roman tax must have amounted to at least this sum, and the Roman silver coinage must have been the usual, if not the obligatory, currency in which to pay it. When Jesus therefore asked his questioners to 'bring a denarius' he was in effect casting the question back at them. If they possessed such a piece, it meant that they used the emperor's coinage, and if they used his coinage they implicitly accepted his authority, and if they accepted his authority they could have no grounds to refuse to pay his taxes. His reply has a brilliance and finality which caused 'amazement' at the time and has inevitably influenced all subsequent discussions of the relationship of church and state; but it must never be forgotten that, when he made it, his interlocutors were holding in their hands a piece of coinage which already committed them to the same answer. The Romans did not think of their coinage as minted for the convenience of their subjects throughout the empire. Its primary purpose was to be a means of paying the army in any part of the world; and in theory it was expected that the coins, after being spent abroad, would be recovered through taxation. In this sense a *denarius*, 16 bearing the image of the emperor, was literally **the emperor's**. By analogy, a human being, made in the image of God, could be said to be **God's**.

18   **Some Sadducees, who say there is no resurrection.** Politically, the Sadducees constituted an influential party. Most of the high priests and important officials belonged to it; and on certain matters of scriptural interpretation

they were opposed to the teaching of the Pharisees. Jesus, with his apparent expertise in the law and his authority as a teacher, will have appeared to them as likely to share the views of the Pharisees; and so they presented him with a question calculated to cast ridicule on a specifically Pharisaic belief.

Apart from the Sadducees, it seems that the great majority of Jews in the time of Jesus believed in an afterlife, and that for most this took the form of a belief in a physical resurrection. But this belief was relatively new. It had become generally accepted only in the last two centuries, and the Old Testament contained at most some faint intimations of it. To support their belief, the Pharisaic interpreters of scripture had to resort to texts in the very latest books of the Hebrew scriptures, such as Daniel, and to appeal to their own tradition of interpretation rather than to any clear evidence in the Old Testament. It was precisely for this reason that the Sadducees differed from them. They denied the validity of the Pharisees' traditional interpretations, and held that, since the first five books of the Old Testament (which they regarded as particularly authoritative) make no mention of it, **there is no resurrection**.

But their question shows them taking a stronger position than this: not only does the law of Moses make no mention of resurrection; it contains provisions which, they could claim, make the idea absurd. The particular provision of the law referred to here is the institution of 'Levirate marriage' (Deuteronomy 25.5–6). This institution belonged to an early stage in Israel's history, when it was regarded as a desirable way of keeping property in one family and of keeping the family name alive. But it could hardly flourish except in a polygamous society (which had virtually ceased to exist among the Jews), and although attempts had been made to give it a high moral significance (the book of Ruth was probably one such attempt), it is unlikely that it was often put into practice in the time of Jesus. Nevertheless, the commandment still stood in the law and may still have been occasionally observed; and the Sadducees were perfectly justified in quoting it to make their point and in weaving a story around it.

23 **"In the resurrection whose wife will she be?"** The absurdity of the conclusion – pointed up by the extreme case of no fewer than seven brothers being involved – was probably a fair point in view of the crudity with which the belief in the resurrection was often held. Paul had to deal with similar misconceptions in 1 Corinthians 15. Writings have come down to us from this period in which the future life is portrayed with the naïvest materialism as a mere continuation, under beatific conditions, of ordinary human existence. Such crude beliefs deserved the Sadducees' ridicule. At the same time there were many thinkers who were ready to formulate their belief in a much more spiritual and refined form; against them, the Sadducees' argument would have had no force. Jesus aligned himself with this more sophisticated

25 view: **"When they rise from the dead, they neither marry nor are given in marriage, but are like angels in heaven."**

Jesus then attacked the Sadducees' own position by quoting a passage from that part of scripture which they accepted as authoritative (Exodus 3.6 – the

26 story of Moses and the burning **bush**). But given that the books of Moses make no mention of afterlife or resurrection, how was this text going to carry his point? Was he going to give it a new and subtle interpretation in the manner of the Pharisees? His commentary on it is so brief that it is not easy to say. As a straight interpretation of the text it seems to us singularly unconvincing: the oft-repeated formula, **the God of Abraham, the God of Isaac, and the God of Jacob**, was not normally understood to have any implication about life after death. But it may be that Jesus was following his more characteristic procedure of drawing attention to the underlying meaning of the words. God was 'the God of Abraham' and of the other patriarchs in the sense that he had led them, protected them and above all promised to them that he would be eternally concerned for their descendants. In early centuries this promise was understood as being fulfilled in the prosperity and (at times) glorious history of the people of Israel. But later, when that history had become anything but glorious and when, in any case, religious interest began to be focused upon the destiny of the individual as much as on that of the nation, the promise had to be understood differently. The promises of God, if they were not being fulfilled in the present, would surely be fulfilled for every righteous Jew in a future life: God had made his promises, not to people who would die and never see their fulfilment, but to those who, in their life after death, could enjoy them. By such reasoning, scripture could be seen to imply the resurrection even if it did not explicitly state it. The Sadducees had

24 understood neither the true sense of **the scriptures nor the power of God**, who could overcome the apparent finality of human death in order to fulfil his promises to **the living**.

28 **"Which commandment is the first of all?"** This question, asked by **one of the scribes** (who would have had a professional interest in the matter), was capable of two meanings. There was the academic question, From what part of the law (if any) could the rest of the law be deduced? In a systematic arrangement of the many individual laws, which law should stand at the head of the list? This was certainly the subject of learned debate at the time. But lurking behind it was a more practical question. The law consisted of a mass of detailed clauses (the Rabbis were soon to calculate the number as 613). Was it equally necessary to keep them all, or were some more important than others? This question was soon to become a crucial one in the church, where gentile converts needed to know how much, if any, of the Jewish code applied to them. In a Jewish community (as Paul insists, Galatians 5.3), there was little option: law is law, and no exceptions are allowed. If Jesus was being challenged to declare a more liberal option the question could well have been hostile.

Jesus' reply gives no ground for legal objection – it can be taken in the academic sense of summing up a system of laws every one of which was

29 equally binding. The first part of it, **"Hear, O Israel: the Lord our God, the Lord is one"**, sounds at first irrelevant, since this is not a 'commandment' at all but a statement of faith. But in fact it is the beginning of the passage which contains the 'first commandment' (Deuteronomy 6.4–5) and which was a basic text for Jewish devotion. It was recited by everyone twice a day, and it was felt to sum up the essentials of the Jewish faith and the Jewish way of life. Therefore it was not inappropriate for Jesus to preface his reply with this introduction: it served to put the first great 'commandment' in the perspective of the Jews' daily profession of faith. But then, to complete his answer, Jesus somewhat unexpectedly added a second 'commandment',

31 taken from Leviticus 19.18: **"You shall love your neighbor as yourself."**

Thus far the conversation had run on lines that need have caused no surprise in scholarly circles. Both these commandments were quite often quoted as being basic to the whole structure of the law of Moses, and, even though we do not happen to know of any other teacher who explicitly paired them as Jesus did, there is no reason to think that simply by putting them together he was doing anything startlingly original. Indeed, Matthew in his version (22.40) ends the conversation at this point and uses it to present Jesus in the rôle of a law-abiding Jewish teacher. Luke (10.29ff.) attaches to it the parable of the Good Samaritan in order to illustrate Jesus' radical interpretation of the second commandment. Mark alone allows the conversation to develop in such a way as to raise the question of how Jesus understood these being the 'greatest' commandments.

32 **"You are right, Teacher."** The scribe agreed with Jesus, but his commentary on Jesus' reply sets it in a totally different light. The keeping of these two

33 commandments was **"much more important than all whole burnt offerings and sacrifices"**. At a stroke, this comment turned the question from a harmless academic one into a controversial practical one. Instead of being an attempt to subsume all other laws (including those relating to the temple ritual) under one or two general principles, Jesus' answer became, in the scribe's commentary, a clear statement that the spirit and basic motivation of the law were **much more important** than the observance of its detailed ritual provisions. This was a message familiar from the prophets, and coheres well with the drift of Jesus' teaching. Mark here allows it to be expressed by a professional, one of those who were normally opposed to him; and Jesus, to show how close this formulation came to his own understanding, reversed

34 his usual judgment on the scribes and said of this one, **"You are not far from the kingdom of God"** – the highest compliment he ever paid to anyone.

There is a further point to be noticed about the narrative. The view of the law which is implied in the scribe's answer, though it could be supported by texts from the Psalms and the prophets, was certainly not that of the legal establishment; but we cannot say for certain that a professional lawyer could not have held it, and we ought probably to leave open the question whether this conversation actually took place as Mark (unlike Matthew and Luke) records it, or whether Mark deliberately constructed it to bring out Jesus' understanding of the Jewish law. There are, however, certain details which suggest that the story may have been edited to suit a different milieu. When the Jewish faith was being commended to educated Greeks and Romans it tended to be presented somewhat differently from the way in which it was discussed among Jews in Palestine. It was proclaimed, first and foremost, as the one great monotheistic religion of the world, as compared with the worship of the many deities of Greek, Roman and oriental religions; secondly, greater stress was laid on its intellectual content than came naturally to traditional Jewish psychology; and thirdly, there was a tendency to play down the ritual side of it, particularly the sacrificial system of the temple. All these three emphases appear in Mark's narrative. Jesus' reference to the daily confession

29 that **'the Lord is one'** and the scribe's paraphrase of it reads remarkably like
30 a conscious defence of monotheism; an intellectual term, **mind** or *understanding*, is added to **heart, soul** and **strength** (the three terms in the text of Deuteronomy); and the conversation ends with a depreciation of the impor-
33 tance of **whole burnt offerings and sacrifices**. This was the kind of language used by Greek-speaking Jews when commending their faith to pagans. If Mark allowed it to influence his record of the dialogue between Jesus and a scribe, it may have been because he realized that the kind of Judaism being preached, say at Rome or Alexandria, was not too different from the
34 religion of Jesus: those who practised it were **not far from the kingdom of God**.

The last of this series of questions is asked by Jesus himself, and in form it is the kind of question that was characteristic of learned discussions both in his time and for centuries after. Given such-and-such a belief, which some infer from the Old Testament, how is a certain text which seems at first sight to contradict that belief to be reconciled with it? The belief concerned was that
35 **"the Messiah is the son of David"**. We have no independent record of **the scribes** saying this; indeed, this kind of speculation about the Messiah was not (so far as we know) much indulged in. The Old Testament nowhere says in so many words that the coming Messiah would be a physical descendant of David, though some passages in the prophets could perhaps be taken in that way (Isaiah 11.1–9; Jeremiah 33.14–18). Nevertheless, the belief must have been held by some, since the gospels themselves, when they show Jesus' ancestry to go back to David, presuppose that this was an important factor in their claim that he was the expected Messiah. Jesus, at any rate, does not question this belief. Rather his question (in the manner of such discussions) drew attention to a text which was difficult to reconcile with it. This text (Psalm 110.1) was subsequently used by the church as a key prophecy of the exaltation of Christ (Acts 2.34; 1 Corinthians 15.25 and many other places). Here, Jesus apparently quoted it to draw attention to a paradox that temporarily silenced his critics. The psalm, which was almost certainly written later than David's time – possibly many centuries later – was nevertheless reckoned

by Jesus' contemporaries among the 'Psalms of David', and it would have occurred to none of them to think it was written by anyone else. Moreover, 36 being in scripture, it was inspired **by the Holy Spirit** and must therefore be taken seriously as the word of God. **"The Lord"** clearly meant God, and **"my"** must mean David's; but who was David's **"Lord"**? There was nothing in the psalm to say; and this was just the kind of obscurity in the sacred text that excited scholarly interest. 'David's Lord' could be a kind of cryptogram for some person who would play a crucial role in the destiny of Israel. Some two centuries after the date of this conversation there is evidence that this person was thought by Jewish scholars to be the expected Messiah. The Christian church evidently drew the same conclusion, finding in this psalm an answer to the question where the risen Jesus now was and why history continued apparently as it had before: this would be so until all Jesus' enemies had been 'put under his feet'. Was 'David's Lord' popularly thought to be the Messiah even earlier? This narrative, if it was not composed after the event (as some believe), seems to presuppose that he was; and in an age when the expectation of a coming Messiah was a feature of many people's religion, it would not be surprising if the cryptogram was interpreted in this way. But if so, it raised a difficulty. How could the Messiah, if he was 'David's son', be addressed by his father as a superior being: 'Lord'? Jesus did not offer an answer, and seems to have been content to leave the question to puzzle his hearers. It was only later that the church began to see an answer in the story of Jesus, whose resurrection and exaltation to the right hand of God made him 'Lord' of all, subject only to God himself.

38 **"Beware of the scribes."** In both Matthew and Luke a substantial section is devoted to an attack on the Pharisees and on the professional experts in the law, the scribes. In Mark, even though there is evident opposition between Jesus and these people, only these three verses (38–40) are devoted to an explicit attack on their character. The real reason to **beware** of them was not, of course, the rather trivial signs of petty ambition and ostentation which are mentioned here, but the legalistic hypocrisy of which these things were a symptom and which Jesus attacks elsewhere (7.6–8). It was presumably because they were particularly striking manifestations of this hypocrisy that Jesus singled out certain instances of arrogant behaviour of which perhaps 40 only a few were guilty. Similarly with the charge that **they devour widows' houses,** a charge which was as old as the prophets (e.g. Isaiah 10.1–2) and which religious groups often used as ammunition against one another. The moral obligation laid on wealthy women to give hospitality to teachers could have given rise to such an abuse, even if not many scribes were guilty of it, any more than Jesus' own acceptance of hospitality from women could be regarded as reprehensible. But if there were even a few cases of it they were sufficient to make Jesus' point. Their ostentatious **long prayers** may have been in lieu of payment to their hostesses or simply another expression of religiosity. Either way, they were another symptom of that hypocrisy of which

Jesus, justly or unjustly (for we know of many admirable religious teachers at the time), accused the whole class of scribes.

41 **He sat down opposite the treasury.** This is not a precise description: the temple had elaborate arrangements for receiving money, both obligatory taxes and freewill offerings. A later report describes thirteen trumpet-shaped receptacles set up in the Women's Court. This gives us a possible location, but still does not explain how Jesus could have seen how much money everyone gave. The narrative, indeed, is in the style of a story deliberately told to point a moral, and it is even possible that it was originally told by Jesus as a story and subsequently projected back as an episode in his life – for similar stories occur both in Jewish tradition and in the religious literature of other cultures. But it gains particular pungency from specifically Jewish attitudes to charitable giving. It was thought by many to be reprehensible to give away too much, lest one became oneself dependent on the charity of others; a fifth of one's capital and a tenth of one's income should be the maximum. Jesus' occasional challenge to give away 'everything one has' was radically opposed to such nice calculations, and is vividly illustrated by the story. One detail requires comment. People were **putting money into the treasury.** The Greek word suggests copper coins, small change for the Roman silver *denarius*. The

42 rich were throwing in handfuls, the widow only **two small copper coins,** in Greek *lepta*, the smallest coin in currency in Palestine. It was little more than a quarter of an inch in diameter and was worth less than a hundredth part of a *denarius*. This coin was unknown in Rome; the smallest coin there was the *quadrans*, which was twice the size of the widow's coin, and Mark may have had his non-Palestinian readers in mind when he added the explanation, **worth a penny** (*kodrantēs*).

Private teaching: an 'apocalypse'

13.1 **"Look, Teacher, what large stones and large buildings!"** This is still the visitor's reaction today. The buildings of Herod the Great can be recognized anywhere in Palestine by the immense rectangular blocks of beautifully hewn stone with which their walls are constructed. The temple, with its surrounding buildings and colonnades, was the greatest of his building enterprises, and not the least spectacular part of it was the huge substructure by which the top of the sacred hill had been extended to form a terrace of some 14 hectares (35 acres). The great east wall of this substructure, which rose vertically from the floor of the valley more than 30 metres (100 feet) below, is in position today and still excites admiration. On the occasion of Jesus' visit it will have been quite recently completed. The exclamation of his disciples as they left the temple area and passed through the gate in this gigantic wall is exactly what one would expect. Indeed, the setting for the long discourse

3 which follows is vivid and plausible. From the Mount of Olives **opposite the temple** one could look down across the steep valley between, and the

whole temple area, one of the most grandiose and impressive architectural achievements of antiquity, lay spread before one's eyes. That it should ever be totally destroyed must have seemed almost unimaginable; yet this is what Jesus had just prophesied. No wonder that he was 'asked privately' about it by some of his disciples.

Yet however realistic the setting, Jesus' answer, which is the longest continuous discourse recorded by Mark, shows signs of being a literary composition rather than the report of words actually spoken. When a master gave 'private teaching' to his disciples it might be merely a matter of clarifying difficult or enigmatic points made in public. (Mark 4 – the parable chapter – provides a good example of this.) But another type of private teaching consisted of esoteric revelations about the ultimate future of the world and of instructions on correctly reading the signs of the times. To impart teaching of this kind, Jewish writers had to hand a well-developed literary form, called (by modern scholars) an 'apocalypse' or revelation. These apocalypses described the approaching end of the world in terms of a supernatural drama, of which the main events were fairly constant but to which new details were added according to the particular intimations of each writer. These additions were themselves nourished by Old Testament prophecies, and could often be interpreted, by those sufficiently instructed to do so, as cryptic references to persons and events of their own time. In the time of Jesus, and particularly also in the second half of the first century CE (the period when the gospels were written), a number of these 'apocalypses' was composed by visionaries who were inspired to see in contemporary events clues to the shape of that final cosmic drama which (they earnestly believed) God was about to initiate. If Jesus gave some teaching of this kind, it need cause no surprise that he utilized some of the elements of traditional apocalypses; and it would be still less surprising if, when that teaching came to be written down, it became further assimilated to the pattern of contemporary apocalyptic writings. There

14 is one clear instance of this in the present chapter: **let the reader understand** is an admonition which could not possibly have occurred in a discourse *spoken* by Jesus; but it is just the kind of hint by which a visionary writer of the period was accustomed to indicate that a phrase or image he had just used was a symbol or a cryptogram for some significant person, place or event of contemporary history. It shows that at some stage Jesus' teaching on the future has been assimilated to the conventions of a written apocalypse.

Not only the form but also the content of Jesus' discourse has been influenced by these conventions. Speculations about the future tended to assume that the ultimate act of the drama, when God would finally manifest his sovereignty and vindicate his elect, would be preceded by a period of exceptional tribulation, when the powers of evil would be unleashed to an unheard-of degree and all but the most faithful and courageous of the saints of God would be tempted to betray their faith. This dark period before the end

8 could aptly be called **the birthpangs** (which was later to become an almost

technical expression for it); and moreover it had a purpose: it would prepare for the impending judgment by putting human beings to a decisive test. Those whose faith was already wavering would lose heart, and those whose grasp
5 of the truth was insecure would be led **astray** (again almost a technical term in this context) by various manifestations of a spirit of deliberate deception. But severe though the ordeal would be, the righteous could take courage.
20 **"For the sake of the elect, whom he chose, he has cut short those days"** – another feature which, if it was not already conventional, was soon to occur regularly in Jewish apocalypses; for the ultimate purpose of these writers was to encourage and sustain their readers in times of acute adversity. Once these calamitous events had got under way the final act could not be long delayed and the righteous could begin to look forward to their promised reward. The important thing was to be able to recognize the stage the drama had reached, to 'read the signs of the times'.

For these reasons it has become customary to call this chapter a 'little apocalypse', with the implication that, since an apocalypse is essentially a literary creation, the teaching it contains can hardly have been given by Jesus in anything like its present form. But at the same time it is important to notice the difference between this discourse and a typical apocalypse. In the Revelation, for example (which is a true Christian apocalypse), the basic pattern is the same – a period of intensified tribulation followed by judgment, a new age and the reward of the righteous. But there the treatment of these themes is totally different. The tribulations are not the ordinary catastrophes which might be encountered in the course of history: they consist of drastic and often supernatural upheavals in the processes of nature, accompanied by – or caused by – desperate conflicts between cosmic and mythological powers; and the climax to which the book builds up is the establishment of a new order by God, an everlasting kingdom in which his chosen people will at last take their rightful place. In short, the scenario is so much larger than life that we seem to be in a world of mythology rather than of history. The style is that of poetry, not of prose. By contrast, the greater part of Jesus' discourse is set firmly within history. The events predicted are all easily imaginable, the warnings which accompany the predictions are serious and practical, and very little space is devoted to the scene which is the *raison d'être* of an apocalypse – the final phase of judgment and reward. For the most part, the nearest parallels are to be found, not in Daniel (a relatively late Old Testament book which contains the first Jewish apocalypse), but in Old Testament prophecy; and the discourse as a whole is more concerned with interpreting the significance of contemporary history (which was an important part of the function of prophets in the Bible) than with painting a cosmic picture of the age to come.

The question the disciples put to Jesus was in any case not a general one about the future of the world, but was quite specific. After Jesus' astounding
4 prophecy of the total destruction of the temple they asked, **"when will this**

30 **be?"** In the course of his reply Jesus gave an equally specific answer: **"this generation will not pass away until all these things have taken place"**. And he was right. In 70 CE (shortly before or after the date when this gospel is likely to have been written) the Jewish Revolt, which had begun four years earlier, was finally crushed. The Romans besieged and captured Jerusalem, set fire to the temple and subsequently levelled it to the ground. That events were already moving in this direction some forty years before could well have been clear to a man of Jesus' prophetic insight.

But the essence of prophecy was not merely to discern the course which history was taking but to set these events in the wider context of God's promises and God's judgment, and to prepare people to see in them the signs of a greater providence. The discourse is an essay in reading the signs of the times, and weaves together predictions of actual events which Jesus may well have foreseen (or which, perhaps, the next generation of Christians may have filled in from their own experience) with some of the traditional elements which the prophets had incorporated in their descriptions of the impending climactic phase of history. To take each detail as it comes:

6 **"Many will come in my name."** Fanatics who claimed to have divine authority to lead the Jewish people in revolt against the Romans had already appeared in Jesus' lifetime and were to appear again before 70 CE. This was the historical form in which the mythological 'spirit of deception' was to appear in the final period before the end, leading people **astray**. Possibly Jesus' own notoriety and death would accentuate the danger: impostors might claim to be Jesus himself, returned from the dead with power.

7 **"Wars and rumors of wars."** An intensification of the political upheavals of which Palestine had always been a victim was a standard feature expected
8 in the last days. Verse 8 is only a slight adaptation of Isaiah 19.2.
9 **"They will hand you over to councils."** 'Handing over' was the expression used almost invariably to sum up the fate suffered by Jesus, which is here extended to his followers. The **councils** would be the local gatherings of elders assembled as a court; the **synagogues** would be where they must expect judicial punishment. **Governors and kings** do not necessarily shift the scene outside Palestine: 'governor' was a usual word for the senior Roman administrator, and those of Herod's sons who still ruled over parts of Palestine by leave of the Romans were commonly known as 'kings'. How far the experience of the early church has coloured these predictions we cannot tell. For instance, they would serve as an accurate description after the event of the things Paul had to suffer; but equally it would not have been difficult for Jesus to foresee that his followers had these trials ahead of them. On the other hand, a wider perspective than was usual in Jesus' teaching is opened up in
10 the words **"the good news must first be proclaimed to all nations"**. It soon became Paul's conviction that this must happen '**first**'; but it took the church as a whole some time to accept that the gospel was intended not merely for the Jews and their immediate neighbours but for the whole Greco-Roman

world; and if Jesus made such a clear statement about it, we must assume that the church did not at first take it as a practical commission but thought that he was predicting some subsequent and perhaps supernatural proclamation that would be made before the end.

12 **"Brother will betray brother to death"** – once again the word is 'handing over', a word that binds several of these predictions together. A prophecy of this kind occurs in Micah (7.6). The Jews set particular store by family solidarity, and this desecration of family ties seemed one of the most horrifying features of the terrible last days.

14 **"But when you see the desolating sacrilege."** The phrase, in the Greek, is virtually unintelligible. It was the deliberately cryptographic translation which the Greek version of the Old Testament offered for a subtle piece of Hebrew invective. In 168–167 BCE Antiochus Epiphanes set up an altar to Zeus in front of the temple in Jerusalem (1 Maccabees 1.54). The author of the book of Daniel (9.27 and elsewhere), by a kind of word-play on the Hebrew equivalent to the title 'Olympian Zeus', called this "an abomination that desolates". Anyone who came across this phrase either in Greek or in Hebrew would think at once of this notorious case of deliberate desecration, and would be led to look for a similar meaning here by the unexpected parenthesis, **"let the reader understand"**. It is probably useless to speculate on precisely what form of desecration Jesus would have had in mind, if indeed, he used this particular cryptogram at all. He could possibly have imagined the ensigns of the Roman eagles, which were regarded by the Jews as idolatrous, being set up as a sign of victory and conquest in the temple precincts. But by the time Mark wrote, one flagrant act of desecration had come so close to being carried out that it could have suggested how Jesus' oracle might be fulfilled. In 40 CE the emperor Gaius (Caligula) attempted to have a statue of himself placed in the temple, thereby nearly causing an insurrection. It may have been the memory of this which led Mark to make the idol sound like a live person (at the expense, in the Greek, of correct grammar): **"set up where it** (literally *he*) **ought not to be"**.

"Then those in Judea must flee to the mountains." An event such as that just mentioned was a real possibility. When it happened, it would certainly be the cue for much violence, and the only course would be immediate flight to the caves and inaccessible places in the mountains where no victorious soldiers or fanatical partisans were likely to follow up fugitives. The haste required is described with conventional but none the less vivid details drawn from peasant life. Inside staircases to the flat roof of one-storeyed houses were not usual. Anyone who was on the roof (where many domestic tasks were done) would have to come down outside before going into the house – and there would not be time to go in. Work in the countryside was done without a coat on – and there would not be time to go home and fetch it. The winter in Palestine sometimes brings rains so heavy that travel is virtually 18–19 impossible – so **"pray that it may not be in winter. For in those days there**

will be suffering": the Greek word (*thlipsis*) is again one that was typically used for the great tribulation which would precede the end and which would be of greater intensity even than the kind of suffering the Jews had so often endured at the hands of conquering or marauding armies; it would in fact be the definitive fulfilment of well-known prophecies of the time before the end,

19 such as that in Daniel 12.1 (of which verse 19 is an almost exact quotation).

22 **"False Messiahs and false prophets."** These would be another manifestation of the spirit of deception which would be at large in these last times before the end, calculated to **lead astray, if possible**, even **the elect**.

24 **"The sun will be darkened."** At this point one might gain the impression that the discourse moves from the realm of reality to that of mythology, from events which can be imagined as taking place in history to cataclysms such as would bring all human history to an end. But the words (which are in any case, a tissue of allusions to Isaiah 13.10 and 34.4 – the imagery was quite conventional) would not necessarily have suggested, as they do to us, a general disintegration of the universe. The sun, the moon and the stars were not thought to be much larger than they look; and their main function (and

25 that of the spirits or powers which were thought to control them, **the powers in the heavens**) was to maintain the regularity of life on earth. The sun and the moon assured the orderly procession of day and night, and the stars (by the principles of astrology, which were widely accepted) regulated not only the seasons but the destinies of human beings. Even a minor dislocation such as an eclipse was thought to be the sign of some extraordinary portent or disaster. *A fortiori*, disorganization in heaven would unleash chaos on earth.

26 **"Then they will see 'the Son of Man coming in clouds'."** This, at last, is the moment towards which the whole process has been tending and introduces the first truly supernatural occurrence, described in the words of Daniel

27 7.13. The presence of **angels** and the gathering of the **elect** continue this, the only truly 'apocalyptic' episode. Paul's description of the same scene in 1 Thessalonians 4.16 perhaps gives a clue to understanding the final phrase: the chosen who are to be gathered **"from the ends of the earth to the ends of heaven"** may be those of the faithful who have died.

28 **"From the fig tree learn its lesson."** In the face of all this, how should people react? Two dangers very soon presented themselves in the early church: first, that of assuming that, since the end had not come at once, it would not come at all in the foreseeable future and that vigilance could be relaxed;

32 secondly, that of becoming distracted by all kinds of speculation about the **day or hour** when these things would happen. Jesus, like other Jewish teachers, may well have had these dangers in mind, even if his words were subsequently adapted to allay the anxieties of his followers. The end would be preceded by signs, just as certainly as summer is preceded by spring. In Europe we might express the comparison differently (and Luke may have been adapting it to European conditions when he wrote (21.29), "Look at the fig tree *and all the trees*"). For us, spring is the time of the return of green life after the

dead colours of winter. But in Palestine, the winter, with its rains, is the one time when the mountains look green: greenness as such is not a sign that 28 **summer is near**. But the fig tree, which is one of Palestine's few deciduous trees, stands strikingly bare in winter and puts on fresh green leaves only in the spring. The transition between winter and summer is rapid and is completed between March and early May. The appearance of leaves on the fig tree is a sure sign that summer is beginning.

29 **"So also."** But how is the comparison to be applied? What in the previous discourse corresponds to the sign of spring, and what corresponds to summer? **"When you see these things taking place, you know that he is near"** – or that *it* is near: as the NRSV footnote indicates, the Greek is ambiguous and does not tell us just who or what is 'near'. Further, the phrase in the 30 next verse, **"all these things"**, is equally vague, and the saying **"this generation will not pass away until all these things have taken place"** only increases the obscurity; for it is clear that there are many things in the discourse which the generation contemporary with Jesus did *not* live to see. We are confronted again by the same difficulties as are presented by the saying in 9.1 (on which see above), and many have inferred either that Jesus was in error or else that he was seriously misunderstood. In fact the same considerations apply here as there. Many of the things which Jesus predicted did actually happen 'in that generation' – civil strife, a famine, persecution of Christians and a terrible war culminating in the siege and destruction of Jerusalem. Moreover, there 26 was a sense in which Christians could claim that they had seen **"'the Son of Man coming in clouds' with great power and glory"**: they were convinced that Jesus had risen from the dead and was now at the right hand of God (Acts 7.56). It is true that the cosmic catastrophes described in the verses quoted from Isaiah did not take place: but they belonged to a traditional form of prophetic utterance and do not represent the heart of Jesus' predictions. The course of events which he foresaw was not on a scale that made all human actions meaningless but was one which demanded vigilance and endurance. If it seemed to involve excessive or senseless suffering, it was to be understood as the essential testing period which must precede that state of affairs for which people longed; if rightly interpreted, it was a cause for encouragement rather than for despair. The important thing was to know how to read the signs of the times. Whether or not the prophesied cataclysms took place, 31 Jesus' way of reading history would still be valid: **"Heaven and earth will pass away, but my words will not pass away."** As for the danger of being 32 distracted by speculation about the exact timing of **that day or hour**, it was something that no human calculation could reveal. God is free to choose his moment. Surprisingly, even **the Son** is excluded from the secret – Jesus never claimed to be able to give privileged information about either life after death or the cosmic scenario. This is, incidentally, the one occasion in this gospel (in striking contrast with the Fourth Gospel) that Jesus is reported to have claimed unique sonship of God. It is possible that the formulation belongs

to the church, anxious to excuse Jesus from an apparent lack of supernatural foresight; but it is significant that the title **Son** occurs in the context of Jesus' human limitations, not of the divine status which the church later came to attribute to him when it used the title 'Son of God'.

33 **"Beware, keep alert"** – this is the only proper reaction. Another brief comparison illustrates it, similar to others which Jesus uses for the same
34 theme. Here, though there are other **slaves** who may also need to be alert, all the emphasis is on the **doorkeeper** whose job it is to be on the watch even at night – an unlikely time for a traveller to arrive, but not for a visitation such as Jesus has been describing. And with that the discourse, which began as private instruction to four disciples, is now declared to be destined for
37 the whole community of Jesus' followers: **"what I say to you I say to all: Keep awake."**

The final days

14.1 **It was two days before the Passover and the festival of Unleavened Bread.** This sentence gives, or appears to give, a precise date; and indeed from this point events move rapidly and in a fairly strict chronological sequence. Passover was a springtime festival at which the slaughter of lambs at the great altar before the temple, and the eating of them at a meal in household groups, were performed as a re-enactment of one of the great moments of the exodus from Egypt (Exodus 12). The festival of Unleavened Bread, on the other hand, which involved removing all old leaven from the house and eating only unleavened bread for the following week, must originally have been connected with the renewal of life at the beginning of each new year. Long before the New Testament period these two festivals had been combined, and the order of events was as follows. The main preparations were made on the 14th day of the month Nisan (which normally fell between March and May, though the Jewish calendar, being lunar, not solar, had frequently to be adjusted). Search was made for leaven and leavened food in all houses, and all that was found was destroyed; and in the afternoon the Passover lambs were ritually slaughtered. After sunset (which for Jews meant the beginning of a new day, so by their reckoning we must now call it 15 Nisan) the people assembled by families or small groups to make a solemn meal of roasted lamb, one lamb having been brought to the altar by each group during the afternoon. At this meal (since the festival of Unleavened Bread was now combined with Passover) all the bread and cakes were unleavened; and the festival continued for a week, during which all bread was prepared without leaven.

Which of these days is Mark referring to when he speaks of the **festival**? Properly speaking neither Passover nor Unleavened Bread began until after sunset, which by Jewish reckoning was a new day, 15 Nisan; but Mark may have been reckoning in the Roman manner (midnight to midnight), in which case both the preparation in the afternoon and the ritual meal in the evening could be described as taking place on the same day, the first day of the festival. It is likely, therefore, though by no means certain, that Mark was counting back from that day which, as we shall see, he believed to be a Thursday. But how far did he count back? **Two days before** suggests to us the previous Tuesday; but when the Greeks and Romans counted days they tended to include the day from which they started counting. If today is Tuesday, tomorrow is the second day, and so Tuesday may be 'two days before' Wednesday, not Thursday. For all these reasons we cannot be sure exactly how Mark allocated the days of what Christians have come to call Holy Week.

Apart from this uncertainty, the sequence of events in Mark is clear and appears to be followed by Matthew and Luke. Jesus celebrated the Passover meal with his disciples in the evening after sunset, was arrested and tried during the following night and early morning, and was executed the same day, which was a Friday. It follows that the Passover festival, properly speaking, took place after sunset on the Thursday, which was therefore the beginning of 15 Nisan by Jewish reckoning. But against this has to be set the evidence of John's gospel that in that year Thursday/Friday was 14 Nisan and Friday/Saturday was 15 Nisan; that is to say, the Thursday evening was only the beginning of the preparation day, 14 Nisan, and the Passover meal was not eaten until after sunset on the Friday, by which time Jesus had been crucified. Admittedly, this scheme suits John's theological interpretation of these events better (Jesus died like a Passover lamb); nevertheless, this discrepancy prevents us from accepting Mark's time-scheme uncritically (it is possible that some forty years later no one any longer knew exactly on which day these things happened); and certain details in Mark's own narrative fit in a little awkwardly. Not the least significant of these details is the planning of the

2 authorities. **"Not during the festival,"** they said.[16] But, according to Mark's account, 'during the festival' was exactly the moment when the betrayal and arrest took place.

3 Meanwhile an episode is introduced which has no exact date. **While he was at Bethany** – the story, or one like it, occurs in all the gospels. In Matthew (26.6–13) its position in the narrative and most of its details are the same; but Luke (7.36–50) places a somewhat similar story much earlier in his gospel and gives it a totally different application; and John (12.1–8) tells a similar story not two but six days before the Passover (and many of the details are different). Evidently the story circulated in more than one form, and it is likely that Mark chose to introduce it at this point and placed his own interpretation on it. If it had no precise date, it at least had a location – **the house of Simon the leper**, about whom we know nothing; was he still a leper

---

[16] It is just possible that the Greek was intended to mean, instead of **Not during the festival**, *Not in the festival crowd.* This would considerably ease the difficulty.

(which would make Jesus' visit to him characteristically bold)? Had he been cured (perhaps by Jesus himself)? Was he even still alive (for it could have been the house which had belonged to him)? But there is some evidence that lepers' houses were concentrated to the east of Jerusalem, which ties in well with the mention of **Bethany** and suggests a basis in historical fact.

It was customary to anoint face, hands and feet with olive oil, especially before any kind of social occasion, and those who could afford it mixed a little perfume with the oil. Perfume was expensive and was sold in bottles of alabaster or pottery with long, narrow necks, so that it would pour slowly. But the woman **broke open the jar**, that is, she broke off the neck and poured
5 out the entire contents at once. This was extravagant. **Three hundred denarii**
4 was what a labourer might earn in a year. The reaction of **some** who **were there** is perfectly understandable.

Jesus' reply needs to be seen against the background of the contemporary Jewish attitude to those 'acts of charity' which were not actually prescribed in the law but were held to be highly meritorious. Giving to the poor was always praiseworthy, and was indeed, expected of those who could afford it: there were certainly opportunities for it every day. But still more meritorious were certain exceptional acts of kindness, such as hospitality to strangers (there is a list of such acts in the parable of the sheep and the goats in Matthew 25). One of the most important of these was that of giving decent burial to a friend or relation; and decent burial might well include anointing the corpse. Compared then with routine acts of almsgiving, the woman's gesture was interpreted by Jesus as a generous anticipation of the burial ritual and
9 therefore as a quite exceptional act of kindness. **"Truly I tell you."** The saying which follows seems straightforward. Wherever the story of Jesus was told some mention was bound to be made of this remarkable act of kindness. Nevertheless, it is curious that the woman has no name (only in John's version is she called Mary) – it seems odd to perpetuate the memory of a good deed but not to record the name of the person who did it; and the phrase, **wherever the good news is proclaimed in the whole world** sounds a little strangely on Jesus' lips (for it is hard to understand why it took so long for the church to accept the necessity of a world-wide mission if Jesus had so clearly predicted it; see above on 13.10). And in any case, the only place where it mattered that there should be **remembrance** of the woman and her good deed was at the judgment that God would pass on her along with the whole world – which was perhaps the sense of Jesus' original saying.

After this interlude the narrative continues from the point reached at the
1 beginning of the chapter, where we were told that the **chief priests and the scribes were looking for a way to arrest Jesus by stealth**. One of the twelve
10 disciples listed in 3.13–19 was ready to **betray him**. The word in the Greek is the one we have met several times when there was a question of 'handing over', and it is arguable that 'betray' is a tendentious translation: whether Judas really 'betrayed' Jesus or merely 'handed him over', perhaps even with

Jesus' agreement, is nowhere stated. Nothing is said here about his motives; but we can infer from the statement that he accepted money for it that at least Mark believed he was a traitor to the cause.

12 **On the first day of Unleavened Bread, when the Passover lamb is sacrificed**. By Jewish reckoning these were two different days. The festival began only after sunset (a new day according to the Jewish calendar, so 15 Nisan) whereas the Passover lambs were slaughtered earlier on the same afternoon (14 Nisan). But Mark's expression, though technically inexact, would have been perfectly intelligible even to Jewish readers: he means the afternoon of 14 Nisan, which (according at least to his information) fell that year on a Thursday and was the time when each family or group of pilgrims made their preparations. Jesus and his disciples had come to Jerusalem along with the thousands of pilgrims who travelled from all over Palestine to attend the festival, and his disciples took it for granted that he would be observing it like anyone else.

The first necessity was to find a room: **"Where do you want us to go and make the preparations for you?"** In earlier times the Passover lamb had been roasted and eaten by all male Israelites over twenty years old in the temple precincts, but by now it had become a more domestic festival and the meal was held in private houses. Nevertheless, although the practice had changed, the theory remained the same: on Passover night the whole of Jerusalem was deemed, by a special dispensation, to form part of the temple precincts. This meant that those who lived in Jerusalem could hold the meal in their own houses, while those who came as pilgrims from outside had to find a room in the city where they could do the same. It appears to have been expected that those who could do so should lend the upstairs rooms in their houses for this purpose, and in this way even the many thousands of pilgrims were apparently accommodated.

13 **"A man carrying a jar of water will meet you."** To a modern reader it sounds as if Jesus had already made arrangements. It was probably as unusual then, as it would be now, to see **a man**, instead of a woman, carrying an earthenware jar of water, and the signal could easily have been pre-arranged. But the episode is remarkably similar to the requisitioning of a colt at the beginning of chapter 11: in neither case does it arouse comment, and yet each is told in such a way that the reader might infer that Jesus was exercising supernatural foresight. Not that it need cause surprise that the room should

15 have been already **furnished and ready**. Anyone who had a large enough spare room was bound to have it filled on that evening and to have provided the necessary tables and couches. But this would still have left the two disciples with many **preparations** to make. A lamb would have to be procured, taken to the temple for slaughter by the priests, skinned and roasted; besides this, unleavened bread, herbs and wine would have to be obtained.

17 **When it was evening, he came with the twelve**. The number of people who shared the same Passover meal was normally between ten and twenty.

These groups might be family groups: married women and male children over twelve years old were allowed to take part (Luke 2.41–2). But equally, men who had come to Jerusalem as pilgrims could make up 'fellowships' for the purpose. The lamb was then slaughtered in the name of each member of the group (theoretically all of them, not just two, should have been present when this was done) and from that moment no further members could be admitted. Jesus and his disciples formed an appropriate group to observe the celebration together.

18 **When they had taken their places.** This is good modern English but fails to convey the implication of the Greek that they were reclining on couches – the Greek or Roman custom which was adopted on special occasions. **"One of you will betray me, one who is eating with me."** Since table fellowship was a particularly strong expression of solidarity, betrayal by one who had shared a meal had long been regarded as particularly base: "Even my bosom friend in whom I trusted, who ate of my bread, has lifted the heel against me" (Psalm 41.9, an example evidently alluded to here). On this occasion, the

20 traitor was **dipping . . . into the bowl** with Jesus. Particularly at the Passover meal, but also at other meals, pieces of bread[17] or vegetable were 'dipped' into a bowl of sweet sauce. If Judas used the same bowl (but there is some doubt about this in the manuscripts: see the NRSV footnote) he must have been lying fairly close to Jesus; but the point of the saying was probably not to help the disciples to identify the traitor so much as to emphasize the table solidarity which the traitor was breaking. As a sin, that was already serious

21 enough. But the narrative sets it in a larger context. **"The Son of Man goes as it is written of him"**: the only passage in scripture that fits this allusion is Daniel 7.21, which (taken with 7.13) hints that the righteous people of God, represented by the Son of Man, must face a period of suffering before their vindication. It was this darker side of his destiny that Jesus was about to fulfil, for which it was necessary that he should be 'handed over', or **betrayed**.

22 **While they were eating.** It may seem surprising that Mark's description of the meal makes no mention of its central feature, the eating of the lamb. But his concern was not to provide a consecutive account of the details of a Jewish observance but to record certain actions and words of Jesus which, though they may have been prompted by the traditional character of the meal, were in themselves something entirely new. The Christian 'Lord's supper', in almost every one of its historical manifestations, has from its inception centred round these actions and words, and when Mark came to record them he can hardly have failed to be influenced by the recital of them which took place every time the supper was celebrated in the church. It is understandable, therefore, that he should have omitted those details of the Jewish observance which had no interest for his Christian readers. Nevertheless, he preserves sufficient indication of the sequence of events during the meal for us to be

---

[17] The translators have assumed that in this case it was bread. See NRSV footnote.

able to place Jesus' innovations in their original context. **He took a loaf of bread**. It is significant that the taking of bread took place after the meal had begun: almost all formal meals began with the host saying the blessing and taking a loaf of bread, which he then divided out among the guests. But at the Passover the supper began with 'bitter herbs' – lettuce and the like – which were dipped into a dish of sweet sauce. This was the moment for the Judas episode which has just been narrated. The breaking of bread seems to have had no fixed place in the meal and certainly did not take place at the beginning. To this extent it is intelligible that Jesus' action should have been **while they were eating**: so far as we know the blessing and breaking, though usual at the start of any other such occasion, had no special place at the Passover meal.

"Take; this is my body." Another feature of the Passover meal, which certainly goes back to the time of Jesus (though it was much elaborated in later times) was that the host – or the father, if it was a family group – had to explain the significance of the special food that was being eaten. The whole meal was seen as a re-enactment of the exodus from Egypt (Exodus 12); and the explanation took the form of a commentary on a passage such as Deuteronomy 26.5–9, where these events are summarized. For instance, the Passover lamb recalled the lamb slaughtered by each family before the flight (Exodus 12.21); its blood stood for the blood that was painted on the Israelites' doorposts so that the punishment of the Lord should 'pass over' them (Exodus 12.27); and the bitter herbs represented the days of bitter slavery which the people had undergone in Egypt. But what did the unleavened bread stand for? This (since it probably did not belong to the original festival) was more difficult, and differing answers were given – in Deuteronomy 16.3 it is called "the bread of affliction". It may have been in this context that Jesus pronounced the words, **"this is my body"**.

What do the words mean? Down the centuries they have been repeated each time the 'Lord's supper' has been celebrated, and Christians have discovered countless meanings through their reflection and their experience. But here there is no suggestion in the text that Jesus was instituting a rite that was to be repeated: the word **"Take"** is the only indication that Jesus even intended the bread to be shared. It is only Paul's version (1 Corinthians 11.24, supported by a doubtful text in Luke 22.19) which states that the bread/body was 'for them' and that the action was to be continued 'in remembrance' of Jesus. And it is only in John's gospel (chapter 6) that we find any discussion of the meaning of the bread itself. If Jesus had been likening himself to a sacrificial victim that is duly consumed by the worshippers, he would surely have used the meat of the lamb rather than bread to carry the symbolism. As it is, we can barely guess what the disciples would have understood by his designation of the bread as his 'body'.

23 Interpretation is easier in what follows. **Then he took a cup**. If the meal was following the usual course of a Passover supper, some time will have elapsed

since the breaking of bread: the lamb will have been eaten and the prescribed explanation given of the meaning of the special food that was served. But the Christian community had no interest in these details (though an echo of them survives in Paul's phrase, "he took the cup also, *after supper*", 1 Corinthians 11.25), and Mark goes straight on to one of the moments at the end of the meal when the host took a cup of wine in his hands, **giving thanks.** The disciples would have found it natural to associate themselves with Jesus in this by immediately drinking with him (possibly from a common cup). But once again Jesus went far beyond any such conventional ceremony by adding

24 words which, this time, give meaning to his action: **"This is my blood of the covenant, which is poured out for many."** This is the language of sacrifice. The most important moment in the ritual slaughter of a victim at the altar in Jerusalem was the shedding of its blood. It was by virtue of the blood poured on the altar that the sacrifice was deemed effective. Certain sacrifices made by the priests were moreover made, not for individual worshippers, but **for many** (though Jesus may have had in mind a larger section of humanity than was envisaged at any Jewish sacrifice); and on one occasion the blood of a sacrifice had been sprinkled upon the whole people of Israel to seal the 'covenant' made with them by God (Exodus 24.8). The Old Testament looked forward to a 'new covenant' of an inner, spiritual kind (Jeremiah 31.31–4), and the work of Jesus was soon to be understood by Christians as the inauguration of this new covenant.[18] The wine, therefore, which the disciples were to drink was interpreted by Jesus as the blood of himself as a sacrificial victim, whose death would be on behalf of many and would seal a new covenant between God and human beings.

25 **"Truly I tell you, I will never again drink of the fruit of the vine."** As it stands here (the position and meaning are different in Luke 22.18), the saying appears to be a simple prophecy by Jesus that he would not live to partake of any further meals at which wine was drunk; and since the narrative implies that he was by now certain of his impending death it can be taken as one more solemn prediction of what was about to happen. But the saying does not stop there. It continues with a rich load of biblical ideas: **"until that day when I drink it new in the kingdom of God"**. The future age was often imagined in terms of a heavenly banquet in which the Messiah would have a place of honour and all things would be made **new**; and Jesus seems to have been deliberately relating the meal he had just shared to the heavenly reality which, he prophesied, would shortly be realized. The one was a foretaste of the other, just as the traditional Passover meal was often interpreted as an anticipation of the coming redemption which God had promised to his people.

26 **When they had sung the hymn.** The Passover meal ended with the singing of the *Hallel*, which consisted of a group of psalms (114–8), and this may

---

[18] The word *new* is inserted in a number of ancient manuscripts: see the NRSV footnote.

well be what is meant here. **They went out to the Mount of Olives.** It seems to have been obligatory for all who kept the festival to remain in Jerusalem or its immediate neighbourhood until sunrise. We can assume that Jesus was conforming with this regulation when, long before sunrise, he left the city, crossed the Kidron valley and approached the lower slopes of the Mount

27 of Olives. **"You will all become deserters."** This is a novel translation of the Greek word *skandalizesthai*, which suggests 'taking offence' or 'falling away from faith'. It partially obscures the relevance of the quotation from Zechariah (13.7, in a form slightly different from any that has come down to us), for this makes the smiting of **the shepherd** (which Jesus appears to be taking as another prediction of his own fate) the cause of his followers' (**the sheep**) being scattered – they do not simply 'desert'. It is remarkable that in the gospels no attempt is made to conceal or mitigate the failure of the disciples to stand by Jesus; on the other hand, it may even have helped them to live it down, so to speak, when an Old Testament prophecy was recalled which made their conduct seem predestined. In any case, all Jesus' predictions seem to presuppose that he was to suffer alone. What makes it all the more poignant is that this denial and desertion took place before the end of the night during which Jesus and his disciples should have been particularly closely bound together by what they had just shared. As on previous occasions in this gospel, Peter is singled out from the disciples, but apparently only to represent them all: **"You will all become deserters"**

30 applies to them all; **"you will deny me"** indicates the particular way in which Peter will fulfil the prediction. **"Before the cock crows twice."** In the east there is often a remarkably regular series of cock-crows well before dawn. The third of the four 'watches' into which the Romans divided the night (and this way of reckoning was known in Palestine – see 13.35) was popularly called 'cock-crow'. Whatever Mark meant by the cock crowing **twice**, the moment was going to be easy to recognize, well before dawn.

28 The section contains one puzzling prophecy. **"But after I am raised up, I will go before you to Galilee."** After the flock had been scattered through the striking down of the shepherd, it would once more gather behind its leader as he moved away northward to Galilee. This, at any rate, is the natural meaning of the words, which are recalled by an angel after the resurrection (16.7). The difficulty is to see in what way, if any, the prophecy was fulfilled. After the resurrection Jesus appeared to the disciples, not in Galilee, but in or near Jerusalem. It is true that Galilee was the natural place for Jesus to return to after his brief sojourn in Jerusalem and that there are two reports in the gospels of a later appearance in Galilee (Matthew 28.16–20 and John 21); but apart from these, all the evidence is that the church began its life, not following its master back to Galilee, but waiting upon his appearances and the manifestations of his power in Jerusalem. Yet Galilee was a symbolic name: it meant 'land of the Gentiles' (as in Matthew 4.15). It is just possible

that this prophecy was understood to mean that after the resurrection Jesus would lead his church far beyond the confines of the Jewish world. And this indeed, took place.

32 **They went to a place called Gethsemane**. The name is likely to mean 'oil press'. John's gospel (18.1) calls it a 'garden' on the far side (from Jerusalem) of the Kidron valley which separates Jerusalem from the Mount of Olives. All the gospel accounts imply that it was somewhere on the Mount of Olives itself. The traditional site, not far from a cave on the slope of the mount facing Jerusalem, fits these data as well as any, and we should visualize a secluded and perhaps enclosed spot not far from the road that led over the Mount of Olives to Bethany. Jesus' purpose in coming to it was to pray, for which he usually preferred to be alone; but on this occasion he allowed near him the three privileged disciples who had earlier been witnesses of his transfiguration.

From this perfectly natural and quiet beginning two altogether unexpected sequences of events unfold. First, Jesus' steady resolution and apparent fore-knowledge of what was about to happen suddenly forsook him. For no rea-
33 son that the gospels explain, **he began to be distressed and agitated** (literally translated, the Greek means *amazed and dismayed*); and his prayer, which we may suppose normally took the form of intimate communion with his Father, was on this occasion an anguished mixture of rebellion and resigna-tion. It may be asked: Did Jesus really pray like this? If the only witnesses fell asleep, how could his words have been heard and remembered? Is it not more likely that a subsequent tradition composed the kind of prayer which Jesus is likely to have prayed, just as ancient historians, from Thucydides onwards, freely composed the speeches which generals or statesmen were likely to have delivered on critical occasions? Certainly this prayer is by no means (in the
34 modern sense) original. **"I am deeply grieved, even to death"**, even if not an exact quotation, recalls both the words of a psalmist whose faith in God is tested to breaking point (Psalm 42.6,12) and the despair of the prophet Jonah when the turn of events had made him feel that he should die rather
36 than endure his vocation (Jonah 4.9). **"Abba"**, an intimate Aramaic word for 'Father', was the way in which the first Christians believed they had been taught to address their prayers to God; and **"not what I want, but what you want"** is a clear allusion to the Lord's Prayer. In short, the materials for com-posing the prayer lay to hand in the spirituality of the Old Testament and the early church, and if it is thought unlikely that any record of Jesus' actual words could have been preserved, there is no difficulty in seeing how they could have been supplied by his followers. But it remains true that the content of Jesus' prayer is startlingly different from what his followers might have been expected to attribute to him unless they had some grounds for think-ing that he had undergone some such agonizing experience during his last hours of solitude in Gethsemane. Moreover, both the letter to the Hebrews (5.7) and the gospel according to John (12.27) offer apparently independent

testimony to some experience of Jesus comparable with that recorded here; and the episode is so unexpected that it seems unlikely that it was invented in its entirety by the church.

The second unexpected sequence of events concerns the disciples. At the
34 outset Jesus merely bade them, without explanation, to **"keep awake"**. It is possible that Jesus was observing the customs of Passover night: if one of the group which had eaten the supper together fell asleep, the table fellowship was deemed to have been broken. Jesus might have bidden them stay awake for the sake of their solidarity with him. But there is no hint of this in Mark's narrative. And when Jesus found that they had nevertheless, fallen asleep – for it was now doubtless late in the night – he rebuked Simon (presumably
38 representing the group) and urged them all again to **"Keep awake"**, this time giving the reason: **"pray that you may not come into the time of trial"**. What 'trial'?[19] The prayer, again, sounds like a reminiscence of the Lord's Prayer: Christians were always to pray, "Do not bring us to the time of trial" (Matthew 6.13). But clearly a special 'trial' is in mind here by which the disciples were threatened. Was it the danger that they would be arrested and executed along with Jesus? Was it the temptation (about to be yielded to by Peter) to flee danger and deny Jesus which constituted their 'trial' and about which they ought to be praying, just as Jesus was praying about his own greater trial? We are not told; nor are we told in what tone of voice Jesus commented on their
37, 38 failure to **keep awake one hour**. As for **"the spirit indeed is willing, but the flesh is weak"**, was this a proverb, wryly appropriate to the situation? Or an indulgent comment by one who suffered no weakness of the flesh himself? Or a comment on human psychology such as we might find in Paul? We do not know. It is true that 'Stay awake' became a common moral exhortation in the early church, that 'Do not bring us to the time of trial' was a prayer which Christians uttered every day and that the power of the spirit and the weakness of the flesh became a familiar contrast in the experience of the first Christian communities. Moreover, 'the spirit is willing but the flesh is weak' is the kind of balanced antithesis which is perhaps more characteristic of literary Greek than (so far as we know) of spoken Aramaic. In short, many would see here tell-tale signs of the subsequent reflection of the church which may have influenced or even created the narrative. And yet it is difficult to see why anyone in the church should have wanted to cast discredit on the disciples by making up the story of their weakness; and if it is true that they failed to stay awake, the rest flows from that. In any case, we are left with an account which, though puzzling in some of its details, is vivid, moving and apparently authentic.

41 **"Are you still sleeping?"** The force of these words depends on the punctuation, and since, when the gospels were first written down, punctuation marks were not much used, it is only from the context that we can tell whether Jesus

---

[19] Traditionally *temptation*: but see above on Matthew 6.13.

was giving a command ('Go on sleeping!'), making an exclamation ('Still asleep!') or asking a question ('Still sleeping?'). Most older translations take the words as a command; more recent ones, like the NRSV, take them as an ironic question commenting on the disciples' repeated failure to keep awake. This has the advantage of leading more naturally into what follows, though there is still considerable obscurity about the Greek word translated **"Enough!"** The most we can say is that there is a note of finality about it. Jesus knows that the **"hour has come"**.

43   **Immediately, while he was still speaking**. It is difficult, in translation, to reproduce the finer points of an author's style without falling into pedantry. But here there is some significance in the Greek word which Mark uses to introduce the next episode: *euthus*, **immediately**; for it is his favourite way of joining one episode to another. The detail is important, because it is at this point that the narratives of all the gospels (including John) converge and begin to move forward together along very similar lines; and this convergence is most easily explained if, in the early church, the account of Jesus' arrest, trial and execution was the first part of the gospel narrative to assume a fairly standardized form, leaving each evangelist little freedom to rearrange it. If such a common tradition existed, it apparently began with Jesus' arrest. It is true that in Mark's account (closely followed by Matthew) the arrest seems to be so closely linked with what goes before that it seems difficult to believe that a new chapter, so to speak, originally began at this point; but the word **immediately** betrays Mark's editorial hand: it could well have been he who joined up the episodes into a single sequence.

   Judas, one of the twelve. There seems to be a deliberate emphasis (as in verse 10 above) on the fact that it was one of Jesus' own disciples who betrayed him: earlier on, Jesus had several times predicted that he would be 'handed over' – the same word as 'betrayed' – but it was not until the Passover meal that he acknowledged that one of his own followers would be the agent. That he was accompanied by **a crowd with swords and clubs** might make it sound as if it was the work of a gang of ruffians, were it not that they were sent by **the chief priests, the scribes and the elders**, who were the three classes of people who made up the Sanhedrin, the supreme Jewish council. This council, though deprived of some of its powers by the Roman administration, exercised legal authority and maintained some kind of police or body of armed men to enforce compliance. It was these men, according to Mark, who arrived with Judas to arrest Jesus.

44   **Now the betrayer had given them a sign**. Evidently there was no intention of arresting Jesus' followers; and there is no explanation in any of the gospels of the need either for identification of the prisoner (who was a public figure)

49   or of armed arrest: Jesus' ironic observation, **"Day after day I was with you in the temple teaching"**, strikes us as fully justified – though it presents us with a slight problem: by Mark's reckoning he had been at most two or three days in Jerusalem teaching in the temple: is this another hint that

45 Mark's chronology may be artificial? As for Judas' kiss: this strikes us as a particularly repellent gesture of betrayal. But this may be a modern reaction. It was customary for a pupil to greet his master with a kiss: when Judas kissed Jesus and called him **"Rabbi"** he was using the ordinary form of greeting and at the same time identifying for the benefit of the armed band the one man in the group who could properly be addressed in this way. Nevertheless, there seems to have been something of a scuffle: the wounding of a slave, which other accounts attribute to a disciple (perhaps to suggest that not all Jesus'

50 followers immediately **deserted him and fled**) is here the work, perhaps

47 accidental, of **one of those who stood near**. The predicted 'handing over' of Jesus, even if it was deliberately carried out in a quiet place by night, was nevertheless witnessed by a substantial number of people.

48   **Then Jesus said to them**. His words are recorded, with slight variations,

49 in all the gospels, and show that he had no thought of resistance. **"Let the scriptures be fulfilled"** summarizes his attitude. Perhaps he still had in mind Zechariah's prophecy of the shepherd being struck (13.7); perhaps he was thinking of the chapter in Isaiah (53) where the servant is 'handed over' – Luke's gospel (22.37) actually gives the quotation, "And he was counted

48 among the lawless", which gives point to Jesus' question, **". . . to arrest me as though I were a bandit?"** The most we can say for certain is that, here as elsewhere, Jesus saw his destiny as one that conformed to the scriptural pattern of the righteous man subjected to undeserved suffering for the sake of the larger purposes of God.

51   Mark alone mentions the **young man . . . wearing nothing but a linen cloth**. From the Greek, we cannot be sure that it was linen – the word could simply mean a garment; but, if it was, it was a sign that he was not poor. The episode is so vivid and unexpected that it has often been suggested that the young man was none other than the writer of the gospel himself. But this is pure speculation.

53   **They took Jesus to the high priest**, where a hearing was held before **the chief priests, the elders, and the scribes**. These three classes made up the Sanhedrin, which had wide judicial powers, and the hearing looks at first sight like a trial. Certainly it has a judicial character – witnesses are called, the defendant is asked for his testimony, a verdict is given. But it also has some irregular features. The council's official meeting place was a building inside (or at least close to) the temple precincts, but on this occasion it was assembled in the high priest's house (verse 54); sittings of the court were permitted only during the day, but this one took place in the middle of the night; capital sentences required confirmation by a further sitting not less than twenty-four hours after the first and no capital case could be heard on the eve of a sabbath or feast day, but in this case the judges proceeded immediately to secure the carrying out of the sentence, the following day was a sabbath, and the night of the hearing was the beginning of the Passover festival. Not all this information about the technical procedure, however, is

reliable. It was first written down and codified over a century after Jerusalem had been destroyed and the council, as a legal authority with judicial powers, had ceased to exist. These later Jewish sources provide us with a picture which may well be idealized and artificial: in the troubled period before the Jewish Revolt, these careful and mostly humane provisions may not have been strictly observed. But there are other reasons for doubting whether what took place was strictly a 'trial' at all. Though the judges condemned Jesus

64 as **deserving death**, this was not necessarily an official verdict, and indeed, they went on, first, to subject him to some extremely unjudicial mockery and beating and then, next morning, to hold a further meeting at which they decided on their course of action. Moreover, by no means all the New Testament writers are agreed that Jesus was formally found guilty in a Jewish court (Acts 13.28,"they found no cause for a sentence of death"), and indeed we know that agreement on a verdict was often difficult to obtain because of the differences between the parties represented. The point to notice is that what these proceedings led up to was not the carrying out of a judicial sentence of death but the decision to 'hand over' Jesus to Pilate (15.1) – an executive, not a judicial, act. In the strict sense, therefore, it may be that this was not a trial at all, but a formal deliberation by those empowered to take the unusual step of 'handing over' a trouble-maker to the Roman authorities. This would explain why, if it was not acting as a court, the assembly was able to break so many procedural rules.

This is not to say that the hearing was free of legal constraints. Genuine evidence was required, and must conform to the normal conditions of being given by at least two witnesses who, when examined independently (and out of each other's hearing) gave identical testimony. This immediately created

56 difficulty: **Many gave false testimony . . . their testimony did not agree**. There was one accusation which, if substantiated, might have been very damaging. The temple was the holiest possession of the Jews, the central shrine of the national religion, the place, above all other, where God was

58 believed to be present with his people. The threat, **'I will destroy this temple'**, could certainly have been interpreted as seriously blasphemous, and there are several reports that Jesus did in fact say something of the kind (Matthew 26.61; John 2.19; Acts 6.14) – though we may doubt whether he meant

59 literally to destroy the temple. **But even on this point their testimony did not agree.**

In the absence of secure testimony, the only course left to the council was to challenge Jesus himself. The high priest's first attempt was simply to get

60 Jesus to incriminate himself: **"Have you no answer?"** But since no charge

61 had been substantiated, Jesus had nothing to gain by replying. He **was silent and did not answer**. The first attempt was a failure.

Surprisingly, the second attempt was successful. **Again the high priest asked him, "Are you the Messiah, the Son of the Blessed One?"** When Mark called Jesus 'Son of God' (as in the first verse of the gospel) he intended the full range of meanings which, by the time he wrote, the church had come to associate with the title. But on the lips of the high priest (who referred to God as 'the Blessed One' to avoid using the divine name), the title may not have meant more than just Messiah, that is, one who claimed to be an emissary of God and whose actions, if done with that assumed authority, would necessarily (if he was an impostor) be blasphemous, as well as possibly illegal. Would Jesus admit to this? At most he had given hints of it, and his understanding of what 'Messiah' involved was clearly very different from that of most of his contemporaries. But when Jesus was asked point blank, Mark reports (unlike the other gospels) that he gave an unequivocal answer,

62 "I am"; and by means of two Old Testament allusions he proceeded to draw out the implications. Jesus' use of the title Son of Man seems in most cases to be a reference to the scene in Daniel (7.13–14) where 'one like a son of man' comes before the Ancient of Days and is given a status of dominion and glory (see above on 2.10). Here the passage is quoted explicitly, with the addition of a reference to Psalm 110.1, "Sit at my right hand . . ." These texts, at the very least, designated a person of divinely ordained authority.

63 At this the high priest **tore his clothes**, a gesture which subsequently became a standard reaction to a formal statement perceived to be blasphemous but may at this time simply have expressed a sense of extreme impa-

64 tience and agitation. **"You have heard his blasphemy!"** By the criteria, at least, of a later age, what Jesus had just said did not amount to the formal offence of blasphemy, for which the death penalty was mandatory; but the pretensions which it implied were certainly serious and, in the tense political situation of the time, could well have seemed to make him **deserving of death**. Even if their decision had been a judicial one, however, it is likely that (as John's gospel tells us, though in a different context, 18.31) they did not have the power to carry out a death sentence – this was normally kept firmly in the hands of the Roman governor. But if they could not execute Jesus themselves, they had to present a case to Pilate for doing so. This was the task of their next meeting. Meanwhile they vented their feelings in a scene of mockery and insult. The gospels all offer slightly different accounts at this point, and it may be that the details were never known to the Christian community (how could they have been?). But certain ideas seem always to be in the background. All the accounts (except that in John) include the

65 sarcastic command, **"Prophesy!"**, which was more than just teasing: a true Messiah would surely have the gift of prophecy, and if Jesus could not there and then give a demonstration of it this would seem to confirm that he was an impostor. Another factor which doubtless influenced the narrative was a prophecy of Isaiah (50.6),

> I gave my back to those who struck me . . .
> I did not hide my face
>   from insult and spitting.

– one of those passages about the 'Suffering Servant' of the Lord which Christians very soon came to see as having been fulfilled in the destiny of Jesus, if indeed Jesus did not make the same connection himself.

66   **While Peter was below in the courtyard**. The high priest's house must be imagined as a substantial building round a courtyard, with the principal rooms (one of which was large enough to hold the whole council) on the floor above, the ground-floor rooms presumably accommodating servants and

54   guards. Peter, we were told earlier, had penetrated right into this courtyard – John's gospel (18.16) provides the explanation that another of the disciples was well known there and was able to get him admitted. He was **sitting with the guards, warming himself at the fire**, which perhaps provided enough

66   light for **one of the servant-girls**, after staring at him, to recognize him. After

68   a brusque denial, Peter **went out into the forecourt** (or *gateway*, that is to say,

69   on the public side of the entrance), where there were **bystanders** who had perhaps been attracted by the news of this unusual meeting of the council. There follow two further denials, the last (a more vehement one) when he was recognized – perhaps by his clothes or, as Matthew reports (26.73), by

70, 72   his accent – as a **Galilean. At that moment the cock crowed a second time**. We cannot be sure whether Mark mentioned the first cock-crow: only some manuscripts give it (at the end of verse 68)[20] and if Peter heard it we wonder why he did not remember what he was doing. At any rate, it is the second cock-crow that makes the scene an exact fulfilment of Jesus' prediction (14.30); and Peter **broke down** – if that is what the mysterious Greek word means: it has been taken since antiquity in a variety of senses from 'covering his head' to simply 'beginning' to weep. It suggests, at any rate, quite violent remorse.

15.1   **As soon as it was morning**. The time for approaching a senior Roman official was the very early morning. His working day began at dawn or even earlier; later in the morning he would have finished his official work and would have been unavailable. Consequently the chief priests lost no time before they **held a consultation** which led to the act which was crucial to the whole story: they **handed him over to Pilate**. Pilate was the governor of Judea from 26 to 36 CE. He had a bad record of tactless and provocative actions aimed at the Jews, but there is nothing in the following narrative to suggest that he acted irregularly. Under Roman law he was obliged to hold a trial before imposing a severe penalty, and this involved taking note of the charges being brought; making sure that the accused was given opportunity to defend himself; deciding what law, if any, the defendant's conduct contravened; giving his verdict; declaring the sentence; and giving orders for it to be carried out. Mark does not attempt to give a systematic account of this procedure; but the points which he records all fit well enough into it. There

---

[20] See the NRSV footnote. It could have been added simply to make sense of the 'second' cock-crow or omitted to bring Mark into harmony with the other gospels.

is no good reason to doubt that a trial along these lines took place, whether or not there were any witnesses present who could relay the facts to Jesus' followers.

2   **Pilate asked him, "Are you the King of the Jews?"** From this question we can infer (what Luke, for instance, makes explicit) that the 'consultation' of the Jewish authorities had resulted in the decision to hand over Jesus on a political charge. A Roman governor, as we can guess from similar hearings in Acts, did not feel willing or qualified to intervene in a matter of Jewish law; and the only charge made against Jesus so far was that of blasphemy, the definition of which was plainly a matter for Jewish jurists. To bring Jesus before Pilate it was necessary to present a charge which would justify his intervention. Jesus had admitted to being the Messiah. This was, in a sense, a claim to be **the King of the Jews**, which, taken in a political sense, could mark

4   the man out as a dangerous rebel. We can assume that the **many charges** the chief priests brought against him centred round this accusation.

   Now there was certainly a sense in which one who claimed to be the Messiah was claiming to be 'the King of the Jews'. The Messiah was the spiritual successor of King David, and some kind of kingship was inseparable from his expected rôle. At any rate, Jesus, when asked point blank, did not deny

2   that there was some truth in the allegation – though his words, **"You say so"**, could hardly be called an explicit admission; indeed, when Pilate remarks

14   later, **"Why, what evil has he done?"**, it is clear that he did not think of Jesus as a dangerous revolutionary. He must have understood – and in John's gospel Jesus explains this to him – that if Jesus aspired to 'kingship' this had nothing to do with political ambition. Nevertheless, he did not omit the regular procedure of giving the accused an opportunity to make his defence.

5   But to his amazement **Jesus made no further reply.** This silence of Jesus, both here and before the Jewish council, is much insisted on in all the gospel accounts. It is true that in both hearings the prosecution had failed to make out a case and Jesus would have had little to gain by trying to defend himself. But there is probably more to it than that. His silence was very soon seen (as in 1 Peter 2.23) as a fulfilment of the 'suffering servant' passages in Isaiah which the first Christians (and possibly Jesus himself) found to be an important clue to the meaning of these events and may indeed, have influenced the narrative:

> He was oppressed and he was afflicted,
>   yet he did not open his mouth;
> like a lamb that is led to the slaughter,
>   and like a sheep that before its shearers is silent,
>   so he did not open his mouth.   (Isaiah 53.7)

Jesus' silence would have been so unusual and unexpected that it could well have stuck in the mind if a witness was present who could pass it on to the

Christian community; but equally it could have been supplied by meditation on this passage of scripture.

6 **Now at the festival he used to release a prisoner for them.** We have no other evidence for this custom in Judea, but it is not inherently improbable. If it existed, it provided Pilate with the possibility of an easy solution: if the people requested the release of Jesus he would be relieved of the task of

7 making a decision in this case. But there was another man **in prison** whom apparently the crowd knew well. **Barabbas** is not a distinctive name – indeed, rather the opposite if it represents *bar-abbas*, 'Father's son'; and Mark does not tell us anything about who the other rebels were or what the **insurrection** was in which they had taken part. (He is the only one of the evangelists to

8 mention it.) Nor does he say whether the crowd **came** (literally *came up*, presumably to the governor's headquarters, which is likely to have been on high ground) to claim their customary prisoner because of their interest in Jesus or in Barabbas. In any case, this early morning 'office hour' of Pilate was the right time for the crowd to present their request, just as it was for the Jewish authorities to bring the case of Jesus. Pilate could have guessed that Jesus was more popular with the people than with his accusers and that

10 he had been brought before him **out of jealousy** (though there has been no hint of 'jealousy' as a factor before). Consequently the fortuitous arrival of people who might be expected to support Jesus may have seemed to give

9 him his opportunity: **"Do you want me to release for you the King of the Jews?"**

Apparently under the influence of the chief priests, however, the people kept to their original purpose (as implied in Mark's account) of asking for the release of Barabbas. It is not clear why Pilate then drew them into Jesus' case. Possibly he hoped that, if they showed themselves sympathetic to Jesus, they would provide him with further reasons for releasing a man who (he may now have been satisfied) was not a source of political danger; and this would give him the gratification of disappointing the Jewish leaders whom

13 (as we know from other sources) he disliked and despised. But they **shouted back, "Crucify him!"** Again Mark gives no explanation. Up to now the crowd had been on Jesus' side. Why this sudden animosity against him? We would not have expected the chief priests to have much influence over popular feelings; but it may be that they had made the crowd aware of the danger of supporting Jesus. Here, after all, was a man who had not denied the charge of claiming to be 'King of the Jews'. Such a claim amounted to insurrection. Did they want to be involved in that? Would they not do better to demand the appropriate penalty, which was crucifixion? If these were the alternatives, it is understandable that they took the chief priests' advice and chose the second: **"Crucify him!"** Without more ado (for in such cases the governor was not bound to any strict procedure), Pilate pronounced Jesus guilty and sentenced him to crucifixion, the penalty prescribed for action taken 'against the Roman people'. As usual, the penalty was carried out straight away; and it

was normal for the accused man to be flogged (as indeed Jesus had predicted he would be) so that he would die more quickly on the cross.

16 **Then the soldiers led him into the courtyard of the palace.** When the Roman governor came up to Jerusalem from his capital (the port of Caesarea) he normally brought with him a company of troops: the word used here (*speira* in Greek, **cohort** in Latin) was the technical name for a company of up to six hundred men. These he will doubtless have lodged in the building which served as his royal residence (or **palace**) and military **headquarters** (for which the Latin name was *praetorium*), and it is no surprise to find them here ready to carry out the sentence passed on Jesus. The soldiers themselves are likely to have been neither Jews (who were not enlisted for military service in Palestine) nor Romans (who were reserved for the regular legions of the Roman army) but non-Jewish local men recruited from Palestine and Syria for the auxiliary forces. They may therefore have had some idea of the religious and political pretensions of a man who called himself 'King of the

17 Jews', and their mockery of the prisoner is quite plausible. They **clothed him in a purple cloak** – the distinctive colour for a monarch in the eastern part of the empire; and, **twisting some thorns into a crown, they put it on him** – not a crown in the modern sense, but an insulting travesty of a wreath such as the emperor's head always bears on Roman coins. So dressed, they greeted

18 Jesus with a parody of a royal acclamation, **"Hail, King of the Jews!"**

20 **Then they led him out to crucify him.** Crucifixion, though generally regarded as a cruel and barbarous form of execution (and administered only to slaves in the Roman homeland), was by no means unknown in Palestine under the Roman administration, being the usual punishment for those who

27 committed violence and insurrection. The **two bandits** who were crucified along with Jesus were typical victims of it – the word had come to be used for members of armed resistance movements; and the fact that Jesus received this penalty proclaimed, as clearly as the inscription placed on his cross, that

26 the charge against him was political: he had claimed to be **"The King of the Jews"**. Few details are given in the gospels about how it was carried out, but the traditional representation of the scene is probably roughly correct. The cross might be in the shape of a T or a †; the prisoner was fastened to it either with cords or with nails (there is a nail through the ankles of a man whose bones were discovered in 1970 near Jerusalem and who was crucified around this time); a peg may have been driven into the upright of the cross to support the body and prolong the agony. Elsewhere in the empire the victims were stripped naked; in Judea the Romans may have respected Jewish feelings and allowed a loincloth. All executions, whether Jewish or

20 Roman, took place outside the city (**they led him out** could mean either out of the praetorium or out of the city), but since crucifixions were intended to serve as warning examples they usually took place not far from a city gate so that many people would be compelled to see them on their way in or out of the city. (John 19.20 reports that the place was "near the city".) The

traditional site of Jesus' crucifixion, where in the fourth century Constantine built a great church, is at a spot which, until the city was enlarged some ten years later, would have lain just outside one angle of the walls, a few hundred metres from one of the gates, in an area which had once been a quarry but now held some tombs. A rocky mound jutted up in this area and still exists inside the present church; by its shape this could have suggested the name,

22 **'place of a skull'**. Of this, **Golgotha** is roughly the Aramaic equivalent and Calvary (*calvarium*) the traditional Latin translation. The identification of this spot with the site of Jesus' crucifixion is by no means certain, but recent archaeological research has made it seem quite probable. In any case, the few precise details which are given by the gospels are entirely consistent with what we know from other sources both about the ancient city of Jerusalem and about the customary procedure at executions in the Roman empire.

21 **Simon of Cyrene.** Mark seldom gives the name of subsidiary characters in his story, but here he gives not only the man's name but his country of origin and the names of his two sons. There were substantial Jewish settlements in North Africa and Simon may have been a Jew who either owned land in Judea (and so could have been **coming in from the country**) or who had come up to Jerusalem for the festival. Why does Mark give the names of his sons? They would have had no significance unless these two men were known to the community for which this gospel was written (they are not mentioned in the other gospels); which means that Mark's church may have counted among its number two people whose father was a witness of the crucifixion – a significant check on his freedom to tell the story any way he liked! If **Rufus** were assumed to be the same Rufus as is mentioned by Paul at the end of his letter to the Romans (16.13), we could go further and locate this community at Rome, where, according to tradition, Mark got his information from Peter. But Rufus is a fairly common name, and Simon's sons could just as well have belonged to the church in North Africa, another place where Mark's gospel is often thought to have been composed. Simon, at any rate, was **compelled** to carry Jesus' cross: the word is technical, meaning that he was 'requisitioned', and does not imply either that he would have offered resistance or that he was identified as belonging to Jesus' movement: the soldiers had a right to impose this on anyone. Criminals on their way to execution normally had to carry their own cross – or rather the cross-beam: the upright would have been in position already – and this is what John's gospel describes (19.17); but a possible way to reconcile the accounts is by the supposition that Jesus may already have been too exhausted to carry it himself the whole way –

22 indeed, the Greek word translated **they brought** him is a rather physical one and suggests that Jesus was dragged or helped along rather than simply led under escort; hence perhaps the need to requisition a helper.

Two more details are given which are perfectly plausible historically but

23 which were soon seen to have symbolic significance. **Wine mixed with myrrh** – that is, with a special flavour – could have been a simple act of

kindness to alleviate suffering: Proverbs 31.6 has "Give strong drink to one that is perishing, and wine to those in bitter distress"; but in Matthew (27.34) it becomes "wine . . . mixed with gall", a reference to Psalm 68.22. Those who

24 **divided his clothes among them** were clearly the soldiers, who had a customary right to them; and that they should have cast lots **to decide what each should take** is perfectly natural. Yet the reader may well have picked up a biblical precedent. The author of a psalm, writing out of a situation very similar to that of Jesus – that of an innocent man brought to the last degree of suffering and humiliation – included the same detail in his description of his own abject circumstances:

> They divide my clothes among themselves,
> and for my clothing they cast lots.
> (Psalm 22.18)

25   **It was nine o'clock in the morning** – literally *the third hour*. The day was divided into twelve hours between sunrise and sunset, and in a country such as Palestine, where the length of days does not vary much more than two or three hours between midsummer and midwinter, this worked well enough. Ordinary citizens did not use an hourglass or water clock to tell the time. They looked at the sun and observed when it was noon (the 'sixth hour'), when it was mid-morning (the 'third hour') and when it was mid-afternoon (the 'ninth hour') – and these are the three times of day most frequently mentioned in the New Testament. Here, when Mark says it was the 'third hour', he means that Jesus was crucified in the middle of the morning, halfway between sunrise and noon, and died in the middle of the afternoon (verse 33). That is to say, he spreads the events evenly over the day. John's gospel follows a slightly different scheme and places the crucifixion at midday.

26   That there was an **inscription of the charge** (which other gospels say was fixed to the cross) is perfectly plausible, even though we have no other evidence for the practice – the nearest parallel is the Roman custom of making convicted criminals carry a notice of their offence through the streets; and since the early Christians were anxious to dispel any accusation that their movement was political it seems unlikely that they would have invented it.

29 **Those who passed by derided him.** Here there were many biblical precedents. Sometimes it was Jerusalem in ruins which was the object of scorn: "All who pass along the way . . . hiss and wag their heads" (Lamentations 2.15); sometimes it was a stricken man who had claimed to be pious and just – "All who see me mock at me; they make mouths at me, they shake their heads" (Psalm 22.7); "I am an object of scorn to my accusers; when they see me, they shake their heads" (Psalm 109.25). Mark uses the conventional vocabulary, but for the content of the taunts he draws on earlier scenes from his narrative – the saying on the temple (14.58), Jesus' 'saving' (that is, healing) the sick, his admission that he was the Messiah (14.62). Jesus was subjected in full

measure to the insults received by the righteous sufferers of Old Testament tradition.

33 **When it was noon, darkness came over the whole land.** An eclipse of the sun is impossible at full moon, but a dust storm could have made the day unusually dark – if indeed, it was a natural phenomenon that Mark meant to describe. But the notion that the sun is 'darkened' at a great king's death was so common in antiquity, and the expectation that the heavenly bodies would vary from their regular courses at a moment of great crisis occurs so often in Jewish imaginative writing, that we cannot be sure that Mark was not intending to give, not a description of the weather, but a symbolic clue

34 to the significance of Jesus' death. The cry **with a loud voice**, on the other hand, appears to be a factual report. The crucial statement in it is that people

35 thought that he was **calling for Elijah**. The first two syllables of this – *eli* – would have been the same as the Hebrew for 'My God'. It was not difficult for his disciples to guess that Jesus was uttering a prayer; and if so, it was likely he was using words from the traditional prayer book – the Psalms. The only question was, which psalm? The word *eli* occurs in several, and in fact different psalms are suggested in other gospels. Here we are told that Jesus was praying the first line of Psalm 22, which is given in Aramaic rather than Hebrew, even though this yields *eloi* rather than *eli*; this would have been more difficult to mistake for Elijah (*eliyya*), but may have been thought a more natural form for Jesus to have used. That Jesus should have felt so

34 **forsaken** by God has been a problem for Christians down the centuries, which seems to have been felt even by scribes or editors who altered the phrase in manuscripts of the text (see the NRSV footnote). But it is important to put the psalm in its context. In the Jewish culture, it was taken for granted that God is just and rewards those who serve him righteously, and that this reward must be visible to others in the form of health, prosperity or honour. If a man was convinced of his innocence before God and yet found himself in extreme misfortune; if, in addition, he fell ill and knew himself to be in danger of death (which people would interpret as punishment for some sin); and if, as was still the case when the psalm was written, there was no faith in an afterlife in which these wrongs could be put right – then, on these presuppositions, his predicament became agonizing. Everyone around him was drawing the obvious conclusion that he must have somehow deserved his fate. He knew this to be false, but unless God acted soon his faith in himself and in the God whom he served would be unable to bear the strain, and his mockers and persecutors would have the last word – and there was not much time left: something must happen very soon! This predicament of the righteous sufferer was the classic way in which the problem of evil was articulated in the Old Testament period, and it finds one of its most eloquent and agonized expressions in the twenty-second psalm, which describes a whole gamut of emotions, from near-despair to a triumphant confidence that, despite everything, God would yet bring good out of the present evil.

It was the conviction of some witnesses of the crucifixion that when Jesus uttered the cry *eli* he was experiencing the acutest form of what we would now call the problem of evil, and confronting it with the spirituality he had inherited from the religious tradition of his own people. He was praying (in his own language, according to Mark) the prayer of the psalmist, **"My God, my God, why have you forsaken me?"**

36 **Someone ran, filled a sponge with sour wine, put it on a stick, and gave it to him to drink.** This seems to have been another effect of Jesus' cry. The sour wine or vinegar was probably the cheap drink which soldiers and labourers carried about with them, and was offered to Jesus in an attempt to revive him. Whoever did so evidently shared the popular belief in an Elijah figure who would miraculously return at a crucial moment of history and wanted to humour what he took to be Jesus' hope of a supernatural saviour. Alternatively the offer was made simply out of an impulse of pity for the sufferer (for exposure and thirst were a significant part of what a crucified victim had to endure). But in recording it Mark may well have had in mind a verse from another of the 'righteous sufferer' psalms, "for my thirst they gave me vinegar to drink" (Psalm 69.21).

37–8 **Then Jesus gave a loud cry and breathed his last. And the curtain of the temple was torn in two, from top to bottom.** These two sentences appear entirely factual, and there is no obvious change of style between them. The
37 first simply reports Jesus' death, using a word of some solemnity (**breathed**
38 **his last**, literally *expired*). The second seems to use a different language altogether. Admittedly it is possible to take it literally. If the darkness was caused by the *hamsin* wind, which quite often blows in from the desert in April and
33 brings with it such a cloud of dust that there is even a kind of 'darkness over the whole land', then a gust of the same wind, reaching gale force, could conceivably have split the heavy curtain which was hung over the main eastern porch of the temple. It is possible therefore that someone familiar with conditions in Palestine would have seen nothing extraordinary about the report – except that the temple was far out of sight of the place of crucifixion and there would have been no means of knowing that the two events were simultaneous. But Mark was not writing for Palestinians, he nowhere mentions the wind, and no one who did not know the country well could possibly have understood how all this was supposed to have happened. Moreover, we know from the letter to the Hebrews (10.19–20) that the curtain of the temple had symbolic value for Christians: it was what had separated the Jewish sanctuary (the special dwelling place of God) from the eyes of all but a few chosen priests, but had now been destroyed by the death of Jesus, who had opened up a new way to the very presence of God for Jews and Gentiles alike. It is not easy for the western mind to take two apparently factual statements ('Jesus died', 'the curtain was torn') in two such different ways; but when Jewish tradition reported, for instance, that at the death of a certain famous rabbi 'the stars became visible in broad daylight', the statement was meant neither

to deceive the credulous nor to be challenged as a scientific impossibility. It was the author's way of indicating the significance of the man who had passed away. So here: Mark gives, in the guise of a bare fact, a hint of the meaning of Jesus' death.

39 **The centurion, who stood facing him,** was the officer in charge of the execution squad. He was certainly not a Jew, but he may well have been a native of the region. The manner of Jesus' death elicited from him the comment, **"Truly this man was God's Son!"** In the mouth of an ordinary Greek-speaking soldier, "God's son" would have been a way of describing any man (particularly a ruler) who seemed endowed with supernatural powers or blessed with exceptional marks of divine favour; and the way in which Jesus died could plausibly have brought this expression to the mind of the centurion. But the Greek words so translated are exactly the same as those ("the Son of God") with which Mark begins his gospel[21]. The saying is thus more than a mere report of a soldier's reaction. That Jesus was the Son of God had become a central article of faith in the church by the time the gospel was written; but here Mark tells us that the fact was recognized immediately after his death – by a Gentile.

40 **There were also women. Mary Magdalene** (Magdala being an identifiable site on the north-west shore of the Lake of Galilee) is known to us from Luke 8.2, and **Salome** appears to be identified in Matthew 27.56 as the mother of the sons of Zebedee. Nothing is known of the other **Mary**: Mark identifies her for his readers by connecting her with two other names which were presumably familiar to his readers. **James the younger** could be James the son of Alphaeus (3.18) – distinguished perhaps by his youth from James the son of Zebedee. Of **Joses** ('Joseph' in Matthew 27.56) nothing is otherwise known.

42 **The day of Preparation** could equally well be translated *Friday* (the word still means this in modern Greek), the day before the sabbath. As soon as darkness fell it would no longer be permitted to do any kind of 'work', and in strict Jewish eyes the land would be 'defiled' (Deuteronomy 21.23) if the body of a Jew was allowed to remain unburied in the place of execution until the next day. A pious and public-spirited citizen might understandably be anxious that consciences should not be scandalized by the sight of Jesus'
43 dead body so close to the city. (**Waiting expectantly for the kingdom of God** was a perfectly appropriate description for such a person: the phrase certainly need not suggest that he was a clandestine Christian, though Matthew seems to assume that he was, 27.57.) Moreover it was esteemed an especially meritorious work of charity to perform the burial rites for one whose own relatives were not present to do it. **Joseph of Arimathea** (which was probably a town about 20 miles north of Jerusalem) therefore **went boldly to Pilate and asked for the body of Jesus.** We do not know how far, if at all, the

[21] See the NRSV footnote.

Roman administration was in the habit of accommodating Jewish scruples in such a matter. The usual Roman practice was to leave the dead bodies exposed and then throw them into a common grave. Victims of crucifixion (depending on the method used) often took more than a few hours to die, and indeed Pilate may have been 'surprised' (a likely meaning of the word

44 translated **wondered**) to know that Jesus had been **dead for some time** and have made certain of the fact before taking any action. Joseph's request was

43 granted, however, and Mark gives a reason: he was **a respected member of the council.** A less influential person (say, a relative of Jesus) might have had no success.

46   **Then Joseph bought a linen cloth.** The Jews did not bury in coffins but wrapped the corpse firmly and laid it in one of the numerous rock tombs to be found outside any town in Palestine. Usually they were family tombs, large chambers in the rock, having a number of cavities carved out of them; and the entrance would often be sealed by a massive stone (in more pretentious tombs shaped like a millstone and rolling into place along a groove in the rock, as can still be seen at the so-called 'Garden Tomb' in Jerusalem). Evidently this one was available for Joseph's purpose; but it is only the other gospels which add that it belonged to him and had not been used before.

16.1   **When the sabbath was over.** By the inclusive reckoning generally used in the ancient world, this Sunday morning was the 'third day' after the Friday on which Jesus was crucified. That Jesus rose from the dead 'on the third day' was the basis for all the preaching of the early church; and we can tell from the sermons and summaries of their faith which are recorded in the New Testament (especially 1 Corinthians 15.3–6, which was already 'tradition' by the time Paul wrote) that they based this startling assertion on the evidence of those who had actually seen the risen Christ, either on the first Sunday or on one of the days that followed. This was the evidence on which the first Christians rested their faith: after his death and burial Jesus was seen by a number of reliable witnesses under circumstances that convinced them, not that they had seen a ghost, or that Jesus had returned from what we would now call a near-death experience, or even that his death had been an illusion, but that he had now entered a new mode of existence of which they had tangible evidence. To describe it they used a term usually reserved for the future destiny that was believed to be in store for all after the end of the present age: with remarkable unanimity they spoke of Jesus having 'risen from the dead'. Now it is true that, according to a widespread belief in the ultimate resurrection of the dead, all were to be called back to life complete with their mortal body – transformed, no doubt, and adapted to a supernatural existence but still recognizably their own: hence the care taken to preserve the bones intact. It followed that if Jesus had indeed, 'risen from the dead' his body must have already undergone this transformation and that his tomb would be empty. But the absence of Jesus' body from the tomb does

not seem to have been regarded as the first or the most important evidence
for the resurrection – it was, after all, capable of other explanations: the body
might have been removed or stolen (and we hear of these explanations in
the other gospels). The whole weight of the Christians' case rested on the
testimony of those who had actually seen Jesus alive, 'risen from the dead'.
To our surprise, Mark's gospel appears to break off just before this crucial
piece of evidence is given. Its last paragraph is a brief account – apparently
the first in Christian literature – of the way in which Jesus' tomb, early on
the Sunday morning, was found to be empty.

Yet we may still ask why this apparently sensational fact was not immediately seized upon and proclaimed. The gospel-writers seem to have been
conscious of this question and to have suggested different answers. Mark
says that the women kept it a secret: [8]**they said nothing to anyone, for
they were afraid**. Luke says that, on the contrary, they told the disciples but
were not believed (24.11). Matthew says that the authorities tried to cover
up the fact by spreading the story that the body had been stolen (28.11–15).
And there may have been a further reason: the evidence of women was not
admitted in a law court. The report brought back from the tomb by the three
women would have had little weight as proof of Jesus' resurrection.

Moreover, Mark's narrative contains some unexpected features. The obli-
1 gation to **anoint** the corpse should have been fulfilled before burial. Possibly
Joseph had been unable to do it; but in any case, the women were doing
more than this by honouring the dead man with **spices** or perfumes – particularly needful, perhaps, for embalming a corpse thirty-six hours after death
– which they would have been able to buy as soon as the sabbath was over the
previous evening. Since they knew that the tomb was closed by a heavy stone
(15.46–7), their project seems strangely unrealistic. On the other hand the
scene which Mark goes on to describe can easily be imagined taking place in
4 a typical tomb. Once the stone had been **rolled back** an aperture would have
5 been revealed. Through this, the women **entered the tomb**, which would
have been a rock chamber with small tunnels opening out of it for individual
burials. They would not have known which of these had been used for Jesus'
burial. But the angel, conventionally described as **a young man, dressed in
6 a white robe**, pointed it out to them: "**Look, there is the place they laid
him.**" The angel then repeated Jesus' prediction about 'going ahead of them
to Galilee' (see above on 14.28), and the scene ends with the understandable
8 **terror and amazement** of the women.

[[According to a number of important manuscripts, **for they were afraid** are
the last words of the gospel. It is unlikely that the following paragraphs, which
occur in some manuscripts, are by the same author. Even in English, the words
which conclude THE SHORTER ENDING, **the sacred and imperishable
proclamation of eternal salvation**, are recognizably un-Marcan: they belong

to the theological language of the church and are quite unlike the spare and sober idiom of Mark's narrative; and THE LONGER ENDING is mainly a summary of episodes that are reported in other places and betrays in its details the hand of a later editor.[22]]]

Did Mark intend his gospel to end on this note of fear and uncertainty, leaving his readers to fill in the rest from their own foundational faith in the resurrection of Jesus? Or has the original ending of his book been accidentally lost? On this question opinion is still divided, and there is little evidence to support a decision either way. Books in the ancient world normally ended in a way we would recognize as intentional, and if Mark meant to finish his work with the words **for they were afraid**, he was certainly doing something unusual. But then this would not be the only respect in which his gospel is, by any standards, a very remarkable book.

---

[22] Verses 9–11: cf. John 20.14–18; Luke 24.11. Verses 12–13: cf. Luke 24.13–35. Verse 14: cf. Luke 24.36–43. Verse 15: cf. Matthew 28.18–20. Verse 16 expresses a later conception of baptism (and the confession of faith which accompanies baptism) as a guarantee of salvation. Verses 17–18: casting out demons and healing the sick are powers given to the disciples in the gospels (Mark 6.7, 13); speaking in strange tongues is described in Acts and the letters of Paul; handling snakes is reminiscent of Acts 28.3–6 and drinking poison without coming to harm occurs in a number of second-century legends. Verses 19–20 are a general summary of the first chapters of Acts.

LUKE

The preface

1.3 **Most excellent Theophilus.** The first four verses of the gospel are what we would now call a 'preface', dedicating the work to a patron. It is the preface to the writings of an author whose name tradition has preserved as Luke, and who may in fact (though we cannot be sure of it) be the same person as 'Luke, the beloved physician' (Colossians 4.14), the friend and companion of Paul. Then, as now, writing a preface showed the work to be a literary project. But this is not characteristic of New Testament writings, which were written for religious rather than literary purposes; it is only here and at the beginning of Acts (which is the second part of Luke's work) that any kind of preface occurs. Luke presents himself, therefore, as someone unusual among New Testament writers: a conscious literary stylist ready to make use of the conventions of the world of letters. His opening paragraph is a smooth and polished piece of Greek prose.

Greek historians took it for granted that their work should begin with a preface (often including a dedication) explaining the writer's purpose and methods. Luke, who certainly felt himself to be writing a chapter of world history, followed the same convention, including also the customary dedication to a personal friend or influential acquaintance. Luke's preface, though it is shorter and less fulsome than most, is entirely in the spirit of his age.

At the same time, its formal character precludes it from giving us much precise information. **Theophilus** could be almost anyone – Greek, Roman or Jew, pagan or Christian, senior civil servant or private gentleman (**most excellent** suggests a person of some rank, but the Greek word was a very
1 general term of respect). The **many** referred to in the opening phrase could be a rhetorical exaggeration of the fact that Mark, and possibly Matthew, had already completed their gospels, or it could be an indication that more accounts of the gospel story were current in Luke's day than have survived to
3 ours. And Luke's decision to write **an orderly account**[1] of these events could be due to a desire to improve on the work of his predecessors, an anxiety to refute false information that might have been coming to the ears of such as Theophilus, or simply a sense that there was need for another 'gospel' based on his own careful research. The language of the preface does not allow us

---

[1] The NRSV (unlike the Revised Standard Version) uses the same words (**an orderly account**) to translate two phrases that are different in the Greek. The first means simply *compile an account*. The second shows that Luke intends to improve on this by writing something more **orderly**.

to decide between these possibilities. But the fact that Luke wrote such a preface at all, and moreover that he extended his work in the 'Acts of the Apostles' to embrace the story of the spread of Christianity from Jerusalem to Rome, shows that he was aware of tackling a more ambitious task than the other gospel-writers and that, unlike them, he had at his disposal many of the techniques and literary conventions of a professional Greek historian.

John and Jesus

5 **In the days of King Herod of Judea.** By contrast with the Hellenistic polish of the preface, and indeed, with the historical precision that Luke shows elsewhere (see especially 3.1), the narrative begins in a way more reminiscent of the Old Testament than of contemporary history books. Herod the Great reigned for over thirty years and died in 4 BCE. So Luke's indication of date is extremely vague. On the other hand, 'In the days of so-and-so, king of Judah' is a standard Old Testament formula for introducing an episode in the history of the Jewish kingdoms, and this is only the first of the many touches by which Luke, in these first two chapters, gives an Old Testament atmosphere to his narrative.[2]

There was a priest named Zechariah, of the priestly order of Abijah. The ritual of the temple in Jerusalem was performed by members of all the families which could trace their ancestry back to Aaron and who formed the priestly class in Jewish society. Twenty-four such families had returned from the exile, each tracing its descent back to one of the grandsons of Aaron (one of whom was **Abijah**), and each of these families, which were a 'section' of the priesthood, still existed as a distinct clan in some part of Judea or Galilee and twice a year took responsibility for a week's duty in the temple. The whole clan took up residence in Jerusalem, and the several families of the clan each took responsibility for one day of the week, casting lots to determine the duty of each individual. Luke was evidently well acquainted with this system and was able to show how it came about that Zechariah was officiating in the 8 temple on a particular day. **His section was on duty,** that is, it was one of the two weeks in the year that his clan attended the temple; **he was serving as priest before God,** that is, it was the day appointed for the family to which 9 he belonged; and **he was chosen by lot** to be the individual who on that day received the coveted privilege (enjoyed only once in a priest's lifetime) **to enter the sanctuary of the Lord and offer incense.**

---

[2] Most of these touches are linguistic and can hardly be reproduced in translation. Sometimes, indeed, the idioms seem more Semitic than Greek, and many believe that Luke's infancy narratives are a translation of a Hebrew or Aramaic original. But phrases characteristic of Luke also occur, and it is at least as likely that Luke, who could in any case, write in more than one style, is here composing the story in language modelled mainly on the Greek translation of the Old Testament. An example is in verse 12, **he was terrified; and fear overwhelmed him.**

Twice a day, morning and evening, a lamb was sacrificed and burnt at the
10 altar before the temple. **The time of the incense offering** came just before this
sacrifice in the morning and just after it in the evening; it was the moment
when the chosen priest left his two assistants outside by the altar and entered
9 **the sanctuary**. This was the first room in the temple proper, being a kind
of anteroom to the Holy of Holies (which only the high priest could enter,
and that on only one day of the year). Here stood a small altar for burning
incense; and the mysterious sanctity of the place, combined with the smoke
of the incense and the complete solitude of the priest, made this moment a
particularly likely one for visions and intimations of the divine. Many stories
are told in Jewish literature of similar experiences in the temple; so much
21 so, that **the people** who **were waiting** outside (probably of his own clan)
had little doubt what had happened when Zechariah stayed so long inside
and was unable to give the customary blessing when he emerged from the
22 sanctuary: **they realized that he had seen a vision**.

13   **"Your prayer has been heard."** A divine intervention, granting the birth
of a child to a woman who had been barren and was now past the age of
child-bearing, was a feature of many Old Testament stories; and these stories
often included the appearance of an angel and a supernatural intimation of
the name the child was to bear. Almost all the details of Luke's narrative (and
much of his actual language) can be found in one or another of these Old
Testament stories, and a comparison with these shows how deeply Luke was
influenced by such precedents – compare especially the promise of the birth
of Isaac to Abraham and Sarah (Genesis 17–18) and the birth stories of
Samson (Judges 13) and Samuel (1 Samuel 1). But this is not to say that his
combination of these elements was due entirely to his imagination. Whether
or not he had reliable information about the circumstances of John the
Baptist's birth, certain facts about his subsequent life must have suggested
to him that it would be true of John, as it had been true of Samson and
certain other Old Testament persons such as the Rechabites (Jeremiah 35)
15 and the nazirites (Numbers 6), that he would be sworn never to **drink wine**;
that, like an Old Testament prophet, **even before his birth** he would be filled
with the Holy Spirit; and that he would be a figure fulfilling many of the
17 prophecies which had clustered round the name of **Elijah** (see above on
Mark 9.11).

Again, that the message was delivered through the angel Gabriel (the angel
messenger *par excellence* since his appearance in the book of Daniel), that
18 Zechariah asked for a sign (**"How will I know that this is so?"**, like Abraham in
Genesis 15.8) and that he was rewarded – or punished – with inability to speak
(like Daniel in Daniel 10.15), are all typical elements of this kind of story;
but this hardly affects the question whether Luke's story is legend or fact. To
convey experiences of this kind, whether true or fictitious, a writer has to use
images and concepts that are at home in the culture. Some eyewitnesses may
22 well have remembered the vivid moment when Zechariah **kept motioning**

to them and remained unable to speak, even if the rest of the story is the writer's attempt to make explicit what was essentially an incommunicable experience.

25 Failure to bear children was keenly felt by Jewish women as 'a **disgrace among their people',** and Elizabeth's thankful reaction is a clear allusion to that of Rachel when, after years of childlessness, she gave birth to Joseph: "God has taken away my reproach" (Genesis 30.23). Why did Elizabeth

24 then remain **in seclusion** for five months? We know of no custom that would have obliged her to do so; but her seclusion gives added point to

26 the surprise of the meeting which took place between her and Mary **in the sixth month.**

Woven into the story of the strange circumstances of John the Baptist's birth is the story of the birth of Jesus. This too comprises a supernatural message and a miraculous birth, but it no longer recalls the stories in Jewish scripture and folklore since it culminates in a happening that was unparalleled in the Jewish culture. It is true that in Greek mythology there are numerous stories of unions between an immortal god and a mortal woman. But Luke's account shows no trace of influence from such sources. The setting is entirely Jewish, and Jewish tradition knew nothing of such things. Every biblical story of a miraculous birth presupposed a human father. So far as Luke's readers were concerned, Jesus' birth was absolutely unique.

Matthew and Luke are the only New Testament writers who explicitly mention it. Matthew simply states it in a single sentence (1.20), with very little comment. Luke, on the other hand, devotes a whole paragraph to it, and his account is clearly intended to give some explanation of its meaning. Mary,

27 he tells us, was **a virgin engaged to a man whose name was Joseph.** 'Virgin' is the traditional translation, and it is true that the Greek word often meant this; but it was also one of the commonest words for 'girl', and there is no reason to think that Luke meant to stress Mary's virginity at this stage of the story – it would be taken for granted in a young woman about to be married. Mary was simply a young fiancée, already legally committed to her future husband but not yet living with him. Unlike Zechariah, who received his vision when performing a ritual act in a holy place, Mary is no one in particular and has done nothing special, and the words of the angel's greeting seem to recognize

28 this: **"favored one!"** – the phrase shows that God has regarded her with exceptional favour, not that there is necessarily anything in her which has drawn this favour upon herself. How will this divine favour be shown? The angel's answer still holds back the critical point: for the present he simply promises to Mary a son who will be qualified to bear the titles and attributes of many of the great figures of Old Testament history and prophecy and

32 who will be a worthy successor of **David,** his **ancestor** through Joseph, his adopted 'father'. (The angel's words are a tissue of Old Testament allusions: compare especially Genesis 16.11; Isaiah 9.7; Micah 4.7). Such promises had been made to women in the past.

34   **"How can this be, since I am a virgin?"**[3] Mary's reaction is puzzling. She was about to be married and could expect to bear a child (unless she was under the age of puberty, which is conceivable); and it is necessary to read a good deal into the text if we are to find there some reason for Mary's finding it hard to believe that she would have a child – that she had made a vow of perpetual virginity, or that she understood the angel to mean that she was to conceive immediately, are far-fetched suggestions that receive no support in the text. But the difficulty is lessened if we ask, not why Mary should have said these words, but why Luke placed them in her mouth. From the narrator's point of view the question has a clear purpose: it is the cue for the angel's

35   decisive declaration that the child is to have no human father at all. **"The Holy Spirit will come upon you."** Matthew says simply that Mary "was found to be with child from the Holy Spirit" (1.18). Luke uses the more poetic and suggestive image of 'overshadowing', suggesting the way in which there would be a sense of God's presence at the moment of conception (the same word is used, for instance, of God's presence resting on the tabernacle in Exodus 40.35): God would himself take the place of a human father, and the child would therefore be, in a unique sense, **"Son of God"**. Mary's apparently naïve question turns the key that unlocks the whole mystery: to have this child she will not require, physically, to 'know a man'.

36   **"And now . . . "** In the Old Testament the recipients of divine promises commonly ask for a 'sign' (as Zechariah has just done). Mary does not ask; but a sign is given. **"Your relative[4] Elizabeth in her old age has also conceived a son."** When Mary had seen this she would have less difficulty in believing

37   that for her, as for Elizabeth, **"nothing will be impossible for God"** – the phrase recalls the reply to the incredulous Sarah when she was given the news that she would have a child in her old age (Genesis 18.14).

39   In response, Mary went **in haste** to visit Elizabeth in **a Judean town in the hill country** – literally *a town of Judah*: Luke is still using Old Testament language, and means nothing more precise than that Elizabeth was somewhere in the mountainous country round Jerusalem and that Mary took the angel's message seriously enough to wish to confirm it by making the three days' journey south from Galilee. This alone would have been enough

45   to elicit Elizabeth's blessing on **"she who believed that there would be a fulfilment of what was spoken to her by the Lord"**. But the coincidence of the baby stirring in Elizabeth's womb at the moment of Mary's arrival

41   gave the scene a new turn. **Elizabeth was filled with the Holy Spirit** – Luke's way of indicating a sudden gift of prophecy – and declared that

44   her baby had not merely stirred but had **"leaped for joy"**. The Greek word used here for 'joy' was rich with scriptural overtones: it suggested

---

[3] Literally, *I do not know* (in the sense of sexual intercourse) *a man*.

[4] The Greek word is too vague for us to be able to say what their relationship was; but it suggests that Mary, like Elizabeth, must have been of a priestly family.

the joy of the people of God in the presence of the long-awaited 'Lord', the Messiah.

46   **And Mary said**. The narrative is interrupted by a song of praise. There was good precedent for this. In Old Testament accounts of a barren woman being granted her prayer for a child the mother often breaks out in a cry of joy and thanksgiving. The finest example is in 1 Samuel 2: when Hannah was at last blessed with a son she uttered a song which fills a whole page of text and which is so similar in style and even content to Mary's that the one can hardly fail to have been inspired by the other. Yet Hannah's great song is not one that only she could have sung. It is mostly a hymn on the justice and mercies of God, with barely a word that bears on Hannah's own situation, so much so that it is quite possible that the verses originally had an independent existence and were only subsequently inserted into the story of Hannah. Much the same could be true of Mary's song here. The greater part of it is concerned with themes which occur again and again in the psalms and in later Hebrew poetry: the fidelity of God to his people and the radical reversal of social values which will one day vindicate the cause of the poor and oppressed against the proud and the rich. Almost every phrase occurs at one place or another in the Greek translation of the Old Testament; there is not a word in it that is distinctively 'Christian', and barely a sentence which is characteristic of Luke. To all intents and purposes the song is a beautiful example of a Jewish psalm, with particular emphasis on the rewards in store for the most humble members of society. As such, there is no reason why it should not have risen spontaneously to the lips of the joyful mother-to-be. But equally (if one concedes that Luke was writing up the scene fairly freely) it could have been inserted by the writer to comply with the convention that the apparently miraculous gift of a child should be answered by a cry of praise such as had been composed in the past to celebrate blessings received by the

52, 53   **lowly** and the **hungry**.

But who sang the song? It was Elizabeth, not Mary, who was in the classic situation of one whose 'disgrace' of barrenness had been taken away, and some manuscripts actually give her name in this verse (see the NRSV footnote). Moreover, there is one point at which the song seems to become personal

48   and to spring from the events which have just been narrated: **"He has looked with favor on the lowliness of his servant."** The word translated 'lowliness' could mean literally *her humiliation*. And who has been 'humiliated'? Not Mary, but Elizabeth. In short, were no name given for the singer of the song (which may indeed, originally have been the case, later copyists adding one name or the other as they thought best), we might be tempted to ascribe it to Elizabeth and regard those few manuscripts which give her name in verse 46 as having correctly divined the original intention of the writer.

The last of these arguments, however, is double-edged. 'Humiliation' is a correct translation in verse 48, but so is **lowliness**, and in so far as the song is a typical expression of that strain of Jewish piety which fervently believed in the blessedness and ultimate vindication of 'the poor', the meek and the humble, the speaker could just as well be anyone (or any group of people) who belonged to that class. Mary, just as much as Elizabeth, is to be imagined as an upright and 'lowly' person to whom God had shown exceptional favour; and the NRSV follows what has been the universal instinct of the church in accepting the traditional ascription to Mary. The song is couched throughout in general but fervent (and socially radical) terms. If it does not allude specifically to Mary's situation, it is nevertheless, a moving expression of what she might have been feeling, and has been acknowledged down the centuries as a profound formulation of Christian values and priorities. Its spirituality, entirely Jewish in origin, has a universal quality which, since early centuries, has won for it an assured place in the worship of the Christian church.

57 **Now the time came for Elizabeth to give birth.** Luke is very soon to recount the circumstances surrounding the birth of Jesus; but the way he has chosen to weave together the strands of the two stories and bring out the parallels between them makes it necessary first to work in the birth of John. The interest of the story lay in the surprising agreement of the child's parents over the name and in Zechariah's sudden recovery of his faculties.
65 These were events such as to make **fear** come **over all their neighbors** and for which Luke continues to adopt a solemn biblical style.

59 **On the eighth day.** This was the normal time for circumcision (Leviticus 12.3), but it is a little surprising to find a Jewish family at this date naming the child (as the Greeks often did) when a week or so old instead of at birth – there may be a hint here of Luke's own more cosmopolitan culture. Nor was it usual to call a male child after its father, even in a priestly family; indeed, it was more common to call it after its grandfather. But, no doubt, if the name 'John' (which had been fairly popular since the time of the Maccabees) had never been given to a member of this family, the sudden consensus of the parents must have seemed striking, particularly since the narrator seems to assume that, since his vision in the temple, Zechariah had been not just dumb but deaf-and-dumb. (In Greek a single word was used for either or both of these afflictions.)

67 **Then his father Zechariah was filled with the Holy Spirit and spoke this prophecy.** Another song of praise, this time with rather more allusion to actual events in the gospel and therefore justly called a **prophecy** – prophesying was regarded by Luke, as by other Jewish writers of the period, as a characteristic manifestation of the Holy Spirit. Perhaps it makes little difference whether the words go back to Zechariah's own inspiration, whether they were composed by Luke, or whether they had an independent existence as a hymn and were incorporated, perhaps with adaptations, into Luke's narrative. This song, like Mary's, is a typical example of Jewish religious poetry, with only small touches added to bring it into line with Christian experience in general and with the story of John in particular. Its style, accumulating

clause upon clause with little regard for logic or syntax,[5] is reminiscent of some of the psalms of the Bible, and still more of the psalms composed during the century before the birth of Christ and known as the 'Psalms of Solomon'. Its language, like that of Mary's song, is impregnated with scriptural idioms, and its content departs little from mainstream Jewish piety. It begins with a typical expression of the ancient Jewish hope that God would 'raise up' a deliverer – for Luke's readers this hope had now been fulfilled by Jesus in a startlingly unexpected form. It goes on to dwell on God's often repeated promises that he would guarantee to his own people a time of safety and peace. And the last two verses return to the theme of the promised Messiah (for

78 whom **the dawn from on high** had become an almost technical expression). Only verses 76–7 bear directly on John, who was to be a prophet, a forerunner
77 and a baptizer for **the forgiveness of their sins.**
80   **The child grew.** Luke had nothing further to record between John's infancy and his public appearance some thirty years later. But he could infer that, being a prophet, he must during that time have become **strong in spirit** (for prophecy was a gift of the Spirit of God) and that his appearance in the wilderness was prepared for by a long ascetic apprenticeship. Since there is a certain similarity between the teaching and activity of John and the ideals and practices of the community which produced the Dead Sea Scrolls, it is sometimes suggested that during his time in the wilderness he came in contact with it. But this remains pure speculation: there is no evidence that he was in any way associated with it.

The birth of Jesus

2.1 **In those days a decree went out from Emperor Augustus.** One of the innovations of Augustus was to replace the existing somewhat haphazard system of taxation in the provinces of the Roman empire by a uniform system based on a census of the population of each province. This policy gradually became effective throughout the Roman empire (which is what Luke means by **all the world**); but we happen to know, independently of Luke's gospel, when it was applied to Judea. Archelaus, one of Herod the Great's sons, ruled over Judea from his father's death until 6 CE, when he was banished by Augustus, and his kingdom became part of the Roman province of Syria. This was the
2 moment to introduce the new system of taxation, and it fell to **Quirinius,** who became governor of Syria in that year, to carry it out. This imposition of direct taxation was extremely unpopular and actually caused a minor revolt. It was the first 'registration' of its kind in Judea, and the violent reaction it provoked was not liable to be quickly forgotten. (Luke in fact refers to it again

---

[5] This is less apparent in the NRSV translation than in the Greek, where the first five verses all belong to a single sentence.

in Acts 5.37.) At the very least, it would have been an obvious moment of crisis by which to date any other event occurring around the same time.

If, therefore, Luke intended at this point to relate his narrative to the wider world and to provide it with a date (as he does much more systematically at the beginning of chapter 3), then this census offered a convenient marker. Unfortunately the date itself (5–6 CE) causes difficulties. In the next chapter Luke states that Jesus was "about thirty years old" when he appeared in public; but the date of this appearance is fixed (by Luke's own reckoning) at 28–9 CE. This is probably only approximate; nevertheless, if Jesus was born in 6–7 CE, he would have been only twenty-two in 28–9, which is rather young for him to be described as 'about thirty'. Moreover, Matthew places Jesus' birth in the lifetime of Herod the Great (that is, before 4 BCE) and Luke himself states that John the Baptist was only six months older than Jesus and was born "in the days of King Herod of Judea" (1.5). Luke's date here (6–7 CE) seems about ten years too late.

But is Luke really concerned about the date at this point, or is he just seeking to indicate that the birth took place in the context of an act of the supreme ruler of the Roman world? At the beginning of this paragraph he is still using
1 scriptural language: the vague phrase **In those days** is typical of the style. His real interest in chronology begins only with the very elaborate dating in the next chapter (3.1–2). His concern with the census here is not so much to give a date as to explain how it came about that Jesus of Nazareth, a Galilean, was born at Bethlehem, a village situated in another part of the country altogether. A census of this kind was normally based on people's actual place of residence, not on their ancestral town; but it could also conceivably have been based on property, and Joseph might have inherited some land in Bethlehem (though, as we shall see, verse 24 implies that he was poor). Was there in fact any such census at the time that Jesus was born? It is unlikely that a Roman census could have taken place when the country was still theoretically independent of Rome under Herod the Great or his son Archelaus; but it is conceivable that one of the Herods initiated something of the kind. Even so, there still remains the difficulty of bringing Quirinius into the picture some ten years before he is known to have held office in the area: the only evidence which has been thought to point to Quirinius having had an earlier term of office is fragmentary and problematical. If Luke is writing serious history at this point we ought perhaps to take his word for all this; but if he is merely working a memory of Quirinius' famous census into his narrative for the sake of giving an approximate date and explaining the strange circumstances of Jesus' birth, then we should perhaps be prepared to admit that (in an epoch when such things were much more difficult to get right than they are now) he fell into error about the some of the details.

7 **She . . . wrapped him in bands of cloth, and laid him in a manger.** The manger is the pivot of the story. Already in the gospel there have been two interventions by angels, and each of them has ended with the promise of a

sign. The third intervention (to the shepherds) will follow exactly the same pattern, but this time the reader knows in advance that the baby will be found 'wrapped in bands of cloth' (as was customary, to keep a newborn child's limbs straight) **in a manger**. Why was the baby in such an unusual place? Luke offers a thoroughly practical reason: **because there was no place for them in the inn**. This seems a strange eventuality in a town where eastern hospitality would normally have assured a welcome, however crowded the place; but it is possible that no one could offer Mary a room to herself for having her baby, in which case a shed or a cave[6] used for sheltering cattle may have been the best the place could provide, thus giving fulfilment to the angel's 'sign'. For what really impressed the shepherds was this miraculous

20 confirmation of the angel's words: it had all happened **as it had been told them**. Nevertheless, Luke works in some deeper significance of the event by

11 putting more words in the angel's mouth. The baby would be a **"Savior, who is the Messiah, the Lord"**, titles which Jesus was given only tentatively during his time on earth but which the church was soon to ascribe to him with conviction; and the event (like the fulfilment of each of the previous 'signs') is the cue for another song of praise, this time quite brief and sung by the angels. One of the main blessings of the age of the Messiah – so it

14 was believed – would be **on earth peace**, to be enjoyed by all whom God had 'favoured' to benefit from it. Previously this could have been thought to mean only the Jewish nation; but Luke was writing for Christians, who now knew that there existed a much wider constituency of **those whom he favors**.[7]

21 **After eight days**. Luke shows himself to be thoroughly conversant with
24 **what is stated in the law** for Jewish parents after the birth of a first male child, and he seems to lay great emphasis (by stating it three times, verses 22, 27 and 39) on the fact that Jesus' parents meticulously fulfilled all the legal requirements. First, after eight days, came circumcision and naming (as with John the Baptist, 1.59). Then, forty days after childbirth (during which she remained at home awaiting her[8] **purification**) the mother had to offer a sacrifice of a lamb (which in the case of poorer people was remitted to **"a pair of turtledoves or two young pigeons"**, Leviticus 12.8), after which the priest declared her 'clean'. A further obligation arose when the child was

---

[6] There is a tradition dating back to at least the second century that Jesus was born in a cave. Constantine's great church at Bethlehem was built over a cave; but this proves little: caves very commonly attracted such traditions. (What else could there have been to mark the spot of such an event?)

[7] The traditional rendering, 'goodwill towards men' (*goodwill among people*), is of a manuscript reading which is less likely to be original (see the NRSV footnote).

[8] **Their** purification is puzzling – so much so that some manuscripts (not mentioned in an NRSV footnote) have changed the word. It was only to the mother that these observances applied. Possibly Joseph and the baby could have been regarded as ritually unclean through contact with her, and needing, therefore, to be present at the temple sacrifice with her.

the mother's firstborn and a male; for it was a very old and strong religious

23 principle in Judaism that **"every firstborn male shall be designated as holy to the Lord"** (Exodus 13.2). In primitive times this probably meant that every family had its priest; but later it was applied only to the descendants of Aaron and Levi (the priests and the Levites), and all other families 'redeemed' their firstborn by paying a tax of five silver shekels (Numbers 18.15–16). But Luke

22 mentions no such payment here. Instead, the parents of Jesus **brought him up to Jerusalem to present him to the Lord.** It looks as if Luke is making a particular point of the rule about firstborn males: this particular child was

23 to be **"holy to the Lord"** in a special sense. It was therefore inappropriate to 'redeem' him from the Lord's service by a payment. He must, on the contrary, be taken to the temple to be 'presented' to the Lord. Thus everything was done that was required by the law – but with a highly significant difference: Jesus was *not* redeemed from special service to the Lord.

25 **Now there was a man in Jerusalem whose name was Simeon.** Two further witnesses are called (one might say) to give their evidence that the birth of Jesus was of exceptional significance. The first was a man **righteous and devout**, qualified by his blameless life, like Zechariah and his wife (1.6), to play a small part in these momentous events. He was also one who was **looking forward to the consolation of Israel**, that is to say, he believed with great earnestness and eagerness that the glorious destiny which God had promised for his people (for which **'consolation'** was almost a technical term) was shortly to come to pass, and like many of his contemporaries he

26, 25 believed that the herald of this would be **the Lord's Messiah. The Holy Spirit rested on him**, giving him not just guidance but the gift of prophecy; and when he recognized that the moment had come for which he had been living, he gave his prophetic testimony in the form of the last of the songs with which Luke adorns this part of the narrative. The song begins quite personally: the

29 sight of the baby gives Simeon his 'dismissal', and he can now die **in peace**. But to sharpen the picture of what the child will be, language and imagery

30 are borrowed from Isaiah: the promised **salvation** (Isaiah 40.5) is not only for Israel but will shine forth far beyond the confines of the Jewish religion to

32 be **a light for revelation to the Gentiles** (Isaiah 42.6; 49.6). Yet this Messiah will by no means conform to the popular image of a figure of power and glory. The story is to have its darker side, and Simeon adds some enigmatic oracles addressed to the parents, which Luke doubtless intends his readers to solve for themselves as the story unfolds.

36 The second witness is **a prophet, Anna.** Luke notes that she was **of the tribe of Asher**, of which the members lived mainly in northern Galilee or in dispersion further east, and was therefore an untypical resident in Jerusalem – perhaps she symbolized the future impact of Jesus on the wider world. It had come to be accepted in official circles that the gift of prophecy had ceased with the last of the Old Testament prophets and would be revived only in the new age with the coming of the Messiah. But in Jesus, Luke is telling us,

the Messiah had come; and so he presents the revival of prophecy as one of the signs accompanying his birth. What this meant was by no means clear to all; but those who were **looking for the redemption of Jerusalem** (another almost technical expression for this new age) would have been alive to the significance of Anna's prophetic words **about the child.**

38

42   **When he was twelve years old.** Nothing is said anywhere else in the New Testament about the years which Jesus spent in Nazareth (though legends soon began to appear in later 'gospels'). But Luke, who has just hinted at the kind of training received by John the Baptist (1.80), provides an anecdote which does the same for Jesus on the threshold of his adult life. To a Greek reader, it would have been axiomatic that these early years would be devoted to education; accordingly Luke reports that Jesus **increased in wisdom,** and the story of Jesus' precocity can be paralleled from the biographies of many famous figures of antiquity. But Jesus' learning would have been of an entirely Jewish character, that is to say, consisting of a deep knowledge of scripture, and there can be little doubt that the questions being discussed by the twelve-year-old boy turned upon the interpretation of certain passages of the Old Testament: Jesus had already learned enough in the local synagogue in Nazareth to be able to hold his own with the scholars in the capital. The occasion was a Passover pilgrimage to Jerusalem, which was often made in family groups; but Jesus' answer to his parents already betrays a loyalty greater even than to his family. For him, the temple was not just 'God's house', it was **"my Father's house".**[9] But this reference to God as 'his own Father', rather than as everyone's 'Father', evidently struck a strange note. Even his parents **did not understand what he said to them.**

52

49

50

John the Baptist

There is now a lapse of time; and in the manner of a careful historian Luke fixes the date at which the story comes on to the stage of world history. The commonly received system of dating throughout the Roman empire was by the year of the reigning emperor. So here: **In the fifteenth year of the reign of Emperor Tiberius** (i.e. 28–9 CE). This sounds, to modern ears, as precise and reliable an indication as one could wish. But in antiquity an accurate chronology was a great deal more difficult to obtain than it is now, and historians often liked to provide some chronological cross-references. Luke's list is not exceptional, though it is unusually detailed, and it also serves to fill out the details of the political conditions of the time. After the death of Herod the Great (4 BCE) his kingdom had been divided into four, each part being governed by a *tetrarch*, which means **'ruler** of a fourth part' (see the NRSV footnote). It

3.1

---

[9] The same Greek words can be translated *about my Father's interests* (as in the NRSV footnote), which would mean that Jesus is being described as already conscious of being his Father's agent on earth.

was this title *tetrarch* which perhaps led Luke, for the sake of completeness, to specify the ruler of each of the four kingdoms. Judea, after the unsuccessful reign of its first tetrarch Archelaus, had come directly under Roman rule in 6 CE and was governed by a Roman official called, first, a *praefectus* and, subsequently, a *procurator*. Pontius Pilate held this office from 26 to 36 CE, and Luke gives him a general title that was used for such officials, **governor**. **Herod Antipas**, son of Herod the Great, became tetrarch of Galilee and Perea at his father's death and remained in power until 39 CE. **Philip**, another of Herod's sons, ruled his tetrarchy in the north-east until 33 CE. **Abilene**, the northernmost part of Herod's original kingdom, lay in the Lebanon, and we know little about its history, but there is no serious reason to doubt Luke's statement

2   that its ruler's name was **Lysanias**. Luke then completes the picture with **the high priesthood**. Only one high priest held office at a time: he normally presided over the supreme Jewish council (the Sanhedrin) in Jerusalem. The high priest in that year was **Caiaphas**; but **Annas**, his father-in-law, had also held the office from 6 to 15 CE and probably still exercised so much influence that Luke may have thought it right to couple his name with that of Caiaphas.

    The word of God came to John. The phrase is an Old Testament one, appropriate to a prophet (compare Jeremiah 1.2). It is one of the touches by which Luke fills in the prophetic side of John's work. The quotation from

4–6   Isaiah (40.3–5) is common to the accounts in all the gospels, though it is given at greater length by Luke; and John's first speech (except that it is delivered to the crowds, not to the Pharisees and Sadducees) runs closely parallel with the version in Matthew (3.7–10). But after this, Luke's narrative takes a different course. From the other gospels the impression might easily be gained that John's preaching consisted entirely of an announcement of the Coming One and an urgent call to repent and be baptized. But it is clear from the fact that his movement lasted long after the appearance of Jesus, and also from the independent account of John which occurs in the historian Josephus, that he must also have given moral teaching. According to Luke, indeed, the crowds

12   called him **Teacher** (as they did Jesus) and evidently expected teaching from him. Luke gives a sample of this teaching here. In part it was not original or surprising. Sharing food and clothing with the needy was recognized as a social obligation and a meritorious act throughout the culture. John's attitude to **tax collectors** and soldiers, however, was unusually liberal. Most of his contemporaries regarded these professions as incompatible with strict observance of the law and as excluded from the true community of Israel. John, by contrast (and here his attitude was closer to that of Jesus), accepted these people, only warning them against the special temptations of their professions – though if tax collectors had taken his teaching literally they would have deprived themselves altogether of their source of livelihood (see below on 18.9–14).

15   **As the people were filled with expectation**. Luke reports the Baptist's proclamation of the Coming One in much the same terms as Matthew, but

sets the scene for it a little more carefully and vividly. Any prophetic figure preaching a radical message in the wilderness was liable to arouse **expectation** about the promised deliverer, and indeed, we know that there was a number of pretenders to this rôle during the century, culminating in the figure of Bar Kochba, who led the last revolt of the Jews against the Romans in 135 CE. It was against this background that John announced the coming of a greater successor, intensifying the atmosphere of expectation but diverting attention from himself to another who was soon to come.

The subsequent fate of John is recounted by Mark and Matthew in some detail at a later stage in their gospels (Mark 6; Matthew 11). Luke is content merely to refer to it (the story was presumably well known to his readers) and, with perhaps a historian's concern to round off a story and draw a moral, he places his summary here. After this, John does not appear again in his gospel: the stage is left clear for Jesus.

21 **Now when all the people were baptized.** Jesus was last mentioned growing up in Nazareth. Here it is simply taken for granted that he was among the crowd who came to John to be baptized, and the vision which accompanies his baptism – which is not something only he saw, as seems to be implied in Mark and Matthew, but is apparently a public event – serves to bring him out of obscurity and indicates that he is now the protagonist of the story.

A genealogy

Who was this Jesus? Luke's previous chapters have indicated that there was something supernatural about his birth – but this was made known to only
23 a few. Who was he in the eyes of ordinary people? Luke answers, **the son (as was thought) of Joseph,** and impressively proceeds to trace his ancestry right back to **Adam, son of God.** A similar genealogy in Matthew (though it offers a quite different list of names for Jesus' immediate ancestors) serves to answer the question: How was Jesus a son of David? Luke's interest is not so obvious; possibly he was using the convention of a genealogy simply to integrate Jesus into the history of his people. (On the genealogy itself, see on Matthew 1.1–17.)

The temptation

Luke's account of Jesus' 'temptation' is very similar to that of Matthew (4.1–11), except that the episodes are in a different order. There are also some slight differences of detail which suggest that Luke may have been less familiar with the geography than Mark and Matthew and found it harder to visualize the
4.1 setting of Jesus' experiences. First, Jesus **returned from the Jordan and was led . . .** Did Luke think that the 'wilderness' was in a different part of the country? In fact, 'wilderness' began close to the Jordan valley, and Mark

and Matthew correctly describe Jesus entering it straight after his baptism. Secondly, according to Matthew Jesus was taken "to a very high mountain". In the wilderness of Judea there are many such mountains which command an immense view over the Jordan valley and would have offered an impression

5 of **all the kingdoms of the world**. But Luke prefers to think of an inner vision – **in an instant**.

Activity in Galilee

Luke evidently knew the tradition that the beginning of Jesus' activity in

15 Galilee was marked by success and popularity: he **was praised by everyone**. But instead of beginning his account with examples of this (as Mark and Matthew did), he placed right at the beginning a notable case of opposition, doubtless seeing this as a foretaste of the ultimate rejection of Jesus by his fellow Jews and as laying down the pattern of Jesus' entire ministry. The episode is recounted by Mark and Matthew at a later stage (Mark 6.1–6; Matthew 13.54–8) and much more briefly.

16 **When he came to Nazareth, where he had been brought up**. Mark and Matthew call it simply his 'hometown', but Luke is careful to maintain consistency with the account he has given of Jesus' birth in Bethlehem: strictly speaking, Nazareth was not his 'hometown' but was only **where he had been brought up**. No followers are with him, as they are in the other gospels. But there the episode comes later in the story; here the disciples have not yet been called. **He went to the synagogue on the sabbath day, as was his custom** – and what follows is consistent with what we know from later Jewish sources about the order of service in a synagogue on the sabbath. After prayers came a reading or readings from 'the law' (the first five books of the Bible). After that, a member of the congregation competent to do so was invited to stand and read a lection from one of the prophets, and then to sit and expound it. Jesus had already made a reputation by his teaching, and when he visited a town it was natural that he should obtain an invitation to give the exposition. Indeed, it is likely that he (like the apostles after him) eagerly accepted such opportunities of proclaiming his message, and the exposition which Luke

15 summarizes on this occasion is doubtless typical of his teaching **in their synagogues** in many other places.

The passage read by Jesus was from Isaiah 61.1–2, with the addition of a phrase from Isaiah 58.6. Whatever its original context, which was probably the period shortly after the return to Jerusalem from exile in the fifth century BCE, in the time of Jesus the passage was certainly understood as a still unfulfilled prophecy of a new age in which the 'jubilee year' (Leviticus 25.10),

19 **"the year of the Lord's favor"**, would bring unprecedented blessings and be inaugurated by the appearance of one 'anointed' for the purpose. Luke gives the passage at some length (following the Septuagint version of the Bible, which gives a slightly different text from the one Jesus would have

used in Hebrew) but offers only the briefest summary of Jesus' sermon –
21 **"Today this scripture has been fulfilled in your hearing."** Yet the force of Jesus' words is vividly captured. In implicitly referring Isaiah's words to himself he was making a prodigious claim. At first this excited admiration –
22 perhaps there is even a note of local pride in the comment, **"Is not this Joseph's son?"** (for so, people thought, he was, 3.23). But then Jesus' words became provocative, and seemed to have a wider target than his neighbours
23 in Nazareth. **"Doctor, cure yourself!"** There is no obvious reason why these people should have thought of casting this well-known proverb in Jesus' teeth, but these were exactly the terms in which Jesus was taunted at the crucifixion (Matthew 27.42) – Luke is evidently using the scene as a trailer for the treatment received by Jesus, not just in Nazareth, but in Jerusalem. Similarly, the Old Testament examples which follow are relevant, not so much to the present episode, as to what was to become a recurring pattern in Jesus' activity, seeking out those whose profession or way of life was thought to disqualify them for membership of the holy people of God, and even extending his concern to those who were not Jews at all. The story of Elijah and the widow of Zarephath is found in 1 Kings 17, that of Naaman in 2 Kings 5. The implication of both these stories was that, in God's saving purpose, it could happen that foreigners might be more favourably placed than Jews;
28 and the result of Jesus' quoting them was that **all in the synagogue were filled with rage.** They evidently intended to put him to death (those among them who were sufficiently learned having perhaps found him guilty of a capital offence such as blasphemy), and to hurl him off a cliff – there are many steep places in the neighbourhood of Nazareth, even though the village was built not on a hill but in a hollow among the hills. Luke suggests something mirac-
30 ulous about his escape: **he passed through the midst of them and went on his way.**

31 **He went down to Capernaum, a city in Galilee.** The phrase is typical of Luke, who does not expect his readers to be familiar with Palestine and is careful to explain that what, to Greek ears, was a barbarous collection of syllables (*ka-phar-na-oum*) was **a city in Galilee.** Whether or not he was familiar with Galilee himself, he probably knew that Capernaum was on the lake and therefore that Jesus must have 'gone down' to it from the mountain village of Nazareth.

31–44 From this point to the end of the chapter Luke closely follows Mark (1.21–34). The only notable difference is that the fever of Simon's mother-in-law
39 is personified: Jesus **rebuked the fever** as he had 'rebuked' the demon in the previous incident. By this touch Luke perhaps wishes to make the whole paragraph into a series of encounters with demons, culminating in their
41 recognition of Jesus as **the Son of God** and **the Messiah.** Jesus' retreat next
42 morning to **a deserted place** serves, as in Mark, to signal the transition
44 from Capernaum to a wider field of work. Luke places this wider field **in the synagogues of Judea.** Strictly speaking, Judea was a long way south of

Galilee, and if Luke means this literally he is in conflict,[10] not only with the other gospels, but even with his own presentation of Jesus' movements, for

5.1 in the very next sentence Jesus is back by **the lake of Gennesaret** (another name for the lake, derived from a district close to Capernaum). But, like other Greek and Latin writers, Luke may be using 'Judea' to mean Palestine in general, and his intention here is probably only to say that Jesus' teaching journeys extended far over Jewish lands.

In the other gospels Jesus had by this time already gathered disciples round him. Luke has not yet mentioned this; but he now tells the story of the calling of the first three disciples, Simon, James and John (who were of course so well known to his readers that they needed no introduction). In Mark and Matthew this was a simple summons followed by an immediate response. But Luke leads up to it with a story which is clearly intended to offer some explanation of the men's instant and surprising decision to follow Jesus – and which also, incidentally, gives early prominence to Simon Peter, who has a particularly important rôle both in this gospel and in Acts. Mark (4.1–2) and Matthew (13.1–3) record that Jesus, when teaching by the lake, liked to put out a little from the shore in a boat. Luke takes the story on from there. The details are entirely lifelike. The best time for fishing was (and still is) at night; and the co-operation of two boats to bring in a heavy haul of fish was regular practice. But what it all led up to was Jesus' word (here

10 addressed only to Simon), **"from now on you will be catching people"**. The story finds a suggestive echo in John 21, where Jesus, this time after the resurrection, again enables Simon to make an exceptional catch of fish. Both stories appear to have been freely written up by the evangelists to bring out a symbolic meaning, and both may go back to what was perhaps originally a single event.

12–14 The narrative of the healing of a leper follows Mark (1.40–45) very closely, only omitting Mark's references to Jesus' anger and sternness (which were perhaps as puzzling to Luke as they are to us). Jesus, indeed, moves more gently in this gospel: instead of being forced to leave the town by the numbers of those pressing upon him (Mark 1.45), it is merely said that, on his own

16 initiative, **he would withdraw to deserted places and pray**.

17–26 The next scene (the healing of the paralysed man) reproduces the words of Jesus almost verbatim from Mark (2.1–12) but shows considerable freedom in the narrative. In part, Luke appears simply to have written the scene

26 in a more polished Greek style – in the Greek, **"We have seen strange things today"** is a fluent and idiomatic expression compared to Mark's "We have never seen anything like this!"; in part also he makes it easier for a non-Palestinian reader to visualize the scene: he sets the story inside one of the large tiled houses of western cities instead of in (or outside) the

---

[10] This apparent conflict led early copyists to make alterations in the text such as that in the NRSV footnote.

flat-roofed, baked-mud houses of the east. But in essential points his narrative follows the tradition preserved in Mark.

In the events and sayings following the call of Levi, Luke has made again only minor alterations: he makes it clear (as Mark does not) that Levi is the

29 host and that the meal is a grand affair – **a great banquet**; and he explains the observance of fasting among the Pharisees as connected with praying. But whereas in Mark (2.13–22) there is only a loose and general connection between each paragraph, Luke has more carefully worked them into the setting of the banquet and, by slight editorial touches, made them more relevant to the Pharisees' complaint that his disciples, instead of following

30 the usual austerities of a religious sect, could be seen to **eat and drink**. The context of the banquet fits the saying on fasting just as well as the context given to it by Mark (an actual fast), and Luke makes no significant alteration

35, 36–9 to the saying, part of which is as puzzling here as it is in Mark. As for the following two sayings (on the patch and the wineskins), the only change is a slight elaboration of the first: in this version, if the new patch is taken from an existing garment (like a custom taken over by the Christians from Judaism?) it spoils *both* garments (doing damage to both the faiths?). And to the similar saying on wineskins Luke adds another, which was in fact a proverb and seems to fit a little awkwardly here: once you have tasted the superior quality of matured wine you cannot go back to the cheap, new stuff. Was this an implicit claim that Jesus' message was the original meaning of the scriptures, which had been distorted by the Pharisees' innovations? Or did Jesus mean that the Pharisees were so wedded to their 'old' tradition that they were prejudiced against anything 'new'? – which would fit the context better but is not the natural meaning of the proverb. (Compare its use in Sirach 9.10).

The two sabbath stories run even closer to Mark (2.23–36). In the first, Luke characteristically adds a detail which makes the story easier to visualize: when

6.1 the disciples plucked some heads of grain they **rubbed them in their hands, and ate them**; and he also omits, as Matthew does, one of the general sayings about the sabbath ("the sabbath was made for humankind", etc.) recorded by Mark – perhaps, like us, both of them found it difficult to understand.

6–11 In the second story the changes are even more trivial, unless it is significant that Luke does not mention Jesus' 'anger' on this occasion: such an emotion did not fit into Luke's portrait of Jesus as it did into Mark's. He also omits the Herodians, who were part of the plot against Jesus according to Mark – indeed, according to Luke (who later on makes the Pharisees seem less united against Jesus than the other evangelists), there was not yet any plot at all.

12 **Now during those days.** Luke now begins to set the stage for a major discourse of Jesus. As in Matthew's Sermon on the Mount, the discourse presupposes a double audience – an inner group of disciples and a large crowd; and the narrative, while still running close to that of Mark (3.7–19), is arranged so as to account for the presence of these two groups. The sequence

begins with Jesus spending the night **in prayer** – Luke insists far more than the other evangelists on the importance of prayer in Jesus' life. Jesus then, out of an existing group of followers (the presence of whom was presupposed in

13 chapter 5) **chose twelve of them, whom he also named apostles.** Even in the less portentous account in Mark, these twelve are clearly listed for the sake of their part in the subsequent history of the church. Luke makes this explicit by stating that Jesus actually called them **apostles.** This was the title by which the founders of the early church became known, and Luke uses it again four times in the course of his narrative. His list corresponds to that in Mark and

16 Matthew, except that Thaddaeus is replaced by **Judas son of James** – a name also apparently known to John (14.22).

The inner group of listeners now being identified, Luke brings Jesus down

17 to **a level place** (which he presumably thought more appropriate as a setting for a sermon than a hill – he seems to have reserved hills for supernatural experiences) and accounts for the presence of **a great multitude of people** by the spread of his fame far to the south and the north-west of Galilee. (By extending it to **the coast** he may even be suggesting that there were Gentiles present.) It was not merely that Jesus had been known to perform miraculous cures; there was **power** in him (recognized also by Mark, 5.30) which could be released if a sick person so much as touched him.

20 **Then he looked up at his disciples and said.** Luke, like Matthew, places a substantial section of Jesus' teaching early in his narrative, and if we compare Matthew's Sermon on the Mount we see at once that here is another version of the same thing. Both begin with 'beatitudes' and end with a parable; Luke's version, though it is much shorter, contains only a few verses which are not in Matthew's; and there is even the same indeterminacy of audience: at the beginning Jesus was seated (as a teacher normally would be) and so was 'looking up' at his disciples; at the end (7.1) we hear that he had been speaking "in the hearing of the people". Yet Luke's 'sermon' is not merely an abridged version of Matthew's. It has its own distinctive tone and in certain details it presents Jesus' teaching in a more radical light.

"Blessed are you who are poor." The first and most striking difference between these beatitudes and those in Matthew is that they are all in the second person: they presuppose an audience of people who are really poor, hungry, weeping and reviled. And this goes with a second difference. In Matthew (5.3,6) the poor are the "poor in spirit", the hungry are those who "hunger and thirst for righteousness". In other words, the blessing is pronounced as a reward for a certain moral and religious disposition. But here the poor are really poor, the hungry really hungry; and the promise is that their condition will be reversed. Doubtless many of the religious or 'spiritual' connotations which are spelled out in Matthew's version (particularly in those beatitudes which Luke omits) are also present here by implication; but now the emphasis (as in Mary's song, the 'Magnificat', 1.46–55), is on the dramatic reversal of fortune which awaits those who are literally poor and in need.

The same emphasis runs through the 'woes' with which Luke balances each of the beatitudes – these do not occur in Matthew's Sermon on the Mount, though rather similar 'woes' appear at another place in his gospel (23.13–30).

24 **"Woe to you who are rich."** This is the logical corollary of "Blessed are you who are poor", but although there was a strain in Jewish piety which was prepared to find a blessing in poverty, it would have come hard to deny that there was a blessing also in wealth. Yet this was Jesus' teaching, embodied here in an unambiguous condemnation of whole classes of society and repeated on other occasions later on. One other detail characterizes the blessed. Unlike

26 **false prophets** who could easily gain people's admiration, they would be like true prophets, persecuted for their faith (as a Jewish tradition had begun to say, see above on Matthew 23.31); and their persecutors would be the descendants of those who had done the same in the past.

27 **"But I say to you that listen."** The rich and prosperous were presumably not in the audience, and little time is spent over denunciations of the world at large. The sermon is for those who are deprived of material prosperity (a very unusual audience to be chosen by an ethical teacher in the ancient world) and who are prepared to follow Jesus. The next sayings are placed under a single bold heading: **"Love your enemies."** In the Sermon on the Mount this radical injunction developed out of Jesus' interpretation of the familiar commandment, to 'love your neighbour as yourself'. Here it is bluntly proclaimed as an ethical principle and illustrated by a series of examples. The examples are familiar from Matthew (5.39–48), but Luke has added some

29 distinctive touches. **"Anyone who takes away your coat"**: evidently a robber who tears off the first garment he can get hold of, not a litigant (as in Matthew)

32 who is prepared to take a shirt as a pledge before he insists on a coat. **"Even sinners love those who love them."** Matthew draws a lesson for the conduct of Christians from the outcasts of Jewish society (tax collectors) or from Gentiles. Luke makes the example more general: simply **sinners**. In Matthew, impartiality is inculcated on the grounds that God dispenses sun and rain impartially on the just and on the unjust. Luke sharpens this, so that 'loving

35 your enemies' can be seen to be a way of imitating the God who is **"kind to the ungrateful and the wicked"**. Similarly, God can be imitated, not (as in Matthew) because he is 'perfect', but – and this is more relevant in the present

36 context – because he is **merciful**; and this quality of mercy is exemplified in

37 the commands, **"Do not judge . . . do not condemn . . . Forgive . . . "**, all of which presuppose that one has suffered some offence but advise against following the normal course of seeking retribution and reparation – not because there may be some advantage in this life from doing so (which would be wishful thinking), but because such generosity secures an even more generous reward in heaven, likened to that of a merchant who crams as much corn as possible, and even more, into his measure.

39 **He also told them a parable.** The word often means a 'riddle', and these two sayings (added to the 'sermon' by Luke) are certainly enigmatic. Both

appear to be proverbs: the enigma is why Jesus used them and at whom he was aiming. Are the 'blind' those who judge and fail to forgive, those who are blind to the force of Jesus' teaching, or (as in Matthew 15.14) those who

40 are his enemies among the Pharisees? Is the equality of disciples with their teacher a warning that they will receive no better treatment than he did (as in Matthew 10.24–5; John 15.20), or a promise that they will become teachers

41–2 like himself? Two more 'parables' follow: the **speck** of sawdust and the **log**

43–4 almost exactly as in Matthew (7.3–5), the fruit metaphor much shortened.

46 Finally there is the same warning about calling Jesus '**Lord, Lord**', shortened again, but with the same challenge (presumably reformulated as a warning to the church): there is no virtue in worshipping Christ without a sincere intention to perform his exceedingly exacting ethic.

47–9 And so, with the same parable of two houses as in Matthew (though Luke perhaps imagines a house near a European river like the Tiber rather than one near a Palestinian wadi), the sermon comes to an end. It contains much less teaching than Matthew's version (though some of what is omitted here appears elsewhere in Luke's gospel), but its tone is both sharper and more general – sharper, because the most radical elements in it are presented without qualification or concession; more general, because the debate between Christians and Jews, which seems often to be in the background of Matthew's presentation, can hardly be overheard in Luke's, and the ethic stands as a guide for life under any circumstances whatever. We may wonder whether Matthew and Luke were each responsible for their own version, or whether two different collections of Jesus' moral teaching already existed before these gospels came to be written. But both versions undoubtedly reflect a teacher of outstanding originality, whose influence has disturbed, not only those of his first followers who undertook to write down his words, but the many generations of those who, in a great variety of ways, have ever since endeavoured to bend their lives to his teaching.

7.1 **He entered Capernaum.** As in Matthew, so in Luke, the great sermon is soon followed by an account of a petition addressed to Jesus by a Gentile. In each gospel the dialogue is virtually identical; but in Luke the story itself is told somewhat differently. In Matthew (8.6) the word used for 'servant' is ambiguous: it could also mean 'son'. But in Luke there is no

2 ambiguity: it is a 'servant', even perhaps a **slave** (the usual NRSV translation of this word), and so he adds the explanation, **whom he valued highly.** In Matthew, again, the point of the episode, with the dialogue it contains, is the comparison between the authority of a military officer over his men with that of Jesus over the world of spirits; but in Luke this point is at most implicit. All the stress is on the character and behaviour of the centurion. He was a friend and benefactor of the Jewish nation; he was so respected that some of their elders were willing to press his case, and at the same time he had too much humility to approach Jesus in person. No Gentile could have been better qualified to gain his petition from Jesus; and Luke

9 doubtless saw all these qualities comprised in the **faith** which Jesus promptly rewarded.

11 **Soon afterwards he went to a town called Nain**. The site of this town is known: it lies just off one of the roads leading from the lake to the coast, on the side of a steep hill. As Jesus approached it from the main road he would have had before him (or so, at least, Luke could have presumed) the principal gate of the town. Out of this gate was coming a funeral procession. Burials normally took place within a few hours of death. The body, wrapped in a linen cloth, was carried from the house on a bier (for coffins were not used) to a family grave cut in the rock; and, since graves were always outside the walls of a town, the procession had at some stage to pass through the gate. This was the moment at which Jesus intervened and performed what was regarded as the greatest of all miracles, that of bringing a dead person back to life (though it was thought to be less difficult if done soon after death). Two such miracles are recorded in the gospels apart from this one: Jairus' daughter (8.40–56; Mark 5.21–43; Matthew 9.18–26) and Lazarus (John 11). Here the story is told quite simply, and there is little to distinguish it from similar stories occasionally told about other miracle-workers in antiquity. On the other hand the reaction of the bystanders was more than mere amazement.

16 **"A great prophet has risen among us!"** Elijah and Elisha, the first great prophets, had performed similar miracles (1 Kings 17; 2 Kings 4): Jesus must be another of the same calibre. Moreover, the raising of someone from the dead could be a sign of the new age that was to come: **"God has looked favorably on his people!"** – the same phrase as in Zechariah's prophetic song after the birth of John the Baptist (1.68). The miracle was seen as a sign of a new phase in their relationship with God.

18 **The disciples of John reported all these things to him.** This episode, with its sayings about John the Baptist, occurs in Matthew 11, where it reads like a digression. By placing it immediately after the account of two notable

21 miracles, and by inserting the note that **Jesus had just then cured many

31–5 people**, Luke knits the same material more neatly into his narrative. In other respects he continues to follow the same order as in Matthew (11.7–19), apart from verses 29–30. This comment, which draws a clear distinction between Jesus' supporters and his opponents, occurs only in Luke's gospel (though it seems to be echoed, in a quite different context, in Matthew 21.32): those

29 who had been baptized by John **acknowledged the justice of God**, that is, they were confirmed in their belief in the validity of that baptism and gave voice to their conviction of having done right. (See the NRSV footnote for another possible translation.) Unfortunately we do not know (since Greek manuscripts had no inverted commas) whether the comment is that of the narrator or is to be attributed to Jesus himself.

36 **One of the Pharisees asked Jesus to eat with him** – evidently a formal meal, since the word translated **took his place at the table** means literally 'lay on a couch', and it was only on more formal occasions that the Jews adopted the

Greek and Roman custom of reclining at table. Moreover, an ordinary family meal would have been held in private; but any kind of large entertainment always attracted visitors other than the invited guests, whether people simply wishing to hear the conversation or beggars hoping for scraps of food. It was

37 only on such an occasion that a woman **who was a sinner** (we are not told in what respect, but it is usually assumed that her sins were sexual) could have gained admission to a Pharisee's house and, finding the guests reclining on couches with their feet stretched out behind them, could have discreetly

38 ministered to Jesus, standing **behind him at his feet.** Jesus' host evidently had little respect for his guest. He had omitted the normal conventions of hospi-

45 tality, failing to greet him with the customary formalities of a **kiss** on the hand or the cheek and to provide him with water for washing his feet. His purpose in inviting him seems to have been, not to honour him as a guest, but to chal-

39 lenge his reputation as a **prophet.** He assumed that Jesus, like himself, would

39 be particular about who was **touching him,** in order to remain ritually 'clean' (particularly before a meal); and he supposed that if he really had prophetic insight he would know intuitively about the personal lives of those with whom

40 he came in contact. Jesus ignored the first point but had **something to say** to him on the second. First, he told a brief and pointed parable, then he drew attention to the signs of powerful emotion in the woman. Actually washing a guest's feet oneself or anointing him with oil and perfume were not courtesies normally offered to guests at a banquet; Jesus was criticizing Simon not so much for his pointed lapse of hospitality as for allowing his disapproval of the woman as a 'sinner' (and perhaps his surprise at the liberty she had taken) to prevent him from noticing her evident sincerity. He did not need to be a prophet to see that her generosity expressed deep feelings of gratitude and love. By contrast, the frigid hospitality of the Pharisee, and indeed his whole

47 way of life, expressed no such response: **"one to whom little is forgiven, loves little"**.

To this extent the drift of the conversation is clear: Jesus wins his point against the Pharisee. But there is evidently more to the story than this; and as soon as we begin to analyse it difficulties and uncertainties appear. A similar story (set in the house of one 'Simon the leper', Mark 14.3) occurs in the other gospels shortly before the narrative of the passion. But Luke has no such story in that place. Has he adapted it to a different purpose here, or were there originally two stories, both involving a woman with a flask of ointment? Did Jesus originally tell the parable on this occasion or has Luke added it to his story? And what is the meaning of his final comment (verse 47)? Had she shown love or gratitude to Jesus before (perhaps on an earlier occasion), or was she suddenly moved now to make this extravagant (some might say outrageous, or else highly symbolic) gesture? At what point had she shown

50 **faith** – when she first heard about Jesus or when she came to the banquet? When was she forgiven? The difficulty is compounded by a problem in the Greek. Its most natural meaning is: 'forgiven *because* she has shown great

love'; that is, Jesus declared that she was forgiven *after* she had shown her
47 love; but it can perhaps also be taken to mean (as in the NRSV) '*hence she has
shown great love*' – this makes the comment match the parable: as between
43 the woman and Simon, it was she who was **the one for whom he canceled the
greater debt**; but in this case she must have been forgiven *before*, and we are
not told when. Sins, in any case, were often called 'debts'; and the word 'love'
must not lead us into thinking that the scene is intended to offer an analysis
of deep emotions. In Jesus' own language such words could mean, not lasting
affection, but the outward expression of loyalty and gratitude. The response
of the pardoned debtors and the generous gesture of the woman could be
described by the same word, only imperfectly represented by *agapē* in Greek
and *love* in English.

8.1   **Soon afterwards he went on through cities and villages**. This marks a new
stage in the narrative: Jesus left the area around Capernaum, where he could
count on the hospitality of friends, and became an itinerant preacher, moving at first from town to town without any explicit strategy until "he set his
face to go to Jerusalem" (9.51). How did he and his disciples live? All the synoptic gospels tell us that the women who witnessed the crucifixion had been
with him in Galilee and "provided for him" (Mark 15.41; Matthew 27.55;
Luke 23.49). Luke (with his particular interest in the women of the story)
alone introduces them at this point, but of those listed by the other gospels he
2, 3 mentions only **Mary, called Magdalene**. **Susanna** is otherwise unknown, but
Joanna reappears as one of those who witnessed the resurrection (24.10). It is
interesting (and was doubtless of special interest to Luke, with his concern to
make connections with secular history) that Jesus' following extended to the
household of **Herod** Antipas, the tetrarch of Galilee. Judging by his name,
Chuza is likely to have been a Nabatean aristocrat holding a senior administrative post (a **steward**) at the court of Herod in Tiberias. His wife **Joanna**
could well have had substantial personal wealth out of which to contribute
to Jesus' needs; but she had gone further: by identifying herself with Jesus'
following she had taken a radical step out of the social world of the court.

    At this point both Mark (chapter 4) and Matthew (chapter 13) introduce
a section devoted to Jesus' parable-teaching and offer some hints on the
significance of this teaching for his work as a whole. Luke follows the same
scheme, but makes much less of it (perhaps because he has so many other
4 parables to fit in later on). **He said in a parable**: only the parable of sowing
is given, followed by two short aphorisms; and although Luke retains the
10 difficult quotation from Isaiah 6.9 (**"so that 'looking they may not perceive,
and listening they may not understand'"**), he gives it in the briefest possible
form and softens the contrast between the disciples to whom it has been
granted **to know the secrets of the kingdom of God** and those who are not
so privileged, whom he vaguely describes as **others**. Some, perhaps many,
may have reacted with the stubborn obstinacy foretold by Isaiah, but no clear
line is drawn between an inner circle and the outside world, and in what

follows there is no suggestion that the disciples are given private instruction. He reserves his full treatment of the Isaiah passage until the very end of his two-volume work (Acts 28.26–7), where he identifies the people from whom God has witheld understanding as that majority of the Jewish race who, though given the first opportunity to hear and accept the gospel message, have persistently rejected it. Meanwhile, the possibility of Jesus' hearers' coming to a full understanding of his teaching remains open: Luke significantly omits the statement in Mark (4.33–4) and Matthew (13.34–5) that Jesus spoke to the crowds *only* in parables.

For the details of the parable, see on Mark 4. Luke has made only slight changes. He appears to have thought that the seed on the footpath would
5   fail to grow because it **was trampled on** and for that reason would ultimately be eaten by the birds. As for the interpretation, it differs from the parallel versions only in that it introduces more of the language (and per-
12, 13   haps of the experience) of the Greek-speaking church, such as **believe and**
15   **be saved, a time of testing, patient endurance** and, most striking of all, **an honest and good heart**, which was virtually a cliché of Greek moral discourse.
16–18   Two unconnected sayings follow, as in Mark (4.21–5). But the sequel is a little awkward. The parable teaching which Jesus has just finished is clearly given out of doors; but when Jesus' family arrives (and no reason is given for their visit, as it is in Mark 3.21), he seems suddenly to be indoors and is told
20   that his mother and brothers are **standing outside**.

Across the lake

Similarly the crossing of the lake has no specific context: it simply happens
22   **one day**, though in other respects the paragraph seems to be a straightforward rewriting of the version in Mark (4.35–41), omitting extraneous details and considerably softening the severity with which Jesus reproves his
26–39   disciples for their lack of faith. The following story of the demoniac runs closely parallel to Mark (5.1–12) and the differences are no more than might have been expected from Luke's attention to stylistic detail. According to a number of important manuscripts he places the episode in the country of the *Gergesenes*. (See the NRSV footnote and the map on p. 129.) Other manuscripts, along with Matthew and Mark, give the names of two cities, Gadara and Gerasa, neither of which is close to the lake. *Gergesa* (if that is what Luke wrote) is totally unknown; all we can say for sure is that Luke cor-
26   rectly understood the place to have been on the east side of the lake **opposite Galilee** – that is to say, in predominantly gentile territory. The devils, however,
31   use the language of Jewish mythology: **the abyss** was the place in which the forces of evil were destined to be imprisoned at the end of time (Revelation 20.1–3).

40–56   In the two interwoven episodes that follow, Luke is faithful to the account in Mark (5.21–43). The few changes[11] he has made are no more than a writer might be expected to introduce in order to make a story his own.

Training the disciples

The departure and return of the twelve are separated, as in Mark 6, by the device of a brief change of scene to the court of Herod. But Luke, though he follows Mark's arrangement, has greatly abbreviated it, having partly anticipated this scene when he concluded his account of the Baptist in 3.19–

9.9   20. The words **"John I beheaded"** are all that is left of the story of Salome's dance. Herod himself is also presented in a more sophisticated light. He is called (as in Matthew) by his correct title of *tetrarch* (**ruler**) and not (as in Mark) by the popular name of 'king', and he is not made to share the naïve view (which is more characteristic of Jewish folklore than of a Hellenistic ruler)

7   that Jesus might be John the Baptist **raised from the dead**. His reaction is more pragmatic: after dispensing with John he now finds himself with another religious reformer to come to terms with. His desire to see Jesus for himself is referred to again in 23.8.

In other respects the narrative in Mark appears to be the model for Luke's

3   account and the differences are few. **"No staff, nor bag"** agrees with Matthew (10.9–10) against Mark (6.9) in forbidding even a staff – perhaps because he saw the main function of a traveller's staff to be self-defence, which might have been inappropriate for the disciples of a teacher who forbade any form of

10   retaliation. The only serious discrepancy in Luke is the mention of **Bethsaida**. This village, which lay on the east side of the mouth of the Jordan, and therefore in the jurisdiction of the tetrarch Philip, had recently become the site for a town of some pretensions. It was hardly a place for withdrawing

12–17   privately, and the feeding miracle which follows (narrated with only small differences from Mark and Matthew) can hardly have been in its vicinity, since

12   it presupposes **a deserted place**. By introducing the name, Luke has made the scene hard to visualize. On the other hand, his approach to the topography of Galilee is rather different from that of the other evangelists. He mentions very few place-names and is usually content to situate the various incidents quite vaguely in the countryside. He is about to omit a series of episodes recorded in Mark, which end with one at Bethsaida (Mark 8.22). His concern may simply be to bring the course of Jesus' progress roughly into line with the narratives he was following, without too much attention to the exact setting of any particular episode.

---

[11]   Some manuscripts omit the reference to the woman vainly spending her livelihood on doctors (see the NRSV footnote), conceivably to remove the aspersion on the profession which Luke was believed to have practised.

18   **Once when Jesus was praying alone, with only the disciples near him.** By inserting the word *only* (which is not in the Greek text) and translating *with him* as **near him**, the translators have attempted to soften the contradiction contained in this sentence. But the contradiction remains, and it is Luke who must bear the blame. What seems to have happened is that Luke liked to represent important experiences in the life of Jesus as taking place when Jesus was at prayer: see, for example, the baptism (3.21) and the transfiguration (9.28). But it was also necessary to have the disciples present for the sake of the conversation which follows; hence '*praying alone, the disciples with him*'. Luke omits much of the detail of this conversation compared with Mark (8.27–30), whose narrative he now picks up again (having passed over the contents of several pages), and still more compared with Matthew (16.13–20), who has some altogether original material to insert at this point. He preserves only the two most significant points: Peter's recognition that Jesus

20   is **"The Messiah of God"** (and Luke for once follows Mark in reporting Jesus'
22   injunction to secrecy on the matter), and the prophecy that **"the Son of Man must undergo great suffering"**.

23   **Then he said to them all.** Again little attention is paid to the actual setting. If Jesus was "praying alone" there can have been no "all" within earshot
23–7 to whom Jesus could have addressed this teaching. But the sayings which (following Mark) Luke now had to record were obviously not part of Jesus' private instruction to his disciples (though Matthew assumed they were, 16.24), and the presence of a larger audience had simply to be taken for granted. Jesus' followers must **take up their cross daily**: the expression 'taking up' or 'carrying' one's cross is one which may have become comprehensible only after the crucifixion (see above on Mark 8.34), and Luke adapts it still more to new circumstances by adding the word **daily**, so making it sound like a constant spiritual exercise. In other respects this sequence of sayings stands

27   much as it does in Mark, including the most difficult of them, **"there are some standing here who will not taste death before they see the kingdom of God"**. Only the final words of Mark's version, "come with power", are omitted; and this omission perhaps made the oracle easier for Luke's readers to interpret. The **kingdom of God**, so long as it did not involve a manifestation of earthly or cosmic power, could be understood as a reality already sometimes present in the activity of Jesus and certainly now experienced in the life of the church. To this extent Jesus' prediction had come true.

     One should not properly use the word 'transfiguration' as the name of the
29   next episode. Instead of 'he was transfigured', Luke writes **the appearance of his face changed**, and notes that this took place **while he was praying**. His account of the scene, while it retains an emphasis on the supernatural glory of Jesus and the two figures who appeared with him, nevertheless adds a few touches to make the sequence of events more comprehensible and logical, at the expense of some of the symbolic meanings suggested by the narrative
32   in Mark (9.2–8) and Matthew (17.1–8). Thus: the disciples **were weighed**

down with sleep. If they had nevertheless, **stayed awake**,[12] they certainly had not taken in the drift of Jesus' conversation with Moses and Elijah, for, a short time later, they were mystified by Jesus' reference to it (verse 45).

31 The conversation had been about Jesus' **departure, which he was about to accomplish at Jerusalem**. The Greek word is *exodos*, which can certainly mean 'departure', but was also used as a euphemism for 'death', and was furthermore an unmistakable allusion to the exodus of Israel from Egypt. Moses had had an *exodos* to fulfil and had died before it was completed; and the force of the disciples' vision was not only (as in Matthew) that Jesus was a new Moses and that (as in Mark) he would shortly be clothed with a glory that was even now momentarily visible in his person, but that meanwhile there was a **departure that he was about to accomplish at Jerusalem**, which would involve his *exodos* – his death. Another touch of rationalization is Peter's suggestion of making three dwellings for these supernatural figures

33 **just as they were leaving him**, hoping (somewhat inappropriately, Luke admits) to detain them; and the disciples' fear is attributed, not so much to the vision (which need not have been particularly frightening), as to their being suddenly enveloped in cloud. Yet the scene retains its otherworldly quality. According to Luke the disciples needed no injunction to secrecy:

36 they **told no one any of the things they had seen**.

37 **On the next day**. It is just possible that Luke thought of the vision on the mountain as having taken place at night (hence the disciples' being "weighed down with sleep"), in which case he may have deliberately added this lapse

38–43 of time. His account of the exorcism is otherwise a much abbreviated version of that in Mark (9.14–29), except for the description of the crowd's reaction

43 at the end: **all were astounded at the greatness of God**. This atmosphere of 'amazement' is built up still further in the next phrase (**everyone was amazed**) and provides the setting for the solemn announcement which Jesus makes to his disciples. The announcement is introduced in strikingly bibli-

44 cal language (**"Let these words sink into your ears"**). Mark reports (9.32) that the disciples "did not understand what he was saying", but offers no reason for their incomprehension. Luke has a simple (if, as it may seem

45 to us, somewhat contrived) explanation: **its meaning was concealed from them**.

46–50 To conclude the section, Luke makes a brief selection of the sayings recorded at this point by Mark (9.34–41), only loosely linking them together, and adding just one new variant on a well-known but startling rebuke given

48 by Jesus to discourage any form of ambitious self-assertion: **"the least among all of you is the greatest"**.

---

[12] The Greek word may also mean *when they were fully awake* (see the NRSV footnote), in which case **weighed down with sleep** would mean that they were really asleep – which is the more likely translation, given their incomprehension later on.

From Galilee to Jerusalem

The next ten chapters form a distinct section of the gospel. It is at this point in the narrative of Mark (10.1) that Jesus begins his decisive journey from Galilee to Jerusalem, and in both Mark and Matthew it is possible, at least approximately, to plot this journey on the map. In Luke, Jesus also begins his journey shortly after the episode of the transfiguration; but the journey is so packed with sayings and events that it becomes quite impossible to visualize the progress made by the travellers or to be sure which route from Galilee to Jerusalem they are supposed to have taken. The journey, in fact, which would normally have taken three or four days at most and which is recorded quite briefly in Mark (it fills less than the whole of chapter 10), becomes a prolonged series of incidents, lasting perhaps several weeks.

If Luke had been a little more precise about Jesus' route, and offered some indication of the places Jesus had reached as the journey progressed, we might have concluded that he was better informed about this phase of Jesus' activity and was therefore in a position to expand his account of the journey. But in fact he is so vague on these matters that we need a different explanation. Practically none of this material appears in Mark, and only some of it in Matthew – where it is set in other contexts. We must imagine that Luke had received a substantial amount of information about Jesus' teaching and activities which had no fixed place in any connected narrative and which he had to work in as best he could. He knew that, at a certain point, Jesus travelled from Galilee to Jerusalem; and this gave him the opportunity to fill out his portrait of Jesus as a travelling teacher (a picture which his Greek and Roman readers would have found familiar, since such teachers were a common phenomenon in the Hellenistic world) by inserting into this journey most of the extra material which he possessed. It may not have greatly concerned him which route Jesus took; all that was necessary was to remind his readers from time to time that Jesus was on the road and to help them to visualize the itinerant life of one who was remembered to have said that he had **nowhere to lay his head**.

There may also be another reason why Luke, though he devotes so much space to the journey, is vague about the route which was actually taken. He may not have known the country intimately, and reliable maps did not exist. He knew that Galilee was a separate region from Judea, and he was well informed about the political differences between them. But both regions were essentially Jewish; and he may not have realized that they were separated from each other by the alien territory of Samaria, so that to go from one to the other it was necessary to travel either through Samaria or round it. He may have visualized Galilee and Judea (as the Roman geographer Pliny appears to have done) as a continuous stretch of country, with Samaria lying alongside it. He knew that Jesus must have entered Samaria at some stage, since one or two episodes clearly belonged there; but whereas in fact a traveller who took

58

241

the route through Samaria would soon have left Galilee far behind, Luke may have imagined that Jesus could have gone back and forth across the border while continuing south towards Judea. If so, he would have felt free to insert the Samaritan episodes at any point he liked.

In any case, it was no ordinary journey. For Jesus, it was a necessary prelude
51 to being **taken up** – a word that could mean simply 'death', but is almost certainly intended here to look forward to Jesus' ascension into heaven (Acts 1.2,11); and it fixed his course as being from now on directed inexorably towards Jerusalem. Luke expresses this in a sentence rich in biblical phrases, and his language leaves no doubt that a new chapter is opening in the story of Jesus. Appropriately, it begins with a moment of rejection; for rejection will be the dominant motif of its ending in Jerusalem. At the same time there is a strong Old Testament flavour right from the start. There was one Old Testament figure in particular – Elijah – who had "ascended . . . into heaven" (2 Kings 2.11). Many thought that Jesus must be this same Elijah,
54 now returned to earth; and the **disciples James and John** (appropriately nicknamed 'Sons of Thunder', Mark 3.17) were probably simply echoing this popular view when they asked permission to do what Elijah had done to his enemies (2 Kings 1.10) and **consume them** by calling down fire from heaven.
52 The scene took place in **a village of the Samaritans**. For several centuries the Samaritans had been something of a race apart from the rest of the Jewish nation. They possessed a different version of the Hebrew scriptures, consisting of only the first five books, and they regarded Mount Gerizim, near their own capital, as the 'chosen place' where God should be worshipped, believing this, and not Jerusalem, to be the true site of the temple. More recently, Samaria had been brought under the same Roman administration as Judea; but relations between the two races were still strained, and, little more than twenty years before Jesus' visit, some Samaritans had caused a crisis by deliberately defiling the temple in Jerusalem at the time of Passover. It was not unknown for them to attack pilgrims on their way through Samaria from Galilee to Jerusalem; and when Jesus sent **messengers ahead of him**, presumably to make arrangements for lodging, the Samaritan villagers were
53 behaving true to form when **they did not receive him, because his face was set towards Jerusalem**. The disciples' reaction was probably equally typical of Jewish prejudices; but Jesus (as several stories in this section show) dissociated himself altogether from the traditional animosity between the two races.[13]
57 Jesus (as Luke will have to remind us again) was on **the road**; and the road
57–62 is the cue for three sayings about 'following'. The first two of these occur also in Matthew (8.18–22) in a slightly different setting but apparently with the

---

[13] It is perhaps surprising that the paragraph ends without any comment by Jesus. Some manuscripts make up for this by adding the words in the NRSV footnote.

same meaning. The third, added by Luke, also has a proverbial sound and (like the others) gains its radical thrust from its context in the narrative.

10.1   **After this the Lord appointed seventy others.** It is clearly stated in the first three gospels that Jesus had a distinct group of twelve disciples and that on one occasion he sent them out on an independent mission; and in the early church the existence of this original group of twelve was taken for granted – not least, no doubt, because it symbolically represented the twelve tribes of the 'new Israel'. Luke alone mentions a larger group and a further mission. The instructions given to them are almost exactly the same as in his own or Matthew's version of the charge to the twelve (Luke 9.1–5; Matthew 10); the only addition is that they are to work with such urgency

4   that they must **greet no one on the road** – oriental courtesies consume a lot

7   of time! – and not get delayed by moving about **from house to house.** After their return they play no further part in the story. What is their significance? Luke was a historian. He knew the importance of the mission to non-Jews in the subsequent history of the church, and he knew that this had been conducted by apostles who were not members of the original twelve. He may have wished to justify the credentials of this larger circle by mentioning

1   the further **seventy.** Alternatively, **seventy** (or *seventy-two*: there is much oscillation between the two in the manuscripts) was an important round number in Jewish legend and history. Genesis 10 lists seventy (or seventy-two) nations in the world; Moses commissioned seventy (or seventy-two) elders (Numbers 11); seventy (or seventy-two) translators had put the Old Testament into Greek under divine inspiration. Any of these factors may have been in Luke's mind; more we cannot say.

13   **"Woe to you, Chorazin!"** This condemnation of cities in Galilee occurs in Matthew 11.20–24, where the context (Jesus being in Galilee) is more

16   appropriate; and the final words to the seventy (**"Whoever listens to you listens to me"**, etc.) are evidently another version of the saying at the end of the charge in Matthew (10.40). They appear also, in a different form and in another context, in Mark 9.37.

17   **The seventy returned with joy.** The mission and return of this larger group are reported quite summarily and in almost exactly the same words as in the case of the twelve (9.1, 10), who had also been given "power and authority over all demons" (9.1). Invocation of the **name** of Jesus could effect an exorcism even if the exorcist was not a follower of Jesus (9.49). The reason was Jesus'

18   victory over Satan. **"I watched Satan fall from heaven"**: the language is traditional (Isaiah 14.12), and the imagery is drawn from Jewish mythology, Satan being destined to 'fall' and 'be bound'. Whether Jesus actually had such a vision or was merely using this dramatic language to convey his conviction of superiority over evil forces we cannot say. The biblical imagery continues with

19   **the authority to tread on snakes and scorpions** (compare Psalm 91.13), the

20   **enemy** being of course Satan himself. The idea of names **written in heaven** – meaning a secure place in the age to come – is a commonplace in the Bible.

21 **At that same hour Jesus rejoiced in the Holy Spirit.** The startling saying that follows occurs in Matthew 11.25–7. Here perhaps it is better in place, since the scene is specifically one in which Jesus is conversing with his disciples; and if Luke was thinking of the seventy as the prototypes of subsequent apostles and missionaries, then he may have found in this saying
22 a validation of their authority: they were those to whom **the Son chooses to**
23 **reveal** the Father. The same may be true of the following saying (**"Blessed are the eyes that see . . . "**), which in Matthew occurs in the parable chapter (13.16–17). Here, **kings** rather surprisingly take the place of "righteous people".

25 **Just then a lawyer stood up to test Jesus.** It is the same question as was put to Jesus on another occasion (18.18; Mark 10.17), and the answer is the same as that given to a slightly different (and perhaps more 'testing') question in Mark 12.28 and Matthew 22.34. This short dialogue in Luke may be a record of a different occasion altogether, or it may be a conflation of the others; in either event, it shows Jesus easily passing the 'test' of whether he had a correct understanding of scripture; Indeed, he and the professional lawyer were in complete agreement – at least so far as the general principles were
29 concerned. But on the practical application of these principles – **"And who is my neighbor?"** – Jesus had something startlingly original to say.

30 **A man was going down from Jerusalem to Jericho.** The long steep descent through the mountains, winding along the courses of the wadis, was a notorious haunt of robbers until quite recent times. The robbery was nothing out of the ordinary; the interest of the story turns entirely upon the response of the other three travellers. We may feel that the response of the first two was strangely inhuman; but their conduct was probably due, not to any lack of human feelings, but to a deliberate choice between conflicting obligations. On the one hand, there was a clear commandment to help any 'neighbour' (normally interpreted as any fellow Jew) whose life was in danger; on the other hand, if the victim was already dead (which, by his appearance, this one presumably might have been), both a priest and a Levite would incur ritual defilement by touching or even by approaching the corpse, and this might prevent them from fulfilling their duties in the temple or from collecting the tithes to which they were entitled. It would probably not have surprised Jesus' contemporaries that in this case caution prevailed over charity:
32 they decided to avoid all risk of defilement and **passed by on the other side.**

We know what Jesus thought of such an attitude: just as it was absurd to invoke rules about sabbath observance as a pretext for refusing to cure a sick man, so it was indefensible to regard rules about ritual purity as more binding than the needs of a half-dead human being on the road. But if this were the point Jesus intended here, we should expect the third traveller to have been a Jewish layman whose simple understanding of the law would have put to shame the casuistry of the professional religious classes. The surprise in the

33 story consists of the fact that the third traveller was **a Samaritan**. It is true that the Samaritans, according to their own version of the law of Moses, were also commanded to 'love their neighbour as themselves'; and it is true that there was a familiar story in the Old Testament about the mercifulness of certain Samaritans (2 Chronicles 28.8–15). But at the time Jesus told this story, Jews and Samaritans hated each other with great bitterness. The Samaritan had every reason for not regarding the Jewish traveller as 'his neighbour'. Yet he did all – if not more than all – that one Jew would feel obliged to do for another.

37   **"Go and do likewise."** This is the only occasion on which the teaching of Jesus is presented as a moral tale, an example to be followed; and 'Go and do likewise' is the moral which countless sermons and exhortations have drawn from Jesus' parable. But is this really the point of it? And is it likely that Jesus, just this once, told a story that was intended to set a moral example? Certainly the Samaritan's behaviour was what, at their best, human beings can be expected to do for each other; but it did not need a parable of Jesus to inculcate such an ideal: people already knew that this is what one ought to do for someone in acute need, and no doubt Jesus' listeners each hoped that, in a similar situation, they would have done as much themselves. They would doubtless have had more sympathy than we have with the priest and the Levite, whom they would have realized to have been under conflicting obligations; and they would have been virtually forced by their Jewish upbringing to regard the concept of 'neighbour' in a somewhat restricted sense and to feel little obligation to come to the aid of any of the traditional enemies of the Jewish race such as the Romans, the Samaritans or indeed most Gentiles. Jesus' choice of a Samaritan, who was prepared to regard a traditional enemy as his 'neighbour', was designed to shock them out of this attitude. If **"Go and do likewise"** are Jesus' words and not those of a narrator keen to find in the story an example of good moral behaviour (as indeed the story has been used for much of its history), then they meant: Treat anyone, of whatever race and background, as your 'neighbour', with all in the way of deserving help and charity which the word implies. If even a *Samaritan* could do so, how much more should you do yourselves? The parable could well have found its target in the exclusive nationalism betrayed by many of Jesus' Jewish contemporaries; but there has never yet been a society or a civilization in which it has no relevance.

38   **A woman named Martha welcomed him into her home.** Hospitality was offered to a visiting preacher as a matter of course; but it is not often that we are given a glimpse of the domestic strains which it caused, or indeed, that any attention at all is given to the women involved. Jesus' hostess Martha (who with her sister Mary probably appears also in John's gospel, chapter
40 11) was **distracted** by her many domestic tasks (the word meets us often in harassed private letters of the period), while her sister took up the position of a listener at the teacher's feet. Jesus' reply speaks for itself: it is an application

of the old adage that it is better to concentrate on one thing than to dissipate one's energies on many (compare Sirach 11.10). But what the moral was for Jesus' contemporaries or Luke's readers is a harder question. Simple fare for visiting preachers? Women's rights in the Christian church? Or simply the very modern tension between domestic chores and 'things that matter'? We cannot tell; but we may guess that for Luke's readers the point probably lay in the one phrase, **listened to what he was saying.** 'Listening to Jesus' words' was the **better part** for anyone to choose, compared with any practical activity.[14]

39
42

11.1   **He was praying in a certain place.** In Matthew (6.7–13) the Lord's Prayer is deliberately contrasted with the lengthy and ostentatious prayers of 'the Gentiles'. Luke gives it a different context. Jesus was a man of prayer (a point which Luke likes to emphasize) and his disciples naturally wished to imitate him: **"Lord, teach us to pray."** Modern instruction on prayer usually concentrates on spiritual preparation and mental and psychological techniques for becoming aware of the presence of God. But whatever experience and methods of prayer the people of antiquity may have had, their teaching on prayer had a different function: it defined the relationship which worshippers had with God, the rewards and benefits which their faith justified them in praying for and the conditions they must fulfil if their prayer was to be accepted. It was in this sense that the Pharisees and other religious groups in Judaism 'taught their disciples to pray': they each used distinctive prayers to formulate their specific beliefs about God and human beings and about the destiny of God's chosen people. We learn from this passage that John the Baptist had composed such prayers; and we are now given Jesus' own instruction, which can be regarded, from one point of view, as a succinct summary of his teaching.

The version in Luke is even briefer[15] than that in Matthew. It is also less Jewish, in the sense that the additional clauses in Matthew can all be paralleled from Jewish prayers of the period and some of the phrases would have been easier for a non-Jew to understand in Luke's version than in Matthew's. Whether this makes Luke's text more likely to represent the prayer which Jesus originally taught (as many interpreters believe) is open to question; but in its brevity it certainly lays bare, even more starkly than Matthew's, the radical economy of Jesus' teaching.

[14] Precisely what the **one thing** refers to has been a puzzle ever since the words were written; hence a number of manuscript variants, one of which is noted in the NRSV footnote.

[15] There was a tendency for copyists to fill out Luke's version with clauses from Matthew's. Later manuscripts therefore offer a text similar to that of Matthew, and this is why older translations such as the Authorized (King James) Version (which was based on late manuscripts) offer virtually the same text in both gospels. See the NRSV footnote, which also records a variant for **Your kingdom come** which, though it is plausible as a Lukan addition, is preserved in only a few late manuscripts.

2   "**Father**". There can be little doubt that this word represents the Aramaic word *abba*, which was an intimate, though still respectful, way for a child to address its father. Jesus' use of it for his heavenly Father was distinctive, and implied both intimacy and reverence. When Christians began to use the same form of address, it became a distinctive mark of their praying: through Jesus, Christians are admitted to an exceptionally intimate relationship with God, such as children have with their father (see below on Romans 8.15). The directness of the opening in Luke, compared with Matthew's more formal address ("Our Father"), expresses that new boldness in prayer which we know to have been characteristic of Christians from earliest times. The next change is Luke's **each day** for Matthew's "today": although the meaning of

3   **daily bread** is still obscure (see on Matthew 6.11), the sense in Luke seems a little more open to the regular use of the prayer *every* day. Finally, Luke uses

4   the normal Greek word for **sins** (instead of "debts"), though he brings back the Semitic concept of debt (in the sense of sin) in the next words: "**everyone indebted to us**".

5   "**Suppose one of you has a friend**". The scene is a Palestinian one-room house, with the family all in bed; the conflict is between the rules of hospitality and mutual aid which would be normal in village life in the east, and the trouble caused to a whole family by such an appeal at midnight. The moral seems to be: a pressing request from a friend, however impor-

8   tunate,[16] will obtain **whatever he needs**. How much greater the efficacy of even an apparently importunate prayer, given the unconditional 'friendship'

9   of God! But does this justify the apparently unconditional promise, "**Ask, and it will be given you**"? As in Matthew, the answer is found in the analogy of a human father, who will hardly refuse food to his children, let alone give

11, 12   them a **snake** or **a scorpion** (a startling addition by Luke) instead of bread and eggs: if God is your father – and that he is so is a premise of the Lord's Prayer and of all Christian praying that begins *abba*, 'Father' – how much more will he grant the prayers of his children! But what prayers? Luke may have been conscious of the obvious objection: surely God does not answer *all* prayers? In Matthew's version the promise seems quite general: God will give "good things" to those who ask him. According to Luke, there is only

13   one prayer which will certainly be answered, that for the **Holy Spirit**.

14–15   **The crowds were amazed. But some of them said**. The only substantial difference between Luke and Matthew (12.22–30) in this paragraph is that in Luke the objectors are not the Pharisees but one section of the crowd: the scene describes, not a deliberate attack by opponents, but a puzzled reaction on the part of some of Jesus' listeners. Luke has also changed one or two details:

---

[16] The word **persistence** translates a Greek word meaning *shamelessness*. The Revised Standard Version has *importunity*.

20   (i) **"If it is by the finger of God."** Matthew has, "by the Spirit of God". Luke's phrase is more biblical: 'finger of God' occurs in Exodus 8.19, 'hand of God' frequently in the Old Testament, and both these expressions are virtually equivalent to 'Spirit' (compare Ezekiel 8.1, 3).

21   (ii) Matthew's 'strong man in his house' has become **a strong man, fully armed,** who **guards his castle**: we should probably think of a local prince, such as one of the sons of Herod the Great; many of their palaces were heavily fortified against insurgents or against attacks by belligerent neighbours from the east.

27   (iii) **"Blessed is the womb that bore you."** This brief exchange occurs only in Luke. The woman's blessing is in perfectly conventional language. Jesus caps it with another, which would again have been unremarkable on the lips of any Jewish teacher. But the reader who was aware of the significance of

28   Jesus and the particular **word of God** which he proclaimed would have seen that the saying had a special point for the disciples and their successors.

For the remaining details, see the comments on the parallel passages in

18, 24   Mark and Matthew: **Beelzebul**, Mark 3.22–7; **the unclean spirit**, Matthew

29   12.43–5; **the sign of Jonah**, Mark 8.11–12 and Matthew 12.38–42; the sayings

33   about **a lamp**, Mark 4.21 and Matthew 6.22–3.

37–52   The two following sections are a striking example of Luke's way of arranging his material (whether or not he took it from the other gospels). The setting, a meal in a Pharisee's house, is due to Luke, and appears to be forgotten as the chapter progresses. The background of the discussion about inner and outer cleansing can be found in Mark (7.1–9), and the various accusations against the Pharisees and lawyers all occur (though in a different order) in Matthew 23. The section ends with a summary account of Jesus' controversies which appears, like the opening, to be due to Luke's editing.

41   In the details, Luke's changes are very slight. **"Give for alms those things that are within"** appears to be an interpretation of the simpler phrase in Matthew (23.26) in terms of the highly regarded activity of almsgiving: avoid a mere show of charitable giving, make sure it comes from the heart! His version

44   of the saying on **unmarked graves** has an authentic Palestinian ring: the Jews took elaborate precautions to avoid the defilement which followed walking over a grave. So also has his introduction of a quotation from scripture (which we cannot place exactly, though it is close to 2 Chronicles 24.19)

49, 52   with the phrase **the Wisdom of God said**. By contrast, the **key of knowledge** is an expression more at home in the world of Greek religious speculation than of Jewish controversy. On the whole, Luke shows himself to be familiar with social and political conditions in the Palestine of Jesus' day, and his recognition that only some of Jesus' accusations were applicable equally to the Pharisees and the lawyers corresponds with the facts better than Matthew's more simplified account.

12.1   **Meanwhile, when the crowd gathered by the thousands**. Luke is evidently anxious to stress the popular interest Jesus had aroused, even to the

248

extent of supposing that the crowd **trampled on one another**. It is all the more unexpected that he offers a selection of sayings (occurring in different contexts in other gospels) directed primarily to his disciples and close followers. The scene with which the previous chapter closed – the Pharisees submitting Jesus to cross-examination – is the cue for the first of these sayings about the **yeast of the Pharisees**. In Mark (8.15) the application is unexplained, but seems to refer to political influence. In Matthew (16.5–12) the 'yeast' is the teaching of the Pharisees and Sadducees. Here it becomes the **hypocrisy** of the Pharisees: what lies behind their profession of piety will be known when all is revealed – doubtless Luke means at the last judgment – and in this context are set sayings on the future revelation of secret things which in Matthew (10.26–7) have a quite different application.

4 **"I tell you, my friends."** 'Friends' is a new word, but clearly refers to an inner ring of already committed followers rather than to the crowd, and

4–9 introduces a series of sayings intended to give encouragement under persecution. Down to verse 9 the sequence is the same as in Matthew 10.66–33. The only significant difference is that the saying in verses 8–9 introduces the

8 figure of the **Son of Man**: here he is not a figure of triumph and glory (as in Mark 8.38) so much as an advocate at the heavenly assize that will be held by

10–12 God with his angels. Verse 10 (on slandering the Holy Spirit) is an abbreviated version of Matthew 12.31–2 (Mark 3.28–30). Verses 11–12 correspond to Matthew 10.19–20 (Mark 13.11).

13 **"Teacher, tell my brother to divide the family inheritance with me."** Disputes about inheritance were complicated by the fact that wills had to be made and executed on principles that could be inferred from certain biblical passages (Numbers 27.1–11; Deuteronomy 21.15–17) and which defined the rights of eldest sons and of other members of the family. At the same time there was a strong instinct to keep the family property so far as possible intact and not to 'divide it' (as this petitioner wanted to do). The lawyers who dealt with such disputes needed, in this and other matters, to be experts in the interpretation of scripture. Jesus had proved himself an expert, and it would have been perfectly normal for **someone in the crowd** to appeal to him to give a judgment on the dispute. Jesus was reluctant, possibly implying that he had received no formal authorization to act in such cases; but the exchange

15 led (at least in Luke's editing) to a general warning about **all kinds of greed**.

16–21 The parable which illustrates it is (for Jesus) unusually philosophical in tone. Instead of pressing on his hearers the demands of a new situation (like most of the parables) it appears to be a dramatic illustration of the age-old truth that man proposes but God disposes. Its impact comes more from the style of telling (the debate of the man within himself, the dramatic divine summons) and from the unexpected use of the catchwords of a philosophical resignation

19 (**"eat, drink, be merry"**) than from the intrinsic interest of the story. The moral – that true riches are non-material – is also an old one. There is a rather similar expression of it in Sirach 11.14–19.

22–31 **"Therefore I tell you, do not worry."** These warnings against anxiety occur in much the same words in the Sermon on the Mount (Matthew 6.25–34), but here are specifically addressed to the disciples, as are the following words,

32 **"Do not be afraid, little flock"** – by no means the only time that Jesus uses this image or exhorts them not to be afraid. The warning against preoccupation with material possessions, which is more elaborately and poetically constructed in Matthew (6.19–21) – and which again is something of a

33 philosophical cliché – is here focused upon concrete actions: **"Sell your possessions, and give alms."** Luke several times emphasizes the degree of actual renunciation and physical poverty demanded of Jesus' followers. Almsgiving was regarded by many as the most meritorious of all 'acts of charity' (though it was the donor rather than the recipient who was said to benefit by it!), but here Jesus is represented as setting no limit to what should be given away; indeed in 14.33 he even says, "Give up *all* your possessions."

35 **"Be dressed for action."** A Christian must be constantly alert: this theme occurs in all the gospels, and is illustrated here by several variations on the theme of servants who are not taken by surprise when their master unexpectedly returns. In Matthew (24.42–51) these illustrations are part of Jesus' explicit teaching about the imminent but still unpredictable hour of crisis and judgment; after which the parable of the ten bridesmaids (whatever its original point may have been) is offered as an illustration of the same theme. Echoes of that parable may perhaps be heard here also. But in this chapter nothing is said about the future crisis except what may be implied

40 by the statement that **the Son of Man is coming**. Indeed it seems that Luke has deliberately shifted the emphasis of this teaching from the prediction of future tribulations and rewards to the inculcation of an alert attitude in the on-going present. Whether the culmination of all things was far or near (and perhaps it was beginning to seem more far than near by the time Luke was writing), the same vigilance was still demanded of Jesus' followers. Of course it remained true that at some time in the future there would be a stupendous reversal of accepted values: the poor, not the rich, would be blessed, the last would be first, the least would be greatest. At such a time one could even imagine the master and the slaves changing places at supper. But now this was no longer a matter only of the future. In the church the paradox had already been experienced. Their Master had come as one who

37 will **serve** (Mark 10.45), and there may even have been a memory of Jesus acting out the rôle of a servant among his disciples (John 13). At this point the master–servant illustration ceases to be a common-sense lesson on vigilance, and points unmistakably to him whom the church came to recognize as its Servant Lord.

41 **Peter said**. Apart from this interjection by Peter (whose question is not directly answered), Luke's one addition to this teaching is the further example

47 of two slaves, of whom one knew, and one did not know, **what his master wanted**. Clearly a new point is being introduced, but we are given no clue how

to interpret it. Different degrees of blame and merit according to ignorance and intention were certainly recognized in Jewish thinking, and the saying seems to have its roots in Jesus' culture. But in its present form it is difficult not to see its relevance to the debate which was soon to begin between Jews and Christians. The Jews, since they possessed the law of Moses, could claim that they knew 'what their master wanted', and most of them tried earnestly to shape their lives accordingly. Even those who did *not* **do what was wanted** could hope to obtain some sort of salvation by virtue of belonging to God's chosen people. On the other hand, the Gentiles (they argued) did not possess the law and so did not know 'what the master wanted'; hence the verdict on them would be infinitely more severe. It was the experience of the church that this judgment must now be reversed: Gentiles might be judged more favourably than Jews, who in reality had not observed the true demands of the law. Indeed, there were sayings of Jesus which suggested that Gentiles might actually be better off at the judgment than many of the Jews.

49 **'I came to bring fire to the earth.'** Fire: a symbol of the Spirit, an image of judgment, an attribute of the Elijah figure whom John the Baptist had predicted and who was to precipitate a moral and religious crisis. The saying is one of those which show Jesus in the rôle of inaugurating a new and crucial phase of history, and it goes on to suggest (as does the baptism saying in Mark 10.38) that his destiny will be an ordeal which will virtually submerge

50 him (which is the original image suggested by the word **baptism**, though
52 it also came to mean a ritual act). **"From now on"**: this note of time, and
51 the replacement of 'sword' by **division**, are highly significant changes to Matthew's version (10.34–6) of the saying about peace. 'Division' within families, in a culture where family solidarity was highly prized, was one of the features of that period of intensified evil which (it was believed) would immediately precede judgment and a new age. Jesus had said (so at least Luke presents the matter) that such division would occur **from now on**. It would not be long before political events began to produce family divisions; but when the church found that the new faith was already tearing families apart, it knew how to interpret these domestic crises: they were signs of

54 the critical new age that was beginning, as surely as, in Palestine, **a cloud**
55 **rising in the west** meant rain, and a **south wind blowing** brought **scorching heat.**

58 **"When you go with your accuser before a magistrate."** This saying in the Sermon on the Mount (Matthew 5.25–6) is a simple everyday illustration of the kind of conduct demanded by Jesus. Luke may simply have added it here for want of a better place; or he may have seen a rather different point in it.

57 It was perhaps in the light of all that has just been said that the **right** thing is not to pursue one's 'rights' but to avoid getting involved in such proceedings at all.

13.1 **At that very time.** Luke writes as a historian, and this is another instance of his concern to tie his story in with what we would call 'secular' history.

Unfortunately his allusions are lost on us. The historian Josephus does not mention either of these events, and we have to reconstruct them as best we can from the little that Luke says about them. If Galileans were 'sacrificing' in the temple, the occasion was presumably a Passover, when thousands of pilgrims came in and had their lambs slaughtered in the temple. This was often the occasion for civil disorders, and Pilate may well have had to use force to restore order even in the temple area, in which case he could well be described as 'mingling their blood with their sacrifices'. That this was news to Jesus is surprising only if we press Luke's chronology: in theory Jesus' journey was not long *before* Passover, and he could hardly have been ignorant of a desecration that had happened the previous year. It is less surprising that the disaster at Siloam is not mentioned anywhere else. The south-east corner of the city walls of Jerusalem stood on high ground looking over the pool of Siloam, and the foundations of a round tower of the period still exist. The accident may have been very much in the news at this time, but would soon have been forgotten had not Jesus commented upon it. The contemporary Jewish explanation of why such calamities befall individuals was very simple (though it was often made more plausible by some subtle refinements): they must have sinned, and this was their punishment. Jesus did not altogether reject this explanation; there were certainly occasions on which he seems to have regarded illness as a consequence of sin. But here he offers an explanation more typical of a prophet: these catastrophes are warnings of the fate which

3 awaits you all – **unless you repent.**

6 **Then he told this parable** – and its theme is the same: repentance. Fruit and vegetables were grown in vineyards alongside the vines, but clearly a tree had to yield fruit if it were to justify the good it took out of the soil. Manuring a fig tree would be a somewhat exceptional measure. But the activity of Jesus was also exceptional, and gave his hearers an exceptional opportunity to repent.

There follows a typical instance of a sabbath controversy provoked by a miracle of healing. Luke has already recorded one such episode (6.6–11), and this one, which has no exact parallel in the other gospels, follows the

11 same pattern but with slightly different details. The sufferer was **crippled** and **bent over**. In modern terms we would think that her condition was one of physical deformity; but it was apparently quite natural to think of this, no less than an obviously mental disorder such as epilepsy, as a case of being possessed by **a spirit**. The cure, then, was exorcism; and there is considerable play throughout the paragraph on the words 'binding' and 'freeing' (the

15, 12 same Greek word is translated **untie** and **set free**). We can detect beneath the surface the mythology of the world of evil spirits: Satan 'binds' his victims, but when he is 'bound' by one stronger than himself (see above on Mark 3.27) his victims are 'freed'. The real interest of the story, however, lies in

14 the dialogue between Jesus and the **leader of the synagogue**. Granted their

17 own premises, it is not obvious why Jesus' **opponents** should have been **put**

to shame. In the following centuries careful regulations were made which permitted Jews to do what was necessary for their animals without infringing the sabbath, and it is likely that similar permissions were already generally accepted. If so, they could well have answered that they did not neglect their animals but that they still kept the sabbath, whereas a permanently crippled woman could equally well have been cured on another day. In his reply, Jesus

16 calls the woman **a daughter of Abraham** – they were talking not just about a fellow human being but about a fellow Jew – and exploits the fact that 'untying' and 'freeing' can be expressed by the same word: if it is legal in one case, so it must be in the other. What put his opponents to shame was perhaps his demonstration by an exorcism that the woman was not (as they might have thought) congenitally deformed. They had failed to see that she was 'bound by Satan', and that her 'freeing' on the sabbath was, to say the least, legitimate.

18–21 The two brief parables of mustard seed and yeast occur (again without any interpretation) in the parable chapters of Matthew (13.31–3) and Mark (4.30–2).

22 **As he made his way to Jerusalem.** Much has happened since we were told that Jesus had set out from Galilee, and much more is to come; we need to be reminded that Jesus is still on a journey, for this journey is in reality little more than a literary framework for a collection of otherwise disconnected sayings and episodes. In this section, as so often, Luke introduces some sayings of Jesus with a question from one of his listeners. His reply and the sayings which follow it are all familiar from Matthew's gospel, but appear in a strangely different combination. The 'narrow gate' of Matthew 7.13 has

24 become a **narrow door**, and the difficulty is, not to 'find' it as in Matthew 7.14, but having found it to **enter** it – for there is a danger of being too late and the door may be shut (as in the parable of the ten bridesmaids in Matthew

27 25). Those who are too late are greeted only with a fierce dismissal, **"Go away from me, all you evildoers"** (a quotation from Psalm 6.8), regardless of their apparent right to enter. Here again Luke offers a different interpretation from that in Matthew (7.22–3), where those excluded are spurious Christian prophets. Here they are Jesus' own society and nation, and this leads to the picture (startling on Jesus' lips, but more easily acceptable in a predominantly gentile church) of Gentiles taking precedence over Jews in the coming banquet in the kingdom of God – a reversal described almost exactly as in Matthew (8.11–12), complete with a phrase which is otherwise entirely confined to

28 Matthew's gospel, **weeping and gnashing of teeth.**

31 **At that very hour some Pharisees came.** Mark says (3.6) that the Pharisees were in league with the partisans of Herod. Were they now trying to drive Jesus out of Herod's territory, or even plotting an ambush together? Or had the Pharisees suddenly become anxious to save Jesus' life? We do not know – though Luke does occasionally make the Pharisees seem better disposed towards Jesus, and in Acts he represents them as initially sympathetic to

Christianity. In any case, Jesus' pointed reply was doubtless remembered for its own sake rather than for the light it threw on his relations with Herod and the Pharisees, though in its setting here it shows that Luke imagined Jesus' journey still to be through the territory of Herod Antipas, that is, through 32 Galilee or Transjordan. He replied, **"Go and tell that fox"**. To the Greeks, as for us, the fox was a byword for cunning; but in Hebrew writings it often stood simply for a puny creature, and Jesus may have been saying, 'Go and tell your little king...' His reply, nevertheless, was very much to the point. Herod wished to put an end to Jesus' activity of **casting out demons and performing cures**. But he did not need to trouble himself. **"On the third day"** – three days was a natural way of referring to any short space of time (e.g. Jonah 1.17) – it would all be brought to its destined end when Jesus had 'finished his work'. The Greek word here has to do with 'fulfilment': what was to be fulfilled was also Jesus' 'way', and this leads on to a saying about the physical destination of 33 that 'way': **"it is impossible for a prophet to be killed outside of Jerusalem"**. This seems to put it very strongly: it was only a fairly recent tradition which asserted that most of the prophets had in fact been killed in Jerusalem (see above on Matthew 23.29). But for Luke, with hindsight, any other destiny for Jesus may have seemed 'impossible'. And there follows, with great appropriateness, a lament over Jerusalem in virtually the same words as in Matthew 23.37–9.

14.1   **On one occasion Jesus was going to the house of a leader of the Pharisees**. The main meal on a sabbath took place after the morning service in the synagogue, and guests were often invited. Perhaps Jesus had been preaching and was invited to the meal afterwards; in any case, his presence was perfectly natural in such a house, and Luke makes it the occasion for a number of sayings to do with feasts and banquets. But first there was a healing miracle to record. Possibly this took place on the street beforehand (which is the sense of **Jesus was going** – but this is only one possible translation: the Greek may 3 mean simply *Jesus went*); but a meal at which other **lawyers and Pharisees** were present would also have been thronged with the usual crowd of hopeful poor, among whom there could well have been **a man who had dropsy**. Jesus' question, **"Is it lawful to cure people on the sabbath, or not?"** probably had a perfectly clear answer in the teaching of the experts present: it was permitted when it was a question of saving life, but otherwise not. The man with dropsy was not in immediate danger, therefore it was not permitted to treat him. Jesus' counter-question does not seem to settle the issue, for falling into a well might be a threat to the life of a child or a beast in a way that dropsy was not. But perhaps what reduced them to silence was the sheer inhumanity of thinking that this principle should be invoked to prevent an immediate cure – and one, moreover, that had involved no action which could be regarded as 'work' forbidden on the sabbath.

7   If what follows can be called **a parable**, the word is being used in a very different sense from its usual one of an illustrative story. Jesus' words amount,

not to a story, but to a piece of moral or social advice in the tradition of conventional 'wisdom' teaching. Proverbs 25.6–7 reads:

> Do not put yourself forward in the king's presence
>   or stand in the place of the great;
> for it is better to be told, "Come up here,"
>   than to be put lower in the presence of a noble.

Jesus' words are a simple dramatization of this ancient maxim, from which, 11 like other moral teachers, he drew a general principle: **"all who exalt themselves will be humbled, and those who humble themselves will be exalted"**. In the context of a social occasion such as a banquet this is sound common sense, and it may seem surprising that Jesus should have troubled to endorse it. But Luke's readers will have been well aware that the principle he drew from it was to have a momentous application. Being 'humbled' and 'exalted' were to be the most significant experiences, first of Jesus, and then of his followers.

12   **He said also to the one who had invited him.** Jesus now proposes a radical revision of normal social practice. Jewish culture was sensitive to the curse of poverty, and when any large party was given it was normal to allow paupers and beggars to be fed on anything that was left over. Moreover many devout Jews made a point of keeping open house to the poor. But Jesus goes even further than this: you must invite the poor, not in addition to your own guests, but instead of them!

15   **One of the dinner guests, on hearing this, said.** Questions about hospitality led the mind naturally to a feast **in the kingdom of God.** This was an image which, ever since Old Testament times, the Jews loved to use for the promised reward of the just and devout of their nation. **"Blessed is anyone who will eat bread in the kingdom"** was a typical 'beatitude': a Jewish teacher might well use it to encourage his students to greater virtue. But Jesus' beatitudes struck a different note: "Blessed are you who are poor" (6.20); and the story which follows illustrates the contrast. The story itself runs more smoothly and plausibly in Luke than in Matthew (22.1–14), whether because of Luke's more careful editing or because he had access to a less complicated version of it. In this form it faithfully reflects Palestinian customs. It was a normal courtesy to send a slave to inform the guests when everything was 16 ready. If the **great dinner** was to celebrate a wedding, the festivities might last several days, and it is quite plausible that the guests should have had other commitments which prevented them from coming at the beginning: they would normally have had nothing to lose by sending their apologies and arriving later. But this is where the story takes an unexpected turn. Instead of keeping their places for them (as would have been usual), the indignant host 21 sent his slave **out at once** to bring in all the poor and disabled he could find. Up to this point the story is not unparalleled: others were told of wealthy and exceptionally generous hosts who filled their house with beggars and

acquired great merit by doing so. The radical note comes only at the end:
24 **"none of those who were invited will taste my dinner"**. The original guests
(who were people of some substance, judging by their business transactions)
would suffer the indignity of arriving at the house and finding that there was
no room for them.

15   To this extent the story is characteristic of Jesus. **"Blessed is anyone who
will eat bread in the kingdom of God!"** – yes, Jesus replies, but this blessedness may be enjoyed, not by you (if you allow other priorities to come first),
but by those whom you least expect. Yet there are signs also that the parable
(for such it is called in Matthew's version) was given another interpretation
in the early church. One of Luke's changes from the version in Matthew is the
21 introduction of a second mission of the slave to **go out into the streets and
lanes**. Possibly this double mission merely underlines the point; but many
have seen it as an allegory: the first Christian mission was to the Jews, the
second went further afield to the Gentiles.

26   **"Whoever comes to me and does not hate father and mother…"** Matthew
(10.37) has "who loves father or mother more", and this is clearly the meaning.
Luke's more violent version (which, unlike the other, includes the wife along
with the rest of the family) may nevertheless be closer to Jesus' own idiom (see
on Matthew 5.43). Moreover the saying in Matthew is addressed to those who
25 are already disciples. Luke, by bringing in **large crowds**, has given this and the
following sayings a different application: this is what you must be prepared
33 for *before* you decide to follow me. Similarly, **"none of you can become my
disciple if you do not give up all your possessions"**. This is the most radical
of all Jesus' sayings on the subject and occurs only in Luke, who seems to
make a special point of it, not just in Jesus' teaching, but when relating the
early church's attempts to put the principle into practice (Acts 2.44; 5.1–
12). But the sequence of thought is interrupted by two little illustrations
which point in a rather different direction. Each of them emphasizes the
need for *calculation*. The wise tower-builder (who could be a smallholder in
the country) 'sits down' to work out the cost first; the wise king (who is also
commander-in-chief) 'sits down' to work out whether he can possibly defeat
an enemy by whom he is outnumbered – and 'sitting down' meant that one
was thinking it out carefully. All this is good sense; but it is oddly at variance
with Jesus' usual message. Where else does he tell us to think twice before
deciding to follow him? We can only speculate on his original meaning; but by
the time Luke wrote, there may well have been some Christians in the church
whose enthusiasm led them into irresponsible ventures and who needed
restraining with what seemed like maxims of more conventional prudence –
34 which is how the saying on **salt** was perhaps also to be understood (on which
see above on Matthew 5.13).

15.2   **"This fellow welcomes sinners and eats with them."** All the synoptic
gospels report that Jesus caused both surprise and offence by consorting
with 'sinners' – that is, with those whose way of life excluded them from

the privileged position which all observant Jews claimed to possess in the economy of God. It was clearly expected of him, as a religious teacher, to be as careful about the company he kept as the exclusive and strictly observant fellowships of the Pharisees. The defence Jesus made on this occasion turned on a small but very important difference between himself and his opponents. It could not be said of the Pharisees, or indeed of Jewish religious thinkers generally, that they did not recognize or value repentance. On the contrary, they took it for granted that a truly penitent person was accepted by God, and they made no objection to 'welcoming' sinners into their company if they had shown genuine signs of repentance (for example, by abandoning their disreputable profession). But it was essential that the sinners should take the initiative: they must first show that they had repented, and only then could they be 'welcomed', either by God or by their neighbours. There was no question of having anything to do with them until they had manifestly abandoned their old ways. Jesus' offence consisted in not having waited for these signs of repentance.

On this occasion Jesus justified his initiative with a group of parables, the first of which occurs also in Matthew 18.12–14 (though with quite a different point). Compared with Matthew, Luke dwells a little more on the moment

5 of finding the sheep: the shepherd **lays it on his shoulders** (the only way

9 of carrying an injured or exhausted animal), the woman **calls together her friends and neighbors, saying, "Rejoice with me"** – for her loss had been serious: a *drachma* was a substantial sum of money, and ten of them would have been her entire dowry or savings. All the emphasis is on the joy which follows finding something that was lost; from which the moral is drawn that

7 there is **joy in heaven** when a single sinner repents. It follows that repentance is not (as the Pharisees might have put it) a matter of making amends for past misdeeds by some ritual act or sacrifice and so rejoining the ranks of the just. It is a matter of the heart, directly responded to by God.

The third parable (for which 'The Prodigal Son' is probably not the best title, since the main emphasis is on the behaviour of the father) illustrates the same point, but takes it a great deal further. A father could either bequeath his property in his will, in which case it was laid down by law how he must divide it between his sons, or else make a gift of it before he died, in which case he was free to dispose of it as he wished, though he was entitled to the produce or the interest until his death. The younger son's request was unusual; but the main part of the property would in any case go to his elder brother, and perhaps he hoped to do better by turning his share into

13 cash (which is what the phrase **gathered all he had** probably means) and setting himself up in business among the Jews of the Dispersion in some foreign city rather than trying to live on a smallholding in the over-populated land of Palestine (where, in addition, he might have to contribute to the support of his father). His taste for **dissolute living**, however, combined

14 with a **severe famine** (which would have sent up the price of food), soon

brought him to total poverty. He hired himself out to a gentile employer – and minding pigs would have been a job particularly repugnant to a Jew – but, even so, his wages were not sufficient to buy himself food at its inflated cost, and he would have been content with the pauper's diet of carob pods. (Three centuries later a rabbi was to say, 'When the Israelites are reduced to carob pods, then they repent.') But even these were jealously guarded for the pigs.

17 So far, the story is a typical rake's progress. Less typical, when he **came to himself**, is the son's confession of guilt; he did not try to justify himself in any
20 way. And less typical still is the reaction of the father: **he ran** – which was very much beneath the dignity of the head of the family – and instead of listening to his request or testing his penitence he dressed him in a robe reserved for honoured guests and, with the gift of a ring and sandals, demonstrated his restored position in the family home. The welcome, the presents, the feast were all tokens of his joy at finding one who seemed lost. The story thus far is a telling illustration of the joy that is the subject of the two preceding parables. But if we may also read off from it a general lesson about the nature of God's forgiveness (and it is irresistible to do so, since it yields such riches in the process), one point in particular seems relevant to Jesus' controversy with his opponents. They laid down all kinds of conditions (genuineness, lastingness, a will to make reparation, etc.) which a sinner's repentance had to fulfil if it were to be accepted. But in the parable it was sufficient for the son simply to return to his father. Similarly, it was not necessary for the 'sinners' with whom Jesus consorted to prove their penitence: it was sufficient that they sought his company.

This already provided part of the answer to those who criticized Jesus for the company he kept. But the parable goes on – though some would argue that the sequel cannot have originally belonged to it. From the point of view of strict fairness the elder son had a genuine grievance. While he had
29 been **working like a slave** for years on his father's estate and for his father's benefit (even if the greater part of the property was now legally his own), his brother, by squandering his share, had deprived himself of the means to make any contribution to his father's support. Surely, therefore, the rewards being given to the younger son were inappropriate and unfair. Once again the father acted with striking generosity. Instead of waiting until his son
28 approached him (as fitted his dignity), he **came out and began to plead with**
31 **him. "All that is mine is yours."** This may have been true in law as well as in theory; if the elder son had already received his far greater share of the property, this was itself a sign of far greater esteem than the killing of a fatted calf for the younger. But the main force of the appeal depended, not
32 on technicalities, but on humanity: **"we had to celebrate and rejoice"**. Jesus' strongest argument against his critics (and it would have been as difficult for the Pharisees as for many of us to disagree with the elder son's objections) likewise depended, not on technical definitions of repentance, but on those

ultimate human values which are a sure guide to the nature of God's dealings with human beings.

16.1 **"There was a rich man who had a manager."** The situation must have been a common one in Palestine, where there were many large estates owned by absentee landlords and administered by managers. But the train of events is puzzling. On the face of it, the manager's action was dishonest, and we

8 are astonished to read at the end that **his master commended the dishonest manager"**. It is true that this last sentence is ambiguous. The Greek for 'master' could also mean also mean *Lord*; in which case the sentence could be, not a continuation of the story, but a comment on it by Luke: '*Jesus commended the dishonest manager*'. But this does not make things any easier. Why should Jesus, any more than the landlord, have **commended** a blatantly dishonest proceeding? The most we can say is that there is perhaps something admirable in making financially prudent decisions or in acting decisively in the face of imminent catastrophe – but such lessons in elementary prudence are hardly what we have come to expect from Jesus' parables.

It may be, however, that the situation presupposed in the parable was not quite what it seems at first sight. The manager had been accused of

1 **squandering** the owner's property. What does this mean? Simply helping himself to more than his due from the revenues would hardly have constituted 'squandering' – the word is that used of the younger son in the previous parable, who "squandered his property in dissolute living". Possibly the manager had been trying to enrich himself by lending out at a high rate of interest large sums from his master's fortune, to the detriment of the proper management of the estate. It is true that among Jews usury was illegal; but there were ways round this prohibition, and a manager who behaved in this way, though he would certainly be 'dishonest', might nevertheless, succeed in keeping on the right side of the law. If he were suddenly to cancel the interest (which could have been payable in oil or wheat), he would earn the gratitude of the debtors and at the same time save his master from any imputation of permitting usury. Alternatively, it may be that the extortionate fees or 'sweeteners' he had been demanding from the tenants had driven them off his master's land, and this had been reported to the landowner in the form of complaints that his land was being 'squandered' by the manager, making it too expensive for them to renew their contracts. In any case, the amount of produce the tenants were already contracted to pay to the landowner would have been known to all the parties, and the bills could not be rewritten unilaterally. But the agent may have banked on his master (who had already shown notable tolerance in not immediately denouncing him) honouring the more favourable terms his agent was arranging. If he did so, both master and manager would gain credit in the community: the master by perforce appearing generous, the manager by having apparently negotiated more favourable terms for the tenants in the

6 nick of time – they must **sit down quickly** – before it became known that he was dismissed and had no authority at all.

8 **"His master commended the dishonest manager because he had acted shrewdly."** If either of these explanations of the parable is on the right lines, the comment becomes plausible. According to one, the master had escaped being involved in usury and the manager had performed the meritorious act of giving loans without interest. According to the other, the master had put an end to extortionate practices on his estate and had acquired a reputation for generosity, while the manager had offered a commendable example of prudence in the face of imminent punishment; he had staked everything on the generosity of his master and thereby also earned favour from his clients. This may well have been the point Jesus wished to make, here as elsewhere. Judgment was imminent: no time must be lost before remitting debts, forgiving offences and throwing oneself on the merciful generosity of God.

Nevertheless, the parable remains obscure. It is possible that its original hearers, being familiar with dealings of this kind, would have followed it without difficulty. But what did Luke think it meant? He adds some sayings which appear to offer no fewer than three interpretations, but two of these are unfortunately as obscure as the parable itself.

(i) **"The children of this age are more shrewd in dealing with their own generation than are the children of light."** The manager was certainly 'shrewd': this is strongly emphasized in the parable. But if this saying is to be seen as anything more than a cynical comment on unpractical pietists, it is necessary to find something admirable in his shrewdness. If in fact it consisted in freely cancelling debts, then, whatever his motives, his conduct could be held up as an example to Christians who, with their infinitely more altruistic standards of behaviour, could hardly afford to be less generous than a **dishonest manager**. But can **the children of light** mean Christians? If we may judge by the Dead Sea Scrolls, this unusual phrase does appear to be one which some religious movements used of their own members. It is perfectly possible that at some stage Christians began to use similar language about themselves.

9 (ii) **"Make friends for yourselves by means of dishonest wealth."** This again seems to refer back to the parable. The manager had 'made friends' by his prompt business action. Christians are to do the same, but in a more lasting sense, in that, instead of ensuring for themselves hospitable houses on earth, they are to take actions (such as generous almsgiving) which will obtain heavenly and **eternal homes** (literally *tents*, appropriate for dwelling near the presence of God). The phrase translated **dishonest wealth** (literally *mammon of unrighteousness*) is a curious one, and may correspond to a Hebrew expression meaning some kind of financial profit that was strictly illegal under the law, though it could also mean any form of worldly wealth.

10 (iii) **"Whoever is faithful in very little is faithful also in much."** This group of sayings simply commends trustworthiness and would be a more

appropriate comment on the parable of the pounds (19.11–27) than on this one; but perhaps it also serves here as a warning against taking the dishonest manager as an example of the wrong kind of 'shrewdness'.

13–18 There is no obvious connection between the sayings that follow, and all except one of them have parallels in different parts of Matthew or Mark: verse 13 = Matthew 6.24; verse 16 = Matthew 11.12–13; verse 17 = Matthew 5.18; verse 18 = Mark 10.11–12 (and, with a significant variation, Matthew

14 5.32). Verses 14–15, however, are found only in Luke. **The Pharisees, who were lovers of money**. It is unlikely that the Pharisees as a class were wealthy; Indeed, we know of several learned ones who were very poor. But there were doubtless some who were not above turning their reputation for sound learning to financial advantage, and many of them may have found means of accommodating their interpretation of the law to the compromises involved in commercial transactions. Much as they praised the virtue of almsgiving, they regarded it as positively undesirable to impoverish oneself by too much generosity, and their attitude to money was certainly a great deal less radical than that of Jesus. Jesus' criticism of them here is a variation of his usual attack on their hypocrisy and recalls his warning in the Sermon on the Mount against practising one's piety before others (Matthew 6.1). Their outward show of strict observance is a cloak for preoccupation with things which attract worldly esteem but are in fact (here we can surely detect Jesus' characteristic fondness for exaggeration) **"an abomination in the sight of God"**.

19 **"There was a rich man"** – unnamed, like most of the characters in the parables (though in the course of time he has acquired a name: 'Dives' is simply the Latin for 'rich man'). Surprisingly, the poor man does have a

20 name: **Lazarus**, which is the Greek form of a common Jewish name, Eleazar. The contrast is carefully drawn: purple and fine linen and daily feasting were marks of ostentatious luxury, while the beggar was a cripple (he **lay**) who had no one even to keep the dogs away from his sores. It is true that it was

21 unusual not to allow beggars even **what fell from the rich man's table**, but nothing is said by way of moral judgment on either the rich man or Lazarus. All we are told is that one was very rich and the other very poor. In the next scene the contrast is equally vivid, though the setting is drawn from contemporary Jewish folklore and popular religion. Whatever might be said in theory about a general resurrection when all would come before God to be judged, ordinary people in Palestine certainly believed (as ordinary people have always believed in many parts of the world) that immediately after death some people go to heaven and some go to hell. Clearly Jesus was not using the parable to give authoritative teaching about life after death.

22 On the contrary, the **angels** escorting Lazarus, the presence of **Abraham** in
24 heaven, the **flames** in hell and the glimpse given to the damned of the better lot they might have had, were all standard features of popular belief. Again there is no moralizing. It is a simple contrast: one is very happy, the other

very unhappy, not because of their virtues and vices, but because of a just reversal of their fortunes. Thus far, the parable is a dramatic presentation of the great change in values proclaimed in Jesus' beatitudes: "Blessed are you who are hungry now, for you will be filled" (6.21), with its corollary, "Woe to you who are rich' (6.24).

The message is stark and clear (especially in Luke's gospel). But can nothing be done? Cannot the rich still be saved? Certainly not after death: it will be
26 too late then, for **"a great chasm has been fixed"**. But suppose a messenger were to be sent to the rich who are still alive to warn them? The parable goes on to deny even this possibility – and here it seems to point to the very heart of Jesus' understanding of himself and the people among whom he worked.
29 **"They have Moses and the prophets."** The Jews might regard themselves as uniquely privileged in having in their scriptures an authoritative guide to the conduct required of them by God. But even to this they could be indifferent – "they may indeed, look, but not perceive" in the words of Isaiah quoted by Jesus on another occasion (Mark 4.12) – so much so that they could still tolerate extremes of wealth and poverty in their own society. No further
30 prompting by God could help the rich who called Abraham **father** to live worthily of their inheritance, not even **if someone goes to them from the dead** – and the parable ends with a tantalizing allusion to another 'Lazarus', who did 'rise from the dead' (John 11 – did Luke know of this?) and to Jesus himself, whose own resurrection at first aroused only incredulity and mockery (Acts 17.32).
17.1   **"Occasions for stumbling"** is a phrase so loaded with biblical meanings that it almost serves as shorthand for a number of distinctive Jewish beliefs. The underlying metaphor is of a snare into which one falls or an obstacle over which one stumbles, and to us this suggests the kind of thing that causes accidents. But the Hebrews seldom thought of things as happening by accident: either someone had deliberately laid a snare, or else it was intended by God that a person should be tripped. And so the metaphor was used of all sorts of catastrophes or dangers which God might lay in the path of his people or of individuals in order to test or punish them (Isaiah 8.14 and elsewhere). Jesus' followers would not be immune from such trials: there would be persecutions from outside, and heresy and schism from within. Such things were **bound to come**. But this would be no excuse for any member of the community willingly to precipitate further trials by thoughtless or malicious behaviour.
2   By **these little ones** who must not be caused to stumble Jesus may have originally meant small children: for a religious teacher of his time, he was exceptionally interested in them. Children must always have been following him about, as they do any unusual person in that part of the world; and Jesus took notice of them instead of ignoring them. But by the time the gospel was written the church was more interested in its own 'little ones', the humble Christians who might stumble over the radical implications of

Jesus' teaching; and this may be how Luke (like Matthew 18.6) understood the phrase.

3 **"If another disciple sins."** Compare Matthew 18.15, 21–2, where the same
4 rule is given as part of the order to be observed by the church. **"Seven times a day"** is equivalent to Matthew's "seventy-seven times" – an unlimited number; but Luke insists that the sinner must clearly and explicitly **repent** in order to be forgiven.

5 **The apostles said to the Lord** is a typically Lukan introduction: the rare occurrence of 'apostles' for the disciples and 'the Lord' for Jesus is character-istic of this gospel. The saying is also recorded in Mark (11.23) and Matthew
6 (17.20); but Luke has **mulberry tree** (or the deep-rooted 'fig-mulberry') instead of 'mountain' – we do not know why.

7 **"Who among you would say to your slave . . .?"** The application of this little parable is obvious from the start. It was a common idiom of religious speech to call oneself God's 'servant' or 'slave', and what was true of the relationship between master and slave would be true, in important respects, of that between God and human beings. The master here is of modest means, having only one slave both to work on his farm and to look after the house. He is under no obligation to put his slave's comfort before his own. Equally, the slave can hardly expect to be 'thanked' for completing his usual routine.

10 **"So you also, when you have done all that you were ordered to do."** What were 'ordered' were the detailed requirements of the divinely given law. There were many of Jesus' contemporaries who believed that they acquired merit by their meticulous observance of these, and failed to realize that the demands of God are more fundamental than can be expressed in any set of regulations about what one **ought to have done.**

11 **Jesus was going through the region between Samaria and Galilee.** This translation of a puzzling Greek phrase (literally *through the middle of*) makes little sense on the map: Samaria and Galilee were next to each other, and there is no 'region between'; possibly the words mean *along the border of*. By now, in any case, since Jesus' 'journey' has lasted through eight chapters, he should have left Galilee and Samaria far behind. But Luke may have had a rather different picture of the geography and imagined that much of Jesus' journey lay close to the frontiers of both regions (see above, p. 241). If so, he would have seen nothing inappropriate in placing a story involving a Samaritan at this point on the route.

12 **Ten lepers.** On the disease and its social consequences, see above on Mark 1.40–45. The lepers were necessarily on the edge of the village and were **keeping their distance** to avoid contact. Jesus' reply to their appeal
14 took the unexpected form of a command to **"Go and show yourselves to the priests"**. The command occurs in Mark's story, (1.44) of the cleansing of a single leper, and we can see the point of it from Jesus' point of view: he may not have wished to come into conflict with the priests by trespassing on their prerogatives. But in Luke's story, what sort of answer was it to the

lepers? They must have known that in their present state they had no hope of being certified 'clean' and readmitted into society – otherwise they would have gone for examination long ago. Jesus' answer could mean only that if they went now they would be sufficiently cured by the time they arrived to be passed as 'clean' – which is just what happened. We can assume that nine of them were Jews, who probably had to go to Jerusalem for the purpose; but the tenth, being a Samaritan, had to go back to find a priest in Samaria.

15 Precisely when he **turned back** (whether before or after he had seen a priest) is not stated. But such details probably did not trouble the narrator, who saw in the story a clear illustration of two points already made elsewhere: first,
19 even a Samaritan can be an example to a Jew; secondly, **faith** is crucial, and far more important than the race to which a person belongs.

20 **Once Jesus was asked by the Pharisees when the kingdom of God was coming.** Given the earnest expectation of a new order of things which (at least in Palestine) ran right through the Jewish religion, and given the fact that this new order was expected to come, not by a gradual advance, but by a sudden divine intervention, the question was an obvious one to put to Jesus and was asked by friends and enemies alike. When asked by the Pharisee, the question may have been intended to elicit a reply which could be regarded as either contemptibly naïve or dangerously incriminating; but Jesus avoided the trap. **"The kingdom is not coming with things that can be observed"** – literally, *by observation*, a word suggesting (among other things) astrological calculation from the conjunction of stars with historical events; and Jesus showed that he agreed with all his learned and responsible contemporaries
21 who tried to discourage this kind of speculation about the future. **"Nor will they say, 'Look, here it is!' or 'There it is!' "**, as if it were likely to be something doubtful or ambiguous, needing careful inspection to check its authenticity. Jesus went on to add a positive answer of his own to the question; but exactly what that answer was is obscured for us by the imprecise Greek in which it is recorded: **"the kingdom of God is among you"** (or *within you* – see the NRSV footnote). Several meanings are possible, and it may be that the preposition in Jesus' own language was equally ambiguous. There are later reports of Jewish scholars themselves debating what was meant by saying that God was 'among' them: did it mean that God saw they were clothed and fed, or that he knew their inmost thoughts? Older translations of Jesus' saying mostly preferred 'within you'. But this suggests an inner spiritual experience, which is something very different from what the Jews (and, it appears, Jesus) meant by the kingdom of God. Jesus seems to have talked of the kingdom both as a future consummation and as an already perceptible reality. Something of his new and rich understanding of the concept probably lurks in this intriguing saying.

22 **Then he said to the disciples.** What follows continues the train of thought about the future, but is now (as in the other gospels) addressed to the disciples. Into the expected drama of the coming of a new age Jesus projected himself in

the rôle of the Son of Man; and when the gospel was written (and indeed long afterwards), Christians were longing for the time when there would be clear signs of either the imminence of the new age or its arrival (either meaning may be intended by the strange phrase, **"one of the days of the Son of Man"**). For some time, in any case, there was a temptation to abandon ordinary

23 occupations and **set off in pursuit** of anything which seemed to promise its advent. There were sayings of Jesus to discourage this (as in Matthew 24.26–7), and the same warning was taken up by Paul (1 Thessalonians 2.1–12). There were also sayings about the darker side of the destiny of the Son of Man which should have corrected any premature preoccupation with his glorious return (see above on Mark 8.31).

26 **"Just as it was in the days of Noah."** The rest of the chapter inculcates an attitude of vigilance and readiness for immediate action which must be maintained in the face of what is to come. The sayings are almost all found (somewhat differently arranged) in Matthew 24. Luke adds to the example of Noah that of Lot (the two were often paired together: see 2 Peter 2.5–8

32 for another example) and gives us the proverb, **"Remember Lot's wife."** The two biblical stories not only warn against neglecting the signs of the times. It is also fatal (doubtless in the Christian life in general as well as at the crucial last moment) to look back (Genesis 19.26)!

18.1 **Then Jesus told them a parable** – ostensibly (according to the narrator) on the rather different subject of prayer, but in reality still connected with the coming of the Son of Man. One of the characters in this little story is called

6 **the unjust judge.** But it is important to see in what sense he was 'unjust'. The

3 setting is a small town. A **widow** – which was a byword for someone reduced to poverty through no fault of her own – had been the victim of some fraud or sharp practice, and was seeking redress from the law. This need not have involved a formal sitting of a court: a qualified lawyer might simply be invited to arbitrate if both parties agreed. But the fact that the widow kept pestering the same 'judge' suggests that she may have been trying to take advantage of the presence of a colonial administrator who might be persuaded to settle a dispute according to the laws observed by the occupying power. In this sense the 'judge', from the Jewish point of view, would be by definition 'unjust' (by virtue of arbitrating without reference to Jewish laws), whether or not he

2 was also an unscrupulous man who **"neither feared God nor had respect for people"**. The scene is easily imagined. The provincial official would hope that if he ignored the widow's request she would go back to a Jewish arbitrator; but in the end, since she went on hanging round his residence day after day, he decided to get rid of her by attending to her case.

What is the point of the parable? Clearly all the emphasis is on the widow (the justice of whose claim is assumed): it is uncomfortable to have to compare the 'unjust judge' in any way with God! And her patience and importunity can be taken as a lesson in persevering with insistent prayer. But Jesus' comments on it have a wider reference. Christians could be certain of the rightness of their cause; but in the face of calumny and persecution they longed for vindication. This was expected to take the form of a reversal of present values, a bringing to light of the things now known only to faith, and the visible establishment of the Christian community as the chosen people of God – in short, the end of the present world order, the judgment and the new age. These things were taking longer to come than perhaps the earliest generation of Christians expected (a disappointment which may underlie the

7 question, **"Will he delay long in helping them?"**). But they must continue
1 to **pray always and not to lose heart**. If even a neglectful and unprincipled
7 human judge yielded at last, how much more certainly would God **grant justice to his chosen ones**! But that moment of vindication would always involve judgment. Anyone who had lost faith (perhaps because of the delay)
8 would have reason to fear it. **"When the Son of Man comes, will he find faith on earth?"**

9 **He also told this parable**. The scene this time is set in the inner quadrangle of the temple, most likely at the hour of the morning or evening sacrifice. At these two times in the day all Jews were bidden to pray, either in the synagogue
10 or wherever they happened to be; but if they were nearby they **went up to the temple** for the purpose and joined the crowd of those who were present at the sacrifice. The Pharisee's prayer probably sounded less objectionable in his own culture than it does in ours. He was not necessarily priding himself on his virtues; rather, he was thanking God for the privilege of being able to lead a life which, both in public and in private, laid him open to no charge of failure to observe the basic laws of the Ten Commandments (he mentions specifically stealing and adultery). Like the rich man of the next parable, he could doubtless have said that he had kept them 'since his youth' (18.21). But he had also gone considerably beyond this. Far from ever failing to observe the annual fast-day, he followed the practice of the more observant groups
12 and fasted **twice a week**; far from ever failing to pay the compulsory tithes on his agricultural produce, he gave away a tenth of all his income – this was to become the recommended level of almsgiving for the pious. In short, his was the typical way of life of a Pharisee, which was one of the most sustained attempts made by any Jewish group to observe both the spirit and the letter of the law in every detail – and he thanked God for it; for thanksgiving, it was said, was the most valuable and meritorious of all forms of prayer. The tax collector, by contrast, was involved in an activity which made such a prayer impossible for him. He lived by raising more taxes from his fellow citizens than he was required to pay to the government, and the element of extortion inherent in his profession branded him in the eyes of Jewish society as for ever 'outside the law'. It was beyond his power to make the kinds of amends (say by changing his profession or giving back the excess by which he lived) which would alone have been regarded as a sign of true repentance and would have allowed him to be readmitted to the society of the just. His prayer was despairing and simple, recalling the opening words of Psalm 51; and later in

that psalm come the words, "a broken and contrite heart, O God, you will not despise". Jesus' parable is a vivid illustration of that classic text of Hebrew

9 spirituality. Luke says that it was aimed at **those who trusted in themselves that they were righteous and regarded others with contempt**. Certainly the Pharisees believed (and not only they) that their way of life was the closest possible approximation to God's will, and tended to regard all who did not follow it as 'sinners'; and this was one of the instances of human pretension which (Jesus taught) was destined to be exposed by that great reversal of values which he proclaimed. In the words of a saying that occurs in a number

14 of different contexts, **"all who exalt themselves will be humbled"**.

15 **People were bringing even infants**. At this point Luke returns to the order

15–30 of events in Mark, and reproduces Mark's narrative (10.13–31) with only a small amount of rewriting. The children who are brought to Jesus for blessing

18 become **infants**; and the 'rich man' of Mark becomes also a **ruler**: he had not only wealth but the responsibility of power – perhaps an additional reason for being unwilling to give everything away. What follows is a succinct version of the corresponding passage in Mark (10.23–31), though once again, as in

29 14.26, Luke includes a **wife** among those who may have to be left behind for the sake of the kingdom.

From Jericho to Jerusalem

31 **"See, we are going up to Jerusalem."** After the long recital of episodes on the journey from Galilee which, though Jerusalem was given at the outset as the destination, gave little feeling of actual progress southward, the narrative now begins to move again and rejoins the scheme of Mark's gospel. But whereas in Mark the narrative is punctuated by three prophecies of the fate awaiting the Son of Man, Luke attributes to Jesus only very general warnings of what is to come (12.49–50; 13.32–3) before reporting this more detailed prophecy. In Mark (10.33–4) the disciples are in a state of fear and amazement. Luke omits this, but adds that it was all foretold **by the prophets** – which was one of the ways in which the early church came to terms with Jesus' humiliation and death and which is particularly emphasized in Luke's account (see, for instance, 24.26). But at the time the disciples had not been able to grasp this: the bearing of these prophecies upon Jesus and his destiny became clear only later. Meanwhile their failure to understand – a failure demonstrated by their subsequent conduct – is to some extent excused (as previously in 9.45) by the

34 suggestion that understanding it was not yet God's purpose for them: **what he said was hidden from them, and they did not grasp what was said**.

After omitting Mark's account (10.35–45) of the dispute over precedence among the disciples (part of which Luke records in another form later, 22.24–

35–43 7), Luke tells the story of the healing of a blind man very much as it is in Mark (10.46–52), though using his own words. He has omitted the name of the beggar (Bartimaeus) and the Aramaic word in which he addressed

Jesus (*Rabbouni*), but he has added a conclusion which he seems to have felt
43 appropriate to a number of Jesus' miracles: **and all the people, when they saw it, praised God.**

19.1   **He entered Jericho.** The Jordan valley between the Lake of Tiberias and the Dead Sea consists of a long, narrow plain which is for the most part dry and treeless. But at Jericho, which lies toward the southern end of this plain close to the mountains of Judea, there is a spring which irrigates the fields and orchards and makes the town a veritable oasis. In the time of Jesus it was a prosperous city, rich in date palms and balsam trees, and the home of a well-to-do Jewish community. It was also the principal eastern frontier town of Judea; Herod the Great had built a winter palace there and it had a large
2 traffic of merchants and travellers. **A man was there named Zacchaeus**, the Greek form of a common Jewish name, Zakkai. The man was a Jew, a wealthy **chief tax collector.** This does not mean a civil servant in the employment of the government; for the government did not collect its own taxes but contracted them out to whichever firm of tax collectors could offer the highest return on a given area. These firms made their money, partly by exacting a slightly higher rate of taxation than they returned to the government, and partly by investing the revenues in business interests before paying over the total assessment. Zacchaeus is to be imagined as the head of one of these companies, perhaps contracted to collect customs dues. In this profession he had enriched himself, but he had also incurred social exclusion, since the principles according to which tax collectors made their living were regarded
7 as incompatible with Jewish law and therefore as rendering the practitioner **a sinner.** Hence **all who saw it began to grumble** when Jesus called him down from his undignified vantage point in the tree and deliberately sought lodging with him. But on this occasion Jesus' initiative was spectacularly vindicated by the immediate repentance of his host. It was always possible for a tax collector to make restitution to all from whom he had exacted more than was due and so to be accepted back into society; and since it was recognized that it was probably impossible for him to identify and repay more than a small number of those whose taxes he had collected, it was considered adequate if he made up the rest by making a proportionate contribution to the public good. The result of his encounter with Jesus was that Zacchaeus immediately resolved
8 to do this – and more. He **stood there** – the word suggests he was making a public declaration – and promised to give away half his possessions (far more than would have been considered adequate) and, to any who could prove that they had been **defrauded**, to pay back the difference, not merely plus 20 per cent (as the law required, Leviticus 6.1–5), but to the astonishing level of 400 per cent. As a result, he and his family would recover their full
9 rights in society – **"salvation has come to this house".** But this sensational act of repentance had taken place because Jesus, instead of shunning him as his pious contemporaries did, had deliberately sought his company, regarding him as one who was 'lost' and could be 'saved'.

11   **They supposed that the kingdom of God was to appear immediately.**
This is Luke's introduction to a parable that, in its main features, is familiar
from Matthew's gospel (25.14–30). There it is presented as an allegory of the
last judgment. Luke gives it a different application. Whatever people thought
about Jesus, there was inevitably a temptation to see in one who gave such
notable signs of miraculous power a harbinger of that new age – the **kingdom
of God** – for which the majority of Jews earnestly waited and prayed; and
Jesus' arrival at the Holy City might have seemed a likely moment for the
promised age to begin. Such crude expectations were politically dangerous to
Jesus in his lifetime, and he certainly did not encourage them; but they lived
on after his death and resurrection, and we know (from the letters of Paul,
for example) that Christian leaders had strenuously to discourage those who
tried to contract out of their normal responsibilities because 'they supposed
that the kingdom of God was to appear immediately'. The question, at any
rate, was still very much alive in Luke's day, and by subtly emphasizing certain
12   details in the parable (the nobleman's journey to a **distant country,** the
17   reward for being **trustworthy in a very small thing**), Luke made the parable
teach a lesson of patience and responsible social conduct. But Luke's version
also has some original features which suggest that the parable already had a
complicated history before it came into his hands. It now contains a by-plot.
12   The capitalist who starts his slaves[17] in business is also a **nobleman** who has
ambitions to **get royal power for himself** (literally, *a kingdom*). This suggests
a historical setting for the story. All 'kings' in Palestine held their kingdoms
with the consent of the Roman emperor; and one of Herod the Great's sons,
Archelaus, had acquired his short-lived 'kingdom' of Judea by making the
journey to Rome in circumstances very similar to those described here, so
much so that Jesus' story may be an allusion to this actual event (4 BCE). But
what has this political episode to do with the story of the three slaves? On the
face of it, very little; indeed, the two fit together so badly that (as is the case in
another parable in Matthew, 22.1–10) what were originally two separate
stories may have at some stage been combined into one. Nevertheless the
political setting of the by-plot has influenced the telling of the main story:
the glittering rewards given to the entrepreneurial slaves seem out of all
proportion to their small-scale commercial successes, all the more so since
the extremely large capital sums mentioned in Matthew ('talents') appear in
Luke as the almost unworkably small asset of one *mina* (*three month's wages
for a laborer,* as the NRSV footnote correctly informs us). This also makes the
detail of giving the third slave's capital to the first seem slightly grotesque –
he had by now become a provincial governor! Hence, perhaps, the protest,
25   **'Lord, he has ten pounds!'** But this leads to another point that Luke saw
in the parable, apart from warning people to expect a delay: the attention

---

[17] Technical difficulties arise from the NRSV translation **slaves.** See above, p. 90n.

you give now to small and humble things will gain you a reward out of all proportion in the kingdom of God. One further detail sharpens the point. In Matthew, the third slave buried his money in the ground, which was often
20 regarded as the most prudent way to keep it safe. But here, he **wrapped it up in a piece of cloth**, which was by no means so prudent. In Luke's hands he
17 has become an example of one who is definitely *not* **trustworthy in a very small thing.**

28   **Going up to Jerusalem** from Jericho involved a walk of some 20 miles up a road which climbed nearly 1,200 metres (4,000 feet) from the plain to the crest of the Mount of Olives. Luke follows Mark (11.1–10) in the details of
29–34 the journey and of the finding of the colt; as in Mark, this episode is doubtless meant to be understood as a confirmation of Jesus' remarkable powers of foresight, not as a piece of prior organization. But Luke gives Jesus' ride a slightly different interpretation. Gone are the branches and greenery, with their Jewish festival associations; the disciples merely throw their cloaks on the ground in front of Jesus, which was the gesture of acclaiming a king (2 Kings 9.13). The Zechariah prophecy (9.9), "Lo, your king comes to you . . . humble and riding on a donkey", which is implicit in Mark's account and is expressly quoted in Matthew, is no more than distantly suggested
38 here; but the word **king** is deliberately introduced into the chanting of the disciples (who take the place of the crowds described in the other versions of the story). Their cry, as in the other accounts, uses the words of Psalm 118.25–6. But Luke has omitted the Hebrew word *hosanna* and added a phrase reminiscent of the angels' song at Jesus' birth. Jesus' ceremonial entry thus becomes, no longer an uncertain recognition by the crowds of the nearness of the Messiah, but a proclamation by Jesus' own disciples of the advent of a divinely commissioned king. And Jesus accepts their acclamation. Using a
40 proverbial phrase, he tells those who question his right to the title, **"if these were silent, the stones would shout out".**

As soon as the procession had come over the saddle of the Mount of Olives, the whole city of Jerusalem would have appeared before their eyes, spread out on the opposite side of the valley, with the immense and magnificent buildings of the temple in the foreground and Herod's citadel commanding the city from its highest point behind. According to popular etymology the
41–4 name 'Jerusalem' meant that it was a 'city of peace'. In the manner of a prophet, Jesus based his lament over the city on the name itself, and, foreseeing the course which events were taking and which his own intervention would do nothing to deflect, he prophesied, not peace, but siege and destruction. By the time Luke wrote, these things had taken place (70 CE); but the details of Jesus' prophecy, though strikingly exact, have not necessarily been rewritten in the light of subsequent history. They can all be found in Old Testament descriptions of sieges and destruction (e.g. Isaiah 29.3; Psalm 137.9; Jeremiah 52): they were already conventional terms for describing a besieged and conquered city. There is no reason to doubt that Jesus foresaw such a fate

coming upon Jerusalem as clearly as Isaiah had before him. It must indeed, have been obvious to any person of vision that the increasing turbulence of Jewish nationalist movements against the Roman occupation could lead only to disaster. Nothing short of a change of heart could avert it. In the person

44 of Jesus, the moment – God's **visitation** – had arrived for such a change of heart. But the opportunity had been, and would be, rejected.

45 **Then he entered the temple.** This episode, told in some detail by Mark (11.15–19) and Matthew (21.12–13), is no more than briefly summarized by Luke. It also presupposes a different chronological scheme. Whereas in Mark it introduces the very last days of Jesus' life, in Luke it introduces a

47 substantial period of activity in Jerusalem: **Every day he was teaching in the temple.**

20.1–8 **One day, as he was teaching the people.** The question about Jesus' authority, which in Mark (11.20–5) follows close upon his violent action in the temple, is placed by Luke in the context of his daily teaching, and so becomes a more general one embracing all his activity, especially perhaps his teaching. For this, the only authority his questioners were prepared to recognize was that which they conferred themselves; but this is precisely what Jesus was challenging when he asked his counter-question about John the Baptist, whose prophetic authority to teach and baptize they did not dare to deny.

9–16 The parable of the vineyard is told very much as in Mark (12.1–12), and Luke's only changes (such as the reduction of the number of slaves to one each time) are probably a matter of literary style rather than of any different understanding of the story. But there can be little doubt that in the 'son' he saw Jesus himself – as indeed, Jesus may have intended. The slight

15 alteration (made also by Matthew, 21.39) that **they threw him out of the vineyard** before killing him is perhaps deliberately intended to suggest Jesus' crucifixion outside Jerusalem (though it is also plausible as a precaution to prevent the produce of the vineyard becoming ritually unclean); and the two scriptural texts which follow, though they have no very clear application to the

17 story, have much to say about the destiny of the Son of God. '**The stone that the builders rejected has become the cornerstone**' (Psalm 118.22) was an image for the miraculous restoration by God of the fortunes of any righteous person or people who had seemed to their enemies ruined and Godforsaken, and it was an image which the early church eagerly added to the complex series of building metaphors with which it strove to express the idea of a Christian community as God's new temple (1 Peter 2.7). But here (as in Acts 4.11) it expresses a straightforward claim that Jesus, though now to be rejected and killed, would subsequently be vindicated and glorified. The continuation

18 (found only in Luke), **"Everyone who falls on that stone will be broken to pieces"**, makes a slightly different point. It is not an exact quotation: the idea, and some of the wording, are drawn from Daniel 2.34 – where a great stone smashes an idol – with possibly also a hint from Isaiah 8.14 ("a rock one stumbles over"). Later Jewish scholars interpreted the Daniel passage as

a prophecy about the Messiah, and this interpretation may have been current in Luke's or even Jesus' time. But, in any case, in their context here these texts clearly express the reverse side of the Son's glorification: all who do not accept him now will then experience, not the thrill of his glory, but the severity of judgment.

20–21.4 The following sections follow Mark (12.13–44) very closely. Luke, like Matthew, has simply added a few narrator's touches in order to keep the action moving. In particular, he connects the question about paying taxes (adding

20 that it was **to trap him . . . so as to hand him over to the jurisdiction and authority of the governor**) with one of the accusations actually made against Jesus before Pilate later on (23.2). One point of detail is corrected. Jesus' answer to the Sadducees in Mark 12.25 ("when they rise from the dead, they neither marry nor are given in marriage, but are like angels in heaven") could conceivably have been misunderstood as a promise of heaven to everyone, good and bad, without distinction. Here the ambiguity is removed: Jesus was

35 speaking only of **"those who are considered worthy of a place in that age"**.

20.5 **When some were speaking about the temple**. The new temple, begun by Herod the Great in 20 BCE, was still not entirely completed; but it was already one of the most spectacular pieces of architecture in the ancient world. Like the great pagan temples that could be seen in many parts of the Roman empire, the temple building had a façade of brilliant white marble and its appearance was enriched by votive offerings, among which was a great golden vine set up over the door by Herod the Great himself. It is these features, which would have been of a kind familiar to any Greek reader, rather than the exceptional size of the masonry (which only those who had seen it could appreciate), that Luke, unlike Mark, singles out for mention.

The same concern to give for his more cosmopolitan readers a less alien character to the discourse, which in Mark (chapter 13) is expressed in a thoroughly Jewish idiom, accounts for some of the detailed alterations which Luke has made. But there are also some more significant changes. The setting itself is different. In Mark, Jesus is presented as a teacher giving private instruction to a chosen group of disciples as they sit on the Mount of Olives overlooking the city and the temple; but here he is giving public teaching in

7 the temple itself. The audience are all who call him **"Teacher"**, and the words in this account are evidently destined for the encouragement of subsequent generations of Christians. Those Christians have experience, not so much

8 of political agitators in Palestine who claimed to be the Messiah (**saying, 'I am he!'**), as of over-enthusiastic preachers in the church who unsettle their congregations by proclaiming, **'The time is near!'** (The phrase occurs only in Luke.) As in the other accounts, a succession of calamitous events

12 is foretold; but **"before all this occurs"** – that is to say, in the continuing experience of the church – those same Christians are to suffer persecution; and in their frequent appearances in the courts (which, for Jews, might be **synagogues** exercising their judicial functions, for Gentiles, the courts

14 of subject **kings** or Roman **governors**) they are not to **prepare** their **defence**
(Luke uses the technical language of Greek courts): Jesus had several times
15 promised them the assistance of the Holy Spirit, here credited with **words**
16 **and a wisdom** that brook no contradiction. **"They will put some of you to
death"**: this had already happened by the time Luke was writing; but there
18 was also a saying of Jesus, **"not a hair of your head will perish"** (compare
Matthew 10.30). How was this to be reconciled with the fact that Christians
had already been martyred? Perhaps along the lines (already traditional in
discussions of martyrdom) that, whatever happened to their bodies, their
19 **souls** would be gained.

But Luke has also made some more significant changes to Mark's account.
It is possible that he was combining what he found in Mark with some other
source; but at the same time certain deliberate touches which he gave to the
discourse show that he had an editorial policy of his own. We may assume that
he wrote his gospel a decade or so later than Mark, when the church, though
still firmly believing in an impending and decisive intervention by God in
human history, had nevertheless to revise its idea of the timing. In Mark, the
question 'When will this be?' was elicited by Jesus' startling prophecy that the
massive temple buildings were to be totally destroyed; and Jesus answered that
all this would take place within their own generation, but must be understood
in the wider context of world history: it would be no isolated catastrophe, but
one of the events in that turbulent period which must necessarily precede the
end. These prophecies were spoken, and probably written down by Mark,
before Jerusalem was in fact taken and the temple desecrated and destroyed by
the Romans in 70 CE. Up to that time, naïve Christians may well have thought
that the end of the present age would follow immediately. But as the years
passed, and as history continued as before, a more subtle interpretation was
required for Jesus' words. A part of what he had prophesied – in particular
the fall of Jerusalem and the persecution of Christians – had already been
fulfilled; but the climax presaged by these events – the last judgment and the
visible coming of the Son of Man – still lay in the future. To be precise (and
9 this appears to be Luke's own formulation), **"these things must take place
first, but the end will not follow immediately"**.

20 **"When you see Jerusalem surrounded by armies."** The historical event
by which Jesus' prophecies were most obviously fulfilled was the siege and
destruction of Jerusalem. At this point Mark and Matthew use the conventionally cryptic language of apocalyptic writing and refer to a mysterious "desolating sacrilege". Luke drops the cryptic convention and makes
the 'desolation' refer explicitly to the siege. If Mark was written before the
event and Luke after it, this might seem a sufficient explanation of the difference between them. But Luke's procedure is by no means just to write
an account of the siege as it happened and put this into Jesus' mouth as a
prophecy. He does not mention any of the things which (as we know from
the contemporary historian Josephus) were particularly notable in the siege

of Jerusalem; his language is entirely that which the Old Testament prophets used to express their premonitions of a similar event and which Jesus may well have used himself when prophesying the fate of Jerusalem. Moreover the catastrophe is not merely prophesied, it is interpreted, and interpreted

22 in a fully biblical manner: **"these are days of vengeance, in fulfilment of all that is written"** (compare Deuteronomy 32.35; Hosea 9.7; Jeremiah 46.10); and the classic consequences – slaughter and captivity – will include the fulfilment of another oracle (Zechariah 12.3 and elsewhere) that Jerusalem

24 would be **"trampled on by the Gentiles"**. Only the last words are cryptic: **"until the times of the Gentiles are fulfilled"**. The foreigners, it would seem, were not destined to trample on Jerusalem indefinitely. Jerusalem (even if only metaphorically) had still a part to play in the salvation of humankind – a hint, perhaps, of that view of world history which is worked out by Paul in Romans 9–11.

25 **"There will be signs in the sun, the moon, and the stars."** All the calamities described so far, however severe, were the kind of thing that could happen in the ordinary course of history. Even the fall of Jerusalem should not be regarded as so unexampled that it was necessarily a sign of the end – Luke, as a historian, and doubtless many of his non-Palestinian readers, found it easier to keep a sense of proportion about it than those more immediately affected. Nothing, in short, that the church had experienced so far was to be interpreted as an immediate presage of the last things. These would be heralded by events of another order, by a serious break in the continuities of the physical world. The portents to be looked for would be in the sky: if the heavenly bodies lost

26 their regularity – and still more if **the powers of the heavens** which controlled those bodies were **shaken** – then disorder must be expected on earth (for most people took a certain amount of astrology for granted: it was the regular movement of sun, moon and stars which guaranteed the orderly succession

25 of cause and effect on earth). **"The roaring of the sea and the waves"**, too, meant more than an ordinary storm. It was believed that only God's firm hand held the sea back from engulfing dry land; if this were withdrawn, a

26 great tidal wave would make people **faint from fear**. It would be signs such as these, and not the familiar vicissitudes of history, which must be read as heralding the coming of the Son of Man. But that coming – and the language of clouds and glory borrowed from Daniel's vision (7.13–14) shows that it would be a moment of vindication – would also put an end to the tribulations

28 of the church; therefore it would be the moment to **"stand up and raise your heads"**.

The tone of all this is comparatively optimistic. As soon as things get really severe Christians can take courage because their **redemption is drawing near**. But it is still necessary to utter warnings. As surely as summer follows the

29 budding of the fig tree – **and all the trees,** as Luke adds for the benefit of his European readers (see above on Mark 13.28) – the portents will be followed by . . . and here Mark and Matthew leave a cryptic blank, which Luke fills

31 in with **the kingdom of God**. In the meantime, however, the apparent delay
of these things must not lead to either cynicism or moral laxity. Jesus had
32 authoritatively predicted that **all things** (however this was to be interpreted)
would take place in **this generation**. Some had already come to pass: possibly
the final phase would take longer. When the final moment came, it would be
a cataclysm not merely in Palestine (as the Jewish idiom in which Christians
35 described it might make others think) but **on the face of the whole earth**.
34 It would be such that **dissipation and drunkenness and the worries of this
life** – which Luke perhaps saw already taking hold of some Christian
communities – would fatally dull the mind: in this state one might be caught
35, 36 unawares, as in **a trap**. All must pray for **strength**, so that, whether or not
one died before the end, one would at all events win the right **to stand before
the Son of Man**. Luke has edited this final exhortation in such a way that it
could serve as the end of a sermon to the church at any time, whether or not
the 'portents' had begun to appear. In a subtle way he has adapted material
that was originally conditioned by expectation of an imminent end to the
needs of a church that was beginning to accept the indefinite continuation
of the present world order.
37 **Every day he was teaching in the temple**. Luke has not yet fallen in with
the careful time-scheme propounded by Mark, but allows a number of days
to elapse before the final conflict. 'Spending the night' on the Mount of
Olives does not necessarily mean camping out. The village of Bethany, where
(according to Mark) Jesus lodged during his last days, lay on the far slopes
of the Mount of Olives.

The final days

22.1 **Now the festival of Unleavened Bread, which is called the Passover, was
near**. Luke's narrative now follows the outlines of Mark's account but also
diverges from it at a number of points. Either he was rewriting the passage
somewhat freely or else he was drawing on a different tradition. In either
event the resultant picture is a new one. The introduction seems aimed, as
often in Luke, at making the events flow in a more natural sequence. There is
no attempt (as in Mark) to offer a date: the festival was simply 'near'; but this
was enough to give urgency to the schemes of the authorities to do away with
Jesus. It is not made clear in the other gospel accounts how Judas' treachery
6 in fact helped them; but Luke makes this explicit: Judas' task was **to betray
him to them when no crowd was present**, despite the fact that Jerusalem
was crowded with pilgrims. He effectively did so by leading the authorities
to the spot where he knew Jesus would go for solitude during the night.
Luke says nothing either of a psychological struggle in Judas or even (like
3 Matthew) of a mercenary motive: he acted under the impulsion of **Satan** –
not the last time in this narrative that human actions are said to be caused by
supernatural agencies.

7   The preparations for the Passover supper, on the day **on which the Passover lamb had to be sacrificed,** are told almost exactly as in Mark; and it follows that Luke, like both Mark and Matthew, thought of this supper as

8   a **Passover meal,** with its special dishes of bitter herbs, roasted lamb and unleavened bread, and with its customary recital of the miraculous deliverance of Israel out of Egypt. This meal was always a formal one. The people in each group that shared it were bound together in table fellowship, which they signified by partaking of the bread and the wine that their host had blessed. Like Mark and Matthew, Luke does not trouble to mention the normal elements of the meal, but singles out certain words and actions of Jesus which made this celebration exceptional. It is in his report of these words and actions that Luke shows how differently he understands the occasion.

15   **"I have eagerly desired to eat this Passover with you before I suffer."** The Greek, like the English, is ambiguous: did Jesus eat with them or not? The

16   phrase in the following verse, **I will not eat it until . . .",** sounds more definite, and seems[18] to settle the matter: Jesus was making a vow of abstinence. However much he may have longed to share this Passover with his intimate group of disciples, when it came to the point he refused to partake of it. If so, his abstinence would certainly have been surprising. Matthew and Mark give no hint of it: the most they suggest is that after the blessing Jesus refused any further wine; the final 'cup' of the formal meal was apparently waived, not only for himself, but probably also for his disciples. Moreover, such abstinence would have been odd in itself on such a solemn occasion. Could Luke really have meant this? Was Jesus really fasting – perhaps (as has been suggested) as a way of interceding for the salvation of his people? In view of the ambiguities already mentioned, it is hard to be sure; but there is one further point which bears on the question. Both Matthew and Mark lay some emphasis on the fact that Judas' act of betrayal was an instance of that base form of treachery which consists in betraying someone with whom one has become intimate through the solidarity of sharing a meal together: Jesus was betrayed by one who was eating with him (Mark 14.18; Matthew 26.23). But if Luke believed that Jesus himself ate nothing at this meal, he needed to make some change at this point; and sure enough we find that Judas is identified,

21   not as one who *ate* with Jesus, but as one whose **hand** was **on the table**[19] with Jesus. There is no mention of eating together.

However this may be, the point serves to focus attention on one respect in which Luke's account is different from any other. This difference is more apparent in the version of the text which is given by a small number of

---

[18] Unfortunately it is not certain that this is what Luke wrote. Some manuscripts have *I will never eat it again,* allowing for the possibility that Jesus did share this Passover meal. See the NRSV footnote.

[19] The Greek means literally *whose hand is with me on the table.*

19 manuscripts and which omits everything between **This is my body** in verse
21 19 and **But see** in verse 21 (see the NRSV footnote). The result is odd in a
number of respects, not least in that it puts the cup before the bread. But it is
precisely this oddity which makes it necessary to take this version seriously
as possibly representing what Luke wrote; for many believe that it is easier
to explain the intrusion of the longer text as a subsequent correction and
amplification of a shorter one than to explain why an original longer one
would ever have been abbreviated. If this is accepted, the only explanation
19 Jesus gives of the bread or the wine consists of the words, **"This is my body."**
But, twice over, Jesus uses the meal itself as a pointer towards a greater reality,
16, 18 **the kingdom of God**. Those who believed in a coming 'messianic age' often
described it in the imagery of a heavenly banquet; and the significance of
this Passover supper then lies in the fact that it was the last that would be
celebrated in the old manner before it was superseded by an experience of
a heavenly reality which would reveal the coming of the kingdom of God.
The main purpose of the present meal (according to this version) was thus
to foreshadow something greater in the near future.

19–20 The longer text, which is accepted by most (but not all[20]) modern translations, preserves this emphasis but brings the narrative much closer to that
in Mark and Matthew; it also reproduces some details from Paul's account
in 1 Corinthians 11.24–5. The usual order is restored of the cup following
the bread, and an interpretation is given of the bread and the cup themselves
which corresponds closely with that in the other accounts. Even so, certain
oddities remain, in particular the extra cup of wine shared by the disciples
before the breaking of bread; but at a Jewish Passover a number of cups were
drunk ceremonially, and the extra cup may be no more than a reminiscence
of one of these.

24 **A dispute arose among them**. It is natural, in the light of centuries of
Christian devotion to the 'sacrament' of bread and wine, to think of the
breaking of bread and the sharing of the cup as the most important, if not
the only important, features of this meal, and of the dispute among those
present (for which the Greek word *philoneikia* has the distinctly unsavoury
associations of ambitious rivalry) as shockingly inappropriate. But this may
not have been Luke's view. Luke saw the Passover supper as the occasion
for a farewell speech by Jesus to his disciples. Such farewell speeches were
one of the conventional devices used by ancient historians to gather together
the last instructions of the hero; Luke himself provides another example in
Paul's farewell to the elders of Miletus at Ephesus (Acts 20.18–35), and the
gospel of John considerably extends the convention when it reports a long discourse of Jesus to his disciples on the night before his death (chapters 14–17).
For the content of the speech, Luke draws partly on sayings which are recorded
in other gospels in different contexts. In particular, the question **which one**

---

[20] The Revised English Bible, for instance, has the shorter text.

of them was to be regarded as the greatest was raised, according to Mark
(10.41) and Matthew (20.24), as a result of an indiscreet request by the two
sons of Zebedee on the way up to Jerusalem. The answer given by Jesus
here is similar to the one recorded in those accounts, but a new detail is the
25 word **"benefactors"**. Some of the Hellenistic kings of the east liked to adopt
this title (*euergetēs*): by their wealth (however acquired), and by the peace
they procured for their kingdoms (however precarious), they were pleased
to describe their rule (however tyrannical) as a benefaction to their subjects.
26 The use of the word here is perhaps ironical; at any rate the **greatest** among
Jesus' disciples must have no such pretensions. As in the versions in Mark
and Matthew, the image invoked for this reversal of the ordinary rules of
27 precedence is that of **the one who is at the table** and **the one who serves;**
but Jesus' final word, **"But I am among you as one who serves"**, though it
rings true of his general manner and intentions, is oddly inappropriate here
where he is to be imagined as reclining at the head of the table. Did Luke
know of the tradition in John's gospel (13.1–20) that, before the meal began,
Jesus washed his disciples' feet?
28 **"You are those who have stood by me in my trials."** This surprising
statement stands in the place of the simple phrase, "you who have followed
me", in Matthew's version of the same saying (19.28). Surprising, because,
taken in its most literal sense, it is not easy to see to what moments in Jesus'
life it can refer. There have been few occasions in the narrative on which it
could be said that the disciples distinguished themselves by their constancy
in moments of trial; and in the 'trials' that were about to begin they first
fell asleep when they might have supported Jesus in Gethsemane, and then
(according to the other gospels, though Luke does not mention this) forsook
him altogether. Unless there had been some 'trials' that are not recorded in
the gospels when the disciples 'stood by' Jesus, we have either to take the
phrase as a very general statement that up to now the disciples have not
actually deserted their often disconcerting master, or else suspect that the
'trials' which certainly tested the loyalty of the early church have been read
back into the experience of the disciples.
29 **"And I confer on you . . . a kingdom."** This translation may be correct;
but it fails to convey the associations of the Greek word, which also stands
for making a *covenant:* it is not so much that Jesus was 'conferring' on them
a kingdom at that moment (which he could hardly do): he was 'covenanting'
himself and them so that they should be members and agents of the 'kingdom'
which was to come. The symbolic description of this is one which has been
used a few verses before, that of the coming heavenly banquet; and, in slightly
uneasy juxtaposition (though feasting in full sight of one's enemies was
traditionally one of the rewards to which the righteous felt they could look
forward, as in Psalm 23.5) a further image is added that belongs, not to the
festivities of the new age, but to the judgment which will precede it. As in
Matthew's version of the saying (19.28), the disciples are promised a part to

30 play in the coming judgment: they will **"sit on thrones judging the twelve tribes of Israel"**.

31 **"Simon, Simon, listen!"** All four gospels record Jesus' prediction of Peter's threefold denial. Matthew and Mark place it a little later, on the walk out of the city to Gethsemane; Luke and John set it in the context of the farewell discourse. Luke, moreover, introduces it with some words which seem, like the rest of the speech, to look further forward into the future. There would certainly be times when it would be the responsibility of any leader of the church to strengthen his 'brothers' (which became almost a standard term for 'fellow Christians'); and by the time the gospel was written Peter would
33 have gone **to prison and to death**. Jesus could have foreseen these things. But in any case, there was a severe test to be undergone in the near future. We have seen that, instead of speculating about Judas' motives in betraying Jesus, the narrative simply ascribed the cause to Satan (22.3). In the same way, there is no psychological reflection on the behaviour of the disciples at Jesus' arrest. This too was caused by Satan. But this time Satan was not
31 permitted to destroy his instruments; he had merely **demanded** to put them to the test (or, as the Greek could mean, *obtained permission*, as he had in the case of Job, see Job 1.12; 2.6). The metaphor used is a strange one, though well in the style of Jesus. Wheat was sifted either in a coarse sieve to separate it from the chaff and other rubbish (in which case the wheat fell through), or else, after threshing, in a fine sieve to separate it from smaller seeds and impurities (in which case the wheat remained in the sieve). Either way it was tested and separated out. The disciples were about to undergo such a test; but because of Jesus' prayer, and with the aid, apparently, of Peter's timely
32 recovery (if this is what the word translated **turned back** means – the Greek word is used for being 'converted', either to one's former state or to a new one) they would – unlike Judas – survive the ordeal.

The last section of Jesus' discourse bears more closely still on what was about to happen. All the gospels record that when Jesus was arrested in Gethsemane at least one of those who were with him was carrying a sword and attempted to use it; John's gospel actually gives the name of the slave who was wounded. This appeared to be incompatible with the instructions which Jesus had previously given to his followers (10.3–4), quite apart from being contrary to the spirit of Jesus' teaching and from carrying with it the danger of trouble with the Roman authorities. But now, perhaps, the circumstances were exceptional and warranted different equipment – or rather, Luke goes on to say, there was a significant Old Testament prophecy which could not
38 be fulfilled unless such preparations were made. **"Here are two swords"** – not enough for serious resistance; but enough (as perhaps Luke was the first to notice) to give fulfilment to some words of Isaiah. One of the first clues which the early church found to the meaning of Jesus' fate (a clue which may indeed have been given by Jesus himself) was the 'suffering servant' of Isaiah 53. But one verse of that prophecy ran, "he . . . was numbered with the

transgressors", literally *the lawless* (53.12). How could this be true of Jesus? In what sense could his disciples be regarded as 'transgressors of the law'? A possible answer lay in the firm tradition that one of them had used a sword in Jesus' defence. From the strict Jewish point of view, simply carrying a sword on the sabbath (and *a fortiori* on a festival such as Passover) was probably forbidden, and from the Roman point of view its use in resisting arrest would have incurred severe penalties. If two of Jesus' disciples had swords on that

37, 38   particular night, this would have been **enough** to make the prophecy **'he was counted among the lawless'** seem to have come true.

39   **He came out and went, as was his custom, to the Mount of Olives.** Luke has a version of the following scene which is rather different from that of Matthew and Mark. The main elements are the same – the words of Jesus'

40   prayer, the disciples falling asleep and the warning about the **"time of trial"**. But all this is told more briefly, and with less obvious criticism of the disciples:

45   Luke suggests that they could not stay awake **because of grief** rather than culpable fatigue. Gethsemane is not mentioned by name: it is simply called

40   **the place**, and rather to our surprise (since Mark and Matthew describe it as an exceptional occasion) we are told that Jesus made a habit of going there

39   **(as was his custom)** – which perhaps explains how Judas was able to find him. But as if to make up for this, Luke (unless it is some later interpolator[21]) offers a description of Jesus at prayer which is quite unparalleled. To pray,

41   Jesus **knelt down**, an unusual attitude: Jews usually stood to pray, sometimes

43   prostrated themselves, and only occasionally knelt. He had a vision of **an angel from heaven** who **gave him strength**. Angels appear quite often in Luke's narrative, but nowhere in a rôle quite like this. Evidently the struggle was exceptionally severe: Luke would probably have thought of it as a struggle between Jesus and the devil rather than as a psychological struggle within

44   Jesus himself; and despite the angel's help, Jesus was in **anguish**. The Greek word so translated is *agōnia,* from which our word 'agony' is derived. It means, not so much an acute conflict of emotions, as an intense anxiety about what is going to happen. Jesus, we should perhaps suppose, was in agonizing suspense whether Satan would after all prevail, and the violent metaphor of 'bloody sweat' (which occurs in Greek literature from the time of Homer) leaves his readers in no doubt of the reality of Jesus' ordeal.

47   **While he was still speaking.** Once again the main points of Mark's narrative are here more briefly told, but with some new details. The kiss, in Matthew and Mark, is simply the means by which Judas identifies Jesus for his captors; here it is the cue for an apparently outraged comment by Jesus.

49   The momentary resistance of **those who were around him** (which is a sequel

---

[21] This appears to be the view of the NRSV translators, who enclose the passage in double square brackets. It is true that it occurs in a minority of manuscripts; but scholars are divided over whether it is more likely to have been added later to explain Jesus' *agōnia* or deleted as making Jesus seem too humanly afraid.

to what was said earlier about providing themselves with swords) is placed, perhaps more logically, before the arrest of Jesus instead of after it, and is followed by a miracle of healing: only Luke mentions this, perhaps to indicate that Jesus did not intend his instructions about carrying swords to be an excuse for violence in his defence. The flight of the disciples is not mentioned – Luke tends to avoid anything which would discredit them; on the other hand, point is given to Jesus' reply to his captors by bringing on to the scene people of some seniority – not just servants and police, but some

52 of the **chief priests** and **elders** (representing the Sanhedrin) and **officers of the temple police** who were responsible for public order in the temple area and would have been the men to take action had Jesus' conduct been in any

53 way reprehensible when he was **"day after day in the temple"**. **"But this is your hour, and the power of darkness."** It was not just that Jesus and his followers were utterly outnumbered; behind the contingent of armed men were supernatural forces of evil which were to be allowed a temporary victory. Satan (euphemistically called 'darkness') had already claimed Judas (22.3), though he was to be denied the other disciples (22.31); he still had some power to exercise before the end.

54 **Bringing him to the high priest's house.** Luke arranges the next events somewhat differently from Mark and Matthew. If we had only his account we should not suspect that there was any formal interrogation during the night. Jesus seems to have been brought to Caiaphas' house simply for safe detention until the early-morning session, and this period of waiting provides the setting for the stories of Peter's denial and of the mockery of Jesus. They

55 **kindled a fire in the middle of the courtyard.** Peter, sitting in the group gathered round it (and not going outside, as in Mark and Matthew), was three times identified. Jesus, meanwhile, is presumably to be imagined as being held by the guards somewhere in the courtyard where he could turn and look at Peter – which may be the climax of the episode, leaving us to

62 imagine Peter's feelings; for the final words of the paragraph, **he went out and wept bitterly**, are exactly as in Matthew and are omitted by a few manuscripts, which raises the possibility that they were added later to bring Luke's account into harmony with Matthew's.[22]

66 **When day came.** At this point Luke's chronology becomes quite different from Mark's, and is in many ways more plausible. The session of the **council** (the Sanhedrin) is described as taking place, not at night, but at the more normal time of early morning – official business in Rome, and still more in the east, was done between dawn and midday – and, for all Luke says, may have been held, not in the high priest's house, but in the usual council chamber. In Luke, no witnesses are called, no evidence is presented. The

---

[22] Surprisingly, there is no NRSV footnote recording this omission. If the words are original, they raise the awkward question whether Luke deliberately used Matthew as well as Mark for his source.

procedure seems to have been simply an attempt to establish from Jesus' own lips whether he admitted to being the Messiah and therefore (in that sense

70 at least) **the Son of God**. Jesus' reply (which is remarkably like the one he gives to a similar question in John 10.25) is at first guarded, as if anything he said would need explanation and qualification; but he then makes the

69 same claim as in the other accounts: the Son of Man **"will be seated at the right hand of the power of God"** (Daniel 7.13); and the implication of this –

70 that Jesus is **the Son of God** – leads to his condemnation (though it is not said on what charge).

23.1 **Then the assembly . . . brought Jesus before Pilate**. Luke offers even less explanation than the other gospels (apart from John's, which almost incidentally provides the clue that the Jews could not officially carry out the death penalty) for this démarche to the Roman authorities. A Roman official did not normally hear cases in dispute between local people, particularly if they concerned matters of local custom and religion, but was prepared to hear charges brought against alleged criminals and trouble-makers. Having heard the charges and questioned the witnesses, it was for him to decide on the nature of the offence and to pronounce a verdict and sentence. This is the procedure which Luke is recording here. The charges sound plausible, and

2 that of **"perverting our nation"** is one that continued to surface in Jewish attacks on Jesus in the following centuries; but the reader will recognize them all as misrepresentations of episodes narrated earlier in the gospel. At any rate, the only one that Pilate seemed willing to consider was Jesus' alleged claim to be Messiah, which Luke qualifies for this purpose as amounting to a claim to be king. If established, this would have constituted a serious charge, and Pilate questioned Jesus on this point. But he apparently did not find Jesus' reply sufficiently incriminating to proceed, and the Jews' further

5 accusation of seditious **teaching . . . from Galilee . . . even to this place** gave him the cue for a different tactic. Galilee was in the territory of the tetrarch Herod Antipas. Pilate was not obliged to hand over his prisoner merely because Jesus' country of origin lay outside his jurisdiction, for the conduct of which Jesus was accused had come to a head in Jerusalem and he had a perfect right to deal with it himself. On the other hand, Pilate had no means of verifying those charges which related to Jesus' activity in Galilee, and he could well have felt that the case would be better heard by the local ruler, who happened to be in Jerusalem at the time. Luke (who is the only

7 evangelist to record this episode) adds that the remission of Jesus to **Herod** was intended and received as a courtesy. We have no independent evidence

12 that they **had been enemies**, though it is not unlikely: Herod Antipas had some influence with the emperor in Rome – it was not for nothing that he had named his capital Tiberias after the reigning emperor – and Pilate's gesture towards his influential neighbour may have been diplomatic.

We know from Josephus where Herod is likely to have been: not in the great palace built by his father, which was now the Roman governor's *praetorium*,

but in the older palace built by the Hasmoneans close to the walls of the
8 temple area. **When Herod saw Jesus, he was very glad**. Hints of Herod's
interest in Jesus were given earlier in the gospel (9.9; 13.31); but the hearing
does not seem to have advanced matters, and it ended once again in a scene
of mockery. Presumably the question of kingship was raised again; Herod
11 evidently regarded it as a joke and sent the prisoner back in **an elegant robe**.[23]

13   **Pilate then called together the chief priests, the leaders, and the people.**
14 Neither Pilate nor Herod having found Jesus guilty **as one who was perverting the people** in the sense of dangerous political subversion, Pilate now
publicly delivered his decision. Having found no serious charge established,
he would let him off with a flogging (which was usual enough in such cases
(Acts 22.25), though here the Greek word is a general one and could mean
no more than a 'warning'). But at this point the crowd intervened to upset
the normal course of justice. Mark and Matthew provide the explanation[24]
that it was customary for Pilate to release one prisoner at the festival – which
also explains incidentally what the crowd may have been doing there: they
had come to claim their prisoner. Luke, apparently assuming this knowledge in the reader, merely represents the crowd as demanding that if any
prisoner were to be released it should be, not Jesus, but a certain Barabbas,
19 who because of his involvement in an **insurrection** against the Romans was
perhaps understandably the more popular of the two – nothing is said here
of any pressure being put on them by the Jewish authorities. Not merely this,
but they clamoured for Jesus' crucifixion, even though neither a Jewish court,
nor Herod, nor Pilate, had pronounced him guilty of a capital offence. The
result of their clamour, according to Luke, was what we can describe only as
23 a miscarriage of justice. **Their voices prevailed**. There was neither fair trial
nor formal verdict; it was the rule of the mob, connived at by the Roman
governor. Luke, by this means, reaches the same conclusion as Matthew and
Mark: it was the Jews who were guilty of Jesus' death, even though the punishment – crucifixion – was one that could have been inflicted only by the
Roman authorities. But his presentation, even if it exculpates Pilate from
direct responsibility for Jesus' death, leaves him with a doubtful reputation
for the administration of justice in his province, and also implies that it was
not so much the Jewish leaders as the people of Jerusalem themselves who
were responsible for Jesus' death.
26   By a very slight change Luke has made the following episode about **Simon
of Cyrene** bear a load of symbolic meaning. Simon does not just 'carry Jesus'
cross' as in Matthew and Mark; he is made to carry it *behind* Jesus, and so

---

[23] **Elegant** is a misleading translation. The Greek word means of any bright colour,
including white, suggesting royalty or luxury. The Revised Standard Version has *gorgeous
apparel.*
[24] The explanation has found its way into some ancient manuscripts of Luke (= verse
17: see the NRSV footnote), but is probably not part of the original text.

becomes the first to fulfil Jesus' demand of his followers, that they should "take up their cross . . . and follow me" (9.23).

27 **A great number of the people followed him**. Luke's interest in **the people** generally, as opposed to an inner group of followers, was perhaps his reason for mentioning this; and it gave him the cue for recording a further saying of Jesus, this time directed towards the women in the crowd,

28 **"Daughters of Jerusalem"**. The tone is prophetic, both in its language and in its intention. The women were weeping, ostensibly for Jesus – it was not unknown for women to be present at crucifixions to administer opiates. But Jesus' prophetic interpretation of their tears was that they presaged the fate of Jerusalem. Jesus had already uttered a similar prophecy about the future and its effects on women: "Woe to those who are pregnant and those who are nursing infants in those days!" (21.23). Here the same thing is expressed in different words, and an oracle from Hosea (10.8) is added, suggesting that the impending catastrophe would be more than a transient disaster. Rather

30 than endure it, people would **"begin to say to the mountains, 'Fall on us!',**

31 **and to the hills, 'Cover us.'"** The speech ends with a proverb: **"if they do this when the wood is green, what will happen when it is dry?"** To give the proverb its most natural application (though we cannot be sure that this is what was intended): if this can happen even to a righteous man and a harmless preacher, what may not happen when there are real revolutionaries at work? – a prophecy that was gruesomely fulfilled during the Jewish rebellion against the Romans, 66–70 CE.

34 **"Father, forgive them; for they do not know what they are doing."** Luke is the only evangelist to record this saying – if Indeed, he did so: a number of important manuscripts omit it, hence the double square brackets in the NRSV. In its setting, the prayer appears to be one for the executioners who were acting under Roman orders: they knew nothing of the issues involved and they must not be held to blame for the crucifixion. But we are doubtless meant to see more in the saying than this. The unconditional and radical character of God's forgiveness is often stressed in the gospel; and in Acts Luke makes it clear that this forgiveness was available even for the Jews, who, through ignorance and failure to understand (Acts 13.26ff.), had allowed their own Messiah to be crucified (Acts 2.36–8). They too had the excuse that 'they did not know what they were doing'.

In his gospel Luke often abbreviates an episode we know from Mark and Matthew and then adds a new element of his own. So here: the mockery is

39–43 described more briefly, but a new light is shed on it by the reactions of the two criminals crucified with him. To one of them, as to all the mockers, Jesus was a false pretender: his impending death proved the absurdity of his claims. But the other was ready to believe that Jesus would, nevertheless, 'come into his kingdom'[25] – that is, that there would be a sense in which the title over Jesus'

---

[25] Or *come in his kingdom*, i.e. as a true king. See the NRSV footnote.

head would be shown to be true. The criminal begged that through Jesus' 'remembrance' of him he too would have a place in that glorious kingdom the Messiah was to inaugurate. 'He got more than he asked for' is an old comment on this passage. Whatever theoretical picture the Jewish theologians drew of the afterlife, involving first a period of waiting, then general resurrection, judgment and apportionment of punishment and reward, there was a much simpler belief about the afterlife which most people held (as they always have) and which Jesus himself was able to use for purposes of teaching (as in the parable of the rich man and Lazarus): the individual would be judged by God and awarded appropriate punishment or reward immediately after death. It is this popular belief which seems to be reflected in Jesus' reply to the

43 criminal, **"today you will be with me in Paradise"**. 'Paradise' was originally the sumptuous garden of a Persian monarch. When the Jews used the word they probably imagined something like the Garden of Eden. Jesus' promise to the criminal was in language he could easily understand: God would grant him the reward of the just. His faith that Jesus was after all a 'king' made him the first to inherit the blessed destiny of all who acknowledged Jesus as Lord.

45 **The sun's light failed.** This is Luke's explanation of the darkness. If he meant that there was an eclipse (which is the usual meaning of the word he uses), his explanation is physically impossible: there can be no eclipse of the sun at full moon (the Passover was always at full moon), and in any case an eclipse lasts only a short time. A heavy sandstorm could have made the sun appear to 'fail'; but, Luke seems anyway to have regarded the darkness as supernatural, like the tearing of **the curtain of the temple**. Mark and Matthew both report that Jesus died with a cry, and interpret it as a prayer drawn from Psalm 22. Luke has another interpretation: it was the prayer from another

46 psalm (31.6), **"Father, into your hands I commend my spirit"**, which was a customary evening prayer before sleep (and so appropriate before death). It is possible that Jesus was heard using this prayer (or at least the word *eli*, which the original Hebrew contains); or perhaps it was an early Christian intuition that Jesus had made his own this serene Old Testament prayer (drawn from another of the 'righteous sufferer' psalms) and prefaced it with his characteristic address to God, **"Father"**.

47 The last word rests (as in Mark and Matthew) with the **centurion**. What impressed him was not the supernatural portents which (according to Matthew) accompanied Jesus' death so much as Jesus' bearing on the cross. But his exclamation is given in a form which would perhaps have come more naturally to a military officer than the theologically pregnant confession ('Son of God') attributed to him by Mark and Matthew: **"Certainly this man was innocent."**

At this the mood of the onlookers seems to change from mockery to

48 sympathy or remorse. With the rather stylized literary expression, **beating their breasts**, the crowd is described as already perhaps regretting its part in the crucifixion and preparing for the repentance which (as Luke will soon

describe in his second volume) will be induced in many of them by the preaching of the apostles.

49   Jesus' **acquaintances, including the women who had followed him from Galilee,** showed their loyalty by remaining within distance until the end. And Joseph of Arimathea, who had dissociated himself from the council's decision, obtained the body for burial from Pilate. Luke has his own explanation for this action. In Mark, Joseph's motive seems to be one of ordinary Jewish piety: no dead body must be left exposed after nightfall. In Matthew, Joseph is a secret disciple and acts out of loyalty to the master. But in Luke, Joseph takes his place among other pious Jews on the fringe of the gospel story
51   who were **waiting expectantly for the kingdom of God** and who, without
50   being disciples, were **good and righteous** (like Zechariah and Elizabeth, 1.6, and Simeon, 2.25); and his goodness and righteousness were shown in his concern to save Jesus from a common grave and to provide him with an honourable burial in a new tomb – one of the most meritorious of 'acts of charity'. In other words, Luke characteristically offers a moral explanation for Joseph's action, which in its main details he records exactly as it stands in Mark.

54   **It was the day of Preparation, and the sabbath was beginning.** This is a very precise note of time:[26] the sabbath began at sunset on what non-Jews would naturally call 'Friday evening'. Luke is carefully building up his effect. The women evidently meant to return, and we are told exactly how they
24.1 spent the intervening time and why they came back only on **the first day of the week** (Sunday morning) – if they had come earlier they would have broken the sabbath commandment. In what follows, the details (including the improbable one that they still hoped to anoint Jesus' body with spices) are as in Mark, but the emphasis is slightly shifted. The main fact in the story
3   is still that the tomb was empty (in this version they actually **went in**); but
4   this only made them **perplexed.** The important point is now the declaration of the angels – two angels have taken the place of one in Mark, but the effect is the same: the essential thing is the angelic vision, not the number of angels. No more than an echo remains of the puzzling promise that Jesus will meet his disciples in Galilee (Mark 16.7; Matthew 28.7); instead, Galilee is mentioned as the place where Jesus was when he uttered a prophecy of his resurrection. And attention is shifted from the mysterious fact of the empty tomb to the enlightening realization that the prophecy had been fulfilled. It was this realization that the women hastened to tell the apostles. Luke does
10   not name them until this point. His list agrees with that of Mark and Matthew except that Joanna (see above on 8.2) takes the place of Salome. Like both

---

[26] The Greek word means *dawning*, and seems an odd way of saying that the sabbath *evening* was beginning. Possibly the reference is to the evening star; or possibly the Greek phrase represents a Jewish idiom which was occasionally used for the beginning of the sabbath at dusk.

Mark and Matthew, he has his own explanation of why their experience did not pass straight into the proclamation of the first Christians: they were not believed; indeed, Peter had to go and see for himself.[27]

13 **Now on that same day.** This story occurs only in Luke; indeed all the gospels, having run closely together in their accounts of the trial and execution, diverge markedly when they come to the circumstances of the resurrection, and it is impossible to fit their accounts into a single coherent scheme. The reason for this may well be that the conviction that Jesus had 'risen from the dead' was not reached at the same time and in the same way by all the disciples, and many different stories about these critical days must have been current; we know from 1 Corinthians 15.5–7 that there were more appearances of the risen Christ than are recorded in the gospels. Each evangelist may have chosen to narrate the particular experiences which seemed to bring out most clearly the meaning of this almost unimaginable event, and we can expect to find a vein of deliberate teaching in the way each episode is narrated.

Luke's story, though the mysterious stranger and his mysterious disappearance give it a slightly eerie atmosphere, is nevertheless precise in its details. The name of the village is given, along with its distance from Jerusalem; and, though there are certain difficulties in identifying it,[28] there is every reason

18 to believe that it existed. One of the two disciples is also named: **Cleopas** (short for Cleopatros, a not uncommon name: he may have been the Clopas who was the husband of a certain Mary and possibly the brother of Joseph, Jesus' mother's husband, John 19.25). Presumably his home was at Emmaus; and the disciples' offer of hospitality rings true for the east: by early evening the main part of the day is thought to be over. The stranger made the proper

28 show of reluctance – **he walked ahead as if he were going on** – but no one liked to be on the road too late in the day (for darkness falls very rapidly in Palestine) and he soon gave in and stayed for a meal. At his sudden departure the disciples could still have had an hour or two's daylight to walk back rapidly to Jerusalem.

The drama of the story is created by Jesus' apparently deliberate incognito;

27 but its significance is concentrated in two points. First, Jesus **interpreted to them the things about himself in all the scriptures.** The various beliefs which Jesus' contemporaries held about the coming Messiah were based on

[27] If indeed Luke wrote verse 12: it is omitted by certain manuscripts.

[28] The present village of Amwas stands on the site of the important Roman town of Nicopolis, some 18 miles north-west of Jerusalem. From the third century this town was firmly believed to be the Emmaus of the gospel, and there are the remains of a large Byzantine basilica there. But the distance does not agree with Luke's figure of sixty stadia (**seven miles**). Another possibility is a village which was called Koloniyeh after the Romans had planted a 'colony' there, but which in Jesus' time had a name like Emmaus. This lies on the Jaffa road, some 4 miles north-west of Jerusalem. If this is the true site, the discrepancy in Luke's 'seven miles' is not too serious.

passages of scripture which could be interpreted as prophetic references to him. But the picture which was usually obtained from these sources was of a powerful figure who would have God-given resources to inaugurate a new age for his people. In the course of his teaching, Jesus had frequently tried to modify this expectation by replacing the traditional figure by another, the Son of Man, and by insisting on the suffering which must precede his vindication and glorification, both for himself and for his followers. Nevertheless he had not succeeded in preparing his disciples for the apparent catastrophe of the crucifixion, which they continued to find impossible to reconcile with any of their existing ideas of what a Messiah should be. It was only after the resurrection that they came to see that Jesus' humiliation and death did in fact 'fulfil' scripture as much as his glorification; or (to put it the other way round) that the scattered passages in the Old Testament about a 'righteous sufferer' pointed to the same person as those which were usually quoted in support of a powerful deliverer. Thus the new faith very soon gave to its adherents a key to understanding the underlying meaning of the scriptures in a way quite different from any held by the Jews; and Jesus is here described as giving his authority to this interpretation.

31 The second point of significance is the moment at which **their eyes were**
30 **opened, and they recognized him.** Jesus was at table with them, he **took bread, blessed and broke it.** These were exactly the actions he had performed at the last supper three days before, and continued to be the distinctive feature of the eucharist in the church. This was the moment at which the two strangely blinded disciples recognized Jesus; and it was the moment at which Christians continued to be particularly aware that their risen Lord was present with them.

They returned to Jerusalem and found that, meanwhile, Jesus had
34 **appeared to Simon** – that is, to Simon Peter. This is confirmed by Paul (1 Corinthians 15.4), though it is not narrated in any of the gospels. Jesus'
37 next appearance is also clearly recorded for a purpose. **They . . . thought that they were seeing a ghost**; and the emphasis on their being able to touch Jesus, and on his evidently quite human appetite, makes it clear that this is no sort of ghost story. Doubtless there were still many people when this gospel was written who thought they could explain away the resurrection appearances (and so discredit Christianity) by suggesting that the disciples had seen nothing more than a ghost. The evidence of the risen Jesus' tangibility is stressed in other places (John 20.27; 1 John 1.1) and continued to be important long after Easter day.

45 **Then he opened their minds to understand the scriptures.** Jesus' magisterial lesson in the right understanding of the Old Testament is repeated, but with an important addition: the message of repentance and forgiveness was
47 to be **proclaimed in his name to all nations.** How this came to be fulfilled is the subject of Luke's next volume, the Acts of the Apostles, and there is no real break in the story. Nevertheless the narrative up to this point has been

along the lines of the other gospels and needs to end, as they do,[29] with Jesus' last appearance on earth. So a brief summary is given of the events which fill the first chapters of Acts,[30] and the gospel ends, as it began, in the temple at Jerusalem. But this is not really the end. The disciples were only to 'begin' from Jerusalem. Luke has still to tell the story of how Christianity reached Rome.

[29] Except perhaps Mark. See above, p. 212, on the possibility of a lost ending of Mark.

[30] Some manuscripts make this summary correspond more closely with the account of the ascension in Acts 1. See the footnotes in the NRSV, and below on Acts 1.1–10.

JOHN

The prologue

The purpose of the gospel according to John is declared, not at the beginning, but at the end, "in order that you may come to believe[1] that Jesus is the Messiah" (20.31).

To anyone (other than a Christian) who understood what was meant by the term 'Messiah', it might have come as a surprise that a book should have to be written for this purpose. The Messiah, by definition, was a figure of power and glory. When he came, it would surely be impossible not to be aware of the fact. His destiny was to restore a kingdom of unprecedented splendour and justice to God's elect people. Once his reign had begun, it would hardly be necessary to write a book to prove that he had come.

Nevertheless, Christians were not deterred from calling Jesus 'Christ' (Messiah) even though the fact that the Messiah had come was not recognized by more than a handful of the human race, indeed not even by the Jews, who prayed for his coming in their daily prayers. For this technical term of Jewish religion seemed the natural way to describe one who had actually been among them on earth, who was now at God's right hand in heaven, and who was the source of new life for his followers. They were able to find Old Testament texts which not only prophesied his glory but also implied a destiny of suffering and rejection; and the more they reflected on the life and teaching of Jesus the better they began to understand the mysterious necessity that "the Messiah should suffer these things" (Luke 24.26) and that his reign was to be, at least for the present, unrecognized by all but a few.

They soon came to realize, however, that Jesus was more than this. He had power, not only over human hearts, but over elemental and demonic forces; he gave meaning, not only to human life and history, but to the whole created order; he belonged, not only to time, but to eternity. But if so, then the problem of his rejection became more acute than ever. If Jesus belonged to the very structure of the world, why did the world not accept him? How could one possibly explain the bitter reality of the crucifixion and the continuing persecution of his followers?

John's gospel is an attempt to answer these wider questions. The technical terms of Jewish expectation which are to be found in the other gospels – Messiah, Son of God, Son of Man – were no longer adequate to convey the depth and universality of the Christian experience. Accordingly, John uses a

---

[1] Or *continue to believe*: see the NRSV footnote on 20.31.

new vocabulary. Jesus is light, and life, and truth – words which belong more to religious poetry than to the prosaic language of narrative or doctrine, and which set Jesus in a much larger frame than could be provided by the traditional categories of Jewish religion. These words need no explanation, though they take on new depths of meaning as they are put to work in the course of the gospel.

The distinctive character of John's gospel is apparent in the way it begins. The other gospels, which had a more modest programme and were mainly concerned to show that Jesus was, in some sense, the Messiah of Jewish expectation, were each content to describe some of the circumstances in which this Messiah made his appearance on earth (though Luke's gospel, in the songs attributed to Zechariah and Mary, at least sets this appearance in a wider context of social change). But John, having so greatly enlarged the scale on which he proposed to tackle his subject, could not regard the story as beginning only with the birth or the first public appearance of Jesus. He needed some way of describing Jesus which would show him to have been an integral element in the created world from the beginning. Jewish thought had already reached towards this conception by affirming that the Messiah would be no afterthought of God (as it were to put right shortcomings that had emerged in his creation) but had in some sense (as 'the Name of the Messiah') existed from the beginning. To express a similar conception, John found another suggestive term which featured in the vocabulary of both 1.1 religion and philosophy: **the Word**.

No single English word conveys the associations which the word *logos* would have had for an educated Greek. It meant far more than a mere unit of spoken language: it included any articulate thought, any logical and meaningful utterance; it was that which gave order and shape to the process of thinking – proportion in mathematics, rational intelligibility in the study of the natural world, an ordered structure in any account of human affairs. It was almost equivalent to 'rationality'. As such, it was a convenient tool for philosophy – the Stoics, indeed, used the term *logos* for the immanent rational principle of the whole universe, the single divine system which (according to their philosophy) underlies the multiplicity of the visible world; and doubtless their use of the word had already begun to influence the everyday speech of countless Greek-speaking people who had never troubled to explore the theoretical system of the Stoic philosophers.

To a Greek-speaking Jew the term had a still wider range of meanings. In the Bible, God's 'word' was not only the means by which (as it might be through a prophet) God communicated with human beings and brought them into obedience to his law; it was also the expression of his relationship with the whole created universe: God said – and there was. God spoke – and it was done. "My word . . . shall not return to me empty, but it shall accomplish that which I purpose" (Isaiah 55.11). God's word was a manifestation of his creative power.

A term which embraced so many ideas could be put to many uses. For Philo of Alexandria, a near contemporary of the author of the gospel, whose life was devoted to the task of expressing the essence of the Jewish religion in terms borrowed from contemporary philosophy, the *logos* became a philosophical entity in its own right and seemed to offer the key to understanding the relationship between the transcendent God of the Bible and the world that is known to human senses. But there is no reason to think that John was addressing his gospel to readers who were accustomed to any particular or technical use of the term *logos*. They spoke Greek, and therefore shared the usual Greek understanding of it as a word with a wide range of meanings to do with the rational use of the intellect. But they were also familiar with Jewish traditions and knew something of the power and vigour associated in the Old Testament with the word of God. They were therefore prepared for this *logos* of John to mean a great deal more than can be expressed in English by 'word'; and it was for John to show, by some specimen phrases, in exactly what sense he wished to apply it to Jesus. The first eighteen verses of his gospel may be regarded as a kind of poetic introduction in which successive stanzas seek to draw out the implications of this single word *logos*.[2]

In the beginning. In the Greek, the first two words of the gospel are the same as the first two words of the Old Testament; and there can be little doubt that this echo is intentional. The first image brought to mind is the moment of creation. But whereas, in Genesis, the sentence continues with a statement about the first thing that happened – "God created the heavens and the earth" – here it goes on quite differently: the Word already **was**. It is as if something is being said, not about creation itself, but about the conditions under which creation was brought about. This was in fact an ancient line of thought. Surely God was not to be imagined as personally attending to every detail of the universe that was being brought into being? The omniscient intelligence which could be seen to underlie all created things, and which indeed made them intelligible to human reasoning, was surely not identical with God himself? – though some philosophers might have said so who denied the existence of any God beyond what is revealed in the rational system of the universe. An answer to these questions had already been supplied in some of the later writings of the Old Testament and Apocrypha: God was assisted at the creation by the figure of Wisdom.

---

[2] These verses are poetical in the further sense that they are more evocative than precise; hence many of them can be translated in more than one way, as can be seen from the NRSV footnotes. Moreover the sequence of thought seems less than perfectly logical; and it is possible (as some have supposed) that the writer did not compose the poem himself but found it already in existence and, in adapting it to his purpose, made changes and additions which interrupted its continuity and disturbed its logic. On the other hand, it is not to be expected of poetry – and certainly not of poetry inspired by the Hebrew scriptures – that it should say things in the order that seems logical to the western mind, any more than that each of the concepts it uses should be capable of exact definition.

The L O R D created me at the beginning of his work . . .
when he marked out the foundations of the earth,
then I was beside him, like a master worker.
(Proverbs 8.22,29–30)

With you is wisdom, she who knows your works
and was present when you made the world.
(Wisdom 9.9)

No Jew would ever have been tempted to think of this 'wisdom' as a separate deity, usurping the honour of the one true God. On the contrary, 'wisdom' provided a way of speaking of God with greater respect, avoiding the somewhat crude and anthropomorphic idea of God actually at work on the details of his creation, and yet conceding that, in the last analysis, this 'wisdom' was nothing other than God himself, though it was God conceived under the particular aspect of the physical and moral laws of the universe. Nevertheless, it was the way of religious poetry to allow this figure of 'wisdom' to take on almost a life of its own. Wisdom was "beside" God (Proverbs 8.30), it "went forth to make its dwelling among the children of men, and found no dwelling" (Enoch 42.2 – an apocryphal Jewish scripture compiled during the second and first centuries BCE). John clearly stands in this tradition when, in his opening sentences, he says similar things about the Word. Yet by using that term (instead of 'wisdom'), he brings this old image of Jewish religious poetry within the reach of a more philosophically minded reader. The Jesus who can be described in such terms is not a figment of the Hebrew imagination but has to do with those essential and rational principles of the universe
3 that must have existed from the beginning: **without him not one thing came into being.**

By a progression which is more poetical than logical, two further ideas
4 are associated with the Word: **life** and **light.** Both of these are developed as the gospel proceeds; but the second serves to lead into the next great
5 theme of the prologue. **The light shines in the darkness.** The concept of light presupposes its opposite. Light would not be recognized if there were no darkness with which to compare it. A scientist would doubtless express the matter differently; but a poet speaks naturally of a light that shines **in the darkness,** and goes on from there to imagine a kind of contest between light on the one hand and darkness on the other, the darkness surrounding the light and trying to quench it. This image is the first hint of the mystery with which the gospel will be concerned: the rejection of Christ by humankind. Christ (we must understand, though it is nowhere stated in so many words) is the Word, an agent of creation, a principle of the universe. As such he is eternal, and can never be **overcome** as a light can; but, just as the concept of light presupposes darkness, so the Word presupposes a world which does not understand and acknowledge. It need be no more paradoxical to say that

the divine Word was not received than to say that a light is surrounded by darkness.

But this raises a new question. If it was of the nature of the Word that, although integral to the created order, it could yet be ignored and rejected by human beings, what assurance was there that it would ever be recognized and acclaimed at all? The answer was that there must be 'witnesses' to it, men and women whose lives, being dedicated to the Word and entirely determined by it, would be powerful arguments for its existence and activity. Here was a way to understand that strange figure who always stood on the

6 first page of the Christian story. **There was a man sent from God, whose name was John** – the sentence is suddenly in the style of the Old Testament, and we are reminded at once of the other gospels, where it is as a man in the tradition of the Old Testament prophets – an ascetic preacher from the desert, with something of Elijah about him – that John the Baptist makes his appearance. He fulfils prophecies, he revives the long-silent gift of prophetic speech, he foretells his greater successor and places him in the flaming scenery of the last judgment – in short, a figure comprehensible only in a culture shaped by the Bible and conditioned by urgent expectation of a new world order that is about to come. But the writer of this gospel suggests a different and less exotic rôle for him, that of a witness: **he came to testify to the light**.

9 **The true light, which enlightens everyone, was coming into the world.** A strictly chronological scheme would yield a different order: Jesus' birth came before the adult witness of his contemporary, John the Baptist. But this is poetry, not history. John's sequence of ideas reflects, not the passage of time, but a movement of thought, a movement from the metaphysical implications of the Word which was 'with God in the beginning' to that moment in time when there was on earth a person – Jesus – whose appearance challenged humankind to accept the Word. The description of the moment of that appearance is the climax of the prologue. But lest it should be thought that its splendour commanded the assent of all who saw it, John first reminds his readers of the point already made: there was darkness around the light; the

10 Word was not received; it required witnesses to commend it. **The world came into being through him; yet the world did not know him.** That was true of the world in general. But certain individuals did recognize and accept him,

12 and these – that is, Christians, those **who believed in his name** – experienced a relationship with God which could be described as that of **the children of God**; for a new sense of the personal and intimate fatherhood of God was one of the distinctive marks of early Christianity.

14 **And the Word became flesh.** John makes no attempt to blunt the edge of this terrific proposition. The man Jesus was now at the right hand of God. That was an easy way of putting it, given the limitations of such naïvely pictorial language. (It was the way most early Christians did put it.) But this exalted Messiah was also – had always been – part of the structure of the

universe, the Word; and all this was somehow concentrated in one individual who fully shared the human condition. John had no alternative but to bring into one sentence words which would normally seem to belong to totally different worlds of discourse: **Word** and **flesh**.

And lived among us. The man Jesus was also the Word. An easier way to conceive of this double aspect of Jesus' person is that adopted by most New Testament writers: the two aspects are assigned to two different periods of time. After (and perhaps also before) his time on earth, Jesus was a figure of glory, seated at the right hand of God, superior to all heavenly and earthly powers. But when he was literally 'among us' he was simply man – a unique and exceptional man, no doubt, but, so far as his humanity went, indistinguishable from other men (except, as one New Testament writer will say, without sin). By contrast, John makes no such clear distinction between the heavenly and the earthly Jesus. Throughout his gospel he invests Jesus with something of the divinity and glory which belongs to the Word, even though this Word became absolutely flesh, even though Jesus was absolutely human. And so here: his brief description of the manner in which Jesus was **among us** contains more than a hint of a presence that was all the time something more than merely human, merely 'flesh'.

He **lived**. The translation is correct, but fails to convey any of the overtones of the Greek word, which originally meant 'dwell in a tent': it was 'in a tent' that God had dwelt when he first accompanied his people across the desert. Moreover, the Greek word recalled a Hebrew expression for the glory of God 'dwelling' on earth. He **lived among us** (or *had his tent-dwelling* among us) is therefore a phrase which, with its Old Testament associations, already suggests a more than human side to the period of Christ's humanity. The following words – **glory**, **grace** and **truth** – are equally charged with meaning by their use in the Old Testament, where they belong to the vocabulary of God's care for his people; yet almost all these words will take on new meaning as the gospel unfolds. For the present they serve as a summary of what it could be said that **we have seen** – that is, not the subjective impressions of one person or a group of people, but the essential double aspect of Jesus' time on earth, to which witness was borne by the whole community of those who had actually acknowledged him, whether after seeing him themselves or after hearing the testimony of others.

15 **John testified to him**. The synoptic gospels present a simpler view of John the Baptist's mission: he prophesied that a greater than himself would come, and a greater did come. But in this gospel John is not so much a prophet as a witness: he was the first to recognize and testify that a greater *had* come. Jesus' later arrival on the scene was such as, in a sense, to put one off the scent. It was John who was drawing the crowds; Jesus only came **after** (perhaps as a disciple, perhaps simply later in time). On the face of it, it was John, not Jesus, who marked the appearance of something radically new. But his real importance was in the testimony he gave that, despite appearances, Jesus was

one who 'ranked ahead of him', of another order altogether: **"he was before me"**.

17   **The law indeed was given through Moses**. This was a basic premise of Jewish religion. From this flowed the tremendous benefits and privileges, as well as the obligations, which the Jewish people believed they had received from God. The law was the expression and guarantee of the 'grace and truth' with which God had consistently treated his people. John boldly modifies this ancient belief: **grace and truth came through Jesus Christ**. Not that Jesus had replaced Moses altogether as the bearer of these benefits: Jesus had not annulled or superseded the law with its duties and privileges. It was rather that he had brought still greater blessings, **grace upon grace**.

18   **No one has ever seen God**. Pagan religions might speak lightly of gods appearing to human beings; but the seriousness with which the Jews took the idea of God forbade any such fantasy. God was far too terrible to be 'seen', at least before the terrifying confrontation at the last judgment. Therefore the Jesus who had indeed been 'seen', despite all the exalted titles given to him, was not in every sense identical with God, even if this gospel can go so far as to call him **God the only Son**.[3] He revealed God only to the extent that human beings could bear it. John uses what in Greek was an almost technical term for the inspired activity of one who imparted truths about God: **he has made him known**. People did not literally 'see' God in Jesus: this would have been inconceivable. But through Jesus they came to 'know' him.

The witnesses to the Messiah

19   **This is the testimony given by John**. Jesus' work and message burst upon the people of Palestine as something entirely new and original; but it had been immediately preceded by a movement which was itself quite out of the ordinary, that of John the Baptist. The gospels differ among themselves in the picture they draw of him, and drop occasional hints that there was a good deal more to say about him than they have chosen to record; and the contemporary historian Josephus also sketches a portrait of him which is recognizably of the same person and yet is seen from a quite different point of view. The main question to which the gospel-writers had to address themselves was this: the movement of John and the movement of Jesus were

---

[3] As can be seen from the NRSV footnote, the evidence of the manuscripts is divided on whether the writer actually called Jesus 'God'. Since the exact relationship of Christ to God was one of the most burning questions in the church in early centuries, it is perhaps not surprising that a verse which has such bearing on it as this one should have been quoted in different forms by theologians of different persuasions, and that these variations should have crept into the text. The version given here is attested by our earliest papyrus manuscripts (second century CE), and must therefore have been current within a century of the writing of the gospel. But another ancient reading, *the only Son . . . has made him known*, makes much easier sense.

each in their own way unique; yet the one came immediately before the other, and there were clear points of contact between them, so much so that it was apparently impossible to tell the story of Jesus without first saying something about John. What then was the connection between the two? Out of what was clearly a mass of tradition about John, the writers of the other gospels selected three points in particular which seemed to point towards an answer. First, John's appearance as a preacher in the wilderness fulfilled an Old Testament oracle about a voice crying, "In the wilderness prepare the way of the LORD" (Isaiah 40.3): his baptizing must be understood as part of this 'preparing'. Secondly, he was the precursor of someone much greater than himself – he had used words like those of the humblest of servants towards his master,

27 **"I am not worthy to untie the thong of his sandal"**. And thirdly (the most obvious point of contact), he had baptized Jesus.

John's gospel, where it uses the same material, uses it in a different way. The verse from Isaiah[4] becomes the phrase with which the Baptist describes

32 himself; and the sayings about his successor, and the description of **the Spirit descending . . . like a dove** (a phenomenon accompanying the baptism of Jesus, according to the other gospels), are all phrased, not as news, but as reminiscences. They describe, not what John did, but what he said. They are his 'testimony'. Accordingly no interest is shown in what was, after all, his main activity – baptizing. This (as we know from both Josephus and the other gospels) was the ritual on which all his teaching was focused, and presupposed an act of profound repentance. But for this writer its significance was that it was the prototype – the first inkling, as it were – of that infinitely

33 more empowering gift offered by Jesus to his followers, baptism **with the Holy Spirit**. Apart from that, John's baptizing was unimportant: this writer barely mentions that John baptized Jesus. For him, the whole importance of John lay, not in his being a baptizer, but in his being the first 'witness' to Jesus the Messiah.

This witnessing rôle is subtly emphasized at the beginning. John, while

28 working at a place called **Bethany across the Jordan**,[5] was accosted by a

19 deputation of **the Jews** from Jerusalem. This strikes us as an odd way of describing the opposition to John and Jesus – after all, Jesus and his disciples were 'Jews' themselves, and the population of Jerusalem was almost entirely Jewish. But in this gospel the other party in virtually every confrontation

---

[4] The verse is quoted, as in the other gospels, in the Greek version of the Septuagint, which puts the messenger, not the 'Lord's way', in the desert.

[5] The site of this **Bethany** had been forgotten even by the time Origen looked for it in the early third century CE, and there was a tendency to insert into the manuscripts the name *Bethabara*, the site of which could still be identified. An early tradition fixed the place of John's baptizing on the east bank of the Jordan, near the ford closest to Jericho, just below the small mountain where Elijah was believed to have ascended into heaven – for John had much about him which recalled Elijah, even though he is said here to have denied that he *was* Elijah.

with Jesus is called 'the Jews', and in each case these 'Jews' are evidently those who carried authority in the religious and legal institutions at the centre of national life. Here, they are represented by some of those concerned with the administration and service of the temple (**priests and Levites**), many of whom will have belonged to the Pharisaic party and could speak also for the

24 influential **Pharisees** in Jerusalem.

20 John's reply to this deputation is introduced by a curious phrase: **he confessed and did not deny it, but confessed.** In the Greek, as in the English, this sentence sounds cumbrous and repetitious. But the verbs would have sounded appropriate in a law court, and their emphatic repetition is surely deliberate. This was John's 'testimony' to Jesus, which he could not give unless he made it absolutely clear that his own rôle, however significant, was not such as could be in any kind of competition with that of Jesus. His questioners (characteristically for this gospel) had asked the wrong question. They evidently assumed that John would claim some special status to authorize his activity, and that this would be along the lines of – even a reincarnation of – one of the great prophetic figures of the Old Testament. But the question they should have been asking was about someone else; John's importance was simply as a witness to a person who was to come.

But this person was not merely one who was to come: he *had* come, though

26 he was one **whom you do not know.** One of the many current beliefs about the coming Messiah was that he already existed and might even already be about on earth, but that he was to remain 'unknown' until the day when he would be revealed. This idea was rich in possibilities for explaining the paradox that

11 Jesus, the Word, **came to what was his own, and his own people did not accept him.** Jesus conformed with the expectation of a hidden Messiah; but the way in which he came to be revealed was totally different from what his contemporaries expected. Indeed, he was hidden, at first, even from his first

31–2 witness: John says twice over, **"I myself did not know him."** There is evidence from the other gospels that John continued for some time to be in doubt about him. At this stage his testimony has to be confined to the statement

26 that this coming one stands somewhere **among you.**

But the next stage of John's testimony (separated by a day's interval) marks an advance: no longer, 'Such a person exists', but, 'This is the person I was

29 talking about'. **"Here is the Lamb of God."** By the time this gospel was written, the phrase had a rich store of meanings. The death of Jesus, occurring as it did in the course of the Passover festival, could be described as the sacrifice of the Passover lamb (1 Corinthians 5.7); and his glorious ascension into heaven is represented in the Revelation as the exaltation of a slaughtered Lamb in heaven (5.6–14). If John the Baptist used this phrase about Jesus he can hardly have foreseen all this, and the only hint of what he could have meant is in the sequel, **"who takes away the sin of the world".** There was no 'lamb' in the Jewish sacrificial system that could have had such atoning power; but the words **"who takes away the sin of the world"** are reminiscent

of just one passage in the Old Testament which describes a servant of God who was "like a lamb that is led to the slaughter" and who "bore the sin of many" (Isaiah 53.7,12). It is even possible that the Aramaic word used by the Baptist was one which meant both 'lamb' and 'servant'. If so, he may have been the first to recognize in Jesus the mysterious servant prophesied in Isaiah 53. But it is perhaps more likely that the phrase, or at least the idea it expressed, had come into Christian use by the time the gospel was written and was placed in the Baptist's mouth as a key part of his testimony. In any case, this is only the first of a series of related images in this gospel. Here Jesus is the Lamb, later he is the door of the sheepfold, and finally he is the shepherd himself.

The third stage of John's witness (again separated by the lapse of a day) is the moment when his testimony was accepted and believed by others who in turn became witnesses to Jesus. All the gospels necessarily place the gathering of the disciples near the beginning of the story; but here the interest is not so much in the fact that certain people decided to follow Jesus, and in the reasons why they did so, as in the building up of a chain of witnesses who, by their individual responses, would corroborate John's and each others' testimony. The first two were disciples of John and immediately recognized Jesus as, at

38 least, a **"Rabbi"** – here as elsewhere John keeps in mind readers unfamiliar with the culture and gives a translation, **Teacher**. Their question, **"where are you staying?"**, showed what they meant by it: a man of fixed abode who gathered a group of students – a kind of 'school' – around him. True, Jesus certainly deserved this title, and much of his work consisted of teaching; and the prosaic question about his lodging received a prosaic answer. But this preliminary testimony was soon overtaken by a more significant one.

41 One of the first two students told his brother, **"We have found the Messiah"** (again considerably translated by the writer). This led to the acceptance of the testimony by Simon Peter and his adherence to the group. In the other gospels the call of these two men takes place beside the Sea of Galilee. Here the setting is quite different, but John's account includes one of the most

42 certain facts in the New Testament: that Jesus gave Simon the name **Cephas**, of which a translation is once more provided: **Peter**.

43 The chain of witnesses continues with **Philip**. Philip appears in the lists of the twelve given in the other gospels. His testimony is much the same as

45 Andrew's: **"We have found him about whom Moses in the law and also the prophets wrote"** – the person, that is to say, to whom so many passages of the Old Testament were believed to point forward, the Messiah, the Christ. It was not in itself implausible that this Messiah should turn out to be identical with a particular man Jesus, of known parentage (**Joseph**) and home (**Nazareth**): many believed that the Messiah would appear *incognito*. But what the next witness, Nathanael, found hard to accept was that this incognito should be so complete. Nazareth was a small, remote place without even a mention

46 in the Old Testament to give a clue to its future distinction. **"Can anything**

good come out of Nazareth?" Nevertheless, his initial doubt soon yielded to recognition, and he was able to give the most comprehensive testimony so

49 far: **"You are the Son of God! You are the King of Israel!"**

Nathanael is not in any surviving list of the twelve, and in fact it is not said here that he became a disciple (though he makes another appearance with the disciples in 21.2). He is brought in, it seems, precisely because of his value as a witness, indeed the last and most decisive witness in the series. Jesus

47 said of him, **"Here is truly an Israelite in whom there is no deceit!"** This was high commendation. First, he was (though Jewish) not one of 'the Jews', Jesus' enemies, but 'an Israelite', that is, an inheritor of the promises made by God to the Israelites of scripture. Secondly, he was 'without deceit' – the essential quality of a reliable witness (Proverbs 12.17, "a false witness speaks deceitfully"). But his testimony was also important because it was independent. He had come to believe in Jesus, not, like the others, through the word of his friends, but by personal experience of Jesus' exceptional powers. For how had Jesus come to know about him? Was it a guess? Had he a gift of prophecy? This time it was Jesus' turn to be a witness. If you wished to give evidence about a scene you had witnessed, you could be asked about the exact place and time. The question might take the form (as in Susanna 54), "Under what tree did you see . . .?" Jesus passed the test, and then went

51 on to cap the series of testimonies with a startling statement of his own: **"you will see heaven opened and the angels of God ascending and descending upon the Son of Man"**.

Here again, the synoptic gospels preserve elements out of which this saying could have been constructed. At Jesus' baptism he saw "the heavens torn apart" (Mark 1.10); immediately after, in the temptation story, "angels waited on him" (Mark 1.13); and there is a number of places where Jesus appears to refer to himself in the same oblique way as the Son of Man. But even if these elements are the material out of which this saying in John's gospel was composed, the result suggests a quite different picture. Jacob "dreamed that there was a ladder set up on the earth, the top of it reaching to heaven; and the angels of God were ascending and descending on it" (Genesis 28.12). Grammatically, the last word in the Hebrew could equally well mean 'on *him*', that is, on Jacob; and in due course Jewish scholars began to be attracted by this possible interpretation. Jacob, after all, was Israel, and the Israel on earth surely had some kind of spiritual counterpart in heaven. Might it not be that the verse in Genesis was intended to illustrate the relationship of the earthly and the heavenly Israel? We do not know how much, if any, of this speculation was going on or would have been known to John, but it is tempting to see a similar train of thought here: the promise to Nathanael was that he, a true Israelite, would see the true Israel in heaven and its true counterpart (Jesus, the Son of Man) on earth. At any rate, the allusion to the Jacob story is unmistakable, and the image is one that emphasizes what (at least for John) was an essential feature of the title 'Son of Man': it meant a figure whose destiny was being played out simultaneously on earth and in heaven.

2.1 **On the third day there was a wedding.** We can fill in a few of the details. Cana was a small town about 9 miles south-east of Nazareth. It was the home town of Nathanael (21.2) and a place visited more than once (according to this gospel) by Jesus. Certainly his family was well known there, for the mother of Jesus was present at the festivities, helping with the domestic

2 arrangements (for only male guests were invited). **Jesus and his disciples had also been invited**, whether because of a family connection or out of a new respect for him as a teacher, in which case it would have been normal to welcome those who had begun to form a regular group of disciples around him. They will have attended, not merely to enjoy the hospitality, but to assist the bridegroom in the formalities and the entertainment, which were a necessary part of the wedding and which usually went on for several days.

On one level, the story simply describes how Jesus saved his host a serious embarrassment. He had arrived with a number of extra guests, but perhaps without bringing the kind of contribution expected of them – food and wine. If so, his action could be understood as a miraculous resourcefulness in the face of an obligation which his chosen way of life made it impossible to meet out of his own resources – the story of the temple tax found in a fish's mouth is on the same lines (Matthew 17.24–7). In any case he acted with great discretion. The other guests were spared the shock of knowing

8 anything about it, and even the **chief steward** (who was probably a kind of head waiter or master of ceremonies) was not in the secret.

Are we to believe that such a thing really happened? Legends of turning water into wine clustered round the pagan god Dionysus and could have attached themselves to Jesus; many such miraculous stories soon began to be told about the boy Jesus, and this episode, when his mother was present, could well have originally belonged to such a collection. The final comment of the steward about good and inferior wine – it is remarkable that the story leads up to a saying, not of Jesus, but of an outsider – could well have triggered a story or even a parable of Jesus, beginning, 'It is was if someone at a wedding, where the wine was running out . . . ', which in due course came to be told as an actual event.

However this may be – and only those who cannot accept the possibility of miracle need be forced to deny that it could be true – the story clearly has not gained its place in this gospel simply as a domestic episode with a

11 miraculous dénouement. John describes it as the first of Jesus' **signs** by which **he revealed his glory**; and there are clear hints of symbolism in a number of

1 the details. It took place **on the third day**, which is by no means an obvious way of linking it to what has gone before, but might make the reader think of the greater miracle of Jesus' resurrection. In the brief dialogue between Jesus

4 and his mother, the sentence **"Woman, what concern is that to you and to me?"** is not just (as it might seem to us) a brusque reply. The tone is slightly

formal ("**Woman**" would have been perfectly respectful, though perhaps a little distant) and the idiom is the same as that used by the demons to Jesus in Mark 1.24 and 5.7, suggesting that he and his mother had more serious

6 concerns in view of an 'hour' that was to come. Again, the **six stone water jars** were nothing out of the ordinary, and their impressive size simply underlines the miraculous abundance of wine created by Jesus; but when John adds the detail that they were of the kind used **for the Jewish rites of purification** we can be sure that we are meant to see a deeper significance: the ritual observances of the Jews were about to give place to the spiritual sacraments of the Christians, which would give new meaning to the ceremonial drinking of wine. Indeed, the saying which rounds off the episode, though it has a proverbial ring in the mouth of the steward, bears more than a hint of a saying of Jesus about new wine (Mark 2.22), and suggests that he had indeed come to offer something new in place of the old rites of the Jewish religion.

12 **After this he went down to Capernaum.** John gives a quite different picture of Jesus' movements from that in the other gospels. There, Jesus makes Capernaum his base for much of his work in Galilee; here, he makes only one brief visit to it. Again, in the other gospels Jesus (after his baptism) makes only one pilgrimage to Jerusalem, the pilgrimage which ends in his death; all the Jerusalem episodes are therefore concentrated in the last few days of his life. But in John's gospel Jesus makes several journeys to Jerusalem – a fairly frequent pilgrimage to attend the great festivals was an obligation he is unlikely to have neglected – and this scheme allows his drastic action in the temple to be placed near the beginning of the gospel instead of towards the end. If we wish to know in what order things actually happened, we have to make our choice between the two versions and allow for the fact that one or other (or both) may have been deliberately rearranged in order to bring out better the significance of each group of events.

15 **Making a whip of cords.** This is one of the details by which John conveys a somewhat more violent scene than the other gospels. With this whip Jesus apparently **drove all of them** out of the temple precincts – a barely credible feat for one man, and we should probably still regard it (as in the other gospel accounts – see above on Mark 11.15–19) more as a prophetic gesture than as an attempted *coup*. When the Old Testament prophets carried out such

16 gestures they added an explanation of their action. Jesus does the same: "**Stop making my Father's house a marketplace!**" – which is a different explanation from that given in the other gospels and appears to be an allusion to the last words in the book of Zechariah (14.21), "there shall no longer be traders in the house of the LORD of hosts on that day" – and Jesus' action proclaims that 'that day' has now arrived. For the disciples, on the other hand, the

17 episode came to have another meaning: "**Zeal for your house will consume me**" is a quotation from Psalm 69.9, and the subject of that psalm is one of the nameless righteous sufferers of the Old Testament: even the man's devotion and piety towards the temple had been held against him. These

words of scripture seemed the perfect comment on Jesus' action and its consequences.

18 **"What sign can you show us for doing this?"** As in the other gospels, the action inevitably provoked a controversy. The reply of Jesus is a saying that is reported by other New Testament writers in other forms and contexts. Speaking sacrilegious words against the temple could be a serious offence (it nearly cost Jeremiah his life, Jeremiah 26.7–19); and the accounts of Jesus' trial suggest that this was one of the charges against him. It caused the evangelists some embarrassment: could Jesus really have threatened to destroy the temple? Mark calls it "false testimony" (14.57); but in the form in which John reports it, Jesus was not so much attacking the temple as claiming that, *if* it were destroyed, he could rebuild it in three days. With characteristic irony John makes the Jews take this literally: the temple had been begun by Herod the Great in 20–19 BCE and was not in fact finished until 63 CE, though

20 the main work may have been completed after **forty-six years** – by, say, 27 CE, which is about the time this conversation might have taken place. It is pedantic to ask whether John knew that the work continued for over thirty years afterwards. The point was simply to contrast the immense labours of the builders with Jesus' apparently grandiose claim to accomplish something comparable in three days. The claim was absurd – taken literally; but of course the Jews, as so often in this gospel, had missed the point. And here the evangelist offers what is likely to have been his own solution to the riddle

21 of Jesus' temple saying: **he was speaking of the temple of his body**, a hidden meaning that would come to light only after the resurrection.

23 **Many believed in his name.** The response to Jesus' 'signs' was positive. How could it be said, therefore, that "his own people did not accept him" (1.11)? The answer would come in the sequel; but meanwhile Jesus was not deceived, for he had a kind of psychic power, which he manifested on more

25 than one occasion, by which **he knew what was in everyone.**

3.1 **Now there was a Pharisee named Nicodemus.** 'The Jews' did not necessarily present a united front against Jesus. Here was one of their 'leaders' who was sympathetic, though he evidently felt it necessary to keep his visit secret,

2 coming by night. He recognized Jesus as a teacher (**"Rabbi"**) like himself, and acknowledged that the 'signs' he performed indicated that he had divine authorization. Nevertheless, his function in the narrative is a humble one. He simply provides the questions and comments that are needed to draw out a discourse from Jesus, and his main contribution is of a kind that often occurs in this gospel, that of the 'idiot question': by understanding a say-

4 ing of Jesus in its most literal and banal sense (**"how can anyone be born after having grown old?"**) he gives the cue for a more subtle explanation from Jesus. Indeed, the whole episode is characteristic of the way in which the writer of this gospel presents the teaching of Jesus, a way that is notably different from that of the other gospels. In them, Jesus' teaching takes the form of brief and memorable sentences, usually evoked by some question or

incident, sometimes running over into a parable or illustration, but never offering a systematic development of a particular line of thought. Even where we find substantial paragraphs entirely devoted to teaching (as in the Sermon on the Mount, or in the discourse on the future) they turn out to consist of collections of sayings, many of which were remembered separately and were brought together only later into a composite discourse. But in this gospel the style of teaching is entirely different. Starting from a particular episode or question or comment, Jesus develops his thought on a particular subject in such a way as both to refute the objections of his adversaries and to deepen the understanding of the gospel's readers. Occasionally his words are reminiscent of sayings recorded elsewhere; but more often they are expressed in the more sophisticated and philosophical idiom which is characteristic of this gospel. Theoretically, it is possible that Jesus spoke like this, and that we have here an authentic recollection of his teaching which is unaccountably missing elsewhere. But this is hardly the most likely explanation. The sayings in the other gospels are pungent, poetic and for the most part easily memorable. Many of them are in exactly the form to be expected in a Semitic language, and it is not difficult to imagine how they could have been preserved in people's memory until they came to be written down. By comparison, the discourses in John are literary and artificial. They are cast in the form of monologues or dialogues such as are familiar from some of the philosophical or religious literature of the time; they are carefully composed around a group of concepts which occur again and again as the gospel proceeds; and they betray a writer composing in his study rather than a teacher responding spontaneously to the questions of his hearers. In other words, it is hard to imagine Jesus delivering the discourses that are attributed to him in this gospel. But neither (in all probability) did he deliver the Sermon on the Mount in the form in which we have it in Matthew. The gospels present us with different attempts to gather the teaching of Jesus into a form which would bring out its meaning and be relevant to the needs of subsequent generations of Christians. The author of this gospel has done this in what we recognize as a more studied and literary way than the others. If, in the process, he has recast it in a somewhat different idiom, it is still possible that he has come at least as near to its essential meaning as any other New Testament writer.

3 **"No one can see the kingdom of God without being born from above."** This saying, introduced by the solemn and distinctive formula which so often goes with a pronouncement of Jesus in this gospel (**"Very truly, I tell you"**) is the substance of the discourse; the rest, in a sense, is commentary. But it contains a significant ambiguity which can hardly be reproduced in an English translation. The word rendered **from above** also means *anew*; and this is how Nicodemus understood it when he responded with his 'idiot question' about the impossibility of being literally 'born again'. Jesus' reply stays awhile with this meaning. The idea that, by committing oneself to a new religion or philosophy, one might be 'reborn', was a familiar one in antiquity and was

immediately adopted in Christianity. The moment when this 'rebirth' took place was obviously baptism (which is actually called 'rebirth' in Titus 3.5).

5 The elements of Christian baptism were the **water**, which symbolized the washing away of sin, and a new **Spirit** which was received; of these, it was the Spirit which (at least for this writer) was mainly responsible for the experience of rebirth. It has already been said in the prologue (1.13) that those who accept Jesus as Christ are born, "not . . . of the will of the flesh . . . but of God". Here the same reality is expressed by means of the psychology of flesh and spirit (see below on Romans 8.5–8). 'Flesh' is the whole human person as it were in its crude state, untouched by God; physical birth by itself can bring forth nothing more. 'Spirit' is that aspect of the personality which is capable of responding to God and which is brought to life when the Spirit of God touches it. The argument is an example of the old philosophical principle that 'like begets like'. If Christian baptism was 'by the Holy Spirit' it

6 evidently caused a rebirth in the human spirit – **"what is born of the Spirit is spirit"**. Whatever Jesus may originally have meant, John makes sense of it in terms of the Christian experience and understanding of baptism.

5 And this seems to yield a clear rule for church life. Jesus said, **"no one can enter the kingdom of God without being born of water and Spirit"**. No salvation for those who are not baptized! But it is characteristic of this gospel to lead us up the path and then show us how wrong we are. This time it is done by a parable. John's gospel contains no explicit 'parables', but there are illustrations which, like the parables in the other gospels, invite one to

8 do some thinking for oneself. **"The wind blows where it chooses"** is one of these. The point of comparison is the freedom and unpredictability of the wind. If you think Christian 'rebirth' happens according to a rule, beware! It is not tied to physical laws and processes like physical birth, but is as sudden, as unpredictable and as impossible to control as a gust of wind. For 'wind', in Greek as well as Hebrew, is the same word as 'spirit'. **"So it is with everyone who is born of the Spirit."**

But this is not all. We still have the second meaning of the phrase to con-

3 sider, **"being born from above"**. This suggests a whole new line of thought. Baptism is something which happens on earth; it does not follow that the

12 person reborn will learn **heavenly things**. But if rebirth is also 'from above', then it must also introduce us to the world above. The clue to this is in Christ himself. Rebirth is faith in Christ; and Christ is a figure who belongs

13 to both worlds. The title which most clearly brings this out is **Son of Man**. It has already occurred once (1.51) with precisely this significance of uniting the two worlds. And here are two more Son of Man sayings that make the same point. This figure is one who is not only a special and perhaps representative Man on earth; he has also a place at the right hand of God in heaven. The Son of Man, by definition, belongs to both worlds; and if Jesus was in fact (as he claimed to be in a number of sayings) the embodiment of this Son of Man conception, then (since John thought of his two rôles as

simultaneous) he was the unique link between the two worlds: **"No one has ascended into heaven except the one who descended from heaven, the Son of Man."** And how was the believer helped by this? The Son of Man sayings in the other gospels throw little light on this question. The Son of Man was to suffer and to die: how then could he help the believer to draw near to heaven and be reborn 'from above'? John's version of these sayings (for that is what

14 verse 14 appears to be) is that the Son of Man must be **lifted up**. This had at least two possible meanings – lifted up on the cross, lifted up to heaven – which could be said to have been fulfilled in what had happened to Jesus. But for the present we are left to grapple with a single image from the Old Testament. To bring to an end an attack of snakes on the people of Israel in the wilderness,

> the LORD said to Moses, "Make a poisonous serpent, and set it on a pole, and everyone who is bitten shall look at it and live." So Moses made a serpent of bronze, and put it upon a pole; and whenever a serpent bit someone, that person would look at the serpent of bronze and live. (Numbers 21.8–9)

The serpent, according to later tradition, was 'raised on high' by Moses; it was a 'symbol of deliverance' for the people (Wisdom 16.6). In the same way (we are to suppose), by 'looking at' and believing in Jesus in the various ways

15 in which he was 'lifted up', the Christian may find deliverance, **have eternal life**, and so be brought by the Son of Man to heaven.

16   **"For God so loved the world."** Is Jesus still speaking? The original text had no inverted commas and so left the question open. Modern translators have to make their choice. Perhaps in fact it makes little difference. The whole discourse is a commentary on some basic affirmations of Jesus, and is more the work of the writer than a transcript of a speech. The writer's task was to show what Jesus meant, and it does not greatly matter how much of the commentary is placed in Jesus' mouth. These final paragraphs introduce a new thought that will be greatly developed later on: that the coming of the Son was a consequence of God's love for the world. But they also deal with a possible misconception. Mention of the Son of Man suggests judgment; for, in the classic Old Testament passage that lies in the background (Daniel 7), it is at God's judgment that he makes his triumphant appearance. But if now

13 (at the time of writing) this Son of Man has already appeared and **ascended into heaven**, does this mean that it is too late for any more rebirth? Are we already lined up for judgment? Is our fate already sealed? The answer lies in a radical reformulation of traditional beliefs about God's judgment. The old conception was of a moment at the end of time when everyone, living and dead, will be summoned to appear before the divine tribunal. To some extent that picture may still be valid; but now, much of what was traditionally thought of as belonging to the ultimate future must be realized as taking place

19 in the present. **This is the judgment** – here and now. It has begun, but it

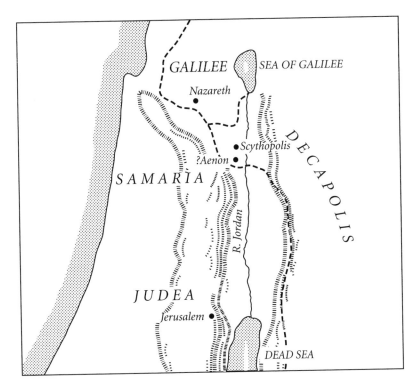

consists in the challenge presented by Jesus: we are judged at the moment when we declare for or against the light. Rebirth, leading to salvation, is still
17 an option for all. In this sense it can be said that **"God did not send the Son into the world to condemn the world, but in order that the world might be saved through him"**.

From Judea to Samaria

22, 23 **Jesus baptized . . . John also was baptizing.** This gospel records a period when both men were apparently doing identical work simultaneously. Such a period is not allowed for in the other gospels; indeed it is implied that Jesus did not begin his public activity until John had been imprisoned (Mark
24 1.14). John's gospel explicitly contradicts this: **John, of course, had not yet been thrown into prison.** There was a period when both John and Jesus were 'baptizers'.

Nevertheless, the activity of these two men was quite distinct. First, with
23 regard to geography: **John . . . was baptizing at Aenon near Salim.** Unfortunately we cannot be sure where this was. 'Aenon' is probably derived from the Aramaic word meaning 'springs', and even in early centuries travellers were unable to locate 'Salim'. By the sixth century two possible sites had been

identified, one of which was at the northern end of that part of the Jordan valley which runs from the Sea of Galilee to the Dead Sea; a third has been suggested in modern times to the north of Samaria. All these sites were well 22 away from **the Judean countryside** where Jesus was baptizing lower down the Jordan valley. The two baptizers were some distance apart, probably in two different political territories.

Secondly, even if they were both baptizing, they were not really comparable. This has already been shown by John's 'testimony' (1.26–30), and the reader is given a further reminder of that testimony here, along with a brief parable: 29 the **friend of the bridegroom** – roughly equivalent to our 'best man' – has a necessary but subordinate rôle on the wedding day. (Jesus uses the same illustration of a wedding to contrast his own activity with that of others 25 in Matthew 9.15.) The conversation arose out of a **discussion about purification... between John's disciples and a Jew.**[6] Doubtless there were many such discussions: the 'baptizing' carried out by both was quite independent of the normal 'purification' rituals of the Jews, but was clearly related to them in some way. John's baptism certainly had some connection with existing ritual; but Jesus, who had turned water intended for ritual purification into wine, had a baptism 'in the Spirit' which gave it an altogether new dimension. It may be also that John's followers were looking askance at the success of Jesus. Whatever John himself may have said, a certain sense of competition may have persisted between the two groups, and if this was still alive at the time the gospel was written it could explain the particular emphasis with which, on several occasions, John the Baptist is made to disclaim any rivalry with Jesus.

Finally the difference is brought out in terms already explored in the previous discourse. Once again there can have been no indication in the original text whether verses 31–6 are intended to be read as a speech of John or as a comment of the writer. This time the NRSV chooses the second alternative. 'Coming from above', 'witness', 'Spirit' and 'judgment' are all concepts which have already been put to use. Here they stand in a new combination and serve to summarize the stage reached so far in defining the status and authority of Jesus, with the additional notion that accepting Jesus' testimony is also certifying (literally, *setting a seal on*) the truth of God 36 that is revealed through him. The only surprise is the word **wrath**, which is never used elsewhere in this gospel. But in other New Testament instances (see especially on Romans 1.18) it occurs with little sense of divine anger or vengeance, but rather seems to stand for the inevitable consequences of sinful acts – which is what this gospel means by 'judgment'.

---

[6] Normally this gospel has 'the Jews', and some manuscripts give this. It has often been thought that the more difficult reading, given here, conceals an early corruption, possibly of *Jesus* or of *those with Jesus*.

In John's gospel the opposition to Jesus always comes from 'the Jews', that is, people of influence in Jerusalem, represented sometimes by the priests or
4.1 chief priests, sometimes (as here) by **the Pharisees**. Exactly what had aroused them on this occasion is not made clear. It has just been said (3.26) that Jesus was baptizing and that crowds were flocking to him; but now a correction is
2 made: **it was not Jesus himself but his disciples who baptized.** This certainly matches better with the other gospels, where it is taken for granted that Jesus was not a 'baptizer'. But in this gospel Jesus certainly had a baptizing period, whether or not he did the actual baptizing himself. (The correction, in fact, is impossible to reconcile with John's narrative and may have been added to by a later editor to remove the apparent discrepancy with the other gospels.) In the face of some sort of threat from the Pharisees, Jesus brought this period to an end and set out for Galilee.

4 **But he had to go through Samaria.** In practical terms this was not absolutely necessary. It was possible to travel from the lower Jordan to Galilee without climbing into Samaritan hill country. But it was common for Jewish travellers (despite the hostility of the Samaritans) to take the higher road through the mountains of Samaria: walking there was very much easier than in the stifling climate of the Jordan valley. Jesus' route was therefore perfectly normal. Moreover, there are several episodes in the other gospels which illustrate Jesus' attitude towards the feud between Jews and Samaritans. In part at least, this encounter in John's gospel has the same intention. But it may also make its point by a subtle contrast with scriptural antecedents. On more than one occasion in the Old Testament a chance meeting at a well led to love
6 and marriage: this well itself, **Jacob's well**, was enough to make one think of the love story of Jacob and Rachel (Genesis 29). There are moments in the course of Jesus' meeting at the well (particularly the woman's protestation that she has no husband) which could be read as hints that the story might have had a similar outcome; and these throw into sharper relief the totally different and unexpected significance of the encounter.

Near the place where the road which Jesus would have taken from the Jordan valley joins the mountain road from Jerusalem, there is a deep well. Archaeological evidence has shown that it was in continuous use between 1000 BCE and 500 CE. There is no other well in the area, and there can be no doubt that it was here that Jesus stopped on his journey. Later in
12 the conversation it is explained why it was called 'Jacob's well'. It was **"our ancestor Jacob, who gave us the well, and with his sons and his flocks drank from it"**. This too fits the spot. Nearby was the ancient city of Shechem (in ruins by Jesus' time), which had particular associations with Jacob (Genesis 33.18–20; Joshua 24.32), and the burial place of Joseph, Jacob's son, is still venerated a few hundred metres away. Even if the neighbouring settlements all had springs of their own (as they have today), the well would have been important for watering herds of cattle and would have been kept in constant
6 use. The tradition that this was **Jacob's well** does not rest on any text in the

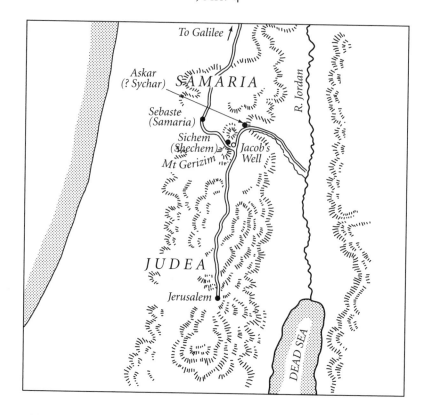

Old Testament but was doubtless already well established in the time of Jesus. It was beyond doubt the same 'Jacob's Well' which is still shown to visitors

5 today. The **Samaritan city called Sychar** is likely to have been on the site of the modern village of *Askar*, less than a mile away; though the name may conceal a reference to Shechem, by then a mere village, which was very much closer.

Why should a Samaritan woman have walked out from Sychar (where

7 there was probably a spring) to **draw water** at this well? It was a very deep well, and it is possible that its water was thought to be exceptionally pure or even medicinal (this was certainly the case as recently as the nineteenth century). At any rate, from this point on the story fits its setting perfectly. Jesus was in Samaria – that is to say, in a country of people who, though closely related to the Jews, had their own customs and religion and were liable to be unfriendly to Jewish visitors. The distrust was mutual, and a generation later it found expression in a decree that all Samaritan women must be regarded by strict Jews as ritually 'unclean'. 'Unclean' persons automatically made their household vessels 'unclean'. It followed that Jews who wished to remain ritually clean could not eat or drink from the utensils of a

Samaritan woman. In John's words (or possibly those of an early editor – not
9 all ancient manuscripts include them), **Jews do not share things in common
with Samaritans**. This was true by the time the gospel was written. That it
was true in the time of Jesus is less certain; but the anachronism (if it is one)
is not serious. Relations were certainly strained between the two races, even
if the decree about Samaritan women was not yet in force.

There was therefore some justification for the disciples' astonishment when
27 they found Jesus **speaking with a woman**. There was no Jewish convention forbidding a man to converse with a female stranger, but proverbial
wisdom warned against the undesirable consequences which might follow;
moreover there was a fairly strong prejudice against the idea of a learned
teacher spending time giving instruction to women. The fact that the woman
was a Samaritan may have made the scene which greeted them even more
surprising.

These problematic aspects of the meeting are soon forgotten, however, in
the light of the conversation which ensues. First, the simple request of Jesus
10 for a drink leads into some teaching about **"living water "**. This expression,
in the Greek, can also mean fresh or running water, so that the woman's
misunderstanding – which could possibly have been meant as a sexual insinuation, though it is also an example of John's characteristic device of the 'idiot
question', enabling Jesus to give further teaching – is not wholly implausible.
Her mind remains on the level of wells and buckets; Jesus is speaking (in
14 words that Jewish writers sometimes liked to use of the law of Moses) of **"a
spring of water gushing up to eternal life"**.

Then the conversation makes a fresh start. Telepathic knowledge (as we
would call it) marked a man as a prophet. If a prophet, then possibly the
Messiah himself – an inference which the Samaritans may have been particularly ready to draw, since they accepted only the first five books of the Old
Testament and the only reference there to a coming one was to a 'prophet like
Moses' (Deuteronomy 18.18). The reaction of the woman was thus typically
29 Samaritan (though many Jews might have asked the same question): **"He
cannot be the Messiah, can he?"**

But again some deeper teaching is worked into the conversation. Just
as, for the Jews, one of the tasks of the Messiah (or at least of a 'prophet
who was to come', 1 Maccabees 4.46) would be to restore the purity of the
temple worship at Jerusalem, so, according to Samaritan belief, the coming
Teacher would reconsecrate the Samaritan sanctuary which now lay in ruins
on Mount Gerizim. For the Jews, the place God 'chose as his habitation to put
his name there' (as Deuteronomy 12.5 puts it) was unquestionably Jerusalem.
But if one referred only to the first five books of the Bible, as the Samaritans
did, there was an equally good case for saying it should be Gerizim, one of
the three great mountains of the country, to which the woman could have
20 pointed with a wave of the hand when she spoke of **"this mountain"**. (She

and Jesus were actually at the foot of it.) Jesus' attitude to this dispute was
22 unashamedly Jewish: **"You worship what you do not know; we worship what
we know."** Even if the Jewish religion seemed exclusive, it was potentially
universal: **"salvation is from the Jews"**. For many Jews, Jerusalem itself may
have been mainly a symbol: it was not the actual city with its temple which was
important, but the deeper realities it stood for. Nevertheless they all felt the
need for a focus to their worship. Their conception of God was transcendent,
but it was still localized. Jerusalem was the place on earth that God had made
particularly his own and which inspired the greatest reverence. To this, Jesus
23 now opposed the concept of worship **in spirit and truth.** By the time this was
written, Christians (few of whom were in Jerusalem) had necessarily begun
to think of their worship as independent of any particular place; but that it
should be 'in spirit' did not mean merely that it required no special sanctuary
or ceremonies, but that it related to God, who is spirit and who therefore has
that freedom and spontaneity which go with spirit or 'wind'. As for 'truth',
the whole gospel is devoted to demonstrating that the truth of God is known
in and through Jesus, who becomes the new focus of worship for Christians,
25 as well as carrying the authority[7] to **proclaim all things** which, even from a
Samaritan perspective, belonged to a coming Messiah.
33 **"Surely no one has brought him something to eat?"** This time it is the
disciples who keep the conversation going by their prosaic misunderstanding
32 of Jesus' words, **"I have food to eat that you do not know about."** But then a
few verses follow which read more like a recollection of some isolated sayings
35 (in the manner of the other gospels) than a continuation of the discourse. **"Do
you not say, 'Four months more, then comes the harvest'?"** This sounds like
a proverb: in Palestine the interval between sowing and harvest was regularly
about four months. But if the proverb was about the need to wait patiently for
the harvest season, Jesus uses it as a foil for saying the opposite. In the other
gospels, as in the Bible as a whole, 'harvest' is a symbol of judgment. People
have seldom seriously expected the last judgment to come inconveniently
soon. When you sow your corn, harvest seems a long time ahead; when you
look at your moral record, the reckoning seldom seems imminent. But Jesus
in his own person was bringing judgment into the present. He was putting
an end to the comfortable sense of delay which belonged to the old way of
looking at things. At the same time, since 'harvest' could also be an image
for the kingdom, he brought the joy of a heavenly reward within the grasp of
human life. This, at least, seems to be the drift of his words. But we have little
to go by, and we are still more at a loss when it comes to the other proverb,
37 **'One sows and another reaps.'** This was usually said from the point of view of
the sower; it was a gloomy recognition of the inherent injustice of things. But
here it seems to be said from the point of view of the reaper and has a cheerful

---

[7] In verse 26 the Greek for **I am he** is simply *I am*, which is a manner of speaking
characteristically used by Jesus in this gospel to claim divine authority, as in 6.35; 8.12; etc.

note. It is possible to think of circumstances in the church to which the saying might have applied by the time the gospel was written. The first 'sowing' of the gospel in Samaria, for instance, was done by a group of 'Hellenists' (Acts 8.4–13); when the Jerusalem leaders arrived, they came in for the 'harvest'. But if Jesus used the proverb, he evidently meant that his immediate followers were to have a part in the 'reaping' that was a prelude to the judgment of the world. This is something that Jesus certainly hinted at elsewhere (Matthew 9.37). But who were the mysterious 'others' who would already have done

38 the hard **'labor'**? The Old Testament prophets, who had repeatedly called for repentance? The Samaritan religious leaders, who had prepared their people for the coming of a prophet-Messiah? A group of Samaritans who had come to believe in Jesus as a result of this very visit? Any of these answers is possible; none is certain.

The Samaritan woman had believed in Jesus because of his apparently

39 psychic powers (**"He told me everything I have ever done"**). He was evidently a prophet and therefore he might well be the awaited Messiah. But after Jesus

41 had stayed with the Samaritans for two days, **many more believed because of his word**. A feat of divination was only the prelude to much more serious preaching, and even the idea that Jesus might be the coming Messiah gave way to the realization that he was a more universal figure, **"the Savior of the world"**.

43   **A prophet has no honor in the prophet's own country**. A saying on these lines appears in all the gospels, but here it has a quite different context. Jesus' 'own country', in the most literal sense, was Nazareth, a village in Galilee; and the other three gospels give the saying (which was probably already proverbial) a setting in an occasion when honour was brusquely witheld from Jesus in his home town (Matthew 13.57; Mark 6.4; Luke 4.24). But the literal meaning was not the only possible one, or even the most plausible one. Here the phrase has a much deeper meaning. Jesus was sent to the Jewish people, the centre of whose religion and national life was Jerusalem. But 'the Jews' (as John usually calls Jesus' influential opponents in Jerusalem, by contrast with the ordinary Jewish inhabitants of the countryside) consistently 'dishonoured' him – this was (according to John) the true application of the proverb. Jesus' **own country** (in the Greek, *patris*, from which we get our word 'patriotic') was the place where, above all, he should have been accepted – Jerusalem. In due course Jesus would deliberately face this hostility.

45 Meanwhile he returned to the more welcoming **Galileans**.

54   John now records **the second sign** done by Jesus, separated by an interlude in Jerusalem from the first, which had also been in Cana. An officer from Capernaum, whose son (or servant) was dangerously ill, is the subject of an episode recorded by Matthew (8.5–13) and Luke (7.1–10). These two accounts each tell the story in a somewhat different way, but both include a dialogue between Jesus and the officer which stresses the officer's exceptional faith; and there is the further point (especially in Luke) that the officer

was a Gentile who showed marked deference to Jesus. In John the story is
46 different again. Instead of a soldier we have **a royal official**, not necessarily of a royal family, but probably an official in the household of Herod
Antipas and therefore just as likely to have been a Jew as a Gentile. Moreover, Jesus' rejoinder to him is reminiscent of the rebuke which Jesus gave
to Jewish people in general, "An evil and adulterous generation asks for a
sign" (Matthew 12.39); despite which the boy's father continued to plead
with him. Thus the interest arising from Jesus' first encounter with a Gentile,
and the whole dialogue that turns on a comparison between the authority
of a soldier and that of Jesus, are absent from John's version. On the other
50 hand there is a similar emphasis on faith. **The man believed the word that**
41 **Jesus spoke to him**, exactly as the Samaritans had **believed because of his**
word a few days earlier, and this initial act of faith, when confirmed by the
miraculous cure (performed at a distance of almost a day's walk) turned into
whole-hearted acceptance. In a phrase that was to become frequent in the
53 later history of the church's mission, **he himself believed, along with his**
whole household.

Healing in Jerusalem, bread from heaven in Galilee

5.1 **Jesus went up to Jerusalem.** In this gospel, unlike the others, Jesus makes
several visits to Jerusalem as a pilgrim: the festivals offered the most natural
2 reason for a Galilean teacher to 'go up'. **By the Sheep Gate there is a pool . . .**
which has five porticoes. Architecturally, five porticoes, or colonnades, is a
puzzling number. But Cyril, a fourth-century bishop of Jerusalem, provides
the solution: 'four ran round the sides, but the fifth, where the crowd of
sick lay, ran across the centre'. In other words it was a double pool, divided
by a colonnade running down the middle. Archaeology has shown John's
information to be correct, at least to the extent of there having been two
pools in the north-east corner of Jerusalem (next to the church of St Anne,
built many centuries later by the Crusaders); but there is no sign of there
having been any colonnades. John may have imagined these, given that this
was the kind of architectural feature he would have been most familiar with in
a city such as Ephesus; and he may conceivably have known another fact that
the excavations have revealed, namely that the pools seem to have been part
of a pagan shrine dedicated to the healing god Asclepius. Something of the
7 atmosphere of this place is conveyed by the man's response to Jesus, **"I have**
no one to put me into the pool when the water is stirred up." Evidently the
pool was thought to have miraculous power, connected with a mysterious
'stirring up' of the water. This could have been the result of a peculiarity
of the spring which fed the pools (at least one intermittent spring, which
produced a kind of siphon action when it failed, has been known to exist in
Jerusalem); and an occasional unexplained eddy in the pool would have been

enough to account for the reverence in which it was held by sick people,[8] who would not necessarily shun the place because of its pagan associations if they thought that there was a chance of a cure – though it is quite surprising to find Jesus there. It may be only an accident that there is still a sheep market in the vicinity; but there is little reason to doubt John's statement that this

2 pool was in some way associated with sheep and was called **Beth-zatha**.[9]

Jesus' cure of the sick man was by any standard remarkable – he had apparently been too ill (through weakness or paralysis) to move himself

5 for **thirty-eight years**. But the story is told, not just as a miracle, but as a meaningful encounter between healer and healed. It begins with a searching

6 question, **"Do you want to be made well?"** After a lifetime as a beggar the man might have been unwilling to face a new way of life. (There is a similar motif in the story of the blind man in Mark 10.51.) The man's answer is relatively

14 trivial, but he is nevertheless cured. Later on, Jesus adds a warning: **"Do not sin any more, so that nothing worse happens to you."** In the other gospels, Jesus' cures are mostly exorcisms: when the demon had been driven out there was always a danger of a worse one coming in, and Jesus was remembered to have made a vivid comment on precisely this danger (Matthew 12.43–5; Luke 11.24–6). Here, it is as if the same idea is translated into terms of a more sophisticated view of disease, though still with the presupposition (which lay deep in Hebrew culture and is sometimes reflected in the sayings of Jesus) that illness may be a divinely imposed punishment for sin.

9 But the story takes a new turn from the circumstance that **that day was a**
10 **sabbath**. It was forbidden to carry any burden on the sabbath; so **the Jews** (who stand, as before, for the authorities in Jerusalem) were correct in saying, **"it is not lawful for you to carry your mat"**. The man, however, disclaimed responsibility: it was, after all, Jesus who had ordered him to do so, and he was perfectly justified in passing on the blame. Moreover, more than 'carrying a

11 burden' was involved: Jesus had **made** him **well**. The real cause of offence was a healing carried out on the sabbath. This is the situation also described in

16 the other gospels: **the Jews started persecuting Jesus, because he was doing such things on the sabbath** – where 'persecuting' translates a word which can equally well mean 'bringing a charge against'. It was certainly the view of some that to heal was a form of 'work' and therefore prohibited on the sabbath unless a life was in danger (which was clearly not the case here). Jesus was impatient of this attitude. Sometimes he simply poured contempt on it in the name of sheer humanity, sometimes he found in scripture a precedent for waiving sabbath regulations. But on this occasion his defence was more

[8] Most of this is made explicit in the additional sentences given in the NRSV footnote. But these sentences, which occur only in some manuscripts, look like an intelligent inference from John's text rather than a piece of independent tradition.

[9] The *district* was certainly called **Beth-zatha**, but some manuscripts give the *pool* another name, such as the more familiar *Bethesda*. See the NRSV footnote.

17 subtle and more far-reaching. **"My Father is still working, and I also am working."** There was certainly a debate in Jesus' time on the implications of Genesis 2.2–3: "God . . . rested on the seventh day from all the work that he had done. So God blessed the seventh day and hallowed it." This, it was supposed, was the origin of the 'sabbath rest'. But could it be the case that God, who is now enjoying his own 'sabbath', does no 'work' of any kind? Surely God is still active! How then does he avoid breaking his own sabbath regulations? Different answers were suggested to this question; but it was generally admitted that there must be some sense in which God is still 'working', and that the prohibition of work on the sabbath does not apply to God in the way that it applies to human beings. Jesus seems to have been alluding to this debate when he said, **"my Father is still working"**; but when he went on, **"and I also am working"**, he clearly implied that the special exemption which applied to God applied also to him. His opponents were

18 quick to scent blasphemy: he was **making himself equal to God.**

This was a serious matter, more serious than breaking sabbath regulations, and one which, if proved, would amply justify the threat of the death penalty. It was true that the Jews claimed a special relationship with God: in a certain sense they were all his 'children' and he was their 'father'. But this did not affect the enormous distance which necessarily separated any human being from God. The claim Jesus had just made, and the form in which he had expressed it (**calling God his own Father,** as if he had a special relationship with him), went far beyond anything a Jew would normally dare to utter. It sounded like a direct assault on the basic monotheism of their faith. Did Jesus claim to be some sort of 'second god'? The question could have been a burning one for John's readers as much as for Jesus' original hearers. Jesus' reply was a preliminary answer to it.

19 **"The Son can do nothing on his own."** In this and the following verse it would be perfectly correct (since the Greek made no distinction) to write 'father' and 'son' without capital letters. When this is done, the saying reads like one of those small parables or comparisons which are characteristic of Jesus in the other gospels. The picture is of a boy apprenticed to his father and learning his trade entirely under his father's supervision. In this case Jesus is clearly applying the parable to himself. Just as a boy apprentice learns all his skill and derives all his knowledge from his craftsman father (and who knows if Jesus was drawing on his own experience as an apprentice carpenter?), so Jesus, far from claiming 'equality' with God, was entirely dependent on him for all he had learnt. But that is only one side of the comparison. The other side is more startling. If Jesus was God's apprentice-son, then Jesus' work was God's work. This would be innocuous enough if it were meant in the general sense that all human beings are doing 'God's work' (though some more than others, and Jesus perhaps to an exceptional degree). But the application Jesus made of it was to a 'work' that would normally be thought to be the

21 prerogative of God alone: **"just as the Father raises the dead and gives them**

life, so also the Son gives life to whomever he wishes". God (it had always been believed) was the supreme judge of humankind; but even this had now
22 been learnt and carried on from him by his apprentice-son: God **"has given all judgment to the Son".** Jesus pretended to no 'equality' with God, he was no 'second god' himself; yet in virtue of all that he had learnt from the Father, he could now carry on his 'work' with the authority of a fully accredited agent to whom as much respect should be paid as to the one who commissioned
23 him, **"so that all may honor the Son as they honor the Father".**

Raising the dead, giving them life, judgment – these terms belonged to the standard picture of the destiny which awaits us all after death: at a given moment, God will 'raise' all who have died, so that they may stand before him for judgment; the righteous he will reward with an everlasting life of felicity, the unrighteous he will consign to an appropriate punishment. To
29 put it in the simplest terms: we are all destined to receive our reward, **"those who have done good, to the resurrection of life, and those who have done evil, to the resurrection of condemnation".** Jesus nowhere explicitly rejects this traditional picture; but in what has just been said he claims to occupy a significant place in it. It appears that he is to exercise on behalf of God the
22 actual administration of the judgment: he is to have **all judgment.** What is the importance of this? Is it simply a redistribution of rôles in that mythological drama which is the way we tend to imagine the judgment of God? Does it mean that in any picture of the last things the traditional representation of the divine Judge at the centre must now be replaced by the figure of Jesus? Doubtless yes – so long as the old picture is kept at all. But in this gospel, Jesus' words, though still using the old language, suggest a different picture altogether.

If one wants to describe two kinds of living as totally different from each other, one can draw a metaphor from the two words 'life' and 'death'. The old, poor kind of life one can call 'death' (we speak ourselves of 'a living death'); the new and splendid dimension one can call 'life', 'real life', or better still, borrowing a term from the traditional picture of the life of the blessed after death, 'eternal life'. In doing this, one is not necessarily denying that the old picture of a final judgment after death is in some sense still valid; but one is deliberately using the old imagery to describe the intensity of a new way of life which is already attainable *before* death.

This seems to be the force of Jesus' words here, at least as John represents
24 them. **Eternal life,** or passing **from death to life,** are ways of denoting a new kind of living; the old imagery is pressed into service to show how radically different this new kind of life is from the old. The traditional concepts are not necessarily cancelled – though the restatement of them in verses 28–9 is completely ambiguous: it could be an endorsement of them or a total
28 reinterpretation of them by using **all who are in their graves** as a metaphor for those still living the old kind of life. But now, the 'judgment' that matters consists in the way one reacts to Jesus: 'eternal life' is what is experienced as

a result of reacting positively. This is all new; and yet it is an expression of
30 the unchanging justice of God: **"As I hear, I judge; and my judgment is just,
because I seek to do not my own will but the will of him who sent me."**

Reacting positively to Jesus, however, meant believing him to be what he
claimed to be; and it was legitimate to ask (as one would ask in a court of
law, and the setting for this whole discourse is that of a legal charge brought
against Jesus) what the evidence was for such stupendous claims. In this
sense, however compelling some people might find Jesus' words, what he
said of himself could not count as evidence: to be believed he must have
independent witnesses. From the strictly legal point of view, it was correct
31 for him to say, **"If I testify about myself, my testimony is not true"** (though
valid[10] would bring out the sense better than **true**). Now the reader knows
that two particular kinds of testimony have already been given, that of John
the Baptist and that of the scriptures. But both of these were cogent only
for those already disposed to believe. Most people saw significance in John's
movement only for a time: he was simply a precursor. They failed to see his
39 lasting significance as a witness to Jesus. As for the **scriptures**, the duty of
'searching' them was recognized by all Jews who took their religion seriously,
and no one doubted that this was the surest way of securing the reward of
eternal life; but the Jews still missed the true meaning of those scriptures
(**"that they testify on my behalf"**) and so failed to come to him who could
offer them 'life' here and now. For anyone who was coming to believe in
Jesus, both these kinds of testimony were exceedingly important. About that
34 of John, for instance, Jesus could **"say these things so that you should be
saved"**. But for those who were so unconvinced as to be actually attacking
36 him, Jesus' appeal was to **a testimony greater than John's**, a testimony more
explicit than that of the scriptures – the testimony of God himself, not in
the form of a crude and dazzling manifestation of the divine (for the Jews
quite rightly thought of God as far too transcendent a being for anyone to
37, 36 have literally **heard his voice or seen his form**), but expressed in the **works**
of Jesus, which testified to the authority of him who performed them and
demonstrated his character as an agent of the one who had **sent** him. It is
of these 'works', and of the testimony which they gave to the reality of Jesus'
authorization, that John's gospel is distinctively a record.
41 **"I do not accept glory from human beings."** Here there is a word-play
which can hardly be reproduced in English. When the Hebrew Bible was
translated into Greek, the Septuagint translators used the word *doxa*, which
means (among other things) 'honour', to translate the Hebrew expression
which in English we usually call 'the glory of God' – a dazzling radiance.
This was an extension of language: it was as if God could be said to have
an 'honour' which (unlike honour in the ordinary sense) is given to him by
no one else, but belongs to him by right and expresses his transcendence

[10] As the word is translated in 8.13.

and power, his 'glory'. Jesus' argument (at least as reported by John) makes deliberate play with this ambiguity. One reason for believing that a certain person is, say, a king, is that people pay him 'honour'. If this kind of honour were being paid to Jesus (which is what his opponents paid to one another), this might possibly convince people of the truth of his claims. But these claims were such that no human 'honour' could validate them. On the other hand, if people had an eye for the kind of *doxa* which is the glory of God they would realize that this was something which did attach to Jesus and showed

43   him to have come as his Father's authorized agent, in his **Father's name**.

45   **"Do not think that I will accuse you before the Father."** If everything depends on how one reacts to Jesus and his message, then it could be expected (given the traditional picture of the judgment, when one's words and deeds will be brought up against one) that Jesus himself would be the 'accuser', saying to God (in effect), 'This person did not accept me.' But this would be to suggest that Jesus introduced a new criterion of judgment – no longer law or lawlessness, good or evil, but for or against Jesus. And yet the criterion is as it always was. Rightly understood, the whole of scripture points to the truth of Jesus' words. Law and sin, good and evil, are to be assessed in the light of that definitive interpretation being given by Jesus of the ancient commands of God as declared in scripture. In this sense, **"your accuser is Moses"**.

6.1   **After this**. A miracle performed by Jesus, in which a great crowd was fed from a small number of loaves and fishes, is told twice over by Mark and Matthew and once each by Luke and John. In all these accounts the main elements of the story are the same: the two episodes that are reported in Mark and Matthew differ only in relatively unimportant details, and Luke appears to follow Mark's first account. The version in John, like that of the second occasion in Mark and Matthew, places the episode on **the other side of the Sea of Galilee, also called the Sea of Tiberias**,[11] but in other respects it comes closer to the first (Mark 6.33–44). A single well-remembered episode evidently forms the basis of these various accounts, even if Jesus, as Mark and Matthew record, actually repeated the miracle on a second occasion. But John characteristically tells the story in his own way, and by a slight shift of emphasis makes it yield a new meaning.

According to all the other accounts, the crowd was hungry, the hour late, the place deserted. A compassionate concern for the crowd's physical needs was the spring of Jesus' action. But John says nothing of this – and indeed the explanation is not even very plausible. Most of Galilee in the time of Jesus was quite densely populated: even on the mountain slopes one could never have

---

[11]   The Greek has the puzzling phrase, *of Galilee of Tiberias*. Tiberias is on the west shore of the lake. It was built by Herod Antipas for his capital city, and its name was intended as a compliment to the reigning emperor, Tiberius. To Gentiles, it would have been natural to call the Lake by the same name. But Jews who had little to do with the new pagan city preferred to call it either by its biblical name, the Lake of Gennesaret (Luke 5.1), or else (as usually in the gospels) the Sea of Galilee.

10 been far from towns, and Jesus certainly had not climbed very high (**there**
 4 **was a great deal of grass in the place**). Instead, John simply records that **the**
    Passover, the festival of the Jews, was near. Our attention is drawn, not to
    the urgent need for food, but to the imminence of an occasion in the Jewish
    year when the food had a specific religious significance. The food Jesus was
    about to provide must not be understood, any more than the Passover lamb,
    merely as a means of satisfying hunger.

12   **When they were satisfied.** Five thousand people had been fed with five
    barley loaves and two fish. This was surely a sufficiently sensational fact
    to make the narrator pause a moment. But John allows it only a passing
13 reference, and hurries on to another point: **from the fragments of the five**
    barley loaves, left by those who had eaten, they filled twelve baskets. Why
    was this so important? On the face of it, it was the feeding that mattered,
    not what was left over. Admittedly the detail is mentioned in all the other
    accounts, and it may have seemed to the writer a necessary part of a story
    of this kind. A miracle performed by Elisha, for instance, included the same
    point (and also has other features in common with this one):

> A man came from Baal-shalishah, bringing food from the first fruits to the
> man of God: twenty loaves of barley and fresh ears of grain in his sack.
> Elisha said, "Give it to the people and let them eat." But his servant said,
> "How can I set this before a hundred people?" So he repeated, "Give it to
> the people and let them eat, for thus says the LORD, 'They shall eat and have
> some left.'" He set it before them, they ate, and had some left, according to
> the word of the LORD. (2 Kings 4.42–4)

    Moreover when Jesus (according to the other gospels) later alluded to this
    miracle, he referred deliberately to this point of bread having been left over:
    "When I broke the five loaves for the five thousand, how many baskets full
    of broken pieces did you collect?" (Mark 8.19). It is important to visualize
    the quantities involved. A modern baker's loaf normally feeds a number of
    people. But the loaves of Jesus' time were the small, round, flat ones still
    used by Semitic peoples. Three of them were needed for one person's meal
    (Luke 11.5). Twenty of them, in the Elisha story, seemed absurdly little to set
    before a hundred people. A basket would hold at least a dozen such loaves,
    if not many more. On this occasion they filled **twelve baskets** with what was
    left over. In other words, even after the meal, they were left with many times
14 more than they started with. We can now see why this detail is the real **sign**
    that is the climax of the story. How much bread the people needed could
    not be calculated. Perhaps (a cynic might have said) they were not hungry.
    But this did not matter. The real evidence of the miracle lay in those twelve
    baskets full of scraps. This was the 'sign' **the people saw.** Moreover, it gave
27 John the cue for the teaching that follows later about **the food that endures**
    for eternal life. Like the water which is "a spring of water gushing up to

eternal life" (4.14), the bread which Jesus gives is always there, even after it has fed multitudes.

14 **They began to say, "This is indeed the prophet who is to come into the world."** At that time the Jewish religion encouraged people to pin their hopes on a figure who 'was to come', even though it allowed a wide variety of opinions on what kind of figure this would be. Speculation ranged from a warrior king to a divinely empowered being who would usher in a new age. One text which was doubtless quoted in this connection was that in which Moses foretold that God would "raise up for you a prophet like me" (Deuteronomy 18.15). Moses had miraculously fed the people with manna, and here was Jesus doing something similar. It was not difficult for the crowd to guess that Jesus was **indeed the prophet.** But this kind of religious excitement could easily spill over into something more political and dangerous. There were several self-styled 'prophets' in this period who promised to show an authoritative 'sign' and then to lead the Jewish people against their Roman conquerors. It needed no more than what Jesus had just done for the crowd 15 to **take him by force to make him king.**

Jesus **withdrew.** In Matthew and Luke the possibility of an earthly kingship was one of the 'temptations' to which Jesus was exposed by the devil at the beginning of his ministry. In all the gospels the point becomes important in the hearing of Jesus before Pilate; and there were earlier occasions on which his words and actions could have had political implications. But this is the only place in any of the gospels where the possibility of a political movement starting around him outside Jerusalem is explicitly referred to. It would have been natural for the evangelists to play down this motif, and John may well preserve here something which the other gospels have deliberately passed over. In any case, the danger (as Jesus saw it to be) provides a convincing motive for Jesus to separate himself from his followers and for his disciples to take to their boat – an episode which comes in this place in Mark (6.45–52) and Matthew (14.22–32).

20 **"It is I; do not be afraid."** All the gospel accounts of this scene contain these words;[12] but the story itself is told by John in a rather a different way. Matthew and Mark leave the reader in no doubt that Jesus miraculously walked across the water. In John the details are not so clear: Jesus could have been in shallow water, since they were evidently near the edge of the lake 21, 22 (**immediately the boat reached the land**). But **the next day,** when the crowd tried to work out what had happened to Jesus, they found his disappearance inexplicable. When the arrival of more boats from the western shore made it possible for them to track down Jesus in Capernaum, this was the first thing 25 they wanted to ask him about. **"Rabbi, when did you come here?"**

[12] **"It is I"** in the Greek is literally *I am*, a phrase which in John's gospel has particular solemnity. See above on 4.26 (footnote).

It looked, then, as if the crowd's motives for pursuing Jesus were curiosity and a desire for more free bread. Jesus ignored the first and poured scorn on the second. The miracle of the loaves was not intended to satisfy physical hunger. It was a 'sign' of something more important, and the crowd had failed to grasp it. To turn the discussion in the right direction, Jesus used a form of

27 words they could easily understand: **"Do not work for the food that perishes, but for the food that endures to eternal life."** They would understand it because it was the familiar choice offered by religious teachers: either 'food that perishes' – that is, the material rewards of this world – or the kind of God-fearing and obedient living which would secure a favourable judgment on the last day and the reward of 'eternal life'. Jesus' next words seemed at first sight to fit into the same picture – **"which the Son of Man will give you"**. In Daniel 7, and possibly in popular belief, the Son of Man was associated with the last judgment; and Jesus seems to be endorsing this scenario when he talks mysteriously of God setting his **"seal"** on this personage. So, missing the real point of Jesus' saying (which becomes clear only later on), they asked him the usual question about the way of life which would entitle them to

28 receive their reward from the Son of Man at the judgment: **"What must we do to perform the works of God?"**

This was a stock question. In the other gospels it is put to Jesus in the form, "What must I do to inherit eternal life?", and Jesus' answer is, "Follow me" (Mark 10.17, 21). Here his answer is similar, though 'following' gives place

29 to 'believing': **"This is the work of God, that you believe in him whom he has sent."**

But how were they to believe? Jesus must do something, give some sign, to show who he was – the same challenge is recorded in Matthew (12.38). Of course (John would have us understand), this is exactly what Jesus had been doing; but his 'signs' had been too subtle, and demanded too much readiness of acceptance, to be understood outside the circle of his followers. The crowd was thinking of something more obvious, such as Moses providing the people in the wilderness with manna (Exodus 16) – a miraculous feat which they may well have thought would be repeated by the coming Messiah.

31 The text, **'He gave them bread from heaven to eat'**, does not occur in the Old Testament in precisely this form (it is perhaps a recollection of such passages as Nehemiah 9.15 and Psalm 78.24). But it serves here as a text which governs the discourse that follows, somewhat in the manner of synagogue sermons of the time (and indeed of sermons ever since). Jesus begins by correcting their interpretation of the first word. **'He'** refers, not to Moses, but to God the Father. (Is there an echo here of the Lord's Prayer, where the 'Father' is prayed to 'give us this day our daily bread'?) Then the **bread:** the manna may have been a supernatural provision of bread, but it did no more than satisfy physical hunger. The text had a deeper meaning than this, just as Jesus' feeding miracle was more than an exceptional supply of provisions.

34 The crowd's unperceptive response, **"Sir, give us this bread always"** – which

showed that they were still thinking about physical needs – is the cue for a
32 discourse on **"the true bread"**.

The metaphor was an old one. In Proverbs 9.5, the figure of Wisdom calls
out, "Come, eat of my bread and drink of the wine I have mixed." Jesus'
35 words clearly draw on this tradition when he says, **"Whoever comes to me
will never be hungry, and whoever believes in me will never be thirsty."**
(There has been nothing about 'water' and 'thirst' in the scene so far.) And
32 there is one more point to be made from the text: the 'bread' was **"from
heaven"**, and Jesus is to explain how he can say, not merely that he has been
38, 42 **"sent"** (as any envoy of God might be) but that he has actually **"come down
33 from heaven"**. He is, in fact, the 'bread' himself, and this bread **"gives life
to the world"**. Here again the crowd had misunderstood: they were thinking
34 of 'daily life' when they said, **"Give us this bread always."** But 'life' here
40 means **"eternal life"**. Normally this would be envisaged only as a gift which
God would give to the righteous after death. This conventional language was
still valid: **"I will raise them up on the last day"** could be no more than
the expected promise that at the last judgment Jesus would secure for his
followers a favourable verdict and a share in the blessings of 'eternal life'. But
by now the reader of this gospel has learnt that afterlife language is also a way
of talking about a new kind of life in the present. **Eternal life** (in this sense)
is attainable now, given belief in Jesus.

44 But who is able to believe? **"No one can come to me unless drawn by
the Father who sent me."** This sounds like the harshest determinism. But
consider how God does in fact 'draw' people: through the revelation of himself
in the Bible. Jesus was witnessed to by scripture: anyone might be 'drawn'
who read Scripture rightly. In this sense, those who came to Jesus and believed
45 were those who **"learned from the Father"** and were themselves a fulfilment
of a prophecy of Isaiah (54.13), **'And they shall all be taught by God.'**

41 **Then the Jews began to complain about him**. Such a claim, from a person
who seemed in so many respects like anyone else, and whose family was
42 well known, provoked incredulity and censure. **"Is not this Jesus, the son of
Joseph, whose father and mother we know?"**[13] Jesus recognized this obstacle
to belief and accepted the consequence that only some would be drawn to
believe. Undeterred, he went on to give a further turn to the idea of 'real bread',
which this time led to a fierce dispute among the Jews themselves (verse 52)
51 and caused many even of his disciples to withdraw from him (verse 66): **"the
bread that I will give for the life of the world is my flesh"**.

This is the climax of the chapter, the point towards which the discussion
has been leading from the beginning. The Christians for whom this gospel

---

[13] Did John know (as Matthew and Luke did) that Jesus had no human father but was
conceived 'from the Holy Spirit' (Matthew 1.18)? It is hard to be sure. The most one can
say is that Jesus' miraculous birth is compatible with John's understanding of his nature.
The present passage, in any case, hardly bears on the question. The Jews merely echo the
general opinion at the time: Jesus was "the son (as was thought) of Joseph" (Luke 3.23).

was written were already accustomed to holding a solemn supper at which the bread and the wine were affirmed to be the body and blood of Christ; and they knew that the institution of this new and distinctive act of worship went back to some explicit teaching of Jesus himself. They will have been prepared

11, 23 by a number of hints earlier on in the chapter to expect such teaching: **Jesus took the loaves, and when he had given thanks, he distributed them . . . after the Lord had given thanks**[14] are phrases which are characteristic of the New Testament accounts of the Lord's supper; and they will have found what

51 they were expecting in the words, **"the bread that I will give for the life of the world is my flesh"**. These words are strikingly similar to those used by Jesus in the other gospels' accounts of the last supper, celebrated by Jesus with his disciples on the night before his death – though this is the only place where **'flesh'** is used rather than 'body'. (The corresponding word in Jesus' own language could have been rendered by either.) Here, however different the setting, the substance of the teaching is the same. Indeed, it seems likely that John chose this point in his gospel to gather together all Jesus' teaching

50 on **"the bread that comes down from heaven"**, the bread which is Jesus' own body and which gives eternal life. In the context of the narrative, this teaching had the effect of still further shocking those who heard it into belief or disbelief. But, for its readers, the whole chapter took on its full meaning only when read in the light of their experience of the eucharist.

59 **He said these things while he was teaching in the synagogue at Capernaum.** After the dramatic series of episodes which led up to the discourse, and nothing having been said to suggest there has been a change of scene, it comes as a surprise that Jesus has in effect been giving a synagogue sermon. At any rate, the sermon is now over, and the remainder of the chapter reports

61 a private conversation. **"Does this offend you?"** Taken literally, Jesus' words about himself as 'bread' to be 'eaten' could well have sounded offensive; and

53 the notion that they should have to **drink his blood** could have seemed an almost deliberate affront to the sensibilities of any Jew, however figurative the language was supposed to be. Jesus does little to mitigate the offence. But

62 he adds a brief pointer to the way his words are to be taken. **"What if you were to see the Son of Man ascending to where he was before?"** It was not as an ordinary man that Jesus could give his flesh to others to eat, but as Son of Man, that is, as a person who belonged to both heaven and earth. There

33 have been hints of this earlier. The bread – or Jesus himself[15] – **"comes down from heaven"**. He belongs (and is soon to ascend) to the realm above, which

63 is also the realm of spirit. **"It is the spirit that gives life; the flesh is useless."** This comes as a surprise after what has been said about Jesus' 'flesh' being

---

[14] This second hint may be due, not to John himself, but to a later editor or copyist anxious to make the allusion more explicit. If so, it would explain why some manuscripts omit the phrase, as recorded in the NRSV footnote.

[15] The Greek could mean either, as the NRSV footnote indicates.

'the bread of life'. But now the context is doubtless different. The contrast between flesh and spirit is characteristic of early Christian psychology (see above on Mark 14.38). The challenge up to now has been to acknowledge that the Word could become 'flesh' in a man, Jesus. But the believer must not remain there: we have now to see that, to receive eternal life through the bread which is Jesus' 'flesh', one must acknowledge that the bearer of that flesh is the Son of Man whose true home is the realm of the spirit.

Nevertheless the shock remained, and many even of those close to Jesus found it too much for them. The rejection of Jesus is necessarily a theme of all the gospels, though they treat it in different ways. Usually there is a clear distinction between the authorities and (later on) the crowds on the one hand, and the disciples on the other. Here the dividing line runs right

67 down the group of disciples themselves: the **twelve** were a remnant of a larger number who had once followed Jesus. (There may be a hint of this in Luke 22.28.) It was only from this time on that there was a sharply distinguished group of twelve disciples corresponding with 'the twelve' of the other gospels.

So Jesus asked the twelve, "Do you also wish to go away?" In Mark 8.27–33 (and in the corresponding passages in Matthew and Luke) there is an important scene in which Peter recognizes that Jesus is the Messiah, the Christ, and in which Jesus then predicts what is to befall him in Jerusalem. This brief dialogue in John contains the same elements.[16] Peter calls Jesus,

69 not 'the Messiah' (as in Mark), but **"the Holy One of God"**. Perhaps there is not much difference: it was the title given by a demon to Jesus in Mark (1.24), and the demons knew who Jesus was. In any case, it was a decisive confession of faith. It marked out who were Jesus' real followers (not by their own merit, but 'chosen' by Jesus) – except, of course, that even in that small

71 group there was one who **was going to betray him.**

In Jerusalem for a festival

7.1 **The Jews were looking for an opportunity to kill him.** This was already reported at 5.18; here it explains Jesus' preference for being out of harm's way in Galilee. But observant Jews would normally make a point of going up

2 to Jerusalem for the annual festivals, and **the Jewish festival of Booths** (or Tabernacles) was the greatest in the year and the one for which Jesus' family would most naturally expect Jesus to make the pilgrimage. It was an autumn festival, to mark the safe gathering in of crops and fruit, and involved setting up token 'booths', or huts made of branches, and there were processions with greenery and fruit. The services and festivities in the temple lasted for a week, and they included certain subsidiary rites such as the ceremonial pouring of

---

[16] An ancient editor or copyist may have recognized this and be responsible for having assimilated Peter's confession to that in the other gospels, hence the variant reading recorded in the NRSV footnote.

water over the altar and the lighting of candles in the court outside the temple. These might well have been the cue for sayings of Jesus about 'living water' or 'the light of the world' (7.38; 8.12). But in John's narrative these allusions, if they were intentional, would have been very recondite, particularly since nothing is made of the 'booths' themselves, which were the best-known feature of the festival. The reader is not invited to find significance in the festival other than as the occasion for Jesus' next appearance in Jerusalem.

But it was an appearance which began in an atmosphere of secrecy. To
3 **his brothers**, who were among those who did not 'believe in him' (the same scepticism on the part of his family is implied in Mark 6.4), it seemed obvious that, unless he was resigned to the obscurity of a provincial existence in Galilee, he must 'show himself to the world' in Jerusalem. But the manifestation of Jesus' true nature to the world (the coming of the Word to "what was his own", 1.11) was more complex than that. A certain secrecy (as is stressed in Mark's gospel) was a necessary condition. Those who recognized him did so because they were able to discern who he truly was, not because his true nature was so blazingly apparent that it could not be denied. Jesus had a
6 **'time'**, and when it was **fully come** he would be prepared for full publicity. But meanwhile his journey to Jerusalem was undertaken after some hesita-
10 tion and **as it were**[17] **in secret**. Popular opinion was already divided about
12 him. The translation, **there was considerable complaining**, does not convey the ambivalence of the Greek. The word is a vivid one for 'murmuring' or 'muttering', and, as the following words show, there were people both for and against; but all had good reason to keep their voices low.

14 **Jesus . . . began to teach**. This immediately raised the question of his
15 authority to do so. **"How does this man have such learning, when he has never been taught?"** Authority to teach normally came to a pupil from a master; but, so far as anyone knew, Jesus had **never been taught**; nor did he ever quote the opinions of other experts, as their teachers would normally do. So where did he get his authority? Jesus' answer was that his authority would be found, not in any formal qualification, but in the teaching itself.
17 All who sincerely resolved **to do the will of God** as it was revealed in the law of Moses would find that this teaching enabled them to do so. The teaching
18 authenticated itself. Instead of giving **glory** to the teacher it gave **glory** to God (and here there is the same play on the double meaning of the word – 'honour' and 'glory' – as in 5.41–4 above).

19 **"Did not Moses give you the law? Yet none of you keeps the law."** The majority of the Jews did not aspire to keep the law in every detail, and by no means all of it could be embodied in a criminal code; but the Pharisees, despising this lack of seriousness, set themselves a very rigorous discipline by which they believed they could avoid even an inadvertent transgression.

---

[17] The omission of *as it were* in some early manuscripts may be authentic. Christians may have very soon found it difficult to believe that Jesus really intended secrecy.

If some Pharisees were present they might well have resented the accusation that they, personally, broke the law; but they would have been ready to admit that the majority of Jews did so in one way or another. Why, in that case, single out Jesus and try to bring a capital charge against him for one transgression? On this occasion a number of 'the Jews' present seem (unusually) to have been sympathetic to Jesus and unaware that proceedings were under way.

20 **"Who is trying to kill you?"** – suggesting Jesus had **a demon** was a way of saying they thought he was mad to be suspecting such serious consequences.

21 But of course Jesus' transgression was a serious one: **"I performed one work"**, and the reference is clearly[18] to the 'work' of healing which Jesus had performed on the sabbath, so setting in motion the proceedings against him (5.16). Breaking the sabbath was an offence against a basic tenet of the Jewish religion, and Jesus' deliberate healing on a sabbath (and instructing the beneficiary to commit another offence by carrying his mat) had aroused powerful opposition. All the gospels contain instances of Jesus apparently sitting light to sabbath regulations (though none so explicitly as John's gospel), and record various lines which he adopted to justify his actions. Here is yet another (of a kind which some Jewish lawyers of the time actually used themselves). Some commandments, such as that to circumcise a baby on the eighth day, inevitably conflicted occasionally with the obligation to 'rest' on the sabbath, but had still to be carried out. An obvious *a fortiori* argument offered itself: if circumcision, affecting only one part of the body, was per-

23 missible on the sabbath, how much more an act of healing **"a man's whole body"**?

But while some were surprised that Jesus should think himself to be in dan-

26 ger at all, others were surprised that he dared make an appearance, **speaking openly**. Certainly the authorities were in a quandary. If Jesus' claims were unfounded, then his sabbath transgression certainly ought to be punished; but if he were to turn out to be really the Messiah, his accusers would have committed the very serious offence of disbelieving one who was sent from God. Could this be the reason for their hesitation? If so, at this stage it seemed hardly justified. Popular belief tended to wrap the coming Messiah in mystery: he would be a person of unknown origin, appearing from some secret recess of the world at the time appointed for him to perform his great work. The known facts of Jesus' home and origin did not fit this picture. Jesus' reply is characteristic of this gospel. The banal question about the village Jesus 'came from' was irrelevant: what mattered was whether (in a much more fundamental sense) he 'came from' God. This was harder to tell.

30 Some judged his claim to be blasphemous, and **tried to arrest him** in order

---

[18] The NRSV omits two small words in the text, which may either go with verse 21 ('you are amazed *because of it*'– so the Revised Standard Version) or with what follows, giving a logical connection: '*Because of this* an exception is made for circumcision on the sabbath.' In the latter case it is clear that Jesus is referring to his *sabbath* work.

to begin new proceedings. Others reflected on the 'signs' he had performed. Once again, there were conflicting reactions to him.

The 'citizens' arrest' had failed – the pre-ordained moment for the decisive confrontation had not yet arrived. Now the authorities, alarmed by reports of Jesus' appeal to a more sympathetic audience, made their arrangements for his formal arrest. This too seems to have been frustrated, this time by some enigmatic words of Jesus. After the event, we can see that Jesus' 'having come' from God implied that he would soon 'go to' God'. But at the time his sayings about 'going' could well have led to speculation that he proposed to leave Palestine – in which, of course, there was an ironic element of prophetic truth: by the time the gospel was written, it could be said that Jesus' mission had indeed included going to the Dispersion to **"teach the Greeks"**.

35

37–8 **On the last day of the festival, the great day.** The festival lasted eight days in all; the last was the sabbath, and was likely to be the best attended and so **the great day.** John's readers are unlikely to have known that it lacked the particular ritual of fetching water and pouring it out on the altar, which took place on previous days; In any case, John gives no hint that this was the cue for Jesus' solemn words, **"Let anyone who is thirsty come to me, and let the one who believes in me drink."**

We have already had an allusion (6.35) to Proverbs 9.5, "Come, eat of my bread and drink of the wine I have mixed." This style of invitation by the figure of Wisdom is echoed in another famous saying of Jesus in Matthew's gospel, "Come to me, all you that are weary" (11.28), and is adopted here by Jesus with overtones of Isaiah's appeal to "everyone who thirsts" to attend to the words of God (55.1). But the quotation which follows is more mysterious. There is no Old Testament text which corresponds; and the thought itself is startlingly crude if taken literally (*out of his belly* shall flow rivers of living water), so much

38 so that the NRSV is probably right to assume a metaphorical meaning, **"out of the believer's heart"**.[19] But there are certainly Old Testament overtones. It was prophesied in Zechariah (14.8) that "on that day living waters shall flow out from Jerusalem", a prophecy greatly elaborated by Ezekiel (47.1–12), who shared the same vision of the arid hills and valleys of Judea being watered by a miraculously abundant spring flowing out of the temple itself – a vivid symbol of the place of Jerusalem in the religious life of the world. Moreover, when Moses struck a rock at Horeb, water came out for the thirsty people to drink (Exodus 17.6), and Paul was to identify this rock in some way with Christ (1 Corinthians 10.4). Any or all of these images might have been invoked, but the saying could not but have sounded obscure. The evangelist adds his own interpretation: water, for Christians, symbolizes the Spirit, and

---

[19] This rendering also involves the assumption that (in the absence of punctuation) the writer intended the phrase **the one who believes in me** to be taken with the preceding sentence, not as part of the quotation from 'scripture'. Nevertheless, it is assumed that 'the believer' is still the subject: "*out of his heart* (or belly)" means **"out of the believer's heart"**.

the saying was not so much about Jesus and his hearers as about those who
39 would follow him and receive **the Spirit**. But Jesus' hearers had no such clue, and the most they could have made of it is that Jesus was announcing a new age, a new source of satisfaction for the needs of the people.
40   Who could make such an announcement? **The prophet** who (like Elijah)
41 was to be the immediate precursor of these things? Or **the Messiah** himself? But there was a problem: Jesus had come **from Galilee**, whereas the Messiah,
42 being a successor to King David, was expected to come from **"Bethlehem, the village where David lived"**. John's readers may have known the answer to this: Jesus was in fact born in Bethlehem, though he was brought up in Nazareth. But Jesus' hearers could not have known it; for them, Jesus, in this respect as in others, both was and was not like the expected Messiah. Indeed this is the theme of the whole scene: the challenge and ambiguity of the
43 person of Jesus. This time it caused **a division in the crowd**. The Pharisees, however, were quite clear in their own mind: his Galilean origin was fatal
52 to Jesus' claims. The scriptures showed that **"no prophet is to arise from Galilee"**. It made not the slightest difference what ordinary people thought. The Pharisees claimed that it was only members of their own movement who made a serious attempt to observe the whole law, and many of them regarded their less devout and disciplined fellow Jews as undoubtedly beyond
49 salvation. **"This crowd, which does not know the law – they are accursed"** was typical Pharisees' language. Even Nicodemus, who, though one of their number (3.1), was sympathetic to Jesus and made a very reasonable point in his defence, was apparently brushed aside.

[[An interpolation

The passage that follows did not form part of the original gospel according to John. It clearly disturbs the sequence of the narrative, and in any case most of the early manuscripts omit it altogether, and some manuscripts have it in a different place. In style it is more like a passage from one of the other gospels (especially Luke, to which one group of manuscripts ascribes it). What appears to have happened is that an isolated story about Jesus was somehow preserved without having been incorporated into any gospel until it was ultimately slipped in at some point where it did not seem inappropriate.

    A great many stories about Jesus circulated in the first few centuries of the Christian era, but were never incorporated in the New Testament and are preserved in the so-called apocryphal gospels. Almost all of them contain miraculous elements and can be recognized as being of considerably later date. By contrast, this one falls well into place beside all that we know of Jesus from the New Testament gospels and seems (so far as we can tell) to reflect the conditions of Jesus' own time. Even if it is impossible to find an original place for it in any of the four gospels, there is little reason to doubt that it preserves an authentic memory of an episode in the life of Jesus.

It is necessary to fill in the background of the incident. The immediate result when a woman was found by her husband to have committed adultery would normally have been that her husband was entitled to divorce her without any financial loss, and that the woman and her family would bear the disgrace of the act. Where there was doubt over whether adultery had been committed, further evidence might be sought or the woman might be subjected to a ritual test (Numbers 5). But in this case we are told that the

8.4 woman **"was caught in the very act of committing adultery"**, so that there was no doubt about the facts, and the divorce would have followed almost automatically. But the fact that there were witnesses to the act opened the way to a criminal prosecution: it was an offence regarded as so serious in the law that it incurred the death penalty (Deuteronomy 22.22). By the time of Jesus this law may not have been often invoked. It is not often that an act of adultery is actually witnessed by two independent witnesses (as the law required), and in any case the courts tended not to impose the death penalty unless they had to – not least because it seems that under the Roman occupation they had lost the power to carry it out. On the other hand, there were certainly sections of Jewish opinion which zealously tried to promote a

3 more rigorous application of the law. Among **the scribes and the Pharisees** who make their appearance in this story there may well have been some

4 who felt that this case of an adulteress **"caught in the very act"** offered an opportunity for applying the law in all its rigour.

These people had therefore constituted themselves as a court (which was perfectly proper for scribes) in the confidence that they were sufficiently expert in the law to reach a valid judgment, and were also prepared themselves, if it were practicable, to pass sentence and impose the prescribed penalty of death. The relevant passage of Deuteronomy did not state exactly how this was to be carried out; but death by stoning was the biblical punishment in comparable cases and is likely to have been the accepted penalty for adultery in the time of Jesus, though it was later changed to the more humane

5 one of strangling. It was therefore fair to say, **"in the law Moses commanded us to stone such women"**.

But in this case zeal for the rigorous application of the law was combined with a desire to compromise Jesus. It was courteous and reasonable (and perhaps prudent) to invite someone who had made a name for himself in expounding the law to give his judgment in such a matter; but against the background of learned opposition to Jesus the case seemed to offer a handle to his enemies. If Jesus recommended the law to be enforced and the death penalty to be carried out, he could implicate himself in an action which might incriminate him with the Roman authorities. If he did not, he could be accused of not taking the law seriously and could be challenged over whether he had any right to expound it. In some such sense as this the narrator may

6 be right in saying that **they said this to test him, so that they might have some charge to bring against him.**

Jesus bent down and wrote with his finger on the ground. It may be that he wrote some Hebrew characters, say the first few words of a clause from the law which bore on the case. It is sometimes possible to read Hebrew words (of which only the consonants are written) in more than one way, and writing would have been a means of drawing attention to an ambiguity. Alternatively Jesus may have been just pausing for thought – his writing on the ground may simply be a vivid touch by which the narrator tells his readers that on this occasion Jesus gave no snap answer.

And no wonder. Not only his own position, but the woman's life, was at stake. When his answer did come, it did not for a moment cast doubt on the binding force of the law on adultery; but by invoking another basic principle of the law Jesus cast the matter in a different light. To convict on a capital charge, the evidence of two independent witnesses was required. To a certain extent their evidence could be checked by examination in court. But in a Jewish court what carried most weight was the known character and probity of the witnesses. The judges required, not so much independent proof of their story, as reason to believe that the witnesses were trustworthy. If the court was convinced, no further questions need be asked: sentence was given and the witnesses had the right and indeed the duty to carry it out by throwing the first stones (Deuteronomy 17.7). In view of this heavy responsibility there were conditions the witnesses had to fulfil before their word could be accepted. Their evidence of the adulterous act had to be first-hand – which would have been unusual; and for their probity to be unquestioned they had to show that they had not been implicated in any way with the crime they alleged or with any other unlawful proceeding. The penalties for giving and accepting evidence when all these conditions were not fulfilled were heavy: both witnesses and judges would be implicated in the grave sin of bearing false witness. Jesus was in effect challenging both those who had claimed to be witnesses of the very act of adultery and those who were ready to accept their testimony. It was all very well to insist on a literal and rigorous application of the law; but had these zealous reformers considered that they must also

7 observe an equally high standard of probity as witnesses and judges? **"Let anyone among you who is without sin be the first to throw a stone at her."**

Jesus had extricated himself and saved the woman. No one now dared to pronounce the death sentence, no one was ready to begin the stoning. In the

11 absence of the witnesses, Jesus was in no position to do so himself: **"neither do I condemn you"**. At this point we can fill in from the other gospels. Jesus was certainly severe on adultery (**"do not sin again"**); but he was equally strong on forgiveness – **"Go your way."**]]

Restoring sight and raising from death

12 **"I am the light of the world."** After water, light. Jesus' affirmations about himself use one great poetical image after another. 'Light' and 'life' were two

of the evocative words used in the prologue: they are about to be explored in the following chapters. Here they simply serve as examples of the kind of thing Jesus was saying about himself. He was making exceptional claims, and the objection of his opponents at this stage was not so much to the language
13 he was using as to his right to make any such claims at all. **"You are testifying on your own behalf; your testimony is not valid."**

When making a claim, one normally needs independent evidence to support it. Jesus' enemies were saying, in effect, that without such evidence his claims could not be seriously considered. But it could happen under exceptional circumstances that no such evidence was available. Suppose, for example, one's title deeds to a property had been lost and there was no other evidence of ownership; in that case a judge or arbitrator would have no choice but to decide whether or not to accept the claimant's 'testimony on his own behalf'. (A similar situation arises today in the case of asylum-seekers who can produce no independent evidence to substantiate their claim to have been persecuted in their own country; the arbitrator has simply to decide whether to accept their word for it.) This was Jesus' defence. His claim rested ultimately on his unique origin and destiny. But the previous dialogue had
14 shown that only Jesus knew what these were. **"I know where I have come from and where I am going, but you do not know."** His case rested on facts to which only he had access. He was in the exceptional position of a claimant whose testimony about himself was the only evidence available. Therefore his testimony was **valid**.[20]
15 **"You judge by human standards"** – that is, by established judicial procedures. One reason why at this point the argument becomes hard for us to follow is that these procedures were different from anything in our experience. We are accustomed to making a clear distinction between judging and giving evidence. Judges, we assume, are utterly distinct from witnesses; their task is to determine impartially whether the evidence given by the witnesses is true. But in Jewish procedure no such clear distinction existed. If the witnesses to an act happened to be also qualified in the law, if they were reputable people, and if their testimony agreed, they could proceed at once to judgment; and, since the penalty for criminal offences was also laid down in the law, there was no need even for a judge to determine the sentence; the witnesses were obliged to see that it was carried out themselves. Thus 'judging' might often include framing an accusation, testifying as a witness, establishing the verdict and carrying out the sentence. This was the situation of the Jews who were 'judging' Jesus on his claims. But this procedure had a further consequence. In a case such as that of Jesus, where there was no independent witness, the defendant could resort to swearing an oath, 'calling God to witness'. This was a serious step to take. A false oath could

---

[20] Most previous translations have rendered this word *true*. But **valid** is also correct and brings out the meaning better.

be expected to attract the punishment of God. But, if taken, it reversed the situation. If the judges failed to believe a statement on oath, it was they who would be guilty of not accepting God as witness, and the defendant would become their judge. This, as we shall see in a moment, is what happened here.

Jesus said, **"I judge no one"** – that was not his intention. But the fact that the judges were now themselves on trial meant that he was in the position of bringing a charge against them. This procedure did require two witnesses ("Only on the evidence of two or three witnesses shall a charge be sustained", Deuteronomy 19.15). Could Jesus provide them? One was himself; who was the other? **"The Father who sent me testifies on my behalf."** Once again the Jews opted for the literal meaning when something much more significant was intended; they assumed that Jesus meant his physical father,[21] in which case Jesus' charge would fail, since one could not call on a close relative to give evidence. But Jesus' real 'father' was God; and to call God as witness was to swear an oath that one's statement was true. It was only the Jews' failure to recognize who Jesus was and who his real father was that prevented them from seeing how serious was their rejection of his claims.

21 **"Where I am going, you cannot come."** When Jesus said this earlier (7.34), his opponents could do no better than imagine that he meant he was leaving Palestine. This time their suggestion was (as it turned out) nearer the mark:

22 **"Is he going to kill himself?"** – but it was still a misunderstanding of Jesus' meaning. Jesus' origin and destiny belonged to a different order of things.

23 One way of putting it was in terms of **from below** and **from above, of this world** and **not of this world**. Admittedly this language, with its apparently philosophical overtones, was not a conventional Jewish one. If asked to think of a world more real than this one, Jewish people would normally talk of 'the age to come' as opposed to 'the present age'. But Jesus, as we have seen, used this futuristic language to speak of present realities: what people expected to come to pass in the future was already a reality for those who could accept it. Another way of putting it was in terms of a 'world above' as opposed to 'this world' below, where death still has its old power and there is no escape from sin without a recognition of who Jesus is.

25 **They said to him, "Who are you?"** Jesus had just used what by now (in this gospel) can be recognized as a characteristic idiom for solemn declarations of his nature, **"I am he."** Literally, the Greek means *I am*, and it was reasonable to ask for the predicate: 'You are *who*?' But the true answer could be expressed only in terms of that world above from which Jesus drew his knowledge and his authority. The Jews knew nothing of that world and had refused to recognize that he was invoking testimony from that quarter when he referred to his 'father', and were therefore necessarily incurring his condemnation

---

[21] The NRSV obscures this by introducing a capital letter into the question: **"Where is your Father?"** (verse 19).

26 ("**I have much to say about you and much to condemn**"). There was nothing

28 more he could say.[22] But all this would be easier to grasp "**when you have lifted up the Son of Man**", – a saying which could only have sounded enigmatic to his hearers, but which the reader now recognizes as the way this gospel describes the crucifixion and the exaltation of Jesus, the Son of Man who belongs to both 'worlds'.

31   **Then Jesus said to the Jews who had believed in him.** In this chapter the opposition of 'the Jews' had not been consistent; some had **believed in him.** But in this case, what difference was it going to make to them? In what sense could it be said that their ancestral religion was incomplete, leaving room for the radical new factor introduced by Jesus? Was not their Jewish inheritance of more ultimate importance than anything that could be added by a new preacher? This question, we know, was to be raised in a sharp form by Jewish groups within the early church – Paul's letter to the Galatians deals with it extensively. It may of course have occurred to some of Jesus' very first Jewish followers; but John can hardly have written this paragraph without being aware how relevant it was to the church of his own day.

33   The argument turned on Abraham. "**We are descendants of Abraham**" was the basic premise of the case for the exclusiveness of the Jewish religion. Abraham had been a man of exceptional faith, piety and merit. In reward for these qualities, God had made great promises to him about his descendants, on the strength of which the Jews believed that, whatever rewards might be in store for other righteous people, they themselves could look forward to life after death and a privileged place in that new order which God ultimately intended for humankind. Of course this was not automatic. It was governed by a 'covenant' which made both personal and national righteousness a condition for inheriting God's promises. Nevertheless, it was a very deeply rooted presupposition that the fact of being a Jew was a key factor in any person's salvation. Again and again in the New Testament we meet the same exclusive claim to special consideration: "**We are descendants of Abraham.**" However hard political circumstances bore on the Jewish nation (and the occupation of Palestine by the Romans seemed to some like virtual slavery), their sense of difference from all other nations remained. Even the Romans showed them exceptional consideration in allowing them to continue the practice of their own exclusive religion. In everything that mattered they felt justified in saying that they had "**never been slaves to anyone**".

To non-Jews this was liable to sound improbable and offensive. It is righteousness, self-understanding, self-control – not belonging to a particular

32 race – which afford confidence and peace of mind in relation to God. "**The**

---

[22] The NRSV translation, "**Why do I speak to you at all?**" (verse 25), assumes that John is using an idiom known only in classical Greek. This is perhaps unlikely, and the more literal rendering in the footnote, "*What I have told you from the beginning*", makes reasonable sense. Jesus has nothing more that he can say.

34 **truth will make you free . . . everyone who commits sin is a slave to sin"** –
such phrases were often on the lips of Greek philosophers. It is perhaps difficult to imagine Jesus using such language himself (though it would probably
have come quite naturally to the author of this gospel). But, in essence, Jesus'
protest against all forms of religious complacency was the same as that of any
Jewish thinker who took the facts of human sinfulness seriously. Indeed, it
was a protest that was written into the Old Testament itself and had recently
found a powerful spokesman in the person of John the Baptist.

The notion of being **"a slave to sin"** is perfectly understandable
psychologically; but Jesus draws a further lesson from it by means of a simple
comparison, which some have seen as another of the 'hidden parables' of
this gospel (see above on 5.19). In antiquity, slaves often rose to positions of
great responsibility in a household and might manage the entire estate. But
35 they had no rights, and could be dismissed at any moment. Only **the son has
a place there for ever**, only the son is always in a position to give the slaves
36 of the household their freedom. Similarly only **the Son** (now legitimately
spelled with a capital letter, though this is a modern convention) could use
the authority given to him by his heavenly Father to set free those enslaved
to sin.

But the same point could be turned against those of 'the Jews' who were
opposed to the new faith – and Jesus seems to continue with his enemies
39 in mind rather than his friends. **"Abraham is our father."** This was spoken as a statement of fact. It was the Jews' guarantee of a special relationship with God. But there were other senses, apart from the purely physical
one, in which one could call a figure of the past one's 'father' (this is Paul's
argument in Galatians 3, on which see below, p. 598). In particular, one
could mean by it that one modelled one's conduct on his. The Jews' present
40 conduct in seeking **to kill** Jesus was sufficient to show that they could not
39, 40 be **Abraham's children** in this more significant sense. **"This is not what
Abraham did."**

Jesus' opponents were ready to accept this more significant meaning of
'father', but they indignantly rejected the suggestion that their conduct did
41 not match Abraham's and so made them **illegitimate children**. Indeed, in
their case the most important sense of the word 'father' was in relation to
God himself. It was on God that they depended for instruction on how to live
their lives, and this instruction had been given through the law of Moses. By
acknowledging this and conforming their conduct with it they could claim
that God was their 'father'. But Jesus claimed to have 'come from God', to
have been 'sent by God', giving him unique ability to understand God's will
43 and to judge the religious pretensions of others. Their failure to **understand**
what he said showed that they had no true understanding of God, who could
not therefore be their 'father'.

On what in fact were these Jews modelling their conduct? They were seeking to kill an innocent man; and they were refusing to listen to a truth which

nevertheless they could not refute. This suggested a different kind of 'father' –
44 **the devil**. The devil had been **a murderer from the beginning** – he had
been the cause of the death of Adam; and one of his most important
rôles, especially in the period immediately preceding the last judgment, was
to mislead those whose faith was weak and, by deceiving them, to bring
them into condemnation: **"he is a liar and the father of lies"**. It was their
'father's' influence on them which made the Jews unable to accept Jesus'
claims.
48 **"A Samaritan"**: to call Jesus this was a studied insult. They were not merely
disowning Jesus as a fellow Jew but were identifying him with their traditional
enemies. **"And have a demon"** – this time more than an insult: they were
turning on Jesus the accusation he was making against them, that they were
acting on behalf of the devil. This sinister explanation of Jesus' words and
deeds is familiar from the other gospels ("He has Beelzebul", Mark 3.22).
Jesus of course denied the charge; but here (as in the other gospels) he
did not thereby take credit for what he said and did. By so speaking and
50 acting he was 'honouring his Father' (which meant also giving him **glory**):
their response to him touched, not Jesus, but God himself, who would pass
judgment accordingly. In the other gospels this is called the one unforgivable
sin. Here the same reality of judgment is expressed by means of its converse:
52 **"Whoever keeps my word will never see death."**
'Death' and 'life' in Jesus' vocabulary had profound religious significance.
Missing this (as usual), the Jews asked the obvious question. Abraham, the
model of righteous conduct, was dead. What sort of 'word' could Jesus utter
53 that even Abraham did not know? **"Who do you claim to be?"** This, in effect,
had been the question all along, but up to this point Jesus' answers had
been tantalizingly ambivalent. He was now about to make a claim that was
decisive. But before doing so he made an important reservation. Any answer
he gave to the challenge would seem to draw attention to himself, whereas his
whole purpose was to draw people, not to himself, but to God. If there was any
54 'honour' or **"glory"** involved (there is the same play as before on the meaning
of this word) it would be entirely attributable to God. The Jews' real error
was not so much that they did not recognize who Jesus was but that they did
not 'know God'. And so Jesus made his reply in terms of that same Abraham
whom the Jews believed to be the key to the history of their relationship with
56 God: **"Your ancestor Abraham rejoiced that he would see my day."** There
was a tradition among Jewish scholars (for which there is evidence not long
after the writing of this gospel) that Abraham was vouchsafed a vision of
things to come. Whether or not Jesus (or John through Jesus) was referring
to this, the implication of the words is clear. Abraham may have been the
key figure of Jewish religious history, but that is not to say he was the last
word in God's self-revelation. The form in which Jesus expressed this, if taken
literally, suggested that he must have been alive in Abraham's time. This, as
57 usual, is how the Jews did take it: how could a man who was **not yet fifty years**

old[23] reach back across the centuries? Understood literally, the proposition was absurd. But at the hands of the writer of this gospel, of which the first sentence proclaimed, "In the beginning was the Word", it was meaningful and

58 true. **"Before Abraham was, I am."** The statement at last brought Jesus into the open: the speaker could belong to no ordinary human category – indeed I A M was the mysterious phrase by which God identified himself to Moses (Exodus 3.14). But to his human judges it seemed axiomatic that only God could make such a statement, and it followed that Jesus must be blaspheming, for which death by stoning was the penalty prescribed in the law (Leviticus 24.16). Technically this may not have been allowed by the Romans, but in practice Jewish judges, who believed themselves to be under an obligation to see the law enforced, may have occasionally taken the risk. Once again Jesus' life was threatened; once again he avoided the threat. This time John offers

59 no explanation: **Jesus hid himself and went out of the temple.**

9.1 **He saw a man blind from birth.** Then as now the spectacle of innocent human suffering posed an acute religious question: how could a good and just God allow such things? The usual answer in Jesus' culture was that suffering and misfortune must be regarded as punishments for sin; and if, as in the present case, it appeared entirely undeserved, there was still the possibility that it was the parents who had sinned and that the son or daughter was bearing the consequences. This somewhat simplistic view needed considerable refinement if it was to account satisfactorily for all the facts, and was by no means accepted uncritically by everyone. Nevertheless the standard reaction to a case of illness or calamity was that the individual, or possibly the parents, must have committed some sin. The disciples'

2 question, **"Who sinned?"**, takes this for granted.

In the other gospels Jesus seems occasionally to make the same assumption.

3 But here he explicitly rejects it. **"He was born blind so that God's works might be revealed in him."** What Jesus was about to do would make this a sufficient explanation in this case and in any other case (such as that of Lazarus in chapter 11) on which Jesus brought his exceptional power to bear. But was it relevant to the innumerable other sufferers who could have no

4 hope of a personal cure by Jesus? The unexpected 'we' in Jesus' reply – **"we must work the works of him who sent me"** – is perhaps a hint deliberately given by the writer that Jesus' saying applied to more than his own miracles of healing: it was addressed to 'us', that is, to his followers in the church who found themselves able to exercise something of Jesus' power over physical suffering and thereby to find a meaning in illness or disability as one of the circumstances under which God makes himself known to human beings. At any rate, this healing would be one of God's 'works', that is to say, a work of a

---

[23] This was understood by many early Christian writers to mean that Jesus was between forty and fifty. But this contradicts Luke's clear statement (5.23) that Jesus was about thirty years old, and in any case does not necessarily follow from **"not yet fifty"**.

different order from the 'work' to which the sabbath rules applied (for this, as in chapter 5, was to be the cause of an official challenge); it could go on being done continuously until that period of **night** when it would seem (but

5 only seem) that human opposition had finally extinguished the **light of the world** that was Jesus.

He spat on the ground and made mud with the saliva. Spittle and mud were quite conventional remedies, though they are better known from pagan than from Jewish sources. Such treatment would normally be followed by careful washing. In Jerusalem there was only one place where fresh spring water could be had: at Siloam, the outlet of the city's only spring. This spring still exists: it runs through the long underground tunnel originally made for it by King Hezekiah and emerges at the lowest point of the old city, at the south-east corner of the city walls. It was the obvious place for a curative washing; but it also had a name which (whatever its true origin) sounded

7 like the Hebrew word for **Sent**. The symbolism would not be lost on the reader: the blind man was cured, not by any magical qualities of the water or the recipe of mud and spittle, but by Jesus, the man 'sent' from God.

14   **It was a sabbath day when Jesus made the mud.** This, as with the cure of the paralysed man in chapter 5, was once again to be the cause of controversy – 'making mud' could be interpreted as 'kneading', an activity forbidden on the sabbath. But at this moment Jesus was absent: the first part of the scene is played out between the man who had been cured and the Jews (this time

15 represented by **the Pharisees**, who were particularly rigorous in their interpretation of the sabbath regulations). As a result the episode moves rapidly, and gives the narrator scope for working in some lively repartee on both sides. One detail, perhaps, betrays his perspective. It is true that in the time

22 of Jesus individuals may have been **put out of the synagogue** for specified periods as a punishment for certain offences; but it is unlikely that this rule could have been applied to people who merely held a certain opinion, such as confessing **Jesus to be the Messiah**. It was only towards the end of the century that the rules may have been revised in such a way as permanently to exclude Christians from Jewish communities. If so, John may be reading back this later development, with the threat that it posed to Jewish Christians, into the time of Jesus. But in other respects his narrative fits its time perfectly.

The point at issue was quite simple. A man born blind had been given his sight – by any standard an astonishing cure, utterly exceptional even

32 among healing miracles (unheard of **"since the world began"** was not a great exaggeration). To the populace this showed that the healer was, at the very

17, 24, 31 least, **a prophet**, certainly not **"a sinner"**, but one who **"worships"** God and

33 **"obeys his will"**. Such a man surely was **"from God"**; and there is a hint that

16 some of the Pharisees were prepared to take the same view: **they were divided**. But 'the Jews' – the main body of Jesus' opponents – saw it differently. To them, the argument, **"How can a man who is a sinner perform such signs?"**, was not entirely convincing. There were other magicians and exorcists about who

achieved remarkable feats but who were far from being sinless. Moreover, by their own principles Jesus had been shown to be a 'sinner'. **"This man is not from God, for he does not observe the sabbath."** These uncertainties made it impossible for them to join in the popular acclamation of Jesus. Their best course seemed to be to cast doubt on what had actually happened. When this

34 failed, they simply resorted to abuse. **"You were born entirely in sins, and are you trying to teach us?"** This again was the authentic Pharisaic tone of voice towards the undisciplined multitude of their fellow Jews, sharpened in this particular case by the fact that, unlike Jesus, they assumed that anyone born blind must be suffering from the sins of the parents.

The man's own acceptance of Jesus was as definite as the Jews' rejection – and this is the climax of the episode so far. The blind man recovering his sight was symbolic: those who had no pretensions that they could 'see' came to believe in Jesus; those who relied on their 'sight' were shown to be 'blind'.

41 Jesus' rejoinder to the Pharisees is full of irony. **"If you were blind you would not have sin."** This was the exact reversal of their presupposition that someone who was blind carried some guilt. The only form of guilt that mattered now was that of those who could not 'see' who Jesus was.

10.6 **Jesus used this figure of speech.** In the other gospels, where it is usually called a 'parable', this kind of 'figure' is among the most distinctive elements in the teaching of Jesus. Some of the parables are complete stories, some are pointed comparisons with familiar scenes for the purpose of illustration. In this gospel Jesus' teaching tends to be more discursive and makes comparatively little use of parables; when it does, they belong to the second kind, that is, they are not so much stories as brief and memorable descriptions of familiar situations drawn from daily life, with an emphasis on certain details which suggest a particular application to the matter in hand. So here: the **figure of speech** consists of a description of Palestinian shepherding. In the evening – or before a storm, or at any other time when protection is necessary – the shepherd may bring the entire flock into the walled courtyard of a

1 house. (The translation **sheepfold**, suggesting fences or hurdles, is mislead-
3 ing.) The door of this courtyard is kept by a **gatekeeper**, who keeps the door closed against any marauder who might try to climb in during the night and open the door from inside; but he opens it to the shepherd when he comes next morning to lead the sheep out to pasture. The interest then shifts to the shepherd (and this may originally have been a second 'figure'). European shepherds drive their sheep from behind; but in the east the shepherd usually walks ahead of his flock. He has special calls which his own sheep know and respond to; indeed he knows his sheep so well that each has a name, just as a farmer in a small farm may have a name for every cow.

The image of a shepherd at the head of his flock occurs again and again in ancient literature. It was an obvious one for the ruler of a people or a general of an army. In Homer, Agamemnon was the 'shepherd of the people'. In the Old Testament the leaders of the people were its 'shepherds', and in Ezekiel

34 (a chapter which has many points in common with this 'figure') those shepherds are subjected to fierce criticism on the grounds of their rapacity and are threatened with being replaced by a new shepherd – David, or a descendant of David – who will make the dispersed flock into a single one, obedient to its Lord (who is God). Had Jesus' comparison been purely in this tradition, it would have contained a thinly veiled attack on the present 'shepherds' of Israel and would doubtless have been easily understood by his

6 hearers. The reason, on this occasion, that **they did not understand what he was saying to them** was perhaps that it did not exploit the obvious theme of good and bad shepherds but concentrated on certain small details, accurately observed from real life, which distinguished the real shepherd from a thief: his free access to the courtyard and his intimate familiarity with the sheep. These details are never mentioned when the shepherd image is used in the Old Testament; and Jesus' hearers did not immediately grasp the point.

The interpretation which is then given makes the comparison bear directly upon the person of Jesus. First (somewhat unexpectedly), one small detail

7 is taken as a clue to Jesus' significance: **"I am the gate for the sheep"** – a pictorial image of the claim he is to make explicitly later, "No one comes to the Father except through me"(14.6): Jesus provides access to the truth with an authority far exceeding that of previous teachers. But there is a more

11 important point of comparison than this: **"I am the good shepherd."** So far, two points have been mentioned which serve to distinguish the shepherd from the thief or impostor: his right to enter the sheepfold and the fact that

14 the sheep are used to him. Jesus refers to one of these again – **"I know my own and my own know me"** – but the thing which fundamentally distinguishes the 'good' shepherd from all others is something that has not been mentioned

11 and which must have caused surprise to his hearers: he **"lays down his life for the sheep"**. Such heroic conduct on the part of a sheep-owner when faced with, say, losing his flock to a wolf, was conceivable (though not usually to be expected); applied to the 'shepherds' of armies or nations it might be called for in times of war. But in what sense could it be said of a religious

18 leader-shepherd that it belonged to his rôle deliberately, of his **own accord**, to lay down his life? After the event Christians could doubtless understand this: his death had indeed been 'for others'. They could also understand how his death could have been of service, not just to those of his own Jewish fold, but to others outside – the Gentiles. But Jesus' original hearers were naturally as bewildered by the idea as they had been by his references to 'going away'.

19 **Again the Jews were divided because of these words.** Until the story was finished and all the clues fell into place, Jesus' words and deeds continued to display a tantalizing ambiguity.

22 **At that time the festival of the Dedication took place in Jerusalem.** Festivals, rather than seasons, offered to a Jewish writer the most natural way of indicating the time of year. Like Luke, who dates important events in the history of the church by reference to the Jewish religious calendar (see below

on Acts 2.1), John separates the various episodes in the story of Jesus by connecting each with a certain festival. Chapter 6 was dated by Passover to the spring, chapter 7 by Tabernacles to the autumn; and now it is Dedication, a winter festival instituted by Judas Maccabeus in 164 BCE to mark the re-dedication of the temple after its profanation by Antiochus Epiphanes. In the eight-day festival there were lights, processions and singing; but John clearly mentions it, not because of anything distinctive about the celebration, but because it gives the episode an approximate date (we should say, 'some time in December'). It was in any case a likely time for Jesus and many other visitors to be in Jerusalem.

It was winter. As an indication of the date this is much less precise. In Palestine there are only two seasons, that of hot, dry, settled weather (roughly from May to September) and that of periodic rainfall (October to April). In Jerusalem, wintry weather – whether it be snow and frost, wind and rain, hail and thunder – can occur at almost any time during the second of these seasons, between long periods of fine days and warm sun. In this sense, 'winter' is half the year. No one would think of dating anything by it. John's words probably mean that it was rough weather; and the other details then

23 fall into place. **The portico of Solomon** on one side of the temple precinct offered protection from rain and wind. Such porticoes were regularly used for teaching and disputations in any city where there were religious teachers and philosophers. They were also used as courts of law; and in what follows, the proceedings (which have had legal features all along) take on a more

24 formal aspect. **The Jews gathered around him** – in the Greek the expression is distinctly aggressive, evoking the picture of an army encircling a besieged city, or (more relevantly) of a court assembled in a semicircle round the accused; and the dialogue follows the same pattern, and uses many of the same words, as that which in Luke's gospel (22.67–71) takes place at the hearing of Jesus' case before a formally constituted Jewish council: Jesus is directly challenged to say whether he is the Messiah, he refuses to give an explicit reply on the grounds of the judges' unbelief, but then makes a claim (in Luke, that he will be seen at the right hand of God, in John, to be 'one with the Father') which makes him appear guilty of blasphemy and liable to the death penalty. All this, in the other gospels, takes place in the course of a hearing before the Sanhedrin and leads directly to the 'handing over' to Pilate and the crucifixion. John places the same material here, and has no record of a further hearing later: its place is taken by a kind of private interrogation before the high priest. That is to say, John uses this occasion rather than the later one to lay bare the issue between Jesus and the Jewish authorities; and its seriousness as a trial is shown by the fact that it could have led to Jesus' immediate execution. Once again, this is averted only by

39 Jesus' strange elusiveness: **he escaped from their hands.**

The scene, nevertheless, is integrated carefully into the pattern of what has gone before. The comparison with the shepherd is developed a little further;

and the discussion of Jesus' credentials is brought to a conclusion. Jesus had made various claims for himself; but the testimony of his words, even though there was a sense in which it was legally valid (8.14), had not been accepted.

25 But there was still another kind of evidence to be considered. **"The works that I do in my Father's name testify to me."** The purpose of these 'works' is

38 now finally defined: **"so that you may know and understand that the Father is in me and I am in the Father"**. In part, this language could be understood in terms of the Jewish procedures of agency: when Jesus did his work he was acting as his heavenly Father's agent, and in law it was said that 'an agent is as his principal'. But the language also belonged to a wider religious culture than that of the Jews: Jesus' relationship with God could not be adequately described within the terms of the Jewish concepts of Messiah or Son of God. His claims could well have seemed to his contemporaries to overstep the sharp line which they instinctively drew between language appropriate

33 to human beings and language appropriate to God: **"you, though only a human being, are making yourself God"**. To this Jesus replied, in effect, that they had drawn the line too strictly. Consider these verses from a psalm:

> God has taken his place in the divine council;
>   in the midst of the gods he holds judgment ...
> I say, "You are gods,
>   children of the Most High, all of you;
> nevertheless, you shall die like mortals."
> (Psalm 82.1,6)

The psalm was originally written against the background of a lingering belief in heathen gods alongside the one true God of Israel. Later interpreters, anxious to banish the idea that any such 'gods' existed, suggested that the beings meant were angels, demonic powers, or even human beings. We do not know what Jesus' hearers would have thought the psalm meant, but whatever view they took they would have been bound to concede Jesus' point that it showed that the word 'god' could be used of some being who is less than God. If so, then it was not so easy to draw the line between language that

36 was and was not blasphemous. Jesus could truthfully say, **'I am God's Son.'** Even if his adversaries did not admit that it was true, they were still on weak ground contesting that it was blasphemous.

40 **He went away again across the Jordan.** For a moment before the final conflict in Jerusalem the contact with John the Baptist's work is renewed and

42 a last tribute is paid to John's witness to Jesus, as a result of which **many believed in him there.** The interlude also prepares for the next scene; for the drama of Lazarus' death depends on Jesus being across the Jordan, a long day's journey from the scene of events.

11.1 **Lazarus of Bethany, the village of Mary and her sister Martha.** The characters in this scene are named and identified – and we receive an unexpected reminder that the readers of this gospel were expected to be already so familiar with the events of Jesus' life that John could point forward to an episode later in the story (12.1–8) in order to identify Mary.[24] The family were friends of Jesus, and it could be expected that he would use his undoubted power to cure one of them of a serious illness. This is in fact what everyone – the two sisters and their friends – assumed would happen; and they were naturally dejected (verses 21, 32), if not cynical (verse 37), when it failed to occur. What no one dared to hope was that anything could be done once Lazarus had died. Raising the dead, though not unheard of, was a rare and exceptional miracle, and Jesus could not be assumed to be able to perform it (though two instances are recorded in the other gospels, Mark 5.21–43 and Luke 7.11–17). Jesus, however, saw Lazarus' illness as an occasion for doing

4 precisely this: **"it is for God's glory, so that the Son of Man may be glorified through it"**. This was to be the spectacular climax of his 'works', but also the opportunity to give a vivid demonstration of the truth of his teaching on life and death.

4 **"This illness does not lead to death"** – the NRSV has introduced a gratuitous possibility of misunderstanding: Jesus is *not* saying that the illness was of a kind that is not normally fatal,[25] but that Lazarus was not going to die (to which the reader will attach a new meaning by the time the story has finished). But it was naturally taken by Jesus' disciples to mean that there was nothing further to worry about, and they were therefore surprised when, two days later, Jesus suggested returning to the neighbourhood of Jerusalem and exposing himself to the danger he had just left behind. Jesus answered

9 them, first, with a parable. **"Are there not twelve hours of daylight?"** Jesus' 'hour' had not yet come; when it did, it would be 'night', the time for 'stumbling'. (But the **light of this world**, though it could mean simply the sun, would have suggested to Christian readers the presence of the one who is "the true light, which enlightens everyone" (1.9), giving security to all who trust it.) Secondly, Jesus had a positive reason for going back, which he grad-

11 ually unfolded to his disciples: **"Lazarus has fallen asleep"**. In Greek, as in English, this was ambiguous. The disciples remembered that Jesus had said that Lazarus' illness was not going to be fatal, and seized eagerly on what seemed like hopeful news (known apparently by intuition to Jesus): falling

14 into a calm sleep was a sign that the fever was passing. **Then Jesus told them plainly, "Lazarus is dead."** Before, the journey seemed pointless because Jesus had said that Lazarus would recover; now, it seemed pointless because he was already dead. Nothing but certain death awaited Jesus in Jerusalem. One at least of the disciples made up his mind what was expected of them.

16 **"Let us also go, that we may die with him."**

---

[24] Two sisters named Mary and Martha are mentioned in Luke 10.38–9, but their 'village' is in Galilee, a long way from Bethany. Nevertheless, Martha is described as 'serving' in 12.2 below, and there is a number of other points of contact with the synoptic gospels.

[25] Literally the Greek means *is not leading* or *will not lead*.

We can reconstruct what had happened. Lazarus had died soon after the sisters sent their message to Jesus. As was usual, he was buried the same day.

38 The tomb **was a cave, and a stone was lying against it.** There are many such tombs in Palestine: they consist of a rock chamber, with small horizontal niches or tunnels hewn out of the sides. The corpse was wrapped in linen and laid on one of these rock shelves. The tomb was then sealed by a large flat stone placed over the entrance until the next burial should take place. The mourning continued for some days. It was a highly esteemed act of charity to visit and console the bereaved. Mary and Martha were naturally surrounded

19 by their friends from the city. (When these are called **the Jews** the word has a completely different connotation from 'the Jews' who were Jesus' religious

17 opponents). **When Jesus arrived, he found that Lazarus had already been in the tomb four days.** There is probably a touch of folk religion in this. For three days, people thought, the soul continued to haunt the body and a return to life might still seem just conceivable. After that, decomposition

17, 39 began and death was irrevocable. We are told twice over that Jesus did not arrive until the fourth day. Unlike the two occasions in the other gospels on which he brought someone back to life, what he was about to do now exceeded the bounds of imagined possibility.

The story is told with considerable dramatic tension, and, unlike the previous miracle stories, receives little commentary. But it contains a characteristic

23 piece of dialogue. Jesus said to Martha, **"Your brother will rise again."** This sounded like conventional spiritual consolation; most people believed in

24 **"the resurrection on the last day"** and it could be reassuring to know that one's dear ones would be there. But this, of course, was a misunderstanding (characteristic of this gospel) of what Jesus meant. Lazarus was to rise again *now*, and this would be more than a miracle of resuscitation: it would demonstrate that the quality of living offered by Jesus to those who believe

25 was such that even physical death could not impair it. **"I am"** – and this time there is a predicate which is the most sensational of all those which Jesus has claimed – **"the resurrection and the life."** Resurrection, an afterlife concept, was being brought into the present in the very person of Jesus. Martha could hardly grasp this; but she did get so far as to make a correct confession of

27 who Jesus was, albeit a limited one. **Messiah** and **Son of God** were titles from her own religious vocabulary. But she may have sensed that this **"one coming into the world"** was bringing something radically new into human experience.

33 Amid the general grief for the dead man, Jesus was **greatly disturbed in spirit and deeply moved.** The first of these phrases translates a word which normally expresses sternness or anger – in Mark 1.43 it is translated 'sternly warning', in Mark 14.5 'scolding'; the second suggests confused agitation. In view of Jesus' apparent confidence about the outcome, was he really just adding his laments to those of the mourners? The question is at its sharpest

35 a moment later: **Jesus began to weep.**[26] The bystanders naturally assumed
36 that this was simply grief: **"See how he loved him!"** But were they right? By
now we are familiar with the way this gospel uses a banal misunderstanding
to lead the reader to a deeper meaning. It is clear from the very beginning
of the narrative that Jesus, far from being disconcerted by Lazarus' death,
welcomed it as an opportunity to show forth the glory of God. It would have
been surprising (however human) if, when it came to the point, he felt it
to be a calamity to be wept over. On the other hand, in all the gospels Jesus
has moments of anger and indignation, usually provoked by the inhumanity
and hypocrisy of people and institutions. The same may be the case here
(and is suggested by verse 33). All these Jewish people (doubtless including
some professional mourners, who would certainly have been less than fully
sincere) professed a belief in the resurrection of the dead, but were weeping
their eyes out as if the death of their friend Lazarus was something tragic and
final. It could well have been this exhibition of almost culpable faithlessness
that moved Jesus to tears of indignation. He was soon to show them how
foolish their weeping had been.

The tension continues to rise with Jesus' command to open the tomb. No
one wished to be confronted with the reality of a corpse decomposing four
days after burial. Could Jesus really perform such a feat? But that was exactly
how Jesus did *not* want them to think of it. It was not he, Jesus, who could do
42 such a thing, but God acting through him – hence his prayer **"for the sake
of the crowd"**. The miracle was intended to persuade them that he was not
acting on his own account: God had **sent** him.

Even this most sensational of all Jesus' actions did not convince everyone.
45, 47 Many **believed in him**; but the continued hostility of others resulted in **a
meeting of the council**, the only such meeting recorded in this gospel. It
is possible to question John's account of this scene on points of historical
detail. If the meeting was a formal session of the Sanhedrin and not just a
hurried conference of influential people (the word translated **council** could
bear either meaning), **the Pharisees** as such would have had no official right
49 to convene it; and the statement that Caiaphas was **high priest that year**
makes one wonder whether John knew that he was in fact continuously high
priest from 18 to 36 CE. On the other hand, in outline the episode is entirely
convincing. All the gospels agree that the 'handing over' of Jesus was the
result of plotting by the Jewish authorities; and one of the most plausible
motives for this action (an unusual one for subject peoples) was fear of what
the consequences might be if someone who was regarded as Messiah were
48 allowed to gather a considerable following: **"the Romans will come and
destroy both our holy place and our nation"**. This had happened by the

---

[26] The Greek means literally *Jesus wept*. The imperfect tense, which is normally used to
express *began to*, is not used here.

time the gospel was written; it could well have happened earlier if a serious insurrectionary movement had got under way under the leadership of a man such as they took Jesus to be.

On the face of it, Caiaphas' advice was sound political sense: the handing over of one scapegoat to the occupying power was a small price to pay for avoiding serious trouble. But what might have been merely the practical wisdom of a political leader was seen by John as an instance of inspired prophesying such as might be expected from the high priest. Jesus did indeed 51 **die for the nation**, but not in the sense of saving it from Roman oppression: it was to make possible a new kind of life. And, John adds, this would also benefit many who did not belong to 'that nation' but would be gathered by 52 Christ into a new community of the **children of God.**

In any case Jesus once more retired from the neighbourhood of Jerusalem. 54 The other gospels do not allow for this withdrawal, and **a town called Ephraim** occurs nowhere else in the New Testament. Ephraim is normally the name of a region, not a town, though a place of this name is mentioned in 2 Samuel 13.23. It can plausibly be identified with an ancient site some $12\frac{1}{2}$ miles north-east of Jerusalem on the edge of the arid range of mountains (**the wilderness**) that fall down to the Jordan valley.

55 **Now the Passover of the Jews was near.** In this gospel all Jesus' visits to Jerusalem have been associated with a festival. His last, which ends in his death, is placed in all the gospels at the time of Passover. But John opens his account a few days earlier than the other gospels with the first influx of visitors – those who, either by living abroad or for some other reason, had made themselves ritually 'unclean' and had to be in Jerusalem for seven days in order to complete the rites of purification which would enable them to approach the temple on the day of the festival. This was a day or two before the main crowd of pilgrims would arrive. It was the moment for the authorities to begin making their plans and for the beginning of popular speculation whether Jesus would take the risk of joining the pilgrimage.

12.2 **They gave a dinner for him.** A somewhat similar episode is recounted in all the gospels. In Luke (7.36–50) it has nothing to do with Jesus' approaching death and burial; the woman who anoints Jesus' feet after washing them and wiping them with her hair is a stranger who intends simply to express her gratitude and love and who thereby gains forgiveness of her sins. In Mark, on the other hand (14.3–9) – who is followed in most of the details by Matthew (26.6–13) – the woman's action is presented as a kind of rehearsal for the anointing which should have been (but in fact was not) administered to the body of Jesus before his burial: as such, it was a notable 'act of kindness' and therefore far more meritorious than an ordinary contribution to the needs of the poor. Most of these elements are present here, and even some of the 3 same phraseology (the rare Greek expression translated **pure nard** is exactly as in Mark 14.3 – though this could be due to copyists having assimilated the two accounts); but the narrative is different in certain respects. First,

2 the characters are all identified. Among the guests was **Lazarus; Martha**
was behind the scenes serving (characteristically, if she was the Martha of
Luke 10.40); the woman who performed the extravagant act of devotion was
3 Martha's sister **Mary**. The shocked reaction which this caused is ascribed,
4 not to the disciples in general, but to **Judas Iscariot**, and gives John an
opportunity to fill in a trait of Judas' character in advance of the betrayal
6 (**he was a thief**). The precision about the people involved goes with a vivid
3 telling of the story. (**The house was filled with the fragrance of the perfume**
is a detail not found in any of the other accounts.) But what meaning did
John find in all this? If he had wished to emphasize Mary's humble service to
Jesus he would surely have mentioned what was in fact the main point of a
similar service performed by Jesus later – the washing of the guests' feet. (John
appears to follow Luke's version in saying that Mary **wiped them with her
hair**, but then confuses things by suggesting she did so *after* anointing them
with oil!) Nor does he make anything of the contrast between the routine act
of giving money to the poor and the exceptional act of kindness of anointing
a corpse (which seems to be the main point of the scene in Mark). The entire
meaning is compressed into a single comment by Jesus – but unfortunately
7 the text is obscure at this point. Literally it appears to mean *so that she may
keep it for my burial*. But in this gospel Jesus' corpse will be anointed, not by
Mary, but by Nicodemus, who brings a hundred times more ointment for the
purpose (19.39–40). The NRSV addition, "***She bought it* so that she might
keep it for the day of my burial**", is no more than a guess at John's meaning;
but whatever the exact sense of the words, Mary's action is evidently seen as
some sort of anticipation of Jesus' death and burial.

The raising of Lazarus, which is recounted only in John's gospel, provides a further motive for the interest and tensions surrounding Jesus at the
moment of his arrival in Jerusalem. But the story of the entry itself occurs
in all the gospels, and only certain details are different here. One significant
13 one is John's statement that the crowd **went out to meet** Jesus and started
their acclamation *before* he mounted a donkey, as if Jesus' commandeering
of a mount was a response to the crowd's enthusiasm, not its cause. Another
difference is that the 'branches' of the other accounts have here become
'palms', such as were brought up from the Jordan valley by pilgrims at certain festivals (though not normally for Passover) and were appropriate for a
religious procession; and the inclusion (as in Luke) of the word **King** in the
crowd's acclamation, in addition to the words from the processional psalm
(118.25–6), points forward to the importance this title will have in the sequel:
17 the crowd's readiness to **testify** to Jesus' 'kingship' is yet another strand in
the texture of 'witness' that has been building up since the beginning of the
14 gospel. In the face of all this, **Jesus found a young donkey** – the story of
its commandeering is completely omitted by John. His disciples may have
thought this was for practical reasons (however startling they may have found
the idea of a pilgrim *riding* into Jerusalem instead of going on foot). If so,

they missed the point yet again: the meaning of Jesus' action (which John says they grasped only later) was to be found in the fact that such an entry had been prophesied and that the 'king' would be more than a political figure 15 (Zechariah 9.9, which is quoted only in summary form compared with the other gospels, even leaving out the significant word 'humble').

If the accounts of this episode in the other gospels contain much the same elements, they leave tantalizing questions unanswered. What did the crowd recognize in Jesus which made them follow the disciples' lead and give him a triumphal reception? Why did the demonstration peter out as suddenly as it had begun? John's account makes it all sound more rational. The crowds acclaimed Jesus because of the sensational raising of Lazarus which they had seen or heard about; and, far from petering out, the demonstration went on 19 for as long as might be expected – for some time it could be said that **"the world has gone after him!"** This popular excitement was of course superficial and transient: the crowd would follow Jesus only so long as the impression 16 of Lazarus' resurrection was fresh in their minds. Even the disciples **did not understand** the sense in which it was appropriate to acclaim this humble, politically powerless man 'king'. In this gospel Jesus' entry into Jerusalem was one more of those moments when his claims were half-accepted, half-rejected, his true nature at best half-understood.

A festival at Jerusalem drew a great crowd not only of Jewish pilgrims: people of other nationalities, whether they were proselytes or merely sympathetic to things Jewish, also made the journey to visit the holy city. It was 20 convenient to call such people **Greeks**, though they might come from almost anywhere in the eastern part of the Roman empire. Their common language would be Greek; and the main thing that was meant by the term was that 21 they were not Jews by birth. Some of them expressed a desire to **see Jesus** – which sounds a simple enough request; but the fact that it elicited from Jesus a series of exceedingly solemn sayings shows that we must be prepared 19 to look for a deeper significance in it. The Jews had said that **"the world has gone after him!"**, meaning simply that Jesus had drawn a crowd. But, taken literally, their words suggested something more sensational. Jesus was attracting not only his fellow Jews but 'the world', that is, strangers and foreigners, people who had no allegiance to the Jewish religion. An example is immediately given in the 'Greeks' who approach Philip. But the readers of the gospel knew that the real fulfilment of these words was the existence of the Christian church, which had by now far outgrown its Jewish origins and was mainly composed of people who were, not Jews, but 'Greeks'.

23 The process by which this was to happen was now beginning. **"The hour has come for the Son of Man to be glorified."** Previous references to the 'hour' have been to show that it had *not* yet come; now the process of 'glorification' was under way. Conventional 'Son of Man' expectation would have construed this as a statement that he was now to be installed, like the figure in Daniel 7, on the right hand of God. But John has been working with a different scenario.

The 'glorifying' of the Son of Man would consist in his being 'lifted up' on the cross: what appeared to be a dark destiny of condemnation and death would in fact be the moment when he was **glorified**. The reader is helped
24 to understand this by a brief parable: **"unless a grain of wheat falls into the earth and dies . . ."** Parables about single seeds growing into fruitful plants occur in the other gospels (see especially Mark 4.26–32), usually illustrating spectacular growth from tiny beginnings. But now there is a new idea: **"if it dies, it bears much fruit"**. The idea that a seed (and indeed nature herself) dies in the dead season of winter and comes to life again in the spring underlies a great deal of religious symbolism. (There is another application of it in 1 Corinthians 15.36–8.) The seed, when it falls to the ground, even if it does not literally 'die', nevertheless enters the yearly cycle of death and rebirth. In this sense it 'dies'; and this enables the parable of **much fruit** being reaped from a tiny grain to relate to that death – the death of Jesus which is also his glorification – which must precede the prodigious growth which is to follow. But this death also conditions the way in which men and women must seek to serve and follow Jesus. In a sequence of ideas very similar to those in Mark 8.34–8 (and elsewhere), the implications for Jesus' followers are spelled out.
27   **"Now my soul is troubled."** All the gospels record a moment before the crisis when Jesus seems to have felt a pang of irresolution. Here the setting is different – Jerusalem, not Gethsemane – but it is clear that the experience being described is the same. We must beware of psychologizing. Jesus' words are chosen, not because these alone exactly describe his emotions, but because (being an allusion to Psalm 6.3–4) they evoke a classical expression of the agony of one whose faith is stretched to breaking point. Both here and on the cross, the traditional language of Hebrew spirituality conveys the sense that Jesus, like countless just sufferers before him, was in a position where circumstances made it excruciatingly hard to continue to believe in God. The admission is unexpected: apart from this one moment Jesus moves with a serene sense of purpose. It is also short-lived. In the other gospels the prayer for deliverance gives place to acceptance: "not what I want, but what you want" (Mark 14.36). Here, the same is said in the distinctive idiom of John's gospel (Jesus' death and resurrection will be his 'glorification'), but also (as in
28 the Gethsemane accounts) with a reminiscence of the Lord's Prayer: **"Father** (the opening of the prayer in Luke's version), **glorify** (meaning much the same as 'hallow') **your name."** And the supernatural answer to this prayer (corresponding perhaps to "an angel from heaven" in some versions of Luke's account of Gethsemane, 22.43) is in effect that the glory already attendant on Jesus is now to be confirmed by that supreme act of glorification by which the Son of Man will be lifted up – on the cross.

Jesus' moment of hesitation was brief. But for others there remained the great difficulty of seeing the glory in the humiliation, of accepting that Jesus' death could be an expression of God's glory. Jesus' teaching had been prepar-
30 ing them for this; now a voice from heaven declared it to be so. **"This voice**

has come for your sake, not for mine." Even this, of course, was ambivalent.

29 Some **said that it was thunder.** But it was the beginning of the events leading up to the crucifixion which would present the decisive challenge to declare

31 for or against Jesus: **"Now is the judgment of this world."** Many would doubtless declare against; but this would not rob Jesus' death of its power. It was a firm Christian belief, supported by a number of Jesus' sayings, that the devil himself (**"the ruler of this world"**) was vanquished by the crucifixion – this is explicitly stated in Hebrews 2.14; and it was the crucifixion which finally broke through the exclusiveness of the Jewish religion and enabled

32 Jesus to **draw all people** to himself.

"Lifted up." The expression is deliberately ambiguous – indeed the macabre pun was apparently quite well known. (It is exploited, for instance, in the story of Pharaoh's two servants in Genesis 40.12–19.) Its most natural meaning was 'exalted', but it could also mean 'lifted up (on the cross) for

33 execution'. John puts his readers wise to the second meaning – **he said this to indicate the kind of death he was to die** – and then tells us that this was in fact the meaning Jesus' listeners seized on and found inconsistent with their

34 belief in a Messiah. **"We have heard from the law that the Messiah remains for ever."** There were various interpretations of those passages in scripture which seemed to point forward to a Messiah; but most interpreters agreed that 'his kingdom would last for ever'. Call him what they would – Messiah in their own terminology, or Son of Man (apparently) in that of Jesus – the one they expected was surely not to be **lifted up** – to die! This, of course, was the question posed by the gospel right from the beginning. How could the Word be rejected, how could the Son of God be crucified? Salvation depended on believing these things. But now it was becoming urgent to declare one's position. In the evening, travellers must not dawdle: they must walk while

36 they **have the light** in order not to be overtaken by darkness. And Jesus was the light.

36 For a brief period Jesus was now off stage: he **departed and hid from them.** John uses this moment to sum up, first the people's response (or lack

37 of it), and secondly Jesus' own message. After **so many signs** performed in their presence these people ought surely to have been prepared to believe. Yet it was the Jews of Jerusalem who would soon be responsible for Jesus being condemned to death, and at the time this gospel was written it was the Jewish nation which was the most unwilling to accept Jesus as Messiah. They were, in fact, the extreme case of the paradox stated at the beginning, "he came to what was his own, and his own people did not accept him" (1.11). Concluding this part of the narrative, John offers two explanations of the paradox, the first theoretical, the second practical. The theoretical one was one that was seized on most eagerly by Christians right from the beginning

38 and may even go back to Jesus himself: **This was to fulfil the word spoken by the prophet Isaiah.** Scripture, rightly interpreted, foretold the rejection of Christ. Isaiah 53 (which begins, **"Who has believed our message?"**), with

its description of a suffering servant who bore the sins of many, was one
40 of the passages most frequently appealed to. Another was Isaiah 6.9, **"He
has blinded their eyes . . . "**, which in all the gospels (though in a slightly
different way in each) is invoked to explain the failure of Israel to accept
and understand Jesus (see above on Mark 4.11–12). However mysterious the
fact of this rejection, and however brutal this explanation might sound, it
remained true that these things were foretold in scripture and must therefore
have been determined long ago by God.

The second explanation was practical. There was a powerful incentive not
42 to acknowledge Jesus: **fear that they would be put out of the synagogue.** In
this form the threat was probably more of a reality at the time the gospel
was written than in the time of Jesus (see above on 9.22). But the general
point was valid at any time, and could be neatly expressed through a play
on words which has already been exploited earlier (see above on 5.41–4).
The same word meant both human 'honour' or praise and divine 'glory'. It
was only to be expected that ordinary, sinful human beings would go for the
43 former: **they loved human glory more than the glory that comes from God.**
44 **Then Jesus cried aloud.** A moment ago we were told he was in hiding,
and now there seems to be no audience, no particular occasion for Jesus'
discourse. But John needs a summary of his claims to set against the summary
of the people's disbelief; and the expression **cried aloud** has overtones of the
law court (see above on 1.15). This was Jesus' final testimony, and all the
ideas it contains have occurred before. But the emphasis is all on one point:
"Whoever believes in me believes not in me but in him who sent me." Jesus
is no independent divinity; he presents no challenge on his own account.
Declaring for or against Jesus is nothing more nor less than declaring for or
against God. That is where he rests his case.

Last words to the disciples

Up to this point the gospel has been wrestling with a paradox. It has illustrated
the ambiguity necessarily involved in the appearance of the Son of God on
earth and the diversity of response which he elicited. It has described the
words and actions by which Jesus sought to confront men and women with
the challenge of his presence and it has recorded the strength of the opposition
he aroused. There were certainly some who did 'accept him'; but the main
emphasis has been on those who rejected him and were soon to bring him
to his death – an emphasis which may well reflect the uneasy relationship of
early Christian congregations with Jewish synagogues at the time the gospel
was written.

Yet the story of Jesus was not only a story of his rejection. By the time this
gospel was written, the Christian church had taken firm root in many parts of
the Mediterranean world; and this church traced its origins to those who in
Jesus' lifetime had given their allegiance to him. By some, Jesus *was* 'accepted';

and to them he gave a great deal in return. As was said in the prologue, "to all who received him . . . he gave power to become children of God" (1.12). The first Christians possessed in common, not only the faith that Jesus was the Messiah, but a conviction of his continuing presence among them, and a relationship with him and with each other which was strong and new. It is with this aspect of Jesus' legacy that the following chapters are concerned.

The other gospels all contain sections of teaching given privately by Jesus to his disciples, but these are usually scattered over the whole course of his activity. Only in Matthew is there a serious attempt to gather this private teaching together into sustained discourses, but these too occur at intervals throughout the gospel. In John, by contrast, all this teaching comes together in the final stages of the story and fills several pages. In part it makes use of themes already introduced in earlier chapters; but in part it works out a new set of concepts, in particular the 'love' which is to bind Jesus' followers together and the way in which his 'going to his Father' will guarantee his continuing presence with them on earth.

In form, also, these chapters are unlike what has gone before: no longer a series of dramatic episodes followed by dialogue, but a long discourse interrupted only by occasional questions from the disciples. It is of course entirely probable that Jesus devoted much of the last night of his life on earth to talking with his disciples. But we must remember that, when John came to write this part of his gospel, he is likely to have been influenced by the historians' convention of writing up a long speech purporting to have been made shortly before the hero's death and summarizing his ideals and the responsibilities he was entrusting to his followers. John's is not the only gospel to make use of this convention: in Luke's gospel, Jesus' last supper is also made the occasion for a parting speech to the disciples (22.14–38). But here the opportunity to gather together Jesus' private teaching at this point is exploited much more systematically, and the moment in Jesus' life which in Mark and Matthew is described simply as a solemn meal and is made to carry only a few important sayings of Jesus becomes here an occasion for the longest discourse of Jesus in the gospel.

In the other gospels this meal is stated to have been a Passover supper, celebrated by Jesus with his disciples according to Jewish custom. In the course of it Jesus spoke certain words over the bread and wine which gave the meal an altogether new significance and made it the origin and prototype of the distinctive act of Christian worship, the eucharist. John says nothing of all this here: he has already put together Jesus' eucharistic teaching in chapter 6. Indeed, the chronology he follows for the last days of Jesus' life makes it impossible for this supper to have been a regular celebration of Passover. From the historical point of view this creates difficulties. The meal he describes is no ordinary one. It was a sufficiently formal occasion for the

13.23 party to be **reclining** on couches round the table; and it was held, not in the afternoon (the usual time for the main meal of the day), but at night. These details would fit a formal party or festivity such as a wedding. It would also fit a Passover supper, which is in fact the only kind of occasion we should expect Jesus and his disciples to have marked with such careful formality. But we are

1 specifically told that this was **before the festival of Passover**, and by John's reckoning Passover night, when a meal of this character would be enjoyed by all the Jews in Jerusalem, was the following night. It is not easy to imagine Jesus deliberately holding his own celebration one day earlier than everyone else (though some have suggested this to get out of the difficulty), and in any case the lambs for these meals were not ritually slaughtered until the following day. But behind this historical difficulty lies a more significant difference of approach between John's gospel and the others. All the gospels agree that Jesus' crucifixion happened around Passover time; but by the time they were written the exact dating may not have been possible to establish. Mark (apparently followed by Matthew and Luke) follows a chronology according to which Jesus was crucified on the day following Passover night, and the effect of this was to give Jesus' last supper with his disciples the character of a Passover celebration. John, however, placed Jesus' supper twenty-four hours earlier, so that his death was simultaneous with the ritual slaughter of lambs in the temple the afternoon before Passover. This made it possible to understand Jesus' death as that of a Passover victim – and this understanding was certainly shared by many Christians (1 Corinthians 5.7); but it necessarily removed any specifically Passover associations from Jesus' last supper. Which version is historically correct we shall probably never know; but it is certain that the church was enriched from the very beginning by the theological associations of both the possible chronologies.

The main element of drama is provided by an action of Jesus which is recorded only in this gospel (though it may be alluded to in Luke 22.27).

4 Jesus **got up from the table, took off his outer robe, and tied a towel around himself.** This was the uniform of the slave whose special task it was to carry out the hospitable act of washing the guests' feet before a formal supper. The act itself was one which a Jew would have felt to be very much beneath his dignity; indeed a Jewish slave was usually spared the task if a gentile slave was available; otherwise it was performed by a woman (as in Luke 7.38; 1 Timothy 5.10). The surprise and shock caused by Jesus' action was voiced by

6 Peter: **"Lord, are you going to wash my feet?"** But, as often in this gospel, this naïve reaction was merely the cue for Jesus to continue the conversation on a deeper level.

On this occasion the deeper meaning is no more than hinted at, and it is not easy to be sure how these hints should be interpreted. The first hint is one

7 which occurs elsewhere in this discourse: **"You do not know now what I am doing, but later you will understand."** One of the themes of these chapters is the connection between the relatively short period of Jesus' activity on earth and the long-term life of the church. **"Later"** meant after the resurrection, the time when Jesus' presence would be known mainly through the Spirit.

In this gospel, water is often a symbol of the Spirit; and Jesus' act of washing his disciples' feet suggests their possession of the Spirit after the resurrection. But we can probably go further. The rite by which Christians received the Spirit was baptism; and all the things which Jesus said about washing his disciples' feet could also be said about the symbolic 'washing' of baptism. It was baptism which marked the solemn moment when the believer could

8, 10 begin to have a **share** with Jesus. It was effective once and for all – **"one who has bathed does not need to wash"**. And since it procured forgiveness of sins it made any other purification ceremony entirely unnecessary: after baptism the Christian was **entirely clean**. All this teaching about the future rite of Christian baptism was elicited by Peter's unperceptive reactions to Jesus' wish to wash his feet. Indeed, it could even perhaps be said (in case anyone wondered whether the disciples had ever been baptized themselves) that this *was* their baptism.

Nevertheless, whether or not Jesus' action had a deeper meaning symbol-

15 izing Christian baptism, it certainly had a direct ethical message: **"I have set you an example, that you also should do as I have done for you."** If Jesus' mastership and lordship could be expressed in such a radical reversal of the usual conventions, the relationship of Christians with one another must be expected to follow a similarly radical pattern of mutual service. So far, Jesus' disciples have been there merely to listen and to question and to make their own decision in the face of the challenge of his work and teaching. But now we are introduced to the ethic which must characterize their discipleship and bind them together. Jesus washing his disciples' feet set a standard for their solidarity with one another; it was also the first and most striking illustration

1 of a theme which runs right through this discourse: **Having loved his own who were in the world, he loved them to the end.**

The scene also provides a fresh application of a proverb-like saying which elsewhere (both in John 15.20 and Matthew 10.24) is intended to show that disciples cannot expect to receive less persecution than their master:

16 **"servants are not greater than their master"**. But here it is clearly meant to silence any protest that washing a fellow Christian's feet is beneath one's dignity. The addition, **"nor are messengers greater than the one who sent them"**, makes the same point, but introduces another model for the relationship between Jesus and his disciples, that of messengers or ambassadors – to maltreat whom is to maltreat the power who sent them – or rather (since this is the technical meaning of the word) of an *agent*. It was a principle in law that agents are 'as' the principal who sent them. This model has already been invoked to elucidate the relationship between Jesus and God (5.23); now (as in Matthew 10.40) it is applied to the disciples: they are Jesus' agents, which should prevent them from acting in any way that does not reflect Jesus' own activity but also assures them that when they are truly about his business they have the blessing of God as well as a share in the rejection that their principal – Jesus – has experienced.

But the scene has a further element of drama, caused (as in the other gospels) by the presence of Judas Iscariot, who was about to betray his master – a betrayal made still more horrifying by the fact that the betrayer had just shared this meal with Jesus and so was to betray, not just a friend, but the table fellowship which such a meal established. **'The one who ate my bread has lifted his heel against me'** (Psalm 41.9) was one of the classic Old Testament formulations of such a betrayal. Jesus was well aware of what was to happen (not the first time he has shown psychic powers), and became **troubled in spirit** – the same expression as in 12.27: Jesus' apparent serenity was by no means unbroken. He then identified the traitor. John allows us to visualize the scene. Jesus lay on his left side with his head towards the table, his right arm free to help himself to food. The disciple on his right was in the same position; his head would have been at about the level of Jesus' chest (which is what the Greek for **reclining next to him** literally means) and he would have been in a better position than anyone to whisper to Jesus. Jesus' gesture to Judas was perfectly natural. Bread was the main implement used at table: one dipped it like a spoon into a common dish, and it was polite to do so for a guest. It could well have escaped the notice of all present except that of the disciple **whom Jesus loved** (the first appearance of this cryptic designation: see below on 21.24); but it was a poignant signal for the traitor to begin his work. Here (as in Luke 22.3) the question why Judas did what he did, which we would tend to explore in psychological terms, is answered quite simply: **the devil had already put it into the heart of Judas,** and now **Satan entered into him.** Jesus offered no resistance, but seems almost to have abetted him, enabling him to slip away without arousing the others' suspicions.

When he had gone out. We can easily imagine that the departure of the traitor relieved the tension and created an easier atmosphere for Jesus to instruct his disciples. But this may have more to do with modern psychology than with the intention of the narrator, to whom the significance of Judas' exit may have been that it finally set in motion the events leading up to the crucifixion. Certainly the repeated emphasis on the moment that had been reached (**"immediately . . . Now"**) suggests a turning point in the story more significant than the fact that the disciples were now alone with Jesus without their one disloyal member.

"Now the Son of Man has been glorified." For some time the reader has been prepared to see in this saying a more subtle meaning than was suggested by the conventional picture of a 'Son of Man' who, after a period of obscurity and suffering, would be exalted to share the visible glory of God. The moment of Jesus' deepest humiliation and final rejection was to be the moment of what in fact was his 'glorification', since the crucifixion itself, followed by the resurrection and the emergence of a church imbued with the Spirit, was that which would enable all humanity to perceive his 'glory'. Once again there is an important proviso: the glory attaching to the Son of Man was not intended for his own glorification in any kind of competition with God: it would be shared in complete mutuality with God's own glory.

33 **'Where I am going, you cannot come.'** To Jesus' adversaries, this had been a riddle they were unable to answer (7.33–6). But even for his disciples the saying caused difficulties. It was natural for them to think that Jesus' progress towards glorification was one on which they would be privileged to accompany him. A period of separation from him, even if temporary, was hard to understand. A full explanation was about to be given; but a

37 false answer had to be disposed of first. Peter said, **"I will lay down my life for you."** Hints have already been given that Jesus' departure would involve him in 'laying down his life' for others; why should not his disciples do the same? The short answer was that they simply were not capable of it. Peter was in fact to deny Jesus (all the gospels contain this prediction, though in somewhat different contexts). No, they would have to be separated from Jesus. The followers would be left without their master. What would hold them together then, and how would their allegiance be known? Part of the

34 answer lay in a **"new commandment"** (new, at least, in the narrative of this gospel, and new in the radical interpretation Jesus was to put on it), **"that you love one another"**.

14.1 **"Do not let your hearts be troubled. Believe in God."** This is the traditional language of faith: it is the spirituality of many of the psalms. But Jesus goes on: **"believe also in me"**. He is not only a decisive new factor in

2 religious belief, he adds something also to belief in life after death. **"In my Father's house there are many dwelling places"** – this much was nothing new: an accepted picture of the afterlife was of a number of different 'places' to which people would be allotted depending on the moral qualities they had shown during their life. But faith in Christ introduced a new element into this picture. The 'dwelling place' of Christians would be such that after death they would certainly be with Christ; and there was a sense in which Jesus' 'going' would be like that of someone going on ahead[27] to make sure of the accommodation and then returning (in a manner about to be explained) –

3 **"I will come again and will take you to myself, so that where I am, there you may be also."**

What then must a Christian do to make sure of coming to that 'place'? What is the 'way' to get there? One of the disciples, Thomas, is made to ask this question in a crudely literal form, as if a knowledge of the geography of heaven were necessary in order to be sure of finding oneself in the right part of it. Jesus characteristically exploits this in order to give a more profound

6 insight: **"I am the way."** Following Jesus guarantees being with him hereafter, just as belief in him guarantees knowledge of **the truth** and a share in eternal

---

[27] Given that the original had no punctuation, translators have to make a choice in verse 2 between a question referring back to a previous saying, such as 12.26 (as in the text in the NRSV), and a statement (as in the footnote).

life. And this 'way' appears to be exclusive: **"No one comes to the Father except through me"** – a text which is eagerly seized on by those who believe they should proclaim Christianity as the only way to personal salvation, but which causes acute embarrassment to those who are more ready to respect the validity of other religious approaches to God. For John's first readers it doubtless expressed their conviction that they were right to insist on the necessity of faith in Christ in the face of the Jews' rejection of Jesus' claims. If so, this is not the only instance of a dogmatic exclusiveness in John's gospel which may well be due to the circumstances of the time and which is incompatible with the larger horizons in which Christianity must now find its place.

8 **"Lord, show us the Father, and we will be satisfied."** The request was natural: instead of constantly straining to glimpse and understand how God was brought near to them by Jesus, the disciples yearned for a direct vision of the Father. But this only showed how little they had grasped of what Jesus was. In him, they had seen and known as much as is possible for human beings in this world. Jesus' words and works constituted the final evidence on which one must base one's faith in God. Jesus' authority – the reason he

10 was to be believed and trusted – was due to his closeness to God: **"I am in the Father and the Father is in me."** But Christians, through their faith, would be equally close. Through prayer they would be able to do things at least as great as Jesus had done, and this would continue his work of bringing others

13 to God, **"so that the Father may be glorified in the Son".**

16 **"Another Advocate."** When (according to the traditional picture) one came before the judgment seat of God, one would find oneself facing formidable charges. Sins which one had forgotten would be brought against one; and the devil (the 'accuser') would be there, seeking to make one appear in the worst possible light. But there would be certain things on the other side. Good deeds might speak in one's favour and outweigh the contrary evidence. To borrow a term from Jewish legal procedure, one would find that one had a *paraclete*, an 'advocate' (the original word *paraklētos* was Greek, but had been taken over into the language in the form *peraqlît*). In a Jewish court a plaintiff or defendant was entitled to enlist the help, not only of a witness to the facts, but of a person of high standing who might give personal support and advise the judges to believe what they were being told. This was not 'advocacy' in the western, professional, sense: the paraclete influenced the judges' decision, not by expertise in the law (this was the judges' business), but by the fact of being a person enjoying the esteem and trust of society. Nevertheless the nearest word in English is probably 'advocate', so long as this is understood in a non-professional sense.

In Jewish writing the most common metaphorical use of the term *paraclete* was in the context of God's judgment on human beings. It was believed that when one came before God one would find one had an 'Advocate' consisting of such things as one's good deeds and the merits of the Jewish patriarchs. But we have seen that, in John's gospel, language that was conventionally used of the last things is frequently brought into the present, and in this passage Christians are promised an Advocate, not only when they come before God after death, but from the very moment that Jesus has left them. Alone of the New Testament writers John uses this title for the Holy Spirit, and it is not too difficult to see why. Christians had been promised that when they found themselves on trial for their faith the Spirit would prompt them with the right words for their defence (Mark 13.11): in this sense, the Spirit would be their 'Advocate'. Moreover, the coming confrontation between Christianity and the world is about to be described as a trial, in the course of which the Spirit will play its part as the Christians' 'Advocate'.

17, 26   But neither of these explanations fully accounts for all the things said of the Advocate here – that it will be **"the Spirit of truth"**, that it will **"teach you everything, and remind you of all that I have told you"**. It is possible that John saw a further possibility in the metaphor. A man of standing who took up a friend's cause before a judge and obtained favourable terms might then find himself in the position of reporting back to his friend, whom he might have to persuade to accept the judgment of the court. He would be in the position of a go-between, interpreting the law (as propounded by the judges) to the individual whose interests were affected. In this rôle he perhaps furnished to John (or to whatever Christian had previously used this title for the Holy Spirit) an illustration of the continuing relationship between Christ and his followers which is one of the principal themes of this discourse.

15   **"If you love me, you will keep my commandments."** This had been the principle of Jesus' relationship with his disciples from the beginning. Faith involves ethics, here as everywhere in the New Testament. These 'commandments' were simply the will of his Father; like an 'advocate', Jesus had been commending them to his disciples all the time he was with them. When he left

16   them there would be **"another Advocate"** to continue the same work (even if Jesus himself was to be their 'advocate' in heaven, 1 John 2.1): he would

26   **"teach you everything"**. In this sense (though only in view of this rather technical function) it is possible to understand a different translation of the word *paraklētos* which was adopted some centuries later by Greek commentators and which found its way into most of the older English versions: 'Comforter'. The Advocate 'comforts' the individual by explaining and so far as possible lightening the weight of the 'commandments' by which the individual is bound. In some such way as this the lives of Christians would continue to be transformed and divinely accompanied even after Jesus' departure. Here was

18   one way of understanding Jesus' promise, **"I will not leave you orphaned; I am coming to you."**

Throughout this chapter the discourse is kept going by questions from

22   different disciples in turn. **Judas (not Iscariot)** is known only from the list in Luke (6.16). His question, **"Lord, how is it that you will reveal yourself to us, and not to the world?"**, presupposes the notion of a Messiah as a figure

who would finally dispel the doubts and ambiguities of religious faith and present all people with a decisive manifestation of the power of God and of the vindication of the righteous. They could perhaps understand how it was that the person of Jesus during his life on earth presented a humble appearance and was greeted by indifference or rejection instead of eliciting universal homage. This period, Jesus had promised, was merely a prelude to his 'glorification'. But now his words seemed to suggest a further period, even after his departure, when things would not be so plain and when faith still would not have given place to sight. And indeed, after the resurrection, the church found itself with the task of explaining why, since Christ was now resurrected and glorified and God's kingdom was a reality, the world seemed to be going on exactly as before and the 'glory' was perceptible only to those who had faith. The answer was that God was now present in a new and unique way in the church. The old concept of a glorious Messiah king, establishing the rule of God by force, had to give place to that of a new relationship

23 between God and human beings, such that **"my Father will love them, and we will come to them and make our home with them"**.

27   **"Peace I leave with you."** 'Giving peace' was a standard formula among Semitic peoples (and others) for greeting or parting. As such, it could be purely conventional, even trivial. It also had social implications: you had to be at least as high in the social scale as the person to whom you 'gave peace' – a beggar could not 'give peace' to a rich man! But Jesus' parting from his disciples was no ordinary leave-taking, since he was promising his continued presence among them, and in an unprecedented form. His 'peace' was therefore far from a conventional formula; it denoted a new experience of reality: **"my peace I give to you. I do not give to you as the world gives."**

31   **"Rise, let us be on our way."** Almost exactly the same words occur in Mark and Matthew just before the arrival of the party sent to arrest Jesus in the garden of Gethsemane. Taken in the same sense here, they suggest that Jesus has done with talking and now resolves to go to meet his fate. This is in fact what happens – but only three chapters later! Many scholars have been tempted to think that something may have gone wrong with John's text and that these words appear in the wrong place. But this is a last resort. It is perhaps better to notice that the apparent anomaly is not uncharacteristic of this gospel. In the first place, it is in John's manner to add a passage amplifying what Jesus has just said, even though the scene itself has come to an end (compare the concluding paragraph of chapter 3). In the second place, the literal meaning of Jesus' words is often a decoy: the real meaning lies under the surface – though in this case what the real meaning of *Arise, let us go from here* might be has tantalized his interpreters from the beginning.

15.1   **"I am the true vine."** Vines grow slowly. In a vineyard in Palestine it was three years before any grapes could be gathered from new plants. They needed constant training and pruning. Any serious damage done to them could destroy in a moment the patient labour of months or years. Tending vines (the occupation of countless Palestinian farmers) naturally suggested itself as an illustration of the care with which God tended his people (Jeremiah 2.21; Isaiah 5), and the sudden destruction of a vine was a poignant image for national calamities (Psalm 80.6–16; Ezekiel 19.10–14). It was characteristic of Jesus to use such a familiar example in his own teaching. The other gospels preserve two parables about vineyards (Mark 12.1–9; Matthew 20.1–16); but it is only here that anything is made of the actual technique of vine growing, and instead of a parable followed by its application we have a direct comparison: the **Father is the vinegrower**, Jesus is the vine and the disciples are the branches.

The solidarity of Jesus with his followers (which is the main theme of these chapters) could be expressed as that of the stem with the vine branches. Everyone knew that there was more to it than just letting the branches grow. Not all the branches would be allowed to survive: there must be constant tending and pruning. It was a metaphor anyone might apply. A ruthless politician, for example, could be said to do some 'pruning' in the state when he eliminated his opponents. So, among Jesus' disciples, the vine-grower (who is God) would do some rigorous selection and training. But the comparison is more subtle, in that the Greek word for 'pruning' has more than one meaning: it can also mean 'cleansing' (see the NRSV footnote). Both meanings are exploited in what follows.

'Pruning' involved two processes: breaking unwanted shoots off the branches and tending the shoots that remained. Some disciples would forfeit their solidarity with Jesus and be pruned off altogether. This would amount to total rejection, for which the penalty was loss of all possibility of new life:

6 **"such branches are gathered, thrown into the fire, and burned"** – traditional language for the last judgment; but John understands this as a thing of the present: it is what people bring on themselves by their attitude to Jesus. Those disciples, on the other hand, who maintained their solidarity with Jesus would still need further tending; and here the other meaning of the

3 word comes into play – they must be **cleansed**. Precisely what this means is obscured by the fact that the discourse is on two levels. In its context it is addressed to the disciples, who, in some sense (though in what sense is not entirely clear, either here or in the previous reference, 13.10), had **already been cleansed**. But on another level it is addressed to the subsequent church, whose members would certainly need 'cleansing', both when they entered it (by baptism) and thereafter (by repentance). The essential thing, in any case, was their solidarity with Christ and with one another; and the essence of this was love and obedience. Given this, Christians would be so much at one with Christ and his Father that prayer would be answered and the remaining term

5 of the comparison would be fulfilled: they would **"bear much fruit"**.

The inspiration for such love could only be the example of Christ himself –

12 **"that you love one another as I have loved you"**. And this in turn was

9 inspired by the love of God: **"As the Father has loved me, so I have**

loved you." An illustration of what such love involved has been given already in the washing of the disciples' feet; it is about to be seen to its full extent in Jesus' own death. **"No one has greater love than this, to lay down one's life for one's friends."** As a general proposition, most people might have agreed. But in the ancient world, 'friendship' was usually defined in terms of mutual advantage: my friends are of value to me and so should I be to them. In what sense, then, did Jesus have 'friends'? The answer could lie only in a new definition of friendship. Jesus had nothing to gain from adopting his disciples as friends. He was their master, and it would have been more natural to think of them as pupils or as **servants.**[28] But now he called them his **friends.** Friends have no secrets from one another: as their friend, he can tell them everything he knows, even his privileged experience of God. He has chosen them for no reason but that he loved them, and we have already been told that "he loved them to the end" (13.1). Love, friendship – these words took on a new meaning in the light of Jesus' relationship with his disciples. All this was implied in his reiterated commandment (which in this sense was a 'new' commandment): **"that you love one another".**

13

15

12

20 **"Servants are not greater than their master."** In 13.16 this saying was given a new application: if their master was prepared to perform a humble service, so should they be. Here, it is given the same meaning as in the other gospels: persecution will come to them as much as to him. But persecution was never regarded in the early church as an avoidable evil, something that might just blow over. Many Christians saw it in terms which they had inherited from the Jewish way of looking at world history: it was a part of that necessary intensification of suffering and testing which the righteous would have to endure before the end. But the experience of Jesus introduced a new dimension. The world, far from spontaneously acknowledging Jesus, had treated him with such indifference or antipathy that it could be said to have 18 **hated** him. So now his continuing presence among his followers would provoke the same reaction of hatred. Jesus' words and works were the ultimate 22 criterion: to reject them was to be guilty of **sin.** In view of what was about to happen, 'hatred' was not too strong a word for this attitude towards Jesus and his Father; it recalled a classic description of such persecution in one of 25 the psalms (35.19): **'They hated me without a cause.'**

Yet not everyone hated. Some believed. How did they come to believe? In Jesus' lifetime they had been persuaded by the witness of such as John the Baptist and (in a sense) by the witness of Jesus himself. Such witness would still be available when people were challenged to believe by Jesus' followers. It would be one of the functions of the Spirit (which has already 26 been described as the **Advocate** in 14.16) to **testify** and so to lend weight to

---

[28] Elsewhere in the NRSV the Greek word for 'servant' is normally translated *slave*; but this would be quite inappropriate here.

the Christians' cause; and of course the disciples themselves would continue
to give powerful testimony, having been eyewitnesses of Jesus' acts **from the beginning**.

The other gospels record detailed prophecies by Jesus of the persecutions and tribulations which would be suffered by the church. Here, Jesus mentions only two. **"They will put you out of the synagogues"** – a hardening of the Jewish attitude towards Christians which seems to have taken place within a few decades of Jesus' resurrection; and **"those who kill you will think that by doing so they are offering worship to God"** – again, the Jews did believe that in some circumstances it was a religious duty to punish blasphemy with death, and in due course they certainly came to regard Christians as blasphemers for paying divine honours to Jesus. These were the dangers which lay before any Jews who became Christians. We can glimpse (in the relatively narrow range of these prophecies compared with those in the other gospels) the specific readership for which John's gospel was written: Greek-speaking Christians, mainly of Jewish origin, exposed to hostile pressure from the Jewish communities in the cities where they lived. The persecution they would be exposed to, like other kinds of persecution which would fall on other parts of the church, was all part of a picture which had been carefully painted in advance by Jesus. To know this was to be kept from **stumbling**.

"Sorrow has filled your hearts." On the human level, the prospect of Jesus' departure on the eve of this period of troubles was a daunting one for the disciples. But in the future, what the followers of Jesus would need most was the conviction that, through all their vicissitudes, they were in the right and had truth on their side. Persecution is intolerable only if you are not sure of that for which you are being persecuted. This would never happen to Christians because of the reality of their experience of the Spirit among them. This Spirit is here again called the **Advocate**; and the scene of its action is again imagined as a law court. Each encounter between the world and the church is like that of two opposing parties before a judge. The world sets out to show (i) that the Christians have sinned (done wrong) in adopting their new faith (which, from the Jewish point of view, involved the blasphemous use of divine titles for Jesus); (ii) that they cannot be in the right after pinning their faith on one who was judicially convicted and punished; and (iii) that Jesus' death was no more than a consequence of due process of law. The appearance of the 'Advocate' on the Christians' side turns the tables on the accusers. (i) **"He will prove the world wrong about sin."** It has already been shown that 'sin' consists in not believing Jesus (15.21–2): it is the accusers, not the Christians, who have 'sinned'; (ii) he will prove them wrong **about righteousness**, in that the resurrection will prove the condemnation of Jesus, allegedly 'right' according to the law, to have been unlawful in the eyes of God, the author of that law; and (iii) he will prove them wrong **about judgment**: Jesus had called God to witness, that is, he had sworn an oath by God, and those who then disbelieved him (behind whom stood the demonic 'ruler of this world') had broken a fundamental rule of 'judgment' in refusing to believe one who testified on oath.

12 **"I still have many things to say to you."** All the gospels report that Jesus gave his disciples some teaching about the conditions under which they would find themselves exercising their discipleship (conditions, it is explained in John, which were the natural sequel of those under which Jesus had done his own work). In Matthew, Mark and Luke these conditions are interpreted in terms of traditional Jewish expectation. Their meaning was to be found in the fact that they formed part of that great drama of inevitable sufferings which would be the prelude to the imminent end of the present world order. Given this traditional picture, it was not difficult to fill in the details of the kind of tribulations which the righteous were to endure. In John's gospel this traditional view of the future is taken less for granted: Jesus, instead of giving his disciples the conventional blueprint, as it were, of what was in store for them, forbore to overwhelm them with predictions of their sufferings (**"you cannot bear them now"**), but promised instead that they would receive

13 enlightenment when the time came from **the Spirit of truth: "he will declare to you the things that are to come"**. One of the ways in which the church experienced the Holy Spirit was as a spirit of prophecy, speaking through individual Christians and predicting events that were about to happen. But we need not suppose that it is only this literal kind of 'prophecy' that is meant here. The essential thing for Christians was to know, not so much what was about to happen, as the meaning of what was actually happening; and this was a classical function of 'prophecy'. Jesus gave a certain amount of teaching on the subject. But the Spirit was to bring a prophetic understanding of

14 events, imprinted with the authority of Jesus (**"he will take what is mine"**), into every situation that would be encountered by the church.

16 **"A little while."** Any reader of the gospel who knew what was about to happen could see one obvious meaning of this pregnant little phrase. In 'a little while' Jesus would be arrested, tried and executed; and in 'a little while' after that he would rise from the dead. We read in the other gospels that Jesus several times predicted his death and his resurrection 'on the third day' (see above on Mark 9.9) and that his predictions were simply not understood by

18 his disciples. On the face of it, this is exactly the situation here. **"What does he mean by this 'a little while'?"**

But this 'little while' was a standard expression in the vocabulary of any Jewish teacher who professed to have insight into the future. If you believed (as most Jews did, and as the first Christians certainly did to an intense degree) that world history was tending towards a climax, then at any moment when faith in the imminence of this cosmic dénouement seemed to be slackening you would recall your hearers or readers to a proper pitch of expectation by reminding them that all this must surely come to pass 'in a little while'. The phrase is in the Hebrew prophets; it is in the Christian book called the Revelation (6.11). Jesus, in this part of the discourse, has been saying something about what the future had in store for his followers. This 'little while' was just what might have been expected: a cryptic reference to the period before the end, when history would at last be hastening towards its consummation. Teaching of this kind about the pattern of the future necessarily sounded cryptic to outsiders. But the intimate disciples of such a teacher would expect to be let into the secret meaning. They would hardly remain content (and their discontent is emphasized by John's repetitious narrative) to have to say, **"We do not know what he is talking about."**

Nor is this the only hint that the paragraph is cast in the mould of traditional esoteric teaching. It was commonly accepted (at least within certain circles of Jewish teachers) that the period before the end would be one of intensified violence and tribulation: the joys of the age to come would be heralded by unprecedented sufferings. To describe this period, a metaphor which suggested itself (and was subsequently quite frequently used) was that of a woman giving birth to her first child: the suffering would be such as she had never suffered before, but it would be short-lived, and the memory of it would be swallowed up in the joy that followed it. The metaphor had been used already in this sense by Isaiah (26.16–18, a passage which has more than one echo in this chapter of John); and in the time of Jesus (or at least very soon after) the 'birthpangs' (Mark 13.8) had become almost a technical expression for the last period of world history. When, therefore, Jesus, in
21 the context of his teaching about the future, elaborated the metaphor of **a woman . . . in labor**, and then described a state of affairs in which prayers would be certain of an answer[29] (one of the expected blessings of the age to come, and also a well-remembered promise of Jesus – "Ask, and it will be given to you", Matthew 7.7; Luke 11.9), there can be little doubt where these
25 **figures of speech** came from. Jesus, here as in the other gospels, was making use of the traditional repertory of those who claimed to have insight into the coming last days of the world and the new age that was to follow them.

But in John's gospel, when Jesus uses language of this kind, it tends to bear a radically original meaning. Things which his contemporaries described as belonging to a future age Jesus showed to be realities which may be experienced here and now. The whole of this section plays upon new meanings of old expressions: both the 'little while' of apparent dereliction and the joy of communion are simultaneous experiences in the life of the Christian. This actualization of traditional hopes becomes explicit towards the end of the
29–30 section. According to the traditional scheme, one of the limitations of life in the period before the end was having to be content with partial vision, partial understanding. The signs of the times were puzzling and ambiguous; one got no nearer to the truth than in 'figures of speech'. But when the end came, the veil would be lifted, the obscurities would be removed. As Paul

---

[29] **Ask nothing of me** may equally well mean *ask me no questions*, a point taken up in the next paragraph. See the NRSV footnote.

puts it, "now we see in a mirror, dimly, but then we will see face to face" (1 Corinthians 13.12). Figures of speech would give place to plain words, the truth would be known no longer through anxious questioning and dimly understood answers but by direct communication. Jesus had already talked many times about 'going to the Father', but had never been understood, even by his own disciples. Now, suddenly, they grasped what he meant, and the truth seemed to burst upon them. It was as if the perfection of knowledge and the clarity of vision which they believed they would have only in heaven

29 were available to them here and now. **"Yes, now you are speaking plainly, not in any figure of speech!"**

31 **Jesus answered them, "Do you now believe?"** Inspired prophecies about the future traditionally included tribulations for the righteous. Nothing Jesus had said must be interpreted as if his followers would be spared them. They

32 would include being **scattered** at the moment of his own arrest – the allusion is to the phrase in Zechariah 13.7, which was seen by the early church as an explanation for the disciples' act of desertion at the critical moment (Mark 14.27). Jesus was exhorting them to bear these things. But traditionally, every exhortation to bear trouble steadfastly was accompanied by the promise of ultimate victory and vindication: in 'a little while' those who were now oppressed and persecuted would triumph. The new factor in Jesus' exhortation was that he did not leave his followers with a mere promise. The victory had already been won. That which made the trouble possi-

33 ble to bear was already possessed. **"Take courage; I have conquered the world!"**

17.1 **Jesus...looked up to heaven, and said.** Since the third century this chapter has been known as Jesus' High-priestly Prayer. It would have been entirely natural for Jesus to have concluded his final words to his disciples with a prayer. Equally, it would have been well in the tradition of historical writing for John to present the last words of Jesus to his disciples (as of any hero to his followers) in the form of a prayer, not least because he must have known the tradition recorded in the other gospels that Jesus prayed with particular earnestness just before his arrest in Gethsemane, and may well have found the present context a more appropriate one for including such material. In either case the impact of this passage is such that few have doubted that it represents faithfully the heart of Jesus' spirituality. In fact, however, this final address of Jesus to his heavenly Father includes rather more than we would normally look for in a 'prayer'. It expresses, certainly, the perfect resolution of Jesus to undergo his destiny – a resolution that had seemed to falter for a moment a short time before (12.27), and was put to the test, according to the other gospels, in Gethsemane; and it contains a number of petitions for his followers (including what appears to be an allusion to the Lord's Prayer,

15 **"protect them from the evil one"**). But – particularly in its opening phrases – it also consists of a solemn summary of what has been said before about the true nature of Jesus and the faith of his disciples; and with the words

19 **"I sanctify myself"** it marks the moment when Jesus may be said to have committed himself irrevocably to his act of sacrifice **"for their sakes"** – for 'sanctify' stands for a word that is perhaps better translated *consecrate* and that reinforces the image of a priest about to present the offering of himself. All this is not quite 'prayer' in the sense the word usually bears. On the other hand, it falls well within the function which a prayer was often held to have in antiquity; that is, not only supplicating and praising God, but defining carefully those beliefs about God and humankind which justify us in attempting to pray at all.

1 **"Glorify your Son."** That Jesus' 'glorification' was to take place on the cross is a paradox that has already been hinted at more than once in John's gospel. But here it is related to a concept more characteristic of the other
2 gospels: **"you have given him authority over all people"**. Jesus was the Son of Man; and it was prophesied that this Son of Man would be installed at the right hand of God and have authority over all the world.[30] **'Eternal life'**, which elsewhere in this gospel is usually defined in terms of 'believing' in Jesus, is here described as a matter of 'knowing God'. To put these ideas together: the Christian is one who 'knows' that the humble Son of Man who was crucified now bears all authority, that the crucifixion was in reality Jesus' glorification, and that to be able to recognize Jesus' 'glory' in that moment is to see something of the nature of God's glory and to enter upon that new reality of living which can be called 'eternal life'. Jesus' time on earth had the purpose of making all this intelligible and credible. But it was something which had always been true. This glory of Jesus, which Christians came to understand through his life and death as well as through his resurrection,
5 had in fact existed (as the very first words of the gospel proclaim) **"before the world existed"**.

The main part of the prayer is for the disciples. They have now reached
8 a decisive point in their apprenticeship: **"they have believed that you sent me"**. They are now to continue in something of the same circumstances under which Jesus himself taught and lived; that is, with the same sense of
14 belonging to two worlds, of being people in this world who yet **do not belong to the world**. The inherent ambiguity of their relationship with the world sets the tone for the prayer which Jesus now makes for them.

He prays first for their safety. This is not just a matter of physical security:
15 the stakes are higher than that. They must be protected **from the evil one**, that is, not just from the danger of suffering and death but from the danger of being forced by these things to renounce their faith and forfeit eternal life.
11 **"Protect them in your name that you have given me."** God's 'name' was an expression used in the Old Testament to indicate that God was believed to be present to a particular degree in a particular place: for instance, God 'made his name to dwell' in the temple in Jerusalem. Jesus' continuing presence with

[30] Literally *all flesh*; see the NRSV footnote.

his disciples would be equivalent to this; and Jesus prays that they would continue to have this protection.[31] If it were objected that Jesus' 'name' had not in fact protected Judas from his fate, the answer was that Judas was a

12 special case, **"the one destined to be lost"** – a traditional phrase (literally *the son of destruction*) for one who, in the current mythology about the future, would appear as a kind of personification of wickedness (2 Thessalonians 2.3); and his special rôle had been amply foretold in **scripture** (13.18).

19 Secondly, Jesus prays that they may be **sanctified in truth**. The metaphor belongs to temples and sanctuaries. Priests 'sanctify' or 'consecrate' themselves by separating themselves from the ordinary and sometimes squalid concerns of the world in order to make themselves fit to draw near to the presence of God in ritual and service. The metaphor, of course, can be used quite trivially: 'consecrating' oneself need mean no more than committing oneself wholeheartedly to a particular task or service. But even then there is a hint of separation: one must free oneself from certain things if one is to be fully available for something else. In this sense, 'consecrated' or 'sanctified' (both meanings belong to the Greek word) was an appropriate word for the disciples who for the sake of Christ no longer 'belonged to the world'. But again, their solidarity with Christ implied that they would share something of the 'sanctification' of him whose priestly service involved utter self-sacrifice.

21 Finally, Jesus prays that **"they may all be one"**. For Christianity, as for any religious or political movement, unity among its adherents was essential for its survival (and indeed, by the time John wrote, the church had been exposed to serious threats to its unity). Jesus' prayer doubtless embraces this functional unity; but it also points to something more fundamental. The intense solidarity between Jesus and his disciples has already been expounded.

21 Here it is developed still further: **"As you, Father, are in me and I am in you, may they also be in us."** The implication of this intimacy of human beings with God is a new unity among themselves; and this is to be experienced, not only among the original disciples, but in subsequent generations of Christians. Jesus may or may not have foreseen such a long history for his followers; but John already knew at least several generations of them.

The whole of the discourse has been exploring the manner in which Jesus would continue to be present with his disciples after the crucifixion and resurrection. Something of heaven, he has been saying, would attend their life on earth. But one could put it the other way round. It was not only that life on earth would be transformed by influences from another world: human beings, while still in this world, could have an experience of heaven. This was

24 the climax of Jesus' great prayer for his followers: **"I desire that those also . . . may be with me where I am, to see my glory."**

---

[31] The sense of verses 11 and 12 is difficult to be sure of, hence perhaps several variants in the manuscripts, one of which is in the NRSV footnote.

Final days

18.1 **After Jesus had spoken these words.** At this point, John's gospel, which up to now has followed a strikingly different sequence of events from the others, suddenly begins to run closely parallel with them – possibly the memory of these final days crystallized more rapidly than other parts of the tradition into a clearly remembered narrative. At any rate, the differences between the accounts no longer lie in the grand design but in the details.

He went out with his disciples across the Kidron valley. The name occurs nowhere else in the New Testament, but we know exactly what it stands for: it is the deep river or wadi which separates the hill on which Jerusalem was built from the range of higher hills to the east which includes the Mount of Olives. John is telling us, therefore, which side of the city Jesus came out of, and when he goes on to speak of **a place where there was a garden** it is obvious that he means the place which appears in the other gospels as Gethsemane, on the slopes of the Mount of Olives. The detail (also hinted at

2 in Luke 22.39) that **Jesus often met there with his disciples** clarifies the rôle of Judas: this was the information he was able to pass on to Jesus' enemies. But this, according to John, is as far as his treachery went. There is no mention of the traitor's kiss, and indeed there was no need to identify Jesus, for Jesus immediately identified himself, using the solemn formula, characteristic of

5 John's presentation of Jesus, **"I am he"** (literally, *I am*, the 'name' of God in Exodus 3.14). This caused some consternation to his captors. Whether or not they originally intended to arrest Jesus' followers as well (a possibility this account leaves open), Jesus insisted that they should let them go, and in so doing gave a practical demonstration of the truth of a promise he had made

9 earlier in general terms (6.39), **"I did not lose a single one of those whom you gave me."** There is no hint here that the disciples disgraced themselves by running away.

3 Jesus' captors are described as **a detachment of soldiers together with police from the chief priests and the Pharisees.** In the other gospels it is clear that they were sent by the Sanhedrin. John's account is less precise. The chief priests *ex officio*, and the Pharisaic party by virtue of their influence, each formed a section of the membership of the Sanhedrin, and John doubtless meant that the police came from that authority. But what about the **detachment of soldiers?** In the Greek, this is the correct term for a Roman cohort consisting of several hundred men. Apart from the fact that such a large contingent seems quite inappropriate to an arrest in a garden, it is a surprise to find Roman soldiers involved at this stage. John may have known, independently of the other gospels, that Roman soldiers were in fact present, or he may have wished to tell the story of Jesus' arrest in such a way as to implicate the Roman authorities right from the start. Alternatively, just as in Mark 6.21 the military men at Herod's court could be called *centurions* (the name for Roman junior officers), so John may have been using military

language rather loosely and have meant, both here and in verse 12, nothing more than a mixed force of Jewish armed men. At any rate, he follows the other accounts in narrating a brief scuffle, but differs in that he gives the names of both the aggressive disciple and the slave; and in Jesus'

11 rebuke – **"Am I not to drink the cup that the Father has given me?"** – makes a suggestive allusion to the scene of Jesus at prayer in the garden (Mark 14.36), which he seems to have known about even though he has omitted it from his own narrative.

13 **First they took him to Annas.** This is a significant departure from the account in the other gospels. Matthew and Mark report that Jesus was immediately brought before a meeting specially convened during the night; Luke describes Jesus as being held in Caiaphas' house until dawn. John introduces a new element altogether with the mention of Annas. Annas had been deposed from the office of high priest, which he had held for ten years, in 15 CE; but he remained a person of influence, for apart from his son-in-law Caiaphas, who was high priest from 18 to 36 CE and has been mentioned earlier (11.49), five of his sons also held the office, and it is not in itself unlikely that he was behind Jesus' arrest and was given an opportunity to conduct a preliminary examination. John, however, combines this new piece of tradition with one that he shares with all the other gospels: the story of Peter's denial. Here too he has a fresh piece of information to offer: Peter's presence in the courtyard

15 was made possible by a disciple who **was known to the high priest.** We are not told who this was; and the fact that Jesus' following included people with connections of this kind is new to us. It does not look, therefore, as if John was simply rewriting the story from the version in Mark. He seems to have had independent information which allowed him to identify some of the characters in the scene.

19 **Then the high priest questioned Jesus.** These are not formal legal proceedings but an informal interrogation. To the high priest's questions Jesus replied (as in the other gospels he replied to his captors in the garden) that,

20 after all his public teaching **in synagogues and in the temple**, such a procedure was pointless. The charges brought by 'the Jews' against Jesus have already occupied several long passages, and John is hastening on to a new issue altogether, that between Jesus and the Roman governor. He pauses only to finish off the story of Peter and to give his own mild and attenuated version (which hinges on Exodus 22.28, "You shall not . . . curse a leader of your people") of the insults suffered by Jesus at the hands of the Jewish authorities. Here it is no more than a single blow struck by an officer; and Jesus replies by

23 insisting on the conditions of a fair trial: **"If I have spoken wrongly, testify to the wrong."**

24 **Then Annas sent him bound to Caiaphas the high priest.** John has already

13 said that Caiaphas was the high priest **that year.** This is correct in so far as Caiaphas was certainly the high priest at that time, but misleading in that it suggests that the office was held for one year at a time – Caiaphas held it

for eighteen years. Possibly John was confused by the fact that a number of high priests did in fact hold office for only one year in the first half of the century, but in any case the 'high priests' were a class of which Annas was an influential member, and John is not incorrect in referring to both men as high priests.

28 **Then they took Jesus from Caiaphas to Pilate's headquarters.**[32] All the other gospels give some account of a session of a Jewish council presided over by Caiaphas, during which Jesus made a statement that was judged to be blasphemous and punishable by death. Whether or not such a session actually took place, John makes no mention of it here. He has already recorded several occasions when the debate with the Jewish leaders took on a legal character and resulted in a charge of blasphemy. Even if John knew that a similar scene took place before Caiaphas, he had no need to delay his readers by repeating it here. The issue between Jesus and 'the Jews' had already been thrashed out; it was to the trial before the Roman authorities that he now wished to give emphasis, and his account of it is a great deal more detailed than that of the other gospels.

The trial scene itself is also conceived somewhat differently. Instead of hearing the case of accusers and accused together, Pilate has Jesus held prisoner inside his headquarters but interviews the Jews outside. The prosecution and the defence are heard in different places, and Pilate, as judge, moves in and out between them. John offers a reason for this: the Jews **themselves did not enter the headquarters, so as to avoid ritual defilement and to be able to eat the Passover.** From an antiquarian point of view we can probably (but not certainly) say that this is correct: the Jews who celebrated the Passover in Jerusalem, and in particular the priests who had ceremonial duties to attend to during the afternoon, were obliged to keep themselves ritually clean beforehand; and the houses of Gentiles were regarded as places of possible contamination. (There was the danger, for instance, that there might be a grave underneath, which would make a Jew ritually unclean for a week.) To this extent, the reason John gives for their remaining outside is plausible, though a little recondite; but it gives us incidentally some precious information in that it clearly dates the Passover festival to the evening following the crucifixion, whereas the other gospels equally clearly place it on the evening before. The day of the week is the same in all the accounts. The question is what day of the month it was. According to the first three gospels, Friday that year fell on 15 Nisan, the day after the celebration of the Passover meal, and Jesus' last supper (on the Thursday) was therefore a Passover. According to John, on the other hand, the Passover had not yet happened on the Friday, and the lambs for the meal were being sacrificed in the temple precincts while Jesus hung on the cross. Both cannot be right; but each version has powerful theological resonances, and it is possible that by the time the gospels were

---

[32] The word John uses is the technical Roman one, *praetorium*.

written no one any longer knew the exact chronology. What was important was that, either way, great significance could be found in the fact that these events took place against the background of the Jewish festival.

In any case, what really needed explaining was, not that the Jews remained outside, but that Jesus was brought inside. It was customary for a Roman magistrate to set up his tribunal in a public place; a special stone platform was often provided for the purpose. Questioning Jesus indoors appears to have been a departure from usual practice. But in other respects Pilate is represented as conforming with normal procedure. It was the duty of a Roman governor to hear charges laid against his subjects, to check their accuracy and to decide on the action to be taken under Roman law. Pilate's
29 first question to the Jews was the normal opening of this procedure: **"What accusation do you bring against this man?"** But their answer was curiously
30 evasive. **"If this man were not a criminal, we would not have handed him over to you."** It is not clear how John means us to understand this; but the fact that they did not immediately bring forward a charge apparently made Pilate assume that the matter was a technical one of Jewish law which the Jews were not disposed to explain to him and on which, in any case, he could not be expected to give a ruling. (This, at any rate, was the reaction of another Roman governor in Corinth on a similar occasion, Acts 18.14–15.) But the Jews replied to this that, even if it was a technical matter, it was a capital case,
31 and they had no competence to carry out the death penalty. **"We are not permitted to put anyone to death."**

This statement provides, almost casually, the answer to the main problem presented by the gospel accounts of Jesus' trial and death. Jesus was crucified, a form of execution carried out only by the Romans; but the blame for his condemnation is placed by all the evangelists, not on the Romans, but on the Jews. How are these two facts to be reconciled? The solution suggested by this statement is that it was indeed the Jews who found Jesus guilty of blasphemy, but that they prevailed on the Roman authorities, in the person of Pilate, to carry out the death penalty. And the clue to this surprising procedure is provided by a chance remark made in John's narrative (and nowhere else in any of the gospels) that at this time the Jews themselves did not have the power to put anyone to death. That this was true is at least probable: it is consistent with what we know of the administration of the provinces of the Roman empire, even if we have no decisive evidence for it in Judea. But it has to be admitted that this single reference to a fact which we find crucial for understanding the trial and execution of Jesus is contained in a brief statement which John records for quite another reason. For him, the fact that Jesus was crucified was not merely the result of historical circumstances: it was the only form of execution which would have been consistent with what Jesus himself had said about the symbolism of his death (12.32). If the Jews had executed him they would have done it by stoning, and this could never have been described as a 'lifting up'. To the mysterious obstacles which had prevented the Jews from summarily doing away with Jesus earlier (7.46; 8.59; 10.39) is now added a purely practical one: officially, they were not allowed to do so by the Roman regulations.

33 We must assume that more passed in the conversation between Pilate and the Jews than is actually recorded here, for when Pilate went inside to examine the defendant he put to him a specific charge (**"Are you the King of the Jews?"**) and admitted that it was one put forward by the Jews. In the accounts in the other gospels, Jesus' reply to the charge, though he never altogether denied it, was always marked by a certain reserve. Here the same reserve is expanded into a definition of the exact sense in which Jesus could admit to being a 'king'. To understand it, we need to remember that the word 'kingdom' need not imply any territorial claims: it is equivalent to 'reign', and on other occasions Jesus had prophesied that, as Son of Man, he would share in the reign, or 'kingship', of God the Father. At any rate, Pilate was soon convinced that, if Jesus' 'kingship' was so other-worldly and operated with

37 abstractions such as **truth**, no action need be taken. He also entertained the hope that he could at the same time exploit the situation by making his release of Jesus satisfy the Jews' customary demand for the release of one prisoner at Passover (see on Mark 15.7). But in this he was disappointed. Instead of being able to get away with releasing the harmless Jesus, he was forced

40 to release one who was a **bandit**, that is, a member of one of the armed resistance groups which constantly harried the Roman occupying forces: **Barabbas.**

19.1 **Then Pilate took Jesus and had him flogged.** Events were still taking a normal course according to Roman justice. The flogging was the Roman equivalent to 'letting him off with a warning'; and the soldiers' mockery, and the public exhibition which followed, may have been a legitimate extension of it. By Roman law Pilate had found Jesus innocent – indeed that no case had been made against him at all. But by Jewish law (the chief priests maintained)

7 Jesus had been proved to have committed blasphemy (**"he has claimed to be the Son of God"**), for which the penalty was death; and Pilate was now being subjected to pressure to carry out the sentence of a Jewish court which that court was not competent to carry out itself. At first Pilate was merely

6 impatient: **"Take him and crucify him"**, he said sarcastically, knowing they had no power even to stone him. But then the strength of the popular agitation

8 seems to have unnerved him; he became **more afraid than ever** and went inside for a further interview with Jesus, doubtless hoping to discover at least some reason why the Jews were so anxious to see the death sentence carried

9 out. His question to Jesus, **"Where are you from?"**, certainly sounded like the opening of a general interrogation. **But Jesus gave him no answer.** This motif of Jesus' silence appears in all the gospel accounts. Here it is made the cue for a brief dialogue about authority and a further indication of where the main responsibility lay for Jesus' condemnation – with the man or men who had 'handed him over'.

In Pilate's final interview with the Jewish leaders the issue once again entered a new phase. Having failed to get their way so far, the Jews brought

12 forward something of a threat: **"If you release this man, you are no friend of the emperor."** 'Friend of the emperor' – *amicus Caesaris* – this is what, under the empire, every Roman official aspired to be: to have the emperor's ear, to be known for one's loyalty. A few years later Pilate was deposed from office at the instigation of one who was more a 'friend of Caesar' than he. At any time, the possibility of reports reaching Rome that he was allowing disloyalty to the emperor among his subjects in Judea would have alarmed him. Finally, therefore, he determined to put the matter to the test: if the crowd showed that they were prepared to acknowledge Jesus as their 'king', clearly the man was dangerous after all and action must be taken.

The scene for this final confrontation is carefully and solemnly set. The

13 Roman governor normally had his **judge's bench** for the purpose of giving judgment[33] in a public place outside his residence. John knows the name of the place. Greek-speaking people called it **The Stone Pavement**: streets and squares paved with massive stone blocks were characteristic of Herodian Jerusalem, and it would not be surprising if there was a particularly fine one outside the governor's house (which was formerly Herod the Great's palace[34]). In Hebrew it was called **Gabbatha**, which probably represents a Hebrew or Aramaic word meaning 'a high place'; and again, in a city built on steep hills, this would be an obvious name for any public square in the

14 higher parts of Jerusalem. John also states the exact time: **it was about noon.** This conflicts with the other gospels, where Jesus is crucified in the morning. John may have had other information; on the other hand, if he knew that on the eve of Passover the sacrificial lambs were slaughtered at the temple in the early afternoon, and if he wished to make Jesus' death carry some of the symbolic meaning of these sacrifices, he may have deliberately pictured Jesus' final condemnation as taking place just in time to have him crucified

16 the same afternoon – another link in the chain of 'handing over' which began with the betrayal by Judas Iscariot.

[33] The phrase **sat on the judge's bench** certainly suggests that he was about to give judgment. But in fact he had given judgment already, and what follows is hardly judicial. Another possible translation of the Greek (NRSV footnote) is *seated him* (Jesus) *on the judge's bench*. This is perhaps less probable; but it would certainly add point and drama to the scene: Pilate would be deliberately challenging the Jews to show their allegiance to a usurper of his own authority.

[34] An impressive area of such paving has been found on the site of one of Herod the Great's buildings in Jerusalem, the fortress-palace called Antonia, which lay next to and defended the temple area. It is tempting to believe that this was the site of Jesus' trial; but unfortunately this identification is far from certain. It is in many ways more likely that Pilate had his headquarters (*praetorium*) in the main palace of Herod the Great, which was situated in a higher part of the city than the Antonia; and in any case the archaeological evidence suggests that the paving at the Antonia dates from the time of Hadrian, a century after the trial of Jesus.

To this extent John's narrative permits us to make a possible reconstruction of the original events. At the same time it is clear that here, as throughout his gospel, John is doing a great deal more than merely recording events as they happened. Like the authors of the other gospels, he has certain points that he wishes to make. Jesus was put to death by the Romans, allegedly as a claimant to the treasonable title, 'King of the Jews'. This was the basic fact known to anyone who knew anything about Jesus at all. But two obvious inferences from this fact needed to be corrected. First, it was not the Romans who were
12 responsible for Jesus' execution. On the contrary, Pilate **tried to release him**.
11 The guilt **of a greater sin** lay at an earlier stage of the process of 'handing over' Jesus, whether at the hands of Judas or of Caiaphas. Secondly, Jesus was not a traitor to Rome. His 'kingship' was not political and therefore his followers need not be regarded as disloyal citizens by the Roman authorities (a point of some importance by the time John's gospel was written). So much is held in common by all the accounts. But the account in John's gospel, though it is in many ways so similar to the others, is at the same time characteristic of him. For he uses it, as he uses many episodes, to clarify some of the concepts used by Jesus. In particular (in view of the title on the cross) there is a conversation between Jesus and Pilate which, whatever may have passed between them (which John could hardly have had any means of knowing), fills a gap in this gospel's presentation of the person of Jesus by explaining the title 'king' and the superiority of Jesus' authority compared with that of Pilate.
17   **Carrying the cross by himself.** John appears not to know the tradition (vouched for by the mention of the man's own sons in Mark's account, 15.21) that a certain Simon of Cyrene was forced to carry the cross for Jesus. It may be, in any case, that Jesus did carry the beam of his own cross at least some of the way until he had to be relieved of it through exhaustion. John may have known of Jesus' saying in Luke 14.27, "Whoever does not carry the cross and follow me cannot be my disciple"; if so, he may deliberately have concentrated on the early stages of the procession, during which Jesus could be described as setting an example for his future disciples to follow.

Much of what follows is familiar from the other gospels. But John adds
20 one new detail: the crucifixion was **near the city** – which is what we would expect. The Romans crucified insurrectionists to set a public example, and, though custom forbade them to do this in the most public places (inside the city), they normally chose a place not far outside, where the victims would be seen by a large number of people.[35] John also gives very plausible details of the inscription (which he calls by the technical Latin name, *titulus*). **Hebrew** can mean (as often in the New Testament) the language actually spoken by the inhabitants of Palestine; Latin was the native language of the Roman

---

[35] The traditional site of the crucifixion, now inside the Church of the Holy Sepulchre, would have been outside the city walls at the time, though it was enclosed within an extension of the walls a few years later.

administrators; Greek was the common language used for official purposes throughout the eastern part of the empire and had been adopted by many educated (and maybe not so educated) people as a second language. Thus publicly displayed, the charge against Jesus could well have seemed to the chief priests a deliberate insult to their nation.

24 **"They divided my clothes among themselves, and for my clothing they cast lots."** This quotation (from Psalm 22.18) occurs in all the gospel accounts, and indeed the whole psalm, with its classic description of the predicament of a righteous sufferer, evidently offered an apt and traditional framework in which to set the remembered details of Jesus' crucifixion. But John seems to have worked out the exact way in which this **scripture** was being fulfilled. In Hebrew poetry the two halves of a line are often intended to balance each other and to yield, not two statements, but two ways of making the same statement. Nevertheless John takes the whole verse quite literally and appears to ask himself how, if the four soldiers shared Jesus' garments by dividing them among themselves, they could also find anything to cast

23 lots about. He found the answer in Jesus' **tunic**, which could have been the only valuable article among the spoils to which the soldiers were entitled: the tunic (*chitōn*) was the long shirt (usually with short sleeves) which was worn under a cloak. Obviously it would have been silly to 'share' this by tearing it up (even if it were not **woven in one piece from the top**, as John

24 painstakingly assures us that it was). Therefore they **cast lots** for it and so fulfilled the prophecy to the letter.

25 **And that is what the soldiers did.** With considerable artistry John builds up a surrounding frame of onlookers before coming to the centre of the picture, Jesus himself. All the gospels refer to the women who were present at the crucifixion, although they differ about the names; only John reports that they were actually near the cross and that Jesus' mother was among them. We do not know who her **sister** was, and so far as the grammar goes she could be the same person as **Mary the wife of Clopas** – the Greek, like the English, is ambiguous. It is perhaps not likely that the sisters would both have been called Mary; but 'sister' could mean 'sister-in-law', and an early tradition named Clopas as the brother of Joseph. (He may also have been the 'Cleopas' of Luke 24.18.) The third woman, **Mary Magdalene**, is known from Luke 8.2. Their

26 presence enables John to record another saying of Jesus, **"Woman, here is your son."** This is evidently more than a last-minute concern for the welfare of a bereaved mother. If it had been merely this it would have been sufficient

27 to say to the disciple, **"Here is your mother."** In any case, the form of address has a certain solemnity. 'Woman' was not rude (as it would be in English), but it was formal (in a way that 'mother' is not). Jesus addressed his mother in the same way at Cana (2.4), and on that occasion too his utterance had a solemn and formal ring. Clearly there is a deeper meaning, and subsequent Christian meditation has found in these simple sentences the germ of many doctrines about the church, about womanhood and about Mary herself. It is

26 certainly possible that **the disciple whom he loved** (whoever he was – this is the only reference to him apart from 13.23, 20.2 and 21.20) stands for more than one individual and represents the whole company of the followers of Christ; if so, the saying falls into line with those great affirmations of Paul that Christians are Christ's 'brothers' and share his sonship.

28, 29 **"I am thirsty."** All the gospels mention that Jesus was offered **sour wine**, and a verse from a psalm that was one of the classic descriptions of a righteous sufferer must have helped to determine the words in which the incident was remembered: "for my thirst they gave me vinegar to drink" (Psalm 69.21).

28 John, too, may well have had this text in mind when he added, **in order to fulfil the scripture**. But he also gave a new slant to the incident. That Jesus should have experienced acute thirst at this moment was virtually inevitable; but this mention of it would be the only reference to his physical suffering in any of the gospel accounts, and John's gospel is not the place where we would expect to find it. On the other hand we are by now familiar with John's technique of using a simple misunderstanding to introduce a deeper meaning. The soldiers assumed that Jesus was expressing physical thirst, and, since sour wine or vinegar is known to have been administered as a restorative, their gesture may have been a humane one[36] (even if this is not the implication of the psalm). But there is good reason to think that John saw a further significance in the episode. Mark and Matthew both record that Jesus uttered a loud cry at this moment, which the bystanders misunderstood as 'Elijah'. Their own interpretation was that Jesus was praying in the words of Psalm 22, "My God (*eli*), my God, why have you forsaken me?" But there is another psalm which begins in Hebrew *elohim eli*:

> O God, you are my God, I seek you,
> my soul thirsts for you.
> (Psalm 63.1)

This appears to be John's interpretation of the same cry. Jesus' 'thirst' was metaphorical: it was an intense longing for God. The misunderstanding consisted in taking the thirst only as a physical need. The need, nevertheless, was there. When it was satisfied, Jesus was able to say his final word, **"It is**

30 **finished"** – which again has more than one meaning. Jesus had several times said that he had a work to complete or 'finish' (4.34; 5.36; 17.4). But the word also means 'fulfil': Jesus' death was not only the finishing or end of his life's work; it was the fulfilment of all that he was destined by scripture to be and do. So saying, he **gave up his spirit** – literally *handed it over*, the last link in the chain which began with the 'handing over' by Judas.

---

[36] A **branch of hyssop** or marjoram (*hyssōpos*) is a totally unsuitable instrument for holding up a sponge full of wine. It was conjectured in the sixteenth century that John must have originally written *hyssos*, meaning *javelin*, and that an easy slip of an early copyist produced the reading in all our existing manuscripts – except one of the thirteenth century which, perhaps by accident, supports the conjectural reading 'javelin'.

31   **The day of Preparation** was Friday, the day before the sabbath. It was laid down in Deuteronomy (21.23) that a criminal executed by 'hanging on a tree' must be buried before nightfall. The sabbath began at dusk, and must not be profaned by dead bodies in public places – especially (as John adds, perhaps unnecessarily) **because that sabbath was a day of great solemnity**, being the first day of the Passover festival. The request of the Jews was therefore reasonable: crucified men did not necessarily die within the first few hours. The 'defilement of the land' (Deuteronomy 21.23) which would have ensued otherwise would have been a serious matter for the consciences of strict Jews who had come to Jerusalem to keep the festival. Execution by crucifixion could be a slow business – sometimes it could take up to thirty-six hours. Breaking the legs of the victims was a recognized way of hastening death – perhaps by asphyxiation if it increased the weight on their arms. (A skeleton has been discovered of a man who was crucified around this time and whose

33   legs were similarly broken.) But Jesus, surprisingly, **was already dead**, so they did not break his legs. Why did John (alone of the evangelists) mention this? We know that many Jews at this time were anxious that a dead person's bones should not be broken (for example, by stoning), since it was out of the bones (as in Ezekiel 37) that it was thought the body would be reconstituted at the

36   resurrection. But John also had in mind a text of scripture, **"None of his bones shall be broken."** It is not quite certain to which text he was referring. Exodus 12.46 reads (of the lamb eaten at Passover), "you shall not break any of its bones". If John intended his readers to have it in mind that Jesus was crucified at the same time as the lambs were being slaughtered in the temple, then this detail may have seemed to add to the symbolism. But the allusion might also be to Psalm 34.20, which describes how the Lord protects the righteous: "He keeps all their bones; not one of them will be broken."

        Instead of having his legs broken, Jesus was stabbed in the side with a

34   spear, and **at once blood and water came out**. This is said to be possible physiologically – a white fluid from the lungs could have been released by the wound, though this would hardly have been visible from any distance. But John, who lays great stress on the reliability of the report, evidently saw more in it than a mere physical phenomenon. Blood was a significant symbol for redemption, and water for cleansing; and there may even be a hint of the Christian sacraments of the eucharist and baptism. Moreover the incident

37   fulfilled another prophecy (quoted also in Revelation 1.7), **"They will look on the one whom they have pierced."** This is a quotation from Zechariah 12.10; and the last chapters of Zechariah provided a number of prophecies which seemed to have been fulfilled in the passion of Jesus – indeed a few verses later (13.1) we read that "a fountain shall be opened . . . to cleanse . . . from sin and impurity", which may well have seemed to give point to the water flowing from Jesus' side.

38   **Joseph of Arimathea . . . asked Pilate to let him take away the body of Jesus.** Different suggestions are made by the evangelists about the motives

of this Joseph. In Mark and Luke, he is a pious and influential Jew, no doubt anxious to avoid the ritual defilement which would ensue if a body were left exposed overnight, or else moved to make some amends for the injustice of the Sanhedrin's action. In Matthew, Joseph is a disciple of Jesus, and John adds to this explanation that he was **a secret one** and that he was joined by another person of influence, Nicodemus, who on his previous appearance (3.1) also appears to have kept his interest secret. They evidently intended to bury Jesus honourably, but they were pressed for time: once the sun had set, their activity would no longer be permissible, it being the eve of the sabbath

31 (**the day of Preparation**). They therefore made use of a new tomb which happened to be nearby in a garden[37] (only Matthew says that it belonged to Joseph). But they did not (as in the other gospels) neglect to anoint the corpse. On the contrary, they brought with them a prodigious quantity of spices for the purpose. Such things were costly, and were normally packed in small jars with long narrow necks so that they could be used sparingly. Since it was usual to anoint a corpse with olive oil, one would have expected them simply to have added to it just a little of the aromatic mixture. Instead, they showed exceptional extravagance, by which John may mean us to understand that the two distinguished but secret disciples gave Jesus a burial worthy of 'The King of the Jews'.

20.1 **Early on the first day of the week.** We would say 'Sunday morning', but there are no names for days of the week in the Bible. The point is not so much to date the episode as to indicate that the sabbath, which forbade all such activity, was now over.

Whatever may have been the case for later generations (and John will have something to say about this later), the faith of the first Christians that Jesus had risen from the dead rested on the conviction that they, or at least certain witnesses whom they had reason to trust, had seen him with their own eyes. But all the gospels tell of a sensational event which preceded any appearance of Jesus: the discovery that the tomb was empty. Exactly how this discovery was made, and why it was not immediately seized upon by the disciples as convincing proof of the resurrection, are questions which receive different answers in the gospels. Clearly there was some uncertainty about the importance of the discovery in view of the fact that it was so soon followed by an encounter with the risen Jesus himself. This gospel, however, seems to present a particularly careful account. John takes for granted many of the details recorded in the other gospels: his readers are evidently expected to know, without having been told, that Jesus' tomb had been sealed with a massive stone, and they are given no explanation of how Mary, having left the tomb in verse 2, is back again weeping there in verse 11 – but presumably

---

[37] The traditional site of the Holy Sepulchre is about 20 metres from the rock of Calvary, and, since the area was certainly not built over at the time, a part of it could well have been under cultivation.

everyone knew the tradition that a group of women (of whom Mary seems to be the single representative here) were the first to see the risen Jesus (Matthew 28.9–10). In other words, John is clearly working with an existing narrative; but not only does he offer certain details which are different and add whole episodes which are new to us: he arranges the material in such a way that it shows a clear progression from simple consternation to assured belief.

This is at its clearest in the first paragraph. The first reaction to the discovery that the tomb had not remained as it was left on the Friday was that of Mary

13 Magdalene. She drew the obvious conclusion: **"They have taken the Lord out of the tomb, and we do not know where they have laid him."** (The women of the other gospel accounts seem to have left their mark on this narrative with the word 'we'.) The second reaction was that of a disciple, and was more perceptive. Here we have a completely new scene, not mentioned in any other gospel, involving an elaborate distribution of rôles between Simon Peter and

2 **the other disciple, the one whom Jesus loved**. From a formal point of view, Peter seems to be given precedence as the first witness (he was, after all, or would at least become, the chief of the apostles). But in reality the decisive reaction belonged to the other disciple. He, like Peter, saw both the linen wrappings and the cloth (such as was wrapped round the head of Lazarus, 11.44) still lying in the tomb. It was inconceivable that anyone stealing the corpse should first have unwrapped it and left the wrappings in a neat pile. Something of a different order altogether must have happened. There were

9 certainly clues (though no more than clues) in **scripture** that might suggest what had happened; but **as yet** they had not been understood. The disciple,

8 however, **saw and believed**.

This is the only occasion in the New Testament on which it is said that someone believed as a result of the empty tomb. It was a vision of the risen Jesus that brought the rest to faith. But this disciple came to believe on the strength merely of a strange fact about the wrappings in the empty tomb. We do not know who this disciple was. He appears, again in close company with Peter, both in chapter 13 and in chapter 21. Whether or not he stands for the author of the gospel (see below, p. 385), he was certainly a person whom the first readers of the gospel knew and whose memory (if he was dead) they revered. His was a powerful example to appeal to: despite such slender and puzzling evidence, he had come to that faith in Jesus' resurrection which was to be the cardinal belief of every Christian.

But now John returns to the pattern set by the other gospels. In Matthew and Luke the discovery of the empty tomb is followed almost at once by supernatural appearances, first to the women, then to the disciples. Here, Mary Magdalene continues to take the place of the group of women, and her vision of angels corresponds with the scene in the other gospels. But this vision still leaves her assuming that there must be some natural explanation of the body's disappearance, so much so that, when Jesus himself appears to her, she immediately (since she does not recognize him) puts the same explanation to the stranger and asks for his help.

16 **Jesus said to her, "Mary!"** That simply addressing her by name was enough to open her eyes is a piece of vivid and convincing reporting. (By general consent John reaches a high level of narrative art in this scene, which is told with a rare simplicity and economy of words.) It is possible that John meant his readers to have in mind some words that Jesus had spoken earlier, "He calls his own sheep by name" (10.3). But there is certainly some serious teaching 17 in the rest of the dialogue. **"Do not hold on to me, because I have not yet ascended to the Father."** In Matthew the women who first saw the risen Jesus "took hold of his feet, and worshiped him" (28.9). This (John may have felt) was to attach the wrong significance to these appearances of Jesus. They were intended to convince, not to excite homage. The reader must not be given the impression that the women, or in this case Mary or indeed any disciple, had been given a chance to know and worship the risen Christ in a way more direct, more personal, than was given to any subsequent Christian believer. The Christ whom Christians worshipped was the Christ who had **ascended to the Father**. If this were imagined in spatial terms, it could be said that Mary and the disciples saw him, so to speak, on his way up to heaven. But the truth behind this naïve form of expression was that Mary's experience, though at that particular place and time it was decisive in convincing her and others of the fact of Jesus' resurrection, was in no way more direct and privileged than that of all Christians when they worship their ascended Lord.

"But go to my brothers." That Jesus' followers are his 'brothers' is implied by a saying recorded in the other gospels (Mark 3.34–5) and is a presupposition of much of the teaching in Matthew's gospel – indeed in Matthew the risen Jesus actually says to the women who have seen him, "go and tell my brothers" (28.10). In this gospel the idea is a new one (though it is perfectly consistent with the earlier teaching about Christians being children of God and friends of Jesus); but even if John was merely reproducing some tradition that Jesus had used this very word, he did not miss the opportunity to draw the consequence: **"my Father and your Father . . . my God and your God"**. For all the unique majesty implied in Jesus' ascension, his followers remained in close solidarity with him. In their relationship with God they were privileged to be his equals, his **brothers**.

18 **Mary Magdalene went and announced to the disciples, "I have seen the Lord."** Each of the other gospels suggests an answer to the question why this news had no immediate effect on the disciples. (See above on Mark 16.8.) John ignores the question. It is as if he is following the traditional pattern of Jesus' appearances – first he was seen by some women (or Mary Magdalene alone), then by the disciples all together – without much attempt to link these appearances together in a coherent narrative. The appearance of Jesus 19 to his disciples in the **evening on that day** takes place exactly as if it were the very first of its kind. This, in any case, was doubtless the appearance that was

remembered as the most important and authoritative of all. Paul mentions an appearance to 'the twelve' (1 Corinthians 15.5); and Luke also gives an account of it which is in many respects similar to this one. John's version has details which are characteristic of this gospel. **"Peace be with you"** is doubtless intended to be understood as more than a formal greeting (along

21 the lines of 14.27); and **"As the Father has sent me, so I send you"** relates back to the teaching on his own and his disciples' mission that was given earlier (17.18). But the scene as a whole falls into place alongside passages in the other gospels. Just as in Luke (24.39) there is much emphasis on the fact that the risen Jesus was no mere ghost, so here the apparition, though

20 he enters through locked doors, shows the disciples **his hands and his side.** Again, the ending of the scene represents a formal commission to his disciples

22 corresponding to that at the end of Matthew's gospel: **he breathed on them and said to them, "Receive the Holy Spirit."** From the very beginning of its existence the church possessed the gift of the Holy Spirit – on this all were agreed. Exactly how and when the gift had been given was not so certain – in Acts 2, for example, Luke gives an altogether different account. In John the gift follows the resurrection immediately, and is described in a distinctive way. According to Genesis (2.7), "the L O R D God formed man from the dust of the ground, and breathed into his nostrils the breath of life". 'Breath' in Hebrew is the same word as 'spirit'; the giving of the Spirit by Jesus lent itself to being described in the same terms: it was a new act of creation.

23 **"If you forgive the sins of any, they are forgiven them."** Jesus, it seems (and this is not at all surprising), was remembered to have given to his disciples – and thereby, it has usually been assumed, to their successors – a definite authority over the lives of their fellow Christians. In Matthew this is expressed in terms of 'binding' and 'loosing' – a somewhat technical idiom (see above on Matthew 16.19). Here the saying has the same form but concerns the disciples' power to forgive sins. John does not elsewhere show interest in the concept of the forgiving of an individual's sins (though this is prominent in the other gospels); but in the life of the church it was certainly necessary sometimes to decide whether the conduct of members made it necessary to exclude them, and authority to do so seems to have been found in this saying of Jesus.

There are traces elsewhere in the gospels that not all the disciples were immediately convinced of the resurrection. In Matthew there is the laconic statement that "some doubted" (28.17). John, alone of the gospel writers,

24 gives a concrete instance. **Thomas (who was called the Twin)** has already been named twice in the course of the gospel (11.16; 14.5); here he is an example of one who refuses to believe without incontrovertible and tangible evidence. When it comes to the point, Jesus' appearance elicits from him what was probably intended to be the most significant confession of faith

28 that had been made by anyone in the gospel: **"My Lord and my God!"** Is this the moment when a Jewish writer (as we assume John to have been) finally

broke the barrier which would normally have prevented a Jew from using the word 'God' of anyone but the one God of heaven and earth? In the following centuries the church, through its doctrine of the Trinity, worked out a way of calling Jesus 'God' that was compatible with the traditional Jewish (as opposed to pagan) belief that God is one alone. In New Testament times this had not yet been achieved; even so, Christians had no doubt that Jesus was far more than any *man*, be it prophet, Messiah or any other exceptional person. We have seen how this gospel portrays Jesus as God's agent on earth; and we have noted the principle that 'a man's agent is as himself'. At this moment, perhaps, Thomas recognized, not that Jesus was God himself (let alone some other god), but that Jesus was representing God in the fullest sense it was possible to imagine: addressing him, he was (as it were) addressing God himself. But of course in this story Thomas is no more than a foil to the true Christian believer. To convince him, Jesus had to make (so to speak) a special appearance. But John was writing for Christians who had come to their faith without demanding an impossible confirmation of it. Jesus' last words are

29 addressed to them: **"Blessed are those who have not seen and yet have come to believe."**

30 **Now Jesus did many other signs . . . which are not written in this book.** The writer now addresses his readers directly. The 'signs', in this gospel, are mostly what we would call 'miracles'; and from a comparison with the other gospels it is quite clear that John has recorded only a small selection of those ascribed to Jesus. The same indeed is true of Mark (1.34); and it is also true that Mark, like John, tended to narrate only those miracles which had a

31 bearing upon *faith*. John now makes this explicit: **But these are written so that you may come to believe that Jesus is the Messiah, the Son of God.** This phrase should have settled the question, For whom was the gospel written? – those who had not yet 'come to believe'. Unfortunately this is far from certain: the crucial word exists in two different forms in the manuscripts (see the NRSV footnote); John may have written that which means *continue to believe*. We cannot tell from this verse alone whether he was writing a missionary book for unbelievers or a treatise for people who were already Christians. Nevertheless it effectively sums up the character of the gospel. The purpose, indeed, was the same as that for which any gospel was bound to be written – to awaken or strengthen faith (or both) in those who heard it and read it. Only the word **life** is distinctive. Almost from the beginning this has been John's most characteristic and emphatic way of describing the benefits and possibilities which are now open to human beings if they will respond with faith to the story he has been telling.

An epilogue

Normally it was only in a preface or an epilogue that a writer addressed his readers about his own book. The last verse of chapter 20 is a typical ending of a book; and any reader would have been surprised to find that another section of narrative follows. This alone would be sufficient to make one suspect that what is now chapter 21 was added after the main work was finished. But

21.1 there are other oddities. The scene is set by the **Sea of Tiberias**. Nothing has prepared us for this. The disciples were last heard of in Jerusalem. Yet we read

3 that Simon Peter said, **"I am going fishing"**, as if he were living the normal life of a fisherman in Galilee. Apart from what looks like an editorial comment –

14 **this was now the third time that Jesus appeared to his disciples after he was raised from the dead** – there is nothing to suggest that the episode follows naturally after the events that have just been related. If its author is the same as that of the gospel (and there is much stress on its authenticity at the end of the chapter) he has chosen a surprising way to continue his work, and though the style is very similar (with just a few points of detail where we would have expected the author of the gospel to express himself differently), and though many of the idioms and ideas are familiar from the gospel, it is tempting to believe that someone else has had a hand in it. The problem is made if anything more difficult by the great emphasis which is placed at the end on the claim that 'the disciple whom Jesus loved' was both an eyewitness and the author. Who was this disciple? And is it claimed that he wrote the whole gospel or just this later addition to it? Perhaps the most we can reasonably say is that chapter 21 is an addition which is unlikely to have been part of the original gospel.

The episode is made up of a number of different elements. The main plot, so to speak, is the story of a group of disciples, now returned to their life as fishermen, who, after a night's unsuccessful fishing, are told by Jesus to try once more; they then make an astonishingly large catch. A story of this kind is told by Luke (5.1–11), who places it near the beginning of Jesus' activity and uses it to explain how Jesus attracted his first disciples. Here it has an unearthly quality, for it is placed after the resurrection and Jesus' sudden appearance is as unexpected as the impressive catch of fish. The real significance, however, is in the by-plots. The first of these turns on a delicate

7 balancing of priorities between Peter and the **disciple whom Jesus loved**, very much as in the discovery of the empty tomb (20.1–9): it was Peter who took action, but it was the other disciple who first recognized (and believed) that the figure on the shore was Jesus. The second by-plot (which is rather loosely integrated into the main plot, since there is no obvious reason why Jesus should have asked for the disciples' catch of fish when he already had other fish laid on the fire) is a meal shared by the risen Jesus with his disciples. This, again, has a parallel in Luke (24.30) and is described in a way which might

13 well be intended to make the reader think of the eucharist: **Jesus came and took the bread and gave it to them, and did the same with the fish** recalls the feeding of the five thousand in chapter 6, which itself is the cue for eucharistic teaching. Besides all this there is a rich load of symbolism. We are told that

11 the net was **full of large fish, a hundred and fifty-three of them**. The writer

hardly intends us to think that someone present counted and remembered the exact number: to give an idea of the size of the catch a round number would have been just as impressive. It was a culture in which the symbolism of numbers had wider currency than it has now. It happens that the sum of the number $1 + 2 + 3 + \ldots$ up to 17 is 153; 17 is $10 + 7$, and ten and seven were both numbers which symbolized totality. This sounds very contrived: but it was spotted at least as early as the fourth century, and it is the kind of meaning (though not necessarily the correct one) which the number is likely to have been intended to convey. And when the author goes on to tell us that **the net was not torn**, we can hardly be wrong in seeing another piece of symbolism. After all, Jesus himself had started the metaphor: "I will make you fish for people" (Mark 1.17). The fish would be the new members, and the net would be the church, which, despite the great number of 'fish', would retain its unity and not be torn apart.

15   **Jesus said to Simon Peter.** Sayings of Jesus which seemed to assign a special place among the apostles to Peter are recorded in Matthew (16.18) and Luke (22.31–2). At the same time, all the gospels faithfully record Peter's threefold disowning of Jesus during the trial. Here Peter's threefold profession of love[38] for Jesus may be intended to balance this threefold denial (which, in this gospel, Jesus foretold directly after a short exhortation to the disciples on the love that was required of them, 13.34–8). Certainly Jesus' final command

19 to Peter, **"Follow me"**, seems to refer back to the same passage, where Jesus said, "You cannot follow me now; but you will follow afterward." But the

15 actual form of the commandment is new: **"Feed my lambs."** Up to now the shepherding imagery has been used only of Jesus. Now it is extended to Peter – and through him (the church soon came to realize) to all who were to bear responsibility for other Christians.

18   **"Very truly, I tell you."** The introduction is solemn; but what follows has a proverbial ring. To walk any distance, a man had to hitch up his long clothes by making a fold over his belt and then fastening his belt tighter. A young man is perfectly independent; but an old man is dependent on others and needs their help to arrange his clothes for him while he stretches out his arms; he may even need to be led on his way. Taken by itself, this reads like a pessimistic aphorism of the kind that is so brilliantly elaborated at the end of Ecclesiastes (12.1–8). What was the application of it to Peter? The writer tells

19 his readers: **He said this to indicate the kind of death by which he would glorify God.** Peter was to find himself as helpless as an old man in the face of those who would put him to death as a martyr for his faith, a death which, like

---

[38] Two different Greek words for 'love' are used in this short dialogue. Jesus' first two questions have *agapaō*, the word characteristically used in the gospel and letters of John for the distinctive love of Christ and Christians. The third question and Peter's answers use *phileō*, which is the commonest Greek word for human affection in general. It is difficult to see any significance in these nuances, which may simply be a matter of literary style, like the variation in the same passage between 'sheep' and 'lambs'.

that of Jesus himself, would 'glorify' God. This comment was clearly written after the event, and is one of our first pieces of evidence that Peter was in fact martyred (probably in Rome, soon after the middle of the first century CE). Tertullian, writing a century or so later, knew (or assumed) that Peter had been crucified (and Origen, a few years later, says that he was crucified, at his own request, head downwards), and saw a prophetic significance in 18 the words **stretch out your hands**. But this goes beyond the text. Taken as it stands, the prophecy says no more than that Peter would not die a natural death.

On two occasions already in these last chapters there has been a careful 20 balancing of honours between Peter and **the disciple whom Jesus loved**. If Jesus had made a prophecy about Peter's death (and, at the time of writing, the death of a Christian martyr was much honoured: it was the most esteemed 19 way of all to **glorify God**), had he not said something also about the other 22 disciple? He had: **"If it is my will that he remain until I come, what is that to you?"** On the face of it, this was less mysterious. For some years after the 23 resurrection it was believed in the Christian **community** (here called literally *the brothers* – none of the gospels uses the word 'church' except Matthew) that, though some Christians might die, others would 'remain until the Lord came'. This disciple, it seemed, was destined to be one of these. But the 'coming' of Jesus did not take place in this way – indeed, it has been one of the themes of this gospel that such naïve language about the future was in reality only a way of speaking about a new dimension of the present. The disciple may have died; and it would have been necessary to draw attention to the oracular ambiguity of Jesus' saying. Correcting this misunderstanding appears to be one of the objects for which this chapter was added to the gospel.

25 The writer provides a new ending, which is little more than a rhetorical flourish such as many ancient authors liked to use. The proper conclusion of this chapter is in verse 24. Peter may have glorified God by his death; but 24 the other disciple gave testimony of another kind: **This is the disciple who is testifying to these things and has written them.** We hear the voice now, no longer of the author, but of the community which used and treasured this book. They believed, rightly or wrongly, that they had the clue to the mysterious phrase, 'the disciple whom Jesus loved'. It was the author himself – of this chapter, or even of the whole gospel (the text will bear either meaning). If this was so, then they had an eyewitness account. The whole of the gospel has stressed the crucial importance of 'witness', **testimony**. This author could not be faulted: **we know that his testimony is true.**

THE ACTS

OF THE APOSTLES

1.1 This book of the New Testament, like the gospel according to Luke, is dedicated to a certain Theophilus. The dedication declares that the gospel was only the **first book** of the total work; what now lies before us is the sequel. The author gave no title to this sequel, and its earliest readers may have been somewhat puzzled to know what to call it. Biographies of popular philosophers sometimes went on to include an account of the achievements of the philosopher's followers; and historians occasionally undertook the history of an institution. But there were also biographical accounts of the achievements of famous men which might be called "The Acts of so-and-so"; and perhaps it is for this reason that, since the second century, this work has been known as THE ACTS OF THE APOSTLES. Nevertheless, the title is not altogether appropriate. Only two apostles, Peter and Paul, are prominent in the story, and only in the second half of the book does one of them (Paul) become the centre of interest. In the first half the real protagonist is the group of early Christians which rapidly grew into the beginnings of a world-wide church.

Greek historians not only wrote a preface to their work as a whole; they often introduced successive books of it by a brief résumé of what had gone before. The beginning of Acts follows this convention and serves to tie the two parts of the work together. It is not explicitly stated that the author is the same in each case; but the style is so similar that it would be hard to doubt it even if it were not implied by the repetition of the name Theophilus, the man to whom both parts are dedicated. This author has been known since very early times as Luke.

The end of Luke's gospel had already pointed forward to a sequel. The disciples were instructed to remain in Jerusalem until they had been "clothed with power from on high" (Luke 24.49), and the first two chapters of Acts describe how this came to pass. Yet even if Luke conceived his two-volume work as a continuous whole, the fact remained that in the first part he had written a 'gospel', that is to say, a book of the same form as the 'Gospel according to Mark', of which he had probably been making use himself. As such, his 'gospel' was likely to have been read and used as an independent work, apart from its continuation; and the author may well have felt the need to give it an ending which would not merely point forward to the sequel but would also stand on its own as a fitting conclusion to his account of the earthly life of Jesus. This he did by his description of Jesus' final moments with his disciples: "While he was blessing them, he withdrew from them and was carried up into heaven" (Luke 24.50). For the purposes of the gospel narrative this brief and solemn moment was all that was necessary. But for the purposes of the continuation it needed some amplification; and this may be the reason why the author, after correctly referring back to the point reached

2 at the end of his gospel (**when he was taken up to heaven**), goes on to narrate the same episode again, adding a number of new points and indeed setting the whole scene in a new light.[1]

3 **He presented himself alive to them by many convincing proofs.** This is the first amplification. The task of the apostles was primarily to bear witness to the resurrection; and lest it should be thought that their testimony was based only on their subjective experiences immediately after the crucifixion, Luke emphasizes that the appearances of Jesus which he narrated at the end of his gospel were no more than a sample of a larger body of evidence. The witness of the apostles was based on **many convincing proofs.** Secondly, the "power from on high" which, at the end of the gospel (24.49), Jesus promised to the disciples is here defined more sharply. The 'power' would be the Holy Spirit, which they were shortly to receive in an experience analogous to baptism and in a way that would fulfil the prophecy of John the Baptist: "I baptize you with water . . . he will baptize you with the Holy Spirit and with fire" (Luke 3.16).

All this represented an incursion of the supernatural into the experience of the disciples such that they (and Christians after them) were bound to ask: Was this now that final and climactic phase of history to which Jewish religious faith had so long looked forward? The disciples are made to ask

6 this question in its crudest form: **"Is this the time when you will restore the kingdom to Israel?"** – as if all that Jesus had taught about the 'kingdom' could be equated with a political change such as the liberation of Palestine from the Roman occupation. Jesus' answer appears to ignore this blatant simplification. First it emphasizes the impossibility of calculating the date of such an event (the same saying occurs in Mark 13.32, but is omitted by Luke in the corresponding passage of his gospel); it then promises two signs which will show that nevertheless a new and significantly different age is dawning: the activity of the Holy Spirit and the mission of the church, beginning from

8 Jerusalem and spreading (after its rejection by the Jews) **to the ends of the earth.**

9 **He was lifted up.** At a certain point the earthly appearances of the risen Jesus came to an end, and the church believed him to be now seated in glory at the right hand of God. The clear impression given by the end of Luke's

---

[1] When placed side by side, the final scene of Luke's gospel and the opening of Acts present a number of discrepancies. The period of **forty days** (1.3) seems impossible to fit into the chronology of Luke 24, and the description of Jesus disappearing into **a cloud** (1.9) is very different from the simple parting recorded in the gospel (24.50). The above explanation presupposes that the two passages are as the author intended them. But if once it is granted that there may have been some alteration or subsequent editing of the text, numerous other explanations become possible, though none has been found entirely convincing.

gospel is that this took place on the same day as Jesus was first seen to have
3 risen from the dead. But here it is stated that there was a period of **forty days**
(a conventional round number) during which Jesus continued to appear
to his disciples, and this is corroborated, not only by the last two chapters
of John's gospel (which seem to presuppose at least a week during which
the appearances took place) but also by the earliest record we have of these
appearances (1 Corinthians 15.5), which lists more appearances than could
possibly have been witnessed in a day or two. It seems that there were in fact
two affirmations which the church felt able to make after the resurrection
of Jesus. First, Jesus had been raised bodily from the dead, not to continue
his former existence on earth, but to assume his destined place at the right
hand of God. His resurrection involved his vindication in glory, and his
place was henceforward 'in heaven'. If one were to think in terms of space
and time, his 'rising from the dead' implied an immediate 'ascension into
heaven', and most Christian writers of the first decades of Christianity looked
upon both as virtually a single event. But secondly, it was an indisputable
fact that during a certain number of days after Easter day Jesus had appeared
to his disciples, both to strengthen their faith and to give them instruction.
How was this possible, if he had already 'ascended into heaven'? The New
Testament writers offer no solution to this question; they simply present the
two facts side by side. In any case, their philosophy made it impossible for
them to conceive of any intermediate state between resurrection from the
dead and a glorious ascension into heaven. Jesus had been resurrected *with
his body*. That body was not now present on earth (at least in any ordinary
sense): it must therefore have 'ascended'. Precisely how Jesus was nevertheless
able to appear to his disciples over a period of weeks is a question which, it
seems, they neither asked nor tried to answer.

Nevertheless one question did demand an answer. Jesus' appearances lasted
only for a limited time. At a certain moment they came to an end. Which
was the last, and how was it known that after that there would be no more of
the same kind? This is a question to which Luke's unpretentious account of
what the church came to call 'the ascension' offers an answer. The reporting
is very sober. There are none of the spectacular phenomena (chariots of
fire and so forth) which accompanied the taking up into heaven of certain
Old Testament figures, both in the Bible (2 Kings 2.11) and in later Jewish
legend. All the emphasis is on the simple fact of a supernaturally attested
10 parting; and the function of the angels (**two men in white robes**, as in the
resurrection narrative, Luke 24.4) is to make clear its finality. The sequence
of resurrection appearances was finished. Jesus' next 'coming' would be that
which he had often foretold himself in the words of an ancient prophecy
about the Son of Man. It would be as decisive and unmistakable as this
disappearance into a cloud; but it would also mean that there would be no
11 need to stand **looking up toward heaven**. This time it would be visible to all,
a cosmic phenomenon.

12   **Then they returned to Jerusalem from the mount called Olivet.** In Luke
24.50 the parting takes place at Bethany, which lay on the far side of the
Mount of Olives, much further from Jerusalem than **a sabbath day's journey**
(a technical term meaning the distance it was permitted to travel on the
sabbath – about half a mile). But the discrepancy may not be serious: Luke
may have thought of Bethany as lying on the Mount of Olives itself (which
he calls **Olivet**), and the way **from the mount** was also the way from Bethany.

Jesus has gone; and from this point the focus of the story becomes the
church in Jerusalem. The basic composition of this church is revealed in two
13 brief scenes. First, in a **room upstairs**, are the leaders: the original twelve (now
14 eleven), **certain women** and Jesus' **brothers**. All these are familiar from Luke's
gospel and constitute the essential nucleus of Jesus' followers. Secondly, out
15 of doors, there are **the believers** (the *brothers*) . . . **about one hundred
twenty persons**. Nothing in Luke's gospel has prepared us for such a **crowd**
of believers. Jesus' last hours with the twelve, his solitary trial and death,
and the gradual recovery of faith by those who witnessed his appearances
after the resurrection, hardly suggest the existence in Jerusalem of a faithful
community of this size. Nevertheless we know (from 1 Corinthians 15.6) that
the risen Christ appeared to a far larger group than Jesus' closest disciples, and
in any case such a group was necessary in order to provide the 'congregation'
of the church, the structure of which Luke is presenting at the outset of
his narrative. The figure of 120 is probably no accident. In Jewish local
government 120 persons constituted the smallest group permitted to have
its own council; and in any case, the number is a multiple of the inner group
of the twelve. Thus Luke presents a picture – perhaps more schematic than
strictly historical – of the composition of the earliest Christian church; and
13 such is the importance that he attaches to it that he gives again the names
of the original disciples (though he has already given them in his gospel,
6.13–16), and then goes on to describe the way in which the place left by the
departure of Judas Iscariot was filled up.

The way this episode is reported is totally unlike anything in the gospel,
15 but is characteristic of the author's method in Acts. **Peter stood up . . .
and said**. This is a formal speech, the first in Luke's work, but now to be
followed by many others. Since the time of Thucydides, Greek historians
had taken it for granted that they might work speeches into their narratives.
Thucydides himself may sometimes have had access to records of speeches
that were actually made; but, where he did not, he freely composed the kind
of speech which he believed would have been made in the circumstances.
Later historians often adopted this convention uncritically and made up
speeches as they went along to put into the mouths of leaders at appropriate
moments: it was a recognized technique for enlivening the narrative and for
bringing out the deeper issues underlying events. It was not required that
these speeches should be based on any surviving record or recollection of
what was actually said.

Luke has already shown, by the style of his opening words of dedication, that he was familiar with the conventions of Greek history-writing, and it would not be surprising if he deliberately composed speeches and inserted them into his narrative for the same reasons. Moreover this point in his work was the natural one for such speeches to begin. Previously (almost from the beginning of the gospel story), the main speaker had always been Jesus, and Jesus' discourses consisted of sayings that must have been reverently preserved in the memory of Christians. The evangelist had no liberty to make up what Jesus might have said; he could only select and edit what people remembered that Jesus did say. But from now on, the speakers were the leaders of the church, and it is unlikely that their utterances were remembered with anything like the same fidelity. It is possible, of course, that there were records, or at least detailed recollections, of some of these occasions and that Luke had access to them; and he may often have been in a good position to know what points a Christian leader made, or was likely to have made, in his own defence against the Jewish or Roman authorities, and what style of preaching the earliest preachers adopted. Nevertheless it is reasonable to allow for the possibility that, on any given occasion, Luke had no information to guide him and, following the conventions of contemporary history-writing, simply composed the kind of speech which would have been appropriate to the occasion.

We shall see signs of this later in Acts. But Peter's first speech is one that he might well have made much as it stands. The treatment of scripture is entirely characteristic of a Palestinian Jew. It was generally believed that, apart from 'the law' (that is, the 'Pentateuch', or Five Books of Moses), which had been delivered directly to Moses by God, the remaining books that had been received into the Old Testament were dictated to their writers by the Holy Spirit. The Psalms, for example, had been given by **the Holy Spirit through David**. Some of these writings, it was realized, may have applied only to the times in which they were written. But the prophets, and many of the psalms, were open to interpretation as clues to the future. The events they prophesied might not yet have occurred, and since it was axiomatic that **scripture had to be fulfilled**, it was one of the preoccupations of those who studied the scriptures to discern in the present, or to forecast in the future, events which could be shown to be the definitive fulfilment of Old Testament prophecies. Luke has already narrated (chapter 24) how the risen Jesus gave instruction on this to his disciples, and we have here an example of the technique being put to use. Psalm 69 was one of the 'righteous sufferer' psalms and contained several verses which appeared to be startlingly exact predictions of the execution of Jesus. If so, then the sufferer's enemies in that psalm could be identified as the enemies of Jesus, and the fate which it prophesied for them could be confidently expected to come to pass. The first of Jesus' enemies to perish was the disciple who betrayed him, Judas; and the circumstances of his death were such that a verse in this psalm also seemed

20 strikingly appropriate, '**Let his homestead become desolate, and let there be no one to live in it**' (Psalm 69.25). The same went for Psalm 109.8, '**Let another take his position of overseer.**'

18 (**Now this man acquired a field . . .**) This parenthesis, recording the manner of Judas' death, appears to be a note added by Luke for the benefit of his readers rather than by Peter for the benefit of his hearers (for Peter would

19 presumably have said 'in your language', not **in their language**); and the NRSV has punctuated it accordingly. It should be compared with the similar note in Matthew 27.3–10. Both accounts give the name **Field of Blood**, but each explains the origin of the name differently. In Matthew, Judas 'hanged himself'; in Acts he has a more gruesome death, which Luke may have borrowed from other literary accounts of the deaths of notable villains – compare especially Wisdom 4.19; 2 Maccabees 9.5–9.

23 **So they proposed two.** Both men had common Jewish names; one of them, like many educated Jews, bore a Roman added name, Justus. It is implied in verse 21 that both had been disciples of Jesus: it may just be chance that there is no mention of them in the gospels. The result of the incident was that the group of twelve was reconstituted and the church began its life with a clear organization. Or so, at least, Luke presents the matter. The letters of Paul, written some decades earlier than Acts, present a less tidy picture.

2.1 **When the day of Pentecost had come.** 'Pentecost' means 'fiftieth' and was the usual Greek name for the Jewish harvest festival, which took place 'on the fiftieth day' after Passover. The festival itself, which involved the presentation of harvest produce at the temple and a day of general festivity, has no obvious bearing on Luke's narrative, but serves to date it by the Jewish calendar. Jesus' crucifixion was at Passover; the church's mission began at the next festival, seven weeks later.

4 **All of them were filled with the Holy Spirit.** This was the 'power from above' (Luke 24.49) for which they had been told to wait; and the manner

3 of its bestowal – **divided tongues, as of fire** – is described in such a way as to seem a direct fulfilment of John the Baptist's prophecy that Jesus would baptize "with the Holy Spirit and fire" (Luke 3.16).

But how could you tell when someone was 'filled with the Spirit'? In the experience of Paul and the later church, the Spirit was seen as responsible for many of the moral and spiritual qualities of Christians, and was therefore a secret and slowly maturing power such that you could not always tell whether a person possessed it. But it was also the cause of some of the more spectacular gifts with which Christians found themselves endowed. One of these was prophecy (for it was indubitably the Holy Spirit which had inspired the prophets of the Old Testament); another was a phenomenon which in Greek was called simply 'tongues'. We cannot always be sure whether this phenomenon was a succession of unintelligible sounds or an actual utterance in a foreign language unknown to the speaker. Paul's references to it usually suggest the former, whereas Luke's narrative here presupposes the latter – even if it sounded to some just like drunken speech (verse 13). But in any case, both were clearly regarded as forms of a miraculous phenomenon called 'tongues'. It was the combination of this gift with that of prophecy

11 (**speaking about God's deeds of power**) which suddenly overwhelmed the apostles and marked the decisive moment at which the Spirit was received by the church.

Or so, at least, the matter is presented here. Luke is the only writer in the New Testament to mention this episode; but that is not in itself a reason to doubt that something of this kind happened not many weeks after the resurrection. But was Luke right in thinking that this was the first time the Spirit was given to Jesus' followers? The author of the Fourth Gospel would not have agreed. According to him, the Spirit was given on the same day as the resurrection took place (John 20.22). It is possible, of course, that the first generation of Christians was not greatly interested in the exact moment at which the Spirit was given: it was sufficient for them to know that after the resurrection the Spirit was there, and was passed on through baptism to all who subsequently became Christians. But Luke, by fastening upon this particularly dramatic manifestation of the Spirit (which may well have been the first of its kind), was able to use it as a kind of precise date for the beginning of his account of the life of the church – a church which, we have been told, had just been constituted in its ideal form: a council of twelve apostles and a 'brotherhood' of 120 men (and doubtless women).

He was also able to present it as significant in another way. Among those who thronged Jerusalem at the festival season were people whose homes or whose places of upbringing lay in countries on all sides of Palestine, from North Africa to Asia Minor, from the Tigris to the Tiber. Most of these people

10 are likely to have been of Jewish origin (unless they were **proselytes**, that is, converts to the Jewish faith), but by living scattered in different countries, they had learnt to use the local languages and dialects. It must not be imagined that they therefore could not have understood one another when they met in Jerusalem, for Greek had become an international language throughout the countries of the eastern Mediterranean. The miracle was not that language barriers had been momentarily overcome and the curse of Babel lifted (for this had been practically accomplished by the Greek cultural revolution started in these countries by Alexander the Great) but that this new message, though still addressed primarily to Jews, seemed already to be clothing itself in languages spoken in remote parts of the world and therefore to be destined for world-wide proclamation.

14 **But Peter . . . addressed them.** Again a set speech, but much longer and more elaborate than the first. Its purpose is to explain the meaning of the extraordinary phenomenon which had just been witnessed, and it does so by setting it in the light of certain Old Testament passages. The first passage is from the prophet Joel (2.28–32), and is given at some length. But the introduction to it contains a significant change. In the Hebrew text, and in

all other versions known to us, the first words of the prophecy are quite indefinite: 'After this . . .' In Luke (or in whatever source he may have been 17 using), these words become **'In the last days...'** This is a small change, but it greatly alters the meaning and gives the prophecy a direct relevance to what has just taken place. Everyone knew what 'the last days' meant: the climactic period immediately before the end, a time both of miraculous happenings and of severe tribulations, of hope and promise for the elect and of foreboding and suffering for the rest of humankind. If the scene which had just been witnessed could be shown to be a fulfilment of Joel's prophecy, then it would follow (from the way in which the quotation is introduced) that this period of 'the last days' had already begun – or rather (since Luke was anxious to make all this easier to grasp for a non-Jewish reader) that the new epoch which began with the birth of the church was the way in which the visionary and sometimes esoteric formulations of Jewish seers were now being given meaning on the plane of history.

The Old Testament nowhere foretold the kind of linguistic miracle which had just taken place. But the phenomenon had been more than this. In various 11 languages the apostles had suddenly, with one accord, begun **speaking about God's deeds of power**. That is to say, they had been seized with the gift of prophecy; and prophecy, for Luke as for most Jewish thinkers, was the characteristic manifestation of the Holy Spirit. Seen in this light, what had just taken place was of a kind to which the Old Testament prophets had certainly looked forward, and the passage of Joel provided an apt commentary on the apostles' experience. As if to underline its message, a refrain is added by Luke 18 (which is not in the original): **'and they shall prophesy'**.

The 'last days', then, had begun, announced by a signal manifestation of the gift of prophecy. What had happened to bring this about? Was this simply the moment God had mysteriously chosen to inaugurate the new age? Or was there something in the immediate past which, if rightly interpreted, could be seen to have been leading up to this moment? The answer was, 22 Yes: **"Jesus of Nazareth"**. Peter's hearers could hardly pretend they had not heard of him: he had been **"a man attested to you by God with deeds of power, wonders, and signs"**. But, far from recognizing him as the anointed 23 representative of God, they had killed him **"by the hands of those outside the law"** (i.e. the Romans, a neat summary of the complicated division of responsibility between Jews and non-Jews that is implied in Luke's account of the trial and crucifixion). And that, they might have thought, would have 24 been the end of the matter. **"But God raised him up."** The principal evidence 32 for this daring proposition was the testimony of the apostles (**"of that all of us are witnesses"**). But it also gained greatly in credibility when it could be shown to be 'in accordance with the scriptures'. This is the cue for the second quotation, Psalm 16.8–11.

To modern eyes there is no mystery about this psalm. It is the song of one who has been providentially delivered from death and who gives thanks

to the God who 'will not abandon his soul to Hades'. But people were accustomed to seeing more in the scriptures than this. The psalms were
25 regarded as prophecy – the phrase **'I saw'** (which is in the Greek version but not in the original Hebrew, which has 'I keep' or 'I have set') is a typical alteration produced by this way of looking at scripture. Moreover, these psalms were unquestioningly ascribed to David. Now the indisputable fact that David had died made it impossible to think that he was in this case prophesying about himself. Therefore it was natural to find in his words a prediction of some future 'freeing from the pains of death' (verse 24 – see the NRSV footnote). Such a miraculous event would hardly have happened to an ordinary person. But David knew (from the prophecy of Nathan, 2 Samuel 7) that his line would not die out (even if the subsequent history of Jerusalem made this seem improbable), and that it would still come to pass
30 that, in a new age, God would **put one of his descendants on his throne**. This descendant of David could only be the Messiah. Evidently, then, when
31 David appeared to predict a resurrection, he **spoke of the resurrection of the Messiah**. That is to say: the fact of the resurrection of Jesus did not only rest on the evidence of the apostles. It too, like the outpouring of the Spirit which had just occurred, had been foretold in scripture.

Peter could thus point to two recent events which had been dramatic fulfilments of Old Testament prophecy. But what had these two events to do with each other? Was there a real connection between the resurrection of Jesus and the outpouring of the Spirit? The answer was twofold. First, it
33 was Jesus himself who **received from the Father the promise of the Holy Spirit** – Luke makes clear Jesus' rôle in this both here and at the end of his gospel. Secondly, Jesus' status after the resurrection was again prophesied in a text to which the early Christians turned again and again, Psalm 110.1:

34–5
> '**The Lord said to my Lord,**
> **"Sit at my right hand**
> **until I make your enemies your footstool."**

– an oracle which clearly David cannot have uttered about himself and which therefore pointed to a Person of the future. And if Jesus (as this prophecy declared) was now 'at God's right hand', anything which came from God (as the disciples' miraculous gift of prophecy did) now came also from Jesus. These events were all part of the same story and witnessed to the same truth. It only remained for those who had seen these things to draw the correct
36 conclusion: **"know with certainty that God has made him both Lord and Messiah, this Jesus whom you crucified"**.

37 **They were cut to the heart.** The Jewish bystanders had been confronted with two uncomfortable propositions. First, a small group of undistinguished Galileans had been the privileged recipients, under their very eyes, of an experience which could plausibly be interpreted as a sign that a new age was beginning; secondly, it appeared that the Jewish people as a whole, far

from being entitled to enter upon the joys of this new age (as they would have expected), had actually forfeited their right to do so by securing the condemnation and execution of Jesus. But Peter's answer (which perhaps also shows traces of Luke's mature reflection on the deeper implications of this question) was encouraging. On the first point, the prophecy of Joel made it quite clear that the new dispensation would be accessible to a far wider

39 circle than this first group of Christians: **"the promise is for you, for your children, and for all who are far away, everyone whom the Lord our God calls to him"** (a sentence compounded of biblical phrases, and drawing also upon the continuation of the passage from Joel already quoted). In other words, it was open to the whole Jewish people to receive the same blessing – and indeed to others: the sentence seems to allow already for the future mission to Gentiles. Secondly, even the complicity of the Jewish people in Jesus' crucifixion was not an insurmountable barrier. For Christian baptism – here mentioned for the first time as the rite of initiation into the church – conveyed the forgiveness of sins (as John's baptism had), and was also the

38 means of receiving **the gift of the Holy Spirit** (which was not the case with John's baptism, but was something new). Christianity, in short, was destined to be a universal religion – though one should not read back a modern universalism into this passage. It was never envisaged that the whole world would become Christian; only that men and women of every nationality would have the chance to join the new community of the elect, and so to

40 save themselves **"from this corrupt generation"** (another biblical phrase: Deuteronomy 32.5).

42 The response was massive; and in a single day the Christian **fellowship**[2] was transformed from a fairly small group of friends into a community to be numbered in thousands. How was this crowd of new members to express its common allegiance to a new faith? Luke answers by giving a sketch of its common life. Two points may be noticed. There are two references to

42,46 **the breaking of bread**, which suggest a technical expression for the Lord's
44 supper; and, as for having **all things in common** – for which there was some precedent: the Essenes are known to have practised a strict form of it in Judea – it appears to have been a provisional answer to questions that are sharply raised in Luke's gospel with regard to Jesus' teaching on wealth and poverty.

So far, the narrative has let the young church appear as a sensational but perfectly legitimate fulfilment of the faith of the Jewish people. The 'last days' foretold by the prophets had begun; the promised outpouring of the Spirit was an undeniable fact; and the way was open for the Jewish people as a

---

[2] Exactly what **fellowship** (*koinōnia*) means in this context is not clear. The Greek text of the last six verses of this chapter contains some unusual idioms, which suggests that Luke may have been transcribing some earlier description of the church's common life, or at least making use of some phrases which had become part of the special language of the early church.

whole, despite their complicity in the execution of Jesus, to repent, to join the new community of believers through baptism, and themselves to receive the Spirit. Indeed, the Christians felt themselves to be so perfectly adhering
46 to the true Jewish faith that **they spent much time together in the temple**. But there was more to it than this. Membership of this new community involved holding certain beliefs about Jesus, who was not just an important figure of the immediate past but whose presence was still felt and whose 'name' was still powerful among them. Specifically Christian (as opposed to Jewish) beliefs began to be formulated; and it was these which produced conflict between the church and the Jewish authorities. The first instance of this arose out of a miraculous case of healing.

3.1   **At the hour of prayer, at three o'clock in the afternoon.** This was the time when a lamb was sacrificed at the altar before the temple, and was observed as one of the two 'hours' of public prayer. In principle, Jews, wherever they might happen to be, would break off their occupations to pray; and those who could do so went to the colonnaded courts of the temple for the purpose. We have just been told (2.46) that the Christian fellowship did this regularly, and it was as a matter of course that **Peter and John were going up to the temple.** Beggars naturally took up their positions at the gates where most people entered. There were eight gates at different points in the wall of the temple enclosure, and two more at the entrances of the two inner courts,
2 which only Jews were allowed to enter. None of these is called **the Beautiful Gate** in any of the descriptions we possess of the temple. A late tradition gives the honour to one gate (part of which still exists) on the east side of the temple enclosure;[3] but this, being comparatively little used, would have been an unlikely place for a beggar to choose. A better place would have been one of the two main gates leading into the inner courts. These gates were of some magnificence; and one of them may well have been called 'the Beautiful Gate'.

The speech by Peter, however, which offers a commentary on the miracle
11 which took place, was given in **Solomon's Portico**, the colonnade which stretched the whole length of the temple area on the east side. The crowd,
9 seeing the former invalid **walking and praising God**, had become aware that a miracle must have taken place; and their natural reaction was to assume
12 that it was an act of God in reward for the exceptional **power or piety** of some individual. Peter corrected this by explaining that there was now a new 'power' in heaven – but not such as to infringe in any way the unique sovereignty of
13 the God of the Jewish faith. God was still **"the God of Abraham, the God of Isaac, and the God of Jacob, the God of our ancestors"**; but he had now

---

[3] The Greek for 'beautiful' is *hōraia*; the Crusaders took this to be the Latin word *aurea*, meaning 'golden', and to this day the gate is pointed out to visitors as 'the Golden Gate'. In the time of Christ its usual name was Shushan Gate.

brought to fulfilment the Old Testament prophecy (Isaiah 52.13) that his **servant** would be 'exalted'. This 'servant'[4] – with all the destiny of rejection and vicarious suffering that is spelled out in Isaiah 53, a chapter quoted at greater length in Acts 8 – was none other than Jesus, whom the people of Jerusalem knew mainly as one who had been condemned as a criminal in the presence of Pilate, but whom the apostles proclaimed to have been raised from the dead. If (as followed from the apostles' experience) this Jesus had really been **glorified**, it followed that he now had "the name that is above every name" (as Paul puts it in Philippians 2.9). Now the sudden cure of the lame man would have been commonly understood as an exorcism – the casting out of a spirit which had kept the sufferer physically captive by paralysis or atrophy of the limbs. The recognized technique of the exorcist consisted in invoking the name (and so the power) of a being more powerful than the evil spirit. Jesus now had the most powerful name in the universe (after that of God himself, which it would have been blasphemous to pronounce), and

6 it was by invoking this that Peter had performed the cure: **"in the name of Jesus Christ of Nazareth, stand up and walk"**. Not that this 'name' could be used mechanically: such a miracle (so at least Luke understood it) demanded

16 **faith** – either the faith of the subject of the cure, or (as the rather involved Greek of the sentence could also mean) the faith of the exorcist who invoked the 'name'.

But the speech is more than an explanation of the miracle. It is also a proclamation of the gospel; and as such it falls into a pattern which (with variations) underlies all the speeches in the early chapters of Acts and which may reflect the way in which the first preachers tended to present their

13 message. It contains all the essential elements – that Jesus was **handed over,**
15 **killed** and **raised from the dead**; but it also leads into some new theological
17 reflection. **"And now, friends, I know that you acted in ignorance, as did your rulers."** Exactly where the responsibility lay for Jesus' death is a question answered somewhat differently in the various gospels, and Luke seems to have had his own explanation: the entire Jewish people had **acted in ignorance**. (This is explicit in a saying attributed to Jesus in some manuscripts of Luke 23.34.) He also has a distinctive approach to offer to the question why Jesus

18 suffered. **"In this way God fulfilled what he had foretold through all the prophets, that his Messiah would suffer."** *All* the prophets? Where does one find such prophecies anywhere in the Old Testament? It is hard enough to find any explicit references to a future Messiah at all, and there is certainly none which tells that the Messiah would suffer – the idea, so far as we know, had hardly been conceived of: it was an inference first drawn by Christians (if not by Jesus himself). What they appear to have done (under the guidance

---

[4] The Greek word can also mean *child* or *son*. But the evident allusion to this passage of Isaiah makes **servant** the most probable translation.

of the risen Jesus, according to Luke 24.27) is to have seen a reference to the suffering of Jesus in the many passages of the Old Testament where a righteous and godly man suffers apparently unrelieved insult, injury and calamity. And given that they were now convinced that Jesus was the Messiah, it followed that all these passages – "**all the prophets**" – could be read as predictions of the fate necessarily endured by the Messiah, Jesus.

Jesus' death, then, had been foretold in scripture. It was destined to happen, and those who allowed it to happen were the unwitting agents of the purposes of God. They had done wrong, but the wrong was not irremediable. There was, however, a new urgency: with the outpouring of the Spirit upon the church, the 'last days' had begun, and the end was not far off. To Jewish thinkers at this time it had often seemed as though the promised consummation of history was a long time in coming. God had promised for his people a new and glorious age: what was preventing it from dawning? One answer was beginning to be suggested: it could not come until there was sufficient righteousness on earth. Only a national repentance could hasten it. And this may be the clue to Peter's challenge to his hearers. Stung by the enormity of their error in acquiescing in Jesus' crucifixion, the Jewish
21 people might now at last repent and so bring nearer **the time of universal restoration** (a somewhat philosophical-sounding term for the expected dénouement). The new age was being inaugurated by that same Messiah,
20 Jesus, whom God had already **appointed** and who now occupied the place of highest honour (after God) in heaven. This time, however, there would be no second chance. Another prophecy which Jesus had fulfilled was an oracle
22 of Moses (Deuteronomy 18.15), '**The Lord your God will raise up for you from your own people a prophet like me.**' A second Moses was another figure who (on the basis of this passage) some thinkers fitted into their scheme of the time before the end; and it seems that some Christians, particularly those represented by Matthew's gospel, saw Jesus in this light. But a stern warning was attached to this figure (Deuteronomy 18.19), made still sterner
23 when combined with a verse from Leviticus (23.29), '**everyone who does not listen to that prophet will be utterly rooted out of the people**'. All of this, with its crucial significance for the Jewish people, could be found predicted
24 in scripture, "**from Samuel and those after him**".
25 '**And in your descendants all the families of the earth shall be blessed.**' This promise to Abraham (Genesis 22.18) was a keystone of the self-understanding of the Jewish race: one day the blessings they enjoyed would be so manifest that the rest of the world would acknowledge them and benefit from them. Perceptive spirits such as John the Baptist had seen that mere membership of the Jewish nation was not enough to guarantee this blessing: there must be repentance as well. The matter had now been brought to a head. They must repent at once, before it was too late – and there is already a
26 hint in Peter's words ("**first to you**") that otherwise the promise might pass to others; it had only been made to the Jews 'first'. Their failure to take this

opportunity is cited as the mainspring of Paul's mission to the Gentiles in the closing scene of Acts.[5]

The temple area, in part of which this scene took place, was under the administration of the reigning high priest, assisted by a number of officials 4.1 such as **the captain of the temple**, a quasi-military officer. It was the sphere of influence of the aristocratic Sadducees, who differed from the more learned 2 party of the Pharisees on, among other things, the question of **the resurrection of the dead**. They denied any possibility of resurrection; this is stated in Acts 23.8 and is one of the few facts known about them. This made them bound to be opposed to the new faith, which vigorously proclaimed **that in Jesus there is the resurrection of the dead**. Luke's account makes them, quite plausibly, the first adversaries of the church. Whatever exactly had been happening in Solomon's Portico, it would not have been difficult for them to have Peter and John arrested on the pretext that they were causing a disturbance within the jurisdiction of the high priest.

The court to which the prisoners would be brought next morning, how-5 ever, consisted not only of the aristocratic **rulers** and **elders**, most of whom could be expected to be Sadducees, but also of **scribes**, many of whom were 6 Pharisees. Luke records that **the high-priestly family** was there in force, and actually names four of them.[6] But the original complaint of the Sadducees 7 was replaced by a much more serious charge. **"By what power or by what name did you do this?"** A cure had taken place in the precincts of the temple and the man who had worked the cure had been heard to invoke a name. To pronounce the name of a pagan deity or alien power in such a place would have been a serious offence. The evidence certainly justified an inquiry by the court.

8 **Then Peter, filled with the Holy Spirit, said to them.** The apostles had received 'power from on high', the Holy Spirit; but this meant, not that they were constantly in an inspired or ecstatic state, but rather (at least as it appears in Acts) that the new power was available to them at moments of need. In his gospel (12.11–12) Luke recorded a saying of Jesus promising the help of the Holy Spirit to all Christians who had to defend themselves in court; and here is the first example of it.

Peter's answer adds little to what he has said in the previous speeches. The 'name' was not that of any pagan deity (for Peter, at the end of his speech, showed that he understood the seriousness of the charge: as a God-fearing

---

[5] The above is but one of many attempts to give a consecutive account of the drift of Peter's speech. But it contains some unusual expressions and fragments of Christian belief, and it may be that it incorporates material which was part of the very early preaching of the church and fits a little awkwardly into the framework of the speech put together by Luke.

[6] Caiaphas, not **Annas** his father-in-law, was actually high priest at the time, but Annas was doubtless influential and still bore the title of high priest. We know nothing about **John** (unless he was *Jonathan*, Caiaphas' immediate successor) and nothing about **Alexander**.

12 Jew he recognized that **"there is no other name under heaven given among**
10 **mortals by which we must be saved"**). The 'name' was that of **Jesus Christ**
of Nazareth. This Jesus was no new or foreign intrusion into the traditional
Jewish faith. Both his resurrection (which the apostles had witnessed) and his
crucifixion (in which this same court had been instrumental) were foretold
in scripture; and to bring home to the court that even their own rejection
of Jesus was foreordained, Peter makes use of another text that came to be
11 much used in the church: '**the stone that was rejected by you, the builders...**
has become the cornerstone' (Psalm 118.22).

13　This speech certainly showed **boldness**, but also an ability to apply scripture which may have seemed surprising in **uneducated and ordinary men**;
but the court's surprise may have been lessened when they realized that
Peter and John had been **companions of Jesus** and so would have received
instruction from their master. The court was in some difficulty over the case.
The defendants had said nothing to incriminate themselves, and the hearing
could not proceed further without witnesses; and although the fact that there
16 had been a **notable sign** was now **obvious to all who live in Jerusalem**, the
21 crowd was hardly in the mood to give evidence; indeed, **all of them praised**
God for what had happened. The court had no alternative but to let the
men off with a caution. This would at least provide stronger grounds for
proceeding against them next time, which was a matter of some importance
in view of the prisoners' defiant question – the classic question of conscience
19 since the time of Socrates – **"whether it is right in God's eyes to listen to**
you rather than to God".

24　**"Sovereign Lord"**. The prayer is hardly one which could have been uttered
spontaneously by the whole group **together**. On the other hand, it does not
follow that it is a free composition by Luke. It may well contain certain phrases
of prayers which Luke had heard used in the church. From the earliest period
of Greek literature down to the collects in the *Book of Common Prayer*, formal
prayers have tended to fall into a certain pattern. First the deity is invoked by
his or her name and title, then certain of the deity's attributes are recalled, and
only then is the actual petition reached. This is exactly the pattern here. In
addition, the language of the opening is drawn from Old Testament prayers
such as that of Hezekiah (Isaiah 37.16–20); and the main part of the prayer is
a quotation from Psalm 2.1–2, which is shown to have been exactly fulfilled
in the events of Jesus' trial and death. In the time of the kings of Judah, the
reigning king was called the Anointed One (the Messiah) and was regarded
as the divinely chosen representative of God on earth. To make cause against
26 him was therefore, in a sense, to set up in opposition to **the Lord** himself. In
later times, when there was no longer a king in Jerusalem, the psalm was read
as a prophecy about the coming Messiah. Jesus, Christians believed, was that
Messiah; and the other references in the psalm could all be filled out from the
27 gospel story. **The kings of the earth** were represented by **Herod** (who appears
only in Luke's narrative of the trial: was this because Luke had this psalm in

mind?), **the rulers** by **Pontius Pilate**; and the psalm, which proclaimed the futility of this opposition, had been strikingly fulfilled in a general sense by the resurrection of Jesus.

It was a common belief in pagan religions (and the idea is found occasionally in the Bible) that when a deity hears a prayer of his worshippers he expresses his approval by a clap of thunder or an earthquake. Luke was writing for readers used to this convention. Whether or not the earthquake actually happened, there can be no doubt about Luke's meaning: God had heard the church's prayer.

32 **Now the whole group of those who believed were of one heart and soul**. The picture of the first Christian community, already sketched in 2.44–7, is
33 now presented in greater detail. Two features of it are singled out: the **great power** with which the apostles were able to give their testimony (which is abundantly illustrated in the episodes that follow), and the unanimity of
32 the whole community, which found expression in the fact that **everything they owned was held in common**. This sharing of all worldly possessions is never referred to elsewhere in the New Testament and it is certain that it never became a permanent or widespread practice in the early church. Paul's letters, for instance, with their frequent exhortations for generous giving, presuppose that members of the church were still in possession of their own property. In his gospel Luke gives special prominence to sayings of Jesus which seem to lay on his followers a total renunciation of material wealth, and it is tempting to see here Luke's answer to the question how such a radical injunction could ever have been put into practice. If so, it is reasonable to ask whether such a drastic experiment in communal living really took place, or whether Luke, in this respect as in others, may not be painting a somewhat idealized picture of the first days of the church. It is unlikely that the first Christian community would have allowed its poorer members to become destitute or go hungry. The Jewish nation as a whole had a strong social conscience about poverty, and generosity to the poor was highly esteemed. It was to be expected that the Christians would take this duty even more seriously; moreover, the old prophecy in Deuteronomy 15.4, "There will . . . be no one in need among you", which had never yet been fulfilled in the history of the nation, could be taken to apply to the 'last days', which had begun at Pentecost. We know from Paul's letters, as well as from Acts 11.27–30, that within a few years the community in Jerusalem became the most impoverished part of the church, and its difficulties might well have begun in the aftermath of a social experiment such as is described here.

Two anecdotes illustrate the principle. The first introduces a figure who
36 subsequently plays a prominent part in the story. **Joseph** was a very common name, and it was to be expected that he would be known by another name as well; but why he was surnamed **Barnabas**, and why Luke says that this meant **"son of encouragement"**, is mysterious. Barnabas was a Semitic name of pagan origin which was becoming not uncommon among the Jews; but, so

far as we know, it did not mean anything to do with 'encouragement'. This Barnabas, at any rate, was a **Levite**, which meant that he belonged by birth to that particular clan which had the privilege of performing certain lesser duties in the temple.

5.1 **But a man named Ananias.** The second anecdote tells as it were the other side of the story, and to the modern reader may seem exceedingly shocking. We are at a loss to understand how it could have been right or admirable for Peter, a disciple of Jesus, to have used his new power to carry out summary execution on a defaulter, particularly since this was in apparent contradiction to the much more humane procedure recommended in Matthew 18.15–17. It is true that the story shows signs of having gained in the telling. Even though burial normally took place shortly after death, it is hardly conceivable that a man could have been buried without his wife's being told, and the repetition of the happening when Sapphira made her appearance strikes us as frankly implausible even if we grant the possibility of Ananias having a sudden and fatal seizure. We are tempted to suspect the hand of a story-teller anxious to heighten the effect of the tale. But even if the original episode was less spectacular and less shocking, we still have to ask why Luke thought it proper to recount it in its present form.

No fully satisfactory explanation has ever been advanced. Nevertheless we must allow for the reaction of Luke's hearers to the story to have been somewhat different from ours. In the first place, we know of two other examples of similar experiments in communal living at about the same period. One was the community which produced the Dead Sea Scrolls. Here, anyone who dissembled the value of the property he contributed was punished with temporary exclusion from the community – certainly a much less serious penalty than death, but still quite severe. The other was an experiment in communal farming which was carried out in Spain. (Our informant is Diodorus Siculus, a Greek historian who wrote only a generation before Luke.) Here, the punishment for keeping anything back for private use was death. Evidently this kind of dishonesty could be regarded as a very serious sin. In the second place, even though the cue for the story was the sharing of possessions, the point which it illustrated was the 'great power' (4.33) of the apostles due to their possession of the Holy Spirit. Peter was able to represent Ananias'

3 deception as a **lie to the Holy Spirit**, and this made it a weighty matter. From early Old Testament times the attitude required of human beings by God was 'faith', that is, a readiness to accept whole-heartedly the demands and promises of God. The opposite attitude was called 'putting God to the test': it consisted of questioning whether God really intended a certain demand or whether he would really fulfil a certain promise. This kind of challenge to God was expressly forbidden (Deuteronomy 6.16, "Do not put the LORD your God to the test"), and Peter was drawing attention to the seriousness

9 of this offence when he asked how the couple had **"agreed together to put the Spirit of the Lord to the test"**. The punishment brought about by Peter

was commensurate with the gravity of the sin. And in the third place, it is possible that Luke approached the story as it were from the other end. The gift of Christ to his church was a gift of a new quality of life, and we know that in the early years it was a cause of bewilderment to Christians when they found that some of their number had died. An explanation that gained some acceptance was that these people must have committed some very serious sin since they joined the church, and that their death was a necessary punishment. (See, for instance, 1 Corinthians 11.30.) Luke has recorded a saying of Jesus to the effect that "whoever blasphemes against the Holy Spirit will not be forgiven" (Luke 12.10). It is possible that the story of Ananias and Sapphira began its life as an attempt to explain why two members of the early church died suddenly within a few days of joining the community.

12   **And they were all together in Solomon's Portico.** These words allow us to form a visual picture of the scene. Any substantial Greco-Roman city possessed one or more 'porticoes' – the Greek word is *stoa* – which consisted of long buildings open on one side, the roof supported by a row of columns. These buildings were the natural centre of social life in the city. They afforded shelter from sun and rain and were convenient for doing business, conducting discussions and holding small meetings. Jerusalem too possessed its *stoas*, particularly in the temple area, where they were under some supervision by the temple police but where, nevertheless, they provided a natural meeting place for many different kinds of people. In Greece it was common to see a small crowd in a *stoa*, gathered round a philosopher – indeed the Stoic school of philosophy got its name from its custom of meeting in a certain *stoa* in Athens. A Greek-speaking reader will have been able to visualize at once the meetings of the first Christian community in **Solomon's Portico.**

    But by now the church was more than a group of like-minded people gathering for discussion and worship. The apostles had miraculous gifts of healing (and a sensational attribute of Peter – healing even by his shadow – gives the narrative an almost legendary character). The community could not be entered thoughtlessly or half-heartedly (witness the story of Ananias

14 and Sapphira), yet **more than ever believers were added to the Lord**, which was doubtless both a consequence of the healing miracles and a reason why

16 their reputation spread so quickly even to **the towns around Jerusalem.**

17   **Then the high priest took action.** The action continues to unfold within the temple area of Jerusalem. This area was under the ultimate control of the high priest. It was administered by another officer of high-priestly family

24, 22 (the **captain of the temple**) and patrolled by **temple police**, who were Levites.

21 The **council** was the Sanhedrin, which Luke suggests gathered in special session with **the whole body of the elders of Israel** (a somewhat archaic phrase in the Greek: it is not clear whether Luke is thinking of a body other than, or larger than, the Sanhedrin). It was primarily a law court, with competence to decide on all cases coming under Jewish law, which included all religious matters. Its meeting place was in, or at least very close to, the temple area;

and the prison was doubtless near by. As on the previous occasion (4.1–3), there was no difficulty in finding a pretext for having the apostles arrested in this area – the only obstacle was public opinion (verse 26) – and Luke once

17 again attributes this action to the jealousy of **the Sadducees**, who could be presumed to object to any movement which seemed to give support to the Pharisees' belief in resurrection. Indeed he seems to have assumed that the Pharisees, the Sadducees' opponents, were at this time fairly favourably disposed towards the church, and he underlines this by reporting that the man who was responsible on this occasion for saving the apostles from a sentence

33 of death was one of the most famous of all Pharisaic lawyers, **Gamaliel**.

19   **An angel of the Lord opened the prison doors.** A supernatural rescue of this kind is described in detail in chapter 12, and Luke does not spoil the effect by anticipating it here. It was sufficient to mention briefly the divine assistance which the apostles received, and the almost comical embarrassment caused to their captors next morning. The narrative returns to sober reporting when it comes to the serious matter of the trial. Neither the personal jealousy of the Sadducees nor the miraculous events of the night before are referred to again. The issue is now one of law and public order.

The legal charge had two points. First, the apostles had disregarded the

28 judicial warning they had received, and were continuing to teach in the **name** which they had been expressly forbidden to pronounce; and secondly, they had been putting it about that the Jews themselves (and therefore the supreme Jewish court) had been responsible for a miscarriage of justice resulting in **this man's blood** (a vivid touch: the judges deliberately avoided pronouncing the name of Jesus, which they had forbidden others to mention). We should now call such charges 'contempt of court', and certainly some such offence existed in the Jewish legal code. But Luke may have been less concerned to record the charge accurately than to give Peter the cue for another direct appeal to the Jewish nation, this time through its leaders. His reply to the charge of disregarding the court's orders is an epigrammatic echo[7] of the

29 defence he made before (4.19), **"We must obey God rather than any human authority."** He then went on to admit the other charge and to expand on it. The Jesus whose 'name' was in question was a person whom the God of the Jews had **raised up**. It was no good saying that, since crucifixion was a Roman punishment, Jesus' death was no responsibility of theirs. Scripture allowed

30 for the corpse of a criminal to be hung on a **tree** (Deuteronomy 21.22), and since the Jewish court had found Jesus guilty and worthy of death, and since the execution had (to this extent) a Jewish as well as a Roman character, the Jewish leaders could not argue that it was no concern of theirs. But this Jesus

31 had now been exalted to be **Leader and Savior**. Not only did this show that the judges' verdict had been entirely wrong, but the words he uttered on the cross were still valid: "Father, forgive them; for they do not know what

---

[7] This comes over better in a literal translation: *We must obey God rather than men.*

they are doing" (Luke 23.34, in some manuscripts only). If they denied this,

32 they would have not only to refute the word of the actual **witnesses to these things**, but to find some other explanation for the manifest power, possessed by believers, which proceeded from the Holy Spirit.

31 But by the time Acts was written, it was clear that this offer of **repentance** and **forgiveness of sins** had been rejected by the Jewish nation – this is one of the themes that runs right through the book; and the reaction of their leaders on this occasion expressed this refusal with apparent finality:

33 **they were enraged and wanted to kill them.** Moderation was advised by the distinguished Pharisee Gamaliel. Two somewhat similar pretenders had made their appearance in recent history, and had been effectively dealt with by the occupying Roman forces. The Sanhedrin could safely follow the same policy with regard to Jesus, who had perished in the same way as the others,

36 and whose following would doubtless soon also be **dispersed**. The idea of the speech is plausible, and Gamaliel may well have recommended a policy

37 along these lines. **Judas the Galilean** was well known: he had been the leader of the famous rebellion which followed the hated census of Quirinius in

36 6–7 CE. **Theudas** was equally well known – but only by the time Luke was writing: his rebellion in fact took place some thirty years after Gamaliel is represented as making this plea for leniency. Luke was fond of linking his narrative to memorable events of contemporary history; but he had not the means which a modern historian possesses of checking all his dates.

40 **When they had called in the apostles, they had them flogged.** This was in itself a severe punishment (on occasion it resulted in death); but the apostles

41 rejoiced. **To suffer dishonor for the sake of the name** was to be a frequent experience. These first apostles were the prototypes of many later generations of Christian leaders.

Up to this point the church in its earliest stages has been depicted as a single, homogeneous community, sharing all its resources in a spirit of enthusiastic generosity and meeting regularly under the leadership of the twelve divinely commissioned apostles. But the next events introduce certain complications. Those who made up the first Christian congregations in Jerusalem evidently belonged to a number of different social and cultural groups, and the existence of these differences was to prove a significant factor in the process by which the church pursued its mission, first to Jewish or mainly Jewish centres outside Jerusalem, and finally to the great cities of the eastern Roman empire.

6.1 **The Hellenists complained against the Hebrews.** Here, for the first time, we are told of two different parties in the church, and the most obvious difference between them appears to have been a difference of language. Although Greek was the official language of the Roman government in Palestine and was probably understood and spoken by most educated Jews, the native language of the Jewish people at this period was Aramaic, and those who spoke it were known as **Hebrews**. But Jewish families who had lived for any length of time abroad were likely to have lost the habit of speaking either Aramaic or the sacred language of Hebrew, and to have adopted Greek as their first language. When such people returned to Jerusalem they continued to speak Greek, not only in their daily life, but also in prayer and worship: they used a Greek translation of the scriptures and attended a synagogue where the service was in Greek. Thus, even though these two groups probably knew enough of each others' language to be able to communicate, there existed in Jerusalem (and doubtless in other places in Palestine) a clear linguistic division between the Jews who spoke Greek (the **Hellenists**) and the Jews who spoke the local dialect of Aramaic. Indeed, the difference probably went deeper than this. With the Greek language went a culture and a habit of mind very different from that of those who were brought up almost entirely on the Hebrew scriptures; and the Jews of the Dispersion, though they may have remained loyally and self-consciously Jewish, inevitably came to understand and practise their ancestral religion somewhat differently from their kinsmen in Palestine. In particular, they are unlikely to have escaped the influence of the more philosophical approach to religion characteristic of Greek culture (which regarded the images and sacrifices of pagan religions, not as a threat, but as primitive and irrelevant), and they may well have found the emphasis on ritual and ceremonial matters, which was characteristic of Palestinian Judaism, difficult to reconcile with their own more ethical and philosophical understanding of their religion. How much of this cultural and religious cleavage between the two groups was in Luke's mind when he called them 'Hellenists' and 'Hebrews' we cannot say: the terms indicate only the languages they spoke. But the potential for cleavage was undoubtedly there, and once Christians began to be recruited from both groups it was inevitable that the church would begin to show different lines of development.

The first signs of discord however, arose (according to Luke), out of a purely practical matter. The Christian community, like any close Jewish community, had a strong social conscience about those of its members who were **widows** and therefore most likely to be destitute,[8] and had organized a **daily distribution**. Complaints were made that the widows from the Greek-speaking community were not receiving their share, and the proposal of the twelve was that the distribution should now be administered more systematically, thereby incidentally lightening their own burden of work. Seven men were appointed and duly commissioned at a ceremony, the form of which was clearly inspired by a well-known scene in the Old Testament (Numbers 11), where Moses, overwhelmed by the number of cases being brought to him, commissioned seventy elders to assist him and transferred to them some of 'his spirit'.

Luke does not tell us how this arrangement was intended to resolve the dispute, or whether it was successful. The seven men appointed were all

---

[8] See below on 1 Timothy 5 for the social status of these widows.

5 presumably Jews (except one, **Nicolaus, a proselyte**) and all bore Greek names; but Greek names were so common even among Palestinian Jews that this does not tell us to which party they belonged. In any case, the narrative can hardly be trusted as an accurate report of the situation. By the time Luke was writing, there existed in at least some parts of the church an order of 'deacons' (*diakonoi*, 'servants') such as is described here; and possibly Luke read back into this episode (as the later church certainly did) the moment when this order was instituted. But in what follows Luke has to admit that two of these new 'deacons', Stephen and Philip, by no means limited their activities to 'waiting on tables,'[9] but were as active and as remarkably endued with miraculous powers as the twelve themselves (8.26–40; 21.8). Moreover, seven, like twelve, was a standard number for the inner council of any Jewish community. These seven may in fact have been the leaders of the growing Greek-speaking section of the church, corresponding with the twelve who presided over the others. Certainly this Greek-speaking group remained sufficiently distinct and sufficiently important to have become victims, independently of the apostles (and presumably the other Aramaic-speakers), of the first serious wave of persecution which hit the church.

7 (Luke mentions, by the way, that **a great many of the priests became obedient to the faith.** He seems to have been particularly well informed about priests and their duties: see above on Luke 1.5–10.)

9 **Some of those who belonged to the Synagogue of the Freedmen (as it was called).** The scene of action now shifts from the crowd of native Jewish Christians gathered in the temple precincts to the more cosmopolitan society of Greek-speaking Jews elsewhere in Jerusalem. After the conquest of Jerusalem by Pompey in 63 BCE many Jewish captives were taken to Rome and sold as slaves. Subsequently they (or at least their children) mostly regained their freedom, either by purchase or as a reward for faithful service. They then became known by the technical name (which Luke transliterates into Greek) of *libertini*, 'freedmen', and those who returned to Palestine seem both to have kept the name and to have formed a distinct community with its own synagogue. Traces of a synagogue which may have been theirs have been found in Jerusalem, and the building could have been a centre for Jews from other parts of the world as well.[10] At any rate, it was with cosmopolitan Jews of this kind, speaking Greek and having, perhaps, some of the religious and philosophical presuppositions that went with Greek culture, that Stephen became involved in debate. But the debate soon turned into something more

---

[9] The word *trapeza*, meaning 'table', was also used for banks and places of financial transactions. It is possible that there is at least some word-play here, suggesting that the seven's rôle was not altogether menial: they may have kept accounts.

[10] The Greek of verse 9, like the English, is ambiguous, and does not make it clear whether this synagogue was also attended by Jews of other nationalities or whether these other nationalities had joined the freedmen on this occasion.

serious, and Stephen found himself, like Peter and the apostles before him,
12 arraigned before **the council** on a serious charge.

Nevertheless, this charge was a very different one from that which had been brought against the apostles. The apostles had been assiduous in their Jewish religious observances, and their behaviour had been entirely correct. Their offence had consisted only in the fact that they had been heard invoking a new 'name'. But Stephen had alarmed even his more cosmopolitan hearers by his overt criticism of the temple itself and of the prescribed observances.

13 Or so, at least, **false witnesses** had alleged. These charges are very similar to those brought against Jesus in the accounts of Jesus' trial before this same council in Matthew (26.59–61) and Mark (14.57–9). Luke omits them in his gospel but brings them in here. Doubtless the charges were trumped up in both cases; in both they were brought by 'false witnesses'. But in Jesus' case they appear to have arisen from a misunderstanding of words Jesus actually used. If we may judge from the speech which follows, the same was true of Stephen.

7.2–53 To the modern reader, Stephen's long speech is exceedingly puzzling. Instead of presenting any kind of defence, it appears to consist almost entirely of a sketch of the history of Israel, drawn mainly from the Old Testament and breaking off unexpectedly when it reaches the time of Solomon. Only a final imprecation directed at the court serves to remind us who has been speaking and what the occasion is. The rest reads like a lesson in biblical history. But to anyone familiar with Jewish literature and Jewish oratory the impression given by it might have been quite different. The Jews did not tire of recounting the main facts of their history. Two of the psalms which they used in their worship (105, 106) contain little else, and there are other, similar, résumés in the prose books of the Old Testament and the Apocrypha (Joshua 24.9; Judith 5). But not all these résumés had the same purpose. Compare Psalm 105 with Psalm 106. The story told in each is much the same; but whereas, in the first, all the emphasis is on the greatness of the favours shown by God to his people, in the second it is on the wilful obstinacy of that people in response to those favours and to the patience of God, who still did not repudiate the promises he had made to them. All depended on the use which was made of the historical facts and upon the emphasis which was placed on the different phases of the story. When a speaker began to make his own résumé of biblical history, his hearers would have been quick to notice small points of detail indicating the lesson the speaker would draw from it.

In this case a Jewish audience would have found Stephen's presentation startling. From Abraham to Joseph the story is told quite conventionally; but with the appearance of Moses, who is the subject of almost the whole of the rest of the speech, a new tone begins to be heard. In the Old Testament, and in Jewish piety generally, Moses was the supreme law-giver through whom the people had received the inestimable benefit of the law under which they lived. But here the point repeatedly made about Moses is that he and

25 his message were consistently rejected by the Jewish nation. **"He supposed that his kinsfolk would understand . . . but they did not understand."**
35, 39 **"It was this Moses whom they rejected." "Our ancestors were unwilling to obey him."** These sentences occur nowhere in the biblical narrative, and indeed, they could not, for they represent a view of Moses as the rejected emissary of God which is totally strange to the Old Testament. If this was really Moses' destiny, it was a destiny very similar to that of Jesus; and the prophecy
37 in Deuteronomy (18.15), **'God will raise up a prophet for you from your own people as he raised me up** (or, *like me*)", which has already been quoted earlier in a speech of Peter (3.22), becomes more clearly than ever a prophecy about Jesus.

From this presentation of the story of the deliverance from Egypt as a repeated national rejection of Moses and all that he stood for, radical con-
41 sequences are drawn. The Israelites' worship of the golden **calf** (Exodus 32), which is made to appear in the biblical narrative as no more than a brief aberration, here marks the climax of Israel's repudiation of Moses and the worship of the true God. As a result (according to this way of looking at the
42 story), God **"handed them over to worship the host of heaven".** We can guess what this phrase would have meant to a Greek-speaking Jew: the idolatrous cult of foreign gods combined with astrology. This, Stephen dares to say, had been the character of all Jewish worship following their lapse into idolatry in the desert; and by way of support he quotes a passage of Amos (5.25–7). In its Hebrew form this text appears to emphasize the purity of the worship of the desert generation compared with the idolatry practised (or perhaps about to be practised) in Amos' own time. But the passage was obscure, and in the fairly free Septuagint translation (which is quoted here),[11] it gave colour to the opposite view, namely that the golden calf was by no means an isolated instance but that other heathen gods were worshipped as well. From that time onwards (this is Stephen's argument), no one could claim that Jewish worship had ever been according to the will of God.

What, then, of the temple in Jerusalem, the place where the traditions of Jewish worship were most jealously preserved according to the norms
44 laid down in scripture? This is the climax of Stephen's speech. The **tent of testimony in the wilderness** had been correctly brought to Jerusalem and
45 remained intact **until the time of David**. This was all that God ever required by way of a sanctuary on earth; anything more was idolatrous. Should Solomon then not have built the first great temple? It was true that David had been dissuaded by the prophet Nathan from undertaking the work himself (2 Samuel 7); and there was a passage from Isaiah (66.1–2, a passage we now

---

[11] The Greek version makes certain changes to the Hebrew text, but the last word, according to all known versions, should be Damascus, not **Babylon**. But the place of the historic exile of the population of Jerusalem had been Babylon, not Damascus, and the change was a pardonable one for a speaker to make.

know to have been composed after Solomon's temple had been destroyed and before another one was built) which could be quoted as a criticism of the very idea of a physical temple for the God of the whole earth. But scripture seemed at least to imply God's approval of Solomon's temple; and the Isaiah passage was normally read as an attack on the idolatrous shrines of the heathen, not on the image-less sanctuary in Jerusalem. It would hardly have occurred to Stephen's audience that Isaiah's words could be taken as an attack on their own most sacred institution. Yet this is exactly what Stephen did – and we must remember that Luke was writing after 70 CE, when the temple had been reduced to ruins by the Romans, and Stephen's interpretation of biblical history began to seem a plausible explanation of the catastrophe.

51　**"You are forever opposing the Holy Spirit, just as your ancestors used to do."** For Stephen's purposes the subsequent history of Israel could be summed up in a single sentence. It had been a succession of similar rejections of the word of God, provoked each time by the appearance of a prophet. The point is made sharper by means of two legends which had recently become widely accepted. One was that (however little the scriptures said about it) *all* the prophets had been persecuted. (See above on Matthew 23.29.) The other

53　was that at Sinai the law had been given to Moses **as ordained by angels**, a clear indication of its divine sanction.[12] The Jews had consistently rejected its

52　spokesmen, from Moses onwards; and now their betrayal and murder of **the Righteous One** (a title for Jesus which occurs only occasionally in the New Testament and subsequent writings) was simply the last and decisive stage in

51　the long history of a people that had consistently shown itself a **"stiff-necked people, uncircumcised in heart and ears"**.

It can be seen at once that this is a very different approach from that of Peter, whose speeches have ended each time with a statement that God's pardon was still offered to the Jewish people. Here, by contrast, the Jews are totally condemned, not only for their treatment of Jesus, but for their stubbornness throughout their history. Did Luke deliberately compose speeches of such a different tenor (as ancient historians often found it quite natural to do)? Or did he possess some record of the kind of speech Stephen made, and incorporate it in his narrative despite its apparently inconsistent doctrine? We have seen that a certain reserve towards the temple institutions and a certain sitting light to Jewish observances might be found among Jews whose first language was Greek and who had been brought up with some Greek culture. Admittedly, Stephen's speech went a great deal further than this, so much so that even the Greek-speaking synagogue took alarm and reported him to the authorities. Nevertheless the speech represents the kind of thinking which could well have been done by a Christian from this comparatively cosmopolitan milieu, and Luke may have heard examples of such preaching.

---

[12]　See below on Galatians 3.19.

Moreover it contains a number of words and idioms which are unusual for Luke and suggest he may have been drawing on some source rather than composing freely as he went along. At the same time, the argument of the speech fits well into the grand design of Luke's history. First, in the preaching of Peter, pardon and salvation are offered to the Jews; when they refuse it, the gospel is taken to the Gentiles. Stephen's speech marks a turning point: Peter's appeal gives place to Stephen's polemic. The result is the first persecution of the church and the extension of the mission field outside Jerusalem to Samaria and beyond.

Yet even if the speech makes sense within the general scheme of Acts, it still strikes us as singularly inappropriate to the occasion. This was Stephen's opportunity to make his defence; instead, he made an attack on his accusers so stringent that they gave up all pretence of giving him a fair trial and delivered him to summary justice. But it is not only the speech which shows that Luke was not attempting to give a completely realistic account of the trial. At the beginning his judges are described as 'those who were sitting in the council' (6.15), that is, in a formal chamber, presumably indoors; but after the speech
55 Stephen **gazed into heaven**: the scene seems to have shifted into the open air and moves rapidly to its climax, when they set about stoning him. One detail, however, is correct and realistic: it was the rule for the first stones to be cast by witnesses against the defendant, and these duly appear when Luke
58 records that **the witnesses laid their coats at the feet of a young man named Saul**. He also seems to have visualized Stephen on level ground, sinking on his knees under a hail of stones. This is probably correct. It was only in the following century that the Jewish penalty of stoning was supposed to take the form of throwing the victim down a cliff and then, if he was still alive, hurling large stones on top of him (which seems to have been the penalty envisaged for Jesus at Nazareth, Luke 4.29).

Whether or not Luke possessed any accurate information about the circumstances of Stephen's death, we can detect his motive for describing it as he did. The death of the first martyr to the faith would appropriately follow the same pattern as the death of Jesus; and so we find that Stephen was arraigned before the same council on much the same charges, and that at the moment
59 of death he uttered much the same prayers: **"Lord Jesus, receive my spirit"** (as in Luke 23.46 – except that the prayer is now addressed to Jesus instead
60 of the Father), and **"Lord, do not hold this sin against them"** (Luke 23.34, according to some manuscripts). The wording in each case is different; but these variations are in Luke's manner. Since Luke often seems to omit a detail from the gospel narrative if he intends to use it in Acts, it is all the more striking that he includes these prayers on at least one of the occasions here. The echo is clearly intentional.

And there is a further echo. In Luke's account of Jesus' appearance before the council, the only statement made by Jesus was "From now on the Son of Man will be seated at the right hand of the power of God" (Luke 22.69).

In these words Jesus proclaimed that he was about to be vindicated. It was Stephen's privilege to have a vision of this vindication having taken place. To describe it he used almost the exact words of Jesus' prediction, including the term **Son of Man**, which otherwise never occurs outside the gospels as a title of Jesus.

56

A brief paragraph records the immediate consequences of Stephen's execution and also prepares the way for the following episodes. **Devout men buried Stephen** – perhaps a deliberate echo of Jesus' burial; **but Saul was ravaging the church** – having become, no longer a mere bystander at the stoning of Stephen (7.58), but a person entrusted (presumably) with strong executive powers by the council, which he used to persecute the church (a piece of information necessary for understanding the story of his conversion in the next chapter). And – which is most important for leading into the next episode – the **severe persecution** which began after Stephen's death was the immediate cause of the spread of Christianity to places outside Jerusalem, some of the Christians having been **scattered throughout the countryside of Judea and Samaria**. The apostles themselves, however, seem to have remained in Jerusalem – this is a presupposition of the next episode (verse 14). Luke allows for this by saying that **all except the apostles were scattered**, which is sufficient for his purpose here, but can hardly give the full picture. Quite apart from the improbability of the leaders being spared while the rank and file were persecuted, we find in 9.31 and 11.1–2 that there is still a substantial church in Jerusalem. Luke has so stressed the unanimity of the church at this stage that he cannot easily allow for different groups within it; but it seems likely that the persecution was aimed particularly at the Greek-speaking element in the church which, as a result of Stephen's preaching, could be accused of open opposition to Jewish institutions, whereas the Palestinian element, under the leadership of the apostles, continued to meet in the temple precincts and to follow Jewish customs, so that there was not yet any clear cause for a breach with the authorities.

8.2

3

1

5   **Philip went down to the city of Samaria.** As it stands, this means the capital of the region, the town that had been rebuilt as a Hellenistic city by Herod the Great and renamed Sebaste (after the Greek form of the name of the emperor Augustus). Its Old Testament name had been Samaria, which Luke may have been deliberately using here.[13] At any rate, the crowds who

6   **with one accord listened eagerly** must be imagined as Samaritans, a race very close to the Jews in language and religion, but socially and politically opposed to them. They represent the first stage in the spread of Christianity outside Jewish territory.

5   Philip **proclaimed the Messiah to them.** He is specifically called 'the evangelist' later on (21.8) – that is, one who proclaimed the gospel. But the side

---

[13] Unless the alternative manuscript reading is correct, which gives *a city of Samaria*, a more natural and appropriate expression.

6 of his activity which is emphasized here is **the signs that he did** (exorcisms and cures), and these brought him into competition with a local magician
9 named **Simon**. The story which Luke tells of Simon first joining the following of one whom he saw to be more powerful than himself, then trying to obtain, not only this power, but the means of transmitting it to others, and finally repenting of his dishonest ambitions, represents a clear contrast between the magic arts practised by not a few notable magicians in antiquity and the authentic activity of the Holy Spirit. But the Holy Spirit had been transmitted to the church only by the Jerusalem apostles; and this seems to
14 be the point of the intervention of **Peter and John** from Jerusalem. Baptism at this time (so far as we know) consisted normally of a single rite, in the
16 course of which converts were immersed in water **in the name of the Lord**
17 **Jesus** and then **received the Holy Spirit** when the minister laid hands on them. But Luke's presentation of church history implied that the Jerusalem apostles were responsible for any advance of the church into new territories; it followed that the rite as administered by Philip (who was not an apostle) must have been incomplete, and that the presence of apostles was necessary before the new converts could receive the Holy Spirit.

But just as Philip was more than a miracle-worker, so there are at least hints in the narrative that Simon was more than a magician. The people were
10 not merely impressed by his magic; they **listened to him eagerly**. He was himself evidently a teacher, making great claims for himself. The title people gave him, **"the power of God that is called Great"**, is a little mysterious, but it suggests at least that Simon claimed divine powers – and this takes us at once into a world different from that of the Jewish Christian preachers and their monotheistic Samaritan converts. It was among pagans that one found people claiming to be divine or to have divine attributes. In any case, we know a little more about this Simon. By the middle of the next century he was widely regarded as the first great Christian heretic and as the originator of all those complicated combinations of mythology and dualistic philosophy which are usually called Gnosticism. Doubtless much that was told about Simon a century later is legendary, and many of the doctrines attributed to him were first worked out well after his lifetime. But there is no reason to doubt that this was the same Simon as the one who appears in Luke's narrative. If so, he was a more formidable rival than a mere magician would have been, and, alongside the simple contest of supernatural power described by Luke, there could have been the makings of a far-reaching philosophical and religious dispute. In this narrative, however, Peter is allowed to dispose of him with the kind of malediction a magician might have used himself,
23 full of biblical phrases: **"you are in the gall of bitterness and the chains of wickedness"** – an almost meaningless formula compounded of phrases such as those in Deuteronomy 29.18 and Isaiah 58.6.
26 **Then an angel of the Lord said to Philip**. It was perhaps natural for Luke to go straight on to this second story about Philip, even though it does not

quite fit into the general scheme: it appears to let Philip steal a march on the apostles in preaching the gospel outside Jerusalem. But the episode is nevertheless, presented as being entirely under divine direction. It is set in

29 motion by **an angel of the Lord** and directed by **the Spirit** (the two seem here almost equivalent as bearers of messages from God); without this guidance,

26 Philip might hardly have thought of going **"toward the south**[14] **to the road that goes down from Jerusalem to Gaza"**. Gaza, until its destruction in 66 CE, was a flourishing city on the trade route to Egypt and lay on the edge of the desert. It had been rebuilt in the previous century not far from the site of the old city, which had been destroyed so thoroughly by the Maccabean army in 96 BCE that it had become almost a byword for a deserted place. For both these reasons, Gaza made one think of 'desert', and this may be why Luke adds a note which, translated literally, means *this is desert* (or **wilderness**). But it is impossible to be sure which word this note is meant to explain. It could be Gaza, which was in some sense 'desert' or 'wilderness'; but, as the story which follows is all about the road to Gaza, not Gaza itself, it seems more likely that Luke meant (as it is here translated) **a wilderness road**. The difficulty is that none of the possible routes from Jerusalem to Gaza goes through desert; at most, there could have been stretches of the descent through the mountains which were, comparatively speaking, a 'wilderness' – and this was perhaps all that was necessary to underline the miraculous nature of the encounter between Philip and the foreign traveller. In any case, the scene can hardly have been set in real desert, since the travellers soon

36 came to **some water**.

The story is vividly told, and there is a strong biblical flavour in the language. The Ethiopian came, not from modern Ethiopia, but from the country to the north of it, lying roughly between Aswan and Khartoum in the Sudan. This 'Ethiopia' represented to the Greeks, and probably to Luke, one of the extreme limits of the world; but its people were well known through trade and politics, and it is recorded that more than one of its rulers was a queen

27 bearing the name **Candace**. That the chief finance minister should have been a **eunuch** would not have been surprising in an oriental court. But why should such a person have gone **to Jerusalem to worship**? He can hardly have been a Jew; but Luke may have thought of him as one of those sympathetic Gentiles who accepted the main principles of the Jewish faith without actually seeking admission to the Jewish community. If so, he was the first gentile convert to Christianity – though the point is not stressed here.

The Ethiopians spoke their own language, but presumably this **court official** also knew Greek, and was reading Isaiah from a scroll of the Greek version. He was reading aloud (in antiquity, silent reading, without even a movement of the lips, would have been very unusual) and Philip, coming close to the chariot, was able to hear what he was reading. The passage

---

[14] The Greek word, like the French *midi*, can also mean *noon*.

was Isaiah 53.7–8. This whole chapter, a description of a certain 'servant' of the Lord who was subjected to unmerited suffering, and whose manner of bearing it was said by the prophet to have been 'for our transgressions and iniquities', was seen by the early church as an important clue to the mean-

34 ing of Jesus' suffering and death. The eunuch's question, **"About whom . . . does the prophet say this?"**, is one which has been debated by scholars since before his time and cannot be certainly answered. But whereas the modern approach is to try to answer the question by analysing the thought of the prophet and determining what his words are likely to have meant at the time he wrote them, a Jewish scholar of the first century CE (and indeed of many later centuries) would have proceeded quite differently. He would have assumed that it was no accident that these verses of Isaiah did not fully explain themselves: they were clearly intended to point forward to – or 'be fulfilled in' – some other significant person through whom God would influence the destiny of his people. The problem was to identify a person in the past, the present or the future whom these words exactly fitted. So far as we know, Jewish scholars had not yet arrived at a convincing answer. But the church was quick to seize on this passage. Jesus' suffering and death had 'fulfilled'

35 it in remarkable detail. It was, in short, an admirable place for **starting** to proclaim **the good news about Jesus.**

36 **"Look, here is water! What is to prevent me from being baptized?"** The eunuch's question was to become an important one as the church began to develop its institutions: candidates for baptism would need to show that they had the necessary knowledge and commitment before they were baptized, and this is probably why some manuscripts insert some words at this point to show that the eunuch had in fact fulfilled these conditions (see the NRSV footnote). But this is not Luke's concern here. The point is the foreigner's readiness to accept the new faith, sealed by immediate baptism. We can imagine how this took place. The two men walked down to the bed of a wadi where water was flowing, and Philip would have cupped his hand in order to pour water over the head of the eunuch (or have immersed him in it if it was deep enough), invoking the name of Jesus Christ. Philip then mysteriously disappeared and was next seen preaching in the towns of the coastal plain,

40 from **Azotus** in the south to **Caesarea** in the north.

9.1 **Meanwhile Saul, still breathing threats and murder against the disciples.** Saul ("also known as Paul", 13.9) becomes the leading character in the second half of Acts, and Luke prepares for this by working in the story of his conversion here. The episode is recognizably the same as that alluded to by Paul himself in Galatians 1.16 and elsewhere, but it is narrated here (and in two other places in Acts, so it clearly seemed of great importance to Luke) in a totally different and much more detailed style; and the immediate sequel in Luke's account is not always easy to reconcile with other statements made by Paul in the same autobiographical passage in Galatians. One is forced to ask how far Luke had reliable sources to go by and how far he had simply to fill in the details as best he could, given the bare facts that Paul was at first a vigorous persecutor of the church, was suddenly converted, but paid only one visit to Jerusalem in the course of his first fourteen years of activity as a Christian preacher. On the one hand, Luke's account of Saul's conversion experience has a number of conventional features – in this respect it is like the visions at the beginning of Luke's gospel – and may have been written up fairly freely by Luke. Paul's own language is more reticent, and comes closer to what we would now call that of mystical experience; but for Luke it may have been more natural, when attempting to describe an essentially incommunicable experience, to use the more traditional scenario of a dazzling light and a heavenly voice. On the other hand, apart from the experience itself, there are details which are not only plausible in themselves but are confirmed by Paul's letters (such as the basket in which he was lowered from the walls of Damascus: Paul mentions this himself in 2 Corinthians 11.33). These details set a limit to the extent to which Luke's narrative can be regarded as due to legend or imagination; at the same time they do not force us to regard the whole narrative as a strictly literal account of what actually happened.

2 **Letters to the synagogues at Damascus.** Damascus was the oldest of the cities of the Decapolis. It was now a prosperous Hellenistic city, but it contained a large colony of Jews. We know that local synagogues had authority over the faith and observance of their members; but we have no other evidence that the high priest in Jerusalem was in a position to procure the arrest and extradition of members of a synagogue of the Dispersion in a city some 150 miles away. Saul's journey to Damascus may, however, suggest a tactical extension of an official policy in Jerusalem to stamp out Christianity (or at least the Hellenists' version of it, such as was represented by Stephen and his subversive preaching). Here we hear for the first time that the new faith was intriguingly called **the Way** (we do not know the source of this expression); and we learn incidentally (what we should hardly have guessed otherwise) that the gospel had already made considerable progress several days' journey from Jerusalem. This makes it likely (though Luke says nothing about a lapse of time) that Saul's conversion took place at least a few months, if not years, after the first preaching of the gospel in Jerusalem.

Paul's own references to his experience use words such as 'glory' and 'revelation'. Luke prefers the more specific and conventional features of a
3, 4 flashing **light** and **a voice**. But whereas in Luke's accounts of visions the speaker is usually an angel, here and throughout the episode it is none other
5 than Jesus himself, the **Lord**. And more than this: **"I am Jesus, whom you are persecuting."** It was implied in some of the sayings of Jesus, as well as in the more systematic thinking and experience of Paul, that Jesus would be in some sense present in his followers and therefore in his church (which Paul called 'his body'). Here, this is taken for granted. In persecuting the church, Paul had been persecuting the very Jesus who was now addressing him. To our minds, the shock of this realization might have been sufficient

to account for his temporary blindness and his refusal to eat or drink. But Luke's reason for mentioning these physical effects may have been different. Some kind of 'sign' regularly followed a message from heaven as if to confirm the authenticity of the experience – Zechariah was similarly struck dumb at the beginning of Luke's gospel. In Saul's case this was temporary blindness,

9 indicating the reality of his supernatural encounter; and that he **neither ate nor drank** should probably be understood as a penitential fast indicating a genuine change of heart. By the time Luke was writing, a comparable fast was probably undertaken by all Christian converts immediately before baptism.

10   **Now there was a disciple in Damascus named Ananias** – the second person in Acts bearing this not uncommon Jewish name (*hananiah*). His **vision** was in reality something heard rather than seen, but this was the case with many 'visions' in the Old Testament. He addresses the speaker simply

17 as **"Lord"**, but knows him to be **the Lord Jesus**. The directions he receives,

11 **"Go to the street called Straight, and at the house of Judas . . .",** are more precise than they appear. Damascus, like other Greco-Roman cities in the near east, was intersected by a main street which ran from one side of the city to the other. It was a mile long, with avenues of Corinthian columns. Officially it was probably named after some emperor or public figure; but it is quite likely that for most people it was simply 'Straight Street'. **Judas** was a common name – for a Jew; but he could well have been the only Jew of this name living in the street. The address is perfectly plausible; but if Luke had to invent it, this would almost have been the obvious one to choose.

13   **But Ananias answered, "Lord, I have heard from many about this man."** Arguing with a heavenly messenger had many biblical precedents, and Luke's purpose in this dialogue may be to say a little more about Saul. First, as a persecutor in Jerusalem he had terrorized the **saints** (the first time this word is used for the Christian community in Acts: it is frequent in Paul's letters).

15 Secondly, **"he is an instrument whom I have chosen"**. We find it natural to speak of Saul's 'conversion'; but the messenger's phrase has a biblical sound, and places Saul's experience alongside that of many Old Testament prophets who underwent, not a 'conversion', but a 'call'. It is Saul's new calling, rather than his 'conversion' from his former way of life, which is the burden of the divine message, and the definition of his future task corresponds with the words he was later to use himself (Galatians 1.16). He was to bring Jesus' name **before Gentiles** – that is, to non-Jews: this was the new and decisive aspect of Paul's divine commission. Luke adds **"and kings"** – a hint of Paul's later arraignments before pagan rulers – as well as **the people of Israel**, for his mission was never to be divorced from that of the other apostles to the

16 Jewish nation. And finally, there was **much he must suffer** – the church was now beginning to understand how it was 'necessary that the Messiah should suffer' (Luke 24.26), and had already had a taste of the kind of suffering, even up to death, which would mark its members as the faithful followers of their Lord. Saul, who up to now had been the one who inflicted suffering,

was henceforward to undergo it no less than others. The word 'suffering' could mean actual death; and Paul had probably already died as a martyr by the time this was written. But his own letters are sufficient evidence of the actual suffering he bore during his lifetime. (See especially 2 Corinthians 11.21–7.)

Ananias was sent to Saul to give him recovery, baptism and the Holy
18 Spirit. **Something like scales fell from his eyes.** The simile seems an odd one (and has no basis in ancient or modern medicine), but it occurs also in the story of the healing of Tobit's blindness (Tobit 11.11–13), and there are other hints in Luke's work that he drew on the book of Tobit for his descriptions of miraculous events. Thus, once again, Luke may either have had access to some source of information which supplied him with the detail, or else he may have used his literary knowledge to fill out the details of the bare facts which he could infer for himself. There are three such facts here: first, Saul certainly recovered his sight; secondly, he was certainly baptized (for all Christians were); thirdly, his subsequent activity showed that he had certainly received the Holy Spirit (which was in any case usually an inseparable part of baptism).

19 **For several days he was with the disciples in Damascus.** It is at this point that the narrative begins to diverge from what Paul says himself in Galatians 1. There we learn that he "went away at once into Arabia" (1.17). Luke appears to know nothing of this, nor of the fact that it was "the governor (*ethnarch*) under King Aretas" who was responsible for the measures taken against Paul in Damascus (2 Corinthians 11.32). But this could be due simply to his lack of information. The discrepancies become more serious in the description of Paul's first visit to Jerusalem. This, Paul tells us, took place 'three years' after his conversion (Galatians 1.18), by which time his story must certainly have been known in Jerusalem and it can hardly have been necessary for Barnabas to explain matters to the apostles. Moreover, Paul says that this visit was an entirely private one, in the course of which he saw only two of the leaders of the church (Galatians 1.18–20). Luke may have known that Paul's stay was quite short, without knowing why. If so, it would have been a reasonable
29 guess that, like Stephen, he had aroused the opposition of **the Hellenists** and had to leave the city rapidly.

31 **Meanwhile the church throughout Judea, Galilee and Samaria had peace and was built up.** By means of this brief summary Luke allows us to glimpse the kind of progress the church was making apart from the episodes he actually records. He has told us nothing about any preaching in **Galilee** (though we can imagine that the recollection of Jesus' activity there would have made it an obvious place for a mission), but he has mentioned that Philip was working his way up the coastal plain of Judea from Azotus to Caesarea (8.40). This and other missionary activities had evidently by now created congregations over quite a wide area, and these are the scene of the events which follow.

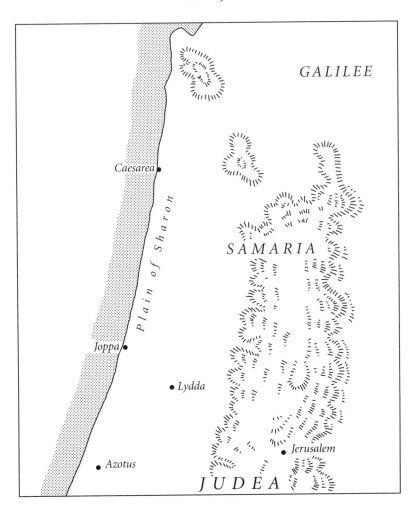

A gospel for Gentiles

32 **Now as Peter went here and there among all the believers.** His tour of the
congregations went as far as **Lydda** (the modern Lod) some 30 miles north-
36 west of Jerusalem and further still to **Joppa**, which lay on the coast at the end
of the same road. These visits were remembered for two miracles, performed
by Peter, which gave new impetus to the spread of the gospel in the area.
35 (**Sharon** was the name of the coastal plain from Joppa to Caesarea.) Both are
33 told with echoes of the miracles performed by Jesus. The cure of **Aeneas** (a
Greco-Roman name, but one that could have been adopted by a Jew) recalls
in a general way the cure of a paralytic in Luke 5.24. (Peter's command to
34 **make your bed** was perhaps more appropriate to an invalid bedridden at

419

home than were the exact words of Jesus to one who had been carried in on a stretcher, "take your bed and go".) But the second miracle has a number of subtle allusions. Bringing a dead person back to life was the most impressive of all miracles. It had been accomplished once by Elijah (1 Kings 17.17–24) and once by Elisha (2 Kings 4.32–7), and echoes of these stories can be heard in Luke's narrative. In his gospel, Luke records two occasions when Jesus performed it (7.11–17; 8.51–6). The second of these occurs also in Mark; and in Mark's version (5.38–43) the actual Aramaic words are preserved which Jesus used, *talitha cum*. In Luke's version only the translation is given, "Child, get up!" But we can hardly doubt that, when he came to write the story of Peter's miracle, the original words were in his mind; for, translated

40 back into Aramaic, Peter's **"Tabitha, get up"** would be *tabitha cum* – the same formula, but for one letter, that was used by Jesus. Yet there is no question of the cure having taken place simply through the recitation of a magic phrase. The reason for it (apart from Peter's exceptional power) was a moral one of the kind which appealed to Luke (compare the healing of the centurion's

36 servant in Luke 7.1–10): much emphasis is laid on the fact that Tabitha **was devoted to good works and acts of charity.**

10.1 **In Caesarea there was a man named Cornelius.** The city of Caesarea, named after the emperor Caesar Augustus, was one of Herod the Great's most spectacular achievements. From a small seaside town he transformed it into the most important port on the coast of Palestine; and when the territory came under direct Roman rule in 6 CE the city was made the administrative capital of Judea and the headquarters of the occupying army. It therefore marks an important stage in the progress of the gospel: from its beginnings in Jerusalem it had spread to the seat of Roman government in Caesarea – just as in the second half of Acts Paul advances the gospel from its beginnings in Palestine and Syria to the centre of the empire at Rome. Politically, Caesarea was the most important city that has yet appeared in the story.

Cornelius, a centurion of the Italian Cohort, as it was called. The regular legions of the Roman army were stationed in Syria. It is known from an inscription that a cohort named *cohors II italica* was stationed in Syria later in the century, and there is no reason to doubt Luke's word that it was on duty at Caesarea in Judea somewhat earlier, even in the brief period (41–4 CE) when it was part of a relatively independent kingdom under Herod Agrippa I. A **centurion** was a junior officer, nominally in charge of a hundred men. To hold this rank a man had to be a Roman citizen, but to serve in the auxiliary forces he did not have to be of Roman descent, and it is no surprise to hear at

24 the end of the story that he had **relatives** in Palestine. His name gives nothing
1 away. **Cornelius** was a family name (Luke strangely does not give him any other: this is equivalent to calling the governor Pontius instead of Pilate); and as a family name Cornelius was common both among Romans and among former slaves who adopted it when they gained their freedom. In any case, Luke is not interested in Cornelius' nationality or antecedents. What he

emphasizes here is his close association with the Jewish community. Just as Jesus' first contact with a Gentile was with a centurion who 'loved the Jewish nation' and had endowed Capernaum with a synagogue (Luke 7.5), so Peter's

2 first contact was with a centurion who was **a devout man** who **gave alms generously to the people** (the parallel is surely intentional). We can be more precise: this man **feared God**, he was one of those 'God-fearers' or gentile sympathizers who were allowed, if not encouraged, to attach themselves to synagogues so long as they respected certain basic Jewish observances such as the sabbath. These were the people to whom Christians were regularly to turn after their message had been rejected by the Jews. Cornelius was the first of many such converts; but his conversion marked an altogether new departure in the policy of the Christian mission, which had so far been directed entirely towards Jews This episode shows how doubts were overcome and assurance given that this new development was intended and validated by God.

Cornelius **prayed constantly to God**. In the Greek the phrase has a slightly technical sound, and we can guess what it means: he had adopted some of the Jewish customs of worship, particularly that of saying his prayers at certain

3 hours of the day. One of these hours was **about three o'clock** in the afternoon

30 (Cornelius says himself that he was **praying** when the vision took place). The

4 angel uses a striking idiom: **"Your prayers and your alms have ascended as a memorial before God."** It was a common notion of Jewish piety that the function of liturgical prayers and of good deeds was to spur God to gracious action by 'reminding him' – bringing 'a memorial' before him – of the deserts of individuals and of the people. The events which follow are to be seen as immediate proof that a gracious act of God was under way. Luke has presented the centurion as (from the Jewish point of view) an exceptionally deserving Gentile; and he even adds the detail that in his household a member of his

7 staff was **a devout soldier**.

The journey from Caesarea to Joppa was about 30 miles. Cornelius' servants may be imagined as having started the same afternoon and covered a certain distance by nightfall, leaving perhaps 15–20 miles to be covered the

9 next day between dawn and midday. **About noon ... Peter went up on the roof to pray.** This is local colour: the flat roof of a Palestinian house, perhaps with an awning to give shade, offered solitude in the middle of the day. On the other hand, Peter would not normally have felt hungry and expected a meal at this hour. The Jews ate in the early morning and again in the afternoon. But the Romans ate at midday – and perhaps Luke was consciously writing for readers used to the houses of Greek and Roman society. The important point was to introduce the vision as coming upon a man who was both hungry and at prayer. To Luke's readers this may have been well conveyed by a time **about noon**.

The background to the vision is Leviticus 11. That chapter makes a distinction between animals that are 'clean' and 'unclean', and forbids the eating of pork and of many smaller birds and animals. These prohibitions were regarded as binding by all Jews; and Peter was reacting as any Jew would

14 when he said, **"I have never eaten anything that is profane or unclean."** That God should have counted any of these forbidden creatures as 'clean' would have seemed an impossible proposition (even though Jesus had said something which was thought to have come near to it, Mark 7.15). It is not said that Peter attempted to take the vision literally and change his eating habits – this would have implied an incredible reversal of ingrained sensibilities. But within a day he was to discover the application of the vision to a matter in which the words 'clean' and 'unclean' were certainly much used: the relationship of Jews with Gentiles.

The characters in the story continue to move under divine guidance: there is to be no question at the end of it of the decision having been Peter's own.

20 Peter might well have had some **hesitation** about accepting the messengers' invitation, even though (as Luke emphasizes once again) their master was

22 a man of exceptional piety – **an upright and God-fearing man.** Strictly speaking, social contact between Jews and Gentiles was severely restricted; but in a city like Caesarea extreme exclusiveness was not practicable, and many Jews treated their non-Jewish neighbours and colleagues with great civility. Nevertheless, there was always a certain reserve: to be too much at ease in gentile society was regarded as a dangerous compromise with pagan and idolatrous customs. Peter was doing no more than his more courteous

23 and liberal contemporaries when he invited the messengers in and **gave them lodging**: this did not oblige him to eat with them or share a room with them. But it was a different matter when he actually went in to Cornelius' house as Cornelius' guest. To be the honoured guest of a Gentile meant being ready to accept a Gentile's ways (though in this case the Gentile concerned was a 'God-fearer' and had presumably distanced himself from pagan customs). Even if there is a touch of exaggeration in it, Peter's statement well expresses

28 what would have been the normal reaction of a Jew in such a situation: **"it is unlawful for a Jew to associate with or to visit a Gentile".** But Peter had had a vision and was directed by the Holy Spirit; he had divine authority for making this new departure in social relations.

Cornelius for his part was inspired by the same deference and humility towards a Jew as his predecessor in the gospel, who had tried to forestall Jesus with the words, "I am not worthy to have you come under my roof" (Luke

25 7.6). He met Peter outside the house, **and falling at his feet, worshiped him** – a gesture immediately repudiated by Peter: worship must be given only to God, even in heaven (Revelation 19.10). There was to be no forwardness on his part to blur the outlines of Peter's radical initiative, an initiative prompted by the Holy Spirit. So the scene was set for a formal encounter: Cornelius with

24, 23 his **relatives and close friends** on one side, Peter with **some of the believers from Joppa** on the other.

34 **Then Peter began to speak to them**. We expect the speech that follows to be a direct appeal to the Gentiles present to repent and believe in Jesus Christ, along the lines of the speeches Peter has already made to the Jews in Jerusalem; and in fact the basic structure is the same as before. But the tone is strangely different. Instead of culminating in a direct appeal to his hearers, this speech of Peter's seems to be more of a recital of known facts than an attempt to persuade those for whom it was all new. Indeed at times it seems to be addressed almost to himself and the Christians who are with him:

36 **"you know the message he sent ... preaching peace by Jesus Christ"**. In the Greek, the whole paragraph is put together in a way that is barely grammatical, and presents an appearance of unexpected disjointedness in the pages of a writer normally as polished as Luke. This could be evidence that Luke had before him some document in Aramaic which was difficult to translate into idiomatic Greek. But the passage also contains words and phrases that are characteristic of Luke's own writing, and possibly the explanation for its unusual construction is to be looked for in another direction. The nearest thing in Luke's writing to this almost ungrammatical heaping of clause upon clause (which is one of the peculiarities of this speech) is to be found in the songs of worship which he has put in the mouths of Zechariah, Mary and Simeon at the beginning of his gospel; and in the rest of the New Testament the closest parallels are some passages of certain letters (such as the opening of Ephesians or Colossians) where the writer adopts the devotional language of public prayer and perhaps even incorporates phrases from prayers already in use in the church. This is the style of Peter's speech here. He is as it were thinking aloud, and the language he uses could be that of the church recalling in its worship the great events of the gospel. The summary of Jesus' life does not follow the usual preacher's emphasis on the death, resurrection and exaltation of Jesus, but is more like a résumé of the gospel narratives that were composed for the instruction of Christians. Peter is rehearsing the facts

34 that were known to all Christians – but from a new angle. **"I truly understand that God shows no partiality."** This was a maxim to which many liberal Jews in the Dispersion might have assented. Outstanding examples of piety among Gentiles would surely not go unrewarded simply because they were not Jews, and for Peter to say as much as this it was necessary only for him to have been impressed by Cornelius' evident piety and holiness of life. But even this would normally have been said with a certain reserve; some advantage

36 still remained with the Jews. God sent the message **to the people of Israel**: it was their possession of the revealed word of God which gave the Jews their unique advantage. But there was now the new circumstance that the message had come through the preaching of **Jesus Christ**; and Jesus Christ **is Lord of all**, Lord not only of those Jews who believe in him but of people of all races. As Paul puts it in his letter to the Romans (10.12) in words that are very close to these, "there is no distinction between Jew and Greek; the same Lord is

Lord of all". The story of Jesus might seem like one of purely Jewish interest –
39 and Luke once again, by talking of **hanging him on a tree**, makes even
the Roman procedure of crucifixion sound like a punishment recognized
in scripture (Deuteronomy 21.22). But its significance, like the message of
43 the greatest of the **prophets**, was universal, for **everyone who believes**. This
was the startling conclusion to which Peter was being led as he went over
the familiar facts of the gospel story; and as if to confirm this conclusion,
before even Peter had finished speaking or his hearers made any sign of being
convinced, there came upon all a dramatic repetition of the experience of
44 Pentecost. But this time the Spirit **fell on all who heard the word**, and 'all'
included the Gentiles. They too were manifestly inside, not outside, the group
47 of chosen people. The next step was a matter of course: **"Can anyone withold
the water for baptizing these people who have received the Holy Spirit just
as we have?"**

Peter himself had been convinced; but he still had to carry the other leaders
of the church with him. As always, it was the practical implications of this
new development which caused most concern. Theoretically, most Jews were
prepared to believe that their religion was ultimately destined for the Gentiles as well as for them, and it need not have been a great shock to the
11.1 apostles to hear that **the Gentiles had also accepted the word of God**:
the gospel had merely accelerated a process which until now had lain in
the inscrutable purposes of God. But the practical implications of this new
development were harder to accept. Were Jewish Christians now to reverse
their ancestral attitudes and receive Gentiles as equals into the church and
into their houses? Their question to Peter voiced their immediate scruples:
3 **"Why did you go to uncircumcised men and eat with them?"** Peter's answer
makes it clear that, far from having taken this questionable initiative himself,
he was obeying a divine summons, the authenticity of which was guaranteed
by the miraculously parallel experience of Cornelius. One could no more
doubt that the Holy Spirit had been given to these Gentiles than one could
doubt the reality of the apostles' experience at Pentecost. Both were equally
fulfilments of the promise of a baptism with the Holy Spirit that Jesus had
18 given just before his ascension (1.5). Only one conclusion was possible: **"God
has given even to the Gentiles the repentance that leads to life."** How this
was to work out in practice is the subject of the rest of Acts.

Antioch and Jerusalem

After Caesarea, Antioch – the third largest city in the Roman empire, the
wealthy and cosmopolitan capital of the province of Syria. Christianity had
of course spread to other places outside Palestine by this time – Luke men-
19 tions **Phoenicia** (the Levantine seaboard north of Caesarea) and **Cyprus** –
but it was still a movement confined to the Jewish communities in those
countries. The place where the next breakthrough was to occur was **Antioch**.

It is certain that the new arrivals from Cyprus and Cyrene moved beyond
20 strictly Jewish circles when they addressed **the Hellenists**,[15] for their mission
19 is clearly distinguished from that which had been to **no one except the Jews.**
Unfortunately the word *Hellenists* is ambiguous. When we met them before
in connection with Stephen they were clearly Greek-speaking *Jews*; and it was
their opposition which caused the first serious trouble for the church. But here
the term must mean Greek-speaking *Gentiles*, for clearly this is the point in
the narrative which marks the transition from a Jewish to a Gentile mission –
hence the crisis that comes before the Jerusalem apostles in chapter 15.
Admittedly Luke records this after he has told the Cornelius story, where
he gives the impression that it was due to Peter that the crucial decision
had been made; but he has to admit that the first serious mission to 'the
Greek-speaking Gentiles' was not conducted by Peter or any of the Jerusalem
20 apostles but by **some men of Cyprus and Cyrene**, one of whom may have
been the Lucius who is mentioned by name in 13.1. Indeed, we know from
Paul's letter to the Galatians (2.11–14) that when Peter visited Antioch he
was not yet whole-heartedly committed to the principle of a gentile church.

Nevertheless Luke's history is written on the assumption that all major
advances were authorized by the Jerusalem church. Barnabas had already
appeared (4.36) as a member of that church; he was also certainly known to
Luke as a close companion of Paul on the first missionary journey undertaken from Antioch (13.4). This made him the obvious link between the two
branches of the church, and Luke suggests that it was his initiative (though
doubtless with the approval of the Jerusalem authorities) that brought to
Antioch the most famous of the apostles to the Gentiles, Paul.

26   **It was in Antioch that the disciples were first called "Christians".** This
is consistent with the developments just described. So long as all Christians
were Jews, they appeared to the outside world as simply a Jewish sect, and
there was no need to distinguish them by a particular name; and since many
Jews believed in some sort of future Messiah or 'Christ', the name 'Christian'
could never have arisen in Jewish circles as that of those Jews who accepted
Jesus as Messiah. (Their name for them, in fact, was usually 'Nazarenes'.) But
as soon as the new religion began to spread to non-Jews, some distinctive
title for its adherents became necessary, not least for the convenience of the
Roman administration, which had to decide how this minority group was to
be treated. The Jews were granted special privileges for the practice of their
religion. Should the same be extended to this new sect, even though some
of its members were not Jews? We have evidence that this question became
acute by the end of the century, and it is likely that it was already an issue
under Nero in the 60s. We do not know whether the Roman government of

---

[15] This is the reading adopted by the NRSV. Virtually all other well-known translations
follow those manuscripts which give *the Greeks*, a much easier reading, which removes any
ambiguity. *Greeks* meant Gentiles.

the province of Syria had already had to tackle the question in Antioch; but it can hardly be an accident that the name given there to the members of this new religion was not Greek but Latin, the language of Roman officials: *christiani*.

27   **At that time prophets came down from Jerusalem to Antioch.** The church had received the gift of the Holy Spirit. This gift was manifested in many ways, and 'speaking in tongues' was by no means the only one. Ever since Old Testament times the principal manifestation of the Spirit was held to be in the form of prophecy. In theory, all Christians had this gift (2.17–18); but in practice certain members of the congregation were found to be particularly gifted and became known as prophets. This is by no means the only time they appear. 1 Corinthians 14 gives some detailed information about them, and there are many other references to them in the New Testament. In part they were the successors of the Old Testament prophets: they had the gift of reading the signs of the times and of discerning, more clearly than their contemporaries, the hand of God in the present and the likely shape of future events – The prediction of Agabus is clearly of this kind. But they also had a wider rôle: they were able to give inspired direction to the church in matters requiring practical decision and to give an inspired lead to Christian prayer and worship. In slightly later times they travelled frequently from church to church and (so long as their gift could be seen to be genuine) they were received as honoured and authoritative visitors.

It follows that we should probably be wrong to think of Agabus' prediction as merely a case of psychic foreknowledge. The early church lived in heightened expectation of the end of the present world order and of the manifest triumph of Christ. Jesus was remembered to have given some teaching on those events of the near future which should be regarded as presaging this climactic time; and it was one of the functions of Christian prophets to relate the facts of contemporary history to this teaching of Jesus and so to help the church to understand the significance of the time in which it was living. Now famines were expected to be one of the 'birthpangs' of the new age (Mark 13.8). Agabus (unless he had true foresight, which is possible) may have heard that there were signs of a bad harvest approaching, and, seeing it in terms of one of the catastrophes of the time before the end, he may have confidently

28   predicted that it would grow into **a severe famine over all the world.** In any event, we can guess that he interpreted the famine as a sign of the times, and we can even hazard a guess at why he was moved to make such a prophecy. In 40 CE the emperor Caligula had threatened to erect a statue of himself in the Jewish temple. This was almost certainly seen by many Christians as 'the desolating sacrilege' (Mark 13.14), the decisive desecration which would herald the last days, and it may well have made the Christian prophets in Jerusalem alert to any other developments which belonged to the traditional picture of this catastrophic age. However this may be, the predicted famine in fact **took place** (as Luke notes) **during the reign of Claudius.** A single world-wide

famine is too simple a picture; but it is certainly true that there was a serious shortage of food in different parts of the empire during Claudius' reign (41–54), and that between 46 and 48 conditions were so serious in Jerusalem that a visiting queen from the east, Helena of Adiabene, is reported to have imported corn from Egypt and distributed it to the local inhabitants. The immediate effect of such shortages was to send up the price of food; and the church in Jerusalem, perhaps impoverished by its early experiment in communal living (2.45), was highly vulnerable.

28   So **the disciples determined that according to their ability, each would send relief.** A much more elaborate collection from the principal churches in Asia Minor and Greece was subsequently organized by Paul in order to relieve the poverty of the Christians in Jerusalem and to express the solidarity of the new churches with their mother church. Luke does not say much about that great enterprise of Paul's, nor (in the fragment of autobiography which we possess in Galatians 2) does Paul appear to allow for a contribution organized at Antioch and delivered to Jerusalem by his own hand (though it is not impossible to identify this visit with one of those which Paul mentions). Since Paul in Galatians is giving a careful account of the journeys he made to Jerusalem, his word must be preferred to Luke's; and in any case, it may be that Luke had only scanty information about the reaction of the Antioch church to Agabus' prophecy, and he may have supposed that, if a contribution was made, it must have been taken to **the elders** (a new name for the Jerusalem leaders) by the two most prominent men in the Antioch church, **Barnabas and Saul.**

12.1   **About that time.** Luke was now faced with the historian's problem of a tale of two cities: important things were happening in both Antioch and Jerusalem, and the two chronicles had to be dovetailed together. Modern historians might take the reader into their confidence with a phrase like 'we must now go back a few years to see what had been happening in Jerusalem'. But Luke's readers were less concerned than we are with exact chronology. **About that time** was a sufficient indication, even if the following events took place a few years earlier than those which have just been recounted.

As must in fact have been the case. **King Herod** (the grandson of Herod the Great, usually known as Herod Agrippa I) was granted the rule of the whole of Palestine in place of the Roman governor in 41 CE, and died in 44, several years before the famine. It seems that, on coming to the throne, he did his best to please his new subjects by actively promoting the orthodox traditions of their religion; and this provides a possible motive – for Luke gives none – why he should have attacked the growing sect of the Christians. If the church was becoming increasingly suspect to the Jewish authorities, Herod could have gained popular support by his persecution. But Luke's purpose seems to be not so much to draw attention to the first

2   martyrdom of an actual disciple of Jesus (**James, the brother of John**) as to mention it as the occasion for a miraculous event in the life of Peter and to

recount the horrible punishment received by Herod for his treatment of the church.

Both stories, whatever their basis in fact, are typical of the kind of divine protection which many new religions in antiquity claimed to receive when threatened by hostile powers; yet the second story (Herod's death) can be confirmed in all essential details from the contemporary Jewish historian Josephus, and the first, though it contains elements that are conventional in such stories (an **angel**, a shining **light**, a gate opening **of its own accord**), is told with such a wealth of plausible detail that it must either contain genuine reminiscences or else be the work of an exceptionally well-informed story-teller. It is dated (like other important stages of the story) by a Jewish festival, in this case that of **Unleavened Bread** (which was almost synonymous with Passover). The **soldiers**, like a regular Roman guard, were divided into **four squads**, each of which was on duty for one of the four watches of the night. The arrangements in the prison are entirely plausible; and psychologically, Peter's trance-like escape, followed by a sudden realization that he was both alone and free, has the ring of truth. The author's intention, however, was not to make the miracle seem more plausible by playing down its miraculous features but on the contrary to emphasize that it was a deliverance so staggering as to be almost incredible. This governs the way he tells the rest of the story. The scene is the **house of Mary, the mother of John whose other name was Mark.**[16] This is the first appearance of Mark, who is soon to have a part to play in the story and whom later tradition came to regard as the author of the second gospel. Luke says nothing to introduce him here: he was presumably well known. The house was substantial: it had a room large enough for many to have **gathered** and a courtyard separated from the street by an **outer gate**. The maid (**Rhoda** was a common name for a slave) was presumably just coming out of the house to answer the knock at the gate when she heard Peter's voice calling across the courtyard from outside in the street. If so, it is understandable that in her excitement, instead of crossing the courtyard and opening the gate, she went straight back inside the house with the news. In this way Luke builds up to the climax. That Peter should actually have escaped seemed so incredible that his friends tried any other explanation first. The maid must be out of her mind. If not, the visitor must be Peter's **angel** – for guardian angels were certainly believed in and were imagined as a kind of counterpart to a human person, and so perhaps (should one appear on earth) might be mistaken for the person being protected. It was only when they saw Peter for themselves that they were prepared to believe that he could have escaped.

"Tell this to James." James, the brother of Jesus, was neither one of the original apostles nor named among Jesus' original disciples. Presumably he

---

[16] John (*johanan*) was his Jewish name, Mark (*Marcus*) his Latin name. Many Jews took a Roman name as a second name, e.g. Joseph Justus (1.23), Simeon Niger (13.1).

was converted after the resurrection. From now on he becomes the leader of the Jerusalem church, and his name appears also in non-Christian writings. Luke says nothing of how he reached this position, or of why Peter was displaced. Evidently the fact of being so closely related to Jesus gave him exceptional authority.

Luke then leads the narrative back to Herod. The sudden death of this king at the height of his powers and in the midst of a successful reign was a phenomenon which few ancient writers would have thought of putting down to chance. Both Luke and Josephus (our other source of information 23 about him) agree that it was the result of Herod's not giving **the glory to God**; and Herod's fatal illness (being **eaten by worms** is a popular, not a medical, description) was typical of the gruesome kind of end by which a tyrant was expected to die. But Luke seems to have had some information 20 which Josephus lacked. The cities of **Tyre and Sidon** lay on the coast to the north of Caesarea, in the province of Syria. They would have possessed sufficient autonomy to negotiate the passage of food supplies; and there is no reason to doubt Luke's circumstantial account of their delegation.[17]

Paul's first missionary journey

The next major missionary enterprise of the church was commissioned, not from Jerusalem, but from Antioch. None of the Jerusalem apostles was 13.1 resident there, but Luke gives us the names of certain **prophets and teachers**, that is to say, men whose particular gift of inspiration, or whose opportunity to acquire first-hand knowledge of the new faith, had raised to a position of authority in the church. Luke has already told us (11.20) that some (such as **Barnabas**) were natives of Cyprus, and some (such as **Lucius**) of Cyrene – though they had come to Antioch from Jerusalem. Among the new names is **Manaen a member of the court of Herod the ruler** – literally the *tetrarch*, that is, Herod Antipas. The Greek word (*syntrophos*) is more specific than 'member of the court', and suggests that Manaen may have been brought up with Herod when he was young (he was now in his sixties) at the court of Herod the Great.

But it was not these men who took the responsibility for the major missionary enterprise which was now to begin from Antioch. The initiative belonged entirely to the Holy Spirit, which came upon them while they were 2 **worshiping the Lord and fasting**. Fasting as a preparation for a religious

---

[17] The statement in verse 25 that **after completing their mission Saul and Barnabas returned to Jerusalem** is puzzling. *From* Jerusalem, which is the reading of some manuscripts, is what we would expect: it leads well into the next chapter, where Saul and Barnabas are in Antioch. But '*to* Jerusalem' is well supported by the manuscript evidence and is adopted (unlike most translations) by the NRSV. It makes little sense in the context unless the words are rearranged to mean, 'after completing their mission for Jerusalem they returned (to Antioch)'.

experience was taken for granted in many religions, and particularly among the Jews. The Christians continued the practice; indeed, it is a recurring pattern, in Acts as in Luke's gospel, that prayer and fasting preceded a com-

3 munication of the Holy Spirit (Luke 3.22; 4.1–2; Acts 9.9, 19). Further **fasting and praying** then preceded the ceremony by which the two missionaries were sent on their way. **They laid their hands on them.** These words could describe either of two different rites which were practised at this time. One was pressing the hands heavily upon another person (an act based on the commissioning of Joshua by Moses in Numbers 27.33): by this a teacher might signify that his authority had passed into a pupil. The other was the much more ordinary act of touching another person in order to bless, to heal or to commission. The church soon gave a new meaning to these solemn acts, seeing them particularly as the means by which the Holy Spirit was transmitted from one Christian to another. Here the rite seems to have been performed between equals, all of whom already possessed the Spirit. It expressed not so much the authority given to Saul and Barnabas to start a new mission as the solidarity between them and those they left behind, a solidarity which kept the missionaries still ultimately dependent (as Luke believed they must have been) upon the church in Jerusalem.

4 **Seleucia** was the port which served the city of Antioch. **Cyprus,** after two hundred years under the Ptolemies of Egypt, was now a Roman province, administered by an official to whom Luke gives the correct Greek title

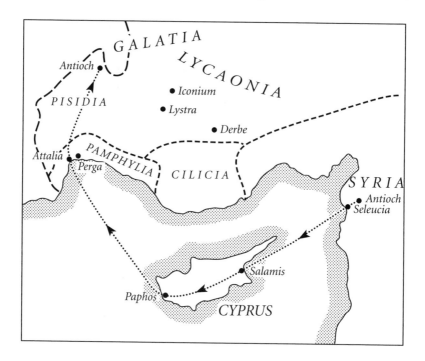

7 corresponding to the Latin term **proconsul**. There were large communities of Jews on the island, and it seems that Paul first addressed himself to

5 **the synagogues of the Jews**. This was in **Salamis**, the largest town in Cyprus, which lay at the east end of the island. But the seat of the Roman government was at the other end, at Paphos, and it was there that the first distinguished convert was made from the pagan world. A notable miracle prepared the way for the conversion of no less a person than the Roman proconsul.

7 This proconsul was a civil servant named **Sergius Paulus**. An earlier stage in the career of a certain *L. Sergius Paullus* (possibly the same man) is recorded in an inscription discovered in Rome. Luke calls him **an intelligent man**, using a Greek word which has to do not so much with native intelligence

6 as with a mature capacity for sound judgment. In his retinue was **a certain magician, a Jewish false prophet**. Several people of this kind make their appearance in the course of Acts, and there is no reason to doubt that there were many people about who made their living by claiming powers of magic and second sight. Christianity soon found itself in serious contest with all kinds of occultism; and this episode is told as if to emphasize its superiority. Luke gives the magician's name in a puzzling way. **Bar-Jesus** (meaning 'son of *yeshua*, Jesus') could well have been a name which Christians preferred not to use of anyone, let alone a magician; and if he was also known by some added name which meant 'magician', this would have been a more acceptable name to figure in the story. Unfortunately the alternative name

7 which Luke offers, **Elymas**, is a mystery. The letters do not seem to stand for any Hebrew or Aramaic word meaning anything like 'magician', though it is possible they disguise some form of a word meaning 'to dream' (the false prophets referred to in Jeremiah (23.25; 27.9) were 'dreamers'; and 'The Dreamer' could conceivably have been this magician's nickname). A double

9 name of a different kind was possessed by **Saul, also known as Paul**. In his letters the apostle always refers to himself as Paul; but up to this point in Acts he has been called Saul. Many Jews used a Roman name in addition to their native one, and often chose one that sounded similar. But Paul (we hear later) was born a Roman citizen, and must have possessed from birth the usual set of three Roman names, one of which was *Paulus*. In that case Saul would have been an extra name, such as many Roman citizens adopted in the eastern part of the empire. It was perhaps the only name he used when he was in Jerusalem. But now that his work had taken him so far afield, Luke gives him his official name, Paul.

The scene between these three men is quickly played out. Paul did not question or challenge Elymas' power; he simply showed his own to be stronger. With a string of biblical-sounding phrases (and more than a hint on his own part of a magician's curse), Paul confronted the magician with a greater authority. This is the climax of the story. But it was not just the miracle

12 which persuaded this distinguished convert: he had been **astonished at the teaching about the Lord**.

13   **Then Paul and his companions set sail from Paphos.** The journey is
summarily reported. Sailing north-west from Cyprus, the travellers landed
14 on the coast of Asia Minor near **Perga**, in the small and undistinguished
Roman province of Pamphylia. **Antioch in Pisidia** was a large Roman town
(though originally founded, like the other more famous Antioch, by one of
the successors of Alexander the Great): it had a famous shrine of Artemis and
a substantial Jewish community. Technically it belonged to the province of
Galatia, and it is possible that the 'Galatians' to whom Paul wrote his letter
belonged to this and neighbouring cities rather than to the region further
north in the centre of the province. At any rate, Paul's visit to it is told in
some detail, and sets the pattern for his activity in other cities of Asia Minor.

   On the sabbath day they went into the synagogue. The proceedings were
exactly as Luke describes them on the occasion of Jesus' appearance in the
synagogue at Nazareth (Luke 4.16–28). Apart from the language – the service
will have been in Greek, not Aramaic or Hebrew – the synagogue abroad
followed the same order of service as the synagogue in Palestine, and it was
entirely natural that a learned visitor such as Paul should have been invited
to give an exposition of the readings from scripture. Indeed, Luke suggests
15 that a particular kind of address was expected of him. The phrase **"any word
of exhortation"** has a technical sound. Some passage of **the prophets** (we are
not told which) had just been read; and the full meaning of Old Testament
prophecies was a subject of constant and earnest speculation. Were there
any signs in contemporary events that God's promises to his people were
about to be fulfilled? Were there any oracles in scripture which could help
the faithful to trace the hand of God in the world around them? Any answer to
such questions would have been eagerly awaited as **a word of exhortation**
that would cheer, encourage or console its hearers. (The Greek word has all
these meanings.[18])

   Paul's speech, like that of Stephen, begins with a summary of Israel's
history; but the treatment is quite different. Only the barest outline is given
of the early period; all the emphasis is placed on the moment when David
22 was made king: **'I have found David, son of Jesse, to be a man after my
heart, who will carry out all my wishes'** (1 Samuel 13.14). The importance of this moment lay deep in the national and religious consciousness.
God was believed to have made a clear promise to David that someone of
23 his **posterity** would reign for ever. On the historical plane, this clearly had
not been fulfilled: the Jewish monarchy had been defunct for centuries. It
was therefore widely believed, with varying degrees of sophistication, that
the promise would be fulfilled on a different plane by the appearance of
a divinely appointed person who would bring about a new era. The Jews
called this person the Messiah, or Christ. For the benefit, perhaps, of a more
cosmopolitan audience, Paul here calls him by the less esoteric title, **Savior.**

---

[18] On the various meanings of this word, see below on 2 Corinthians 1, p. 564.

But the meaning is the same. God's promise to David was still valid; and the theme of Paul's 'exhortation' was that the promise had now been fulfilled in the person of Jesus.

This, of course, seemed paradoxical. Jesus was not merely unknown to the great majority of Jews in the world: those who had come in contact with him had actually allowed him to be put to death. Nevertheless, that entirely Jewish and evidently inspired figure, John the Baptist, was barely **finishing his work**, preparing for a successor far greater than himself, when the heralded person appeared – and that person was Jesus; and even the crucifixion, if described as a death on **the tree**, could be seen, not as a pagan form of execution, but as the fulfilment of an ancient text (Deuteronomy 21.22) that could only now be fully understood. It was their failure to understand, even though the texts were **read every sabbath**, that caused **the residents of Jerusalem and their leaders** not to **recognize him** – so much so that they even 'condemned' him, or at least made the decision to 'hand him over',[19] despite the fact that **they found no cause for a sentence of death** – it seems to have been Luke's view, unlike that of virtually all the other New Testament writers, that Jesus was *not* formally found guilty and sentenced to death by the Jewish authorities (compare Luke 18.32 with Mark 10.33, and Luke 22.71 with Mark 14.64). That is to say, their part in Jesus' execution, whom they had recognized to be innocent of any capital offence, was an aberration; it did not necessarily either discredit Jesus or permanently disqualify the Jewish nation from being the destined recipient of God's promises. It could still be said by Paul, a Jew in the company of Jews,[20] that **"to us the message of this salvation has been sent"**.

"David . . . both died and was buried, and his tomb is with us to this day." So, in his first speech after Pentecost, Peter clinched the argument that the historical David could not be the person in whom great prophecies of immortality and eternal dominion would be fulfilled (2.29). The same might have appeared to be true of Jesus, for **they took him down from the tree and laid him in a tomb**. But it was not so: **God raised him from the dead**. And the proof was, first, the testimony of **witnesses** (among whom Luke does not let Paul mention himself: the message is told very much as one of the original apostles might have told it); and secondly, the fulfilment of scripture.

---

[19] The word translated **condemning** need mean no more than *deciding*; otherwise it seems in contradiction with the following clause, **they found no cause for a sentence of death** (verse 28).

[20] Verse 25 includes **others who fear God**. This phrase could be used to refer to any pious monotheists, Jews and non-Jews alike; but the term 'God-fearers' seems also to have had a more technical use, describing those Gentiles who were allowed to associate themselves with the synagogue in return for observing certain Jewish customs. This is the meaning the phrase normally has in Acts. But here it is evidently Luke's intention to present Paul's speech as primarily an appeal to the Jews, which was followed by an appeal to non-Jews only after it had been rejected by the Jews. The phrase here cannot be intended to draw attention to non-Jews in the audience.

33 The first text cited, **'You are my Son'**, is from Psalm 2.7. Since the opening verses of this psalm had been so clearly fulfilled by the manner of Jesus' trial and execution (see above on 4.25–6), another verse of it could now be invoked to prove that, far from being merely the condemned criminal which he appeared, Jesus was God's **Son**. The second text, though clear enough in the original Hebrew, was mysterious in the Septuagint Greek version (quoted

34 here): **I will give you the holy promises made to David** (Isaiah 55.3). What were these 'holy promises'? In the Greek the phrase is even more mysterious than it appears in this translation: *the holy things*. What were these 'holy things'? To solve a puzzle of this kind it was a usual technique to introduce another text where the same word or phrase occurs. Hence the third quo-

35 tation in this series (Psalm 16.10) which runs, **'You will not let your Holy One experience corruption.'** This verse has already been shown to refer to Jesus in an earlier speech in Acts (2.27). It also contains the same keyword ('holy') as the quotation from Isaiah. Therefore (according to this method of interpretation) the *holy things* in the Isaiah passage must mean Jesus, who was thereby proved to have been 'given to you', that is, to the Jewish people. Certainly that people had grievously sinned in rejecting this Jesus; but the

38 promise was being made good by the fact that **by this man forgiveness of sins**

39 **is proclaimed to you** – that is, to **everyone who believes** (we seem to hear for a moment the authentic tones of Paul's own preaching: justification by faith alone). The sermon ends with a quotation from Habakkuk 1.5, which is a warning that, for all that the promise was intended primarily for the Jews, they could still forfeit their right to it if they showed themselves to be, not

41 'believers', but **'scoffers'** – which is exactly how things were in fact about to turn out.

On this first sabbath, those who were convinced by Paul's teaching were

43 **many Jews and devout converts to Judaism**. But a week later, as a result of the

45 **jealousy** of the Jewish community, Paul and Barnabas took the decisive step

46, 44 of **turning to the Gentiles**. The scene is described impressionistically. **Almost the whole city** suggests a huge open-air meeting, perhaps in the theatre, or else in the neighbourhood of the synagogue. The Jewish community had turned against the Christian preachers, and the message was now being acclaimed by the Gentiles. Who these Gentiles were, and what opportunity they had to listen to the preaching and prepare themselves for their joyful acceptance of it, are questions Luke does not answer. His concern is simply to present a first and vivid example of what was to become a regular pattern in Paul's work – Jewish rejection followed by gentile acceptance (a pattern of

51 which there were hints even in the ministry of Jesus, Luke 4.14–30). **So they shook the dust off their feet**, a gesture well understood in Jewish society

50 (Jesus recommends it in Matthew 10.14), in answer to the **persecution** being stirred up by the Jews against them. But this was more than a personal reaction of impatience. The pattern of Jewish rejection and gentile acceptance

46 was according to the will of God. "**It was necessary that the word of God**

should be spoken first to you" – necessary, that is, on several counts: the whole story had started among the Jews; Jesus had proclaimed his message primarily among Jews; Jesus was the Jewish 'saviour' or Messiah; and the Jewish people were the foreordained inheritors of the promises of God. But when all this had been rejected by the Jews, the necessity of an approach to the Gentiles was equally apparent. It was implied in a prophecy of Isaiah

47 (49.6), **'I have set you to be a light for the Gentiles'** – a prophecy already used by Luke at the beginning of his gospel (2.32). By the Jews it would have been taken as describing the ultimate destiny of their own people, to be fulfilled by their faithfulness to their own religion and ethics; but for Christians it seemed to authorize an immediate mission to the Gentiles. And since this mission was foreordained in the purposes of God, it could now be said of

48 Gentiles, and not only of Jews, that some of them **had been destined for eternal life.** In view of the immense growth of the church in gentile lands by the time he was writing, Luke could safely put these tremendous claims in the mouth of Paul on this first occasion of his 'turning to the Gentiles'.

14.1 **The same thing occurred in Iconium.** This city lay nearly 100 miles southeast of Antioch. Luke has little to say about Paul and Barnabas' work there[21]

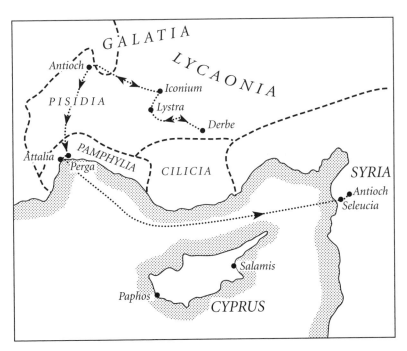

---

21 In the Greek of this paragraph they are not named but referred to simply as *them*, or as **apostles** (which is unexpected: normally the title is reserved for the Jerusalem leaders) or **brothers.**

beyond the fact that it followed the pattern established at Antioch of a powerful resistance stirred up against the apostles among the Gentiles by the Jews.

6 He hurries on to their arrival in cities south and east of Iconium, **Lystra and
Derbe**; for at Lystra there was a sensational event to record.

8 **In Lystra there was a man . . . crippled from birth.** The description of
the healing falls into line with similar stories in the gospels and with Peter's
miracle in Acts 3. Fixing his eyes on him, and using a formula borrowed
10 from scripture (it can hardly be an accident that the words **"Stand upright
on your feet"** are an exact quotation of Ezekiel 2.1), Paul effected the cure
11 in the manner of an authoritative exorcist. But the reaction of **the crowds**
introduces us to a different world altogether. The city would have had the
outward appearance of a typical Greco-Roman town in Asia Minor. The
official languages were Latin and Greek, and the official religion included
the cult of the main Greek deities such as Zeus, carried on in temples that
were doubtless built in the Greek style, one of which lay just outside the walls
and close to the monumental gates of the city. But among themselves the
inhabitants would still have spoken their native language, and doubtless it
was their own local gods that they continued to worship under the forms of
the imported Greek religion. Seeing the miracle that Paul had performed,
they did not (as Jews or other more sophisticated Roman citizens might have
done) think of Paul and Barnabas as men specially endowed by God with
miraculous powers. More credulously, they thought their visitors might be
gods themselves, walking the earth in a way that had formed the subject of
countless pagan myths (and perhaps of one in particular which was set in
12 their own part of the country). Paul, the spokesman, would be **Hermes**, the
messenger of the gods; and since the king of the gods was believed often
to disguise himself as a human traveller (in order to test the hospitality
offered to strangers), Barnabas could well be **Zeus** himself. Accordingly they
13, 11 hastened to **offer sacrifice**. But their shouts were all in their native **Lycaonian
language**, and it was some time before Paul and Barnabas realized what was
happening.

14 **They tore their clothes.** A non-Jew might have reacted simply with a
modest disclaimer. But to **the apostles** it seemed far more serious. The Jews
had a deep horror of being involved in pagan worship of any form. Indeed,
the main reason why they kept themselves apart from gentile society was to
avoid any possibility of being implicated, however indirectly, in idolatrous
observances or of contacting the ritual 'uncleanness' which might attach
to gentile houses. Paul and Barnabas now found themselves at the centre of
preparations for a pagan sacrifice. Their sensibilities outraged, they **tore their
clothes,** one of the most expressive gestures in the ancient world, and one
which Jews were liable to make when they heard the name of God profaned.

15 **"We are mortals just like you."** This was the message they had to get across
18 quickly if they were to restrain the crowds from **offering sacrifice to them.**
But curiously (as it seems to us) the rest of their speech seems hardly to bear

on this at all: it is a brief sermon advocating the worship of the one true God. That God is the creator of all things (a basic Old Testament proposition, here borrowed from Exodus 20.11), and that he can be known through his creation, was one of the stock arguments used by Jewish writers against pagan religion; and **"turn from these worthless things to the living God"** was a typical Jewish appeal to the gentile world. This kind of argument scarcely seems what the situation demanded here; but its significance comes from the scheme of Acts. This is the first report that Luke gives of Christians publicly addressing Gentiles. The approach they used to Jews has been abundantly illustrated, particularly by Stephen's speech (chapter 7) and Paul's first speech (chapter 13). Their approach to a fully non-Jewish world will be represented in detail by Paul's speech in Athens (chapter 17). What we seem to have here is a fragment of the same argument. This, Luke may be suggesting, is enough to give a flavour of the way Paul and Barnabas are likely to have spoken to the pagan crowds in Lystra.

But however pagan the city, the course of events (so at least Luke believed) was the same as before. **Jews came there from Antioch and Iconium**, and set in motion that hostile reaction against the church which it seemed to be the destiny of the Jews to provoke. Paul barely escaped with his life, after which his work in the region is only summarily described. The return journey was used for consolidating the new churches. They also **appointed elders for them in each church.** 'Elders' (*presbyters*) sounds like an official title, and indeed, it soon became one of the three orders of ministry in the church. How much of this later technical meaning Luke intended when he used the word here we cannot be sure. He may have meant no more than that some of the senior members ('elders' in the sense of older people) were entrusted with the responsibility of leadership.

Attalia (the modern Antalya) was the main port on this part of the coast of Asia Minor. On their return, Paul and Barnabas reported back to the church in Antioch. A decisive new stage had been reached: Christianity had been preached direct to the Gentiles. But this (Luke insists again) was not a personal decision by any apostle: it was God who had **opened a door of faith for the Gentiles.** The implications of this for the church in Jerusalem are the subject of the next chapter.

The terms of gentile admission

Christianity was born as a Jewish religion. Jesus was a Jew, and there is more than a hint in his teaching that he intended his message, at least primarily, for Jews. His first followers were also all Jews, and for the first few years their work consisted entirely of trying to convince their fellow Jews that the Jesus whom they had personally followed was the Messiah, or Christ, who had long been awaited. They expressed their message in entirely Jewish terms. Indeed, one of their strongest arguments was that the recent facts of which they were witnesses provided the essential clue to understanding the meaning of the Jewish scriptures. It followed that the Jesus whom they proclaimed was the saviour, first and foremost, of the Jewish people.

Yet by the last decades of the century (when Acts was probably written), the majority of Christians were Gentiles. How had this happened? As a historical development it is not hard to understand. There was a large number of Gentiles in the Greek-speaking world who were well acquainted with Judaism. They found in the Jewish faith a pure and exalted conception of God combined with a high and exacting ethic, such as they seldom found in the many religious cults of Greece and Asia Minor. But they also found in the Jewish religion a disturbing exclusiveness. They were welcomed to listen in the synagogue, but they were not permitted to share the social life of the Jewish community, and the only way in which they could advance further was by submitting to what they might well have regarded as a barbarous rite – circumcision – and by taking on themselves all the observances which constituted the Jewish way of life. By contrast, Christianity seemed to offer them as pure a religion and as exacting an ethic, but with none of the ethnic exclusiveness of Judaism.

For the original Christians of Jewish descent, on the other hand, this matter of the admission of Gentiles to the church raised questions both of principle and of practice. As Jews, they had been brought up to believe that theirs was a uniquely privileged race, to which God had promised exceptional blessings. Were they now, just because they had become Christians, to accept Gentiles as members of the same elect community as themselves? All their lives they had shunned social contact with Gentiles lest they should unwittingly be involved in pagan worship. Were they now to sit down beside Gentiles at table for the Lord's supper? They had always regarded the law of Moses as their one defence against the prevailing immorality (as they saw it) of the pagan world. Were they now to allow the Christian community to be one in which this law was no longer to be regarded as binding? These questions were brought to a head at different times in different places. At Antioch, for instance, the question of table fellowship seems to have been the most urgent one, since almost from the beginning there was a large number of Gentiles in that church. In Jerusalem, where a gentile Christian must have been a rare phenomenon for some time, the question was rather one of principle. Should Gentiles be admitted to the church? Should the Christian mission be carried into gentile lands? Some of the phases of this controversy are referred to in Paul's letter to the Galatians. Luke presents it (perhaps a little schematically, since the details of his narrative are sometimes difficult to reconcile with Paul's account) as an issue that was debated and settled once and for all at a meeting in Jerusalem. Church historians call this meeting the Council of Jerusalem. It may be calculated to have taken place in or around 49 CE.

The main point of principle – whether or not Gentiles should be admitted to the church – had already been settled by the incontrovertible fact that the gift of the Holy Spirit, which was the distinctive possession of the Christian community, had been imparted in full measure to Gentiles as well as to Jews. This had been the clear meaning of Peter's experience in Caesarea (chapter 10), and was the decisive point he made in his speech at the council. It was doubtless this, in reality, that made it impossible for the original Jewish church to close its doors altogether to gentile converts. But there were still the practical questions to be settled of table fellowship and the requirements of the law of Moses. On these they had some precedents to guide them. Similar questions were being debated in orthodox Jewish circles. One school believed that there was literally no salvation for human beings apart from the Jewish people, and that the only hope for Gentiles was to undergo the rite of circumcision (or a purifying ritual in the case of women), enter the Jewish community and lay upon themselves the full observance of the law. But another school was more liberal. According to this, God must be believed to accept the piety and good works of those Gentiles who genuinely turned from paganism to worship the one true God, even if they did not take the ultimate step of integration into the Jewish community as proselytes. It was doubtless this more liberal opinion which led to the welcoming of Gentiles in the synagogues, and along with it went a somewhat more flexible attitude towards social intercourse between Gentiles and Jews. But this attitude, though more humane and accommodating, still involved laying certain obligations on gentile sympathizers who wished to be associated with the synagogue. They must, of course, distance themselves as far as possible from every kind of pagan worship; they must try to observe the sabbath and the Jewish festivals; they must abstain from certain forbidden foods; and they must accept some basic moral principles which could be deduced from the law of Moses. If they did this, it was not necessary for them either to be circumcised or to adopt in full the Jewish way of life. The advocates of this attitude were able to find some precedent for it in scripture (the 'Noachic covenant', made by God with Noah, was for all human beings, not only for the Jews, Genesis 9), and appear to have drawn up some kind of code regulating the conditions to be observed by gentile adherents of the synagogue. Unfortunately, we do not know exactly what such a code would have consisted of at this date. But it is fairly clear (despite considerable obscurities in Luke's account) that the decision of the Christian council in Jerusalem was modelled on a code of this kind.

15.1   **Then certain individuals came down from Judea**. These were evidently from the strictest party among Jewish Christians. Their teaching was that of the first school of thought mentioned above: **"Unless you are circumcised according to the custom of Moses, you cannot be saved."** It may seem surprising that such an illiberal point of view should have been represented in the Jerusalem church. But Luke has already mentioned one Pharisee (Gamaliel, 5.34) who was sympathetic to the church, and by now it seems that a number

5   had become **believers**. Among the Pharisees were certainly to be found some

of the most exclusive groups in Judaism, and the presence of members of this **sect** in the church may well have led to a movement to exclude uncircumcised Gentiles. At any rate, representatives of this strict view had now appeared in Antioch, and this caused a deputation, which included Paul and Barnabas, to leave for Jerusalem. They took the route southward along the coast, and established on the way that they had the whole-hearted support of the Jewish Christian churches outside Jerusalem. Luke emphasizes that differences of opinion on this matter were confined to Jerusalem; again, when we compare his account with that of Paul in Galatians 1–2, we can see that he has somewhat simplified the picture.

6   **The apostles and the elders met together.** The structure of the Jerusalem church had evidently changed since it first appeared as a group of twelve apostles leading a growing number of new converts. In chapter 6 Luke described the appointment of seven additional ministers; and the terms he now uses allow for a further development. Alongside the original apostles (of whom at least one had been killed (12.2) and others may have been dispersed), there were now **elders**. Once again, however, we cannot be sure whether Luke is here using the word 'elders' (*presbyters*) in the technical sense which it acquired later (it is the term from which the English word *priest* is derived). It could mean simply 'the senior men', the persons, that is, who would naturally be able to assume responsibility in the church once the original group of apostles began to be dispersed.

From the letter to the Galatians, one would have expected it to have been Paul who presented the case for gentile Christianity. But Luke clearly sees the divine authorization of the gentile mission having taken place, not in Paul's recent journeys from Antioch, but in Peter's experiences in Joppa and Caesarea (chapter 10). It is Peter, therefore, who appears as the spokesman for the liberal point of view, and he bases his argument on that same episode (which is fresher, perhaps, in the memory of the reader of Acts than it would have been in the minds of the Christian leaders some ten or fifteen years after it took place). In this event God had shown his approval of the admission

8   of Gentiles by **"giving them the Holy Spirit, just as he did to us"**. Peter's language may reflect the arguments subsequently used by the gentile church in its controversies with Jewish synagogues. To Jewish scruples that non-Jews must be held at a distance because they were ritually 'impure', Christians could

9   reply that God had made such scruples irrelevant by **"cleansing their hearts by faith"**. To Jewish reliance on their law as their one defence against pagan immorality, Jewish Christians (some of whom, perhaps, had previously made

10   little attempt to be strictly observant Jews) could retort that it was **"a yoke that neither our ancestors nor we have been able to bear"**. Salvation (this is very much the language used by Paul in his letters) is not by observance of

11   these onerous requirements but **"through the grace of the Lord Jesus"**.

13   **James replied.** In the early chapters of Acts, the leader of the church is Peter – which is what, indeed, Jesus seems to have predicted (Matthew 16.18).

440

But by now (we do not know why), the leadership seems to have passed to one who was not one of the original twelve, but who was perhaps regarded as having a special claim to authority by virtue of being the brother of Jesus: **James**. Luke gives no explanation of this change; his narrative simply takes it for granted. It is James who now makes the speech which forms the basis of the church's policy, and it is James who appears as the leader of the church when the action returns to Jerusalem later on (21.18). Right at the start his speech bears what may be a touch of local colour: he calls Peter, not even by his original name in its Greek form (Simon), but in the form it would

14 have had in his native language (**Simeon** – the only time this form occurs except in 2 Peter 1.1). James, Luke may wish us to understand, was speaking in Aramaic. But the impression is superficial, for the speech as it stands could never have been composed in any language but Greek. The first point made in it is that the evidence offered by Peter is a fulfilment of scripture. The passage quoted is Amos 9.11–12 (along with a fragment from Jeremiah 12.15), and it runs here very much as it does in the Septuagint translation of the Old Testament into Greek. But it happens that at this point the Septuagint translators misread the Hebrew original. Among other mistakes, they took what in Amos is an oracle about "the remnant of *Edom*" as an oracle about

17 **'all other peoples'** (*adam*). This mistaken translation suits James' purpose admirably. But the historical James is unlikely to have been familiar with this version and certainly could not have used it if he was speaking in Aramaic. Luke is unlikely to have possessed any transcript of the speech originally made by James. Instead he is likely to have followed the historian's convention of composing the kind of speech which he believed James would have made. There is no reason why he should have noticed, or regarded as important, the fact that his Greek text of Amos diverged significantly at this point from the Hebrew original.

The principle, then, that Gentiles were intended by God to be admitted into the church was established by the events Peter had recounted and by Old Testament prophecy. The church must move in the direction indicated by the more liberal Jewish thinkers; the strict exclusiveness of the Pharisaic party was untenable in this new situation. But there remained the question of what obligations should be placed upon these gentile converts. Granted that they were neither to be circumcised nor to be subjected to the full observance of the Jewish law, it was still axiomatic (from the Jewish point of view) that some rules should be laid upon them to make sure that when they became Christians they would make a clean break with pagan idolatry and pagan morals. This would ease the scruples that some Jewish Christians were bound to feel at having free social intercourse with them. The formula suggested owed something to scripture. Certain clauses of the Mosaic law were expressly said to be binding even on non-Jews resident in Palestine (for instance the prohibition on 'eating blood' instead of kosher meat, Leviticus 17.10). These provided a precedent for elaborating a code of conduct for

Gentiles who would be in close association with Jewish Christians. Such a code was bound to include a reference to the two aspects of the pagan way of life which the Jews found particularly offensive: idolatry and sexual immorality. Both these were included in James' proposal; but, as the NRSV footnote shows, there is considerable disagreement among the manuscripts at this point and it is not clear what further provisions were intended.[22]

21 **("Moses has had those who proclaim him."** The last sentence of James' speech is obscure. If his proposal seemed too liberal, he might be answering them by pointing out that the Gentiles in question always had the opportunity to hear and observe more of the law of Moses if they wished. If, on the other hand, it seemed too strict, he could be saying that anything less would be inconsistent with a proper respect for the law which was in fact publicly **"read aloud every sabbath in the synagogues"** throughout the Jewish Dispersion. This seems to be an occasion when we are now too far removed from the world of Luke's time to be able to catch the tone of voice of the speaker.)

22 **With the consent of the whole church.** Luke describes the council on the model of a Greek democratic assembly. Speeches are made (though on this occasion all on one side), the matter is put to the assembly, and a resolution is recorded. Of the envoys, nothing more is known of **Judas called Barsabbas**, though he may have been a brother of the Joseph Barsabbas mentioned in 1.23; **Silas** appears again in the next chapter. Both are Jewish names; but, among Romans, Silas might well have been known as Silvanus, and we meet a Silvanus in Paul's letters to the Thessalonians and in 1 Peter.

23 **With the following letter.** This is one of the few occasions when an actual document is quoted in the New Testament. (There are several in the book of Ezra.) It has the form and style of the many official letters which have survived, written on papyrus or recorded in inscriptions. But, as with speeches, so with letters: if a historian had no access to the original document, he was perfectly free to compose the kind of letter which would have been written under the circumstances. The fact that this letter is written in careful and idiomatic Greek, combined with one or two phrases from the Greek Old Testament, suggests that in its present form it is more likely to be a composition of Luke than of the Jerusalem apostles. Moreover it ties in with the episode at Antioch with which the chapter began in a way that suggests the hand of a skilful historian. At the same time, Luke may well have seen some document of the kind, and have reproduced, for instance, its address to gentile Christians

---

[22] There is the further complication that the word '**blood**' is ambiguous. It could refer to the blood in meat and be a regulation about food (in which case it seems unnecessary to add **and from whatever has been strangled**), or else, in Greek as in English, it could mean 'murder'. But murder (which was unlawful in any case) comes oddly in this list, which is mainly concerned with ritual observances; and the variations in the manuscripts may be due to a desire to make the list more general, more ethical and more in line with other moral codes which are concerned with such things as bloodshed and sexual immorality. Some manuscripts even add to the list a form of the Golden Rule (Matthew 7.12).

in Antioch and Syria and Cilicia, despite the fact that he has not yet mentioned the founding of any churches outside Antioch itself. In any case, the letter serves his purpose well. It allows him to repeat (with that slight stylistic variation he is fond of) the formula which was the most important result of the episode, and to emphasize once again that this whole matter of the Christian mission to the Gentiles was by no means the personal decision of certain church leaders but the direct result of divine guidance. By slightly

28 modifying a familiar bureaucratic expression, he can write, **"it has seemed good to the Holy Spirit and to us"**.

31 In Antioch, **they rejoiced at the exhortation**. On the practical level their rejoicing was understandable: the immediate crisis had been resolved. But

32 Luke twice uses a word (translated both **exhortation** and **encourage**) which suggests something more than this. It is the same word as was used of Paul's great speech at Pisidian Antioch (13.15), and had an almost technical meaning. Specifically, it was the 'encouragement' which came from being able to show that the prophecies of the Old Testament were being fulfilled in contemporary events. This could well have been the kind of 'encouragement' given by **Judas and Silas, who were themselves prophets**. We may imagine them, not merely communicating the Jerusalem decision, but demonstrating how it fulfilled the many Old Testament prophecies which stated that the people of Israel would one day, in some way, be "a light to the nations" (Isaiah 42.6, quoted in Luke 2.32).

Philippi, Athens and Corinth

Throughout the first half of Acts, the progress of the gospel has been represented as an advance of the church into different regions, directly authorized by the leaders in Jerusalem, or else (in the latest instance) conducted under the supervision of the daughter church in Antioch. But now the picture changes. 'The Acts of the Apostles' becomes 'the acts of Paul', and his movements are no longer dependent on the decisions of a central authority. To this extent, Luke's account describes a new phase in the Christian mission.

36 It begins with what we would now call a pastoral visit: to **"visit the believers . . . and see how they are doing"**. This second visit included a journey

41 through the country lying between Antioch and central Asia Minor (**Syria and Cilicia**), which was mentioned in the decree of the Council of Jerusalem (15.24), even though Luke does not record Paul's original mission to it.

37 Meanwhile, **Barnabas** and **John called Mark** (on whom see above on 12.12) revisited Cyprus. Luke has to admit that this was not an agreed plan to work

39 in separate areas but was the result of a **disagreement** that was **sharp**. This is the only case of a serious dispute which Luke records in the early history of the church (Paul's letters are very much more candid). Doubtless the crisis at Antioch was too vividly remembered to be passed over. A dispute at Antioch in which Barnabas was involved also rankled in Paul's memory

(Galatians 2.11–14); but in Paul's account it turned on the question of Jewish observances, and his real opponent was Peter. If the same episode lies behind Luke's narrative (and it is difficult to think there could have been two such notable disputes between Paul and Barnabas at Antioch), Luke has made it turn on the much less inflammatory issue of the personal reliability of John Mark.

16.1   **Timothy** is well known from many references to him in Paul's letters.

3   But the information that Paul **had him circumcised because of the Jews** is unexpected. Paul was strongly opposed to any pressure exerted on gentile Christians to receive circumcision; this is the principal theme of the letter to the Galatians, and in one place he strongly repudiated the suggestion that he had ever advocated circumcision (Galatians 5.11). On the other hand, he continued to respect the scruples of those who followed a strict Jewish way of life, and it may be that Timothy presented something of a special case.

1   The son of a Jewish mother, even if **his father was a Greek**, was technically Jewish and therefore obliged to be circumcised. Timothy's family may have drifted away from Judaism (Luke's narrative in 14.9 suggests there may have been no Jewish community at Lystra), and the obligation to circumcise him had not been carried out. At Lystra he was probably regarded as a Gentile. But, once he began travelling with Paul to cities where there were Jewish communities, his position might have become more difficult: he might have been recognized as a Jew who had failed to observe one of the most basic commandments. It may have been for this reason that Paul, as a special case,

3   **took him and had him circumcised.**

6   **They went through the region of Phrygia and Galatia.** From being a pastoral visit, the journey soon turned into a new missionary venture; but Luke still insists that it was carried out under divine guidance – **having been**

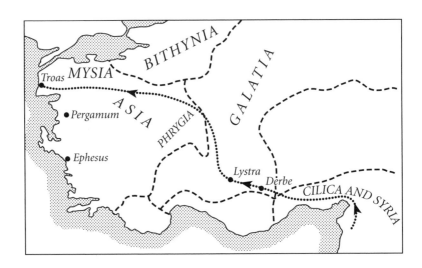

forbidden by the Holy Spirit to speak the word in Asia. The natural sequel to the work done so far might have seemed to be to press on to the great Greco-Roman cities of Ephesus and Pergamum, which were the commercial and administrative centres of the province of Asia. In these there were substantial Jewish communities, and the missionaries could expect to find a ready hearing among Greek-speaking citizens who were already sympathetic to the Jewish religion. Instead, the Spirit led them further into the interior of Asia Minor. From there, their obvious objective would have been the Hellenistic cities in Bithynia and Pontus on the shores of the Black Sea (where there were in fact Christian churches before the end of the century, 1 Peter 1.1). But before they got there, their real destination was revealed to them: the port of Troas on the Aegean coast. This was a long journey – at least 500 miles – and must have taken many weeks. In the course of it there must have been many occasions when the gospel was preached and churches founded (18.23). But Luke is here giving only the briefest summary in order to prepare for a dramatic new phase in the mission; and the few geographical details he offers are no more than a rough guide to the route actually taken by Paul and his companions.[23]

Divine prompting this time took the form of a dream-vision; as a result they
10 **immediately tried to cross over to Macedonia** – in the sense, presumably, of looking for a ship that would take them. The narrative now becomes notably precise about travel movements and ports of call; and at the same time it unexpectedly drops into the first person: **we immediately tried.** The writer seems suddenly to have joined the travellers, to leave them again as suddenly two paragraphs later and to reappear briefly on two subsequent occasions. This occasional 'we' is a puzzle that has still not been resolved. On the face of it, the author seems to have been one of the party but to have alluded to the fact only haphazardly, or else to have been present intermittently and to have discreetly drawn attention to his presence only when he was actually there. Either way, there are difficulties; and in any case there are other possibilities. Luke may have had access to some travel diary (whether his own or someone else's) and have dropped almost unconsciously into the first person when he used it as a principal source; or else he may have deliberately made use of the literary convention that a good travel story should seem to be vouched for by someone who was present. Whatever the explanation, the effect is that the

---

[23] Which may in fact be all that Luke was able to give, unless he knew the country well. In any case, some of the expressions in this paragraph are ambiguous. On Galatia, see below, p. 589. Phrygia lay to the west of Galatia and most of it was inside the province of Asia. But Luke says that they did not go to Asia. Either, therefore, they went through a part of Phrygia outside the borders of Asia, or else by 'Asia' Luke means, not the whole Roman province, but a smaller region round the great cities near the coast. **Passing by Mysia** is also difficult, since it is hard to see how they could have reached Troas without going through Mysia or Asia.

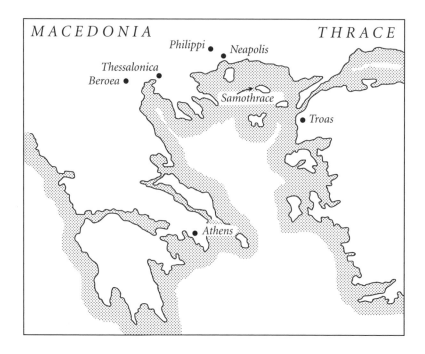

writer now appears as one who can claim to have some personal knowledge of the events described.

11   **Troas** – the island of **Samothrace** – **Neapolis** (the port serving Philippi): this was the most direct sea route, and their ship did well if it accomplished the crossing (as Luke implies) in a mere two or three days. From Neapolis the

12 road inland to **Philippi** could have been covered in a few hours. Once there, the travellers found themselves in a city rather different from any they had worked in so far. Philippi had a history as a Greek city going back at least as far as Philip of Macedon, the father of Alexander the Great. But in 42 BCE, after the famous battle outside its walls between Octavian (later Augustus) and Mark Antony, it had become a **Roman colony**, which meant that it was used as a place for settling Roman soldiers on their discharge from the army. As such, it retained a strongly Roman character. Latin was spoken alongside Greek, and the civil administration followed the Italian instead of the Greek model. This difference of atmosphere is reflected in the details of Luke's narrative. It was a peculiarity of the province of Macedonia that it was divided into 'districts', and the description of Philippi as **a leading city of the district of Macedonia**, even though it may not be quite accurate as it stands,[24] nevertheless, uses the correct technical terms. Justice in the city was

---

[24] The Greek is awkward at this point and the manuscript reading uncertain (see the NRSV footnote). It is possible that Luke gave the city its correct administrative title but that this was misunderstood and distorted by the copyists.

administered by two senior officials known as *duoviri*, for which a popular
20 Greek equivalent was *stratēgoi*, **magistrates**; and these had police officers
under them known as *lictores*, for which Luke again gives the correct Greek
35 equivalent (here translated **police**). The magistrates had the power to hear
20 charges brought by citizens against one another on such matters as **disturbing**
21 the **city** and **advocating customs** that were **not lawful**,[25] and to inflict minor
punishments, apparently including prison. But Paul was a Roman citizen, and
therefore exempt from the summary justice of local magistrates. In this first
encounter between the Roman authorities and the church, the authorities
were publicly shown to be at fault. The point was important if it was one of
Luke's intentions to show that the Christian religion at no time constituted
a threat to law and order in the Roman empire.

For most of the chapter, however, these official institutions remain in the
background. The story begins, as usual, with Paul seeking out the local Jewish
community. But this appears to have been very insignificant. Only some
13 **women** gathered on the sabbath, and a rather unexpected phrase (**where we**
supposed there was a place of prayer) suggests[26] that there was not even a
regular synagogue but only an agreed 'place of prayer' by the river, which was
14 over a mile outside the city (unless a smaller stream is meant). **Lydia** may or
may not have been Jewish (**worshiper of God**, as we have seen, could mean a
gentile sympathizer). Her native city, **Thyatira** (in a part of Asia Minor also
known as Lydia), was famous for its purple-dyeing industry. **Purple cloth**
was a luxury, and any dealer in it was likely to be well off and to have a
house large enough to accommodate guests. As a result of her conversion
and her hospitality, the Christian missionaries became established; and we
know from Paul's letter to the Philippians that in the course of their stay they
built up a loyal and flourishing church.

But Luke hurries on to the end of their visit. The immediate cause of
16 this dramatic episode was **a slave-girl** who was possessed by **a spirit of**
divination. Most cases of spirit-possession in the New Testament are set in a
Jewish context; but this spirit was **of divination**, that is to say, it performed
fortune-telling in the style of the Greek oracle at Delphi (Luke uses a technical
Greek word for that oracle – *pythōn*: the girl may have been a ventriloquist)
and it used language that was pagan as well as occasionally Jewish for God
17 (**the Most High God**), just as in a notable case in the gospel (Luke 8.28).

---

[25] We are surprised to hear that the customs of the Jews or of any other race were in
themselves unlawful for Romans. It was not the customs, but certain activities they might
lead to, which were normally punishable. But the government of a Roman colony may
have been particularly anxious to maintain the Roman way of life, and Luke's version of
the charge may reflect the spirit of the place rather than the legal code that was actually in
force.
[26] But we cannot be sure: **place of prayer** was a phrase quite often used (though not
elsewhere by Luke) to describe a synagogue building; equally it could have been an outdoor
shrine used by pagan monotheists, worshippers of 'the Most High God'.

18 But spirits of any kind could be exorcized **"in the name of Jesus Christ"**. In a pious Jewish community, such an exorcism would have caused awe and rejoicing; but pagans saw less evil in the presence of such spirits and their reaction was frankly materialistic.

The arrest, punishment and imprisonment of Paul and Silas are recounted in plausible detail. But their release – a miracle comparable with the release of Peter in chapter 12 – is told in the manner such stories demanded. There
24, 26 are touches of exaggeration (**the innermost cell, all** the doors were opened, **everyone's** chains were unfastened); there are conventional miraculous features (the prayers and singing answered by **an earthquake** – compare 4.31); and there is an irrational haste in the jailer's movements which is humanly understandable and adds greatly to the drama of the story, but would have been odd behaviour for someone responsible for the whole jail. But the point, for Luke, was that Paul and Silas were miraculously released (as was to be expected when God was so clearly behind their work – Paul's letters show that he was not always so fortunate!), and he told the story in the way that seemed most appropriate. He was also able to make the episode something more than merely spectacular: it resulted in the conversion and baptism of
33 the jailer and **his entire family.**[27]

17.1 **Paul and Silas had passed through Amphipolis and Apollonia** – that is to say, they took the *Via Egnatia*, the great Roman road that led right across northern Greece to the Adriatic. After a few days' travelling they reached the most important city in Macedonia, **Thessalonica**. We know something of their work there from Paul's letters: Paul spent long enough in the city to found an important church (1 Thessalonians 1.6–10), to sustain himself by doing manual work (2 Thessalonians 3.8), and to receive contributions to his physical needs from Philippi, 100 miles away (Philippians 4.16). It is evident that Luke has telescoped his narrative, so that what was really a stay of several months reads like a short visit of a week or two. Moreover, while Paul tells us that the Christians in Thessalonica were persecuted by their pagan fellow citizens (1 Thessalonians 2.14), Luke maintains that on this occasion the real instigators of the trouble were the Jews, and that Paul's work there conformed
2 with the usual pattern: first (**as was his custom**) he addressed himself to the synagogue, but the fruit of his preaching was to be seen in the conversion of
4 **a great many of the devout Greeks** (the 'God-fearers' who were welcomed in the synagogue) **and not a few of the leading women**, with the result that the Jews soon launched a jealous attack on him. This attack used more subtle tactics than any that had been made on him in Asia Minor. Thessalonica was a 'free city', which meant that its courts had more freedom of jurisdiction than in most cities of the Roman empire (Luke may have known this, since

---

[27] This passage has been frequently appealed to in discussions on the question whether, in the early church, children and infants were baptized as well as adults. But the phrase, which means literally *those who belonged to him*, is too general to decide the question.

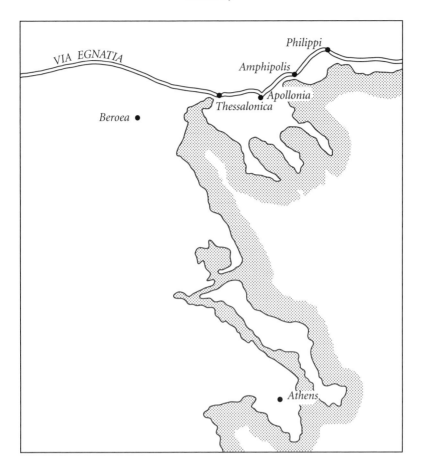

6 he knew the unusual name by which the **city authorities** were known in Thessalonica: *politarchs*). If the machinery of Roman justice could be turned against Paul and Silas there, this could prove a real setback. The first plan was
5 to bring them before **the assembly**, where the crowd could be worked upon to bring specific charges against them. But since they could not be found, all that could be done was to bring before the magistrates a certain **Jason** (who could have been either a Greek or a Jew who had assumed a Greek name), along with some other converts. The charges they brought were calculated
6 to arouse Roman apprehensions. **"People who have been turning the world upside down"** was the kind of language the emperor Claudius had made fashionable when he instituted punitive measures against the Jews (he had accused them of 'stirring up hatred throughout the world'): these Christians, therefore, with their Jewish type of religion, might be a recrudescence of the
7 same evil. **"They are all acting contrary to the decrees of the emperor"** – we do not know what this accusation was based on, but it sounded damaging

enough; and **"saying that there is another king named Jesus"** this was the most serious charge. All the gospels report that the charge against Jesus, that he was or claimed to be 'King of the Jews', was publicly displayed and could not be denied, and it was not always easy to explain that his kingship was 'not of this world'. There was therefore a serious *prima facie* case against these men. But the men could not be found. The authorities took the only course

9 open to them: they took **bail from Jason and the others**, binding them over to guarantee the good conduct of their guests. But it would be in the interest not only of the safety of Paul and Silas but also of the convenience of the local government if they left the city (for the jurisdiction of one city did not extend to another). Which is what they were immediately persuaded to do.

10 **Beroea** (today called *Verria*) lay off the trunk road, some 50 miles from Thessalonica. Exactly the same pattern was repeated, except that the Jewish

11 opposition was not local (for the Jews there were **more receptive** – the Greek word suggests greater *civility*) but was stirred up by the same Jewish instigators who had caused trouble in Thessalonica. Once more Paul prudently left the area. Luke seems to be in error about Timothy's movements. According to Paul he accompanied him to Athens and only later returned to Thessalonica (1 Thessalonians 3.1–2).

16 In Athens, **he was deeply distressed to see that the city was full of idols**. This was a typical Jewish reaction to the city, which was still the cultural and intellectual centre of the ancient world; and Paul's famous speech to the Athenians is for the most part an attack such as any courageous and well-educated Jew might have made on the beliefs and practices of paganism. Athens, since its subjugation by Rome in the previous century, had lost all vestiges of its former political power; but its art and architecture remained an impressive monument to its past glory, its streets continued to be embellished by the lavish buildings of munificent patrons, and the sheer abundance of its temples and altars and statues, even compared with other flourishing Greco-Roman cities, could well have **distressed** the sensibilities of a pious Jew seeing it for the first time. To this extent the scene is absolutely true to life. Nevertheless, we cannot be sure that Luke had actually been to Athens himself or that he had any detailed information about Paul's activity there. The things he tells us about Athens are the things any educated person knew about it. Its fame now rested, first on its philosophical schools, and secondly on the many religious cults that flourished there and which even Roman emperors found occasion to attend. These cults certainly gave the Athenians the reputation of

22 being **extremely religious . . . in every way**. As far as public observances such as sacrifices and festivals were concerned, the Athenian religious institutions were zealously maintained and offered a serious target for attack by any convinced monotheist. But the religion of educated Greeks was something a good deal more sophisticated; and this they learnt, not by frequenting the temples, but by furthering their education in that other institution for which Athens was famous, the schools of philosophy. It was philosophy rather than

religion (though the dividing line was hard to draw, since most philosophies assumed the existence of God) which moulded the principles and ideals of educated Greeks and Romans. The Stoic view of life was the most popular, and had become almost the official philosophy of the Roman empire. It strongly affirmed the moral values of respectable Roman citizens and it provided powerful intellectual arguments for a belief in God. But its vitality was due in part to the continual dialogue which went on between its exponents and the leaders of other philosophical schools. Athens was the centre of this

17 dialogue. Philosophers met constantly in **the marketplace**[28] under the great colonnaded porticoes (or *stoas*) built by foreign kings and benefactors – the *Stoics* actually got their name from this activity. It was doubtless often said,

21 somewhat cynically, that **all the Athenians and the foreigners living there would spend their time in nothing but telling or hearing something new**. But this was a superficial impression. Luke also knew (as all educated people knew, whether or not they had actually been there) that serious philosophical issues were constantly discussed. He presents Paul's appearance in the city as a challenge to all that Athens stood for, its religion and its philosophy, its temples and its cults.

How was Paul equipped to address himself to such people? On the one hand, the severe monotheism he had inherited from his Jewish upbringing commended itself to many serious-minded Greeks who were much attracted to this aspect of Jewish religion. On the other hand, Paul was now a Christian,

18 and so was expounding this monotheism in terms of **Jesus and the resurrection**, a name and a concept that were so alien in sound that his hearers assumed that he was **a proclaimer of foreign deities.** (This was the famous charge that had been brought against Socrates.) Yet he possessed, like many educated Jews, a sufficient smattering of Greek philosophical concepts to be able to express his beliefs in terms that his hearers could understand. They, for their part, would sense that this was very superficial philosophy, and Luke, using a rare and expressive Greek word, says that they called him a **babbler** – the original Greek word suggests a bird picking up seeds wherever it can find them – and their first impression of Paul may well have been of a man mouthing philosophical jargon without much understanding of what it meant.

19 Nevertheless, they did not dismiss him out of hand, but **brought him to the Areopagus.** *Areopagus* is the name of a small hill ('Mars' Hill') near the Acropolis in Athens. In classical times a select city council met there, and took its name from the hill; but, though it had great prestige, its actual power was insignificant. It was only under Roman rule that it became the most important assembly in the government of Athens. It was still called the Areopagus, though it may now have met in some part of the *agora*, close to

---

[28] The word is *agora*, the major public space in a Greek city, which was suitable for many activities other than the exchange of goods.

the main civic buildings. It is possible that this council, or some committee of it, supervised the teaching of philosophy and that it was normal for a new teacher to be presented to it. But, even without such detailed knowledge, it is not difficult to see why Luke should have chosen the Areopagus as the setting for Paul's self-defence. He knew that this was the name of the most important civic assembly in Athens; and he knew that the hill where it met (or rather, used to meet) was the site of a historic Athenian tribunal. By using the name, he achieved his purpose of making it seem that Paul's speech was made at the very centre of Athenian public life.

When presenting the gospel Paul usually began with the Old Testament: rightly interpreted, the scriptures could be shown to proclaim the coming of one who would be the Saviour, not of the Jews only, but of all humankind; and that Saviour had now come in the person of Jesus. But this approach was appropriate only when his hearers were either Jews or Gentiles who were already familiar with the Jewish religion (the 'God-fearers'). How would Paul have addressed himself to Athenian intellectuals who knew nothing of these scriptures, and who were accustomed to seek God, not by meditating on the history and traditions of a particular race, but by means of philosophical enquiry? Luke (whether or not his information went back to Paul himself) has already given a short answer to this question in Paul's only other recorded speech to a gentile audience, that at Lystra (14.15–17); the speech in Athens is more elaborate but follows the same pattern. The language and arguments that Paul uses are those that had already been worked out by Greek-speaking Jews to commend their religion to people whose culture was Greek. Two points were frequently made in such Jewish apologetic. First, the statues and images and diverse cults of pagan religion were unworthy of God: God

24, 29 **"does not live in shrines made by human hands . . . we ought not to think that the deity is like gold, or silver, or stone, an image formed by the art and imagination of mortals"**. Secondly, even though the Jews alone had received in their scriptures the authentic revelation of the true God, all human beings could have some intimation of his nature, and indeed the poets and philosophers of Greece had often glimpsed the truth about him. As Paul said at Lystra (14.17), "he has not left himself without a witness in

27 doing good". And so here: **"he is not far from each one of us"**. In other circumstances these points could easily have been made by quoting from the Bible; but they were also implied by some widely held tenets of philosophy – indeed Paul would have carried the Stoics in the audience with him until he reached the specifically Christian part of his argument; and the whole of Paul's speech, in the manner of sophisticated Jewish preachers, is a subtle mixture

24 of Bible and philosophy. Thus: (i) God **"made the world and everything in it"**: this is the theme of the opening of Genesis and a recurrent motif in Hebrew poetry (compare especially Isaiah 42.5, where many of the same expressions occur); but Stoic philosophy also proclaimed that God is the

25 creator of all. Again, (ii) God is not **"served by human hands, as though**

he needed anything" – a criticism of the routine of temple sacrifices which occurs often in the prophets and psalms (compare especially Psalm 50.12),

26 but was also a commonplace of Greek philosophy. (iii) **"From one ancestor he made all nations to inhabit the whole earth."** Hebrew thought conceived this mythologically: all human beings were descended from Adam, who was directly created by God. But the phrase in the Greek (*from one* – see the NRSV footnote) was equally acceptable philosophically: the Stoics laid stress on the unity of humankind. (iv) **"He allotted the times of their existence and the boundaries of the place where they would live."** The Jews, again, invoked certain myths: God created the world in a certain number of 'days' and laid down a plan for its existence which could be reckoned in 'weeks' of years; moreover (a myth which lies under the surface in parts of the Old Testament), in the course of creation he had subdued the forces of chaos and pushed back the sea so that it should not trespass on the **boundaries** of inhabited land (Psalm 74.13; Jeremiah 5.22). But the Stoics, though they did not share these myths, believed equally strongly in the succession of epochs and the providential ordering of the earth's surface which made some parts fit for human habitation. In all this, Greek philosophy and Jewish religion stood so close together that we cannot always tell which phrase belongs to the Bible and which to popular philosophy.

But Jewish preachers tended to go further than this. The sages of Greece were (they naturally held) inferior to Moses; but they often had glimpses of the truth and could be quoted to support the Jewish case (some even said that they had learnt it from Moses). Even the supreme pagan deity had a name, *Zeus*, which (in one of its grammatical inflections) suggested 'to live', just as the name of the God of Israel suggested 'to be'. It was therefore

28 self-evident to Jews and Gentiles alike that **'in him we live and move and have our being'**, just as both believed (even if in somewhat different senses)

29, 28 that **"we too are God's offspring"** – **"as even some of your own poets have said"**. The quotation is from a poet-astronomer of the third century BCE called Aratus; but this does not show that either Paul or Luke was well read in Greek literature. The verse is quoted in at least one other Jewish writer, and the line in question was doubtless proverbial long before Aratus included it in his poem. It was probably just another stock example of the kind of old Greek wisdom which, some Jewish preachers argued, showed that all human beings have some intimation of the true God.

But from this point the argument could go in one of two ways. God had not left any human beings "without a witness" (14.17); therefore (so one school would argue) the guilt of the Gentiles was all the more evident. They could not plead ignorance; they must bear the full severity of God's judgment on them – this is the line taken by Paul in the first chapter of Romans. Alternatively, a more liberal and optimistic conclusion could be drawn. The fact that God had revealed himself, even if only partially, to the whole of humankind surely meant that he must intend something better for them than damnation. Even now, if they turned to the pure worship of the God of Israel, the Gentiles could still be saved. This is the tone of the

30 speech here: **"God has overlooked the times of human ignorance"**, so now is the time to **repent**. This appeal must often have been heard from Jewish preachers: in their mouths it meant, 'Turn away from the idolatrous religion and debased morals of the pagan world and accept the austere worship and ethic of Judaism.' But here Paul proceeded differently: he offered as a motive for repentance some precise information about the imminence of God's judgment and began to prove this part of his argument, not by general considerations, but by reference to a particular and unheard-of event: the

32 raising of a human being from the dead. At this, **some scoffed**, and no wonder. Philosophy could not entertain such a dubious method of proof. It was, as Paul subsequently wrote to the Corinthians, "foolishness to Gentiles" (1 Corinthians 1.23).

Paul's argument, then, is of a kind that may often have been heard in Jewish propaganda: this was how an educated Jew might have addressed educated Greeks on the subject of the Jewish faith. Only in the last few words is any reference made to the new factor introduced by Christianity. Paul may indeed, have adopted this style of preaching on occasion (though from his letters we should hardly have guessed it); but Luke certainly believed – perhaps in the light of the experience of later Christian preachers – that this was the kind of argument Paul must have used when addressing the Athenians. At any rate, he has certainly used his literary skill to make the form of the speech appropriate to the occasion. It contains a number of expressions and idioms which belonged to the language of cultivated Greeks; and it makes brilliant use of a technique still used in sermons, that of starting from something

23 well known to the audience. No altar bearing the exact inscription **"To an unknown god"** has ever been found, and none may have existed bearing exactly this wording. But it was well known that, especially in Athens, altars were occasionally erected to nameless gods when none of the 'known' gods seemed to be the appropriate one to pray to in a particular emergency; and one of these (or even possibly an altar, which is known to have existed nearby, to the nameless 'Most High God') was perhaps a sufficient cue for the vivid introduction to the theme of the whole speech: **"What therefore you worship as unknown, this I proclaim to you."**

34 **Some of them joined him and became believers**. Paul's visit to Athens was not a failure, but neither was it a great success. He left behind him individual converts, but we do not hear of the existence of an Athenian church before the middle of the next century. The sophisticated city with its intellectual pursuits cannot have offered an easy opening for Paul's message.

18.1 It was otherwise with **Corinth**, which was no longer a Greek city in the sense that Athens was, even though it was now the administrative centre of the province of Achaia. Corinth had been virtually destroyed in the wars of the second century BCE and lay deserted until it was refounded as a Roman colony by Julius Caesar. Its new citizens were more Roman than Greek; but its atmosphere was essentially cosmopolitan. It was a great trading centre. Ships from the east unloaded at the isthmus rather than make the risky voyage round the Peloponnese. Their cargoes were then carried across and re-embarked in the Gulf of Corinth. With this trade came settlers from all over the Mediterranean. There was a substantial Jewish community, and there were cults of eastern deities (involving, it was said, much immorality). Corinth, in short, was more like the cities Paul knew in Asia Minor than like Athens. His work there produced a flourishing church, of which we gain a vivid picture in 1 Corinthians.

2   Luke's narrative touches Roman history at two points. **Claudius had ordered all Jews to leave Rome.** This is confirmed by an independent historian, Suetonius. Claudius' reign (41–54) began with a declaration of a policy of toleration towards the Jews and their worship. But later – possibly as a result of divisions within the Jewish community caused by the arrival of Christianity in Rome – the emperor moved against them. **Priscilla** (a diminutive of *Prisca*) and **Aquila** we know to have been a well-to-do couple (see below on Romans 16.3); they were perhaps prominent enough at Rome to fall immediate victims to Claudius' edict. They may indeed already have been Christians. The second point of contact with secular history is the

12 reference to **Gallio.** This person is well known. He was the elder brother of the philosopher and dramatist Seneca, and he is proved by an inscription to have been **proconsul** (the correct title for the governor of a Roman province) of Achaia around 51 CE. These two historical references make it certain that Paul's arrival in Corinth can be dated between 49 and 51.

3   **By trade they were tentmakers.** Cloth of goats' hair, used for tents and coats, was one of the industries of Paul's native Cilicia. The same trade may have been possible in Corinth; alternatively the Greek word may bear the more general meaning of 'leather-worker'. There was nothing unusual in a Jew as learned as Paul practising such a trade. Jewish scholars usually regarded it as wrong to receive payment for their services to the community and often supported themselves in quite humble professions. Paul, moreover, prided himself on being financially independent of the churches he founded; and the reason why, after the arrival of Silas and Timothy, he is specifically said to have

5 been **occupied with proclaiming the word** (the Greek expression suggests he would have had time for little else) may be that these men brought with them contributions from other churches towards his physical needs.

Despite this slower and more settled pace, the progress of Paul's work

4 in Corinth followed the usual pattern. First he preached **in the synagogue;** but when the Jews refused to accept that Jesus was the expected Messiah he solemnly absolved himself of any further responsibility towards them and

7 made his base with a gentile **worshiper of God** – one of those who attached themselves to the synagogue (and in this case actually lived **next door**). But

8 this time the hostile reaction of the Jews was delayed. Even an **official of the**

synagogue (who would have had responsibility for its worship and upkeep) **became a believer**; and in a vision Paul was instructed not to fear opposition
11 but to stay to consolidate and extend the new church. As a result, **he stayed there for a year and six months.**

A serious clash with the Jewish leaders was bound to come in the end, but when it did so, it left Paul and his church for the first time unharmed. This was entirely due to the attitude of the Roman authorities; and Luke seems to present the distinguished Roman administrator as a typical representative of what he took the correct Roman policy to be. Far from being a public
17 menace, Christianity deserved to attract **no attention** from the government.

A grandiose rostrum (which is the literal meaning of the word here trans-
12 lated **tribunal**) has been excavated in the main square or *agora* of ancient Corinth, and is possibly the place from which the proconsul gave his judgment. It was for Gallio to decide whether the charges brought before the defendant constituted an offence under Roman law. The Jews' charge against Paul is not implausible: certain kinds of religious proselytizing were cer-
13 tainly **contrary to the law** in the Roman sense. But for Jews 'the law' usually meant their own law; and this is how Gallio preferred to take it. This allowed him to decline to hear the case. What followed sounds like a riot; but once the case was handed back to the Jews there was nothing to stop them
8, 17 pursuing their own legal procedures. If another leading **official of the synagogue** had become a Christian – and a Christian Sosthenes is mentioned at the beginning of Paul's first letter to the Corinthians – it would doubtless have been possible for them to frame a charge against so prominent a renegade and to carry out the prescribed sentence in the public square of Corinth, within sight of the proconsul's rostrum. But the text is not clear at this point.
17 Those who **seized Sosthenes** may have been Gentiles (some manuscripts actually read *the Greeks*), and the riot may simply have been a case of popular anti-Semitism.
18 After this relatively long stay in Corinth, Paul **sailed for Syria.** The capital of Syria was Antioch, whence Paul had originally set out on his travels (15.36), and the direct route would have been to the port of Seleucia which served Antioch. But it may be that Paul could not find at **Cenchreae** (the port on
19 the east side of the isthmus of Corinth) a ship bound for Syria. **Ephesus,** on the other side of the Aegean, was by no means out of the way, and the crossing made possible a preliminary visit to a city where he was later to found an important church. But the next stage of the journey involved a
22 substantial détour. There were many ports nearer to Antioch than **Caesarea.** But Caesarea served Jerusalem, and when Luke says simply that Paul '**went up**' from there, he is using an almost technical expression, meaning (as the NRSV translates it) that he took the road up the mountains **to Jerusalem.**
18 His reason for doing so may be that he had been **under a vow.** When Jewish people placed themselves under a vow, they committed themselves to remain ritually clean, to abstain from wine and to allow their hair to grow (these

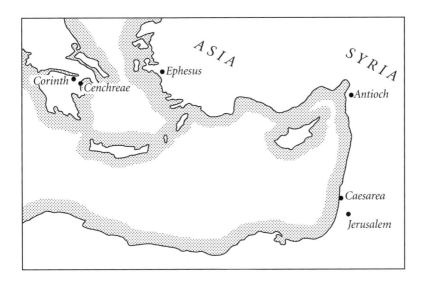

three disciplines were based on Numbers 6). Vows of this kind were taken for various periods, never less than a month, but sometimes for much longer; thus one might take a vow until one had completed a particular enterprise – it was a way of strengthening one's resolution and (it was believed) acquiring merit in God's eyes. When the period of the vow was completed, the growth of hair was cut off and presented, along with other offerings, at the temple in Jerusalem. This procedure is described below in 21.24, but the brief reference here implies that Paul had made a vow of this kind before or during his travels, and that his embarkation at Cenchreae marked the moment when the period of the vow came to an end. He was now free to cut his hair and drink wine; but he still had to make the prescribed offerings in Jerusalem. This would explain his circuitous route to Antioch via Caesarea.

Luke has now only one more stage to record in Paul's missionary activity. Paul founded no more new churches; but he spent some years building up
23 churches which already existed. Some of these, such as those in **the region of Galatia and Phrygia**, he had founded himself (16.6); but in Ephesus, where he was to be active for some time, he found Christianity already established. This presented a new situation in the pattern of Paul's work; and Luke endeavours to clarify Paul's relationship with this important church by observing (or assuming) that a curious and incomplete form of Christianity was established there before Paul's arrival and that Paul had to introduce some necessary corrections.

Until now, each church had been founded either by, or with the authority of, one of the Jerusalem apostles or by Paul himself; and the legitimacy of each new serious departure in missionary policy had been proved by an irrefutable manifestation of the gift of the Holy Spirit (2.4; 8.16–17; 10.44).

So, at any rate, Luke presents the history of the early church. But Christianity at Ephesus had begun rather differently. Among the first missionaries there, 24 Luke mentions only Priscilla and Aquila, who came from Rome, and **a Jew named Apollos, a native of Alexandria**. The situation (at least according to Luke's scheme) was irregular: the Ephesian church had been founded independently of the apostles and needed to be brought into conformity with the Christian tradition which stemmed from Jerusalem. This is what Paul did, and the precedent for his action seems to have been an episode such as that in Samaria (8.4–17), where the presence of apostles was required for the Holy Spirit to be received. Paul was an apostle, and it fell to him to make up the deficiency in the same way. But in this case the matter was more complicated. There had been Christians in Ephesus at least since the arrival of Priscilla and Aquila (18.18). Since then, Paul had returned by sea to Antioch 19.1 and had **passed through the interior regions** before he **came to Antioch**, a long journey that must have lasted several months. During all this time, was the Christianity that was flourishing in Ephesus such that the converts were without that gift which was the distinctive mark of any Christian community, the Holy Spirit? Luke says that it was, and suggests that the reason had to do with their baptism. Two kinds of baptism are mentioned in the gospels, that of John the Baptist (which was a rite symbolizing repentance) and that of Jesus (which was carried out by his followers and conferred the Holy Spirit). If the Christians in Ephesus were still without the Holy Spirit, this could perhaps best be explained by the fact that their baptism was only of the first kind. Luke describes how Paul put this right with the appropriate act of laying on his hands; and he accounts for the rise of the previous anomalous situation by the activity of a certain preacher named Apollos, who, at least until he was 18.25 instructed by Priscilla and Aquila, **knew only the baptism of John**, and had presumably started to build up the church on an inadequate foundation.

This explanation may be logical; but the reality may have been somewhat different. We know Apollos from 1 Corinthians 1–3. Luke's description of 24 him, **a native of Alexandria ... an eloquent man, well-versed in the scriptures**, suggests a type we can recognize. It was at Alexandria that some Jewish scholars made the most consistent attempt to interpret the Old Testament with the help of Greek philosophy. In the voluminous works of Philo we possess an impressive example of this, but there were certainly others who followed the same method. If Apollos was one of them, he might well have seen less importance in a cultic rite such as baptism, and he would certainly have been a very different kind of preacher from Paul, who seldom expressed his faith in philosophical terms; and the disagreement between the two men, which can be detected in 1 Corinthians, may well have arisen from this difference of background. But did Apollos really have such a serious misapprehension about baptism and the gift of the Holy Spirit? There is nothing in 1 Corinthians to suggest it. Moreover there are inconsistencies in Luke's account. How could Apollos have received instruction from Priscilla and Aquila and still not have understood about the Holy Spirit? Some have suggested that this passage is evidence for a continuing group of followers of John the Baptist who had some influence on the church; alternatively, Apollos, evidently a brilliant preacher, had presented the gospel in a much more Hellenized form than Paul and something had to be done to bridge the gap. It may have been out of some recollection of these disagreements that Luke constructed his somewhat schematic account of Paul's part in shaping the life of the church in Ephesus.

19.8, 9   **He entered the synagogue ... some stubbornly refused to believe.** Given that (according to Luke's account) there had been a new start in the life of the Christian community in Ephesus, Paul's work could be shown to have conformed with the usual pattern: first, an approach to the Jews, and only when that failed, a wider mission to the Gentiles. The transition is emphasized by a vivid detail. The synagogue was the centre, not only of Jewish worship, but of that whole culture and education which the Jews strove to keep intact from the influence of pagan customs and beliefs. By contrast, Ephesus boasted a number of magnificently endowed buildings (such as still dominate the ruins of the city) devoted to instruction in philosophy and general education in

9   Greek culture. When Paul reacted to Jewish opposition by **taking the disciples with him** to the **lecture hall of Tyrannus**, the significance of the move was apparent: one who **argued daily** amid pagan surroundings and images was no longer preaching a religion intended only, or even mainly, for Jews.

10   **This continued for two years.** Ephesus was the most important city in which Paul had yet worked. It was the commercial capital of the Roman province of Asia, which embraced the whole of the western part of Asia Minor with its many wealthy cities. It was an important port and a famous religious and cultural centre. Having been rebuilt on a grand scale during the Roman period, it had a population of perhaps a quarter of a million. Clearly it presented an important field for mission. Luke says summarily that **all the residents of Asia, both Jews and Greeks, heard the word of the Lord**. This grandiose claim was not wholly exaggerated. We hear from Paul's letters (Colossians 4.13) of three cities inland where churches were founded (of which Colossae was one); and by the time Revelation was written six other great cities in the province had churches. What Luke does not mention (either because he did not know about it or else because he saw no reason to record it) is that during this time Paul also revisited Corinth. Ephesus may also have been the place where he underwent imprisonment. In short, his activity must have been intense.

There follows an account, however, not of missionary achievements but of

11   more or less sensational episodes. **God did extraordinary miracles through Paul.** Paul – and this may be why Luke mentions it – was not to be imagined as in any way inferior to the other apostles in supernatural power: what Peter

12   could do with his shadow (5.15) Paul could do through even indirect contact with his body. The narrative then leaves Paul for a moment and describes the

power of the new religion over all its competitors (Ephesus was probably a centre for magical arts). Exorcism in particular, though it was esteemed to be more reputable than magic, used unmistakably magical techniques. It consisted of discovering the name and status of the demon and then 'adjuring' it

14 (a technical term) by the name of some superior power. A **Jewish high priest**, by virtue of his office, was privileged to utter the sacred name of the true God (which was religiously avoided by all other Jews). The sons of such a person, by making unscrupulous use of this secret knowledge, might well have had some success as exorcists, since the divine name was believed to have unique power. But they would doubtless have used many lesser names besides; and hearing of the potency of a certain name, 'Jesus', in this connection, they would naturally have added it to their repertory. Luke's anecdote is a dramatic pendant to the stories of exorcism in the gospels. There, the spirits had recognized in Jesus an exorcist of supreme authority. Here, while still recognizing the same

15 authority (**"Jesus I know"**), the spirit challenges the irresponsible use of that authority and demonstrates the reality of its own power (and by implication the power of Jesus whom it acknowledges) by a typical demonstration of violence, such that (like the crowds which witnessed Jesus' exorcisms)

17 **everyone was awestruck**. From the historical point of view, the only dif-

14 ficulty in the story is that we know of no high priest called **Sceva** (a Latin name) – but the exorcists' father may have been an impostor also. In any case, Luke has successfully conveyed an atmosphere of charlatanry. Exorcism practised without due authority had been shown to yield before the power of the new religion. As for ordinary magic, its practitioners publicly repudiated their arts in one of those orgies of book-burning by which the great cities of the Roman empire periodically attempted to check the superstitious credulity

19 of the time. Books being expensive, their value (**fifty thousand silver coins**) was equivalent to the cost of hiring a hundred and fifty workmen for a year.

From Ephesus to Jerusalem and Rome

21 **Now after these things had been accomplished**. The phrase is a significant one. Christ had been triumphant in the province of Asia; Paul's work there was done. It was no longer a matter of being harried from place to place by the Jewish opposition; Paul was now free to take the initiative himself. Accordingly he **resolved in the Spirit** (perhaps a deliberately ambiguous phrase – it could also mean 'made up his mind', indicating his freedom to obey divine guidance) **to go through Macedonia and Achaia**; and, as if to

23 emphasize his freedom to make his own plans, it is recorded that **he sent two of his helpers** on ahead of him. All this dispels in advance any sense of compulsion which might have been conveyed by the turbulent episode which follows. At the same time, a hint is given of the destiny which is to

22 determine Paul's movements for the rest of Acts: **"After I have gone there, I must also see Rome."**

23   **About that time no little disturbance broke out**. We know from Paul's letters that his stay in Ephesus was by no means peaceful. It was almost certainly in Ephesus that he underwent a nearly fatal illness (if that is what his enigmatic words mean in 2 Corinthians 1.8–9), and he was also involved in some public confrontation which nearly cost him his life ("I fought with wild animals", 1 Corinthians 15.32). One might have expected Acts to fill in the details; but Luke's narrative is either concerned with a quite different disturbance or else gives it a quite different character. Either way, it is a fitting climax to this part of Acts: the contest between Christianity and the greatest religious cult of Asia Minor. For Ephesus' most famous monument was its temple of Artemis, which had been rebuilt in the fourth century BCE and was one of the architectural wonders of the ancient world. To the Ephesians, Artemis was far more than the huntress-goddess of classical Greek mythology. She was the greatest divinity in Asia and represented the power of fertility. She was worshipped at countless shrines in the countryside, and her temple in the city was a place of impressive sanctity and wealth.

   This temple was served by officials with various exotic titles, one of which was a Greek word meaning literally 'temple-maker'. An inscription proves that a 'temple-maker' around this time was called Demetrius. It is possible that this is the same Demetrius as in the narrative here, and that Luke, knowing Demetrius' official title, misunderstood it and assumed that he

24 must have been **a silversmith who made silver shrines of Artemis**. But this Demetrius may equally well be another man of the same name who really was a silversmith, for the manufacture of small models of temples was quite common, and it may be only an accident that no such models of the Ephesus temple have ever been found. In any case, this Demetrius was one whose interests were directly affected by any falling away in the observance of the cult of Artemis. His harangue to his fellow artisans has a prophetic ring. Very soon after Luke was writing, a Roman governor in Asia Minor was to complain that, as a result of the spread of Christianity, the pagan temples were becoming deserted. But the arguments Luke attributes to Paul are not

26 so much Christian as Jewish: **"gods made with hands are not gods"** was one of the stock phrases of Jewish polemic against pagan idolatry. This is the first touch by which Luke suggests that an agitation which could have been (and indeed may have been) a serious blow for the Christian church was rather an outburst of popular anti-Jewish feeling by which, in the end, the Christians were barely affected.

29   **People rushed together to the theater**. This theatre is still well preserved. In the course of the first century CE the stage buildings underwent massive alterations, and we should probably imagine them surrounded by scaffolding. But the auditorium, an immense semicircle cut into the hillside, with tier upon tier of seats holding over twenty-five thousand people, must have appeared very much as it does today. It was the natural place, not only for

drama, but for any large meeting of the city populace; and, once the crowd had gathered there, it was for any orator who could be found to explain the emergency and suggest a course of action. Demetrius had mysteriously disappeared, and the only attempt at giving some direction to the demonstration

33 was made by a certain **Alexander**, who was presumably a spokesman for the Jewish community and attempted to **make a defence** (a further hint that the attack was primarily against Jews, not Christians). But his appearance was the cue for a burst of frank anti-Semitism. It is easy to imagine the terror that the endless chanting of the crowd would have inspired in any Jews who happened to be present. The church, on the other hand, seems to have been

31 barely represented. Paul himself had been persuaded to keep away by **some officials of the province of Asia** (Luke calls them *asiarchs*, which was the correct title for those entrusted with responsibility for the official religion): they were evidently sufficiently well disposed towards the Christians and towards Paul to make sure that he should not get implicated. If any of Luke's readers had heard of a riot at Ephesus and had jumped to the conclusion that it was Christians who caused it, Luke was careful to correct such a damaging misapprehension.

But there was another side to the affair. Ephesus still retained its old Greek constitution, under which an assembly of the citizen body could function as a parliament. This privilege was allowed to them somewhat grudgingly by their Roman rulers, and in fact came to an end a few generations later; and the rest of the scene is played out under the shadow of the stern power of Rome. The assembly of rioters could easily have been misconstrued in official reports as an abuse of democratic powers; and the speech of the senior city executive

35 (whom Luke correctly calls by his title of *grammateus*, **town clerk**) is devoted entirely to warning against this danger. Emergency assemblies (such as this had become) could be called only when serious danger threatened the life of the city. The official religion of Ephesus was surely not in danger: some symbol or image of the goddess was venerated which, it was believed, **fell from heaven**,[29] and the city therefore possessed the unique honour of being **temple keeper of the great Artemis**. There was no allegation of blasphemy or of damage done to the holy places. There could therefore be no emergency, and the speech ends by outlining the proper course of action which should have been taken if some individual had a serious grievance. To hear civil disputes

38 between citizens, regular **courts** were held before the Roman governors (the

39 **proconsuls**); **anything further** – that is, anything affecting the community as a whole – could be brought in due course before **the regular assembly** of the citizen body. The speech fits the occasion perfectly. This is exactly how we would expect the Ephesian town clerk to have warned the people

---

[29] This appears to be the meaning of the technical Greek word used here. Some Greek cults were certainly believed to have begun in this way, but we have no other evidence that this was the case at Ephesus.

against conduct that might lead the Roman authorities to deprive them of their privileges. But that, in Luke's narrative, is the end of the matter; and the implication is unmistakable. The whole thing was trumped up, the mob had been irresponsibly roused, and it all came to nothing. The only people who came under suspicion were the Jews; the Christians were actually under official protection. There was no more than this to the famous incident at Ephesus. The church was on the right side of the law. It was only incidentally

23 that anyone could say that **no little disturbance broke out concerning the Way.**

20.1 **He left for Macedonia.** Ephesus to Macedonia was a long and complicated journey whether by sea or by land; but Luke gives us none of the details. His narrative of Paul's movements is remarkably sketchy until the mysterious 'we' suddenly reappears in verse 5: whoever is speaking (see above on 16.10) seems to have spent the interval at Philippi and to have rejoined Paul and his party only when they called at Philippi on their return journey eastwards. After this the travel diary becomes as detailed as before. But the single sentence,

2 **When he had gone through those regions,** is all that Luke tells us about Paul's travels after leaving Ephesus. These must in fact have lasted for at

3, 2 least eighteen months. He then spent **three months** in **Greece** (which could mean anywhere south of Macedonia, and in this case almost certainly means Corinth). For all this we have to rely on Paul's letters, from which it seems likely that at least one of his motives for going on from Corinth to Jerusalem, if not the most important one, was to pay over the financial contributions which he had so painstakingly collected for the needs of the church in Jerusalem. (See especially Romans 15.22–26.) This is a possible explanation for his circuitous

3 return journey and for Luke's statement that **a plot was made against him by the Jews.** This 'plot' may have been an attempt to waylay him when he was carrying the money. If Paul had sailed on a ship plying direct from Corinth to a port in Syria, he and his consignment of silver coins might have been at risk. His return overland **through Macedonia,** though it was much longer, had so many different stages (not to mention the perhaps deliberate splitting up of his party at certain points) that a planned ambush would have been much more difficult. But this is speculation: Luke says nothing about it. The purpose of this last part of Acts is simply to show the stages by which Paul reached Rome. It may be significant that the members of Paul's escort are all listed with the countries they came from: they may have been emissaries of the various churches that had contributed to the collection. But again, Luke says nothing about this. In his narrative their names and countries serve merely to reflect the geographical range of Paul's missionary

4 work. **Sopater son of Pyrrhus** may or may not be the same as the 'Sosipater' mentioned in Romans 16.21; **Aristarchus** has been mentioned in 19.29; **Secundus** is unknown; **Gaius from Derbe** (apparently not the Macedonian Gaius of 19.29) is naturally paired with **Timothy,** who came from Lystra (which was near Derbe in central Asia Minor); **Tychicus** (Colossians 4.7;

2 Timothy 4.12) and **Trophimus** (21.29) were **from Asia**, by which Luke probably means from Ephesus.

5 At Philippi the party split into two: some **went ahead** by land to Troas, 6 while Paul and at least one companion **sailed from Philippi after the days of Unleavened Bread**. The dating, as usual in Acts, is by the great Jewish festivals; and in fact the seasons fall exactly as one would expect. The three months Paul spent in Greece were presumably in winter, when sea voyages were seldom risked. Sailings were resumed in the spring, and Paul would have embarked for Syria at the earliest opportunity had he not changed his plans and taken the land route north to Philippi. This brought him to **the days of Unleavened Bread** or Passover, which fell each year some time in March or April and left him another six weeks before the next great festival to 16 complete the rest of the voyage to Jerusalem (**he was eager to be in Jerusalem, if possible, on the day of Pentecost**). Even allowing for changing ships once or twice, this was quite a feasible programme, given normal Mediterranean sailing conditions in early summer.

7 **On the first day of the week**. If Luke had been using the Jewish way of reckoning days from sunset to sunset, we would have to take this as Saturday evening (the beginning of the first day after the sabbath). But we must assume he was using Roman reckoning; for by the time he was writing, if not long before, Christians regularly held their weekly assembly some time on Sunday, the day of the resurrection. In that case the episode which follows took place on Sunday night, in the context of the customary breaking of bread. It is hard to be sure whether the story is intended to be read as a miracle. Falling 9 **to the ground three floors below** would not necessarily have been fatal (the house, like many others in antiquity, had a ground floor and two upper floors without being excessively high): the words **was picked up dead** could mean 'as if dead'. If he was really dead, Paul would have accomplished a feat which would have placed him in the very first rank of miracle-workers. But the reaction of the others was relief and comfort, not amazement, and it may be that Luke means no more than that Paul helped the boy to recover from shock and bruises.

13 Troas and **Assos** lay on opposite sides of a slight promontory. The main party went round by ship; Paul for some reason (perhaps splitting the party again for greater security) crossed by land. After that the ship made its way south, stopping each night at one of the islands that lie off the coast of Asia 14, 15 Minor: Lesbos (of which **Mytilene** was the capital), **Chios** and **Samos**. Calling at Ephesus would have involved a substantial delay, and Paul had deliberately boarded a ship which took the more direct route towards Palestine. There was one more port of call on the mainland, however: the historic city of **Miletus**. This marked Paul's final departure from the province of Asia, and Luke records it as a moment of great solemnity.

17 **The elders of the church** at Ephesus could hardly have been summoned to Miletus within fewer than four or five days (the distance by road was in the

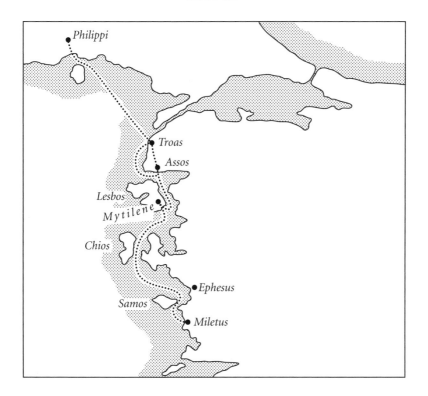

order of 40 miles); but Ephesus had been the scene of Paul's longest single period of continuous work, and his desire to say a formal farewell is perfectly plausible. If his ship had to spend a few days in the harbour anyway, it would have been natural for Paul to make contact with his friends. At the same time, Luke clearly had a historian's interest in the scene. He had reached the end of Paul's missionary work. It was a moment for summing up what had been achieved before beginning what was to be a very different chapter in Paul's life. A convenient model for such a summing up lay ready to hand. Ancient writers liked to put into the mouths of their heroes a farewell speech. Luke had done this for Jesus in his gospel (the discourse at the last supper, 22.21–38). This brief pause at Miletus now gave him the chance to do the same for Paul. Some such scene may well have taken place: Luke may even have been there. But we must allow for the possibility that, as a conscious literary artist, he deliberately elaborated it in order to fix in the reader's mind a clear picture of Paul's personality and achievements.

A hint that this is so is provided right at the outset. The description of Paul's activity in Asia rings absolutely true of every church he founded and 19 can be substantiated in many cases from Paul's letters. The **"plots of the Jews"** have been a recurring theme. But curiously enough, one place where there has been no mention of them is – Ephesus! Clearly Luke has generalized: Paul's whole missionary experience is the subject here. Similarly with Paul's glimpse into the future. This is an accurate foretaste of the story Luke still

22 has to tell, and yields a vivid picture of the sense both of divine guidance (**"as a captive to the Spirit"**[30]) and of the personal self-sacrifice which animated Paul as he neared Jerusalem. If we ask how Paul knew in advance of his

23 **imprisonment and persecutions**, the answer is that the **Holy Spirit** testified to him **in every city** – Luke gives an example of this happening through a

24 prophet a little later on the journey (21.7–14). **"But I do not count my life of any value"** – a sentence that has notable echoes of the way Paul talks about his motivation in Philippians 3.7–11.

The speech so far has been a fragment of Paul's biography; but in what follows the real subject is the church that is being addressed. This church may be Paul's own foundation at Ephesus; or it may be the church of Luke's day, a generation or so later, for which Luke is deliberately compiling a summary of the principles which governed Paul's work. In either event we are in a difficulty, for we cannot do more than guess at the issues which caused the

26 writing of such sensitive words. **"I declare to you this day that I am not responsible for the blood of any of you."** Who was accusing Paul of this? In what sense could Paul have been charged with actually shedding people's blood? The early Christians certainly regarded expulsion from the church as tantamount to death; and in Corinth, if not elsewhere, Paul had occasionally recommended expulsion (1 Corinthians 5.5). Is such a case in mind here? Is it the fate of Jews in general which is meant, to whom Paul had said, "Your blood be on your own heads" (18.6)? Or is it some subsequent schism in the church which had led to violence and for which the ultimate blame was being laid at the door of some ambiguity in Paul's original teaching? We do not know. But

29 in what follows the case is perhaps a little clearer. **"Savage wolves will come in among you, not sparing the flock."** The metaphor is obvious enough, and was used by Jesus himself (Luke 10.3). Only a few generations after Paul's time it came to be used frequently in Christian writings, and always referred to heretical teachers. Paul may well have foreseen the emergence of such teachers, and indeed in his letters he sometimes had to confront them. But by the time Luke wrote they were certainly a reality, and amid the conflicting loyalties within the church at the time of writing it may have been useful to record Paul's repeated warnings. For Paul's farewell speech at Miletus could

28 be read as a timeless reminder to those who had to **shepherd the church of God** and who are described here by a word which was soon to become

---

[30] The same Greek word is used for the 'Spirit' of God – the **Holy Spirit** – and the 'spirit' in human beings: distinguishing one from the other by a capital letter is a modern convention. Hence the alternative translation in the NRSV footnote. For the relation between these two senses of 'spirit', see below, p. 507.

the official title of the senior minister in the church: **overseers**, in Greek *episkopoi*, bishops.

33 **"I coveted no one's silver or gold or clothing."** This seems an even stranger piece of self-defence: why should Paul have been accused of such a thing? Yet there are hints in his letters that his enemies had found reason to cast suspicion on his handling of the money collected for the church in Jerusalem. Moreover we know that a fierce debate raged round the issue whether or not a preacher was entitled to be supported by the church. On this, Paul's view was that in principle a minister should be provided with board and lodging; and in support he quoted a saying of Jesus to the effect that "those who proclaim the gospel should get their living by the gospel" (1 Corinthians 9.14). Nevertheless in his own case he believed he had good reasons to decline it; and he could cite his own record of hard manual work with his
34, 35 **own hands**, not merely to prove his point, but as **an example** to the church of the way in which all members should be prepared to work in order to **support the weak.** This too he clinches with a proverb-like saying attributed to Jesus (though nowhere recorded in the gospels, and certainly said by others besides Jesus), **"It is more blessed to give than to receive."**

Even if the later interests of the church have influenced Luke's composition of this speech, its tone is still faithful to the sadness, the foreboding and the sense of inexorable purpose with which Paul must have taken leave of his converts; and Luke allows the same tone to permeate his brief account of

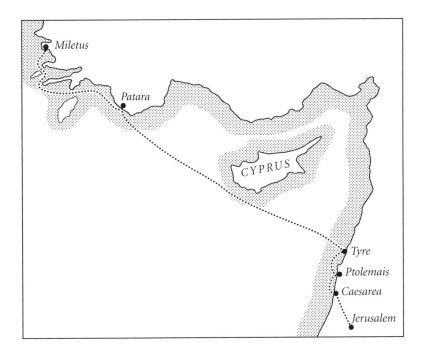

the remaining stages of the voyage. The ship ran easily before the prevailing north-westerly wind and made the usual stops on the way round to the
21.1 mainland port of **Patara**. A different ship – possibly a larger one – then took the travellers on the much longer stage across the open sea from Patara to the coast of Palestine. (The narrative here has some good nautical terms such as
3 **came in sight of** – in Greek a technical expression for sighting land.) They
3, 7 stopped at two ports, **Tyre** and **Ptolemais**, before they reached Caesarea; and at each they found Christian churches to greet them (though their foundation has not been mentioned in Acts). At Caesarea there were links with the past:
8, 10 **Philip the evangelist, one of the seven** (6.5; 7.4–13), and **a prophet named Agabus** (11.28), who, in the vivid style of Old Testament 'acted prophecy' (compare Isaiah 20), brings to a climax the series of prophetic warnings by which the tension has been built up during the journey.
17 **When we arrived in Jerusalem**. The main purpose of this visit we know from Paul's letters: to hand over the collection which had been raised in the gentile churches for the needs of the Jewish church in Jerusalem. Luke seems to have known about this collection and alludes to it later (24.17). Its purpose was twofold: to express the solidarity of the gentile churches with the parent church and to bring assistance to the impoverished Christians in Jerusalem. One aspect of this purpose – expressing solidarity – is in fact the subject of Luke's narrative, even though he makes no mention of the collection itself, which was the main purpose of Paul's journey.

Meanwhile a further threat had arisen to the solidarity between Jewish and gentile churches. On a previous occasion (chapter 15) the question had been how far, and under what conditions, Gentiles could be admitted to the church without at the same time becoming full Jewish proselytes. This had been settled by a decree (which is mentioned again here). The new cause of dissension was the question of the proper conduct of Jews who had become Christians. How far was it right for them to abandon strict Jewish observances in order to live in close community with their gentile fellow Christians? How far was the full observance of the Jewish law still binding upon them, now that they had come to place their confidence, no longer in their faithfulness to the Jewish way of life, but in Christ? We know that Paul was deeply involved in this question. For him it was a matter of principle, and he grappled with it in his letters to the Galatians and the Romans. As for the practical implications, there had been a serious dispute in Antioch about the freedom with which the Jewish Christians there, with the approval of Paul, had been sharing meals with gentile Christians (Galatians 2.11–14), and it is understandable that strict Jewish Christians should have been attacking his
21 policy on the grounds that **"you teach all the Jews living among Gentiles to forsake Moses"**. But they may have been exaggerating when they said that **"you tell them not to circumcise their children or observe the customs"**; for, from all that we know about Paul, we may doubt whether he went so far as to discourage circumcision *for Jews*.

Paul's arrival in Jerusalem brought this question to a head. In a scene reminiscent of the earlier council (chapter 15), he was given a hearing before

18 **James** and **all the elders.** This time there was no argument: this was Paul's last visit to the Jerusalem church, and Luke would surely have been unwilling to describe it as anything but cordial. Nevertheless, the suggestion was made that Paul should demonstrate his allegiance to Jewish institutions by publicly assisting certain Jewish members of the church to fulfil their obligations to the temple. The expense involved was considerable: each had to provide three sheep for the prescribed sacrifice (Numbers 6.14–15). Luke does not say whether Paul paid for this out of his own pocket or whether the money came from the collection. (It would have been a signal instance of solidarity if the gentile Christians had been prepared to see their money used for such a purpose.) His object is simply to show that Paul's conduct was visibly correct by the strictest Jewish standards. The four men under vow may have been in

24 real financial difficulties. If he were to **pay for the shaving of their heads** (and presumably the other expenses involved in completing their vow) he might rescue them from an embarrassing situation – this kind of help was highly regarded as an act of kindness. Further, by publicly associating himself with the ritual, Paul would have given ample proof that he was still an observant Jew himself.

26   The details of **the completion of the days of purification** seem a little confused. A vow of this kind has already been mentioned (see above on 18.18). It was temporary, and was terminated by shaving the head and making a substantial offering. While the vow was in force it was necessary to remain ritually 'clean'. Unless they had become 'unclean' by accident (which would have meant that they had to follow elaborate rules of purification before they could complete their vow), the four men would have been ready to enter the temple as soon as their offering was available. Paul, on the other hand, had just returned from abroad and was therefore by definition 'unclean'. Before he could accompany the men to the temple he had to go through a ritual of purification for himself, once on the third day after his arrival and once on the seventh day. Luke's narrative makes it sound as if the four men under a vow had also to be purified. On the basis of what we know of the rules in force at the time, this is unlikely. Either Luke has expressed himself obscurely, or he was not well informed about the details of these observances. What is

27 clear is that it was in the course of these rituals that **the Jews from Asia** (who had doubtless come, like Paul, for the festival and recognized an Ephesian

29 Gentile, **Trophimus,** among Paul's followers) found a pretext for stirring up violent opposition against him in Jerusalem.

28   **"Fellow Israelites, help!"** The trouble began in the temple; and we can fill in some of the details. The large colonnaded terrace which surrounded the temple area was open to all. In the centre were the buildings and courts which only Jews could enter. Around this central area was a balustrade, on which were fixed prominent notices in red letters, forbidding entry to all Gentiles

on pain of death. A rumour that Paul had deliberately introduced a Gentile past this barrier was the immediate cause of the disturbance. Such an act would have been regarded as unpardonably provocative. The statement that

30 **all the city was aroused** may not be more than a slight exaggeration.

The gatherings that thronged this temple area, particularly at festival seasons, could very quickly turn into a riot. For this reason a substantial part of the main Roman garrison in Jerusalem (consisting of a cohort of up to a thousand men) was stationed in the Antonia fortress, which had been built by Herod the Great on a commanding position at the north-west corner of the temple area, with its own flight of steps leading down into the colonnaded terrace. A force of soldiers was always on duty there to cope with public disorders. Luke's account of the riot fits these arrangements at every point.

The Roman officer naturally assumed that Paul was yet another of the insurrectionaries who frequently aggravated the burden of keeping the peace

38 in Judea. We know that there was in fact an **Egyptian** who had led a large following into the wilderness about ten years previously with a view to organizing an attack on Jerusalem and was still at large; and we also know that there were many **assassins** (*sicarii* – 'men with daggers') in Jerusalem during the years immediately preceding the Jewish Revolt of 66 CE, particularly during festivals. Luke's narrative may have confused some incidents that were originally separate; but in any case, the purpose of Paul's short dialogue with the Roman officer is to show how far he was removed from any such movement. A foreign insurrectionary could have been presumed to be an uneducated man, unable even to speak Greek correctly. Paul, by contrast, was able to conduct a civilized conversation in Greek, and could point with pride to his upbringing in one of the leading centres of intellectual life in

39 the eastern Mediterranean: Tarsus in Cilicia – **"an important city"**, as Paul adds, using the idiom (literally, *no mean city*) of a well-read man. His manner and background apparently persuaded the soldier that he should be given permission to **speak to the people**.

The suspicion that Paul had brought a pagan into the sacred precincts of the temple had been the immediate cause of the riot. This was of course unfounded; but it was a symptom of a much more deep-seated suspicion of Paul which, according to Luke's narrative, was beginning to obsess influential Jews in Jerusalem and which eventually left the Roman administration with no choice but to send Paul to Rome for trial. This suspicion arose, quite simply, from the fact of Paul's missionary work among Gentiles. Christian Jews had come to accept that Christianity, for all its roots in Jewish culture and history, was to be a universal religion (though Luke allows us to see some of the difficulty they had in doing so); but to ordinary people in Jerusalem this could have seemed nothing less than a dangerous and shameless attack upon their inherited assumption that their religion was the unique possession of the Jewish people. Paul's speech, which has clearly been written up by Luke to elucidate this first direct confrontation between Paul and the Jews, is a formal

22.1 **defense** against any such interpretation of his work. From the very outset, it stresses Paul's complete solidarity with his own race. Luke even notes the language in which it was delivered: not Greek (for, although this was the common language of Jews throughout the world and the language in which Paul wrote his letters and worked out his theology, it was also the language of that pagan culture from which the Jews were anxious to protect their own
2 traditions), but **Hebrew** (which for this purpose almost certainly means Aramaic). The speaker was in every sense a Jew, by birth, by upbringing and
3 by his education **at the feet of Gamaliel**, one of the most famous of Jewish
5 scholars. He could even call upon **the high priest and the whole council of elders** to testify to his zeal in trying to stamp out the Christian heresy. After this there had been his conversion, which has already been narrated (9.1–19). Luke lets the story be repeated here, with a few minor variations of detail
12 and style; but the ending has a significant new twist. **A certain Ananias**, who was Paul's first personal contact in Damascus, is described as **"a devout man according to the law and well spoken of by all the Jews living there"**. That is to say, even Paul's supernatural experience of the risen Jesus did not separate him from the company of observant Jews; indeed, this new turn in his life
14 could be described in biblical terms: it was **"the God of our ancestors"** who had chosen him and given him his mission to proclaim **"the Righteous One"** (another occurrence of this rare title for Jesus, as in 7.52). So much so, that he might have expected his mission to be among his former Jewish friends. But his natural expectations had been overruled by a vision in the temple (which has not been mentioned before, and is not easy to fit into the known
21 history of Paul's early years as a Christian): **"Go, for I will send you far away to the Gentiles."**

But all this made no difference. Paul may have been as Jewish as any of his hearers and have received his divine summons in the very temple he was accused of desecrating; but a deliberate mission to found gentile communities calling on the name of the God of Israel was still incompatible with Jewish religious assumptions, and the moment he referred to it the uproar began again. To the Roman officer it was clear that Paul, for whatever reason, constituted a threat to public order, and he was perfectly correct in taking
24 police action and ordering him to be **examined by flogging**. And there the matter might have ended, but for Paul's revelation (dramatically held back to this moment by the narrator) that he was a Roman citizen.

Those who were citizens of Rome by birth enjoyed certain privileges wherever they lived or travelled in the empire. They were exempt from the taxes paid by provincial subjects, and on any criminal charge they normally had the right to be tried at Rome and to be protected from any summary execution of justice on the spot. These privileges constituted a valuable reward which could be given to provincials for services rendered to the state, and it was a perquisite of the emperor to confer the citizenship on anyone he wished. In due course, certain professions and offices began to entitle a man to apply for citizenship. In particular, officers in auxiliary regiments could often obtain it, and indeed would need to do so if they were to rise to the rank of commanding officer – *tribune* – in charge of a cohort. It is therefore no

28 surprise that this officer had done so, or that he had had to pay **a large sum of money** (presumably in bribes) to get his name high enough on the list. On becoming a Roman citizen he had correctly added the name of the reigning emperor, Claudius, to his own name (23.26); indeed, his full Roman name now signalled his civic status. Paul's position was different: he was a citizen by birth. This means that his father, in Tarsus, had acquired the citizenship in some way before he was born. Nevertheless, Paul, at least when he was among Jewish people, lived as a Jew and presumably both dressed as a Jew and was known, not by his full Roman name, but only by his local name, Saul (or Paul). In order to enjoy the privileges of citizenship he had to claim them, and even if necessary prove his right to them, by producing some document or referring to the municipal archives in Tarsus. Here he simply makes the claim; and it gives a sensational new turn to the proceedings.

After this the tribune had to proceed carefully. He could not discharge his prisoner for fear of further riots; but neither could he impose a warning punishment on him because of Paul's status as a Roman citizen. He therefore tried to get the Jews to present their grievance against Paul in an intelligible form. This is the point of the following scene. The Jewish council – the Sanhedrin – had only limited powers under the Roman government, but it was still an autonomous body with its own meeting place (somewhere in or near the temple precinct) and its own rules of procedure. As the official deputy of the Roman governor (who was resident in Caesarea), the tribune

30 was presumably empowered to order **the chief priests and the entire council to meet**. But proceedings took an unexpected course. Why did the high priest order Paul to be struck on the mouth? For speaking out of turn? For not using a sufficiently respectful form of address? For making a statement he regarded

23.5 as untrue? And why did Paul **"not realize . . . that he was high priest"** (for so far as we know it was always the high priest who presided)? Because he was short-sighted? Or because he thought the man's conduct unworthy of his high office? These questions can be answered only by guesswork; possibly Luke had to reconstruct the scene out of only scanty information. But he was

3 able to make two points: first, the council acted **in violation of the law** in allowing the prisoner to be struck before the verdict (Leviticus 19.15: "You shall not render an unjust judgment"): secondly, Paul's retaliation was in the manner of a prophet: **"God will strike you!"** In point of fact, Ananias was murdered a few years later. Luke may have known this, and seen Paul's speech as an inspired prophecy. If so, it became even more impressive if Paul delivered it as it were blindfold, without realizing to whom it was that he was speaking – this is a possible explanation of Luke's account of the episode. At the same time, Paul's unawareness was also his defence against the charge

5 that he had clearly infringed the law (Exodus 22.28, **'You shall not speak evil**

of a leader of your people'). Despite the formal offence involved in insulting the high priest and prophesying his death, Luke was anxious to show that
1 Paul was correct by Jewish law and had reason to claim that he had **a clear conscience.**

It is certainly true that the Jewish council at this period contained two main
7 parties. The **Sadducees** were the conservative and more aristocratic element; they still exercised considerable influence in Jerusalem, but they were being gradually displaced by the Pharisees, whose social background was more
9 middle class. Among the Pharisees was a number of **scribes** who held seats in the Sanhedrin alongside the Sadducees. Apart from the social and cultural differences between them, there were differences of religious belief. The Sadducees accepted as binding only what was literally stated in the law of Moses; the Pharisees, on the other hand, recognizing that it was impossible to apply the ancient law to all aspects of contemporary life and activity, professed to have a tradition of interpretation which enabled them to lay bare its meaning and relevance. One result of this was that they claimed to be able
6 to support from scripture the widespread popular belief in **resurrection**, whereas the Sadducees, finding no support for it in the law books (virtually the only relevant texts are in the book of Daniel, which they would not have held to be authoritative), regarded the belief as false. Luke adds that they
8 also denied the existence of any **angel, or spirit.** This we did not know, but it follows from their literal approach to scripture that they could not accept the beliefs on such matters which had arisen only recently. Moreover, the Pharisees claimed that their tradition of interpretation was sometimes confirmed by a heavenly voice or apparition; and this, of course, the Sadducees rejected.

How far a session of the council would in fact have degenerated into a rowdy dispute between the parties on a matter of doctrine is hard to say. But in the early chapters of Acts Luke has already shown that the Pharisees had something in common with the Christians, and the fact that Paul's message
6 was a particular form of the hope (which they shared) of **the resurrection of the dead**, and that his teaching had been inspired by a vision like that
8 of **an angel, or spirit** (such as the Pharisees believed sometimes endorsed their own teaching), might well have commended him to the Pharisaic party and enabled him to exploit the inherent rivalries within the council. At any rate there was no formal charge forthcoming from the meeting to help the Roman officer; meanwhile, Paul was strengthened by a divine intimation that all these vicissitudes were no more than a necessary stage in the process that would eventually bring him to Rome.

Unless he were to release him unconditionally, the tribune now had no choice but to refer Paul's case to the only person in Judea who had the right to hear a serious criminal charge against a Roman citizen, the Roman governor. If he still had any doubts about it (or if Luke's readers were still wondering why the Roman authorities acted as they did), all doubt was dispelled by
13 the story of the Jews' **conspiracy.** The discovery of the plot through Paul's

nephew led the tribune to take exceptional security measures. Paul was given an enormous escort – according to Luke, who fills his account with technical military terms,[31] it amounted to a substantial part of the garrison of Jerusalem; and the two-day journey to Caesarea, where the governor resided, was begun during the night, so that by daylight the party was well over half-

31 way to Caesarea at **Antipatris**. There is certainly a touch of exaggeration in all this. The probable site of Antipatris is more than 35 miles from Jerusalem.

23 The soldiers, starting at **nine o'clock** (three hours after sunset), could hardly have got so far by dawn next day, and the infantry certainly could not have made the return journey within twenty-four hours of setting out. Similarly, Paul's escort seems out of all proportion to the danger of ambush by forty conspirators. But if Luke wanted to give an impression of a display of military strength and urgent preparation by the Roman authorities for Paul's protec-

26–30 tion, he has certainly succeeded; and by adding the text of an accompanying letter from the tribune he has described the whole episode as formally correct according to official Roman procedures. So far as the content goes, the letter could perfectly well be a transcript of the one Lysias actually sent; but if Luke did not have access to official archives he could have composed one along the lines of a standard bureaucratic letter of this kind.

It was the policy of the Roman empire in this period to allow routine matters of administration and law enforcement to be undertaken by local courts and officials; but capital charges, and any case which seriously affected the maintenance of public order, were always heard before the provincial governor himself. In such cases, the charges were brought by private individuals, and the defendant was given an opportunity to reply. When he had heard the evidence (which might be presented by a professional advocate), the governor, usually with the help of a panel of magistrates, decided what kind of offence was involved. If the defendant was an ordinary subject, he then pronounced verdict and sentence; but if the prisoner was a Roman citizen, the case might have to be referred to Rome.

35 The official residence or **headquarters** (*praetorium*) of the governor of Judea was the palace built by Herod at the port of Caesarea. Normally the governor would probably have dealt with cases arising in Jerusalem on the occasion of one of his visits there; but Luke has just shown why it was necessary to take special measures in Paul's case. Granted these exceptional circumstances, and perhaps also because Paul was a citizen of another province altogether (**Cilicia**), the governor's reaction was entirely correct according to the official procedures. **"I will give you a hearing when your accusers arrive."** Antonius Felix cuts a shabby figure in the pages of other historians of the time. Provincial governors were normally Romans of good family; but Felix was the son of a slave or a freedman and had won his position entirely

---

[31] One of these terms occurs nowhere else in Greek literature until five centuries later and we do not know its meaning. **Spearmen** (verse 23) is no more than a guess.

through influence at the emperor's court. He was governor of Judea from around 53 to 55 CE, and his period of office was marked by considerable popular unrest. Luke hints at his venality (24.26); but in other respects Felix's conduct of the case appears to conform with what was expected of a person in his position.

24.1 **Five days later** Paul's accusers duly arrived, bringing with them a professional **attorney, a certain Tertullus**. Luke's description of the proceedings uses the correct legal terminology, and the two speeches are elegant miniature specimens of formal advocacy. Each begins (as was standard form) with complimentary words addressed to the judge. In Tertullus' case, the compliments refer to the governor's achievement in keeping the peace and to

2 specific **reforms** – probably revisions of the legislation affecting his subjects. Then, following the advice of the teachers of rhetoric, the speaker craved the indulgence of the judge for 'detaining' him in this way and proceeded with his case. We possess a large number of documents preserved on papyrus which record hearings of this kind, and many of them similarly reproduce the oratorical flourishes in the opening (which were nevertheless supposed to be relevant to the matter at issue: here the reference to **peace** is clearly pointed, given the rioting which had occurred). They then go on to give a concise summary of the speaker's arguments. This appears to be the case here; and, once again, there is no way of knowing whether Luke had access to an official record of this kind or whether he composed these summaries himself. In either event, the words in which the Jewish advocate brought his

5 charge are carefully chosen. **"We have, in fact, found this man a pestilent fellow, an agitator among all the Jews throughout the world."** This was the language of contemporary anti-Semitism (as in 17.6 above): it was exactly what was needed to make the governor uneasy about Paul as a potential

2 threat to the **peace** of his province (and so to the record of his own tenure of office). But Paul's reply, which is by no means technically inferior to the speech of the professional lawyer, showed this charge to be mere rhetoric. The original disturbance of the peace in the temple had been alleged by

19 **some Jews from Asia**, who had now disappeared. Paul was on strong ground when he said that, if this charge were to be sustained, the original accusers would have to be present: we happen to know that the Roman government was becoming increasingly impatient of informers who failed to appear in person to substantiate their charges. Moreover his own reason for being

17 in the temple at that time was exemplary – **"I came to bring alms to my nation and to offer sacrifices"** (a hint that Luke knew about Paul's collection from the gentile churches, even though he does not explicitly mention it).

5 As for the other charge, of being **"a ringleader of the sect of the Nazarenes"**, there was nothing in this of a criminal character. Even the Jewish council had found it mainly to be concerned with a belief, a form of which many

15 of them held themselves, in **"a resurrection of both the righteous and the unrighteous"**.

The prosecution's case was evidently not proven; and Felix was still fol-
22 lowing the correct procedure when he **adjourned the hearing, with the
comment, "When Lysias the tribune comes down, I will decide your case."**
Lysias was the one independent witness still available to support the charge
that Paul constituted a threat to public order, and nothing more could be done
until his evidence was heard. Meanwhile Paul remained in prison, possibly for
27 **two years.**[32] This was not unheard of: provincial governors were not obliged
24 to do prompt justice. But Luke drops a few hints about Lysias' motives: **his
wife Drusilla, who was Jewish,** was also the sister of King Agrippa II, and
had left her former husband in order to marry the Roman governor, a Gen-
25 tile. Paul's discourse about **justice, self-control, and the coming judgment**
may have touched on this affair (just as John the Baptist had lectured Herod
Antipas on a similar misalliance) and so have caused Felix to become **fright-
ened.** At the same time Luke represents him as sympathetic to Christianity
22 (he was **rather well informed about the Way**), and also as hoping to pick
up a bribe. These conflicting interests could well have encouraged him to
prevaricate until the end of his term of office. He could then either quickly
settle the matter by releasing Paul or else pass the case on to his successor.
In the end he chose the latter course: a retiring governor could always be
accused at Rome by provincials whom he had misgoverned; and Felix may
27 well have had reason to want to **grant the Jews a favor** by leaving Paul in
prison.
27   Little is known about **Porcius Festus** beyond the bare fact that he succeeded
Felix as governor of Judea around 55 or 56 CE. In this narrative he represents,
like his predecessor, the correct Roman attitude to a case such as Paul's. It
was natural that the Jews, having failed with his predecessor, should make a
renewed attempt to have Paul brought out of prison to face their charges as
soon as the new governor arrived; it was equally natural that Festus should
insist on a new formal hearing at his own residence in Caesarea. This hearing
was as inconclusive as the previous one. What was Festus to do? The reason for
his unexpected suggestion that he should, after all, hold the trial in Jerusalem
is probably the fact that the governor was assisted by some sort of **council**
of advisers. The case against Paul seemed to turn on questions of Jewish law
and religion. If he transferred the case to Jerusalem he could presumably
recruit advisers from Jewish experts there, and so be better briefed to form a
judgment. But this, of course, would have been to load the proceedings heavily
against Paul, and Paul was fully within his rights to refuse. As a Roman citizen
he was entitled to demand that his trial should be held in Rome. This was
the moment to claim the privilege. Festus immediately granted the claim; his
only remaining responsibility was to draft a report to go with the prisoner.

---

[32] **After two years had passed** may mean only that Felix had completed his two-year
term of office.

The courtesy visit of some Jewish royalty gave him the opportunity to get some expert assistance in this difficult task.

20   For the governor was, as he admitted himself, **"at a loss how to investigate**
16 **these questions"**. On the question of procedure he was in no doubt: **"it was not the custom of the Romans to hand over anyone before the accused had met the accusers face to face and had been given an opportunity to make a defense against the charge"** – this we know to have been correct. Therefore it would have been wrong for him to have handed Paul over to the Jews. But when he attempted to carry out this procedure, no charge
19 was presented that he could handle: the matter seemed to turn on **"certain points of disagreement about their own religion"**. Festus' language betrays frank bewilderment; and Luke's account of his confession of this to Agrippa may reflect the difficulty which, by his own time, Roman administrators had begun to feel when they tried to understand the relationship between Christianity and Judaism and the disputes which were breaking out between the two.

23   **Agrippa and Bernice** are the most distinguished persons yet to have appeared in Acts. Agrippa II, a great-grandson of Herod the Great, had been a youthful companion of the emperor Claudius, and his influence at court helped him to obtain various kingdoms in the Middle East. Bernice (*Bernikē*), his sister, married two other petty kings of Herod's family in succession, and ultimately became the mistress of Nero's successor Titus. At this time they were both quite young – well under thirty – but they were already famous and influential. Luke makes the most of this. They **came with great pomp . . . with the military tribunes and the prominent men of the city**. Paul's last speech of self-defence was made to the very greatest in the land. In their presence even the Roman governor was careful to use correct and deferential
25 language when referring to the emperor – **"his Imperial Majesty"**.[33] The ostensible occasion of the meeting was an examination of Paul's case before the prisoner was despatched to Rome. But in the end nothing came out of it which could have been of much use to the governor; and in fact Luke lets it be the opportunity for Paul to make his last and most elaborate statement of his position, no longer to the Roman governor (who had confessed it was beyond him), or to the Jews of Jerusalem (who were now his sworn enemies), but to someone who occupied a middle position between the two, a person of Jewish background but owing allegiance to the world of high Roman society
26.3 rather than to the leaders of Judaism, a sympathetic expert in **all the customs and controversies of the Jews**, who was nevertheless not committed to taking the side of Paul's Jewish enemies. This illustrious person and his distinguished retinue were the audience for Paul's final presentation of the new faith, which was already beginning to penetrate sophisticated society

---

[33] This title (in Greek *Sebastos*, in Latin *Augustus*) began to be used in the reign of Claudius. The reigning emperor was now Claudius' successor Nero.

throughout the eastern part of the empire and was no longer – if it ever had
26 been – what could be described in idiomatic Greek as **"done in a corner"**.

A legitimate development of the Jewish religion – this is how Paul defended
his new faith. Yet his speech is carefully crafted to persuade a sophisticated
and cultured audience. It obeys many of the rules of ancient rhetoric, and
begins with the usual polished and pointed compliments. Paul then presents
5 his credentials: it was well known that he **"belonged to the strictest sect
of our religion".** As regards observances he had been irreproachable; and
as regards belief he was still, as the Pharisees were, committed to expecting
7 God's promises to the legendary **twelve tribes** of Israel to be fulfilled in a new
age inaugurated by the resurrection of the dead. Just as Jesus had challenged
the Sadducees (Mark 12.26–7), so Paul challenges his mainly Jewish audience
8 here: **"Why is it thought incredible by any of you that God raises the dead?"**
It was only on the character and timing of this new age – according to Jews still
in the future, according to Christians already coming about – that Christians
differed from the majority of Jews.

This difference, however, was crucial, so much so that Paul had begun
9 by doing **many things against the name of Jesus of Nazareth.** Only his
experience on the road to Damascus led him to see his error. This experience
is related here for the third time. As before, there are small variations in
the details. (This seems to be a feature of Luke's style.) For instance, the
14 audience is told that the supernatural voice spoke **in the Hebrew language**,
using the Aramaic form of Paul's name (*saoul*) – though in order to bring
home to them the force of the voice's message it is put this time in the
form of a Greek proverb, **"It hurts you to kick against the goads."** But
the important change is in the sequel. There is no mention of temporary
blindness, of Ananias, of Paul's baptism and other practical consequences.
Instead, the voice outlines Paul's future mission in language drawn partly
from Old Testament prophecies (compare especially Jeremiah 1.7; Isaiah
35.5; 42.7, 16), partly from the formulas which Christians soon began to use
when confessing their faith (compare Colossians 1.13–14; Ephesians 2.1–
2). The experience, as we know from Paul himself, convinced him that his
17 distinctive mission was to **the Gentiles** (Galatians 1.16; 2.8), and he ends
the autobiographical section of his speech by giving a summary sketch of his
missionary work. It was this approach to the Gentiles that had aroused such
violent Jewish opposition. But Paul could show that this was no more than
22 a fulfilment of the great prophecies of the Old Testament. He was **"saying
nothing but what the prophets and Moses said would take place"** – adding
only the distinctive Christian interpretation of certain prophetic texts to the
23 effect that **"the Messiah must suffer".**

Before he could come to the customary peroration, Festus impatiently
intervened, doubtless finding the argument (from a Roman official's point
24 of view) excessively academic, or even frankly unbalanced – **"You are out of
your mind, Paul!"** But Paul had his eye on Agrippa, who could be assumed not

26 only to be following the argument but to have some personal knowledge **of**
27 **these things** (perhaps even of Christianity). **"Do you believe the prophets?"**
Agrippa could hardly deny it – they were part of the scriptures read every
sabbath. The question was how one understood them. The difference between
Jews and Christians could be reduced to this one point: was or was not Jesus
the Messiah who was promised by the prophets? Agrippa is made to see that
this was indeed the crux of the argument: if he yielded to it he would be
28 open to Paul **"quickly persuading"** him to become a Christian.[34] This is the
thrust of the whole speech, the point which Luke probably especially hoped
would be grasped by his Roman readers. Paul ultimately arrived at Rome as
a prisoner. Was he a criminal? The highest authorities in Judea had found
no substance in any criminal charges against him. Everything turned on
the interpretation of the scriptures. King Agrippa agreed with the governor:
32 **"This man could have been set free if he had not appealed to the emperor."**
27.1 **When it was decided that we were to sail for Italy**. The responsibility of
escorting Paul on the long journey to Rome was given to a military officer,
a centurion of the Augustan Cohort, named Julius. (The privileged title
Augustan was given to some detachments of the Roman auxiliary forces,
including one that is known to have been in Syria during the first century
CE.) He had a squad of soldiers with him (27.31), and his task was to secure
a passage for the whole party on any ship which was going in the right
direction. This centurion seems to have been correct and courteous towards
Paul. He allowed him substantial freedom of movement, both at the first port
3 of call (**Sidon**) and later in the journey. He also apparently consented to Paul
2 bringing some friends with him: **Aristarchus** (who has been mentioned
before, 19.29), and the person (perhaps the author) who lies behind the
mysterious 'we', which reappears here from 21.17.

The route of the sea journey depended on the course of whatever ship was
available, and the courses which the ships took can be understood only in the
light of the fact that the prevailing wind in the eastern Mediterranean comes
from the north-west. If, as on this occasion, the ultimate destination also lay
in the north-west, then for any sailing ship the voyage was bound to involve
considerable détours and a lot of tacking. From Caesarea the first stage was
covered in **a ship of Adramyttium** (a port near Troas in north-west Asia
Minor), bound for ports in the province of Asia. This was the right direction
(north-west), but there could be no question of sailing straight across the sea
4 into a head wind. The closest course a ship could set was due north (**under
the lee of Cyprus**, which gave some protection) until it reached the southern
5 coast of Asia Minor, **off Cilicia and Pamphylia**. It could then take advantage
of different winds coming off the land and sail or tack westward, not too far

---

[34] Both the manuscript reading and the meaning of the Greek phrase are uncertain (see
the NRSV footnote). The sentence could also mean, "*You are almost persuading me* (or:
you almost believe) *that you have made me a Christian.*"

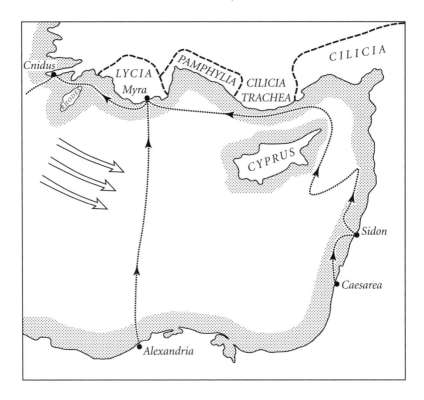

from the coast, but avoiding the deep bays and inlets (which is what must be meant by **across the sea**). In this way the ship carrying Paul reached an important port in the south-west corner of Asia Minor, **Myra in Lycia**.

6   It was nothing out of the ordinary to find in Myra **an Alexandrian ship bound for Italy**. Rome was provisioned largely by corn from Egypt, which was carried by a fleet of large cargo ships. But the course of these ships was also determined by the prevailing wind. To sail directly north-west across the open sea from Alexandria was normally impossible. The prevailing wind came from precisely that quarter, and so the ships, sailing as close to the wind as they could, were forced to go due north to the coast of Asia Minor. Myra was one of the ports they could reach. From there they would creep westward along the coast and among the islands, making use of the land winds; but this part of the journey was notoriously difficult, and a stop was usually made at Cnidus or Rhodes.

7   **We sailed slowly for a number of days and arrived with difficulty off Cnidus** must have been typical of many sailors' diaries. After this, the direct route westward across the Aegean was impracticable (the southern promontories of the Peloponnese were notoriously hard for a sailing ship to round) and an easier course was to sail south-west as far as Crete. The prevailing

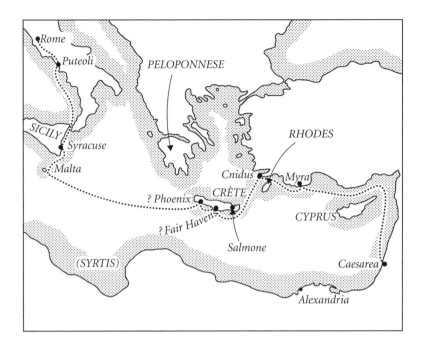

wind made it impossible to sail along the north side of the island, but on the south side there was some protection from the prevailing wind, less danger of being blown on to the rocks, and more chance of local southerly winds.

On this occasion, however, even **under the lee of Crete**, progress was slow. 8 **A place called Fair Havens** (if it existed: Luke may conceivably have invented it in the absence of better information) would have been a harbour **near the city of Lasea**, somewhere along the south coast of Crete; and we are 12 told that it **was not suitable for spending the winter.** This unsuitability was 9 now the only reason for continuing the voyage. **The Fast had already gone by** – this was a normal Jewish way of saying that it was already the closed season for sailing. (The one Jewish fast-day in the year was associated with the Day of Atonement, which fell around the autumn equinox.) The ship must find a harbour for the winter; the rest of the voyage would be put off 13 until the spring. **A moderate south wind** seemed to offer an opportunity to 12 sail westward along the coast and make for the harbour of **Phoenix**, which was presumably known to provide good protection against winter storms.[35] But on the way the ship was caught in a north-easterly gale, which was so powerful that there was little the crew could do but allow the ship to run before it, keeping as far north as possible so as to avoid ending up on the

---

[35] The site of this harbour has been identified, with some probability, close to Cape Myra in south-west Crete. Exact identification is difficult, since the coastline has altered as a result of severe earthquakes.

17 notorious quicksands of **Syrtis**, off the coast of Africa. After a fortnight's battering in the open sea[36] the ship struck land at Malta, some 500 miles to the west. It was clumsily beached and broke up on the shore. No lives were lost.

Reduced to this bare outline, the story is unremarkable. Despite the storm, the ship actually followed the usual course taken by transports from Alexandria, and in the long run the only difference for the passengers was that they wintered in Malta (another regular port of call on the route) instead of in Crete. But a severe storm in a sailing vessel, ending in shipwreck, is not the kind of experience that is quickly forgotten, and if Luke was one of the party this is sufficient explanation why he should have filled out the narrative with so much detailed description. The chapter abounds in what were evidently nautical terms, not all of which we can understand. **To undergird the ship**, for example, is assumed to mean 'frapping', that is, passing heavy ropes under the ship and tightening them on a windlass to protect the hull from strain in a heavy sea; and when **they lowered the sea anchor and so were driven**,[37] we can only guess that they were doing what was necessary to keep the ship on some sort of course, for to have run straight in front of the north-easterly gale at any speed would have taken them straight to the shallows of **Syrtis**, whereas in fact they succeeded in keeping more or less due west. But we cannot be sure that this is the correct meaning of the various terms, or that Luke had so much technical knowledge himself. He may simply have wished to colour his narrative with nautical-sounding language, without checking his facts with a professional sailor.

Nevertheless, while most writers who described a storm at sea made the most of its terrifying violence, Luke's narrative is remarkably restrained. There is no exaggeration, no dramatizing. The interest is concentrated on the person of Paul, who made some unexpected interventions. First, he appeared

10 simply to offer amateur advice – **"I can see that the voyage will be with danger and much heavy loss"** – and was naturally overruled by the professionals.

23–4 Secondly, he had a vision which gave him grounds to encourage the ship's

31 company. Thirdly, he caused the soldiers to interfere with the sailors' use of the dinghy – rightly or wrongly: if he was wrong about the sailors' intentions he could have been responsible for the loss of the dinghy and perhaps even indirectly for the loss of the ship; but it is true that a panic-stricken stampede for any form of lifeboat was a feature of shipwrecks, then as now. Fourthly,

35 at what seemed to be almost the critical moment for action, **he took bread; and giving thanks to God in the presence of all, he broke it and began to eat** – words which may mean no more than they say, but which certainly

---

[36] **The sea of Adria** (verse 27) included, not just the modern Adriatic, but the open sea between Greece and Sicily.

[37] The Greek means literally *letting down the gear*, and could refer just as well to sails or ballast.

have overtones suggesting the actions of the president at a Christian eucharist. Whether or not these interventions were prudent from a practical point of view, they have a clear function in the narrative: the hand of God was guiding events, bringing the whole crew to safety and ensuring that Paul would duly reach Rome.

28.2 **The natives showed us unusual kindness.** The touchstone of civilization in the Roman empire was language. If people spoke Latin or Greek they belonged to a world which, thanks to the achievements of Alexander the Great and the Roman government, now possessed a single Greco-Roman culture. Otherwise they were simply 'barbarians' – *barbaroi* – here translated **natives.** Malta, now part of the Roman empire, was originally a Phoenician colony, and local people probably still spoke only their own language. Luke therefore describes the scene as a typical encounter between 'Greeks' and 'barbarians' – compare the events at Lystra in 14.8–18, where the natives are also described as speaking their own language. Yet the reaction of these

4 people to Paul with a viper **hanging from his hand**[38] shows that Luke credited them with much the same beliefs as Greek people had, if only a little more naïve. All Greeks believed in a providential or divinely enforced **justice,** and most were prepared to allow for the possibility that a god might visit them *incognito.*

7 **The leading man of the island,** literally *the first man:* we know from inscriptions that, here as elsewhere, Luke has used a correct local title for this official. **Publius** was a common Roman first name, and we cannot identify him further. The almost casual miracle of recovery from the snake bite is

11 followed by a series of healings through laying on of hands during the **three months** that they had to wait in Malta for the sailing season to open (usually February or March). There was no difficulty in getting a passage: Malta lay on the usual route between Alexandria and Rome, and the **Alexandrian ship with the Twin Brothers as its figurehead** was doubtless another of the corn transports **that had wintered at the island** and was now ready to leave. (The name of the ship was typical – and could have been invented if Luke did not know it: the Twin Brothers, Castor and Pollux, were believed to be protectors of ships at sea and were particularly revered in Egypt.) It was not difficult

12, 13 to tack across the prevailing wind to **Syracuse** and on up to **Rhegium.** After that, a south wind gave them a good speed – about 5 knots – up the coast of Italy to **Puteoli,** near Naples. This – now called *Pozzuoli* – was the principal port serving Rome until very shortly after this date. The last lap of the journey was by road along the Appian Way, a march of less than a week. Paul found

---

[38] This is what Luke appears to be saying; but vipers do not hang on the hand they bite. Perhaps it is simply Luke's way of making it clear that, however difficult it may be to see usually, on this occasion everyone distinctly saw the snake biting Paul, so that there could be no doubt about the apparently miraculous outcome.

himself already in the company of Christians, and groups came out to meet him at two points along the way, about 43 and 33 miles from Rome.

16 **When we came into Rome**. The last section of the book has the effect of summing up Paul's final position with regard to the Romans on the one hand and the Jews on the other. **Paul was allowed to live by himself, with the soldier who was guarding him**, and an impressive picture of the consideration shown to him by the Roman authorities is built up until the end. Even though he was technically in custody, he was able to pursue his work of

31 teaching **without hindrance** – the word was often used in legal documents and is placed emphatically at the end of the closing sentence of the book. It may well have been intended as a final proof that Paul was at no time regarded as a serious criminal by the authorities, and that therefore (by implication) the religion he preached must not be imagined to present any kind of threat to public order.

The Jews, however, behaved true to the form described many times before. We know that there was a large and influential Jewish community at Rome, grouped around a number of synagogues. What is described here is a formal confrontation between its leaders and Paul; and it is carefully shown that Paul started with an absolutely clean sheet: no information had yet reached Rome

21 to his discredit (no one had **spoken anything evil** about him) and he for his

19 part had **no charge to bring** against his nation. His efforts to convert them

25 should have had every chance of success. But no, **they disagreed with each other** and began to leave. This is evidently taken as tantamount to rejecting the gospel. There could be no explanation for their refusal to listen other than that this was the will of God; and the authority for this explanation lay

26–7 to hand in a passage of Isaiah (6.9–10) which had been used by Jesus himself in somewhat similar circumstances (Luke 8.10) and is here quoted at some length. The episode was a further justification – if any were needed – of what

29 had been the principle of Paul's whole missionary policy: "**this salvation of God has been sent to the Gentiles**".

He lived there two whole years. It is certain that Paul was put to death in Rome, and there are allusions in letters by him or ascribed to him to at least one period of imprisonment (here or elsewhere) and to his own uncertainty as to the outcome of an impending trial. But we have no means of knowing either the date of his death or its immediate cause. It may have followed the trial to which the events in Acts have been tending, or Paul may have been acquitted and then imprisoned again on a new charge. In any event, given the distance between Jerusalem and Rome, it could well have been some months before his accusers arrived, and there is no reason to doubt Luke's statement that things dragged on for a full two years. The only serious question is why Luke ends his work at this point. To our minds it seems to leave matters very much in the air. We would dearly love to know what happened to Paul, and since it is likely (though of course not certain) that Acts was written well after his death, we find it hard to forgive Luke for not telling us about it. It is possible, of course, that he planned or even wrote a continuation; but it may also be the case that our modern presuppositions about how the book ought to have ended are mistaken. The main protagonist of Acts was not intended to be Paul but the church; and Luke has recounted the church's progress from its first small beginnings in Jerusalem to its world-wide presence a few decades later. He has described the sustained Jewish opposition to it and its eager reception by Gentiles; and he has emphasized the tolerance and consideration so often shown to it by the Roman authorities. He has now told how its greatest missionary finally reached the capital of the empire, technically a prisoner, but in fact able to continue teaching and preaching

31 **with all boldness and without hindrance**. And he may well have felt that, if he was to leave this momentous achievement clearly impressed upon the minds of his readers, this was the place to end.

LETTERS

The first thirteen letters in the New Testament are, or purport to be, from the correspondence of Paul. They tell us, as letters should, who was the writer and to whom they were written. In Acts, we possess a brief biography of Paul which (as we can see from Paul's own letters) tells us only some of the facts and is not always easy to reconcile with what Paul says himself. But from this biography, and from occasional pieces of information scattered in the letters themselves, we can make a rough outline of Paul's travels and gain some picture of the circumstances which caused him to stay a relatively short time in each of the churches which he founded and to keep in touch with them afterwards by correspondence. In the case of the letters to Corinth, we can be more specific: these letters were written while Paul was in Ephesus between 51 and 54 CE. For the rest, we do not know for certain where and when they were written, beyond the fact that none of them is likely to have been written earlier than 45 or later than 65 (the probable date of Paul's martyrdom in Rome). Nor do we know when and how they were collected and how far, if at all, they were rearranged by a subsequent editor. Some of them may even have been written by his followers after his lifetime. But these questions are relatively unimportant. The essential thing is that we possess in these letters a number of unquestionably authentic documents which bear witness to the first generation of the church's existence.

For the most part the letters were addressed, not to individuals, but to churches, and were probably intended to be read aloud to the assembled congregation. They were all elicited by particular questions which had arisen, and they cannot be fully understood unless an attempt is made to reconstruct the circumstances of the recipients, to understand the arguments which Paul had to refute and to lay bare the unspoken presuppositions which Paul shared with his converts. But the result of such an enquiry is not merely a better understanding of a particular crisis or difficulty in the progress of the early church. It was part of Paul's genius that he saw the wider implications of each problem he was confronted with, and his answer to them often involved an exposition of fundamental perceptions of the Christian faith. The letters are real letters, and the issues they deal with belong to a particular period in the history of the church. Yet they have a depth and generality which have given them an interest far beyond their own time and place; indeed they soon became, and have remained, among the primary documents of the Christian religion.

The character of the remaining letters is somewhat different. The letter to the Hebrews is hardly a 'letter' at all, but a treatise by an unknown writer addressed to an unknown church or group of Christians. The other seven are all (in some sense) 'letters', but, though the name of the writer is usually given, it is true of most of them that we do not know in detail to whom they were written. The letters of John (and indeed the Revelation, part of which is also in the form of letters) are real letters, in that they were clearly addressed to readers or hearers in a particular area, and in each case the author had some personal acquaintance with those to whom he was writing. But the rest, being apparently addressed to almost any Christians who might read them, are 'letters' only in a rather special sense; consequently it has been customary since early times to refer to them as the 'catholic' (meaning 'general') letters. James and 1 Peter may have been what we would now call encyclicals, written from the centre of authority to Christian churches over a wide area; while 2 Peter and Jude are more like 'open letters', that is to say, messages for a wide public dressed up (as was not uncommon for ancient writers) in the form of a letter. With them, we can perhaps see Christian writing beginning to conform with contemporary literary conventions. But for the rest, the LETTERS of the New Testament seem to have given new life and content to the hackneyed conventions of Greek and Jewish letter-writing. Like the gospels, they represent something strikingly new and original in the literature of their time.

THE LETTER OF PAUL TO THE
ROMANS

Romans, like most of the New Testament 'letters', is a real letter, in the sense that it was written to particular people for a particular reason – it is not (as some literary 'letters' were) a treatise or essay dressed up in letter form. It begins and ends with the customary greetings (though Paul always gives these a distinctive Christian content) and refers to matters that were clearly already under discussion. To understand it, we have to make some effort to reconstruct the situation, even though we do not possess the other side of the correspondence and have very limited knowledge (from Acts and from Paul's other letters) of the circumstances which caused Paul to write to a church which he had never yet been able to visit.

But this letter is also more than just a fragment of Paul's correspondence. Romans is the nearest thing we have in the New Testament to a theological treatise (apart perhaps from the letter to the Hebrews); and it is as such that it has been regarded throughout much of the history of the church, providing arguments for the protagonists in some of the most earnest debates which have taken place between churches and between believers. It is the combination of this theological content with Paul's evident concern for the well-being and right belief and conduct of a particular church which gives this letter its unique character among the writings of the New Testament, and for this reason it has always been given pride of place among his letters and placed first in the series, even though it was probably the last of his surviving letters to have been written – probably when he was still in Greece, preparing to go to Jerusalem (Acts 21) around 56 or 57 CE.

Christianity had reached Rome several years before this letter was written. Its adherents were both Jews and Gentiles – Jews had been expelled from Rome under the emperor Claudius but had recently been allowed to return by Nero. Tensions between the two groups can be detected in the letter, and the great questions of law and grace with which it is concerned seem to have arisen mainly because of disputes over Jewish observance and privilege within the (perhaps predominantly gentile) Christian community. But whether or not Paul had been informed about the details of such disputes in communities that he had not yet visited himself, he characteristically does not let the discussion founder among the accusations and counter-accusations of the local parties but raises it to a level where the matters at issue touch the very heart of the Christian faith.

The greeting

A typical Greek letter in the ancient world began: 'From MM . . . to NN, greetings (*chairein*)'. Jewish people had their own variation on this, in that instead of saying 'greetings' they liked to say 'peace' (*shalom*). A combination of the two is found in most of the New Testament letters.

Paul's letters are all real letters, addressed to particular individuals or churches, and they all make use of this conventional formula, even if (as here) they cram a great deal of extra Christian matter into the simple framework. But Paul also makes one very significant change to the formula itself. Instead of 'greetings' (*chairein*) he writes 'grace' (*charis*) – which is almost a pun: the two words are derived from the same Greek stem. This may originally have been a conscious manipulation of a familiar expression to make it yield a rich Christian meaning – a device that Paul was fond of. Whether Paul invented this one, or simply adopted it as an already accepted form of greeting between Christians, we cannot say. In any event, it occurs in the opening of many other New Testament letters.

1.1–7 The whole of the first paragraph – seven verses – forms one long sentence: **Paul . . . To all God's beloved in Rome . . . Grace to you and peace.** But the conventional formula is broken into by a massive parenthesis, sparked

1 off by the word **gospel**, and going on to explain what Paul means by being **an apostle**. The first part of this parenthesis, concerning the 'gospel', has a strikingly solemn ring, and is often thought for this reason to be a fragment of an early Christian confession or creed, inserted by Paul (perhaps with a few personal alterations) into his opening greeting. This confession contains

3 two fundamental propositions about Jesus. **According to the flesh** he was a particular man, a descendant of King David and therefore qualified, at least

4 to this extent, to be the expected Jewish Messiah, or Christ. **According to the spirit of holiness** – that is to say, not as a matter of empirically verifiable fact like his ancestry, but in a manner which presupposed the activity of the Holy Spirit making this reality known to those ready to believe it – **he was declared to be Son of God** when, after the apparent defeat and humiliation of the crucifixion, he was gloriously vindicated **by**[1] **resurrection from the dead.**

5 The second part of the parenthesis relates to Paul himself: **through whom we have received grace and apostleship.** 'Grace' is a word to which Paul attaches a rich load of meaning. There was a word in Hebrew which described the whole of God's gracious dealings with his people. It has no exact Greek or English equivalent: the usual translation is 'mercy'. These 'merciful' dealings had now reached a climax in the story of Jesus Christ, and to describe this transcendentally merciful gift of God, along with all the acts of divine mercy

---

[1] The Greek word translated **by** has more than one meaning. It might also be rendered *after* or *as a result of.*

which had led up to it in the course of the history of the Jewish people, Paul used another Greek word which stressed the free generosity of God: *charis*, of which one of the usual meanings was 'grace' or 'favour'. At the same time, the effect on a believer of this tremendous sign of God's favour was a new power, a new quality of living, a new radiance of personality; and this too could be expressed by the same word *charis*, which also meant 'grace' in the subjective sense of 'graciousness'. All these ideas may be present here in the single word **grace**. **Apostleship** too was a word with considerable resonance. The basic meaning of the word *apostolos* was one 'sent out' on a mission. It was used in Jewish circles for any official or commercial agent, and also for the accredited emissaries of the high priest in Jerusalem. It belonged to the calling of all Christians that they were 'sent out' to preach the gospel; but this was true to a particular degree of that original group of men who had witnessed the resurrection and who had received an explicit commission to undertake the founding of the first Christian communities. Paul, though his calling had been somewhat later and the circumstances of it exceptional, was nevertheless, soon recognized (though apparently not without some opposition) as one of these specially authorized apostles; but what marked off his apostleship from that of the others was that it was **to bring about the obedience of faith among the Gentiles**, which meant (the explosive element in Paul's commission) among non-Jews.

All under judgment

8 **First, I thank my God**. Most of Paul's letters proceed straight from the opening greetings to an expression of thanksgiving for the vitality of the church to which he was writing. The only peculiarity here is that the church at Rome was not one he had founded or for which he had a personal responsibility. He had not yet been to Rome and he had not met the Christians there. His thanks were, in this case, for the good report of their faith – **proclaimed throughout the world**, a pardonable exaggeration in a phrase intended primarily as a compliment; and his prayers for them, and his longing to see them, were a natural expression of his desire to be more closely associated with a Christian community which had sprung up at the centre of the civilized world.

    Nevertheless, Paul evidently felt a certain urgency in addressing himself
13 to the Roman Christians. **I have often intended to come . . . in order that I may reap some harvest among you**. Not that Paul could have added to his own successes by preaching to an already existing Roman church; but he
11 could hope to 'reap some harvest', not only by finding means to **strengthen** them, but by encouraging a greater inclusiveness of membership and settling, once and for all, the problem he had already encountered in his own churches: the relationship and social contacts between Jews and non-Jews
14 within a single Christian community. In this sense he was **a debtor** (that is, under an obligation) to the whole gentile world, **both to Greeks and to**

barbarians – 'barbarians' meaning anyone (from a Greek point of view, which Paul seems to be adopting here to place himself alongside his gentile hearers and readers) whose language and culture were not Greek or Latin. Rome would have held many such foreigners, among whom there would also have been the extremes of **the wise and the foolish**.

The tension between Jewish and gentile Christians, which caused the first great crisis the church had to undergo, was the ostensible occasion of the letter to the Romans and can be overheard in almost every chapter of it. Yet Paul characteristically did not treat this problem on a practical level, as if it were merely a question of how these people were to live together amicably. He saw in it a threat to the central truths of the Christian faith. It could be solved only by an acceptance of the crucial proposition that the gospel was

16 not for a particular race or community but **for everyone who has faith**. But this in turn raised still wider issues. Jewish people might instinctively feel that God had made special promises to their own people: how could Gentiles be admitted to salvation on the same terms without making God seem to be abandoning his promises and becoming 'unrighteous'? To answer this, Paul had to speak, not only of the subjective **faith** of the believer (now equally valid whether in Jew or Greek), but also of the way in which the advent of this

17 new faith had **revealed** something new about God: the true working out of his **righteousness**. The guiding Old Testament text for his argument, which contains the two principal terms in question, was Habakkuk 2.4: **"The one who is righteous will live by faith."**

18 **For the wrath of God is revealed**. This sentence, and the sentence before, both contain the word **revealed**. The new factor introduced by Jesus Christ is one that 'reveals' something which was not understood before. The pos-

17 itive side of this is a new understanding of God's **righteousness:** by virtue of what has been achieved in Jesus it is now possible to see how a righteous God can offer salvation to sinful human beings without impairing his own righteousness. This is the essence of Paul's gospel and is explained more fully later in the letter. But there is also a negative side to this divine righteousness:

18 **the wrath of God**. This phrase, in Paul as in other Jewish writers, is not used as a way of ascribing a human kind of 'anger' to God; it is rather that the evil deeds of human beings necessarily have moral consequences and incur a retribution that is sanctioned by God – 'divine retribution' is another possible translation that is adopted in some modern English versions. In any case, the truth which underlies the phrase is that, if God is righteous, the consequences of unrighteous deeds must necessarily be visited upon the per- petrators. The important point for Paul's argument is that this in fact can be seen to happen. It is not the case (as righteous people have so often despair- ingly concluded) that 'the unrighteous flourish'. Whatever may be the case for individuals, if you look at whole societies you can see only too clearly the consequences of immorality: on that scale, God's 'righteousness' is certainly 'revealed'.

For proof of this, Paul had only to draw on the widely held presuppositions of both Greek philosophy and Jewish religion. It was common ground to both Jewish and Greek thinkers that the prevailing immorality of contemporary society was rooted in a failure to accept a true understanding of the nature of

19 God. The existence of God could hardly be denied – **what can be known about**
21 **God is plain.** Only those who had **senseless minds** could fail to recognize the Creator in his works, and the inevitable consequence of this failure was
28 a **debased mind** which led people to do **things that should not be done** (literally, *that are not fitting,* a phrase made popular by Stoic philosophy). The long list of vices in verses 29–32 has many parallels in the religious and philosophical literature of the ancient world.

So much was common ground – and an immediate source of these ideas for Paul may have been the Wisdom of Solomon, a late Jewish writing much influenced by Greek thought (compare especially Wisdom 13.1, "All people who were ignorant of God were foolish by nature", etc.). But Paul, with his strict Jewish background, instinctively brought still severer criticism to bear on the gentile world. Two features of Greek life particularly shocked the Jews: first, the crude idolatry associated with the innumerable statues of deities – which were not in fact taken too seriously by the majority of educated

23 Greeks, but were regarded with horror by Jewish people as exchanging **the glory of the immortal God for images resembling a mortal human being or birds or fourfooted animals or reptiles** (words deliberately reminiscent of Psalm 106.20, for this primal sin – worshipping a golden calf – had also been committed by the people of Israel); and secondly, the Greeks' acceptance of openly homosexual relationships, which had no counterpart in Jewish culture. These, from the Jewish point of view, were the characteristic vices of the gentile world. Any Gentile who sought association with a synagogue was expected to renounce them. Paul sketches them somewhat luridly; but he is only giving a characteristically Jewish turn to an argument that would have

18 been widely recognized as valid. The consequences of the **wickedness of those who by their wickedness suppress the truth** about the righteousness of God were clearly to be seen in the idolatry and sexual immorality of the pagan world. In this sense, the negative side of God's righteousness was 'revealed'.

2.1 **Therefore you have no excuse, whoever you are.** This sudden turning upon an imaginary conversation partner might have been less of a surprise to Paul's readers than it is to us. It was a well-known technique of philosophers (going back ultimately to Plato) to present their teaching in the form of a dialogue, enlivening it by introducing the cut-and-thrust of debate with an imaginary opponent; and this style of writing (technically known as *diatribe*) might be adopted by anyone trying to present a serious philosophical or religious argument – we have many examples of it in the popular lessons in philosophy given by the Stoic philosopher Epictetus, a near contemporary of Paul. The surprise would have lain rather in the identity of the imagined opponent. At first this opponent might appear to be anyone who tried to take the high moral ground in the face of pagan immorality in order to **judge others**; but given that the whole gentile world has apparently come under the condemnation of the previous paragraph, the only part of humanity left that could claim this independent moral status was the Jewish nation – and that this is indeed the opposition Paul has in mind soon becomes clear. Up to this point Paul would have carried most Jews with him in his argument.

2 When he says, **"we know that God's judgment on those who do such things is in accordance with truth"**, the 'we' clearly denotes those people who would normally believe that they themselves were *not* under this judgment. They would have taken it for granted that wrongdoing inexorably attracts God's punishment – witness the quotation from Proverbs (24.12, an aphorism

6 which occurs often in later Jewish literature), **he will repay according to each one's deeds**. But Jewish people would also have believed that being a Jew gave one a certain superiority in moral and religious matters, even a measure of immunity from this inexorable judgment. Equipped with the divinely given law of Moses (which provided remedies that atoned for the offences which people inevitably commit), and following a divinely ordained way of life that was zealously observed by Jewish communities throughout

1 the world, they felt some justification for **passing judgment** on the rest of the world. Could they not point to their own history, which showed the

4 marks of God's special favour, **the riches of his kindness and forbearance and patience?**

The surprise for them, therefore, would have been to find that they were cast in the rôle of objectors whom Paul (himself a Jew but now also a Christian) proceeds to attack with the same weapons as he has used against the Gentiles. More searching arguments against the presumed privilege and immunity of the Jews will come later in the letter. Paul's manner at this point is rhetorical and sweeping. Jewish history is ambivalent: it can be read in more than one way (**God's kindness** may not be so much a mark of his favour as a warning **meant to lead you to repentance**). The Jews' proud possession of the law has not prevented them from committing exactly the offences they condemn in others. Their own conduct has even been such

24 as to bring their religion into disrepute (**"The name of God is blasphemed**
11 **among the Gentiles because of you"** – a quotation from Isaiah 52.5). **God shows no partiality**, and such conduct can expect no exemptions. The Jews cannot even claim that the law, as a moral standard, is unique to themselves.
14 Its moral principles are instinctively acknowledged by all. Even **Gentiles, who do not possess the law, do instinctively[2] what the law requires.**

Jewish men bore in their body a physical sign of the privileges and immu-
25 nities they believed were theirs: **circumcision**. Without this sign, no man

---

[2] Literally, *by nature*, a phrase which in this context has caused centuries of discussion on the question whether Paul had a 'natural theology' and believed that all human beings have 'by nature' a knowledge of God and of his moral demands.

could qualify for membership of the chosen people of God; with it, no one who observed the divinely given law would be consigned to eternal punishment. Paul, though brought up himself as a strict Jew, had now come to deny that a mere outward rite could have such power. **Circumcision indeed is of value if you obey the law**. So much would have been agreed. No one took circumcision to be a charter for law-breaking. But in so far as it was a symbol of belonging to a race and a community that prided itself on being protected from the consequences of immorality by its code of law, it seemed to give an assurance of being, in principle, on the right side of judgment. "Even if we sin", wrote the author of the Wisdom of Solomon (representing the thought of many Greek-speaking Jews) "we are yours, knowing your power"(15.2). But what if the actual offences of Jewish people were as grave as those of Gentiles? On what grounds could circumcision be expected to provide exemption from the judgment which an impartial God must be expected to pass on *all* law-breaking? Was there not a distinction between 'true Jews'
28, 29 and those who are Jews only **outwardly**? Was there not a **real circumcision** which was a **matter of the heart**, and which was the only ground on which a human being could receive **praise . . . from God**? Such questions had been raised in the past by the prophets. Paul is compelled by 'his gospel' (verse 16) to raise them in a still sharper form.

3.1   **Then what advantage has the Jew?** The 'diatribe' style continues: the imaginary interlocutor now raises a question that troubles the argument throughout Romans. It is a question that touches Paul personally, and the extent of the trouble it causes him can be seen in the two answers he gives to it in quick succession. **What advantage has the Jew?** In verse 2 the answer is,
2, 9   **Much, in every way**. But in verse 9 we have the opposite: **Are we any better off? No, not at all**. It seems impossible to clear Paul of some inconsistency.[3] Nevertheless, these verses dispose of some too-easy solutions to the problem.
2 The Jews, after all, have the law of Moses (**the oracles of God**), which is a definitive revelation of the justice and faithfulness of God. Of course it has not always been kept. Perhaps it never could be. But this is no reason for tearing it up and starting again with the gospel. The law cannot be cancelled without impugning the very justice and faithfulness of God. No amount of human sinfulness, no apparently contrary events in human history, can affect the truth of God's word or the eternal validity of his commandments. It is always human beings who are in the wrong, not God. If God were, as it were,
4 put on trial, so that he had to be **proved true**, even confronted with the reality of a deep sinfulness throughout his creation he would still be **justified**, that is, proved just, vindicated as entirely consistent with his own standards of justice. (The quotation is from Psalm 51.4.)

---

[3] The punctuation of verse 9 is uncertain and there is more than one possible meaning (see the NRSV footnote). It is also possible to translate *not altogether* instead of **not at all**. But the apparent inconsistency belongs to the whole context.

The law, then, retains its validity; and the Jews have both the privilege and the responsibility of access to this special revelation of the will of God for human beings. No amount of failures on their part can invalidate the advantage which this gives them. But again, this advantage gives them no

9 security – in respect of God's judgment they are no **better off**. Scripture itself
19 (which Paul can refer to as **whatever the law says**, though what he has given us is in fact a cento of quotations mainly from the psalms[4]) shows that **the whole world** (that is, Jews no less than Gentiles) **may be held accountable to God**. Of course there is advantage in knowing how God wills his human creatures to conduct themselves. But the effect of this, for Jews as well as

20 Gentiles, is **the knowledge of sin**. The defence that one has done **the deeds prescribed by the law** carries no weight on its own. Human beings remain essentially unrighteous in the sight of God. The problem for Jews is just as acute as for the rest of humankind. It may be summed up in the question: how is it possible for those who are justly condemned for their offences to have any continuing relationship with a perfectly just God?

The righteousness of faith

21 **But now**. There is now – this is Paul's 'gospel', the 'good news' he has to impart – a new answer, a new factor in the relationship between God and his human creatures, which is **apart from law**, and yet (as will be shown in the next chapter) consistent with the scriptures, **attested by the law and the**

22 **prophets**. The **righteousness of God** – which in Hebrew thought is more than 'justice': it is the just and yet faithful and compassionate way in which God maintains his unbreakable relationship with his people – **has been disclosed** by the creation of a new human possibility. God remains just; but a function of his justice is that he now has the means to give us, despite our sin, the possibility of restoring our relationship with him.

How has this happened? The short answer is: **through faith in Jesus Christ for all who believe**.[5] That is to say, what determines God's relationship with human beings is no longer a code of law, with its attendant system of penalties and sacrifices to atone for transgressions, but **faith in Jesus Christ**, a new human response to God made possible by the gospel. This, as we shall see, has its own ethical consequences (a standard of behaviour equivalent to the law) and its own assurance that offences can be remitted. But for the purpose of the present argument (which is what the whole of the first three chapters

---

[4] See above, p. 2, on this sense of the term 'law'. The texts quoted here are Psalms 14.1–3; 53.2–4; 5.9; 140.3; Isaiah 59.7–8.

[5] An alternative translation, *through the faith of Jesus Christ*, is grammatically possible, as it is in a number of other instances of the same phrase in Paul. The meaning would then be that it was Christ's faith, or faithfulness, in undergoing the crucifixion which created the new situation, rather than the faith of those who believe. But the sense here runs more easily if it is the believer's 'faith' which is in question.

have been leading up to), the really significant thing about it is that it does not depend on membership of the Jewish race and the observance of the norms of Jewish community life: it is **for all who believe**.

The sentences that follow contain a summary of this new set of beliefs, briefly expressed with the help of some technical religious terms. These terms are introduced as if they are already familiar to Paul's readers, and serve to sum up truths with which they are already familiar – it is the kind of summary, in fact, which may well have been already used in their worship, and may here be being quoted or adapted by Paul. Its implications will be worked out in chapters 5 to 8 of the letter. Meanwhile, by way of a kind of theological shorthand, three expressions are used which are rich in metaphorical resonance:

24   (i) It was **through the redemption** – a word which evoked the act of God by which his people had been liberated from the bondage in Egypt, like slaves being 'redeemed' by a payment to their masters (only in this case there was no payment!). Sinners are similarly 'redeemed' from the slavery which their sins lay upon them.

25   (ii) It was achieved by Christ's being **put forward as a sacrifice for atonement**. In the Jewish legal system, ritual offences could be atoned for by offering an animal sacrifice. On the Day of Atonement a sacrifice was offered for the whole nation in the Holy of Holies itself on the lid of the Ark of the Covenant, the 'mercy seat' (which is one of the meanings of the technical word *hilastērion* that is used here – see the NRSV footnote). This whole sacrificial system had now been superseded by the 'sacrifice' of Christ: his **blood** – that is to say, his death – was now the effective means[6] of forgiveness to which the old sacrificial system had pointed forward; and this forgiveness was not now obtained by carrying out the correct ritual sacrifice, but was **effective through faith**.

(iii) God had **passed over** the sins previously committed. The word used here does not occur anywhere else in Paul's letters (or indeed, in the New Testament) – another sign, perhaps, that Paul is quoting an early Christian formula. The existing sacrificial system allowed for no such 'passing over': every offence must be answered for by paying a penalty, and a general remission for all members of the Jewish people depended on the correct performance of the annual ritual of the Day of Atonement. Christ's sacrificial death had now replaced this ritual, and its effect was to create the possibility of a new relationship with God, for those outside as well as those inside the Jewish nation.

All of this has profound consequences for Christian life and faith, and these will be worked out later. But here the purpose of reciting these new factors in God's relationship with human beings is quite specific: it is to show that

---

[6] The familiar translation, *by faith in his blood*, is grammatically possible but is less likely to be correct.

God **did this to show his righteousness.** The real subject here is 'theodicy': the question is about God, not about us. How can God be 'righteous' – faithful, just and compassionate in his relationship with human beings – and at the same time deal 'righteously' with their sinfulness? The answer is by introducing a new criterion, a new standard for exercising judgment: no longer the law as a code of commandments and a system for atoning, but a 'law of faith', with a new code of conduct that comprises and indeed exceeds the old law, and with the assurance of forgiveness, of being 'justified', **by his grace as a gift.**

24

27   **Then what becomes of boasting?** A Jewish person has already been described earlier as one who 'boasts in the law' (2.23). Paul's reasoning has led to the conclusion that all such boasting **is excluded**; but he still has one more argument to bring forward. **God is one** – this was a proposition recited every day by Jews in their prayers. It was the distinctive affirmation of the Jewish faith, one of the very few truly monotheistic faiths known to the ancient world. But even for Jews this affirmation was not without its difficulties. When they thought of God, they thought of him as the God of Israel, the God of their fathers. He was the God who had a special relationship with the Jewish people, a relationship that had been demonstrated again and again in the course of biblical history. But if he was the one and only God, it could not be the case that he was **the God of Jews only**. He was the creator of all humanity, and therefore he must be in some sense **the God of Gentiles also**. This was where the difficulties began; for it seemed obvious to Jewish thinkers that the Gentiles neither acknowledged the one true God nor received from him the gracious treatment he bestowed upon the Jews. In what sense, then, was he the God of the Gentiles? The question was embarrassing, and received a variety of answers. But on Paul's premises it was perfectly simple. Once it was recognized that the Jews could appeal to no special relationship with God, there was no difficulty in seeing how God could be the God of Jews and Gentiles alike. For both, the only possible relationship with God (their 'justification') was established **on the ground of faith** (or, by a very slight change of phrase which appears to be no more than a matter of style, **through that same faith**). And this 'faith' was not merely a subjective attitude towards God, but a system of belief which included an assurance of forgiveness and an exalted standard of ethical behaviour. It included, in fact, all that – and more than – the law had ever offered. Hence it was not in opposition to the law, as if to **overthrow** it, but it 'upheld' the law by giving it a new basis. It could be called **the law of faith**.

30

29

30

31

27

4.1   **What then are we to say was gained by Abraham?** We know that the shocked reaction of Jewish people to any suggestion that they had no privilege in the sight of God was, "We have Abraham as our ancestor" (Matthew 3.9; compare John 8.33). Instinctively, they would introduce into the argument their physical descent from Abraham. The figure of Abraham was the foundation of all Jewish thinking about their nation. To Abraham, and through Abraham to his descendants, God had given a promise in the form of a 'covenant': if those who were the 'children of Abraham' kept their side of the covenant (that is, observed God's law), they could look forward to the 'inheritance' which had been promised from the beginning to the Jewish people. This 'advantage' of the Jews was axiomatic; the story of Abraham guaranteed it. And Paul, himself physically a 'child of Abraham' (**our ancestor according to the flesh**) now turns to answer this inevitable Jewish protest.

To demonstrate an inherent superiority to any Gentile a Jew had only to quote from Genesis, chapters 15 and 17. These chapters showed how Abraham had received a blessing (15.5–6; 17.7–8), and proved that this blessing would pass to all his descendants on condition that they were duly circumcised (17.10–14). Why had Abraham received this signal blessing? Subsequent Jewish interpretation took the line that it was because Abraham had spontaneously carried out all the precepts of the law (even though these were written down only in the time of Moses, many generations later), and that, to receive the blessing in full, his descendants must do the same. And 'descendants' was understood quite literally. The strictest schools of Jewish thought admitted only physical descendants, to the exclusion of all non-Jews. A more liberal school conceded that Gentiles, by becoming proselytes, might also have a share in the blessing; in which case the fact that Abraham himself was circumcised so late in life was taken as a sign that he was in some sense 'the father' of all those who, like him, observed the whole law, even if they were gentile converts and were themselves circumcised only late in life.

It was this second view which Paul, as a Jew, probably once held himself; but he now develops it in a highly original way. He starts from a text taken 3 from the same chapters of Genesis, **"Abraham believed God, and it was reckoned to him as righteousness"** (15.6). But his interpretation is quite different from the usual Jewish one. He concentrates attention on the single expression, "**reckoned to**". This, he argues, would not be an appropriate word for the payment of wages that had been earned or of a reward that had been deserved. True, the verb itself, in Greek as well as in English, does not settle the matter. But it was a recognized technique among Jewish scholars to determine the meaning of a word in one place in scripture by reference 6 to its meaning in another place. So here: Paul quotes Psalm 32.1–2 (**'David'** 8 is assumed to be the author of all the psalms), **"blessed is the one against whom the Lord will not reckon sin"**. In this text[7] the word 'reckon' cannot mean 'pay as a reward for certain acts'. The subject is a sinner, and yet he is **blessed**. What must have happened is that God, instead of 'reckoning sins against him' (which would be 'reckoned' in the sense of adding up for the sake

---

[7] The meaning is clearer in the Greek, which may be literally translated *whose sin the Lord does not reckon.*

4 of awarding a penalty), counted to him **as a gift** a blessedness which he had not earned by any deeds of his own. And this gives the sense of 'reckoned' in the Genesis passage. Abraham had not done anything to deserve his attribute of righteousness: God had simply 'reckoned him' as righteous in response to

5 his **faith**. The conclusion drawn from this passage by Paul is thus the exact opposite of that which was usually drawn by Jewish interpreters. It was not Abraham's acts of obedience, but only his faith, which made him the great prototype of all whom God 'counts' as righteous.

Secondly, Paul attacks the idea that it is necessary to be a physical descendant of Abraham, or even a circumcised proselyte, to have Abraham as one's 'father'. Abraham's fatherhood must be understood (as some Jews already partly recognized) not literally but metaphorically: he is the prototype of a

11 particular kind of relationship with God, he is **the ancestor of all who believe**. This gives the key to a passage that had always given trouble to Jewish expos-

17 itors (Genesis 17.5): **"I have made you the father of many nations"**. So long

1 as 'fatherhood' was understood literally (**according to the flesh**), this was bound to be a puzzling verse: at most it could be taken to indicate a gracious extension of 'descent' to those Gentiles who became proselytes and received circumcision – that is, who followed Abraham in keeping the whole law. But if this 'keeping the law' was the criterion, there would be no advantage in

15 having Abraham as father; for, as has been shown already, **the law brings**

14 **wrath** (or retribution). The fact that everyone breaks the law prevents **the adherents of the law** from being **heirs**; indeed, they have the same status as everyone else: the only difference for the Gentiles is that, having no law, they cannot even recognize their transgressions as a **violation** of the law. No, having Abraham as 'father' is of use only if the fatherhood is understood

11 metaphorically. He is **the ancestor** (the same word as 'father' in the Greek) **of all who believe ... and who thus have righteousness reckoned to them**. Indeed, it is arguable that Abraham's decisive act of faith took place **before he was circumcised** precisely in order to demonstrate that he was the prototype for all, circumcised and uncircumcised alike.

Abraham's 'faith' can be more sharply defined: it was faith in the power of God to bring about a specific and seemingly impossible event, the birth of a son in old age to Abraham and his wife Sarah (Genesis 15–18). The God in whom we must have faith is a God who does the seemingly impossible.

17 He **gives life to the dead** (as in the resurrection of Christ) and he **calls into existence the things that do not exist** (as at the creation). Abraham's true 'descendants' are those who have faith in a miraculous act: in God

24 having **raised Jesus our Lord from the dead**. The significance of this act is encapsulated in a formula which may have already been in use when Paul

25 wrote: he was **handed over to death for our trespasses** (an allusion to Isaiah 53.12) **and was raised for our justification** (which, in effect, is the subject of the next chapters).

The new Adam

5.1 **Therefore, since we are justified by faith.** So far the argument has moved on a theoretical plane. Paul's agenda has been theological: to show how it is possible to hold two apparently incompatible beliefs: (i) that God is 'righteous', and (ii) that a relationship with this righteous God – 'justification' – is possible for inherently unrighteous human beings, even though "there is no one who is righteous, not even one" (3.10). Moreover, – and this is the cutting edge of the argument – this relationship is available to all, not just to members of the Jewish race. Paul's gospel is a newly revealed solution to this paradox: "now . . . the righteousness of God has been disclosed" (3.21).

But at this point Paul passes from theological implications to practical
2 consequences. The new relationship with God – **this grace in which we stand** – brings with it a new range of moral and spiritual resources, giving us grounds for confidence (enabling us to '**boast**'), and rhetorically listed by Paul as a kind of chain reaction starting with suffering and ending with hope; and its reality is guaranteed by an experience which is evidently shared by
5 all the churches to which Paul writes: that of **the Holy Spirit that has been given to us.**

How has Christ's death and resurrection procured such tremendous consequences for Christians? This act of God in Christ may perhaps be understood
6 as comprising two stages. One stage is already completed: **Christ died for the ungodly.** That one man's death could have consequences of this order was not an unintelligible idea. Innocent and pious men had been martyred for their faith in Jewish history, particularly during the Maccabean wars in the early second century BCE, and Jewish thinkers had begun to interpret their deaths as a vicarious sacrifice. These exceptional acts of heroic endurance and death could be understood as being in some sense 'for others'. But these 'others' – the beneficiaries, so to speak, of such sacrificial deaths – were always thought of as the righteous people of God; and these righteous people, who by their own piety were trying to hasten the coming of the kingdom of God, felt assisted in their efforts by the heroism of certain of their forerunners, which (they believed) would predispose God to act in favour of his people as a whole. In this sense there had been some examples in Jewish history of
7 the proposition that **perhaps for a good person someone might actually dare to die.** But Paul's argument has shown that there are no 'good persons'. Christ's sacrificial death for others cannot be explained as an act of heroic piety enhancing the general piety of others. It is entirely *sui generis*, it is
6, 8 not for the good but for **the ungodly**, for those who **still were sinners.** The only possible explanation for it is that it is an act by which **God proves his love for us.** But if this is the true explanation, and if God has indeed shown
10 such love towards us, it follows that we have now been **reconciled** to God – Paul introduces a new word in place of the more judicial or forensic concept

11 of being 'justified'. Moreover, we can now **even boast in God** – a word expressing pride and confidence: we can now be sure that God, instead of being inexorably severe to us in judgment, will be "for us" (8.31). All this has been effected by Christ's sacrificial death. It now belongs to the past; it is the first stage of God's act in Christ.

But this first stage is immediately followed by a second, which is not past but present, and which involves our response to what has been done for us. 10 After having been reconciled by Christ's death, we shall **be saved by his life** – a continuing process which transforms the life of the believer. More will be said about this second stage in what follows. The important point for the present is that these stages cannot be separated.

To return to the first stage: Paul offers an interpretation of Christ's death in terms of the story of Adam. Today's reader may ask: Did he think of this story as history or as myth? But this is probably an inappropriate question. Jewish people of his time would not have doubted for a moment that the opening chapters of Genesis contain a true record of creation; on the other hand, they would not have had the modern preoccupation to check historical records against 'facts'; they would have been more interested in the meaning of the story than in its 'historicity'. Moreover, a general, almost mythological, significance was already built into the story, in that in Hebrew the name Adam means 'human being'; and so one finds, in Jewish literature of about the same period as Paul, generalized and almost psychological interpretations of the story, such as this one from the book known as 2 Baruch: 'Each of us has become our own Adam.'

Paul's use of the story shows the same ambivalence. It is both a universal 12 parable and a particular moment in history. It is universal, in that **sin came into the world through one man**; for the main current of Jewish teaching was not that Adam's physical nature had been changed after his disobedience, so that his descendants literally inherited from him a body subject to sin and death (though it is of course possible that Paul believed something of the kind, and the slightly ambiguous language of verse 12[8] has given rise to severe doctrines of 'original sin'), but that in Adam could be seen the primal representative Man whose sin was the sin of all humanity. To this extent Adam was a timeless and universal figure. But he was also a particular man of a particular time. He represented a particular moment, as it were, in human history. Adam's sin was the first sin: the sin of disobedience. It was only later that the law of Moses was given as a kind of paradigm of all possible forms of 20 disobedience (**law came in, with the result that the trespass multiplied**). The function of the law was to mark the next stage in human history by breaking down the sin of Adam into all its possible varieties. But Paul wishes to set 'sin'

---

[8] The phrase translated **because all have sinned** can bear the meaning *in whom all have sinned*; and this has given rise to the doctrine that human sinfulness is the direct result of the 'original sin' of Adam, and even that we all bear a measure of *guilt* for it.

in a wider context than that of actions prohibited by the Jewish law. He goes back to the first moment, the master sin of Adam. Even in the early period
14 **from Adam to Moses,** when the law had not yet 'come in' (a word which in Greek suggests a secondary intrusion: Paul probably uses it to relegate the law to a subordinate place in the sweep of his universal anthropology), all human beings were already the successors of Adam in the sense that their lives were conditioned by sin (whatever its precise form) and terminated by death.

But the function of Adam in Paul's argument is not so much to account for sin (for there would have been nothing new in this for most of his readers) as to explain Christ. If the Adam of Genesis represents every sinner, he may also be **a type of the one who was to come** and who would represent the new humanity which God has now 'justified' despite its sin. This usage seems to lean towards the universal Adam of myth; but the 'new Adam' is Christ,
15 and Christ is in no sense mythical: he is a particular person, **the one man, Jesus Christ.** And so, when the parallel between Adam and Christ is being worked out, Adam too is treated, like Christ, as a particular historical figure,
18 so that **one man's trespass** (Adam's sin) can be compared with **one man's act of righteousness** (Christ's willing death, which leads to **justification and life for all**). So particular are the two events that a kind of arithmetical comparison is possible, showing the immense excess of God's grace which was needed to balance the equation.

And yet the whole force of this somewhat technical excursus lies not in its inferences from two particular figures of history but in its universal application. 'Adam' is humanity – all of us. The condemnation of Adam resulted in his death. Because of the solidarity of the whole of humanity with Adam –
14 Adam is all of us – **death exercised dominion,** we are all mortal. But the new Adam, **the one who was to come,** is related to us in the same way. Christians have the same solidarity with Christ as human beings in general have with
18 Adam. With Christ they receive **justification** and new **life,** instead of continuing sin and death. The way this solidarity is achieved and appropriated is the subject of the next chapter.

If, to this extent, we may understand the act of God in Christ in two stages, we may say that the first is already completed and consists of the historical events of Christ's death and resurrection, and that the second follows from his continuing activity among his people. To concentrate on the first of these stages at the expense of the second is to open the way to a serious misunderstanding. It is to suggest that the new relationship with God which is acquired through faith in Christ lays no moral obligations on believers: they will be 'justified' whatever they do; indeed, that the more they sin the more striking a demonstration this will give of the 'righteousness' of God who, despite everything, 'justifies' them. It seems to lead to the shocking
6.1 conclusion that a Christian should **continue in sin in order that grace may abound.**

The moral struggle and the law

The charge that Paul's preaching was libertarian, and simply did away with the old moral restraints without providing any new ones, seems often to have been made in his lifetime; and indeed it is arguable that he laid himself open to it. He appeared to make the observance of the laws governing the life of a Jewish community of no account for Christians, and yet not to put any new moral code in their place. It is true that his letters contain substantial sections devoted specifically to moral instruction; but even so, the emphasis is primarily upon the reality of a Christian's new relationship with God, the freedom of the Christian life, and the fact that God's grace is given freely, not in reward for conduct or actions of a particular kind but solely in response to a believer's faith. It is easy to see how such preaching could have been misconstrued, and how Paul could have been accused of encouraging Christians to **continue in sin**.

Paul here answers the charge. He has already tried to show that he is not disputing the importance of the law ("we uphold the law", 3.31), and in any case the Christians have a moral code of their own. But the real answer lies in the fact that it is impossible to separate the two stages of salvation, the

3 historical fact of 'justification' and its present consequences. **Do you not know**, Paul asks (which suggests that they may never before have thought of their baptism in quite this way), **that all of us who have been baptized into Christ Jesus were baptized into his death?** Being 'baptized' into Christ may have been, in part, a powerful metaphor: it meant taking up his cross and sharing his suffering. But there was also an obvious symbolism in the rite itself. Baptism involved complete immersion: new converts stepped down into a river or pool and the water closed for a moment over their heads. It

8 was a ritual death: they **died with Christ**. This was the first stage of salvation. But of course you could not stop there! The convert did not remain under the water to drown, any more than Christ remained in the tomb. A second stage

5 followed: **if we have been united with him in a death like his, we will certainly be united with him in a resurrection like his**. For us, this resurrection lies in the future; but the certainty of it transforms life in the present. The newly

4 baptized emerge from the water in order that they may **walk in newness of life**. The second stage of salvation is present and continuing: it involves a new

10 unity with Christ, who **lives to God**. And this unity with Christ lays a new ethical foundation for life here and now.

2 In which case it makes no sense to think of committing sin. **How can we who died to sin go on living in it?** Today we might express this change by saying that conversion is a matter of moral transformation: the convert is psychologically different, and the former sinful way of life no longer holds any attraction. But to a person of Paul's background a psychological analysis of this kind would not have seemed to do justice to the seriousness of our moral predicament. Paul, like many philosophers since Aristotle, recognized

an irrational element in the human make-up which leads us to do wrong even when we clearly see what is right and are determined, in principle, to adhere to it. To do justice to this irrational element in terms of moral philosophy or of simple psychology is not easy; and many of Paul's contemporaries saw the issue, not as a matter of the moral or psychological nature of the individual, but as a struggle played out between objective forces of good and evil, fighting for control of our will. To put it crudely, it was as if we sin, not through some irrational propensity of our own, but because of some external force working upon us that we are not strong enough to withstand.

Exactly how this struggle was thought of varied from one culture to another, and even among the Jews there were different views. One school of thought imagined two conflicting impulses within us; another represented human beings as subject to alien forces, a good and a bad 'spirit'. But all these approaches to the problem of moral failure had in common a tendency to personify moral concepts and to think in terms, not of habits and dispositions, but of objective powers to which the human will is subject. There are

9 clear examples of this in the present passage. That Christ **will never die again** may be taken as a literal statement of fact. But the same thing can also be stated in terms of personified realities: **death no longer has dominion over him**. Here the point could be brought out by writing 'death' with a capital letter. To say that we shall die is doubtless equivalent to saying that we are 'under the dominion of death'; but the second formulation implies that there is a personified power, Death, that holds us in subjection. Similarly with sin.

6 'Sin' means a certain form of intention or action. To be **'enslaved to sin'** may be no more than a metaphor: certain kinds of conduct, if they become

12 habitual, can 'enslave' us. But a sentence like **do not let sin exercise dominion in your mortal bodies, to make you obey their passions** is more than metaphorical: 'sin' has become personified. It is an objective force working upon the will of the individual. It too could be spelt with a capital letter: Sin.

This tendency to think in terms of personified forces influencing our moral conduct explains some of the language in which Paul expresses the consequences of Christ's death and our participation in that death. By virtue of our unity with Christ, who literally 'died', there is a sense in which we

6 'die' also. Physically we are still alive, but we can say that **our old self was crucified with him**; and this 'death' transforms our relationship with sin. It

7 was a commonplace in Jewish thinking that **whoever has died is freed from sin**. Imagine 'sin' in a law court, demanding his due: once a person is dead and is no longer there to answer in court, sin gets no redress. Or think of death as the penalty of sin: once this penalty is paid, sin can demand nothing more. Either way, sin loses its power over human beings at the moment of their death; and if there is a sense in which Christians have 'died' with Christ,

11 they can now be said to be **dead to sin** and liberated from its power.

To put it another way – a way that brings us closer to the conclusion that

1 it is absurd to imagine that a Christian can **continue in sin**. Imagine sin,

12 not as a claimant in a law court, but as a king over the **mortal bodies** of
16 human beings, as a master to whom we are all **slaves**. Once again death –
the 'death' which we have undergone in unity with Christ – liberates us
from this master, this king. The way in which sin exercised this mastery was
through the law; now that slavery to sin has been brought to an end, the
law becomes irrelevant. But this was exactly the point being made by Paul's
critics. If there was no law, what was there to control conduct? The answer
lay in a consistent application of the same analysis of moral conduct in terms
of external influences bearing upon us. We are not morally autonomous.
13 Our bodies are **instruments** of whatever power is in control. If sin loses its
mastery, some other power must take its place. For Christians there could
be no doubt what this power would be: **present your members to God as
instruments of righteousness.**

To a Jew, 'presenting oneself to God' normally meant only one thing: a
determination to obey the law in its entirety. But Paul has been arguing that
the law is an expression of the mastery of sin. Therefore Christians must
have some other means by which to fashion their conduct so that it accords
with God's will and with the standards of their new life. Indeed, they have a
moral code of their own. Paul seems to be referring to such a code when he
17 mentions a **form of teaching to which you were entrusted**. Precisely what it
consisted of at this date we do not know. Presumably it was based partly on
explicit moral teaching of Jesus and partly on existing moral standards. But
it must certainly have been sufficiently specific and comprehensive to refute
the charge that Christians, because they no longer observed the Jewish law,
19 were continuing to live a life of **impurity** and **greater and greater iniquity**.
By obeying this new form of teaching, they could acknowledge the control
19 of God in their lives and bring their **members** to a degree of **sanctification**
which would refute any charge of what, from the point of view of the Jewish
moral code, might be described by the metaphor of **impurity**.

It follows, then, from this analysis of moral conduct, that the act of God
in Christ cannot consist merely in liberation from the mastery of sin. That
stage involves another. The mastery of sin gives place to a new mastery. A
crude way of stating it would be that one has been freed from one slavery
only in order to enter another. But then (it could be said by an objector), at
20 least **when you were slaves of sin, you were free in regard to righteousness**.
What was the advantage of being freed from one if it meant being bound to
another? The answer is obvious. It lay in the rewards attached to each: in the
21, 23 one case **death**, in the other **eternal life**.
5 Unity with Christ, not only **in a death like his**, but **in a resurrection like
his** – this is the mechanism by which we achieve the status of 'righteous' before
God; this is the process which, since it embraces the two stages of salvation,
13 enables us to present ourselves to God **as those who have been brought from
death to life**, and our members to him **as instruments of righteousness**.
This is Paul's answer to those who accuse him of excusing Christians from

observance of the law and of any comparable moral standards. Through unity
22 with Christ we are **freed from sin**; but we are also **enslaved to God**.

Paul adds a further illustration of the way in which the death of Christ may
be understood to entail our liberation. It is addressed specifically to those
7.1 **who know the law** – in this case clearly those who are familiar with Jewish
matrimonial law (since Roman law was more permissive). A wife's legal duty
to her husband was terminated by her husband's death. This was normally
the only way (other than by a divorce initiated by the husband) in which
a Jewish woman could become free to contemplate marriage with another
3 man; otherwise she would be **called an adulteress**. Similarly, one's duty to
observe the law was terminated by one's own death (this was a familiar Jewish
cliché). Now a Christian, through being identified with Christ's death, has
4 (in a sense) 'died'. Not only this, but that 'death', having been **through the
body of Christ**, has the same consequence for the Christian as the husband's
death has for a wife: it enables us to **belong to another**, in this case **to him
who has been raised from the dead**; and at the same time all obligation to a
previous law has been terminated. In each case a death is necessary, and the
result of that death is both the end of an obligation and the beginning of a
new relationship – this, at least, is the main point of comparison: if applied
strictly, Paul's example (in which it is not the dead husband but the wife who
is liberated) clearly does not work out in all its details.

But this illustration raises once again the awkward question (which recurs
throughout the letter) of the continuing validity of the law. It was said earlier
that we "died to sin" (6.2). It is said now that we have **died to the law**. Does this
7 mean that **the law is sin**? Paul has already had to make good the claims of the
Mosaic law to be an authentic revelation of the justice of God (chapter 3).
He now has to clarify the connection between law and sin, lest his argument
should seem to lead him to the paradoxical conclusion that the law given by
God has been wholly harmful in its effects and has now been made obsolete.

That there is a connection between law and sin is admitted. Sinful passions
5, 7 are **aroused by the law**, in that **if it had not been for the law, I would not
have known sin**. For example – and two views are possible about what Paul's
example consists of. One view is that he is referring to his own boyhood: the
full obligations of the law were not laid on a Jewish boy until he was thirteen
9 years of age. '**I was once**' would then refer to those early years in which the law
did not have to be fully observed. To that extent it could perhaps be said that
a young boy **was alive**, and that when he became an adult fully accountable
10 to the law he (in a sense) **died**. But this explanation is somewhat forced.
The other view, which seems more probable, is that the example depends,
once again, on the figure of Adam (who was everyone, and so 'I'). Between
9 Adam and Moses there was a stage when the law did not yet exist (**I was once
7 alive apart from the law**). But the subsequent commandment, **"You shall
not covet"**, had in fact already been given to Adam in the particular form,
"You shall not eat of the fruit of the tree" (Genesis 3.3). Adam's reaction to

8 this commandment (and so 'my' reaction) was **all kinds of covetousness**. Thus sin (now personified), **seizing an opportunity in the commandment, deceived me** (an evident allusion to the serpent in Genesis 3.13: 'me' is again Adam). Sin, therefore, is not itself law; but law gives the opportunity to sin. Thus Paul can still maintain that the law is good and permanent. It was sin that caused 'my' death: the law, represented in the Adam story by the particular commandment not to eat of the tree, and then by the more

12 general commandment against covetousness, is **holy and just and good**.

    The tendency to personify sin, which was already apparent in the previous

17 chapter, now becomes explicit: **it is no longer I that do it, but sin that dwells within me**. Sin has become an independent source of action, an *alter ego* in conflict with my true self, and the next few verses passionately portray the symptoms of moral struggle in terms which are as comprehensible to modern psychology as they were to both Jews and Greeks in the ancient world. The only difference is that the root cause of the struggle is identified as a demonic entity named 'sin'.

    This sudden essay in psychology is not entirely unprepared. It follows upon a distinction, alluded to already in this chapter and worked out more fully in the next, which came naturally to Jewish thinkers; the distinction between 'flesh' and 'spirit'. This distinction was not a way of dividing up human beings into their component parts (like 'body' and 'soul'), but of distinguishing the motives, conduct and ambitions of which they are capable. 'Flesh' covers the whole range of human conduct which is governed by merely selfish motives. Its propensities may be grossly sensual (such as fornication) or subtly emotional and intellectual (such as idolatry and party intrigues: see the list in Galatians 5.19–21). It is that part of our nature that is directed towards all that is purely human and is in no way open to the influence of God. 'Spirit', on the other hand, is that which enables us to respond to the commands and initiatives of God. These two terms are distinct, but they are not themselves in conflict. They merely define the area in which a conflict might take place. Paul has to go further than this to identify the protagonists in the struggle which he experiences within himself. On the one side, he

8.4 suggests, is the 'I' which can enter the new life of **the Spirit**, that is, which has responded, however imperfectly, to the promptings of God. On the other is the power which seems so often to gain control of the rest of my nature (my

2 'flesh'): the power of **sin**.

    All this is characteristically Jewish psychology. Paul goes a little way towards translating it into terms which a Greek reader would find easier to understand.

7.22 He allows that a person's 'spirit' is roughly equivalent to the **inmost self**, and that the word 'law' also means 'principle'. In these terms the conflict is one

23 between two principles or 'laws', one of which is **of my mind** – some might call it 'reason' – the other which **dwells in my members**. To this extent the conflict can be expressed in concepts familiar to Greek-speaking readers, as between the reasoning power of the mind and the unreasonable impulses of

the body. But Paul does not linger in this terminology; for the Jewish way of expressing it is essential when it comes to understanding the rôle of the Spirit of God in the next chapter.

It seems to follow from the whole run of the chapter that Paul here uses the first person as a way of describing the human condition: 'I' is everyone. But there can be little doubt that Paul is also writing from experience. Everyone's struggle is Paul's own struggle. It has often been felt that this creates a difficulty. The analysis (it is said) is appropriate enough in general, but surely not to a Christian enjoying the new freedom that has been obtained through Christ. If Paul is offering us autobiography, it must surely belong to his experience before his conversion; he would describe his present state quite differently. The difficulty is to reconcile this view with the last sentence of the chapter, in which, after giving thanks to God for his rescue from **this body of death**, he still describes himself as **a slave to the law of sin**; and critics have even been led to suggest that this sentence must have been displaced in the manuscripts from its correct position a few lines higher. But this is an arbitrary solution. It is better to recognize (for it is consistent with Christian experience as well as with Paul's argument) that a continuing moral conflict is a part even of the liberated life of a Christian. Paul had reason to utter the warning, "do not let sin exercise dominion in your mortal bodies" (6.12). The liberation is not yet complete; the Christians' experience of a new quality of living is but a foretaste of a new form of existence altogether which they will experience only at the resurrection. Meanwhile the realities of human psychology and the sins of the 'flesh' have not changed. What *has* changed is the consequence of this general sinfulness: no longer slavery to law leading to God's condemnation, but a new relationship with God, a new 'righteousness', a complete 'justification'. And this change is momentous enough to warrant the exclamation, **Thanks be to God through Jesus Christ our Lord!**

Life in the Spirit

8.1 **Therefore now.** These two words mark the point which the argument has reached: it can now be taken as agreed that there is **no condemnation for those who are in Christ Jesus**. The fact is established; but how is it to be understood? So far, two interpretations have been offered, one drawn from the biblical story of creation (our solidarity with Adam is superseded by our solidarity with Christ, chapter 5), and one from the symbolism of baptism ('dying' to sin with Christ in order to begin a new life with him, chapter 6). A third interpretation is now offered on the basis of the distinction that has just been alluded to between 'spirit' and 'flesh'.

2　　**For the law of the Spirit of life in Christ Jesus has set you free from the law of sin and death.** Paul has just been arguing for the continuing validity and sanctity of the law: how can it suddenly have become something from which we have to be liberated, **the law of sin and death**? It is true that

the word 'law' can also mean 'principle', so that we have to be on our guard
before assuming that Paul is referring to the Jewish law every time he uses the
word. But in this paragraph it seems that the 'law', being almost personified
3 (**weakened by the flesh**, and so forth), stands consistently for the Jewish
system of commandments and atoning sacrifices; in which case we have to
2 ask how this same law can somehow be understood as **both the law of the
Spirit of life and the law of sin and death.** To which the answer seems to
be that the same law has two quite different manifestations according to the
motivation and quality of the way of life of those who observe it. A code
4 of law in itself is a dead thing. It comes alive only when it is **fulfilled** by a
2 community of people living their lives according to its spirit. **The Spirit of
life in Christ Jesus** is the law having come to life in the spontaneous conduct
4 of those who **walk not according to the flesh but according to the Spirit.**

This is not to say, of course, that by choosing to live in a certain way (by
choosing 'spirit' instead of 'flesh') we are able to procure our own liberation.
To think this would be to forget the first stage of our salvation, the fact that
3 it was God who took the initiative **by sending his own Son.** It is true that it
is only by our 'faith' that we can be said to be **in Christ Jesus**; but our faith
is only the human and subjective side of the equation: there is an objective
side also. Quite independently of us and of our response (and in no sense
deserved by us), something has been done for us by God.

Precisely what it is that God has done, and how this affects human beings, is
not easily said in a single sentence. Previously, Paul has made use of metaphors
from the Jewish sacrificial system (3.25). The same imagery seems to underlie
his very compressed phrase, **to deal with sin.** Whether or not this is explicit
sacrificial language (the alternative translation, *as a sin offering*, is equally
problematical), the Jewish sacrificial system is certainly in the background:
part of the law's provision was to 'deal with sin' by means of 'sin offerings' to
atone for all inadvertent sins (Leviticus 4). But if Christ could be described
as such an offering, his sacrifice was infinitely more effective than that of any
sacrificial ritual. He came **in the likeness of sinful flesh.** The effect of this (if we
may apply the argument that is worked out in Galatians 3) was to undermine
the authority of sin – and here, once again, 'sin' becomes an independent
personification of the power that makes human beings commit evil deeds.
Until then, sin had invariably dragged those who 'walk according to the flesh'
into death and condemnation. Its claim on human beings (who are naturally
'in the flesh') had never been contested and could be regarded as legally
established. But now, by raising from the dead one who was **in the likeness of
human flesh**, God has given a decisive demonstration that condemnation and
death are not the inevitable verdict and sentence passed on the descendants of
Adam. By this one great exception, the hitherto uncontested claim of sin has
been challenged: God has **condemned sin in the flesh.** And this reverses our
whole situation, including our relationship with the law. Before, our 'flesh',
being under the dominion of sin, made it impossible for us to obey the law,

and so the law could do us no good: it could provide only the standard by which we would be judged and found guilty. But now the claim of sin that it could always bring us into condemnation under the law has been disposed of, and the law can become what it always was potentially, a means by which

4 **the just requirement of the law might be fulfilled in us.**

9   **But you are not in the flesh.** After this extensive discussion of the way in which being 'in the flesh' is a cause of condemnation for all human beings, it is time to say something of that alternative condition which has now been made possible: being **in the Spirit.** In English it is customary to use a capital letter to distinguish the Spirit of God from the 'spirit' in human beings; but Greek had no equivalent convention and we have to make our way as best we can through Paul's various references to 'spirit', deciding in each case whether he means Spirit or spirit (see the NRSV footnote). And we have to cope with a further complication: the 'Spirit' is normally the Spirit of God; but it seems that it can also be the **Spirit of Christ**; and this in turn seems to be equivalent to Christ himself being 'in us', assuring us that the Spirit of God **dwells** in us. It may not be possible to give a completely consistent account of Paul's terminology here; for in any case the terms overlap. To have the Spirit (of God) entails responding to God in that part of one's nature that is 'spirit';

5 and equally it is only the mind that is set **on the things of the Spirit** (or *spirit*) that will make room for the Spirit of God; and that same indwelling Spirit

11 will be the agent which will transform our **mortal bodies**, giving them the **life** that is promised by the resurrection.

9   **You are in the Spirit.** This sounds like a statement of fact; and indeed, there is no suggestion that Paul has to convince his readers of the reality of their new life in the Spirit. And yet it is not automatic. They may be 'in

12 the Spirit', but they are also **debtors**, they have an *obligation* to live by the

13 Spirit. The promise that they will **live** – that is, have the kind of new life which comes from 'walking according to the Spirit' – is conditional upon

14 their willingness to be **led by the Spirit of God.** The Spirit, in fact, is both an experienced reality and an invitation to bring more and more of daily living into its sphere. One way in which it was experienced was in prayer. In Aramaic, *abba* was a respectful but intimate way of addressing one's father. It was certainly not the usual way for a Jew to address God, who would normally use the less personal and proprietary form, 'Our Father'. But the Christians,

15 when they prayed, found themselves crying, **"Abba! Father!"** They would hardly have done this of their own accord: all their religious instincts would have deterred them from assuming any kind of intimacy with God. It must therefore have been the Spirit which inspired them to do so. And the Spirit would have done so only if this prayer was correct – that is, only if God were now in some special sense their 'Father' and they in some special sense his 'children'. Now in Jewish law a man could adopt a child simply by calling it 'my son' or 'my daughter'. In this sense the Spirit is **a spirit of adoption**; it

16 bears **witness with our spirit** (providing the evidence of two witnesses, as

required in a Jewish court) to the act of adoption by which we have become **children of God** and formally entitled to the inheritance that we share with Christ, the Son of God.

This distinctively Christian form of prayer – *abba* – may go back to Jesus himself, who is reported to have used it in a moment of extreme suffering

17 (Mark 14.36). It can now be used by us, but only on the same condition – **if, in fact, we suffer with him**. Not that Paul was bidding Christians to go out

18 and look for suffering deliberately: they already had enough in **the sufferings of this present time**. But these sufferings are made endurable by hope, hope of **the glory about to be revealed to us**. There is a 'glory' to come, as yet

19 unrevealed, which will transform not only ourselves (**the revealing of the children of God**) but **the creation** itself. The key to this grand conception lay in the creation story in Genesis. Not only the condition of humankind, but the evident disharmony of nature itself, was the result of Adam's sin: "cursed is the ground because of you" (Genesis 3.17). It was Adam's sinful

20 **will** that had made it **subjected to futility**.[9] But this curse, this subjection, was not final or permanent; it was a stage on the way to something better,

22 like **labor pains** before the birth of a child. The present condition, not just of human beings but of the whole creation, must be seen, not as its final

19 form, but as a stage on the way to a greater future: **the creation waits with eager longing**. And this future will come about through **the revealing of the children of God**: human beings, now restored to their proper relationship with God their Father, will reverse the 'futility' that was the result of Adam's

21 sin and restore the **freedom** of creation.

Thus it is hope on this cosmic scale, not just for ourselves but for the whole created order, which is a vital component of our new condition, enabling us

25, 24 to endure **with patience – for in hope we were saved**. But even if the future glory can be grasped only by hope, there is a present experience which gives

23 us confidence: we have **the first fruits of the Spirit** – a metaphor Paul uses a number of times: once the first fruits are gathered, there is no longer any doubt of the coming harvest. These 'first fruits' are experienced already, not

26 least in prayer. **The Spirit helps us in our weakness** – and here there must again be doubt whether we should use capital letters each time *spirit* occurs; for the experience of prayer taking place at a deep level, almost in spite of ourselves, evidently involves our own 'spirit' as well as being evidence for the

27 presence of the Spirit of God, who **intercedes for the saints** – that is, for all Christians – praying for them and in them.

28 **We know that all things work together for good**[10] **for those who love God** – but not as a *result* of their loving God. As if to forestall this suggestion,

---

[9] This is by no means the only possible interpretation of the Greek. **The one who subjected it** could be God, and the words **in hope** could go with the previous clause: *who subjected it in hope; because the creation itself will be set free* (so the Revised Standard Version).

[10] Neither the text nor the translation is certain: see the NRSV footnote.

Paul stresses that the initiative has been God's, in that it was part of his **purpose** from the beginning. Christians who now have come into this new situation and experience the Spirit are not a sudden innovation in the divine
29 economy: God **foreknew** them and **predestined** them to be **conformed to the image of his Son.** Logically, this has a negative side (which has been seized on by those interpreters who have found here the basis of a severe doctrine of 'predestination'). Those whom God did *not* foreknow are presumably without hope of salvation. But Paul may not have been thinking of this logical corollary here. His words may be intended simply to guard against any suggestion that the new situation has been created by ourselves: it was all in God's original **purpose.** The emphasis is on the positive side: we have been **conformed to the image of his Son,** so that we can take our place with him in **a large family** of human beings, Christ being simply **the firstborn** among
30 a new community of brothers and sisters. **Predestined – called – justified – glorified:** these are the stages of a seamless process which owes everything to the gracious initiative of God.

31   **What then are we to say about these things?** This part of the letter ends with a direct and confident application of theology to life. If it is true that God has done all this for us, what (even in the difficult circumstances in which the Roman Christians may be finding themselves) can any longer cause alarm? If there are accusations, the highest authority is there to secure acquittal:
33 **it is God who justifies.** If there is a court hearing, there is a new advocate
34 to plead the Christians' case, **Christ Jesus . . . who indeed, intercedes for us** from his supremely exalted place **at the right hand of God.** No matter
36 how severe the persecution – in the words of a psalm (44.22) **"we are being killed all day long"** – we belong with the long line of righteous sufferers who fill the pages of scripture. But all those sufferers could merely hope;
37 whereas **in all these things we are more than conquerors;** and the chapter ends with an impressive roll-call of all the powers and influences that are now unable to harm us – not only persecution by human beings, but the psychic and demonic powers of the universe, the 'heights' and 'depths' of astrology,
39 metaphysics and popular superstition. None of these things can **separate us from the love of God in Christ Jesus our Lord.**

The destiny of Israel

Paul's 'gospel' has now been stated: salvation is for all through faith in Christ, "apart from law" (3.21). But it was one thing to state this magnificent impartiality of God as a theoretical proposition; it was quite another thing to bring the matter down to a personal level and admit that it involved a moral and
9.3 spiritual judgment on one's **kindred according to the flesh.** Yet this, from the Jewish standpoint, was the clear implication of the universal gospel of Christ; and Paul, personally caught in the logic of his own argument, makes

2 no attempt to hide his feelings: **I have great sorrow and unceasing anguish in my heart**. What had become of God's promises made to the Jews? Had God now rejected his chosen people? In the short term, the problem seemed insoluble, and the anguish remained. But in the longer perspective of world history, an answer might yet be found. This is the theme of the following three chapters, the longest discussion of a single issue anywhere in Paul's correspondence.

The list of the Jews' religious privileges is impressive: they had all the riches contained in their scriptures, both the institutions of law and cult, and
4 **the promises** originally made by God specifically to his own people. They
5 also had among their ancestors **the patriarchs**, who (they believed) by their impeccable obedience had built up a balance of credit with God on which their physical descendants could still draw; and now it was one of themselves whom God had appointed to fulfil the rôle of saviour, first of the Jews and then of the whole world; and this rôle had for centuries been associated with the title **Messiah** (anointed one, Christ). Rich indeed, was this inheritance – and Paul breaks off to utter, like any religious Jew, his grateful acknowledgment of the goodness of God, who is **blessed for ever**.[11]

Yet the Jews had rejected their own Messiah; salvation had gone to others. What had gone wrong? Had God gone back on his promises? Was the glory and the privilege an illusion all the time? Was the Old Testament a fraud?
6 No, this was inconceivable: it could not be **as though the word of God had failed**; and indeed, one way out of the difficulty was suggested by scripture itself.

6 **Not all Israelites truly belong to Israel**. We should notice the subtle change of terminology. Throughout this section Paul speaks, not of 'Jews', but of 'Israel' or 'Israelites' (literally, *those of Israel*). That is to say, his argument is not about the empirical entity of the Jewish race now scattered around the world, but about Israel, the 'people of God', who are defined, even in scripture, not purely by race but by the fact of having been called by God and subjected to a certain history. He has already made a distinction on general grounds between those who are inwardly Jews and those who are Jews only outwardly (3.28–9). He now turns to the concept of 'Israel', and invokes the narrative of Genesis to prove that mere physical descent from Abraham was not a sufficient condition for claiming to be an 'Israelite'. Abraham had two sons, Isaac and Ishmael. But Ishmael was only Isaac's elder half-brother, and his mother was Egyptian: his descendants therefore were not true Israelites. (To be recognized as a Jew it was necessary, as it still is, to

---

[11] It is uncertain how the text of verse 5 should be punctuated (see the NRSV footnote). Grammatically, the most natural run of the words yields the sense given in the main text. But it is usually thought unlikely that Paul would have so boldly given the title 'God' to Christ, and this is avoided by placing a full stop after **Messiah** and reading the following words as a conventional Jewish prayer of blessing.

7 have a Jewish mother.) Only **through Isaac** would Abraham's descendants
8 be **named** (Genesis 21.12). And since Isaac was a child of **promise** (for Sarah was long past the normal age of child-bearing, and God had to intervene with a miracle before she could give birth to Isaac, Genesis 18.14), the principle of 'promise', rather than of natural genealogy, was introduced into the history of Israel from the start.

This example did not, however, take one very far. Since Ishmael's mother was Hagar, a foreign slave-girl, he could hardly claim to belong to Israel anyway. A better example was furnished by the next generation. Isaac and Rebekah had two children, twin sons, yet only one of them, Jacob, became
13 a patriarch in Israel (Genesis 25). The other, Esau, was **"hated"** by God (Malachi 1.3 – in the sense, at least, of not being 'loved' by him as Jacob was), and the Edomites (his presumed descendants) duly became the object of centuries of Jewish hatred. This second example was decisive proof that God's creation of his people Israel did not depend on physical heredity but involved a principle of selection. And we have been prepared by the argument of earlier chapters to expect that this principle of selection had nothing to
12 do with **works** or merit. It was entirely a matter of free election, **his call**.

But this last example, if it proved the point in question, opened up new problems. If God could choose one of a pair of twins and reject the other
11 **even before they had been born**, one must ask: does God abide by any
14 principle at all? Is he entirely capricious? **Is there injustice on God's part?** Paul has two answers to this ancient paradox. First, the key to God's purpose
15 is not caprice but **mercy**. God singles out those on whom he **will have mercy** and **compassion** (Exodus 33.19). It is true that this singling out inevitably appears unjust to those who are *not* so singled out but are used as the necessary villains, so to speak, in the drama of God's merciful purposes. An example is Pharaoh, whose heart God deliberately 'hardened' (Exodus 9.12,16) in the interests of a greater design. But this design was itself an expression of God's 'mercy' to his own suffering people. It was not 'unjust' simply because it caused suffering elsewhere.

But from the point of view of the unfortunate foils to God's gracious purposes this answer is plainly unsatisfactory. If some are to be rejected and punished through no apparent fault of their own, but merely because their suffering is necessary for the working out of God's grand design, does this not undermine moral responsibility? The point is raised by another imaginary
19 objector in a passage that returns to the 'diatribe' style: **"Why then does he still find fault? For who can resist his will?"** Paul's second answer to the paradox is one that was classically expressed by the prophets (Isaiah 29.16; 45.9; Jeremiah 18.6): the creator, like the potter, is free to do what he likes with his creatures. It is not for them to call him unjust; for only he, and not they, know the purpose for which he created them. This image certainly enjoins a proper reverence towards the inscrutable purposes of God; but it hardly removes the apparent injustice inflicted on those who are arbitrarily

22 made into **objects of wrath**. Paul, however, introduces a mitigating factor. God's purpose does not always involve immediate action. It may be worked
23 out over a long period. For the sake of **the objects of mercy** God may endure
22 **with much patience the objects of wrath**. God's justice is not simply black and white. Even Pharaoh was allowed a long period to go his own way before his **destruction**.

In fact, of course, the problem arises as soon as one begins to talk about God's purpose of election. If God 'called' some, it follows that he did *not* call others. The creation of any identifiable people, of any 'Israel', inevitably implies that some people will not be in it; and if the principle of selection is nothing to do with merit or deserving (as Paul has insisted), but only with faith in what God has done, those who are excluded will have a sense of injustice. But against the background of the argument at the beginning of the letter, that humanity as a whole is under condemnation, the rescue of *any* from this condition is an act of mercy; and Paul now brings this conclusion to bear on the question of 'Israel'. If such are the principles by which God defined the membership of Israel in Old Testament times, these are exactly
23 the principles which have created the Christian church. His **objects of mercy**
24 must include Christians, and these have been **called, not from the Jews only but also from the Gentiles**. Two verses of Hosea (2.23; 1.10), which originally expressed God's restoration to peoplehood of the former Israel which had ceased to deserve this privilege, are quoted (as they are in 1 Peter 2.10) as prophecies of the 'new Israel' which is the Christian church. This new people is now made up in great part of Gentiles; and that tiny minority of the old Israel which has also entered the church appears to give effect to the important principle, to be found in Isaiah, that God's purpose will be
27 achieved if **only a remnant of them will be saved** (Isaiah 10.20–22).

From the Jewish point of view, this election of Gentiles to be members of Israel could hardly be expected to seem acceptable. It was they, the historic
30 Israel now represented by the Jewish people, who did **strive for righteousness**, in contrast to the Gentiles who (they thought) showed no such moral effort. But they had made the error of supposing that their end could be
31, 32 attained by virtue of these efforts and their physical ancestry alone, by **law** and **works**. They had failed to reckon with the fact (demonstrated in chapters 3 and 4) that the key requirement for a relationship with a just and merciful God is **faith**. The new situation, in fact, was well illustrated by a composite image which the early church found by combining two passages of Isaiah (28.16 and 8.14 – the same combination occurs in 1 Peter 2.6). A piece of masonry, left lying on the ground by the builders, may seem at first sight to be no more than an obstacle to stumble over; looked at more closely, it may be recognized as the stone which may crown the whole structure, the 'very head of the corner'.

God is righteous, but God is selective. These apparently incompatible propositions have now been reconciled, in so far as God's selectivity has been shown to be governed, not by caprice, but by that aspect of his righteousness which is his mercy shown towards the entire human race. It must now be asked (for this is a question asked by every religion): Is there no way in which this merciful treatment may be earned?

One obvious way of earning it might seem to be by religious zeal. This the historic Israel had shown in abundance. **I can testify that they have a zeal for God.** But their zeal for God had taken the form of creating a community defined by its observance of law. By so doing, they had believed that they could **establish their own** righteousness and claim a special relationship with their righteous God. The error involved in this belief has already been demonstrated; but Paul now sums it up in a phrase that has caused intense controversy through the centuries: **Christ is the end of the law.** At first sight this looks like a total rejection of all that the law stood for. But in fact the phrase exploits the ambiguity of the word 'end' (*telos*). Christ puts a temporal end to the law, in that he opens a new era in which observance of the law is no longer the decisive criterion for salvation. But he also reveals the destined 'end' or purpose of the law; he 'fulfils' it, in that he has dethroned the power ('sin') which robbed it of its usefulness and has made possible a spontaneous obedience to all that God demands. This new possibility of **righteousness** is no longer to be sought in a community governed by legal observances, but simply in **everyone who believes.**

The difference between observance and faith can be illustrated by a contrast latent in the Old Testament itself. Compare Leviticus 18.5, **"the person who does these things will live by them"** (where the emphasis is on *doing*) with Deuteronomy 30.11–14:

> Surely, this commandment that I am commanding you today is not too hard for you, nor is it too far away. It is not in heaven, that you should say, "Who will go up to heaven for us, and get it for us so that we may hear it and observe it?" Neither is it beyond the sea, that you should say, "Who will cross to the other side of the sea for us . . .?" No, the word is very near to you; it is in your mouth and in your heart for you to observe.

There is at least a hint here that something is given to human beings before ever they start 'doing' anything; and Paul adapts this passage to the Christian experience. No human 'doing' has created the new situation. The appearance of the Son of God on earth was not the result of anything we did: no human effort was needed to **bring Christ down.** The resurrection was entirely God's action: there was nothing we could have done to **bring Christ up from the dead.** That the word was **"on your lips and in your heart"** would normally have been taken to mean that one constantly meditated on the law (speaking it aloud) and brought one's heart into obedience to it. But the words could also be read as a description of that **faith** which is now the one condition of belonging to the new 'Israel'. All that now matters is that one **should confess with** one's **lips that Jesus is Lord** (when, for instance, one is on trial for one's faith), and believe in the heart **that God raised him from the dead**. This 'word of faith' is something utterly different from the long and exacting discipline of 'doing' the law. Yet it guarantees that one will be 'saved' – that one will

11 not **be put to shame** (a phrase from Isaiah 28.16, referring to the future judgment before God). What had been proclaimed as a general principle of rescue from the terrors of that judgment by the prophet Joel (2.32) –

13 **"Everyone who calls on the name of the Lord shall be saved"** – now has a new and startling connotation. We have just been reminded that we confess Jesus as 'Lord'. Calling on *his* name now has saving power. Moreover, there

12 is new force in the word *everyone*: no longer only the Jews, but – **there is no distinction between Jew and Greek; the same Lord is Lord of all.**

But how are they to call . . .? Rather abruptly, Paul appears to meet a possible objection. It might be said that the Jews – perhaps it was true of the majority of those at Rome – had had no chance to hear this gospel of Jesus

14 Christ. There may have been no one **to proclaim him** (almost a technical term, in the Greek, for preaching the gospel); or, if there were, they may not

15 have been officially **sent** (another almost technical term for commissioning an agent or representative). How could they know that the proclaimer was to be trusted? But – to take the last point first – there is evidence in scripture (Isaiah 52.7) that those who **bring good news** authenticate themselves (their

18 feet are **beautiful**, welcome); and to answer the first point, Psalm 19.4 (**"Their voice has gone out to all the earth . . ."**) could be taken as a prophecy that the outreach of the gospel preaching would be universal: the Jews must have heard it, or at any rate would soon do so. The fact is, not that they have not

16 heard, but that **not all have obeyed the good news**. As Isaiah had prophesied (53.1), they had not **believed** the **message**. And this failure to respond, with the threatening consequence that salvation may go to others, is foreshadowed

19 in many passages of scripture. Paul quotes **Moses** (Deuteronomy 32.21) and

20 **Isaiah** (65.1–2).

11.1 **I ask, then, has God rejected his people?** The argument of these chapters would seem to entail that he has. But at this Paul recoils. **By no means!** – the phrase occurs several times in a similar context (3.6; 3.11 and again here at verse 11), and Paul uses it to reject what he feels to be an outrageous conclusion: *God forbid!* (the rendering in older versions) catches something of the force of the Greek phrase. And in fact Paul can suggest two ways out of the difficulty. One has already been alluded to (9.27): the biblical doctrine that

5 so long as **a remnant** of faithful people continued to exist, God's promises to Israel could still be fulfilled even if the majority had been disqualified. This doctrine was illustrated by the story of Elijah (1 Kings 19): it made no difference if the entire nation had gone after false gods so long as there were

4 **seven thousand** left who were still faithful. The principle now had a new application. God had not rejected his people, since a tiny 'remnant' of them

1 had accepted Jesus Christ – among whom was Paul (**I myself am an Israelite**). But this remnant, unlike the previous 'remnants' in the history of Israel, was

5   **chosen by grace**. It had done nothing to deserve its election. It must not be
6   imagined that the salvation of this remnant had been **on the basis of works**:
7   it had not been earned by any merit acquired through observance of law.
This would be contrary to all that has been said about salvation depending
on faith: **grace would no longer be grace**.

But this 'remnant' explanation accounted only for that small number who,
like Paul, had become Christians. The question still remained, what of all
the rest? It could not be denied that any doctrine of the divine selection of
some implied the rejection of others; and there were abundant prophecies
in scripture of the fate in store for those who were **hardened** (the word takes
us back to the example of Pharaoh that was used earlier, 9.17). Paul quotes
8, 9   two: Isaiah 29.10 and Psalm 69.22–3. But Paul could not accept that the
failure of all except a small remnant meant the complete downfall of the rest
11   of Israel. That they had **stumbled** did not necessarily mean that they had
'fallen' – an implication which Paul again finds shockingly unacceptable (**By
no means!**). In the short term, this **stumbling** (for which Paul uses a stronger
expression, literally *transgression*) had resulted in the immense benefit of
salvation coming **to the Gentiles**: the universal scope of the gospel might
never have been realized had it not come into conflict with the exclusive
ethos of the historic people of Israel. But this need not be the end of the
matter. A chain reaction had been set up, and this would ultimately impinge
again on Israel, which had started it by its misguided rejection. The effect
of gentile Christianity would be to **make Israel jealous**; as a result, their
12   **inclusion** (like making up the full complement of a ship's crew, which is one
of the meanings of the word Paul uses) would result in a still greater benefit
for all.

This line of thought suggested a second explanation; and possibly Paul was
constrained to put it forward, not merely by his natural feelings of solidarity
with his own people, but by a patronizing and complacent attitude which
had been taken up by the gentile Christians in Rome over against their Jewish
fellow members. Therefore he addressed this explanation specifically to them:
13   **Now I am speaking to you Gentiles**.

Paul, as he had often said, was primarily **an apostle to the Gentiles** (and
therefore had a particular mission to a church such as that in Rome). But this
did not mean that he had abandoned his own people or had given up hope
for them. It was only in the short term that it might appear that salvation had
simply passed from the historic Israel to the Gentiles. In the long term it was
impossible to suppose that anything had changed in the destiny of God's own
people. Of another nation it might be said simply that their history had a
brilliant beginning but that it had all come to nothing. But the history of Israel
15   was of a different order. Their **rejection** of the gospel had been the trigger
for the mission to the Gentiles; but this did not mean that the Gentiles *alone*
were to constitute the new Israel; indeed, the long-term purpose of Paul's
14   work was to make his own people **jealous** and at least to start the process

of re-integrating them into the true people of God – **and thus save some of them**. With such beginnings, it was inconceivable that their history should

16 come to nothing. Just as it was believed that an offering from **part of the dough** made holy all the bread that was offered (Numbers 15.20–1); and just as a tree, once consecrated, did not have to be reconsecrated every time a new branch grew, but **if the root is holy, then the branches also are holy**, so the fact that the Gentiles who had accepted the gospel were now 'holy' did not mean that the parent stem was holy no longer. Indeed, the situation of the gentile church over against the old Israel had an analogy in nature. The normal growth of a wild olive tree can be altered by grafting in shoots from a cultivated olive, so that the tree begins to bear fruit. The Gentiles were in

17 this situation: they had been **grafted** in among the branches of the parent tree, and they must not imagine that they could either exist independently of that tree or be regarded as superior to it. Moreover, if the analogy were pressed, it became a vivid parable of God's gracious treatment of them. The

24 grafting had been **contrary to nature**: wild olive shoots had been grafted into the cultivated olive instead of the other way round! Against all expectation, and entirely owing to the gracious purposes of God, the Gentiles had been made part of a new composite growth which would fulfil the promises made to 'Israel'. The moral for them, whenever they were tempted to scorn their

18, 20 unconverted Jewish neighbours, was clear: **do not boast, do not become proud, but stand in awe**.

25   **I want you to understand this mystery**. The rejection of the gospel by the historic Israel was certainly **a hardening**: as in the case of Pharaoh (the particular example of 'hardening' mentioned in 9.16–18), it was the necessary

28 dark side of God's favour shown to others – **they are enemies of God for your sake**. But in this case it was part of a larger design. Israel had been 'chosen' – **as**

29 **regards election they are beloved** – and nothing could alter the fact: **the gifts and the calling of God are irrevocable**. But before the true 'Israel' could be

25 brought into existence, there was a **full number** of Gentiles to be made up, the 'crew' needed its full complement from that quarter. Then – and only then –

26 **all Israel will be saved**. This is the ultimate answer to the personally agonizing question from which Paul started. But it also provides striking confirmation of Paul's understanding of the true nature of humanity's relationship with God. Had the Jewish people, instead of rejecting the gospel, calmly accepted Jesus as Messiah, it might have appeared that their salvation still depended on their own privileged history and their faithfulness to a way of life determined

30 by law. But their present phase of **disobedience** (in respect of which they had been shown to be no different from anyone else) meant that when they

31 ultimately came to **receive mercy** they would receive it on the same basis as the Gentiles, as a free and gracious gift. Only in this way would those ancient prophecies be fulfilled which appeared to predict the coming of a

26 Messiah who would deliver and purify **all Israel**: "Out of Zion will come the Deliverer" (Isaiah 59.20–1).

Paul has reached the end of his great argument; and he breaks off once again (as he did at 1.25) with a brief hymn of praise built out of Old Testament phrases. (See especially Isaiah 40.13). When the letter was read aloud, its
36 hearers will doubtless have responded: **Amen.**

Christian morality

This final section of the letter follows not so much on the previous one but on the argument which reached its climax at the end of chapter 8. Salvation has been procured by the act of God in Jesus Christ; but a response is still required from the believer before that salvation can become effectual. In chapter 6 this response was described in terms of a continuing solidarity and unity with the
12.1 risen Christ. Here it is commended under the metaphor of **a living sacrifice** – not the old ritual sacrifices of the temple, but our *reasonable* worship (a more literal translation than **spiritual worship**: the word implies a deliberate and thought-out dedication of mind and body). This involves nothing less than
2 a moral and intellectual transformation and a new capacity to **discern what is the will of God.** All this follows logically from Paul's analysis of salvation.
1 And so he begins, **I appeal to you therefore, brothers and sisters.**

The chapter contains a series of specific moral instructions, delivered with that particular authority which Paul believed he possessed by virtue of his
3 apostleship (**by the grace given to me**). Some of these instructions are particularly relevant to the common life of the Christian community. We know from 1 Corinthians 12 how the 'gifts of the Spirit' (some of them newly inspired, some an intensification of existing talents), though they were one of the marks of an authentic church, could lead to rivalry and disorder. In his first letter to Corinth, Paul had worked out his answer (which is only
5 hinted at here) in terms of being **one body in Christ**, from which it follows that **individually we are members one of another.** This means that all such gifts are to be exercised for the good of all; there is no superiority of one
3 over another; the only criterion of an individual's merit is **the measure of faith that God has assigned.** It makes no difference if some of the 'gifts' are
6 obviously God-given, such as **prophecy**, while others are more routine capac-
7 ities for the needs of daily life, such as *diakonia* (here translated **ministry**; it means anything from technical Christian 'deaconship' to specific services performed by some members of the community for others). Whatever they are, they must be exercised single-mindedly, without pretension.

By no means all these injunctions express a distinctively Christian morality. Many of them can be found in some form or another in the Old Testament,
19, 20 and two of them are actual quotations: Deuteronomy 32.35 and Proverbs 25.21–2. But amidst this conventional moral teaching, most of which would have sounded familiar to Greeks and Jews alike, occur injunctions which may suggest that the church was already subject to some degree of harassment or persecution and which have unmistakable echoes of a more radical ethic

14, 17   characteristic of Jesus: **Bless those who persecute you; Do not repay any-**
21   **one evil for evil; overcome evil with good**. The church did not create a new moral code. It borrowed from what was best in the society around it. But just occasionally we can overhear the radicalism of the Sermon on the Mount.

13.1   **Let every person be subject to the governing authorities**. Had the Roman Christians been in trouble with the government? Were their communities already regarded by the authorities as a danger to society or even illegal? Had they been tempted to keep their heads down and withdraw from normal social activities? Or was civil obedience simply one of the standard sub-headings of the Christian moral code? We do not know. But, at least until the persecution launched against them by Nero several years after the writing of this letter, we have no evidence that the Roman state posed any serious threat to the life of the church. Indeed at this period the main adversary was usually the local Jewish community, and the narrative of Acts claims that the Christians sometimes actually invoked the protection of the Roman government against Jewish attacks. At any rate Paul firmly recommends that they avoid anything which might provoke trouble from the authorities. When he supports this by saying that **those authorities that exist have been instituted by God**, he is aligning himself with a well-known philosophical view, namely that the order which should be maintained in civil society reflects the order that has been imposed by God on the cosmos. But it was also an understanding of the nature of secular power that could be found in the Bible (most explicitly in Daniel). Most Jews in the Dispersion adopted the same attitude, even though in Palestine there were some notable groups who were fanatically opposed to Roman rule. The evidence of the New Testament and of early Christian literature shows consistently that the Christians were deliberately law-abiding even while they fiercely resisted all attempts to make them conform with pagan emperor-worship. In particular, Paul exhorts

6   the Roman Christians to **pay taxes**: we know that at this time in Rome some indirect taxes were particularly severe, and the small Christian communities might have made themselves vulnerable by joining the outcry against them. And apart from this prudential reason for paying taxes, they may well have known that Jesus himself advised giving "to the emperor the things that are the emperor's" (Mark 12.17).

    Obligations towards the state lead into obligations towards society in
9   general: **your neighbor**. It was a well-known subject of discussion among learned Jews how the law could be **summed up** in a single commandment. Jesus, we know, took part in such discussions and reached his own conclusion: love of God and love of neighbour. Paul, like a number of early rabbis – and in view, perhaps, of the context, which is that of social ethics – uses only the second part of this. All law, at any rate so far as it affects soci-ety, can be **summed up in this word, "Love your neighbor as yourself"**. Living by this rule (which underlies much of the moral teaching in this

and the previous chapter) means that one will automatically be **fulfilling the law.**

This section of moral admonition has proceeded logically from the argument of chapters 5–8. For good measure, Paul adds a motive for good conduct which was doubtless (as it has been ever since) a more commonplace one in the church than Paul's highly sophisticated reasoning: the nearness of the

12 end of the present age and the judgment of God on every individual: **the night is far gone, the day is near.** One might have expected the urgency of this challenge to have decreased as the years passed and as the expectation of the first Christians for an immediate return of Christ began to wane; yet throughout the New Testament the same call recurs: 'The end is at hand . . . *therefore* be sober and vigilant.' Paul is here adopting one of the distinctive notes of early Christian moral teaching. Nevertheless, at the end of the

14 chapter he returns to his deeper argument: **put on the Lord Jesus Christ –** a metaphor which may have reminded his readers of their baptism, when they were 'clothed' with Christ (Galatians 3.27) and were thereby initiated into a new moral life, but which also suggested taking on a new rôle, a new character. Either way, there could be no doubt that their new existence in Christ entailed profound moral consequences.

Taboos and observances

Christians (as Paul has been arguing throughout the letter) are people who have come to see their relationship with God as dependent, not on belonging to a community that followed strict legal observances, but on 'faith' – on believing in Jesus Christ and in all that God has done for humanity through him. Gentile Christians might find this a welcome liberation from pressure exerted by Jewish communities to adopt Jewish observances; and some Jewish Christians may have similarly welcomed being released from a régime which they now felt to be irrelevant or irksome. But for others the life-long practice of these observances may not have been so easy to discard. If one had always thought of some foods as 'unclean' (pork, for example, or any meat associated with pagan sacrifices – see below on 1 Corinthians 8), it might be difficult to face them if they were served at the table of a fellow Christian who was a Gentile. Similarly, a life-long pattern of rest and family celebration on the sabbath and on other holy days might make it difficult to take part in social activities arranged by Gentiles who had no such background.

It is evident that these difficulties had begun to trouble the common life of the church in Rome, with its mixed membership of Jews and Gentiles. The

14.1 tension was between those who were 'strong' and those who were 'weak' **in faith,** and here 'faith' – this fundamental term of the Christian religion – is used in a way that defies exact translation into English: those who are 'weak in faith' are not so much people who have begun to doubt the truth of the gospel as those who lack the *conviction* to overcome old habits and taboos. Some members of the community (doubtless mainly Jews) had solved the immediate problem by becoming vegetarians and abstaining from meat altogether, unable to put their consciences or their deeply ingrained squeamishness to rest in any other way; whereas others (doubtless mainly Gentiles, though some Jews may have come to share Paul's indifference to such matters) had

2 come to **believe in eating anything**– an unusual phrase in the Greek which might equally mean to *have the conviction* (or *faith*) *required to be able to eat anything*. And similar scruples – or perhaps an ascetic movement in the church – seem to have led to different views on whether it was right to

21 **drink wine**. These differences were evidently causing serious damage to the

3 community, in that some were beginning to **pass judgment** on their fellow Christians or even to **despise** them for their 'weakness'.

14   In the matter of principle, Paul was absolutely clear in his own mind: **I know and am persuaded in the Lord Jesus that nothing is unclean in itself** – and the words 'in the Lord Jesus' suggest that he may be appealing to something that Jesus possibly taught himself (Mark 7.19);[12] it was certainly an important principle in the history of the early church (Acts 10.15). But he also recognized the powerful psychological factors at work in such things: **food is unclean for anyone who thinks it unclean**. It followed that, for the sake of the common life of the community, those who felt emancipated from such scruples must show consideration to those who could not yet bring themselves to share the same freedom; and Paul devotes this part of his letter to a strenuous defence of the need for mutual understanding and tolerance.

   Paul bases his argument on a number of grounds. (i) There is the general point that all Christians, both the 'weak' and the 'strong', are people

3, 4 whom God has **welcomed**: it is not for Christians to **pass judgment on servants of another**. (ii) Both traditional observances and freedom from

6 such observances may be practised **in honor of the Lord**. A Jew observed the sabbath, not for personal convenience or to acquire religious merit, but for the glory of God; similarly, Jewish meals were normally preceded by the saying of grace – **they give thanks to God**. But it is equally possible for those who adopt a different practice to do so **in honor of the Lord**.

5 The essential thing is absolute honesty with oneself: **Let all be fully convinced in their own minds**. If the effect of Christ's dying for us was that

8 we can even **die to the Lord**, it follows that we must be able to **live to the Lord** in every detail of our lives, whatever religious traditions or customs

13 we observe. (iii) It is the plain duty of Christians not to **pass judgment on one another**, which may again be a recollection of words of Jesus (Matthew

11 7.1), but is here illustrated by a composite quotation from Isaiah 49.18 and

17 45.23. (iv) **The kingdom of God is not food and drink**, which was perhaps not quite so obvious to a Jewish believer as it seems to us, since the ritual

---

[12] Though it is far from certain that Jesus addressed the issue so directly: see above on Mark 7.19.

cleanness of foods and liquids was of great importance in the Jewish concept
of a life regulated by religion. (v) All such matters must be subordinated to
19 the **mutual upbuilding** of the community (*oikodomē*, an important word
in Paul's understanding of the church, see below on 1 Corinthians 14.2–5).
Any decision in these matters may be right so long as it is followed with
22 **conviction**. This is undoubtedly the sense in this context of the Greek word
for *faith*, which Paul uses here; and yet it is not only acting from a lack of
23 conviction which is **sin**, but manifesting an absence of that **faith** which is the
basis of Christian identity altogether. (vi) Finally, it is Christ himself who has
15.3 given us an example: **For Christ did not please himself.** Christ's whole tenor
of life fulfilled a pattern adumbrated in such passages of the Old Testament
as Psalm 69.9, **"The insults of those who insult you have fallen on me."** The
righteous sufferer of that psalm, in his agonized complaint to God, found
that even his faith in God was being held against him by his enemies. Such
a notable fulfilment of one prophecy (and of many others which seemed to
prefigure the events of Christ's life and death) could only mean that other
promises contained in scripture would shortly be fulfilled. This was the source
4 of **encouragement** (almost a technical word in this context – see above on
Acts 13.15), which Christians might find in the Old Testament and which
would give them grounds for **steadfastness**.

But in so far as all these practical problems sprang from the basic difficulty experienced by Jews and non-Jews, with their different religious and
social backgrounds, in accepting one another as equals and forming a single
community without prejudice or privilege, the ultimate solution could be
found only on the level of the main argument of the letter. Part of the work
8 of Christ was to **confirm the promises given to the patriarchs** – the historic
Israel was by no means to be abandoned (chapters 9–11); but at the same
9 time it was **in order that the Gentiles might glorify God for his mercy** when
they received a promise of salvation "apart from the law" and without the
condition of joining an observant Jewish community (chapters 1–4). It was
10 the old vision come true: **"Rejoice, O Gentiles, with his people"** (Deutero-
9 nomy 32.43; Paul introduces this with Psalm 18.49 and continues his string
11, 12 of quotations with Psalm 117.1 and Isaiah 11.1, 10). The greatest spur to
agreeing in lesser matters was the great purpose that God was working out
7 for both peoples together. In a word, **Welcome one another, therefore, just
as Christ has welcomed you.**

Personal projects

14 **I myself feel confident about you.** The letter suddenly becomes personal. Paul
is evidently aware that there were some at Rome who might have resented his
15 forceful language. **I have written to you rather boldly by way of reminder** –
the sentence sounds deliberately apologetic. Of course the Christians at Rome

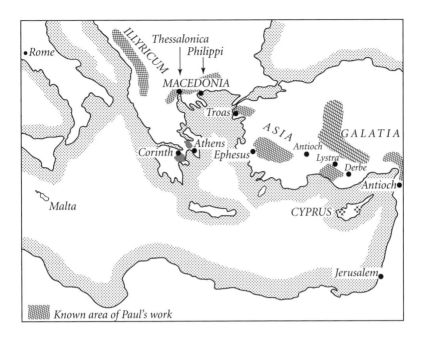

Known area of Paul's work

14, 15 were well able to **instruct one another**; but Paul – **because of the grace given to me by God** – possessed an authority which none of them could claim for themselves; and moreover his apostleship, with its special commission
16 **to the Gentiles**, made it peculiarly incumbent on him to address himself to problems experienced by churches like that at Rome which had a substantial gentile membership.

No one, after reading the narrative in Acts, would question the claim –
17, 19 Paul's '**boast**' of his work – that his ministry had been made effective **by the power of signs and wonders, by the power of the Spirit of God**. But what about the next sentence? **From Jerusalem and as far around as Illyricum I have proclaimed the good news of Christ**. The part of the world in fact covered by Paul's preaching (so far as we know from his letters and from Acts) can best be seen by a glance at the map. Jerusalem (which he had visited several times since his conversion) and Illyricum on the eastern side of the Adriatic represented the geographical limits of his work; but in what sense, after having evangelized no more than a few cities and territories in the intervening area, could he be said to have **fully proclaimed** the gospel, so
23 much so that he had **no further place . . . in these regions?** Not, clearly, in an exhaustive geographical sense. The explanation is probably more theoretical. Jesus had said that before the end "the good news must first be proclaimed to all nations" (Mark 13.10). Yet in the first century the end was expected quite soon; therefore the proclamation 'to all nations' must have been understood somewhat symbolically: so long as there had been some preaching in each

province of the empire, and a substantial number of people had come within earshot of it, Jesus' prophecy would be deemed to have been fulfilled. Paul may even have thought that the completion of his own preaching at representative points throughout the civilized world would contribute to bringing about the end – hence, perhaps, his determination to reach Spain, which was regarded as the westernmost part of the known world (though there is no certain

19 evidence that he ever succeeded in doing so). In any case, the statement **I have fully proclaimed the good news** (the Greek word stresses *completion*) is probably intended less as a claim to have covered a continent than as a statement that his work had advanced the world-wide progress of the gospel **as far around as Illyricum**. The pattern of his pioneering work was laid

21 down for him in a prophecy of Isaiah (52.15), which Paul clearly felt was being fulfilled each time he brought the gospel to a place where no one else

20 had been before him to lay a **foundation**.

But meanwhile he had to complete a task which had already occupied

26 him for some years: the raising of money for **the poor among the saints at Jerusalem**. On this collection, which is mentioned in a number of Paul's letters, see below on 2 Corinthians 8. It seems that, by the time Romans was

28 written, the collection had reached a point at which Paul could make plans to deliver the proceeds to the Jerusalem church in person.[13]

The last paragraph of the section throws a little light on Paul's relations with Jerusalem. The later part of Acts shows that Paul had indeed something

31 to fear from **the unbelievers in Judea**; but he evidently felt some anxiety also about his likely reception by the Jerusalem church.

Commendation and greetings

16.1 **I commend to you**. Letters of commendation for travellers or for candidates for appointments were as common in the ancient world as they are today. Paul here commends a certain **Phoebe**. He describes her as a *diakonos,* a word which may already have been a technical term meaning 'deacon' or 'deaconess' (though the existence of an order of deaconesses at this early period cannot be proved), or may simply be a way of saying that she had given of her time and money in the *service* of the congregation at Cenchreae (the port on the east side of the Isthmus at Corinth).

Paul then proceeds to send his personal greetings to some individuals at Rome. It may seem surprising that he should have been acquainted with so many in a church he had not yet visited. But there was much travelling to and

3 from Rome. The Jewish couple **Prisca** (called by her more correct Latin name *Priscilla* in Acts 18) and her husband **Aquila** are a good example. Expelled from Rome under the edict of Claudius around 50 CE, they had settled in

---

[13] This is the most likely meaning of the puzzling Greek expression, *to have sealed to them this fruit* (see the NRSV footnote).

Corinth, then moved to Ephesus (1 Corinthians 16.19) and were now back in
5 Rome, apparently in sufficient affluence to be able to accommodate a **church in their house**.

13 Nothing is known for certain of any of the other persons named. **Rufus** could be the same man as the son of Simon of Cyrene mentioned in Mark 15.21: if he was a person well known at Rome, and if the tradition is correct that Mark's gospel was compiled at Rome, his appearance in both passages 10 would be explained. Again, **Aristobulus** could be Herod the Great's grandson, who is known to have lived and died at Rome, and whose **family** or household might well have contained both Jewish and gentile converts to Christianity; 11 and **Herodion** suggests a member of the same household who was also possibly a distant relative of Paul.[14] But all this is speculation. All that we can say for certain is that most of the names are such as might have been met 9 with in any Greco-Roman society, though some (such as **Stachys**) are rare 12, 15 ones; many of them are typical slaves' names (**Persis, Philologus**), and the list suggests a socially mixed and cosmopolitan society such as one would expect the church in Rome (though not necessarily only in Rome) to have 7 been. Within it Paul recognizes two **apostles**, both Jews, one with a Greek name (**Andronicus**), one, like Paul, with a Roman name (**Junia**[15]). Evidently he could use the term 'apostle' in a wider sense than that implied in the early chapters of Acts (where it denotes one of the twelve). These two became Christians even before Paul himself, they had suffered imprisonment with Paul for their faith, and they may have been responsible for the first bringing of the gospel to Rome.

16 **Greet one another with a holy kiss.** Paul's letters were probably intended to be read to the assembled congregation immediately before the celebration of the eucharist; and this phrase may well be an allusion to the 'kiss of peace' which the hearers of the letter were about to exchange with one another. This 'kiss of peace' formed part of Christian worship from at least the mid-second century, and may have already been customary in Paul's time.

After a very direct and personal piece of advice – inspired perhaps by some specific and disquieting information he has received from Rome – Paul 21 associates some of his friends with his closing greetings. **Timothy** was one of his constant companions, and one of his fellow countrymen (not necessarily **relatives**[16]). **Lucius** may be the Lucius of Cyrene of Acts 13.1; **Sosipater** the Sopater of Acts 20.4; and **Jason** the Jason of Acts 17.5–9 – but none of these 23 identifications is certain. **Gaius** is doubtless the Corinthian of 1 Corinthians 1.14; **Erastus** was evidently an influential person.

---

[14] The Greek word for **relative** may mean nothing more than *compatriot*.

[15] Most older versions take this as a form of a man's name (*Junias*), so avoiding the implication that there could have been a female apostle. But linguistically the female name **Junia** is far more probable.

[16] See footnote 14 above.

The final paragraph sums up much of the argument of the letter in the form of an ascription of praise to God (as in 1.25; 9.5; 11.33). It refers to a

25, 26 **revelation** that was implicit down the ages but **is now disclosed** in a manner which embraces **all the Gentiles** as well as the Jews for whom it was first prophesied. But it is not certain that it originally formed part of the letter. If one may judge from the style, it may not even be from the hand of Paul. In some manuscripts it occurs at the end of chapter 14, in some at the end of chapter 15, and in some it is omitted altogether. These curious variations in the manuscript tradition over where and how the letter should end (see the last footnote in the NRSV) suggest that the letter may have existed from the beginning in more than one version, and even (since some manuscripts omit the words 'in Rome' in 1.7,15) that it may have been originally written to some Christian community other than that in Rome – possibly Ephesus. But it is also possible that the manuscript tradition suffered derangement at an early stage. In any case, there is no compelling reason to doubt the traditional view that the letter was destined, at least in the first instance, for the Christians in Rome.

CORINTHIANS

The ancient city of Corinth, built on the isthmus dividing mainland Greece from the Peloponnese, enjoyed notable prosperity by reason of its commanding position with a port on each side. It had been destroyed by the Romans in 146 BCE but refounded by Julius Caesar two centuries later, and had soon after become the capital of the Roman province of Achaia (the whole of central and southern Greece). Because of its commercial importance it had a cosmopolitan population which included a Jewish community – an inscription proves the existence of a synagogue; and the religious and cultural life of the city was typical of the Roman and Hellenistic world, with temples and institutions dedicated to the deities of classical mythology as well as a few of foreign provenance. The constant traffic of seafarers and others through the ports also gave it a persistent reputation for immorality.

The founding of the church at Corinth by Paul around 50 CE is described in Acts 18. Shortly afterwards Paul spent some time at Ephesus (Acts 19). These two chapters of Acts provide the background for what has come down to us as Paul's 'First Letter to the Corinthians'. But this letter was evidently not the beginning of the correspondence. Paul had already had occasion to write to the Corinthians once before (5.9), and had received a letter from them (7.1). He had also received information from members of the Corinthian congregation who had visited him at Ephesus (1.11; 16.17). This letter is therefore in reality at least Paul's *second* letter to the Corinthians, and contains both a reply to theirs and some comments on the information he had received from their emissaries. Much of the difficulty of interpreting it lies in the fact that we do not possess the earlier stages of the correspondence; it is not always easy to see precisely what questions, complaints or difficulties Paul was addressing, or what was the nature of the opposition which was causing dissension.

The first six chapters are concerned mainly with some serious matters of life and conduct in the church, which Paul had heard about through his informants. The remaining chapters appear to answer, one by one, points made by the Corinthians in their letter to Paul.

Salutation

The opening of the letter, as in Romans, follows the conventional form: **Paul . . . To the church of God that is in Corinth . . . Grace to you and peace.** But, as usual, Paul makes this conventional framework carry a good deal of Christian matter. In Romans, he adds a long parenthesis concerning his own apostleship. Here, he is content with only a brief statement about himself (for the Corinthians, unlike the Romans, knew him well), and inserts instead some words about the Corinthians: that they are not a self-appointed congregation, but owe their existence and their 'sanctification' (which means

2 being set apart by baptism) entirely to the fact that God has **called** them **to be saints** – that is, not necessarily people of outstanding virtue (Paul never uses the word 'saint' of a single individual), but members of the 'holy people of God' and part of the universal fellowship of Christians. Paul also associates

1 himself with a colleague, a certain **Sosthenes,** who appears in Acts 18.17 as a prominent Corinthian Jew.

True wisdom and false divisions

The conventional letter structure continues (as it might today, when we begin, 'I am glad to hear that . . .') with an expression of thanksgiving; but

4 the style is of a Jewish prayer: **I give thanks to my God always . . .** The conduct of the Corinthian church comes under a good deal of criticism in the course of the letter, but Paul begins diplomatically by conceding that

5 there is much to be thankful for. They have been **enriched** through their adherence to Christ in **speech and knowledge of every kind** – not in the worldly accomplishments which these words usually denote, and which Paul

7 will disclaim for himself later on, but in **every spiritual gift**: the word is *charismata*, 'charisms', from the same root as the 'grace' (*charis*) of God which they have received; and these gifts, unlike ordinary 'speech and knowledge' (which, being their own accomplishments, might make them complacent),

8 will be a source of confidence to them that they will be **blameless on the day of our Lord Jesus Christ** – a 'day' not only of glory but of judgment; and Paul, at least when he wrote this letter, certainly expected this day to dawn in his own lifetime and constantly urged others to be prepared for it.

There was no doubt, then, of the Corinthians' gifts; but equally (from a Christian point of view) their conduct had shown serious deficiencies, and

10 Paul adopts a tone of urgent remonstrance: **Now I appeal to you.** He has been

11 informed **by Chloe's people** (about whom we know nothing) that there are **divisions** and **quarrels** among them – at least, that is how he regards the fact (even if the Corinthians did not think it so serious) that the names Paul, Apollos, Cephas and Christ were being used as some kind of party labels. The Corinthians will have known at once what he was referring to; for us it

12 has to be guesswork. We have no other evidence that **Cephas** (which is how Paul normally refers to Simon Peter) ever visited Corinth, though we cannot say that he did not. **Apollos,** on the other hand, was certainly a well-known person there (3.6; 6.12), and Acts (18.24–19.1) gives this information about him: that he was a scholarly Alexandrian Jew, that he had been associated with John the Baptist's movement, and that he carried on the work of preaching in Corinth after Paul had left. What sort of groups or tendencies these men could have given their names to, and how a separate group could have called

itself that of **Christ**, are questions which the names alone do not allow us to answer. But something may be learnt from the way Paul approaches the matter.

Paul does not take the side of any of these groups against the others – not even the one which bears his own name – but instead attacks the whole idea of a congregation divided by allegiance to personalities. What would it matter (he asks ironically) who baptized them? The idea was futile: even Paul himself, though he had founded the church and although one of the parties bore his name, had done no baptizing – or at least only in a very

16 few cases, such as **the household of Stephanas**, who were among his first converts (16.15). Moreover, there could be no competition: Paul knew that his apostolic commission may have been to preach, but it was not to preach with

17 **eloquent wisdom**. This phrase is significant. The words appear frequently in the next few chapters, and point almost unmistakably in the direction of the rhetorical skills which any public speaker was expected to show and which Paul, by his own confession, conspicuously lacked. It looks, then, as if the parties or slogans which caused divisions in Corinth were to do with disagreements about the proper way to preach the gospel (with or without appropriate rhetorical presentation) rather than with differences in its actual content. This preoccupation with style rather than with message would have been characteristic of the culture of a city such as Corinth, where philosophers and orators were keenly compared with one another as exponents of the skills of rhetoric. But any such concern about the manner as opposed to the content of Christian preaching was a dangerous diversion: if people started thinking about the gifts and personality of the preacher instead of about what was preached, the gospel would be **emptied of its power**.

18 In any case, Paul's concern is to show that **the message about the cross**, both in its content and in the manner in which it is proclaimed, is something totally other than the intellectual concepts and rhetorical conceits to which people were accustomed in Corinth. He uses three arguments.

First, look at the preaching itself. From the lack of rhetorical skill with which it was presented, and from its apparent lack of philosophical content, it could well have appeared **foolishness**; but those who saw it as such condemned themselves to be among **the perishing**, whereas those who recognized that it was the way in which **the power of God** was manifested were those **who are being saved**. That God had deliberately bypassed the accom

20 plishments of the **wise ... the scribe ... the debater of this age** (Paul seems to have had Jewish learned people in his sights as well as pagans) should not have been unexpected: it was foretold in a prophecy of Isaiah (29.14); and this leads on to a word about the content of this apparently uncouth message for which the word **wisdom** could also do duty. For the word meant, not only the skill of the accomplished persuader (which was not the sort of 'wisdom'

21 which would ever enable one to **know God**), but also an attribute of God himself – not the 'wisdom' of philosophy that aspired to define God in a

concept, but 'wisdom' in the Jewish sense of God's fundamental design in fashioning and maintaining the universe, eliciting an answering 'wisdom' in the human being who learns to accept it. According to this quite different
23 'wisdom', the message of **Christ crucified** could be commended on its own
22 terms. True, the learning of the Jews could make nothing of this. **Jews demand signs**; that is to say, if a revelation of God's nature was to be accepted as true, it must be authenticated by some significant happening; whereas the cruci-
23 fixion of this alleged Messiah seemed an insurmountable **stumbling block.**
22 Equally, for Greeks who **desire wisdom**, that is to say the truth expressed in intellectual terms, the claim that the divine nature could be revealed by an
23 ignominious execution was obviously **foolishness.** The message, in fact, was unprecedented both in form and in content – and in this lay its power.

Secondly, look at the intellectual calibre of the Corinthian Christians. If the doctrine of the cross had been principally an intellectual discovery, and if its preaching had been open to judgment according to the standards of rhetoric, the congregation would hardly have consisted from the beginning of such undistinguished members as in fact it did. And if it was not because of
27 their intellectual distinction or persuasive powers that God **chose** them, but rather the reverse, then the important theological point follows (which Paul
29 expresses in a striking Old Testament idiom): it was **so that no one might boast in the presence of God.** It is precisely those who have no pretensions to 'wisdom, power and nobility' that God has chosen to be recipients of a message which relies on none of these things. Their attributes are now of a quite
30 different order: **righteousness** (in the specifically Christian sense expounded by Paul in, for instance, Romans 3.21–8; 2 Corinthians 5.21), **sanctification** (probably again the fact of having been baptized) and **redemption** from sin. All this proceeds from Christ, who is the only possible source of our self-esteem; and since Christ now bears the title of the 'Lord' of the Old Testament,
31 the words of Jeremiah are appropriate: **"Let the one who boasts, boast in the Lord"** (9.24).

Thirdly, look at Paul himself and the manner of his preaching. He had
2.1 renounced any attempt at **lofty words or wisdom** – the resources of the
4 skilled orator; he had not tried to make his message **plausible**; he had none of the self-confidence of the trained public speaker. There had been nothing in his discourse that could have made any appeal on the level of philosophical 'wisdom' or persuasive presentation. If his hearers had been moved by it and
5, 4, 5 come to **faith,** this was entirely the work **of the Spirit** and of the **power** of God working through the weakness, not the strength, of human beings.

But, as we have seen, the word 'wisdom' also had a positive rôle to play in the argument. For gentile readers it may have suggested a secret and esoteric knowledge accessible only to initiates – and this would certainly not have been conveyed by rhetorical arguments; but, more importantly, it had strong resonance, in Jewish culture. In the later books of the Old Testament, 'wisdom' had assumed great importance as an almost personified attribute of God: it (or 'she') had been present at the creation of the world, it provided a clue to the pattern and future destiny of the universe and it was an authoritative guide for moral behaviour (see especially Job 28; Proverbs 7–9;

6 Sirach 24). It was a wisdom of this kind that **the mature** – those who had fully

7 accepted the preaching – had received. It was something **secret and hidden** – a phrase which in the Greek includes the word *mystērion*, a secret design that had always been God's purpose, **decreed before the ages**, and which was now revealed to Christians for their **glory**. But this was something quite different

6 from **a wisdom of this age**, such as politicians and military men might believe

8 they possessed **(the rulers of this age)**, for it was such people who had been on the wrong side (so to speak) at the time of the crucifixion, and their 'wisdom' evidently gave them no insight into the hidden purposes of God.

7 The true wisdom, being a 'mystery', was something God had **decreed** long

9 ago, as scripture attested;[1] and it was **revealed**, not through philosophical or esoteric reasoning, or by means of carefully honed argumentation, but

10 **through the Spirit.**

The point is reinforced by an argument that is partly philosophical, partly psychological. It was a commonly accepted maxim that, among conscious beings, only like knows like. In the case of human beings, only the human

11 consciousness (here called for the purpose of the argument **the human spirit**) can know **what is truly human**. In the case of God, **no one comprehends what is truly God's except the Spirit of God.** So how can human beings know anything of God? Only if they have God's Spirit in themselves – which is precisely the gift that Christians have received. And this knowledge, being derived from a quite different source from that of human wisdom, also requires a different form of transmission, not by human eloquence, but by the persuasiveness that belongs to the Spirit: those who transmit it are

13 **interpreting spiritual things to those who are spiritual** (or rather, according to an alternative translation in the NRSV footnote, *interpreting spiritual things*

15 *in spiritual language*). This places them apart from anyone else's **scrutiny**, for the criteria which must be applied to this message are not drawn from the standards of human 'wisdom'. Is this not presumptuous? Do not the

16 scornful words of Isaiah apply (40.13), **"Who has known the mind of the Lord?"** But the Christian can answer that what was said of 'the Lord' in the Old Testament can now be said of Christ, and Christians, by virtue of their union with Christ (a spiritual and even psychological reality) **have the mind of Christ.**

Where then do the Corinthian Christians stand? Do they have this wisdom? Clearly they did not reject the original message, for they have become

3.1, 3 Christians; they are **in Christ.** But the **jealousy and quarreling** among them, attaching themselves to individual leaders such as Paul or Apollos, shows

---

[1] It is not clear whether Paul's quotation is a rough paraphrase of a passage such as Isaiah 64.4 or is drawn from some lost apocryphal writing.

that they still think on the level of 'human wisdom'; they are people **of the**

4, 1 **flesh . . . merely human**, instead of **spiritual people**. But not totally: their failure to understand springs not from perversity but from immaturity – and

2 Paul uses the philosophical cliché of infants not yet **ready for solid food**.

To help them advance, Paul gives them a common-sense reason why they should not attach importance to individual preachers. These men – Paul, Apollos, perhaps others who had influence in the church at Corinth – were

9 simply **servants**, agents of their conversion to the faith according to God's assignment. Paul gives two analogies, both quite conventional (they occur in Jeremiah 1.9–10): gardening and building. In either case the actual gardeners or builders are a secondary factor. All that matters is who gives the growth (God) or what the foundation is (Jesus Christ). Not that this makes the servants' work any less responsible. The quality of each builder's work will be

13 laid bare on **the Day**; and the conventional Jewish imagery of fire associated with the day of judgment is now worked into the building analogy (even if it does not quite fit in every detail). Yet even the incompetent builders,

15 though all their work may be lost, will **be saved** (for failure will not exclude them totally from the company of Christians). On the other hand there is another side to this building analogy. It was a Christian commonplace that

17 the church is a new, 'spiritual' temple. So anyone who **destroys** this building (or damages it in any way, as the Greek could also mean) will receive, at the same judgment, a far harsher sentence.

18 It is now possible to understand the difference between being **wise in this age**, and being 'wise' with the wisdom of God. That the pretensions

19 of **the wisdom of this world** would be an obstacle rather than an aid was not a new thought: verses from Job (5.13) and a psalm (97.11), though originally directed more against the cunning and unscrupulous than against the philosopher or the orator, are pressed into service to reinforce the point. Everything that is merely human – leaders like Paul and Apollos, along with

22 other more important factors of the human condition such as **life or death** – is of small importance compared with the spiritual reality of belonging to Christ.

The perspective from which the Corinthians had been judging and comparing those who had preached among them was 'of this age', that is, they not only judged by secular standards but they were ignoring the factor of the coming judgment of God. Even a clear conscience, such as Paul claims

4.4 for himself (**I am not aware of anything against myself**) is provisional: not

5 until the judgment will **things now hidden in darkness** be revealed. And this applied not only to the preachers – they were merely examples, a warning

7 equally to their hearers, among whom there could be no competition: **What do you have that you did not receive?** (The point is driven home with a

6 proverb: "**Nothing beyond what is written**"; but unfortunately we do not know what it means.)

But there is also a side-effect of the Corinthians' trust in the dialectics of 'worldly wisdom' which rouses Paul to some words of bitter irony. Philosophers might claim to be truly rich, even to be 'kings' (which Paul clearly feels is a travesty of the Corinthians' actual situation). If this was the sort of superiority to which they were aspiring, then let Paul contrast this with his own understanding of what it meant faithfully to follow Christ. People with gifts of reasoning and eloquence expected to be admired; but

9 Paul was a **spectacle**, not of heroic prowess, but such as might be seen in a Roman theatre (the word he uses is *theatron*) when convicted criminals were put to death. Like a Stoic philosopher, Paul can list the things he has been enabled to endure. (He does this several times in the Corinthian correspondence.) But in his case it is not philosophy that sustains him: others might call it 'foolishness', but for him it is a deeper reality which has led him to take physical endurance and deliberate non-retaliation to extremes hardly contemplated even by the most ascetic philosophers. Such a comparison with

14 their own standards might well have made the Corinthians **ashamed**. But this was not Paul's purpose; he had put himself forward as an example for

17 them to imitate, not of superior virtue or asceticism, but of his **ways in Christ Jesus**. Evidently the situation in Corinth was in stark conflict with principles such as these; and Paul urges them to reform. He bases his appeal on the

15 unique relationship he has with them, that of a single **father** as opposed to their many **guardians** (literally *pedagogues*, on which see below on Galatians

17 3.24); and he is also sending his most trusted fellow worker, **Timothy**, to see to the matter in person. He is aware – and this is the first time he says

19 so openly – that some of the Corinthians are **arrogant**, and maintain their self-importance when he is absent. But such arrogance derives, again, from their talk – that is, from their reliance on eloquent arguments. By contrast,

20 there is a **power** in the preaching of the kingdom of God which Paul, when

21 he comes, will administer either in correction or in support, **with a stick, or with love in a spirit of gentleness**. It is for them to choose which it shall be.

Sexual immorality

5.1 **It is actually reported**. Divisions and party quarrels were only a part of the disquieting news brought to Paul by his informants. There had also been a serious case of **sexual immorality**. Both Jewish law (Leviticus 18.8) and Roman law forbade a man to marry his stepmother; and any sexual relationship with a stepmother (even after the father's death) would doubtless have been regarded as equally immoral. Yet the Corinthian Christians, per-

2 haps mistakenly thinking themselves above both law and convention (**you are arrogant!**), were complacently tolerating such a relationship in their midst. Paul does not discuss the case or consider whether there is any further enquiry to be made, but sternly lays down the procedure to be followed. A

solemn assembly of the whole congregation, at which Paul will be present in
3 his **spirit**, must pass sentence of excommunication – just as a Jewish court
would have imposed banishment (Leviticus 18.29), a punishment which had
the effect (it was believed) of denying the culprit the protection of the community from the retribution that God would exact for the crime. This was
5 likely to be death, and could be said to be administered by **Satan**. This punishment may sound to us extreme (and 'un-Christian'); but it may have been
seen as the lesser evil; for, after retribution, the sinner's **spirit** might qualify
for salvation **on the day of the Lord.**

So much for the offender. But this act of excommunication was equally
necessary for the church, which might otherwise be corrupted by the presence
6 of the offender in its midst. A familiar proverb makes the point: **a little yeast
leavens the whole batch of dough.** But Paul then develops this into a piece
of complex Christian imagery. A metaphor for describing the work of Christ
was furnished by the Passover. Christ was crucified at Passover time (indeed,
according to John's gospel, at the exact time when the Passover lambs were
slaughtered); he could therefore be described as a **paschal lamb**, and the
Christian life as a Passover festival. But – to carry the metaphor still further –
this festival opened a period when only unleavened bread was eaten. All the
old yeast had to be cleared out and a fresh start made in baking. In the same
way, the Christian 'Passover festival' must be observed by making a clean
8 break from **the yeast of malice and evil.**

This leads Paul to mention a point which had come up earlier in the
9 correspondence. In a previous letter it seems that he had told them **not to
associate with sexually immoral persons.** This had been (perhaps deliberately) misunderstood by the Corinthians, who had replied that to do this
10 they would **need to go out of the world**, that is, to have no further contact
with people outside the church. Paul now explains what he meant: he was
not talking about the citizens of Corinth in general – he doubtless knew of
their reputation for immorality – but about fellow Christians. No one who
committed acts of this kind – and Paul uses a conventional list of vices to
extend the category beyond sexual offenders – should be admitted to the
11 congregation: they should **not even eat with** them (for table fellowship, in
that culture, implied more than mere acquaintance). An injunction that was
frequently laid on the Israelite community was to this extent applicable to
13 a Christian congregation also: **"Drive out the wicked person from among
you"** (Deuteronomy 13.5 and elsewhere).

Litigiousness and sexual purity

Paul had also heard of another moral lapse. In Jewish communities in the
Dispersion, and also in religious and other unofficial associations which
abounded in the Greek-speaking world, it was normal for disputes to be
settled within the community – from the Jewish point of view, any other

6.1 court, not being bound by the law of Moses, was a tribunal of **the unrigh-teous**. By taking one another to court before gentile judges, Christians were falling below the standards even of other societies; and this was all the more inexcusable in that they were now united with Christ, and Christ would have a place alongside God on the day of judgment. They were therefore destined
2 to be a part of the tribunal that would **judge the world** – and not only the world: since Christ was above all other orders of creation, they would even
3 be judging **angels**. On these grounds alone, their conduct was reprehensible. But then it is as if Paul suddenly recollects the radical teaching of Jesus (as
7 in Matthew 5.39), which excludes any claim for redress whatever: **Why not rather be wronged?** And in any case, the grievances would not have arisen had not at least one party in each case been falling below the moral stan-
9 dards of those who claimed to **inherit the kingdom of God** – and Paul again recites a conventional list of offences.[2] Of course the congregation included
11 people who had done such things. But since then they had been **washed** by their baptism and so **sanctified** and **justified** – terms that belonged to Paul's standard vocabulary for describing the status of the Christian before God.
12 **"All things are lawful for me."** A Greek manuscript had no quotation marks, and we cannot be sure whether Paul is giving his own or someone else's opinion. The NRSV is probably right to take this as a slogan used by the Corinthians. It does not mean that they thought that they were 'above the law', but rather that their new religion released them from some of the social and moral constraints of pagan and indeed Jewish society. In the same way, Stoic and Cynic philosophers claimed that their philosophy gave them a moral code independent of law or convention. If so, then Paul is prepared to agree, but with two vital qualifications. First, all behaviour in the church must still be governed by what is beneficial for all – he will develop this point later (10.23ff.). Secondly, there is a danger that if the constraint of conventional morality is removed, then improper desires and habits may take over: **I will not be dominated by anything**. An obvious example is greed. It is all very well to say – and this seems to have been another of the Corinthians' slogans –
13 **"Food is meant for the stomach and the stomach for food"**, as if such things were nothing to do with religion or morals (this was also a popular philosophical position), and the slogan might be a useful one to use against taboos and food laws such as were practised in Judaism. But this did not mean that *any* bodily function was a matter of indifference; it certainly could not be used as a licence for sexual permissiveness. For whatever might be said about the stomach, the whole body was quite another matter. Christianity was not a religion concerned only with 'soul' or 'spirit': Christians' solidarity

---

[2] The words translated **male prostitutes** and **sodomites** have given rise to much discussion. Their range of meaning can perhaps be indicated as follows: the first are those who submit (voluntarily or involuntarily) to homosexual practices, the second are those who deliberately indulge in them.

with Christ was a quite physical matter, for it was their **body** (conceived as an integral complex of flesh, mind and spirit) that was **for the Lord** here and now, and was also that which would be the subject of our resurrection (like that of Jesus) in the future. Indeed this solidarity with Christ involved the whole

15 person to such an extent that one could say that we are actually **members** (or *limbs*) **of Christ**; so much so, that Christians have a new and decisive reason to shun one of the sins which were most sternly condemned in Jewish ethics:

18, 16 **fornication**. The words in Genesis (2.24), **"The two shall be one flesh"**, imply, at the least, that sexual intercourse creates a very close relationship between a man and a woman; and if the man is a Christian and the woman a prostitute, this relationship would implicate Christ in prostitution. In this

18 sense, fornication affects the body in a way no other sin does: **the fornicator sins against the body itself.** And since a Christian is united with Christ's body, it follows that fornication is a sin against Christ.

And there is a further point to be made. It was said earlier (3.16) that the Christian community is the 'temple' of God and his Spirit. But this is also true of the individual. It was impossible for anyone educated as a Jew to separate (as a Greek thinker might do) 'body' from 'soul' or 'spirit'; in Hebrew psychology the person was an integrated entity. It followed that a

19 Christian's body was **a temple of the Holy Spirit** which must not be profaned.

20 Moreover, **you were bought with a price**. The metaphor is probably from purchasing or redeeming slaves. The purchaser does not buy or free only part of the slave, the slave's 'will' or 'soul', as if this were detachable from the body. No, the transaction affects the whole person. The vaunted 'freedom' of the Christian is a new relationship of the whole person with the one who has freed us; **therefore glorify God in your body**.

Marriage, divorce and social status

7.1 **Now concerning the matters about which you wrote.** Apart from the disturbing reports he had heard about Corinthian church life, Paul's main reason for writing seems to have been a letter he had received; and the rest of 1 Corinthians is devoted mainly to answering that letter point by point. Precisely why the Corinthians had written, and whether their questions were in the form of protests against his previous teaching or of requests for clarification and further guidance, we cannot be sure. But at this point the correspondence gives us insight into some of the moral problems which were besetting a Christian community in a pagan and cosmopolitan society.

The first topic has to do with relations between the sexes. **"It is well for a man not to touch a woman."** This reads, again, like a slogan being cited by the Corinthians (so, at least, the translators have taken it), presumably applying to sexual intercourse. Some Christians may well have been adopting an extreme sexual asceticism, which Paul does not necessarily disapprove

2 of, but the reality is that there have also been **cases of sexual immorality,**

married people having apparently made a vow of continence within marriage and then having broken it by going to prostitutes. Far better, then, to maintain normal marital relationships – and Paul prescribes a reciprocity in them which is in the very best philosophical and religious tradition of the ancient

6 world. But he does this **by way of concession**. His own preference is somewhat different. He had no wife himself (though, as an orthodox and devout Jew, it would be surprising if he had not once been married), but regarded

7 celibacy (and presumably continence) as **a particular gift from God** which was not necessarily given to everyone; and this leads him on to the question whether Christians who were unmarried should contemplate marriage or not.

8–9   The first consideration follows from the ascetical principle with which the paragraph began. Complete abstinence (such as many philosophers recommended for the sake of a contemplative life) could be practised only by those who, like himself, were unmarried. Those who wished to practise it

10–11 should therefore remain as they were. What about those who were already married? Following the same principle, should they seek separation (in the case of the wife) or divorce (in the case of the husband)? But against this stood the Lord's ruling against divorce (which Paul evidently knew in much the same form as it has in Mark 10 and Matthew 19). And although Jesus

12–16 when he gave this ruling presumably did not envisage the problems of mixed marriages in which only one partner is a Christian, yet Paul feels justified (on his own authority, not that of Jesus) in extending the prohibition of divorce, and of remarriage in the case of a wife who separates, to marriages of this kind. For, in the first place, the conversion of one parent makes the

14 whole family into a Christian household (it is made **holy**), and this is bound in some way to involve the other partner; and secondly it is always possible that the unbelieving partner might be 'saved'. The only exception allowed (known in subsequent controversies over divorce as 'the Pauline exception')

15 is if the **unbelieving partner separates**. The peace of a Christian household is not to be threatened by a desperate attempt to hold on to a non-Christian partner.

17   **However that may be.** Paul now digresses a little in order to place the whole matter in a wider context. The background here may be the conditions which might be imposed on converts to Judaism: beginning a new life in their new religion, they might be exhorted, if not compelled, to leave behind any of their former possessions and commitments that might be tainted with paganism (everything from a wine cellar to a wife!). Should Christians do the same? Moreover, the time was believed to be short: Paul was about to discourage marriage for this reason. Either of these motives could have tempted new Christians to abandon their ordinary occupations and social obligations. Paul's rule in all the churches had been sternly opposed to anything of the kind. Neither Jews nor Gentiles should seek to change their

21–4 social or ethnic identity, and even slaves should remain content with their

condition.[3] Any agitation of this kind would result only in their becoming
23 once more **slaves of human masters** and would be incompatible with the
dearly bought freedom of those who had exchanged all human subservience
22 for the service (or 'slavery') **of Christ**. So in general (and not only with
24 regard to marriage), **In whatever condition you were called ... there remain
with God.**

This principle is relevant when Paul comes to his third topic, the question
of celibacy. Here (by contrast with the question of divorce) there is no saying
25 of Jesus to appeal to: **I have no command of the Lord**. But Paul can still
40 give a trustworthy opinion (authorized, as he says later, by **the Spirit of
God**). It follows from what he has just said that all should 'remain as they
are'. Not merely should the married remain married, but the unmarried
should remain unmarried. But now a further reason for this is introduced.
26 The time Christians were living in was one of **impending** (or the Greek
could mean even *present*) **crisis**. The pressing imminence of the end of the
present world order (as it seemed to Paul and doubtless to many Christians
at the time) placed a question mark over all human conditions, possessions
and institutions – even marriage, which could not be expected to continue
unchanged into the new age. If one was to take this prospect seriously, one
must be prepared to look upon even marriage as something provisional.
29 In this sense (and despite what Paul had said earlier, 7.3), **those who have
wives** should be as **those who have none** – just as they should have a certain
almost philosophical detachment from human grief, human joy and human
30 **possessions**, and in general be as free as possible from practical anxieties –
35 though all this is said without the intention of imposing any **restraint** on
them. Neither the inclination of his own temperament, nor the asceticism
of some of the Corinthians, nor even the imminence of the Day, should be
allowed to turn celibacy into an absolute rule.
36 Woven into this discussion is a further topic introduced by the word **fiancée**
or *virgin*. Here we are at a loss to know exactly what was at issue. The Greek
word *parthenos* certainly means 'a virgin'; but it could also have a considerably
wider meaning, including almost any young, unmarried woman; it could
be a way of referring to a daughter or to a fiancée. What is Paul talking
about here? The traditional view, accepted by most until the end of the
nineteenth century, was that the paragraph is about the problems of parents
in a Christian community. With the prospect of an early end to the present
world order, should they marry off their 'virgin daughters'? In this case
the word **marry** in verse 36 must be transitive, meaning 'marry off' (which
would be perfectly good Greek). But it then becomes difficult to see what
not behaving properly, or having 'strong passions', has got to do with it.
A second possibility is that *parthenos* means **fiancée**, and that the question

---

[3] Whether or not they should seize a legitimate opportunity to gain their freedom is a
detail which the obscurity of Paul's Greek conceals from us. See the NRSV footnote.

was whether a betrothed man should proceed to marriage. This appears to be the solution adopted by the translators of the NRSV, but it too runs into difficulties, for it is hard to see in what sense the man should **keep her as his fiancée** when resolved *not* to marry her. A third view, which is more speculative but makes better sense of the text, is that *parthenos* here means a kind of 'partner in celibacy'. It is assumed (on this view) that couples in Corinth were entering into a kind of 'spiritual marriage', without either the legal form or the physical intimacy of normal marriage, and that this relationship had been subject to the inevitable strains involved in such relationships. Experiments of this kind certainly took place in Christian communities in later centuries; it is not impossible that they had already begun at Corinth. If so, we may suppose that Paul, on his own principles, was not opposed to such 'spiritual marriages'; but if the Corinthians, out of asceticism, were thinking it sinful to turn such a relationship into a real marriage, Paul's reply was that if anyone's physical desires make it necessary to take this course, he **does well**.

Finally, the same reasoning is applied to widows. For the sake of peace in the community (7.15), they should certainly not remarry outside it, but choose a husband who is a Christian (**in the Lord**). Better still (as in the case of unmarried men), they should not remarry at all.

Food sacrificed to idols

The next subject about which the Corinthians had written to Paul was one which arose out of the ordinary circumstances of life in a city such as Corinth. There were many temples and altars dedicated to the various gods of Greek religion, and these demanded frequent sacrifices of animals. But only a small part of these was actually burnt on the altar; the rest was disposed of in one of two ways. Either, at the time of the sacrifice, one might invite one's friends to come to the temple and dine off the sacrificial meat, or else the meat, after the sacrifice, was returned to the trade to be retailed in the meat market.

By the ordinary citizen all this was taken for granted: it formed an accepted part of social life and marketing arrangements. But for the Jewish community in a pagan city this connection of meat with worship could not be a matter of indifference. Indeed, the Jews coined their own word for it: *eidōlothyta*, **food sacrificed to idols**; and they had a clear policy towards the whole question. Their religion forbade them to join in any social gathering in a pagan temple, and indeed greatly limited their social life with Gentiles altogether; and their scruples about kosher meat prevented them in any case from buying their meat in the ordinary market, and so protected them from the danger of eating anything which had been contaminated by pagan worship.

What was to be the attitude of non-Jewish Christians? On the one hand, they now shared with the Jews their faith in the one true God, and this was clearly incompatible with any real participation in pagan worship; on the other hand, they shared none of the Jews' scruples about sharing meals with Gentiles or about the kind of meat they ate. To have adopted the Jewish policy would have cut them off from much social contact outside the church and would have complicated their shopping in the meat market. Yet some policy was necessary, since simply to ignore the associations with 'idols' involved in normal social life was clearly something that not all their members could cope with.

Paul deals first with the question of invitations to meals in pagan temples. The Corinthians had taken the line that it was best for them to go on as before, and had used certain arguments in support of this (**"all of us possess**
4 **knowledge"**, **"no idol in the world really exists"**, **"there is no God but one"**).[4] Paul was broadly in agreement with these propositions. The worship of the many **idols** of the Greeks and Romans could be of no significance to
6 Christians, who had superior 'knowledge' of **one God, the Father** (and here Paul adds some somewhat metaphysical-sounding attributes such as would have been familiar to educated Corinthians, but building a new factor, **the Lord, Jesus Christ**, into the conventional religious formulas). Even though for many of them – and certainly for Paul – the universe was peopled with supernatural beings such as angels and demons, and so the words 'gods' and 'lords' might well mean something, yet this did not affect the fact that there was in reality only **one God**, infinitely superior to all such beings.

But this 'knowledge' – and the word could be used of varying degrees of philosophical or mystical religious illumination – did not necessarily solve
1 the problem; indeed, there was a danger that it **puffs up**, to the detriment of the mutual **love** which should 'build up' the Christian community. The relationship between Christians was far more important than the intellectual justification of their policy, and the Corinthians' simple solution to the
9 problem was in danger of becoming **a stumbling block to the weak**. Not all their members had reached the same point of enlightened 'knowledge'. Long association with heathen practices had made it impossible for some of them to be present at sacrifices without some sense of involvement; for them, it
10 was better to stay away, and the spectacle of their fellow Christians **eating in the temple of an idol** might put them under pressure to do what they conscientiously believed they should not do. Therefore, although Paul was
8 prepared to agree with another of their slogans, that **"food will not bring us close to God"** and is therefore a matter of indifference from a religious point of view,[5] there might be unfortunate consequences for the Christian fellowship. The overriding principle must be the one he stated at the outset:
1 only **love builds up**. Paul would rather take the extreme step of becoming a

---

[4] Once again (see above on 6.12), it is assumed by the translators that some of the sentences in this paragraph are slogans that the Corinthians used themselves.
[5] This is the clear implication of the slogan, which may have included the following phrase (see the NRSV footnote).

13 vegetarian than risk causing one of those to fall who belong to the Christian
12 **family**.[6]

Paul's self-defence

9.1 **Am I not free?** Suddenly – and this outburst is indeed so sudden that some
have thought this must be an addition to the original letter – Paul begins
to defend himself. Clearly he has been under attack; and he addresses much
3 of this chapter against those **who would examine me**. (The word in the
Greek has a strong legal resonance: *bring a charge against me* would capture
the meaning.) There are two points on which he appears to be sensitive: his
freedom (which is relevant to the question just under discussion) and his right
to be called an apostle; and we shall see that these two points are connected.

First, his apostleship. This could hardly be denied by the Corinthians. As
1 with all the apostles, it rested primarily on his having seen the risen **Jesus our
Lord**; but it may be that Paul's vision, so unlike the others' experience, and
which he himself describes as "to one untimely born" (15.8), was regarded by
some as not fully authentic. If so, there was a second mark of authenticity. His
apostleship had been confirmed by its fruits: the Corinthians themselves –
2 and the growth of the church among them – were **the seal of my apostleship
in the Lord**.

So much, in general terms, the Corinthians could hardly dispute. But there
seems also to have been a specific accusation. Paul (as we are told also in Acts
18.3) did not expect the Corinthian congregation to provide for him, but
earned his own living or relied on support from elsewhere. This he did by
personal preference; but it appears that his practice was not in line with that
5 of the **other apostles (and the brothers of the Lord**, Paul adds: we know
from Acts that one of Jesus' brothers – whether a full brother or a half-
brother – namely James, became a leader of the Jerusalem church; and there
is a later tradition that other relatives came to hold positions of authority).
They, apparently, felt entitled to support from their congregations, both for
themselves and for their wives. This difference of practice between Paul (and
perhaps his fellow worker Barnabas) and the others seems to have provided
his opponents with an argument against him: if Paul were a real apostle,
surely he would enjoy the same material privileges as the other apostles; but
in fact he had to earn his own living; therefore he could not be a real apostle.

Paul attacks both the premise and the conclusion of this argument. The
reason the other apostles received support from their congregations was not
any privilege which belonged to the office of 'apostle'; it was a matter of what
8 we would call 'natural justice'. Ordinary **human** analogies (from military
service or agriculture) proved the point; but there was also the authority of

---

[6] Literally, *brothers* (see the NRSV footnote). The translation **family** is a slightly misleading designation for the Christian community.

9 scripture: **"You shall not muzzle an ox while it is treading out the grain"** (Deuteronomy 25.4). There is no doubt that this clause from the law of Moses was originally intended to be exactly what it seems, a humanitarian regulation to protect domestic animals in a threshing mill, and so of little relevance to the point at issue. But learned interpreters were loath to believe that anything in the divinely given law had such a limited application – **Is it for oxen that God is concerned?** There must be a meaning of more immediate relevance

10 to human beings – **It was indeed, written for our sake.** So understood, it yielded the point for which Paul was arguing, that genuine work of any kind entitles the worker to a reward. In this respect he was obviously on all fours with the others. It was by virtue of their work, not their office, that they could claim support; and so, of course, could he. And if it were to be said that this

14 applies only to manual work, and that those who **proclaim the gospel** were

13 in a different category, what about priests **in the temple**, who also have a right to the provision of food? And was there not a command of Jesus to the same effect? – an allusion, perhaps, to a saying of Jesus such as that recorded in Matthew 10.10, "laborers deserve their food".

There could be no question, therefore, but that Paul had as much right as anyone else to material support. His opponents were quite wrong on their facts. But they were also wrong in their conclusion. Paul had come to his

15 own decision and acted of his own free will: **I have made no use of any of these rights.** And this was not a mere preference: it was a passionately held matter of principle. So urgent had been Paul's commission to preach the gospel that his entire self-confidence, his **boasting**, rested on the reality of

16 this **obligation.** Had this preaching been on his own initiative, he might have claimed payment; but for something laid on him as a commission he *must*

18 be free to **make the gospel free of charge** – and this brings him back to the second question, that of his 'freedom'.

Paul's conduct, especially with regard to Jewish observances, and also perhaps with regard to the Gentiles' problem of 'food sacrificed to idols', may have seemed at times inconsistent; and possibly this inconsistency was at the root of some of the charges laid against him, and made it the more difficult for him to give a clear ruling on matters of practical conduct. Paul does not deny this apparent inconsistency; on the contrary, he justifies it

19 on the grounds (i) that he is **free with respect to all** – that is, like every Christian, free from religious taboos and ordinances, and (ii) that he has

23 been exercising this freedom not for his own sake but for the **sake of the gospel.** His willingness to accommodate himself to the scruples of others has brought him even to the point (which should particularly touch the Corinthians, and shows how they, too, ought to behave) where he can say,

22 **To the weak I became weak, so that I might win the weak.**

Not that this can have been easy. A person brought up as a strict Jew could hardly feel indifferent to the habits, customs and religious ordinances which had governed the greater part of his life. In the same way, the Corinthians could not expect to be able to accommodate themselves to their more scrupulous fellow Christians without serious self-discipline. But if athletes (a popular comparison in rhetoric) were prepared to **exercise self-control** for a mere wreath of leaves (the only prize given at Greek games), how much more should Christians be prepared to do for an **imperishable** wreath!

Warnings from scripture – respect of conscience

10.1 **I do not want you to be unaware.** The tone becomes somewhat more severe. It may be that the Corinthians, with all their 'knowledge' and 'freedom', had allowed themselves to slip into a false sense of security. They were instructed to believe, as Paul certainly did at the time when he wrote this letter, that the present world order was coming to an end: they were the people **on whom the ends of the ages have come**, they were singled out for acquittal and reward on the day of judgment, and they possessed a supernatural assurance of their privileged destiny in the rites of baptism and eucharist. But – **watch out that you do not fall**. Paul has a warning for them derived from his reading of certain passages of scripture.

The basic narrative referred to is contained in Exodus 13–17. The people of Israel (Paul's physical ancestors, but also, in a sense, the spiritual ancestors of Christians) were preserved during their flight from Egypt by means of certain supernatural events. They were preceded (or 'covered', according to Psalm 105.39) by a pillar of **cloud** (Exodus 13.21), they miraculously **passed through the sea** (Exodus 14), they were supplied with the **spiritual food** of manna (Exodus 16) and with **spiritual drink** out of the rock at Horeb (Exodus 17; Numbers 20.11). This narrative had for some time been the subject of much scholarly elaboration. Exactly how the people of Israel had passed through the sea, for example, was a question only sketchily answered by the biblical account, and later interpretations of the story made it into a kind of ordeal by water, a symbol (as it seemed to Paul, and perhaps to other Jewish interpreters) of that baptism which was one of the ways in which a proselyte was received into the Jewish community. In this sense, it could be said that they **all were baptized**, and this, though it was **into Moses** and not 'into Christ', was a clear foreshadowing of Christian baptism. Similarly, the story of the rock had received considerable elaboration. It not only provided people with water to drink – even in the Exodus account it was no ordinary rock, so **spiritual rock** is not a misdescription – but it came to be thought of, like the pillar of cloud, as a symbol of the concern of God for his people, which **followed them** and provided **spiritual drink** in the form of divine wisdom. This kind of speculation made of the rock a powerful symbol of the gifts of God to his people; and Paul was only taking this line of thought a stage further when he made it stand for the greatest of God's gifts: **the rock was Christ** (one of several hints in Paul's letters that he ascribed to Christ some form of pre-existence). In this way he found clear precedents in the

Exodus narrative for the Christian sacraments of baptism and perhaps – in view of what follows – eucharist.

6 **Now these things occurred as examples for us** – literally *types*, that is to say, not just literary parallels and warnings but significant moments of the past pointing forward to some subsequent events. The people of Israel

5 received these supernatural blessings; nevertheless, **they were struck down in the wilderness** (Numbers 14.16 and elsewhere). Their sins (i) of desiring

7 evil (Numbers 11.34), (ii) of idolatry (**"the people sat down to eat and drink, and they rose up to play"** is a quotation from the story of the golden calf,

8 Exodus 32.6), (iii) of **sexual immorality** (Numbers 25.1, 9), (iv) of putting

9, 10 *the Lord*[7] **to the test** (Numbers 25.5–6), and (v) of readiness to **complain** (Numbers 14.36–7), were all duly punished – and for the last punishment Paul uses the biblical expression **the destroyer** (as in Exodus 12.23). All these,

11 then, served as an **example**, or as *types*, a warning to those others who would also receive supernatural blessings and would also stand under imminent

13 judgment – **they were written down to instruct us**. So no **testing** will be any excuse for Christians to commit such sins, nor will they be able to plead that

14 what they are going through is unprecedented or unendurable. **Therefore** (to take from this list the particular temptation involved in the original question (8.10) of "eating in the temple of an idol") **flee from the worship of idols**.

So much by way of a general warning against associating with heathen worship. But there is a more specific issue. Christians had their own sacred

16 meal, one which involved an intense degree of **sharing**, both with one another and in the **blood** and **body of Christ**. This 'sharing' was something new and distinctive, and is the key word throughout the paragraph. (The NRSV

18–20 obscures this by translating it **partners** in the following verses.) Yet it was not altogether without precedent or analogy. In the Jewish religion the sacrifices

18 in the temple made those present into **partners** – literally *sharers* – **in the altar** (which is an oblique way of saying, 'sharers with God'). What about pagan sacrifices? Surely the same principle could hardly apply; if it did, it would seem to imply that an idol was more than an idol, and had some supernatural existence in which the worshippers could 'share'. Certainly it had no real existence; but Paul's stress on 'sharing' makes the resemblance rest, not so much on that to which the sacrifice is made, as on the fellowship involved in the shared act of sacrificing. This shared act can never be, so to speak, neutral. If it is not offered to God it becomes demonic. At the receiving end

20 there may be, not nothing, but **demons**, whose existence is acknowledged in scripture (Leviticus 17.7; Deuteronomy 32.17 and elsewhere). 'Sharing' in such circumstances cannot avoid this implication; therefore it is incompatible

---

[7] Some important manuscripts read **Christ** instead of *the Lord*, and this is preferred in the NRSV text. It is certainly more difficult (and therefore perhaps more likely to be the original reading): the thought must be that if the rock was Christ, they could be said to be 'tempting Christ' if they behaved in the same way. *The Lord* was in any case an early Christian title for Christ.

21 with partaking of **the table of the Lord,** and is a clear instance of that sin described in Deuteronomy 32.21, "They made me jealous with what is no god,
22 provoked me with their idols", to which Paul's question, **are we provoking the Lord to jealousy?** is a clear allusion. It follows that for Christians to join in the temple meals of their pagan friends is incompatible both with the reality of their new sharing in the Christian eucharist and with the Old Testament insistence on the avoidance of idolatry.

Paul is now ready to give a ruling on the remaining questions raised by 'food sacrificed to idols'. He quotes once again (as above, 6.12) the Corinthi-
23 ans' slogan **"All things are lawful"**, which in this, as in the matter of sexual morals, is their main argument for permissiveness; and once again he accepts it, but with the qualification that it is still more important not to do anything
26 that will not **build up** the unity of the congregation. **"The earth and its fullness are the Lord's"** (Psalm 24.1), so that a Christian when shopping at the meat market may buy anything: no one's conscience should be troubled. Equally, Christians may continue to accept invitations to dine at the houses
27 of pagan friends: their 'freedom' allows them to eat **whatever is set before** them. But if on such an occasion the host or a fellow guest explicitly points
28 out that the food has been **"offered in sacrifice"** (the term used here is one which a pagan would have used, not the Jewish term used above in 8.1), then
29 it becomes necessary to consider questions of other people's **conscience,** such as the inferences which might be drawn from such public participation by Christians – which is different from suggesting that Christians' own consciences should be troubled. In other words, the principle of 'freedom' must
32 always be qualified by another equally important one: **Give no offence to Jews or to Greeks or to the church of God.** Paul himself has set an example for them to follow, as Christ set an example for him.

The ordering of worship

The next topic is the ordering of public worship. The Corinthians seem to
11.2 have said in their letter, by way of justifying their own practice, 'we remember you in everything and maintain the traditions as you handed them on to us'; and Paul begins with a gracious acknowledgment of their protestation. But at the same time they had apparently been permitting women to attend services, and even to pray and to prophesy in public, with their heads unveiled. We know very little about the background to this. In the Jewish world, and to a large extent in the pagan world, women customarily had their heads covered in public; that they did not do so in the Christian assembly – possibly when they were carried away 'prophesying' – is surprising. Paul was clearly shocked by it, and felt the need to give a ruling. Unfortunately, his arguments are even more obscure than the matter in question. They may be tentatively set out as follows.

(i) Despite the Christian conviction that the sexes are equal before God 11.3 (Galatians 3.28), there is still a certain order of preference: just as **God is the head of Christ**, so man is the head of woman (or **the husband is the head of his wife:** the Greek words could mean either).

(ii) An argument from custom: if shaving off the hair is a disgrace for a woman (as it is not for a man), then taking off the veil is equivalent, and also 6 **disgraceful.**

8–9 (iii) An argument from scripture: the second Genesis account of creation seems to imply the priority of man over woman (2.22); the first makes man the 'image' of God, his reflection or glory (1.26–7; as a matter of fact, this account includes both male and female!); by analogy, the woman, who proceeds from 10 the man, is the 'reflection' or 'glory', not of God, but of man. In addition there are angels to be reckoned with: either the evil angels of Genesis 6, or good angels such as some may have believed were present at Christian worship. In either case, the veil would be necessary, to ward off the evil angels or to show proper respect to the good ones.[8]

(Verses 11–12 are parenthetical: a concession that, despite these conserva-11 tive arguments, **in the Lord** – that is, for Christians – the sexes are interdependent.)

14 (iv) An argument from **nature** (of a kind popular in Stoic philosophy): 15 long hair is natural for women (their **glory**); so, presumably, are veils.

16 (v) An appeal to universal practice, followed throughout the churches: **we have no such custom.**

But Paul has also heard about a much more serious breach of good order 18 in the Corinthians' worship. The **divisions** which are besetting the whole membership of the church are also in evidence at their services; and although 19 there is a sense in which **there have to be factions** – in that, before Christians can take their place beside Christ at the imminent judgment, their community will need already to have been tested and sifted by their own disputes to make clear **who are genuine** – yet such divisions should not interfere with worship. 20 The particular abuse Paul has in mind concerns **the Lord's supper** – and this is the earliest account we have of the Christian eucharist. It appears that at this stage it was a real supper, supplied by members of the congregation; hence the possibilities for that social injustice, selfishness and insensitivity which Paul had heard about. But it was also much more than this. Paul reminds them (or even teaches them, if they had not realized it before) that 23 it was a direct continuation of that supper which the Lord Jesus held **on the night when he was betrayed**; and the tradition which Paul appeals to, and for which he claims the Lord's authority, corresponds essentially with the accounts given by Mark, Matthew and (in one version) Luke. One detail is

---

[8] The meaning of **authority** here is obscure: literally, the Greek can mean either 'on her head' or 'over her head', hence the NRSV alternatives.

24 peculiar to this passage and the longer text of Luke:[9] the words, **"Do this in remembrance of me."** The precise significance of the word here translated 'remembrance' (*anamnēsis*) has been the subject of centuries of discussion, but at least this is clear (and clearer here than in the gospel accounts): the supper was intended to be continued in the Christian congregation, and its significance was determined by the words spoken on that original occasion; so

26 that to hold the supper was to **proclaim the Lord's death until he comes.** The rite was therefore quite different from any mere love feast or fellowship meal, such as existed in both Jewish and pagan religion; and the consequences

27 of taking part **in an unworthy manner** – that is, in a state in which the partaker does not 'discern' that the bread is more than just bread – were correspondingly serious. Indeed, it appears from this and other passages that in this early period all Christians were expected to continue in life and

30 health until the imminent 'coming' of the Lord. If any had become **ill** or **died**, the explanation might well lie (Paul suggests) in their irreverent behaviour at the eucharist. Yet even such instances of divine judgment could be beneficial as a warning to other Christians of the dire consequences of such behaviour.

Diversity of gifts in a single body

The next topic on which Paul had to answer the Corinthians was that of

12.1 **spiritual gifts.**

From chapter 14 it is clear that in Corinth there was one mode in particu-

10 lar in which the reality of the Spirit was experienced, namely **various kinds of tongues,** that is, a form of trance in which the worshipper was inspired to utter words that were more or less unintelligible or else in a foreign language unknown to the speaker. This experience had become so common in the Corinthian church that it was assumed to be almost a condition of membership; and Paul may have had occasion previously to give some warning about it. The phenomenon was disturbingly similar to the kind of thing that was known to occur sometimes in pagan worship when people were

2 **enticed and led away to idols,** and so could not always be distinguished from idolatrous practices. In any case, it did not guarantee the presence of the Spirit. If, for instance, it should take the form of uttering the exact converse

3 of the Christian profession (**"Let Jesus be cursed!"**) – something that has occasionally been experienced even in modern charismatic communities – then the utterance clearly could not be under the influence of **the Spirit of God.** But before developing this point further, Paul devotes the next two chapters to putting the matter in a wider context. Speaking in tongues was by no means the only way in which the Spirit was manifested (even if it was the most spectacular). The Corinthians had an altogether too limited

---

[9] See above on Luke 22.19.

4 conception of the Spirit and must be introduced to a much richer one: **there are varieties of gifts, but the same Spirit.**

For the full Christian experience of the Spirit is one of diversity. Just as in
5 the one church, with its one Lord and God, there are varieties of **services** and
6 **activities,** so with the Spirit: there is not just one possible form of the gift,
7 but **to each is given the manifestation of the Spirit for the common good** – that is to say, not for personal distinction, but (as Paul is about to explain) for the good of the whole congregation. (The phrase translated **the common good** was a standard one in civic life.) Many different kinds of gifts (which the Corinthians doubtless possessed, but had not associated with the Spirit)
9, 10 are in fact exercised **by the same Spirit,** and their particular gift of **various kinds of tongues** does not even come very high on the list.

To drive the point home, Paul uses an analogy which was popular among philosophers of his day: the members of any human society are related to one another like the limbs of a body. The analogy was commonly used to illustrate the interdependence and relationship of the various members; and this is a sufficiently relevant point (especially as it touches the treatment of weaker
24 or **inferior** members) for Paul to devote a few lines to it here. But there is another, and from the Christian point of view more significant, implication. The body analogy would make little sense if all the members of the body
19 were identical – if they all had the same function or the same gifts. **If all were a single member, where would the body be?** If, then, the Christian community is one of interdependent members like a body, then there must
4 be, not just one gift, but **varieties of gifts.**

But is the Christian congregation like a body? And if it is, what has this to do with the Spirit? May not the analogy simply show that from the point of view, say, of administrative organization or social status the congregation does indeed consist of different kinds of people closely dependent on one another? It might still be the case that the Spirit manifests itself in one gift only – which, as we shall see, is what the Corinthians appear to have believed.

By way of answer, Paul shows that the body analogy is more than a rhetorical commonplace: it applies to the Christian congregation in a quite special – some would say 'mystical' – way. When Christians are baptized, one of the consequences is that they are brought into a close unity, not just with one another, but with Christ. As a result Christ, present as he is in a congregation of Christians who have been united with him through baptism, is like a body
12, 27 with **many members.** To put it still more boldly: **you are the body of Christ.** And anyone who doubts that this involves the Spirit need only recall the
13 nature and circumstances of every baptism. Baptism is not only **into one body,** it is in **one Spirit.** To use another metaphor (which unfortunately we cannot interpret with certainty: its most common use was for water being poured into different channels for irrigation, and the Spirit was often compared with a downpour of rain), **we were all made to drink of one Spirit.** This means, of course, an end to all racial and social barriers – a point very

precious to Paul (Galatians 3.26–8), though not strictly relevant here; but it also means that the Spirit is given to us all, not just to those who have the gift of tongues. The congregation, therefore, if it is to be in a true sense a body, 4 the 'body of Christ', can be expected to exhibit **varieties of gifts.**

28 How does this work out in practice? **God has appointed in the church first apostles, second . . .** – and there follows a whole list of the different offices and gifts which (we may suppose) were in fact exercised in the congregation. Since all these could be expected to be present in the community, it would be absurd if all the members had one and the same gift and function. Moreover the gift to which the Corinthians attached so much importance – speaking in **tongues** – comes right at the bottom of the list.

31 **And I will show you a still more excellent way.** Over against the Corinthians' pride in their 'knowledge' and 'freedom', Paul has had occasion to invoke a still more important principle, that of 'building up' the community (10.23) and of showing consideration for all its members, including the weakest. He has already once called this principle, quite simply, 'love' (8.1); and he now 13 devotes a chapter to a distinctively Christian understanding of it. In form, the passage, which is complete in itself and only loosely attached to its context, is not unlike other rhetorical exercises in praise of a particular virtue, and it is possible that Paul was drawing on or adapting some existing models for his own essay on the theme. Yet, though there is no Christian 'theology' in the sense of defining the relationship between the gift of love on the one hand and God, Christ or the Spirit on the other, there are distinct echoes of Jesus' teaching – where else would Paul have got the unprecedented idea of giving away *all* his possessions? And many have felt that the description of love's patience, kindness, long-suffering and so forth could have come only from a deep Christian experience ultimately inspired by Jesus himself. However this may be, the passage has a lyrical grandeur and psychological depth which has justly made it one of the best-known and best-loved texts in the entire Bible.

It is often felt that the old English word *charity* is still a better translation of the Greek word *agapē*. An almost decisive objection to this, at least in a modern translation, is that in contemporary speech the word has quite the wrong associations, to do with charitable institutions and charitable giving. On the other hand, it is certainly true that when the early Christians used the word *agapē* it was a far less common word and had a far narrower range of meanings than our modern word 'love' – it had no sexual connotations, for example. So far as the evidence goes (which tells us only, of course, about literature: we do not know what words people used colloquially), the word did not belong to ordinary speech at all, the commonest expressions being *erōs* (which was predominantly sexual love) and *philia* (friendship). *Agapē* occurs occasionally in the Greek version of the Old Testament; but it seems to have been only among Christians that the word became important, and if we wish to learn its meaning we have to go to the New Testament itself. It occurs most frequently in the gospel and letters of John, where it denotes the self-giving love of God towards human beings as expressed in Jesus Christ and the response of human beings towards God and one another. The word, in fact, is not a term of psychology, but is part of the Christian vocabulary. It derives its meaning from the act of God in Christ, and it shows its Christian character by the fact that it is entirely without the self-interest which philosophers taught was inherent in friendship, and is untouched by any of the mixed motives often associated with the words 'love' or 'affection'.

1 Compared with this *agapē*, not only speaking in **the tongues of mortals and of angels** (doubtless a reference to the 'various kinds of tongues' on which
2 the Corinthians prided themselves), but **all knowledge** (another Corinthian
3 pretension), the most reckless generosity, and even the exotic and desperate act of self-immolation (*giving one's body to be burned*[10]) – any one of which might be thought to be sufficient to mark out the true Christian – were relatively insignificant.

4–7 The next paragraph consists of a carefully composed series of short clauses, of each of which the subject is this 'love'. As a result, love seems to become almost personified – much as, in the later books of the Old Testament, the concept of 'wisdom' is almost endowed with an independent existence of its own and is made to say, for example, "I have good advice and sound wisdom; I have insight, I have strength" (Proverbs 8.14) – a passage which may well have been in Paul's mind here. We do not know – and perhaps there is little point in trying to guess – what led Paul to write in this way. Some have thought that the passage describes conduct that could have been inspired only by Jesus; others, that Paul was deliberately showing love to be the exact opposite of all those failings for which he had to criticize the Corinthians; others again, that he was simply adapting an existing pagan or Jewish hymn. Whatever the explanation, the passage remains a psychologically telling and (so far as we know) brilliantly original account of authentically Christian motivation.

---

[10] An early variant reading, **so that I may boast**, is adopted in the text of the NRSV in the place of *to be burned*, which is accepted in most earlier translations. It is true that voluntarily giving one's body to be burnt is a surprising notion. What could Paul have been thinking of? Cremation was alien to the Jewish culture, so he could not have been imagining an ordinary suicide or a heroic exposure to the risk of death. Even in the pagan world, deliberate self-immolation was virtually unheard of, and the few instances which were known involved motives (in Heracles' case, to escape the still worse torment of a poisoned shirt; in the case of his occasional imitators, a desire for literal or metaphorical immortality) which were not such as to appeal to Paul. It is conceivable that he had in mind stories of Indian ascetics who deliberately immolated themselves in fire – such stories certainly circulated in the Greek world. But in any event the notion would have been startling to his readers. The alternative reading, **that I may boast**, may be preferable, even if it seems a banal anticlimax to this series of radical options. It could have been altered by editors or copyists in the following centuries, when 'handing over their bodies to be burnt' had become a well-known act of Christian martyrs.

8   **Love never ends.** Up to this point it has been a matter of straight comparison: 'love' over against all other phenomena associated with a life touched by religion. But now there is a new dimension: what will survive into the new age to which Christians look forward? Will it be the gifts on which the Corinthians prided themselves – **prophecies and tongues**? A criterion is to hand. The new age will be one in which everything comes to completion;
10   therefore only **the complete** will survive into it. The partial realities of knowledge and prophecy bear the same imperfect relation to the complete
11   reality which is to come, as childish ways of speaking and thinking do to adult
12   ways, or dim and enigmatic reflections[11] in the metal mirrors of antiquity do to directly seen objects; but in the new age, knowledge will be 'complete', **we will see face to face** (as Jacob saw God 'face to face', Genesis 32.30). It follows that all 'partial' phenomena, such as the more obvious and sensational gifts which the Corinthians were so proud of, will come to an end.
13   By contrast, there are just three things that **abide** and will continue into the ultimate future: (i) **faith** – which is here quite different from the act of will that 'removes mountains' (verse 2): it is used in the full religious sense of total self-commitment of the person to God; (ii) **hope** – which includes the thing hoped for (like "the hope laid up for you in heaven", Colossians 1.5), and so necessarily belongs to the coming age; and most of all (iii) **love**. Paul may not have just invented this triad, for it seems to underlie other passages in his letters (1 Thessalonians 1.3; 5.8; Colossians 1.4–5), and it may already have been a familiar formula in the church. But all three pass the test of being 'complete', and together they form the basic constituents of that part of Christian life and experience which (unlike so much of what the Corinthians set store by) is of enduring value. **And the greatest of these is love.**

Having talked of these 'varieties of gifts' in general, and of that 'love' which is the greatest of them all, Paul now brings the discussion back to the point from which it started: the undue importance attached by the Corinthians to
14.2 speaking **in a tongue**. What has been said in praise of love is not intended to
1   depreciate **spiritual gifts altogether**; on the contrary, they are something one should **strive for**. But even among these gifts, speaking in tongues cannot be given pre-eminence, for it is unintelligible to others – one could even[12] be
2   divulging secret **mysteries** and yet not be understood by anyone but God; therefore it does not meet the essential requirement (as love supremely does)
3   of **upbuilding** the congregation. By this standard, a higher place is held by the less spectacular but ultimately more valuable gift of 'prophesying'; for

---

[11] The Greek means literally *in a riddle* (see the NRSV footnote), which was often used figuratively; we might say, *enigmatically*. Here the dimness of a mirror may be meant, but strangely the ancients tended to be more impressed by the *accuracy* of a mirror than by its inadequacy.

[12] The translation **since they are speaking mysteries** may not be correct. 'No one hears, *even if . . .*' may be what is meant.

prophecy, though it was also an inspired form of utterance, was by definition intelligible to its hearers.

Nevertheless, Paul is careful not to disparage a gift which often so obviously does proceed from the Spirit. He does not recommend its discontinuance or suppression, but only that so far as possible it should be accompanied by
5 someone who interprets. In the absence of such interpretation it may be as meaningless as the untutored strumming of a musical instrument. Again, praying and praising God is done not entirely by human effort but by the Spirit within us (Romans 8.15; Galatians 4.6); and although this receives
6 striking demonstration if the form taken by these prayers and praises is **in tongues** (as Paul knows from his own experience), yet even in his own case
19 he would rather speak five intelligible words **to instruct others**. The gifted
13 Corinthians must **pray for the power to interpret**, that is (probably) to give articulate form to their 'foreign' sounds; they must learn to pray and sing,
5 not only under inspiration, but at the same time **with the mind**, so that an
16 **outsider** may not feel excluded from their worship but can say **the "Amen"** in the right place. The real significance of the phenomenon can be inferred from
21 scripture (or **the law**, as Paul can loosely call even a quotation from one of the prophets). Paul quotes Isaiah 28.11–12 in a Greek version otherwise unknown to us. This version contained the phrase **"people of strange tongues"**, which Paul seems to have seen as a reference to 'speaking in tongues' and to contain a warning that it will not gain the attention of God's people, though (he
22 concedes) it may have value in impressing **unbelievers** – though they are perhaps more likely to assume that the speakers are out of their mind! But believers, and those who may be brought to faith, must be addressed not in tongues but in prophecy. It is the searching and convincing character of prophecy, rather than the spectacular but unintelligible flow of tongues, that
25 will force from the visitor the scriptural confession, **"God is really among you"** (Zechariah 8.23).
26 **What should be done then?** Paul is now ready to give specific instructions about the ordering of worship. The overriding principle must be **building up**; and this dictates a strict control of speaking in tongues, a careful ordering of different individuals' contributions, and mutual agreement on how to
34 work peacefully together. One other instruction is added: **women should be silent in the churches**. It is not clear how this is to be reconciled with 11.5 above, where it seems to be assumed that women may 'pray or prophesy' in church. Paul seems to be reverting to the conventional view that women should on all occasions **be subordinate**, and simply cites the practice of
33 **all the churches:** the Corinthians have no right to set a different standard themselves. Moreover, in respect to any authority claimed by those who have
37 special spiritual gifts, Paul invokes his own authority based on **a command of the Lord** – a mysterious reference, since it is unlikely that Jesus said anything
38 relevant to this particular issue. Yet it is made in all earnestness: **anyone who does not recognize this is not to be recognized** – a possible translation of

these obscure Greek words, which are perhaps more likely to mean that such a person *will not be recognized* by God at the judgment.

The resurrection of the dead

15.1 **Now I would remind you.** The reason Paul now introduces a summary of the basic facts of the Christian faith, with a strong emphasis on the evidence for
12 the resurrection, emerges a little later when he asks, **How can some of you say there is no resurrection of the dead?** A statement to this effect must have stood in the Corinthians' letter to Paul, and he now devotes a long chapter to his reply. Once again, we are at a disadvantage in that we do not possess both sides of the correspondence and can only guess at the real cause of the Corinthians' difficulties.

The 'resurrection of the dead' was the specifically Jewish doctrine that at the last judgment all those who have died will be resurrected bodily (hence the careful preservation of their bones) in order to receive the appropriate sentence of punishment or reward. The righteous will then receive a new body which will enable them to enjoy the everlasting felicity prepared for them. This doctrine was taken over into Christianity with only slight modifications. When Jesus appeared alive after his death, his followers seem immediately to have recognized this extraordinary event as *resurrection*, that is, as both an anticipation of their own resurrection after death and also a means by which, through their closeness to him in his risen life, they could experience here and now something of the reality of their own future resurrection. At the time this letter was written, they seem also to have believed that they would live to see the general resurrection, when they would share with Christ the office of judging the rest of the world. To this extent the Christian faith proclaimed a new understanding; but the concepts and terminology in which it was expressed were entirely Jewish.

Not all Jews subscribed to the doctrine of resurrection. We know, for instance, that the Sadducees roundly denied it (Acts 23.8), on the grounds that it was not plainly written into the Old Testament. But it is not likely to have been such ultra-conservative Jews, now become Christians, who were denying it at Corinth. It is much more probable that the question was raised by members of the Corinthian congregation who came from a Greek background and found the Jewish way of looking at life after death both crude and improbable. They would have been more familiar, perhaps, with the philosophical doctrine of the immortality of the soul, and the Jewish concept of a literal 'raising up' of the physical body would have made little sense to them; and some of them may well have thought that it was by no means an essential part of the Christian faith. Moreover the assumed imminence of the day of the Lord may have made the question seem somewhat academic. They would still be alive, so they believed, at the end of the age (unless they forfeited this hope in some such way as Paul refers to above, 11.30), and some of them evidently imagined that they would pass unchanged into the new age – if indeed, they had not already done so: a naïve belief which Paul explicitly counters with the statement that **flesh and blood cannot inherit the kingdom of God.**

50

Paul begins his reply by reminding them of his original preaching to them and of the faith to which they had committed themselves. From a historical point of view the passage is of great importance in that Paul tells us that this was what he had in turn received; that is to say, this formulation of the Christian faith is earlier than any existing writing of the New Testament and is evidence for the earliest stage of Christian belief. The concise way it is set out also suggests that it may have been a kind of summary of the faith – a 'creed' – already in use in the church. But in the context of Paul's argument its salient points are as follows.

3
(i) **Christ died for our sins in accordance with the scriptures.** It was already a basic tenet of the Christian faith that the crucifixion was not a tragic miscarriage of justice but had taken place according to the will of God and could be found to have been foretold in the scriptures. To our minds, Isaiah 53 seems the only passage in the Old Testament which can be read as foreshadowing this event and as offering a clue to its significance. But although this passage was quoted in the early church (see especially 1 Peter 2.22–5), it is not necessarily the only one referred to here. Many other passages seemed to have gained their true meaning, or to have been 'fulfilled', in particular episodes in the suffering and death of Jesus.

4
(ii) **He was buried.** The story is told in all the gospels, proving the physicality of the resurrection which left an empty tomb.

(iii) **He was raised on the third day in accordance with the scriptures.** Again, there is no explicit prediction of this in the Old Testament. But the first Christians were quick to find hints of it in such passages as Hosea 6.2 or Psalm 16.10 (Acts 13.35).

5
(iv) **He appeared to Cephas, then to the twelve.** One of the qualifications of an apostle was to have witnessed an appearance of Christ after the resurrection. Accounts of such appearances occur at the end of the gospels and can be used to fill out this summary. But Paul also mentions appearances which are not otherwise recorded. The most significant of these is the appearance to James, the brother of Jesus, who had by now assumed the leadership of the Jerusalem church but who was clearly not a disciple of Jesus before the resurrection. It was presumably this appearance which turned him from an unbeliever into a church leader (and probably also an 'apostle', though the language both here and at Galatians 1.19 is ambiguous on this point). In the

8
same way, as the last and most dramatic of the series (**as to one untimely born**), Paul also was made an eyewitness and apostle – the full story is told three times in Acts and clearly alluded to by Paul in Galatians 1 – and his apostleship had been confirmed by the success of his missionary work; or

10
rather – Paul hastens to add – by **the grace of God that is with me.**

Thus the miracle by which Paul had become an eyewitness and an apostle was a part of that single sequence of events which included the resurrection of Christ and which together were the basis of the preaching of the gospel.

11 Of this there was only one possible version. **So we proclaim and so you have come to believe.** It followed that to deny any part of it would be to make the

14 whole **proclamation** (the word picks up what Paul says he 'proclaimed' at the outset) **in vain**, along with their **faith.** And this gives Paul his first point against those who say there is no resurrection of the dead.

His next arguments may be set out as follows.

16 (i) A *reductio ad absurdum.* **If the dead are not raised, then Christ has not been raised.** But this conclusion is incompatible with the apostles' basic proclamation and with the Corinthians' own belief about Christ; it would also undermine the credibility of the apostles, who had proclaimed that it was God who had raised Jesus and who would then be shown to be giving false evidence about God. Not only that, but it would be a doctrine of despair. If Christ were still dead and buried, there would be no sense in which Christians could now be united with him, and so no release from their old state of being

17 in their **sins**; and Christians who had died could expect no better destiny than Christ himself. Verse 19 is ambiguous in the Greek (*only* may go with

19 **for this life** or with **in Christ**), but its purpose is clearly to underline the misery of a hope that is bounded by the limits of human existence. Clearly,

16 then, as applied to Christ, the proposition that **the dead are not raised** must be false.

But this is only half the answer. Christ may have been raised from the dead, but it does not follow that there is a resurrection for others. Paul has still to prove that 'resurrection' is a valid concept for humankind and not for the Son of God alone. To do this he uses

(ii) the argument from solidarity. This is essentially the same point as is elaborated in Romans 5, though there is a slight difference of emphasis. In both passages the skeleton of the argument is the same. Just as our solidarity with Adam produced (and still produces) death, so our solidarity with Christ, who has been raised from the dead, procures for us a new resurrection life. In Romans, where the subject in hand is Christian living, this is applied mainly

22 to the present. Here it is applied to the future: in Christ **all** (by which Paul presumably means all Christians) **will be made alive.** Paul's concern in this paragraph is not with Christian living in the present, but with the future hope which is rooted in a present experience of solidarity with Christ and which therefore guarantees the reality of a future resurrection. Paul expected this hope to be realized quite soon; and this leads him into a digression.

The final culmination of history is not to be thought of as a single event but

23 as an ordered process, **each in his own order.** Christ himself is **the first fruits** – his resurrection, that is to say, is a sure sign of the imminent resurrection of others, just as the first handful of ripe grain is a sign of the harvest that must soon be gathered. The present time is that brief interval; **then, at his**

coming – the word used is *parousia,* meaning the ceremonial arrival of a king or the glorious self-revelation of a divine being; it probably had not yet acquired the technical sense Christians were soon to give it of Christ's 'return' – **at his coming** the promised resurrection will take place of those

24 who **belong to Christ. Then** – and we expect further categories, such as those who are not Christians; and this passage has sometimes been interpreted as if it offered a kind of phased programme for different classes of humanity. But in fact it is more likely that Paul here moves into mythological language. What supervenes is **the end,**[13] when the subjects become, not human beings, but God, Christ, and those angelic or demonic entities which peopled the universe of Jewish (and often Greek) speculation: **every ruler and every**

26 **authority and power,** and finally the personified figure of **death.**

25–8 What Paul appears to be doing is working into the conventional Jewish scheme of the general resurrection a Christian interpretation of two passages from the psalms. The passages are these:

> The LORD says to my lord,
> "Sit at my right hand
> until I make your enemies your footstool."
> (Psalm 110.1)

> You have given them dominion over the works of your hands;
> you have put all things under their feet. (Psalm 8.6)

The first of these passages was seen by Jews as referring to the coming Messiah, and was used in argument by Jesus himself (Matthew 22.44), and then on many occasions in the second half of the New Testament; the second was also regarded by the early Christians as a prophecy about Christ (Ephesians 1.22; Hebrews 2.6–9). Both seemed to imply a period when the whole created universe would be gradually brought under the lordship of Christ; and Paul (like the apocalyptic writers of his time) conceives of this part of the drama as being played out on a metaphysical stage, with an appropriately metaphysical

28 climax: **so that God may be all in all.**

After this digression Paul comes abruptly back to the point with his third argument to prove that there is a resurrection of the dead.

(iii) An argument from Christian practice. We know nothing more about

29 baptism **on behalf of the dead,** beyond the fact that certain forms of it lingered on in the church for some centuries. Presumably the Corinthians (and maybe others) believed that by a kind of vicarious baptism they could bring into the promised kingdom relatives and friends who had died before the coming of the gospel. (A similar practice still continues among the Mormons.) Paul does not comment on this practice. He merely remarks that the fact that they were doing it presupposed a belief in the resurrection.

---

[13] It is possible that the word *telos,* which normally means 'end', could also mean *the rest* (as in the NRSV footnote), which would support the interpretation that Paul is giving a phased programme for all humanity.

(iv) An argument from Paul's own sufferings. If there were no resurrection beyond this life, the old saying (which occurs in Isaiah 22.13 but was of course

32   also a commonplace in both Greek and Latin), **"Let us eat and drink, for tomorrow we die"**, would be a valid philosophy of life; in which case there could be no sense in the Herculean dangers and hardships Paul had endured, which could be likened to fighting **with wild animals.** (This is likely to be metaphorical: no one who was put to the wild beasts in the arena was likely to survive to tell the tale!)

Possibly in the same series belongs

33–4   (v) a moral argument. The imminence of the day of resurrection and judgment was a powerful spring of Christian moral conduct, and was often invoked to inculcate sobriety, alertness, decency and the like (see above on Romans 13.12). Those who denied the resurrection might thereby be removing this moral pressure and affecting the morals of their fellow Christians. Paul here quotes a line from a comedy by the Greek playwright Menander, which had doubtless, like many other lines from his plays, become proverbial.

35   **But someone will ask, "How are the dead raised?"** Paul's arguments may have proved that there is life after death; many from a pagan background might have agreed. But the problem remained of the excessively physical nature of the belief in resurrection. **"With what kind of body do they come?"** Even Jews were sometimes puzzled by the question, and some cast doubt on the doctrine for this reason. Accordingly, Paul suggests answers to the problem that are drawn both from Jewish and from Greek culture.

37–8   (i) The analogy of the seed, which receives a new **body** when it grows into a plant. This analogy was used by Jewish scholars.

39   (ii) Ancient medicine recognized different kinds of **flesh;** popular cosmol-
40   ogy recognized different kinds of heavenly **bodies**, each with its own **glory** (which in this case probably means its particular degree of brilliant light).

(iii) The creation story (Genesis 2.7) suggests a distinction between bodies
44   that are **physical** and those that are **spiritual.** When God breathed breath
45, 47   into Adam he made him **"a living being"**, meaning that Adam, **a man of dust**, was now, like the animals, breathing, alive. But the life given by Christ
5, 47, 46   (**the last Adam**) is **from heaven**, and so, **spiritual**; and we, by our solidarity
48   with this second Adam or **man of heaven**, will receive a 'spiritual' body as opposed to our old 'physical' one.

These distinctions offer possible ways to conceive of a bodily resurrection without having to adopt a crudely realistic scenario of the coming age. They also preclude the suggestion (apparently made by some Christians in Corinth) that those who survived to Christ's coming would pass unchanged into the kingdom of God. On the contrary, a change of 'body' was part of
51   the **mystery** – the word here has its Jewish sense of the mysterious plan or design of God, which Paul can now reveal. According to this, some would indeed be alive on the day: **We will not all die.** But, whether alive or dead, when the moment comes **we will all be changed.** A new kind of body, such

as the previous analogies may help us to conceive of, will be given to all; and,
52 drawing on the conventional Jewish imagery of the last day (the **twinkling of an eye, the trumpet**), as well as on the popular philosophical distinction
53 between **perishable** and imperishable, **mortal** and immortal, Paul gives a vivid picture of the imagined future.

54–5 Two prophecies (Isaiah 25.8; Hosea 13.14) will then be fulfilled; and the words of the second, **"Where, O death, is your sting?"**, serve to relate this awesome vision of the future to the present reality of Christian living. What did the prophet mean by death's **sting**? In Greek (and Paul is quoting from a Greek version of the Hebrew) it meant the goad used on an animal, or an instrument of torture used on human beings. In this somewhat free quota-
56 tion, Paul takes it to refer to that factor in human life – **sin** – which carries the penalty of death and which is seen in its full enormity and power when exposed by its opposition to **the law**. Over both these (in a manner expounded
57 at length in Romans 5), God **gives us the victory through our Lord Jesus Christ**.

This brings Paul to the end of his argument. It was impossible to deny the resurrection or to do without the concept; for it is absolutely basic to the Christian faith. Nor was there any need to be put off by the crudity and naïvety with which the concept was often presented: many Jewish thinkers had worked out a perfectly credible account of it, and pagan thought also offered useful analogies. Moreover, Christianity had introduced a new note of relevance and urgency. For Christians, resurrection was more than a concept:
58 it was an imminent event for all. **Therefore, my beloved** – and this was a standard Christian exhortation every time the promise and the seriousness of the end were mentioned – **be steadfast, immovable**. As the building metaphor in chapter 3 made abundantly plain, if it is **in the Lord your labor is not in vain**.

The collection – future projects – final greetings

One more question that the Corinthians had put to him remained to be
16.1 answered. We know that Paul had committed himself to raise a **collection** from his churches for the Christian community in Jerusalem. The necessity for this may have begun with a real shortage of food there, driving up prices (Acts 11.27–30), and it subsequently became a standing obligation of the gentile churches towards the parent church in Jerusalem (Galatians 2.10; Romans 15.26). The question bulks larger in 2 Corinthians (8–9), but it seems that the Corinthians already had queries, if not complaints, to put to Paul about it. They had been told about the collection and doubtless accepted it in principle; but they were perhaps proposing to do nothing about it for the time being, and – if we may read back a hint of the accusations brought against Paul later on – they may have had doubts about the uses to which the money would be put and the reliability of those who would deliver it. Paul

had apparently already given directions to another group of congregations in Galatia, and he now repeats them here: the Corinthians must start laying money aside regularly, and they can certainly send their own representatives to help deliver it if they wish.

This leads on to Paul's immediate plans. He is at present in Ephesus (doubtless the stay described in Acts 19) and plans to stay until after the summer
8 festival of **Pentecost.** He will then travel, not by the direct route across the
5 sea, but all the way round by land – **passing through Macedonia** – which will mean that he can hardly be in Corinth before the autumn, by which time
6 the season for travel by sea will be nearly over and he may even **spend the winter** with them.

The commendations which follow are more than mere formalities. Paul has
10 promised to send **Timothy** (4.17),[14] who will have the difficult and delicate task of restoring order in the Corinthian church. Perhaps it was particularly in view of his youth (see 1 Timothy 4.12) that Paul felt he must warn them not
11, 12 to **despise him. Apollos,** an important figure in the Corinthian church and presumably particularly popular with the party that bore his name, appears to have been prolonging his absence, and Paul has to make a kind of apology for him.

15   It is some indication of the disorder at Corinth that **Stephanas,** one of Paul's
17 first converts, and two other men otherwise unknown to us (**Fortunatus and Achaicus**), had not been receiving the respect they deserved in virtue of their seniority and devoted work. It was their visit to Paul in Ephesus which had alerted him to the disquieting state of affairs in Corinth, and he now finds it necessary to make a personal appeal for a warm reception for them when they return.

19, 20   On **Aquila and Prisca** and on the **holy kiss** (the kiss of peace), see above on Romans 16.3 and 16.16. As was usual (see on Galatians 6.11), Paul adds a greeting in his **own hand**, along with three phrases which may be intended to mark the transition from the reading of the letter to the beginning of the celebration of the eucharist.

(i) A formula of exclusion from the congregation of anyone unsympa-
22 thetic to the faith, who should be **accursed** – literally, *anathema*. Compare Revelation 22.15.

(ii) *Maranatha*, a phrase in Aramaic which seems to have occurred in the worship of the first Christians. Paul leaves it in the original language. It may mean either an invocation (**Our Lord, come!**) or (less likely) a statement of faith (*Our Lord has come*). It also occurs (in Greek) as an invocation at the end of Revelation (22.20), where, as here, it is followed by
23   (iii) the 'grace'.

---

[14] The verb in 4.17 is ambiguous: it can mean either *I sent* or *I am sending* – see the NRSV footnote there.

THE SECOND LETTER OF PAUL TO THE
CORINTHIANS

We do not know how the first letter to the Christians in Corinth was received, or whether Paul paid the visit he promised them. Acts is silent on these questions, and our next letter from the correspondence is so taken up with more recent matters that the questions raised in 1 Corinthians are barely referred to. Indeed, after that letter was written, Paul's relations with the Corinthian church evidently went through a difficult period. Some member of the church had committed a serious offence, and the Corinthians had failed to punish it in the way demanded by Paul. This had led to a direct challenge to Paul's authority; and Paul, fearing that a personal visit from himself at such a juncture might merely cause pain and embarrassment, sent a stern letter by the hand of Titus; but he was not at all sure how this would be received, and he spent an anxious period of waiting, unable even to carry on with his missionary work in northern Greece, until Titus eventually rejoined him with the news that the Corinthians had yielded to his authority.

Paul's side of this story is told in the course of the first two chapters and in part of chapter 7 of 2 Corinthians. At the end of his account of it he frankly expresses his relief at the way things have turned out, and his tone is as cordial as anywhere in his letters. The difficulty comes when we compare this with the rest of the letter. Apart from two chapters about the raising of funds to alleviate the poverty of the Christians in Jerusalem (8 and 9), and an isolated (and almost certainly misplaced) paragraph of moral teaching (6.14–7.1), the remainder of the letter reveals Paul on the defensive: in the earlier chapters he labours to establish the true basis and continuing validity of his apostleship; in the last four chapters he feels himself forced to dwell (even though it is against his principles to do so) on his own superior qualifications for the work; and he concludes with a direct and outspoken attack on his opponents and with a threat to the Corinthians that, unless they own his authority in the meantime, he will be forced to put the matter to the test by confronting them in person.

These differences of mood and purpose are so striking that they demand explanation. In some passages, where Paul seems to change rapidly and repeatedly from one frame of mind to another, the differences can perhaps be explained as due to the tension and agitation which he had recently been undergoing. Indeed he tells us at the outset that he had recently endured some physical crisis (perhaps a severe illness) which had nearly cost him his life and which must have had serious consequences for his work and his reputation. But there are certain sections, in particular the last four chapters, which it is hard to believe were written in the same circumstances as produced the serene sentiments of chapter 7; and many critics believe that the only solution to these difficulties is to assume that what we now know as the SECOND LETTER TO THE CORINTHIANS is a collection of different letters (or parts of letters) written by Paul at various stages of the trouble with the church at Corinth and assembled by some later editor without regard to the order in which they were originally written.

Whether or not the several parts of the letter were composed at the same time, it is clear that for the most part they are connected with the same crisis, and some are certainly influenced by Paul's recent physical setback. The moment of rebellion against his authority had been accompanied by a many-sided attack on his credibility as an apostle. Men whom Paul calls 'false apostles' (or, with bitter irony, 'super-apostles') had been alleging that Paul was deficient in spiritual gifts and personal authority; that he had no letters of recommendation; and even that he had been defrauding the church. Precisely who these men were, where they came from and what doctrine they preached are difficult to determine. Part of the difficulty is caused by a fact which also gives the letter its interest and value for us today. Paul seldom comes down to the level of his adversaries to refute them point by point. If he did, we should probably be able to infer more about them. Instead, he fights on a ground of his own choosing and demonstrates, by implication, the falsity of his opponents' pretensions by an analysis, based on his own experience, of the true nature of an apostle's calling. He also scotches any criticism arising from his physical tribulations by appealing to his own recent and unprecedented discovery that suffering can have a positive value as a means of entering more fully into that relationship with Christ which is at the heart of his gospel.

The greeting

1.1 Paul, an apostle of Christ Jesus ... to the church of God. The greeting follows the usual form without any notable expansion; but this time it is addressed, not to Corinth only, but to all **throughout Achaia.** The Roman province of Achaia, of which Corinth was the capital, included the whole of Greece south of Thessaly and Epirus. Did other churches already exist in that area, apart from Corinth? We have no reason to think so – unless Paul's preaching in Athens (Acts 17) had led to the growth of a Christian community there. It is therefore likely that the greeting was intended to embrace all members of the Corinthian church, including any who happened to live outside the capital.

Paul's afflictions

3 Blessed be the God and Father of our Lord Jesus Christ – a stereotyped beginning which occurs also in Ephesians and 1 Peter and which is a Christian adaptation of the commonest of all Jewish prayers, 'Blessed be God, who . . .' The particular attribute of God for which Paul gives thanks here is: **of all consolation**. The Greek word (*paraklēsis*, from the verb *parakaleō*) is impossible to translate into English. Its basic meaning is any form of urgent address. If I need your help, I can 'appeal' to you (the modern Greek word for 'please' is *parakalō*). If I think you are doing wrong, I can 'remonstrate' with you. If I find you sad, I can speak to you insistently to encourage you, I can 'console' you. It is this last meaning which is most appropriate here, and receives great emphasis (the words 'console' and 'consolation' occur nine times in this short paragraph). Indeed, it is more than a pious phrase: it is a datum of Christian experience and, as the letter will show, it is an important factor in the mutual relationship of the apostle with his churches.

According to Jewish religion, God was certainly a 'God of consolation'. But this 'consolation' was embodied primarily in the prophets, the Messiah, the ultimate destiny of Israel – these things were 'consoling' because they gave grounds for hope, and it is hope which makes bearable the tribulations of the present. God's 'consolation', therefore, took the form of directing the eyes of the sufferer towards a promised future. This conception is often found in the New Testament, for example in Romans 15.4 (where, however, the same word is translated 'encouragement'). But in this passage, and often throughout the letter (though not in the previous one), the real substance of God's consolation is brought out of the future into the present. It is found to consist, not of hope merely, but of a present experience. How does this happen?

5   An answer is suggested by verse 5. **Just as the sufferings of Christ are abundant for us** – literally, 'overflow for us': the image is of a vessel that has to be filled up to the brim (Paul uses it again in Colossians 1.24 when he writes, "I am completing what is lacking in Christ's afflictions"), but is filled so generously that it overflows and the surplus can be collected or allowed to water the ground all about. The sufferings that Christians endure (and Paul is about to say something about his own) are not to be thought of as an adventitious calamity which might have been avoided, but as a necessary part of their destiny; indeed, there is a kind of quota of sufferings that has to be undergone before the end comes, and these sufferings form a continuous series with those of Christ, such that the 'consolation' which made it possible for Christ to endure them overflows, **through Christ**, into his followers and is 'abundant' for them. Moreover, this consolation 'through Christ' is an experience which Christians can communicate to one another:

6   **if we are being consoled, it is for your consolation**. Paul will say something later on about the positive dimension he has personally discovered in his suffering 'with Christ'; here he affirms that this is not just a resource for himself but something he can share with them and which enables him to say

7   that, whatever befalls them, his hope for them is **unshaken**.

564

It is in this perspective that Paul wishes to place the trials he has recently
8 gone through. We have no other information about what he calls **the
affliction we experienced in Asia**. Evidently it was a recent experience,
about which the Corinthians are assumed not to know anything. It was also
extremely serious: **we were so utterly, unbearably crushed that we despaired
of life itself.** If it was an illness (which is perhaps more likely than extreme
persecution), we might expect to be told some details; but in antiquity the
conventions were different: it seemed less important to describe the symptoms and physical conditions of an illness than to dwell on its causes and
consequences. The consequences of a near-fatal illness would have been of
extraordinary significance for Paul. Not merely would it have deprived him
of work for his livelihood (and he prided himself on his financial independence), it would have aroused suspicion among both friends and enemies
that he had something on his conscience for which he was being punished,
and would also have shattered his own expectation (clearly expressed in 1
Corinthians 15) that he would certainly be among those who would live to
see the return of Christ. It would have been an experience which touched
the very heart of his faith in God, and which could be surmounted only with
the resources of a well-nurtured faith – a number of verbal allusions show
that Paul instinctively used the vocabulary of the prayer which opens Psalm
116. His deliverance was not something for which he could take any credit
himself. It had been due to God alone, and his continued survival would
depend on the prayers of his friends.

12   **Indeed, this is our boast.** The contradiction with what has just been said
about 'relying on God, not ourselves' is only apparent. The Greek word
translated 'boast' – *kauchēsis* – had a larger range of meanings than any
English word. Its normal usage was certainly pejorative, expressing any kind
of boasting, over-confidence or excessive pride – Paul could certainly have
been criticised if he seemed to be taking credit for his stamina in overcoming
his affliction. But there was also a perfectly proper kind of pride which
arose from the confidence that God had done great things for his people,
or even (as here) from a sense of one's own integrity; and this too could
be called *kauchēsis*. Paul uses the word a great deal in this letter – no fewer
than twenty-three times. His opponents had evidently been behaving in a
way well described by the first group of meanings: they had been boasting of
advantages or of superior talents which were either fictitious or irrelevant, and
they may have been drawing unwarranted inferences from Paul's misfortune.
Their excessive *kauchēsis* was to be one of the main objects of Paul's attack.
Paul, on the other hand, had a consciousness of the commission God had
given him and of his own integrity in carrying it out – and now of God's
endorsement of this by delivering him from a premature death – which
furnished him with a genuine and proper *kauchēsis* of his own to set against
the inflated and objectionable *kauchēsis* of his opponents. The word is thus

made to do duty for the attitude of both sides in the dispute; and, in addition, it derives a still more serious meaning from being projected into the context 14 of the ultimate judgment to be passed on human beings. On **the day of the Lord Jesus,** Christians were to come before God supported by each other; it would be the relationship of trust which held between them on earth which would enable them to stand with a certain confidence (*kauchēsis*) before God. What mattered far more than the present misunderstanding between Paul and his friends in Corinth was the deep relationship between them which would come to light at the last day.

Meanwhile, however, there was misunderstanding in plenty. People had been reading between the lines of Paul's letters, and in particular had been criticizing his travel plans. We last heard of these plans at the end of 1 Corinthi-16 ans (16.5): **I wanted to visit you on my way to Macedonia, and to come back to you from Macedonia.** We cannot say for certain whether or not this plan had been carried out before the present letter was written, though Paul certainly did pay a visit to Macedonia. Starting from Ephesus, he will have had two possible routes. He could either go mainly by land round the Aegean; or he could cross the sea to Corinth and then proceed north, either overland, or up the coast by ship. The second route was the one he had planned to take,

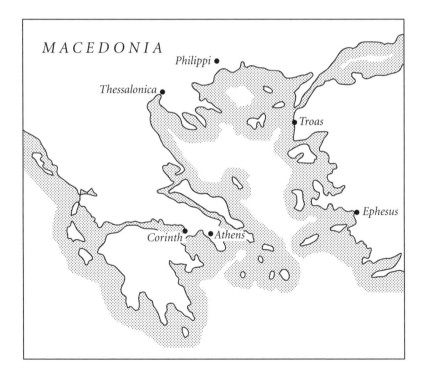

in order to have a chance to visit the Corinthians both before and after his journey to Macedonia.

15 So much is fairly clear. Less clear is why he calls this plan **a double favor,**[1]
17 and why he should have been accused of **vacillating** and of planning **according to ordinary human standards.** Nothing in the text suggests that he vacillated by *changing* his plans: it seems to have been the plans themselves that aroused criticism – possibly they seemed over-ambitious, particularly if Paul had promised to place no burden on his hosts but to visit them *gratis,*
15 as a **favor** (which might then have become impossible due to his state of
17 health). Planning by **ordinary human standards** would presumably involve reviewing various possible courses of action and their practical and financial implications, and then saying **"Yes, yes"** to some and **"No, no"** to others. But this, Paul protests, was not his way at all. The project, for instance, of going all the way to Macedonia was not adopted as a result of weighing alternatives and balancing yes's against no's: it was a command of God to which only one
20 response was possible: **"Yes."** There was no negotiation, no vacillating. Just as Jesus Christ's whole being was a 'yes', an affirmation of the certainty of God's promises, so Christians, by virtue of having been baptized into union
21 with Christ (for which **anointed** is doubtless a metaphor), and of possessing
22 the Spirit (for which **seal and first installment** are certainly metaphors), are
20 taken up into this affirming response of Jesus. Their very **"Amen"** in their worship expresses their solidarity with Christ Jesus in giving glory to God:
17 thus their actions and plans, far from being inspired by **ordinary human** motivations or negotiations, are simply their response to the commands of God, which they make by virtue of their intimate union with Christ.

23 Nevertheless, Paul did in fact change his plans: **I did not come again to Corinth.** How was this to be squared with what has just been said?

It was to spare you. In 1 Corinthians Paul insists more than once that in anything affecting the relationship between Christians there is one overriding principle – 'love', or 'building up', or care for the 'weak'. And so here: this was the principle that had made him change his mind. If it had been necessary for him to go to Corinth to give instruction in the faith,
24 doubtless he would have gone at once. But this was not the case: **you stand firm in the faith**, and there could be no question of Paul's 'lording' it over them in respect of something which was so much their own possession. No, the relationship could only be one of joyful partnership – **we are workers with you for your joy** – in which case, to have undertaken the visit at that

---

[1] Difficulties of translation increase the obscurity of these verses, which indeed have caused difficulties since early times, producing variations in the manuscripts (see the NRSV footnote). The Greek for **double favor** means literally *a second favour* (alluding perhaps to a 'favour' given by means of a previous visit); and the word translated **vacillating** should perhaps be rendered *my (well-known) irresponsibility* or even *my (well-known) anxiety not to be a burden.*

moment would have been pointless, since such was the estrangement between
2.1 them that it could have resulted only in something **painful**.[2]

Instead, Paul wrote them a letter. Unless (as some believe) 2 Corinthians
10–13 originally formed part of it, we do not possess this letter, and we
know nothing more about it than can be inferred from this chapter and from
4 chapter 7 below. It was written, we learn, **out of much distress and anguish**
12 **of heart**, so much so that Paul was unable to settle down to **proclaim the**
good news of Christ at Troas or to find any relief in Macedonia (7.5) until he
had received an answer. What was really at stake (as Paul eventually confesses
in 7.12) was not 'the one who did the wrong' or 'the one who was wronged' –
the specific cause of all the trouble at Corinth – but whether the Corinthians
9 were **obedient** to Paul **in everything**. The issue must have been a test case:
Paul had laid down a certain course of action to be followed, and remained
in suspense until he knew whether he had been obeyed.

This test case was possibly the same as, or more likely one similar to, that
on which Paul had already legislated in 1 Corinthians 5. A certain offender
6 had been sentenced by **the majority**. Now that his punishment was complete,
it was necessary for the congregation to show that they forgave him and to
welcome his return by 'reaffirming' their love for him. If the procedure was
similar to that recommended in 1 Corinthians 5, we may suppose that the
offender had been excommunicated but had now shown signs of penitence,
and that instead of being permanently 'handed over to Satan' (1 Corinthians
5.5), he could now be forgiven and formally readmitted. This course of action
11 would incidentally deprive **Satan** of the satisfaction of having gained a victim,
and it should have been taken for granted that Paul would support it.

But this is to anticipate the end of the story. In the last paragraph of this
chapter Paul recalls something of the relief with which he finally received an
14 answer to his letter. **Thanks be to God** – the recollection of any success or
good fortune was enough for Paul, as for other Jewish writers, to respond with
a brief exclamation of thanksgiving; but he enlarges it with two metaphors.
First, he is like a captive in a triumphal procession, being led by God in the
cause of Christ: he can no more take credit for his success in this matter than
a prisoner of war can take credit for the success of his captors. Secondly,
15 he is **the aroma of Christ,** which is both like the incense which is offered
to God **among those who are being saved**, and also a deadly fragrance to
those who are perishing. For just as some fragrances which are pleasant to
humans are noxious to animals (the ancients had noticed this), so it is one
of the mysteries of religious truth that, though it may be offered to God
like incense, a 'sweet savour', it may repel other human beings and lead to
their rejection of it. A heavy responsibility indeed, for the preacher; and if

---

[2] The Greek here is ambiguous. It can mean either **another painful visit** or 'another
visit, this time a painful one'. The phrase cannot be used to prove that there had already
been one such visit.

16 Paul's opponents in Corinth had been saying that they were **sufficient for these things** (or 'competent', as the same word is translated at 3.5), they must realize what they were claiming. One absolutely essential quality of preachers

17 was that they should **speak as persons of sincerity**. If teachers of religious or philosophical truth were known to be making their living out of it, they would be suspected of adapting their message to what people wanted to hear and of being **peddlers of God's word** – a standard criticism of such people since the time of Plato. Paul, unlike even other Christian apostles, accepted no fees or maintenance for his preaching: on these grounds, at least, he could lay claim to absolute sincerity. An adverse reaction to his preaching would amount to the rejection, not of the messenger, but of the message.

If this was the case, it could hardly be necessary for Paul to start all over again 'commending' himself by producing his credentials. Why then does

3.1 he introduce the matter of **letters of recommendation?** It is tempting to use this as a clue to the nature of the attack that was being made on him: were his opponents equipping themselves with formal letters (perhaps from the Jerusalem authorities) and criticizing Paul for not having done so? Very possibly; but we cannot be sure that Paul did not introduce the idea himself for the sake of a metaphor he was about to use, one that would have appealed to the English metaphysical poets: his 'letters of recommendation' came not from any human authority but from Christ; they were written, not on papyrus, but on the human heart; they consisted of the churches he had founded, whose very existence validated his apostleship – as he was fond of saying (compare 1 Corinthians 9.2).

But this metaphor suggests another. The Old Testament knew of a divinely authored 'letter': the laws given by God to Moses, which were written on

3, 7 **tablets of stone**. But this 'letter', **chiseled in letters on stone tablets**, was that old covenant or old dispensation which, Paul had come to realize, had no power to save: it was a **ministry of death** – indeed, the Old Testament prophets themselves had looked forward to a new dispensation under which the law of God would be taken out of the realm of objective commands and duties and would become a spontaneous motive of conduct, 'written on the heart' and taking effect through the agency of the Spirit (see especially Jeremiah 31.31–3; Ezekiel 11.19). And the qualitative difference between conduct regulated by law and conduct inspired by the living Spirit could be expressed in a trenchant

6 aphorism: **the letter kills, but the Spirit gives life**. But the same metaphor also had a more immediate application. If the Corinthian church could be described as a document of this new relationship between God and human beings, as a result of which their conduct was not law-directed but Spirit-inspired, then it provided all the 'credentials' a preacher could need; but it no

5 more argued for any special **competence** in the messenger than the character of a letter argues for the competence of a postman. If Paul's opponents were laying claim to some special kind of qualification for exercising authority in the church and criticizing Paul for his lack of it, the effect of Paul's metaphor

was to show that in this matter of dispensing a new, spiritual, covenant no preacher could say that 'we are **competent of ourselves**'. On the contrary, **our competence is from God.**

The metaphor of the two 'letters' or covenants – one on stone, the other in the heart – serves to make a further point. The agent of the first covenant was Moses; and at the time when it was given, Moses was invested with an 7 unearthly **glory** which was actually visible to those who saw him. The account is in Exodus 34.29–30:

> As he came down from the mountain with the two tablets of the covenant in his hand, Moses did not know that the skin of his face shone because he had been talking with God. When Aaron and all the Israelites saw Moses, the skin of his face was shining, and they were afraid to come near him.

Yet, despite the splendour of its inauguration and the shining it gave to the face of the messenger, the divinely given law failed to provide assurance 9 of salvation and became **the ministry of condemnation**. Its efficacy was 7 provisional; the glory came to be **set aside**. There was now a new dispen- 8 sation, the **ministry of the Spirit**. How much greater, then, must be the **glory** of this new dispensation, and what a radiance there must be in the face of the messenger who brings such a 'letter'! Much of 2 Corinthians is concerned to show that this was indeed the case. Paul's ministry (he would be the first to admit) had been attended by reverses and tribulations of various kinds; recently he had even been brought to the point of fearing for his life (1.10). His opponents had apparently been fastening on these tribulations as evidence that he lacked proper authority. But, unlike the glory of the divine presence on Sinai, which was with Moses only temporarily, 11 the glory of the Spirit remained with Christians: it was the glory of **the permanent**.

The narrative in Exodus continues with a curious detail:

> When Moses had finished speaking with them, he put a veil on his face; but whenever Moses went in before the L O R D to speak with him, he would take the veil off, until he came out; and when he came out, and told the Israelites what he had been commanded, the Israelites would see the face of Moses, that the skin of his face was shining; and Moses would put the veil on his face again, until he went in to speak with him. (Exodus 34.33–5)

What was the point of the veil? In the biblical narrative it seems to be assumed that the 'glory' was too dazzling to be looked at directly, and the veil was for the protection of the people. But the passage remains a little puzzling; and it was characteristic of the style of learned interpretation of scripture in Paul's time to find hidden meanings in any curious detail. So Paul offers a 12 quite different point for the veil: it was **to keep the people of Israel from** gazing at the end of the glory that was being set aside.[3] And he goes on to liken this to the inability (as it seemed to him) of the Jewish people right

14 up to his own day to see the true meaning of scripture. **Their minds were hardened**, so that all they could see in it was what he boldly called **the old covenant** (or 'old testament', a way of referring to the Hebrew scriptures that has been universally followed by Christians ever since, see above, p. 2). He could then go on to say that Moses, by removing the veil whenever he went

16 in to speak with the Lord, symbolized what happens when a Christian **turns to the Lord** who is also the Spirit; for this Spirit has made possible a new reading of scripture and brought into effect a new, 'spiritual' covenant, of which Paul is a minister. Only in Christ, in other words, does scripture yield its true meaning, enabling the 'veil' to be removed. And this in turn allows Christians to become more and more like Moses at the times when the veil

18 was removed, **being transformed . . . from one degree of glory to another**. And from this Paul may well have wished his readers to infer that no physical infirmity or affliction (such, perhaps, as he had recently undergone) could affect the validity and 'glory' of the message he had to impart.

Paul's authority, then (unlike, we may suppose, the authority being claimed by his opponents), does not depend on any 'competence' of his own, but upon

4.1 a **ministry** with which he has been entrusted by God. He has nothing on his

2 conscience (**the shameful things that one hides**) which would make him to blame in any way for what has happened to him; and he has never resorted to the subtle arguments (involving **cunning** and 'falsifying') which often arouse

1 suspicion of insincerity. Despite everything, **we do not lose heart** – a phrase, in the Greek, which suggests at least an element of physical lassitude that had to be resisted. Paul's conduct, in fact, both with regard to his methods of preaching and with regard to the chequered course of his ministry, has been

2 entirely candid: **by the open statement of the truth we commend ourselves**. The reason some of his hearers have not believed is not (as some of the opposition may have been saying) any distortion of the message on his part,

4 but their blindness – or rather, because Satan (**the god of this world**) has blinded them. And it is a crucial form of blindness; for the light which God

6 originally created **"out of darkness"** (Genesis 1.3), and which had always served as a powerful symbol of the coming of salvation to Israel (Isaiah 9.2), is now gloriously present as **the knowledge of the glory of God in the face of Jesus Christ**.

7 But we have this treasure in clay jars. The image would have been familiar: earthenware jars (as we know from Qumran and elsewhere in the Middle East) were used for storing and hiding not only precious manuscripts but

---

[3] The NRSV translation here is a paraphrase. Literally the Greek means *to gaze at the end of what was passing away* – which is an odd way of referring either to the 'glory' or to the old covenant. Possibly it refers to Moses' face, which was aging and might seem inappropriate for reflecting the divine glory, whereas the glory imparted by the new covenant could be reflected by Christians permanently, whatever their physical condition.

also gold and silver coins. The jars were useful for the purpose, but had little value in themselves. They were therefore a good metaphor for the bearer of the gospel message. Being ordinary household objects, no one would think of crediting them with special qualities by virtue of what they contained; similarly, bearers of divine truth must not take credit for what they bring. But there is a further point. These jars were essentially fragile, breakable, disposable. Paul's body, similarly, had been tested almost to destruction – and a list of these afflictions follows (the first of several in this letter), in the style, it seems at first sight, of a philosopher who is keen to show how his philosophy enables him to bear such treatment. But the following words show that Paul is using this philosophical commonplace for a quite different purpose. Indeed, a new thought is introduced that is nothing less than a leap

10 forward in Christian experience and understanding: **carrying in the body the death of Jesus**. The Greek here is virtually untranslatable. Paul uses a word (*nekrōsis*) which means the condition of a corpse; and this condition was thought to begin even before death took place. We might translate, 'the dying and death of Jesus'. Paul's suffering, in other words, could be described as a manifestation of what Jesus had endured; and as Jesus' dying and death had issued in the new life of resurrection, so this physical suffering of a Christian, even if it resulted in physical death, could be seen as a making

11 **visible** of the **life of Jesus**. To press home this conjunction, Paul adds that **we are always being given up to death for Jesus' sake** – 'being given up' is the same word as 'being handed over', the standard expression for what befell Jesus in the events leading up to the crucifixion. What we have here, in other words, is a filling out, from excruciating personal experience, of Paul's image of the Christian as being 'crucified with Christ' (Galatians 2.19).

12 **So death is at work in us**. The whole paragraph has been an explication of the radically new concept of suffering as, not a debilitating reverse, but an access of new life in the body of a Christian believer. One would expect the second half of this sentence to complete the picture: 'but at the same time life is at work in us'. Unexpectedly, Paul writes, **but life in *you***. It is as if, at this point, Paul shies away from the idea that this new evaluation of suffering is something which merely deepens his own experience and enables him to answer those of his critics who were drawing conventional conclusions from it. It is of universal significance: the benefits of this radically new concept that his own suffering was taken up into and transformed by the suffering of Christ are not for him alone, but for everyone with whom he can share this

15 revolutionary insight: **Yes, everything is for your sake**.

13 **"I believed, and so I spoke"** – hardly, one would have thought, a significant or memorable phrase to quote from scripture. But it comes from the same psalm (116.10) as Paul alluded to earlier when describing his sufferings in chapter 1, and which was still evidently in his mind. It was the psalmist's 'faith' which had enabled him to express his confidence in deliverance; so it is **the spirit of faith** which enables Paul to set his own sufferings in the

perspective of a progression towards the resurrection life he would share with
15 all Christians, with ever-increasing **thanksgiving, to the glory of God**.

16 **So we do not lose heart**. The phrase is emphatic, and is repeated verbatim
from the beginning of the chapter, using again a rather rare and expressive
word for 'losing heart'. Evidently there was much that might have discouraged
him – not least, we may suppose, his recent physical sufferings. The usual
way for a pious person of Jewish background to explain the sufferings of
the innocent (as Paul knew himself to be) was to express the conviction that
God would reward the sufferer in the next life. This was Paul's usual way of
putting it (Romans 8.18; 1 Corinthians 15.30–2), and he resorts to it again
17 here: **this slight momentary affliction is preparing us for an eternal weight
of glory**. But not before he makes one more effort to convey the radical new
understanding of suffering which has recently come to him. He does so in
terms of what sounds more like Greek than Hebrew psychology. Philosophers
16 were accustomed to the distinction between our **outer nature** and our **inner
nature**, and would have found nothing surprising in the proposition that the
'outer' might 'waste away' without harming the 'inner', so long as the latter
was protected by a careful philosophical discipline. Hebrew thought did not
normally work with this distinction (though it was of course aware that things
happen 'inside' a person which are not visible 'outside'), and Paul does not
use this exact formula elsewhere. But even if he was consciously using this
philosophical cliché, he gave it an entirely new meaning. It was not just that
the 'inner nature' might be such as to be unaffected by physical suffering:
it could actually be **renewed** by it – Paul uses what seems to have been an
unusual word for a concept which was unprecedented. Possibly for the very
first time in religious thought and experience, suffering was being seen, not as
a negative phenomenon – a punishment, a form of discipline, something to
be stoically endured – but as something that could have positive value. To use
another philosophical commonplace: this value belonged to the realm, not
18 of the **seen**, but of the **unseen**, and as such was part neither of the temporary
present nor of the still awaited future. It was an already experienced reality,
and it was **eternal**.

5.1–10 The passage which follows is a particularly difficult piece of Greek and has
been interpreted in a number of different ways. The fact that there is some
reference to the afterlife, and to the danger (or advantage) of an interim
period of 'nakedness' between death and the general resurrection, may make
it appear that Paul here turns to give some teaching on these things in the
light of Christian belief. But these matters lie rather wide of the argument as
it has developed so far, and the fact that a new chapter begins at this point is
not a reason for thinking that Paul is changing the subject. (Chapter divisions
were not introduced until at least a thousand years after Paul wrote.) Indeed,
the very first words of this chapter indicate the opposite.

1 **For we know**. This sentence, and the two which follow it, begin with
the word 'for', which strongly suggests that we are being given, not a new

topic, but an explanation of what has just been said – which would not be surprising, given the radically new understanding of suffering which Paul has introduced. Moreover, we should not expect what follows to advance new ideas: to help us understand the previous paragraph, Paul does not break further new ground but reminds us of what **we know**. The body, he has been saying, is a frail thing like an earthenware jar. You do not judge the value of treasure by the vessel which contains it; no more should you judge the truth of the gospel message by what you see happening to a person's body. But suppose – and perhaps at this time Christians were not reckoning with the possibility seriously enough, since the majority of them expected to live to see the return of Christ – suppose we do not just nearly die, but that the all-too-breakable earthenware jar is actually broken! Suppose (to change the metaphor to one that was familiar to philosophers, who thought of the immortal soul as weighed down by the temporary 'tent dwelling' of the body) **the earthly tent we live in is destroyed**: 'we know', says Paul, that we are already in possession of something which makes even that event insignificant. What is this possession? It can of course be described only metaphorically. It can be called **a building from God**; and the words, **not made with hands**, suggest a building of a particular kind. The holy 'tent' where the Israelites worshipped during their wanderings in the desert became in due course the temple of solid masonry in Jerusalem. But for Christians this temple too had been superseded by one 'not made with hands' (Mark 14.58; Acts 7.48; Hebrews 9.11): Paul's first way of describing the Christian's most precious possession is by a metaphor suggesting the life and worship of the church.

2 But then the image changes. This **heavenly dwelling** is also something with which we can be **clothed**; and the explanation of this startling mixture of metaphors seems to be that 'being clothed' was almost a technical expression for baptism, the moment at which the believer 'puts on' Christ (Romans 13.14) or 'is clothed' with Christ (Galatians 3.27) and becomes a member of 'the dwelling not made with hands', the community of believers here on earth but which is also 'heavenly', a reality to be entered into after death.

For in this tent we groan. In the Greek the connecting particle is even more emphatic; we could paraphrase it as, 'And here is another part of the explanation.' For what has been said so far, though it affirms the faith of Christians in the reality of their solidarity with Christ in baptism and church, a solidarity that continues after death, does not throw light on the new understanding of suffering which Paul has just proclaimed. We get closer to this with the words **in this tent we groan**. We may gain tremendous assurance from our experience of Christ in the church, but we are still left both with moral choices for which we are responsible and with physical dangers and tribulations which may oppress us, and we naturally yearn for the heavenly counterpart of this new existence which we shall enter after death – we are **longing to be clothed with our heavenly dwelling**. But, for the morally accountable person, there can be no automatic assurance of this destiny. The

3 question is how we shall **be found** – an almost technical expression for the moment when we will appear before the judgment seat of God. We hope that we shall be 'clothed' – that is, that our incorporation into Christ was real and certain, and that we would not be found unprotected, **naked**.[4] Indeed,

4 during this life (**while we are still in this tent**) we strive to consolidate our existence 'in Christ' and in his church (**to be further clothed**). But we can

5 do so with assurance, for we have been given **the Spirit as a guarantee**.

6 **So we are always confident**. This is the point of this difficult paragraph: to give assurance that neither extreme suffering nor even premature death can invalidate the Christian experience. Of course it is true that our earthly existence **in the body** involves separation from Christ compared with the unity we shall have after death. Our confidence, therefore, does depend on

7, 8 **faith**, not **sight**, and of course **we would rather be** in that future state, **at home with the Lord**. But we are confident, because neither suffering nor death can be any kind of disqualification; indeed, death is the transition to that state of closeness to Christ in the heavenly church-dwelling which is what we are yearning for and seeking to strengthen and deepen in our earthly church-dwelling here and now. For there is nothing automatic in this future

10 destiny. We remain morally accountable; **all of us must appear before the**

9 **judgment seat of Christ,** and **so we make it our aim to please him**. This is as true as it ever was (something Paul often had to insist on in the face of accusations that he was promising 'free grace' regardless of moral principles). But no physical affliction, not even death, when endured by the innocent, can in any way affect the confidence we have in being 'renewed' by Christ.

It has often been noted that the foregoing paragraphs seem to display a certain inconsistency. At one moment, "we groan"; at the next, "we are always confident". Why does Paul's mood seem to swing so rapidly? It is possible that the reason was personal and psychological: because of his private troubles and his anxiety over his churches, his confidence may have ebbed and flowed even while writing the letter. But it may be that the apparent inconsistency is no more than an acute form of a tension which is always present in the Christian life. On the one hand, there is a legitimate assurance of salvation: Christians, through their baptism, have 'put on Christ', they have received the Spirit as a 'guarantee' of the heavenly dwelling which awaits them. On the other hand, none of this diminishes the individual's responsibility to walk worthily in this new way, to follow the promptings of the Spirit and to be morally accountable for the good and evil we have done. Moral standards still

---

[4] This interpretation, which is only one of many that have been proposed, is easier if the alternative manuscript reading in the NRSV footnote is adopted, *when we put it on*.

3 The version in the text, **when we have taken it off**, suggests that at death we may have to leave off this 'clothing' until we are judged fit to 'put it on' again in heaven, though we may be able to acquire *some* clothing in the meantime which will prevent us from having to stand before God 'naked'.

apply, and our confidence and assurance must ever be tinged with a serious awareness of the impending judgment of God.

11   **Therefore, knowing the fear of the Lord, we try to persuade others**. Those in the business of 'persuading others' are usually orators. Their rhetorical skills may often involve being, as we say, economical with the truth, if not actually misrepresenting it. But Paul has not only renounced these skills; he conducts his defence in **the fear of the Lord**, in statements whose truth cannot be faulted even by God. Similarly, in addressing his fellow Christians, he is relying, not on considerations which might 'commend' him personally, but on facts which will be recognized by their **consciences**, facts which give grounds, not for shame or embarrassment (given his recent reverses), but for a proper pride or 'boasting' (*kauchēsis*, see above on 1.12). They will then

12   have a standard by which to measure the pretensions of his opponents (**those who boast in outward appearance and not in the heart**).

And here he introduces a new and very personal factor which will have

13   considerable significance later on. **If we are beside ourselves**. This is nothing to do with anger (as the English phrase might suggest), but denotes an experience we would now call 'mystical', essentially incommunicable, and therefore a matter entirely between the mystic and God. By contrast, when Paul is in his **right mind** – meaning, not sanity as opposed to madness, but the full possession of his rational powers which mystical experience places in abeyance – then all that he says must be taken seriously by those to whom he is writing. Yet the experience, even if it has reached an intense mystical form in Paul's case, is one which lies at the heart of the Christian life. Christ's death

14   is appropriated by believers in such a way that one can say that they have **died**

15   with him (we carry his dying and death in our bodies, 4.10); they **live no**

17   **longer for themselves . . . there is a new creation**. Henceforward, therefore, our judgment of one another will not be by the standards of the world,

16   drawing conclusions from material reverses or physical weaknesses – and at one time Paul may have been tempted to think of the crucified Jesus in this way, an object of shame, contempt and scandal.[5] The only thing which can now carry weight is the reality of this new experience of intimacy with God

18   through Christ, which Paul here (unusually) describes as **reconciliation**. And

20   this allows those who bring this message to be described as **ambassadors**. It was as if an erring son had to be 'reconciled' with his loving father. A go-between or 'ambassador' was required, one who had no share of the guilt

21   (**who knew no sin**) but could share the weight of the estrangement (be so involved with the 'sin' that he could be said to be **made . . . to be sin**) so that the son could be reconciled and re-established in his father's favour. This

---

[5] The Greek means literally *even if we once knew Christ according to the flesh*, from which it has often been inferred that Paul may have actually known Jesus before the crucifixion. But there is no other evidence for this, and the argument as interpreted here suggests that Paul is talking of judgment by human standards as opposed to the new standard created by Christian experience.

was what Christ had done for us – **so that in him we might become the**
20 **righteousness of God** – and it was now for us to become his **ambassadors**
in our turn, bringing the same possibility to others.

6.1 **As we work together with him.** If the notion were of an equal partnership,
'working together with God' would sound pretentious, indeed blasphemous.
But there is a sense in which ambassadors, or agents, 'work together' with the
one who sends them; now that Paul has established that this is the nature of the
Christian's calling, it is time to stress its urgency: Paul uses the word *parakaleō*
for this urgent insistence (see above on 1.3), and calls in aid a passage from
2 Isaiah (49.8) to stress that this is now **the acceptable time.** But why is he
1 afraid they might accept this grace **in vain?** The answer seems to come in
3 verse 3: they must not regard anything he has been through as an **obstacle**
to accepting the validity of his message. If he were a philosopher, he might
well take pride in the series of afflictions which his philosophical training had
4–5 enabled him to endure – and the list of them which he gives here is typical of a
philosopher's defence; it becomes a bit more specific only when he mentions
beatings and **imprisonments** (which he certainly endured, 11.23–5; Acts
16.23; etc.) and those self-imposed hardships of **labors, sleepless nights,**
hunger, which resulted from his chosen style of ministry. But then the list
6 turns into something else: **purity, knowledge, patience . . .** – these things
are the equipment provided, not by philosophy, but by religion; and the
paradoxes with which he rounds off the list, though they have a flavour
of Cynic philosophy (for a Cynic might well have claimed to be **poor, yet**
10 **making many rich**), evidently arise from the very ethos of the Christian life;
9 moreover, **dying, and see – we are alive** echoes the experience which he told
us nearly cost him his life just before he wrote this letter (1.10).

All this has involved self-examination and self-exposure, a strenuous
demonstration that Paul has nothing to hide and nothing to apologize for. If
12 there is still **restriction** or constraint in their relationship, it is on their side,
13 not his. It is for them, like him, to **open wide their hearts.**

A fragment on church discipline

There is now an abrupt break in the argument. The short section 6.14–7.1
seems to have no connection with what comes before or after it, and if it were
omitted the letter would run on smoothly from 6.13 to 7.2.

Furthermore, the content of this short paragraph is unexpected. It consists
of a piece of dogmatic moral instruction for Christians, couched in strikingly Jewish terms. (The tone is reminiscent of the discipline enjoined in the
14 Dead Sea Scrolls.) **Do not be mismatched with unbelievers.** The metaphor
is of setting two different beasts, say an ox and an ass, under the same yoke,
and the application intended could well be to the question of mixed marriages between Christians and non-Christians. But the language seems to be

inspired less by the practical inconveniences of such unions than by a characteristically Jewish horror of close contact with heathendom and idolatry. 'Unbelievers' are described not (as they are in 1 Corinthians 7) as persons who might still be influenced for good, but as embodiments of **lawlessness**

15 and **darkness**, indeed as **Beliar** himself (a current Jewish name for Satan).

16 The Christian, on the other hand, is **the temple of . . . God** (an idea found elsewhere in Paul); and a veritable mosaic of scriptural phrases is used to stress the incompatibility of the two. The paragraph ends, in language that

7.1 sounds a little unlike Paul (the phrase, **of body and of spirit**, for instance, does not bear quite the meaning he usually gives these two words), with a personal exhortation to avoid **every defilement**. This could certainly have an application in a Christian context, but it sounds uncharacteristically exclusive and sectarian for a Christian writer.

In view of all this it is hard to allay the suspicion that the paragraph did not originally belong here. Where it originally belonged, how it got inserted here, and whether it is by Paul at all, are questions to which no convincing answer has been found. One possibility may be mentioned among many that have been suggested: that it is a fragment of a letter to which Paul refers in 1 Corinthians 5.9, when he writes, "I wrote to you in my letter not to associate with sexually immoral persons."

Relief at the outcome

2 **Make room in your hearts for us.** These words repeat and continue the appeal made in 6.13. Paul has had to go on the defensive, and he once more protests his innocence, using words that may allude to specific charges made against him but which may equally well be drawn from the conventional repertory of the innocent man forced to show that his afflictions have no sinister explanation. But if Paul is innocent, does this mean that his correspondents are guilty of a damaging misunderstanding? Paul hastens to reassure them: his relationship with them is far too close and valuable to be put at risk in

4 this way. All he has done is spoken with great directness and frankness,[6] and this must not be allowed to impair that precious shared **consolation** which, as he has shown, has been the fruit of his **affliction**.

But to return to the misunderstanding itself: Paul picks up the story from the point at which he broke off at 2.13. There he explained the extreme anxiety he had felt while waiting for news of how his stern letter had been received: he had been able to do no useful work in Macedonia, and his agitation had

6–7 continued until Titus eventually brought his report. Now he describes his

---

[6] The NRSV translation, **I have great pride in you**, misrepresents the meaning. The Authorized (King James) version rendering, *with boldness of speech*, is more accurate.

8–13   relief, and seeks to allay any lingering bitterness his letter may have caused by pointing out the benefits which have proceeded from it. Once again the
13   key word is 'consolation' or **comfort** (*paraklēsis*), which has born fruit also
13–16   in the unaffected relief and joy felt by Titus.

The collection

Feeling, perhaps, that relations between himself and the Corinthians were now at last sufficiently cordial for the matter to be reopened, Paul turns (or at least the letter turns – see below) to the matter of the collection which he was raising from all his churches for the 'poor' Christians in Jerusalem. He has already alluded to this at a previous stage in the correspondence (1 Corinthians 16); at that time it seems that the Corinthians had already agreed to it in principle, but were being slow in doing anything practical about it; and during the period[7] of misunderstanding we may assume that the matter had to be shelved. But now the time was ripe to raise it again, and the next two chapters are devoted to it.

These two chapters also have a further purpose, which gives them a more formal character. The matter was to be handled by Titus and two 'brothers'; and in order that these representatives should be received as fully authorized to act on his behalf, Paul appears to be sending them with a 'letter of rec- ommendation' – or rather two such letters, since chapter 9 seems to make a new start – which in style and vocabulary has at times an official, almost bureaucratic, character. It is tempting to think that each of these chapters was originally such a letter which, shorn of its opening greetings and concluding farewells, an early editor inserted into 2 Corinthians at a point where they did not disturb the argument. This would explain some of the oddities; but these chapters also display some connection with what has gone before, and it is equally possible to read them as a continuation of the letter, written somewhat *in the style* of a formal letter of recommendation, and occasionally using official-sounding language in order to cover the embarrassment which Paul always felt when having to speak about questions involving money. (For a notable example, see the concluding paragraphs of the letter to the Philippians.)

However this may be, chapter 8 begins with a distinct echo of chapter 1. Paul's first tactic for exciting the generosity of the Corinthians is to
8.1   appeal to the example of **the churches of Macedonia**, which have suffered

---

[7] The repeated phrase, **last year** (8.10; 9.2), is the nearest indication we have of how long this period lasted. Unfortunately, we do not know at what time of year this letter was written, or whether Paul would have reckoned by the Jewish new year (in the autumn) or the Roman one (January), so that **last year** may mean anything from six to eighteen months previously.

2 **a severe ordeal of affliction** comparable with (though presumably not so life-threatening as) the 'affliction' Paul had recently suffered himself (1.8), but which (like Paul) have recovered sufficiently to manifest **abundant joy**. Despite their **extreme poverty** (which might have gained them exemption from making a contribution), they have shown a **wealth of generosity** in
4 begging for **the privilege of sharing in this ministry** and so encourag-
6 ing Paul to send Titus to Corinth to **complete this generous undertaking**. (A number of these words – 'privilege', 'sharing', 'ministry', 'favour' – are familiar in civil-service administrative language, useful for avoiding any direct reference to sums of money, but also invested by Paul with a load of Christian meaning, especially **this generous undertaking**, which in the Greek is the same word as *grace*).

8 **I do not say this as a command**; but Paul presents it as a strong obligation on grounds of comparison with others, of Christian faith and of expediency.

(i) Comparison with others: the point of mentioning the Macedonians was clearly to shame the Corinthians by the comparison. They must not be outdone by **the earnestness of others** (another civil-service word – 'earnestness' or 'zealousness' was a quality much desired among administrators).

(ii) Christian faith: it was a Christian obligation because of the example
9 of Christ himself and his **generous act** – once again the word means literally 'favour' or *grace*. That is to say, though Christ was **rich** in his unique relationship with God, **he became poor** in that he took human form (Philippians 2.5–11); and Christians who profess to follow him must be ready to follow the same pattern with their material possessions for the benefit of others.

13–15 (iii) Expediency: whether or not the Christians in Corinth were in fact better off than those in Jerusalem, no heroic sacrifices were being asked of
12 them. **The gift is acceptable according to what one has – not according to what one does not have.** If they were better off, however, Greek philosophers and lawyers laid stress on the dangers of social 'inequality': citizens should
13 enjoy equal rights and benefits (**a fair balance**). An illustration could be
15 found (Paul was not the only Jewish writer to do so) in Exodus 16.18: when manna was gathered in the desert, God saw to it that no one had too much or too little.

And now for the 'recommendation' itself. Titus was already well known and hardly needed further commendation. But he was Paul's man; and there seems to have been criticism about the way Paul proposed to handle the actual conveyance of money to Jerusalem. In 1 Corinthians 16.3 he had to
23 give assurances that representatives (here called **messengers** or *apostles*) of
18, 22 the donor churches would be present. Here he names two others who will share the responsibility – or rather, he most puzzlingly omits to name them. Who these two men were who were of such high reputation that they would silence all criticism, why Paul leaves them unnamed (if indeed, he did in the original – the names could have been erased from subsequent copies), and why indeed, there should have been any need for further recommendation

of Titus, are matters quite unknown to us. But their arrival is intended to put the Corinthians on their mettle and to justify Paul's 'proper pride' or
24 **boasting** about them.

9.1 **Now it is not necessary for me to write you about the ministry.** This is, to say the least, unexpected. How can Paul say it is 'superfluous' (the literal meaning of the word translated **not necessary**) when he has just done exactly this and is about to do it again? The assumption that this was originally another 'letter of recommendation' solves this problem, but leaves us with another: why should Paul have needed to write a second letter to the
2 same addressees (the solution that **Achaia** means the country as opposed to the city of Corinth is hardly defensible), and why should he need to cover the same ground again? It may after all be easier to take the opening sentence as a pure formality, as we might say, 'I am sure I do not need to remind you that . . .', and accept that Paul felt he needed to press his point still further. The real difficulty is that after using the Macedonians' generosity as an example to shame the Corinthians in chapter 8, he now appears to say the exact opposite, claiming to have held up the Corinthians' **eagerness** as an example to the Macedonians. But it may be that, as Paul suggests in 8.10–11, the Corinthians really did have a remarkable 'eagerness' to help at the beginning, and this could have impressed the Macedonians; the problem was that, though they were **ready** to contribute in the sense of being willing to do so, they had not kept it up and were now falling behind and becoming 'unready', so that the Macedonians, who had responded so magnificently, could be held up as an example to *them*. Their initial enthu-
5 siasm should have resulted in a **bountiful gift**, a **voluntary gift** (the same word in the Greek in each case), not in the need to 'extort' money like a tax.

6 **The point is this.** Instead of appealing, as he often does elsewhere, to distinctively Christian motives such as love, self-sacrifice and compassion, Paul follows up his argument with a string of conventional maxims. **The one who sows sparingly will also reap sparingly** recalls Proverbs 11.24: it has
7 the sound of popular country wisdom. **God loves a cheerful giver** recalls
9 Proverbs 22.8, but was probably also a popular proverb. The quotation in verse 9 is from Psalm 112.9: the **righteousness** (which is the same word as 'charitable activity' or *benevolence*) of the generous giver **endures for ever**;
10 and the God who recognizes this 'righteousness' is also he who **supplies seed to the sower and bread for food** (Isaiah 55.10) and so will himself **increase the harvest of your righteousness** (Hosea 10.12). But the Corinthians' action will also have profound Christian significance beyond merely meeting a
12, 13 particular need **(the needs of the saints)**: it will be proof of their **obedience** to the demands of the gospel and a veritable 'overflowing' of generosity such as is appropriate when one is genuinely giving thanks to God with the
15 spontaneous enthusiasm with which Paul ends his appeal: **Thanks be to God for his indescribable gift!**

Paul's self-defence

At this point there is a sharp change. The preceding chapters, including the 'letters of recommendation' (if such they are), were evidently written when relations between Paul and the Corinthian church had become once again confident and affectionate. The tone was serene, and even the delicate subject of the collection could be broached without fear of causing offence. But with the beginning of chapter 10 it is as if such a period of calm and reconciliation had never been. Paul seems to be reduced, once again, to defending himself against damaging imputations and to mounting a fierce attack against his opponents, who now for the first time come out of the shadows into the light of day. If in earlier chapters it was hard to tell whether they really existed or whether Paul was making a rhetorical point by imagining them as more vocal than they were, there is now no doubt of their reality and little difficulty in reconstructing the nature of their attacks.

For these reasons many critics have concluded that the last four chapters of 2 Corinthians are a separate letter (possibly the one written "out of much distress", referred to in 2.4) and were placed in their present position by a later editor. Yet it is possible to think of reasons for the change of tone: Paul's mood may simply have changed overnight before completing his letter, he may have just received disturbing news from Corinth, or he may even have been influenced by the rhetorical convention of placing the most impassioned part of an appeal at the end of a discourse. The fact that these chapters have been handed down to us as part of the one letter, and that there is no external evidence of any kind to suggest that they were ever separate, is a strong inducement to try to make sense of them as they stand.

10.1 **I myself, Paul, appeal to you.** Certainly this is a new start; but it has a distinct echo of the beginning: the word **appeal** (*parakaleō*) is the same as that which was almost a theme word throughout the first chapter (there used in its meaning of 'console'). Moreover, just as there the appeal was 'through Christ', so here it is **by the meekness and gentleness of Christ** – the latter word meaning something more like 'magnanimity', undeserved kindness towards enemies and persecutors. And these enemies at once make themselves felt in the first of the charges which Paul addresses: they are saying that he is humble – the word in this context suggests servile acquiescence – and dares to speak his mind only at a distance (presumably through his letters). And

2 a second charge follows, **acting according to human standards** (literally *according to the flesh*), which could either be a harking back to the criticism made of his plans (1.17) or a new accusation, say of worldly motivation and judgment (such as using his recent physical setbacks as a pretext for making new demands), or even of profiting personally from the collection. Whatever

3 it was, Paul spares it no further words. In one sense we are all 'fleshly' (**we live as human beings**), but in this particular battle Paul claims to have weapons

4 of **divine power** – and he continues the striking military metaphor to the end of the paragraph.

But the metaphor must not be pressed too far. Paul's authority was not
8 given to him for creating destruction (**tearing you down**) as in a siege, but for
7 **building you up**. If his opponents were saying, 'We **belong to Christ**', how could they possibly do so more than he does himself? They were pretending
10 that Paul was reduced to trying to exert his authority at one remove, by **his letters**, and were making capital out of his confessed lack of rhetorical skills. The obvious way to refute this was to come in person and demonstrate the power of his personality – something he has been reluctant to do in order to act rather with the 'gentleness of Christ'.

But it is only momentarily that Paul condescends to come down and fight on his adversaries' own ground. If he were to accept the standard by which
12 they **classify or compare** him with themselves, he might quite possibly not measure up to it – he might be found lacking in certain skills which they regarded as essential qualifications for holding authority. But what is the validity of this standard? It merely shows that **they measure themselves by one another**, they have set their own standard themselves. Paul's claim to authority, by contrast, depended on no such subjective standard. His field
13 of action was one God had **assigned** to him. But even this, it seems, had been misrepresented. His opponents appear to have been saying that it was they who were really responsible for the growth of the church in Corinth and that Paul's field, if he had one at all, did not extend to Corinth, which was **beyond limits**. In reply, Paul can simply point to the fact that he was
14 **the first** to bring the gospel to them; and if, as he hopes, the Corinthian church becomes more firmly established, he will be able to go further on
16 from there, still without trespassing on **someone else's sphere of action**. All this boasting of his opponents is beside the point. The only proper ground for boasting (*kauchēsis* again, see above on 1.12), for 'proper pride', is not what we do ourselves but what God does through us. (Verse 17 is a quotation from Jeremiah 9.23–4.)

Nevertheless, even though it was beside the point to claim any personal qualifications for the task of preaching the gospel, and even though it would
11.1 have been **foolishness** (in view of all that has been said) for Paul to try to 'recommend himself', yet he could not resist pointing to certain things which in any normal contest would have shown him to be at least the equal of his opponents. He was not, after all, concerned only about his own status; he had an anxious concern and affection for the Corinthian church, which he thought of as presented by himself to Christ as a 'bride' (much as an Old Testament prophet might see Israel as 'betrothed' or 'married' to God), but
3 now in danger of seduction, like Eve, from **a sincere and pure devotion**. We cannot tell how real this danger of seduction was, but Paul presumably had reason for his fears. At any rate, if some other preacher was trying to

modify Paul's gospel, saying that Jesus was not like that at all, or that the spirit which the Corinthians thought they had received was not the real Spirit, then the Corinthians were apparently not reacting against their sug-

4 gestions with the firmness they should: **you submit to it readily enough.** To have had such success, these preachers – and now for the first time they come out of the shadows and we cannot doubt their existence – must indeed

5 be **super-apostles**! But had they in fact any excellence which Paul did not possess? Perhaps they had one: a facility for rhetorical speech. Paul did not pretend to compete with this; indeed he regarded it as, if anything, an imped-

6 iment in the way of imparting the true **knowledge** he had shared with them (1 Corinthians 2).

Before pursuing the 'foolishness' of listing some of his own qualifications, Paul had to defend himself against yet another accusation, that of preaching

7 **free of charge.** This has already formed the subject of a substantial section of 1 Corinthians (chapter 9), where it appeared that Paul's unwillingness to conform with the usual practice of claiming remuneration was exploited as a reason for doubting his authority. Here, the attack seems to have had its basis in social attitudes. Some people certainly thought that any teacher would be demeaning himself if he did manual work to support himself instead of relying on the hospitality of others. This was not actually what Paul had been

9 doing: he had contrived not to **burden anyone** (he uses a colloquial expression which might be rendered 'sponge on anyone') by receiving support from the congregation in Macedonia. (This is referred to in Philippians 4.10–18.) This too could perhaps be criticized. Why was he prepared to accept support from one congregation and not another? Did it suggest that he lacked confidence

11 in the Corinthians? Was it **because I do not love you? God knows I do!** At

10 any rate, with an emphatic oath (**As the truth of Christ is in me**) he affirms he had no intention of changing his policy in this matter, at least in Achaia. If he were to do so, it would put him on the same level as his opponents – and it seems as if the very thought of this riled him so much that he began

13 to say what he really thought of them: **false apostles, deceitful workers.** If

14 even Satan could disguise himself as **an angel of light**, so his **ministers** could

15 masquerade as **ministers of righteousness.** These agents of Satan would have an end to **match their deeds.**

After this digression, Paul returns to the little 'foolishness' for which he asked indulgence at the beginning of the chapter and which allows him to

16, 19 **boast a little.** If the Corinthians are so **wise** that they can put up with the arrogance and insults and exploitation inflicted on them by his opponents (he permits himself this much irony), then surely they can put up with a mild piece of foolishness from Paul, who is ready to admit, to his shame, that he

21 was **too weak** to indulge in such behaviour!

Now for the moment of 'boasting'. Paul can meet any of these opponents on their own ground – and for the first time we get some solid information

22 about them. They are **Hebrews, Israelites, descendants of Abraham** – three

different ways of describing their Jewishness (the exact nuances are lost on us: see below on Philippians 3.5–6), which is of course no greater than Paul's.

23 They also claim to be **ministers of Christ**, which implies a claim to be acting in Christ's name and with his authority. To this Paul replies with a vivid sketch of what this 'ministry' has meant in his own case, which shows him to be in a completely different league from them. With a lack of modesty of which he is painfully aware (or with the risk of appearing to claim a philosopher's indifference, which is not his purpose) – **I am talking like a madman** – he recites an impressive catalogue of the afflictions he has endured. In part these are quite general: **labors** and dangers such as might be cited as tests of anyone's stamina. But in part they are specific and show little sign of rhetorical exaggeration; indeed, had circumstances not forced this confession out of him we should never have known more than half of what he endured. From Jewish courts – to which he must have voluntarily submitted himself in order, as he said, "to win Jews" (1 Corinthians 9.20) –

24 he had received the maximum penalty short of death: **forty lashes minus one.** (In Deuteronomy 25.3 the maximum prescribed is forty, but thirty-nine had become the usual number, allegedly to avoid breaking the law by accidentally giving one too many; and the punishment was normally given for an offence against rules of religious purity.) By the Romans, despite his Roman citizenship which should have protected him, he was three times

25 **beaten with rods.** (One of these occasions is recounted in Acts 16.22.) From the Jews again he **received a stoning**, a punishment (perhaps for blasphemy)

23 which usually resulted in death; and that he was **often near death** receives an illustration in Acts 14.19.

A philosopher might have listed all this to prove the strength of his stamina in the face of adversity. Paul's purpose is the opposite. His opponents might take that line; but for him his survival speaks of the power of God sustaining him and a divine commission which no physical adversity could frustrate. The list ends, therefore, not with a climax of Herculean labours, but with a

28 most unstoical confession of **anxiety for all the churches**, involving an acute identification with their moments of weakness and indignation, and with the report of an incident, also recorded in Acts (9.24): being smuggled out

32 of a city in a basket was hardly something that could do him credit! **King Aretas** was king of the Nabateans, a desert people, from about 9 to 39 CE. His capital was at Petra, deep in the desert towards the Red Sea, but his empire certainly extended as far north as the region of Damascus. The city itself was technically under Roman administration until the death of Tiberius in 37 CE, but it is reasonable to accept the evidence of this passage that Aretas had some sort of **governor** or *ethnarch* there at this time, who could be persuaded by the Jews to try to arrest Paul.

12.1 **I will go on to visions and revelations of the Lord**. Continuing his 'boast' – the things he could legitimately take pride in – though still aware that, even if he is obliged to do it, **nothing is to be gained by it**, Paul goes on to say something about what we would now call a 'mystical' experience. Such experiences are essentially incommunicable; but Paul's inherited religion and culture gave him certain resources for describing it. A number of accounts of visionary experiences have survived from his period; and one feature they have in common is that the writer never allowed himself to appear as the subject of them: he either ascribed the experience to a figure of the distant past, such as Moses or Isaiah, or he wrote pseudonymously under a biblical name

2 such as Enoch or Daniel. Paul shows a similar reticence: **I know a person** – and we need have no doubt that this person was Paul himself. He is reticent also about the form the experience took: **whether in the body** (the experience of being lifted bodily into another world like Enoch) **or out of the body** (the more common type of interior vision). Such reticence makes it impossible

5 to **boast** of the experience (though the reality of the experience itself was something in which there could be a proper 'confidence'). Beyond this, Paul can use only the conventional language of Jewish visionaries who, writing of such experiences, would often describe them as a kind of progression through a series of 'heavens', sometimes three, sometimes four, sometimes seven, of

4 which the last would offer a vision of **Paradise**. More details than this would amount to **things that are not to be told** – the authentic inability of the mystic to convey such experience in any but highly symbolic form. But this much was sufficient for Paul to make his point. If his opponents were claiming to have had some supernatural authorization for their mission, his account of his own experience, however reticent, should be a sufficient answer, without incurring the charge of going in for the kind of 'boasting' which they did.

Yet there was a danger for Paul: an experience of this kind might have

7 made him so **elated** that he would begin to take credit for it or to use it to claim some superiority. The sense of this danger perhaps helped him to come to terms with what he describes as **a thorn . . . in the flesh**. This is a vague metaphor covering almost any form of illness or even harassment by others, but it clearly caused Paul humiliation, embarrassment and pain. By calling it **a messenger of Satan** he evidently identified it as a temptation sent to try him; and his resistance to it was strengthened by an answer to his prayers that affirmed the understanding of suffering that had been growing in him

9–10 throughout his sufferings: that **"power is made perfect in weakness"**, and that all the afflictions that he has listed – **weaknesses, insults, hardships, persecutions, and calamities** – if endured for the **sake of Christ** (and, we might add, in close communion with Christ, as in 4.10–12), are the means by which a Christian may be strong with **the power of Christ.**

11 **I have been a fool!** Indeed, this 'boasting' was not only foolish, it was irrelevant to the point at issue. If any evidence were needed of the apostle's status it should have been looked for, not in the man himself, but in the fruits of his work: **you should have been the ones commending me**. Whatever Paul's personal shortcomings (**even though I am nothing**), the very existence of the Corinthian church, and the supernatural experiences which had taken

place there (and which had thrown up some of the problems which are the
12 subject of 1 Corinthians), were the sufficient **signs of a true apostle**. Was
there anything they did *not* receive from their founding apostle – except
perhaps the privilege of giving him material support? And by way of this
ironical exception, Paul returns to the charge he has already dealt with more
than once in chapter 11 but which still seems to rankle in his mind: that
he had refused financial assistance from the Corinthians. He continues to
14 refuse it: this third time he would **not be a burden** on them (or 'sponge
on them', the same colloquial expression as before), and he has yet another
argument to support his policy. He sees himself as the Corinthians' 'father'
(1 Corinthians 4.15). Children, although they should certainly support their
elderly parents (Paul's argument is a little precarious here), should not lay
up capital for them – that is the parent's responsibility, who should hand on
the family fortune, not receive it from the next generation. Which leads to
a deeper consideration. It is not only money that one can 'spend': one can
'spend oneself' – which is exactly what Paul has been doing for them.

Paul had never asked for money: that was common ground. Damaging
inferences had been drawn from this, which Paul had shown to be false. But
there was still one particularly offensive suggestion to attend to: that he had
16 been **crafty** and taken them in **by deceit**, recouping his expenses through
his assistants. By way of reply, it was sufficient to recall the arrangements
18 he had made. **Titus** was surely above suspicion; and the fact that there was
another **brother** with him (apparently a reference to one of the authorized
representatives mentioned in 8.18) should have been enough to scotch any
suggestion of malpractice.

19   **Have you been thinking all along that we have been defending ourselves?**
Paul can hardly deny that he has been on the defensive, and that his arguments
may have sounded like those of one pleading his cause at a trial. But if there
is a trial, it can only be in the conscience, **in Christ before God**. So far as the
Corinthians are concerned, Paul's only interest is dictated by the principle
governing his relations with all his churches: all must be for the sake of
building you up (an almost technical expression that occurs quite frequently
in 1 Corinthians). The last thing he wants is for the dispute to blow up into
20 a spate of personal animosities (**quarreling, jealousy** and so forth: Paul uses
a typical moralist's list of such consequences); but equally he fears that his
next visit might bring things to a head and cause a rupture with those who
21 should have **repented** of what was evidently unacceptable conduct, in which
case Paul would have to **mourn over** them as persons lost to the church and
lost, therefore, from the salvation that was offered them. This would amount
to a kind of failure, which Paul would feel as a stroke by which God would
humble him.

If this second possibility – of humiliation – has been correctly interpreted
(and the whole paragraph is by no means easy to understand), Paul never-
13.1 theless, seems willing to confront it. The basic rule of legal procedure quoted

from Deuteronomy (19.15) would not be mentioned unless the situation between them was still like a trial. Doubtless Paul's opponents could summon at least two witnesses; but now that Paul has proved himself innocent, the blame falls on his critics and he becomes the prosecutor, needing inde-

3 pendent witnesses to support his case. Hence the unusual expression, **Christ is speaking in me**. Paul's 'weakness' had been taken as proof that he was not speaking with the power of Christ; but once it is understood that Christ can

4 be recognized as much in weakness (for he was **crucified in weakness**) as in power (manifested in his resurrection life), then it must be acknowledged that Paul was not alone, but all the time had Christ with him and, with such a 'witness' beside him, would be an invincible prosecutor if his third visit was to become a trial of the Corinthians.

5   Such an encounter would certainly put them to **the test**; but of course it would not be a real 'trial' – the metaphor must not be pressed too far. The question was whether Christ was really 'in' them, and to answer this it was necessary to bring both weakness and strength into the equation, just as (as Paul has been arguing all through the letter) his own 'weakness' had not been a sign of failure or disqualification but a manifestation of the 'strength' of Christ in him. The whole purpose of the letter was to bring them to this deep Christian understanding, so that his visit could be entirely in the interest,

10 once again, of the overriding principle of **building up**.

12   On the **holy kiss**, see above on Romans 16.16. Once again, the ending seems to contain echoes of the church at worship. The last sentence is one of the very few 'trinitarian' formulas in the New Testament (placing together God, Jesus and the Holy Spirit), though each element of the formula occurs

13 separately in other places. **The communion of the Holy Spirit** is the translators' choice out of several possibilities. The Greek word *koinōnia* (usually translated 'fellowship') means something like 'common participation' in the Holy Spirit, with perhaps a hint that this participation creates in itself a new kind of community or 'communion' among Christians. No single translation can do justice to the richness of the phrase.

THE LETTER OF PAUL TO THE
GALATIANS

This letter, like the letters to the Corinthians, was evoked by a particular crisis in the relations between Paul and one of the churches he had founded. Something had been going wrong for some time before the letter was written, and this was not the first time that Paul had intervened (4.13). There was pressure from outside the church and there were factions within it, and the atmosphere was such that charges of various kinds had been levelled at Paul. So much, at least, is evident from the letter; but since we have no other record of the various exchanges which took place, and since the narrative in Acts makes no mention of this crisis at all, a great deal remains mysterious and it is impossible to know exactly what was happening and what arguments and accusations Paul had to confront.

We cannot even be sure who THE GALATIANS were. Since the third century BCE, when an invasion of Gauls from central Europe (in Greek: *Galatai*) had finally secured an area for settlement in the centre of Asia Minor, *Galatia* had been the name currently used for the territory of these invaders. But in 25 BCE the Roman province of Galatia was created out of lands that included not only the original Galatian heartland but also (for political and administrative reasons) parts of Pisidia and Lycaonia to the south. It then became correct, at least from the point of view of the Roman administration, to call the southern cities (Pisidian Antioch, Iconium, Lystra and Derbe) 'Galatian'.

We know nothing from Paul's own letters of his movements in the central part of Asia Minor (the ethnic 'Galatia'). Acts provides a somewhat vague report of a journey through "the region of Galatia" during Paul's second missionary journey (16.6; 18.23); but it gives much more detailed information about his work in the southern cities during his first journey (chapters 13–14), so that although these cities were 'Galatian' only in a technical sense, it is possible and in many ways tempting to think that it was to the Christians there that this letter was addressed.

Bound up with this uncertainty about the destination of the letter is the question of its date. If the northern area ('ethnic Galatia') was its destination, then it must have been written some time after the events of Acts 16–18, which brings us down to at least 52 CE (close to the time of the writing of the letter to the Romans, with which it has some points of contact). On the other hand if the southern cities were the home of Paul's 'Galatian' churches, it could equally well have been written several years earlier; indeed, it could be Paul's earliest extant letter. And this wide range of possible dates makes it difficult to relate the incidents mentioned in the letter to other known episodes in Paul's

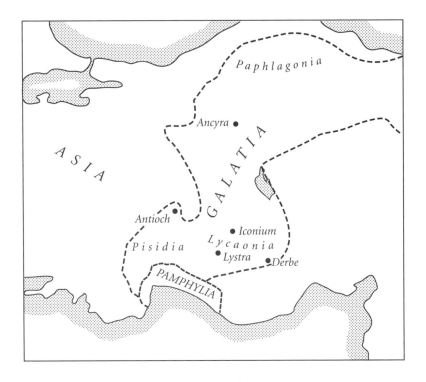

life. Even the fragments of autobiography in chapter 2 present difficulties, for some of them are also recorded in Acts but in such as way as to make it difficult to reconcile the two accounts.

None of this prevents the main argument of the letter from being followed in its own right, and all the circumstances do not have to be reconstructed before it can be understood. Nevertheless, it may be helpful to read the letter with some picture of the Galatian church and its problems in mind, even if there is no reconstruction on which all can agree. It appears that the Galatian church was under pressure from Jewish influences but itself consisted mainly of Gentiles. Even those who had recently yielded to some pressure to conform with Jewish observances were by no means all originally Jews by birth and had only recently been circumcised as proselytes. On the other hand the argument of the letter, with its detailed references to the Old Testament, can have been intelligible only to people who were already familiar with the Jewish religion and the Jewish scriptures. Where were such Jewish-minded Gentiles to be found? The answer seems to be that they were those described in Acts as 'God-fearers', that is, what we might call associate members of the synagogue in any cosmopolitan city of the Greco-Roman world. These gentile associates, who seem to have existed in considerable numbers, were not admitted to full membership or even full social contact with the Jewish community, but they were permitted to attend the synagogue in order to hear scripture read and to learn about the Jewish religion and way of life. In return, they were asked to observe certain moral standards and to respect the Jewish sabbaths and holy days.

It was among such people that Paul made his earliest converts. The Christian preaching had a natural attraction for them. It offered a religion no less exacting and exalted than Judaism, but without the same restrictions on social contact with their gentile friends and neighbours and, above all, without the objectionable requirement of circumcision. The narrative of Acts shows Paul on a number of occasions turning away from an unwelcoming Jewish community to this non-Jewish group who proved readier listeners.

But suppose the Jews of the local synagogue saw their following of sympathetic (and perhaps financially generous) gentile associates being suddenly drawn away into a separate movement. It would not be surprising if they began to put considerable pressure on the renegades to return and, having returned, to accept circumcision as an irrevocable sign of their allegiance. Equally, it would not be surprising if many of the Christians, subjected to pressure and even harassment from the synagogue community (and perhaps also from fellow Christians who were themselves Jewish), felt tempted to purchase a quiet life at the price of accepting the synagogue's conditions. This would, after all, oblige them only to accept certain outward observances. They would still be free among themselves to confess Jesus as Lord – or so they believed, and this seems quite plausible when we consider the very wide range of beliefs held at the time by law-abiding Jews.

This, at least, is one possible reconstruction of the situation which elicited Paul's letter. To Paul's converts the issue may have seemed merely a practical one to do with outward observances. But to Paul it appeared to strike at the very heart of the Christian experience of freedom and new life. And so he addressed them on the level, not of practical expediency, but of theological truth. His argument rises above the local dispute between church and synagogue and has been justly prized throughout the history of Christianity as a classic formulation of some of the central tenets of the Christian faith.

The background

1.1–3 **Paul an apostle**. The opening of the letter, as in the letter to the Romans, follows the conventional structure: **Paul . . . To the churches of Galatia: Grace to you and peace.** (For the distinctively Christian adaptations of this formula see above on Romans 1.1.) But Paul expands it here by working into it two specific claims. The first concerns himself: he is **an apostle** (possibly some people were disputing this, or at least were questioning whether his apostleship was equal in authority to that of others), and his authority has

1 been conferred by **Jesus Christ and God the Father;** the second reads like
3, 4 a credal statement about **the Lord Jesus Christ.** That Christ **gave himself for our sins** was a fundamental belief which we find in a number of slightly different formulations in the New Testament. But that this was **to set us free from the present evil age** sets the formula in the context of the widespread Jewish assumption that the present age is one in which evil powers have a temporary ascendancy, soon to be brought to an end when God brings in the new age. The decisive Christian modification of this scheme consisted in recognizing that in Christ the moment of release has already begun.

6   **I am astonished.** Normally at this point there would be an expression of thanksgiving for the gifts and achievements of the Christians to whom Paul is writing. But this letter has to deal with a crisis and comes straight to the point. Certain persons have been proclaiming **a different gospel.** Not that any gospel (in the technical Christian sense of the word) is possible other
7 than the **gospel of Christ:** this 'gospel' is the *good news*[1] that the expected Messiah has come, and to deny this would be to deny the possibility of any such 'gospel' at all. No, these persons have been trying to **pervert the gospel of Christ** – strong language, and later in the letter we shall see what prompted it: they were deliberately failing to see its practical and moral implications. And this is serious: any such interpretation of the gospel, even if it has the apparent authorization of a divine messenger, must be recognized as an
9 acute danger to the church. Indeed, whoever the messenger, **let that one be accursed!** – literally *anathema*, a Jewish expression for expelling a guilty person from the sacred community.

Strong language indeed, – and understandable if this had been a rhetorical
10 attempt by Paul to *persuade*[2] people to support him or even to 'persuade' God of the rightness of his cause. (The author of some of the psalms had cursed his enemies in much the same way.) But to **please people** is no part of his agenda. The issue is much more serious. His orders come only from the master (**Christ**) of whom he is a **servant** or *slave*, as does the authority of the gospel he has proclaimed. This is what he is now about to demonstrate.

The story of Paul's conversion is told three times in Acts (chapters 9, 22 and 26). Here it is simply alluded to – but that it is the same experience
12 is shown, first by the word **revelation**, a technical word for the kind of vision and commission received on the Damascus road, and secondly by the account of what went immediately before it: as in Acts, Paul was violently
13 **persecuting the church of God and was trying to destroy it.** But here, Paul tells us something of his motivation – his powerful commitment to **Judaism**, a somewhat technical way of referring to his strict observance of the Jewish

---

[1] As it is usually translated in the NRSV.
[2] *Persuade* is the literal meaning of the Greek word. The rendering in the NRSV, **seeking human approval** – like that in many other translations – seeks to soften Paul's startling idea that he might be thought to be trying to 'persuade' God.

14 way of life; and a **zealous** concern that no deviation should be allowed from the practices elaborated in ancestral **traditions**. To this he adds an emphasis on two further points: first, that he had received an experience comparable with the call of an Old Testament prophet, not random but predestined (verse 15 contains allusions to Isaiah 49.1 and Jeremiah 1.5); and secondly, that the call, as in the two Old Testament passages, was specifically a call to preach

16 **among the Gentiles**. In other words, it was not so much a 'conversion' as a 'call' or 're-call' to proclaim the true meaning of the Jewish scriptures in a more universal way than could ever have been conceived of by a zealous proponent of 'Judaism'. Such was the impact of the revelation of God's **Son**, whom Paul was often to speak of as being *in* him as well as revealed **to** him.[3] And such was the self-authenticating nature of the vision that it needed neither confirmation nor elucidation by the Jerusalem apostles – we shall see how important it was to Paul to stress his independent authority – and instead

17 he **went away at once into Arabia**, possibly to begin preaching, but more likely for a period of withdrawal and meditation on the shattering experience he had undergone. (This period of withdrawal is not mentioned in Acts. The word **Arabia** could denote anywhere from the desert in the immediate neighbourhood of Damascus to the shores of the Red Sea. Much of it was in the Nabatean kingdom of Aretas, who is mentioned in 2 Corinthians 11.32.)

18 **Then after three years**. This must correspond with the visit described in Acts (9.26–30), for both accounts presuppose that this was Paul's first visit to Jerusalem after his conversion. The two accounts describe the visit from different points of view, but are not irreconcilable. The author of Acts evidently did not fully appreciate Paul's purpose in going to Jerusalem; and Paul had no interest in recounting all that happened there. At any rate, Paul says that his motive for the journey was **to visit Cephas** (his usual name for Simon Peter). The exact sense of the verb translated **to visit** is uncertain. It could mean 'to get information from' or 'to get to know'. We can certainly assume that there were things and people Paul would want to learn about. But it was important for his argument to use a word which did not imply that he took instructions from any of the existing apostles – hence his protestation,

20 **before God, I do not lie!** Unlike that of Acts, his account is of a strictly private

19 visit: apart from Peter he claims that he saw only **James the Lord's brother**, who was soon to become leader of the Jerusalem church and who seems already (though the Greek is as ambiguous as the English) to be counted as one of the apostles. At any rate (whether or not there were more meetings, as Acts suggests), the point being emphasized and reiterated with an oath is that despite this visit Paul had remained entirely independent of the Jerusalem

21 church, and that up to his return to Tarsus in **Cilicia** (Acts 9.30) and Antioch

22 in **Syria** (Acts 11.25) he remained **unknown by sight to the churches of Judea**, who came to know of his extraordinary conversion only by hearsay.

---

[3] The Greek means literally *in*, but translators assume that it could also mean **to**.

2.1   **Then after fourteen years.** Attempts to reconstruct the history in the light
of Acts now run into difficulties. The next visit recorded in Acts (11.29–30;
12.25) is the mission of Paul and Barnabas to Jerusalem with an emergency
contribution from Antioch for the relief of "the believers living in Judea" in
a time of famine. Since Paul is also clearly describing his next visit, the two
should correspond. They can certainly be made to do so, but this relatively
early dating (before 49 CE) creates other problems, and most interpreters
prefer to assume some error in the order of events in Acts and to identify the
visit to Jerusalem described here with that which resulted in the council of
Acts 15, with which indeed, it has some striking resemblances. But here too
there are serious differences between the two accounts, and it becomes difficult to understand the episode in Galatians 2.11–14 if the decision recorded
in Acts 15 (not to impose circumcision on gentile Christians) had already
been taken and promulgated. Either way, complete harmonization seems to
be impossible.

For our purposes, more important than the details of a historical reconstruction is Paul's description of his own part in the episode. First, it was
2   undertaken **in response to a revelation** – that is, not at the behest of any
human authority in Jerusalem or anywhere else. Secondly, the visit was not
in order to receive instructions from other apostles, but to 'lay before them'
his own practice of proclaiming the gospel **among the Gentiles**; it was not
a matter of submitting to their judgment but of making sure that his efforts
(likened to **running** a race) would not be nullified by a serious disagreement
in the church – would not be **in vain**. Thirdly, a key factor in the visit was the
1   presence of **Titus**, whom Paul brought along with him as well as Barnabas
(about whom we hear a good deal in Acts: he was a wealthy and generous
man from Cyprus, who accompanied Paul at various stages of his work).
Titus was a Greek, that is to say a non-Jew, and Paul may have taken him
along as a living example of what had hardly yet been seen in Jerusalem: a
non-Jewish, uncircumcised Christian! It is perhaps not surprising that there
were evidently Jewish Christians in Jerusalem who took it for granted that the
social and religious problems which would arise from this could most easily
be solved if all such converts were to be circumcised as Jewish proselytes.
4   And those who were **secretly brought in** to the deliberations (and Paul's language here uses some sharply antagonistic expressions) evidently sought to
'compel' this to take place.[4] But this would have amounted to a direct assault
6   on Paul's **freedom . . . in Christ Jesus**, and was not endorsed by **the acknowledged leaders** – Paul stresses that those who supported him were not just a
9   rival party but were **acknowledged pillars** – he often likened the church to
a building – and he gives their names: **James**, the brother of Jesus; **Cephas**
(Simon Peter); and **John,** presumably the son of Zebedee, one of the original

---

[4] In Greek, as in English, **was not compelled to be circumcised** is ambiguous. It could
possibly mean that, though not compelled to be, he *was* circumcised.

disciples, who was a constant companion of Peter (Acts 3.1 and elsewhere)
6 and evidently respected as a leader. These leaders **contributed nothing** to
Paul's account of his work: the word seems carefully chosen to emphasize
9 their acknowledgment of the correctness of his strategy; they **recognized the
grace that had been given** to Paul, evidenced by the success of his mission;
and they affirmed their **fellowship** with him, that is, the unimpaired unity
of the church (*koinōnia*), by a gesture which assured Paul that he had not
'run in vain'. As a result, Paul and Barnabas were officially entrusted with
responsibility for the mission to the Gentiles, while the Jerusalem apostles
10 continued their work among Jews. The only condition was that the new gentile churches should express their solidarity with Jerusalem by maintaining
the traditional Jewish religious practice of charitable giving and should send
financial relief – a task which we know that Paul subsequently took very
seriously (2 Corinthians 8; Romans 15.25–7), and which he may even have
begun already.[5]

Paul's strategy, then, had been formally recognized as legitimate and fruitful – in theory. But it had practical consequences which, even if hardly yet
experienced in Jerusalem (where a non-Jewish Christian like Titus was a
rarity), might present an acute problem wherever (as in a city such as Antioch)
the young church was likely to consist of Jews and non-Jews together. Many of
the Jewish Christians will have been brought up to regard sitting at a gentile
table as impermissible (since they could not be sure that the food conformed
with their standards of ritual purity). How could they now share meals
(particularly perhaps the Lord's supper) that were offered to them by
Christians of quite different backgrounds? Paul's own experience in such
4 churches had convinced him that the solution was what he called **the freedom we have in Christ Jesus** – Jewish food laws should be no barrier to social
and religious life in a mixed community; and Peter, perhaps encouraged by
his experience in the house of Cornelius (Acts 10), adopted the same liberty
12 when he visited Antioch: **he used to eat with the Gentiles.** But – in theory
at least – there was another solution: if all the Christians who were not Jews
were to become proselytes and be circumcised, it would then be permissible
for the most scrupulous Jewish Christians to eat with them and the problem
14 would disappear. This solution, that Gentiles should **live like Jews,** was evi-
12 dently being promoted by an influential party in Jerusalem (**certain people
from James**), and the arrival of this party at Antioch precipitated the crisis
described in verses 11–14.

Paul rejected this solution outright, not merely because it would soon
have become unpractical anyway, but because of his conviction that it was
14 inconsistent with **the truth of the gospel.** When Peter, clearly alarmed by the
12 reaction of the conservative visitors, **drew back and kept himself separate**
13 from some of the common meals – a course which Paul describes as **hypocrisy**

---

[5] The tense of the Greek verb is again ambiguous. See the NRSV footnote.

in view of his former 'living like a Gentile' – Paul vigorously attacked him
on the grounds that this traditional Jewish 'separateness' would have had the
14 consequence of 'compelling' the gentile Christians to **live like Jews** – literally
to Judaize, that is, to adopt the full rigour of a scrupulous interpretation of
the Jewish food laws or even to go the whole way and become proselytes
through circumcision. We do not know whether Paul's view prevailed with
Peter on that occasion; but from many hints scattered through the letter
we can infer that there was a group of Christians in the Galatian church
who had been tempted to follow the same line, doubtless seeing it merely
as a matter of practical expediency in a mixed community. But Paul saw
it as a policy charged with theological significance, a direct challenge to
the truth of the gospel; and the following chapters are a sustained attempt
to alert the non-Jewish Galatian Christians to the danger of taking it too
lightly.

But first[6] – and by way, perhaps, of a rhetorical transition to his main
theme – Paul has something to say about the proper attitude of Jewish Chris-
16 tians (like himself) to the scrupulous keeping of Jewish observances (**the
works of the law**). From the point of view of an observant Jew, all Gentiles
were 'sinners' in the sense of being outside the community of those who
were assured of their salvation by reason of their birth and their way of life.
But the Christian faith was that this was irrelevant to the question whether
a person is 'justified' or 'righteous' in the eyes of God – only **faith in Christ**
had this significance. The fact that one was born a Jew should therefore make
no difference.

But the reality was more complicated. Jews who had become Christians
doubtless varied in the degree to which they insisted on ritual purity; but their
new faith did not compel them to give up their observances or cut themselves
off from their former friends, and they will have had an instinctive reluctance
to live in a way that had formerly seemed, by definition, 'sinful'. In this sense,
17 some of them might even have said that Christ was **a servant of sin**, allegiance
18 to him forcing Jews to live in this 'sinful' way. But this, Paul argues, is to **build
up again** that very faith in observances and privileged ethnicity which faith
in Christ had superseded; it is to 'transgress' a far more basic principle. The
fact of becoming a Christian (as Paul demonstrates at much more length in
the letter to the Romans) is a kind of 'death' to previous ethnic and ritual
convictions. What may appear, in Jewish eyes, to be a 'sinful' disregard of all
that goes with observance of the law is in fact a new life, entered on by dying
with Christ to that same law and being governed, no longer by any such law,
20 but by **faith in the Son of God.**

---

[6] There are no inverted commas in a Greek manuscript, and it is possible that verses
15–21 (or part of them) are a continuation of Paul's retort to Peter. The NRSV text rejects
this possibility (but allows for it in a footnote). In any case, Paul's argument is addressed
to Jewish Christians, real or hypothetical.

Faith and freedom

3.1 You foolish Galatians! Paul now turns directly to his readers. They have
been **bewitched**, that is to say, they are evidently under some sinister kind of
3 pressure to compromise over Jewish observances (matters essentially of **the
flesh**, to do with requirements of the Jewish law) and have already yielded
ground. To show them their error, Paul appeals to a fact of their Christian
5 experience they cannot deny: they received **the Spirit**, even to the extent of
having **miracles** take place among them; and he asks them twice over whether
this was the result of **doing the works of the law** (in which case why did it
not happen to all observant Jews?) or of the new departure they had made
1 once Paul's public preaching had brought Christ crucified vividly 'before
5 their eyes' and they had come to 'belief in what they had heard'. This word
'belief' is the key to what follows; for if the answer to Paul's question is that it
was the result of 'belief' (which of course it was – the question is a rhetorical
7 one), then Christians are **those who believe** and are therefore **descendants**
(literally, *sons*) **of Abraham.**

Why does Paul introduce Abraham at this point? When addressing non-
Jewish Christians one would think he could have used a simpler argument:
in Christ they had no need of Jewish ordinances in order to appear
'righteous' before God, and therefore no need to be integrated into the Jewish
understanding of history which made Abraham so important. But for Paul,
and perhaps also for his Galatian converts who had long been attracted by
Judaism, it was not so easy to abandon this historical connection and all the
theology which went with it. Abraham was the key figure in the history of
God's chosen race and, through him, of all human beings. He was the symbol
of God's concern for human beings in terms of a promise, a covenant and
an assurance of salvation. All this had been expressly conferred upon him
and, through him, upon his descendants – that is, the Jews and also (in the
view of many) to some degree upon those who associated themselves with
the Jews by adopting the same way of life and many of the same observances.

But there was a further reason. These Christians in Galatia (as we can infer
from the fact that they could follow this argument at all) were familiar with
scripture and had accepted it as a guide to belief and conduct. Paul needed
to show that what he was arguing for was compatible with what Genesis said
about Abraham and his 'descendants', and indeed, was actually implied by it.
The relevant passages are in Genesis 12–17. In the course of these chapters
it is repeatedly stated that God made his promise to Abraham and to his
'descendants', but also that his descendants would inherit the promise only if
they observed certain conditions, among them being duly circumcised. "Any
uncircumcised male who is not circumcised in the flesh of his foreskin shall
be cut off from his people" (Genesis 17.14). The implication of these chapters
seems quite clear: the promise was made only to the physical descendants
of Abraham, and to them only on condition that they were circumcised.

Jewish thinking allowed that this could be extended to proselytes, that is, Gentiles who were circumcised. But gentile Christians who were distancing themselves from Jewish observances appeared to be excluded.

But Paul can offer a different interpretation. As the fundamental text, he
6 takes Genesis 15.6: **Abraham "believed God, and it was reckoned to him as righteousness"**; and along with this a second text (which is a combination of Genesis 12.3 and 18.18 but which recurs in slightly different forms several
8 times in Genesis), **"All the Gentiles shall be blessed in you."** The first of these makes 'believing' the fundamental attribute of Abraham from which the blessing flowed, and the second promises the blessing to others – **all the Gentiles** – who (like the Galatian Christians) are certainly not Abraham's
9 'descendants'. But at this point Paul introduces his interpreter's key. **Those who believe**, he writes – and he has just said that Christians are what they are by virtue of *believing* – are the *sons* of Abraham. Of course the natural
7 meaning of this word was physical **descendants**, as NRSV translates it. But there was also a less literal meaning. A common idiom in Palestine was to speak of (for instance) a 'son of peace', meaning a 'peaceful man'. Equally it was an acceptable Greek idiom to speak of a 'son of Plato', meaning a Platonic philosopher. So, a 'son of Abraham' could mean an Abraham-like man. In which case the text could be taken as a promise, not to Abraham's physical descendants, but to those who became Abraham-like in believing; that is, to Christians; and if these Christians were Gentiles (as they were in
8 Galatia), then the second text would also be fulfilled – **"All the Gentiles shall be blessed in you."**

Jewish interpreters might well have jibbed at this line of thought. They were accustomed to thinking of Abraham's 'believing' – his *faith* – in terms of *faithfulness*, since this was the quality he showed most conspicuously under the various trials to which he was subjected. Moreover, the word translated **Gentiles** (or *nations*) would normally have been taken by them to mean the tribes or 'nations' of Israel. But their main objection is likely to have been that by this reasoning Paul appeared to be demoting from its prime place in Jewish self-understanding the entire system of ordinances and observances which constituted their ethnic identity and way of life. For they were, in this
10 sense, people who **rely on the works of the law**; and Paul's argument seems to strike a note of extreme paradox when he claims that they were therefore **under a curse**. It used to be assumed that Paul regarded it as impossible to keep the law in its entirety, and, since any transgression might attract a curse, it followed that everyone must be deserving this curse one way or another. But this assumption runs counter to what he says of himself before his conversion (in Philippians 3.6, for example, where he describes himself as 'blameless'), and is not an attitude that any Pharisee of the time is known to have taken. On the other hand, to 'rely on the works of the law' meant to believe that belonging to the Jewish community, which regulated its life
12 by the law of Moses, was a sufficient guide to blessedness (**"Whoever does**

the works of the law will live by them", Leviticus 18.5), even though it also meant placing oneself at risk of prescribed penalties (which in extreme cases meant being 'cursed'); and those sects or parties which adopted a particularly rigorous form of observance might equally use the word 'cursed' of those who took the law less seriously than they did. (There is a clear case of this in John 7.49.) But in any case the converse of being cursed was being 'justified' or being found 'righteous' by God. Paul's Christian theology centred on the proposition that this justification or righteousness in the eyes of God came only from faith in Christ. But the argument here is about scriptural texts; and

11 he can quote one to make his point: **"The one who is righteous will live by faith"** (Habakkuk 2.4).[7] Christ, of course, was a Jew living in a Jewish society in which he was bound to the observances of the law. Moreover we know that many criticized him for his apparently relaxed attitude to some of them and might well have called him (in this sense) 'cursed'. Even if not in life,

13 scripture showed that in death he was certainly 'cursed': **"Cursed is everyone who hangs on a tree."** (Deuteronomy 27.26). Christ shared, therefore, the curse that reputedly hung over all (such as the gentile Christians) who in the eyes of strict Jews failed to observe all that the law required. But since Christ had been raised and vindicated by God one could say that he had **redeemed us from the curse of the law**, and thereby removed any obstacle to Gentiles' receiving the promise made to Abraham, a promise that was appropriated

14 by believing – **faith** – and confirmed by the gift of **the Spirit**.

But here an objection could be made. Paul's case against the necessity of full conformity with the ordinances of the law had rested so far on his interpretation of a key text concerning Abraham. But so far as the law was concerned it could surely be said that the decisive figure was, not Abraham, but Moses. The promises made to Abraham might indeed have been a response to faith and not to observance of laws. But it might also have been provisional: the final disposition of God was surely not fully known until the moment when the complete law was given to Moses. Paul's answer to this objection involves

15 a play on the Greek word *diathēkē*, which normally meant a **will** (in the sense of 'last will and testament') but which in the Septuagint translation of the Hebrew scriptures was used in the special sense of the 'covenant' made by God with his people. Taking the word in its usual sense of **will**, Paul points out that, once a will has been **ratified** and the testator is dead, no alteration can be made. Therefore, since God's promise to Abraham is called in scripture a 'covenant', which is also a 'will', it could not be altered by the subsequent dispensation of the law given to Moses. True, God does not die, and can hardly be thought of as making wills. But from the fact that the same word

17 could do duty for both, Paul could infer that the **covenant** made by God

---

[7] This is ambiguous in Greek; see the NRSV footnote. Doubtless the ambiguity was intended by Paul.

with Abraham had at least this in common with a 'will' – that it could not be invalidated by subsequent legislation.

(The argument is interrupted by a parenthesis which seems bewildering to a modern reader, since it involves a highly technical method of interpretation. It was by no means taken for granted that the meaning of a text of scripture always lies on the surface: there might also be a hidden meaning that was at least as important. One of the signs which was believed to indicate the presence of such a hidden meaning was any kind of grammatical irregularity, such as a singular noun when a plural might have been expected (or vice

16 versa). Now in fact the word **offspring** here was perfectly intelligible in a passage such as this (Genesis 13.15 and elsewhere) as a collective noun denoting the physical descendants of Abraham. But Paul (somewhat arbitrarily, as it seems to us, but consistently with this method of interpretation) chose to regard this noun as a less natural expression than the plural, **offsprings**, and therefore as an indication that there was a hidden meaning. By this method (which would have been regarded as legitimate by many Jewish scholars) he was able to declare that the singular noun **offspring** looked forward to **Christ**, so providing a scriptural proof that Christ was the recipient of the promise.)

19 **Why then the law?** Paul has been arguing that receiving the promise depends neither on physical descent from Abraham nor on belonging to the community whose life is regulated by obedience to the law, but only on faith; and he is now ready, in the light of this, to reveal to the Galatians the seriousness of what they would be doing if they were to yield to the pressure being put upon them to conform with the observances prescribed by the law of Moses. But first he has to answer a question that is raised by his argument so far – **Why then the law?** It would almost seem as if the whole system that controlled the Jewish way of life – ritual, sacrifices, diet, festivals and the rest – has been bypassed altogether, losing its whole value and function. But this is by no means Paul's intention, and he suggests a number of reasons for ascribing value to 'the law'.

(i) **It was added because of transgressions.** In Romans (4.15; 5.20) Paul goes so far as to say that the law actually makes sin worse by detailing possible as well as actual transgressions. But here the intention is more positive, and we can assume that **because of transgressions** is a reference to the fact that the law not merely was a code of conduct but also enshrined an elaborate system of sacrifices and offerings by which **transgressions** could be atoned for.

(ii) It was in place **until the offspring would come to whom the promises had been made** – that is, it was provisional, but not for that reason invalid.

(iii) **It was ordained through angels by a mediator.** This was standard Jewish theology: in Paul's time it was an accepted tradition that angels were present at the law-giving on Sinai (possibly to communicate its moral provisions to other nations), and no one doubted Moses' rôle as 'mediator'. This

degree of divine authorization made it impossible to devalue the law. Nor,
20 on the other hand, did the fact that this mediation involved **more than one party** in any sense impinge on the fundamental Jewish doctrine that God is one – there was nothing divine about the mediators.

For these reasons Paul can argue that the law has, or at least has had, a necessary function and is not invalidated by the new state of affairs brought
21 about through Christ. **Is the law then opposed to the promises of God? Certainly not!** Life in Christ was a new life, so different from the old that it could be called being 'made alive'. If law and all that went with it in the Jewish way of life could **make alive** in this sense, then it could certainly claim to assure its adherents of **righteousness** before God. But in fact it was a way of living that took its character from the very nature of the sinful world as
22 scripture diagnosed it to be – **the scripture has imprisoned all things under the power of sin.** It was only by receiving the promise made to **those who believe** in Christ Jesus that a genuinely new life could be lived in the midst of such a world.

And Paul had a further argument, or rather illustration, to support this positive but provisional view of the law.
24 (iv) **The law was our disciplinarian** is not quite what the Greek means. The word is *paidagōgos*, 'pedagogue', and meant a tutor (usually a slave) who was put in charge of his owner's children to accompany them back and forth to school and generally to supervise their conduct. The children owed obedience to this tutor until they came of age; and Paul finds the analogy with the function of the law so striking that he comes back to it in chapter 4. But for the present he moves rapidly forward to his conclusion, which takes him beyond questions of scriptural interpretation into new realms of social analysis. If the condition of becoming (in this new sense) children of Abraham and receiving the promise made to them is, not observance, but **faith** in Christ, then those who have made such an act of faith and confirmed it by
27 being **baptized into Christ** (that is, to use what was certainly a standard Christian metaphor, being **clothed . . . with Christ**) have entered a new society in which all human divisions and barriers – even the fundamental one between Jew and Gentile – have been superseded by a new unity: they
28 are **all** – and this **all** is very emphatic, both here and in verse 26 – **all one in Christ.** The old divisive distinction between Jew and Greek has been abolished – indeed, as if this were not enough, Paul enlarges on his theme far beyond the point required by his argument: *all* distinctions, whether social (**slave or free**) or even natural (**male and female** – an astonishing suggestion in the ancient world) are abolished in this new unity in Christ.

One further point rounds off the argument and returns to the point of
29 departure. The key passage of scripture talked of **Abraham's offspring**, which was always assumed to mean those who belonged to the Jewish covenant. But Paul has demonstrated (by reasoning that may have seemed highly technical) that this phrase had a hidden meaning, namely 'Christ'. But Christians **belong**

to Christ. Therefore they are the true **offspring** of Abraham, to whom the promise was made.

The incompatibility of this new faith with submission to the observances practised by a community in obedience to law can be illustrated still further.

24 Paul has already likened the law to a *paidagōgos*, a **disciplinarian** responsible for the conduct and safety of the children of a family. He now picks

4.1 up another point of comparison with the status of children as **minors**. It made no difference how certain a child might be of ultimately inheriting the family possessions and privileges; during the period of minority, in which the father had total authority over all members of the household, there was little distinction between the children and the slaves in the house. Indeed, the children, like the slaves, were viewed in law as part of the property, with

2 **guardians and trustees**, until such time as the father had set a **date** for their

3 emancipation into freedom. **So with us**. Up to now the comparison has been with a Jewish community in its subjection to the ordinances of the law. But now Paul appears to speak for those of his converts who had never had that experience but who (he claims) were **enslaved to the elemental spirits of the world**,[8] that is, to the pseudo-philosophy, astrological determinism or even sheer superstition which governed the lives of all but the most enlightened pagans, and from which they needed the release offered by the coming of Christ, as surely as the Jewish people (who were 'under the law') received their true inheritance only when they, too, became people of faith rather than of obedience.

And if the reality of this release needs further proof, an argument is to hand from Christian experience. If you find that your prayer (or rather the

6 prayer of the Spirit praying within you) is addressed to God as **"Abba"**, the Aramaic word for **"Father"** used by Jesus himself, then this proves that you

7 are a child of God and therefore (unlike a slave) also **an heir**, due for release from all tutorship and all dominion from outside. (There is a fuller treatment of this theme in Romans 8.14–17.)

9   In which case – **how can you turn back again?** The pagan's submission

8 to superstitious observances (in respect to beings which **by nature are not gods**) is equivalent to the obligation imposed by the Jewish way of life to

---

[8] The meaning of this phrase is a puzzle. The argument would run more simply (since the Jewish law would be the subject throughout) if the alternative translation in the NRSV footnote were adopted and the phrase *the rudiments of the world* could be taken as a reference to the rudimentary principles of the law. But the Greek words mean literally *elements of the natural world*, a scientific or philosophical term for the basic constituents of the physical universe, also used sometimes to refer to the stars. Enlightened minds would hardly have thought of these as imposing 'slavery'; but popular belief (and we have evidence for this at a later period) may well have regarded these 'elements' as the agents of supernatural or demonic powers to which all human beings are subject. It seems that Paul's thought here embraces two kinds of 'slavery', both of which are brought to an end by Christ: slavery to law and slavery to superstitious fear of the 'elements'.

10 observe **special days, and months, and seasons, and years** (the sabbaths, new moons and festival days of the Jewish calendar). The Galatians' previous servitude may have come to an end; but their present willingness to adopt Jewish observances is a relapse into similar enslavement all over again. If they persevere, they will nullify their newly obtained freedom, which for
11 Paul would amount to his work being completely **wasted.**

12   The letter now becomes more personal: **Friends** (literally *brothers*) was the most intimate word in Paul's vocabulary for the fellow Christians for whom he was responsible. But the passage is tantalizingly obscure, partly because we do not know enough of the circumstances to understand all the allusions, partly because some of the Greek phrases themselves are ambiguous. **Become as I am, for I also have become as you are.** The key to this seems to be what Paul has said on another occasion (1 Corinthians 9.22), "I have become all things to all people": in order to work effectively among Gentiles Paul has been prepared to conduct himself as if he were not Jewish. He would expect the gentile Galatian Christians to show a similar freedom in refusing to yield to pressure to conduct themselves in ways insisted on by Jews. There follows a reference to a former visit – and again the Greek is ambiguous: the word
13 translated **first** can also mean *previously*: we cannot be sure which visit he means or how many there had been. Evidently he had been forced by illness to abandon some more ambitious journey and to preach to the Galatians instead. What the illness was we do not know: people in that culture did not go in for describing their symptoms in the way we do, and the expression
15 **you would have torn out your eyes and given them to me** was as likely to be a metaphor then as it is now. But *any* serious illness tended to have social consequences. It could be taken to mean that the sufferer was being punished by God and must therefore have committed a serious sin and should be shunned; or even that he was possessed by an evil spirit and
14 should be kept at a safe distance – the words translated **scorn or despise** are very strong, with even a hint of 'spitting at' a person in such a sinister condition. In this sense Paul's illness had been a **test** for them: would their reaction be the conventional one of cold-shouldering, or would they accept that the illness was just one more of the hardships Paul suffered for their sakes? In the event they had welcomed him cordially: far from regarding him as possessed, they had recognized that he was a trusted messenger or **angel of God**, an authorized agent of **Christ Jesus** (for in law an agent was reckoned to be 'as' the one who sent him). What a contrast with the present
16 state of their relationship! **Have I now become your enemy by telling you the truth?**

And now we hear something of the group or party that is putting such pressure on the Galatians – and again the language is tantalizingly allusive.
17 The phrase **make much of** (literally *be zealous for*) can have a good or a bad meaning, and Paul exploits both. His opponents appear to be showing their 'zeal' by trying to **exclude** the other Galatian Christians, presumably

by arguing that they will be 'excluded' from God's people unless they conform with the observances prescribed by the law and regulated by the synagogue; and their hope is that the Christians will show a similar 'zeal' by acceding

18 to their demands. It is admirable, Paul replies, **to be made much of**, but it depends for what purpose. Not for the only time (1 Corinthians 4.15),

19 he uses the image of childbirth to describe his work of preaching – **until Christ is formed in** them. Will he have to do it all over again? Have these

20 people been taking advantage of his absence? **I am perplexed about you** – the word is another strong one, meaning to be bewildered, to see no way out: such was the effect on Paul of their readiness to yield to these people's pressure.

21 **You who desire to be subject to the law.** Evidently the Galatian Christians have already gone some way towards accepting the conditions and observances involved in joining the Jewish community, and Paul now mounts a further attack on this attitude by an argument based on **the law** itself – that is, scripture: 'the law' was a correct name for at least the first five books of the Hebrew scriptures. The passage in question consists of those chapters in Genesis (16–21) which tell the story of how Abraham, despite his wife's barrenness, finally acquired an heir, first by his slave Hagar (who bore him a child

23 in the ordinary course of nature, and so **according to the flesh**) and then (late in life, and so **through the promise**) by his free-born wife Sarah. Normally this story was taken quite straightforwardly: the Jews regarded themselves as descended from Abraham and Sarah; the tribes supposed to be descended from Abraham's union with Hagar were outside the covenant. But Paul turns the usual interpretation upside down, and makes the Jews the descendants of Hagar, and the Christians (including Gentiles) the descendants of Sarah.

24 He achieves this feat by treating the story as **an allegory**, that is to say, by taking each character in it as a symbol of something else (a method he seldom used but which was brought to a fine art by his near contemporary Philo of Alexandria). The key to the symbolism is the antithesis slavery/freedom. Hagar was a slave woman. She could therefore be regarded as a symbol of the law and of the covenant given with it on Sinai (which, as the earlier argument

25 has shown, was a kind of 'slavery'), and also of **the present Jerusalem** which, either because it was under Roman occupation (in which case this would be one of Paul's rare political allusions), or because it represented a people governed by the Mosaic law, was also **in slavery**. All three are linked by the common tie of 'slavery': they belong 'in the same column' (a metaphor which

25, 26 underlies the word translated **corresponds**). In the other column stand, first, Sarah (who is **free**); secondly, the new covenant of freedom (which Paul does

24 not explicitly mention, but his reference to **two covenants** shows that he has

26 it in mind); and, thirdly, **the Jerusalem above**, the Jerusalem that is to come; and all this is confirmed by the fact that Isaiah, when using language entirely appropriate to a childless wife such as Sarah (54.1), was in fact prophesying

about the new people or new Jerusalem that was to come in the future
27 (54.11–12). So two columns emerge:

Slavery	*Freedom*
Hagar	Sarah
Sinai: covenant of the law	new covenant
the present Jerusalem	the future Jerusalem

Thus by his allegorical interpretation of scripture Paul finds further support for his conclusion. The true sons of Abraham are those who live in freedom under the new covenant of faith and are members of the new Jerusalem; the Jews, by contrast, are still labouring under the slavery of the law and are no better off than the 'Hagarenes' and other tribes supposedly descended from the slave woman Hagar.

Paul scores one further point from the same narrative in Genesis, though this time by a more direct application of the biblical text. The sequel of God's miraculous promise to Sarah was the birth of a son, Isaac, who was born as
23 the result of **the promise**, as opposed to Hagar's son, who was born in the normal course of nature, **according to the flesh**. Now our existing texts of
29 Genesis (21.9) do not say that Hagar's son **persecuted** the boy Isaac; they say that he 'played with him' or 'laughed at him'. But the Hebrew word is a little obscure, and it seems that Jewish scholars were tending to take the word to mean 'persecuted', which then gives more point to Sarah's request
30 which follows in Genesis: **"Drive out the slave and her child."** And this gives Paul one more proof that he is correct in identifying the Christians with the descendants of Sarah, the Jews with those of Hagar; for just as Hagar's son persecuted Isaac, so the Jews are now persecuting the Christians.
31 **So then, friends, we are children, not of the slave but of the free woman.**
5.1 The correspondence has been established by two separate arguments. **For freedom Christ has set us free**, and so placed us decisively in the 'freedom' column. The moral is obvious: **do not submit again to a yoke of slavery**.

But the Galatians, it seems, did not think of it as 'slavery' at all. To them, the issue may have seemed to be one merely of avoiding trouble by consenting to Jewish demands and adopting the Jewish way of life with its various observances. Even if this did involve the irksome rite of circumcision, marking them irrevocably as members of the Jewish community, they were still binding themselves only to outward and practical obligations. There was a wide range of religious belief in any Jewish congregation, and they could surely continue to hold their distinctive Christian beliefs and practise their own sectarian forms of worship. Surely it would be an exaggeration to call this 'slavery'?

But if this is what they were thinking, they had been grievously (perhaps even deliberately) misinformed. Paul now repeats his conclusion with great
2 emphasis and evident personal feeling (**Listen! I, Paul, am telling you . . .**). For the first time we can tell from his own words exactly what was at stake: his

converts were under pressure **to be circumcised**, that is, to identify themselves totally and irrevocably with the Jewish community, and were being led to

4 believe that by so doing they would be **justified**, acceptable to God, in the same sense as the Jews believed themselves, by virtue of being Jews, to be the chosen people of God. Had they realized that if they did this they would

3 be **obliged to obey the entire law**, which meant to adopt the Jewish lifestyle in its entirety, submit to the jurisdiction of the synagogue and conform with all the required observances? Such an action would result in Christ's

2 being **of no benefit** to them, for the 'benefit' of Christ existed only in the community of those who acknowledged him, a community of hope, based

5 on **faith** and **the Spirit**, in which racial and ethnic distinctions were now irrelevant. Membership of this new, inclusive community could not possibly be combined with a deliberate application to join one which distinguished itself by the highly exclusive qualification of circumcision.

The direct and impassioned tone continues; but Paul now turns his attention away from the whole congregation to the individual person or per-

9 sons who have been exerting the pressure to conform. Proverbially (**A little**
10 **yeast...**), even one person would be sufficient to 'confuse' them, though this
8 'persuasion' would be of a totally different kind from that which originally
10 converted them; and this person would **pay the penalty**. As for the sugges-
11 tion (which we can assume was made by his opponents) that Paul was **still preaching circumcision**: we do not know what made this seem plausible, though it is true that Paul's own example of being 'all things to all people' and conforming with Jewish scruples when he was among Jews might occasionally have looked like an invitation to gentile Christians to do the same. But it could be scotched by a simple observation of fact. It was being claimed by some of the Galatians (see below on 6.12) that accepting circumcision was a way of escaping persecution – presumably from the Jews. But Paul was **still being persecuted;** his preaching of the cross was still an **offense** (presumably because it made circumcision and observance irrelevant). He could not possibly be advocating circumcision – and the suggestion that he was doing so was itself so offensive that he indulges in a rare moment of invective: those who were recommending circumcision should go one step

12 further and **castrate themselves**!
13 **For you were called to freedom.** This is not a general statement about the human race, like 'All are born to be free'. It refers to the specific liberation, whether from the pattern of Jewish ordinances or from the constraints of pagan superstition, which followed from becoming a Christian. The **freedom** is that which has been at stake in the entire argument so far. But this same freedom also had a moral aspect, to which the letter now turns. The Jews naturally thought of their law as a bulwark against the immorality of the pagan world. The Christians to whom Paul was writing had doubtless been associated for some time with the synagogue before coming to their new faith, and so had come to accept the standards of moral behaviour which the

Jewish community expected and which its law enforced. If they had now left this community, what was to prevent them from relapsing into their former immoral ways? The very frequency with which Paul had to utter warnings

21 about this (**I am warning you, as I warned you before**) suggests that this was a real danger. From the point of view of theology – Christian identity and 'justification' – Paul was on strong ground. But from the point of view of moral behaviour the position might seem a dangerous one. And so now, as a consequence of his whole argument, he has to turn his attention to moral

13 questions. **Do not use your freedom as an opportunity for self-indulgence**.

If, for Christians, the standards and observances imposed by a community that fashioned its life by the law of Moses were no longer obligatory, what was there to take their place? What would guide their behaviour and enforce moral standards? It was a question to which Paul often had to return. Here he offers two answers. The first is very brief, and something of a paradox. The old slavery has gone, and has been replaced by – another slavery! **Become slaves to one another** – a challenging metaphor, given the pride of all free citizens in *not* being slaves but being free – which is Paul's radical Christian

14 interpretation of the **single commandment** by which (as many agreed) **the whole law is summed up**. The same point is made at greater length in Romans 13.8–10. Here Paul draws an alarming picture of the opposite behaviour: of

15 what happens if people **bite and devour one another**!

The second answer is more far-reaching. It presupposes an analysis of

16 human conduct in term of **the Spirit** and **the flesh**, which is worked out at greater length in Romans 7 (see above, p. 507). This analysis is not a matter of straight psychology, for the Spirit is not an ordinary human source of inspiration available to anyone, but is a gift of God directly dependent on the acknowledgment of Jesus as Lord. Once received, it becomes a new and dominant factor in moral conduct and works against **the desires of the flesh**. It offers, in fact, an empirical answer to the question: What guide and motive in moral conduct will take the place of membership of a community disciplined by a comprehensive law?

Lists of vices and virtues were a standard resource in moral philosophy and moral teaching, and we possess many examples, both serious and relatively trivial. We should probably not look in these verses for distinctively Christian moral insight. Paul's lists can be paralleled from both pagan and Jewish sources, and it appears that he could have drawn on both (though the prominence given to sexual immorality has a Jewish tone). What is distinc-

22 tive is the source of the virtues: they are **the fruit of the Spirit** – that is to say, not the result of high moral aspirations or of strict law-abidingness, but a consequence of accepting the new guidance and dynamic which are now

24 available to **those who belong to Christ Jesus**, who can be said (in a bold metaphor) to have **crucified the flesh with its passions and desires,** and who are in the grip of a new kind of motivation altogether – the Spirit. This view of the Spirit may have been Paul's own. Whereas elsewhere (for instance in

Acts) the Spirit is typically the source of supernatural guidance, prophecy, ecstatic utterance or other exceptional powers, here it is seen as responsible for much less sensational gifts and qualities. It is the distinctive motivation for the whole of Christian moral conduct. The standards and excellences which flow from it make the restraints of law and convention superfluous.

23 **There is no law against such things.**

The lists of vices and virtues are followed by some positive moral teaching. Again, we should probably not expect it all to be distinctively Christian 6.2 (though the **law of Christ**, fulfilled in 'bearing one another's burdens', goes some way beyond standard morality). Several of these jerky sentences are 7 known to have been proverbs (**you reap whatever you sow**, for instance), and others have a proverbial ring; and verse 6 simply reiterates a principle, which seems to have been generally accepted in the early church (as elsewhere), that teachers should be paid. Paul is not working out a new moral code, but rather recommending one that is for the most part already accepted. But there is a 8 difference: the motivation is new – **the Spirit.**

Postscript

11 **See what large letters.** The clearest evidence about the mechanics of Paul's correspondence comes in 2 Thessalonians 3.17. Like other letter-writers, such as Cicero and Augustine, he seems to have dictated his letters, sometimes adding a final greeting in his own hand (which was evidently larger than the copyist's, at least on this occasion). This time he adds not so much a greeting as a final urgent appeal, couched in such direct and personal terms that we gain further insight into the danger threatening the Galatian church.

12 His opponents are now described as **those who want to make a good showing in the flesh** by persuading the gentile Galatian Christians to be circumcised. If they achieved this, there would be a tangible ('fleshly') demonstration of the firm commitment which these converts had made to identify themselves completely with the Jewish community even while professing 13 their Christian beliefs: the infiltrators would be able to **boast** of their success in procuring the Gentiles' acquiescence in the physical rite of entry to the community – circumcision. By so doing they would also, it seems, escape 12 being **persecuted for the cross of Christ**: evidently they were being harassed, presumably on the grounds that they were conniving with a community that was claiming much of the Jewish religious heritage but refusing to be integrated into it by accepting circumcision. Who were these people? Their identity is obscured by a tantalizing ambiguity in the text. Paul appears to call 13 them **the circumcised**, which would be a natural way of referring to Jews who had become Christians – though apparently, if they were Jews, their life-style had not been one that would satisfy the standards of a rigorous Jewish party: they were people who **do not themselves obey the law**. But the Greek word

means literally *those who get themselves circumcised*, and if this is interpreted strictly it must mean that Paul's opponents were gentile Christians who had yielded to Jewish pressure to become proselytes, and were now trying to get others to follow suit – perhaps quite a small group; but the passion with which Paul has attacked them shows that their arguments had made a considerable impact on the congregation.

14   The word **boast** recalls Paul to one of his deepest theological convictions. A Christian has no grounds for boasting – or confidence[9] – save **the cross of our Lord Jesus Christ**. Jewish people (including at one time himself, as he says with some pride in Philippians 3) had good reasons for this kind of 'boasting': their race was one singularly favoured by God, and it was understandable that gentile Christians should have been attracted by an invitation to be more closely associated with it. But all such racial and ethnic distinctions, along with the observances that went with them, had been superseded by the new

15 community created by the cross of Christ, which was nothing less than a **new creation**.

16   And so Paul's greeting to this torn and harasssed church is a conditional one – he can give it to them only if they **follow this rule**, the principle of inclusiveness which follows from the universal salvation gained in Christ. Such is the true destiny of any people (and possibly he is including here also the historic Jewish people) who can be called **the Israel of God**.

17   The **marks** which Paul bears could be almost any distinctive scar. The meanings of the Greek word[10] include a soldier's tattoo, a ritual branding given at a pagan temple or a mark burnt on to the skin of a slave. Paul might mean the 'branding' of his Christian baptism; he might be speaking figuratively of his interior life; or (perhaps most likely) he may be describing the physical sufferings his body had endured in Christ's service as **the marks of Jesus**. But whatever he meant, he probably intended it to be understood as the antithesis of the all-too-physical 'mark' which his opponents were advocating and which was the practical issue to which the whole letter is devoted: circumcision.

[9] The Greek word is difficult to translate. See above on 2 Corinthians 1.12.
[10] *stigma* (**mark**). The word **branded** does not occur in the original and has been added by the translators.

THE LETTER OF PAUL TO THE
EPHESIANS

Paul knew the church at Ephesus well. He spent more than two years there (Acts 19–20) – probably longer than he spent in any other single city during his missionary work. One might therefore have expected his letter to this church to be particularly intimate and personal. But in fact this LETTER TO THE EPHESIANS is the least personal of all those attributed to Paul. There is little to suggest that the writer was personally acquainted with his correspondents – indeed the impression given by such verses as 1.15 and 3.2–4 is that he had never met them; and it is difficult to believe that the letter could really have been written by Paul to his friends at Ephesus. A further peculiarity of the letter is that, compared with Paul's other letters, it has little in the way of a precise purpose or occasion. There is plenty of solid teaching in it about the church, about the unity of all Christians, about the institutions of marriage and slavery and about the fight against supernatural powers; but, even if one may occasionally suspect a particular danger or heresy to have been in the writer's mind, there is no point at which the letter is addressed to a specific situation or problem. The tone is throughout general, never particular, and the letter, apart from the brief personal greetings at the beginning and the end, reads more like a homily or a circular letter than a document from a missionary's correspondence. Add to this the fact that the words 'in Ephesus' in the first verse are omitted in a number of manuscripts, and it is difficult to resist the suspicion (which was voiced already in the second century) that this writing, though it has now been given the form of a letter to the Christians at Ephesus, began its life as a message of more general interest to a wider Christian public.

The letter, of course, purports to be by Paul and to have been written when he was in prison, presumably in Rome (1.1; 3.1; 6.19–22). But this does not necessarily settle the question of authorship. In antiquity, both among Jews and among Greeks, the writing of literary works under the name of a distinguished predecessor was not regarded in the same light as it would be now. Deliberate forgery was certainly not approved of if it were done for personal gain or reputation; but if it were felt, for instance, that certain ideas of the master's which he had not committed to writing but which were remembered by a disciple ought to be given permanent form, a book might be written which preserved them as accurately as possible and which could then legitimately appear under his name if it was so far as possible in his style. A generation or so later, when the circumstances surrounding the production of the book had been forgotten, it might be included in good faith among the collected works of the master, even though, in the process of composition, certain points of style or context may have made their appearance which betrayed a later hand. Many such cases are known from antiquity, and several of the New Testament 'letters' may have originated in this way. Among the letters attributed to Paul, Ephesians is one of those which, since the rise of modern critical scholarship in the nineteenth century, has most frequently come under this kind of suspicion.

There is a number of minor peculiarities in the letter – its formal structure, its style, its vocabulary – which distinguish it from the other letters of Paul. But the most remarkable feature is its relationship with Colossians. Several paragraphs use almost identical language; only Colossians, out of all the New Testament letters, offers any parallel to the sometimes convoluted style of Ephesians; and the number of verbal resemblances is so great that many believe that the author of Ephesians must either have had Colossians fresh in his mind or have had an actual copy of it in front of him.[1] There are also reminiscences in Ephesians of other passages in Paul's writings. Now these facts, however difficult to explain, do not make it impossible that Paul was the author; but it is widely held that the best explanation is that the letter was composed by an early Christian who was steeped in Paul's writings and whose ideas were a legitimate development of those expressed by Paul, particularly in his letter to the Colossians. The letter may then have been included in the collection of Paul's letters and addressed to the Ephesians, either because it was genuinely intended for that church and neighbouring churches in Asia, or else because Paul's surviving correspondence lacked any letter to that important church. It is also possible that the writer had in his possession some genuinely Pauline material to incorporate in his own work.

The result, however, is by no means slavish imitation. The writer of this letter, whether Paul or another, may have drawn freely on the language of Colossians, but he made it carry a new and different message. What is said here about the church – its nature and its place in the divine ordering of creation – is unique in the New Testament, and there are many other passages in which, though the language is more or less familiar, the thought is strikingly original. The questions raised by the origin and purpose of this letter, the strangeness (at times) of its style and its curious ties with Colossians, though they have preoccupied generations of critical scholars, are ultimately of little importance beside the richness of ideas and language which is found in it.

The church on earth and in heaven

The greeting, which follows the usual Christian pattern (see above on Romans 1.1), does little more than name the writer and the recipients. The writer

---

[1] Theoretically the converse is also possible: Colossians could have been modelled on Ephesians. But that Ephesians was written after Colossians is on the whole an easier hypothesis.

1.1 is described as **an apostle of Christ Jesus by the will of God** – a status which is claimed without discussion here, but which could not always be taken for granted: it evidently had to be defended when Paul wrote the first verses of Galatians; and the recipients are called **the saints who are in Ephesus and are faithful in Christ Jesus**[2] – a manner of speech (*in* Christ Jesus) which perhaps assumes knowledge of Paul's conception of Christians as 'members of Christ's body' or as persons who, like himself, are 'in Christ'.

3 **Blessed be the God and Father of the Lord Jesus Christ, who . . .** This is a Christian adaptation (which occurs also elsewhere: 2 Corinthians 1.3 and 1 Peter 1.3) of one of the commonest of Jewish acts of prayer: 'Blessed be God, who . . .', and is the formal peg on which the whole of this paragraph is hung. In 2 Corinthians 1 the burst of praise is evoked by the experience of God's 'consolation' given in this present life to Christians undergoing tribulation. Here the motive is a promise of a different kind: **spiritual blessing in the heavenly places**. Christians have an eternal destiny, to be fulfilled not only on earth but in heaven (for which **the heavenly places** is one of this author's characteristic expressions). That is to say (and this is an important theme of the letter), they are to share in Christ's ascendancy over all supernatural and demonic powers which may be held to influence life on earth: they are to take their place above all such beings in heaven.

This high destiny is expressed in terms borrowed from the language used by Jewish people about themselves. To the Jews, it was axiomatic that they had been chosen above all other races of the world to receive a unique inheritance; and when they reflected on the question when this divine act of choice had taken place, it seemed logically necessary to push the moment of choosing as far back in history as possible – indeed even beyond its beginning. But then, in the formless time before the world was created, how could God have made a choice? What object could have existed for God to point to and say, *That* is what I choose? One answer was found in the person of the Messiah, who was thought of as a divinely appointed person of the future, and whose main function would be to usher in the new age of Israel's blessedness. That such a person should at some moment make his appearance and fulfil his prescribed destiny was no afterthought – it was intended by God from the very beginning. Indeed, God had determined who this person would be. As later Jewish thinkers were to put it, the 'name of the Messiah' was one of the things which existed before the world began. But if God had chosen the 4 Messiah **before the foundation of the world** he must also have chosen the people whom the Messiah was to deliver. There was a sense in which God had chosen Israel 'in' the Messiah.

---

[2] See the NRSV footnote. Not all the early manuscripts include the words *in Ephesus* (see above, p. 610) and there is some confusion about how the words **saints** and **faithful** are connected grammatically.

All this could now be given a new interpretation in the light of Christ. Jesus was the Messiah (that is, the Christ), and Christians were the true Israel. It was as represented by Christ that God, even before history began, had chosen his new people for their destiny: **he chose us in Christ before the foundation of the world**. This high destiny is described first in terms borrowed from Jewish religious language. **To be holy and blameless** is the imagery of temple sacrifices, transferred to a relationship with God **in love**.

5 Moreover, they were to be destined for **adoption as his children** – though no longer because, like the Jews, they belonged to a particular nation which was accustomed to regard God as its own particular 'father', but **through Jesus Christ, according to the good pleasure of his will**: and the equivalent of their

7 **redemption** – the standard term for the transaction by which God delivered Israel from Egypt – was a sacrifice made by Christ. And since the death of a sacrificial victim seemed a necessary condition for any such radical change in a people's status before God, it could be said that it was **through his blood** that this new people of God had received **forgiveness of** their **trespasses** (a common enough concept, but here expressed by a word, **forgiveness**, which is surprisingly rare in the New Testament).

8 **With all wisdom and insight**. All these clauses are loosely attached to one another in the Greek text. Here the meaning might best be brought out by adding '*along with* all wisdom and insight' – that is to say, these are not attributes of God but gifts to mortals by which they can now discern

9 **the mystery** of God's will. The essence of this 'mystery' – a word with a very specific meaning in Jewish thought – was that it was the secret purpose of God for his people and for the world, hidden from human beings and glimpsed, if at all, only by rare and privileged seers. (Daniel was the first and virtually the only Old Testament figure to have expressed his experience in this way, see Daniel 2.) Christians were now to have this privileged insight; for the 'mystery' had become intelligible **in Christ**, who had revealed the

10 divine **plan** – a striking word in the Greek, usually meaning the 'stewardship' or 'management' of a household or an institution. God could be said to have a similar managerial responsibility for the long-term flourishing of the universe stretching right through **the fullness of time**, and the new insight of Christians into this 'plan' offered the key to understanding both **things in heaven and things on earth**.

In Colossians, the significance of Christ for understanding the created order is worked out on a cosmic and metaphysical scale. In Ephesians, similar language is used for a more limited end. If the purpose of God was to **gather up** all things in Christ, this meant that former divisions and barriers between human beings were now made obsolete. One such cause of division seems to be hinted at by the unexpected appearance of a distinction between two

12 partners in this outpouring of praise: **'we'**, which evidently means the author (necessarily Jewish) and perhaps, with him, the first generation of Jewish

13 Christian believers; and **'you'**, who are later identified as 'Gentiles' (2.11). The

overcoming of this division between Jews and Gentiles was one of the most dramatic changes brought about by Christ. Jewish people (with whom the author appears to identify himself at this point) had long looked forward to a glorious fulfilment of their destiny, and most had associated this fulfilment with the coming of a Messiah (a 'Christ'); but they had always thought of this 14 **'inheritance'** as something reserved to themselves, to the necessary exclusion of all other nations, so accentuating the religious and social exclusiveness of their culture. But the newly revealed Messiah or Christ of the Christian faith 13 cut right across this distinction. Gentiles (**you also**, for this writer) were now to share this heritage as much as any Jews – indeed both alike, when they became Christians, were already experiencing a new force in their lives which guaranteed their future destiny and could be described as a mark put upon them by their new owner, **the seal of the promised Holy Spirit.**

The whole of the foregoing paragraph consists, in the Greek, of one continuous sentence. The pivot is the opening formula, "Blessed be God, who . . .", and the rest is a tangle of subordinate clauses creating, more by accumulation than by any logical sequence, a sense of the magnitude of blessings for which God is to be praised. As such, it presents the most extreme example in the New Testament of a style which occasionally appears elsewhere (particularly in Colossians) and which bears the marks of the language of worship: its somewhat general and repetitive phrases are like those of someone leading extempore prayer; they build up a strongly devotional atmosphere. This thanksgiving, or 'blessing', is followed (as so often at the beginning of New Testament letters) by a prayer which is more personal, though it continues in the same richly loaded style and is still in fairly general terms. Usually such prayers include a number of petitions and have a practical slant; but here the prayer, drawing on the language of the great paragraph of praise which 17 precedes it, is almost entirely for a certain kind of knowledge – **a spirit of wisdom and revelation**. A possible reason for this may be that the author had in mind a situation somewhat similar to that which seems to have elicited the letter to the Colossians. There may have been a tendency in the church to suggest that Christ offered only limited power and limited knowledge, and that there were other powers and other mysteries abroad which could not be mastered without stronger resources than Christ alone could supply. But in any case a sense that human life is constantly threatened by demonic powers and malign supernatural forces (often explained in terms of 'fallen angels') was so widespread in this culture that there could be no real confidence in the saving power of Christ unless he was demonstrably superior to all such 20–1 forces. In the face of this, the author appeals (as early Christians so often did) to the first verse of Psalm 110:

> The LORD says to my lord,
> "Sit at my right hand
> until I make your enemies your footstool."

22 and to Psalm 8.6:

> You have put all things under his[3] feet.

These words, they believed, declared the truth about Christ in the present and the future. They proved that his place was above all other powers, not only in the present order of the universe, but also (using standard Jewish
21 terminology) **in the age to come.** Not that Christ is thereby removed in lofty majesty from creation; on the contrary, he is organically related to it in that
22 his exaltation is **for the church.** And the church, according to a profound
23 theological idea worked out elsewhere by Paul, **is his body.** Indeed, such is his intimate identification with it that it is through the church that he fills the universe and provides the key to its meaning – such seems to be the drift of the last sentence of the chapter, which (at least to modern ears) seems more impressive in sound than precise in meaning.

The prayer appears to be complete; but the same unstructured and devotional style continues – the first seven verses of chapter 2 are virtually one sentence – with an elaborate summary of the new status of Christians before God, which is the basis for their thanksgiving. Indeed, the paragraph reads almost like a summary of the main theme of Romans. Not only Gentiles
1, 3 (again addressed as **'you'**) but Jewish Christians also (**'all of us'**), by reason of the standard of moral conduct they all displayed, lay under the dreadful judgment of God (Romans 1–2). And yet, even when we were all in this
5 condition (Romans 5.8), God **made us alive together with Christ** (Romans 6.11), not because of anything we had done or deserved, but entirely **by grace**
8 (Romans 3.24), a free **gift of God.** It was not the result of 'works', such that
9, 10 anyone **may boast** (Romans 3.27–8); but at the same time we are **created in Christ Jesus for good works** – our moral standards must be at least as high as before (Romans 8.12).

All this is familiar Pauline theology; but at two points it breaks new ground.

(i) In both Romans and Ephesians the general state of humankind, as it was before the advent of Christ, is described in straightforward moral and
3 psychological terms. **All of us once lived among them in the passions of our flesh, following the desires of flesh and senses** is typical of the language of both letters. But Ephesians adds another dimension, which is at most hinted at in Romans. Immorality is thought of, not only as endemic in human beings (**by nature children of wrath**), but as originating outside, inflicted by demonic powers. Such powers were believed to exist in
2 the space immediately above the earth (**the power of the air**) and their

---

[3] In Psalm 8.6 the NRSV has "under their feet" instead of 'under his feet', This is the result of translating 'man' and 'son of man' as "human beings" and "mortals". The original Hebrew and Greek texts and all literal translations have the singular, 'under *his* feet'.

ruler was, of course, Satan. The means by which Satan and his under-
lings worked upon human beings was through an evil **spirit** which inclined
them to immorality (a similar idea, in the form of a perpetual inner contest between a good and an evil spirit, occurs in the Dead Sea Scrolls); and
although the effect might now be called psychological, the ultimate cause
was widely thought to be a personified manifestation of evil working upon
us from outside ourselves. This conception is of some importance later in the
letter.

6   (ii) **And raised us up with him.** This is exactly what is said in Romans
6.5–11, where it is the intimate solidarity of Christians with Christ, not
only in his death, but in his resurrection, which explains the quality of the
spiritual life they now enjoy and gives them a sure hope for the future.
But here the idea is taken a stage further. Our union with Christ extends
beyond the resurrection to the ascension: God **seated us with him in the
heavenly places** – another dimension of the Pauline experience of being **in
Christ.**

The magnitude of the change brought about by Christ could be seen also
in the light of its social consequences. Gentiles were not only (in Jewish
eyes) proverbially prone to moral laxity; they suffered racially from a radical

11   disadvantage. When Jews called Gentiles **"the uncircumcision"** they meant
far more than the empirical fact that Gentiles (unlike Jews and some other
Semitic races) belonged to a culture in which this physical rite – **made in
the flesh by human hands** – was not practised. They meant that the Gentiles
were deprived of all those advantages and privileges which the Jews deemed
themselves to possess – even the Gentiles' worship of many 'gods' and many

12   'lords' (1 Corinthians 8.5) left them **having no hope and without God in
the world.** With regard to the coming judgment, Jews believed that their
principal ground of confidence was membership of **the commonwealth of
Israel** (the writer uses strikingly political language – Gentiles might think
they had another 'commonwealth', that of Rome). From this Gentiles were
barred. There was no means by which (in words taken from Isaiah 57.19)

13   those who **once were far off** could be **brought near** to this salvation. But
the shedding of **the blood of Christ** had changed all this. Christ, being the
very essence (verse 14) and maker (verse 15) and proclaimer of peace (verse

14   17), had **broken down the dividing wall, that is, the hostility between
us.** It is sometimes thought that the key to this metaphor is the balustrade
in the temple area in Jerusalem, which marked the point beyond which
Gentiles could not go on pain of death (see above on Acts 21.29). Another
possible source of the metaphor is the 'fence' of subsidiary regulations and
observances with which Jewish lawyers came to surround the law, so defining

15   in ever more detail the exclusive identity of the Jewish people – **the law
with its commandments and ordinances.** But in any event the metaphor
is readily understandable. The racial barrier between Jews and Gentiles had
been finally broken down through the creation of a new community in which

16 **both groups**, now reconciled to God and to each other,[4] overcame their
   former hostility. The result was a completely new community, a new solidarity
   between people who had formerly been deeply estranged. Gentiles, who had
19 always been made to feel, in their relations with Jews, like **strangers and
   aliens**, had now become **citizens with the saints and also members of the
   household of God**. This new community could be described as a building,
20 still in progress from its inception by **the apostles and** (doubtless Christian)
   prophets, founded upon Jesus Christ, and superseding the Jewish temple as
22 **a dwelling place for God.**
   There is, then, one particular result of the work of Christ which receives
3.6 special emphasis in this letter: **that is, the Gentiles have become fellow heirs,
   members of the same body, and sharers in the promise**. But this is also a
   key to the career of Paul. It is clear from the letter to the Galatians (1.15–
   16), as well as from Acts (25.17–18), that Paul's experience on the road to
3 Damascus (his **revelation**) was not merely a personal conversion to Christ
   but included an explicit commission to preach to the Gentiles. This writer
   does not dwell on this aspect here, but refers his hearers and readers to
   some previous account of it – **as I wrote above in a few words**. This is the
   translators' interpretation of a Greek idiom which means literally *as I have
   already written briefly*. Is Paul asking the reader to refer back to an earlier part
   of the letter (**above**)? Or does he mean that he had already written a letter
   which they had not yet seen but might soon be able to read? – possibly the
4 letter to the Colossians, which certainly sets out Paul's **understanding of the
   mystery of Christ**. What was this 'mystery'? On the face of it, the new gospel
   was as Jewish as the environment out of which it came, and at first it was
   difficult (even for the church) to believe that it was addressed to anyone but
   Jews. Paul's commission to preach to the Gentiles would have seemed quite
   incompatible with the special destiny of the Jewish people that seemed to be
   presupposed in the scriptures, were it not for what has been called earlier in
   the letter (1.10) a divine "plan for the fullness of time". Here it is called **the
   mystery of Christ**, that is, the radically new invitation, at best only dimly
5 presaged in the Hebrew scriptures, but now **revealed to his holy apostles
   and prophets by the Spirit,** that was to be extended to the Gentiles to share
   in the inheritance, the community and the promises hitherto reserved to the
   Jews. It was the proclaiming of this new era in the evolution of the Jewish
   religion that had been Paul's particular task and privilege; but it had also led
   him into confrontation with strict Jewish factions, who had subjected him
1 to severe penalties and even, it seems, had him thrown into prison – **This is
   the reason that I Paul am a prisoner.**[5]
   But Paul's vicissitudes are not the point here, and the writer returns to
10 his main theme, which is the ultimate destiny of Christians in **the heavenly**

---

[4] The construction of the Greek sentence is ambiguous, as the NRSV footnote shows.
[5] Unless the phrase is metaphorical. See the NRSV footnote.

places (a frequent and characteristic phrase in Ephesians). And the startling
9 and original thought now appears that this long-hidden **mystery** (the open
invitation to Gentiles) is not only something to be proclaimed and experi-
10 enced among human beings, but is also, as a reflection of **the wisdom of God
in its rich variety**, to be made known at the supernatural level **to the rulers
and authorities in the heavenly places**; and this (since the church now shares
Christ's exalted position in that supernatural sphere) is to be done **through
the church.**

In the light of this high destiny, the prayer for the church, begun in 1.17
and since somewhat interrupted, is resumed and concluded with greater
14–15 precision. It is addressed to **the Father, from whom every family in heaven
and on earth takes its name** – a solemn phrase which, in the Greek, exploits
the fact that 'father' and 'family' are both words derived from the same root;
16 and it asks again that, along with being **strengthened in your inner being
with power through his Spirit**, they may be endowed with a love that will
19 make them aware of the true dimensions of **the love of Christ**, and may be
able to comprehend that ultimate mystery which is here again, as in 1.23,
impressively rather than clearly expressed in terms of **the fullness of God.**
The prayer ends with an elaborate ascription of glory to God.

Moral implications

The remainder of the letter, like the final section of many of Paul's letters,
consists almost entirely of moral teaching. Ephesians is exceptional only
in that, between the opening prayers and thanksgivings (which are greatly
extended in this letter) and the concluding ethical passages, there are no
paragraphs devoted specifically to doctrinal or practical questions; and the
absence of any central section concerned with specific problems is one of
the strongest reasons for thinking that this letter, unlike all those which are
certainly attributed to Paul, was written (whether by Paul or by a follower)
without any particular church or particular situation in mind. On the other
hand the devotional material in the first part of the letter, despite its somewhat
diffuse and exalted character, contains a fair amount of solid doctrine. It
reverts again and again to the theme of the new unity between human beings
(especially those of different races) which has been made possible in Christ;
4.3 and this theme of unity – **the unity of the Spirit in the bond of peace** –
leads naturally into the first moral exhortation: an attitude of humility and
peaceableness is essential if this new possibility of unity is not to be frustrated
by ordinary human shortcomings. Indeed, this unity is desirable not merely
for the sake of the community: unity of worship and unity of worshippers are
a reflection of the essential unity, the oneness, of God himself, who (according
to a standard religious formula which occurs also in 1 Corinthians 8.6) is
5 **above all and through all and in all.**

But what will this new community be like? Must unity mean uniformity? Are all its members to have the same function and the same gifts? The answer to this question is already familiar from 1 Corinthians 12: the one Spirit has a variety of gifts to impart, and the unity of a Christian community is like the unity of a body with all its different organs. It consists in the interdepen-
11 dence of different gifts and responsibilities, enabling some to be **apostles, some prophets, some evangelists, some pastors and teachers.** (The last two are an addition to the list in 1 Corinthians 12.28, reflecting perhaps a slight change in the needs and development of the church.)
8 The point is proved, as so often, by a quotation from scripture, though in this case the application is complicated. Psalm 68.18 runs (in both the Hebrew and the Greek versions):

> You ascended the high mount,
> leading captives in your train
> and receiving gifts from people.

These words were doubtless addressed originally to a victorious king return-ing to Jerusalem; but a later Jewish tradition came to interpret them as refer-ring to Moses ascending Mount Sinai in order to receive the law, and in so doing it seems to have made current a version of the text somewhat closer to that which is quoted here, substituting 'giving . . . to' for 'receiving . . . from'. According to this text with its interpretation, the 'gifts' became, not the spoils of conquest, but the blessings proceeding from the law. It is possible that this tradition (for which we have evidence only a century or so later) was known to Christians at an early date, who then applied the words, not to Moses, but to Christ. This, at least, would explain the otherwise puzzling change from 'received' to **gave**; and if the victorious king of the psalm was now taken to be Christ, the highly idiomatic phrase, **made captivity itself a captive** (of which the meaning may amount to *made many captives*), could refer, either to Christ's supremacy over all supernatural powers, or even, perhaps, to his 'captive' following, those who had now become bound to him as Christian converts. But the point which the text is quoted to prove is different. It is to prove that Christ gave to the church, not one gift, but a variety of gifts; and the proof is in the words, **"he gave gifts to his people"**. But first it has to be shown that the subject of the verse is neither a king of Israel, nor Moses, but Christ;
9 hence the importance of the first words of the quotation. **"He ascended"** suggests a previous descent. Who could be meant, who both ascended and descended, if not Christ? For Christ, having been from the beginning up above with God, **descended into the lower parts** of the heaven-and-earth universe[6] before ascending once again to that position of supremacy over all

---

[6] It is unlikely that a writer of this date would have known the doctrine that later was called Christ's 'descent into hell'. If he did, he could have been alluding to it with the phrase **the lower parts of the earth.**

which has been described in 1.20–23. Given this way of thinking and this method of interpretation, the passage could be claimed, like many others in the Old Testament, to be a prophecy of Christ. In which case it proved that the church had received, not just one uniform gift for all, but a plurality of

11 **gifts.**

These 'gifts' have so far been associated with particular ministries in the church: different people are gifted for particular forms of service in the com-

12 munity. But the **work of ministry** is not confined to these office-holders: it is for **the saints**, who together are engaged in **building up the body of Christ**. The quality of character required for this task is here summed up in

13 the notion of **maturity**:[7] Christians are exposed to the dangers of competing

14 attempts to formulate belief (**every wind of doctrine**) and a diabolical deceitfulness in their midst – this is strong language, but (perhaps deliberately) too general to be applicable only to what may have been going on either in Paul's time or in that of a later author. These dangers would be serious if Christians behaved like **children**, prone to be swayed by any strong personality. They

15 must therefore make sure they **grow up in every way**, not just taking Christ

13 as their model and inspiration (**to the measure of the full stature of Christ**), but finding their strength and unity through incorporation into the church,

16 which is his **body**. This is a powerful metaphor (indeed in 1 Corinthians 12.13 it is more than a metaphor; it expresses a real experience), and the language here is an elaboration of the same metaphor as is used (to slightly different effect) in Colossians 2.19.

17 **Now this I affirm and insist on.** The moral exhortations now continue in earnest. There are some striking similarities between the language of these paragraphs and that of other passages in the New Testament, and many of the sentiments can also be paralleled in both Jewish and Greek literature. The explanation appears to be that the early church needed an ethical code which could be taught to new converts whatever their background. The teaching of Jesus did not provide such a code: his precepts were for the most part more like a radical challenge to received ideas than like a new code of conduct, and there are very few explicit references to them outside the gospels. To meet their immediate need for practical instruction, the Christians drew on the best ethical standards and traditions of their culture, whether Jewish or Greek – indeed the two had much in common – and wove them into their own pattern of moral teaching without any attempt to label each according to its origin. The resultant code, even though it contained little that was distinctively Christian or radically new, was endorsed by the church as a

---

[7] Translated literally, the last words of verse 13 mean, *to the perfect man* (in this case a true masculine, perhaps referring to the 'perfect man', the second Adam, who is Christ), *to the measure of the stature of the fullness of Christ.* **Maturity** is the NRSV interpretation of *the perfect man*, perhaps justified by the contrast with 'children' in the next verse.

guide to the way of life now required, and any part of it could be urged as
17 being inherent in the new faith – that is, **in the Lord.**

You must no longer live as the Gentiles live. It is clear from what was
said earlier (1.12–13) that the letter was written by a Jewish Christian writer
to gentile Christians. With regard to Gentiles, the prevalent Jewish assumption was that, without the advantage of the Jewish law and with no generally
accepted moral code of their own, Gentiles were bound to fall into the vices
characteristic of a pagan civilization. So here: verses 18–19 use the conventional language of Jewish attacks on the pagan way of life, and the tone is
similar to that which Paul adopts, for the same purpose, in the first chapter of
Romans. But Christian moral conduct, though it did not require adherence
20 to the Jewish law, ought not to be exposed to such criticism. **That is not
the way you learned Christ** – a striking and original phrase which appears,
from what follows, to mean that the act of accepting Christ as Lord (i.e. the
moment of baptism) involves, not only a course of instruction showing that
21 **truth is in Jesus** (which the writer, with a touch of irony, assumes they have
surely received), but also – and in this perhaps they had not been so successful –'putting away' the old nature and 'being renewed' and 're-clothed',
so that the whole pattern of conduct is changed. The language here is all
familiar from what Paul says about baptism in Romans 6 and Colossians 3.

26   The next exhortations follow no particular order. **Be angry but do not
30 sin** is an allusion to Psalm 4.4. **Do not grieve the Holy Spirit of God** is
an Old Testament idiom (Isaiah 63.10) but takes on a special meaning for
Christians, since their baptism (already called a 'seal' in 1.13) places them
in a new relationship with the Spirit as well as giving them a foretaste and
32, 5.2 guarantee of their future destiny. For **forgiving one another** and living **in
love**, the example of Christ himself is appealed to (which is surprisingly rare
in the New Testament), not so much with reference to what may have been
forgiving and loving in his character, but because of the implications of his
self-offering in death, which is described in the sacrificial language of such
scriptural passages as Exodus 29.18. Among the vices to be shunned (since
5, 3 they disqualify for **inheritance in the kingdom of Christ and of God**) is
greed, (or 'covetousness') which this writer, along perhaps with many of his
Jewish contemporaries, had begun to regard as the contemporary expression
5 of the old biblical sin of idolatry (**one who is greedy (that is, an idolater)** –
as in Colossians 3.5).

At verse 6 the writer seems to have a specific danger in mind against which
6, 11 he must warn his hearers or readers: deception by **empty words ... unfruitful
12 works of darkness ... what such people do secretly.** It is possible that what
are being attacked are certain rites and doctrines which were clothed in
secrecy and so attracted suspicions of immoral practices (as Christianity
itself subsequently did); but even here the words are too general for us to
get a clear picture. The point of the paragraph, in any case, is to introduce
8–9, 11 a new metaphor, that of **light** and **darkness**, to emphasize the transparent

goodness which should characterize the Christian life. And to support it there
14 is a quotation (**it says**), not, this time, from any known part of scripture, but
from what appears to be a very early Christian hymn. After this, the paragraph
returns to general moral exhortation, and in two places (verses 16 and 19–20)
comes very close to Colossians (4.5 and 3.16).

At verse 21, the injunctions fall into a distinctive pattern. One of the ways
in which moral teaching was given in antiquity was according to the various categories of domestic relationships – how husbands should behave to
wives, fathers to children, masters to slaves and so forth. The New Testament
writers on more than one occasion appear to make use of this conventional
scheme (see below, p. 740) and for the most part the moral guidance is equally
conventional, reflecting the standards recommended by enlightened philosophical teachers. But occasionally also they introduce a new and distinctive
insight derived from their Christian faith. So here, under the general heading,
21 **Be subject to one another out of reverence to Christ** (which was a guiding
principle in Christian communities: Galatians 5.13; 1 Corinthians 16.16),
a Christian version of this conventional type of instruction is introduced,
beginning with wives and husbands.

That women should be 'subject' to men in general, and wives 'subject'
to their husbands in particular, was taken for granted in both Jewish and
Greek society, and there is little in the New Testament to suggest that the
early Christians thought otherwise. It is true that women did occasionally
assume some independent responsibility in the church (as indeed, they did
in pagan society), but for the most part the submission of wives to husbands
could be represented as the sign of 'God-fearing' women. It would have
been natural to say that they submitted 'in the fear of God': the phrase,
out of reverence to Christ, means literally *in fear of Christ*, and is a simple
Christian adaptation of a familiar expression. That Christian wives should be
similarly submissive hardly needed demonstration, and is taken for granted
33 throughout this section, which ends with a repetition of the same formula, **a
wife should respect her husband** (literally, *should fear her husband*). But since
all forms of mutual submission are such an important feature of relationships
within the church, the author takes the opportunity to strengthen the point
by setting it in the context of the essential submission of the church to Christ.
We have already been reminded that being a member of the church is being
23 a member of Christ's 'body'. In that body, Christ is necessarily **the head**.
Obedience to Christ is therefore the obedience which the limbs of the body
owe to the head. But it was also an accepted figure of speech (as we can see
from 1 Corinthians 11.3, though we do not know where the idea came from)
that **the husband is the head of the wife**. By a natural analogy, the submission
of church members to Christ, their 'head', could be invoked to provide a new
model for the normal submission of wives to their husbands.

But what about husbands in relation to their wives? How could the general
principle of mutual submission apply to a relationship which was taken for

granted as one of dominance and superiority? Here the strikingly original thought is introduced that, if the submission of wives could be likened to that of church members (his 'body') to Christ, the appropriate behaviour of husbands to their wives might similarly be modelled on Christ's relationship to the church; and this was one, not of dominance and superiority, but of love:

25 **Christ loved the church and gave himself up for her.** The consequences of this act of self-sacrifice for the church are briefly summarized: Christ's death

26 made possible Christian baptism (Romans 6) which, by virtue of **washing of water** and (perhaps) the invocation and instruction which accompanied the rite (**by the word**), made the church what it could never be by its own

27 efforts, **cleansing her** and making her **without blemish** – the metaphor is

28 of an animal fit to be accepted at the altar in the Jewish sacrificial system. **In the same way** – and here is the surprise. Why should Christ's love for the church be a model for human husbands? The answer is found in that verse of Genesis (2.24) which was quoted by Jesus as the basis for his own view of

31 marriage: **"the two will become one flesh"**. This shows that the husband's wife is, in a sense, his 'body'. This means that he should treat her at least as well as he treats his own physical body. But more than this: what holds of Christ's loving and self-sacrificial treatment of his 'body', the church, may

32 hold also of the husband's treatment of his 'body' – his wife. **This is a great mystery.**[8] Here the word does not seem to have its special meaning of 'hidden divine plan', but the more general one of 'secret meaning': the intimacies

31 of married life, alluded to in the biblical phrase '**one flesh**' and hardly to be spelled out in public, are boldly used as a model for understanding the intimate love shown by Christ for his church; and this, in turn, becomes a new and arresting model for the way in which a husband should love his wife – so arresting that this passage is quoted or alluded to in virtually every form of the Christian marriage service.

The same principle of 'submission' applies more obviously to children and slaves. In the case of children (who had little opportunity *not* to obey

6.2 their parents) it is reinforced by the Fifth Commandment (Exodus 20.12). Submission could hardly be demanded of fathers towards their children, but there is a corresponding duty to avoid unreasonable treatment of them

4 (which would justly provoke them **to anger**) and to ensure that they had the **discipline and instruction of the Lord.** And in the case both of slaves

5–9 and of their masters, the fact, once again, of their submission to Christ as their heavenly master was a principle that should influence their mutual relationships. The institution of slavery itself is, of course, not questioned; but it did not affect the fundamental equality of all human beings before

9 God, who (in a phrase from 1 Chronicles 19.7) shows **no partiality.**

---

[8] In the fourth century CE the word was translated into Latin as *sacramentum*, one of the meanings of which is what the church came to call a 'sacrament': hence the doctrine, held for many centuries, that marriage is a sacrament and therefore 'indissoluble'.

10   **Finally, be strong in the Lord.** The moral teaching of the previous paragraphs – mostly fairly conventional but with some highly original Christian
insights – has assumed that it lies within the will of human beings to respond
to such exhortations. But this writer (as has already appeared above, 2.1–2)
thinks of moral conduct as a struggle not merely with human weakness and
12   depravity but as **against the cosmic powers.** Evil, according to this view of
things, is an objective and external force, a superhuman power which bears
upon human beings from outside and brings them into involuntary subjection. In unsophisticated Jewish circles (as we can see from the gospels)
this force was identified quite simply with Satan and his attendant demons.
But the popular philosophies and religious speculations of the time offered
to the more cultivated thinker a wide range of concepts for describing this
objective and personified power of evil. There was the late Jewish myth of
the 'fallen angels'; there was the popular world-view which saw the space
between heaven and earth as peopled with spiritual beings, some benign, but
mostly malignant and in revolt against God; and there were the doctrines of
astrology, which invested the heavenly bodies with ineluctable power over
human destinies. The author draws freely on such concepts. In 2.2 he spoke
of "the ruler of the power of the air". Here, he paints a still more sombre
picture of human beings pitted against **the cosmic powers of this present
darkness, against the spiritual forces of evil in the heavenly places.** The
letter began with a vision of the destiny of the church to be raised in unity
with its Lord to a position high above these supernatural powers; and this
great destiny is in the course of fulfilment. Yet meanwhile the powers are still
abroad, and Christians, like all human beings, are exposed to their influence.
For this struggle their own strength is inadequate, and they are urged to put
13   on **the whole armor of God.** The metaphor is magnificently worked out; and
19   by means of the last term in the exhortation – **pray also for me** – a gentle
transition is made to the personal remarks and greetings which were to be
expected at the end of a letter.
21–2   These personal matters are almost identical (though briefer) with those
at the end of Colossians (4.7 – see the comments there), and raise in a sharp
form the question of the relationship between the two letters. The final wish
23   for the church – **peace . . . and love with faith** – is more elaborate than in
any other letter by Paul, though it uses phrases characteristic of him.[9]

---

[9] The last words mean literally *in immortality*, which the translators have linked with
'love': **an undying love.** But other constructions are possible, and Paul never uses the word
in greetings elsewhere.

PHILIPPIANS

The events surrounding Paul's first visit to Philippi are dramatically told in Acts 16 and are also referred to by Paul (with some indignation) in 1 Thessalonians 2.2. Despite this violent beginning the Philippian church had evidently taken root and flourished; and although Paul was able to make it only one, or possibly two, subsequent visits (Acts 20.1–7; 2 Corinthians 2.13), it more than once provided him with generous financial support, and its record of faith and loyalty is apparent from this, the warmest and most affectionate of Paul's surviving letters.

The city of Philippi was the first on the Egnatian Way leading from Asia to the Adriatic (see the map on p. 449). It was not large, but had received the distinction of being re-founded by the emperor Augustus in 31 BCE as a Roman colony, which meant that almost the entire upper class were Roman settlers, speaking Latin rather than Greek and enjoying a number of civic and financial privileges which made them enthusiastically loyal to Rome. Their culture and their religion dominated the city, even though it contained a substantial population of indigenous Greek-speaking inhabitants as well as a very small Jewish community – too small, certainly, to have built itself a synagogue (Acts 16.13), but possibly large enough to have exerted some pressure on the Christians.

It is clear from the text that Paul wrote this letter when he was in prison awaiting trial. The traditional view is that this was his final period of captivity in Rome, and that Philippians, like Colossians and Philemon, therefore belongs to his last years; and this provides a reasonable explanation of the circumstances alluded to in this letter. On the other hand the journey from Rome to Philippi was a long one (about 800 miles by road); yet messengers had passed between Paul and the Philippians at least twice before this letter was written (2.25–6); and since we do not know the details of his earlier imprisonments (such as Paul alludes to in 2 Corinthians 11.13) we cannot rule out the possibility that the letter was written from a place much nearer Philippi, such as Ephesus; in which case it could belong to an earlier period in Paul's life.

The greeting

The opening of the letter follows the conventional letter-writing form in its Christian adaptation (see above on Romans 1.12). **Paul and Timothy** are named as the joint senders, with no reference to their status or authority (for once Paul does not even call himself 'apostle'), but with the challenging designation **servants** (the Greek has the still more startling word *slaves*).

1.1

Those addressed are **the saints in Christ Jesus who are in Philippi**, not persons of especial sanctity (as is clear from the amount of moral exhortation later in the letter) but simply members of the 'holy people' of God constituted by the church. But there is a remarkable addition: **with the bishops and deacons**. The Greek words used here are the same as those which subsequently became the names of established orders of ministry within the church; but we do not know whether they had already become precise terms by this time, or whether they were still fairly common words suggesting a less formal mode of authority (as in the NRSV footnote). It was not until early in the second century that a threefold ministry of bishops, presbyters (priests) and deacons was established in any part of the church, and it did not become universal until the beginning of the third. During the first decades of its existence the church's organization was certainly not uniform. According to Acts the church in Jerusalem was governed, first by apostles, and then by 'elders' (*presbyters*); in Corinth there do not seem to have been any defined office-holders at all; and only in the letters to Timothy and Titus do the titles 'bishop' and 'deacon' reappear. The most we can say is that some sort of precursors of the later bishops and deacons may have already been established at Philippi.

The example of Christ

Thanksgiving for the record of the church to which he is writing and prayer for its continuing progress stand at the beginning of many of Paul's letters: the pattern and many of the words are the same, for instance, in Ephesians 5 and Colossians. The tone here is particularly warm. Their **sharing in the gospel** may be a reference specifically to the material contributions they have made to Paul's work (4.15–16), but must also mean that they have played a part themselves in the growth of the church. In any case, Paul goes on to mention other reasons for his gratitude, particularly the solidarity they have 7 shown with him in his present critical circumstances (the words **defense and confirmation** may be a deliberate allusion to his impending trial); and he expresses his confidence that their faith is such as to remain unshaken 6, 8 until the coming **day of Jesus Christ**. Moreover, Paul longs to see them **with the compassion[1] of Christ Jesus** – not, that is to say, as if he imagines his own emotions to be like those of Jesus himself, but rather with that depth of feeling which is due to the unique relationship which now holds between Christians and especially between Paul and his converts.[2]

Meanwhile, Paul is in prison. The word *praetorium* might have been hoped to yield some indication of where Paul was. If it is being used in its proper

---

[1] Literally, *in the bowels of Christ Jesus*, a way of saying 'with an emotion that affects one's deepest inward parts'.

[2] There are details in this passage which are a little ambiguous – see the NRSV footnotes. But the general sense is clear enough.

13 sense, it denotes the **imperial guard**, and makes it most likely that Paul is imprisoned in Rome; but it can also mean the governor's residence in an imperial province such as Judea (hence its correct use in Jerusalem, Acts 23.35), in which case the prison might have been in, say, Caesarea. In any case, his imprisonment might have been regarded by many as a serious setback in the progress of the gospel. Paul, on the contrary, could claim that it had been in the main a source of encouragement, even if some of his personal rivals had taken advantage of his absence in prison to advance their own

18 reputation, proclaiming Christ **out of false motives**. What did that matter? **Christ is proclaimed in every way.**

But Paul was not just in prison: he was facing the prospect of a trial on a capital charge. Nor was this merely a matter of his personal condemnation or acquittal. What was at stake was his reputation for truth and innocence, not just in human eyes but in the eyes of God. In the same way Job, brought near to the point of death by his misfortunes, had been anxious above all that he should not die in disgrace: convinced of his innocence, his most earnest prayer was, not for an escape from death, but for this innocence of his to be recognized. 'The issue of it all will be my salvation', he said, 'in that no deceit shall come into God's presence' (Job 13.16 in the Greek version of

19 the Septuagint). Paul, by alluding to this verse (**this will turn out for my deliverance** – the allusion is clear in the Greek) placed his own ordeal in the same perspective. The important thing was not whether he was released or

20 condemned, whether he lived or died, but only that he would not be **put to shame in any way**, and that, whichever way the human judgment went, Christ would be **exalted now as always**. Through the prayers of the Philippians

19 and through **the help of the Spirit of Jesus Christ** he was confident that

18 this would be the outcome; so he could say, **Yes, and I will continue to rejoice**.

But suppose he was in fact to die, had he personally no fear of death? Paul was not one to take lightly the reality of judgment after death, nor did he assume that he had already arrived at a point where he could be totally assured that it would be favourable (3.12–14). But at the moment of writing

21 his consciousness of union with Christ was so intense (**to me, living is Christ**) that, brushing aside all theoretical scenarios of an interval between death and resurrected life (such as that in 1 Corinthians 15), he seems to have envisaged his own death as an immediate escape into a still closer relationship with Christ. Did this mean he positively looked forward to being condemned to

22 death? On the contrary, there was too much **fruitful labor** that he could still undertake if he lived for him to be able to accept death without a qualm. To convey this tension, Paul writes as if the choice was actually in his own hands. We can hardly imagine that he contemplated suicide (though his language has echoes of the freedom Socrates felt to choose his own death). Conceivably (if his imprisonment was an earlier one and not in Rome) he could have had the choice whether or not to declare his Roman citizenship and so have his

trial postponed – as he did when arrested in Jerusalem (Acts 22.27). But the intensity of his language is perhaps sufficiently explained by his own inner conflict. An almost mystical exaltation at the thought of a still closer experience of Christ in death had to contend with a very real confidence that his life would be spared and that he would be released to continue his work

26 with the Philippians and **share abundantly** in their **boasting** (or *confident jubilation*) **in Christ Jesus.**

27 **Only . . .** The following paragraphs (1.27–2.18) amount to a brief sermon addressed to the Philippians of which the theme can be summed up in a single sentence: **live your life in a manner worthy of the gospel of Christ.** Normally Paul uses a turn of phrase which has a Jewish resonance: 'walk' – for the manner of 'walking' (*halakah*) was a technical term in Jewish moral discourse. Here he speaks a language more familiar to the Philippians: 'exercise your citizenship' (the literal meaning of the word translated **live your life**). They would often have been exhorted to do so worthily of the status of the Roman colony to which they belonged; now they must conform with the much greater demands of the gospel. First, the Christian life is painted in the colours of a battle or an athletic contest (both would have been familiar metaphors in Philippi): their unity and teamwork (**striving side by side with one mind**) would be crucial for their defence of the faith. Secondly, their constancy would make increasingly clear the line of demarcation between themselves and their opponents who, the more they stood in opposition, the more they

28 would condemn themselves to **destruction** – for if the final judgment was a reality, their continued opposition must leave them with no prospect of salvation (the same point is made more elaborately – and we might say more ruthlessly – in 2 Thessalonians 1.6–10).

Who were these opponents? Later in the letter we hear of a Jewish pressure group (3.2). But here it seems more likely that Paul is referring to the kind of pagan opposition which he had originally encountered himself in Philippi and which may have been still continuing against the church there. And this was not just an unfortunate phase of suffering which they must endure until it blew over. As Paul had discovered in his own case (and it was a revolutionary discovery), there was a positive side of suffering, in that it could be borne 'for' Christ, and could be a means (as he says later, 3.10) of "becoming like him".

2.2 Paul's second argument is a highly personal one: **make my joy complete.** Life in Christ is an experience binding men and women closely together (on

1 the force of the word **consolation** see above on 2 Corinthians 1.4); and it inevitably makes Christians particularly sensitive to the shortcomings as well as to the excellences of their fellows. So Paul begs that his own joy in their fellowship and constancy (which suffuses much of this letter) may not be impaired by any backsliding from the mutual love and personal humility which are part of the Christian ethic. There was a well-known motto among early Jewish teachers: 'Let another's honour be as your own.' Christians must

4 go even further than this: **look not to your own interests, but**[3] **to the interests of others.**

Thirdly, there is the example of Christ himself – but here a rather loose expression in the Greek makes it difficult to know whether Paul means us 5 to copy a disposition that **was** in Christ Jesus (looking back to his life on earth) or to follow up in our lives the implication of being 'in' Christ, whose life story had a particular character of humility, obedience and exaltation (see the NRSV footnote). Either way, there is no doubt that Christ is being appealed to as providing the ultimate motivation for the Christian ethic.

6–11 The passage that follows has a marked poetical quality, and even a kind of symmetry of construction, which has suggested to many interpreters that it may have been a transcription of an existing poem, hymn, or liturgical text. Not that Paul could not rise to great heights of eloquence himself; but the poetical form, combined with certain peculiarities of diction and doctrine, make it plausible to suggest that the passage may have existed in some form before Paul incorporated it here, and indeed, may be evidence for a very early stage of Christian reflection and worship. On the other hand, even if this is the case (and there is no external evidence to show that it is), Paul gives no indication that the words are not his own, and we must assume that he deliberately chose them to convey precisely the message he wished to impress on his hearers and readers.

The theme of the passage is the humility and obedience of Christ. But these are not presented as if they were marks of Jesus' character that might be illustrated by known episodes from his earthly life. Rather, they are key principles of Jesus' nature and destiny. The story is taken up (as at the begin-6 ning of John's gospel) long before his human birth. He was **in the form of God**, that is, indistinguishable from God; but if (in this sense) he was 'equal' with God, this was not something to be **exploited:**[4] it did not prevent him[5] 7 taking on the 'form' that was the very opposite of God's form, namely **human likeness**, and that in its most demeaning category, **the form of a slave.** Fur-ther, the humility and obedience involved in this willing identification with 8 human beings extended **to the point of death:** there was no question of being 'caught up to heaven' beforehand like Enoch or Elijah; and not merely this, but the death was of the most cruel and humiliating kind, normally reserved for slaves and rebels – **death on a cross.**

---

[3] Some manuscripts, which are followed by many modern translations, reduce the radical force of this by inserting the word *also*: **but** *also* **to the interests of others.**

[4] The Greek word is *harpagmos*, and there has been much debate over its meaning. So far as the word goes, it could mean the act of 'grasping', the possession of something 'grasped', or the fact that the object still needed to be 'grasped'. The meaning given here is that accepted by the majority of scholars today.

[5] The word **though** has been introduced by the translators. Paul's words (literally, *being in the form of God*), allow for the possibility that it was not *despite*, but *because of*, being in the form of God that he 'emptied himself'.

This, beyond anything which a merely human being could perform, was supreme obedience, supreme humility; this was the example which the Philippians must take to heart if their own conduct was to be worthy of their name as Christians. But the passage continues beyond this immediate application – and perhaps this is the clearest indication that it existed in
9 some form before Paul made this use of it. **Therefore** – an emphatic word in the Greek, beginning what looks like the second strophe of a poem and thereby showing that this was the important thing about Jesus, the key to his nature and saving work, the answer to what had happened to him after the crucifixion – **Therefore God also highly exalted him** and gave him the paramount honour which, in Isaiah (45.23), God reserves to himself: "To me every knee shall bow, every tongue shall swear." Yet this exalted position, above all earthly, infernal and even heavenly beings, was no usurpation by
11 Jesus: it was **to the glory of God the Father**.

All this has profound theological and metaphysical implications, not least in that it appears to ascribe 'pre-existence' to Christ. But these are not developed here. It may also owe much to ideas which were implicit in Jesus' use of the title 'Son of Man', or to the 'suffering servant' motif in Isaiah 53 – not to mention more remote antecedents which have been suggested by scholars.[6] But, if so, these lie far beneath the surface. What is before us is a brief poetical statement, such as a hymn or an act of worship might have contained, and it is possible that this is one way in which the earliest Christians sought to express the significance of the life and death of Jesus. At any rate it is significant that Paul speaks in this way of Christ, not as an example of divinely inspired human virtues, but as exhibiting in the broad sweep of his destiny the obedience and self-humiliation of one whose status of equality with God did not prevent him from descending to the depths of human suffering and ignominy, and who only then was awarded his place of supremacy under God in the whole created universe. It was obedience and humility on this divine and cosmic scale to which Paul was appealing when he wrote that the Philippians should have 'the mind of Christ'. In the past their obedience was perhaps shown sufficiently in obeying Paul's personal authority when he was present with them. But this more profound obedience was some-
13 thing they had to **work out** themselves – or rather that God would be **at work** creating in them, enabling them **to will and to work for his good pleasure**.

The last section of this short sermon, like the first, is placed in the perspective of the coming day of judgment. When that day comes, Christians must be sure that their conduct has been such as to assure them of a place on

---

[6] One widely accepted suggestion is that the passage draws on the myth of Adam, whose sin was precisely to 'snatch at equality with God' (Genesis 3.5 – though in fact it was Eve who was first tempted to do so): Christ, the second Adam (Romans 5), resisted the identical temptation.

15 the right side: not (as the scriptural phrase has it, Deuteronomy 32.5) **in the midst of a crooked and perverse generation,** but as **children of God without blemish.** Indeed, not only do they already have a radiance and a message which distinguish them from all others (**like stars in the world**), but on that same day of judgment they will stand to the credit of Paul himself when he

17 too is called to account. Paul may die before that day: the metaphor which he uses, being based on pagan sacrifices as much as on anything Jewish (pouring out 'libations' was a standard feature of any sacrificial system), could be a way of speaking of his whole ministry as much as of his death. In any case, whatever his own sacrifice, it will be an integral part of the sacrifice they are offering themselves. It need neither separate him from them nor impair their mutual joy.

Two envoys were to maintain contact between Paul and the Philippian

19 church. One, **Timothy,** had already been entrusted with a delicate mission to Corinth (1 Corinthians 4.17), and is here given an eloquent testimonial (pos-

25 sibly one of the immediate pretexts for this letter). The other, **Epaphroditus,** belonged to the Philippian church, and had recently been extremely ill. In Paul's culture such an illness was liable to have serious implications: it could be thought that the sufferer had done something to deserve God's punish-

26 ment, and his 'distress' at the possible reaction of the Philippians may have been more than merely concern that they would be anxious about him: he may have been genuinely nervous about meeting them again and having to defend himself from unfounded suspicions. Hence Paul's enthusiastic com-

28 mendation, that they might **rejoice at seeing him again** and that Paul also should be **less anxious.** What he had been through must be seen as no kind of slur on his character but as an honourable consequence of his self-sacrificial service.

3.1 **Finally, my brothers and sisters.** The commendation of Timothy and Epahroditus was evidently a main purpose of the letter, which looks as if it is now coming to an end – indeed, the word translated **rejoice** could actually mean *farewell,* though the phrase itself, **rejoice in the Lord,** has a distinctively Christian sound and is rather more than a conventional formula. But there was still a serious issue to deal with which possibly caused Paul to change his mind and continue.

Breaking with the past

By way of transition, Paul inserts some rather colourless words, of which the exact relevance is obscure (**to write the same things . . .** what things?). Possibly the sentence was something of a cliché, a trite way of apologizing for returning to a familiar topic (the Greek words form an almost perfect line of verse).

2 But it is a topic that sharply changes the tone of the letter. **Beware of the dogs.** Whenever Jews said this they were usually expressing contempt of

non-Jews (much as Jesus did, though perhaps somewhat more playfully, in Matthew 15.26). But here Paul turns the expression on its head and uses it to attack opponents who are evidently Jews themselves. Indeed, his attack is very bitter: and it would surely have been only under extreme provocation that Paul, a Jew, could have called circumcision *mutilation* (the literal meaning of his words, which were sometimes used of self-mutilation in pagan rites). What had provoked him to this? There has been no hint so far of Jewish opposition in Philippi – such persecution as there had been seems to have come from the pagan side. But the kind of Jewish pressure Paul had to cope with in the Galatian church may have made him especially sensitive to the danger to which any of his gentile churches might be exposed; and this virulent passage may have been written more as a warning against what might happen than as a defence against an actual threat.

In any event we can probably overhear the kind of propaganda which a Jewish party, whether inside or outside the church, would use against gentile
3   converts. **It is we who are the circumcision,** says Paul; from which we can infer the terms in which these opponents are likely to have been taunting the Christians. 'You do not have circumcision, you have no temple and no sacrifices, you have no religious tradition in which you can "boast" or put your confidence.' To which Paul replies, 'We are the true circumcised, we have all the things you are proud of – but not in the same sense as you have them: we place no trust in externals, we **have no confidence in the flesh.'** (For other examples of a reply to this propaganda, see Colossians 2.11; 1 Peter 2.5–10.)

If this was the answer that ordinary non-Jewish Christians were encouraged to give, it may well have seemed to their Jewish oppressors somewhat evasive, as if, lacking the advantages which the Jews possessed, the Christians were reduced to pretending that they had the equivalent in their own religion. In Paul's mouth, on the other hand, the argument was formidable. He, if anyone, could argue from strength.
5   (i) He was **circumcised on the eighth day** – the regular time for this ceremony (compare the circumcision of Jesus, Luke 1.59), without which no male could be regarded as a true Israelite;

(ii) **a member of the people of Israel,** the historic people of God;

(iii) **of the tribe of Benjamin:** membership of a 'tribe' or family network was important to Romans as well as to Jews. Paul's Jewish namesake, King Saul, was a Benjaminite;

(iv) **a Hebrew born of Hebrews:** the word 'Hebrew' distinguished those Jews who maintained their cultural links with the language that was still spoken in some circles in Palestine.

So much for his ancestry. His conduct and way of life before his conversion to Christianity were equally irreproachable.

(v) **As to the law, he was a Pharisee,** that is, one of those who believed that no part of the Mosaic law was outmoded but that it was all capable of being interpreted in such a way as to be practicable in their own day, and who went to great pains to bring their lives into conformity with its detailed requirements.

6 (vi) **As to zeal, he was a persecutor of the church.** Correctness of life according to the law was one thing; 'zeal' was another. Those who belonged to such movements in Judaism were not just concerned for their own correctness; they were zealously opposed to any serious deviation by others from the traditional Jewish way of life. Hence such a person might be led to persecute a breakaway movement such as the church.

(vii) **As to righteousness under the law, he was blameless.** Parties such as the Pharisees prided themselves on their scrupulous observance of the law, particularly with regard to ritual cleanness. If they transgressed, they made use of the ritual provisions for atonement.[7]

Paul, therefore, could meet his Jewish opponents on their own ground. His Jewish credentials would stand comparison with those of anyone, a fact which he did not hesitate to exploit whenever he found himself in dispute with the Jewish authorities. But at the same time he was capable of behaving in an exceedingly un-Jewish way: when in the company of gentile Christians he would behave as if he were a Gentile (as he tells us himself, 1 Corinthians 9.19–23). His Jewish opponents might well have asked: Was he or was he not going to continue to call himself a Jew? Equally, his Christian friends might have wondered why, despite all this talk of 'having no confidence in the flesh', Paul was in fact still ready to appeal to his Jewish parentage, his circumcision and his former Pharisaic way of life. To this question Paul now gives an unequivocal answer. He has mentioned these things only for the purpose of the argument, in order to silence the taunts which the Jewish opponents were aiming at uncircumcised Christians. His real opinion of them he expresses

8 in strong language: **I regard them as rubbish.**

What was it that Paul regarded as of such overwhelming value that he was prepared to 'write off' all his previous assets? (The accountancy language

7 of **loss** and **gains** seems deliberate: it is not that these things had no value in themselves but rather that Paul had found something else so much more worth having that he could dispense with them.) What was it that cancelled out all the advantages of race and upbringing that his fellow Jews set such store by? It is not sufficient to answer, 'His Christian faith'; for his opponents evidently thought of Christianity as a system of beliefs that could be held in addition to reliance upon the external observances of the Jewish religion, whereas Paul was speaking of something which made these obsolete. Part

9 of the answer was the **righteousness** that **comes through faith in Christ,** a concept which is not elaborated here but is defended at length in Romans

---

[7] The view, which until recently was widely held in Protestant scholarship, that Paul suffered from a sense of guilt for not being able to observe the law in its entirety, has never fully come to terms with this verse.

and Galatians and which excluded all reliance upon the external observances
8 of the law. But Paul also gives another, much more surprising, answer: **the surpassing value of knowing Christ Jesus my Lord**. Only here does Paul speak in such intimate terms of 'knowing his Lord'; and we must ask: In what sense did Paul claim to 'know' Jesus, and know him, not just as 'the Lord' of the Christian confession (2.11), but in a personal way as **my Lord**? Not, it seems, in the sense that he had been acquainted with Jesus on earth – this seems very unlikely, and even if he had[8] he certainly attached no importance to it. His 'knowledge' sounds more like the kind associated with many popular forms of religion (later called 'gnosticism', from *gnōsis*, knowledge) in which the supreme object of all rites and ceremonies was to come to 'know' the deity in what we might call a mystical sense. But for Paul, this 'knowing' had its roots in the Bible, not in mystical religion. The biblical conception of 'knowing God' meant having a relationship with him which was marked by faithfulness and obedience, and was almost equivalent to 'being known' by him (Galatians 4.9). It involved an experience (whether personal and unique, as on the Damascus road and on other occasions in Paul's life, or more
10 generally shared by the Christian community, as in Romans 6) of the **power** – the reality and efficacy – of Jesus' **resurrection**, a sense of solidarity with Jesus in his **sufferings**, and the hope of ultimately entering the resurrection life oneself.

In some Greek religions the devotees were promised 'knowledge' as a result of certain initiations, having obtained which they would be 'perfect'.
12 Paul makes a passing reference to such language: **not that I . . . have already been made perfect** (the literal meaning of the words translated **reached the goal**); and this might have aroused a similar expectation: after initiation by baptism, Christians might feel they had been 'made perfect'. But of course this was not so – not even in Paul's case, though he, under threat of death, could plausibly claim to have followed Christ to the limit. Yet the analogy of initiation into a 'mystery religion' was not without its value. In the Christian
15 life some will be more **mature** than others – Paul seems deliberately to use another form of the word meaning *made perfect* in verse 12. Those who have not yet got so far may **think differently**, but so long as their progress is maintained they too will soon reach the point at which God will **reveal** to them what at present is known only to those who are **mature**. Meanwhile, whatever stage we have reached – and the metaphor now has shifted from religious initiation to running in a race – there is no excuse to slacken our
16 efforts: **let us hold fast to what we have attained**.
17   **Join in imitating me.** Had it not been for the explanations just given, Paul's 'example' might have seemed to point in more than one way. He was ready enough to make a point of his impeccable Jewishness, but equally

---

[8] 2 Corinthians 5.16, "even though we once knew Christ from a human point of view", literally *according to the flesh*, is not evidence for a personal meeting. See above, p. 576n.

ready to feel himself not bound by Jewish observances; and he used language about 'knowing Christ' which could suggest that he belonged to a class of superior initiates and had already achieved a kind of 'perfection'. But now, having dispelled any such misunderstandings, Paul could offer himself as an example. An example of what? Certainly of resolute independence over against any pressure the Jewish party might exert on Christians. But his sudden reference to **enemies of the cross**, whose influence seems more to be in the direction of encouraging licentiousness and the satisfaction of physical appetites, suggests that he is concerned for the general moral health of the congregation. Philippi, with its strong Roman connections, was a city where

20 **citizenship** was greatly prized: it involved civic duties and responsibilities, but also advantages and privileges. Christians were not setting themselves up as a rival focus of citizenship; rather, they had a higher loyalty and a more profound source of confident expectation. This did not mean that their physical body, with its appetites and temptations, was irrelevant. On the contrary, it was the material out of which the **Savior, the Lord Jesus Christ**, would fashion a new body on the day of his coming, one that would

21 be **conformed** to his. This meant that not only in faith and expectation, but

4.1 also in moral discipline, they must above all things **stand firm**.

2   There follows a brief paragraph on domestic matters: a quarrel between

3 two women in the church, an appeal to an unknown **companion** to help in settling it, and a reference to other faithful members of the church, including one (**Clement**) with a Roman name, **whose names are in the book of life** (a conventional expression: see below on Revelation 3.5).

Financial matters

4–9 And here the letter appears to be coming to an end, with a series of loosely connected exhortations and expressions of affection, all characteristic of the specially warm relationship which existed between the writer and the recip-

10–19 ients. But a further section is added (possibly as an afterthought, or even a separate letter placed here by an editor) by way of thanking the Philippians for their financial generosity. The passage is very laboured, and goes to great lengths to avoid speaking directly of any sum of money. There can be no doubt that the Philippians had made generous contributions to Paul's support during his earlier travels (4.16) and had now sent a fresh instalment with Epahroditus (2.25); and we might have expected him to use this opportunity to thank them profusely. But evidently it was not so simple. Paul prided himself on his financial independence, and must not give the impression that he depended on their generosity; if he said too much they might either think that their previous gifts had been inadequate or else that he still wanted more; so he goes out of his way to deny both implications, and shows considerable embarrassment (real or feigned) at having to accept anything at all. Hence

11 the protestations that, personally, he could stand any degree of poverty (**I**

have learned to be content with whatever I have was a cliché of popular philosophy), and hence perhaps also the rather surprising piling-up of technical

17–18 business language (**. . . the profit that accumulates to your account. I have been paid in full**) in order to conceal his embarrassment behind a formal mode of speech. To round it off, he describes the Philippians' gift, not just as a piece of financial generosity, but in the cult language of the Jerusalem temple as **a fragrant offering, a sacrifice acceptable and pleasing to God**.

While Paul was in prison (whether in Rome or elsewhere) the people he saw most of were presumably soldiers and junior civil servants, many of whom would have been technically 'slaves of the emperor'. Evidently Christianity

22 had already spread to many of those who (in this sense) belonged to **the emperor's household**.

COLOSSIANS

Outside this letter there is no mention in the New Testament of the city of Colossae, and from the letter itself it is clear that Paul had never been there. The church had been founded by an assistant of Paul's named Epaphras, who appears to have been a native of the city; and to the question when this happened the most likely answer can be found in the account in Acts of Paul's stay in Ephesus. His work there "continued for two years, so that all the residents of Asia, both Jews and Greeks, heard the word of the Lord" (19.10). Colossae, with Laodicea and Hierapolis, made up a group of three small cities some 100 miles inland from Ephesus, in the valley of the river Lycus. Christian communities had taken root in all three of them (4.13), and the obvious time for this to have taken place is during Paul's activity in Ephesus.

From the last sentence in the letter it appears that Paul was writing in prison, and it has generally been assumed that the imprisonment referred to is that which Paul underwent while awaiting trial in Rome. As with Philippians (which was also written from prison), there are reasons for doubting this: Rome was too far away from Asia for some of the contacts mentioned in these letters to have been maintained, and Paul himself mentions other 'imprisonments' (2 Corinthians 11.23) – there may well have been one at Ephesus (1 Corinthians 15.32). But in any case, the question hardly affects the interpretation of the letter. Wherever Paul was, he had received a visit from the original founder of the church (Epaphras), and also from Onesimus, a slave from Colossae, about whom Paul also wrote a letter to the slave's owner, Philemon. He was clearly in close contact with this church and had many personal acquaintances among its members (4.10–17). It was as the result of fresh news brought by Epaphras that he felt the need to write this letter.

The trouble that had overtaken the Colossian church was less to do with conduct (as in Corinth) than with belief. The Christians in Colossae had been exposed to "philosophy and empty deceit" (2.8), and the immediate purpose of the letter was to warn them of the dangers of such ideas and to strengthen their understanding of the true faith. It was probably in answer to this 'philosophy' that Paul developed a conception of the nature and work of Christ which is on a grander scale, and has wider metaphysical implications, than virtually any other passage of the New Testament. The only other writing that comes close to it is the letter to the Ephesians; but this has in other respects such close similarities with Colossians that the one must in any case, be in some way dependent on the other (see above, p. 611). It is because of this remarkable extension of Paul's thought, as well as for certain technical reasons, that this letter (like Ephesians) is sometimes thought to have been written by a follower of Paul rather than by Paul himself.

The cosmic supremacy of Christ

After the opening greeting the letter proceeds with the usual thanksgivings and prayers. But in this letter (as in Ephesians) the prayer is greatly extended; indeed, the language of almost the whole of the first chapter has a devotional ring, and even the great theological statements which it contains on the place of Christ in the universe are set in the framework of the prayer. This devotional intention may explain the style of the chapter, which is diffuse and elaborate to a degree that is rare in the New Testament.

The immediate subject for thanksgiving was the reputation of the church at Colossae: its members had shown clear evidence of possessing that same 1.4–5 triad of Christian virtues – **faith, hope** and **love** – which are the subject of the great thirteenth chapter of 1 Corinthians. But the Colossian church was not alone. Its progress needed to be seen in the context of the 'world-wide' spread of the gospel (Paul evidently saw the remarkable growth of churches around 6 the eastern Mediterranean seaboard as symbolic of their ultimate presence **in the whole world**). And the preacher who first brought this gospel to Colossae 7 was now acting on their **behalf**[1] in reporting back to Paul some tangible act 8 of their **love in the Spirit** (the only time the Spirit is mentioned in this letter). Possibly they had made a contribution to his collection for the needs of the church in Jerusalem, which Paul had urged on all his churches.

The prayer itself is very similar to that in Philippians (1.3–11), but with a greater emphasis on the practical outworking of their faith. The religion of those who had been troubling the church in Colossae was strong in specu-9 lation but perhaps weak in practical conduct; and Paul here insists that **the spiritual wisdom and understanding**, which was certainly to be desired, 10 must nevertheless go together with **every good work** and be sustained by a 11 patient endurance, of which the source was God's **glorious power**.

At this point Paul's intercession for those to whom he was writing returns to 12 **giving thanks**. The normal form which thanksgiving took in all Jewish prayer and worship (as in most religions) was that of a recital of the gracious acts and attributes of God. Thus the remarkable passage that follows is essentially a summary of the immense benefits which flow from the person and work of Christ. The sequence of short clauses, which all follow on from the initial pronoun **who**, and which in the Greek are bound together grammatically in a single movement of thanksgiving and praise, shows traces of deliberate symmetry and rhythmical pattern and dwells upon the supremacy of Christ in the church and in the whole universe. In the course of it the thought extends further than the usual range of New Testament conceptions of Christ and

---

[1] Many of the oldest manuscripts read *on our behalf* instead of **on your behalf**.

opens up a cosmic perspective; and the language draws on the vocabulary both of Jewish and of Greek speculative thinking to an extent otherwise unexampled in Paul. There are many possible explanations for this somewhat surprising language. It may have been already adopted into the worship of the church; it may be a conscious correction of the speculations of the heretics; it may be an adaptation of originally non-Christian concepts and formulas to the needs of Christian theology; it may be the result of Paul's searching (or possibly that of one of his followers, if the letter is not by him) for means to express something with more far-reaching metaphysical implications than he normally ventured upon; or it may be a combination of several of these. But whatever the explanation, the passage represents a significant advance towards formulating the nature and work of Christ in a way that was to be worked out in more detail by the church theologians of the following centuries.

Giving thanks to the Father, who has enabled you to share in the inheritance of the saints. This is the first of God's gracious acts for which thanks are to be offered, and up to this point seems to reflect the language a Jewish Christian might naturally use towards a gentile congregation: because of their faith in Christ they had entered the 'inheritance' formerly promised only to Jews. But the immediately following words widen the perspective. The contrast of darkness and **light** is part of the standard language of religious conversion: these gentile converts had received more than simply integration
13 into the Jewish inheritance, they had moved from the realm of **darkness** into the realm of light, which, for Christians, is experienced as **the kingdom of** God's **beloved Son**. This was more than a mere advance in knowledge or understanding (as possibly the heretics in Colossae would have claimed). The Jewish religious outlook (like that of many religions and philosophies) tended to think of this darkness, not just as ignorance, but as an evil **power**
14 from which the believer might be 'rescued' by means of **redemption, the forgiveness of sins**. These were natural and familiar terms in which to express the 'redemption' effected by Christ.

But now the canvas is enlarged. Christ is to be understood, not only in the context of redemption, but in that of creation; he is Lord, not only of those who are redeemed, but of the whole universe.
15   **He is the image of the invisible God.** This is an unmistakable allusion to Genesis: the first man and the first woman were created 'in the image of God' (Genesis 1.27), and Christ is the perfect example of what all human beings were created to be. But the sentence is also a paradox. If God is 'invisible' (as religious philosophy would normally maintain), how can there be an 'image' of him? Paul's answer is given elsewhere: God can be known, or 'imaged', in his creation. "His eternal power and divine nature, invisible though they are, have been understood and seen through the things he has made" (Romans 1.20). And if this so-called 'natural theology' is to be brought into harmony with the special revelation of God which comes through faith in Christ, it

follows that Christ himself, if he is indeed God's 'image', must stand behind the created universe, either (like the figure of Wisdom in Jewish writings) because he is conceived of as having assisted at the moment of creation, or else (like the divine rational principle believed by Stoic philosophers to underlie the physical world) because he is the key to understanding the universe – and either or both of these lines of thought are suggested here by

16 the phrases **in him . . . through him and for him**. All of which is of more

15 than theoretical importance. It makes Christ the **firstborn** (which means with absolute primacy, not just in time, but in rank and dignity), superior to **all creation**, and in particular to those beings which in popular belief – and indeed in some philosophical systems – occupied a sphere far above the human race (though inferior to God), and from which humans must expect

16 protection by any true saviour – **thrones or dominions or rulers or powers.** (On these beings see above on Ephesians 6.12.)

It is a little surprising, amid these tremendous conceptions, to find the

18 interest suddenly focused upon that comparatively small entity, **the church**; indeed, some have thought that this is an indication of an author other than Paul introducing what could be called a Pauline idea, that of the church as Christ's 'body'. But when Paul uses this image in 1 Corinthians 12, he does so to express the unity of the church's individual members despite the different functions which they perform within the single Christ-filled organism. Here the same metaphor is used, but for a quite different purpose: Christ does not so much fill the body as preside over it, like a **head** presiding over a physical body. He has achieved this supremacy through the resurrection: having been the **firstborn from the dead** he is now the head of that community, the church, to which the same resurrection is promised and by which it is already, in a sense, experienced. But although this reference to the church may seem something of an intrusion into an account of the cosmic stature of Christ, it has wider implications which may earn it its place here. Death, in Paul's thought, is sometimes personified as a cosmic power (1 Corinthians 15.26); and Christ's victory over death in the resurrection is therefore also of cosmic significance. For the universe, despite its origin in the act of a single creator, is now a place of strife and alienation, not only on a human level, but also on the level of those superhuman powers already mentioned which exert their influence on human beings and are in rebellion against God; and so the bold,

19 even paradoxical, conception can be advanced that he in whom **all the fullness of God was pleased to dwell**, and who underlies and presides over the entire created universe, has also, through his sacrificial death, been an instrument of reconciliation between God and the warring elements in creation, so liberating humankind (through the church) from their baneful influence.

The highly wrought poetical style of the thanksgiving now gives place to

21 more personal prose addressed to the reader or hearer. **And you who were once estranged.** The Colossians themselves (though the language might be applied to all who have been converted to faith in Christ) had been objects

of the same great act of reconciliation. They (like all non-Jews in Jewish eyes, like all humankind in Paul's eyes) were formerly **hostile in mind,** part of the cosmic rebellion against God; and the reconciliation effected by Christ, even if it was on a cosmic scale, had the immediate consequence for them that at the imminent judgment, instead of being inevitably condemned for their

22 evil deeds, they would now, by virtue of Christ's physical self-sacrifice (**in his fleshly body**) be 'presented' before God as sharers in the innocence and

23 perfection of the divine victim himself. **Provided that** – and, as usual after any reference to the judgment, the necessary warning is given (see above on Romans 13.12) – **you continue securely established and steadfast in the faith.** The epoch-making event recorded in **the gospel** may have a cosmic dimension; but it is equally crucial for the life and conduct of the Christian church, just as it has been for Paul, its **servant.**

The thanksgiving, with its recital of the gracious acts of God, has touched on immense concepts which nevertheless are of crucial significance to the church. Now a transition is made to more personal matters. The world-wide growth of the church has not been achieved without effort and pain; and Paul, as a principal agent of this growth, has borne a heavy share of it. But he does not for one moment describe this as just the inevitable down-side of the Christian vocation. On the contrary, a Christian's sufferings may have profound significance and value. What the church endures may be described

24 as **Christ's afflictions,** as if the suffering of Christ is continued in his 'body', the church; and indeed, there is necessarily more of this to come, there is as it were a quota of suffering that must be 'completed' before the end and which can be accepted with **rejoicing,** given that it is **for the sake of . . . the church,** enabling the church to be truly Christ's **body.** In this sense it can be said that there is still something **lacking in Christ's afflictions**: like a vessel not yet full, more has to be poured in before all is 'complete'.

Apart from all this, Paul's task, assigned to him by God (for the divine

25 origin of his **commission** is one of the things Paul is most certain of) can be

26 expressed thus: to make known **the mystery.** The Greek word is *mystērion,* and to a Greek reader it conveyed a specific meaning. In the so-called 'mystery religions' the things of God were indeed a 'mystery', a secret open only to those who had undergone certain rites of initiation and could attain to esoteric knowledge of the divine. Such a 'mystery' was by definition never to be divulged; it was a secret accessible only to the initiated (and Paul may be

28 borrowing this language when he uses the almost technical term 'mature' in verse 28 – see above on Philippians 3.8–16). But knowledge of the God of Israel was never 'secret' in this sense. He revealed himself in a multitude of ways, and if people failed to respond, it was not because of their lack of sophisticated religious knowledge but because of their blindness or their hardness of heart. When, therefore, towards the end of the Old Testament period (in the book of Daniel), the word *mystērion* was taken into the religious vocabulary it acquired a quite different meaning. There were indeed things to

do with God that were 'secret', but these were not attributes of his nature that were known only to the initiated: they were stages in his purposes for the world that had not yet been revealed. An inspired visionary might occasionally be given a glimpse of them; but in principle they remained 'secret' until such time as it would be God's pleasure to disclose them. They were something **hidden throughout the ages and generations**; but unlike the Greek idea of a *mystērion* they were not intended always to remain hidden from all save a few initiates. They were now – and this is the gospel – disclosed to God's people, **the saints**. And the particular aspect of this 'secret' which is stressed here is that God's purposes (against all expectation from the Jewish point of view) were working themselves out among the Gentiles, and that even of a non-Jewish congregation such as the church at Colossae it could be

27 said that they were the place where it was possible to see the **glory of this mystery**.

2.2 Thus Paul's prayer for the Colossians comes to this: that they **may have the knowledge of God's mystery, that is, Christ himself**; if they know Christ they need have no ambition to explore other avenues of knowledge besides, for in

3 him **are hidden all the treasures of wisdom and knowledge**. This needed to

4 be said; for clearly the Colossian church was in danger of being deceived **with plausible arguments**. What these arguments were we shall have to infer as best we can from the paragraphs which follow, where Paul advances counter-arguments. Meanwhile Paul assures the church at Colossae, and the nearby

1 church at **Laodicea**, of his lively concern for their welfare. If the local agitators had been suggesting that Paul's teaching could be disregarded because it came from a man who had no real connection with the churches concerned, Paul could reply that even if he had never been able to see them face to face he

5 was close to them in another way: **I am with you in spirit**.

Certain indications of what these rival teachers were saying can be gleaned

8 from the following section. That it could be called **philosophy and empty deceit** does not tell us much: these words may be simply counter-propaganda; but that it was **according to human tradition** made it quite different from Christianity, for which the 'tradition' went back to Christ himself, the Son of God, who was also the key to understanding the word of God in the scriptures. What was this 'human tradition'? It is identified with **the elemental spirits of the universe**. Whatever the precise meaning of this phrase (see above on Galatians 4.3), it clearly belonged to the vocabulary of a speculative type of religion far removed from Christianity; and it is a reasonable guess that the opponents, even if they did interpret scripture in the light of the coming of Christ, nevertheless used their interpretation as material for constructing a system in which Christ held only a secondary place. Hence Paul replies by recapitulating the great affirmations of the prayer of thanksgiving in chapter 1.

9 **In him the whole fullness of deity dwells bodily**. The word *bodily* (derived from *sōma*) may have a range of meanings, from 'physically' to 'in reality'; but whatever the precise sense of it here the intention of the phrase is clear:

there is nothing in heaven or on earth with a power or an importance equal
8 with Christ. Any true 'tradition' must therefore be **according to Christ.**
11 **In him also you were circumcised.** Why this sudden mention of
circumcision? It is possible that the opponents had taken over another slogan of Jewish anti-Christian propaganda: 'You have not been circumcised,
therefore you do not belong to God's people.' But the writer may also have
had another reason to introduce circumcision as an image. For a gentile
proselyte entering Judaism, circumcision was a decisive moment, marking
a distinct change in life-style and allegiance. Christian baptism was this and
more: being **spiritual** (literally *made without hands*, like the new 'temple' that
was the church), it was of far more significance than the physical rite, and
involved a new religious experience and a moral renewal. Paul can apparently
take for granted the interpretation of baptism which we read in Romans 6:
it was a 'putting off' of the old nature (**the body of the flesh**), a 'burying'
with Christ in his death and a 'raising' to new life with the risen Christ. It
13 also spelled the forgiveness of **all our trespasses**; and in a brilliant metaphor
Paul relates all this to the cross. The essence of sin – **our trespasses** – is the
failure to fulfil our obligation, our 'debt', to God. Debts are recorded in some
14 kind of bill or document which imply **legal demands** for repayment. But
the cross was the place where God had effectively erased the obligation by
nailing up, and so cancelling, the evidence. Not only this: the cross was also
the instrument of that victorious act of reconciliation already alluded to in
the previous chapter, by which the cosmic powers were brought into subjection. In another vivid image,[2] Paul imagines them as captives following
some Roman general who, having returned to Rome after victories abroad,
15 would display them as a **public example** in his triumphal procession.
   What had these two tendencies, one towards religious and philosophical
speculation, the other towards Jewish observances, to do with each other?
On the face of it, very little. But almost at once the same combination occurs
16 again. **Do not let anyone condemn you in matters of food and drink or
of observing festivals, new moons, or sabbaths.** Evidently the Colossian
Christians were being molested by people who insisted on the observance
of Jewish festivals and food laws (including abstention from **drink**: a few
strict Jewish groups did practise abstinence) – things which were at most a
17 preparation for and foretaste (**a shadow** compared with the reality) of **what
is to come,** whereas for Christians the reality of the new age was already
experienced as belonging **to Christ.** Yet in the very next sentence we hear of
18 people who insist on **self-abasement and worship of angels, dwelling on
visions.** These people could hardly have been practitioners of an orthodox
Judaism. Religious observances were not usually thought of as a kind of **self-
abasement,** nor was **angel-worship** encouraged; and **visions** were routinely

---

[2] Unfortunately the Greek of verse 15 is obscure and ambiguous, and we cannot be sure
of the details of this image.

suspect, particularly if they made the visionary **puffed up** as a result of what might, after all, be no more than **a human way of thinking**. None of these could have any place in the Christian community in its organic relationship

19 with Christ, who is **the head** of the body. But neither would they normally be present in the Jewish community. Again, in the very next verse, Paul refers

20 for the second time to the pagan and speculative concept of **the elemental spirits of the universe**, and then goes on immediately to talk about orthodox rules of ritual purity ('tasting' is clearly to do with ritually unclean foods, 'handling' and 'touching' with ritual uncleanness contracted from contact with 'unclean' objects and persons). Since, three times over, the language of Jewish observances and the language of speculative religion are brought so closely together, we have to conclude that the opponents were people who were interested in both. How could this have been so? It is time to draw together the scattered clues bearing on their identity and beliefs.

It is evident, in the first place, that they were intellectuals. Paul has to warn the Colossians against their "philosophy and empty deceit" (2.8). The objects of their speculations were such things as "the elemental spirits of the universe", and they attached importance to the power of supernatural beings. To answer them, Paul had to insist again and again on the supremacy of Christ in the universe, his victory over cosmic powers and his central position in the whole pattern of creation. The opponents were clearly much preoccupied with those powers and influences, which were widely believed to inhabit the regions between heaven and earth and to exercise a baneful influence over the lives and destinies of human beings; and in that hierarchy of being and power it appears that they assigned only a subordinate place to Christ.

We know what this kind of speculation led to from the systems of the so-called 'gnostic' thinkers, who arranged all these beings, along with a series of philosophical abstractions, in a kind of ascending hierarchy, and accounted for the origin of this hierarchy by means of an elaborate mythology. Christ and the Creator usually held a place in the hierarchy, but not necessarily the highest place. Salvation was held to consist in an ascending scale of knowledge (*gnōsis*) by which the soul could be released from subjection to the forces operative at the lower end of the hierarchy and rise to the freedom of the superior beings.

Our written evidence for the existence of speculative systems of this kind is all at least a century later than the writing of this letter. How much of it had already developed by Paul's time we do not know; but that the speculations of his opponents ran on somewhat similar lines is in itself quite likely. And if it is asked where such thinkers found the materials for their speculative and mythological theories, the answer is (of course): all over the place – in science, in astrology, in philosophy, in existing religious beliefs. They were doubtless also interested in the Jewish scriptures, which furnished them with many persons and events which could be incorporated in their mythology.

How did they get to know these scriptures? Only by hearing them read in the synagogue. And they could hear them in the synagogue only if they were either Jews themselves or else Gentiles whom the Jews welcomed into the synagogue in return for observing certain Jewish ordinances such as those relating to sabbaths, festivals and food laws. This, apart from any discipline they may have gone in for themselves to do with abstinence or 'self-abasement', would explain why they sought to interest the gentile Christians of Colossae in the observance of **festivals, new moons, or sabbaths.**

16

If this is correct, it is possible to gain a clearer picture of the trouble-makers at Colossae and to understand why Paul had to warn the Colossians not only against this form of speculative religion but also against being persuaded to adopt Jewish observances. His opponents, perhaps taking advantage of his failure to visit Colossae and alleging that he was uninterested in the churches of that area, had been trying to use the gospel of Jesus Christ as just one, and not even the most important, element in a larger speculative system of their own, and had also perhaps been encouraging the Christians to adopt the ascetic practices which went with it. At the same time they had been putting pressure on them to conform with the demands of the Jewish law to the extent of being admitted to the synagogue regularly, so that they could acquire for themselves a deeper knowledge of the scriptures and of traditional Jewish interpretations of it. The mistake here (Paul replies) is twofold. First: such people, **puffed up without cause by a human way of thinking,**[3] are **not holding fast to the head.** Paul's conception of the church as Christ's 'body' is rich in applications. In 1 Corinthians 12 it is used to explain how a variety of people with a variety of gifts can constitute a harmonious and unified society; in 1.18 above it is brought in to explain the relationship of the Christian community to him who is also supreme over all created things; and here it suggests that belonging to the church, as to a living and growing organism directed by its 'head', is an actual source of power and knowledge, making superfluous all the speculations of rival religious thinkers.

18
19

The second mistake is that of attaching any importance to observances such as those to do with ritual cleanness. The appeal here may possibly be to a saying of Jesus: "Do you not see that whatever goes into a person from outside cannot defile, since it enters, not the heart but the stomach, and goes out into the sewer?"; on which Mark comments, "Thus he declared all foods clean" (Mark 7.18–19). The words used here are different; but the phrase **things that perish with use** makes the same point, and the verse of Isaiah (29.13, following the Greek version of the Septuagint), which is echoed in the words **simply human commands and teaching,** is also quoted in the same context in Mark (7.8). At any rate, Paul seems[4] to be rejecting these

22

---

[3] Literally *by the mind of his flesh.*

[4] The Greek of verse 23 is extremely obscure, and no translation can be relied on to convey Paul's meaning.

ordinances for much the same reason as Jesus does. He admits that such practices may have a certain spurious air of usefulness. But in reality they are
23 **of no value in checking self-indulgence.**

The new life in Christ

Paul now moves away from the abstruse topics into which his opponents have drawn him and allows the rest of the letter to take the form of a sermon on moral behaviour. The link with what goes before is baptism (a "spiritual
3.3, 1 circumcision", 2.11). In baptism Christians have **died** and have been **raised**
9 to life **with Christ**; they have **stripped off** – the same Greek word as is translated *put off* in 2.11: almost a technical expression for the consequences of
10 baptism – **the old self with its practices and have clothed yourselves with the new self** – another almost technical term: after baptism the candidate put on a new white robe. This moment in their lives (as Paul is careful to insist when he gives the matter full treatment in Romans 6) lays moral duties on them. In view of ordinary human weakness (and plenty of this lies below the surface of these paragraphs), this is something to which Christian preachers have to return again and again.

1   **Seek the things that are above.** This is standard religious language: there is a 'higher' and a 'lower' world, and human beings are free to choose between them. Speculative religion tended to think in terms of an ascending scale of *knowledge*, with little direct consequence for moral behaviour. But the implication of being **where Christ is** is that not just intellectual understanding but moral conduct is renewed. Moreover the Jewish and Christian, as opposed to the pagan, way of thinking of reality was not as a realm *spatially* 'above' so much as one *temporally* future: it was 'the age to come'. But, for Christians, this future age had already dawned, they already had access to **the things that are above**, though these were not yet fully present and visible. Hence
3 the life they had already entered through baptism was still **hidden.** Its full
4 manifestation must await the time when Christ **is revealed.**
5   The opposite of all that is 'above' is **earthly**; and some kinds of behaviour so obviously belong to 'the earth' that there is no need to explain why they
6, 5 may attract **the wrath of God.** They are to be **put to death** as part of the 'dying' which goes with baptism. The lists of virtues and vices which appear in the New Testament letters are usually fairly conventional, and the fact that here they are in groups of five is perhaps a further sign that the lists were already stereotyped. Yet there is also a distinctively Christian ring. In Christ,
10 the **image** of the **creator** takes on a new meaning of human solidarity; for baptism not only brings moral regeneration but also (as the great argument
11 in Galatians 3 labours to prove) breaks down the old divisions of race (**Greek and Jew, circumcised and uncircumcised**), of education (**barbarian** means without Greek culture, **Scythian** is a byword for the totally illiterate) and of social rank (**slave and free**). Moreover there is a new motive for mutual

13, 15, 16   forgiving: **the Lord has forgiven** *us*![5] **Love, peace, wisdom, gratitude** – these are to be the marks of the new life lived out in the Christian community, not
17   just in its worship, but in **everything**.

18–4.1   **Wives . . . husbands . . . children . . . fathers . . . slaves . . . masters.** This way of setting out moral standards and duties was quite conventional for moral teachers and philosophers (see below, p. 740). Christian writers made use of it, sometimes simply endorsing the received wisdom (though with a Chris-
3.18   tian motivation: **in the Lord**), sometimes introducing specifically Christian teaching into the list. In Ephesians (5.22–33) the section on husbands and wives is elaborated to expound a new conception of that relationship; here, as in 1 Peter 3, it is the relationship of slaves and masters which is placed in a distinctively Christian light. Christian slaves (evidently there were some)
24   **serve** – literally, *are slaves to* – **the Lord Jesus Christ**; and the implications of this are developed more fully in 1 Corinthians 7.21–4. Here, the fact that the same Greek word can stand for both *Lord* and *master* sharpens the point that, since both have a 'master' in heaven who is also 'the Lord', neither can take their position as a pretext for wrongdoing of any kind.

Christian conduct

4.3   In the pagan world, to **declare the mystery** would be an oxymoron: 'myster-ies', by definition, were known only to the initiated and were *not* to be revealed to anyone. But in Paul's culture the 'mystery' was the purpose of God which it was the particular privilege of the Christian to understand and experience and which it was Paul's task to make known – even **in prison** (how he might do so is described in Philippians 1.12–18). But not only Paul's. All Christians shared the same responsibility, which demanded 'wisdom' in their approach
5   **toward outsiders**, an alertness to make the most of every opportunity (**of**
6   **the time**), and a graciousness, even seasoned with wit (**salt**), in response to serious questioning.

Personal greetings

7   Of the people with whom Paul was in touch while in prison, two, **Tychicus**
10   and **Aristarchus**, were his companions on his last journey from Greece to
9   Palestine (Acts 20.4). Another, **Onesimus**, was a slave and is the subject of
10   the letter to Philemon. **Mark** appears to have been reconciled with Paul after
11   the dispute recorded in Acts 15.37–9. **Jesus who is called Justus** is otherwise unknown: like Paul (Saul) he had both a Jewish name (Jesus) and a Roman
12   name (Justus). **Epaphras** has already been mentioned (1.7) He seems to have been the first to bring the gospel to Colossae and to have had a relationship

---

[5] **The Lord** may refer to God forgiving us through Christ, or possibly (as some manuscripts make explicit) to Christ himself forgiving.

with the church there (and with the neighbouring churches of Laodicea and Hierapolis) similar to that of Paul with the churches he had founded

14 himself. **Luke, the beloved physician**, is the Luke to whom the third gospel

15 and Acts are traditionally ascribed. **Demas** is otherwise unknown. **Nympha** is a Greek name for a woman, but in some of its forms (such as the one used here) it is indistinguishable from the masculine name *Nymphas*, and there is some uncertainty in the manuscripts about this person's sex. She (or he) was evidently well-to-do and had a house large enough to accommodate the meetings of the congregation. The following sentence indicates that some of

17 Paul's letters were intended to be read in more than one church. **Archippus** was a common name, and we know nothing about this person, or about the **task** entrusted to him.

18 On greetings in Paul's **own hand**, see above on Galatians 6.11.

THESSALONIANS

Thessalonica was the capital of the Roman province of Macedonia. It stood, like Philippi, on the Via Egnatia, the great road across northern Greece which linked Rome with the east; and its population, though predominantly Greek, included a Jewish community (Acts 17.1).

Since much of the letter is inspired by Paul's personal recollections of his visit to Thessalonica, it is possible to reconstruct most of the circumstances from his own words. The account in Acts 17 adds little to our knowledge, and is not always consistent with what Paul says himself; but it does help us to decide the place and (within certain limits) the date of writing. According to

1.1 Acts, the only time when **Paul, Silvanus, and Timothy** were all together was during Paul's eighteen-month stay in Corinth (Acts 18.5); and this period, since it followed soon after Paul's visit to Thessalonica, seems the most appropriate one for the writing of a letter that is full of vivid reminiscences. If this is correct, and if this letter was written while Paul was in Corinth (say in the year 50 or 51), then it has some claim to being the earliest of Paul's surviving letters, indeed the earliest complete writing in the New Testament.

Thanksgiving and prayer

The first three chapters conform, in effect, with the usual form of opening and consist of thanksgiving leading into prayer; but the sequence is broken by a long section of personal reminiscence and self-vindication, and the prayer itself is not reached until 3.11.

2 **We always give thanks to God for all of you** – and for two things in particular: first, the evident fruits of Paul's preaching among the Thessalonians, who had already exhibited the characteristic Christian triad of

3 **faith, hope** and **love** (1 Corinthians 13.13; Colossians 1.4–5). Such results proved that the preaching was not just an exhibition of one individual's

5 power of persuasion **in word**, but was **in power and in the Holy Spirit**; and to have produced them the preachers must have had more than human resources: **you know what kind of persons we proved to be among you for your sake**. And this example was contagious: Paul's second reason for giving

6 thanks was the Thessalonians' subsequent loyalty to their new faith **in spite of persecution** (of which we get an idea in Acts 17.5), which was worthy of Paul himself – or rather, as he hastens to add, worthy **of the Lord**. This had already achieved widespread fame. For as a mainly gentile community they had taken the decisive step (as seen from the Jewish-Christian point of

9 view) of having **turned to God from idols**; and in the phrases which follow we may be reading a standard summary of the essentials of their new faith.

To continue his missionary work after the violent end to his stay in Philippi (Acts 16), Paul had travelled on to Thessalonica (17.1–4). This information

2.1 from Acts is confirmed by Paul's own words: **our coming to you was not in vain . . . though we had already suffered and been shamefully mistreated at Philippi**. He goes on to remind the Thessalonians of the conditions under

2 which he had worked among them – **in spite of great opposition**. The language indeed becomes so pointed that we may suspect he was anxious to scotch some insinuation that had come to his ears about his conduct at Thessalonica; or it may just be that he is contrasting his own methods with those of travelling philosophical teachers who were notoriously suspect of

3 working from **impure motives**. At any rate, he makes it clear that at Thessalonica he had adhered strictly to his normal practice of being financially independent of the churches to which he brought the gospel, either by work-

9 ing for his living (**we worked night and day, so that we might not burden any of you**), or else by securing contributions from existing churches. But it seems that this policy, by comparison with that of the other apostles, tended to arouse criticism. It was suggested on more than one occasion that Paul must be lacking in confidence and authority if he did not claim the financial support due to him as an apostle. Paul was evidently sensitive on this subject and devoted a surprising amount of space to it in his letters (see especially 2 Corinthians 11.7–11). It may have been the same anxiety which made him

7 say here, **we might have made demands as apostles of Christ**. In this case he defends his practice on the grounds of the particularly intimate relationship –

11 that of **nurse** or of **father** towards children – that had grown up between himself and the Thessalonians and to which the whole tone of the letter bears witness.

Paul's third reason for thanksgiving lay in the results of his preaching,

13 which they had accepted **not as a human word but as what it really is, God's word**. In consequence of this, the Thessalonian church had already received its share of persecution. There is some discrepancy here with the account in Acts (17.5–9), where it is stated that the opposition came from the Jewish colony in Thessalonica. Possibly this had been so in the very early stages, or possibly the writer of Acts assumed that events in Thessalonica had conformed with the pattern which he regarded as characteristic for the foundation of Paul's churches – immediate opposition from the Jewish community followed by a rapid spread of the gospel among gentile converts. However this may be, the opposition which the Thessalonians had to meet

14 when this letter was written was from their **own compatriots**, who were following the example of the persecution of Christians set by the Jews in Palestine. Here Paul uses remarkably strong language: not only does he bor-

15 row terms that were used in gentile anti-Semitic propaganda (**they displease God and oppose everyone**), but he makes the Jews entirely responsible for the death of Jesus (whatever part the Romans may have had in it) and even

of **the prophets.**[1] His prophetic denunciation of them, involving their total[2] condemnation, is in marked contrast to his later more reflective treatment of the matter in Romans 9–11.

According to Acts, Paul was forced to leave Thessalonica by night and take refuge in the neighbouring city of Beroea. From there he went first to Athens and then to Corinth, while Timothy and Silvanus (Silas) remained behind at Beroea until they received Paul's command to join him in Corinth (17.15; 18.5). Paul's own evidence shows this to be not quite accurate. Timothy did not stay in Beroea but accompanied Paul to Athens; but such was Paul's

3.1 anxiety that by this time he **could bear it no longer.** He had been forced to leave Thessalonica at a few hours' notice. He had had no news about the church there, how far it had taken root and withstood the troubles it was in when he left. He had not been able to take any of the opportunities which

2.18 presented themselves to return (**Satan blocked our way** could mean anything from missing a boat to encountering malicious obstruction), and had finally sent Timothy instead. Moreover, his anxiety was not just that of anyone for separated friends: it had a more serious aspect, in that Paul knew himself to be accountable to God for the churches he had founded, and any neglect on his

19 part would be severely judged before the Lord **at his coming.** The good news which Timothy brought on his return caused him correspondingly intense joy and prompted him to write the present letter.

3.11 After this long digression the prayer for the church is at last resumed and
13 rounded off with another glance at the future – **the coming of our Lord Jesus.** This 'coming' would be a moment of judgment. In the Old Testament (as in Zechariah 14.5, to which this verse doubtless alludes) God was sometimes thought of as coming to pass judgment, not alone, but in company with beings who were already (as it were) on the right side of judgment and so could take part in the judging. Who these beings were – whether righteous men and women or supernatural spirits – remained an open question among interpreters. But the ideas fitted well into the Christian expectation of the Lord Jesus' coming **with all his saints** – for Christians had been promised a place on the tribunal at the last judgment (1 Corinthians 6.3).

The Christian life-style

4.1 **Finally** – though this turns out not to be the end, but leads on to other matters – Paul devotes a paragraph to teaching he has already given on how

---

[1] It is not stated in the Old Testament that any of the prophets were killed; but legends had been growing up of their violent deaths at the hands of their fellow countrymen. Alternatively the word may refer to *Christian* 'prophets', some of whom may already have been martyred.

[2] The Greek phrase (*eis telos*) can also mean 'utterly' or 'finally'.

Christians **ought to live**. It is clear from the letters of the New Testament that a tradition of this moral teaching was developed in the early years in order to clarify and where necessary supplement the ethical demands of Jesus. This was particularly necessary for gentile Christians in view of the traditional Jewish prejudice that the Gentiles, having no 'law' in the Jewish sense, had nothing to prevent them from leading immoral lives. Christians had to show that they lived by a moral standard at least as exacting as that of the Jews. One of the commonest charges against gentile morals was in the area of sexual

3 relationships; and this Paul takes up here, warning the church to **abstain**
5 **from fornication** and not to yield to **lustful passion, like the Gentiles who do not know God** (this last phrase is scriptural, as in Psalm 79.6; Jeremiah 10.25). The reason he gives here (though there were many others he might
3 have given, see 1 Corinthians 7) is that the **sanctification** attributed to and
4 demanded of Christians implied mastery over their **own body**.[3] Impurity has
6 of course also social consequences which would be intolerable in a Christian
8 community;[4] but the real objection is not social but religious: **whoever rejects this rejects not human authority but God**.

Another danger about which Paul has to sound a warning is one which seems to have arisen from the earnest expectation held by Christians at this time of an early return of Christ. More will be said about this in the following paragraphs. Meanwhile the danger referred to is that of reacting to the prospect of imminent cosmic change by giving up normal work and social obligations on the grounds that they belonged to a world order that was passing away. There are signs that the church had a number of members

11 who became **dependent** on others in this way. Paul's advice is **to mind your own affairs, and to work with your hands**.

The coming of the Lord

The question now to be discussed is not the general and perennial one of
13 what happens to **those who have died**, but a particular and urgent one precipitated by the unexpected death of some members of the church at Thessalonica. The first generation of Christians seems to have believed that the Lord's coming would take place in their lifetime and that they would then be given a place beside him in judging the world – this belief has already been expressed several times in the letter. The premature death of some of their number was not allowed for in this scheme. When it happened, it could

---

[3] The word translated **body** means literally *vessel* or *utensil*. This may be an idiomatic way of talking about the human body as opposed to the 'soul' which it 'contains'; but it is also possible that the phrase is used idiomatically to mean 'sexual organ' or even possibly 'wife' (as in the NRSV footnote).

[4] There is doubt about the meaning of verse 6. The Greek words translated **in this matter** could also mean any matter in dispute, or even a sexual affair.

sometimes be explained as the result of some sin or blasphemy which the dead person had committed – this explanation was apparently accepted in the church at Corinth (1 Corinthians 11.30). But at Thessalonica no such explanation was to hand, and the Thessalonians must have conveyed to Paul their unhappy question: could they be sure that those of the faithful who had already died would still share their own glorious destiny? In reply, Paul gives a rare account of his beliefs about the future in store for Christians.

His answer is, first, quite general: they should not **grieve as others do who have no hope**. This, of course, was an overstatement. The majority of Jews probably believed in ultimate resurrection from the dead; and a number of Greek religious and philosophical schools taught some kind of existence after death. But it was certainly true – as the gravestones of the period bear eloquent witness – that, in any Greco-Roman city such as Thessalonica, most ordinary people shared the traditional view of a dark and formless underworld in which the dead enjoyed at best a bleak and shadowy existence; and very few would have had any expectation of an afterlife comparable in intensity with that of the Christians. By contrast, the Christian faith was centred on the resurrection of Jesus, as a result of which those who believed in him were

14 assured of a similar resurrection to new life. **We believe that Jesus died and rose again . . . God will bring with him those who have died**. It followed, not from any particular scheme of the last things, but from the most fundamental doctrine of Christianity – Christ's resurrection – that all Christians who had died would themselves rise to a new and glorious life with him.

But although this might certainly be agreed in principle, it did not answer the anxious personal questions of those who expected to be alive when the Lord came but had seen others die in the meantime. The majority of Chris-

15 tians (it was then believed) would remain alive **until the coming of the Lord**. What about those who had prematurely died? How would they be able to take their rightful places in the final drama?

By way of answer, Paul claims to be able to refer to **the word of the Lord** – possibly the promise which Jesus was understood to have made that some of his followers would certainly be still alive when the kingdom of God came "with power" (Mark 9.1). Paul's imagining of this final moment of history has

16 three elements: first, the conventional motifs of **archangel's call** and **God's trumpet**, which routinely appear in Jewish apocalyptic writing; secondly, the ceremonial of the arrival (the *parousia*) of a king or emperor outside a city: he would have his own entourage of courtiers but would be met by distinguished representatives of the place, who would come forward to greet him – similarly the 'coming' of the Lord could be imagined as taking place

17 a certain distance from the earth, with people rising up to meet him **in the air**. Thirdly, the experience would be like that of a heavenly vision: the Greek word for **caught up** was regularly used for what we would now call mystical experiences. But apart from these elaborations, the basic scheme was one that had certainly been endorsed by Jesus: the Lord would shortly come to

judge the whole world, and Christians, instead of being among the multitude who were to be judged, would take their places as a kind of tribunal at the side of the judge. It would make no difference that some had already died. This was how those words of prophecy, already alluded to in 3.13, were to be fulfilled: "Then the LORD my God will come, and *all* the holy ones with him" (Zechariah 14.5).

5.1   **Now concerning the times.** These Christians expected the end to come soon, so it is not surprising that there should have been speculation about exactly when it would happen. Such speculation went on even among the Jews, though it was discouraged by responsible thinkers. Jesus, too, recognized the danger of trying to pin it down in time or place (Luke 17.20–21). It was true that the day might be heralded by certain signs and portents; but not in the sense that anyone could use them to calculate the date and make plans accordingly. On the contrary, it would be sudden. It would come, as they might remember Jesus had said himself (which is what Paul may mean

2 by a phrase which in the Greek has a slightly technical sound, **you yourselves know very well**) – it would **come like a thief in the night** (Matthew 24.42–

3 3); and Paul adds two other indications of its suddenness: first, **when they say, "There is peace and security"** (which was the propaganda of the Roman empire), **then sudden destruction will come upon them**; and secondly it will be **as labor pains come upon a pregnant woman.** And the proper response to this threatened suddenness is expressed, as so often, in terms of light, vigilance and sobriety, with a brief allusion to the metaphor of heavenly armour which is so brilliantly developed in the last chapter of Ephesians.

Final advice

Among the miscellaneous injunctions with which, as so often, the letter ends, it is notable that Paul, as in 1 Corinthians 16, makes an appeal for proper respect to be paid to the leaders of the church. These leaders are described by two terms which belong together inseparably, if paradoxically, in the concept

12 of Christian ministry: service (**those who labor among you**) and leadership (**have charge of you**). There is also reference to another topic to which Paul had to pay attention in Corinth (and we have seen that this letter may well have been written from Corinth) – the proper management of inspired utterances

20 and **words of prophets** (or *prophecies* by members of the congregation).

26   On the kiss of peace (**a holy kiss**), and on the general character of the ending, see above on Romans 16.16.

THESSALONIANS

The greeting with which this letter begins is almost identical with that of 1 Thessalonians, and gives the impression that the two letters must have been written from the same place and within a short time of each other. And indeed, they are very similar in other respects also – so similar, in fact, that it has often been doubted whether they could originally have been intended for the same congregation, or even whether they could both have been written by the same author; for how, it is said, could anyone have written two letters within a short space of time to the same people and used whole sentences in the second letter which are taken almost verbatim from the first? At the same time there are notable differences between the two letters. The treatment of questions about the "coming of our Lord Jesus Christ" runs on different lines, and in the second letter the tone is somewhat more severe. The problem is to explain both the similarities and the differences.

Various explanations have been proposed. One is that Paul, soon after writing the first letter, received news from Thessalonica which caused him to write off again at once while phrases from the first letter were still running in his mind. Another is that the two letters were originally written to go by the same messenger to two different (though probably neighbouring) congregations. A third is that the second letter was written by an imitator who was anxious to give circulation to a somewhat stricter doctrine of the coming judgment than Paul himself had expressed.

All these explanations are plausible, none is fully convincing. Nor is it impossible to take this letter for what it purports to be, Paul's second letter to the Thessalonians. He could have heard, not long after writing the first letter, about the irresponsible behaviour of some members of the Thessalonian church (3.11), and have deemed it necessary to correct some mistaken ideas which were current about the second coming of Christ (2.1–2); and the fresh news he had received may sufficiently account for the different tone of the second letter. As for the similarities, it is significant that they are concentrated in two contexts: first, in the greetings and prayers, for which a fairly conventional and stereotyped vocabulary was already emerging; and secondly in the section on the necessity (felt by the apostle) to work for a living – a topic to which Paul reverts a number of times in his correspondence and for which he tends to use a standard terminology. These two factors may go some way to explaining how Paul could have written both letters to the same recipients within a short space of time.

The judgment at Christ's coming

The initial section of thanksgiving and prayer has distinct echoes of the first
1.3 letter: the Thessalonians' **faith** and **love** are again singled out (though the
triad is not completed with 'hope'). And again there is a digression before the
prayer is taken up in 1.11; but here the subject is different – not a record of
5 the church's influence and endurance, but a short discourse on **the righteous**
4 **judgment of God,** sparked off by a mention of the **persecutions** to which
the church had been subjected. Traditional language was to hand to describe
the fearsomeness of God's judgment, both in the prophets (compare Isaiah
66.15, "For the L O R D will come in fire . . . to pay back his anger in fury")
and in recent apocalyptic literature. What is striking here is the way in which
the same imagery is applied to Christ, who takes on the role of judge and
administers his justice with unmitigated severity. The view that all who reject
the gospel will inevitably receive such merciless punishment was not often
expressed so starkly either by Paul or by other early Christian writers (though
Matthew's gospel attributes sayings of this kind to Jesus). Its appearance here
may possibly have been prompted by a particularly intense experience of
persecution.

2.1 **As to the coming of our Lord Jesus Christ and our being gathered to-**
gether to him. This doctrine was discussed in much the same terminology in
the first letter and could presumably now be taken as read between Paul and
his correspondents. But it had apparently undergone a new and dangerous
2 interpretation. Some were alleging that **the day of the Lord is already here**.
One can see how the teaching of Paul, and indeed of the church as a whole,
could have given rise to such an interpretation. The 'day' was declared to
be imminent; signs of its coming had already appeared; Christians, under
the influence of the Spirit, were having experiences which could be described
as a foretaste of the age to come. It would not have been difficult to take all
this as a sign that the decisive event – the 'day' – had already happened. A
sudden upsurge of those remarkable experiences of the Spirit which were a
feature of church life at Corinth, or a sensational increase in the membership
of the church, might easily have predisposed some people to interpret some
manifestation of **spirit**, some **word,** or some **letter** purporting to be from
Paul, as evidence that the moment had arrived; then, thinking that the final act
of history had been completed, they might abandon their normal occupations
and wait for God to bring down the curtain on the drama.

Paul's answer is not (as we might have expected) that one only has to
look at the present state of things to see that they bear no resemblance to
the conditions that will prevail in the new age. Instead, he explains that
the 'day' *cannot* have come yet since certain things have got to happen *first*.
He had already given some teaching on these things in the course of his
5 original preaching at Thessalonica (**Do you not remember that I told you**
these things when I was still with you?) – and this is the cause of most

of our difficulties. The language used about such things tends in any case, to be somewhat cryptic; and when, in addition, Paul is not attempting to give any fresh teaching but is merely reminding his hearers of something he has told them before, it is hardly surprising that we have some difficulty in following him.

The background to Paul's exposition is not too hard to reconstruct. The 'day' cannot come without judgment; and one reason the judgment cannot yet come is that it is not yet sufficiently clear on whom the judgment should fall. The rejection or reception of the gospel is one criterion that has been mentioned: those who decisively reject it and persecute the church have already secured their condemnation. But this criterion will not do for everyone: there will be too many borderline cases. If men and women, confronted by the good (whether or not in the form of the gospel), continue to prevaricate or remain simply indifferent, it could be that they have not yet been seriously put to the test. There is not yet any decisive proof of their guilt, in which case they are not ready for judgment. Hence the belief (widely held in Paul's culture) that before the end there would be an intensification of evil, a stepping up of calamities, forcing men and women to show their true nature. In particular – and here a concept is borrowed from popular Jewish mythology – people would be exposed, not just to the challenging truth of

9–10 the gospel, but also to a positive force of deception – **signs, lying wonders, and every kind of wicked deception** – which would lead astray all who were not fully committed to the truth and so would draw a clear line between those who were to be saved and those who would be lost. Only when a series of unprecedented tests of endurance had completed this process would the time be ripe for the final judgment.

So much is fairly clear; but Paul fills out his picture of the future with a more complex mythology, only part of which is familiar from surviving Jewish writings of the time. It was a frequent theme of so-called 'apocalyptic' writers that immediately before the end there would be a final and decisive confrontation between the forces of good and the forces of evil, in which evil would be represented by a single supernatural individual and would create, in that embodiment, an unprecedented degree of disorder and suffering.

3 This is the context of such phrases as **the rebellion, the lawless one, the one destined for destruction**. In the year 40 CE the emperor Caligula threatened to set up a statue of himself in the holiest part of the temple in Jerusalem, and this may have given fresh actuality to the old prophecy (Ezekiel 28.2; Daniel

4 11.36) that this personification of wickedness would even take **his seat in the temple of God, declaring himself to be God**. There are also faint traces in the Old Testament (Job 7.12; Amos 9.3) of an ancient myth (not uncommon in other middle-eastern religions) that this evil monster had existed since the beginning of the world and was held in prison by some force which was

6 **restraining** him until **his time comes**; and this idea reappears elsewhere in the New Testament (Revelation 20.2). But even if this myth was in Paul's

mind (which is far from certain), it does not take us very far, for we are still
7 left without any clue to the meaning of the cryptic expression, **the one who now restrains it**. Since early centuries it has been suggested that Paul was referring to the rule of law maintained by the Roman empire, which prevented
8 the incursion of **the lawless one**. But Paul is deliberately expressing himself in coded language which only the Thessalonians could have understood. Without the explanation he had given them we shall never know for certain what he meant.

The thanksgiving and prayer which follow are strongly reminiscent of the
13 previous letter (especially 1 Thessalonians 3.11–13). The phrase **chose you as the first fruits for salvation** places the Thessalonians in the first phase of the great harvest of the 'saved' that was to come; but some early manuscripts (see the NRSV footnote) give **chose you** *from the beginning* **for salvation**, a concept that occurs in Ephesians (see above on Ephesians 1.4).

Warning against idleness

3.1 **Finally, brothers and sisters.** We expect the warm exhortation which follows to be the end of the letter; but there is another matter Paul needs to give a
6 warning about: **believers who are living in idleness**. Whether this was the result of the particular misapprehension about the 'day' which was dealt with in chapter 2, or whether it was some people merely taking advantage of the community to indulge their natural laziness, Paul takes the opportunity of
8 appealing once again to the example he himself tried to set. **With toil and labor we worked night and day, so that we might not burden any of you** (a phrase which is almost a cliché in this context: compare 1 Thessalonians 2.9;
9 2 Corinthians 11.9); and his reason for doing so was **not because we do not have that right** – a point on which he was sensitive – **but in order to give you an example to imitate**. To clinch the matter, he presses into service what
10 is likely to have been already a proverb: **Anyone unwilling to work should not eat**.
17 On greetings in Paul's **own hand**, see above on Galatians 6.11. The reference earlier to "a letter, as though from us" (2.2) perhaps explains his anxiety to authenticate his own letters in this way.

THE FIRST LETTER OF PAUL TO
TIMOTHY

The three letters which follow are addressed, not to churches, but to two of Paul's colleagues, Timothy and Titus; but this does not mean that they were originally part of a personal correspondence. On the contrary, Timothy and Titus are addressed, not as friends and partners in Paul's missionary activity, but as men who hold long-term responsibility for their respective churches in Ephesus and Crete, and to whom it is appropriate to send instructions about the correct ordering of church affairs. They are addressed, in fact, in their capacity as established pastors; and these three letters, which are notably similar in tone and presuppose similar conditions in the churches to which they were written, have been known since the eighteenth century as THE PASTORAL EPISTLES.

The letters purport to have been written by Paul and were accepted as genuine by the church from at least the end of the second century. But in recent times their authenticity has been questioned. The language and style can be seen on a first reading to be different from those of the other letters attributed to Paul; the structure and the concerns of the churches addressed seem to reflect a later stage of development than one would expect to find in the period of Paul's main correspondence; and the writer's presentation of the Christian faith has an unexpectedly steady, settled quality. For all these reasons it is widely believed that the letters must have been written by an imitator some decades after Paul's death, with the purpose of adapting the Pauline message to a somewhat different situation in the churches, and of giving the authority of an apostle to a form of church organization which had not yet developed when Paul was alive but of which (it was felt) he would certainly have approved had he lived to see it.

An explanation of the same kind has been suggested for the origin of the letter to the Ephesians (see above, pp. 610–11); but there the problem is simpler. That letter consists, in effect, of a treatise: it is given the form of a letter only by the addition of opening and closing greetings and of a very small amount of personal matter. Here, however, there is a comparative wealth of personal details. If these three letters were not written by Paul himself, the imitator must have been anxious to make his work look as convincing as possible by introducing (either from imagination or from some source now lost to us) fragments of the kind of correspondence Paul might have been expected to exchange with his friends. If this is really what happened, however, it is all the more surprising that these details do not fit easily into the biography of Paul as we can reconstruct it from the other letters and from Acts. To take only the most obvious examples: nothing is known from the New Testament about any journey made by Paul to Crete, or of a winter spent (or intended to be spent) on the Dalmatian coast at Nicopolis (Titus 3.12); there is no period in Paul's missionary work up to his imprisonment in Rome which would have allowed for Timothy to assume long-term responsibility for the church in Ephesus; and the vivid personal touches in 2 Timothy 4 are impossible to reconcile completely with the known events of Paul's life immediately preceding his trial at Rome. If, therefore, the letters are the work of an imitator, this writer must either have invented fresh episodes in the life of Paul without caring to match them with what could be known from existing letters, or else have assembled fragments of real biographical value but without regard for their true sequence, so that the picture as a whole is a different one from that which emerges from the other documents.

These details are, of course, no less of a problem if the letters are genuinely by Paul. The traditional explanation is that Paul must have been released after the imprisonment at Rome which is recorded at the end of Acts, have travelled widely for a few years, and then have been once more imprisoned, tried and put to death. Outside these letters there is virtually no evidence that Paul had such a spell of freedom (though we know from Romans that if he were able to he intended to travel as far as Spain). If the letters are authentic, we have to assume a further chapter in the life of Paul to accommodate the movements they mention – in which case it is possible to argue (as some have done) that the undoubted differences of style and content between these and other letters of Paul are due to the fact that Paul wrote the Pastorals somewhat later in life than the other letters.

From Paul to Timothy

1.1–2 **Paul ... To Timothy.** All the New Testament letters begin with a distinctively Christian elaboration of the basic opening formula, 'From X . . . To Y: Greeting.' A greatly extended example is the beginning of Romans; here it is much shorter, but concentrates on Paul's status and authority as an apostle.

3 **When I was on my way to Macedonia.** The only departure of Paul from Ephesus to Macedonia of which we know anything from other sources is that recorded in Acts 20.1–5. But that Paul then left Timothy in Ephesus is hard to reconcile either with the account in Acts or with Paul's own letters to the Corinthians. Like other such references to travel in the Pastorals, this one is virtually impossible to fit into the known biography of Paul. In any case, it has no bearing on what follows: the danger which Timothy is urged to resist is one which reappears several times in the Pastorals in much the same form, and may have been prevalent in several churches at the

4 time these letters were written. It arose from too much studying of **myths and endless genealogies.** The phrase, though familiar from the polemical language used by philosophers of the time, is not precise enough for us to be able to say precisely what the danger was. It appears from what follows that the trouble-makers, though they probably were not Jews themselves (unlike

those in Crete, Titus 1.10), were interested in the Jewish scriptures, and their 'myths and genealogies' may have been similar to the fantastic mythologies which later speculative thinkers constructed out of Old Testament material (see above on Colossians 2). This was far removed from the disciplined approach to scripture which was implied by **divine training**[1] **that is known by faith**.

In 1 Corinthians 13 Paul describes 'love' in memorable terms as the greatest of all God's gifts, exceeding in value even those spectacular manifestations of the Spirit which had so excited the members of the church in Corinth. Here the analysis is tamer and less original: love is described as if it were the necessary psychological consequence of a certain kind of behaviour and 5 belief. The phrase **a good conscience** is not nearly so frequent in the New Testament as its currency in English would lead one to expect, and it occurs only in the later writings. Indeed the idea was something fairly new in Greek moral thought. 'Conscience' itself, in a fully moral sense, was a concept which appeared only a century or two before the time of Christ, and it was normally used only in a negative sense, as equivalent to the consciousness of having done wrong. Its opposite (the consciousness of *not* having done wrong) and of 'conscience' as a guide to determine the difference, did not play an important part in moral analysis until later centuries, and its emergence in a passage such as this is more likely a relic of the Jewish concern for 'cleanness' from any acts that were regarded as sinful or impure – hence the biblical phrase used here, **a pure heart**.

Above all, faith must be **sincere**. What the erroneous teachers were guilty 7 of was its opposite, hypocrisy. They were **desiring to be teachers of the law**, but had no idea of the law's functions and limitations. It was a matter of debate in antiquity whether laws had the capacity, not just to restrain criminal behaviour, but actually to make people better. For Jewish thinkers this was hardly an issue: the law of Moses clearly presented a moral ideal alongside its detailed provisions, and whole-hearted obedience to it was seen as a way to salvation. But this author seems to be thinking of 'law' in 8 the more limited sense of the criminal code, which is certainly **good**, but hardly a sufficient foundation for the moral behaviour of the Christian. The speculative teachers may have meant more than this by 'law' – possibly they were recommending slavish obedience to Jewish observances, possibly they were devising an elaborate code of their own for which they made great claims. The writer accepts the necessity of basic legal prohibitions. But these can be used only **legitimately** – literally, *according to law*. The conduct of a person of faith must surely have a different orientation.

The possibility of a good conscience, the description of the law as 'good' – these sentiments would have come strangely from the author of the letter

---

[1] The word translated **training** could also mean *plan*, indicating the unified and consistent message of scripture as opposed to mythological speculations.

to the Romans. There are also two phrases in this paragraph which belong
10 especially to the language of the Pastorals. One is **sound teaching**, which
occurs frequently in these letters but in no other New Testament writing.
It was a common enough phrase in the mouths of moral philosophers, but
seems (at least for Paul) a curiously tame way of describing the revolutionary
11 truths of the gospel. The other is **the blessed God**, an unusual expression
in the New Testament but one that was at home in the language of Greek-
17 speaking synagogues (as was **the King of the ages** a few verses below). It is
small details such as these which build up the impression that the Pastorals
stem from a somewhat different cultural and religious milieu from that of
the other letters of Paul.

When Paul refers to his own conversion in other letters, he does so in order
to defend his status as an apostle. Here the intention is more general: Paul's
conversion is put forward for the inspiration and encouragement of others
who were conscious of previous sins and had now entered the church. It did
not matter what outrages they had committed in the past, provided only
that (unlike the persistent heretics who had had their chance of learning the
13 truth) they too realized that they had **acted ignorantly in unbelief**.

15 **The saying is sure and worthy of full acceptance.** This formula occurs at
least three times in the Pastorals, and its function seems to be to alert the
reader to the fact that the writer is citing a standard Christian doctrine. The
only difficulty is that, since Greek manuscripts had nothing corresponding to
quotation marks, it is not always clear which words belong to the quotation
and which to the writer's commentary. Here, however, it is fairly obvious
that the quotation is the single proposition, **Christ Jesus came into the
world to save sinners**. It was presumably a sentence frequently used in the
worship or the teaching of the church; and here it is applied to Paul (**sinners –
of whom I am the foremost**), thereby presenting Paul's experience as a model
16 for all who **would come to believe in him for eternal life**.

We have no other information about the circumstances of Timothy's first
association with Paul, though Acts 13.1–3 may be an example of the kind
18 of **prophecies** meant here, validating the appointment of a church minister
20 with the evident authority of the Holy Spirit. Another of **Hymenaeus**' errors
is mentioned in 2 Timothy 2.17. About **Alexander** we know nothing, unless
he is the coppersmith of 2 Timothy 4.14. 'Turning over **to Satan**' presumably
meant excommunication: Satan still had his power over those outside the
church (see above on 1 Corinthians 5.5).

Prayer and discipline in the church

2.1 **First of all, then.** The first chapter has been in the nature of an introduction;
the writer now turns to his main agenda, which begins with instruction for the
common life and worship of the congregation. There is nothing surprising
2 in the early Christians' having offered prayers for **everyone, for kings and**

all who are in high positions. (The word 'kings' probably covers both the Roman emperor and the vassal kings, such as the Herods, whom the Romans allowed to rule in the eastern territories.) Even though there were moments when the church had cause to regard the Roman administration as an agent of the devil, it was always conscious of the benefits, in the form of a **quiet and peaceable life,** which the power of the empire made possible, and was glad to follow the example of the Jews, who regularly offered prayers (and even, in the temple, sacrifices) for the welfare of the emperor. We happen to possess a prayer[2] which was used by Christians towards the end of the first century and which includes the words, 'Give them, O Lord, health, peace, concord and stability, that they may exercise without offence the rule you have entrusted to them.'

4 Such prayers were not only good in themselves; they helped to combat any tendency to isolation and exclusiveness which all too easily crept into Christianity. God **desires everyone to be saved.** Taken out of context, this statement raises acute difficulties. It is hard to reconcile, both with the observed fact that many people apparently are *not* 'saved', and also with the realization, which occasionally comes to the surface in the New Testament, that some people are, it seems, *not intended* to be 'saved'. But here the purpose is probably not so much to lay down an absolute rule as to answer those who took the view that some classes of people were *a priori* outside the scheme of salvation. The Jews, for example, tended to believe this of most non-Jews, and the kind of speculative thinkers who are alluded to in these letters may have believed it of all who could not qualify for salvation by pursuing the right kind of 'knowledge'. Christians, by contrast, were to think of salvation as in principle available to all; and so there was good reason to pray for **everyone.**

5 **For** – and the point is supported by a sentence which looks like a fragment of an early creed. Concise formulations of faith usually come into existence when there is some heretical tendency abroad which needs to be refuted. Was a particular heresy in mind here? The significant statement seems to be, not just that **there is one God** (which was fundamental to Judaism and Christianity and any other monotheistic religion), but that **there is also one mediator.** Much religious speculation in the first and second centuries CE was concerned with the question of 'mediators' between the supreme, inaccessible God and the earth-bound existence of human beings. Jewish writers might describe Old Testament figures such as Moses or Enoch in this way (there is a striking example in Galatians 3.19); or they might think of supernatural beings such as angels, or of abstractions such as 'wisdom', as fulfilling this function. More speculative thinkers might postulate a whole series of such entities mediating between God and humans. It is against such a background that we should probably understand the significance of the unusual phrase, **one mediator** (whether it was the writer's own or, as suggested, a

---

[2] First Letter of Clement, chapter 61 (written from Rome about 96 CE).

quotation from an existing creed): no 'mediator' must be imagined to exist save Jesus Christ. The rest of the passage uses normal New Testament vocabu-

6 lary. That Christ **gave himself a ransom for all** appears to be an echo of Mark 10.45. **This was attested at the right time** is the translators' interpretation of a puzzling Greek phrase which means literally *the testimony in their own times.*

8 We are now given a few glimpses of the customs of the early church. Jews and Greeks alike normally prayed with hands 'lifted up'; and the Christians

9 evidently did the same. They also accepted with little modification (though if Paul is the author we might have expected him to be a little more radical) the place accorded to women in ancient society. It is true that the context here seems to be that of meetings of the congregation for worship; but what is said about the conduct and dress appropriate for women is the kind of thing which was commonplace among popular teachers of the time, and most of what is said is applicable to the status of women generally as this was understood in the culture to which the writer belonged. This inferior status was taken for granted. Even if the church was a place where women seem occasionally to have discovered a new freedom and new opportunities, this writer clearly

10–12 feels obliged to restate the conventional view, and he supports it by his only venture into biblical interpretation, one that would not be out of place in later rabbinic writings. Adam and Eve, in Jewish thinking, were thought of both as historical persons and as type-figures representing the whole human race (see above on Romans 5.12). So here: as a matter of history Adam was created first, but (since Adam is also representative Man) this priority over Eve is shared by all his male descendants. Equally, it was Eve who first yielded to the deception of the serpent, and this implicates all her female descendants.

14 What is surprising is the statement that **Adam was not deceived**. This seems to contradict Genesis 3, which gives equal responsibility for their disobedience to both. But we know that a later Jewish interpretation of the story took 'deceived' in the sense that the serpent actually seduced Eve sexually. If this was in the writer's mind (though we cannot be sure that it was), it would explain why he found support for the superiority of men over women in this part of the story. Yet there is one thing – this was a commonplace of both Greek

15 and Jewish thought – which gives women a unique status: **childbearing**. This (since it was so important for the flourishing of any community, including the church) went some way to compensate for their Eve-like susceptibility; and this may be all that is meant[3] by the maxim, **she will be saved through childbearing**. But in Christian language 'saved' meant a great deal more

---

[3] These words have caused difficulty since early times. Some Latin fathers, feeling a difficulty in the notion that childbearing 'saves', suggested that it was not *any* childbearing, but Mary bearing the child Jesus, that brought salvation; and this has found its way into some English versions.

than this, and the writer hastens to avoid misunderstanding by adding the qualification (with a certain grammatical clumsiness) that, for Christian salvation, it was necessary that **they** (women in general? husband and wife?) **continue in faith and love and holiness**.

3.1 **The saying is sure.** The phrase is identical with that in 1.15 and 4.9, and appears to be one which the writer regularly used to indicate that he was quoting a well-known article of faith. But here the formula seems inappropriate. There is nothing in the paragraph which precedes it or that which follows it (and we cannot be sure whether the phrase looks forward or backward) which reads like a fragment of doctrine. The sentence that follows appears to be a popular maxim[4] to do with noble ambition; but it can never have been an ordinary proverb in its present form, since it contains a specific and highly technical term, here translated **office of bishop**. The origin of this term in the Christian vocabulary is obscure: it means literally a kind of *oversight* (see the NRSV footnote), sometimes attributed to God, sometimes designating an official responsibility in a secular organization. But by the middle of the first century the word 'overseer' had become the title of a Christian minister (Philippians 1.1), and was soon to be that of the leader of a congregation or of more than one church in a region: a *bishop*. By the time this letter was written it seems already to have become the title of the leader of a church or group of churches.

The chapter goes on to give a list of the qualities which are to be expected
8 both in a bishop and in the **deacons** – another word which by this time had become a technical term for an office in the church, though in ordinary Greek usage it meant one who performs comparatively menial tasks such as waiting at table. It can be seen at once that there is very little difference between the two lists; and in fact the qualities required in both of them are very similar to those which would have been looked for in the holder of any responsible office in the ancient world. In other words, what we are being given is not (as we might have hoped) a picture of the specific offices of bishop and deacon, with the duties and abilities required of each, but a fairly conventional account of what the persons ought to be like who would be entrusted with any responsible office in the church. The end of the paragraph
11 contains two ambiguities (see the NRSV footnotes). The term **women** could mean the wives of deacons, women who *are* deacons, or just any women in the congregation (perhaps the least likely option in a section concerned
12 with particular offices). **Married only once** could mean not divorcees, not marrying again after the death of a first wife, or even not taking advantage of the Jewish legal possibility (seldom used) of polygamy.

---

[4] Some manuscripts actually have the variant, *The saying is commonly accepted* (see the NRSV footnote). But if the following words were originally a popular maxim, a general word for 'leadership' must have been replaced by the particular term, **office of bishop**.

These qualities, though applicable in many walks of life, are listed here
15 in order to show **how one ought to behave in the household of God**. This
is a traditional image for any religious community, and is often used in the
Old Testament for the people of Israel; but the Greek word for 'household'
is the same as the Greek word for 'house', and the image leads easily into the
more familiar idea of the church as a 'building'. The physical building which
the church was most often said to replace was the temple at Jerusalem; but
here it is just possible that another building was in mind. The temple of
Artemis at Ephesus was one of the largest and most famous of the ancient
world (it became one of the 'wonders of the world') and will have been, for
most Ephesians, the most impressive religious monument they had ever seen.
This too the church replaces; and the classical architecture of that temple
may have suggested to the writer the two architectural terms, **pillar and
bulwark**.

16 **Without any doubt**. This phrase introduces what seems likely to have
been an independent summary of **our religion** (or part of one, since salient
facts such as Christ's death are not mentioned. On the meaning of **mystery**,
see above, pp. 641–2). The lines fall into a discernible formal pattern, and
since each phrase looks more like a statement of belief than an attempt to
advance fresh teaching, it seems likely that the writer is quoting an existing
hymn or creed rather than composing something new. Each line is a succinct
statement about Jesus Christ, and they can be set out in either three or (as
here) two stanzas:

I (i) **Revealed in flesh** summarizes Jesus' time on earth, making it quite
clear that Jesus (as some were liable to deny) was completely human.

(ii) **Vindicated in spirit** is more allusive. Outwardly, it could be said that
Jesus' life and work had been a failure, and some might interpret this failure
as God's judgment passed against Jesus. But the Christian faith was that this
was not so. God had not condemned Jesus. On the contrary, he had accepted
him and endorsed all that he did. By his resurrection and exaltation, and by
the power now released in the church, God had **vindicated** him (or *justified*
him). Yet this vindication was apparent only (as we say) to the eye of faith.
Jesus was not yet vindicated in such a way that "every eye will see him"
(Revelation 1.7) – that belonged to the future. Meanwhile he was vindicated
in spirit – that is to say (and here a number of interpretations are possible)
that it was only by 'the Spirit' that one could know that God had vindicated
Jesus (1 Corinthians 2.10–16); or, that one was led to believe by the mighty
acts performed by the Spirit through the church; or again, that it was in
the spiritual sphere, not yet in the fully visible and material sphere, that the
vindication had taken place.

(iii) **Seen by angels** possibly continues this thought. Something that had
taken place 'in spirit' could not yet be 'seen' by mortals, but only by supernatural beings such as angels.

II The second stanza sums up the mission of the church:

(i) It had been Paul's constant source of pride and confidence that the gospel had now been preached, not to the Jews only, but **among Gentiles**.

(ii) Jesus' prophecy of a world-wide proclamation was already, in a sense, nearing fulfilment **throughout the world** (see above on Romans 15.19).

(iii) The complement to this, and its justification, was that Jesus was **taken up in glory**.

Opposition and how to meet it

4.1 **Now the Spirit expressly says.** When the early church found itself confronted by persecution, heresy and counter-propaganda it did not regard these things as either unexpected or menacing. Jesus had said that such things were bound to happen before the end could come (Mark 13.7), and the church therefore tended to see its tribulations as a necessary part of the pre-ordained pattern of history that would immediately precede the end. Moreover it was a common theme of contemporary Jewish 'apocalyptic' writing that the final age of world history would be marked by an intensification of evil. Thus, although we cannot identify the prophecy alluded to here in any known writing, we can recognize a belief which was widely held both inside and outside the church and which found expression in many writings believed to have been inspired by **the Spirit**. This view of the ultimate phase of history tended to be expounded in vivid and mythological terms. It was believed, not simply that people by their own nature would get worse and worse, but that objective forces of evil would progressively take control of human minds and bodies. The phrase translated **in later times** was almost a technical term for this final age (see the NRSV footnote), which would be characterized by **deceitful spirits and teachings of demons** (compare the "lying wonders" and "wicked deception" of Satan in 2 Thessalonians 2.9–10), and by the fact that some people would already have become committed servants of the devil, their 2 **consciences** (the word here is equivalent to 'consciousness') having been **seared** (the image is of branding a slave).

What were these subversive doctrines? The readers of the letter will have recognized them without difficulty; we have to infer them as best we can. 3 In the first place, their promoters were ascetics: **They forbid marriage and demand abstinence from foods**. Those philosophers who regarded everything in the material realm as evil, and saw the liberation of the soul from all earthly limitations as the true purpose of life, tended naturally to discourage their followers from assuming the cares of married life. Detailed descriptions of such philosophies are available to us only from the second century CE, but it is intrinsically probable that the interest in 'myths and genealogies' discussed above had a similar tendency and carried with it the same kind of asceticism. This seems, at any rate, a more likely explanation of why these people 'forbade marriage' than any pressure from a Jewish party, for Jewish people normally regarded marriage as an obligation and only one sect is known which actually discouraged it. **Abstinence from foods** is more difficult to pin down. There were many possible motives for it. It could have been another instance of asceticism inspired by philosophy; but equally it could have been the influence of any religion, including Judaism, which held certain foods to be ritually unclean. Whatever form it took in Ephesus, it is attacked in this letter in terms that would be at home in any of Paul's polemics against Jewish observances. It is stated in Genesis (1.31) that God saw that his creation was good; and this is invoked as making invalid any religious or social prohibitions. **Those who believe and know the truth** (that is, Christians) may partake of any food, provided only (as in Romans 14.6; 1 Corinthians 10.30) that they 'say grace'. And grace, according to Jewish custom and doubtless also among Christians, included a verse of scripture.

5 Thus the food was **sanctified by God's word and by prayer.**

6   The word translated **instructions** is not so severe as to imply that Timothy must exercise firm authority. His rôle is rather to teach people as **a good servant** (the word is the same as that rendered *deacon* earlier on, but although it had become an official title in the church it still had its ordinary Greek sense of one who performs menial tasks for others). These admonitions were to spring, not from any new Christian insight, but (and this is characteristic of the atmosphere of the Pastorals) from **the sound teaching that you have**

7 **followed.** By contrast, the teaching of the heretics sounded like **profane myths and old wives' tales** – the last phrase was a stock term of abuse that rival philosophers used against each other. **Train yourself in godliness.** The athletic metaphor was a commonplace, but this writer also sees its dangers. On the one hand, he was warning against those who were turning this training into an excessive asceticism; on the other hand, athletic achievement tended to take an unduly prominent part in the Greek system of education, and serious-minded pagan thinkers were often induced to point out its limitations in terms very similar to those used here.

9   **The saying is sure.** The phrase indicates a quotation; but once again it is hard to be sure where we should put the quotation marks. The following sentence continues the metaphor of a race or athletic event (the primary meaning of the word translated **struggle** is to do with competition in athletics).

10 On **Savior of all people**, see above on 2.4.

   The following paragraphs return to questions of church order and afford a glimpse into the circumstances in which Timothy (or any church leader) might have to learn to exercise authority. It was natural to regard seniority as a qualification for leadership (which would go some way to account for the emergence of the word 'elder' as a title of office in the church); and one's youth might make it harder to get one's authority accepted. One's

13 responsibilities would include **the public reading of scripture** (the Greek says simply *reading*, but reading was normally done aloud, and what else

would the church official have read?), **exhorting** (which may have had its technical meaning of expounding scripture to show how it was being fulfilled) and **teaching** (which was evidently of particular importance in view of the dangers one had been alerted to). The authority to do all this stemmed from **the laying on of hands.** There are several descriptions in Acts of the ceremony by which hands were laid on Christian ministers to commission them for particular tasks, on occasion under the guidance of **prophecy**, as in Acts 13.1–3. It was with the same gesture that Moses commissioned Joshua (Numbers 27.22–3) and the people of Israel commissioned the Levites (Numbers 8.10); and the church, inspired perhaps by these precedents, and perhaps also by the similar 'ordination' of rabbis which was by this time an accepted institution, had come to recognize the rite as one which conferred a spiritual **gift** on its ministers. But we must not too hastily read back into this passage the form which was subsequently taken by Christian 'ordination'. 2 Timothy 1.6 refers to an occasion when Paul alone laid hands on Timothy, without the assistance of **the council of elders** (*presbytery*, apparently a technical word).

Widows and elders

5.1 **Do not speak harshly to an older man.** This introduces a section which is concerned not so much with church officials as with certain categories of church members; hence the Greek word here is likely to have its general meaning of 'older man', rather than the more technical meaning of *elder* or *presbyter* which it clearly has in verse 17. There follows a surprisingly extended section on 'widows', an important element in any congregation both as contributors of **good works** and as vulnerable individuals often needing help and support. Women married young in the ancient world; they were free to do so soon after puberty, and there was a correspondingly high risk of their being widowed quite early in life. Often they would marry again, or they might have grown-up children to support them. But equally often they fell into real poverty. In addition, they had little protection in law and their difficulties made them proverbially unfortunate members of society. The charitable support of needy widows was recognized as an obligation in any Jewish community, and the same was certainly true in the church; indeed this was held to be one of the most meritorious activities of religious people (James 1.27). But for any community which took this responsibility seriously it was essential to distinguish between those widows who were really in need and those who had other means of support; and it may be this which caused this writer to insist on the distinction between widows in general and **widows who are really widows.** It was the prime duty of a widow's surviving family to **provide** for her, not only for social reasons but because this was the spirit of the Fifth Commandment ("Honour your father and your mother", Exodus 20.12) and was **pleasing in God's sight.**

But there was another distinction to be made, this time with regard to the widow's seriousness as a religious person. Some young widows may well
6 have seemed to live **for pleasure**, whereas the 'real widow' would be one who devoted herself to prayer and good works. And with this in mind the
9 writer proposes a range of qualifications for a widow to be **put on the list**. Judging by these qualifications, and by the fact that there is a reference to
12 some sort of **pledge** which had been made to Christ, the 'list' seems to be not so much a register of those in material need as a roll of active and dedicated church women entrusted with specific duties. This is the only reference to such an institution in the New Testament, but there is some evidence for its existence in the following centuries, and the conditions for belonging to it are
9 what one would expect for such an 'order' – being **not less than sixty years old**, of irreproachable married life (*wife of one husband*[5] can mean either not having remarried after the death of her husband or not having been
10 divorced and remarried), having **washed the saints' feet** (a customary act of hospitality), and generally having done **good in every way**. The paragraph is a little confusing only because it appears to refer to widows in three senses:
3 (i) in the ordinary sense of any bereaved wife; (ii) those who are **really widows**
9 in need of material support; and (iii) the **list** of widows who had a special status and responsibility in the congregation.
17 The writer then turns again to **elders**; but this time they clearly cannot be just 'older men', since they have specific duties and receive **honor**. This is almost certainly a discreet way of describing a stipend, which is apparently to be adjusted according to merit. Paul uses the same passage of scripture
18 (**"You shall not muzzle an ox"**, Deuteronomy 25.4) to support the principle that "those who proclaim the gospel should get their living by the gospel" (1 Corinthians 9.14); but there he says nothing about 'double stipends': his concern is whether they should be paid at all. The other saying quoted here – **"The laborer deserves to be paid"** – was used by Jesus (Luke 10.7). But this writer is not necessarily thinking of Jesus' teaching (which in any case was in a different context). The sentence has a proverbial ring and may have been endorsed rather than invented by Jesus.
One of the leader's responsibilities was hearing charges brought against elders who, by virtue of their public position, were perhaps particularly vulnerable. They were entitled at least to the protection customary under Jewish law: a charge had to be substantiated by more than one witness (Deuteronomy 19.15). But once a charge was proved, they (or indeed, any Christian: it is
21 hard to know exactly to whom verse 20 applies) must be judged **without prejudice**. One way of avoiding scandal was of course to exercise great care
22 in the choice of those who were to be appointed in the first place – **Do not ordain anyone hastily**. But the Greek means literally *Do not lay hands on*

[5] See the NRSV footnote.

anyone hastily, and we cannot be sure that 'ordination' is meant rather than, say, temporary commissioning or even absolving from sin.

23 **No longer drink only water.** Whether it was a personal trait of Timothy's or the influence of over-ascetic groups which prompted this warning we do not know. The medicinal qualities of wine were well known – as Plutarch aptly put it, 'the most useful of drinks and the pleasantest medicine'.

6.1–2 Christian congregations certainly included both slaves and free, which could well have created tensions, particularly where both slaves and their masters were together in the church. Christianity was not to be a pretext for disrespect; and it was many centuries before Paul's radical hints ("There is no longer slave or free" Galatians 3.28) became a motive for real social change.

Instructions to Timothy

3 **Whoever teaches otherwise.** The writer now sets up a contrast. On the one side are **the sound words of our Lord Jesus Christ** – and we have no idea to what extent there was already some tradition of his 'words' such as we find in the gospels; but in any event he places them alongside **the teaching that is in accordance with godliness**, which is likely to mean a widely accepted religious ethic. On the other side stand teachers with the very worst motives:

4 **a morbid craving for controversy and for disputes about words;** and even worse – like any freelance wandering philosopher they hope to make money

5 out of their teaching, **imagining that godliness is a means of gain.** Such a mercenary attitude needs no refutation; but the idea of 'gain' puts the writer in mind of what was probably a current philosophical maxim about

8 religion in general (being **content with** was a familiar Stoic catchword), and the critique of worldly wealth which follows includes a number of sayings that sound proverbial.

11 **But as for you, man of God.** The remainder of the letter consists of a personal message to Timothy, who, by virtue of his particular office and responsibilities, merits the title given to Moses, Samuel and many other Old

12 Testament figures, **man of God. Fight the good fight of the faith.** The Greek word (*agōn*) means not a battle but a contest, and the metaphor, like many others in the New Testament, derives from athletics. **You made the good confession.** This phrase has a precise and technical flavour, and must refer to some occasion in Timothy's life. Was it his ordination? Or a trial in which he was arraigned for his faith? Since there were **witnesses** we should probably think of his baptism: Timothy is being reminded of the vows he made on that public occasion. But the word 'confession' leads on to the example of Christ

13 on a very different occasion. If **before Pontius Pilate** is a correct translation, the allusion is to some moment (it is impossible to say exactly which) in Jesus' trial. But the Greek words could also mean *in the time of Pontius Pilate* (which reappears as 'under Pontius Pilate' in the Apostles' Creed), in which case the reference is a general one to Jesus' bearing throughout his passion and death.

But here, as so often in the New Testament, the ultimate motive of Christian steadfastness is the expectation of the imminent coming of Christ in glory –

14 **the manifestation of our Lord Jesus Christ** – and if it was asked (as perhaps it was being increasingly asked at this time) when that 'manifestation' would

15 come to pass, the answer was essentially that given by Jesus himself: **at the right time**. And in a string of phrases which probably derive from the worship of Greek-speaking synagogues, God is praised with the traditional attributes both of the Lord of the Old Testament and of the divinities of Hellenistic religions.

After some conventional thoughts on wealth and its dangers, the letter ends with a postscript (in the manner, for instance, of Galatians 6.11–18), underlining the most urgent point made in the letter. (On the metaphor

20 underlying **guard what has been entrusted to you**, see below on 2 Timothy 1.12.) Just as, in the following century, when this kind of thinking became more powerful and systematic, many religious systems claimed to offer a kind of '**knowledge**' which would enable the soul to rise above the realm of earthly things, so, we may assume, the false teachers in Ephesus made

21 similar claims for their own speculations. In so doing, they **missed the mark as regards the faith**.

TIMOTHY

The greeting

The greeting is very similar to that of the first letter and follows the same standard form, leading into thanksgiving. But what follows has a particularly personal warmth and intimacy which is sustained throughout the letter. Timothy is addressed as **my beloved child**.

1.2

Thanksgiving and encouragement

5 What binds them particularly together is Timothy's **sincere faith** which he has inherited from his grandmother through his mother. It may seem surprising that in this instance the faith has already been transmitted over three generations, as if the grandmother had been converted to Christianity first, followed by the mother and then finally the son. But we notice that Paul

3, 5 says that he worshipped God as his **ancestors did**, and since **Eunice**[1] (and presumably **Lois**) were Jewish (Acts 16.1), then Timothy's 'faith' may (like Paul's) mean the devotion to God which he showed as a Jew before his or their conversion to Christianity. All three generations may have been models of that traditional Jewish piety which Christianity inherited and only partly modified.

Timothy's faith and piety, then, had long been habitual to him. In addition

6 he had received, by the **laying on** of Paul's **hands**, both a commission and a **gift of God** enabling him to perform it. But this too, for all its supernatural origin, was something which (as modern experience will endorse) could in due course be taken for granted and lose its potency unless one were periodically to **rekindle** it by an effort of will; and to assist this process of 'rekindling', the writer devotes a few words to the Spirit which is imparted with the 'gift'. As is explained, for instance, in Romans 8, the function of the Spirit in human conduct is to introduce a new motivation, and the kind of

7 qualities which it inspires are not **cowardice** but **love** and **self-discipline**; and this relates the 'gift' to that aspect of the Christian life that really demands

8 these resources: **testimony about our Lord**.

To what does a Christian testify? The main headings of the testimony are set out in terms which can be paralleled with (or may in fact be drawn from) other

9 Pauline writings. (i) The phrase **not according to our works but according to his own purpose and grace** is a basic Pauline proposition, though expressed

---

[1] Pronounced *Eu-ni-kē*.

without the usual contrast between works and 'faith'; (ii) the long perspective of this salvation, beginning **before the ages began** and now manifested in a decisive revelation, is familiar from Ephesians and Colossians; and (iii) 1 Corinthians 15 provides a full commentary on the statement that Christ Jesus

10 **abolished death.** The only words which belong to a slightly different world are (i) **the appearing,** a word much used in pagan religion for the appearance of a god on earth, and occasionally used for Jesus' 'appearing' at his glorious return, but never elsewhere for his time on earth; (ii) **Savior,** which was soon to become a standard title for Christ, just as it was already for the gods of many contemporary religions and indeed for great benefactors such as the Roman emperor claimed to be; but it was never used by Jesus himself, and is rare in Paul. Its occurrence here and three times in the letter to Titus may be an example of the way in which Christianity, which was at first preached in the more restricted idiom of Palestine, gradually assimilated the terminology of a more cosmopolitan society.

12–14   The following three verses are dominated by a new metaphor (though it was hinted at in 1 Timothy 6.20), that of entrusting something precious to another person for safe keeping. Both Greek and Roman law defined the conditions under which a sum of money or a valuable object might be placed on deposit: the person who accepted the deposit was obliged to keep it intact and return it on demand. Other translations (including the Revised Standard Version) have taken the Greek to mean the same in both verse 12 and verse

14   14: the **treasure** is the gospel, which must be 'guarded' – that is, untainted by

12   heretical teaching – **until that day** when Christ returns. But the main text of the NRSV opts for a different meaning in verse 12: that which is 'entrusted' is (presumably) the *church*, which Paul entrusts to God to be 'guarded'.

15, 16   Nothing further is known about **Phygelus** and **Hermogenes. Onesiphorus** had evidently shown particular loyalty to Paul during Paul's imprisonment (or one of his imprisonments) and continued to do so when he arrived in Rome. It is not clear whether he was still alive. If not, this is the first example of Christian prayer for the dead (for which there is plenty of evidence a century or so later). The prayer itself sounds conventional – the clumsy double use

18   of **the Lord** may be a sign that the writer is somewhat carelessly adapting an existing (perhaps Jewish) prayer.

The charge to Timothy

The metaphor of the 'deposit' is taken up once more. Timothy received the

2.2   treasure of 'sound teaching' (which he now has to **entrust** to others) on a solemn occasion, **through** (which must mean 'in the presence of') **many witnesses.** What was this occasion? Possibly his baptism; but more probably the moment of his commissioning or 'ordination', which had placed him in a position of special responsibility. What this required of him is illustrated by three further comparisons. Timothy has been 'enlisted' by God for service,

4 and must not be **entangled** in any lesser loyalties; like an athlete, he can be disqualified if he breaks the rules of the race; like a farmer, he can lay first claim to the crop only if he has been working for the harvest himself.

8   **Remember Jesus Christ.** There were various ways of summing up the gospel. **Raised from the dead, a descendant of David** states the barest essentials (Romans 1.3–4 is a similar formulation). Another way was to summarize the *consequences* of Christ's life, death and resurrection; and the summary is introduced with the formula which this writer uses each time he appears

11 to be quoting some well-known article of the faith: **The saying is sure.** This time it is clear where the quotation begins and ends; and from the structure of the next two verses it seems that we are being given, once again, a fragment of an early hymn or creed which puts together, without much sense of logical connection, a number of familiar Christian propositions. **If we have died with him, we will also live with him** is reminiscent of Paul's exposition of

12 baptism in Romans 6; **if we endure, we will also reign with him** is similar to Romans 8.17 and reminiscent of words ascribed to Jesus in Luke 22.28–9; and **if we deny him, he will also deny us** recalls a well-attested saying of Jesus (Matthew 10.33; Mark 8.38). But the last clause seems to go on to contra-

13 dict what has just been said: **if we are faithless, he remains faithful.** Is not being 'faithless' the same as 'denying him'? But the Greek word for 'being faithless' does not create the same problem as the English. It means, not 'if we renounce our faith', but 'if we waver in our faith'. When this happens to us (as happen it will), we are sustained by the thought of the 'faithfulness' of God, who has made us a promise in Christ and cannot allow it to come to nothing without 'denying himself'.

   Timothy's constancy, devotion and hold on sound teaching are now set in a context that makes these qualities especially relevant. In the first letter, the heretical thinkers who were causing trouble in Ephesus were characterized by their interest in "myths and endless genealogies" and by their tendency to indulge in unnecessary ascetic practices. Here they reappear in much the

14, 16 same guise, **wrangling over words** and indulging in **profane chatter.** Two of

17 them are named. (One of whom, **Hymenaeus,** was mentioned in 1 Timothy

18 1.20.) And their error is specified: they are **claiming that the resurrection has already taken place.** Many people who were accustomed to Greek ways of thinking must have found the Christian teaching on the resurrection of the body at some moment after death (which the Christians had inherited from their Jewish background) both strange and naïve, and have been tempted to reformulate it in terms more congenial to their culture. Paul had to face precisely this difficulty in 1 Corinthians 15. Here the proposed reformulation may have taken its start from the experience of baptism. Christians, when they were baptized, 'rose' with Christ. This, in orthodox Christian teaching, was a metaphorical way of speaking; at most, it was a foretaste of that future 'resurrection' when they would rise in bodily form to sit with Christ at the last judgment. But the heretics perhaps hoped to avoid the apparent naïvety

of this teaching by concentrating on the foretaste to the exclusion of the future consummation. They held that what was meant by 'resurrection' was simply a new quality of life which flowed from conversion and baptism, and that it was therefore unnecessary to believe in what they may have felt to be an exotic concept of future 'resurrection'. It was sufficient to point to what had already been experienced. All that a sophisticated Christian could be expected to understand by 'resurrection' had already taken place.

The writer attacks this view in a way that makes him very different from the Paul of the earlier letters. Instead of seeking to refute it by counter-arguments (as Paul would certainly have done), he appeals to the strength and solidarity of the church which is entrusted with the true teaching. In a metaphor which appears frequently in the New Testament, the church is likened to a building of

19 which God has laid a **firm foundation** and of which Christians are the living stones. The building is imagined as bearing inscribed upon it the text, **"The Lord knows who are his."** This comes from the story of Korah (Numbers 16.5), who was the Old Testament prototype of all apostates, and the words, spoken as a threat by Moses to Korah, were an appropriate warning to any Christian who was tempted to depart from the sound teaching entrusted to the church. A second 'inscription' is added, this time more freely constructed out of biblical phrases and expressing a more general warning. The metaphor

20 is then given a new twist. The building is now **a large house**, and Christians are the various **utensils** in it. But not any utensils – **special** ones, with a

21 special obligation to serve God, **the owner of the house.**

A personal word for Timothy: being young, he may be subject to wayward

22, 23 **passions**; but he is also warned, once again, against **stupid and senseless controversies** – not, this time, because of the errors of doctrine they may lead to, but because of their moral consequences. The kind of discipline he

24 must exercise (as was said in 1 Timothy 4.6) is that appropriate to **the Lord's**

26 **servant**: its very gentleness may save others from **the snare of the devil.**

As in the previous letter, the growth of heresy and immorality is seen, not as a passing hazard to the growth of the young church, but as a necessary

3.1 feature of the distress of **the last days.** The examples of human depravity which follow are listed in terms which were probably quite conventional; on the other hand, the subversion caused by some of the women in the congregation, is a detail which may well be drawn from the actual experience of the

8 church. **Jannes and Jambres** are the names which tradition gave to two of Pharaoh's magicians, who performed miracles identical with those of Moses (Exodus 7.11) but were powerless to avert the fate coming upon Egypt.

10 **Now you have observed my teaching, my conduct.** Paul does not hesitate to offer himself as an example to be followed; but the emphasis here is on

11 his **suffering – What persecutions I endured!** – and all Christians must be prepared to be similarly persecuted for their faith. **The things that happened to Paul in Antioch, Iconium, and Lystra** seem to belong to the earlier period of his work (Acts 13.50; 14.5–6, 19). Timothy's home was in the region of

Lystra (Acts 16.1) and he might well be expected to know what Paul suffered there.

15 **From childhood you have known the sacred writings.** 'Sacred writings' was the term which Greek-speaking Jews frequently used for what we call the Old Testament; and these 'writings' were as important for Christians as they were for Jews; indeed for the first generations of Christians they were the *only* 'scripture'. Admittedly, the Christians had a new revelation by which to interpret these writings, and often drew quite new meanings from them;

16 but they certainly regarded them as **inspired by God**, and made use of them (though probably not 'all' of them – **all scripture** must mean scripture as a whole) for the teaching of both morals and doctrine and for **training** – here this writer uses a word (*paideia*) which was a key term in the Greek theory and practice of education.

All these injunctions are now summed up with a fresh note of urgency in

4.1 view of the expected **appearing** of Christ. As so often in early Christian moral teaching, belief in an imminent day of judgment is a powerful stimulus. The period immediately preceding the last days was to be marked by an upsurge of evil and apostasy (see above on 1 Timothy 4.1–2); and when this writer says

3 that **the time is coming** he is evidently not brooding on a distant future but is pointing to the premonitory signs already manifest in the present. Those

4 who **turn away from listening to the truth and wander away to myths** are not merely a danger to be resisted; they are themselves a signal that the crisis is near.

6 **As for me.** The letter suddenly becomes very personal – so personal that, whether or not Paul is the author of the whole letter, it is often felt that these verses at least must be a genuine fragment of his correspondence, worked in here (possibly with invented additions) by a later writer. The sacrificial metaphor, **being poured out as a libation**, occurs in Philippians 2.17; while the athletic one, which is common both in Paul and in other contemporary writers, bears an emphasis rather unexpected for Paul – not so much on the contest itself as on the reward at the end of it. The prize for

8 the winner in the Greek games was a garland or 'crown'; and **the crown of righteousness** suggests a reward for the long discipline of a righteous life – though Paul would characteristically have stressed that this 'righteousness' was not something one could ever earn by one's own efforts but was a free gift of God's grace, reserved not for Paul alone but for **all who have longed for his appearing**.

Personal matters

The main part of the letter has consisted of advice and instructions to Timothy in Ephesus, and seems to presuppose that he has permanent responsibility

9 there. Nevertheless, Paul is now anxious for a visit from him. **Do your best to come to me soon.** Paul has only one companion left. The rest, for one reason

or another, have dispersed. It is possible to fit all these movements into the period of Paul's first (and only recorded) imprisonment in Rome. **Demas, Luke, Mark** and **Tychicus** were all with Paul when he wrote Colossians (also from prison) and all but one of them could by now have left him. **Crescens** is otherwise unknown;[2] **Titus'** presence in **Dalmatia** on the Adriatic coast may have been to follow up Paul's preaching "as far around as Illyricum" (Romans 15.19). The only real difficulty is Paul's stay at **Troas**. He can hardly be referring to the occasion when he was waiting for news from Corinth several years before his imprisonment at Rome (2 Corinthians 2.12), and none of his recorded journeys after that took him to Troas. The easiest explanation would certainly be that, if Paul was released from Rome, he made a journey back to Asia, in the course of which he could have visited both Troas and Miletus.[3]

16 Exactly what stage in the proceedings is meant by **my first defense** would be uncertain even if we could be sure that these were genuine words of Paul. It seems unlikely (in view of the closing scenes of Acts) that Paul would have been left with so little support during his first trial in Rome; therefore (on the traditional view) the trial in question must be a second one, which, unlike the first, led to his being put to death. Such a trial (according to Roman practice) could well have begun with a preliminary hearing before a magistrate at which Paul would have made his **first defense**. If this hearing was not final (as would appear to have been the case here), the hearing would have been adjourned to a later trial; and Paul looked forward to this more public occasion as

17 an opportunity for the **message** to be **fully proclaimed** – Paul expressed a similar hope in Philippians 1.12–18. Meanwhile the immediate danger had passed; Paul had been **rescued from the lion's mouth**.

19 **Prisca and Aquila**: see above on Romans 16.3.

Onesiphorus: already mentioned at 1.16 above.

20 **Erastus**: possibly the same as in Acts 19.22 (where he worked with Timothy).

Trophimus: an Ephesian, according to Acts 21.29.

21 **Eubulus, Pudens, Linus** and **Claudia** are not mentioned elsewhere in the New Testament, though there is an early tradition that the second bishop of Rome, after Peter, was named Linus.

---

[2] An early tradition, however, makes him the founder of the church at Vienne, near Lyons in Gaul, and the Greek word for **Galatia** can also mean 'Gaul'.

[3] The word **parchments** in verse 13 translates a word of Latin origin which means literally *membranes*. It was used for leaved parchment notebooks, which were coming into use at the time, and it has been argued that it might have been on these that the gospels were first written.

THE LETTER OF PAUL TO

TITUS

We know nothing of a journey by Paul to Crete, nor of the founding of a church there, but we must assume that by the time this letter was written there was a settled Christian community on the island. The letter is addressed to Titus, whom we know from other letters and from Acts to have been one of Paul's principal assistants, and to have been entrusted with missions of some delicacy. Here, though he still seems to be regarded as quite young and inexperienced, he is in charge of the church in Crete, and the letter, though addressed to him, is clearly intended for the church as a whole. For the most part its tone is not personal but formal and authoritative.

Opening greetings

The formality is stressed at the outset by the long parenthesis, which inter-
1.1, 4 rupts the normal structure of the greeting (**Paul ... To Titus**,[1] see above on Romans 1.1), and rehearses the qualifications of the writer to give authorita-
1 tive instructions to the church **for the sake of** its **faith**, its **knowledge of the**
2 **truth** and its **hope**[2] – this last resting on a promise made by God **before the ages began** (an idea developed in Ephesians, see above on Ephesians 1.4).

Good order in the church

The historical situation we are to imagine is that Paul, after preaching the gospel in Crete and making a number of converts, left to Titus the task of organizing the young church and appointing its officers. The qualifications which he then laid down are repeated here, presumably to serve as a guide in all future appointments. The qualities to be looked for in candidates for office are very similar to those listed in 1 Timothy 3 and are of a general character: this is the sort of person that anyone who holds responsibility in the church ought to be. The only difficulty in the paragraph is that at the outset it is
5 concerned with the appointment of **elders**, but two verses later is speaking
7 of **a bishop**. Do both these titles belong to the same office? This supposition would make sense of this passage but would raise difficulties elsewhere. In 1 Timothy, for instance, the bishop is treated separately from the elders; and

---

[1] **My loyal child**: the Greek word means rather *true, legitimate, genuine.*

[2] This translation, which follows the Revised Standard Version, is only one possible way of taking the Greek. Another may be found in (for instance) the Revised English Bible: *apostle of Jesus Christ, marked as such by the faith of God's chosen people and the knowledge* etc.

in the subsequent order of the church the bishop and elders were quite dis-
5 tinct. It is possible that the confusion arises from the phrase **appoint elders**.
The natural meaning of this is to 'appoint men to the office of eldership'. But
it could also mean, 'appoint elders' (i.e. older or responsible members of the
church) 'to certain offices in the church', one of which is the office of bishop.
But the phrase is ambiguous, and does not allow us to reconstruct with any
certainty the constitution of the church in Crete or elsewhere.

10 **There are also many rebellious people.** Just as in Ephesus one of the main
responsibilities of the leader of the church was to protect the congregation
from the influence of teachers who wove elaborate speculative systems out
of a combination of Old Testament and Christian materials (see above on
1 Timothy 1.4), so in Crete Titus is warned against a similar danger, that
14 of people **paying attention to Jewish myths or to commandments of those
who reject the truth.** Here, **Jewish myths** can hardly mean any part of the Old
Testament, for no Christian would ever have thought of the Old Testament
as anything but a divinely inspired book. The phrase must be an allusion
to fanciful interpretations of the Old Testament such as we find in later
Jewish literature or in the systems of the so-called 'gnostic' thinkers of the
following century. As for **commandments of those who reject the truth**,
these may have been observances pressed upon them by the synagogue or
rules of asceticism and ritual purity devised by these speculative thinkers for
themselves – rules which the Christians could disregard on exactly the same
15 grounds as they disregarded the observances of the Jewish community: **to
the pure all things are pure** (as Paul had said in Romans 14.20, possibly
appealing to a remembered word of Jesus, Mark 7.15).

11 To this extent (and also because they do it **for sordid gain**, compare 1
Timothy 6.5), the trouble-makers in Crete are very similar to those described
in 1 Timothy. But there are two respects in which they seem to be unlike the
10 heretics in Ephesus. First, they are **of the circumcision** – that is to say, having been converted from Judaism they are now presumably dissatisfied with
Christianity and propose to construct their own more ambitious religious
philosophy; and secondly, they are Cretans – and Cretans are proverbially
liars! The proverb in question was originally a line of verse attributed to
Epimenides, a philosopher of the sixth century BCE. He is here called a
12 **prophet**, doubtless because it was felt that he had rightly predicted the
character which the Cretans would still have some centuries later.

The Christian way of life

As in the other Pastoral letters, the defence to be presented against these
subversive influences is not (as it might have been in an earlier letter of
Paul) a pugnacious counter-attack or even a careful restatement of Christian
beliefs, but simply that firm hold on essentials which is once again called

2.1 **sound doctrine** (a word characteristic of these letters, see above on 1 Timothy 1.10). And since this 'sound doctrine' is as much ethical as theoretical, the writer goes on to describe the Christian way of life as it is to be lived out by different groups within the Christian community. This kind of systematic presentation of moral duties is familiar from other New Testament letters (see below, p. 740) and occurs frequently in early Christian literature. In Ephesians and Colossians, however, the groups singled out are those represented in a domestic household – husbands, wives, children and slaves. Here, the groups are those to be found in the congregation as a whole – the older men, the older women, the younger men and the slaves. As so often, the qualities demanded of them (as of the church's leaders) are those which were expected of respectable people anywhere in the Greco-Roman world. Only occasional

2 touches, such as the **faith, love** and **endurance** of the older men, betray a distinctively Christian ethos.

Yet even if these moral standards were nothing out of the ordinary, there was something new about Christian motivation. In Paul's earlier letters this

11 new factor was called simply the Spirit; here it is **the grace of God**. There, the Spirit was described as working directly upon a person, assuming control, as it were, of every aspect of conduct and bringing forth 'fruits' or a 'harvest' of qualities to which human beings, unaided, can hardly aspire. Here, the metaphor is less dramatic and is perhaps appropriate to a more gradual evolution of the Christian character. The grace of God is thought

12 of as something which is **training** us – the word (related to *paideia*) was a basic one in the Greek theory of education, according to which this 'training' was a process by which the naturally unruly body and mind were 'trained' until they functioned according to their true potential. This training was of course supervised by tutors – and the psychological effect of the grace of God is described as fulfilling precisely the tutor's function, providing a constant stimulus to endeavour, and training mind and body to be **self-controlled, upright, and godly.** A further motive is suggested by the phrase **the present age**, which always implied, both in Jewish and in early Christian writing, that the present order is temporary and will be succeeded by 'the age to come', a radically new era promised long ago by God. Christians now had their own vision of this future age and expected it to dawn very soon; its imminence was often invoked as a spur to calm, sober and vigilant conduct. It would be the

13 moment of **the manifestation of our great God and Savior, Jesus Christ**[3] – and the following summary of the achievement of Christ is full of scriptural echoes. To **redeem us from all iniquity** is the 'ransom' metaphor frequently used of the deliverance of Israel from Egypt and invoked in a saying of Jesus

---

[3] Notice the NRSV footnote. There are very few places in the New Testament where Christ appears to be actually called *God*. Though closely associated with God the Father, he is also usually distinguished from him. Many translators therefore favour the other possible translation which is given in the footnote.

(Mark 10.45); and to **purify for himself a people of his own** expresses the Christian understanding of the church as the new Israel, the people for whom the Old Testament promises were ultimately intended. (The allusion here is to such passages as Exodus 19.5; Deuteronomy 14.2; Ezekiel 37.23.)

3.1 **Remind them to be subject to rulers and authorities** – the usual early Christian attitude: see above on Romans 13.1.

8 **The saying is sure.** Each time this phrase occurs in the Pastorals it seems to point to a quotation or article of belief well known to the church. Here, the passage referred to must be the paragraph immediately preceding it, which is a summary statement of Christian belief such as might have been recited in a hymn or a creed. On more than one occasion (see, for instance, the first chapter of Romans or Colossians 3.5–7), Paul used what may seem almost excessively sombre colours to portray the state of humankind before its redemption through Christ; and the same vivid contrast seems very soon to have entered the ordinary vocabulary of the church. The contrast served to

4 throw into high relief the **goodness and loving kindness of God our Savior** (words, in the Greek, which were more often used of human benefactors than of God, and which may be a sign that the church was coming under the influence of the language of a more cosmopolitan society). Inspired

5 only by his own mercy (**not by any works of righteousness that we had done** – good Pauline teaching), God had overlooked the years of unregeneracy, and the moment when this act of mercy became effective for the individual believer was the moment of baptism, here uniquely called **the water of rebirth.** Admittedly, the idea of 'rebirth', whether of the individual or of the whole created order, was quite a common religious one. When the Christians adopted it, they made it specific by relating it to the water of baptism and to the **renewal** effected **by the Holy Spirit.**

It was Christ's command that those who sinned against the community should be treated with patience (Matthew 18.15–17 is the severest passage on the subject). But if an individual, after two warnings, persisted in heresy, then this was no ordinary sin: the offender was one of the predicted and inevitable signs of the last days, an instrument in the hands of the devil. Therefore only

10 one course was possible: **have nothing more to do** with such a person.

12 **Nicopolis** was the name of several towns: the one in north Greece is most

13 likely to be meant. **Tychicus** appears in 2 Timothy 4.12; **Apollos** may be the famous preacher of Acts 18.24. The letter was evidently intended to serve as a

12, 13 letter of recommendation for two travelling Christians, **Artemas** and **Zenas the lawyer** (neither is otherwise known), who may have been its bearers.

THE LETTER OF PAUL TO

PHILEMON

A runaway slave, in the Greek world, might take refuge in the house of someone whom he had met at his master's and beg his new protector not to send him back. If he made a good impression, he might be a cause of some embarrassment to his protector, who would either have to keep the slave against the wishes of his former master or send him back to certain punishment; and if the two men were friends this might be a genuinely difficult decision. We happen to possess two letters of the Latin writer Pliny which are concerned with precisely this dilemma. Pliny solved it by sending back the culprit with a carefully worded letter in which he asked his friend to receive the slave kindly. This letter of Paul appears to be of exactly the same kind.

The culprit in question was certainly a slave. But what exactly had he done? It has traditionally been assumed that he had run away from his master Philemon and taken refuge with Paul, who had converted him to Christianity; but the only evidence for this is the sentence in which Paul says that he was 11 **formerly useless** to Philemon – and he evidently chose this word, not because it described exactly how Onesimus had behaved, but because it was a pun on his name (*onēsimus*, 'useful').[1] It is quite conceivable that he had not run away at all, but that Philemon had sent him on some errand to Paul (who was in prison), in the course of which he may possibly have been involved in some shady dealings – Paul may be referring to something of the kind in verse 18. But the important point was that Paul had formed a close and trusting relationship with the slave and wanted his master, a fellow Christian, to treat him accordingly.

Yet the letter is not a piece of purely personal correspondence. It appears to have been written at the same time as the letter to the Colossians, and the greetings at the beginning and the end (with the addition of an otherwise 2 unknown **Apphia** and of Philemon himself) make mention of almost the same names. It looks, then, as if Philemon lived at Colossae; and this is confirmed by the statement in Colossians (4.9) that Onesimus also belonged there. In writing to Philemon, therefore, Paul addresses him not merely as an individual friend but as a representative of the Colossian church; and, like his letter to that church, this letter begins with thanksgiving and prayer, using a number of the same phrases as occur in the opening paragraphs of Colossians.

---

[1] There may be a still more subtle pun: the word for 'useless' (*achrēstos*) would have sounded exactly the same as *achristos*, 'not a Christian', and if this was intended it may be that Onesimus had done nothing wrong at all.

The transition to personal matters is made in verse 8. Writing as an apostle
8 to a member of the church, Paul could have used a tone of authority – **I am
bold enough in Christ to command you to do your duty**. But he prefers to put
the matter as tactfully as he can, appealing only to his own relative impotence
9 as an **old man**[2] and a prisoner. The complication here, which makes this a
very different case from that of an ordinary delinquent slave, is that Paul
has converted Onesimus to Christianity (a process which Paul more than
10 once compares to becoming **father** to a child, as in 1 Corinthians 4.15). This
makes it harder for Paul to part with him, since he now has a personal tie with
11 him, and his new faith has made him (as his name would suggest) **indeed
useful**. But Paul would not wish to keep him without his master's willing
12 consent; and so he is **sending him** back; and the rest of the letter is a plea
that the faith they now share may cement a new relationship of trust between
16 them, Onesimus becoming **more than a slave, a beloved brother**. As for any
19 financial liability (possibly even to purchase his freedom), Paul's **own hand**
is surety for making up any debt if required.

Philemon's answer is not preserved, and we do not know the sequel. Early
in the second century there was a bishop of Ephesus named Onesimus; but
that it was the same Onesimus, reformed and given his freedom and then
growing up to a position of authority in the church, is no more than an
intriguing possibility.

---

[2] The word translated **old man** is barely distinguishable from that meaning *ambassador*,
which is adopted in many standard translations.

HEBREWS

As early as the second century CE this writing was referred to by ancient authors under the title 'To Hebrews'. If, at that date, they knew any more about it – who was the author, why it was written – they have not told us. Indeed, even this title tells us nothing we could not have inferred for ourselves. Whoever was originally intended to read the letter must have been familiar not only with the Jewish scriptures and institutions but also with current Jewish methods of interpretation: without a 'Hebrew' background it would have been difficult to follow the argument. It would seem to follow that the first readers were Jewish Christians – either Jews or proselytes. But even this conclusion is not certain. They could conceivably have been Gentiles who had spent many years attending a Jewish synagogue without actually converting to Judaism (like the probable recipients of Paul's letter to the Galatians: see above, pp. 590–1). The traditional title, TO THE HEBREWS, is therefore not certainly correct. But so far as it goes it is a reasonable guess.

It is less obviously appropriate to call the work a LETTER. It is true that it ends, as letters should, with some personal greetings; but at the beginning, where one normally looks for some indication of who is writing and to whom, there is nothing of the kind. The work begins like a treatise, and we are a long way into it before the tone becomes sufficiently personal to give the impression of a man writing to his friends. If it is a 'letter' at all, it is a 'letter' only in that rather special sense (more familiar then than now) of a literary work intended for wide circulation but adopting (though in this case only towards the end) the conventional form of a letter. The style, moreover, with its careful exposition of scripture and its free use of rhetorical techniques, is recognizably that of a sermon. At most, one might say that it is a sermon that may have been inspired by particular circumstances and that a particular congregation was in view when it came to the ending.

Who wrote it? Until the fourth century CE most people were ready to confess that they did not know. It was then perhaps by way of taking the line of least resistance that the church began to attribute it to Paul. The only other letters as extended as this one were by Paul, and the argument in Hebrews is on a scale that would have been worthy of the author of Romans. Nevertheless, there are striking differences, both in style and in content: the Greek is more sophisticated and polished than Paul's, and the evident interest in temple ritual suggests an author of a quite different background. It is only the somewhat uncritical tradition of the church (which in any case has not been unanimous) that provides any basis for continuing to regard Paul as the author. Other candidates have been proposed. Barnabas was suggested in the third century, Apollos in more recent times. But this is little more than guesswork.

The letter itself gives little away. The recipients have undergone persecution and have the prospect of more coming to them; and they are warned several times of the danger of falling away from the faith (and possibly reverting to their former Jewish loyalties). But this was a situation like that of many Christian congregations in the first few decades of their existence. As for the author, perhaps the most distinctive thing about him (apart from his literary style) is his use of the Old Testament. Not only does he comment on larger sections of scripture than any other New Testament writer, but he makes it the basis of his entire understanding of the 'priesthood' of Christ and of the necessity for a new dispensation that makes the old temple ritual obsolete. But even this does not tell us a great deal about him. The most we can say is that, he could have been a Jewish Christian, possibly of a priestly family (hence his interest in the temple ritual), who lived in any city of the empire where the dominant language was Greek.

Around 96 CE the letter was quoted by Clement, the bishop of Rome. Can we say how much earlier than this it was written? Much of it consists of a discussion of the Jewish sacrificial system and the light it throws on the sacrifice of Christ. On the face of it, this should make it easy to tell whether the author was writing before or after 70 CE, when the temple in Jerusalem was destroyed by the Romans and the Jewish sacrificial system came to an end. But even this clue leads nowhere. The author had an academic mind. If he wished to know the details of the work of the priests in Jerusalem he did not enquire into the ritual which was performed there in his own day; he simply went into his library and consulted the law of Moses, which laid down the pattern of priestly service that was still observed in Herod's temple. The actual performance of this ritual in his own day seems to have held little interest for him – in this respect he was a typical educated Jew of the Dispersion. Even if he was writing shortly after it came to an abrupt end with the fall of Jerusalem, it is quite possible that he would not have referred to the fact. He drew the entire inspiration for his argument from his study of scripture. From the narrative of Exodus he gained his overpowering sense of the seriousness and awesomeness of the presence of God; and out of the detailed regulations in the law concerning the arrangement of the sanctuary and the function of the high priest he developed his understanding – the most systematic and suggestive in the New Testament – of the true nature and destiny of Christ.

The Son and his priesthood

1.1 **Long ago God spoke to our ancestors**. The opening paragraph is a carefully composed piece of Greek. Its style and vocabulary show that the author was not merely a Jew who happened to write in Greek: he was a man well educated in Greek culture. Nevertheless, he took for granted in his readers a world-view that was distinctively Jewish, and in particular an understanding of history that was conditioned entirely by the Old Testament. At a certain time in the past God had revealed himself to the human race by means of the law given to Moses on Sinai. This law, which was the unique possession of the Jewish people, gave them a moral and religious code by which to regulate their lives and contained the promise of a secure and glorious destiny for the community which observed it. The perfect keeping or 'fulfilment' of this law was the state of affairs for which the world was created and towards which all history was tending.

But the empirical facts of history and human psychology made it impossible to think of the law as the sole channel for God's influence in the world. The Jewish people down the centuries had again and again failed to observe it faithfully; and, as the years passed, this archaic code of law became ever more difficult to adhere to as the one standard of moral and ritual perfection. Some guidance was needed as to how the original divine imperatives could still be carried out, some fresh impulse to revive the people's moral earnestness.

Such guidance and such an impulse had in fact been given. God had not been silent since the time of Moses. It was true that people differed about the way in which God had spoken. The Pharisees, for example, believed that God had inspired the learned tradition of interpreting scripture which they practised themselves, and that the 'oral law' had as much authority as the written law. In Alexandria, on the other hand, it was through the insights of Greek philosophy that thoughtful Jews sought to discern the contemporary relevance of their ancient law. But on one aspect of the question they were mostly agreed. There had been a period in Jewish history (roughly from the establishment of the monarchy to the return from exile, the tenth to the sixth centuries BCE) when the divine guidance had been clothed in a particularly challenging form. **God spoke . . . by the prophets,** who, by the oracles they uttered and by the example of their lives, demonstrated the kind of religion and the kind of morality which would fulfil the spirit and the intentions of the law.

It is to this stage in God's dealings with his people that the writer refers in his opening words. After the law itself, the prophets had represented the most powerful and important phase in God's self-revelation. But it had taken place (all would agree) **in many and various ways** – the Greek words suggest incompleteness as well as variety. Indeed no one could claim that the prophetic revelation had been final and exhaustive. By contrast, Christians could now point to a revelation that, though it by no means superseded the law of Moses (for this too was the authentic word of God), gave a new and decisive turn to the relationship between God and human beings, and showed for the first time the true meaning of much in scripture which had formerly been indeterminate and obscure. Through what had been **spoken to us by a Son,** old truths could now be seen in a radically new light.

2   **In these last days.** The phrase means more than just 'a short time ago'. The 'last days' was a term for that glorious future to which, according to the Jewish way of looking at history, all things were tending. But the coming of Christ seemed to Christians to be an event of such a decisive kind that they could think only that it marked the transition between the two ages. They must now be standing at the threshold of the **last days.** For there was no longer anything incomplete in the revelation of Christ. The Son was **the appointed heir of all things.** Until you know who is to be the heir you cannot understand why the father shapes the inheritance as he does; but as soon as the heir is known you can see the purpose of each part of the inheritance. Now that we know that Christ is the **heir** to the universe we can, for the first time, understand the purpose of the universe itself, a purpose which has been there from the beginning, since it was **through** Christ – that is to say, with reference to him as the guiding principle and purpose of creation – that God **created the worlds.**

To be so completely involved in the purpose of all created things, this Son must stand very close to God himself – and the writer uses a metaphor of reflected light and a metaphor from the minting of coins to express this near-
3   identity. Yet he was distinct: **he made purification for sins,** an individual act on the level of humanity, which will be explained in terms of the function of a priest; and at a definite moment of time he **sat down at the right hand of the Majesty on high** – a clear allusion to the opening of Psalm 110, a verse which this writer, along with the early church as a whole, regarded as an inspired description of the destiny which Jesus fulfilled after his resurrection from the dead: 'The LORD says to my lord, "Sit at my right hand until I make your enemies your footstool" ' (the verse is quoted or alluded to in the New Testament more often than any other text from the Old Testament).

One point in this summary of the nature and destiny of Christ is taken
4   up for special treatment: he is **superior to angels.** Why is this so important? Possibly there were some among the listeners who were inclined to place angels too high on the scale of heavenly beings, and who failed to see that Christ was far superior to all such intermediaries between God and human beings. We know that in some circles of Judaism people were inclined to worship angels and might be rebuked for it by the orthodox; and if such people had become Christians they might have been tempted to think of Christ as just 'another angel'. Alternatively, it was an accepted doctrine among Pharisaic Jews that God might send "a spirit or an angel" (Acts 23.9) in order to reveal or endorse a new interpretation of scripture, and some Christians may have been following the same line by thinking that Christ was one of this series of revelatory 'angels'. In any case, whatever the reason, the writer now devotes the first part of his discourse to proving that Christ is immeasurably superior to any angel.
5   **To which of the angels did God ever say . . . ?** This sets the pattern of the following argument. It is based entirely on scripture. Words spoken to angels

are compared with words spoken to the Son, and the difference between them demonstrates the inherent superiority of the Son. This procedure was quite straightforward so far as angels were concerned: there was a number of texts explicitly about angels. But what about the Son, the Christ? This was more difficult; for the Old Testament writers did not directly foretell the Christ whom Christians worshipped; they merely used language – sometimes about God, sometimes about some human being – which later generations came to regard as prophetic of a Messiah who was still to come in the future and which Christians now believed to have been completely fulfilled and explained by the person of Jesus Christ. It is to such passages as these that the writer appeals. His readers must have already been accustomed to reading these texts as prophecies about the Messiah. Without this clue they could hardly have followed the argument.

"You are my Son; today I have begotten you" (Psalm 2.7). The words are echoed in the gospel account of Jesus' baptism, and the whole psalm is one of those which seemed to the early church to have been most startlingly fulfilled by Jesus. The fact that it was originally addressed to a king of Israel was not important: its real meaning was now finally disclosed by Christ.

"I will be his Father, and he will be my Son" (2 Samuel 7.14). This was part of God's promise to King David, transmitted by the prophet Nathan. On the face of it, the promise was no more than a metaphor: God intended to show particular favour to one of David's immediate descendants. But we know (from the Dead Sea Scrolls) that at least one Jewish sect had no hesitation in reading the text as a prophecy about a 'son of David' who was still awaited – the Messiah, the Christ. This writer evidently assumed that his readers were accustomed to taking it in the same way.

6   "Let all God's angels worship him" (Psalm 97.7). In the original Hebrew this verse reads, "all gods bow down before him" – the poem is about the absolute supremacy of God compared with the worthless idols of the heathen. In the Greek version (the Septuagint), the translators, bothered perhaps by the implication that there exist any gods but the one God, rephrased the verse in the form quoted here. But in both versions it is God himself whom angels (or 'gods') must worship. How does this help the argument? – there is nothing whatever here about the Son. To see the force of it we have to read on. Verse 11 of the same psalm runs (in the Greek), 'Light dawns for the righteous.' This was regarded in many Jewish circles as almost a technical expression for the coming of the Messiah. Therefore (so the argument may have run) if the end of the psalm was about the Messiah, so were the earlier verses. "Let all God's angels worship him" could be read as a prophecy about the Messiah, the Son – the firstborn (that is to say, receiving the highest honour from his father), and one who had existed in some sense (as many believed) since the beginning of the world.

So far all the quotations have been in the column of the 'Son', showing his superiority. But what does the Bible say about 'angels' that could be set

7   in the other column? Only one text is offered: **"He makes his angels winds, and his servants flames of fire"** (Psalm 104.4); and instead of searching for more, the writer immediately turns to others that can be placed in the Son's

8   column. **"Your throne, O God, is forever and ever"**. This psalm text, like Psalm 2, was originally addressed to an actual king. It is court poetry: the king is literally praised to the skies, so much so that it appears that he is actually given the terrific title 'God'.[1] But the kings of Israel had never lived up to this high vocation; and these extravagant words of scripture therefore began to be taken to refer to a figure of the future. Who this figure was is given away

9   by the last sentence of the quotation: he was **anointed**, which means that he was the 'anointed one', the Messiah, the Christ – that is (in this writer's language) the Son. Once again scripture is shown to prove that this Son was given the highest honour of all.

10   **"In the beginning, Lord, you founded the earth"** (Psalm 102.25). This is the most puzzling of the series. The psalm speaks of God the Creator – the language and the context leave no possible doubt of this. But for Christians the word 'Lord' was ambiguous. God was 'Lord', but so was Jesus. There is slight evidence to be found in the Septuagint translation of the psalm that this part of it was already, in the century or so before Christ, being interpreted as a prophecy about the coming Messiah. If so, it is a little easier to understand how this writer, and perhaps his readers, felt able to take the 'Lord' of these verses as referring to Christ instead of to God the Creator – particularly since Christ was believed (like the figure of 'Wisdom') to have been in some sense present at creation himself. It was perhaps on the basis of this interpretation that he was able to place this passage in the 'Son' column, proving the absolute superiority of Christ to the angels.

13   **"Sit at my right hand until I make your enemies a footstool for your feet"** (Psalm 110.1). No Christian would have doubted that these words referred to Christ. Had not Jesus himself used them of the Messiah (Mark 12.35–7)? And did they not explain where Christ had gone after the resurrection? With this quotation, already alluded to in verse 3, the series of proof texts in the 'Son' column is rounded off. In the 'angels' column, by comparison, there

14   is nothing more to add but that they are **spirits in the divine service** – this follows from Psalm 104 already quoted; and it may have been the experiences of the earliest Christians, such as those described in the first chapters of Acts, which caused the writer to add that these angels are **sent to serve for the sake of those who are to inherit salvation**.

2.1 **Therefore we must pay greater attention**. It is characteristic of this author to break into his argument by addressing urgent admonitions to his hearers.

---

[1] Whether this is really so has been uncertain almost since the psalm was written. Ultimately it is a question of punctuation, and there was no punctuation to speak of when these words were first written. A different punctuation would yield the meaning given in the NRSV footnote.

Angels, he has just shown, are inferior to Christ; yet according to a tradition which, though not in the Old Testament, was believed by many, it was they who had transmitted the law of Moses: they had been entrusted with a legal

2 **message** which demanded obedience on pain of **a just penalty.** *A fortiori*, if

3 Christians had received **through the Lord**, who is here evidently Christ Jesus and therefore a being far superior to the angels, a message that ensured their

1 **salvation**, how much more must they **pay . . . attention** to any possibility of **transgression?** And if it were said that the angels made the law valid by witnessing to it, here again the gospel of the Son was superior: God himself

4 had **added his testimony** through the remarkable events which had marked the early history of the church.

On no possible timescale, then – even that of the future – could it be said that the angels were superior to Christ; for he was superior to everything under God. And yet this Christ was also Jesus (the first time this name has been mentioned) who had suffered and died on the cross. How were these two things to be held together? By way of an answer, we are offered another extended quotation, this time from Psalm 8.4–6 (though the author

6 introduces it as if he were vague about the source). **"What are human beings that you are mindful of them?"** The psalm is in praise of the dignity given by God to humans: this is its clear meaning. But to this writer (as to most scholarly Jews of his time) a passage of scripture did not necessarily mean only what it appeared to mean on the surface. Any curious feature or inconsistency in the language could be regarded as a clue which might lead to a deeper

8 meaning underneath. And so here: **"subjecting all things under their feet".** If the passage were really about human beings in general, this would be simply untrue: **we do not yet see everything in subjection to them.** Therefore the word translated 'human beings' (which in the Greek is singular, *man*[2]) must refer to someone in particular. Who was this? The psalm offered a further

7 clue: it was someone who was **"for a little while[3] lower than the angels".** This sounds like a hard riddle – but not for Christians, who do see in **Jesus**

9 someone who **for a little while was made lower than the angels,** and then went on, through his suffering and death, to be **crowned with glory and honour** at the right hand of God; for his tasting of death took place, not by way of tragedy or defeat, but as part of a greater design, by **the grace of God.**[4]

---

[2] The Greek word for *man*, unlike the English word, embraces both sexes, and the fact that it is singular makes the author's argument possible. The NRSV routinely avoids using *man* in this generic sense, but by using the plural **human beings** here it obscures the argument. In the following phrase the word **mortals** translates *son of man*, which may possibly have inspired Jesus to use the title of himself – a person who was for a little time lower than the angels but would then be crowned with glory and honour.

[3] The phrase is ambiguous in the Greek: it probably meant originally *a little lower*, but could reasonably be interpreted as meaning **for a little while lower.**

[4] The variant *apart from God* occurs in some manuscripts. It may have been hard for some early editors or scribes to accept that the crucifixion happened **by the grace of God,**

Jesus, then, was superior to the angels, even though there was a period when he was 'lower' than they, a period which involved suffering and death. This much has been shown to fulfil scripture. But it has still to be shown what were the purpose and meaning of this suffering. The clue is in the words **for everyone**. The image which is now to be elaborated, and which will give the key to this part of Jesus' work, is the image of a *priest*.

To perform the function of a priest at the temple in Jerusalem did not demand any qualities of character or spirituality: it was necessary only to be a member of a priestly family, to be without any physical deformity and to undergo certain rites of purification. The purpose of the priesthood was simply to perform the ritual connected with the sacrifices in the temple. This the priests did on behalf of the people as a whole; and the ablutions and rites of cleansing which they underwent before performing their duties were designed to make them ritually pure, or 'perfect'.

If Jesus were to be likened to such a priest, he must be shown in some sense to have fulfilled similar conditions. First, he must be 'perfect' – that is, fully qualified by something corresponding to the ritual of purification; and the manner of this 'perfecting', which was unprecedented for any known priests

10 but which is here said to be **fitting** (the word belongs to Hellenistic religious philosophy) for the one whose priesthood was to have such immense effect, was the unprecedented one of enduring **sufferings** – this will be elaborated

9 in what follows. But secondly, he must have been able to represent **everyone**. This he could do only if he had as much solidarity with those whom he represented as the Jewish priestly families had with the rest of the Jewish race.

11 It was axiomatic that **the one who sanctifies and those who are sanctified all have one Father** – or at least that they are *of one* (the literal meaning of the Greek: **Father** has been introduced by the translators), belonging to one 'family' in the human race. Did Jesus, who was 'superior to angels', have the

16 required solidarity with this family – the new 'family' of **Abraham**? He did; and this is proved again by some texts from scripture. The force of these texts

12 depended on knowing the Christian interpretation of them. The first, **"I will proclaim your name to my brothers and sisters"** (Psalm 22.22), is from a psalm which (according to Mark and Matthew) Jesus actually recited on the cross (Mark 15.34), and which contained many apparently exact prophecies of his sufferings. No Christian would doubt that the speaker in the whole of the psalm was Christ. Therefore the psalm could be quoted to prove that Christ had human **brothers and sisters**. In much the same way, several verses in the eighth chapter of Isaiah seemed to contain clear allusions to the Christ who was to come (Immanuel, the "rock one stumbles over", 8.8,14). Therefore if verses 17 and 18 of that chapter included the words "I will wait

13 for the L O R D . . . **I will put my trust in him . . . Here am I and the children**

and this would explain the alteration. Yet *apart from God* also makes sense. Christ went to his death deliberately, of his own personal will, even if it was God's will that he should die.

whom God has given me", it could be assumed that Christ was the speaker, whose relationship with God, like that of any human being, was based on 'trust', and that the words proved his solidarity with all 'children' of the same family. All this showed that in this respect, as well as that of 'perfection', he was fully qualified to be a 'priest'.

But into this idea of priestly 'perfecting' is introduced a factor that breaks
10   out of the conventional 'priest' imagery altogether: Christ was made **perfect through sufferings**. No such experience was demanded of the Jewish priest, indeed rather the opposite. The difference can be seen most clearly in the case of the high priest on the Day of Atonement (the case which, as we shall soon see, dominates the imagination of this writer). For a week before this day the high priest had to isolate himself from all social contacts lest any chance meeting should make him ritually 'unclean'. He had to be so far as possible totally insensitive to personal or family ties so that no private concerns should interfere with his performance of the great ritual act upon which, once a year, the whole Jewish people depended for its sense of continuing favour with God. Jesus' priesthood was totally different. Instead of being dispassionate
17   and aloof, he was **merciful and faithful**. His solidarity with his brothers and sisters involved entering into the darkest corners of their experience; he was
10   not just their priest, he was also **the pioneer of their salvation**. By treading
14   the path of life right up to death he was able to **destroy the one who has the power of death, that is, the devil**. (This is the author's one excursion into the mythological manner of speech such as we have in Romans 6.12–19.)
17   His solidarity with human beings meant not only that he could perform **the service of God** on their behalf (which was the function of any priest); it
18   meant that he was **able to help those who are being tested**, up to, and even beyond, the moment of death. It is true that his function could be defined
17   like that of the high priest as being **to make a sacrifice of atonement for the sins of the people**. But the means by which he did this – the suffering which it involved for him – were such as to give new content altogether to the concept of priesthood.

The requirement of faithfulness

3.2   This high priest **was faithful** – a new idea, and one which plays an important part in the letter. For an illustration of what this means, the reader is referred to a passage in Numbers (12.7–8) where God is speaking of Moses: "Not so with my servant Moses: he is entrusted with (or *faithful in*) all my house." But here the passage is quoted in indirect speech: **Moses also "was faithful in all *his* house"**. This makes the pronoun *his* sound ambiguous: it could be misinterpreted to mean that Moses was faithful in his *own* house. So the writer has first to dispose of this possible misunderstanding. Every house has its owner; and 'his house' could certainly mean 'the owner's house', that is (in
3   this case), 'Moses' house'. But every house also has a **builder**, and 'his house'

could equally well mean the house of the man who **built** it. And since God

2 is **the builder of all things**, 'his house' could mean **God's house** – which is the meaning here.[5]

This little misunderstanding disposed of, it is possible to use Moses' having been **"faithful in all God's house"** as a pointer to the nature of Jesus' faithful-

5 ness. Jesus was superior to Moses as a son is superior to a **servant**. But Jesus

6 also has a house (the startling metaphor is introduced without apology: **we are his house**) and this 'house' is the setting in which he exercises his faith-fulness, just as God's house was the setting in which Moses exercised his own, lesser, faithfulness. This gives some idea – though more about this will follow – of the sense in which Jesus, the high priest, is 'faithful'.

7 **Therefore**. The connection is emphatic. Christ is faithful; we have become

14 **partners of Christ**; *therefore* we too must be faithful. Characteristically, the author turns aside from his main argument to give a moral exhortation; indeed he has prepared for it by pointing out that we are not automatically 'Christ's house': we have to **hold our first confidence firm** in order to be so. He makes his point by a long quotation from Psalm 95. The second line of

8 this yields an immediate lesson: **do not harden your hearts**. But the bearing of the rest of it on Christian belief and practice depends, again, on a detailed and rather technical process of interpretation.

16 **Now who were they who heard and yet were rebellious?** It was essential to fix exactly who was being referred to in each of the verses of the quo-tation before a moral could be drawn. It was obvious enough that those who **were rebellious** were the whole of the desert generation, whose various 'rebellions' are recounted in Exodus. But to whom, then, were the verses addressed? This was a more difficult question, and could be answered only

11 when the whole passage was considered. The key was in the last words, **"They will not enter my rest."** This implied, surely, that someone else would. The

4.8 obvious candidates were the very next generation, those whom Joshua had brought into the promised land (which was often described by the same word, 'rest'). But the psalm under consideration implied that the 'rest' had still not been entered when the psalm was written, and the psalm was believed

7 to have been spoken **through David much later**, that is, some centuries after the time of Joshua. The 'rest', therefore, must have meant something other than the historical possession of the promised land. What it meant

4 could be shown from another passage of scripture, **"God rested on the sev-enth day from all his works"** (Genesis 2.2). It might be thought that this referred only to God's own 'rest' which he enjoyed after the creation. But

3 the words of the psalm, **"They shall not enter my rest"**, showed that this 'rest' not only belonged to God but was also a future reality intended as

9 a kind of **sabbath rest** for the **people of God**. The psalm, therefore, was

---

[5] The NRSV has obscured this. The Greek in each case has simply *his* (not **God's**), and it is essential to know this in order to follow the argument.

addressed to the future inheritors of this 'rest'. The option to enter it was still open.

What were the qualifications for entering? This could be answered from the same psalm. It was said of the desert generation,

3.10
> "They always go astray in their hearts,
> and they have not known my ways."

19 In other words, **we see that they were unable to enter because of unbelief**. The opposite, 'belief' (or 'faith', the same word), was the particular attribute of those who believe in Christ and are partners with the faithful high priest. This faith would guarantee their entering – but only so long as they held fast 4.11 to it and did not **fall through such disobedience as theirs**. This passage of exposition ends, as it began, with a powerful moral exhortation.

12 **Indeed, the word of God is living and active.** The **word**, in this brief poetic stanza, may be taken to embrace the whole of the divine revelation: the original law given to Moses, the sporadic guidance given through the prophets, and the definitive revelation given in the Son. As such, it is of the strongest possible moral force and penetration. Any failure to obey is at least as serious as it ever was.

A high priest according to the order of Melchizedek

14 **Since, then, we have a great high priest.** Once a year the Jewish high priest **passed through** the outer sanctuary which any priest was entitled to enter, on through the curtain beyond it, and into the Holy of Holies itself. This 'passing through' was the key moment of his priesthood; it was the atoning act for which the high priesthood existed. The high priest of Christians has similarly **passed through** – but now in a different and more profound sense: **through the heavens**, to the throne of God himself. Yet he is still in solidarity 15 with human beings, having been **tested as we are** – and something will be said later about the sufferings which constituted this 'testing' – **yet without sin**, which is probably not so much a statement about Jesus' psychological make-up (as we might naturally take it) as about the fact that the testing[6] caused no swerving from the path of perfect obedience to God. Both by virtue of his closeness to all human beings in the testing to which they are exposed, and also by his perfect access to God, he fulfils the traditional functions of priesthood in a new and definitive way. As a result, it is now possible for us to 16 **approach the throne of grace with boldness** – a word which is used several times in this letter to express the confidence which Christians may now feel in their relationship with the awesome God of the Jewish faith.

[6] The Greek word can also mean *tempting*. But the modern psychological associations of this word make it inappropriate in this context.

Jesus' high priesthood, then, was on a level which far transcended any earthly institution; yet there were still one or two points of correspondence with the Jewish high priesthood which strengthened the comparison. According to a strict interpretation of scripture (though this was not always observed in the politics of later times) every high priest had to belong to the Aaronic

5.1 family and be duly *appointed*[7] for **things pertaining to God**. Now it was known that Jesus did not belong to the high-priestly family. Did he therefore seize the high-priesthood (such things happened in Jewish as well as

4 pagan history), instead of being **called by God**, as Aaron and his descendants

5–6 were? On the contrary, the two psalm verses which form the basis of the whole argument (2.7 and 110.4) show that he became both Son and priest by divine appointment. Secondly, the high priest was very much like other human beings, conscious of their ignorance and weakness, and able not to be

2 **excessively moved**[8] by it but rather to acknowledge his own share of the sins

3 for which he must **offer sacrifice**. Was there anything to correspond with this

7 in Jesus' life? The writer tells us that there was. **In the days of his flesh, Jesus offered up prayers and supplications, with loud cries and tears**. The image is still that of a priest, 'offering up' prayers for himself and others, but is filled out here with what appears to be a historical reminiscence. The gospels do not report any episode in Jesus' life which exactly fits this description. Jesus prays in a general way in the manner of a high priest in John 17, and in Luke 22.32 he refers to a prayer which he has previously offered for one of his disciples. But the only place where an actual struggle in prayer is described is in the episode at Gethsemane. There, we can well imagine that he prayed **with loud cries and tears**; and there are several points of contact between Luke's account of this episode (22.39–46) and these verses in Hebrews. But the natural meaning of the statement in Hebrews that **he was heard** would be that, being threatened with death, Jesus prayed and was delivered in answer to his prayer. In Gethsemane, on the other hand, his prayer was not answered, or at least not in this sense: he was *not* delivered **from death**. It is only by assuming that the prayer alluded to here was a prayer to be delivered, not from death, but from the usual consequences of death, that the two descriptions can be made to match. Possibly some other episode was in the writer's mind which happens not to be recorded in the gospels; or possibly he was thinking of Jesus' **reverent submission** on the cross – where he did indeed, utter a loud cry and offer a prayer to God. But this uncertainty does not affect

8 the point being made: **he learned obedience through what he suffered**, a jingle of Greek words which had become something of a philosophical cliché but which threw light on an otherwise paradoxical point made earlier: it was

---

[7] The NRSV has for some reason introduced a new and less accurate translation of this word: **put in charge**.

[8] See Leviticus 21.10–12: the high priest must restrain any violent show of emotion. The word used in the Greek is a philosophical cliché for moderating anger and grief, and is not well conveyed by the traditional translation, **deal gently**.

9 not by any of the prescribed ritual acts, but by suffering, that Jesus was **made perfect** as a priest.

10 **According to the order of Melchizedek**. This mysterious figure, who suddenly appears and as suddenly disappears in the narrative of Genesis 14, provoked much speculation among Jewish scholars, and the writer is about to devote a substantial discussion to him. But first, in the style of an orator who knows how important it is to keep the listener's attention, he breaks off from the main argument to administer some strongly felt words of reproof, warning and exhortation. Are his readers any longer fit for a lesson of this kind? The deeper meaning of scripture could be known only to those who had advanced some distance in the knowledge of God. Mere beginners had

12 to remain at the level of the literal meaning of the text, **the basic elements of**

13 **the oracles of God**. The knowledge of good and evil – **the word of righteousness** – was not expected of young children: were the readers of this letter in danger of reverting to a similar moral infancy, they who ought by now to be

12 **teachers** themselves?

But the writer does not propose to treat them as such. He is not going to

6.1 be **laying again the foundation**. It is tantalizing to try to discover from this passage exactly what this 'foundation' consisted of and how new converts to Christianity were given their first instruction. The difficulty is that we do not know for certain whether these particular converts were Jews or Gentiles before their conversion. If they were Jews, then the 'foundation'

2 was presumably distinctive Christian teaching; but although **laying on of hands** sounds sufficiently like the rite by which Christians received the Holy Spirit, the plural **baptisms** is a curious way to refer to Christian baptism, but well describes the ritual washings which were a prominent part of Jewish religious practice. If they were Gentiles, then much of the initial instruction must have been indistinguishable from the teaching that was given to any gentile 'sympathizer' who was interested in Judaism, and nothing in the list is so obviously Christian that it could not also describe a course in the elements of Judaism. To either faith, most of these things were fundamental. But the

1 writer refuses to treat his hearers as novices; he is concerned for a **perfection** (in the sense of *maturity* or completeness) which took all this for granted and pressed on to a higher stage of knowledge and understanding.

4 For these are people who have **once been enlightened**; and the danger is not so much that they will make no further progress as that they will be

6 found to have actually **fallen away** – not, probably, in the sense of a lack of faith or conviction (for this kind of introspective reflection on religious belief was less common in antiquity than it is now), but by a standard of moral conduct which might seem not to square with the Christian faith, or even – and this seems to be the danger constantly in the mind of the writer – by abandoning their new Christian allegiance and rejoining the synagogue. In the early days of the church such lapses posed a problem. Christians were people who, having been baptized, had been forgiven their

former way of life and entered a new phase of their existence. It made no sense for them to return to old ways or old loyalties. Yet this happened, and it was hard to know what to do about it. After baptism, was further repentance possible? Should offenders be pleaded with until they repented or should they be expelled from the church? If, after entering the church, they then renounced it and rejoined the Jewish community (which seems to be the force of the startling expression **crucifying again the Son of God and holding him up to contempt**), could they be readmitted to the church? Different answers to these questions are given by different New Testament writers, and it was some time before it became generally accepted that the pattern of inevitably sinning and repeatedly being forgiven is inherent in the Christian life, even after baptism. But if the particular problem that faced this writer was that of apostasy from the community and return to the ranks of its Jewish opponents, it is understandable that he should have taken a particularly firm line. There is a limit in practical terms to the number of times a person may move from one community to another: having left the synagogue once and then returned to it, people could hardly expect to be received a second time into the Christian community; hence the stringency of the judgment – more severe than anywhere else in the New Testament –

4   **it is impossible to restore again to repentance those who have once been enlightened.** Indeed, the writer does not find it necessary to argue the point. He merely supports it with an illustration somewhat in the manner of a

8   parable of Jesus. Earth which, after cultivation, produces only **thorns and thistles** cannot expect anything better than being **cursed** and **burned over**.

The warning is a strong one; and the writer follows good rhetorical practice by following it up with a reference to the good things in his hearers' record,

10   their **work** and their **love**. Unfortunately his words are very general: he may have had in mind specific acts of certain Christians, or he may have been merely paying a formal compliment to the church; his words help us very little as we try to picture the community he was addressing. It was a matter

12   of seeing their Christian life as a response of **faith and patience** to God's **promises.** All that had been promised to Abraham in the way of blessings and salvation was now theirs to **inherit.** And this enables the writer to give positive

16   encouragement. Could God's promises be relied on? In human terms, the greatest assurance that a statement was true was given when the statement was made on oath; for this meant 'calling God to witness', which no one would risk doing unless sure of the truth of what was being said. In this

17   case God himself **guaranteed it by an oath** (the words of the oath are from Genesis 22.16–17). Admittedly it was an unusual oath, for it did not say by whom or by what it was being sworn, or who or what was being 'called to witness'. But this was because there is nothing greater than God, and therefore nothing other than himself by which God could swear. Here, then, to support

18   the promise were **two unchangeable things**, God himself and his oath, **in which it is impossible that God would prove false.** This hope is like an

19 **anchor** – an obvious enough metaphor; but it becomes startling when it is mixed with another drawn from the image of the high priest entering the Holy of Holies on the Day of Atonement. The promise – the anchor, the Melchizedek-type high priest, Jesus himself – **enters the inner shrine behind the curtain**.

7.1 **This "King Melchizedek of Salem"**. The writer now returns to the project he had interrupted of expounding the text relating to this mysterious personage. The relevant verses of Genesis are as follows:

> "After his [Abram's] return from the defeat of . . . the kings . . . King Melchizedek of Salem brought out bread and wine; he was priest of God Most High. He blessed him . . . and Abram gave him one-tenth of everything" (Genesis 14.17–20)

Nothing is known about Melchizedek beyond what is stated in these verses, which seem to preserve some recollection of an ancient pre-Israelite king of 'Salem' (probably Jerusalem), whose religion included the worship of a 'God Most High' (and so was not too far from that of the Jews), and who was permitted by custom to be both king and priest. This enigmatic figure gave Jewish interpreters some trouble. It was almost an axiom of many Old Testament writers that the same person could not be both priest and king: the priesthood went back to Aaron and was instituted by the law of Moses; but the kingship was a later creation, and the king must not presume to claim the rights of a priest. The appearance of this Melchizedek, who was both a king and a 'priest of God Most High', and who also received such reverence from Abraham, was therefore something of an embarrassment. To this writer, on the other hand – as to the speculative thinkers in the sect that produced the Dead Sea Scrolls, where there is also some discussion of him – he was a godsend. He wished to present Jesus under the image of a high priest. But

14 Jesus did not come from a priestly family (**our Lord was descended from Judah, and in connection with that tribe Moses said nothing about priests**), and he was also in some sense a king. How could he be a priest? The answer was given by the precedent of Melchizedek and by the promise in Psalm 110 that Melchizedek would have a successor.

The point is made by means of a careful commentary on the text of Genesis. First, what could be gathered about Melchizedek himself?

(i) He was certainly a king: this was proved both by his name (which in

2 Hebrew suggested **"king of righteousness"**) and by his title, **king of Salem** (which was also suggestive, since *salem* was a form of the word *shalom*, meaning 'peace').

3 (ii) **Without father, without mother**. The most important qualification for any Jewish priest was his genealogy: there must be no doubt that he belonged to the right tribe and family. Nothing is said anywhere in the Old Testament about Melchizedek's ancestors; yet he was a priest. Indeed the fact that not even his birth or his death is mentioned could be taken as a

sign that he had no ordinary **beginning of days nor end of life** – in short, a unique and exceptional king-priest, **a priest forever**, whose function in the Old Testament narrative could now at last be understood: he pointed forward to Christ (**resembling the Son of God**).

Secondly, two actions of Melchizedek are recorded: he received a tithe from Abraham, and he gave Abraham his blessing. Each of these was significant.

(i) The priests and the Levites – all those who served the sanctuary in Jerusalem – were entitled to receive a tenth part of all agricultural produce. This tithe was laid down in the law: it was a right which certain of those

5 **descended from Abraham** had over the rest. Melchizedek was certainly not one of those privileged descendants; yet he apparently had the right to tithe Abraham (who represented the entire Jewish people that was to come, including the priests and Levites). This demonstrated a greatness far exceeding that of any regular priest.

(ii) A similar greatness was proved by the blessing he gave to Abraham; for

7 **it is beyond dispute that the inferior is blessed by the superior**. Melchizedek was greater than Abraham himself! Moreover, as we have seen, Genesis says

8 nothing about Melchizedek's death, from which it could be inferred that **it is testified that he lives**. This puts him in a different category altogether from **those who are mortal**.

This commentary on the text of Genesis has highlighted the fact that being a king and having no priestly ancestry did not disqualify Melchizedek from being a priest. Could this be applied to Jesus? Would there ever be such a priest again? The answer was given by the one other text in the Old Testament which mentions Melchizedek:

> The LORD has sworn and will not change his mind,
17 > **"You are a priest forever according to the order of Melchizedek."**
> (Psalm 110.4)

It was taken for granted that this was a psalm of King David, and that the words must therefore have been spoken to some other figure of the future, long after the promulgation of the law of Moses. It proved, therefore, that a priest of this exceptional type, who was not allowed for in the law, was still to be expected. Here then was a precedent for Jesus' priesthood. But the text had another implication: the new priesthood would supersede the existing

18 one; it involved **the abrogation of an earlier commandment**. And since the existing Aaronic and Levitical priesthood was an integral part of the law, this could mean only that the law itself was to be superseded. The writer will show later that this too was in accordance with scripture: the law contained

19 the promise of its own obsolescence. Here he merely alludes to the point: **the law made nothing perfect**.

Two more phrases in the psalm are significant:

21 (i) **"The Lord has sworn."** An oath was given to the future successor of

20 Melchizedek, but not to the existing priests, who **took their office without**

an oath: another proof of the superiority of Jesus' priesthood and of his
22 authority to initiate **a better covenant**.

21, 24   (ii) **"A priest for ever."** Jesus would be one who **holds his priesthood**
16 **permanently**, so making obsolete the **legal requirement** according to which
a series of men succeeded one another in the office after the death of each
holder.

26   **For it was fitting that we should have such a high priest** – and here it is
a question, not of Jesus' 'qualifications' (these – his sufferings, his solidarity
with human beings – can now be taken as demonstrated), but of his present
status. In order to perform the great ritual of the Day of Atonement,[9] the
high priest in Jerusalem was separated from all possible contact with 'sinners'
28 for a week before. So Jesus, **who has been made perfect** – that is, who has
26 performed the equivalent of all ritual purifications – is now **separated from
sinners**, in the sense that his place is now in heaven, far away from all that
might profane the presence of God. This might seem a fatal separation from
27 those whom Jesus' priesthood was intended to save. But no, Jesus has **offered
himself**, and this great priestly act enables him to dispense with any further
25 separation and to stand in the presence of God uniquely privileged to **make
intercession** for human beings.

The heavenly sanctuary

8.1 **Now the main point in what we are saying is this.** The difficulty in the idea
that one person could be both priest and king has been resolved by means of
the figure of Melchizedek. But a further difficulty remains. The same psalm
which contains a reference to Melchizedek begins with the words, "Sit at
my right hand until I make your enemies your footstool" (110.1). It was
taken for granted by Christians that these words referred to Christ (they are
quoted again and again in the New Testament). It follows that Christ, the
Melchizedek-type priest-king, is now in heaven, with a rôle that looks more
kingly than priestly. In what sense is he still a priest? Priests surely belong
to the sanctuary on earth (whether the 'tent' of the book of Exodus or the
actual temple in Jerusalem which was its successor). But Jesus cannot belong
4 there – for in that temple **there are priests who offer gifts according to the
law** – and in any case, his place is now in heaven. He is definitely still a priest:
3 the condition of priesthood – that one must have **something to offer** –
was certainly fulfilled in his case (by his own self-offering). What kind of
'sanctuary' can there possibly be in heaven for this new high priest to be able
to exercise his priesthood there?

---

[9] The writer slightly confuses the picture by mentioning the sacrifices that were made
day after day. These were normally performed by the ordinary priests, but the high priest
could do so if he wished. Normally, however, he reserved himself for the annual ritual of
the Day of Atonement.

The answer is in another verse of Exodus (25.40). On Sinai, Moses had been given detailed instructions about the construction and furnishing of the tent in which God was to be worshipped. The instructions ended with these

5 words: **"See that you make everything according to the pattern that was shown you on the mountain."** The literal-minded reader might take these words according to their plainest meaning: Moses was to follow carefully the instructions he had just been given. But Jewish scholars, brooding on the word 'pattern', found a deeper meaning in it. Moses, they believed, must have been 'shown the pattern' of an ideal sanctuary, of which the earthly sanctuary which he constructed was no more than an imperfect copy. Scholars whose background included some Greek philosophy imagined this ideal sanctuary to be a kind of microcosm of the universe, and in the actual details of Moses' tent (and subsequently of the temple) they found symbols of the great principles underlying the physical world; while those whose culture was more narrowly Jewish assumed that the ideal sanctuary was a future reality that God would one day bring into existence on earth, the present sanctuary being but a kind of rough draft of what was to come.

This writer comes somewhere between the two. The terms he uses to describe the relationship between the earthly and the heavenly sanctuaries are terms familiar from Greek philosophical language – s**ketch and shadow,**

2 **true tent** – a way of speaking about the distinction between appearance and reality that goes back ultimately to Plato. But the realities he describes in these terms are not philosophical at all. For him, the heavenly sanctuary is not an abstraction, but a real sanctuary with a real priesthood. And this answers the question how Jesus can be thought of as a 'priest' in heaven.

Before this answer is worked out in detail there is one more point to be made. It has already been said that a new priesthood must involve replacing the existing set of laws (for the old law included the regulations governing the old priesthood). But the law was also an expression of the 'covenant' made between God and his people. It followed that the new priesthood of Christ implied also a new covenant, replacing the old – and this too was confirmed

13 by scripture. Jeremiah had spoken of a **"new covenant"** (31.31–4), and this
8–12 phrase alone (which the writer cites in its full context) proved that the original covenant was never intended to last for ever.

9.1 **Now even the first covenant had . . . an earthly sanctuary.** The writer
2 describes it as a **tent**: that is to say, he bases his description on scripture rather than on the temple of masonry which existed in his own day and which was built on the same pattern. Like many other ancient sanctuaries, the sacred tent described in Exodus consisted essentially of two rooms separated by a
3 curtain (**the second curtain**). The outer room – **the Holy Place** – was entered directly (again through a curtain, and only by priests) from the courtyard outside. The inner room – **the Holy of Holies** – had no outside door and could be entered only from the outer room. The outer room contained the articles
4 necessary for the regular services during the year, including **the golden altar**

of incense (it is strange that this writer seems to think of this altar as being in the inner room: he may be thinking of it as a necessary adjunct of the annual ceremonies in the inner room, or he may have been simply misled by a certain ambiguity in the description in Exodus 30.1–10). The contents of the inner room were more mysterious, for they were seldom seen. Originally they were trophies of Israel's earliest history. By the writer's time they had mostly disappeared.

5 **Of these things we cannot speak now in detail.** For many Jewish thinkers each of these objects had a deeper meaning; indeed the whole sanctuary was conceived as a microcosm of God's creation. But this writer has no time for such speculations. The objects he has listed are no more than

6 **preparations.** Far from having a cosmic significance, they accentuate the provisional arrangement of the sanctuary. The Holy of Holies, where God was believed especially to be present, was a dark, inner room separated from worshippers by an outer room given over to the daily routine of **gifts and sacrifices.** But these were concerned only with ritual requirements relating

10 to clean and unclean **food and drink** and various forms of **baptisms** or

9 ablutions, none of which could **perfect the conscience of the worshiper** or bring anyone nearer to the presence of God. The arrangement constituted, in effect, a permanent barrier between the people and the inner sanctuary where God might be most directly encountered. So long as it remained in force it could be said that there was no access to the presence of God, the

8 **way into the sanctuary** had **not yet been disclosed.** If at all, it was trodden only by the high priest on one occasion in the year; but even the ritual of that great Day of Atonement was unable to effect lasting reconciliation with God.

11 **But when Christ came.** The question from which the whole discussion started was, In what way could Christ be thought of as a 'high priest' in heaven? The answer has been suggested by an account of the existing (or recently existing, if Hebrews was written after the temple's destruction) arrangements of the sanctuary – arrangements described rather as they are laid down in the book of Exodus than as they may actually have existed in Jerusalem in the writer's own day. These arrangements were defective – they

9 could not **perfect the conscience of the worshiper.** But in any case, they were only a copy of the 'pattern' shown to Moses on the mountain (8.5). This meant that they pointed forward to a new and better kind of sanctuary altogether. This was the sanctuary in heaven where Christ would now exercise his high priesthood; and the fact that this new high priest had come showed that the old sanctuary was obsolete and the new one in operation.

Yet even if it was obsolete there were important analogies to be drawn with the new sanctuary. The old functioned by means of animal sacrifices.

12 In the new, Christ sacrificed himself – **his own blood.** A priest sacrificing himself is of course a paradoxical idea – it almost tears apart the whole priest metaphor. But there are three ways in which the paradox can be shown to be significant.

(i) The sacrifices of the old sanctuary were not useless: they were the means

13 by which the **flesh is purified – the sprinkling of the ashes of a heifer** was the means of cleansing one of the most serious forms of ritual uncleanness, that caused by contact with a dead body. But if animal sacrifices were the means of purifying the body, Christ's self-sacrifice, being infinitely more effective,

14 could be claimed to **purify our conscience.**

(ii) If there was now a new covenant in place, a death must have been

15–21 necessary to inaugurate it. The argument here (like that of Paul in Galatians 3.15–18) depends on a kind of pun. The 'covenant' made by God with his people was rendered into Greek by the word *diathēkē*, which usually meant 'will' or 'testament'. This made it appear as if a covenant, like a will, could come into force only after a death. Now of course God, the author of the covenant, does not die. But the original covenant was in fact sealed by death – the death of sacrifices: to this extent it was like a will. In which case it could be expected that the new covenant would also be established by a death. Here was another way of expressing the meaning of the death of Christ.

(iii) The sacrifices which took place in the earthly sanctuary were not

23 meaningless, but they purified only **the sketches of the heavenly things.** This presupposed that the heavenly things themselves would need purification, for which **better sacrifices** would be needed. The heavenly sanctuary is still a real sanctuary, with a real sacrifice; but that sacrifice, the death of Christ himself, is of another order altogether, able to accomplish all that the earthly high priest could never do.

This reference to death highlights the greatest difference between the old sacrifices and that of Christ. Animal sacrifices were performed again and

26 again. If Christ's sacrifice had been in the same category **he would have had to suffer again and again** – which is obviously absurd. Indeed, unlike the offerings of the Levitical priests, which dealt only with ritual uncleanness and the expiation of particular offences against the law, the offering of Christ

27 was once for all and cancelled **the sins of many.** The old realities remain: **it is appointed for mortals to die once, and after that the judgment.** But the sin which made death and judgment to be feared has now been atoned for by Christ's death (with a finality that could never have been achieved by the ritual of the Day of Atonement), and the judgment itself will be transformed,

28 for it will be the moment when Christ will **appear a second time ... to save those who are eagerly waiting for him.**

10.1 **Since the law has only a shadow of the good things to come.** It has already been shown (by a passage from Jeremiah, 8.8–13) that the law has been made obsolete by the new high priest; and the same point is now made in popular philosophical terminology: it is a shadow and **not the true form of these realities.** Moreover it can be proved by reflecting on that part of the law concerned with ritual acts and sacrifices. For the law provides for **sacrifices that are continually offered year after year.** What clearer indication could there be that these sacrifices are useless? For when these sacrifices are offered

(and the writer seems once again to have the Day of Atonement in mind)

3 **there is a reminder of sin year after year**, as if the sacrifice of the previous year had had no effect at all. Clearly this could not be the ultimate state of

5–7 things – and the proof, once again, is found in scripture: Psalm 40.6–8.

5 **When Christ came into the world, he said.** *Christ* is an addition by the translators: the Greek text has merely, 'When *he* came into the world' – an enigmatic introduction which belongs, once again, to the kind of private language which scholars like this writer felt able to use when interpreting scripture. Psalm 40 was originally the song of a pious worshipper who had been mercifully delivered from misfortune and who saw that his sense of gratitude to God must be expressed in the form of something more personal and demanding than the prescribed ritual of sacrifices and offerings. But to those accustomed to find deeper meanings in scripture the psalm was full of

7 suggestive phrases. **"See, God, I have come."** (40.7). Who had come? Why, he who 'was to come', the Messiah. But the Messiah had not yet come. Therefore the psalm must be a prophecy, it contained the words he would say when he finally did come. This whole chain of reasoning[10] is presupposed in the highly condensed phrase, *when he came into the world, he said.*

Many of the prophetic writings protested against attaching undue importance to the ritual of sacrifice – Jesus himself quoted Hosea 6.6, "I desire mercy, not sacrifice" (Matthew 9.13). But, taken as an authoritative utterance of one who 'was to come' into the world, these verses of Psalm 40 were more than a protest: they actually annulled the former law with its system of sacrifices and established a new dispensation, under which the one sacrifice

10 was **the offering of the body of Jesus Christ once for all**. In that offering, 'the will of God' took the form of Christ's obedient self-sacrifice; and the effects of that sacrifice are that we too **have been sanctified** – once again a cultic image: we have been made fit to enter the presence of God.

This offering, unlike its shadowy counterparts in the old system, was **once for all**. This finally removes the difficulty of conceiving how a single person could be both priest and king at the same time. A priest's place is at the altar, a king's is on his throne: how could Christ be both? The answer is now quite

12 simple. *First,* Christ **offered for all time a single sacrifice for sins**; *then* **"he sat down at the right hand of God"**. The two acts followed each other, and we do not have to try to imagine them as being simultaneous. Now at last we know how to put together the two verses of Psalm 110 (1, 4) which have been

---

[10] Traces of this reasoning are to be seen in the Septuagint translation of the psalm into Greek, which is the version always used by this writer. The original Hebrew version was probably intended to mean, 'As it is written for me (to do) in the scroll (of the law), I have come to do your will.' But by rendering this, 'As it is written *of* me', the Septuagint translators implicitly identified the speaker with one whose coming was foretold in scripture. They seem also to have frankly misunderstood the sentence they rendered **a body you have prepared for me**. The original meant something like, 'you have given me attentive ears'. But this mistranslation yielded a valuable point to the Christian interpreter.

running right through the letter: "Sit at my right hand, until I make your enemies a footstool for your feet", and "You are a priest forever, according to the order of Melchizedek".

15 **And the Holy Spirit also testifies.** One more text ties up the argument (Jeremiah 31.33–4). This text has already been quoted to prove that there
17 will be a new covenant (8.8–12). It ends, **"I will remember their sins and their lawless deeds no more."** If the promise of a new covenant has now been fulfilled, this last clause must have been fulfilled also. It follows that
18 the old system of making **a** sacrificial **offering for sin** no longer has any validity.

Take a final glance at the old system. Outside the temple are the arrangements for ritual cleansing by blood sprinkled on the people (Exodus 24.8) and water ablutions. Inside the temple, in the outer room, are the furnishings required by the priests for their daily rituals. At the far end is the curtain which none could pass through (on pain of death) save, once a year, the high priest, who alone had the right and the duty to enter that awesome inner
22 sanctuary. All this is now superseded: it is the heart that is **sprinkled**; the former ablutions are replaced by the **pure water** of Christian baptism; and
20 the **curtain** no longer forbids access to the presence of God: a **way** through has been opened by means of Jesus' **flesh**,[11] that is, the highly physical experiences of suffering and death by which Jesus performed his high-priestly
19 offering. All this gives us **confidence** (a key word in this writing: see above on 4.16) **to enter the sanctuary** – but now the writer characteristically changes his tone of voice: no longer doctrinal teaching but moral exhortation. And without so much as a pause for breath he comes straight to a particular
25 point where his hearers had been at fault – **neglecting to meet together**. This is hardly to be understood as mere slovenliness in attendance at church. The stakes are far higher. The Greek word suggests 'abandoning', failing to stand firm with fellow Christians in times of adversity – and a sketch of such times follows a few lines further on. Once again we detect the pressure Christians were under to leave the church and rejoin the Jewish community, a step of enormous consequences given the expected imminence of the **Day** of judgment.

The seriousness of this judgment is a fixed point for both the Jewish and
27 the Christian faith. **A fury of fire that will consume the adversaries** is a typical Jewish phrase for it, and both the idea and the imagery were taken over into Christianity. For the Christian as for the Jew, **a fearful prospect of judgment** remains for those who fall away from faith and obedience. This author differs from other New Testament writers only in the greater

---

[11] It is not clear, in this rush of metaphor, whether it is the way or the curtain which is described as the 'flesh' of Jesus – the Greek can be taken either way. In solidarity with him, we either burst through the limitations of flesh to life beyond (in which case his flesh is the curtain, as in the NRSV); or else, united with him, we come to be where he now is (in which case his flesh is the way).

26 stringency with which he regards apostasy or moral laxity in Christians. **If we wilfully persist in sin . . . there no longer remains a sacrifice for sins.** This was indeed a dramatic change for those who had been converted to Christianity from Judaism. Formerly, every offence against the law could be atoned for by a prescribed sacrifice, and offenders would then resume their place in society. Christians no longer had any such provision for dealing with their sins: they were thrown directly upon the judgment, the mercy and the forgiveness of God. In other parts of the New Testament a distinction is made between (for instance) the sin against the Holy Spirit and all other sins (Mark 3.29), or between sins that are and are not 'mortal' (1 John 5.16–17). Does this writer expect the same condemnation for all sins? His language, here and elsewhere, certainly suggests that he does. But the parallel he draws with the Mosaic law shows that it is principally grave offences that he has in mind. The death penalty was attached only to such sins as idolatry and murder (Deuteronomy 13.6–9; 19.11–13). An offence of equivalent gravity
29 was that of those who had **spurned the Son of God, profaned the blood of the covenant . . . and outraged the Spirit of grace.** We might today be inclined to give these words a psychological meaning and to interpret them as a kind of interior disloyalty to the faith. But the author will have intended them in a more tangible sense. The issue was that of belonging either to the Christian community or to a Jewish or pagan one which had explicitly rejected Christianity and attempted to discredit it through slander and contempt. Under conditions of persecution (such as are about to be described), solidarity with the church was crucial. If one stood away from it, one would be forced to renounce it altogether in words that amounted to blasphemy and profanation. For such apostasy God remained as severe a judge as he ever had been under the old system of the law. There were plenty
30 of texts in the Old Testament to underline this severity. Two are quoted here, from Deuteronomy 32.35–6.[12]
32   **Recall those earlier days.** The Christian church did not escape persecution for long – the description here is presumably typical of what they were
35 subjected to. Under persecution Christians needed to hold on to **confidence**
36, 39 (which has been one of the writer's main themes), to **endurance** and to **faith.** Faith is another of the themes, and is about to receive fuller treatment: it is a deep and many-sided attitude. But the easiest way for an early Christian writer to encourage it was to point to the imminence (as it then seemed) of the day of judgment and the vindication of the righteous. This suggested a text that was often appealed to in Jewish circles to encourage those who were tempted to doubt the promises of God: Habakkuk 2.3–4. This text also
37–8 contained some suggestive words about faith – a term which (somewhat differently understood) played an important part in the reasoning of Paul

---

[12] The first is quoted also in Romans 12.19, though for a rather different purpose. In each case the quotation is a free one: perhaps these texts had almost become proverbs.

(see above on Romans 1.17) and forms a link with the great sermon on faith that follows.

11.1   **Now faith is ...** What is faith? For us it can have a wide range of meanings – faith in ourselves or other people, in leaders, in our country, in certain procedures, but also (and for many people primarily) faith in God, faith in Christ. For Paul, the word takes on its full meaning only when it denotes the relationship between a believer and Christ. But for this writer the word is more general. He does not reflect on all possible different kinds or objects of 'faith'; for him the word simply reflects a choice between religious and philosophical alternatives. One alternative is a thoroughgoing pragmatism: you base your life on things as you see them; you do not concern yourself with any metaphysical realities that may lie behind appearances or with any expectations of a future state of affairs better than the present; everything you do is a calculated response to the world around you. The other alternative is simply 'faith'. For the sake of **things hoped for**, which give you **assurance**, and of **the conviction of things not seen**, you live a life different from that of the pragmatist. Because you believe that there will be some ultimate, otherworldly reward, you go beyond ordinary proverbial wisdom and are prepared to suffer exile, suffering, even death. Your decisions are not made on the basis of material advantage: you set your heart on realities that are known only to faith.

In other cultures these basic questions presented themselves differently. The alternative to pragmatic common sense was not always thought of as faith in a future heaven or an underlying reality. The most widely followed philosophy of the time – Stoicism – taught detachment from worldly concerns and offered the philosopher an inner peace and security far superior to anything that could be gained from the comfort and enjoyment of the senses. Here, the antithesis was not between pragmatism and faith but between pragmatism and a philosophical discipline of detachment. Or again, Paul's experiences as a Christian led him to discover that the meaning of present sufferings was to be found not merely through a promised reward in heaven but rather through the sense of intimacy with Christ, the inner transformation of the person, that was effected by the suffering itself. Here again, the issue was not so much between pragmatism and faith as between the values of this world and the values of a faith-based experience which embraced both this world and the next.

But for most Jewish thinkers the choice was quite simple. Either the visible world is all that is, or else we must believe that God exists, that God makes demands, and that God rewards (in this world or the next) those who are faithful to those demands. The alternatives were simply faith and no faith. Not that faith was an easy option. It is all very well to say that God rewards those who fulfil his demands; but is this borne out by the facts? The Old Testament is full of stories of men and women who made great sacrifices rather than disobey the will of God; and every Jew felt inspired by the heroes and martyrs of the Maccabean period, who had steadfastly faced torture and death rather than abandon their religious principles. But had these people received their vindication and their reward? The answer was no – not yet. The faith of the Jewish people was that the promises made by God would be *ultimately* fulfilled, that God would *in the end* pronounce his universal judgment and vindicate his elect, and that the men and women of faith would *then* receive their rightful reward. The present was the time when that faith was tested; the time of vindication and reward still lay in the future.

Christians inherited the same view: the alternatives were still faith and no faith. If they were being persecuted they would have the same temptation to opt for the easier way out. But no, they must have 'endurance' and 'faith', and they could be encouraged by the classic examples of faith given by those great figures in Jewish history who had unswervingly adhered to the will of God in the face of all the discouragements that materialistic common

2 sense and ruthless enemies could devise. It was **by faith that our ancestors received approval**. But there was a difference. For the Jewish heroes the reward still lay in the future. As the writer says at the end of his sermon, they

39 **did not receive what was promised**. But for Christians the period of reward had already partly begun. They still needed faith – that is the point of the whole discourse – but whereas previous generations could see only a distant prospect of reward, Christians stood on the very threshold.

Accordingly, this writer did not have to look for his examples of faith in the fresh annals of the Christian church. He could point to any of the great figures of the past who had consistently obeyed the commands of God rather than the promptings of expediency. He could search the Old Testament for them; or he could take his examples from that more recent period when Jewish history (recorded in the books of the Maccabees) seemed to have attained a high point of nobility and glory, the Maccabean resistance to the paganizing oppression of Antiochus Epiphanes. In point of fact he probably did not need to work out his own list of heroes. Jewish writers were fond of singing the praises of the great names of their history, and he could borrow from the work of others. This list happens to be by far the longest example in the New Testament (the letter of James, in a somewhat similar passage (2.21–6), mentions only Abraham and Rahab), but it is less ambitious than that in Sirach 44–50.

The list could start almost anywhere in the Bible. But right at the beginning there is a statement of faith: "in the beginning God created the heavens and the earth". This was the ultimate and basic faith held in common by all those

2 **ancestors** who are about to be mentioned and by their successors down to the present day. The known universe was not a meaningless phenomenon, or (as some religions pretended) a battleground between competing gods or evil powers: it was the deliberate creation of the one God. To put it in terms that we would associate with philosophical theology, but which may

3 be[13] no more than a recognition of the power of the **word of God: what is seen was made from things that are not visible.**

4 The list begins with **Abel.** "The LORD had regard for Abel and his offering, but for Cain and his offering he had no regard" (Genesis 4.4–5). The text gives no explanation of God's preference; a certain arbitrariness seemed characteristic of God's dealings with human beings at this early stage in their history. But later Jewish thinkers were not content to leave it at that. There must surely have been something about Abel and his offering which made God have regard for him and not for Cain. Our author assumes without question that it was his faith: **through this he received approval as righteous.** In the Genesis narrative God subsequently said to Cain, "Your brother's blood is crying out to me from the ground!" (4.10). This may explain the sentence, **through his faith he still speaks.**

5 "Enoch walked with God; then he was no more, because God took him" (Genesis 5.24). This enigmatic verse gave rise to much speculation. It seemed that Enoch, like Elijah (who was carried up to heaven), did not die. Why was he spared the normal fate of mortals? Genesis said only that he "walked with God" – or **pleased God,** as it appeared in the Greek version always used by this writer. What exceptional character or quality was there here to explain such a prodigious exception to the common condition? Differing answers were given; but our author again takes it for granted that it was faith, for

6 **without faith it is impossible to please God.**

7 **Noah:** again there had been a shift of emphasis in biblical interpretation. In Genesis (6–9) Noah represents the means by which God allowed the world of living things to survive the punishment that was to be inflicted on the entire human race. But later thinkers began to reflect on the response of Noah himself. He had been given the apparently absurd command to build a huge ship in the middle of dry land. That he did so was proof of amazing faith in God. And, as it turned out, he was right and the world was wrong: **he condemned the world.**

8 **Abraham:** it was traditional to think of Abraham as the subject of a whole series of 'tests' by which God made him the perfect progenitor of the Jewish race and an object lesson of faith. The last and most demanding of these

18 tests was the command to sacrifice his only son Isaac (Genesis 22), **of whom he had been told, "It is through Isaac that descendants shall be named for you."** This was the supreme test of faith: Abraham passed it and was rewarded with promises of a unique destiny. Before this, our author mentions other instances of Abraham's faith: his obedience when called to leave his native country (Genesis 12.1,4), and his acceptance of a nomadic existence. This acceptance, which characterized not only Abraham but his whole family and his people, was a clear sign of living by faith, not by short-term self-interest.

---

[13] The NRSV footnote offers one alternative translation; but the Greek words may also mean *that which is seen came into being by means of what is not seen* (i.e. the word of God).

15 **If they had been thinking of the land that they had left behind, they would have had opportunity to return**. But in fact they were sustained by God's promise of a land of their own in the distant future. Indeed our author goes further and spiritualizes this promise: ultimately their faith was not even in something as tangible as that part of the earth's surface they were to inherit, 10 but in the remote vision of a perfect society, a **city that has foundations,** 16 **whose architect and builder is God**, a country that is **a heavenly one**.

One more Abraham example is given: both Abraham and Sarah were 12 past the age for begetting and bearing children – in this respect they were **as good as dead** – when Isaac was conceived; nevertheless, God promised them a tremendous posterity (**"as many as the stars of heaven"**, etc., Genesis 22.17 and elsewhere). In point of fact, Genesis records that both Abraham and Sarah laughed at this promise instead of believing it (17.17; 18.12). But what Jewish thinkers remembered was that their race was the result of a supernatural promise made to Abraham and Sarah, who in the end accepted their responsibility and thereby gave another example of faith.

20 **Isaac**: for us the interest of Isaac's two blessings in Genesis 27 depends on the deception that had been played upon him by Jacob: this is the dramatic climax of the scene. But it could still be said that Isaac could not have given such a blessing at all unless he had had faith in his vision of the future.

21 **Jacob**: the same goes for Jacob's blessing of each of Joseph's sons (Genesis 48). The detail that he was **"bowing in worship over the top of his staff"** is an echo of a different incident (Genesis 47.31), where in fact the word 'staff' is a misreading by the Septuagint translators. The correct Hebrew word means 'bed'.

22 **Joseph**: it is natural to wish to be buried in the place where one's own people live. Joseph's desire to be buried in Palestine (Genesis 50.24–5) was a clear proof of his faith in God's promise to Abraham that his people would one day return there.

23 **Moses**: After Abraham, Moses is the key figure of Israelite history, and is associated with a number of acts of faith. First, **his parents**. In the Hebrew version of Exodus, only his mother is credited with defying the king's edict to kill all male offspring (2.1–3). But in the Greek version (the Septuagint) and in subsequent tradition both parents take credit for showing the faith required to believe that the boy had a future. (That he was **beautiful** is not necessarily the meaning of the Greek word, which suggests refinement of character: the parents would have needed 'faith' to discern this when he was a baby.)

Moses himself is cited for three acts of faith. It is true that he abandoned 24 his status as **a son of Pharaoh's daughter** (which would have carried wealth and influence) in order to take up the cause of the Hebrews; but according to Exodus the immediate cause of this was the fear of being caught after killing an Egyptian (2.11–15) – and some manuscripts have actually added this reference to the text (see the NRSV footnote). This writer, however, takes

a longer view. Ultimately Moses preferred to share the still obscure destiny
25 of his people rather than **to enjoy the fleeting pleasures of sin**. The choice
26 was a decisive one. On the one hand **the treasures of Egypt** were proverbial;
on the other hand there would be **abuse**, and abuse of no ordinary kind.
Abuse was what Christians were now suffering **for the Christ**, which is a
possible meaning of the Greek phrase; but literally the words mean *abuse of
the Christ (the anointed one)*, which is an idea with a long history. Psalm 69.9
and Psalm 89.51 were both passages that recognized that a righteous man –
even one whom God had chosen and 'anointed' – might have to suffer abuse;
and the destiny which lay before Moses would involve similar suffering and
27 **abuse**. Seeing **him who is invisible** is of course a contradiction in terms; and
though Moses is occasionally credited with exceptional intimacy with God
(as in Numbers 12.8), the passage in Exodus (33.18–23) insists that even
Moses could not see God's 'face'. God is invisible – this was an axiom for
Jewish saints and Greek philosophers alike. Hence Moses' actions were the
28 result of faith, not of sight. Finally, Moses **kept the Passover**: he responded
to God's instructions to sprinkle the doorposts of the Israelites with blood
without knowing whether this would give protection from **the destroyer** –
he acted **by faith**.

Two more episodes from the saga of Israelite history are adduced as exam-
29 ples of faith, shown this time by the whole people: the crossing of the **Red**
30 **Sea** and the conquest of **Jericho**. Last in the list of individuals – somewhat
31 surprisingly – comes **Rahab**. The story of Rahab is in Joshua 2. She was a
prostitute and a heathen – two serious disqualifications for appearing in a list
of honourable figures of Jewish history. But later speculation fastened upon
the fact that she, alone of **the disobedient** (that is, the people of Jericho,
who were *unbelievers* – see the NRSV footnote), had made a true confession
of faith: "The LORD your God is indeed God in heaven above and on earth
below" (Joshua 2.11). Rahab became the prototype of all who turned from
paganism to faith in the one true God; she began to appear in the ancestry
of King David himself (Matthew 1.5) and to be revered as the mother of
prophets and priests. Her popularity in Jewish tradition sufficiently explains
her appearance in the series here.
32 The stories of **Gideon, Barak, Samson** and **Jephthah** are in the book of
Judges; those of **David** are in 1–2 Samuel and 1 Kings; those of Samuel in
1 Samuel. In the earliest period the exploits of such people were mainly
in the form of military achievements against overwhelming odds: through
33, 34 faith they **conquered kingdoms . . . became mighty in war and put foreign
armies to flight**, though their faith might also be said to have informed their
33 administration of **justice** and enabled them to direct policy according to
God's **promises**. (An allusion to two notable miracles, one of Elijah (1 Kings
35 17), one of Elisha (2 Kings 4), seems to be slipped in with the words, **Women
received their dead by resurrection**.) Later, faith was more characteristically
shown in the resistance of the pious to all threats and tortures which might

have made them abandon their ancestral faith. The literature of this later
33 period began with the book of Daniel. Daniel himself **shut the mouths**
34 **of lions** (Daniel 6); Shadrach, Meshach and Abednego **quenched raging**
fire (Daniel 3). In the Maccabean wars there were many heroes of faith
whose fortitude became enshrined in history and legend and who inspired a
whole literature of martyrdom. Even the great prophets of the Old Testament
began to be credited with feats of endurance and with martyrs' deaths (such
37 as Isaiah, who, legend said, was **sawn in two**). With so many examples to
32 choose from, the writer could do no more than summarize: **time would fail**
me to tell . . .

The author of one of the psalms, appalled and bewildered by the fact that
so often the wicked appear to flourish, had been tempted to abandon his
faith. A sudden thought brought him up short:

> If I had said, "I will talk on in this way,"
> I would have been untrue to the circle of your children.
> (Psalm 73.15)

The fact that so many people in the past had chosen God, not the world –
that is, had shown faith – was one of the strongest supports an individual
could have in making the same choice. All these figures of the past had given
12.1 their 'witness' that the decision of faith was the right one. And so now: **we**
are surrounded by so great a cloud of witnesses. We Christians should not
falter for one moment in choosing the way of faith rather than the way of
material self-interest and compromise.

But then the metaphor changes. The 'witnesses' become a dense cloud of
spectators seated round a stadium while the athlete lays aside **every weight**
(an image that suggests laying aside **sin**) and stands at the starting line,
inspired by the example of one who is now seated in a place of honour,
2 having been the first to undertake the full course (**the pioneer**) and complete
it (**the perfecter**). The witnesses have not yet received the prize; their faith
has not yet been vindicated. But Jesus inspires, not merely as one who has
had the resolution to make the choice of faith, but as one whose faith has
been triumphantly justified. It was **for the sake of**[14] **the joy that was set**
before him – which could be grasped only by faith and hope – that he chose
the bitter alternative and **endured the cross, disregarding its shame.** But
(unlike all previous witnesses) he has already taken possession of what lay
ahead. To quote Psalm 110.1 again, he **has taken his seat at the right hand**
of the throne of God.

3 For Christ, the cost of this steadfast and uncompromising **hostility against**
4 **himself from sinners** was death. The Christians' **struggle against sin** – which

---

[14] The Greek can be taken in two ways. It has often been felt that Christ can hardly
be said to have suffered **for the sake** of the joy ahead, and that the alternative meaning,
instead of the joy, is preferable (see the NRSV footnote).

probably means the struggle against harassment by others as well as any struggle within themselves against the impulse to betray their faith – is not yet so acute: **you have not yet resisted to the point of shedding your blood.** Their suffering has not yet approached the point of martyrdom. There are places in the New Testament where the problem of suffering is tackled in a deep and original way: the suffering of a Christian is a sharing of Christ's suffering, a renewal of the inner person, a condition of true discipleship. But here this author is content to use an old and familiar argument to explain

7 the relatively mild suffering his hearers have undergone: **what child is there whom a parent does not discipline?** We are God's children; therefore we must expect God's fatherly discipline. The argument makes use of proverbial

5–6, 11 wisdom (Proverbs 3.11–12) and Greek moralizing (**discipline always seems painful**); it ends with a return to the metaphor of the stadium. The athlete needs strength, endurance and determination to run straight down the

13 course; and the equivalent of going **lame** in the Christian life is likely to have been the danger of apostasy. A single renegade from the community could

15 be a **root of bitterness** – the image is taken from Deuteronomy 29.18, where it applies to someone who turns aside from the worship of the one true God. The health and peace of the whole church could be threatened by it.

No middle position was possible. To leave the church was to relapse into a

16 way of life that gave priority to material interests and made one an **immoral and godless person.** Where in the Bible could one find an example of such a lapse? The figure of Esau suggested itself, who **sold his birthright** (Genesis 25.31–4) – which was tantamount to renouncing his membership of the people of God – and whom later tradition painted in the colours of the

17 most persistent immorality. Moreover, **he found no chance to repent**, his apostasy was irrevocable; in this respect too he could serve as a warning to the Christian apostate, for whom likewise (as this writer has already twice insisted) there was no possibility of return.

18 **You have not come.** The awesomeness of God is a reality that is taken with intense seriousness, not only in the temple arrangements which have been the subject of much of the argument, but throughout the Old Testament. He is **a blazing fire, and darkness, and gloom, and a tempest.** Remember the awesomeness which accompanied the law-giving on Sinai, in which this majestic God disclosed his demands on human beings (Exodus 19.16–23).

21 Even **Moses said, "I tremble with fear."** But now set against this the new

22 situation created by Christ. **You have come,** not to Mount Sinai, but **to Mount Zion and to the city of the living God, the heavenly Jerusalem,** a symbol of the ultimate and glorious society which God will one day bring into being. God is no longer simply an awesome presence, keeping all creatures at their distance by the blazing fire of his sovereignty. He now holds court in heaven, surrounded by **innumerable angels** (his dedicated worshippers

23 since the beginning of time) and **the assembly of the firstborn** – perhaps the recipients of God's first promises to his people; but now also by **the spirits**

of the righteous made perfect, that is, those with a complete qualification to stand in God's presence. But is this heavenly and holy society, this great symphony of consecrated worship, any more accessible to ordinary human
24 beings than the blazing fire of Sinai? Yes, because of **Jesus, the mediator of a new covenant**. Sinai, and the law proclaimed there, has been superseded. Jesus has offered his own life; and his blood, instead of crying out for vengeance like Abel's (Genesis 4.10), is a means (foreshadowed by the **sprinkled blood** of the old ritual) of making others pure and admitting them to the presence of God.

Is this really so? Does this new state of affairs now exist? Scripture may not give explicit proof of it, but there are many texts which suggest it by
26 implication. Haggai 2.6 is one: **"Yet once more I will shake not only the earth but also the heaven."** If heaven and earth – the whole world of appearance – can be 'shaken' in a final cosmic catastrophe, there must be some reality
28 which endures, **a kingdom that cannot be shaken**. It makes sense to talk of transience only if somewhere there is permanence by which to measure it.

So **let us give thanks** – yes, but not forgetting that God is still to be taken with immense seriousness; he is to be worshipped with **reverence and awe**. The old covenant may have gone, but there is a new one that is equally
25 binding. The old law may have been superseded, but there is still **one who warns from heaven**. We may have new privileges in the face of the dread realities of majesty and judgment, but these realities still remain. It is still awesomely true, as it was when Moses spoke the words (Deuteronomy 4.24),
29 that **our God is a consuming fire**.

Moral exhortations

13.1 **Let mutual love continue.** The author seems to turn rather suddenly to moral exhortation, and adds a series of injunctions similar to that which forms the conclusion of a number of New Testament letters. Some have thought that this last chapter may have originally been a separate document belonging to another letter; hence the personal greetings at the end of it, of which there has been no hint in the previous chapters. But others are more impressed by points of contact with what has gone before, and observe that it is in the author's style to let his argument lead to earnest moral instruction, which would in any case form a natural peroration to a composition of this kind. The injunctions themselves are not original or even distinctively Christian: they belong to the common stock of moral teaching in antiquity.
2 **Do not neglect to show hospitality.** This was a virtue highly esteemed by both Jews and pagans, and there were stories in the literature of both which showed how dangerous it might be to neglect it: in Genesis 18–19 Abraham and Lot offered solicitous hospitality to their mysterious visitors, who did indeed turn out to be angels; and in Homer it was a commonplace that a stranger from over the mountains might always be a god in disguise.

3   **Remember those who are in prison**. Again, this was a duty taken for
granted in popular Stoic ethics, and for much the same reason as is given
here; and it features in the list of 'acts of kindness' which Christians are to
do for one another in Matthew 25.31–46.

4   **Let marriage be held in honor by all**. Adultery and sexual promiscuity
were regarded in the Jewish culture as among the most flagrant sins of the
pagan world: they never felt any doubt that **God will judge fornicators and
adulterers**.

5   **Keep your lives free from the love of money**. This again was a popular
philosophical principle: **be content with what you have** is a phrase that
owes something to the Stoic ideal of 'self-sufficiency'. It was also strongly
endorsed by Jesus on the grounds that God provides all that is needful. The

5   two quotations here make much the same point. The first is a paraphrase of

6   a passage such as Joshua 1.5; the second is from Psalm 118.6.

7   **Remember your leaders**. This again seems to have been one of the regular
themes of Christian ethics that was based on general moral principles. It
occurs in similar contexts elsewhere (Galatians 6.6; 1 Thessalonians 5.12).
The **outcome of their way of life** is not necessarily a way of saying that
they were martyred for their faithfulness – there is little evidence for such
persecution at this time – but means rather that their teaching had a visible
effect on their own lives.

The series is now interrupted by a solemn sentence of the kind that Chris-

8   tians may well have used in their worship: **Jesus Christ is the same yesterday
and today and for ever**. It might seem more natural to have made this affirmation about God: so, in Revelation, it is God "who is and who was and who
is to come" (1.8). Here it is boldly transferred to Jesus Christ, perhaps with
the difference that 'yesterday' means, not 'existing from eternity', but a short
time ago when he was among his followers.

9   **Do not be carried away by all kinds of strange teachings**. Evidently the
writer was aware of some specific danger, but we have no clue to its nature.
'Strange teachings', from the point of view of people steeped in Jewish and
Christian traditions, must refer either to a fringe sect of Judaism or to people
influenced by some frankly pagan cult or philosophical speculation; and
regulations about food could indicate that some were tempted to return
to the Jewish community with its food laws,[15] or else that the fringe group
practised some particular kind of abstinence (which was not uncommon).

10   **We have an altar**. All the temple imagery in this letter has been inspired
by one part of the temple only, the Holy of Holies, the place where God's
presence was imagined at its most intense, and to which only the high priest

---

[15] The Greek is less precise than this translation. Literally it means, *by the grace of God,
not by foods*. It is possible that these people could have been recommending, not abstinence,
but eating a certain kind of food that was claimed to give 'grace', or even consuming a
certain kind of sacrifice.

had access. Now suddenly we are in the great courtyard outside the temple, where people brought their offerings to the altar. At this altar the sacrifices were performed by the priests, who could be described as **those who officiate in the tent**, since they also had duties in the Holy Place, or outer room, of the temple; and the priests had the right to reserve some of the meat from the sacrifices for themselves (Leviticus 6.16; 7.6). Now Jesus, we have seen, could be thought of as a high priest. That is to say, he had nothing to do with the altar where the ordinary priests functioned and where they had **the right** to certain privileges; his office was performed entirely in the Holy of Holies, to which they had no access. But Jesus the high priest was also his own offering; and this again was nothing to do with the priests and their daily sacrifices at the altar; it was the Day of Atonement offering, of which the blood was

11 **brought into the sanctuary by the high priest** and the carcasses **burned outside the camp**. All of this procedure could be described as a sacrifice, or

10 indeed, as **an altar**: it was this which had brought Christians into the presence of God. But if it was in some sense an 'altar', it was not the great altar in front of the temple, served by the priests. Hence the Levitical priesthood no longer had any significance (a matter of importance for any Christians who were yearning for the security of the old sacrificial system). But there was a further respect in which the old ritual foreshadowed the new spiritual reality. Part of the ordinance for the Day of Atonement ceremonies runs as follows (Leviticus 16.27): "The bull of the sin offering and the goat of the sin offering, whose blood was brought in to make atonement in the holy place, shall be taken outside the camp . . . and . . . consumed in fire." Like the sacrificial victims

12 in that ceremony, **Jesus also suffered outside the . . . gate.**[16] It might seem more natural to say 'outside the city' or 'outside the walls', where Jesus was in fact crucified. But this writer is meditating all the time, not on what actually happened in the Jerusalem temple, but on the description of the ritual as it stands in the law. That description presupposed a nomadic people whose sanctuary was still a tent and whose dwelling was still a 'camp'. It was that original ritual which prefigured the death of Jesus; and so the writer goes

13 on, **Let us then go to him outside the camp**. Indeed, the picture of the early worshippers living under canvas, their possession of lands and cities still a promise for the future, suggested another point of comparison: Christians

14 too have **no lasting city, but we are looking for the city that is to come**.

13 The exhortation could be a perfectly general one to follow Christ, to **bear the abuse he endured** and to renounce attachment to material things. But it has a sharper edge if there were some Christians tempted by the security of rejoining their former Jewish community. The Master they followed, the new high priest, had suffered 'outside the camp'. It was there, in similar exclusion

---

[16] The NRSV has added the word **city**, which is not in the Greek and which obscures the fact that the writer is thinking of the ritual as described in Leviticus, not as it was in a later period in Jerusalem.

from their ancestral environment, that Christians must **go to him**. And if they were yearning for the old sacrificial system (which may have been the case with some, though we cannot be sure), they might reflect on the ancient
15 prophetic message that the true sacrifice is **praise to God, that is, the fruit of lips that confess his name** (compare Hosea 14.2 and Psalm 50.14 – a psalm imbued with prophetic concern for inward motivation rather than outward ritual). And this interior 'sacrifice' also had ethical implications:
16 **Do not neglect to do good . . . for such sacrifices are pleasing to God.**
17 **Obey your leaders.** Obedience to the leadership of the church was a regular topic among the moral exhortations which tended to be gathered at the end of New Testament letters (compare Romans 16.19; 1 Corinthians 16.16; 1 Thessalonians 5.12–13). The tireless concern of the leaders of churches and their sense of responsibility for their people come vividly out of Paul's letters (see especially 2 Corinthians 11.28; 1 Thessalonians 2.19–20).
18 **Pray for us.** The words are perfectly conventional, and bring us little closer to the personality of the author.
20 **Now may the God of peace.** Some kind of formal benediction occurs at the end of a number of New Testament letters. This one has some conventional Christian phrases which do not occur otherwise in the letter – including this writer's only allusion to the resurrection and to the shepherding presence of Jesus in the church – but also refers back to the new **covenant** that has been
21 one of his principal themes. The solemn **Amen** was probably the cue for the hearers to respond with their own 'Amen'.

A personal farewell

22 **I appeal to you, brothers and sisters.** These final verses are the only ones that make what has so far sounded like a discourse or a sermon look like a letter. They tell us nothing about the author and very little about the time and place at which he wrote. Indeed they are so general that it would not have been difficult for a later editor to add them to the treatise in order to give it the appearance of a letter, so that we cannot even be sure that the little they tell us is authentic. Yet they fit well with what has gone earlier. The writer calls his work a **word of exhortation**, and indeed, one of its features has been the way in which the argument breaks off from time to time to exhort its hearers to follow the Christian path in morals and faithfulness. But there is also a more technical meaning of the word. In Acts 13.15 Paul is invited to give a 'word of exhortation' in the synagogue, and in response he expounds scripture in a new, Christian sense. This is exactly what our author has been doing, even if only **briefly** (what seems to us a quite lengthy discourse was nevertheless, much less than the subject might have required); and the result is the 'encouragement' (another meaning of the same word, *paraklēsis*) that comes from the realization that the promises contained in scripture are now at last being fulfilled.

23 **Our brother Timothy has been set free.** There is a famous Timothy in the New Testament, the recipient of two letters from Paul. If this is the same one, it is news to us that he was ever in prison. But there may well have been other Christians of this name.

24 **Those from Italy send you greetings.** Again, this means nothing to us. But there is one frail link by which this letter can be attached to a known fact of history. Clement of Rome, writing to the church in Corinth in about 96 CE, quoted the letter to the Hebrews. This makes it seem likely that the letter was written to Christians in Rome; in which case it would have been natural for the writer, whoever he was, to convey the greetings of Italian expatriates to their friends at home.

A LETTER OF
JAMES

Author and recipients

1.1 **James** was a common name (it was the Greek equivalent of the Hebrew name Jacob), and there are at least five men who bear it in the New Testament alone. But this James writes with authority and has apparently no need to explain who he is: his mere name is enough to command attention. Only one of the men called James in the New Testament held such a prominent position in the church. This was James, the brother of Jesus, who became the leader of the church in Jerusalem.

Is this letter from his hand? No other James has ever been suggested, and it was as a document bearing the authority of the Lord's brother that the letter was given a place among the writings of the New Testament – though it was several centuries before it became firmly accepted. But in modern times serious doubts have been felt. Could a man of James' relatively humble Galilean background have written such sophisticated Greek? Is it likely that Jesus' own brother would have been content to write to the churches without mentioning any of the central beliefs of the Christian faith such as the crucifixion or the resurrection? Is the somewhat Hellenized Jewish culture displayed by the author what one would expect from one who had the reputation of maintaining an orthodox Jewish way of life in Jerusalem even after he was converted to Christianity?

Not all these doubts are justified. We know too little about the extent to which Greek was used in Palestine to be sure that James could not have acquired sufficient fluency to compose – perhaps with some help – a work of this kind. The author did not have to repeat well-known facts of the Christian faith if they were not relevant to what he was trying to say. And his language about 'the law' is not necessarily unorthodox. Moreover, it has to be said that he makes more allusions to Jesus' teaching than can be found in any other New Testament letter, and the situation presupposed is by no means improbable for the church in Jerusalem some time before James' death in 61 CE. It is therefore not impossible that the author was James, and that this is one of the earliest, rather than one of the latest, writings in the New Testament. But even if the letter may have been written after James' lifetime and is therefore pseudonymous, this is not to say that it was not written in good faith. A later author could well have had means of knowing the kind of teaching which the real James would have given and, having an authoritative message for his fellow Christians, would have found it natural to claim the authority of one of the great apostles of the recent past.

The letter is addressed to **the twelve tribes in the Dispersion**. Then as now, the word *diaspora* was a technical term for the Jewish people 'dispersed' outside Palestine. But the letter is intended, not for Jews, but for Christians. That is to say, the word *diaspora* is being used in a new sense: the Christian church was the new **twelve tribes** of Israel, the true successor of the historic Jewish nation; and the Christians, like the Jews, were 'dispersed' in many countries round the eastern Mediterranean. Now the old *diaspora* – the Jewish Dispersion – looked to Jerusalem as its spiritual centre, from which it received periodic exhortations to remain true to the ancestral faith and to observe the cycle of religious festivals according to the calendar that was still regulated there. These exhortations took the form of circular letters emanating from Jerusalem and addressed to the Jewish people, either in certain areas (such as Egypt), or else throughout the world. Three such letters can be found in the Apocrypha: the 'Letter of Jeremiah' and the two letters in the first two chapters of 2 Maccabees. It is quite possible that a Jewish Christian leader, moved by the Spirit to address his fellow Christians at large, and aware of possessing a certain authority over the whole church, deliberately chose the form of a Jewish encyclical letter as he began his message to the new *diaspora* of scattered Christian congregations.

Religion and morals

2 **My brothers and sisters**. This paragraph sets the tone for the whole letter, which contains moral exhortations only loosely bound together, with little real progression of thought but with considerable literary artifice. Sometimes

4, 5 the link is a single word: **lacking** occurs in two consecutive sentences, and the

, 6; 6, 7 words **ask** and **doubting/doubter** link the following ones into a complete paragraph. The topics are for the most part commonplaces of Jewish moral instruction, with an occasional stylistic device or illustration drawn from

2 a more cosmopolitan culture. That **trials** are good for the character, that

5 **wisdom** (in the sense of discerning the will of God rather than in any sophisticated philosophical sense) is given by God to those who sincerely desire it, and that prayer must be full-hearted and unwavering, are sentiments which can all be found in, for instance, Proverbs (2.6), Wisdom (11.9) and Sirach

6 (1.28; 2.1–5); while the image of a heaving sea **tossed by the wind** belongs to the common stock of Greek literary similes. Indeed teaching of this kind would have caused little surprise to a wide section of Greek-speaking Jewish society, and it has even been suggested that the 'letter' was originally a Jewish writing, simply adapted to Jewish use by the addition of 'the Lord Jesus Christ' in two places (1.1; 2.1). Nevertheless in the course of the letter there are certain phrases which sound distinctively Christian; there are several almost unmistakable references to sayings of Jesus; and even in this paragraph the teaching of Jesus on prayer is almost perceptible in the background (Mark 11.23–4; Matthew 7.7–11). Perhaps the most likely explanation is that, when

Christianity took root among mainly Jewish communities, the social and moral life of those communities continued without much change: the traditional morality of the synagogue needed only slight adjustment to bring it into line with Christian teaching. It is to such a community of Jewish Christians that this writer may have belonged, and the vigour of his language suggests that he was keen that their conduct should be at least up to the standard expected in any God-fearing society.

9, 10   **The believer who is lowly . . . and the rich.** We may assume that the church contained both; and it was evidently necessary to counter any intrusion of worldly values which might create social distinctions where there should be none. The writer could draw on a critique of such distinctions which he inherited from the Old Testament. In certain strands of Jewish religious thought, 'poor' had become almost synonymous with godly, 'rich' with materialistic and oppressive (see above on Matthew 5.3). True religion, according to this tradition, was preserved by the 'poor' or **lowly**; and in a new age God would make this apparent by 'raising up' the poor and 'bringing low' the wealthy and proud. This reversal of ordinary, worldly values (which was part of Jesus' message) was earnestly believed in by Christians; and if there were wealthy people among them, even they could 'boast' (meaning 'have confidence') in now being among those who would receive a reward. The influence and allurement of riches threatened to blur this insight; but reflection on the transitoriness of material possessions helped to keep it clear. Isaiah (40.6–7) had used the suddenness with which (in Palestine) spring vegetation can be turned brown by summer heat as a vivid illustration of the transitoriness of life. The same metaphor would serve for material possessions.

12   **Blessed is anyone who endures temptation.** This translation obscures the fact that the word rendered 'temptation' is the same as that used for 'trials' in verse 2. Indeed 'trial' or 'testing' is probably the better translation here, since it is standing this sort of test which qualifies for **the crown of life**, in the same way as an athlete competing for a crown or garland has to withstand the rigorous testing of the contest. But the ambivalence of the word allows the author to proceed naturally to genuine psychological 'temptation', and to

13 deal with an excuse which people often made when they succumbed to it, **"I am being tempted by God."** It was a serious excuse. Since the time of Homer, belief in God or the gods often seemed to take responsibility away from ourselves and ascribe it to the divine power which was in control of everything and therefore was the cause of our being exposed to evil desires and motivations. But such fatalism was alien to both Judaism and Christianity. A good example in Jewish literature of a protest against it is in Sirach 15.11–12. Here, the author uses an argument which is again a play upon words. In Greek, **God cannot be tempted by evil** can also mean 'God is untouched by evil'. This proposition would have been generally agreed: God has nothing to do with evil. It follows that he would never put evil temptations in anyone's

path – **he himself tempts no one** (a conclusion which has caused much trouble since early centuries: God certainly 'tested' – the same word as 'tempted' – Abraham and others in the Bible story). The real culprit is the distorted
14 **desire** of the flesh, which may even lead (the writer adds rhetorically) to
15 **death**.
16   **Do not be deceived** is an expression common enough in this type of writing. It may go with what has just been said; but the same phrase is used by Paul in Galatians (6.7) to introduce a proverb, and in 1 Corinthians (15.33) to introduce a popular saying quoted from a Greek poet. Here it could
17 serve as an introduction to the following sentence. In Greek, **every generous act of giving, with every perfect gift** are words which make up an almost perfect line of verse. It may be that the writer is quoting part of a familiar maxim ('All giving is good and every gift is perfect') and then, by taking the grammar in a different way and by adding the words **is from above**, making it give fine expression to the Jewish aphorism that God is the author of all good things. The word 'above' was perhaps sufficient to bring to mind the concept of God the Creator, **the Father of lights** (presumably the heavenly lights of sun, moon and stars, as in Genesis 1.14–16); and this gave rise to the further thought that, unlike the heavenly bodies which rise and set and go into eclipse, **with God there is no variation or shadow due to change**.
    That God (in various ways, such as through the law of Moses) revealed a
18 **word of truth** and that his people were **a kind of first fruits of his creatures** were ideas that would have been familiar to any Jewish reader. But the particular combination of these ideas here has a less Jewish sound and perfectly expresses the Christian convictions that (i) God has declared the **truth** in the gospel, (ii) he has created the possibility of new **birth** in conversion and baptism, and (iii) that the church is a kind of **first fruits** of humanity (Revelation 14.4). This is one of the verses where the Christian vocabulary seems
21 unmistakable. The same goes for **the implanted word that has the power to save your souls**, which can hardly mean anything but the Christian gospel, though it is embedded in a sequence of fairly conventional moral injunctions.
25 The same probably also goes for **the perfect law, the law of liberty**. It is true that some Jewish thinkers (influenced perhaps by the prevalent philosophical notion that obedience to a true philosophy makes one free) regarded the law of Moses as a means towards moral and spiritual freedom, even though it was just as often referred to as a 'yoke'. But Christians were no longer bound by this law: in this sense they were 'free', though it was a freedom inspired and regulated by a new law, that of love. This law too demanded attention and obedience: the case of those who are **hearers who forget** is as old as morality itself, though it receives a particularly vivid illustration in the Sermon on the Mount (Matthew 7.24–7).
26   **If any think they are religious**. Most Jews would have agreed that the mere
27 outward forms of religion are inadequate: serious charitable concern (**to care for orphans and widows in their distress** was one of the classic Jewish 'good

works'), and an earnest effort to adhere to a godly way of life, uninfluenced by the contamination of the secular world, were essential components of any true religion – and certainly of Christianity.

Impartiality, faith and works

2.1 That the congregation was committing **acts of favoritism** was a serious charge. It suggested that they were conforming with a world where the rich subtly influence the course of justice and the settlement of disputes, and where social distinctions are allowed to divide the community and distort its judgments. The basic argument against such behaviour was one that has been
5 touched on already (1.9–10). **Has not God chosen the poor in the world?** The faith of the 'poor' in the Old Testament that they were the chosen of God had now been decisively endorsed by Jesus. This made it unthinkable that the church should begin to reproduce the structure of secular society and allow special privileges to the rich. But there was also a more practical reason. However welcome such people might be in the congregation, they represented a class whose members (society being organized as it was) were constantly seen as plaintiffs in the courts, claiming against debtors, evicting tenants, suing for compensation – in short, using their influence to further their own interests under the cloak of the law. In all such cases the defendants were usually 'the poor'. Moreover, many of the rich might actually be
7 contemptuous of **the excellent name** of Jesus Christ. People had a class solidarity. Christians might welcome the rich into the church; but they must beware of admitting with them the social distinctions and injustices they represented.

It was against the whole Jewish tradition to select any particular com-
8 mandment from scripture and call it **the royal law**. It was an axiom of Jewish interpreters that all the laws of the code were of equal weight. True, some laws were more general than others and could be regarded as basic principles which implied a whole series of particular laws. But this was a question of logical arrangement, not of a greater or lesser degree of importance attaching to the laws themselves. From the strict Jewish point of view it was reasonable to regard **"You shall love your neighbor as yourself"** as a law which summed up a great many other laws, but not to suggest that other laws were therefore less binding than this one. Jesus, we are told, was prepared to enter the academic discussion about the 'greatest commandment in the law' (Matthew 22.34–40); and the church, following his teaching, continued to regard 'Love your neighbour as yourself' as a summary of the whole Jewish law. But to anyone untrained in this strict tradition it seemed natural to take such a principle, not as a technical summary of the Jewish law, but as a moral standard which replaced the detailed commandments of the law of Moses. There are signs that this was beginning to happen in Mark's account of Jesus'

teaching on the subject (see above on Mark 12.28–34); but here, the process is clearly complete. The Christians had taken this single commandment from scripture and made it into what philosophers called **the royal law**, a universal moral principle which allowed them to dispense with the detailed ordinances of the Jewish legal code.

Up to a point this was a valid understanding of Jesus' teaching. But it also had the danger of breeding a certain moral insensitivity. Certain sins, which a Jew might avoid because they were explicitly forbidden in the law, might be committed by Christians simply because they did not recognize them as sins.

9 Such a sin was the **partiality** of which the writer has been complaining. A good corrective was to take a fresh look at the detailed commandments in the law, the same law as that from which Christians had culled their overriding moral principle, " you shall love your neighbor as yourself" (Leviticus 19.18). A few verses earlier in Leviticus (19.15) came the sentence, "You shall not render an unjust judgment; you shall not be partial to the poor or defer to the great." The two laws came almost as close together as two of the Ten Commandments, and there was no great distinction of seriousness between,

11 say, **adultery** and **murder** (both were in theory punishable by death); and even when the punishments were less severe, from the religious point of view a person was just as much a sinner whatever transgression had been

10 committed. **For whoever keeps the whole law but fails in one point has become accountable for all of it.** This characteristically Jewish reverence for the law in all its particular clauses had its dangers, and was justly criticized by Jesus. But there was a useful lesson to be learnt from it. 'Loving one's neighbour' was no excuse for subverting justice with partiality. The Christian

12 **law of liberty** made no less extensive moral demands than the Jewish law of Moses.

'Talking of judgment' (a modern idiom which catches the connection between this verse and the last), it was as true in Christian as in Jewish thinking that those who show mercy will receive mercy, according to the

13 maxim, **mercy triumphs over judgment.**

The whole letter up to this point has been concerned, directly or indirectly, with sincerity and single-mindedness in religion and with the need to bring outward actions into accord with inward convictions. Moreover in any Jewish environment great store was set by 'acts of charity' (to "care for orphans and widows" has already been said by this writer to be at the heart of true religion, 1.27), even though such 'good works' were not specifically commanded in the law. It seems surprising, therefore, that anyone in the congregation should

14 seriously have been saying that they **have faith but do not have works.** If the response of those who professed to be Christians to those who are

15 **naked** and lack **daily food** was to turn them away unclothed and unfed, surely anyone could see that their religion meant nothing: such 'faith' was

17 **dead.**

725

18   **But someone will say** – and it seems that some people really did have
an objection to this obvious proposition. There were plenty of religious
philosophies about in the Greek-speaking world which concentrated upon
intellectual 'knowledge' of God (which was, after all, a kind of 'faith') and paid
little attention to morality or 'good deeds'. Moreover, Paul's great argument
in Romans and Galatians 3, that the basis of Christian salvation is not good
deeds but faith (by which, of course, Paul meant a good deal more than a
mere profession of religious belief), may have made a considerable impact
on the church, and have reached some congregations in the simplified form
(which Paul would never have intended) that good deeds were irrelevant and
all that mattered was some kind of 'faith'. Certainly the argument here uses
the same terminology as Paul, and has often been thought to be directed
specifically at him. But either of these tendencies might have thrown up an
17   objection to the common-sense proposition that **faith by itself, if it has no
works, is dead**.

In any case, it may not be necessary to look so far afield for an explanation. It
was logically possible to drive a wedge between faith and good deeds: the one
did not seem necessarily to imply the other. But this writer has an ingenious
answer. To introduce it he deliberately adopts the style of a popular lesson
18   in philosophy (technically known as a *diatribe*). In this style, **someone may
say** was a standard way of introducing a possible objection which the writer
20   wished to demolish in order to set his own position in a clearer light; and **you
senseless person** was an equally conventional way of pouring contempt on
an imaginary opponent. This brief dialogue is wholly artificial and literary. It
is a typical example of the way in which popular philosophers liked to press
home a point.

The point which this writer wished to make is quite clear (even though
there is much uncertainty about the details: Greek manuscripts had little
punctuation and no quotation marks, and it is impossible to tell from the
language alone where the interjections of the objector begin and end). Every
day Jews would begin their prayers with the statement of faith that "The LORD
is our God, the LORD alone" (Deuteronomy 6.4). Theoretically, it could be
argued that this 'faith' guaranteed salvation: there was no need of good works
19   as well. But it could be replied that even **demons** do as much (as is taken
for granted in, for example, Mark 1.24). But demons, far from being saved,
actually **shudder** before God. Therefore faith of that kind alone could not be
sufficient for salvation.

The argument is strengthened by two biblical examples. The Jews cherished
the memory of great figures of the past who had acted, not from ordinary
human and materialistic motives, but from 'faith' (see above, pp. 708–9).
The greatest of these was Abraham, and the most spectacular example of his
21   faith was his readiness to offer **his son Isaac on the altar** (Genesis 22.9–12).
Admittedly this did not seem to support an argument about 'works'; indeed

scripture itself seemed to lay the emphasis on 'faith' (which is why the verse
23 was so important for Paul in Romans 4): **"Abraham believed God, and it
was reckoned to him as righteousness"** (Genesis 15.6). But common sense
would show that Abraham had to perform certain actions to prove that he
22 really had this faith – **faith was brought to completion by the works**. And the
same went for other heroes of biblical history who were celebrated for their
25 faith, such as **Rahab** (see above on Hebrews 11.31). Ultimately they were all
justified not just by a form of belief – their 'faith' – but by the actions which
26 demonstrated that this faith was alive; for **faith without works is . . . dead**.

The roots of conflict

3.1 **We who teach**. In the church, as in the synagogue, teachers were important
and respected. Their prestige attracted many to follow the same career, but it
was necessary to remind the aspirants of the frightening responsibility they
would bear and which not many were fit to undertake. The writer can speak
with authority as a teacher himself (the only thing we know for certain about
him); and he bases his warning on a weakness which is common to all but
which is particularly serious for teachers: the uncontrollable nature of the
tongue.
5   Plenty of similes were available to illustrate the way in which **a small
member** may have disproportionate influence: the bridle of a horse, the
rudder of a ship. These were commonplace comparisons, and perhaps the
writer did not pause to consider that they did not fit his argument perfectly:
bridles and rudders are used for constructive purposes, whereas what he
wanted to illustrate was the destructive influence of the tongue. But his third
5 simile – **a small fire** setting a whole forest ablaze– was perfectly to the point
and leads into a whole chain of images. The tongue is not just *like* a fire; it *is* a
6 fire, kindled in **hell**. What then does it burn? A common expression was the
'wheel of fortune': here the writer rather mysteriously adapts the expression
to refer to the whole of natural life (or of *birth*, see the NRSV footnote).
Thinking rather literally of a wooden wheel, he could combine this with
his fire metaphor and say that the tongue **sets on fire the cycle of nature**.
Normally, fire purifies. But not so the tongue, which is the quintessence of
wickedness, with a touch of hell-fire about it.
10   **From the same mouth come blessing and cursing**. To a Jew, cursing
was something that was occasionally required as a religious duty, and the
phenomenon of a tongue capable of both blessing and cursing might not
have caused concern. But Jesus taught that cursing was always evil, and
to a Christian this fickleness of the tongue seemed something unnatural,
something which (as Stoic philosophers liked to put it) prevented one from
being true to one's own nature even to the extent that water and plants are

true to theirs. The tongue seemed to offend, not just against morals, but against the laws of nature.

13 **Who is wise and understanding among you?** Being a follower of a new religion almost inevitably involves claiming to know the answers to old questions, to have a new and deeper understanding of God and the world. The dangers of this kind of intellectual 'wisdom' are the subject of the first few chapters of 1 Corinthians. There, Paul seeks to meet them by a radical critique of philosophical wisdom and rhetorical skill. Here, the writer is content to insist that Christian wisdom must never be purely intellectual and must be accompanied by **gentleness** (or *meekness*, as the word is translated in 1.21);

14 otherwise it leads (as Paul saw so clearly) to **bitter envy and selfish ambition.** By contrast, there exists a true wisdom to which Christians can legitimately

17 aspire, **the wisdom from above** (a Jewish way of saying, 'from God'). The characteristics of that wisdom are listed in many Jewish writings (compare especially Wisdom 7.22–5). One of them is peace-making; and this leads to

18 a general maxim about those who **make peace.**

4.1 **Those conflicts and disputes among you.** It was a commonplace of moral philosophy that it is the aggressiveness of sensual desires that is the root cause

2 of human conflicts and quarrels. This writer agrees, and adds a brief piece of psychological analysis:[1] his point is a general observation about human nature, and if he seems to be going rather far in suggesting that the people he is addressing might actually **commit murder** for the sake of satisfying their desires, it may be that he (somewhat in the manner of Jesus, Matthew

1 5.21–2) is simply drawing attention to the gravity of these **cravings** which always *might* lead to serious crime. The argument then turns to religious practice. It was firm Christian doctrine that prayers are answered, but only if they are offered for the right reasons and the right objects. There are traces of this reasoning in the gospels. Here, the failure of certain prayers is put down

3 to praying **wrongly,** that is, with evil intention. Sensual desires can pervert even one's prayers.

4 **Adulterers!** This sudden accusation is even more startling in the Greek, which reads *Adulteresses!* It is hardly likely to have been meant literally; and people who knew the Bible were familiar with the idea that forsaking the worship of the one true God is again and again likened to sexual unfaithfulness. In the Old Testament the classic expression of this unfaithfulness was idolatry. In the writer's time it was more naturally called **friendship with the world,** which amounted in his eyes to **enmity with God** – a radical antithesis which seems to be his own formulation.

5 **The scripture says.** This quotation occurs nowhere in the Bible or any known apocryphal writing. Possibly it comes from some lost writing which for a time was included in scripture; and without their context the words are

---

[1] There are several possible ways of punctuating the Greek text in verse 2. See the NRSV footnote.

barely translatable.[2] The most one can say is that they seem to presuppose yet another psychological explanation of sin, according to which there is a 'spirit' in human beings which begins its life in all innocence and is capable of responding to the Spirit of God, but is liable to be corrupted by evil desires or by a 'bad spirit' warring against it. But now there was a new factor which effectively altered the balance: as a result of Christ's death and resurrection the Christian receives **grace**. The concept was a new one; but the word itself could be found in the Greek version of the Old Testament, for instance in the passage quoted here from Proverbs 3.34: **"God . . . gives grace to the**
7 **humble."** And this leads naturally to another injunction: **Submit yourselves therefore to God**.

The remaining sentences in the paragraph are all broadly relevant to the same theme, and were doubtless the kind of injunctions a Christian preacher would often give. But then a note is struck which to our ears is unexpected:
9 **Lament and mourn and weep**. We need to be aware of the biblical overtones. The style is that of an Old Testament prophet addressing the proud, the arrogant and the wealthy and prophesying their speedy discomfiture. The writer adopts this tone to ridicule the easy complacency and cheerfulness of the wealthy. God is shortly to bring about a reversal of social values. The only way to be sure of salvation is to join the ranks of the 'poor' who make
10 up the church. **Humble yourselves before the Lord, and he will exalt you**. This writer may have a certain bias against the rich as such (as we shall see in chapter 5); but basically he has the faith which underlies Jesus' beatitudes.
11 **Do not speak evil against one another**. This is more than a piece of conventional moral advice. The 'law' which now determines the conduct of Christians is the 'royal law', 'Love your neighbour as yourself.' To speak evil of another is not only against this law; it implies that one is above the law and can make one's own judgment. This could be serious: it could involve
12 usurping the place of the **one lawgiver and judge who is able to save and to destroy**, and who alone has the right to **judge your neighbor**.

Practical wisdom, patience and healing

13 **"Today or tomorrow we will go to such and such a town."** The style is conversational: this is evidently the kind of thing that was often heard in the street. Possibly it was sometimes heard also in the Christian congregation. At any rate, it gave the writer a cue for a little sermon. Such a thoughtless
16 sense of security amounted to **arrogance** and **boasting** and to forgetting
15 one's human condition. What one ought to say is, **"If the Lord wishes . . ."**

---

[2] The Greek words do not make it clear whether **spirit** is the subject or the object. The NRSV supplies **God** as the subject. But **jealously** is not an appropriate adverb for God. One of the possible alternatives is *the spirit which he (God) has made to dwell in us has jealous yearnings*.

Greeks and Romans constantly said, 'If it be God's will', as do Muslims today; but (so far as we know) it was not a common expression among the Jews. For once, the Christians could learn a moral lesson, not from their Jewish forebears, but from their heathen neighbours.

5.1 **Come now, you rich people.** A critique of riches could be pitched in more than one tone of voice. There was, first, the simple observation that all material possessions are precarious and transient: clothes can become

2, 3 **moth-eaten,** silver and gold can become **rusted** – not of course literally (these metals are physically imperishable), but as symbols of wealth and prosperity. So much was ancient wisdom, though Jesus too used the same image (Matthew 6.19–20). But the moralist could also adopt a sharper, more prophetic tone. When the rich get richer the poor get poorer: the amassing of wealth involves injustice; its 'rusting' is **evidence** against those who should have distributed it more generously to the poor. Depriving workmen of their wages was a social injustice very strongly condemned in the Old Testament (a judgment endorsed by Jesus when he quoted the maxim, "Labourers deserve their food", Matthew 10.10); yet cases were doubtless known of it happening. It could stand as a typical example of the injustices committed by the rich which would bring their own inevitable retribution. The very **rust** of their hoarded wealth (which should have been distributed as alms) was a fiery poison (another meaning of the word for 'rust') that would be visited on their flesh. And there was more. The attitude of the rich had been well described in the Wisdom of Solomon: "Let us oppress the righteous poor man . . . because he is inconvenient to us . . . let us condemn him to a shameful death" (2.10–20). Their oppression of the poor could even be described as

5 **a day of slaughter.**[3] But the 'poor' were also the righteous. They had no
6 means to **resist;** but the biblical hope, now confirmed in the gospel, was that the tables would soon be turned, the righteous vindicated and the rich condemned.

8 **The coming of the Lord is near.** By now the 'coming' had become virtually a technical term for Christ's return in glory. Of course this would be accompanied by judgment, and the phrase could mean no more than the 'coming' of God at the end of the age, as was prophesied, for instance, by Habakkuk (2.3), and was always a call to examine one's behaviour. (This writer uses
9 the image of the Judge **standing at the doors** to warn his readers not to **grumble against one another.**) But for Christians the 'coming' was that of Christ, and was a prospect giving hope and consolation. The appropriate
8 response to this prospect was therefore to be **patient.** Their model should
7 be the farmer waiting for **the precious crop from the earth.** In Palestine

---

[3] The Greek is compressed and ambiguous. The 'day of slaughter' could be hyperbole for their willingness to see the poor die; or it could be the day of judgment when they themselves would be condemned to death. Many interpreters have seen a reference to Christ in the **righteous one** of verse 6; but the context suggests a more general meaning.

and Syria all farming depended on the rainfall. After the long dry summer, nothing could be done until the autumn rains had moistened the ground sufficiently for ploughing and sowing. This usually happened in October, but was sometimes delayed until late November, and the patience of the farmer could be sorely tested as he waited. The season of rains then lasted until March or April; but the success of the crop depended on some good showers after the dry season had begun. So **the early and the late rains** were as much a proverbial preoccupation of the Palestinian farmer as the monsoon for the Indian. If this writer did not know this from experience, he would have noticed the phrase many times in the Bible.

10 If, then, the lesson to be learned was of **suffering and patience**, an exemplary pattern was provided by **the prophets who spoke in the name of the Lord**. That many of the prophets were persecuted and martyred does not appear from the Old Testament, but by the time of Christ legends had grown up to this effect (see above on Matthew 23.30). Their names occurred in lists of Jewish heroes, as did also that of Job. The main part of the book of Job, as it now appears in the Old Testament, consists of a highly wrought debate in the course of which Job could hardly be described as a model of patience. But this debate was the creation of a great thinker and literary artist, who attached it somewhat loosely to the simple folk-tale which is told in the first and last chapters. It is clearly the Job of the folk-tale, rather than of the literary work,

11 who is in mind here. The point is clinched by two references to scripture: **we call blessed those who showed endurance** (Daniel 12.12), and **the Lord is compassionate and merciful** (a formula which occurs in many places, such as Psalm 103.8).

12 **Above all, my beloved**. If this sentence occurred in a logically constructed argument, we should have to conclude that the prohibition of swearing was the most important thing the writer felt he had to say. But in fact it is an isolated injunction, with little connection with the rest of the chapter, and we can probably take 'above all' with a pinch of salt. He is simply asking his readers to pay special attention to the danger of swearing. In Judaism, swearing was a serious matter. If one swore an oath that was found to be false, the punishment was severe. Yet swearing is natural, particularly in moments of anger; and in some legal situations it was actually necessary. Many moralists and religious leaders warned against it. It was a rule of the law of Moses that all oaths must be by the name of God (Deuteronomy 6.13); but it was thought that the consequences might be less serious if one said **by heaven** or **by earth** or used some other phrase which referred only obliquely to God. It was not difficult to expose the casuistry of this – as Jesus did (Matthew 5.33–7). Jesus was not the only Jewish or pagan thinker who was severe on swearing; but it seems more likely that this writer took his radical prohibition of swearing from the teaching of Jesus than from any other source, since most people, and certainly Jews, regarded oaths as a necessary feature of the legal system and as a natural (even if undesirable) habit of ordinary speech.

13   **Are any among you suffering?** The vivacious style is again that of a popular lesson in philosophy: this is how people of a certain persuasion ought to live.

14   But the answer to the question **Are any among you sick?** breaks right out of these conventional generalities and gives us a glimpse of the organization of the early church. Among the Jews, visiting the sick and praying for them (or **over them**) was a highly esteemed act of charity, and was virtually an obligation for relatives and close friends. But there were also certain people whom the sick person might actually **call for**, such as a noted man of prayer or a physician – though this last was a comparatively late development: Jewish religion regarded sickness as a consequence of sin; the only cure, therefore, lay in the forgiveness of God, and the only proper course for the sick was to throw themselves on the mercy of God. The first and only positive thing which is said about physicians in the whole Bible is in Sirach 38.1–15 (written around 180 BCE); and even there the diagnosis and cure are closely associated with prayer. Healing, that is to say, was essentially a religious process; and there was at least one Jewish sect in the time of Christ which practised both the arts of medicine and what we would now call 'spiritual healing'.

Evidently the church had a similar approach to sickness and had its own ministry of healing. Jesus had healed sick people; and his followers continued to exercise this power of healing, in which the main factor (as in the stories in Acts) was the invoking of the name of Jesus. We learn from this passage that the responsibility for responding to the sick person's call lay with **the elders of the church**; and that, just as Jesus used the outward gestures of medicinal cures (Mark 7.33; John 9.6), so the church practised **anointing them with oil** as part of its rite of healing. (There is another reference to this in Mark 6.13.) It is also a presupposition of this passage (as of many of the accounts of Jesus' healing miracles) that sickness is closely associated with sin and that recovery

16   is conditional on being forgiven. **Therefore**, says this writer, **confess your sins to one another** – this is essential if prayer for healing is to be effective. Another condition for success (for perhaps it was already necessary to have an explanation ready in case of failure) was that the prayer should be made by one who was **righteous**. But this was not an impossible condition. One of the great men of faith of the past, Elijah (who was a healer and about whom many details were supplied by popular legend as well as by the Bible), was

17   after all **a human being like us** – and the Greek word (literally *being of like feeling*) suggests that he too had human frailties.

The last topic of the letter (as of 1 John) is the problem of Christians defecting from the church. The seriousness of this can be gauged from other passages in the New Testament (1 Corinthians 5.1–5; Hebrews 10.26–31), where a basic Christian presupposition comes to the surface: inside the church was salvation and eternal life, outside was the risk of death and condemnation.

20   Bringing back a straying member was therefore rescuing **the sinner's soul from death**. It was possible to think of apostates as agents of the devil, or at least as persons within the devil's power, and to dismiss them with fear and

hatred. But more often the **wandering** was not so serious and Christian love dictated a different course. Here, as in 1 Peter 4.8, an old proverb seemed relevant (whatever its precise meaning):

> Hatred stirs up strife,
> but love covers all offenses.
> (Proverbs 10.12)

THE FIRST LETTER OF

PETER

A chosen people – their conduct and their suffering

1.1 **Peter, an apostle of Jesus Christ.** There is only one Peter among the apostles, or indeed in the entire New Testament, and the letter purports to come from his pen. This in itself does not settle the matter. The Second Letter of Peter makes the same claim; but the church has always, with good reason, hesitated to accept it as the work of the apostle. The first letter bears much better credentials. It breathes the authentic spirit of early Christianity and it expounds the central principles of the faith with a seriousness and authority comparable with those of Paul. Admittedly, it is not easy to see how it could have been written by the Galilean fisherman who was a disciple of Jesus. It is composed in polished Greek, such as could hardly have been commanded by a Jew who from childhood had not spoken Greek as his first language; its frequent quotations from and allusions to the Old Testament are from the Greek translation of the Septuagint, which Peter is unlikely to have known, at least until late in life; and the symbolic reference to the place of writing as 'Babylon' (5.13) makes it likely that the letter was written, not before 64 CE (the likely date of Peter's death), but after the conquest of Jerusalem in 70 – it was only then that Jewish writers began to liken Rome to the historic Babylon which had similarly sacked Jerusalem six centuries before. All these facts would be easier to explain if the letter was written by a person of considerable standing in the church (presumably in Rome), who felt inspired to address his fellow Christians as the apostle might have done, and who found it natural to invest his letter with the authority of Peter. Yet none of these arguments is decisive. It is still possible that the author was the apostle Peter himself.

To the exiles of the Dispersion. This form of address places the letter in the tradition of the encyclicals which were issued from Jerusalem to the Jews of the Dispersion (see above on James 1.1). These Jews, who greatly outnumbered those in Palestine, were for the most part not full citizens of the countries in which they lived: they were *resident aliens* (a technical term: they were not necessarily **exiles**, as the word is translated here). Some of the Christians in the Roman provinces may have had the same status; but others must have been indigenous inhabitants, in which case the description of them as 'resident aliens' must be metaphorical. Just as the Jews of the Dispersion had an ethnic loyalty which transcended their political status in the empire, so Christians had a new solidarity with one another which made it natural to think of themselves as not fully belonging to the countries in which they lived, as 'aliens'.

The letter is written, not from Jerusalem, but from Rome, and is addressed to distant Christians scattered over a wide area in the four Roman provinces of **Pontus** and **Bithynia** (which formed one province), **Galatia, Cappadocia** and **Asia**. Between them these covered the whole of Asia Minor apart from the small coastal strip south of the Taurus mountains. The Christian additions to the usual formula of greeting continue to make play with Jewish religious

2 terms. Like the Jews, Christians believed themselves to have been **chosen and destined by God the Father**; like them, they were **sanctified** – though not now through ritual acts related to the service of the temple in Jerusalem, but in a way that affected their inmost being – **by the Spirit**; and they were **to be obedient . . . and to be sprinkled** – a difficult phrase[1] which may have its background in some words of Exodus. When Moses read to the people the book of the covenant, they responded, "We will be obedient," and he then "took the blood and dashed it on the people" (Exodus 24.7–8). Christians are now to be obedient to the new covenant in Jesus Christ and are saved by his blood shed on the cross.

3 Thanksgiving to God is, first, for **a new birth into a living hope**. The expression is unusual, though the idea appears in several strands of Christian thinking (Titus 3.5; John 3.1–8), and is not far from the Jewish notion

4 that a convert is 'newly born'. Secondly, this new birth is **into an inheritance** – another traditional Jewish expression, now transformed into a Christian concept. When the Jews talked of their 'inheritance', they meant, first of all, a peaceful and prosperous existence in the land of Palestine; but, with a deepening of religious ideas and with the increasing insecurity and world-wide dispersion of the Jewish nation, it was reinterpreted as a reward promised in a future age or even in an afterlife. But, however it was conceived, it represented a conviction, common to all Jewish people, that they were reserved for a unique and privileged destiny in the purposes of God. Christians now believed that this inheritance had passed to them. Its full realization must

5 await **the last time**; meanwhile they were **being protected by the power of God** so long as they had **faith**; and their **salvation** was both already experienced and to be awaited in faith and hope – an almost paradoxical tension between present and future that could be expressed by the phrase **ready to be revealed in the last time**.

All these concepts, in part distinctively Christian, in part adaptations of Jewish ones, are worked into an opening paragraph which carries the usual

2 form of Christian greeting (**May grace and peace be yours**) and the very com-
3 mon exordium, **Blessed be the God and Father of our Lord Jesus Christ!**
6 (2 Corinthians 1.3; Ephesians 1.3). Only with the mention of **various trials** does the letter become more specific. The nature of these trials will become

---

[1] Both the grammar and the logic are obscure. An alternative translation is *to the obedience shown by Jesus and to the sprinkling of his blood*. Some have thought that the 'sprinkling' is an allusion to Christian baptism.

clearer later in the letter. Meanwhile, it was an insight of ancient Jewish
7 wisdom that tribulation can purify the character just as **gold, . . . though
perishable, is tested by fire** (Wisdom 3.6; Sirach 2.5); but this author sharpens the point: compared with a Christian's faith, even gold – the precious
residue from a refiner's fire – can be called **perishable**. The second source of
8 encouragement is more distinctively Christian. **Although you have not seen
him, you love him**. A modern reader tends to think of Jesus on earth: how
easy to love him if (like the historical Peter) one had actually seen him! But
in the letters of the New Testament there is very little harking back to Jesus'
presence in Galilee and Jerusalem. The Jesus who is loved and longed for is
the Jesus who at present is known only by faith, but who will one day be
7 **revealed** in glory so that all may see him for what he is. Meanwhile his relationship with Christians is one of trust and love. This is enough to transport
8 them **with an indescribable and glorious joy**. Christian salvation belongs to
the present as much as to the future.

A further source of encouragement for Christians in their trials was the fact
that Christ had suffered before them and that they could find the sufferings
of Christ and their glorious outcome foretold in scripture. Sayings of the
prophets which had for so long seemed to point to some remote event in
the future now took on their definitive meaning in the light of the Christian
experience. Some, indeed, though spoken by a prophet in the first person,
seemed to have been so perfectly fulfilled by Christ that one could speak of
11 **the Spirit of Christ within them**. (A good example is the series of quotations
in Hebrews 2.12–13.) Those prophets were inspired to cast their utterances
in the form of oracles about the future. To understand them, Christians
were no longer dependent on the efforts of learned interpreters. They now
12 had preachers who brought them, with the **good news** of the gospel, the
key to all that had been foretold in the past. Even **angels**, who were usually
thought to have access to the secret purposes of God, did not have that perfect
understanding of the divinely ordained shape of human history which was
now the possession of Christians.

13 **Therefore**. The readers have been bidden to fix their eyes on what is to
come, the salvation which is to be revealed. As so often in the New Testament,
a reference to the 'last time' has a serious moral import: **prepare your minds
for action; discipline yourselves** – the warning can be paralleled from many
other passages (see above on Romans 13.12). Here it goes with renouncing
the ways of the past, and the nature of this past throws precious light on
14 the background of this letter's recipients: **the desires that you formerly had
in ignorance**. A Jewish writer could well have spoken in this way to gentile
proselytes: while the Jews had the divinely given law to show them what kind
of moral conduct God demanded, Gentiles lived in 'ignorance', and so were
given to the fulfilment of sensual and even unnatural desires (Romans 1.18–
24). The same tone could be used when speaking to Christian converts from
paganism: they too had emerged from a life of ignorant immorality into one

governed by the law of Christ. But would Christians have spoken like this to Jewish converts? Certainly they had been 'in ignorance' of the significance of Jesus Christ; but the ignorance referred to here is to do with morals; and the high moral standards enjoined in the Old Testament were something of which Jews certainly were not 'ignorant'. The readers and hearers of this letter, then, seem more likely to have been pagan converts than Jewish ones, at least for the most part.

Christianity was a new and distinctive way of life, totally different from paganism, but different also from Judaism. Yet much of its ethos was inherited from the Jews. It aspired, like the Jewish faith, to form in its followers a standard of 'holiness', a character which would bring them closer to God.

16 Both faiths found inspiration in passages such as Leviticus 19.2: "You shall be holy, for I the LORD your God am holy".

17 Invoking God as **Father** was standard form in a number of religions and taken for granted in Judaism. What the author is about to say about the need for **reverent fear** applies to any religious person approaching God in prayer. But a particularly intimate form of address to God as 'father' (*abba*) seems to have come spontaneously to the lips of Christians through the inspiration of the Spirit (Romans 8.15) and to have been used and taught by Jesus himself (Mark 14.36; Luke 11.2). Such apparent intimacy with God could easily breed over-confidence, and it may be that Christians were in particular need of being reminded that God is also **one who judges all people impartially according to their deeds**.

The writer's purpose, as we can see by now, is principally a moral one. He is exhorting his readers to live by the standards of their faith and warning them of the consequences of licentious behaviour. To do this, he reminds them of important articles of their belief or of expressions (such as 'Father')

18 which were constantly on their lips. Another such expression was 'ransom', the price paid for a person's freedom. This was an Old Testament metaphor, often used in the church (1 Corinthians 6.20; 1 Timothy 2.6) and (according to Mark 10.45) by Jesus himself, as a means of describing the effects of his death. A prisoner ransomed or a slave freed by the payment of a sum of **silver or gold** might not feel under any strong obligation to lead a righteous life afterwards. But if the ransom was a human life – if it was paid with

19 **precious blood** – then it would be unthinkable to put such an expensive freedom to immoral use. Surely Christians were in precisely this situation. Their freedom had been bought by **the precious blood of Christ**. His death could be understood, both as the ransom for human beings, and also as that of **a lamb without defect or blemish**, a perfect offering for the sins of all, such as no temple sacrifice could ever be.

20 **He was destined . . . but was revealed**. These neatly balanced clauses sound like a well-honed statement of belief about Christ, such as might even have been said or sung by Christians in their worship; there is a hymn on similar

21 lines in 1 Timothy 3.16. **Through him you have come to trust in God**. If the

Christians who are so addressed were pagans before their conversion, this was an apt description of what had happened to them. Through Christ, they had learnt for the first time what it was to be able to **trust in God**. But even Jewish converts, whose ancestral religion had also been a call to **trust in God**, had now come to a new possibility of 'trust'. Previously, one might say that their trust had often been *despite appearances*: it seemed that it was the ungodly who flourished, and there was little to show that the 'trust' of those who believed in God was justified. But Christ had changed all that: **God . . . raised him from the dead and gave him glory**. After that, no Christian could doubt that God was on the side of his own. There now existed a new and decisive ground for faith and hope.

22–3   **You have purified your souls . . . You have been born anew.** These expressions would have been particularly pertinent to people who had recently been converted and baptized, and it is possible that at least some parts of the letter were originally written to be read aloud when a baptism of converts had just taken place. However that may be, the symbolism of baptism seems to have been much in the author's mind, and one of his main purposes was to remind the recipients of the kind of conduct which necessarily followed from their baptism and their Christian profession. Right at the start he had reminded them that they had been "sanctified by the Spirit to be *obedient* to Jesus Christ" (1.2); and here the nature of that obedience is made explicit: it is **genuine mutual love** – *philadelphia*, brotherly and sisterly love, the only form of social relationship which is appropriate to those who have become, in a new sense, 'brothers and sisters' through their rebirth into Christ. This

24–5   rebirth was through **the word of God**; and the word of God, as a passage of Isaiah proves (40.6–7), **endures forever.**

That religious truth to the newly converted is like milk to a newborn infant was a common enough metaphor in both the Jewish and the Greek

2.2   worlds. Metaphorically, milk is **pure,** unlike the devious natural instincts of the heart, and **spiritual**, appropriate to the mind and soul and not to the sensual appetites. A century later it was even worked into the symbolism of Christian baptism: the newly baptized were given milk and honey to drink. The Bible is full of such sensuous imagery. Psalm 34 is often in this writer's

3   mind. Here he alludes to verse 8: "O taste and see that the LORD is good."

4   **Come to him, a living stone.** In isolation, this seems a very strange expression; but the author goes on to show how he arrived at it. Jesus himself was believed to have quoted Psalm 118.22, "The stone that the builders rejected has become the chief cornerstone", as an illustration of the dramatic reversal which would follow his rejection by his own people (Mark 12.10). If this were put together with two 'stone' metaphors from Isaiah, one (28.16) of

6   a **cornerstone chosen and precious** to **whoever believes in him,**[2] the other

---

[2] The fact that the Greek pronoun can mean either **him** or *it* helps the reader to see the application to Christ.

8 (8.14) of **a stone that makes them stumble,** then it was a short step to see this 'stone' as an eloquent image for the 'living' Christ, who continued to be the source of life for those who believed but to make still more confounded the destiny of those who refused to believe. (The fact that the same combination of texts from Isaiah occurs in Romans 9.33 suggests that these passages were frequently quoted together in the early church.)

The image of a living stone leads on to another image which had wide
5 currency among the early Christians. The church was **a spiritual house,** replacing the masonry temple in Jerusalem, its members were **like living stones,** and the sacrifices offered in it were no longer sacrificial animals but **spiritual sacrifices.** That is to say, the church replaced the old institutions of Judaism, and gave a new meaning to words and concepts that had belonged to the historic people of Israel. A classic description of this people was in Exodus 19.6: "a priestly kingdom and a holy nation". True, in Jewish history, royalty and priesthood had always been vested in certain individuals; but these individuals exercised it as representatives of the people as a whole, a
4 people which believed itself to be **chosen** from among other nations as a special kind of 'kingdom' and to have the task of offering a unique 'priestly' service to God. All these ideas found their fulfilment in the new community of Christians; but, paradoxically, this community was largely composed of men and women who, being Gentiles, had long been regarded by the Jews as necessarily disqualified from playing any such rôle in history. Yet even this
10 paradox could be illuminated from scripture. Hosea, in his vivid representation of the infidelity of the chosen race, had talked of Israel being called by God 'Not my people', and of the possibility that, when it repented, 'Not my people' would once more be called 'My people' (Hosea 1.8; 2.23). The Gentiles had always been 'Not my people'. It could be seen as the true fulfilment of Hosea's prophecy when, by entering the church, they became 'My people'.

11 **Abstain from the desires of the flesh that wage war against the soul.** This was a cliché of popular ethics and was as old as Plato. Strictly speaking, it was not a correct Christian or Jewish way of putting it: in Paul, for example, 'spirit', not 'soul', constitutes the higher level of human nature. But here the writer was concerned, not to give a Christian doctrine of the human being, but to advise his fellow Christians on their moral life, and he used the current moral jargon of his time. Nevertheless, the reasons he gave were specific. They were **aliens and exiles** – which, as we have seen (1.1), meant that, whether or not they were actually 'foreigners' in the countries where they lived, they stood apart from the general population much as the Jews did. Indeed, just as Jews made no distinctions among the non-Jews by whom they were surrounded, and called them all 'Gentiles', so Christians felt themselves a race apart and
12 could use the same term, **Gentiles,** for everyone else. But this, of course, made them highly vulnerable to moral criticism. We should not be surprised to hear that they were being maligned **as evildoers.** They must take care to avoid giving any pretext for such accusations; but they could not expect

vindication on their own account: they must wait for **God when he comes to judge.**

13 **Accept the authority of every human institution.** Civic obedience, good order in society and firm household management were values at the heart of civic life in the Roman empire. The small Christian communities may have felt they stood apart from pagan society in important respects, but this did not mean that they should show lack of respect to its laws and institutions; indeed it may be that this writer was particularly conscious of the dangerous consequences which might follow if they failed to perform the usual duties of a citizen. At any rate, he shows no sign of wishing to criticize or subvert the established order, whether it be the Roman administration, the institution of slavery or the conventions of married life; and in order to encourage civic obedience he makes use of a pattern of instruction that was as old as Aristotle. Greco-Roman society was built on the conviction that the government of the state and the management of individual households belonged closely together. Good order in one supported good order in the other; and education in citizenship was formulated by teachers and philosophers according to the various categories of relationship which supported civic and domestic life. The substance of what follows conforms faithfully with this pattern, but with one or two distinctive additions. **Accept the authority of** is considerably more emphatic in the Greek than in this translation (it means literally, *submit to*) and occurs no fewer than three times in this short section: evidently the Christians are being encouraged to be *particularly* orderly and law-abiding. All is to be done, not just out of a spirit of conformity, but **for the Lord's**

16 **sake**; and the precious **freedom** of which Christians are now conscious (their service being to God, not to any human institution) must never be **a pretext for evil.**

The civic aspect of this obedience is dealt with briefly. The colonial régime

13 under which they lived was under the supreme authority of **the emperor,**

14 who appointed provincial **governors** to keep order and administer justice. (The function of a legal system in antiquity was often thought to be to reward **those who do right** as well as **to punish those who do wrong.**) Obedience to these authorities need not go against the grain. It was recommended even in scripture:

> My child, fear the LORD and the king,
> and do not disobey either of them.
> (Proverbs 24.21)

In domestic affairs, the relationship in which 'submission' was most evi-

18 dent and necessary was that of household **slaves** with their masters. Hence, perhaps, this writer places it first in the list. (The word he uses for 'slaves' is specifically one for household servants.) Evidently some slaves had become Christians; and it was necessary to warn against allowing this to be a pretext for insubordination. There is a similar warning in the comparable lists of

domestic duties in Ephesians (6.5–8) and Colossians (3.22–5), and in each case it is supported with a distinctively Christian piece of teaching. Here, it is the cue for one of the most profound passages in the letter. The situation in mind was one of the perennial topics of comedy and casuistry: a

19, 18 servant who is **suffering unjustly** under a master who is **harsh**. Christian teaching went along with that of many moralists: one must be obedient even

20 if, having behaved well, one has to **suffer for it**. But in recommending this more demanding option, the writer has a motive to offer of great power: the slave's situation is exactly that of Christ himself. Through such an experience Christians may draw closer to their heavenly Lord.

21   **Leaving you an example.** The idea that Christians are to follow the example of Christ has become a commonplace of Christian teaching, but this is one of the very few places where it occurs in the New Testament. For the most part, early Christian writers concentrated on Christ's death and resurrection; distinctively Christian conduct was inspired by the implications of these fundamental facts. But this writer appeals to a slightly earlier moment in the story: Jesus' trial. He does not describe it in detail; indeed, the phrases

22, 24 **"He committed no sin, and no deceit was found in his mouth"** . . . **He himself bore our sins . . . by his wounds you have been healed** all occur in Isaiah 53, the chapter describing the afflictions of a nameless 'suffering servant', which was found by the early church to throw precious light on the meaning of Jesus' suffering and death. But at the same time he works in something new, which could well be an actual recollection of Jesus' trial,

23 stemming from an eyewitness or from the gospel tradition. **When he was abused, he did not return abuse; when he suffered, he did not threaten.** These words have no precedent in the Old Testament: they seem to describe what actually happened to Jesus, and are summed up in a striking phrase, **he entrusted himself** (literally, *he handed over*) **to the one who judges justly.**

21 Slaves, who were to **follow in his steps**, must have a similar confidence in the face of unjust masters. But this encouragement is incorporated in a further spelling out of Christ's destiny. His trial had been followed by the crucifixion, a penalty not allowed for in the Old Testament. But, at a stretch, one could call the cross a *tree* (see the NRSV footnote), which did appear as an instrument of punishment in Deuteronomy (21.23). With this, it was possible to fill a gap which is left in that chapter of Isaiah. It is not said there, though it seems to be implied, that the 'servant' was actually killed. But if he was, it would have been by a scriptural punishment – on a tree. By adding this detail the writer completes the prototype sketched by Isaiah and finally fulfilled by Christ. With a slight strain on the grammar of the original phrase, he inserts his

24 addition, **in his body on the cross** (the *tree*), after Isaiah's words, **he bore our sins**. The resulting statement is compressed and suggestive: **He himself bore our sins in his body on the cross.**

25   **For you were going astray like sheep.** The metaphor of straying sheep, standing for a people which has lost its sense of moral direction and so fallen

into sin, appears for a moment in the same passage of Isaiah (53.6). This writer takes it a stage further. The opposite of straying sheep is a compact flock purposively following its shepherd. Jesus was such a **shepherd.** (The idea is worked out in John 10, but occurs also in Hebrews 13.20 and was doubtless familiar to Christians.) He was also a **guardian**: the word is that which was subsequently used for the highest order of ministry in the church (*episkopos*, bishop), but it already had a long history as a word for describing God's care for his flock. Jesus, the shepherd, had now assumed God's historic guardianship of his forgiven people.

3.1   **Wives, in the same way**. A section addressed to wives forms part of the similar sections in Ephesians and Colossians, and there is a paragraph on the same theme in 1 Timothy 2.9–15. The topic was conventional, and Christians seem to have accepted without question the usual view, generally promoted by moral teachers, that wives should be submissive to their husbands and that they should concentrate on purity of character rather than on outward adornments. To this our author adds a particular reason for submissiveness. If a husband was a non-believer (and the problem of 'mixed marriages' between Christians and non-Christians seems to have arisen generally in the churches, not just in Corinth, 1 Corinthians 7.12–16), then the proper attitude of the wife was neither to seek a separation nor to assume any kind of superiority,

2, 1   but to persevere in **purity and reverence** by which the husband might be **won over**. As for obedience in general: just as it was possible to regard Christian men as 'sons of Abraham' by reason of their Abraham-like faith (see above on

6   Galatians 3.7), so Christian women could be called **daughters** of Abraham's wife Sarah if they imitated Sarah's bearing towards her husband. For us, who have only the Bible to go by and not the later traditions and legends by which Jewish readers interpreted it, the comparison seems bizarre, for the only place in the Old Testament on which Sarah's conduct can be judged is Genesis 18.12, where her response to an angel's message is anything but obedient. But Sarah, like other Old Testament figures, had since come to be regarded as a model of virtue, and so was a suitable example for Christian wives to follow by 'doing good'. Why the author adds **and never let fears alarm you** is less clear. Possibly it is the wives of non-believers who are still in mind. Their husbands might be expected to react angrily to their wives' new faith, for households were generally expected to share the same religious practices.

7   The series is completed by a brief word to **husbands**. This (like Paul's treatment of the same theme in 1 Corinthians 7.3–6) stands in the very best tradition of Greek and Jewish domestic morals. For all that wives remain socially subordinate, they are nevertheless deserving of **honor** for their unique part in the domestic order, and also – and here is a shaft of true Christian light – because they are **heirs** (literally, *fellow heirs*) **of the gracious gift of life**, a phrase never used elsewhere but clearly summing up the new dimension given to life by the Christian faith.

8   **Finally.** In conclusion, a general exhortation is given to all in the church on the kind of life Christians should seek to live together. The church did not attempt to evolve a completely new code of behaviour. Many passages in the Old Testament which offered a definition of the righteous life could serve as examples of godly living. Psalm 34 was one of these. It has already been

10–12   alluded to once (2.3), and here several verses are given (13–17). It enunciates the basic standards of the common life; upon this basis Christians could build their own distinctive society, of which one of the more radical principles was

9   **Do not repay evil for evil** (as in 1 Thessalonians 5.15; Romans 12.17), **but, on the contrary** – and this is a radical note which echoes the Sermon on the Mount (Matthew 5.43–8) – **repay with a blessing.**

13   **Now who will harm you if you are eager to do what is good?** In the case of the Christian communities this was more than a rhetorical question. From

16   what the writer goes on to say about their being **intimidated** and **maligned**, it is clear that, even if some Christians may have got into trouble through their own fault, the fact of being a movement that deliberately promoted a way of life in some ways different from that of their pagan and Jewish neighbours inevitably made them vulnerable to malicious questioning and slanderous gossip. Their situation, in fact, was like that of the prophet Isaiah, who was warned by God not to 'walk in the way' of the people around him and who

14   was strengthened by the words, **Do not fear what they fear,**[3] **and do not be intimidated** (Isaiah 8.12 in the Greek version of the Septuagint).

16   But however much they practised **gentleness and reverence** when challenged about their beliefs, and however carefully they kept their **conscience**

17   **clear**, it is evident that they were in real danger of suffering **for doing good.** What would be their support in this situation? One answer was offered by what looks like an echo of Jesus' own 'beatitude' (Matthew 5.10, "Blessed

14   are those who are persecuted for righteousness' sake"): **if you do suffer for doing what is right, you are blessed.** But there was a deeper source of strength

18   in the fact that **Christ also suffered**; and the passage that follows is solemn, stylized and allusive, such as might have been part of an early Christian hymn (its opening is strikingly similar in form to the hymn in 1 Timothy 3.16) – perhaps even one sung at the time of a baptism (given the reference to baptism in verse 21).

The passage begins with a basic statement of belief in the efficacy of Christ's death: Christ **suffered for sins once for all, the righteous for the unrighteous** – this is the basis of Paul's great argument in Romans 6. It goes on: **He was put to death in the flesh, but made alive in the spirit** – a way of referring to the crucifixion and resurrection which leads into a quite different formulation of the consequences of both. The underlying question is still the same: How have Christ's death and resurrection affected the human condition? The answer

---

[3] This is probably the meaning of the phrase in Isaiah, but as quoted here it can be more naturally taken to mean *Do not fear their fear*, that is, 'Have no fear of them.'

depends on what one thinks is the cause of human sinfulness. If the cause is in ourselves, then Christ's work must have been such as to change our inmost being. But many believed that the cause is also outside ourselves. There are evil powers, demons and spirits working on us and persuading us to do evil. Our salvation is ineffective if Christ has not defeated and disarmed these dark forces which are responsible for our human predicament.

To show how Christ had in fact overcome these powers of evil, it was necessary to accept a certain amount of mythology. The evil spirits which work upon human beings were not thought of as timeless elemental forces: they had a history, and their history explained their present activity. A popular version of this history was that the spirits had originally been in heaven, that they had 'fallen' soon after the creation of the world, and had then wrought such havoc on earth that God was compelled to put an end – by means of the flood – to the generation of human beings whom they had corrupted, and

19 20 to restrain all but a small number of these spirits by having them 'bound' **in prison.** Nevertheless, God saved **a few** human beings from the consequences of the spirits' influence by bringing them to safety **through water.**[4] He had **waited patiently** in the hope that someone would be found who did not deserve the fate incurred by humankind in general; and that person was Noah with his family. But the descendants of Noah were still subject to a certain amount of evil influence from these spirits. It remained for Christ to deliver the *coup de grâce.*

18 **He was put to death in the flesh.** This might have seemed like a victory for the forces of evil, an assertion of the supremacy of Death. But – he was **made alive in the spirit.** Death was made impotent by the resurrection; in that moment the forces of evil were overwhelmed. All that remained was to communicate this to the spirits, and Christ is imagined as doing precisely

19 this: he **went and made a proclamation to the spirits in prison** before taking his place at the right hand of God.

The issue in the realm of spirits and evil forces was decided. But how did this affect human beings? How were they to be rescued from the still continuing consequences of the activity of these spirits on earth? The answer

21 was prefigured in the story of Noah itself. Safety was available once again 'through water' – this time the water of **baptism.**[5]

---

[4] **Through** could have more than one meaning. It could mean that they were physically brought 'through' water until they reached dry land, or that the water which punished the rest of the human race was also their means of salvation.

[5] The definition of baptism offered in verse 21 is puzzling. That it is quite different from bodily washing is clear enough. But that it should be **an appeal to God for a good conscience** seems to contradict the usual Christian understanding of baptism as something given and effected by God, whether or not the convert has a 'good conscience'. But the Greek sentence is very compressed and its meaning is uncertain. The word translated 'appeal' also occurs in legal documents in the sense of a *pledge* or undertaking. This yields the meaning of baptism as 'a pledge or commitment made from a good conscience'. See the NRSV footnote. On the concept of 'conscience', see above, p. 661.

(This interpretation knits the passage into its context and does reasonable justice to the very compressed and allusive language. But many other interpretations are possible. The most famous, and one of the oldest, is that which connects this passage with the later Christian doctrine of Christ's 'descent into hell'. On this view, Christ used the brief period during which he was buried to visit the underworld and preach the gospel to the 'imprisoned spirits' – the deserving dead – who thus had the opportunity to repent.)

4.1 **Since therefore Christ suffered in the flesh.** This seems to be a third approach to the problem of the innocent suffering of Christians. That Christ's suffering (and not merely his death and resurrection) has power to help a Christian in adversity is an idea that is prominent in this letter and was worked out with reference to slaves in chapter 2.18–25. Here it is related to what has just been said by means of the proposition **whoever has suffered in the flesh has finished with sin.** Taken literally, this is plainly untrue. To make sense of it, we must either suppose that the author is alluding to the discipline which is necessarily involved in bearing suffering and which is a protection against sin; or else that a Christian's suffering can be identified with the suffering of Christ to such an extent that it becomes a kind of 'death' from which Christians are liberated by their baptism. At any rate,

3 the Christian profession meant a complete break with the **licentiousness** (as both Jews and Christians always saw it) of unredeemed pagan life. Non-

4 Christians might **blaspheme** this attitude. They might accept that there is an

5 ultimate moral judgment which would demand **an accounting**; but when they saw Christians still exposed to the common lot of death, and especially when they saw them suffering and even dying for their faith, they might ask sarcastically what use their Christianity had been to them. What was the use

6 of it, if believers died all the same? Why was the gospel **proclaimed even to the dead?** To this, Christians could reply that, **though they had been judged in the flesh as everyone is judged,** their faith was gloriously justified in that they shared the victory over death, the resurrection, the 'being brought to life in the spirit' (3.18) of Christ himself: they would **live in the spirit as God does.**

(This last sentence is again open to different interpretations: that the gospel was preached **even to the dead** is reminiscent of 3.19, "[Christ] made a proclamation to the spirits in prison", and many have tried to work out a connection between the two. The interpretation given above is only one of the many that have been proposed.)

7 **The end of all things is near.** This conviction is voiced again and again in the New Testament. In a literal sense, it was not justified: the end did not come. Yet there is little evidence that this delay disturbed the faith of the church. The serious expectation that the present was about to give way to a new age was characteristic of Christianity throughout at least the first century of its existence and has remained so (though usually in a more sophisticated form) ever since. Moreover the New Testament writers were careful to draw

the right conclusions from it. They urged that it should not be thought of as a pretext for irresponsible excitement or for failure to fulfil one's social responsibilities. On the contrary, they invoked it as a spur to prudent and moral behaviour. Almost every time it is mentioned in the New Testament it leads into an exhortation to vigilance and sobriety. **Be serious and discipline yourselves** is a typical example.

What follows paints a distinctive portrait of the Christian community. Love, hospitality and service were three key words of Christian conduct. Most of the ideas can be found in Paul's letters (love, 1 Corinthians 13; hospitality, Romans 12.13; service, 2 Corinthians 8.4): they were doubtless a common factor in Christian teaching throughout the early church. The writer adds one piece of proverbial wisdom: **love covers a multitude of sins.** In isolation this sounds like a weighty statement about the power of love to procure forgiveness. But it should be read in its original context:

> Hatred stirs up strife
> but love covers all offenses.
> (Proverbs 10.12)

In this form the maxim is a simple one: in an atmosphere of hatred the smallest offences are magnified; in an atmosphere of love they are immediately 'covered' – overlooked, forgiven, cancelled. The proverb certainly circulated in the early church (it occurs also in James 5.20).

Intensified harassment?

12 **The fiery ordeal that is taking place.** What is this? Earlier references to harassment or persecution have suggested that it was, at most, a possibility to be taken seriously. Here it seems to have broken out in earnest. It is possible that the writer has just heard of the crisis and hastily adds a postscript to his
11 letter – the previous verse, with its **Amen**, might have been intended to be the end of the letter (compare the ending of Jude). On the other hand, there are many more cases where this kind of formula occurs in the middle of a letter; and moreover, it is hard to be sure how literally we ought to take a phrase
12 like **fiery ordeal**. In our minds it arouses a picture of arson and violence, and even perhaps of the emperor Nero burning Christians alive in Rome. But if it is taken as a metaphor it need be nothing so dramatic. At the beginning of the letter the writer compared the relatively minor harassment suffered by the church with the assaying of gold by the refiner's fire. The analogy was a very old one, and provided one of the ways in which innocent sufferers could find meaning in their sufferings. Following the same line of thought, the writer may still have only sporadic and relatively mild harassment in mind when he speaks of a 'fiery ordeal'.

The resources and encouragement available to a Christian to cope with innocent suffering are one of the principal themes of the letter, and this writer

explores them with particular earnestness. At this point he goes further even
than in the previous passage on the innocent suffering of slaves: it is not only
13 that Christ suffered *for* us (2.21), but Christians are **sharing Christ's suffer-**
ings in such a way that they will also share the joy which is to be their sequel.
14 They are also already **blessed** – and there seems to be a reminiscence of Jesus'
words, "Blessed are you when people revile you and persecute you . . . on
my account" (Matthew 5.11), as well as of his promise that, when his followers found themselves under attack, the Spirit would tell them what to say
(Mark 13.11).

Once again the point is made that Christians must not lay themselves open
to any charges that might legitimately incur penalties from the state. This
time there seem to be echoes of the prophet Malachi:

> The LORD whom you seek will suddenly come to his temple . . . who can
> endure the day of his coming? . . . he is like a refiner's fire . . . he will purify
> the descendants of Levi and refine them like gold and silver . . . swift to bear
> witness against the sorcerers, against the adulterers. (3.1–5)

17 The 'temple' of the Lord is now his **household** (one word in the Greek does
for both) – that is, the church. The Levites who served the Jerusalem temple
have been replaced by a new priesthood (2.5), which is now undergoing
12, 17 the refiner's fire, the **fiery ordeal.** The **judgment** which was the theme of
Malachi's prophecy is about to begin, and it will follow the pattern Malachi
foretold. Those in **the household of God** will be the first to be exposed if they
are found guilty of anything criminal, from murder to mischief-making. This
is sufficient warning for Christians; for those outside the church the prospect
18 is still more sombre. As a verse of Proverbs puts it (11.31), **"If it is hard for the**
righteous to be saved, what will become of the ungodly and the sinners?"
5.1   **I exhort the elders among you.** The letter has already had one section
addressed to different groups within the community. It now has another, and
5 this time the distinction is between the **elders** and those **who are younger.**
This was perhaps a more natural grouping than it might seem now: most
of the Greco-Roman cities of Asia Minor had highly organized guilds and
associations of 'older men' and 'younger men', and a similar tendency to form
separate societies within the whole may have been present in the church. It
was also doubtless true of the church, as of most institutions, that in its
early stages the responsibility for leadership lay mainly in the hands of those
who were older and more experienced (or some of them). At any rate, it is
no surprise that this appeal to the elders is concerned with the exercise of
authority.
1   The author writes as an **elder** himself (literally, *a fellow elder*). His authority
to write to the churches must have been due to a position enjoying considerable respect in the church at large; but he prefers to dwell on the dignity and
responsibility which he shares with other 'elders'. **A witness of the sufferings**
of Christ would be a particularly appropriate description of the apostle Peter,

who was an eyewitness of many of the last events of Jesus' life, and so would have come naturally from the pen either of Peter himself or of one wishing to invest the letter with Peter's authority. But it also had a more general meaning. The sufferings of Christ were continued in the church (Colossians 1.24), and a 'witness' of them might be anyone who was caught up in those sufferings and who believed (like any Christian) that this would guarantee a share in **the glory to be revealed.**

Christian leaders are 'shepherds', pastors: the church took the metaphor from the Old Testament and enriched it with overtones which had sounded through much of the teaching of Jesus (see above on John 10). The pattern for
4 their shepherding was set by Christ himself, **the chief shepherd.** In practice, the task may have turned out to be onerous, and some may have required
2 some **compulsion** to undertake it; it may have been attended by some material rewards which even attracted some by the prospect of **sordid gain**; and it bestowed a rank and sphere of influence which some may have coveted as
3 an opportunity to **lord it** over others. Such motives must be far from those who were to be **examples to the flock.**
5 This 'submission' (the word translated **accept the authority of** is again the one that means *submit to*) was no more than was taken for granted in ancient society, but was also an example of that **humility in** their **dealings with one another** which should characterize all members of the church. Humility
5 is often commended in the Old Testament (there is a quotation here from Proverbs 3.34), but it came into its own as a general principle of conduct in the Christian fellowship, a necessary condition of their exaltation by God in the future.
8 **Discipline yourselves; keep alert.** Not only violence, but stealth and deceit, were the weapons of the church's enemies. Now, at the end of the letter, these enemies are identified as agents of **the devil**, who is active wherever the Christian church exists. The pattern is everywhere the same. The writer
10 closes his exhortation in words that recall his opening (1.5–6): **for a little while** there will be suffering; but in the future a share in the unimaginable glory of Christ.
12 **Through Silvanus.** Writing a letter of this length in antiquity usually meant dictating it to a member of the household and then entrusting it to a personal messenger. Silvanus (the Latin form of the name which appears as Silas in Acts) was a companion of Paul's; he is mentioned in the opening of Paul's letters to the Thessalonians, and he may have assisted Paul in one of these ways. We did not know that he was also a companion of Peter's. Whether he was or not, the name could easily have suggested itself to a writer who wished
13 to imagine whom Peter would have had as a secretary or a messenger. **Mark** was also (for a time) a fellow worker with Paul. A later tradition has it that he was with Peter in Rome and stood in a close relationship with him which could well have been metaphorically described as being Peter's **son.**

Your sister church in Babylon. A Jewish 'letter to the Dispersion' would properly have been sent from Jerusalem, a Christian one from some other major centre. Since the exile, Babylon had stood in the minds of Jewish people as the archetype of any great pagan city, and after the destruction of Jerusalem by the Romans in 70 CE they began to see Rome as the new 'Babylon'. This makes it probable that the writer of this letter was in Rome. Everyone would have known what he meant when he referred to *she who is* in Babylon: the church in Rome.

14   On the **kiss of love**, see above on Romans 16.16.

PETER

Like the First Letter of Peter, this letter claims to have been written by the apostle, in this case shortly before his death. But a number of factors makes it difficult to accept that Peter could really have been the author. For one thing, extensive use is made of phrases and ideas which appear in the Letter of Jude – would the historical Peter have borrowed from a fellow apostle? For another, there is a reference to the letters of Paul, which seems to presuppose that there already existed a collection of them bearing the authority of scripture (3.15–16) – and this is unlikely to have been the case in Peter's lifetime. In addition, the sophisticated style and Hellenistic character of the letter are not what one would have expected from a Galilean companion of Jesus. It seems therefore probable that the letter is one of those which appear to have been written after the death of their supposed authors and which supported their claim on the attention of Christians by invoking the authority of one of the apostles. In this case, if it was written from Rome, Peter's would have been the most appropriate name and authority to invoke. It can be plausibly dated to the last part of the first century CE. By the end of the third century it had been hesitantly accepted into the canon of the New Testament.

Examples from the past

It begins, like other similar writings of the New Testament, in the conventional form of a letter ('From A to B, greeting'), but, as usual, with Christian additions. It was from **Simeon Peter**. The apostle is usually called *Simon*, which is the Greek equivalent of the common Jewish name Simeon. By using the form **Simeon** the writer may have wished to give a particularly Palestinian flavour to the opening. But there may also have been another reason. Simeon was one of the original patriarchs of Israel; and a popular form of Jewish writing was that of a 'testament' or farewell discourse, purporting to be the final words of a patriarch just before his death, but containing moral instruction appropriate to the time of writing. This literary form (which has continued in use down the centuries) was a convenient way of invoking the authority of a leader of the past for teaching that was relevant to the present. Accordingly, this writer represents Peter as expecting his death to **come soon**; and just as in Jewish works of this kind the patriarch was made to recall some of the events of his life (recorded in the Old Testament) before proceeding to the message he wished to give, so Peter is represented as recalling a significant moment in his own life, his presence on the **holy mountain** when Jesus was transfigured (Matthew 17.1–8). Formally, the writing begins as a letter, addressed generally to all Christians; but the convention is not kept up: there are no personal greetings and no salutation at the end. The model the writer is using is not so much a 'letter' as a 'testament'; and he may have felt it particularly appropriate to introduce Peter as *Simeon*, the name borne by one of the patriarchs who was credited with having left a 'testament'.

Nevertheless, if the literary model was Jewish, the language and phraseology reflect a culture shaped more by Greek religion. This may have helped to overcome the diffidence which any Jewish writer would have felt in calling Jesus God alongside the one true God,[1] and may have made it seem more

1 natural to call him **Savior** – a title which was borne by both pagan gods
3 and pagan rulers (see above on 2 Timothy 1.10). Phrases such as **divine power, godliness, glory and goodness** belong to the vocabulary of Hellenistic
4 religion; and the process of escaping from **the corruption that is in the world** and becoming **participants in the divine nature** was recognized to be the object of many philosophies in the Greek-speaking world. The chain of virtues in verses 5–7 is a rhetorical device found in both Jewish and Greek literature. In short, the style is that which might be expected of an educated
5, 7 Hellenistic Jew; though the prominence given to **faith** and **love**, by their position at the beginning and end of the chain, betrays this writer's Christian priorities.

As for his understanding of his faith, it has already a certain conventional rigidity compared with that of the first generation of Christians. For him,
11 **the eternal kingdom of our Lord and Savior Jesus Christ** evidently means a blessed state in the future, for which Christians may qualify by the cultivation of certain kinds of behaviour: a Paul or a John would hardly have described the distinctive elements of the Christian life in terms merely of the expectation of better things to come in the afterlife. Again, he seems no longer to share the exhilaration of the first Christians in their discovery that Old Testament prophecies were now fulfilled in the person and destiny of Christ. For him (and this is a point to which he returns at the end), scripture, including what we would now call the New Testament, may have been one of the sources of the church's faith, but was also dangerous material in the hands of
20 undisciplined interpreters: **no prophecy of scripture is a matter of one's own interpretation**. He recalls Jesus' 'transfiguration'; but not as a moment when the human Jesus was suffused with heavenly glory so much as an occasion
17 for an authoritative statement of Jesus' true nature, the **Majestic Glory** of God having pronounced, **"This is my Son."**
2.1 **But false prophets also arose among the people**. We read in the New Testament of a number of occasions on which the church was confronted with the problem of false prophets (see above on Matthew 7.15). It was guided, not only by the predictions which Jesus had made on the subject, but by Old Testament precedents. It suits this writer's purpose to see **false teachers** as

---

[1] It is not certain that he did so. The Greek of verse 2 can also be translated as in the NRSV footnote.

the same phenomenon – part of the predestined ordeal which the church would have to face; and he proceeds to attack them in a way characteristic of the later writings of the New Testament, that is to say, not by arguing with his opponents but by representing them as such a serious danger that his readers must cease to have anything to do with them. This approach makes it difficult for us to gain any clear picture of these false teachers until, in chapter 3, we read of their scepticism on the particular question of the expected end of the present world order. Meanwhile the writer is not afraid to generalize

2–3 and perhaps to exaggerate. He accuses them of being dissolute, mercenary and insubordinate – but these accusations were so commonly levelled at heretics that they do not much help us. The situation is complicated by the fact that throughout this chapter the writer seems to have had before him the letter of Jude.[2] Many of the phrases used there appear again here, and most of the Old Testament examples are the same. The only specific charges against the heretics concerning their teaching which are made in this

10 chapter have clear echoes of Jude: they **despise authority**, they **slander the glorious ones** (on which see below on Jude 8). Even these heretical errors, therefore, must have been of a fairly general nature if more than one writer could have made them the subject of a letter addressed to Christians in general.

Having identified these heretics as the predicted diabolical enemies of the church, it was not difficult to find traditional colours in which to paint their inevitable retribution. For his first example he follows Jude in quoting the myth of the fallen angels; but like the author of 1 Peter (3.18–20) he refers to the biblical account of the flood to reinforce the argument, and

5 draws a contrast between **Noah, a herald of righteousness** and the **world of**
6 **the ungodly**. The traditional object-lesson of **Sodom and Gomorrah** again
7 comes from Jude, but the contrast with **Lot, a righteous man**, is another of his own additions – and to us a surprising one, since Lot was by no means entirely righteous in the story in Genesis 19, and it was only Abraham's intercession which saved him; but Lot was another of the Old Testament figures whom later tradition included in a list of the righteous. The clearest case of dependence on Jude is in verses 10–11: the language is almost the same, but this writer, just as he drops all reference to the book of Enoch, also leaves out the (perhaps, to his mind, not sufficiently well-attested) story of Michael's restraint when disputing with the devil over Moses' body (Jude 8–9), even though without that story it is hard for the reader to make any

11 sense of the statement that **angels . . . do not bring against them a slanderous**

---

[2] This, of course, is not certain: Jude may have copied 1 Peter. But some literary dependence is undeniable, and it is on the whole easier to imagine the author of 2 Peter expanding and generalizing what he found in Jude than the author of Jude sharpening the point of what he found in 2 Peter. In any case, neither quotes the other verbatim, and it is possible that both worked independently on similar material.

15 **judgment from the Lord.**[3] His last example, that of **Balaam**, is an expansion of the reference in Jude, based on the story in Numbers 22.

But the heretics are not merely in error; they are guilty of moral laxity. To press this home the writer attacks them in the same terms as Jude but

13 adds some lurid touches of his own. To **revel in the daytime** was thought to be a particularly degenerate kind of self-indulgence. Exactly what their **dissipation** at table amounted to we cannot tell, though it is tempting to accept the alternative reading recorded in the NRSV footnote and to see here, as in Jude 12, some allusion to irreverent behaviour at Christian love feasts.[4]

22 The section ends with two proverbs which, if taken strictly, suggest that there was something natural about the apostasy of these heretics – despite the cleansing of their conversion they were returning to their bad old ways

19 as a dog does to its vomit or a pig to its mud-bath. They were such **slaves of corruption** that it was almost inevitable that they should have gone back to their old ways.

The promise of his coming

3.1 **This is now, beloved, the second letter I am writing to you.** Possibly the writer had composed a previous treatise which is now lost; possibly he had read and wished to refer to 1 Peter (though he makes no other allusion to it). Or possibly the phrase (like that in Jude 3) was simply meant as an apology for not covering the whole of the topic. In any case, this introduction allows the writer to return to the convention of a 'testament'. According to this, teaching which was relevant to the present gained authority by having been

2 given at a significant moment in the past – by the **holy prophets** of the Old Testament and in the tradition handed down by the **apostles** (from whom, despite the opening claim to be writing as an apostle himself, this writer feels so far removed as to call them **your apostles**).

3 **In the last days scoffers will come.** That the church would have to contend with an intensification of both heresy and immorality was accepted by Christians as a necessary part of the divine project: the ordeal was a preordained element of **the last days**, the period in which the church now believed itself to be living. To this extent the statement simply echoes others which occur elsewhere in the New Testament (see especially 1 Timothy 4.1). But here the writer sees an important connection between heresy and immorality. One of the arguments most commonly invoked to persuade Christians to be sober and morally correct was the imminent coming of the Lord and the last judgment. 'The Lord is at hand, therefore be sober, be vigilant' is a recurrent

---

[3] The verse is in any case obscure, and there is some confusion in the manuscripts. See the NRSV footnote.

[4] It is possible that there is a deliberate pun. The two Greek words *apatai* (**dissipation**) and *agapai* (love feasts) sound quite similar.

theme in the New Testament and is reiterated here. It followed that any who doubted or denied the imminence of the end lacked moral motivation and might be particularly liable to indulge **their own lusts**. The scoffing question 4 **"Where is the promise of his coming?"** had to be dealt with, not just as an error of belief, but as a source of moral decline.

This phrase, **the promise of his coming**, suggests to a Christian reader the glorious return of Jesus Christ in the last days. This had apparently been predicted by Jesus himself and was earnestly expected by his followers to take place within their own lifetime. But now a whole generation of Christians – **our ancestors** – had **died**. What could be more natural than that people should scoff at a religion which made such promises? Was it not discredited if the promises remained unfulfilled?

And yet, so far as we can tell, this is not how it worked out. The books of the New Testament were written over a period which covers more than half a century of the church's existence. Paul's earliest letters show that he confidently expected the coming within his own lifetime; yet there is little evidence in writings which may date from a whole generation later that its unexpected delay seriously troubled the faith of Christian people. Indeed this is the only place in the New Testament where the question, **"Where is the promise of his coming?"** is explicitly raised. It is of course quite likely that in the second or third generation of the church the question did become acute for some people, and we ought not to be surprised to find it discussed in a letter which probably belongs to a comparatively late period. But it is strange that the writer does not attempt to answer it by appealing to the promise of Jesus himself or to the consistent expectation of the church. His answer, in fact, runs on such different lines that it may well be that we have misunderstood the question.

His coming (*parousia*) is a phrase which was certainly used of the return 12 of Christ; but it could also mean **the coming of the day of God**, that is, the 4 last judgment and the end of the present world order. Again, **our ancestors** could certainly have meant the previous generation of Christians; but the more natural meaning of the phrase is the patriarchs of the Old Testament. In which case the scoffers' question may not be about the return of Christ at all; it may have been simply a general attack on the basic view of history which is presupposed in the Bible and in all subsequent Jewish and Christian thinking. History, in that culture, was always pictured as one great and developing movement leading towards the final judgment of God and the establishment of a new age. It may have been this whole conception which the scoffers, influenced perhaps more by Greek philosophical thinking than by the Bible, intended to call into question when they pointed to the huge span of Israel's history and observed that **"all things continue as they were from the beginning of creation!"**

If so, this writer's counter-arguments become more comprehensible. He points out, first, that the scoffers had a false view of the historical facts recorded in the Bible. The water of the deluge represented a preliminary (and almost decisive) judgment on the world by God, as a result of which he nearly allowed it to revert to the elements out of which it had been created. But this near-destruction was not the end of the story. It was a widely held belief, both in eastern religions and in western philosophy, that the universe would ultimately be destroyed by water *and* by fire. One half of this prediction had been fulfilled by the flood; but the destruction by fire must still lie in the future. **The elements will be dissolved with fire . . . the heavens will be set ablaze** – these propositions were accepted by many thinkers who reflected on the probable end of the world. The scoffers were factually incorrect when they said that **all things continue as they were from the beginning.** They had overlooked the fact that the first stage of the destruction had already taken place in the time of Noah, bringing closer the inevitable second stage of total dissolution by fire.

The second argument sounds at first more philosophical: **with the Lord one day is like a thousand years, and a thousand years are like one day**. To us, this seems self-evident. God's timescale, we say, is not ours. In the measureless span of eternity the few thousand years of human history have little significance. It is possible that this is what the writer meant here. It was absurd, he may have been saying, to complain that the end had not come after only a few decades, when by God's reckoning only a few days had passed. But the notion of world history extending over many millennia is a modern one. History, it was usually supposed, had lasted some three or four thousand years. How much longer would it continue? The question was often pondered by philosophers and others, and the answer given usually presupposed a total duration for world history (or at least for this cycle of it) of about seven thousand years. Jewish people had a special reason for refining this estimate. It is stated in Genesis 1 that God created the world in six days, and this was interpreted to mean that God had imposed a similar arithmetic on history: **one day is like a thousand years** – an interpretation confirmed by Psalm 90.4, which could be taken to mean (in either Greek or Hebrew) 'in your sight **a thousand years are like one day**'. The answer to the scoffers, therefore, could be read off from the account of creation in Genesis. Creation was based on a seven-day 'week'. Six thousand years was the maximum for world history; the seventh thousand – the 'rest' period – would be something new, preceded by judgment. On this timescale history still had some hundreds of years to run: there was no cause for 'scoffing' that the end had not come. But at the same time one could not be sure. At some stage God might "cut short those days" (Mark 13.20). In view of this it was quite possible that the end might come tomorrow – **like a thief**, as Jesus himself had said (Matthew 24.43–4; 1 Thessalonians 5.2).

For a Jew the question could never be academic: the end, with its expected accompaniment of fiery chaos among the heavenly bodies, meant judgment. Still less could it be so for a Christian, who could now see new substance in

13 God's **promise** to his people and could look forward to the inauguration, through Christ, of **new heavens and a new earth**. The end was now a prospect to be looked forward to with faith and hope. The longer one had to wait for

9 it, the more it was tempting to complain that the Lord was **slow about his promise**. The complaint was as old as the prophet Habakkuk (2.3), who had replied to it by simply stressing the need for faith. Another answer, which could also be found in scripture, was that the delay was a sign of God being **patient** with us, allowing us more time to repent before the judgment. This

15 answer – to **regard the patience of our Lord as salvation** – was in fact used by Paul (Romans 2.4), as this writer points out. Moreover, a third answer was becoming popular in Jewish circles around this time: the end was delayed because not enough people were living God-fearing lives, so that it was

12 possible to be **hastening** it on by keeping one's own conduct irreproachable.

16   We might agree that some things in Paul's letters are **hard to understand**, and our reaction would probably be to wish that he had expressed himself less obscurely. But, until the rise of critical scholarship in recent centuries, an obscurity was not necessarily regarded as a defect. On the contrary, it might be a sign that the passage contained a particularly rich and subtle meaning which it was the task and privilege of the qualified interpreter to tease out. This was the positive side. But here the writer is more concerned with the danger that heretical teachers would interpret these passages in such a way as to support their own teaching. Instead of finding salvation there, they would **twist** them **to their own destruction**.

JOHN

Both parts of this title raise questions. Is this really a 'letter'? And who was 'John'?

The first question arises from the opening, "We declare to you what was from the beginning". This is not how one would expect any letter, ancient or modern, to begin; nor is there any greeting at the end to make up for the lack of one at the beginning (as there is in Hebrews, the only other New Testament 'letter' which begins so abruptly). The document is certainly not a 'letter' in the ordinary sense. Neither, apparently, is it a letter in the literary sense (which was widely accepted in the ancient world) of a piece of religious or philosophical writing dressed up in the form of a letter; for such 'letters' always had at least the conventional greetings at the beginning and the end. The writer starts straight in on his subject, and at first sight he appears to be writing a treatise or a sermon. Yet a few lines further down he begins a new paragraph with the words, "My little children, I am writing these things to you." There is nothing conventional or literary about this: we are reading a real message written to a real congregation. A pastor is appealing to his flock; and for some reason unknown to us he does not make his appeal in person but writes it down and sends it to them. It is as if we are overhearing a conversation which has already been going on for some time. The writer takes a great deal for granted in his hearers or readers, and uses a characteristic idiom which was doubtless familiar to them and which we recognize as belonging to the same world as the gospel of John. To outsiders it would have sounded strange and esoteric. It is essentially a private piece of writing, destined for particular people at a particular time. It uses a limited vocabulary and concentrates on a small number of themes. Yet it conveys some of the central truths of the faith in such a way that it has won a secure place in the Christian scriptures since at least the beginning of the third century CE.

The main thing which the writer seems to have taken for granted in his readers is a knowledge of John's gospel. The opening of the letter contains unmistakable allusions to the opening of the gospel, and the whole argument centres round abstract words such as 'light', 'truth' and 'love', which are nowhere defined and which yield their full meaning only to someone who has encountered them in the gospel. On every page the style and vocabulary are reminiscent of the larger work; and it is not surprising that within a hundred years of its composition the church came to assume (in the absence of any indication in the document itself) that this 'letter' is from the pen of the author of the gospel.

Yet this tradition is by no means certainly correct. It is impossible to regard the letter as simply a kind of continuation of the gospel. Certain small points of style and thought are notably different; the idiom has a less Jewish flavour than the gospel – there is virtually no explicit reference to the Old Testament, for example; and the situation addressed is not at all the same as that for which the gospel was written. The gospel's purpose was expressly stated: "so that you may come (or *continue*) to believe that Jesus is the Messiah" (20.31). But in the letter, that belief is assumed: it is written to those who "believe in the name of the Son of God" (5.13). The issue now is the danger of schism or heresy within the church. This is reflected even in the writer's way of addressing his people. Sometimes he writes in his own person: the writer is 'I', the church to which he is writing is 'you'. But sometimes he is so conscious of a division in the church between those who are faithful and those who hold false beliefs that he deliberately identifies himself with one party against the other. 'We' then becomes the true church, 'you' the dissidents; and the purpose of the letter is that "you . . . may have fellowship with us" (1.3). It is not impossible to imagine the author of the Fourth Gospel addressing himself to such a situation, say at the very end of his life, when tensions of this kind had begun to show themselves in the church; but it is perhaps more likely that the letter was written, not by the evangelist, but by the leader of a church in which the Fourth Gospel had already been known and studied for some time and had given rise to some misunderstandings which needed to be warned against or corrected.

Life, truth and love

1.1 **Concerning the word of life**. This phrase provides, as it were, the centre of gravity in a paragraph that is loosely constructed of short phrases, strung together in a way that defies both grammar and logic. In itself, the 'word of life' is a vague expression. It seems to promise, if anything, a philosophical discourse. But a reader familiar with John's gospel would have been able to fill out its meaning. In the gospel, Jesus was 'life', he was also (implicitly) 'the Word'. But now the transmission of that 'life' to new members of the church involved an exposition of who and what Jesus was, and this exposition could also be called **the word of life**. This 'word' could take different forms. The task of a gospel was to portray the person of Jesus during his earthly life – and this, for the recipients of this letter, had already been done in the gospel of John. This writer adds nothing to that. But the Jesus who was known from the gospel was continuous with the Christ who now enlivened the faith of Christian believers: in an important sense, Jesus was present among Christians in the church – and in part this letter seems to have been written as an answer to those who questioned this continuity and who did not see much importance in the historical Jesus for the reality of their religious faith. It is from this point of view that the writer now proposes to speak about Jesus. The 'word of life' is no longer concentrated in the story of one person; it has been prepared for in the prophet's vision of a truth that only some would be able to 'see' or 'hear' (Isaiah 6.10, a passage which has echoes in what follows), and it is diffused, so to speak, in the post-resurrection experience of Christians. This experience, though rooted in the historical person of Jesus, is something that is still developing. It can therefore no longer be defined (as in the gospel) in purely personal terms, as a certain 'he' who made the whole experience possible; it is now a more complex reality, involving a certain amount of abstraction: it is an 'it'.

This new point of view imposes a different timescale. In the gospel, the person of Jesus ('the Word') was there "in the beginning" (1.1). The same phrase is echoed here: **what was from the beginning**. But the subject of the sentence is no longer just the person of Jesus: it is the total reality experienced by the church, of which Jesus was the historical revelation but which was also there from the beginning of all things in the purposes of God. It was true that the 'beginning' of that experience was the moment when Jesus first began to be believed in – perhaps the resurrection, perhaps the first preaching by the apostles. But if any heretics were claiming that they had grasped a new reality more significant than that which was now accessible to all members of the church, it was sufficient to answer that what the church believed in was no second-hand discovery made by the present generation, but was there **from the beginning**.

Let us assume (as most scholars do) that the letter was written around the end of the first century of our era. Few, if any, Christians survived who had actually 'seen' Jesus. In the Fourth Gospel the testimony of eyewitnesses is of

2 great importance. But in the letter the perspective has changed. **We have seen it and testify to it** is not a claim to have actually seen Jesus; it is still about 'it', that is, about **the life** that **was revealed**, which began with the physical appearance of Jesus but which is still continuing in the form of a prolongation of his presence on earth in the experience of the church. For in the language of Jesus himself, to 'see' can mean to understand, to appropriate deep within oneself. Moreover, each generation of Christians receives this inheritance, this possibility of 'seeing', from the previous generation: every Christian has an intense solidarity with all those who have gone before. In this sense they are at one with those individuals who literally 'saw', 'heard' and 'touched' Jesus. But since then Jesus has been present in the church in ways almost as tangible; and it is to this experienced reality, which began as a personal apprehension of the earthly Jesus and continues as an awareness of his continuing presence among them, that the Christians of this writer's generation **testify**.

5 **This is the message**. Again, the form of this 'message' – **God is light** – sounds abstract and philosophical; it is devoid of that particularity which usually goes with statements of Christian belief. It is true that the hearer or reader was expected to have in mind those great statements in the Fourth Gospel to the effect that Jesus is 'the light of the world'. But this writer is saying something much less original: not Jesus, but God, is 'light'; and this was familiar religious language. On a human level, one's existence is

conditioned by alternating periods of darkness and light. By night one has to grope and guess. By day one can see and explore to the full the possibilities of life. On the religious level the same contrast readily suggests itself. Without God, one is groping in darkness. With God, one can see where one is going. And for many religious thinkers the idea extended to a radical distinction between the things of this world – the realm of darkness – and the things of God, who is 'light'. It followed that throughout one's physical existence

6 one was **walking in darkness** unless one had means to escape from ordinary human limitations and share the life of God. But neither Jews nor Christians normally entertained any such radical dualism. For them, darkness and light signified, not separate realms, but two ways of living in the world as it is. For this writer the contrast is not metaphysical but ethical: **walking in darkness** is simply immoral behaviour. It is this, and not the world as such, which is incompatible with **fellowship** with a God who is 'light'. Not that one can 'walk in the light' just by intending to do so: Christians are not people who claim they can be good and godly just by turning over a new leaf. On the contrary: the powerful metaphor of the Jewish sacrificial system still applies:

7 **the blood of Jesus his Son cleanses us from all sin**. Neither pretending to be without sin, nor pretending that sin does not matter, is compatible with what this writer understands to be the meaning of the general proposition

5 that **God is light**.

2.1 **I am writing these things to you so that you may not sin**. The danger does not seem to have consisted in the ordinary temptations of the flesh – though a few fairly conventional warnings about these occur later on – but in the insidious view that sin does not matter. We can guess who held this view.

4 Someone who says, **"I have come to know him"**, is a familiar character in the history of the early church. 'Knowing' God (*gnōsis*) was the professed ideal of a popular kind of religious philosophy. This took many different forms and adopted many different speculative systems, but always tended to represent the true aim of life as an attempt to free oneself from the evil environment of the visible world by means of 'knowledge' of the real and the good. In this kind of religion – which is now usually called 'gnosticism' – to 'know God' was to be saved; and since this salvation was held to consist in rising above the realm of earthly things to a knowledge of purer things above, it was not unusual for these 'gnostics' to regard the body and its passions as quite unimportant and to pay little attention to morality. It was certainly true of some of them that, according to their principles, sin had no importance. These were evidently the kind of people who were menacing the unity of the church to which this letter was written. It was to check the spread of their

1 influence that the author found it necessary to say, **I am writing these things to you so that you may not sin**.

But if anyone does sin. It was one thing to refute a religious doctrine that might lead to immorality. It was quite another thing to pretend that Christians, any more than anyone else, were immune from the tendency to sin. The church was not a community of people who never sinned (which would be impossible), but of people who had reason to believe that their sins were no longer a permanent cause of estrangement from God. The conviction that, in Christ, something had happened which fundamentally transformed one's relationship with God was characteristic of Christians right from the beginning. It was not easy to put into words, and a number of different metaphors was used. One of these exploited the image of a law court. At the last judgment Christians would find that someone was there to plead their cause – **an advocate**. This advocacy, in John's gospel, is one of the rôles of the Spirit. But here (following another line of thought which is hinted at in the gospel, 14.16) the 'advocate' is Jesus himself. Another metaphor was drawn from the Jewish sacrificial system and was well accepted in the church (though it is not actually used in John's gospel). The author has already

2 alluded to it in 1.9; here he spells it out: **he is the atoning sacrifice for our sins.**

4 **Whoever says, "I have come to know him", but does not obey his commandments.** We may assume that some people *were* saying this; but the writer has already argued that this is an impossible position: religion and morals are not separable; the mark of true religion is obedience to God. In the Jewish religious tradition this was taken for granted. The self-revelation of God had taken the form of a code of law which they must obey, and it was axiomatic that anyone who professed to stand in any relationship with God must **obey his commandments.** At first the church unquestioningly adopted the same principle. All Christians were bound by the law of Moses: this obligation was presupposed in the teaching of Jesus as recorded in all the gospels, including that of John. But the opening of the Christian religion to Gentiles brought change; and here we seem to have moved a long way from the Jewish ethical tradition. The readers of this letter seem to have been more used to philosophical preachers than to Jewish rabbis; and here, almost for the first time in Christian literature, the ultimate moral standard appealed to is not the law, nor even the generally accepted moral code, but the example

6 of Jesus: we **ought to walk just as he walked** (and the word 'walk' was a standard term for moral conduct).

The essence of the example given by Jesus was love. When Jesus gave his disciples the command to love one another, it was, in a sense, something quite new (John 13.34). To this writer, surveying the growth of Christianity

7 since its origins, it was already **old**: it was something they had had **from the beginning**. It was the standard of conduct that had always been demanded of Christians. To use again the metaphor of light and darkness, it was this kind of mutual love that constituted 'living in the light'. Yet there was more to it than metaphor. Mutual love was part of that whole new experience of living which was indeed so new that it could be described as the beginning of that 'new age' to which so many religious thinkers had looked forward. In the

8 language of that traditional expectation it could be said that **the darkness is**

passing away and the true light is already shining. The present was a new age; and a commandment which had so much to do with the inauguration of that new age must itself be in some sense **new**.

12   **I am writing to you, little children**. This is how the writer likes to address his readers in general. But to our surprise he now singles out two groups
13   within the congregation, **fathers** and **young people**, to speak a special word to each; and then he repeats the pattern again with only very slight changes. Why he does this we do not know. The message for each group is not obviously appropriate only to them (though it may be that 'young men', having stronger passions, could be said to have scored a greater victory over the devil – **the evil one** – by mastering them). Nor does the section seem to play any part in the argument; it comes after a point that is complete in itself and before a
17   piece of perfectly conventional wisdom (**those who do the will of God live forever** is drawn from a store of Jewish or Christian maxims). The distinctive values that Christians live by are the forgiveness of sins, the knowledge of the Father and the Son, and a will and capacity to resist evil. Here these propositions are simply woven into a balanced refrain.

18   **You have heard that antichrist is coming**. The church inherited from Judaism a characteristic way of looking at history. The present age was nearing its end, and God would shortly bring into existence a new age fraught with blessings for his elect. But before that could come to pass there would be a period of intense tribulation. The forces of evil would make a last desperate stand, the elect would be subjected to unprecedented trials and the violence of this final struggle would be such as to leave those who survived with no more opportunity to compromise: events would force them to take one side or the other, and by the time the hour struck for judgment the sheep would have been effectively divided from the goats. In this scenario the forces of evil tended to be personified in the form of some monstrous being who was destined to have a brief spell of freedom and power before his final overthrow; and when, in any period of acute distress, Jewish visionaries represented the events of their own times as signs of the imminent end, they were not slow to identify the nation or ruler particularly responsible for their sufferings with that dreadful being in whom, in the last days, the power of evil was to be concentrated.

The church (doubtless following the example of Jesus himself) made use of the same visionary scenario and adapted it to its distinctive Christian beliefs. It seldom regarded its own vicissitudes as mere strokes of ill fortune that might soon give place to better times. Instead, it interpreted them as necessary events in that climactic stage of history in which Christians were now living: **the last hour**. Among such events was the emergence of heretics and schismatics. This had already been foreseen and experienced; but this is the first time we read of such people actually leaving the church and forming a separate sect. Their defection is seen by the writer as **antichrist** – a term not met before, but clearly representing the traditional monster of Jewish speculation about the last days, the personification of evil forces now ranged against the true Christ. This figure, the writer seems to be saying, must now be understood in a new way, not as a single king or emperor, but as a type: **many antichrists have come**. The fact that these people had actually 'gone out' from the church – apparently an unprecedented instance of apostasy at that time – meant that they were truly cast as personifications of ultimate evil, as 'antichrists' signalling that this was **the last hour**.

Strong language: what had these people done to deserve it? It has already appeared that, by their indifference to questions of conduct, they posed a threat to the morals of the church. We are now told where their doctrine was

22 wrong: they denied that **Jesus is the Christ**. It is difficult at first to imagine how people who denied this could ever have been Christians at all; but from hints later in the letter we can piece together the kind of beliefs they may have held. They were Christians in the sense that they believed the Christ had come; but for them 'the Christ' was only a mythological symbol for a spiritual reality. The man Jesus was no essential part of their faith; at most he was an example of a general truth, a lay figure in a drama that must be played out ultimately in terms of philosophical abstractions. Their way of looking at things hardly allowed for a proposition as starkly concrete as that which the church proclaimed, that "Jesus Christ has come in the flesh" (4.2). They denied that Jesus is the Christ in the sense that they denied that the abstract concepts they associated with 'the Christ' could be identified with a person as particular and human as Jesus.

The apostle Paul would have attacked this error with argument and shown why the heretics were wrong. This writer also had his arguments, though of a less sophisticated kind: the heretics did not care about morality, and no doctrine which gave rise to immoral conduct could possibly be true.

23 Moreover, as was clear from John's gospel, **no one who denies the Son has the Father** ("No one comes to the Father except through me", John 14.6). But his main line of attack is one that is more characteristic of some of the later writings of the New Testament: no argument is necessary; the truth is in the keeping of the church; those who are in the church can be sure that what they are taught is the truth; those who separate themselves from the church separate themselves also from the source of truth. Here this is expressed by

27 means of a new image: **anointing**. Since the name 'Christ' itself meant 'the anointed one', it is understandable that his followers should have thought of themselves as also 'anointed'. But from 2 Corinthians 1.21–2, where Paul speaks of God's having "anointed us, by putting his seal on us and giving us his Spirit", we can infer that this was a possible way of referring to baptism: by this 'anointing' Christians were brought into solidarity with Christ, the Anointed One. Moreover, this 'anointing' (or baptism) was the moment when they received the Holy Spirit which (as John 14.26 puts it) would 'teach them

20 everything', so that (as this writer puts it) they would all **have knowledge**. But the heretics (presumably) had also been baptized. Could they not also

claim the same guarantee of the truth of their doctrines? The answer must be that this writer intends by 'anointing', not just the moment of baptism, but also that subsequent experience of the Spirit's guidance and of solidarity with the Son which, though it certainly followed baptism, also depended on remaining within the fellowship of the church.

Let us assume that the heretics were saying that the important thing is to 'know' God; what the body does – what people call 'sin' – is less important. Our author has not yet finished with this dangerous error. It was a familiar turn of speech to call people metaphorically someone's 'children' if their character and conduct were like those of their 'father'. For example, those who called themselves 'children of Abraham', as the Jews did, ought to behave as Abraham did (John 8.39). In the same way, since most religions allowed that human beings are in some sense 'children of God' (Paul quotes a pagan poet saying this in Acts 17.28), it followed that, since God
3.8 is righteous, his 'children' must be righteous too. Conversely, **everyone who commits sin is a child of the devil** – and here, as in John 8.44, there is a hint of another possible way of understanding what Christ has done: we sin because an external force of evil, the devil, makes us sin; Christ, by overthrowing this force and destroying **the works of the devil**, has rescued us from sin.

So much followed from common speech and was already a serious argument against the heretics. If they said sin does not matter, how could they claim (as they presumably wished to claim) to be 'children of God'? But in the Christian vocabulary (which the heretics had also learnt) the term **children of God** meant a great deal more. Not only John's gospel, but the teaching of Jesus as recorded in all the gospels, made much of this. Being a 'child of God' meant having a new relationship with God through Jesus Christ. It was a new status, a new kind of living, which did not come to all human beings as of right, but had been given to Christians through the sheer grace
1 of God: **See what love the Father has given us.** One way of describing what this meant for Christians was in terms of the traditional picture of the last things: at the judgment (which, for Christians, would be the moment when
2, 2.28 Christ is definitively **revealed ... as he is**) Christians would **have confidence and not be put to shame.** But this writer has a much bolder definition to offer than this of what it means to be a 'child of God'. It is not something
3.1 we shall be called only on the last day. It is something that **we are** – here and now. This must not be imagined as a crudely obvious change in a person's appearance or character; even Jesus himself was not recognized as the Son of God by **the world** (a clear allusion to a frequent theme in John's gospel). Rather it is a new intimacy with God: Christians (as much as the heretics) can claim to 'know' God, and this, on the familiar philosophical principle that 'like knows like', means that already in the present life, and
2 much more hereafter, Christians are **like him**, they have something in common with God. Sometimes this 'something' is called the Spirit, sometimes

it is described in terms of union with Christ or of a just status, as it were, before God. Here a term is used that had resonances in popular philosophy as well as suggesting an almost physical relationship: **God's seed abides in them**.

9

This was more than mere words. Describe it how they would, Christians knew that something had changed and that this change had brought them closer to God. But being closer to God necessarily involved being further from that which is abhorrent to God, namely sin. There could be no dispute about what this meant. 'Sin', admittedly, was a religious term; but its conse-

4 quences were often indistinguishable from ordinary wrongdoing. In fact, **sin is lawlessness**. This was the final answer to those who were saying that moral conduct does not matter. That new closeness, or likeness, to God which went with being a Christian was totally incompatible with an immoral life. To put

9 the matter in its simplest form: **those who have been born of God do not sin**.

All this was logical enough, and was a powerful argument against the heretics. But as a full description of the Christian life it needs considerable qualification. It may be true that the new kinship with God which comes from being a Christian is incompatible with sin; but the fact is that Christians, like anyone else, go on sinning – indeed, it has already been said with great emphasis that "if we say that we have no sin, we deceive ourselves" (1.8). An analysis of the Christian life has to do justice to two apparently contradictory facts. One is that Christians are no longer subject to the power of sin; the other is that they continue to sin. The tension between these two can be resolved only by the conviction that when Christians sin a new factor is present which rescues them from estrangement from God. The writer does not enlarge on

3 the nature of this new factor here, but he makes two allusions to it. **All who have this hope in him purify themselves, just as he is pure** – where the metaphor is drawn from cultic sacrifices which were believed to 'purify' the

5 sinner in more than just a ritual sense; and Christ **was revealed to take away sins** – perhaps an echo of Isaiah 53.12, a passage which had helped Christians to understand how the death of the righteous one could atone for the sins of others.

The contrast in this passage has been between doing right and committing sin. But the Christian commandment is not just that we should do right but

11 that **we should love one another**; and the opposite of this is not just a sinful absence of love but active hatred. The Bible likes to paint things in black and white. Just as Jesus rated anger on a level with killing, so this writer makes

15 the choice as sharp as possible: love or hate. And **all who hate a brother or sister are murderers**.

Is the choice really so stark? Is the alternative to love nothing less than 'murder'? Two examples are given to support this extreme use of language. The first comes from the beginning of the human story in the Bible. It is written there (Genesis 4.4–5) that God accepted Abel's offering but not

Cain's, after which Cain murdered his brother Abel. But no explanation is given for the feud; nothing is said to show why God preferred Abel's offering and rejected Cain's. Subsequent Jewish tradition (for example in Wisdom 10.3), not content with this silence, filled in the reason: Abel was just, Cain

12 was unjust. As this writer says of Cain, **his own deeds were evil and his brother's righteous**. Abel then began to figure in lists of Jewish saints (as in Hebrews 11.4), Cain in lists of villains. From such a list (since he is not in the habit of quoting scripture) this writer may have drawn his example. Or else he may possibly have known a learned interpretation of the episode in Genesis, according to which the devil, in the form of the serpent, seduced Eve, who gave birth to Cain (**who was from the evil one**). In any event, the story suited his purpose admirably. It was the archetypal example of wrongdoing and hatred leading inexorably to murder.

13 The second example is only hinted at. **Do not be astonished . . . that the world hates you**. In this writer's perspective, and perhaps already in the experience of these Christians, there was a sharp division between the church and the world. If the church was being persecuted there may have been a real danger of death. The contrast may not have been overdrawn: inside the church was mutual love; outside was a hatred of Christians which could lead to their death.

In John's gospel the new life experienced by Christians was described as being as different from the old as life is from death. This writer uses the same

14 imagery: **we know that we have passed from death to life because we love**
15 **one another** – and this new life can also (as in the gospel) be called **eternal life**. It was possible, of course, to misunderstand the 'love' which made such life possible. Some might be tempted to think of it as a mere friendliness, a

18 superficial matter of **word or speech**. But Christ had created a new standard
16 of love, in that **he laid down his life for us**. Nothing less was demanded of Christians – though (the writer adds, with an eye to the more prosaic routine of daily life) it need not always take such an extreme form. It comes into

17 action just as much when there is simply **a brother or sister in need**.

22 Certain things about God would be agreed by all: we must **obey his commandments and do what pleases him**; there will be occasions when we know
20 in our **hearts** (today we would say, in our consciences) that we are not doing right, so that our **hearts** (again, our consciences) **condemn us**; and in any case, we shall be found out: **God is greater than our hearts, and he knows everything**. So much was common ground (it was certainly good Jewish theology). What was the new factor introduced by Christianity? The Greek in this paragraph has some grammatical problems and is far from clear. But the answer seems to be very much in terms of what is expressed more fully in John's gospel. The 'commandment' is both that we should love one another

23 and **that we should believe in the name of his Son Jesus Christ**. This will
21 give us reassurance and **boldness before God**, and also confidence that our
24 prayers will be heard. In this way we shall **abide in him** – this has been a

theme of the letter; but at this point a new factor is introduced that has not been mentioned before: **the Spirit**. And this leads on to the discussion of Spirit and spirits in the next chapter.

4.1 **Test the spirits**. In the early church, as we can see it in the pages of the New Testament, Christians were distinctly aware of having received a new power, a new quality of living, which they identified as the Spirit of God. The precedent for this was in the Old Testament, where the Spirit was understood to be responsible for people speaking or acting in a way which showed that the initiative was not their own but God's. The classical manifestation of this phenomenon was prophecy: prophets were inspired to proclaim their insight into present and future events, and their words, though they were still the personal utterances of an individual prophet, were recognized to have the authority of an oracle proceeding from God. Similarly in the church: the fact that the Spirit was once more active among human beings was proved most spectacularly by Christians speaking words – sometimes 'in tongues' – which could not be other than supernaturally inspired (although, as Paul argued in 1 Corinthians 12, there were many other ways in which the Spirit might be experienced).

The reality and objectivity of this experience was denied by no one; and yet, like so much in the Christian life, it was ambiguous. Just as, in the Old Testament, warning had to be given against prophets whose words seemed to be supported by signs of supernatural inspiration, yet whose message must be rejected because it was idolatrous (Deuteronomy 13.1–4), so in the church there was a danger of **false prophets**. But there were now new ways of understanding this phenomenon. For one thing, it had become accepted in some Jewish circles to speak of humans being influenced by two 'spirits' within them, one of good and one of evil (the Dead Sea Scrolls use language very close to that which we find here); and since the Spirit of God could be assumed to work through lesser spirits (just as the devil could), the good 'spirit' in human beings could be thought of as a manifestation of God's Spirit. Moreover, the Christians' conviction that they were living in the last days gave new significance to the 'bad spirit'. Its heightened activity in others could be understood as one of the tribulations to which the church would

6 necessarily find itself exposed in these last days. A **spirit of error** would be sent to test the faith of the elect, separating the sheep from the goats in preparation for the final judgment. Only those whose faith was sound and sure would remain safely within the fold. The spirit of error would take the shape of a spurious manifestation of the real Spirit; it would ape the **spirit of truth** which inspired authentic prophecy among Christians. Indeed, this

3 was one of the ways in which the ultimate evil would be personified: **this is the spirit of the antichrist**. Behind it was the devil, and normally human beings were very much in the devil's power. But Christ had overcome the

4 devil, therefore Christians need not fear the devil's agents: **you are from God, and have conquered them**.

How were these false prophets to be identified? They gave themselves away if they said what was contrary to the Christian faith. That faith, the writer
2 has argued, depended on the proposition **that Jesus Christ has come in the flesh**. A version of Christianity that did not do justice to the full humanity of Jesus and to the identity of Jesus with 'the Christ' could not be proclaimed by a true prophet; and that, it seems, was precisely the doctrine which was being preached by the heretics, who denied "that Jesus is the Christ" (2.22). Once their doctrine could be shown to be false, it made no difference if they supported it by means of what appeared to be supernatural prophetic utterances. On the contrary, the very power of their prophesying showed that they were agents of a diabolical spirit of error, they were manifestations of the antichrist. The fact that they might be widely listened to was nothing for Christians to be alarmed by. It was merely another instance of the mysterious
5 truth that **the world** did not accept Jesus and still does not accept his followers.
7 **Beloved, let us love one another**. On its own, this might have been merely a general exhortation to behave lovingly – we might suppose that the writer had heard of notably unloving conduct in the congregation. But here the concept of 'love' is woven so closely into the texture of the writing that the words have a deeper significance. In the first place, the word for love is *agapē*, which Christians seem to have coined to express an altogether new concept of 'loving'. For them, it meant something very demanding: following the example of Christ, if need be to the point of laying down one's life for another. This 'love' is one of the dominant themes of the letter; but so far, in chapter 3, it has been introduced in a rather negative way: a Christian must love, because *not* to love is to sin, and a sinner cannot know God. But now this love is given a positive definition. **Love is from God**; and the nature of
10 this divine love has been demonstrated in the sending of God's Son **to be the atoning sacrifice for our sins** (the sacrificial metaphor that was used earlier, in 2.2). In other words, it is God's loving initiative towards human beings, not the merely human love by which we try to respond to it, which sets the standard by which we must recognize what love really is. Therefore loving is in effect the medium through which we know God.

Now 'knowing God' was what the heretics claimed to be expert in. Their idea of religion was to discover more about him and to rest in the satisfaction of a secure understanding of his nature. Such a religion had no strong ethical implications: it did not follow that one must behave in a particular way. But against this our writer sets a proposition which he now expresses in its
8 most direct and radical form. **God is love**; therefore 'knowing God' involves having something of this love in oneself and expressing it in one's relations with others. God cannot be known by means of concepts, let alone direct
12 experience: **no one has ever seen God**. Knowledge of God comes only **if we love one another**.

How was this known? Not by philosophical speculation, but by two data of experience. One was the Spirit, a new force in Christians' lives which argued for the reality of their faith. The other was that original encounter of the

14 first Christians with Jesus, **the Savior of the world**, an encounter so vividly remembered and so faithfully handed down to their followers that this writer

16 could say (as he said at the outset) that **we have known and believe** (literally, *have believed*, suggesting access to first-hand testimony, as in 1.2, "we have seen it and testify to it").

Consider the traditional picture of the last judgment. We appear before God, who is totally other, totally just and good. Immediately, we are made bitterly aware of our own sin and inadequacy. We know that our whole life (apart from a few gracious moments which may speak in our favour) has disqualified us from receiving anything but a stern verdict; and so, in those moments of life when we take stock of all this beforehand, we are necessarily afraid. But suppose now that God is *not* totally other; suppose that there

19 is something in common between the love with which God **first loved us**, and the love towards God and our fellow human beings with which we

17 respond to God's love. It will follow that, by virtue of this love, **as he is so are we in this world**.[1] At the judgment we shall not come before one who is totally other, terrible and transcendent, but one with whom we already share something fundamental. Our past life, instead of being mercilessly held up to the standard of God's justice, will be seen to have embodied already something of God's love. And so we shall have **boldness**. Meanwhile

18 we need no longer live our present life with a fear of ultimate **punishment**: to the extent that we love, and that the love of God already dwells in us, the verdict on us at the judgment is settled in advance: **perfect love casts out fear**.

20 **Those who say, "I love God," and hate their brothers or sisters**. There has never been a time when some Christians did not do this (the word 'hate', which sounds so strong to us, was an idiomatic way of saying 'fails to love'); but we may assume that it is again the heretics, with their different doctrine of God, that the writer has in mind. He has three arguments to bring against this attitude – though he deploys them briefly and with little care for logical order.

(i) A straight argument from psychology: **those who do not love a brother or sister whom they have seen, cannot love God whom they have not seen**.

21 (ii) An appeal to the teaching of Christ himself – **the commandment we have from him**.

5.1 (iii) An argument by analogy: **everyone who loves the parent loves the child**. This is an observation (perhaps an optimistic one, but with some justification) about ordinary human life. Christians are God's children. To claim to love God therefore involves loving his children, one's fellow Christians.

---

[1] The text is not easy to interpret at this point. The pronoun **he** in verse 17 might more naturally refer to Christ; but then it is hard to understand how we already *are* in this world 'as he is'.

3   **For the love of God is this, that we obey his commandments.** What are
God's 'commandments'? A Jew would have answered without hesitation: his
commandments are in the law of Moses, and by keeping this law one expresses
one's love towards God. But this law, though a privilege and a guide, was also
called a 'yoke'; there was a sense in which it was **burdensome**: the world
(subject to the devil) constantly placed obstacles in the way of fulfilling it.
But for a Christian this law had been superseded by a code based entirely
upon love; and the unity which this forges with Jesus Christ, through faith,
4   enables the believer to share the **victory that conquers the world.**
6   **This is the one who came by water and blood.** This is symbolic language,
unintelligible to outsiders, full of meaning to those within the church, for
whom water and blood had come to stand for profound realities. 'Water'
meant baptism, the rite by which they had become Christians and received
the Spirit; 'blood' was the sacrificial death of Christ, represented by the wine
of the eucharist. In the life of the church these were continuing realities; they
were part of the Christians' objective experience. As such, they were also
(along with the Spirit) what we would now call 'proofs' of their faith: they
'testified', like witnesses that could be called in court, to the truth of what they
professed. But they were more than symbolic rituals or subjective experiences:
they were rooted in two decisive historical events, the baptism and crucifixion
of Jesus. The heretics, it seemed, disbelieved in the full humanity of Jesus;
and one form which such disbelief certainly took in early centuries was the
view that the man Jesus became united with the divine Christ at his baptism,
but that the crucifixion involved only Jesus, the divine Christ (who could not
suffer) having left him before it took place. If this was the kind of deviant
view which the author of this letter had to contend with, we can understand
his insistence that Jesus Christ came, **not with the water only but with the
water and blood.** But this is guesswork. All that we can say for certain is that
there must have been some reason for insisting so much on both. In any case,
he quickly returns to his main point. Water, blood and Spirit are objective
7   realities in the church. As such, they **testify**, like witnesses in court, to the
historical facts on which the Christian faith is based. In a Jewish court of
law witnesses had to pass two tests. First, did they agree with one another?
Secondly, were they the kind of persons whose word could be trusted? The
8   'witnesses' to the Christian faith pass both tests: **these three agree**; and as for
9   their reliability, **this is the testimony of God.**[2]

A key word in this paragraph is **testimony**. The content of this testimony
11 is given at the end: **God gave us eternal life** – this is one of the basic themes

---

[2] In verse 7, after the words **there are three that testify**, the Authorized (King James)
Version has the words given in the NRSV footnote. This insertion occurs in no Greek
manuscript, but appears occasionally, from the fourth century onwards, in manuscripts
of Latin translations of the Bible. It is now universally agreed to be a relatively late inter-
polation into the Latin text.

of the whole letter. It was proclaimed right at the beginning (1.1), and a final reference to it here rounds off the argument. But the original subject of the paragraph is not the content of the testimony but the way it is given. How does God 'give his testimony' to the facts of the Christian religion? We have seen: through those objective signs of his presence – his 'witnesses' – which are experienced by Christians in the form of baptism, eucharist and Spirit. It follows that to accept this testimony is to let it become part of oneself –

10 Christians **have the testimony in their hearts**. To reject it is to refuse to believe the witness – to have made God **a liar**.

13   **I write these things to you who believe in the name of the Son of God**. The letter, that is to say, is addressed to those who have remained faithfully in the church, holding the true faith about Jesus. About the others – those who have deviated from the faith – it has used language of the utmost severity; it has even called them personifications of evil, 'antichrist'. It would have made for a clear and simple picture if a line could have been drawn between these heretics and those who had remained faithfully within the church. But the reality was more complicated: the line of division was blurred. There were Christians who were neither fully in the church nor definitely out of it. In this situation Christians had a clear duty to pray for their wavering brothers and sisters – for the efficacy of Christian prayer, given certain conditions, is taken for granted in this letter (3.22), as it is in John's gospel and indeed in many

16 traditions of Jesus' teaching (Mark 11.24). If the sin was **not a mortal sin** – that is to say, if the fellow member had not yet definitively left the church, which was the community of those who have 'life' – then there was hope for the sinner. On the other hand, **there is sin that is mortal**. Christians might go so far in the way of the heretics that their sin was no longer just a case of

17 **wrongdoing** such as could be remedied through forgiveness and cleansing (1.7; 2.2), but placed them irrevocably outside God's family, in the realm of 'death'.

(This is an interpretation which knits the passage into the context of the letter as a whole. But the writer may have had some quite specific 'sin' in mind of which we know nothing. Jesus' saying about the sin against the Holy Spirit (Mark 3.28–9) shows that some sort of grading of sins into forgivable and unforgivable was known to early Christianity; and the problem of Christians who committed the grave sin of apostasy was a serious one for, for instance, the writer of the Letter to the Hebrews. The Jewish system certainly distinguished between deliberate and involuntary offences, and was moving towards a further classification according to the gravity of the offence. But the systematic classification of sins into 'mortal' and 'venial' is a much later development and is hardly anticipated in this passage.)

Nevertheless, apart from these borderline cases for whom the Christian

19 could pray, the line between the church – **God's children** – and the rest of the world was sharply drawn. Outside, men and women were by definition sinners; they lay **under the power of the evil one** – for it did not come

naturally to think of the world as a neutral environment: all human beings are exposed to the forces of evil that are rampant in **the whole world**, from
18 which there is protection for Christians only so far as **the one who was born of God protects them**.

18–20 **We know ... We know ... And we know ... so that we may know ...** These sentences sum up the main points made in the letter. But there could hardly
21 be (at least for us) a more unexpected ending than the words, **Little children, keep yourselves from idols**. It is not just that the letter ends without any of the usual greetings and salutations. This final warning seems quite unrelated to anything that has gone before, and sounds more appropriate to a Jewish writing than to a Christian one. The worship of 'idols' was what Jewish observers tended to find most repugnant in their heathen neighbours, and they insistently tried to protect themselves (and all who sympathized with Judaism) from the dreaded contagion of it. It may be that in the early years of Christianity the same warning had to be sounded: the images of pagan gods and goddesses which adorned every Greco-Roman city were possibly a source of dangerous distraction from the pure religion of the Christian as much as of the Jew. But, taken literally, it will have been a warning only to the simple. More sophisticated spirits, whether of Jewish or Greek background, did not attach much importance to images and statues of diverse gods. God, they knew, was known by the heart and the mind, not by sight or touch. And so the old cry of Jewish prophets and preachers – **keep yourselves from idols** – was reinterpreted by more cultured writers as a warning against the 'idolatry' of things such as money or ambition. At the same time, the word **idols** – *eidōla* – was a technical term of popular Platonic philosophy: it meant the transient appearance of things as opposed to eternal realities. The letter has been speaking the language of people who may have been more at home in the jargon of popular philosophy than in the catchphrases of Jewish religion. To them, all the pretensions, all the seductive 'knowledge' of the heretics could be caricatured, in a parting shot, as mere appearance, **idols**.

JOHN

Warnings from an elder

1 **The elder to the elect lady.** In form, this is exactly the way a letter was expected to begin: 'From A to B, greetings.' Indeed, unlike the First Letter of John, this and the Third Letter are more like the actual letters of their time than almost any other writing of the New Testament. They are both of the right length to fill one side of a sheet of papyrus, and they both have a beginning and an end typical of the conventions of letter-writing in the ancient world. Yet there is a difference between them. The Third Letter is evidently part of a personal correspondence between individuals; but the Second Letter, though it follows the same conventional form, puts it to a different use. It is not a private letter at all, but open one. And the salutations and greetings (as in the letters of Paul) are adapted so as to carry a load of Christian meanings.

To this extent the writing has the form of a letter rather than the reality of one; and this may give the clue to the opening. The **lady**, if a real lady, would have a name. It is possible that there is a name concealed in the word **elect**: *Eclecta* (the Latin form of the Greek word) is a known first name. But the fact that there is no personal message in the letter makes it more likely that this is a symbolic 'lady', for she has 'children' and a 'sister', similarly unnamed. The symbolism is fairly obvious. Just as on a Roman coin a female figure or goddess often represented a city or a nation (like the British 'Britannia'), so for a Christian writer a 'lady' could stand for a particular church, her 'sister' for a neighbouring church. It is the same convention as in 1 Peter 5.13, "your sister church" (in Greek, *syneklektē*). In both cases the symbolic lady is called 'elect'. A Christian reader would doubtless have picked up the symbolism without difficulty.

In this way, the conventional formula, 'From A to B', is turned into a symbolic device for addressing an open letter to a church. The rest of the formula is similarly adapted to Christian use. Not only is the usual Greek
3 word (*chairein*, 'greeting') replaced by its Christian equivalent (*charis*, **grace**) and combined with two other religious words (**mercy, and peace**), but the whole phrase is transformed from a conventional expression of good wishes into a statement of Christian hope, with a reference also to two themes which are dominant in the gospel and all the letters of John, **truth and love**.

Thus the whole salutation, like the opening of many of Paul's letters, is a
1 piece of conscious literary artifice. What then of **the elder**? Is this intended to stand for just any senior person in the church who might be sending such a letter? We might be tempted to think so, were it not that the opening of 3 John, which is not in the least artificial or symbolic, uses exactly the same

term, 'the elder'. To the first readers of that letter, this was evidently sufficient to identify the author: it must therefore have been a fairly distinctive title. Now by the end of the first century CE the word 'elder' (*presbyter*) had become a title for one of the orders of ministry in the church. Every church had its 'elders', who came next in seniority after the bishop. By this time a church official could hardly have referred to himself simply as 'the elder' – there were too many of them for this to be a distinctive title. Indeed, from the very first appearance of 'elders' in the church there seem to have been more than one of them in each place. This was not, however, the only use of the word. A man became an 'elder' (or 'senior'), not just as an official title, but by reason of advancing years and experience. In the New Testament period it was a distinction in itself to be old enough to have known some of the eyewitnesses of the events of Jesus' life or of Christian beginnings. Early in the second century a certain Bishop Papias knew of a John whom he called 'the elder', evidently meaning that this John had been a Christian long enough to remember the first generation of Christians. The same John may or may not have been the author of this letter; but this reference to an 'elder' suggests that the most likely explanation of **the elder** here is that the title designates a man of some seniority in his own church, whose advanced years made him a unique contact with the early days of Christianity and who thereby possessed the authority to write the two letters which begin, "The elder to . . ."

Did the writer of this letter also write the First Letter and the gospel of John? That he did so has been the tradition of the church since early times; but there are the same difficulties here as have been mentioned in connection with 1 John. In particular, these letters are not so much an extension of the thought of the gospel as its subsequent application to particular situations in the church; and this letter is at one remove further from the gospel in that it applies, not the thought of the gospel itself, but the formulation of it that we find in 1 John – it is even possible that it was written first and

5 that 1 John is an expansion of it. Thus the first exhortation, **let us love one another**, is a summary of the teaching in 1 John 2.6–8; and the description

7 of the **deceivers** matches the treatment of the same theme in 1 John 2.18–19. As in 1 John (2.22–3), the point at issue between the author and the heretics is the doctrine that **Jesus Christ has come in the flesh**; the **deceivers** (almost a technical term, as in 1 John 2.26) did not acknowledge that the saviour figure, whom Christians recognized as the promised Christ or Messiah, had **come in the flesh**. We may guess that the heretics were insisting that this saviour was a heavenly figure, far above fleshly manifestations: in this sense

9 they were 'going beyond' the specific realities of Christian belief. We can perhaps overhear a certain anxiety (similar to that expressed in the letters to Timothy and Titus) to preserve the church's beliefs intact against the inroads of such recklessly adventurous thinkers.

In 1 John much is said about the danger which is constituted by such
10 heretics. Here we are told what action should be taken. **Do not receive into
the house or welcome** any such person. This sounds less than Christian; but
we must remember the background. Heresy and false doctrine were seen by
the church at this time, not as something which it could contain and defeat
by argument and persuasion, but as a manifestation of evil that must be
expected to assail the faithful during this critical phase of history. There were
of course Christians who were borderline cases, wavering between truth and
error: these it was proper to pray for (1 John 5.16). But on the whole the
heretics betrayed their true colours as malicious opponents of the church:
7 they were **the deceiver and the antichrist**. Moreover, they were particularly
dangerous when they descended on the church from the outside. Giving
hospitality to travelling fellow Christians was an absolute obligation in the
church; and any visitor who was a 'prophet' had a special claim on such
hospitality. The problem of the abuse of this hospitality by 'false prophets'
soon became a pressing one; and it is perhaps understandable that when (as
in this case) there seemed to be a clear criterion by which to judge whether the
teaching of such a visitor was true or false, and when the heresy in question
had manifested itself as a diabolical menace to the church, it seemed right
for all to protect themselves by excluding the visitor.

12   **I hope to come to you.** This is the one personal note in the letter – an
excuse, perhaps, for not (or not yet) writing a more comprehensive statement
of belief such as is in 1 John.

THE THIRD LETTER OF
JOHN

A testimonial and its rejection

1 **The elder to the beloved Gaius.** The opening, the prayer for Gaius' physical and spiritual health, the expression of pleasure at news recently received: all these can be paralleled in numerous private letters in Greek which have been preserved on papyrus in the sands of Egypt. The author is writing exactly as people frequently wrote to their friends in the ancient world. At the same time he is **the elder**, a senior and distinguished Christian (see above on

4 2 John 1); and he is writing to one whom he calls one of his **children**, that is (if we may assume that he uses this figure of speech the way Paul does), to a man whom he converted to Christianity himself or who once belonged to his flock. He uses a term in his greeting which, as in English, may be entirely conventional (meaning 'truly') but which evidently has a particular Christian resonance for him: **in truth.**

3 The writer is in touch with some fellow Christians (**friends**[1]) who have been making a missionary journey and who depend for their sustenance (as

7 was normal in the church), not on the **non-believers** to whom they may have been preaching, but on the hospitality of other Christians. Gaius has been host to some of these, and has treated them so well that the report of it has

6 come back to the elder. It only remains to **send them on** for the next stage of their journey (which presumably involves a certain expense) – and this is one of the reasons for writing the letter. Another is the common one of

12 sending a testimonial. This is for a certain **Demetrius**. The testimonial tells us little about him; somewhat obscurely, the writer once again works in his theme word, **truth.**

8 Hospitality to travelling **co-workers**, letters of commendation from one church to another: these things were part of the normal life of Christian communities. That they were subject to abuse we know from the previous letter and from many other references in early Christian literature. It would not be surprising if some church leaders occasionally went too far in the direction of forestalling abuses and deprived deserving Christians of the welcome and hospitality which they deserved; and this could well have led to friction with the church from which the visitors came. The elder, it seems, had written a letter commending some of his own people to the leader of

9 another congregation named **Diotrephes**; but his letter had not been heeded, and his people had been given much the same treatment as he himself had recommended should be given to heretics (2 John 10). Exactly how the two

---

[1] The Greek word means *brothers*, a standard term for fellow Christians.

men stood to each other we do not know. The elder was clearly a figure of authority in his own congregation but may not have been equally respected elsewhere. Diotrephes he describes as **one who likes to put himself first**, a description which must have been intended to be derogatory – he may have been the official head of the local church, but he had shown inappropriate arrogance and spitefulness. What would have happened when the two men confronted one another we do not know. It is possible that this quarrel between them was characteristic of a period in the history of the early church when the leadership of men like the elder, whose memory stretched back to the first generation of Jesus' followers, was passing to an elected group of younger men; but this is guesswork. In any case, the elder is not asking Gaius to take any action. He is merely citing the case of Diotrephes as an example emphatically not to be followed. By his conduct, Diotrephes has

11 shown himself up as **evil**, which means (according to the argument of 1 John 3.6) that he is one who **has not seen God**.

JUDE

The author and his readers

1 **Jude ... brother of James.** Since there is a letter of James in the New Testament, claiming to be the work of the James who was a brother of Jesus, it is natural to assume that this *Judas* or J U D E (so called in English Bibles, presumably to distinguish him from Judas the traitor) is the Judas who is also listed among Jesus' brothers in Mark 6.3 and Matthew 13.55. Judas was a common Jewish name at the time. To distinguish himself from others, this writer discreetly identifies himself as the brother of the leader of the church in Jerusalem. This would have been enough to endow his message with some authority in the church.

What was said above (p. 270) about the authorship of the letter of James applies equally here. This writer uses idiomatic Greek but draws freely on the stock of a Jewish education, even showing knowledge of the Hebrew of the Old Testament. This is hardly the kind of learned accomplishment to be expected of a member of an artisan family in Galilee – though of course it is not impossible that he acquired these accomplishments later in life. Moreover, the situation to be combated, which is to do with sophisticated distortions of Christian belief, and the arguments used to warn against it, are more characteristic of the later writings of the New Testament than of the first

17 generation of Christians. Again, the injunction to **remember the predictions of the apostles** might come more naturally if the apostles already belonged to a previous generation – though again the author could have been much younger than Jesus and have been writing towards the end of a long life. In short, once we have accepted that some New Testament letters may have been written under assumed names, that attributed to 'Jude' may well be one of those which sought to gain authority and a wide circulation by claiming to have been written by one close to Jesus; but there is no decisive argument either way.

1 **To those who are called.** The address is quite general, and there is no personal salutation at the end. We are told as little about the recipients as about the author. Evidently the writing is a 'letter' only in the formal sense: in reality it is more like a sermon or a treatise, addressed to any who care to read it.

Predestined trials of the church

One of the conventions of such a 'letter' was to begin with the circumstances, real or imaginary, which caused it to be written. Here these circumstances

4 appear to be quite specific: **certain intruders have stolen in**. The church, here as perhaps elsewhere, was in danger of being influenced by the views of a certain group from outside, and the writer saw in this influence such an insidious danger to the faith that he felt it necessary to identify its proponents in the light of scriptural types and prophecies and to warn his fellow Christians to be on their guard against their subversive teaching.

What was this teaching? We are badly placed to discover, for the author's concern was not to describe it accurately but to warn against it by identifying its proponents as dangerous heretics. He wished to portray them in such dark colours that faithful Christians would no longer be tempted to yield to their influence. Yet certain features stand out from his attack. Their beliefs apparently led them into **licentiousness** (which, from a Jewish point of view, seemed an inevitable consequence of contact with some forms of pagan philosophy and religion); and this tendency to immorality was enhanced by the fact that they **deny our only Master and Lord, Jesus Christ**. Denying Christ's 'mastery' presumably meant rejecting the ethics which followed from his teaching – though the words could also be taken to imply[1] a radical reinterpretation of Christianity such that Jesus Christ, and even God himself, might be given only a subordinate place among the powers of the universe.

The writer does not attempt to argue with them – and this is one of the features of this letter which suggest a relatively late date for it. The church was now not so much exploring the implications of its Christian discipleship as

3 conscious of possessing **the faith that was once for all entrusted to the saints**. This was no longer something to be discovered in practice and developed in theory, but something to be defended against all attempts to adulterate or distort it. That it would come under such dangerous influences was not

4 open to doubt: the false teachers were **people who long ago were designated for this condemnation**. And the main part of the letter is devoted to a demonstration of the way in which scripture and other inspired writings foretold the danger and offered typical examples of its occurrence.

For this purpose a tradition of Jewish reflection on certain texts lay to hand. The author first gives three instances from the distant past of the kind of punishment which was visited on the disbelieving and the disobedient.

5 First, there were those of the desert generation **who did not believe** – this example is used both by Paul (1 Corinthians 10.1–12) and by the author of the letter to the Hebrews (3.16–19). Secondly, there were the fallen angels

---

[1] See NRSV footnote. The lack of punctuation in the manuscripts makes it possible to take **Master** to mean God, in which case their beliefs may have resembled those of later Gnostics (see above, p. 760) who believed in a divine power superior to the creator of the world and might have been said to 'deny' that the man Jesus was identical with the divine Christ.

6 **who did not keep their own position** but ended up **in eternal chains in deepest darkness:** the author here draws, not on the Bible as we know it, but on a later book, attributed to Enoch, which identified as angels the 'sons of God' who lay with mortal women (Genesis 6.1–4). These angels thus became responsible for the wickedness on earth which caused God to send the flood, and were themselves given eternal punishment. Thirdly, there was the example of Sodom and Gomorrah, which may have been particularly relevant to the immorality of the heretics; this again was proverbial and was much elaborated in later Jewish writings.

These examples are now applied to those who threaten the church's life
8 and faith. First, there is a hint of their activities: they are **dreamers**, meaning that they claim to receive supernatural revelations in their dreams. Then, they **defile the flesh, reject authority and slander the glorious ones.** One might have hoped that these three charges would have been specific enough to afford a clear picture of them. The first item is almost certainly another allusion to their sexual immorality; but the second is ambiguous. It could mean a disrespect for authority in general, including the 'lordship' of Christ (as in verse 4), or for particular authorities such as those in the church. The third is equally allusive. The **glorious ones** are almost certainly angels; but what it meant to **slander** them, and why these people should have done so, is mysterious. The angels referred to may have been good or bad, higher or lower powers in the supernatural hierarchy. Possibly they were those, mentioned by Paul, whom some believed to have mediated the law of Moses, in which case their slander of them would have been part and parcel of their indifference to law and moral standards. But in any case, the word **slander** (literally, *blasphemy*) leads on to another example. There was a Jewish legend that, when Moses died, the archangel Michael was about to take charge of his body and give it the unique privilege of special, unlocatable burial, when he was challenged by the devil, who claimed that, since Moses had murdered an Egyptian (Exodus 2.11–12), his body, like any other murderer's, belonged to the devil. But even then the archangel did not retaliate by 'slandering' the
9 devil, but left the judgment to God: **"The Lord rebuke you!"** Similarly (perhaps) the heretics should refrain from attaching blame even to supernatural powers. That they did so was part of what would lead to their inevitable punishment.

Three more Old Testament incidents provided models or 'types' by which
11 to recognize these people's behaviour for what it was. **Cain**, in Jewish legend, had become a proverbial example, not just of murder, but of enticement into every kind of sin. **Balaam**, originally guilty merely of disobedience to God (Numbers 22), had become a traditional type of one who corrupts others **for the sake of gain**; and Korah was remembered, not just for his rebellion against Moses and Aaron (Numbers 16), but also as a teacher who inveigled others into disobedience to divine commands.

The degree to which these dangerous heretics had penetrated the Christian community becomes clear when we read that they were attending its
12 **love-feasts.** Whether or not these were what we would now call formal celebrations of the eucharist (for this is the first use of *agapē* with this meaning), they were certainly important moments in the common life of the church; and the presence of those who could be described as proverbial villains and deceivers destined for destruction was at the very least a 'blemish' (if not more: the word means literally hidden *reefs*, threatening shipwreck). Their actions are a caricature of reverent participation or of Christian 'shepherding' (see the NRSV footnote). Their futile destiny could be described in well-worn images of clouds that bring no rain to thirsty lands or trees that bear no fruit in an orchard. Their pretentious formulations had no more
13 substance than **wild waves of the sea;** and their end would be that of the planets, which some Jewish thinkers (though many knew better) imagined to be **wandering stars, for whom the deepest darkness has been reserved forever.**

To conclude his demonstration that the heretics were a predestined source of danger for the church, the writer gives his first and only explicit quotation
14 of a text. But the text is not from scripture. It is from the book of **Enoch**, a work which was compiled during the second and first centuries BCE and was never accepted into the canon of the Old Testament. Much of it is in the form of visions which Enoch, **in the seventh generation from Adam** (Genesis 5.21–4), is alleged to have been given of the future; and this writer, like many of his contemporaries, believed these prophecies to have been inspired. (His
15 account of the fallen angels also alludes to them.) The **harsh things** spoken against the Lord, which are mentioned in the prophecy, are interpreted as the
16 typical utterances of these **grumblers and malcontents**, whose contempt for law and morality led them to **indulge their own lusts** and may have involved **flattering people** for the sake of financial gain.

In fact, however, there was more recent and (for Christians) even more authoritative prophecy that could be invoked to identify the heretics. Again and again the 'apostolic' writings of the New Testament told their readers to see in such movements, not a chance hazard for the church, but a predicted
18, 17 and unmistakable feature of **the last time.** Examples of such **predictions** are in Acts 20.29–30; 1 Timothy 4.1; 2 Timothy 3.1–5. They are this writer's final argument for his concluding admonitions. The most important of these is that his readers should stand firm in their faith; but they are also told how they should relate to those whose doctrines and way of life are threatening it. Some must be shunned because their heresy is irrevocable (and even contagious, like physical excrement on clothes); others might still be saved. Two other letters (James and 1 John) close with advice on this subject; but here the obscurity of the writer's Greek (as well as some confusion in the manuscripts) makes it impossible to be sure what his advice is.

Ascription of praise

24 **Now to him**. Instead of any personal greetings, the letter ends with an ascription of praise, following a Christian form which appears at the end of a number of letters. (Romans 16.25–7 is a striking parallel.) It may be a fragment of the kind of language that was already familiar in the worship of the church.

THE

REVELATION

TO JOHN

In its very first words this book announces itself as a 'Revelation' (*apocalypsis*), and within a hundred years of its composition this became the title by which it has been known ever since. The idea behind the word is as old as religion itself. There have always been certain men and women who have claimed that in the course of some supernatural experience divine mysteries were 'revealed' to them; and the religions of Greece and Rome, as of Egypt and the Middle East, produced numerous books of which the writers (whether under their own or assumed names) claimed to have fallen into a trance, to have seen inexpressible visions and to have been instructed by heavenly voices, apparitions or angels in the meaning of the mysteries they had seen or heard. To this extent there would have been nothing surprising in the appearance of such a book in a collection of the literature of the Christian religion. Nevertheless this book, though it was published and probably originally written in Greek, owed more to a particular Jewish tradition than it did to any precedents in the Greco-Roman world. To a Jewish thinker, the ultimate mystery to be revealed was not (as it might have been to a Greek philosopher or mystic) the reality lying behind the appearance of the physical world, or the destiny of the individual soul after death, or even (as was of great interest in an age much preoccupied with astrology) the pattern inexorably fixed on history by the movements of the stars. The ultimate mystery, from the Jewish point of view, was the future – the state of affairs for which creation had been destined by God and which alone gave meaning to the present. Partial glimpses of that future, in so far as it affected their own nation, had been given to the prophets of the Old Testament, who had used them as precious clues by which to interpret the times in which they lived and to give authority to the warnings they felt bound to give to their people. More recently (that is, in the second century BCE and again in the later part of the first century CE), Jewish books had been written which worked upon these partial glimpses and developed them into more elaborate pictures. The visionary authors believed themselves to have received an insight into the future, not just of Israel, but of the whole of creation. They took no credit for this. We know the names of none of the authors: they all attributed their insight to a figure of the remote past such as Moses or Enoch, and claimed that it was only now that these mysteries could be divulged, since only now had history reached the moment at which they were destined to be fulfilled. This type of writing (which modern scholars have called 'apocalyptic' because of its resemblance to this *apocalypse* in the New Testament) began in earnest with the book of

Daniel, a collection of stories and visions which, though associated with a national hero of a previous age, appears to have been written in such a way as to seem to throw light on the sensational vicissitudes and rebellions of the Jewish people under their Hellenistic rulers at the time of writing (second century BCE) and to provide hope and consolation amid their sufferings.

In due course the book of Daniel was incorporated in the Hebrew scriptures. A number of similar books was written in the following centuries under the names of famous figures of Old Testament history, but none of these was accepted into the Hebrew canon, and we do not know how widely they were read. They have survived only because there was keen Christian interest in them. Indeed for Christians this kind of writing assumed great importance. The conditions which had made the visions of Jewish seers seem partial and tantalizing were now dramatically altered. The new epoch of history, which for them had lain in an imprecise future, was now inaugurated by Jesus Christ; and the difficult and subjective process of elucidating ancient and mysterious prophecies had given place to direct and authoritative teaching. Jesus himself had shown the way; Paul and other New Testament writers no longer felt any doubt about the basic shape of things to come (however uncertain the date of such events might be); and here at the end of the New Testament

1.1 was the definitive **revelation** given by God to Jesus Christ. Christians were in a position to complete and supplement the fragmentary insights of their predecessors. There existed now, not just dreams and oracles and visions, but a definitive and final 'revelation'. The claim contained in the first words of the book was as new as the religion which made such a claim possible.[1]

Nevertheless to the modern reader his book may well appear as the most obscure in the New Testament. One reason for this is that the task which it attempts is one which stretches language to its limits, and the writer's prose (which is often barely grammatical) has for the most part the freedom and scope of visionary poetry. But a more obvious reason is that the author used the forms of speech and imagery which came naturally to him for the purpose but which now seem to us exotic and desperately allusive. His idiom starts from the language of the prophets: indeed, he calls his book a

3, 1 **prophecy** (and himself God's **servant**, a traditional title of a prophet), and the great visions of his predecessors – particularly Ezekiel – were constantly

---

[1] The title at the head of the page, THE REVELATION OF JOHN, stands at the beginning of all the manuscripts (sometimes with the addition of 'the theologian', rendered in the Authorized (King James) Version as 'the Divine'). But it is unlikely to have been put there by the author, who defines the nature of his book rather differently. The new circumstance was not that a certain John had suddenly been privileged to see what no one had seen before (in which case he probably would not have revealed his identity), but that Jesus Christ had come to reveal all things and that John had been chosen to be the human recipient of the revelation. To this extent the traditional title, The Revelation of John, is not exact. The NRSV has changed it (somewhat arbitrarily) to THE REVELATION TO JOHN. In any case the title was probably simply affixed as a convenient way of referring to the book by its first word and the author.

present to his mind. His imagery is drawn from the accumulated stock of visionary pictures which Jewish seers had been elaborating ever since the composition of the book of Daniel, and his prose is a tissue of allusions to scripture. Whatever the nature of his visionary experience may have been, his description of it was conditioned by the literary resources which he had inherited. The work is one of extreme originality and power; but its shape and its presentation are determined by the logic of the traditional elements out of which it is composed.

The author

Who was the person who describes himself by no other name or title than **John**? We know nothing about him beyond the very little that he reveals of himself in the book. A tradition that goes back to the second century CE identifies him with the author of the gospel and letters of John. Certainly he writes to the churches of Asia with considerable personal authority, and there are echoes of the language of the Fourth Gospel: both works may well have arisen in the same part of the world. But since both the style and the content of Revelation are totally different from that of John's gospel (and indeed, from anything else in the New Testament), it is hard to believe that the same man wrote both. The most which the evidence allows us to say is that the work was written by a Jewish Christian who was familiar with a few of the ideas in John's gospel, who was held in respect by certain churches in Asia Minor, and whose name was John.

Yet even though we know so little about the author, we can catch something
2 of the mood in which the book was written. John had **testified**, a word (related to *martyr*) which was beginning to take on a heavy meaning for Christians: their **testimony** might have to be given at the risk of their lives. Persecution had evidently not reached the intensity it was to have in the early second century – there is little evidence for serious persecution outside Rome before
9 that – but the author speaks of **persecution** and **patient endurance**, and it is usually thought that he was on the island of Patmos because of having been exiled for his faith. In any event his book had a serious purpose. He had no intention of merely satisfying his readers' curiosity about the future. His book was meant to be read aloud, presumably during the worship of the churches to which it was addressed, and was for their warning and encouragement. Like so much of the exhortation found in the New Testament, it received its urgency from the fact that the final stages of history, prophesied for so many centuries, had now been precipitated by the coming of Christ. John's vision
3 gave him particular authority to proclaim that **the time is near**.

The salutation

The form of what John had to impart was still further conditioned by the circumstances in which he wrote. Whatever the eventual circulation of his

book might be, he intended it in the first instance for certain churches which were known to him personally. Consequently he began with the address
4 and salutation which would have been normal in a letter: **John to the seven churches that are in Asia: Grace to you and peace.** But at the hands of Christian writers these conventional greetings were often transformed into something more significant. So here: John first introduces (with, in the Greek, a flagrant disregard of grammatical correctness) a solemn formula, based perhaps on Exodus 3.14 ("I AM WHO I AM"), but extended into the past and the future to take account of God's presence in all stages of history: **him who is and who was and who is to come.** Next (his mind already forming a visual image of the court of heaven) he speaks of **seven spirits who are before his throne** – angels, he might have called them, since it was angels who (in the Jewish picture of heaven) stood closest to God; but angels were 'spirits', and spirits were an intelligible symbol for the Spirit of God. Finally
5 he invokes **Jesus Christ**, and robes him with titles that had their literary origin in scripture (Psalm 89.27; Isaiah 55.4; etc.) but which were now full of Christian meaning – and this is characteristic of the style of Revelation. The Old Testament is seldom explicitly quoted, but phrases from it occur in
6 every paragraph. Thus, **a kingdom, priests serving his God and Father** is
7 from Exodus 19.6, **coming with the clouds** from Daniel 7.13, and the rest of verse 7 from Zechariah 12.10. But these allusions are not mere padding from existing scripture: along with distinctively Christian phrases (such as
5 **him who loves us** – an expression characteristic of John's gospel) they are combined in a texture that is fresh and arresting.
8   **Says the Lord God.** So spoke the Old Testament prophets; and this book
3 calls itself a **prophecy.** But Alpha and Omega are the first and last letters of the Greek, not the Hebrew, alphabet. God is first and last: the idea is Hebrew as much as Greek (Isaiah 44.6), but it appears here in Greek dress. This writer (it appears from his grammar) seems to think in Hebrew – or more probably Aramaic – but he wrote for people who knew only Greek.

The place and the time

9 **I, John.** The author now introduces himself – and this makes his book unlike all surviving Jewish 'apocalypses', which are attributed by their anonymous authors to figures of the remote past. He shares with the churches some experience of **persecution**, but we cannot be certain that this was the cause of his being on Patmos. It is true that the Roman emperors banished political enemies to lonely islands, and provincial governors could do the same; but we know of no one punished in this way who was not a fairly influential Roman citizen. John may have been exiled there (as was the view of some early Christian writers), he may have taken refuge there from some form of harassment, or he may simply have retired there for meditation. However this might be, Patmos lies close off the coast of Asia, a small and thinly populated island,

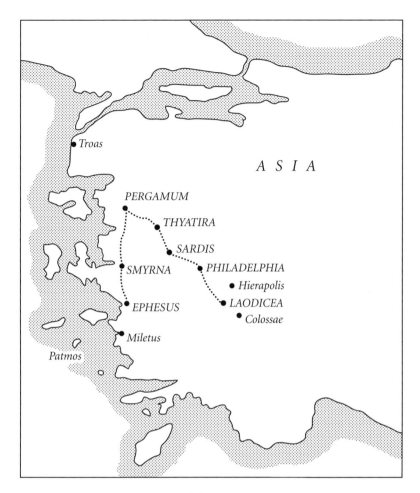

appropriate (to our minds, at least) for a visionary experience. His experience
10 **in the spirit** was **on the Lord's day**, an expression which became standard
for 'Sunday' a century or two later, the day which Christians celebrated as
the weekly festival of the resurrection of Jesus, as opposed to Saturday, the
Jewish sabbath.

This is all that the author says about himself and his circumstances. From
now on he becomes simply the reporter of heavenly visions and messages,
all of which, nevertheless, have the authority of being what was announced
11 at the beginning as "the revelation of Jesus Christ". **"Write in a book what
you see."** This is significant. The word translated **book** means a scroll: John
was not merely to take notes (which he would have done on wax tablets or
possibly a leaved notebook), but was to compose a document that would fill
a scroll of papyrus. This was then to be sent to **the seven churches.** These
were in cities that all lay in an approximate circle, between 25 and 50 miles

from one another. Why John was to write to just these seven (when there were certainly others in the area which were at least as important) we do not know. His mind certainly worked in sevens, and seven messages to seven churches fit well into the plan of the work. It is also true that a messenger, charged with delivering the letter to each of the churches, would most conveniently have started from Ephesus, and the main roads would have brought him to each of these cities in the order in which they are mentioned. But beyond this, the selection of these seven seems arbitrary. It may just have been that these were the churches for which John believed he had a message.

12   **I saw seven golden lampstands**. The scenery of John's heavenly visions is provided by the temple in Jerusalem – which was itself believed to be a replica of a heavenly original (see above on Hebrews 8.5). In the outer room of the temple stood a great golden lampstand with seven branches. A Jewish prophet's vision of heaven naturally tended to include this lampstand (as in Zechariah 4). But John saw, not one, but seven separate lampstands – a symbol with a secret meaning which is explained at the end of the chapter: each stood for one of the churches which, for these Christians, now replaced the Jerusalem temple. But of course not only these seven. Seven was a perfect number, representing the totality of all the churches. With this symbol is

16 combined another: **in his right hand he held seven stars**. These were perhaps the planets: they signified dominion over all the nations of the world. But they too had a secret meaning. Stars, in ancient cultures, were not thought of as inanimate: they controlled much of what happens on earth and were themselves controlled by angels or spirits. And the angels of these stars, being

20 seven, also signified **the angels of the seven churches** – for, just as nations or their rulers were held to be under the control of some supernatural power (an angel or a demon, as the case might be), so each church must also have its angel in heaven.

13   **In the midst of the lampstands I saw one like the Son of Man**. The Jerusalem temple contained no image: the presence of God was suggested by the dark awesomeness of the place. But it was a fundamental Christian belief that Jesus had now fulfilled Psalm 110.1: he had 'sat down on the right hand of God'; and this human presence within the majestic splendour of an image-less God was foretold in Daniel, where there is a vision of 'one like a *son of man* coming with the clouds of heaven' (7.13, as in the NRSV footnote). Jesus was this Son of Man (he had apparently used this title of himself); and the Daniel passage, enriched with details from other prophetic texts (especially Daniel 10.5–6; Ezekiel 9.2; 43.2), provided the model for John's vision of Christ in heaven. For the most part the vision is described in concrete visual terms; but towards the end the words become more symbolic than descriptive. The

16 **seven stars** mean dominion, the **sharp, two-edged sword** means the power of his word.

18   **"I was dead, and see, I am alive for ever and ever."** This does more than merely identify the heavenly Son of Man with Christ: it describes the

characteristic pattern of Christian experience. The prototype was Christ's
own death and resurrection, and here it is symbolically re-enacted by John,
17 as he falls down **as though dead** and is revived. Though it meant a great
deal more than this, it meant at least that Christ had 'conquered death'
(1 Corinthians 15.26, 57), or – to use a different image – that he now held
18 **the keys of Death and of Hades.**

A message for Ephesus

2.1 **"To the angel of the church in Ephesus write."** John has been told to write
down what he sees and to "send it to the seven churches" (1.11). Accordingly,
the book begins and ends in the form of a letter addressed to a group of
churches. But just as a letter to a particular church might single out one
class of people within that church for a special message (1 John 2.12–14), so
this letter has a special message for each of the churches within the group.
Each of these messages contains a warning appropriate to the condition of
the church addressed. The actual circumstances of the Christians in, say,
Ephesus or Smyrna seem to have been vividly in the author's mind while
each message was being composed.

Yet in each case the message is addressed, not to the church itself, but to **the
angel of the church**. 'Angel' meant 'messenger', and it is conceivable that here
it is simply an enigmatic way of referring to the person in each church who
would have the task of imparting John's message to the congregation. But
elsewhere in Revelation angels are always angels, and so they almost certainly
are here. In that case, why warn an *angel* about the dangers of heresy or inertia?
The clue probably lies in a way of thinking much influenced by astrology.
Stars controlled human destinies. But the stars in their turn were controlled
by spirits or angels. We have been told that the seven stars in John's vision
were "the angels of the seven churches" (1.20). Therefore what happened
in these churches would ultimately depend on the angels who controlled
the seven stars. According to this way of thinking, it made little difference
whether the Spirit spoke to the church on earth or to its angel in heaven; and
it was more in keeping with the tone of the rest of the book that the messages
should be written as if addressed to heavenly beings.

It was proper that **Ephesus** should stand first in the list. It was the chief
port of Asia, its largest and most prosperous city (its surviving ruins cover
many acres), and it was the place where the courier would have begun his
journey. The letter begins diplomatically by giving credit where credit is due;
and this was not just a matter of having high moral and religious standards.
The question was whether the church had withstood the particular trials
which were destined to appear in the 'last days'. One of these was the activity
2 of false prophets, or (as they are called here) false **apostles**, men who tried
to claim authority for their teaching, not just because it was inspired, but
because of their supposed position in the apostolic church. This proved to

be unsettling to the church in many places, and is mentioned elsewhere in early Christian writings; but it was always understood as one of the necessary tribulations which had been foretold by Christ himself (Mark 13.22). Against this danger the Christians in Ephesus had shown a firm front. They had also

6 resisted heresy, which took the form in some of these churches of **the works of the Nicolaitans**, about which more will be said later (see below on 2.14–15). But – possibly as a result of closing ranks and becoming over-critical of others – they had been less vigilant against another danger that had also been

4 foretold (Matthew 24.12): **you have abandoned the love you had at first.** A

5 church which failed to put its Christian love into practice (through **works**) would lose its place in the court of heaven. Christians were called, not to an easy life, but to warfare – warfare against Satan (whose power is evoked by a reference to the Paradise story) – and in this their destiny was (to use a word that occurs several times in these messages) to 'conquer'.

A message for Smyrna

Travelling due north from Ephesus the messenger would have come next to

8 another of the great ports of Asia Minor, **Smyrna**. It was a prosperous and beautiful city, and it is possible that the famous skyline of its public buildings, encircling a small table mountain that rises sheer out of the plain, inspired the phrase **the crown of life**. We get the impression of a struggling community,

9 rich only in its possession of faith, and subjected to persecution by **those who say that they are Jews and are not**. There was evidently a Jewish community in Smyrna. It would be in keeping with John's style to refer to it enigmatically. In Paul's language, true Jews were those who recognized Jesus Christ. John sharpens the contrast: those who did not do so were no longer 'the Lord's assembly' or 'synagogue' (Numbers 16.3), but a monstrous perversion of it –

9 **a synagogue of Satan.** Alternatively, those behind the persecution may have been renegade Christians who had become associates with the synagogue or even proselytes, and so could only 'claim' to be Jews. (This was apparently the situation Paul had to deal with in Galatia: see above on Galatians 6.13.) In either event, we can infer the kind of persecution involved from the word **slander.** These people, by informing on the Christians, could have had them brought before a Roman court as apparently disloyal citizens – it was only Jews who were exempt from the duty to offer sacrifices to the emperor. If they refused to do so they were liable to punishment. A famous case of this took place in Smyrna a few decades later, when the aged bishop Polycarp was burnt to death for refusing to participate in emperor-worship and the Jewish community turned out in force to watch. Something less than martyrdom

10 seems to have been expected here. **For ten days you will have affliction** – that is, not for long (ten days was a conventional expression for a short time, as in Daniel 1.12,14): the author did not envisage a long persecution or one pushed to extremes. Prison might be only detention awaiting trial.

But there was always the danger of Christians yielding to the pressure of their persecutors and compromising their faith, either by 'claiming to be Jews' or by performing the required act of pagan worship. The Christians of Smyrna are warned, **Be faithful until death**. The alternatives are more than just survival or death. The faithful will receive 'life' in the full sense which that word has in John's gospel. Even if this involves the ultimate penalty on

11 earth, the martyr is safe from **the second death**, which (as in 20.14) means the verdict passed at the last judgment on those who have lost their claim to share in the life to come.

A message for Pergamum

12 **Pergamum** was the most impressive city in Asia Minor. It had been the capital of the most wealthy of the successors of Alexander the Great, and the centre of a substantial empire. With its temples, its library, its theatre and civic buildings, all built on the terraced summit of a rocky hill that dominates the country for miles around, it was a monument of Hellenistic culture and wealth. Its immense altar to Zeus was one of the wonders of the ancient world: its foundations are still visible, covering an area of about 36 metres (40 yards) square, and its famous sculptures survive in a museum in Berlin. All this passed to the Romans in 133 BCE; but the city, though shorn of its power, kept something of its civic splendour. The Roman governor made it his principal residence, and the cult of the Roman emperor received its first sanctuary in Asia when a temple in Pergamum was dedicated to Augustus.

13 John calls Pergamum the place **where Satan's throne is**. Many things may have contributed to this image: the hill on which the city was built, the great altar in its midst, the palace where the Roman governor lived in state. But it was more than a metaphor. The pagan rulers who surrounded the small Jewish nation and oppressed the Christians were not thought of (at least in Jewish writing of this kind) as merely human powers. They were ultimately controlled by demonic forces. In the last analysis, they could be overthrown, not by human forces, but only by God himself: the real contest was between God and the devil. Behind the Roman power stood Satan himself. Where this power was concentrated in the person of the Roman governor and in the cult of the official Roman religion, it was more than a figure of speech to say that this was **where Satan's throne is**.

The Roman governor had the power of life and death over all his subjects who were not Roman citizens. Technically this was known as *jus gladii*, the

12 right of the sword. John was delivering a message from **him who has the sharp two-edged sword** proceeding from his mouth (1.16). That is to say, the word of Christ stood over against the authority of Rome. To what extent did the two come into conflict? Part of the difficulty of interpreting Revelation is that we cannot be certain when it was written; and in any case, we have very little evidence for persecution before the second century. At an earlier date there

seems to have been no systematic persecution; but it was doubtless possible
to get Christians brought before a Roman court on some pretext, and once
there they might be challenged to participate in the ritual of offering sacrifice
before the statue of the emperor. Under some such pressure one Christian in
13 Pergamum, **Antipas**, had lost his life rather than compromise with his faith.
The rest are complimented on **holding fast**.

But the real danger came, not from the state, but from those same
15 **Nicolaitans** whom we have already met at Ephesus (2.6). They were evidently a heretical group within the church. We know nothing more about
them. Irenaeus, writing about a hundred years later, states that they were followers of the Nicolas of Antioch who is mentioned in Acts 6.5. This may be
correct, but it tells us nothing about the nature of the heresy. The recipients
of the letter will have known all about it, but were evidently not sufficiently
aware of its dangers, and John uses a parallel from the Old Testament as a
caution. The well-known story of Balaam and his ass is immediately followed
in Numbers 25 by an account of how the people of Israel were seduced by
Moabite women into performing acts of heathen worship. Later in Numbers
(31.16) there is a passing reference to the fact that it was Balaam who insti-
gated these women; and the story of how he did so was much elaborated in
14 later traditions. When John referred to **the teaching of Balaam** it is likely to
have been this story which came to mind. The result of Balaam's teaching
had been that the Israelites were led to compromise with heathen religions.
The result of the Nicolaitans' teaching might be that Christians would be led
to compromise with the demands of the official religion of Rome.

17 **Manna** had been the supernatural food of the people of Israel in the
wilderness (Exodus 16), and it was natural to assume that it would also be
the food of the elect in heaven. Some traditions existed which went further:
the manna of the future would be literally the same as that eaten by the desert
generation. A piece of it (so such stories ran) had been **hidden** in some place
on earth and would be brought out at the beginning of the new age.

John's second image for the prize of constancy is more obscure. Small
stones were used for many purposes: as voting papers in a ballot, as tickets
for admission to a large entertainment, as counters for calculating, as tokens,
as charms. A white stone could mean acquittal or election (the opposite of
our 'blackball'), it could be a sign of good fortune or a badge of success.
Any stone with writing on it could have various religious or magical uses.
Acquittal after trial, victory over persecution, admission to heaven, the power
of a 'name' over evil – any or all of these ideas could have been evoked by a
white stone.

A message for Thyatira

The courier carrying the letter must now be imagined as taking the important road which led south-east from Pergamum through the remaining four

18 cities to which the letters are addressed. **Thyatira**, though it had an important political history in the Hellenistic period, was an undistinguished place
in Roman times, and seems to have been mainly a centre of industry and
commerce. There is a reference to its purple dyes in Acts 16.14, and there is
evidence that it had a remarkable number of trade guilds – it is possible that
an issue which faced the Christians there was whether they could belong to
these pagan guilds without compromising their faith.

Like the church in Pergamum, this church had a good record but was
20 threatened from within. **You tolerate that woman Jezebel.** Once again the
heresy is painted in Old Testament colours. Jezebel's worst crime had been
that of introducing foreign cults (2 Kings 9.22); **fornication** was a standard biblical metaphor for deserting the worship of the one true God. In
true prophetic style John carries the metaphor through: the heretics are a
23 harlot who has lovers and **children**; and all will be involved together in her
punishment. This is deliberately highly coloured language. The Christians in
Thyatira may not be aware of the danger they are in. As in Pergamum, so here:
it is hard to know what doctrines or practices lie behind the biblical language.
'Fornication' almost certainly stands for a permissive attitude in associating
20 with pagan cults (possibly in the guilds). On the other hand, **to eat food
sacrificed to idols**, though it could also be metaphorical, may mean exactly
what it says. We know that this was an issue at Corinth (1 Corinthians 8),
24 and it may be significant that the phrase **I do not lay on you any other burden** is one which was used in a formal instruction to Christians about the
extent to which they should separate themselves from pagan society (Acts
15.28): John may be saying that they must be sensitive about the meat they
buy but that they need not adopt the social exclusiveness of a strict Jewish
community. There is one further clue to the nature of the heresy: **what some
call "the deep things of Satan".** It is possible that some prided themselves
on their knowledge of pagan religion and called it satanic; but it is more
likely, and more in keeping with John's style, that the phrase is a deliberate
parody of one of their doctrines. "The depths of God" (1 Corinthians 2.10)
were something into which Christians claimed to have insight through the
Spirit. The heretics may have claimed an insight into different and esoteric
'depths', which John ridiculed by calling it an insight into **the deep things of
Satan.**

Amid all this metaphor and word-play, is there any significance in the fact
20 that the woman Jezebel also **calls herself a prophet?** It could be merely an
ironic piling on of biblical attributes. Yet the problem of people claiming to
be prophets certainly existed in the early church, and the leader of the heresy
may well have been one of these.

28 **To the one who conquers.** This, like all the messages, ends with a promise.
The words come from Psalm 2.8–9. They were originally addressed to a king
of Israel, promising him victory in battle. But for a long time the psalm
had been regarded as a prophetic description of the destiny of the Messiah,

who would one day come to inaugurate an age of glory for his people. The church then seized on the passage as a statement of the ultimate sovereignty of Jesus Christ, a sovereignty in which (as Jesus had promised) Christians were destined to share.

I will also give the morning star. What this stands for in John's symbolism is stated explicitly only at the very end of the book (though some might have recognized it as a code name for the Messiah): it is Christ himself (22.16).

A message for Sardis

3.1 **Sardis** had once been an illustrious city, but suffered a severe earthquake in 17 CE, from which it recovered only by the munificence of the Roman emperor. It was now once again a flourishing commercial centre, and had a sizeable Jewish community. Nothing is said of the church having any difficulties either with its pagan or with its Jewish neighbours; indeed, it may be that it had reached accommodation with them too easily, and so incurred the charge of being 'dead'. It was a phenomenon that was to be common enough in the later history of the church: the original zeal had departed, and only an apparently flourishing exterior remained. The reprimand takes the form (as often in the New Testament) of a warning of an imminent reckoning,

3 the 'coming' of Christ as judge. The warning that this will **come like a thief** is attributed to Jesus in the gospels (Matthew 24.43) and repeated by Paul (1 Thessalonians 5.2). In view of this impending 'coming', the summons to Christian faith and morals is always to **wake up** (as in Matthew 24.42).

5 **White robes**, both for Jews and Romans, represented purity and celebration. The majority in the church, it seems, still had to **conquer** their half-heartedness and lack of zeal if they were to qualify to wear them and to have their names entered in **the book of life**, ready for the day of judgment. Only then would Jesus acknowledge them before his Father – a clear allusion to another saying of Jesus (Matthew 10.32).

A message for Philadelphia

7 **Philadelphia** was the next substantial city on the route. It had been founded in the second century BCE by Attalus II Philadelphus, one of the kings of Pergamum, as a vantage point for the further spread of Greek culture into the interior of Asia Minor; but it had been one of the worst victims of the earthquake of 17 CE, from which it never fully recovered.

The beginning of each of the messages takes an element from the description of the heavenly Christ in 1.12–20. For Philadelphia, the phrase selected is "I have the keys of Death and of Hades" (1.18); but the metaphor of a key immediately goes its own way and governs the drift of the whole message. First, it recalls a passage of Isaiah (22.22): "I will place on his shoulder the key of the house of David; he shall open, and no one shall shut; he shall shut, and no one shall open." When this was written it was a prophecy that a certain Eliakim would become the king's chief minister in Jerusalem. But subsequent interpreters saw more in it than this; and to a Christian it seemed to be fulfilled definitively in Jesus Christ. Moreover, the word 'key' suggested a door; and a 'door', in Christian language, was almost a technical expression for an opportunity to preach the gospel (Acts 14.27 and elsewhere). The church

8 in Philadelphia, however weak, had such an opportunity: **Look, I have set before you an open door.**

This church, unlike that of Sardis, had not allowed its relative weakness to lead it into compromise with either paganism or Judaism; but they had clearly come under some pressure, particularly from the Jewish community

9 which, as in the message to Smyrna, John calls a hypocritical **synagogue of Satan.** It was a frequent theme of Old Testament prophecy that their enemies and oppressors would one day recognize that the Jews were those whom God **loved** and would **come and bow down** at their feet (Isaiah 60.14 and elsewhere). Christians now believed themselves to be the 'true Israel' and could invoke the same prophecies in their own favour, even against those who were, or claimed to be, the historic Jewish people.

10 **I will keep you from the hour of trial.** This trial, or test, is what Christians must constantly pray to be spared (as in the Lord's Prayer, Matthew 6.13). Doubtless it can take many forms in the experience of each individual; but in the early church the decisive 'trial' was thought of as a moment in the final stage of history, the ordeal that was **coming on the whole world to test the inhabitants of the earth.** The main part of Revelation is in fact a description of this ordeal in its universal – even its cosmic – aspect. But this did not take away from the seriousness of local and particular ordeals that might fall upon individuals and churches – only they must always be seen, not as a bad time that might blow over, but as part of, or at least a sign of, that ultimate ordeal from which God had promised that his elect would be saved.

One of the ways in which Christians conceived of the church, whether they were thinking of its empirical existence and structure on earth or its ultimate place in heaven, was as a building composed of living stones, a spiritual temple replacing the old one of masonry in Jerusalem. To be firmly knit into

12 the fabric of this building, like **a pillar,** was an assurance of salvation. On such a pillar might be written the name of the builder or of the city's founder or even of the city itself – the imagery leads the mind to the **new Jerusalem** that will be described at the end of the book.

A message for Laodicea

14 **Laodicea,** Hierapolis and Colossae formed a cluster of cities in a valley about 100 miles from Ephesus. When Paul wrote his letter to the new church at Colossae, he asked that it should be read also "in the church of the Laodiceans"

(Colossians 4.16). It can hardly be an accident that John's phrase, **the origin of God's creation**, echoes Paul's words in Colossians 1.15: either Paul's letter was still being read in Laodicea, or else the kind of language it used had become part of the Christian vocabulary in those cities.

The message comes from **the Amen**. This was a Hebrew word with which the Christian congregation was accustomed to respond in worship. There was a sense in which Christ could be thought of as an 'Amen' to the promises of God (the idea is worked out by Paul in 2 Corinthians 1.19–20). But the word *amēn* itself was usually understood to mean 'in truth': this is the force of it when it occurs in a characteristic phrase attributed to Jesus, "Very truly (*amēn*), I tell you" (e.g. John 3.3). Christ, then, was truth, the **faithful and true witness**, who would vindicate his followers at the judgment.

Laodicea was renowned for its wealth, its wool industry and its medical school. The church, it seems, had identified itself with the city's fame and prosperity and so had lost hold of its own distinctive values – this is the one church in the seven about whom John has nothing good to say. Instead of 18 material wealth it should have **gold refined by fire** – a proverbial expression for the effects of suffering on a noble character. Instead of the glossy woollen garments which were the pride of Laodicean industry it should have the **white robes** of innocence and purity. And instead of the eye ointment which was used in the Laodicean medical school it should find something which would improve its spiritual vision.

All these symptoms of accommodation to the non-Christian world are 16 summed up in a single vivid image: **you are lukewarm, and neither cold nor hot**. As a figure of speech, 'lukewarm' may already have been proverbial (as it is now). But in this setting it may have had a sharper edge. The hot water of the neighbouring springs at Hierapolis was good; and cold spring water was good. But the city of Hierapolis had neither, and lukewarm water (so ancient doctors said) was of use only to make one vomit. So here: **I am about to spit you out of my mouth.**

19   **I reprove and discipline those whom I love.** This was proverbial wisdom (Proverbs 3.12 – see above on Hebrews 12.5–11), one of the stock answers to the problem of evil: suffering is imposed by God on those whom he loves in order to test and strengthen their character. The converse is then also true: if those whom God loves are not suffering there must be something wrong with them. The comfortable existence of the church in Laodicea was a sign 19 of a dangerous inertia. The message is urgent: **Be earnest, therefore, and repent.**

The joys of the age to come were often pictured both as a heavenly banquet and as a period of world dominion for the elect. Both these images are used here, but with a mass of Christian meanings. Christians must be ready for the return of their master at any time, "so that they may open the door for him as soon as he comes and knocks" (Luke 12.36). But the heavenly feast is anticipated by the supper which Christians already celebrate in the

20 eucharist, when Jesus may be conceived as one who already 'comes and eats' with believers.

A vision of the Lamb

4.1 **After this I looked.** Up to now the only part of his vision that John has revealed has been that in which he saw "one like the Son of Man" (1.12); the setting, so far as it has been sketched in at all, has been suggested only by the great seven-branched lampstand which stood in the temple in Jerusalem. Now the scene shifts: the central figure, though he is not named or described, is sensed to be God himself (the Hebrew prophets show similar reserve about God's actual appearance). John concentrates on describing what surrounds that awesome heavenly presence. Yet his imagery is still controlled by things seen or heard of on earth. At the beginning of his vision he was in the outer room of the temple, the Holy Place, where a priest entered every day to offer incense and tend the sacred lights. Facing him in that Holy Place there was a door (with a curtain over it) leading to the Holy of Holies, the mysterious inner sanctuary where God himself was believed especially to dwell, and where only once a year the high priest was privileged to enter. John was now about to penetrate further: **there in heaven a door stood open!** What lay beyond that door in the earthly temple in Jerusalem? In recent centuries probably nothing at all. The sacred objects which were kept there had disappeared with the destruction of Solomon's temple in 586 BCE, and the Holy of Holies was simply an empty room of darkness and mystery. But John's imagination was nourished, not by the actual temple as it existed in Jerusalem, but by the traditions preserved in scripture (in this respect he stands close to the writer of the letter to the Hebrews). According to these, the Holy of Holies contained the ark – a wooden chest in which were stored the tablets of the law (Exodus 25.10–22). This was the symbol of God's presence, his 'throne' (Isaiah 6.1; Ezekiel 43.7). Over it stood statues of winged, sphinx-like creatures, the 'cherubim' of the original sanctuary (Exodus 25.18–20) and of Solomon's temple (1 Kings 6.23–8).

But these were only the raw materials. Out of them John forged some-
6 thing new. As in Ezekiel's vision (Ezekiel 1), the cherubim become **four living creatures**; but here each one has its own personality. As in Isaiah's vision, and using similar words (Isaiah 6.3), these creatures sing the praises of God; but here the praise of these creatures alone is not enough, and another biblical picture becomes fused with that of the temple. "The LORD of hosts will reign on Mount Zion and in Jerusalem, and before his elders he will manifest his glory" (Isaiah 24.23). The inner room of the temple becomes the heavenly throne-room where God holds court among the angels and spirits who worship him. The twenty-four families of priests who officiate
4 in the outer room of the temple are replaced by **twenty-four elders**, the
5 seven-branched lampstand by **seven flaming torches** (perhaps seven

archangels, perhaps simply a numerical symbol for the Spirit of God); and one more feature of Solomon's temple, the huge basin (or 'sea') of bronze (1 Kings 7.23–6), which stood in the courtyard and served for ablutions but which may also have been symbolic of the primordial ocean from which all

6 creation began, reappears transformed into what seemed **like a sea of glass, like crystal.**

5.1 **Then I saw . . . a scroll.** Scrolls of papyrus were used for a variety of purposes – books, letters, legal documents. But there can be little doubt what sort of scroll is meant here. A contract or a will was sometimes written out in full on one side of a sheet of papyrus; the sheet was then rolled up to form a scroll and tied round with narrow papyrus strips. Each witness added his seal to secure the knots, and a summary of the contents was written on the outside of the roll so that it could be identified without being opened. Examples of this have been recovered from the sands of Egypt. The first thing suggested to John's readers by a scroll with several seals and written **on the inside and on the back** (i.e. of the rolled sheet) would certainly have been a legal document of this kind. If such a scroll were produced in a law court, only respected and qualified persons could break the seal and use it as evidence. Christians thought of Christ as their 'advocate' in the heavenly court, ready to produce decisive evidence on their behalf. It was in this sense

4 that they would have recognized Christ as the one who was **worthy to open the scroll.**

But since, in real life, a scroll could be other things besides, so in the vision there were many possible meanings of the symbol. Those of John's readers who were familiar with Ezekiel's vision would have been expecting a scroll of prophecy, containing words of "lamentation and mourning and woe" (2.10): and here, sure enough, the seer was about to witness catastrophic events which were all written beforehand in the book of God's purposes; the opening of the scroll was a symbol that this inexorable sequence of events was about to begin. But there was another image: in a synagogue, the president would take one of the scrolls of scripture from its case and present it to some qualified person who would read and expound it. In exactly this way Jesus had once accepted a scroll in the synagogue at Nazareth and had declared that the words he read from it were now fulfilled in his own person (Luke 4.16–21); and it was a part of the Christian faith that only in the light of Christ could the Old Testament be rightly understood, only through him could the secrets of the scrolls of scripture be known. None of these images must be pressed too hard. This scroll was no ordinary one. It had no fewer than seven seals, and the breaking of each seal, not the reading of the contents, was to be a signal for a spate of catastrophes on earth. Nevertheless, all these ideas may have been present in the background.

The being who was found **worthy to open the scroll** is described first in two Old Testament phrases which were often taken to be prophetic allusions

5 to the Messiah: **the Lion of the tribe of Judah** (Genesis 49.9) and **the root**

of David (Isaiah 11.1). But John's vision of him takes a new and startling
6 form: **a Lamb standing as if it had been slaughtered**. According to John's
gospel (1.29), Jesus was called by John the Baptist 'the Lamb of God', and
was crucified while the Passover lambs were being slaughtered in front of the
temple. Moreover some New Testament writers saw in Jesus the fulfilment
of the mysterious oracle in Isaiah about one who was "like a lamb that is led
to the slaughter" (53.7). To this extent the idea of Jesus as a lamb was not
wholly new; but it was at most a metaphor that helped to throw light on the
meaning of his death. Here the metaphor has turned into a vivid and almost
paradoxical image. The Messiah whom Jewish thinkers thought of as a lion
now appears as a lamb. To us, the animal suggests weakness and vulnerability,
the helplessness of Jesus' unresisting progress to the cross. But, just as the
cross was also a symbol of Jesus' victory over death, so John's image of the
lamb bears the conventional marks of power. In the Old Testament a horn is
a symbol of power: in the visions of Zechariah (1.18) and Daniel (7.7–8; 8.3)
horns appear on the heads of the beasts which have temporary dominion
over the world. Writing in the same tradition, John portrays the Lamb as one
with **seven horns**, the number seven meaning (as usual) that his dominion is
total; and the **seven eyes**, perhaps suggested by another vision of Zechariah
in which the seven lamps on the lampstand are "the eyes of the LORD, which
range through the whole earth" (4.10), stand, he tells us, for the **seven spirits
of God** – for Jesus and the Spirit are one.

   Even if features of the synagogue and of the law court crowd in for a
moment with the appearance of the scroll, the scene is still the heavenly
8 temple. The elders, like psalmists, were each **holding a harp**, and like priests
in the temple they held **golden bowls full of incense**, which were a readily
understood symbol for **the prayers of the saints** (as in Psalm 141.2). But the
9 form of their worship was a **new song**. The traditional language of Jewish
praise was not enough: the Lamb was a new object of worship in heaven
who had effected something decisively new on earth, and a new vocabulary
of praise was needed. Each phrase of the song can be elaborated from other
pages of the New Testament: the idea of 'ransom' by blood combines that of
sacrifice with that of redemption (Mark 10.45); **every tribe and language and
people and nation** represent the universality of Christ's work, transcending
the inevitably nationalist emphasis of Judaism (Matthew 28.19; Luke 24.47);
10 and the kingdom of **priests** is a picture of the church that features in 1 Peter
2.9–10. But John is not concerned here with the precise meaning of these
concepts. He uses them only as headings under which to organize the praise
of Christ. When the circle of worshippers widens to include, first, myriads of
angels who throng the courts of heaven, and then the whole order of created
things, the words of the song become quite general. The object of worship is
God with the Lamb; but the language is also such as might have been heard
at the procession of a Roman emperor or in the temple of a pagan god: it is
the universal language of praise.

Breaking the seals

6.1 **Then I saw the Lamb open one of the seven seals.** Heaven, for this writer (and indeed, for the whole tradition of Jewish writers in which he stands), is not a place remote from the world where there is opportunity for undisturbed felicity and praise. It is in heaven that the future of the world is prepared; a revelation of heaven is a revelation of the secret destinies which are working themselves out on earth. What the writer sees are symbolic actions – the breaking of seals, the blowing of trumpets, the pouring out of bowls – which are the heavenly counterpart of predestined events in human history. These symbolic moments come in groups of seven; and the seventh of each group prepares for the next sevenfold catastrophe. The visions, that is to say, proceed according to their own logic, not in a strictly temporal sequence, but each leading to an intensification of the previous scenario. Yet they never lose contact with realities on earth.

And so here: the breaking of the seals is the signal for the first cycle of calamities. These are described in terms borrowed in part from John's own prophetic understanding of contemporary events, in part from his inherited

8 presuppositions about the destined course of world history. **Sword, famine, and pestilence** and **the wild animals of the earth** were traditional scourges by which God was believed to punish a disobedient world (Ezekiel 14.21). To symbolize these in heaven, a vision of Zechariah provided the vocabulary (1.8; 6.1–8): sometimes four horses, sometimes four chariot teams of differently coloured horses, were sent to patrol the earth. But instead of simply fitting these to the four traditional scourges, John seems to have worked in some

2 allusions to contemporary events. A horse on which the rider **had a bow** could have been understood as a reference to the cavalry of the Parthians. This nation was a constant threat to the eastern frontier of the Roman empire, and won an important battle against Rome in 62 CE. Mounted bowmen formed the most distinctive and dreaded part of the Parthian army. The **white horse** and the **crown** (or victor's garland) would have been an appropriate symbol for the victory of these dreaded forces. To this extent John may have made the traditional scourge of 'the sword' come alive in the threat of successful barbarian invasions into the territory of the Roman empire.

But the sword could also mean civil war: that fellow citizens would slaughter one another was one of the grisly predictions which belonged to the Jewish predictions of the last days. There had been a bitter experience of this in the last days of the Jewish rebellion which ended with the sack of Jerusalem in

4 70 CE. For this, **another horse, bright red** was a fitting symbol.

Food shortages afflicted the Middle East several times during the first

6 century and made for very high prices. A **quart of wheat** was an average ration per person per day, and a whole **day's pay** (literally, *a denarius*) would have been a prohibitive price for all but the rich; working people would have had to make do with **three quarts of barley**. They would have survived

(if it did not go on too long); and, since serious damage would not be done to olive trees and vines (which take years to replace), this was the kind of famine which, though severe, could be endured. Nevertheless, it was seen by Christian prophets as one of the signs of the critical times that lay ahead (Acts 11.27–8).

7 **A pale green horse.** John has made a rough equation between the first three horses and the traditional afflictions experienced by his contemporaries. For
8 the fourth, we expect 'pestilence'; and indeed, **Death** could stand for this. But when we are told that **Hades followed him** we realize that this horse is a more comprehensive symbol, standing for the other three and for all the traditional scourges that were to come. And whereas perhaps any of the other three might have been evaded by most people, cumulatively they might take their toll to the extent of **a fourth of the earth.**

All these were calamities that might be encountered in the ordinary run of history. John and his readers could well have experienced such things themselves: their significance lay only in a certain intensification which made it possible to see them as moments in the final drama of world history. But there was also a more particular tribulation which had begun to oppress the minds of Christians. Persecution of the church had already resulted in
9 martyrdoms: people had been **slaughtered for the word of God and for the testimony they had given.** This raised two questions. First, what was the point of their death? Jewish writers, reflecting on the persecution of the saints of their own faith (particularly the heroic martyrdoms of the Maccabean period), had for some time been describing them as a 'sacrifice', that is to say, a means by which the suffering of a few could ward off the suffering of many. Christians seized on the same idea (see Paul's use of it in Philippians 2.17); and John exploits it here by filling out his description of heaven with one more feature of the Jerusalem temple, the great altar which stood before it and on which animals were sacrificed, their blood (representing their life) running **under the altar.** The sacrifice of these martyrs was the reality symbolized by the old Jewish ritual.

Secondly, when and how would these martyrs be vindicated and avenged? This question may appear to be one which conflicts sharply with Christian principles of forgiveness and reconciliation; but it may seem less objection-able when seen against the background of a distinctive approach to the prob-lem of evil. It is a fact that the righteous suffer, and often their suffering is inflicted because of their beliefs. If the righteous meet misfortune and death, the world may judge them to have been hypocrites or victims of self-delusion; but if the God in whom they believe is just, surely he is bound to save those who believe in him and have faithfully served him. If not, it would seem to follow, either that the righteous are not what they claim to be, or that God himself is unjust. This dilemma afflicted many pious believers as they prepared to meet their death amid the taunts of their enemies. If they must die, they prayed for vindication, either now or in the future. If God were just, he must surely turn the tables on their persecutors. He must force them to acknowledge that their victims were in the right and that they were in the wrong. This would doubtless involve something that looks very like revenge: it would only be by suffering some of the pain which they had inflicted on others that the unrighteous would be brought to acknowledge their error. But (at least at its best) this very human longing for vindication was not necessarily vengeful. It was a postulate of faith: the God whom the sufferer believed to be just must surely at some stage be seen to be just. In the end he must surely come down unmistakably on the side of those who served him faithfully, whatever the consequences for their enemies.

This way of thinking must be borne in mind through much of the violent imagery of Revelation. It throws some light, for example, on a phrase which
16 occurs later in this chapter, **the wrath of the Lamb**. The Lamb, we know, is Christ; and Christ, surely, is not to be thought of as wrathful. But the word 'wrath' has not quite the same nuance in the New Testament as it has in ordinary speech. In Romans 1.18, for instance, the word means, not the personal anger or revenge of God, so much as the inevitable consequences of human wrong-doing in any world which is ultimately subject to divine justice. If God was in Christ, and Christ was nevertheless crucified by human beings, the total opposition to God which this implied must one day be made clear to them – a terrifying reversal which (according to these presuppositions) might be called **the wrath of the Lamb**.

And so here: it is promised that the martyrs would indeed be vindicated – but not yet. Revelation not only dramatizes the end of history and makes it seem imminent; it also takes account of a necessary delay: the period of
11 waiting would be **a little longer** (almost a technical expression in this kind of writing, see above on John 16.16). The sacrifices of the martyrs were necessary, and there were more of them to come. (The idea of a number to be made up like a quota occurs also in Colossians 1.24.) Meanwhile the martyrs already possessed their **white robe** of purity, victory and service.
12 **There came a great earthquake**, accompanied by a cataclysmic disordering of the heavenly bodies. The sky was widely thought of as a kind of tent stretched over the earth, from which the sun, the moon and the stars were suspended. These heavenly bodies controlled the seasons and much else on earth. Conversely, a major break in the regularity of earthly seasons and processes would be reflected in (and caused by) disorder in the heavens. In
14 this vision the sky itself **vanished**. A person reading a scroll of papyrus would hold one end in each hand. When it was finished it would be rolled up and put away. It would be like this with the sky: instead of being stretched out overhead it would be 'rolled up', leaving nothing in its place, and **every mountain and island** – normally the most obvious and permanent geographical points by which to orient oneself – would be **removed from its place**.

At this point the reaction of all classes of human beings (which here include
15 such suggestive titles as the **magnates** or senior courtiers of eastern kingdoms,

and the **generals** of the Roman army) is painted in colours freely drawn from the Old Testament: compare Isaiah 2.10; Hosea 10.8; Joel 2.10–11. They recognize at last that such things are not just an inexplicable catastrophe of nature but that they constitute God's judgment on themselves.

Unexpectedly, there is now a delay before the opening of the seventh seal. Equally unexpected, perhaps, for some of the early Christians was the delay before the coming of Christ and the inauguration of a new age. The church in Asia Minor must have experienced some of the tribulations that have just been described; but it had also had periods of relative prosperity, peace and security. The secular mind might think of these periods as a return to normal; but to a prophet, who discerned in the course of history signs of that final stage when the sufferings of humankind would necessarily be

7.1 intensified, they might have seemed *ab*normal, an exceptional **holding back** of the inexorable sequence of destruction and judgment. Why were there such pauses? The delay of the breaking of the seventh seal is an opportunity to glance at this question. The end would come suddenly, like a thief in the night (1 Thessalonians 5.2); and yet certain things were destined to happen first – the gospel had to be preached throughout the world, the number of the elect had to be made up. That is to say, any respite must be understood, not as a time for relaxation, but as an opportunity to spread the gospel further and as a merciful extension of the time in which men and women might avoid the retribution coming upon them by declaring themselves to be unambiguously on the side of the righteous. An image lay to hand in Ezekiel's vision of a man, armed with pen and ink, being instructed by God, "Go through the city, through Jerusalem, and put a mark on the foreheads of those who sigh and groan over all the abominations that are committed in it" (9.3–4). Those who were so marked would be spared from the imminent catastrophe. John uses the same image but replaces the ink mark by a seal: being 'sealed' seems already to have become an accepted metaphor for becoming a Christian through baptism (Ephesians 1.13).

4 **Out of every tribe of the people of Israel**. To speak of the actual Jewish people as 'the twelve tribes of Israel' would have been sheer antiquarianism: the tribal organization had disappeared at an early stage in Old Testament history, and by the first century only a few of the tribes retained any distinct identity. But the Christian church was encouraged by at least one saying of Jesus (Matthew 19.28), as by Paul (Galatians 6.16), to think of itself as the 'new Israel', the true embodiment of the people of God to whom the divine promises had been made. It was natural, therefore, to describe it in terms, not of contemporary Judaism, but of an ideal Israel such as could be discerned

5–8 in the earlier books of the Old Testament. The order, and even the names, of the twelve tribes vary in the Old Testament lists. John's order is different from any of them, and he omits Dan altogether, apparently replacing him by Manasseh (perhaps because there was by now a legend that Antichrist would arise from the – now extinct – tribe of Dan). But the symbolism is easy. The church is the new Israel, its members are a perfect multiple of the twelve tribes of remote history, organized as battalions of Christ's messianic army – yet (as will be emphasized in a moment) not victorious in the conventional sense, but conquering only by their suffering in the 'great ordeal'.

9   A surprise comes with the further **great multitude**, which decisively disproves any presumption (such as certainly existed in parts of the early church) that some association with the Jewish community was necessary for salvation: they were **from every nation**. All these people are privileged to take part

15–17 in the worship of heaven, magnificently painted in Old Testament colours.

13   The motif of the dialogue with **one of the elders** is in Zechariah 4.1–5, the

15–17 description of heavenly felicity is in Isaiah 49.10; 25.8 (to mention only a few such passages). But at the centre stands a Christian affirmation in startlingly

14   paradoxical symbolism: **they have washed their robes and made them white in the blood of the Lamb**. The martyrs' robes were stained with blood. They now have white robes, obtained, not by their own heroism or their own righteousness, but because of their faith in Christ crucified: the purifying **blood of the Lamb**.

    The sequence of calamities accompanying the breaking of the seals has been interrupted by a moment of 'holding back'. The afflictions visited on humankind have not yet been catastrophically severe; there is a time of waiting, during which the roll of the new people of God will be made up, while some who have already met suffering and death are assured of their glorious destiny in heaven. But this delay was to be short-lived: it was not a time for relaxation or complacency. Accordingly the sequence of seals is now resumed: one more is still to be broken, the last. And that, one might have thought, would be the end of the drama: after the earth had received such punishment,

8.1 could there still be more in store? And so, with the opening of the **seventh seal**, one expects the final cataclysm. It does not come. Instead, **there was silence in heaven**. The climax of this sequence turns out to be the prelude to a further sequence. For this is John's design (or the pattern of his visions). Revelation contains three of these cycles of seven symbolic events in heaven signalling seven series of catastrophes on earth. It is hardly possible to set them end to end, as if John were writing a consecutive history of the end of the world. Rather he is composing sets of variations on a single sevenfold theme. And so here: the seventh seal is a cue for a new development, this

2   time announced by the archangels, **the seven angels who stand before God**, by means of **seven trumpets**.

    That there were periodic spells of silence in heaven was an idea that was not strange to Jewish thinkers: how otherwise could the prayers of God's servants ever be heard amid the continual worship which surrounds the

1   throne of God? John allows only **about half an hour** (unlike others, who thought of a day or a night at a time) – presumably he wanted to stress the

3   imminence of the next sequence of events. This was enough to allow **the prayers of all the saints** to rise like incense – an age-old simile which took

the mind, once again, to the temple in Jerusalem, where every morning and evening a priest entered the Holy Place and offered incense on **the golden altar**; at the same time, one of the seven Levites appointed for the task blew a blast on his trumpet which (it was piously said) could be heard as far away as Jericho. This earthly ritual was a faint copy of the heavenly liturgy; it furnished some of the elements out of which John built his account of his vision of this dramatic moment in heaven. And he adds one thing more: the prayers of God's people were answered. How did they know? Because God

5 gave the usual sign: **peals of thunder, rumblings, flashes of lightning, and an earthquake**. A similar sign is recorded in Acts 4.31.

6   **Seven trumpets**. In Jerusalem a trumpet was blown, not only in the course of the regular temple worship, but also (like church bells before the age of radio and sirens) to announce any exceptional calamity. The first four angels' trumpets are signals for natural, but not yet supernatural, calamities: a third of the world suffers, the disasters are as severe as can be conceived. They certainly merit their place among the portents of the end; but they do not yet (unlike what is to come later) exceed the bounds of human experience.

    Language to describe these disasters was ready to hand in the Bible. Three

7 of the plagues which Moses brought upon Egypt – hail, blood and darkness (Exodus 7–10) – provide the framework; fire is added, perhaps from Joel

8, 10 2.30, the blazing mountain from Jeremiah 51.25. The poisoning of rivers and streams in a time of great heat was a calamity prophesied by Jeremiah (9.15;

11 23.15) and taken up in more recent Jewish writing. **Wormwood** is a bitter plant and was thought to be poisonous; this would be the immediate cause; but the remote cause (in an age much given to astrology) would be assumed

10 to be the influence of an evil **star**.

    Were such things happening at the time of writing? If, as is quite probable, Revelation was written after 79 CE, when the sudden eruption of Vesuvius engulfed the city of Pompeii with molten lava, filled the air with sulphurous dust and destroyed the ships in the gulf of Naples, then John's hearers, from the reports they had heard of the catastrophe, would have had no difficulty

8 in picturing **something like a great mountain** being **thrown into the sea**. John was not the only Jewish writer whose imagination was kindled by that event.

13   The cry of an eagle – **"Woe, woe, woe"**, which in the Greek (*ouai*) sounds not unlike the call of a bird – accompanied each of the last three trumpet blasts. This extra note of terror goes with an extra dimension of evil which attends these final plagues: demonic forces conspire with natural disasters.

9.1 Here the images melt into one another. First, **a star that had fallen** – but the stars were believed to be controlled by angels or spirits, one of whom,

2 descending with the star, could unlock **the shaft of the bottomless pit**. This is mythical geology: in the primordial conflict between God and chaos, the unwanted waters of the ocean, along with destructive elemental forces, were finally imprisoned far below the earth. Their only escape was through a

shaft of which God held the key. To open this shaft was to threaten the earth with a new onslaught from the forces of destruction which had been so long suppressed. What rises first is **smoke**; but the cloud of smoke turns into a cloud of locusts – a swarm of these creatures can look like a cloud against the sun. Locusts – as the prophet Joel observed in his terrifying description of a plague of them (2.4–5) – have something in their appearance which makes one think of horses. So, in John's vision, they turn into almost human cavalry,

9 the metallic sound of their wings being like **the noise of many chariots with horses rushing into battle**. Not only this, but they are also like centaurs; and since the centaur of the zodiac (Sagittarius) was sometimes depicted not only

7, 8 with the traditional bow (**equipped for battle**) and long hair (**like women's**

10 **hair**) but with the tail of its neighbouring sign Scorpio (they had **tails like scorpions**), it is possible that what started in John's mind as one of the plagues on Egypt – the locusts – became fused (through Joel's description of them as horses) with a more sinister influence suggested by the sign of the zodiac, able to afflict humans as well as vegetation and lasting the full **five months** which lie between the beginning of Scorpio and the end of the year. That is to say, these are not locusts at all, but demons in insect form, marching under

11 one of the signs in the heavens. They have **as king over them the angel of the bottomless pit**, the power which commands all the suppressed evil of the universe. Shunning his true name, John gives an equivalent in both Hebrew and Greek. **Abaddon** occurs in Job 26.6 and other places in the later books of the Old Testament; the Greek equivalent means simply 'the destroyer'.[2]

13 **The sixth angel blew his trumpet.** The ceremonial in heaven continues with a trumpet blast and **a voice from the four horns of the golden altar** (it was a characteristic of an altar in ancient Israel to have a 'horn' or vertical

14 projection at each corner). The counterpart on earth is the release of **the four angels who are bound at the great river Euphrates**. The kingdoms of the earth were believed to be ultimately controlled by supernatural powers – angels, spirits or demons. The river Euphrates was the eastern frontier of the Roman empire; it had also been for many centuries the north-east frontier which separated Syria and Palestine, first from the Assyrian empire, and then from the Parthian. The most dreaded enemies of Israel had always come 'from the north', and awesome descriptions of these northern warriors are a frequent theme of the prophets. The menace had reasserted itself in recent times: the Parthians had inflicted humiliating defeats on the Romans in 53 BCE and again in 62 CE. Their immense forces of cavalry (poetically

16 inflated here to **two hundred million**) consisted of mounted bowmen who

19 shot with deadly accuracy both when charging and when retiring (**the power of the horses is in their mouths and in their tails**), and they had become a symbol of the incalculable military power of the barbarian hordes of the east

---

[2] The Greek word (*apollyōn*) may also have pagan associations. The god *Apollo* was normally beneficent, but was occasionally thought to be an agent of pestilence and destruction.

who were constantly threatening the frontiers of the Roman empire and the way of life of all who lived within them. To the Romans, the Parthians were a military problem. To a visionary in the Jewish tradition who was convinced of the imminent fall of Rome as a punishment by God for the iniquities of Roman rule, they represented one of the most obvious means by which this fall would be brought about. It was not that the Parthians were not yet strong enough to attack: the delay was rather to be understood as another instance of God deliberately holding back the forces of destruction until the predestined moment. That moment, in John's vision, had now come. The image of the Parthian cavalry is elaborated into a free description of mythical beasts, representing the innumerable horsemen and deadly weapons of the nations of the east.

20   **The rest of humankind.** The attack from the east might be a blow to Roman dominance of the world, but would it affect the fundamental paganism of Greco-Roman culture? To the Jew, and also the Christian, the most offensive thing about this civilization was its polytheism, its mulitudinous statues and temples and the unashamed materialism and sexual permissiveness which went with so much of pagan religion. To describe all this, Jewish writers used the one word 'idolatry', and applied to it all the polemics they found in the Old Testament against heathen religions which (unlike the pure worship of the Jews) seemed to be directed towards **the works of their hands** (Psalm 135.15–17 seems to be particularly in mind here, but there are many similar passages in the Bible). They also saw in their pagan neighbours certain vices

21   which were particularly abhorrent to Hebrew culture, especially **sorceries** and **fornication**. Any real change of heart in the world at large must surely involve a change of heart over these basic moral and religious matters. The purpose of this revealing of 'God's wrath' (Romans 1.18) was to encourage such a change of heart. But John, having seen no such change of heart resulting from the disasters of his own lifetime, had realized that even the intensified tribulations of the future might not alter the idolatrous tendencies of the majority of the human race.

All this time John has enjoyed the privilege of a seer transported into heaven. From that vantage point he has witnessed both the sequence of symbolic ceremonies carried out in the heavenly liturgy and their corresponding eventualities on earth. He has had insight, not only into the course of human history, but into its meaning within the grand purposes ('the mystery', 10.7) of God. But now, in the heavy and ominous pause which precedes the final trumpet blast, John is apparently once more on earth, his powers of vision temporarily limited like those of other prophets. Before, when he saw a

10.1 **mighty angel** holding a scroll, he was in heaven and was allowed both to witness the unsealing of the scroll and to be aware of the corresponding events on earth. But now he is back on earth – it might be in Patmos – and he sees **another mighty angel coming down from heaven.** The building up of thunder clouds as seen across the sea could well have suggested his

description of this angel, and when at last the thunder comes it is the voice
3 of the divine messenger, **like a lion roaring** – the metaphors were traditional
(Psalm 29.3–9; Hosea 11.10; Amos 1.2). But not all that a human being hears
from God is communicable. Paul, in an experience of Paradise, heard "things
that are not to be told, that no mortal is permitted to repeat" (2 Corinthians
12.4). John likewise is forbidden to write down the thunderous words from
2 on high. Instead, he has to be content with **a little scroll**. He is, after all,
7 one of God's **servants the prophets**. He stands alongside other Christian
prophets in succession to the great prophets of the scriptures. The question
mark which had always hung over the prophecies of these men was not so
much 'Was their vision true?' as 'How much longer would it be before it
6 came to pass?' John's experience is an answer to this question: **"There will
be no more delay"** – a message delivered by the angel with a portentous oath
modelled on Daniel 12.7.
9 **"Take it, and eat."** As a metaphor, the word of God that tastes sweet in
the mouth is common enough in the Bible. The more elaborate picture of
a prophet actually eating the words of a book before prophesying occurs in
Ezekiel 3.1–3 and is closely reproduced here. The book of destiny can never
be read straight off. It has to be digested and meditated on before it can be
communicated. The experience, for the prophet, is precious. As Ezekiel put
it, "in my mouth it was as sweet as honey". But this message, when reflected
10 on, was an ominous one; and John adds, **my stomach was made bitter**.
11.1 **I was given a measuring rod**. After the destruction of Solomon's temple in
586 BCE, two prophets, Ezekiel (40.3) and Zechariah (2.1–2), received visions
of measurements being taken for a new temple. For each, it was a symbolic
reassurance that the religious life of Israel would soon be re-established. Not
long before John was writing, the temple had once again been destroyed in
the war against the Romans. In the tradition of his prophetic predecessors
John received a vision of its replacement.

But the new temple to which Christians looked forward was not a localized
masonry structure but a body of people, the church. For them, 'temple' and
'altar' had become metaphors: the new temple created by Christ consisted
entirely of human beings, of **those who worship there**. Yet one feature of
the old temple could not be absorbed, even as a metaphor, into the new. In
Jerusalem, the central area containing the temple building and the immediately surrounding courtyards was accessible only to Jews: it was thought
too holy to be profaned by gentile feet. But the immense terrace around
this area, though still part of the temple precincts and under the authority of the priests, was open to all: Gentiles could enter freely and mingle
with Jewish worshippers. This arrangement was symbolic of the relationship
between Judaism and the world. In the Roman empire the Jewish religion
was officially sanctioned and Jewish worship continued without opposition
in gentile cities, sometimes actually attended by gentile sympathizers. Yet it
retained a very clear boundary between Gentiles and Jews, just as prominent

notices near the temple in Jerusalem forbade Gentiles to enter the sacred areas. Quite different was the situation of the new temple – the church – in the pagan world. Just as the old temple had now been exposed for gentile

2 feet to **trample over**, so the new temple possessed none of the old security of the Jewish religion. Both pagan and Jewish society were opposed to it and sometimes persecuted it. There was no **court outside** where Christians and non-Christians could mingle peacefully together. No city or building or institution now enjoyed the respect from the pagan world which Jerusalem and its temple had once received. The heathen were trampling **the holy city** (the phrase is from Isaiah 63.18) with no respect for any place set apart to the God of Israel, who was also the God of the Christians. Christians now, like the Jews in the war of 66–70 CE, saw their very identity threatened. It was the time that had been foretold, of great tribulation.

How long would it last? John was writing to his anxious fellow Christians. His purpose was like that of other Jewish writers in the same tradition: to give his hearers hope and courage; and he used the same coded language. What they had to express was their conviction that the period of distress was finite; it had an end to it, therefore it could last only a certain time, a given number of years, months and days. But not, obviously, a random number. God had imposed a pattern on time when he created the week of seven days. Any significant period of history must be reckoned in sevens, or fractions of sevens. Daniel, predicting the length of oppression under Antiochus Epiphanes, had opted for a half-week – "a time, two times, and half a time" (12.7). What were these three-and-a-half 'times'? Days, months, years? Probably Daniel deliberately left the symbol open. The point was that the period was certainly finite and would certainly betray, even in its arithmetic, the providence of God. John here uses the same idiom. **Forty-two**

3 **months . . . one thousand two hundred sixty days** sounds more precise than Daniel's formula. But it represents the same symbolic half-week of years: it is any period that is moving swiftly to its end in God's pre-determined timescale.

If everything holy is to be trampled underfoot, how will the church survive? What will be the manner of its existence? Here a new theme is introduced, that of *witness*. The destiny of the church is to bear witness – witness to faith in the power of Jesus' resurrection and in his continuing presence in the church. In a Jewish court, evidence would normally be accepted only on the word of two persons. The church is therefore pictured in the form of, not one, but **two witnesses**. Its heavenly counterpart in John's original vision (1.12) is a set of lampstands like the seven-branched candlestick that stood at the door of the inner sanctuary of the temple. Think of the church as two witnesses and you may think at the same time of its heavenly counterpart:

4 **two lampstands**. Alternatively, think of the **two olive trees** which Zechariah saw in his vision on either side of the lampstand (4.3–13). These represented the two 'anointed ones' (4.14) who, as king and priest, were to lead the people

of God – and Christians, John said at the beginning (1.6), are both kings and priests. This is their appearance in heaven. On earth their counterparts are
3 two prophets, **wearing sackcloth** as a constant challenge to repentance. Yet they are more than ordinary prophets. They have the attributes of Moses and
6 Elijah – Moses, who had **authority over the waters to turn them into blood, and to strike the earth with every kind of plague** (Exodus 7–12); Elijah, who was a man of fire (2 Kings 1) and had the **authority to shut the sky** and prevent rainfall (1 Kings 17). They stand, that is, for the prophetic witness of the church, and also perhaps for a new 'law and prophets', the rule of life which the church proclaims and the inspiration by which it is led.
7 Will their evidence be taken seriously? Not before **the beast that comes up from the bottomless pit** – the superhuman force of evil that has been held in check until now – **will make war on them and conquer them and kill them.** Indeed, they will suffer the last indignity of being refused burial and will lie exposed to the gaze of their enemies for more than the three days during which, people said, the soul might return to the body (see above on John
8 11.39). The city which allowed such a thing – whether Jerusalem where **their Lord was crucified** (one of this writer's rare references to a specific historical event), or a city of the Roman empire, or even Rome itself – deserved the 'prophetic' and proverbially evil name of **Sodom** or that of **Egypt**, the place of Israel's bondage until their deliverance by Moses. It had even indulged in a shameless celebration of the murder, an ironic mirror image of the celebration which Jews still recalled in an annual festival commemorating
10 their revenge on their persecutors in Persia, when they exchanged **presents** of food with one another (Esther 9.22).

But these prophets were Christian martyrs whose death would be followed
11 by resurrection as surely as that of Jesus – **after the three and a half days** is only a slight adjustment of the 'after three days' of the gospel message to fit the sevenfold pattern; and their resurrection is described in terms of the dry bones receiving **the breath of life**[3] in Ezekiel's vision (37.1–10). This time it would be a public event, visible to all their enemies and confirmed by a destructive earthquake. The prophets of old had not been heeded; but this
13 time the challenge to repentance was irresistible: **the rest were terrified and gave glory to the God of heaven.**
15 **Then the seventh angel blew his trumpet.** This is evidently the climax, the end towards which the sequence of trumpets (and the briefer series of 'woes' which double the last three trumpets) has been tending. Yet this ending is not accomplished in a moment. It is not a shapeless cataclysm effacing all that has gone before, but expresses a reasoned judgment on the whole of history. To be understood, there are several aspects of it which

---

[3] In Greek the same word *pneuma* stands for 'breath' and 'spirit', and the expression here, like *pneumatikōs*, 'spiritually', in 11.8 (see the NRSV footnote), may be due to the fact that in Revelation the Spirit is experienced principally as the spirit of prophecy.

have to be explained – which is the task undertaken in the second half of Revelation.

But first John must describe what takes place in heaven; only then can he reveal the corresponding events on earth. This time it is a hymn of praise. God is king, but his kingship has not yet been fully recognized on earth. Christians, like Jews, pray 'Your kingdom come', not doubting that God is already on his throne, but expressing their faith that his kingship will one day be acknowledged, not just by those who already worship him, but by all humankind. The seventh trumpet is the signal that this is at last coming to pass; and its immediate sequel is a burst of praise from the worshippers in heaven: what has been prayed for has at last been brought about.

15–18 Some of the words for such a hymn were suggested by Psalm 2, which was originally the triumphal enthronement song of a king of Israel, the 'anointed king' of the Lord, but which seemed to the early church to contain numerous prophecies of Christ; others by other psalms and passages of scripture (see especially Psalm 115.13). The essential elements of this final establishment of God's kingship are all there: the judgment is given, the righteous are recompensed for what they have suffered at the hands of the wicked, and the destructive forces of evil that have long seemed to hold the field are finally eliminated.

Another way of putting this – or another moment in the heavenly vision – was to imagine the splendour of God fully revealed to all human beings. Suppose you were in the temple in Jerusalem and had before you the curtain which hid from view the dark, innermost sanctuary where God was believed especially to dwell, the Holy of Holies. The curtain, the darkness, the mystery symbolized the effort of faith required to believe in the lordship of God. But imagine now the curtain removed, the darkness turned to light, so that the divine presence becomes visible to all; and then transfer this vision from the 19 Jerusalem temple to the eternal realities of heaven. **God's temple in heaven was opened**. Originally the innermost sanctuary had contained the **ark of his covenant**, the symbol of God's faithfulness towards his people. It is this aspect of God – his merciful faithfulness – which is placed before human eyes even at the moment of judgment.

Portents in heaven

12.1 **A great portent appeared in heaven**. No one in antiquity who looked at the heavens saw a mere mass of undifferentiated stars. Each constellation had its name, and the regular movements of the heavenly bodies were known and understood. Indeed it was essential to understand them. It had long been realized that the rising or setting of certain stars was a sign of the beginning of certain seasons, a signal for ploughing, sowing or harvesting; and in the last few centuries before Christ the conviction that events on earth are controlled by the movements of the heavenly bodies grew into a complex astrological science which spread throughout the empire from its home in Mesopotamia and exercised a powerful hold on people's minds. John's vision of portents in heaven signalling catastrophic events on earth was not far from this way of thinking, and here the connection becomes almost explicit.

In astrology, each constellation had its own character. Named after some god or hero in Greek mythology, each presented a still shot, so to speak, from an old story: Orion for ever bore his sword, Andromeda her chains. The timeless myths of classical antiquity were caught in action as eternal pictures in the heavens. It was perhaps because of these pagan associations that Jewish and Christian writers seldom borrowed astrological motifs. Yet astrology was part of the surrounding culture. No symbolic discourse could totally ignore it, and its images and mythical associations could be subtly exploited for Jewish or Christian purposes.

It is likely, therefore, that John's description of **a woman clothed with the sun** was suggested, at least in the first instance, by the virgin of the zodiac in the season when the sun rises in that constellation. In a complete chart of the zodiac, the sun and the moon would belong equally to all the signs. But in the period of Virgo it would have been natural to think of **the moon under her feet** (for the moon rises in the same quarter as the sun) and **a crown of twelve stars** indicating her sovereignty in the heavens. Who, then, was this **woman** in the sky? Pagan writers connected Virgo with various myths; but John, a Jewish Christian, drew upon the scriptures. One figure in particular suggested itself: the 'daughter Zion'. This of course was not an individual: it was the personification of an idea, a poetic code name both for the inhabitants of Jerusalem and for that ideal of society cherished by the great prophets. One day, they believed, the people of Israel, or a remnant of it, would become fully obedient to the will of God and fully responsive to the demands of its high destiny. A nucleus of the righteous would at last be established in Jerusalem worthy of the promises which God had made to the Jewish people. This nucleus they called the 'daughter Zion'.

"Writhe and groan, O daughter Zion, like a woman in labor", the prophet Micah had cried (4.10), as he saw the citizens of Jerusalem carried off into exile in Babylon, and with them (as it seemed) all hope of the perfect nation of the future. And the same metaphor could be elaborated: if her suffering was like birth pangs it would bring forth a child (Isaiah 66.7–9), the suffering would be the very process which would create the community of the future. So far the Old Testament; but for a Christian the image took on new life. The church was the true Israel, the community in which God's ancient promises were destined to be fulfilled. In the 'daughter Zion' it could see itself, in her birth pangs its own tribulations. **She was crying out in birth pangs, in the agony of giving birth.** John sees in the sign of Virgo a still shot from the continuing drama of the sufferings of the church on earth But there was more to it than this. Even if the 'daughter Zion' now symbolized the new community which was founded by the death and resurrection of Christ, she still represented the historic people of God out of which Christ himself had been born: she had already (in the person of another Virgin) given birth to a momentous child – so momentous that there must surely have been some special conjunction in the heavenly bodies to signal so great a revolution in human affairs. Matthew's gospel expresses this astrological necessity in the story of a new star recognized by astrologers from the east (2.1–2). John puts it more dramatically in terms of a mythical conflict in heaven

3 between Virgo on the one hand and on the other **a great red dragon**, who is
9 also the serpent that deceived Eve (Genesis 3.13). He is **the Devil and Satan**, who stands behind the powers and kingdoms of the world, and so is pictured
3 with **horns** and **diadems**; he has a tail sweeping through the sky and, as in a
4 vision of Daniel (8.10), is throwing stars down **to the earth**. The myth itself was almost universal. Again and again in classical and oriental literature we read of a god or hero whom some power of evil tries to eliminate in infancy but who is snatched away and kept safe until he is of an age to fulfil his great destiny. The myth had a biblical embodiment in Moses, who was saved as a baby from destruction by Pharaoh; and it had now been acted out in the story of Herod's attempt on Jesus and of Joseph and Mary's flight to Egypt (Matthew 2.13–15). In a more fundamental sense it was fulfilled when Jesus, through the crucifixion and resurrection, was snatched from the power of the devil and was established as the one who (to quote Psalm 2 again) was to
5 **rule[4] all the nations with a rod of iron**. But the woman herself – even if to our minds Virgo seems to be taking on the character of the Virgin Mary, the actual mother of Jesus – still represented the people of God. That people
6 (now the church) was to live in **the wilderness** during a spell of persecution which would last (as we have been told earlier) for a symbolic period of three and a half years, **one thousand two hundred sixty days**. All this mythology – now rendered true and meaningful in the facts of the Christian story – John reads off from the symbolic constellations in the sky.

7 **And war broke out in heaven** – a startling idea to the modern mind, which thinks of heaven as a place of everlasting peace and felicity. But the tradition in which John is writing, and the whole drama of his visions, presupposes that the violent cataclysms of this crucial stage of history on earth are signalled by equally potent symbolic portents in heaven. Moreover the final contest between the church and the pagan world was not to be thought of as one merely between human beings. Behind each side stood supernatural forces – the risen and enthroned Christ on the one hand, the Devil on the other; and the real war would be fought out in heaven. The archangel Michael was believed to be the heavenly patron of Israel, and therefore of the church, the new people of God; and the idea of a final battle between Michael and Satan was an old one (Daniel 12.1). John has only to combine it with the image of

---

[4] The word translated **rule** means literally *to shepherd*, another case of John's paradoxical mixing of images: the power of the Lion is in a Lamb, his rod of iron is a shepherd's staff.

the mythical dragon, who was also the serpent that tempted Eve in the Garden
9 of Eden (Genesis 3.13), the **deceiver of the whole world**. The image was a
rich one: it may have evoked the mythical monster, the Leviathan, which
was responsible for chaos at the beginning of God's creation and had to be
restrained until the final conflict; and there were also pagan associations:
some gods were represented either as serpents or as threatened by serpents
in infancy. But no myth suggested that Satan had been prevented from being
active on earth. Some believed that he had been **thrown down** from his
original place in heaven at the beginning of the world's history. But this was
nothing to the ravages he would cause on earth in the last days. His original
fall (if it took place) was no more than a rehearsal for his decisive overthrow
at the end.

In a strict chronological scheme this would make difficulties. The Devil
is defeated, yet he is still at work. The victory is decisive, yet there is more
fighting to come. One must ask: Why this repeated prolongation of the battle?
The answer lies deep in the faith of the early Christians. Sin, persecution,
error, were not just thought of as permanent elements of our condition
which we can be helped to overcome by faith in Christ: they were caused
by supernatural forces outside ourselves, and what Christ had done for us
could be described as a victory over those forces: if Christ had defeated the
Devil, the Devil could no longer prevail over a human determination not
to sin. Now this was precisely what Christ had done on the cross; and his
followers, through their solidarity with him, were now immune from the
fatal consequences of sin. Nevertheless error, sin and death were still rife in
the world. That is to say, even if the Devil had been defeated he could still
do a great deal of damage. John's vision therefore allowed for various stages
in his final elimination. The first stage was his expulsion from the heavenly
10 court, where, in his rôle of **accuser**, he had been trying to bring incriminating
11 evidence against Christians. His expulsion was caused both by **the blood of
the Lamb** (the sacrifice of the crucifixion) and by the counter-**testimony** of
all those who had been willing to die rather than compromise their faith –
for they did not cling to life even in the face of death. All this is a cue for
10–12 another triumph song in heaven. But there was still another stage to come of
the Devil's defeat, his death throes, so to speak, in his place of punishment:
12 **"woe to the earth and the sea, for the devil has come down to you with
great wrath"**.

To describe this stage John returns to his zodiacal image of the woman and
the dragon. When we last heard of the woman (who is now the church) she
had "fled into the wilderness" (verse 6). The story is picked up again at the
14 same point, John adding only that she had reached her refuge by means of **the
two wings of the great eagle.** (Virgo was often depicted with wings in art; and
astrology might say that she was rescued from the claws of Scorpio by Aquila,
the eagle. But John's image is more likely to have come from the Bible: Israel's
flight from Egypt is described in Exodus as "on eagles' wings", 19.4.) As for the

16 picture of the earth swallowing the river which the dragon **poured from his mouth,** we have no means of knowing whether John was drawing on some myth that is now lost, interpreting patterns among the stars (such as the end of the Milky Way), or simply working into his vision a phenomenon that he or others may have seen, a river disappearing underground. The important thing, at any rate, is the explanation the vision offers for the tribulations of the church: they represent the last spasms of the Devil's fury.

18 **Then the dragon took his stand on the sand of the seashore.** All that the church suffered was ultimately traceable to the Devil. But the dragon was a symbol for evil in general; more specific symbols were needed to stand for what had precipitated the particular kinds of suffering the church had to undergo. The Devil, after all, had demonic agents. Accordingly, John imagines the dragon on the seashore, calling up an assistant from the sea.[5]

13.1 **And I saw a beast rising out of the sea.** Behind the rulers of heathen powers stood demonic forces. The churches in Asia Minor (like John himself in Patmos) were under Roman rule, and if they suffered, it was in Roman courts, in Roman prisons and (if it came to that) by Roman executioners. Rome, therefore, was the Devil's agent, and John had next to show how Rome itself would be involved in the Devil's ultimate defeat. Some might say that there were good things to say for Roman rule – peace, stability, ease of travel. But these, if real, were of small account beside its extortion and its idolatry, which seemed to Christians so monstrous that they would inevitably bring fearful punishment on Rome.

John's vision starts, once again, from the book of Daniel (7.1–7). In Daniel's "vision by night . . . four great beasts came up out of the sea", the last with ten horns; and later he was told that the four beasts signified four successive empires, and the ten horns ten kings who reigned over the last of these empires. John here combines the four beasts into one, for only one empire, that of Rome, was now of significance in world history. The **ten horns** (as he tells us in 17.12–13) are ten of the vassal kings whom Rome allowed to reign in its name over parts of the east; and he adds that it had seven **heads** representing (as we also learn in 17.9–10) both the seven hills of Rome

3 and seven emperors. **One of its heads seemed to have received a death-blow, but its mortal wound had been healed.** The career of Nero, who had launched the first serious persecution of Christians in Rome and had even murdered his own relatives (including his mother), and who had apparently committed suicide in 68 CE, had struck particular horror into many minds, and a somewhat superstitious fear persisted that he had not died at all but had fled to the Parthians east of the Euphrates and would one day return at the head of an immense army. In any event, his death had been followed by a period of civil war, when the future of the empire itself seemed in

---

[5] Some manuscripts offer a reading which makes John say of himself, *I stood by the sand of the seashore.* This is easier to intepret but less likely to be correct.

doubt. These events were enough to have caused a memorable break in the succession of 'heads', a scar which might well show on the mythical monster which represented the empire. But the monster had recovered: Vespasian had been securely placed on the throne of the empire and people were ready to celebrate the apparent invincibility of the 'beast'. Moreover the whole episode, with its recovery from death – literal, some had feared, in the case of Nero, metaphorical in the case of the empire – was a symbol of the way in which the death and resurrection of Christ might receive a diabolical travesty in secular history.

5   We are still in the period of **forty-two months**, the symbolic three and a half years during which the church's suffering was to last. Throughout that time Rome would be **allowed to exercise authority**. Throughout that time, therefore, there would continue that particular feature of Roman imperialism which caused the greatest offence to Jewish and Christian sensibilities. The

6 beast **opened its mouth to utter blasphemies against God**. We can guess what this means. Beginning with Julius Caesar, Roman emperors had been 'deified', that is, given the status and worship due to a god, usually after their death, but more recently even during their lifetime. Their official titles began to include the word 'divine': *augustus* itself, when rendered into Greek, meant 'worshipful'. In most of the cities to which John was writing, temples had been built by the allegedly grateful populace to these deities, a mockery of God's true **dwelling** and of those who had sacrificed their lives rather than renounce their allegiance to the one true God. All this, to passionately monotheistic Jews and Christians, caused the greatest scandal. But the Jews were permitted to practise their own religion in peace. They were not forced to assent to the worship of the emperor. Not so the Christians. Any who found themselves in a court of law might be put to the test and told to offer a sacrifice before a statue of the emperor. Refusing to do so, they might lose their lives. It was only faithfulness under these extreme circumstances which marked a person as

8 one whose name had been **written from the foundation of the world in the book of life of the Lamb**. The rest would have compromised, and consented to worship the beast. Resistance was no easy option – a proverbial-sounding verse from Jeremiah (15.2) thrusts home the message that the saints would

10 require **endurance and faith**.

The policy of encouraging an emperor cult came ultimately from the emperor himself, that is, from the distant source of authority which John

1 saw as **a beast rising out of the sea**. But its execution lay in the hands of local officials, whether the Roman provincial governor or the regional councils responsible for the organization of the cult. These local authorities were doubtless at least as potent a source of fear to the churches as was Rome

11 itself, and could aptly be represented by **another beast that rose out of**

13 **the earth**. This beast's activities are described in biblical terms: **even making fire come down from heaven to earth in the sight of all**, as Elijah the prophet did (1 Kings 18.38) – but of course these pagan authorities are a parody of

prophets; and there may also be an allusion here to those false prophets who we know existed and who may have added their delusive influence to complicate the agonizing decision Christians had to make in the face of demands to conform with the cult of the emperor. The symbol of the beast may stand for pressures within as well as from outside the church.

One of the ways in which a ruler impressed his sovereignty most forcibly on the minds of his subjects was by the issue of coinage bearing his image and his title. Throughout the Roman empire – even in Judea, where such images

17 were thought to be blasphemous – every transaction to **buy or sell** meant handling imperial coins. Ordinary citizens constantly held in their hands a head of the emperor surrounded by an inscription giving his titles. These included one which the Jews found particularly objectionable: AUGUSTUS, which in Greek reads *SEBASTOS*, 'worshipful'. This was grist to the mill of

16 John's visionary imagination: holding a coin was like being **marked on the right hand** – or, to still more sinister effect, on **the forehead**, a diabolical parody of the 'seal' on the forehead received by God's own people (7.3).

The letters of both the Greek and Hebrew alphabets served as numerals, and it was a well-known procedure to add up the letters composing a proper name for the purpose either of creating a code name – i.e. a number standing for the name – or of finding another phrase with the same numerical value which would reveal a hidden meaning in the name. A Roman historian tells us that there was a popular lampoon in the reign of Nero which found the value of the letters of the emperor's name in Greek to be that also of a phrase meaning 'he killed his mother'. John is doubtless doing something similar here (for his hearers have not only to recognize the number as a name but

18 must show **wisdom** and **understanding** to see its meaning). Since there have already been fairly clear allusions to Nero in this passage, the identification would probably not have been difficult (though it was not until the nineteenth century that a scholar came up with the solution: the Greek form of Nero's name and title – *nērōn kaisar* – transliterated into Hebrew adds up to 666). But this number, which struck ancient mathematicians as unusual (it is 'doubly triangular'), and which might also have seemed symbolic of *in*completeness (each digit being one short of seven), was a challenge to anyone disposed to find a hidden meaning – as it has been ever since.

14.7 **The hour of his judgment has come**. John has been recounting his visions of all those things that must come to pass before the end. He is now ready to present his picture of the end itself. No one would have doubted what this end consisted of: it was the moment of judgment, and there were well accepted conventions for describing it. The reality to be expressed was a simple one. At the judgment, the righteous would be rewarded and the unrighteous would be punished, and any visual picture which represented both sides of this reality would necessarily bring on to a single canvas both the reward and the punishment. Jewish writers of a certain mentality drew the naïve (and immoral, as it seems to us) conclusion from this juxtaposition that one of the joys of the blessed in heaven would be the spectacle of the torments inflicted on those who were once their enemies and persecutors, and that an additional torment of the wicked would be the sight of the righteous, whom they had once despised, now enjoying their heavenly reward (Jesus makes use of this image of folk religion in his parable of the rich man and Lazarus, Luke 16.19ff).

John, whose vision follows the same conventions, was perhaps too sophisticated a writer to include the motif of the righteous gloating over the condemned. But, if the reality of judgment were to be taken seriously, some condemned there must be. No representation could do justice to the seriousness of God's judgment unless it depicted a dreadful punishment for them. To this extent John was bound by the conventions within which he wrote. The resultant scene has an element of horror from which the Christian reader 10 may recoil. Words like **wrath** and **anger**, when applied to God, seem incompatible with the revelation of God's love and mercy in Jesus Christ. Yet just as the idea of God's 'choosing' certain men and women logically implied that some were *not* 'chosen', and were therefore apparently victimized for the sake of those who were, so the idea of God rewarding the righteous logically implied a very different future for those who persevered in wickedness. Biblical language, in any case, tends to paint in black and white. The opposite of reward is punishment. Using such language and inheriting such a tradition, John was perhaps less free than a modern writer would be to temper the necessary severity of God's judgment with faith in his ultimate mercy.

1 **There was the Lamb, standing on Mount Zion!** One side of the picture (so to speak) – the place of those acquitted by God's judgment – was often represented as a new Jerusalem. Mount Zion, the hill on which the oldest city of Jerusalem had been built, became, even in the Old Testament, a symbol for an ideal city of the future. The new feature in John's vision was the Lamb standing there – new, that is to say, not only because a Messiah who was also a weak and vulnerable 'lamb' was a startling new Christian concept, but because this was a new rôle for the Lamb: he was now to be a king among his own people. In the words of a psalm (2.6) that was doubtless running in John's mind, "I have set my king on Zion, my holy hill." **And with him were one hundred and forty-four thousand.** We know who these were from chapter 7: they were the new Israel, who bore the names of Christ and God on their foreheads instead of the name of the beast. They alone could join in the 3 worship of heaven. They had been **redeemed** – this metaphor for the saving work of Christ has occurred already in 5.9 ('redeem' and 'ransom' translate the same Greek word). But there is also a hint that their lives and deaths were 4 to benefit others. They were **as first fruits for God and the Lamb**, which means that a still greater harvest was to come (the "great multitude . . . from every nation", 7.9). What was it in their conduct that produced these great consequences? We might say, their faith in Christ. But in their

5 case this faith had been put to the test, and **in their mouth no lie was found** – they did not compromise their faith with so much as a word of
4 homage to pagan gods; they were **blameless. These follow the Lamb wherever he goes** – a straightforward description of Christian discipleship which may lead to suffering and death. But the previous sentence is more puzzling: **It is these who have not defiled themselves with women, for they are virgins.** If this is taken literally, it implies that John, in the midst of his sweeping description of universal judgment, suddenly chose to concentrate on that very small section of Jesus' followers who practised celibacy – and so it has often been understood. But – apart from other difficulties – this would hardly be in keeping with John's symbolic language. He has just described the great company of the faithful as the new Israel, organized like an army in battalions of twelve thousand men. The historical Israel, in its early days, believed it should maintain its army when on active service in a state of ritual and sexual purity (Deuteronomy 23.9–10; 1 Samuel 21.5). Here was another symbol. In the Bible, any participation in pagan religion was called 'fornication'. It was surely from this, even under compulsion to worship the Roman emperor, that the righteous had kept themselves chaste, like **virgins.**

6   **Another angel flying in midheaven.** One side of the judgment picture is complete, the other – more gruesome – side is still to be painted. But John has something to place in between. All that has gone before is preparation for judgment, and, logically, the verdict on each human being must now be given. But in defiance of such logic John introduces a last chance. The final catastrophes of world history show the imminence of judgment; but **an eternal gospel** is still proclaimed up to the very last moment – eternal because, unlike the transitory blessings promised by secular authorities in their bulletins of 'good news', this proclamation has eternal validity. A constructive reaction from any of the inhabitants of the earth (no distinction here between
7 Jew and Greek) is still possible: **"Fear God and give him glory."** The gospel is eternal, it is open to humankind to be saved until the very moment when judgment is passed. Between his two panels of reward and punishment John sets a final opportunity of decision.

But it is none the less the very last moment. The angel with the gospel is only one of three: the next two follow immediately with the verdicts passed on
8 God's enemies. **"Fallen, fallen is Babylon the great!"** Babylon, the greatest enemy of Israel in the past, was a Jewish and Christian code name for the greatest city in the contemporary world: Rome. It was Rome which bore responsibility for the oppressive paganism and idolatry of the entire civilized world. It was she who had **made all nations drink of the wine of the wrath of her fornication** – a tumbled combination of Old Testament images which compresses into a few words both the allurement of paganism and its terrible consequences. The ultimate fall of Rome seemed inevitable to anyone who stood in the tradition of Jewish prophecy (and John elaborates the theme

later). Meanwhile here was a new factor in the circumstances leading up to God's judgment. When Rome fell, it might be easier for all to accept the eternal gospel: everyone would see the hollowness of the alternative promoted by Rome.

Finally, the third angel, announcing the punishment of those who, despite everything, continue to **worship the beast and its image. The wine of God's wrath, poured unmixed into the cup of his anger** may be good Old Testament language (Psalm 75.8; Isaiah 51.17; Jeremiah 25.15), but it sounds shockingly vindictive in a Christian book. Yet we have to remember that retribution for evil deeds was and is a valid Christian concept. Since his justice demands it, God must allow it. We may accept this as an abstract proposition; it shocks us only when expressed (as was more natural for biblical writers than it would be for us) in personal terms: the 'wrath' or 'anger' of God.

The whole vision might be understood as a commentary on a message which John is now explicitly told to communicate to the churches: **"Blessed are the dead who from now on die in the Lord."** In the face of deaths and threats of death suffered by their own number, this was what they most needed to hear. Paul, after giving to the Corinthians his own vision of the end, summed up in these words: "Therefore, my beloved, be steadfast, immovable, always excelling in the work of the Lord, because you know that in the Lord your labor is not in vain" (1 Corinthians 15.58). John in his vision has seen the promised rest which follows the labour, and can offer what is virtually the same reassurance. Christians' labour cannot be lost, **for their deeds follow them**.

But the messages of the angels did not by any means exhaust the repertory of images which John had inherited for describing his vision of the imminent judgment. Another key element was Daniel's vision of the vindication of the righteous: "I saw one like a *son of man* coming with the clouds of heaven" (7.13, as in the NRSV footnote). This **one like the Son of man** was now, to any Christian writer, Jesus himself; and Jesus had connected his 'coming in the clouds' with a final harvesting: "Then they will see 'the Son of Man coming in clouds' with great power and glory. Then he will send out the angels, and gather his elect from the four winds, from the ends of the earth to the ends of heaven" (Mark 13.26–7). This suggested a new piece of imagery for one side of the picture: the gathering of the righteous into the harvest of their reward. But what of the other side? A prophecy of Joel furnished a powerful image:

> Put in the sickle,
>   for the harvest is ripe.
> Go in, tread,
>   for the wine press is full.
> The vats overflow,
>   for their wickedness is great.
>
> (3.13)

It is possible that in John's mind the two harvesting images – that suggested by Jesus' words and that suggested by Joel – both stood for the same horrifying reality on one side of the picture: the ultimate judgment on the obdurately wicked. But it seems, nevertheless, as if he was deliberately keeping them
15–16 separate by allotting the reaping of the grain harvest to the Son of Man (whom we must recognize as Christ), and the gathering of the grape harvest
17 to **another angel** (even though Christ is said to tread the wine press himself later on, 19.15); that is to say, he was still elaborating the traditional picture of judgment, with the gathering in of the elect on one side and the punishment of the wicked on the other. At any rate, he leaves us in no doubt about the meaning of the second image. The order is given by the angel
18 who has **authority over fire** (where perhaps a more literal rendering, 'over *the* fire', would be clearer, since the fire in question is certainly the traditional fire of punishment); and the **great wine press of the wrath of God**
19 is quite unambiguous: the metaphor is worked out at length in Isaiah 63.1– 6. We, being more squeamish, might prefer to say that God 'allowed' the wicked to be punished. But John's imagination was both more vivid and more logical. If God 'allowed' it, then he took full responsibility for it and could just as well be pictured carrying it out himself. The image of the wine press was not of a punishment somehow carried out independently of God: it was the instrument of his justice, **the great wine press of the wrath of God**.

John adds a further grisly detail that was probably already traditional
20 in this context. The **wine press was trodden outside the city**: Joel's vision (3.12) was in the 'valley of Jehoshaphat' (which means 'the Lord judges'). This was often imagined as the Kidron valley, which separates Jerusalem from the Mount of Olives. The valley is at the head of a long wadi which winds down through the mountains for many miles until it reaches the Dead Sea. In the summer it is dry; but after a spell of heavy rain in winter it can become a raging torrent. The immense wine press outside Jerusalem is imagined as discharging its gory liquid down the valley in such quantities that horsemen could only just ford the stream – an image that was used by Jewish rabbis to describe the horror of the sack of Jerusalem by the Romans in 70 CE. In one of Ezekiel's visions (47.1–12) great springs of fresh water rose from under the temple in Jerusalem, filling the valleys, sweetening the stagnant Dead Sea and flowing on south through the desert towards the Red Sea some 200 miles away. John may have been consciously suggesting a gruesome parody of this theme; but, somewhat unexpectedly, he adds an estimate of the distance the river flowed: **about two hundred miles**. He may have been imagining its course all the way to the Red Sea, or he may have known that this is about the length of the historic land of Israel. But in any case, his interest was probably, once again, in the number itself. **Two hundred miles** is a correct but prosaic translation. John actually says, *one thousand six hundred stadia* (as in the NRSV footnote). We can guess that this number (a multiple of ten and four)

had some significance for him and his hearers, though we no longer hold the clue to his arithmetical symbolism.

15.1   **Then I saw . . . seven angels with seven plagues.** In what manner John saw them is about to be told. But to anyone even slightly versed in the scriptures, the word 'plagues' suggested, not just natural calamities, but a scourge visited on a particular people for the ultimate benefit of others. Through Moses, plagues had afflicted the Egyptians to the benefit of the people of Israel. These **last** plagues, which symbolized the final phase of God's judgment on the world, were to follow a similar programme. Immune

2   from them now were **those who had conquered the beast** and who were **standing beside the sea of glass**, which was described earlier as part of the landscape of heaven (4.6), but was now **mixed with fire**, perhaps because it was not just water for purification, but an ordeal, like the Red Sea (its redness enhanced until it was 'fiery'), through which the original saving act of the exodus had taken place. Their reaction to the plagues being visited on others echoed the Song of Moses after the deliverance from Egypt (Exodus 15): Moses saw in that deliverance an event which redounded to the glory

3   of God and filled whole nations with awe. But now it was **the song of the Lamb**, since the deliverance had been through Christ; and the greater the deliverance, the more the effect that could be expected on the nations which witnessed it: when those who served God (and not the beast) were delivered,

4   it was God's **judgments** that were revealed. Plagues were necessarily visited on someone; some people must suffer from them. But in biblical thinking (even if there is logically little room for the thought at this stage in Revelation, since there is not supposed to be anyone left who could be an onlooker), the justification for such punishing afflictions was the effect they had on others. To put it in thoroughly scriptural language (and the whole song is a tissue of Old Testament phrases), **"All nations will come and worship before you, for your judgments have been revealed."**

The plagues, then, were to be no orgy of indiscriminate destruction but an expression of God's justice; and this determines the symbolism that follows. John repeats from chapter 4 the dramatic image of the opening of the door or curtain that concealed the innermost sanctuary of the heavenly temple – or, if one thought of the ideal description in Exodus (29.42) rather than of its actual

5   realization in the temple in Jerusalem, of **the tent of witness** (as the 'tent of meeting' was translated into Greek). But this time the feature of that sanctuary which was probably most in mind was the ark of the covenant, containing the tables of the law which Moses wrote at the dictation of God. This law was the definitive expression of God's justice; and the final vindication of God's justice involved the full sanction of the law upon those who disobeyed

6   it. Hence the mission of the **seven angels with the seven plagues** who were

7   given **seven golden bowls full of the wrath of God.**

16.1   A further series of **seven** may cause us surprise at this point, when everything seems to be tending towards its final end. But for John (as for any biblical writer) the end meant judgment; and the ultimate judgment on humanity must be seen to be appropriate to the various atrocities that human beings have committed. The point is made explicit after the third bowl has been poured:

6   **"because they shed the blood of saints and prophets,**
                        you have given them blood to drink"

7 – a judgment endorsed by **the altar**, which is soaked with the blood in question (6.9). The point becomes even more obvious as the plagues proceed from the physical environment to specific political entities (see below). Doom, if it is to be seen as a function of God's justice, must be analysed into its component parts. But there is also a literary reason for a further series of seven. It allows the seer scope to take as his model the plagues visited on Egypt
2, 4, 13 (**a foul and painful sore**, water turned to **blood**, **frogs** and immense
21 **hailstones** all occur in Exodus 7–10), and it also enables him to match the effects of the seven trumpets (8.6–11.15) with another intensified series. Previously, repentance was still possible, but this time the possibility seems to
11 have been rejected: people **cursed the God of heaven because of their pains and sores, and they did not repent of their deeds**. The moment had come for executing justice: there could hardly be another appeal for repentance.

    After the first four general plagues, which affect the natural environment indiscriminately (though, as we have seen, with a certain rough justice, the mark of the beast turning to sores, the shedding of blood punished by drinking it, and possibly the burning of Christians by Nero producing a scorching
10 sun), the punishments become focused on political entities. The **darkness** of the Egyptian story is here visited on **the throne of the beast**, which we know from chapter 13 to be both the cult and the authority of the Roman emperor – any eclipse was believed to herald disaster, and possibly this darkness is an allusion to the period of anarchy and disputed succession which followed the
12 death of Nero in 68 CE. The **great river Euphrates**, as in the trumpet series, is the eastern frontier of the empire where Parthian troops were constantly thought to be massing for a final assault on Rome. Part of the necessary preparation for the end was the removal of this natural barrier so that the way might be open for **the kings from the east**. For perhaps it was not easy to conceive of the final visitation of God's justice taking place simultaneously in widely distant places. One needed to be able to imagine the kingdoms of the world gathered in one place for the final verdict. But what would produce this extraordinary and comprehensive gathering? Why, a great battle
14 involving everyone, a **battle on the great day of God the Almighty**. But of course the kings and emperors would not naturally commit themselves to this all-or-nothing confrontation on a gigantic battlefield. To get them there, demonic powers of persuasion would be needed. True to the character of the contending powers – dragon, beast and false prophet (13.14) – out of their mouths come **demonic spirits, performing signs** and with the ability to

assemble the kings for battle. Where would this great battle take place? What site more natural than one of the great and tragic battlefields of Jewish history, Megiddo (Judges 5.19; 2 Kings 9.27; 23.29)? Zechariah, in a prophecy much meditated on by John, used this evocative name (12.11); but John, perhaps to

16 make his geography more solemn and mysterious, calls it **Harmegedon**, and tells us that this is Hebrew. We can construe the word: *har-megiddo* means 'Mount Megiddo'. But we protest: Megiddo is (as battlefields must be) in a plain, the great plain between Samaria and Galilee. The only mount in the neighbourhood is Carmel. Perhaps John simply wished to work in Carmel as well, with its associations of the punishment of the prophets of Baal and the vindication of the true prophet Elijah (1 Kings 18).

15 (**See, I am coming like a thief!**" We are suddenly reminded that all of these visions are part of a letter to the churches. All attention has been on the future; but John's hearers still have to cope with the present and must beware of any temptation not to stay awake or to be in any sense **exposed to shame**.)

17 "**It is done!**" Three syllables of a Greek word (which suggest by their sound – *ge-go-nen* – a clap of thunder) bring the drama to a close. People in

18 Asia Minor had experienced catastrophic earthquakes, but this one was **such as had not occurred since people were upon the earth**. They had doubtless

21 suffered from terrible hail, but not from **hailstones, each weighing about a hundred pounds** (45 kilos). Mountainous islands had been known to disappear in the Aegean through volcanic eruptions, but this was to be a complete redrawing of the map of the world.

Yet even the series of seven plagues did not give John scope to show exactly how God's justice was visited upon the greatest offenders. In particular, he

19 needed to emphasize that God did not forget **great Babylon** – always the symbol for the city of Rome – and made her drink the **wine-cup of the fury of his wrath**. After the general description of the end of the kingdoms of the world the next two chapters provide as it were a close-up of this particular and crucial scene of the drama.

The judgment on the great whore

17.1 "**Come, I will show you the judgment on the great whore**." The Old Testament prophets, contemplating the capitals of their powerful neighbours at their moment of greatest influence and wealth, were the first to coin this metaphor. Tyre (Isaiah 23.16–17), Nineveh (Nahum 3.4), and even Jerusalem itself in moments of religious infidelity (Isaiah 1.21), were each described as a **whore**; the word suggested both a religious permissiveness and promiscuity, contrasting with Israel's uncompromising worship of the one true God, and a state of material luxury never to be emulated with the modest resources of the Jewish nation and always suspect as a source of economic inequality and corruption. It epitomized the paganism, the idolatry, the moral laxity and the affluence based on social injustice which so forcibly struck Jewish people when they observed the great cities around them. To some, these features might have seemed an alluring attraction and a symbol of enduring power. But the prophets knew better: these things were essentially sinful and attracted inexorably the judgment of God. Their writings contain elaborate prophecies of the inevitable downfall of such cities – prophecies which were fulfilled as the splendour of each one passed away and gave place to another.

Contemplating the Rome of his own day, John stood in the tradition of these prophets. From Isaiah he took the pattern of a vision seen in the
18.2 wilderness, at the end of which it is proclaimed, **"Fallen, fallen is Babylon"** (Isaiah 21.9); in Ezekiel 26–8 he found the model for a dirge over a city (Tyre) of "abundant wealth and merchandise" (27.33); from the great oracle of Jeremiah predicting the fall of Babylon (51.6–14) he took the image of a
17.1, 4 woman by the **many waters** of the Euphrates, **holding in her hand a golden**
2 **cup** from which **the inhabitants of the earth have become drunk**. But John was not merely working like a prophet with powerful metaphors. He was not just describing Rome as a whore; he claims to have had a vision of an
5 actual whore which he then interpreted as **Babylon**, meaning Rome. He saw
3 her **sitting on a scarlet beast**, which we recognize from a previous vision (chapter 13): this symbolized Rome's apparently invincible military might. To this is now added all Rome's economic allurements and her idolatries: the
4, 5 woman is clothed in imperial **purple and scarlet**, and **on her forehead was written a name**, just as (we are told) it was the impudent custom of harlots in Rome to advertise themselves by wearing their names on a band across their foreheads. The name was a **mystery**, challenging interpretation – so clearly not the 'Babylon' of history, but the **mother of whores** of the present. For Babylon, long after the fall of its empire, remained the prototype of the luxury and power of any great imperial city. In John's day the rôle of Babylon was manifestly played by Rome, and Rome had all the typical attributes of such a city to an unprecedented degree. She also had a new one of particular
6 horror to Christians: **she was drunk with the blood of the saints and the witnesses to Jesus**. The persecution by Nero in 64 CE, when a number of Christians was burnt alive, fully justified this gory image; and doubtless 'the blood of the saints' included all those other righteous sufferers who had fallen victim to that evil régime.

In the manner of the author of Daniel 7, John tells us he was astonished at
7 the vision, and records the interpretation given by an angel. **"I will tell you the mystery of the woman."** To a certain extent there was no mystery. The woman was Rome, and the beast she was riding (as we know from chapter 13) was Rome's military power. ("Who is like the beast, and who can fight against it?" 13.4.) The **seven heads and ten horns** were the succession of her emperors and vassal kings. In that sense, the symbols were easy to read. But this did not exhaust their meaning. There was a deeper 'mystery' hidden

among the familiar attributes of Rome which it was important for John's hearers to know.

For example: they may have known what the beast was; what they did not 8 know was that it could be described as one that **was, and is not, and is about to ascend from the bottomless pit and go to destruction**. That is to say, the empire was the embodiment of an old myth, the myth that the monster of evil and chaos, which had been subdued when the earth was created and would remain imprisoned for most of the world's history, would have a brief period of terrible freedom before the end. The beast symbolized a fearful pattern in the destiny of Rome: her present power was as nothing to the absolute power and absolute terror she would wield in the last phase of her history, to the astonishment of all human beings except those who had received a revelation of these things and were invulnerable in Christ.

9   Or again: **the seven heads are seven mountains on which the woman is seated**. One hardly needed to be told this. Everyone knew that Rome was built on seven hills. But – **also, they are seven kings** (or emperors: the same Greek word served for both). That is to say: the succession of emperors conformed with John's pattern of symbolic numbers: it was finite and was moving rapidly towards the end of the series. It was not in the style of this kind of writing to work out exact correlations with historical events (and in any case, John's hearers may well not have been able to say exactly how many Roman emperors there had been), and it is unlikely that John was committing himself to the extent of saying, for example, that Domitian or Trajan was certainly to be the last or the last but one.[6] What he is far more likely to have been doing is saying that the series, like the periods of world history, would inevitably fall into a pattern of seven – a symbolic 'week' – and that (however it worked out exactly) the end would not be slow in coming. Moreover the pattern was to reveal a significant peculiarity: John has already shown that he was aware of the prevalent almost superstitious awe at the memory of the reign of Nero. Nero could return: he would be an 11 embodiment of the mythical beast that **was and is not**, and **is an eighth**, and was still to have a period of destructive freedom before the end. John turns this popular dread of a reincarnation of Nero to the advantage of his scheme: the series of Roman emperors will be brought to an end by an anarchic power, a demonic parody of death and resurrection.

12   **"And the ten horns that you saw are ten kings."** The beast in Daniel's vision had ten horns, each signifying a king (7.24). The same symbolism fits John's vision, since Rome allowed vassal kings to hold territories in the eastern parts of the empire; and these kings also, like the emperor, tended

---

[6] There had certainly been more than seven emperors by the time John wrote. It would be possible to bring the seventh down to his time by omitting some from the list (such as the three contending emperors of 68–9 CE) but no historical correlation is fully satisfactory, and it is not very probable that John intended one.

to adopt blasphemous titles like 'saviour' or even 'god'. They were therefore an integral element of the beast; and so long as the empire lasted they would
14 necessarily pursue Rome's policy towards the Christians and **make war on the Lamb** before they in their turn would be forced to submit to the Lamb's rule.

How would the whore meet her end? In terms of the metaphor, she would receive the traditional punishment of the adulteress and the prostitute: she
16 would be made **desolate and naked**. As a city she would be pillaged and burnt. As an imperial power she would succumb to an eventual revolt of all the eastern kingdoms against her tyranny – for their subjection, after all, had been unnatural and would last only so long as was necessary for God's overriding purpose – the 'mystery' – to be fulfilled.

It remained to return from symbols to reality and to describe the physical ruin of the city. John may never have seen Rome; but he will have known of its size and magnificence, and will have been aware what a fantastic picture
18.17 of destruction was involved in his prophecy that **in one hour all this wealth** would have been **laid waste**. Once more he drew heavily on passages of Isaiah, Jeremiah and Ezekiel that described the doom of earlier cities. The
2 picture of ruins infested by beasts and demons is from Isaiah 13.20–1; the
4 warning to **come out** before it is too late from Jeremiah 51.6; the notion of
6 divine justice paying the wicked city back in her own coin occurs often in the
7–8 prophets, and the **double** payment is suggested by Isaiah 40.2; the boasting
9–19 words followed by retribution are a theme of Isaiah 47.7–9; the idea of the lament of kings, merchants and shipmasters is worked out in Ezekiel 27;
21 and the casting of a stone into the water as a symbol of the city's final end is modelled on Jeremiah 51.65. None of these passages is quoted verbatim. They are merely the materials which John used to describe his tremendous vision of the sudden doom of the greatest city the world had known. Logically, not all these elements fitted the stage reached in the drama: there should no longer have been any kings or merchants surviving to raise a lament on the fall of Rome. But this was hardly a consideration. A lament was what John needed in his picture and the mourners were an artistic necessity. The total effect of the description of his vision was quite properly more important to him than a rigid adherence to the formal progression of the drama.
19.1 **A great multitude in heaven.** The worship in heaven, of which John becomes aware at intervals throughout the series of visions, is partly timeless, partly a response to the events taking place on earth. In this chapter there are both elements. **"Hallelujah!"**, a Hebrew phrase that occurs in some of the psalms and means 'God be praised', became a formula of Jewish and then
4 Christian worship. The same goes for **"Amen"** (the two occur together in the Hebrew at the end of Psalm 106); and another of the antiphonal responses
5 takes the form of a psalm verse, **"all who fear him, small and great"** (Psalm 115.13). It was natural to think of the heavenly worship as using the language in which God had for centuries been praised on earth. But the heavenly song

is also adjusted to fit the moment which has been reached in the drama
2 on earth. **"He has judged the great whore"** – the hymn of praise has been
called forth by this latest manifestation of the reality of God's just judgment.
To us, justice and vengeance seem two different and incompatible things,
and we are shocked when the hymn goes on, **"and he has avenged on her
the blood of his servants"**. But the matter may have seemed different to
John. The suffering of the righteous was for Hebrew thought the nub of the
problem of evil. If those who inflicted it seemed to escape any penalty, it
became agonizingly difficult to continue to believe in the absolute justice
of God: somehow, some time, God must surely come down on the side of
his righteous servants, either by bringing their persecutors to recognize their
error, or else (if that failed) by inflicting on them an appropriate punishment.
This ultimate punishment – the decisive execution of God's justice when all
appeals for repentance had failed – was seen as a kind of 'vengeance', not so
much an expression of personal vindictiveness as a necessary consequence
of the incontrovertible justice of God.

The last stanza of the hymn introduces a fresh group of images which recur
7 throughout the remaining chapters of the book. **The marriage of the Lamb**
is an image with strong biblical associations. Ideally, God's relationship with
his people was always intended to be like that of husband and wife – perfect
mutual trust and fidelity sealed in a 'covenant'. That relationship was at last to
be realized in the union of Christians with Christ. For the wedding, the bride
must have white clothes, signifying innocence (there is doubtless a deliberate
contrast here with the gaudy robes of the harlot); and we have heard how she
will obtain them: in an early vision of heaven John described the process in
a startling oxymoron, "they have washed their robes and made them white
in the blood of the lamb" (7.13) – hence it has often been thought that the
8 explanatory note (the fine linen is **the righteous deeds of the saints**) betrays
the hand of a later editor who had a less firm grasp of the necessity of Christ's
sacrifice for the purification of the faithful. The marriage supper itself would
be how Christians might conceive of that spiritual banquet prepared for them
9 in heaven – the image runs through much of Jesus' own teaching. **"Blessed
are those who are invited to the marriage supper of the Lamb"** might sound,
in another context, simply like a Christian version of a religious truism: it
is good to be one of those who are saved. But here it is pronounced with
particular solemnity: **"These are true words of God."** To those who were
standing firm in their ordeal it gave reassurance; to those who were wavering
it was a warning: they might lose their place among the blessed.
10   **Then I fell down at his feet to worship him.** Falling down before the
feet of an angel in fear and amazement was a common motif in this kind
of writing. Less common, but still in the tradition, was a warning against
actually *worshipping* the angel. John repeats the little episode in 22.8. Possibly
there was a tendency to angel-worship in the churches which he wanted to
rebuke (though he does not mention this in the opening letters) – something

similar seems to have been happening among the recipients of the letter to the Hebrews (see above, p. 688). Possibly John intended a contrast with the worship of the beast: Christians were not *even* to worship an angel who brought divine revelation. Or possibly he merely wanted to emphasize the ultimate authority of his visions: **the testimony of Jesus**, which was the possession alike of the angel and of his fellow servants who had **the spirit of prophecy**, came directly from God, and only God was a fit object of worship.

The millennium

11 **Then I saw heaven opened, and there was a white horse!** At the centre of John's heaven there is always the ineffable presence of God himself; but associated with him is the ascended Christ, who also shares the mystery
12 of God's true name and nature (**a name inscribed that no one knows but himself**). In many of the visions this figure of Christ is implied rather than described, and we are kept in mind of him only by the worship by which he is surrounded. But from time to time he comes into the foreground, clothed in a form which expresses some aspect of his status and power. Most often he is the Lamb, an image that serves to keep his sacrifice continually before the hearer's mind. In this chapter there is a new symbol, that of a white horse and
11 its rider. The name **Faithful and True** refers back to a previous description of
10 Christ (3.7), who is both witness (for he gives **testimony**) and judge – the two
11 were not so distinct in John's culture as they are in ours: **in righteousness he judges and makes war** – for a judge (who could also be a witness) had the further responsibility of seeing that his sentence was carried out.

A white horse signifies a conqueror, and the further aspect of Christ which is now to be revealed is that of his sovereignty over all nations. A prophecy in one of the royal psalms is now being fulfilled:

> "I have set my king on Zion, my holy hill."
> . . . I will make the nations your heritage,
>   and the ends of the earth your possession.
> You shall break them with a rod of iron.
> (Psalm 2.6–9)

Yet it has been fulfilled in a totally unforeseen way. Temporal power was firmly rejected by Jesus (it is described as a temptation of the devil in Matthew 4 and Luke 4), and his victory was won only through his own death (of which
13 his **robe dipped in blood** is a recognizable symbol, the same blood which
14 made the clothing of his followers **white and pure**, as in 7.14). So, when his sovereignty finally becomes manifest at the end of history, the crudely military language of the psalm has to be reinterpreted. The rider bears on his head
12 **many diadems**. The diadem – a jewelled band across the brow, like (but also totally unlike) the name-band on the forehead of the whore – was the badge of an oriental king (as distinct from the wreath worn by the emperor); two

diadems were occasionally worn to signify the possession of two kingdoms,
15 the rider's **many diadems** show him to be a universal ruler. But the **sword**
of his conquest is (as in 1.16) a sword proceeding from **his mouth**: it is (as
13 one of his names testifies) **The Word of God**, an instrument, that is to say,
not of military power but of righteous judgment – the metaphor is also used
in Hebrews 4.12. For another prophecy lies below the surface along with
Psalm 2:

> With righteousness shall he judge the poor,
>   and decide with equity for the meek of the earth;
> he shall strike the earth with the rod of his mouth,
>   and with the breath of his lips he shall kill the wicked.
>   (Isaiah 11.4)

It is true that his kingship inevitably involves the condemnation of those
15 inexorably opposed to him – **he will tread the wine press of the fury of the
wrath of God the Almighty** (see above on 14.19). But the weapons of his
conquest and his rule are those by which he won his victory on the cross. It is
these that have won him the title that, in the Old Testament, was reserved for
16 God alone: **"King of kings and Lord of lords".** (John is perhaps imagining a
statue inscribed with the subject's name when he says, a little obscurely, that
on his robe and on his thigh he has a name inscribed.)

The figure of the conquering rider is now added to the picture that began
to be painted in chapter 16 of all the nations of the earth mustered for battle
at Harmagedon. The battle turns into a final encounter with Christ; and
John lets his imagination work on the scene of the battlefield when it is all
over – for the gruesome details he could draw on a similar vision in Ezekiel
21, 17 29.17–20. The feast of the vultures that were **gorged with their flesh** was **the
great supper of God**, a terrible parody of the marriage supper of the Lamb.
Such was the inevitable end of the human combatants. But their ranks had
20 been led by supernatural agencies, the **beast** and the **false prophet**, for whom
a special place of destruction was reserved, **the lake of fire that burns with
sulfur.**

Yet there were still aspects of God's justice which needed to be fitted into
the scheme. Divine justice must not only be done, it must be seen to be
done. If the obdurate enemies of God, who continued until the end to inflict
suffering on the righteous, were to be punished simply by being consigned to
death and oblivion, this still left a certain unfairness in the reckoning: were
those who had been unjustly deprived of recognition, and even of their basic
human rights, to be given no recompense, no vindication, before the end of
everything? To put it another way: already in the present age Christ was being
proclaimed as Lord. He had a rule or kingship which, though denied by the
world, was a reality which his followers both acknowledged and shared. To a
cynic who questioned the reality of this lordship it was natural to reply, 'You
may not see it now, but one day you will.' Christians were destined to be

kings as well as priests (1.5). To give substance to this title it was necessary to look forward to a future period of history when the physical rule of kings and armies would give place to a different kind of authority, vested in the persons of Christian martyrs and acknowledged by those who had previously despised it. But John's drama seemed not to have allowed for this stage: the forces of evil had been steadily gathering momentum until their final overthrow, and now (we would have thought) history had come to an end. It was too late for a Christian epoch.

It was perhaps with something like this in mind that John, just before bringing the drama to a close, found space for a Christian millennium. The concept of a millennium was not a new one. Several Old Testament prophets looked forward to a new period of history in which God's people would enjoy a just, peaceful and prosperous existence under the rule of an 'anointed one' or Messiah. But in more recent times the practical possibility of such a destiny for Israel had disappeared; there was a growing belief in an afterlife and in the reward of the righteous after death, and the ideal messianic kingdom became something of an abstraction, belonging to another world altogether. Yet a hankering for the old ideal of a restored and purified political kingdom remained; and some tried to combine the two beliefs by postulating a limited period of messianic kingship on the old model which would precede the last judgment and the reward of the blessed. To enjoy this millennium, those

20.4 counted worthy of it – **those who had been beheaded for their testimony** (*martyria*) **to Jesus** – would be resurrected before the rest of humanity. After

6 that would come the judgment, with a **second death** (meaning final relegation to a place of punishment) for all the unrighteous. How long would this kingdom last? A thousand years was not an arbitrary figure. God created the world in six days, and it was thought by many that each 'day' represented a thousand years (see above on 2 Peter 3.8). It followed that the last thousand (the seventh) would be the world's sabbath, the glorious period to which all history was tending.

2 **He seized the dragon . . . and bound him**. If (as many believed) the final period before the judgment (and before the millennium) was to be one of unprecedented tribulation, the question could be asked: What was restraining the powers of evil in the meantime? The notion of there being some 'restrainer' (2 Thessalonians 2.6), of the strong man being 'bound' (Matthew 12.29), of the forces of chaos having been placed under strict limits at the creation, was quite widespread. But this did not prevent **the Devil and Satan** from doing a good deal of damage: for the Christian millennium they must be altogether banished, even though their final destruction must await the end of all things.

After this interlude John was at last ready to round off the history of the world with the final destruction of the forces of evil and the judgment passed on all humanity. The imagery is furnished by a vision of Ezekiel (chapters 38–9). Again and again in Israel's history conquering armies had approached

Palestine from the north and had been recognized by the prophets as instruments in the hand of God, punishing the Hebrew people for their sins. But now, at the end of time, these hosts, and the supernatural powers behind them, would in their turn be defeated. Ezekiel had called these invaders by the already almost legendary name, 'Gog, of the land of Magog'. John, echoing several of Ezekiel's phrases, gives them a still more legendary sound by

8 calling them **Gog and Magog**. They represented the final spasm of the Devil's power, and their defeat was his ultimate elimination.

Finally, the judgment. The reality of this ultimate verdict cast by God upon the life of every human being, and the justice of his sentence, was not doubted by any Christian (though it received some reinterpretation in the Fourth Gospel), and the imagery in which it was pictured remained fairly constant. John had little new to add, and he makes his account quite brief.

13 All the dead had been placed by **Death** in the shadowy underworld of Sheol, or **Hades** – this was the almost universal belief in the ancient world. The only exceptions were those who had died at sea (there was some speculation about what happened to the bodies of the shipwrecked). But all alike were brought for a judgment that was based upon a carefully kept record of their deeds. It only remained to dispose of the forces of physical death themselves –

14 **Death and Hades**. These too were cast into the fiery oblivion reserved for all the wicked. As Paul put it (1 Corinthians 15.26), "The last enemy to be destroyed is death."

The new Jerusalem

21.1 **Then I saw a new heaven and a new earth**. The Hebrew prophets never imagined that one day things might take a turn for the better and that human beings would gradually advance towards a new age. The events around them were significant, not of human progress, but of God's judgment on human sin. The world was not as God intended it to be; but neither would it become so merely by human effort. What was needed was a new act of creation.

John had now reached this point in his vision. Justice having been done, and seen to be done, on all those elements of the old order which constituted an offence against the will of God, the decks were cleared for the creation of a new order. **The first heaven and the first earth had passed away** – we might have thought it would be sufficient to do away with the earth; but in antiquity the picture of the universe was integrated by astrology. Events on earth were governed by movements in heaven. Doing away with one meant doing away with the other, and a newly created earth would require a new heaven to regulate its destiny. Moreover, the earth was thought of as hemmed in on all sides by sea and as resting on waters imprisoned beneath it. This element, in the old order, was the place of the chaotic forces of evil. In the new order it had no function. So **the sea was no more**.

So much was easy to state negatively: it was not difficult to see what would *not* belong to the new order. But John's vision was addressed to the positive question of what *would* belong to it. In this, he was influenced, as always, by those who had seen similar visions before him. The new age, however different it might be from the old, was never thought of as a completely fresh start. There were elements in the present which pointed forward to it and might even be incorporated in it. The ideal of human life – God dwelling among his people and his people living in the peace, the purity and the justice demanded of them – had for centuries been symbolized by the city of Jerusalem. In Jerusalem there was a great precinct around the central sanctuary of the temple which only those could enter who were members of the chosen people and who had been cleansed from ritual impurity. Round that there was a still larger precinct which people from any nation could enter, and from it they could catch at least a glimpse of the central building symbolizing the holiness of God. Around this precinct again stretched the city, the capital of a nation of people whose lives were oriented towards the God who was worshipped in their midst. In theory, this city was a microcosm of God having his dwelling among human beings. In practice (as the prophets insisted again and again), it was nothing of the kind: the worship might be hypocritical, the institutions unjust, the people disobedient to the divine law. More than once both temple and city had been destroyed, and both stood in ruins when John was writing. But the old ideal remained: whether one was a Jew or a Christian, one's vision of human destiny was likely to be clothed
2 in the form of **the holy city, the new Jerusalem**. Some even said that the historical city of Jerusalem was but an imperfect copy of the true Jerusalem existing in heaven. All that was necessary was for the archetype to come **down out of heaven from God**.

Given this almost inevitable frame for his final tableau, John proceeded to paint his vision in colours that he found already used by the prophets. One source of his inspiration was Isaiah 65.17–19:

> For I am about to create new heavens
>   and a new earth;
> the former things shall not be remembered
>   or come to mind.
> But be glad and rejoice forever
>   in what I am creating;
> for I am about to create Jerusalem as a joy,
>   and its people as a delight . . .
> no more shall the sound of weeping be heard in it,
>   or the cry of distress.

These verses dominate John's first paragraph; what he adds is the principle
3 which governs the whole vision: **"See, the home of God** (literally *the taber-nacle*, the sacred dwelling) **is among mortals"** – the fulfilment of a hope expressed again and again in the prophets (Ezekiel 37.27; Zechariah 8.8; etc.),

but stated in its most generous form: not among people of one particular race or allegiance, but quite generally among all **mortals**.

Before proceeding with his description John has a particular message for his hearers or readers, signalled by the same instruction as he had for each 5 of the churches at the beginning: **"Write this"** – and the message is one of reassurance. The joys of the new Jerusalem are not a theoretical reality of the 6 distant future: in one thunderous word it is declared, **"It is done!"** (*ge-go-nan*, compare 16.17). All that was said at the beginning about the nature of 7 God (**"I am the Alpha and the Omega"**, as in 1.8), and the reward of **those who conquer,** is already true; what remains is only its perfect fulfilment in the new Jerusalem. To use an image hinted at earlier (7.16) and worked out 6 in detail in John's gospel (4.7–15), **"To the thirsty I will give water as a gift from the spring of the water of life."** How much of humanity was ultimately destined to share these blessings is a question which is never directly answered (though there are suggestive hints scattered through the book). But there 8 would always be an irreducible remainder of those for whom the **second death** was reserved. Partly they were those whose courage had failed them, the apostates from the church, **the cowardly, the faithless;** partly they were those who were irremediably implicated in those crimes and vices[7] which (from the Jewish and Christian points of view) were characteristic of the pagan world.

9 **"Come, I will show you the bride."** The poetry of John's final vision must be allowed to speak for itself. What determined his choice of words was what he actually saw: his recollections of the visions of previous prophets served only to fill out some of the details. It is not difficult to trace the sources of his imagery in the Bible; but in every case he has used his sources so freely that the result is entirely his own.

12–14 (i) The city was to accommodate the true Israel, a re-embodiment of the legendary twelve tribes. This imposed a pattern of 'twelves' on the architecture (as in Ezekiel 48.30–5). It was only necessary to add a further 'twelve' that 14 was very important in Christian history, **the twelve apostles of the Lamb.**

15–17 (ii) The convention of an angel revealing dimensions by measuring them out before the eyes of the seer is in Zechariah 2.1 and Ezekiel 40, and has already been made use of earlier (11.1). The city would be of immense size – necessarily, since it was to accommodate 'the nations'. Jewish writers had been prepared to extend the boundaries of the imagined new Jerusalem as far as Damascus to give it the necessary size. John's more inclusive city would be far larger, and his dimensions, if taken literally, would make it the size of 16 a continent. But this prosaic calculation (like the modern equivalent, **fifteen hundred miles**, prosaically introduced into the translation) obscures the

---

[7] The **polluted** are those involved in the 'abomination' of idol-worship. A similar and more extended list of those who must be excluded from inheriting the kingdom of God is in 1 Corinthians 6.9–10.

obvious symbolism being used by John (indeed when he tells us that the
17 **human measurement** was also that of the angel we may be sure that the
numbers, like the number of the beast in 13.18, are rich in symbolic meaning).
His figure is *twelve thousand stadia*, another multiple of twelve, and the
city had the perfect measurement of a square. Indeed John adds a third
16 dimension: **its length and width and height are equal**. A cubic city strains
our imagination, and is probably not what is intended. We have been told
10 that the vision is of a **great, high mountain**: the earthly Jerusalem was 'a
city set on a hill', and its heavenly counterpart is imagined as covering an
immense mountain and surrounded by a an exceptionally high city wall
17 of **one hundred forty-four cubits** – again a multiple of twelve, the image
perhaps inspired by Herod's immense retaining wall for the esplanade of the
Jerusalem temple, which still stands to this day.
18–21 (iii) An exiled prophet in the sixth century BCE, prophesying the restoration
of the ruined city of Jerusalem to a state of ideal peace, justice and prosperity,
had written:

> I am about to set your stones in antimony,
>   and lay your foundations with sapphires.
> I will make your pinnacles of rubies,
>   your gates of jewels,
>   and all your wall of precious stones.
>   (Isaiah 54.11–12)

The theme lent itself readily to elaboration. Another essay in it – written
nearly three hundred years before Revelation – can be found in Tobit 13.16–
17. John's description stands in the same tradition, though here it is combined
with the symbolic twelvefold structure of the city. A further recollection
which may have been in John's mind is that of the 'breastpiece' (a kind of
shallow box) which was attached to the high priest's garments and which
was studded with twelve precious stones, each one symbolizing one of the
twelve tribes of Israel (Exodus 28.15–21); a later Jewish tradition held that all
21 these came from Paradise. As for the gates made each from **a single pearl**, the
comparatively recent pearl trade from the Red Sea had prepared the oriental
mind to imagine the possibility of ever larger pearls; and the brilliantly white
marble masonry of some classical buildings, emulated by Herod's temple in
Jerusalem, could have suggested, if one half closed one's eyes, the shimmering
brightness of immense pearls.
22 (iv) **I saw no temple in the city**. A large part of Ezekiel's vision, which was
so much in John's mind, had been taken up with the details of a new temple
replacing the one that had recently been destroyed in Jerusalem. It would be
this which set the standard, so to speak, for the purity and holiness of the
nation. In John's time the temple was once again in ruins; but in his vision of
the new Jerusalem John dared to extend the holy precinct over the whole city.
All that the temple stood for would be diffused throughout every part of it;

there would be no need for a central shrine, any more than a lamp is needed
27 when the sun is shining. The barrier excluding anything **unclean** would no
longer be set up around a small temple courtyard but would be at the city
boundaries: for all citizens would be in a constant state of holiness. Even if
logically there were no longer any of the world's population left outside it,
24 the old dream of the prophets that **kings of the earth will bring their glory
into it** remained a powerful image for its new moral and religious stature.

(v) Ezekiel dreamed of a restored Jerusalem making the desert fertile by
a river of water that flowed under the temple: on either side would grow
trees bearing fruit every month of the year and "leaves for healing" (47.1–
12). The picture was already an idealized one; but John has (as we would
22.1 say) spiritualized it still further. The river is **the water of life**, such as Jesus
2 promised to those who believe in him (John 4.14), the trees are each a **tree
of life** such as grew in the garden of Eden (Genesis 2.9) and are reserved for
3, 21.27 God's **servants**, those who are **written in the Lamb's book of life**.
22.6 **"These words are trustworthy and true"** – this was the formula by which
the final vision was introduced (21.5) and which now marks its end. The
promises and warnings are spoken on the very highest authority, that of
God himself; and the channel by which they reach human ears is the inspiration of **the prophets**, assisted in a case such as John's by an angel. But
the prophets of the past, however urgent their message, could never guarantee that their words would be immediately fulfilled. John's informant –
who appears to be both God and Christ – gives an absolute assurance:
7 **"See, I am coming soon!"**

The time is near

With this, the writer seems to re-establish that direct relationship with the
recipients of his letter which seemed almost to have been forgotten in the
torrent of visionary revelations. First, he repeats the little episode in which
he is forbidden to worship the angel – possibly because something of this kind
continued to be a danger to the churches (see above on 19.10). Secondly, he
distinguishes himself sharply from the Jewish writers who have preceded him
and whose work he seems to know. They wrote anonymously and couched
their prophecies in the form of visions vouchsafed to great figures of the past,
but only now to be revealed; hence the supposed author of centuries before
would have to instruct his visions to be 'sealed up' until the prophet appeared
who could reveal them. But John writes in his own name, and his visions
concern the present and the immediate future: the convention of 'sealing
up' is irrelevant. Indeed, even the time for human change and repentance is
11 exhausted. **Let the evildoer still do evil** . . . Throughout the book there has
10 remained an opportunity to repent. But now **the time is near** – it may be too
late.

Warnings and promises

A constant feature of Christian (as of biblical) prophecy was its serious moral tone. It was never intended either to satisfy idle curiosity or to breed complacency by dwelling on the joys in store for the elect. What it read off from the future was always in some form or another a judgment on the present. Its immediate message, therefore, was the necessity of vigilance and faithful-

7 ness here and now. Hence the stern moral note sounded here: **Blessed is the one who keeps the words of the prophecy of this book**. The last judgment would draw the line finally between the good and the bad; but the line was already being sketched in. The finality could be described in terms of the

14, 15 new Jerusalem: inside would be those **who wash their robes**. **Outside are the dogs** – this was Jewish language for pagans, taken over into Christian parlance to describe all who persevered in error and vice. Before contemporary Christians were confronted with the end, there would doubtless be many opportunities for repentance; but if they looked around them attentively they could already see the materials for judgment being assembled, the attitude of the 'evildoer' beginning to harden. The message of the prophecy must be

11 taken to heart as a solemn warning to **the righteous still** to **do right**. The coming of Christ, however confidently it might be yearned for by Christians, always contained a threat as well as a promise. When he came, he would

12 **repay according to everyone's work**.

There are signs at the end of some of Paul's letters that they were read out when the church was assembled, and that the ending was a signal for the congregation to begin the service. In the same way, when one reaches the end of Revelation, it is as if the music of praise has already begun. The worship is 'antiphonal' – that is to say, to each of the sentences spoken by the leader the congregation makes its response. The leader may be speaking in his own person, bidding the people to prayer and praise, or he may be reciting scriptural texts and hallowed phrases of worship, in which case the real speaker is understood to be God, Christ or the Spirit. Either way, there is no need to distinguish: it is all part of a single act of worship. If there seem to be almost bewildering changes of speaker in these last few verses, this atmosphere of worship needs to be kept in mind.

This is more than speculation. The end of 1 Corinthians contains, first, an injunction to separate from the congregation anyone who is there for dishonest reasons ("Let anyone be accursed who does not love the Lord", 16.22); secondly, a formula of prayer in the original Aramaic (*marana tha*, 'Come, O Lord'); and thirdly, the 'grace'. The same three elements occur here. First, a warning: prophecies of this kind were easy for an unscrupulous impostor to interrupt and distort; therefore, on any occasion when the book was read, it was particularly false prophets who must be threatened with exclusion. Secondly, there is the same formula of prayer (though given only

20 in Greek: **Come, Lord Jesus!**) And thirdly the 'grace'. The form of worship is

evidently the same in each case; indeed, here the language of worship pervades
16 the whole epilogue. Jesus bears titles such as befit the object of worship, **the root and the descendant of David** (a variation on the expression in 5.5), **the bright morning star** (as in 2.28). He offers, in the very moment of being
17 worshipped, **the water of life**. Above all, in this book devoted to assuring Christians of the glorious destiny which awaits them, Jesus is heard voicing
20 the greatest assurance of all: **"Surely I am coming soon."** And the response of all who are moved by the Spirit to lead the congregation, the response of
17 the whole church on earth (**the bride**), the response of **everyone who hears**, is that of a people prepared and expectant: **"Come."**

Old Testament References

14.2	718, 760

Joel

2.1	86
2.4–5	806
2.10–11	803
2.28–32	392, 395
2.30	805
2.32	517
3.12	821
3.13	127, 820

Amos

1.2	808, 809
1.9–10	49
5.25–7	409
9.3	657
9.11–12	441

Jonah

1.3–6	128
1.17	254
4.9	195

Micah

4.7	216
4.10	812
5.2	16
7.6	184

Nahum

3.4	824

Habakkuk

1.5	434
2.3	717, 730, 756, 780
2.3–4	707
2.4	491, 599

Haggai

2.6	715, 753

Zechariah

1.8	800

1.18	799
2.1	834
2.1–2	808–9
2.6	86
4	736, 786, 788
4.1–5	804
4.3–13	809
4.10	799
4.14	809
6.1–8	800
8.8	833
8.23	554
9.2–4	49
9.9	76, 166, 348
11.12	93
11.12–13	97
12.3	274
12.10	377, 736, 786
12.11	824
13.1	377
13.7	194, 198, 365
14.4	169
14.5	651, 654
14.8	328
14.21	302

Malachi

1.3	514
2.14–16	156, 159
3.1	48, 105, 106
3.1–5	747, 797
4	19
4.5	64, 106
4.5–6	150

Apocrypha

Tobit

11.11–13	418
13.16–17	835

Judith

5	408

Index